(handwritten) Questions = Talk to [...]
at his carpet store
(Athens)

② In the Plaka eat at Byzantino Restaurant near Syntagma

LET'S GO

Greece

■ Let's Go writers travel on your budget.

"Guides that penetrate the veneer of the holiday brochures and mine the grit of real life."
—*The Economist*

"The writers seem to have experienced every rooster-packed bus and lunar-surfaced mattress about which they write."
—*The New York Times*

"All the dirt, dirt cheap."
—*People*

■ Great for independent travelers.

"The guides are aimed not only at young budget travelers but at the independent traveler, a sort of streetwise cookbook for traveling alone."
—*The New York Times*

"Flush with candor and irreverence, chock full of budget travel advice."
—*The Des Moines Register*

"An indispensable resource. *Let's Go*'s practical information can be used by every traveler."
—*The Chattanooga Free Press*

■ Let's Go is completely revised each year.

"Only *Let's Go* has the zeal to annually update every title on its list."
—*The Boston Globe*

"Unbeatable: good sight-seeing advice; up-to-date info on restaurants, hotels, and inns; a commitment to money-saving travel; and a wry style that brightens nearly every page."
—*The Washington Post*

■ All the important information you need.

"*Let's Go* authors provide a comedic element while still providing concise information and thorough coverage of the country. Anything you need to know about budget traveling is detailed in this book."
—*The Chicago Sun-Times*

"Value-packed, unbeatable, accurate, and comprehensive."
—*Los Angeles Times*

(handwritten) Exchange @ $100 to Drachma at Athens Airport

Let's Go Publications

Let's Go: Alaska & the Pacific Northwest 1999
Let's Go: Australia 1999
Let's Go: Austria & Switzerland 1999
Let's Go: Britain & Ireland 1999
Let's Go: California 1999
Let's Go: Central America 1999
Let's Go: Eastern Europe 1999
Let's Go: Ecuador & the Galápagos Islands 1999
Let's Go: Europe 1999
Let's Go: France 1999
Let's Go: Germany 1999
Let's Go: Greece 1999 **New title!**
Let's Go: India & Nepal 1999
Let's Go: Ireland 1999
Let's Go: Israel & Egypt 1999
Let's Go: Italy 1999
Let's Go: London 1999
Let's Go: Mexico 1999
Let's Go: New York City 1999
Let's Go: New Zealand 1999
Let's Go: Paris 1999
Let's Go: Rome 1999
Let's Go: South Africa 1999 **New title!**
Let's Go: Southeast Asia 1999
Let's Go: Spain & Portugal 1999
Let's Go: Turkey 1999 **New title!**
Let's Go: USA 1999
Let's Go: Washington, D.C. 1999

Let's Go Map Guides

Amsterdam	Madrid
Berlin	New Orleans
Boston	New York City
Chicago	Paris
Florence	Rome
London	San Francisco
Los Angeles	Washington, D.C.

Coming Soon: Prague, Seattle

③ Athens on Kydatheneon St (Plaka)
go to Brettos (Oldest distillery
for ouzo Try his Raki
buy + metal canister of ouzo too
for friend

Let's Go Publications

Let's Go

Greece

1999

④ Jewelry = On Plaka on Adrianou
St (near cross of Kydatheneon +
Adrianou) Byzatium Jewelry
cheap + good wised

Christian Reed Lorentzen
Editor

Penelope Carter
Associate Editor

Saadi Soudavar
Associate Editor

Magic Travel Svcs Specialists
in Athens to Rome Tel
01 323 7471
magic@magic.gr http://www.magic.gr

Researcher-Writers:
Brady Gunderson
Ashley Kircher
Jeremy Kurzyniec
Michele Lee
Nick Stephanopoulos

St. Martin's Press ❧ New York

Packing Pg 23

HELPING LET'S GO

If you want to share your discoveries, suggestions, or corrections, please drop us a line. We read every piece of correspondence, whether a postcard, a 10-page email, or a coconut. Please note that mail received after May 1999 may be too late for the 2000 book, but will be kept for future editions. **Address mail to:**

Let's Go: Greece
67 Mount Auburn Street
Cambridge, MA 02138
USA

Visit Let's Go at **http://www.letsgo.com**, or send email to:

feedback@letsgo.com
Subject: "Let's Go: Greece"

In addition to the invaluable travel advice our readers share with us, many are kind enough to offer their services as researchers or editors. Unfortunately, our charter enables us to employ only currently enrolled Harvard-Radcliffe students.

Maps by David Lindroth copyright © 1999, 1998, 1997, 1996, 1995, 1994, 1993, 1992, 1991, 1990, 1989, 1988 by St. Martin's Press, Inc.

Distributed outside the USA and Canada by Macmillan.

Let's Go: Greece. Copyright © 1999 by Let's Go, Inc. All rights reserved. Printed in the United States of America. No part of this book may be used or reproduced in any manner whatsoever without written permission except in the case of brief quotations embodied in critical articles or reviews. For information, address St. Martin's Press, 175 Fifth Avenue, New York, NY 10010, USA.

ISBN: 0-312-19484-6

First edition
10 9 8 7 6 5 4 3 2 1

Let's Go: Greece is written by Let's Go Publications, 67 Mount Auburn Street, Cambridge, MA 02138, USA.

Let's Go® and the thumb logo are trademarks of Let's Go, Inc. Printed in the USA on recycled paper with biodegradable soy ink.

Contents

About Let's Go

THIRTY-NINE YEARS OF WISDOM

Back in 1960, a few students at Harvard University banded together to produce a 20-page pamphlet offering a collection of tips on budget travel in Europe. This modest, mimeographed packet, offered as an extra to passengers on student charter flights to Europe, met with instant popularity. The following year, students traveling to Europe researched the first, full-fledged edition of *Let's Go: Europe*, a pocket-sized book featuring honest, irreverent writing and a decidedly youthful outlook on the world. Throughout the 60s, our guides reflected the times; the 1969 guide to America led off by inviting travelers to "dig the scene" at San Francisco's Haight-Ashbury. During the 70s and 80s, we gradually added regional guides and expanded coverage into the Middle East and Central America. With the addition of our in-depth city guides, handy map guides, and extensive coverage of Asia and Australia, the 90s are also proving to be a time of explosive growth for Let's Go, and there's certainly no end in sight. The maiden edition of *Let's Go: South Africa*, our pioneer guide to sub-Saharan Africa, hits the shelves this year, along with the first editions of *Let's Go: Greece* and *Let's Go: Turkey*.

We've seen a lot in 39 years. *Let's Go: Europe* is now the world's bestselling international guide, translated into seven languages. And our new guides bring Let's Go's total number of titles, with their spirit of adventure and their reputation for honesty, accuracy, and editorial integrity, to 44. But some things never change: our guides are still researched, written, and produced entirely by students who know first-hand how to see the world on the cheap.

HOW WE DO IT

Each guide is completely revised and thoroughly updated every year by a well-traveled set of over 200 students. Every winter, we recruit over 160 researchers and 70 editors to write the books anew. After several months of training, researcher-writers hit the road for seven weeks of exploration, from Anchorage to Adelaide, Estonia to El Salvador, Iceland to Indonesia. Hired for their rare combination of budget travel sense, writing ability, stamina, and courage, these adventurous travelers know that train strikes, stolen luggage, food poisoning, and marriage proposals are all part of a day's work. Back at our offices, editors work from spring to fall, massaging copy written on Himalayan bus rides into witty yet informative prose. A student staff of typesetters, cartographers, publicists, and managers keeps our lively team together. In September, the collected efforts of the summer are delivered to our printer, who turns them into books in record time, so that you have the most up-to-date information available for your vacation. Even as you read this, work on next year's editions is well underway.

WHY WE DO IT

We don't think of budget travel as the last recourse of the destitute; we believe that it's the only way to travel. Living cheaply and simply brings you closer to the people and places you've been saving up to visit. Our books will ease your anxieties and answer your questions about the basics—so you can get off the beaten track and explore. Once you learn the ropes, we encourage you to put *Let's Go* down now and then to strike out on your own. You know as well as we that the best discoveries are often those you make yourself. When you find something worth sharing, please drop us a line. We're Let's Go Publications, 67 Mount Auburn St., Cambridge, MA 02138, USA (email: feedback@letsgo.com). For more info, visit our website, http://www.letsgo.com.

How to Use This Book

Traveling through the lands of the northeastern Mediterranean, you are walking in the footsteps of philosophers, conquerors, archaeologists, kings, apostles, writers, generals, classicists, and saints. Of course, our job here at *Let's Go* is to help you enjoy the majesty while avoiding any tragedies of your own. To that end, we have comprehensive practical information on each town that you may visit. From hospitals to hotels, cops to cafes, we give you the addresses and phone numbers you need to make your visit smooth.

This year's edition sees some major changes from past editions—when you get right down to it, we've become a different book; the transition from *Greece and Turkey '98* to *Greece '99* added 150 pages to the Greece section, with which we've almost doubled our breadth of coverage in Nothern Greece, entirely overhauled and expanded the chapter on Athens, bringing you around each of the city's neighborhoods, and significantly deepened our nightlife, sights, and practical listings in the Greek islands and mainland.

In addition to actual new points of coverage, *Let's Go: Greece 1999* is even more user-friendly in a number of ways. The part we'd like to draw your attention to first and foremost is the introductory historical and cultural material. Never has Greek life, from the dawn of civilization to the present, been so carefully distilled into a Let's Go needs-to-know package of wisdom. We've added, in addition, a glossary of Greek terms, covering essential terms for art, food, and travel experience, and expanded the Greek phrases listings.

Planning a trip to Greece and Cyprus is a good way to learn the difference between theory and reality. In theory, ferries leave on time, buses arrive as scheduled, and pensions are open. In reality, the ferry from Andros got cancelled because not enough passengers bought tickets, the bus from Nafplion to Thessaloniki took an extra 15 hours, and the pension owner is on vacation in May. This doesn't mean that your trip won't be the most stimulating, exciting, beautiful, and entertaining one you've ever taken; it just means that you need to be flexible and work with a rough itinerary rather than a firm one. Responding to this aspect of travel in Greece and Cyprus, we've concentrated, above all, on making sure that we offer as much general information as is humanly possible, to help you decide where to visit and how to enhance your trip once there. As always, be sure to check out the **Essentials** section at the beginning of the book, as well as the **Appendix** for quick reference.

Within each city, we offer information on orienting yourself; practical information like the hours and location of the post office and tourist police; several lodging recommendations; our favorite restaurants, bakeries, bars, and clubs; and the most interesting sights in the area. Virtually every listing in our book has a telephone number, so if you get lost in, say, Athens, you could call a grocer to ask how to get from the tourist office to the *plateia*. Please note that listings of hotels and restaurants are ranked in order of the researchers' preferences.

We hope you love Greece and Cyprus as much as we have. Παμε—Let's Go!

A NOTE TO OUR READERS

The information for this book was gathered by *Let's Go*'s researchers from May through August. Each listing is derived from the assigned researcher's opinion based upon his or her visit at a particular time. The opinions are expressed in a candid and forthright manner. Other travelers might disagree. Those traveling at a different time may have different experiences since prices, dates, hours, and conditions are always subject to change. You are urged to check beforehand to avoid inconvenience and surprises. Travel always involves a certain degree of risk, especially in low-cost areas. When traveling, especially on a budget, always take particular care to ensure your safety.

Maps

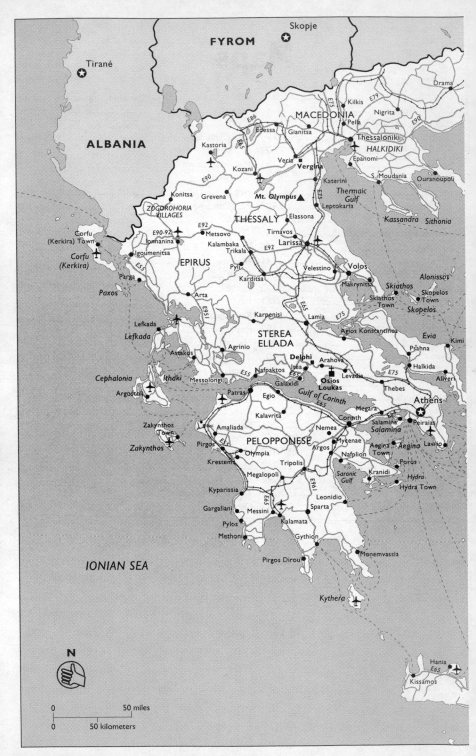

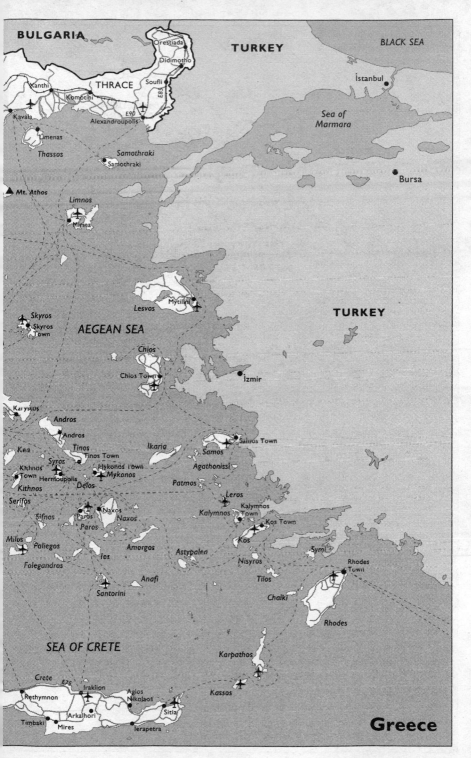

BULGARIA

TURKEY

BLACK SEA

Orestiada

Didimotho

İstanbul

Xanthi   THRACE   Soufli
Komotini

E85

Kavala

E90

Alexandroupolis

Limenas

Thassos

Sea of
Marmara

Samothraki
Samothraki

Bursa

▲ Mt. Athos

Limnos

Mirina

Lesvos   Mytilini

TURKEY

Skyros

Skyros
Town

AEGEAN SEA

Chios

Chios Town

İzmir

Karystus

Andros

Andros

Ikaria

Samos Town

Kea

Tinos

Tinos Town

Samos

Syros

Agathonissi

Kithnos
Town   Hermoupolis   Mykonos Town
Mykonos

Patmos

Kithnos

Delos

Serifos

Leros

Sifnos   Paros   Naxos
Paros   Naxos

Kalymnos   Kalymnos
Town

Kos Town

Milos   Paliegos

Amorgos

Astypalea

Kos

Syml.

Folegandros

Ios

Nisyros

Rhodes
Town

Anafi

Tilos

Santorini

Chalki

Rhodes

SEA OF CRETE

Karpathos

Crete   E75

Rethymnon   Iraklion   Agios
Nikolaos

Kassos

Timbaki   Arkalhori   Sitia

Mires   Ierapetra

Greece

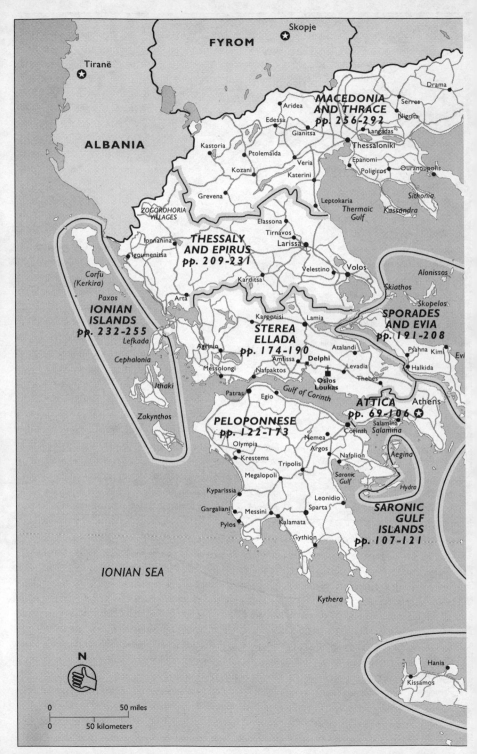

FYROM

Skopje

Tiranë

ALBANIA

MACEDONIA
AND THRACE
pp. 256-292

Aridea
Edessa
Gianitsa
Kastoria   Thessaloniki
Ptolemáida   Langadas
Kozani   Veria
          Katerini   Epanomi
Grevena   Poligiros   Ouranoupolis

Drama
Serres
Nigrita

Leptokaria
Thermaic
Gulf

Sithonia
Kassandra

ZOGOROHORIA
VILLAGES
                    Elassona
                    Tirnavos
Ionnanina   Larissa
Igoumenitsa

THESSALY
AND EPIRUS
pp. 209-231

Velestino   Volos

Corfu
(Kerkira)

Paxos

IONIAN
ISLANDS
pp. 232-255

Arta

Karditsa

Karpenisi   Lamia

STEREA
ELLADA
pp. 174-190

Alonissos

Skiathos

Skopelos

SPORADES
AND EVIA
pp. 191-208

Lefkada

Cephalonia

Agrinio
Messolongi
Nafpaktos

Amfissa   Delphi
Osios
Loukas

Atalandi
Levadia
Thebes

Psahna   Kimi

Evi
Halkida

Ithaki

Patras   Egio

Gulf of Corinth

ATTICA
pp. 69-106   Athens

Zakynthos

PELOPONNESE
pp. 122-173

Olympia
Krestems
Megalopoli

Nemea
Argos
Tripolis

Nafplion

Corinth   Salamina
           Salamina

Saronic
Gulf

Aegina

Hydra

Kyparissia
Gargaliani   Messini
Pylos   Kalamata

Leonidio
Sparta

Gythion

SARONIC
GULF
ISLANDS
pp. 107-121

IONIAN SEA

Kythera

N

Hania
Kissamos

0   50 miles
0   50 kilometers

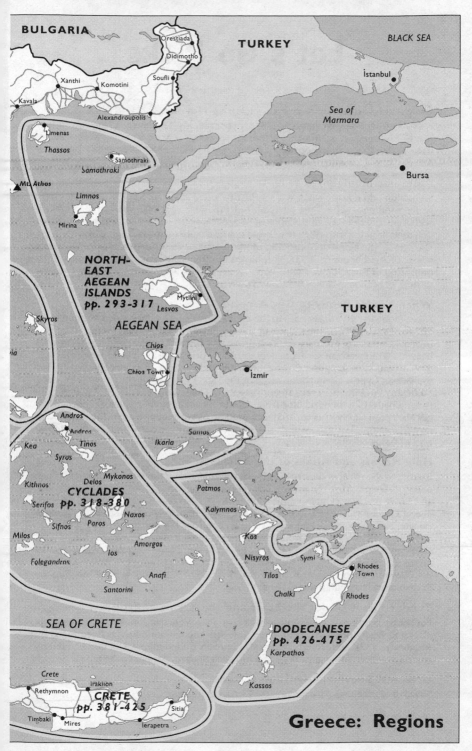

Greece: Regions

Let's Go Picks

Best Archaeological Sites at which to Murder. . .
. . . your daughter—**Mycenae** (p. 128) . . . your father—**Thebes** (p. 174) . . . your husband—**Mycenae** . . . a Minotaur—**Knossos** (p. 389) . . . your mother's lover—**Mycenae** . . . Persians—**Thermopylae** (p. 189) . . . your mother—**Mycenae**.
  Let's Go: Greece cannot recommend murder.

Dionysiac Indulgences
If you don't do it now, when will you? Party naked at **Ios** (p. 327). The streets aren't really winding—you're just partying with the jet set at **Mykonos** (p. 318). Party within puking distance of the ancient agora at **Kos** (p. 442). The British football set don their drinking shirts for a rowdy old colonial night of imbibing on **Corfu** (p. 232). On Cyprus, the island of Aphrodite, Dionysus' still has a substantial following on the coasts of **Agia Napa** (p. 492). You haven't gotten your Nordo-Bacchic mojo fully motivated in the Sporades until you've tossed back a few rounds of *ouzo* among throngs of Scandinavians at **Skiathos Town** (p. 192).

When You're Ready to Get Ascetic
Hike among the 20 monasteries in the exclusively male and monastic community on **Mt. Athos** (p. 277), a throw-back to the heyday of the Byzantine Empire. The sky-high monasteries of **Meteora** (p. 218) prove that elevation really can get you closer to heaven. Whitewash never had such an otherworldly purity as at **Hozoviotissa** (p. 359) on Amorgos. Emperor Constantine's mother bestowed **Stavrovouni** (p. 491) to the men of Cyprus along with a piece of the Holy Cross. Architectural wonder, natural beauty, and Inner Peace, all congregate at **Osios Loukas** (p. 177). Wander the twisted paths past the vivid blue frescoes and glittering mosaics, plus the exalted Virgin Mary icon, at **Mystras** (p. 165). It would be worth visiting even if the nuns didn't give free samples of their yogurt—whenever you're in Spetses, stop by the **Monastery of Agios Nikolas** (p. 121).

Holy Haunts and Altars of the Ancients
Journey to the navel of the earth and seek the guidance of the world's foremost pagan oracle at **Delphi** (p. 179). A lusty Zeus was once infused in the roots of a giant oak, and a holy oracle was built on this spot; try to pick up on some of the god's whisperings at **Dodoni** (p. 227). You just can't ask for more than an island-sized archaeological site, Apollo worship, and the chance to confront the five great cats at **Delos** (p. 325). Seek mystical healing from Asclepius and rehabilitate yourself watching a Classical drama at the theater of **Epidavros** (p. 138). Run in the footsteps of the champions of the ancient games at **Olympia** (p. 148). Trek to the Temple of Aphrodite, once the religious center of Cyprus, and you'll be walking in the footsteps of much of the Roman world through **Peleopaphos** (p. 498).

Tender Kisses Under the Stars and the Arrow of Eros
Pucker up between Mediterranean waves and the Venetian fortezzas of **Iraklion** (p. 382) and **Rethymnon** (p. 396). Duck into the ancient aqueduct at **Epta Piges** on **Rhodes** (p. 437), then emerge when you're ready for a dunking. Get down and dirty among *malakas* and mangy dogs in **Syntagma Square, Athens** (p. 75).

Greasiest Souvlaki and Gooiest Gyro
Savas in Monastiraki, Athens (p. 86). **Thraka** in Iraklion, Crete (p. 386).

ESSENTIALS

You may feel overwhelmed in the colorful sea of American, German, Japanese, and other tourists at the most renowned destinations in Greece and Cyprus. Yet if you can see the "must see's" without getting lost in the crowds, there are also secluded beaches, remote mountain trails, and quiet ruins to be discovered.

Although it's important to plan ahead to get the most out of your vacation, in Greece you'll need to be flexible with your itinerary. Ferry schedules change with the winds and without notice, national holidays pop up unannounced, bus drivers strike for a day, and everything takes longer than you'll anticipate.

Summer is high tourist season in Greece and Cyprus; beaches lined with discos enter Dionysiac overdrive, and the hot sun frames the remains of ancient cities now populated by tourist hordes. If you feel annoyed by crowds or taxed by the frantic pace of summer travel, consider visiting during the off season (Sept.-May), when inexpensive airfares are easier to obtain and lodging is cheaper; a few facilities and sights may close down, but residents are often more receptive and the weather is far less oppressively warm. Even during the winter months, some areas continue to be mild, though winter does tend to be the rainy season in most of Greece (especially Athens). Greece also has winter sports, with ski areas at Mt. Parnassos, Mt. Pelion, Metsovo, and Troodos. Refer to the climate chart in the appendix for average temperatures and rainfall.

USEFUL INFORMATION

■ Travel Organizations and Agencies

If you don't know where to begin, write a few polite letters. Calling offices directly (or faxing, if you have the means) may be necessary if you're in a rush. In most countries, citizens may receive consular information sheets, travel warnings, and public announcements at any passport agency, embassy, or consulate.

GOVERNMENT INFORMATION OFFICES

Greek National Tourist Organization (GNTO)

Australia, 3rd Fl., 51 Pitt St., **Sydney,** NSW 2000 (tel. (02) 9241 1663; fax 9235 2174).

Canada, 1300 Bay St., **Toronto,** ON M5R 3K8 (tel. (416) 968-2220; fax 968-6533; http://www.aei.ca/gntomtl); 1233 rue de la Montagne, Suite 101, **Montréal,** PQ, H3G 1Z2 (tel. (514) 871-1535; fax 871-1498; email gntomtl@aci.ca).

U.K., 4 Conduit St., **London** W1R DOJ (tel. (171) 734 5997; fax 287 1369).

U.S., Head Office, Olympic Tower, 645 Fifth Ave., 5th Floor, **New York,** NY 10022 (tel. (212) 421-5777; fax 826-6940); 168 N. Michigan Ave., 6th floor, **Chicago,** IL 60601 (tel. (312) 782-1084; fax 782-1091); 611 W. Sixth St. #2198, **Los Angeles,** CA 90017 (tel. (213) 626-6696; fax 489-9744).

Cyprus Tourism Organization (CTO)

Cyprus, P.O. Box 4535, CY1390, **Nicosia,** Cyprus (tel. (2) 33 77 15; fax 33 16 44; email cto@cyta.com.cy).

U.K., 213 Regent St., London W1R 8DA (tel. (171) 734 9822; fax 287 6534; email cto lon@ctolon.demon.co.uk).

U.S., 13 E. 40th St., **New York,** NY 10016 (tel. (212) 683-5280; fax 683-5282; email gocyprus@aol.com; http://www.cyprustourism.org). Offers *Travelers Handbook*.

TRAVEL ORGANIZATIONS

Council on International Educational Exchange (CIEE), 205 East 42nd St., New York, NY 10017-5706 (tel. (888)COUNCIL (268-6245); fax (212) 822-2699; http://www.ciee.org). Work, volunteer, academic, internship, and professional programs. Identity cards, including ISIC and the GO25; *Student Travels* (free).

Federation of International Youth Travel Organizations (FIYTO), Bredgade 25H, DK-1260 Copenhagen K, Denmark (tel. (45) 33 33 96 00; fax 33 93 96 76; email mailbox@fiyto.org; http://www.fiyto.org). Members include schools, educational travel companies, national tourist boards, hotels and hostels. Sponsors GO25 card.

International Student Travel Confederation, Herengracht 479, 1017 BS Amsterdam, Netherlands (tel. (31) 20 421 2800; fax 20 421 2810; email istcinfo@istc.org; http://www.istc.org). Includes: International Student Surface Travel Association (ISSA), Student Air Travel Association (SATA), IASIS Travel Insurance, and the International Association for Educational and Work Exchange Programs. Offers ISICs.

■ Travel Advisory Services

GOVERNMENT TRAVEL ADVISORY BUREAUS

Australian Department of Foreign Affairs and Trade (tel. (02) 6261 9111) offers travel information and advisories at their website (http://www.dfat.gov.au).

Canadian Department of Foreign Affairs and International Trade (DFAIT) provides advisories and travel warnings at its website (http://www.dfait-maeci.gc.ca). Call them at (613) 944-6788 from Ottawa or (800) 267-8376 elsewhere in Canada. For their free publication, *Bon Voyage,* call (613) 944-4000.

United Kingdom Foreign and Commonwealth Office. Official warnings are on-line at http://www.fco.gov.uk; you can also call the office at (0171) 238 4503.

United States Department of State. For official travel advisories, call their 24-hour hotline at (202) 647-5225. Check their website (http://travel.state.gov) for travel information and publications. Other publications, such as *A Safe Trip Abroad,* are offered for a small fee; call the Superintendent of Documents at (202) 512-1800.

COMMERCIAL TRAVEL ASSISTANCE

Travel Assistance International by Worldwide Assistance Services, Inc. (http://www.worldwide-assistance.com) provides its members with a 24-hour hotline for travel emergencies and referrals in over 200 countries. Their Per-Trip (starting at US$21) and Frequent Traveler (starting at US$88) plans include medical (evacuation and repatriation), travel, and communication services. Call (800) 821-2828 or (202) 828-5894, fax (202) 828-5896, email wassist@aol.com, or write them at 1133 15th St. NW, Suite 400, Washington, D.C. 20005-2710.

The American Society of Travel Agents provides extensive informational resources, both at their website (http://www.astanet.com) and in their free brochure, *Travel Safety;* send a request and self-addressed, stamped envelope to 1101 King St. Suite 200, Alexandria, VA 22314.

■ Tourist Media

Sometimes you've got to take things into your own hands. These sources may help.

USEFUL PUBLICATIONS

Forsyth Travel Library, Inc., 1750 East 131st St., P.O. Box 480800, Kansas City, MO 64148 (tel. (800) 367-7984; fax (816) 942-6969; email forsyth@avi.net; http://www.forsyth.com). Mail-order service offers a wide range of maps and guides for rail and ferry travel in Europe; rail tickets and passes; reservation services.

Hippocrene Books, Inc., 171 Madison Ave., New York, NY 10016 (tel. (212) 685-4371; orders (718) 454-2366; fax 454-1391; email hippocre@ix.netcom.com; http://www.netcom.com/~hippocre). Free catalogue. Publishes travel reference books, travel guides, foreign language dictionaries; guides to over 100 languages.

European Festivals Association, 120B, rue de Lausanne, CH-1202 Geneva, Switzerland (tel. (22) 732 28 03; fax 738 40 12; email aef@vtx.ch). Free booklet *Festivals* lists dates and programs, including music, ballet, and theater events. To receive the booklet, enclose 5 International Reply Coupons for postage and address request to Dailey-Thorp Travel, Inc., 330 West 58th Street, New York, NY 10019-1817.

INTERNET RESOURCES

Today, you can make your own airline, hotel, hostel, or car rental reservations on the Internet, and connect personally with others abroad. **NetTravel: How Travelers Use the Internet,** by Michael Shapiro, is a useful guide to planning by Internet (US$25).

On the World Wide Web, **Search engines** (services that search for web pages under specific subjects) can aid the search process. **Lycos** (a2z.lycos.com), **Alta Vista** (www.altavista.digital.com), and **Excite** (www.excite.com) are among the most popular. **Yahoo!** is more organized; check out its travel links at www.yahoo.com/Recreation/Travel. Check out the **Let's Go web site** (www.letsgo.com) and find our newsletter, information about our books, a list of links, and more. Let's Go lists web sites specific to certain aspects of travel throughout the Essentials chapter.

Microsoft Expedia (http://expedia.msn.com) has everything you'd ever need to make travel plans on the web—compare flight fares, look at maps, make reservations. FareTracker, a free service within Expedia, sends you monthly mailings about the cheapest fares to any destination.

The CIA World Factbook (http://www.odci.gov/cia/publications/factbook/index.html) has tons of vital statistics on the country you want to visit. Check it out for a number-packed Greece overview.

Shoestring Travel (http://www.stratpub.com), an alternative to Microsoft's monolithic site, is budget travel e-zine that features listings of home exchanges, links, and accommodations information.

Cybercafe Guide (http://www.cyberiacafe.net/cyberia/guide/ccafe.htm) can help you find cybercafes worldwide.

■ Alternatives to Tourism

Because most visitors see Greece, Turkey, and Cyprus only through the eyes of a tourist, those who go in order to study or work can expect a particularly unique and rewarding experience. There are several general resource organizations for those interested in alternatives to tourism.

STUDY

Foreign study programs vary tremendously in expense, academic quality, living conditions, degree of contact with local students, and exposure to local culture and languages. Many colleges have offices that give advice and information on study abroad. Talk to recent participants in these programs in order to judge which is best for you.

College Year in Athens (tel. (01) 726 0749) runs a one-semester or full year program for undergraduates (usually juniors), which includes travel as well as classroom instruction (in English). The program has two tracks, one in Ancient Greek civilization and one in Mediterranean area studies. Scholarships available. Students are housed in apartments in Athens's Kolonaki district. 3- to 6-week summer programs and 3-week language programs on Paros. From the U.S. call (617) 494-1008 or write to College Year in Athens, P.O. Box 390890, Cambridge, MA 02139.

The Athens Centre, 48 Archimidous St., Athens, Greece 11636 (tel. (01) 701 2268; fax 701 8603; email athenscr@compulink.gr), offers a modern Greek language program. Semester and quarter programs on Greek civilization in affiliation with U.S. universities. Offers 4- to 6-week summer Classics programs, a yearly summer theater program, and Modern Greek Language programs in June and July on Spetses island.

Beaver College Center for Education Abroad, 450 S. Easton Rd., Glenside, PA 19038-3295 (tel. (800) 755-5607 or (888) BEAVER 9 (232-8379); fax (215) 572-

2174; email cea@beaver.edu; http://www.beaver.edu/cea/). Operates summer, semester, and year-long study abroad programs in Greece (and other countries), as well as offering a Peace Studies program. Applicants must have completed three semesters at a university; graduate study programs also available. Call for brochure.

Council on International Education Exchange, 205 E. 42nd St., New York, NY 10017 (tel. (888) COUNCIL (268-6245); fax (212) 822-2699; email info@ciee.org; http://www.ciee.org), sponsors over 40 study abroad programs throughout the world. Contact them for more information (see **Travel Organizations** on p. 3).

WORK

Finding work in Greece and Cyprus is difficult. Job opportunities are scarce and the governments try to restrict employment to citizens and visitors from the EU. Be persistent; the informality of local life will work to your advantage. Friends can help expedite work permits or arrange work-for-accommodations swaps. Students can check with their universities' foreign language departments, which may have connections to job openings abroad.

For long term employment in Greece, you must first get a **work permit** from your employer; permits are available at the **Ministry of Labor,** 40 Pireos St., Athens 10437 (tel. (01) 523 3110). Make all arrangements and negotiations before you leave home.

Arrive in the spring and early summer to search for **hotel jobs** (bartending, cleaning, etc.). Most night spots offer meager pay. Check the bulletin boards of hostels in Athens and the classified ads in the *Athens News.* Another possibility is farm labor. The **American Farm School** runs a summer work and recreation program in Greece for high school students. Write to 1133 Broadway, New York, NY 10010 (tel. (212) 463-8434; fax 463-8208; email NYO@amerfarm.com; www http://afs.edu.gr); or P.O. Box 23, GR-55102, Thessaloniki (tel. 30 (31) 471 803, 471 825; fax 472 345).

The brightest prospect for working in Cyprus is probably **teaching English.** Students with university credentials might fare quite well, but having your credentials verified can take some time. Various organizations in the U.S. will place you in a (low-paying) teaching job, but securing a position will require patience, because teaching English abroad has become enormously popular in the past few years. Before you arrive you must find an employer who can assert that you are particularly suited for your position, due to unique academic interest or experience.

You may receive room and board in exchange for your labor if you seek to **volunteer** in Greece or Cyprus. Opportunities include archaeological digs and community aid projects. Organizations that arrange placement sometimes charge high application fees in addition to the workcamps' charges for room and board; you can sometimes avoid this extra fee by contacting the individual workcamps directly. Listings in Vacation Work Publications' *International Directory of Voluntary Work* (UK£9, postage UK£2.50) can be helpful.

The Archaeological Institute of America, 656 Beacon St., Boston, MA 02215-2010 (tel. (617) 353-9361; fax 353-6550; email aia@bu.edu; http://csa.brynmawr.edu/ aia.html), puts out the *Archaeological Fieldwork Opportunities Bulletin* (US$16 non-members), which lists over 250 field sites throughout the world. This can be purchased from Kendall/Hunt Publishing, 4050 Westmark Dr., Dubuque, Iowa 52002 (tel. (800) 228-0810).

Office of Overseas Schools, A/OS Room 245, SA-29, Dept. of State, Washington, D.C. 20522-2902 (tel. (703) 875-7800; fax 875-7979; email overseas.schools@dos.usstate.gov; http://state.gov/www/aboutstate/schools/). Keeps a list of schools abroad and agencies that arrange placement for American teachers.

DOCUMENTS AND FORMALITIES

In the midst of your marvelously exciting vacation dream plans, you'll need to remember to arrange a number of legal matters associated with traveling, including your **passport, visa, customs,** and **identification documentation.** Assembling these can mean filing applications several weeks or months of advance of your planned departure date. Remember that in many cases you are relying on government agencies to complete these transactions. In case these agencies deem your applications inadequate and return them, you must leave enough time to re-submit them. Demand for documentation—especially passports—is highest between January and August.

U.S. citizens may find additional information (including publications) about documents, formalities and travel abroad at the Bureau of Consular Affairs homepage at http://travel.state.gov, or at the State Department site at http://www.state.gov.

■ Embassies and Consulates

GREEK

Embassies

Australia, 9 Turrana St., Yarralumla, Canberra, ACT 26000 (tel. (02) 6273 3011; fax 6273 2620).

Canada, 7680 MacLaren St., Ottawa, ON K2P 0K6 (tel. (613) 238-6271; fax 238-5676).

Ireland, 1 Upper Pembroke St., Dublin 2 (tel. (3531) 6767 2545; fax 661 8892).

South Africa, 1003 Church St. Athlone, Arcadia, 0083, Pretoria (tel. (2712) 437 3513; fax 434 313).

U.K., 1a Holland Park, London W113TP (tel. (44171) 229 3850; fax 229 7221).

U.S., 2221 Massachusetts Ave., N.W., Washington, D.C. 20008 (tel. (202) 939-5800; fax 939-5824; email greece@greekembassy.org).

Greek Consulates

Australia: 366 King William St., 1st Fl., **Adelaide,** SA 5000 (tel. (08) 8211 8066; fax 8211 8820); Stanhill House, 34 Queens Road, **Melbourne** Vic 3004 (tel. (03) 866

4524; fax 866 4933); 15 Castlereagh St., Level 20, **Sydney**, NSW 2000 (tel. (02) 9221 2388; fax 9221 1423); 16 St. George's Terrace, **Perth**, WA 6000 (tel. (08) 9325 6608; fax 9325 2940).

Canada: 1170 Place du Frère André, 3ème Etage, **Montréal**, QC H3B 3C6 (tel. (514) 875-2119; fax 875-8781; email congrem@citenet.net); 365 Bloor St. E, Suite 1800, **Toronto**, ON M4W 3L4 (tel. (416) 515-0133; fax 515-0209); 688 West Hastings, Suite 500, **Vancouver**, B.C. V6B 1P1 (tel. (604) 681-1381; fax 681-6656).

New Zealand, 57 Willeston St., 10th Fl., Box 24066, **Wellington** (tel. (04) 473 7775 or 473 7776; fax 473 7441).

U.S.: 2211 Massachusetts Ave. NW, Washington, D.C. 20008 (tel. (202) 939-5818; fax 234-2803); 69 East 79th St., **New York**, NY 10021 (tel. (212) 980-5500, fax 734-8492); 650 North St. Clair St., **Chicago**, IL 60611 (tel. (312) 335-3915 or 335-3916; fax 335-3958); 2441 Gough St., **San Francisco**, CA 94123 (tel. (415) 775-2102 or 775-2103; fax 776-6815); 12424 Wilshire Building, Suite 800, **Los Angeles**, CA 90025 (tel. (310) 826-5555; fax 826-8670); 86 Beacon St., **Boston**, MA 02108-3304 (tel. (617) 523-0100 or 523-1083; fax 523-0511); Tower Place, Suite 1670, 3340 Peachtree Rd. NE, **Atlanta**, GA 30326 (tel. (404) 261-3313, or 261-3391; fax 262-2798); 1360 Post Oak Blvd., Suite 2480, **Houston**, TX 77056 (tel. (713) 840-7522; fax 840-0614); World Trade Center, 2 Canal St., Suite 2318, **New Orleans**, LA 70131 (tel. (504) 523-1167; fax 524-5610).

CYPRIOT

High Commissions or Embassies

Australia, 30 Beale Cr., Deakin-Canberra ACT 2600 (tel. (02) 6281 0832, fax 6281 0860).

U.K., 93 Park St., London W1Y 4ET (tel. (0171) 499 8272; fax 491 0691).

U.S., 2211 R St. NW, Washington, D.C. 20008 (tel. (202) 462-5772; fax 483-6710).

Consulates

Canada: Toronto, 365 Bloor St. E., Suite 1010, Box #43, **Toronto**, ON M4W 3L4 (tel. (416) 944-0998; fax 944-9149); 2930 Rue Edouard Mont Petit, Suite PH2, **Montréal**, QC H3T 1J7 (tel. (514) 735-7233).

▓ Passports

Citizens of the United States, Canada, the United Kingdom, Ireland, Australia, New Zealand, and South Africa all need valid **passports** to enter Greece and Cyprus, and to re-enter their own country. If you plan a long stay, you may want to register your passport with the nearest embassy or consulate.

Notify them or the police immediately if your passport is lost or stolen. Your consulate can issue you a new passport or temporary traveling papers—sometimes you can get your replacement within 24 hours, while other times it may take weeks to process, and it may be valid only for a limited time. To expedite its replacement, you will need to know all information previously recorded and show identification and proof of citizenship. Any visas stamped in your old passport will be irretrievably lost. In an emergency, ask for immediate temporary traveling papers that will permit you to re-enter your home country.

Your passport is a public document belonging to your nation's government; you may have to surrender it to a foreign government official, but if you don't get it back in a reasonable amount of time, inform your country's nearest mission. Before you leave, photocopy the page of your passport that contains your photograph, passport number, and other identifying information. Carry one photocopy in a safe place separate from your passport and leave another copy at home. These measures will help prove your citizenship and facilitate the issuing of a new passport if you lose the original. Consulates also recommend carrying an expired passport or an official copy of your birth certificate in a part of your baggage separate from other documents.

In general, apply through **passport offices** and **diplomatic missions** (Embassies and Consulates) overseas; in some countries, applications are also available at **post offices, travel agencies,** or **courthouses.** To expedite the application process, call ahead for an appointment. Allow up to three months; express service available for an additional charge in some countries. Parents usually apply for passports for under-age, unmarried children; in a few countries children may be included on the parent's passports.

Australia Apply at a **passport office** (located in Adelaide, Brisbane, Canberra City, Darwin, Hobart, Melbourne, Newcastle, Perth, and Sydney), a **post office,** or an **Australian diplomatic mission** overseas. For more information, call toll-free (in Australia) 13 12 32, or visit http://www.austemb.org. Adults AUS$120.

Canada Application forms available at all regional **passport offices, Canadian missions,** many **travel agencies,** and **Northern Stores** in northern communities; overseas, contact the nearest Canadian **embassy** or **consulate.** For additional info, contact the **Canadian Passport Office, Department of Foreign Affairs and International Trade,** in **Ottawa,** ON, K1A 0G3 (tel. (613) 994-3500; http://www.dfait-maeci.gc.ca/passport); in **Toronto,** (416) 973-3251; in **Vancouver,** (604) 775-6250; in **Montréal,** (514) 283-2152; travelers may also call (800) 567-6868 (24hr.). For further information, contact the **Consular Affairs Bureau** in Ottawa (tel. (800) 267-6788 (24hr.) or (613) 944-6788), or refer to the booklet *Bon Voyage, But...,* free at any passport office (or from **InfoCentre** at (800) 267-8376 within Canada, or (613) 944-4000). Adults CDN$60 plus CDN$25 consular fee.

Ireland Pick up an application at a local **Garda station** or request one from a **passport office** (Passport Express Service available) or write to either the **Department of Foreign Affairs,** Passport Office, Setanta Centre, Molesworth St., Dublin 2 (tel. (01) 671 1633; fax 671 1092), or the **Passport Office,** Irish Life Building, 1A South Mall, Cork (tel. (021) 272 525; fax 275 770). Adults IR£45.

New Zealand Applications available from **travel agents** and **Department of Internal Affairs Link Centres** in the main cities and towns; overseas, look to New Zealand **embassies, high commissions,** and **consulates.** Forward applications to the **Passport Office,** P.O. Box 10526, Wellington, New Zealand. Higher fees apply at nine overseas posts including London, Sydney, and Los Angeles, offering both standard and urgent services. For more information, hit http://www.govt.nz/agency_info/forms.html. Adults NZ$80.

South Africa Apply at any **Home Affairs Office** or **South African Mission.** Current passports less than 10 years old (counting from date of issuance) may be **renewed** for free until December 31, 1999. For further information, contact the nearest Department of Home Affairs Office. Adults SAR80.

United Kingdom Applications available at **passport offices** (in London, Liverpool, Newport, Peterborough, Glasgow, or Belfast), main **post offices,** many **travel agents,** and branches of **Lloyds Bank** and **Artac World Choice.** The London office offers same-day, walk-in rush service; arrive early. The **U.K. Passport Agency** can be reached by phone at (0990) 21 04 10. Adults UK£31.

United States Passports may be **renewed** by mail or in person for US$55. Apply for a **new** passport at any **federal or state courthouse** or **post office** authorized to accept passport applications, at a U.S. **embassy** or **consulate** abroad (given proof of citizenship), or at a **U.S. Passport Agency** (located in Boston, Chicago, Honolulu, Houston, Los Angeles, Miami, New Orleans, New York, Philadelphia, San Francisco, Seattle, Stamford, or Washington, D.C.; check the telephone directory or the local post office for addresses). For more information, contact **Passport Services,** 1425 K St., N.W., U.S. Department of State, Washington, D.C. 20524, or the U.S. Passport Information's **24-hour recorded message** (tel. (202) 647-0518). Citizens may wish to contact the **Overseas Citizens Services,** Room 4811, Department of State, Washington, D.C. 20520-4818 (tel. (202) 647-5225; fax 647-3000).

■ Visas

Citizens of the U.S., Canada, EU members, Australia, and New Zealand do not need to get a visa ahead of time to visit **Greece.** Non-EU members will be automatically granted leave for a three-month stay (not valid for employment). South Africans need a visa. Apply to stay longer at least 20 days prior to the three-month expiration date at the **Aliens Bureau,** 175 Alexandras Ave., Athens 11522 (tel. 011 30 642 3094), or check with a Greek embassy or consulate.

Bona fide tourists with valid passports from Australia, Canada, Great Britain, Ireland, New Zealand, and the U.S. do not need a visa to enter **Cyprus** for stays of up to 90 days; South Africans and Turks do need visas (fee: C£5). It is suggested that tourists wishing to stay longer first leave and then re-enter.

■ Customs

ENTERING

You'll need to let the authorities know if you're bringing devices of unusual value or currency above US$1000. The obvious objects of organic hazard (agricultural products, raw meat, etc.) are prohibited. Don't try to sell things in Greece and Cyprus; authorities expect tourists to leave with everything they brought except their money.

GOING HOME

Upon returning home, you must declare all articles you acquired abroad and pay a **duty** on the value of those articles that exceed the allowance established by your country's customs service. Goods and gifts purchased at **duty-free** shops abroad are not exempt from duty or sales tax at your point of return. If you plan on bringing back an exorbitant amount (e.g. more than 200 cigarettes) of anything (e.g. cash, goats, *ouzo*, classicists) contact the Customs Service of your home country. The usual laws of possession apply to such controlled substances as cigarettes, alcohol, or narcotics; foodstuffs and animal products usually must be declared upon arrival.

Australia Contact the Regional Director, Australian Customs Service, GPO Box 8, Sydney NSW 2001 (tel. (02) 9213 2000; fax 9213 4000), or visit http://www.customs.gov.au.

Canada Write to Canadian Customs, 2265 St. Laurent Blvd., Ottawa, ON K1G 4K3 (tel. (613) 993-0534), phone the 24hr. Automated Customs Information Service at (800) 461-9999, or visit Revenue Canada at http://www.revcan.ca.

Ireland Information available from The Revenue Commissioners, Dublin Castle (tel. (01) 679 27 77; fax 671 20 21; email taxes@iol.ie; http://www.revenue.ie), or The Collector of Customs and Excise, The Custom House, Dublin 1.

New Zealand Consult the New Zealand Customs, 50 Anzac Ave., Box 29, Auckland (tel. (09) 377 35 20; fax 309 29 78).

South Africa Consult the free pamphlet *South African Customs Information*, available in airports or from the Commissioner for Customs and Excise, Private Bag X47, Pretoria 0001 (tel. (12) 314 99 11; fax 328 64 78).

United Kingdom Contact Her Majesty's Customs and Excise, Custom House, Nettleton Road, Heathrow Airport, Hounslow, Middlesex TW6 2LA (tel. (0181) 910-3602/3566; fax 910-3765; http://www.open.gov.uk).

United States For more information, consult the brochure *Know Before You Go*, available from the U.S. Customs Service, Box 7407, Washington, D.C. 20044 (tel. (202) 927-6724), or visit the Web (http://www.customs.ustreas.gov).

■ Identity Documentation

When you travel, always be prepared to carry on your person two or more forms of identification, including at least one photo ID. A passport combined with a driver's license or birth certificate usually serves as adequate proof of your identity and citizenship. Many establishments, especially banks, require several IDs before cashing traveler's checks. Never carry all your forms of ID together, however; you risk being left entirely without ID in the event of theft or loss. Also bring several extra passport-size photos that you can attach to the sundry IDs or railpasses you will amass, and make several photocopies of the IDs you carry.

YOUTH, STUDENT, & TEACHER IDENTIFICATION

The **International Student Identity Card (ISIC)** is a widely accepted form of student identification. Flashing this card can procure you discounts for sights, theaters, museums, accommodations, meals, train, ferry, bus, and airplane transportation, and other services. Ask about discounts even when none are advertised. It also provides insurance benefits, including US$100 per day of in-hospital sickness for a maximum of 60 days, and US$3000 accident-related medical reimbursement for each accident (see **Insurance,** p. 18). In addition, cardholders have access to a toll-free 24hr. ISIC helpline whose multilingual staff can provide assistance in medical, legal, and financial emergencies overseas (tel. (800) 626-2427 in the U.S. and Canada; elsewhere call collect (44) 181 666 9025).

Many student travel agencies around the world issue ISICs (see **Travel Organizations,** p. 1); it's also available via the web (http://www.ciee.org/idcards/index.htm) in the U.S. When you apply for the card, request a copy of the *International Student Identity Card Handbook,* which lists by country some of the available discounts. The card is valid from September to December of the following year and costs US$20, CDN$15, or AUS$15. Because of the proliferation of phony ISICs, many airlines and some other services require additional proof of student identity, such as a signed letter from the registrar attesting to your student status that is stamped with the school seal or your school ID card. The **International Teacher Identity Card (ITIC)** offers the same insurance coverage, and similar but limited discounts. The fee is US$20, UK£5, or AUS$13. For more information on these cards, consult the organization's website (http://www.istc.org; email isicinfo@istc.org).

Federation of International Youth Travel Organizations (FIYTO) issues a discount card to travelers who are under 26 but not students, known as the **GO25 Card,** offering many of the same benefits as the ISIC. Most organizations that sell the ISIC also sell the GO25 Card (http://www.go25.org). To apply, you need a passport, valid driver's license, or copy of a birth certificate, as well as a passport-sized photo with your name printed on the back. The fee is US$20. Information is available on the web at http://www.ciee.org, or through travel agencies (see **Travel Organizations,** p. 3).

■ Driving Permits and Car Insurance

If you plan to drive a car while in Greece, you must, according to law, have an **International Driving Permit (IDP)**. You can usually rent a moped with a valid national license from your home country. Although some car rental agencies don't require the permit, it may be a good idea to get an IDP anyway, in case you're in a situation (e.g. an accident or stranded in a smaller town) where the police do not know English.

Your IDP, valid for one year, must be issued in your own country before you depart; AAA affiliates cannot issue IDPs valid in their own country. You must be 18 years old to receive the IDP. A valid driver's license from your home country must always accompany the IDP. An application for an IDP usually needs to include one or two photos, a current local license, an additional form of identification, and a fee.

Australia Contact the local **Royal Automobile Club (RAC)**, or, in NSW or the ACT, the **National Royal Motorist Association (NRMA)**. (RAC tel. (08) 9421 4271; fax (08) 9221 1887; http://www.rac.com.au). AUS$15.

Canada Contact a **Canadian Automobile Association (CAA)** branch office in Canada. CAA, 1145 Hunt Club Rd., Suite 200, K1V 0Y3 Canada. (tel. (613) 247-0117, ext. 2025; fax (613) 247-0118; http://www.caa.ca). CDN$10.

Ireland Drop into the nearest **Automobile Association (AA)** office or phone (tel. (1) 283 3555; fax 283 3660) for a postal application form. IR£4.

New Zealand Contact your local **Automobile Association (AA),** or the main office at P.O. Box 5, Auckland (tel. (9) 377 4660; fax 302 2037); procedural information at http://www.nzaa.co.nz. Add NZ$2 return postage if mailed abroad. NZ$8.

South Africa Visit your local **Automobile Association of South Africa** office. For further information call (11) 799 1000, fax 799 1010, or write P.O. Box 596, 2000 Johannesburg. SAR28.50.

U.K. Visit your local **AA Shop,** call (1256) 49 39 32 (if abroad, fax (44-1256) 460 750), or write to AA 5 Star Post Link, Freepost, Copenhagen Court, 8 New Street, Basingstroke RG21 7BA, for a postal application (allow 2-3 weeks). For further information, call (44) 0990 448 866 or visit http://www.theaa.co.uk/travel. UK£4.

U.S. Contact the **American Automobile Association (AAA)**. Travel Agency Services Department, 1000 AAA Drive (mail stop 28), Heathrow, FL 32746 (tel. (407) 444-4245; fax 444-4247). You do not have to be a member of AAA. US$10.

Most credit cards cover standard **insurance.** If you rent, lease, or borrow a car, you will need a **green card,** or **International Insurance Certificate,** to prove that you have liability insurance. It is available through some travel agencies, at border crossings, or through the car rental agency (most include coverage in their prices). Even if your insurance applies abroad, you will need a green card to prove it to foreign officials.

SAFETY, SECURITY, AND FINANCIAL FORESIGHT

■ Medical Preparations

In Greece, dial 166 for **first aid,** 106 for the local **hospital.** See **Emergencies,** p. 33.

Greece and Cyprus require few medical preparations. Greece requires no specific **inoculations,** but you may want to make sure your tetanus, hepatitis, rabies, and polio vaccinations are up to date. Carry up-to-date, legible prescriptions or a statement from your doctor, especially if you use insulin, a syringe, or a narcotic. While traveling, be sure to keep all medication with you in your carry-on luggage. Be aware that all medications containing **codeine** are banned in Greece.

ESSENTIALS

If you wear glasses or contact lenses, carry a copy of your prescription and pair of glasses. If you heat-sterilize your **contact lenses,** you should consider switching temporarily to a chemical system, as your heater will not work properly without a converter, and the availability of equivalent devices in Greece is slim. **Allergy** sufferers should find out if their conditions are likely to be aggravated in the regions they plan to visit, and obtain a full supply of any necessary medication before the trip, since matching a prescription to a foreign equivalent is not always easy, safe, or possible.

Those with serious medical conditions (e.g., diabetes, allergies to antibiotics, epilepsy, heart conditions) may want to obtain a stainless steel **Medic Alert** identification tag (US$35 the first year, and $15 annually thereafter), which identifies the disease and gives a 24-hour collect-call information number. Contact Medic Alert at (800) 825-3785, or write to Medic Alert Foundation, 2323 Colorado Ave., Turlock, CA 95382. Diabetics can contact the **American Diabetes Association,** 1660 Duke St., Alexandria, VA 22314 (tel. (800) 232-3472), to receive copies of the article "Travel and Diabetes" and a diabetic ID card, which carries messages in 18 languages explaining the carrier's diabetic status.

Before you leave, write in your passport the names of any people you wish to be contacted in case of a medical emergency, and also list any allergies or medical conditions you would want doctors to be aware of. You may choose to assemble a compact **first-aid kit** (containing such things as bandages, aspirin or other pain killer, moleskin, a decongestant for colds, motion sickness remedy, medicine for diarrhea or stomach problems, sunscreen, insect repellent, and burn ointment). However, **pharmacies** *(farmakeia)* are ubiquitous and there's one open 24 hours in nearly every town, so you will likely have access to remedies and advice for any more serious complaints near at hand. Pharmacies in Greece and Cyprus have sophisticated staff with more prescribing power than you may be accustomed to elsewhere.

REGION-SPECIFIC HEALTH DATA RESOURCES

United States Center for Disease Control and Prevention (based in Atlanta, GA), maintains an international fax information service for travelers; call 1-888-232-3299. CDC information is also found at http://www.cdc.gov. The CDC publishes "Health Information for International Travelers" (US$20), disease, immunization, and general health advice; send a check or money order to the Superintendent of Documents, U.S. Government Printing Office, P.O. Box 371954, Pittsburgh, PA, 15250-7954, or order by phone (tel. (202) 512-1800) with a credit card.

United States State Department compiles Consular Information Sheets on health, entry requirements, and other issues. See http://travel.state.gov.

Overseas Citizens' Services (tel. (202) 647-5225; fax 647-3000) provides quick information on travel warnings. Contact them by phone or fax, or send a self-addressed, stamped envelope to the Overseas Citizens' Services, Bureau of Consular Affairs, #4811, U.S. Department of State, Washington, D.C. 20520.

American Red Cross provides general health information, and publishes a First-Aid and Safety Handbook (US$5); write or call The American Red Cross, 285 Columbus Ave., Boston, MA 02116-5114 (tel. (800) 564-1234; M-F 8:30am-4:30pm).

TRAVELERS' MEDICAL SUPPORT SERVICES

Global Emergency Medical Services (GEMS) has products called *MedPass* that provide 24-hour international medical assistance and support. For more information call (800) 860-1111 (8:30am-5:30pm); fax (770) 475-0058, or write 2001 Westside Drive, #120, Alpharetta, GA 30201.

International Association for Medical Assistance to Travelers (IAMAT) offers a membership ID card, a directory of English-speaking doctors around the world who treat members for a set fee schedule, and detailed charts on immunization requirements, various tropical diseases, climate, and sanitation. Membership is free, though donations for further research are encouraged. Contact chapters in the **U.S.,** 417 Center St., Lewiston, NY 14092 (tel. (716) 754-4883, 8am-4pm/EST; fax (519) 836-3412; email iamat@sentex.net; http://www.sentex.net/~iamat); **Can-**

ada, 40 Regal Road, Guelph, ON N1K 1B5 (tel. (519) 836-0102) or 1287 St. Clair Avenue West, Toronto, ON M6E 1B8 (tel. (416) 652-0137; fax (519) 836-3412); or **New Zealand,** P.O. Box 5049, Christchurch 5.

Avoid purchasing unnecessary travel insurance, but if your regular insurance policy does not cover travel abroad, you may wish to purchase some additional coverage. With the exception of Medicare, most health insurance plans cover members' medical emergencies abroad; check with your carrier to be sure (see **Insurance,** p.30).

■ Personal Safety

There is no sure-fire set of precautions that will protect you from all situations you might encounter when you travel. Trust your instincts: if you'd feel better somewhere else, move on.

Always carry extra money for a phone call, bus, or taxi. A self-defense course will give you more concrete ways to react to different types of aggression. **Impact, Prepare,** and **Model Mugging** can refer you to local self-defense courses in the United States (tel. (800) 345-KICK), Vancouver, BC Canada (tel. (604) 878-3838), and Zurich, Switzerland (tel. 411 261 2423). Prices range from US$50-500. Women's and men's courses are offered.

■ Specific Concerns

WOMEN TRAVELERS

Women traveling in Greece are likely to experience verbal harassment, which can be just as intimidating as physical abuse. Look as if you know where you're going (even when you don't) and consider approaching women or couples for directions if you're lost or feel uncomfortable. Your best answer to verbal harassment is no answer at all (a reaction is what the harasser wants). **Dress conservatively,** especially in rural areas. If you spend time in cities, you may be harassed no matter how you're dressed. In crowds, you may be pinched or squeezed by oversexed slimeballs. Wearing a conspicuous **wedding band** may help prevent such incidents.

If unwanted attention becomes physical, you should scream "vo-EE-thee-ah" (help) or "as-te-no-MEE-ah" (police). Make getting away your first priority. Don't hesitate to seek out a police officer or a passerby if you are being harassed. A **Model Mugging** course will not only prepare you for a potential mugging, but will also raise your confidence and your awareness of your surroundings (see **Personal Safety,** p. 13).

Consider staying in hostels which offer rooms that lock from the inside or in religious organizations that offer rooms for women only. Communal showers in some hostels are safer than others; check them before settling in. Stick to centrally located accommodations and **avoid solitary late-night treks** or metro rides. **Hitching** is never safe for lone women, or even for women traveling together. Choose train compartments occupied by other women or couples; ask the conductor to put together a women-only compartment if he or she doesn't offer to do so first.

Women face unique **health concerns** when traveling. Women traveling in unsanitary conditions are vulnerable to **urinary tract and bladder infections,** diseases which cause a burning sensation and painful and sometimes frequent urination. Drink tons of vitamin-C-rich juice, plenty of clean water, and urinate frequently, especially right after intercourse. Untreated, these infections can lead to kidney infections, sterility, and even death. If symptoms persist, see a doctor. If you often develop **vaginal yeast infections,** take along enough over-the-counter medicine, as treatments may not be readily available in Greece and Cyprus. Women may also be more susceptible to **vaginal thrush** and **cystitis,** two treatable but uncomfortable illnesses that are likely to flare up in hot and humid climates. Wearing loosely fitting clothing and cotton underwear may help. **Tampons** and **pads** are sometimes hard to find when traveling;

pack your favorite brands. For more health tips, refer to the women's health guide *Our Bodies, Our Selves* (published by the Boston Women's Health Collective.)

Reliable contraceptive devices may be difficult to find while traveling. Women on **the pill** should bring enough to allow for possible loss or extended stays, as well as a prescription; those who use a **diaphragm** should bring enough **contraceptive jelly. Condoms** are available in nearly all pharmacies, though brands and quality vary.

Women overseas who want an **abortion** should contact the **National Abortion Federation Hotline,** 1775 Massachusetts Ave. NW, Washington, D.C. 20036 (tel. (800) 772-9100; open M-F 9:30am-12:30pm and 1:30-5:30pm), for information on the availability of and techniques for abortion in other countries. For information on contraception, condoms, and abortion worldwide, contact the **International Planned Parenthood Federation,** European Regional Office, Regent's College Inner Circle, Regent's Park, London NW1 4NS (tel. (0171) 487 7900; fax (0171) 487 7950).

Other resources that might be helpful include:

A Journey of One's Own: Uncommon Advice for the Independent Woman Traveler, by Thalia Zepatos, (US$17). Interesting and full of good advice, with a bibliography of books and resources.

Active Women Vacation Guide, by Evelyn Kay (US$17.95; shipping is free for *Let's Go* readers). Includes listings of 1,000 trips worldwide offered by travel companies for active women and true stories of women's traveling adventures. Blue Panda Publications, 3031 Fifth St., Boulder, CO 80304 (tel. (303) 449 8474; fax 449 7525).

Adventures in Good Company: The Complete Guide to Women's Tours and Outdoor Trips, on group travel by the same author (US$17), is available from The Eighth Mountain Press, 624 Southeast 29th Ave., Portland, OR 97214 (tel. (503) 233-3936; fax 233-0774; email soapston@teleport.com).

Handbook For Women Travelers, by Maggie and Gemma Moss (UK£9). Encyclopedic and well-written. Available from Piatkus Books, 5 Windmill St., London W1P 1HF (tel. (0171) 631 07 10).

OLDER TRAVELERS

Senior citizens are eligible for a wide range of discounts on transportation, entertainment, restaurants, and accommodations. If you don't see a seniors price listed, ask. Agencies for senior group travel (like **Eldertreks,** 597 Markham St., Toronto, ON, Canada, M6G 2L7; tel. (800) 741-7956 or (416) 588-5000; fax 588-9839; email passages@inforamp.net; http://www.eldertreks.com) are growing in popularity.

BISEXUAL, GAY, AND LESBIAN TRAVELERS

Greeks and Cypriots have a relatively tolerant attitude toward homosexuality. Though legal, homosexuality as a declared lifestyle is still socially frowned upon.

In Greece, Athens in particular offers a variety of gay bars, clubs, and hotels. For further information, consult the multilingual **Greek Gay Guide,** TΘ 4228, Athens 10210 (tel. (01) 381 5249; English speaker M-F 7-9pm). The islands of Hydra, Lesbos, Paros, Rhodes, and Mykonos also offer gay and lesbian resorts, hotels, bars, and clubs.

Giovanni's Room, 345 S. 12th St., Philadelphia, PA 19107 (tel. (215) 923-2960; fax 923-0813; email giophilp@netaxs.com). An international feminist, lesbian, and gay bookstore with mail-order service that carries the publications listed here; they accept email orders as well.

International Gay and Lesbian Travel Association, 4331 N. Federal Hwy., Suite 304, Fort Lauderdale, FL 33308 (tel. (954) 776-2626 or (800) 448-8550; fax (954) 776-3303; email IGLTA@aol.com; http://www.iglta.org). An organization of over 1350 companies serving gay and lesbian travelers worldwide. Call for lists of travel agents, accommodations, and events.

Spartacus International Gay Guides (US$32.95), published by Bruno Gmunder, Verlag GMBH, Leuschnerdamm 31, 10999 Berlin, Germany (tel. (49) 030 615 0030; fax 030 615 9007; email bgvtravel@aol.com). Lists bars, restaurants, hotels, and bookstores catering to gays. Available from Lambda Rising, 1625 Connecticut Ave. NW, Washington D.C., 20009-1013 (tel. (202) 462-6969).

Women Going Places is a women's travel and resource guide geared toward lesbians, which emphasizes women-owned enterprises. Advice appropriate for all women. US$15 from Inland Book Company, 1436 W. Randolph St. Chicago, IL 60607 (tel. (800) 243-0138; fax (800) 334-3892), or a local bookstore.

DISABLED TRAVELERS

Greece and Cyprus are only slowly beginning to respond to the needs of travelers with disabilities; those with severe physical disabilities will run into difficulty. Even the most renowned sights, including the Acropolis, are not wheelchair accessible. A few hotels, train stations, and airports have recently installed facilities for the disabled; most of the archaeological sites throughout the region are still not wheelchair accessible. However, some cruise ships that sail the Greek islands are equipped to accommodate those with disabilities, and special air transportation is available aboard Olympic Airways to many of the larger islands.

Facts on File, 11 Penn Plaza, 15th Fl., New York, NY 10001 (tel. (212) 967-8800). Publishers of *Resource Directory for the Disabled,* a reference guide for travelers with disabilities (US$45 plus shipping). Available at bookstores or by mail order.

Moss Rehab Hospital Travel Information Service (tel. (215) 456-9600, TDD (215) 456-9602). A telephone information resource center on international travel accessibility and other travel-related concerns for those with disabilities.

Directions Unlimited, 720 N. Bedford Rd., Bedford Hills, NY 10507 (tel. (800) 533-5343; in NY (914) 241-1700; fax (914) 241-0243), arranges individual and group tours and cruises for the physically disabled. Group tours for blind travelers.

Flying Wheels Travel Service, 143 W. Bridge St., Owatonne, MN 55060 (tel. (800) 535-6790; fax 451-1685). Arranges trips in the U.S. and abroad for groups and individuals in wheelchairs or with other sorts of limited mobility.

The Guided Tour Inc., Elkins Park House, 114B, 7900 Old York Rd., Elkins Park, PA 19027 (tel. (800) 783-5841 or (215) 782-1370; fax 635-2637). Programs for those with developmental and physical challenges and those requiring renal dialysis.

DIETARY CONCERNS

Vegetarians should have no problem finding suitable cuisine. Most restaurants have vegetarian selections on their menus, and some cater specifically to vegetarians. *Let's Go: Greece* often notes restaurants with good vegetarian selections in city listings. Vegetarian dishes in Greece and Cyprus include succulent fruits, colorful salads, tasty breads, *fasolia* (beans), *spanakopita* (spinach-filled pastry), and *tyropitakia* (cheese-filled pastry). In Cyprus, *meze* appetizers are plentiful. In summer, fresh produce abounds in the outdoor markets; vegetarians find plenty of fresh vegetables, fruits, and interesting cheeses.

In Greece or Cyprus, travelers who keep **kosher** will find synagogues or kosher restaurants difficult to find. Strict observers should consider preparing their own food.

The International Vegetarian Travel Guide was last published in 1991 (UK£2). Order back copies from the Vegetarian Society of the UK (VSUK), Parkdale, Dunham Rd., Altringham, Cheshire WA14 4QG (tel. (0161) 928 0793). VSUK also publishes other titles, including *The European Vegetarian Guide to Hotels and Restaurants.* Call or send a self-addressed, stamped envelope for a listing.

The Jewish Travel Guide lists synagogues, kosher restaurants, and Jewish institutions in over 80 countries. Available through Vallentine Mitchell Publishers, Newbury House 890-900, Eastern Ave., Newbury Park, Ilford, Essex, U.K. IG2 7HH (tel. (0181) 599 8866; fax 599 0984); or in the U.S. from Sepher-Hermon Press, 1265 46th St., Brooklyn, NY 11219 (tel. and fax (718) 972 9010; US$15 plus shipping).

TRAVELERS WITH CHILDREN

Greeks and Cypriots adore children. Expect a stream of compliments, advice, candy, and substantial discounts on transportation throughout Greece or Cyprus. Children under two generally fly for 10% of the adult airfare on international flights (this does not necessarily include a seat); children from two to 11 are discounted 25%. Family vacations will be most enjoyable if you slow your pace and plan ahead. Be sure that your child carries some sort of ID in case of an emergency or he or she gets lost, and arrange a reunion spot in case of separation when sight-seeing.

Backpacking with Babies and Small Children (US$9.95). Published by Wilderness Press, 2440 Bancroft Way, Berkeley, CA 94704 (tel. (800) 443-7227 or (510) 843-8080; fax 548-1355; email wpress@ix.netcom.com; http://wildernesspress.com).
Travel with Children, by Maureen Wheeler (US$12, postage US$2.50). Published by Lonely Planet Publications, 150 Linden St., Oakland, CA 94607 (tel. (800) 275-8555 or (510) 893-8555, fax 893-8563; email info@lonelyplanet.com; http://www.lonelyplanet.com). Also at P.O. Box 617, Hawthorn, Victoria 3122, Australia.

TRAVELING ALONE

There are many benefits to traveling alone, among them greater independence and challenge. Without distraction, you can write a great travel log, in the grand tradition of Henry Miller, Lawrence Durrell, and Don DeLillo. As a lone traveler, you have greater opportunity to meet and interact with natives. On the other hand, you may also be a target for robbery and harassment. Lone travelers need to be well-organized and look confident at all times. Maintain regular contact with someone at home who knows your itinerary. Some organizations can find travel companions for solo travelers.

American International Homestays, P.O. Box 1754, Nederland, CO 80466 (tel. (303) 642-3088 or (800) 876-2048). Lodgings with English-speaking host families.
Connecting: News for Solo Travelers, P.O. Box 29088, 1996 W. Broadway, Vancouver, BC V6J 5C2, Canada (tel. (604) 737-7791 or (800) 557-1757; http://www.travel-wise.com/solo). Bimonthly newsletter with member reports, solo tips, travel companion ads, and advice and lodging exchanges. Membership US$25.
Traveling On Your Own, by Eleanor Berman (US$13). Lists information resources for "singles" (old and young) and single parents. Write to Crown Publishers, Inc., 201 East 50th St., New York, NY 10022 (tel. (212) 751-2600).

■ Money Matters

CURRENCY AND EXCHANGE

Before leaving home, exchange US$50 or so for Greek or Cypriot currency. You'll pay a higher exchange rate but will save time and exasperation, especially if you arrive in Greece or Cyprus when the banks are closed. When exchanging currency, you'll usually lose money due to commissions and high exchange rates; exchange in fairly large sums in order to minimize the loss.

> A note on prices: throughout the guide, prices quoted were effective in the summer of 1998. Since inflation and exchange rates fluctuate considerably, be advised that listed prices could rise by an additional 10-30% by 1999.

Greek *drachmes* are issued in both paper notes (100, 200, 500, 1000, 5000, and 10,000dr) and coins (5, 10, 20, 50, and 100dr). If you're carrying more than US$1000 in cash when you enter Greece, you must declare it upon entry in order to export it legally (this does not apply to traveler's checks). You can bring up to US$445 worth of *drachmes* into Greece. In addition, no more than 20,000dr can be taken out of the country when you leave. It is not difficult to exchange money in Greece. Commission-free ATMs are located in most major cities.

US$1 = 303 Greek Drachmes (dr)	**100dr = US$0.33**
CDN$1 = 206dr	**100dr = CDN$0.49**
UK£1 = 497dr	**100dr = UK£0.20**
IR£1 = 421dr	**100dr = IR£0.24**
AUS$1 = 189dr	**100dr = AUS$0.53**
NZ$1 = 158dr	**100dr = NZ$0.63**

SAR1 = 81dr   100 dr= SAR1.24
TL 100,000 = 113dr   100dr = 88,472TL
C£1 = 572dr   100dr = C£0.18

The main unit of currency in the Republic of Cyprus is the pound (£), which is divided into 100 cents. Coins come in 1, 2, 5, 10, 20, and 50 cent sizes; bank notes in denominations of £1, 5, 10, and 20. Cyprus imposes no limit on the amount of foreign currency that may be imported upon entering the country, but amounts in excess of US$1000 should be declared on Customs form D (NR). No more than £50 in Cypriot currency may be brought into or taken out of the country.

US$1 = C£0.52 (Cypriot Pounds)	**C£1 = US$1.90**
CDN$1 = C£0.34	**C£1 = CDN$2.96**
UK£1 = C£0.87	**C£1 = UK£1.14**
IR£1 = C£0.74	**C£1 = IR£1.35**
AUS$1 = C£0.30	**C£1 = AUS$3.36**
NZ$1 = C£0.26	**C£1 = NZ$3.85**
SAR1 = C£0.14	**C£1 = SAR7.17**
100GRdr = C£0.17	**C£1 = 418GRdr**
TL10,000 = C£0.02	**C£1 = TL533,943**

TRAVELER'S CHECKS

Traveler's checks are one of the safest and least troublesome means of carrying funds. They are widely accepted in major tourist destinations in Greece. Some agencies or banks provide services in addition to the usual refund, such as toll-free refund hotlines (in the countries you're visiting), emergency message services, and stolen credit card assistance when you buy your checks. (Members of the American Automobile Association, and some banks and credit unions, can get American Express checks commission-free; see **Driving Permits and Car Insurance,** p. 11). **American Express** and **Visa** are the most widely recognized.

Remember to keep your check receipts separate from your checks and store them in a safe place or with a traveling companion. Record check numbers when you cash them, and leave a list of check numbers with someone at home. Ask for a list of refund centers when you buy your checks. Never countersign your checks until you are ready to cash them, and always bring your passport with you when you plan to use the checks. Contact one of the major agencies listed below for more information.

American Express: Call (800) 25 19 02 in **Australia;** in **New Zealand** (0800) 44 10 68; in the **U.K.** (0800) 52 13 13; in the **U.S. and Canada** (800) 221-7282. Elsewhere, call **U.S.** collect (801) 964-6665. Cardmembers can order by phone (tel. (800) ORDER-TC (673-3782)). Online offices (http://www.acxp.com). 1-4% fee.

Citicorp: Call (800) 645-6556 in the U.S. and Canada; in Europe, the Middle East, or Africa (44) 171 508 7007; elsewhere call U.S. collect (813) 623-1709. 1-2% fee.

Thomas Cook MasterCard or Visa: from the U.S., Canada, or Caribbean call (800) 223-7373; from the U.K. call (0800) 622 101 free or (1733) 318 950 collect; elsewhere call (44) 1733 318 950 collect. 2% fee. **Capital Foreign Exchange** (see **Currency and Exchange,** p. 16) also sells Thomas Cook traveler's checks.

Visa: Call (800) 227-6811 in the U.S.; in the U.K. (0800) 895 078; from anywhere else in the world call (44) 1733 318 949 collect.

CREDIT CARDS

Credit cards are widely accepted in larger businesses in major tourist destinations in Greece. Major credit cards—**MasterCard** and **Visa** are the most often welcomed—can be used to extract cash advances from associated banks and teller machines in local currency at the wholesale exchange rate, which is generally 5% better than the retail rate used by banks. All such ATM transactions require a **Personal Identification Number (PIN),** which credit cards in the United States do not always carry; you must ask your credit card company for a PIN before you leave.

Credit cards are also valuable in an emergency—an unexpected hospital bill, ticket home, or loss of traveler's checks—and may offer insurance or emergency assistance.

American Express (tel. (800) 843-2273) has a US$55 annual fee, but offers a number of services: cashing personal checks at AmEx offices; Express Travel Service providing assistance in changing reservations, baggage loss and flight insurance, sending mailgrams and international cables, and holding your mail at an AmEx office; and a 24-hour hotline with medical and legal assistance in emergencies (tel. (800) 554-2639 in U.S. and Canada; U.S. collect (202) 554-2639 elsewhere).

Visa (Telephone Assistance Center (800) 336-8472) and **MasterCard** are issued in cooperation with individual banks and other agencies; ask about additional services.

CASH CARDS

Cash cards (a.k.a. ATM cards) are perhaps the easiest method of getting cash in Greece; *Let's Go: Greece* lists ATM machines in all but the tiniest towns. You can probably access your own personal bank account whenever you need money. Do some research before relying too heavily on automation, and memorize your PIN code. Check with your bank at home before you leave. If your PIN is longer than four digits, ask your bank whether the first four digits will work, or whether you need a new number. ATMs get the same wholesale exchange rate as credit cards.

There is often a limit to the amount of money you can withdraw per day (usually about US$500). Computer networks sometimes fail. Keep all receipts—even if an ATM won't give you your cash, it may register a withdrawal on your next statement. Many ATMs are outdoors; be cautious and aware of your surroundings.

The two major international money networks are **Cirrus** (U.S. tel. (800) 4-CIRRUS (424-7787)) and **PLUS** (U.S. tel. (800) 843-7587 or http://www.visa.com). Cirrus charges US$1-5 per transaction to withdraw internationally.

GETTING MONEY FROM HOME

An **American Express** card allows its cardholders to withdraw cash from their checking accounts at any of its major offices or representatives' offices (up to US$1000 every 21 days); call U.S. (800) 227-4669. Elsewhere call collect (336) 668 5041.

Money can be wired abroad through international money transfer services operated by **Western Union** (tel. (800) 325-6000); money may be available in an hour. Some people also choose to send money abroad in cash via **Federal Express** to avoid transmission fees and taxes. FedEx is reasonably reliable; however, this method may be illegal, it involves an element of risk, and it requires that you remain at a legitimate address for a day or two to wait for the money's arrival. In general, it may be better to swallow the cost of wire transmission and preserve your peace of mind.

In emergencies, U.S. citizens can have money sent via the State Department's **Overseas Citizens Service, American Citizens Services,** Consular Affairs, Room 4811, U.S. Department of State, Washington, D.C. 20520 (tel. (202) 647-5225; nights, Sundays, and holidays 647-4000; fax (on demand only) 647-3000; email ca@his.com; http://travel.state.gov on the web).

■ Insurance

Remember that insurance companies may have time limits on filing for reimbursement, and usually require a copy of the police report for thefts and doctor's statements and receipts for medical expenses before they will honor a claim. Always carry policy numbers and proof of insurance. You may consider buying extra **travel insurance**, which generally covers medical problems, property loss, itinerary changes, and emergency evacuation. Beware of buying unnecessary travel coverage—your regular insurance policies may well extend to travel-related medical problems and property loss with the exception of items of unusual value, and travel insurance may only be useful if the cost of potential itinerary changes is greater than you can absorb.

Although **medical insurance** (especially university policies) often covers costs incurred abroad, **Medicare's** very limited "foreign travel" coverage is valid only in Canada and Mexico, not in Greece. Canadians should check with the provincial Ministry of Health or Health Plan Headquarters for details about the extent of their coverage. **Homeowners' insurance** (or your family's coverage) often covers theft of belongings and travel documents (to a limited extent) during travel.

ISIC and **ITIC** provide basic insurance benefits, including US$100 per day of in-hospital sickness for a maximum of 60 days, and US$3000 of accident-related medical reimbursement (see **Youth, Student, and Teacher Identification, p. 9**). **Council** and **STA** offer a range of supplement plans, with options covering medical treatment and hospitalization, accidents, baggage loss, and even charter flights missed due to illness (see p. 3). Most **American Express** cardholders receive car rental insurance (collision and theft, but not liability) and ground travel accident coverage of US$100,000 on flights purchased with the card. For customer service, call (800) 528-4800.

INSURANCE COMPANIES

Check with each insurance carrier for specific restrictions and policies. Most of the carriers listed below have 24-hour hotlines.

Access America, 6600 West Broad St., P.O. Box 11188, Richmond, VA 23230 (tel. (800) 284-8300; fax (804) 673-1491). Covers trip cancellation/interruption, on-the-spot hospital admittance costs, emergency medical evacuation, sickness, and baggage loss. 24hr. hotline (if abroad, call the hotline collect at (804) 673-1159 or (800) 654-1908).

Avi International, 30, rue de Mogador, 75009 Paris, France (tel. 33 (0) 1 44 63 51 86; fax 40 82 90 35), caters to the youth traveler, covering emergency travel expenses, medical/accident, dental, liability, and baggage loss. 24hr. hotline.

The Berkely Group/Carefree Travel Insurance, 100 Garden City Plaza, P.O. Box 9366, Garden City, NY 11530-9366 (tel. (800) 323-3149 or (516) 294-0220; fax (516) 294-1095; info@berkely.com; http://www.berkely.com). Offers two comprehensive packages and a trip cancellation/interruption deal. 24-hr. hotline.

Campus Travel, 105/106 St. Aldates, Oxford OXI IDD (tel. 01865 25 80 00; fax 01865 79 23 78). Per-trip packages to those with ISIC cards or under 35. 24hr. hotline.

GETTING THERE

Greece and Cyprus are accessible from Europe and Middle Eastern countries by airplane or boat—Greece, also by road and rail. Greece borders Albania, Bulgaria, Turkey, and the Former Yugoslav Republic of Macedonia. Cyprus lies 64km from Turkey, 160km from Israel and Lebanon, and 480km from the nearest Greek island.

■ Budget Travel Agencies

Students and people under 26 ("youth") qualify for enticing reduced airfares. These are rarely available from airlines or travel agents, but instead from student travel agencies which negotiate special reduced-rate bulk purchase with the airlines, then resell them to the youth market. Return-date change fees also tend to be low (around US$35 per segment through Council or Let's Go Travel). Most flights are on major airlines, though in peak season some agencies may sell seats on less reliable chartered aircraft. Student travel agencies can also help non-students and people over 26, but probably won't be able to get the same low fares.

Let's Go Travel, Harvard Student Agencies, 17 Holyoke St., Cambridge, MA 02138 (tel. (617) 495-9649; fax 495-7956; email travel@hsa.net; http://hsa.net/travel). Railpasses, HI-AYH memberships, ISICs, ITICs, FIYTO cards, guidebooks (including every *Let's Go*), maps, bargain flights, and a complete line of budget travel gear. All items available by mail; call or write for a catalogue.

Council Travel (http://www.ciee.org/travel/index.htm), a division of **CIEE** (see p. 3), specializes in youth and budget travel, offering discount airfares and railpasses, hosteling cards, low-cost accommodations, guidebooks, budget tours, travel gear, and ISIC, youth GO25, and ITIC identity cards (see p. 9). U.S. offices include: Emory Village, 1561 N. Decatur Rd., **Atlanta,** GA 30307 (tel. (404) 377-9997); 2000 Guadalupe, **Austin,** TX 78705 (tel. (512) 472-4931); 273 Newbury St., **Boston,** MA 02116 (tel. (617) 266-1926); 1138 13th St., **Boulder,** CO 80302 (tel. (303) 447-8101); 1153 N. Dearborn, **Chicago,** IL 60610 (tel. (312) 951-0585); 10904 Lindbrook Dr., **Los Angeles,** CA 90024 (tel. (310) 208-3551); 1501 University Ave. SE #300, **New York,** NY 10017 (tel. (212) 822-2700); 953 Garnet Ave., **San Diego,** CA 92109 (tel. (619) 270-6401); 530 Bush St., **San Francisco,** CA 94108 (tel. (415) 421-3473); 1314 NE 43rd St. #210, **Seattle,** WA 98105 (tel. (206) 632-2448); 3300 M St. NW, **Washington, D.C.** 20007 (tel. (202) 337-6464). **For U.S. cities not listed,** call 800-2-COUNCIL (226-8624). Also 28A Poland St. (Oxford Circus), **London,** W1V 3DB (tel. (0171) 287 3337), **Paris** (146 55 55 65), and **Munich** (089 39 50 22).

　　STA Travel, 6560 Scottsdale Rd. #F100, Scottsdale, AZ 85253 (tel. (800) 777-0112 nationwide; fax (602) 922-0793; http://sta-travel.com). A student and youth travel organization with over 150 offices worldwide offering discount airfares for young travelers, railpasses, accommodations, tours, insurance, and ISICs. In the U.S., offices include: 297 Newbury St., **Boston,** MA 02115 (tel. (617) 266-6014); 429 S. Dearborn St., **Chicago,** IL 60605 (tel. (312) 786-9050); 7202 Melrose Ave., **Los Angeles,** CA 90046 (tel. (213) 934-8722); 10 Downing St., Ste. G, **New York,** NY 10003 (tel. (212) 627-3111); 4341 University Way NE, **Seattle,** WA 98105 (tel. (206) 633-5000); 2401 Pennsylvania Ave., **Washington, D.C.** 20037 (tel. (202) 887-0912); 51 Grant Ave., **San Francisco,** CA 94108 (tel. (415) 391-8407); **Miami,** FL 33133 (tel. (305) 461-3444). Also at 6 Wrights Ln., **London** W8 6TA (tel. (0171) 938 47 11 for North American travel); 10 High St., **Auckland** (tel. (09) 309 97 23); 222 Faraday St., **Melbourne** VIC 3050 (tel. (03) 349 69 11).

■ By Plane

> Whenever flying internationally, pick up your ticket well in advance of the departure date, so you have time to fix any problems. Have the flight confirmed within 72 hours of departure. Arrive at the airport at least three hours before your flight.

The price you pay for airfare varies widely depending on whom you purchase your ticket from and how flexible your travel plans are. Always get quotes from different sources; an hour or two of research can save you hundreds of dollars. Call every toll-free number and don't be afraid to ask about discounts, as it's unlikely they'll be volunteered. Knowledgeable **travel agents**, particularly those specializing in traveling to the Mediterranean, can provide excellent guidance.

　　Understanding the airline industry's byzantine pricing system is the best way of finding a cheap fare. Very generally, **courier fares** (if you can deal with restrictions) are the cheapest, followed by tickets bought from **consolidators** and **stand-by** seating. **Last minute specials,** airfare wars, and charter flights can often beat these fares.

　　Students and others under 26 should never pay full price for a ticket; many airlines offer **senior traveler clubs** or airline passes with few restrictions and discounts for their companions as well. **Sunday newspapers** often have travel sections that list bargain fares from the local airport. Outsmart airline reps with the phone-book-sized *Official Airline Guide* (check your local library; at US$359 per year, the tome costs as much as some flights), a monthly guide listing nearly every scheduled flight in the world (with fares, US$479) and toll-free phone numbers for all the airlines which allow you to call in reservations directly. More accessible is Michael McColl's *The Worldwide Guide to Cheap Airfare* (US$15).

　　There is also a wealth of travel information to be found on the Internet. The **Air Traveler's Handbook** (http://www.cs.cmu.edu/afs/cs.cmu.edu/user/mkant/Public/Travel/airfare.html) is an excellent source of general information on air travel. Groups such as the **Air Courier Association** (http://www.aircourier.org) offer information about traveling as a courier and provide up-to-date listings of last-minute opportunities. **Magic Travel Services** in Athens (tel. (01) 323 74 71; fax 322 2021;

email magic@magic.gr; http://www.magic.gr) offers inexpensive flights and long-distance bus service, particularly between Athens and Rome.

Most airfares peak between mid-June and early September. Midweek (M-Th morning) round-trip flights run about US$40-50 cheaper than on weekends. An "open return" ticket can be pricier than fixing a return date and paying to change it.

Even if you pay a **commercial airline's** lowest published fare—usually the **Advance Purchase Excursion Fare (APEX)**—you may waste hundreds of dollars. However, APEX fares provide confirmed reservations and allow "open-jaw" tickets (landing in and returning from different cities). Lots of restrictions apply; book early. Most airlines in the world are heavily regulated, which means that their published fares may be significantly more expensive than other, less conventional options.

Although ticket prices are marked up slightly, **bucket shops** (retail agencies that specialize in getting cheap tickets) generally have access to a larger market than would be available to the public and can also get tickets from wholesale consolidators; a dealer **specializing** in travel to the country of your destination will provide more options and cheaper tickets. The **Association of Special Fares Agents (ASFA)** maintains a database of specialized dealers for particular regions (http://www.ntsltd.com/asfa). Look for bucket shops' tiny ads in the travel section of weekend papers, be a smart shopper, because among the many reputable and trustworthy companies are some shady wheeler-dealers. Get a full receipt. Kelly Monaghan's *Consolidators: Air Travel's Bargain Basement* lists of consolidators by location and destination (US$8 plus shipping); contact the Intrepid Traveler, P.O. Box 438, New York, NY 10034 (email info@intrepidtraveler.com).

Always try to contact specialists in your region. For general services to destinations **worldwide,** try **Airfare Busters,** (offices in Washington, D.C. (tel. (202) 776-0478), Boca Raton, FL (tel. (561) 994-9590), and Houston, TX (tel. (800) 232-8783); **Cheap Tickets,** offices in Los Angeles, CA, San Francisco, CA, Honolulu, HI, Seattle, WA, and New York, NY (tel. (800) 377-1000); **Interworld** (tel. (305) 443-4929, fax 443-0351); and **Travac** (tel. (800) 872-8800; fax (212) 714-9063; email mail@travac.com; http://www.travac.com). For a processing fee, depending on the number of travelers and the itinerary, **Travel Avenue,** Chicago, IL (tel. (800) 333-3335; fax (312) 876-1254; http://www.travelavenue.com), will search for the lowest international airfare available (5% rebate on fares over US$350). To **Europe,** try Rebel, Valencia, CA (tel. (800) 227-3235; fax (805) 294-0981; email travel@rebeltours.com; http://www.rebeltours.com) or Orlando, FL (tel. (800) 732-3588).

On **charter flights,** tour operators contract with an airline (usually one specializing in charters) to fly extra loads of passengers to peak-season destinations, for discounts. Charter flights fly less frequently than major airlines, and tend to make refunds particularly difficult. Schedules and itineraries may also change at the last moment.

Many consolidators such as **Interworld, Rebel, Travac,** and **Travel Avenue** (see **Ticket Consolidators** above), also offer charter options. Don't be afraid to call every number and hunt for the best deal. Eleventh-hour **discount clubs** and **fare brokers** offer members savings on travel, including charter flights and tour packages. **Travelers Advantage,** Stamford, CT (tel. (800) 548-1116; http://www.travelersadvantage.com; US$49 annual fee), specializes in European travel and tour packages.

■ By Ferry

Ferry travel is a popular way to get to and travel within Greece and Cyprus; their ports can be reached by sea from a seemingly unlimited number of points, and finding a boat agency to facilitate your trip should not be difficult. Make reservations, especially in high season. Be warned that **ferries run on irregular schedules.** Check in at *least* two hours in advance; late boarders may find their seats gone. If you sleep on deck, bring warm clothes and a sleeping bag. Bicycles travel free, and motorcycles are transported for an additional charge. Don't forget motion sickness medication, toilet paper, and a hand towel. Bring food and drink to avoid high prices on board.

The major ports of departure from **Italy** to Greece are Ancona and Brindisi, on the southeast coast of Italy. Bari, Otranto, and Venice also have a few connections. If coming from the north of Italy, be aware that gassing and theft are not unheard of on the overnight trains from Rome to Brindisi. Some ferry lines offer free deck passage on a space-available basis, but all passengers still need to pay the port tax (L10,000, or $6.25, in Brindisi) and, in high season, a supplementary fee of L19,000 ($12). Boats travel primarily to Corfu (10hr.), Igoumenitsa (12hr.), and Patras (20hr.). Prices range L50,000-105,000 ($31-66); in low season L22,000-45,000 ($13-29). For schedules from Greece to Italy, see Patras (p. 140), Cephalonia (p. 251), Corfu (p. 232), or Igoumenitsa (p. 220).

From Çeşme, **Turkey,** an **Ertürk** ferry offers service to Chios (May-June 3-4 per week, July-Apr. 1 per week). Prices are one-way $25, same-day return $30, open round-trip $35. **Rhodes** is connected by ferry to Marmaris (one-way 10,000dr, round-trip 12,000dr), as well as to Limassol, **Cyprus** (17hr., 2 per week, 18,500-22,000dr), and Haifa, Israel (36hr., 2 per week, 28,500-33,000dr).

■ By Bus

Although trains and railpasses are extremely popular in most of Europe, the long-distance bus networks of Greece are more extensive, efficient, and often more comfortable than train services. You may wish to contact one of these agencies:

Eurolines, 4 Cardiff Rd., Luton LU1 1PP (tel. (01582) 40 45 11; fax 40 06 94; in London, 52 Grosvenor Gardens, Victoria (tel. (0171) 730 82 35); email welcome@eurolines.uk.com; http://www.eurolines.co.uk). Eurolines Pass offers unlimited 30-day travel between 30 destinations (under 26 and over 60 UK£159; ages 26-60 UK£199) or 60-day (under 26 and over 60, UK£199, 26-60 UK£249).

Eurobus UK Ltd., Coldborough House, Market St., Bracknell, Berkshire RG121JA (tel. (01344) 300 301; fax 860 780; email info@eurobus.uk.com; http://www.euro bus.uk.com). Buses, with English speaking guides and drivers, stop door-to-door at one hostel or budget hotel per city, and let you hop on and off. In the U.S. contact Commonwealth Express (tel. (800) EUROBUS); in Canada contact Travel CUTS (see **Budget Travel Agencies,** p. 39).

Magic Travel Services buses between Athens and Rome (see **By Plane,** p. 20).

■ By Train

Greece is served by a number of international train routes that connect Athens, Thessaloniki, and Larissa to most European cities. Eurail passes are valid in Greece, and may be a useful purchase if you plan to visit other European countries as well; they are also valid for ferries from Italy to Greece. However, the Greek rail system is one of Europe's most antiquated and least efficient. Count on at least a three-day journey from Trieste or Vienna to Athens.

■ Packing

He who would travel happily must travel light.

—Antoine de St. Exupéry

Pack according to the extremes of climate you may experience and the type of travel you'll be carrying your luggage through, be it a multi-city backpacking sojourn or a week-long stay in one place. Before you leave, imagine yourself walking uphill on hot asphalt with your full pack for three hours—this should give you a sense of how important it is to pack lightly. A good rule is to lay out only what you absolutely need, then take half the clothes and twice the money. The less you have, the less you have to lose (or store, or carry on your back).

LUGGAGE

It's easy to keep track of your bags if you choose one primary piece of luggage. If you plan to cover most of your itinerary by foot, a sturdy **frame backpack** is unbeatable. **Internal-frame packs** are usually more compact, mold better to your back, keep a lower center of gravity, and can flex adequately on difficult hikes that require a lot of bending and maneuvering. **External-frame packs** are more comfortable for long hikes over even terrain, since they keep the weight higher and distribute it more evenly. Look for a pack with a strong, padded hip belt to transfer weight from your shoulders to your hips. Good packs cost anywhere from US$150 to US$500. Be wary of excessively low-end prices and don't sacrifice quality. Toting a **suitcase** or **trunk** is fine if you plan to live in one or two cities and explore from there, but a bad idea if you're going to be moving around a lot. Make sure it has wheels and consider how much it weighs even when empty. Hard-sided luggage is more durable but more weighty and cumbersome. Soft-sided luggage should have a PVC frame, a strong lining to resist bad weather and rough handling, and seams that are triple-stitched for durability.

In addition to your main vessel, a small backpack, rucksack, or courier bag may be useful as a **daypack** for sight-seeing expeditions, and can double as an airplane **carry-on.** An empty, lightweight **duffel bag** packed inside your luggage may also be useful. Once abroad you can fill your luggage with purchases and keep your dirty clothes in the duffel. In order to keep your valuables with you at all times, you may choose to guard your money, passport, rail pass, and other important articles in a **moneybelt** or **neck pouch,** available at any good camping store. The moneybelt should be tucked into the waist of your pants or skirt, and should not be bulky or brightly colored. See **Material Security,** p. 13, for more information on protecting you and your valuables.

CLOTHING

When choosing your travel wardrobe, aim for versatility and comfort. Avoid fabrics that wrinkle easily. Always bring a jacket or wool sweater. Stricter dress codes (especially for women) may call for something besides shorts, t-shirts, and jeans.

Regarding footwear, think *sturdy.* Well-cushioned **sneakers** are good for walking nearly everywhere, though you may want to consider a good water-proofed pair of **hiking boots** if you plan to do serious trail hiking. A double pair of socks—light silk or polypropylene inside and thick wool outside—will cushion feet, keep them dry, and help prevent blisters. **Break in your shoes before you leave.** If you have room, consider a pair of dress shoes and a pair of flip-flops for protection in the shower.

Do not leave home without a waterproof jacket and a backpack cover (if you're carrying a pack). Gore-Tex® is a miracle fabric that's both waterproof and breathable; it's all but mandatory if you plan on backpacking. Avoid cotton as outer-wear, especially if you will often be at the mercy of the elements.

Let's Go: Greece attempts to provide information on laundromats in the **Practical Information** listings for each city, but it may be easiest to use a sink. Bring a small container of detergent, a rubber ball to stop up the sink, and a travel clothes line.

MISCELLANEOUS

No matter where or how you're traveling, it's always a good idea to carry a **first-aid kit;** other useful items include umbrella, sealable plastic bags (for damp things and spillables), alarm clock, waterproof matches, sun hat, moleskin (for blisters), needle and thread, safety pins, sunglasses, a personal stereo (Walkman) with headphones, pocketknife, plastic water bottle, compass, string (makeshift clothesline and lashing material), towel, padlock, whistle, rubber bands, toilet paper, flashlight, cold-water soap, earplugs, insect repellant, electrical tape (for patching tears), clothespins, maps and phrasebooks, tweezers, garbage bags, sunscreen, vitamins. Deodorant, razors, tampons, and condoms may not always be available or affordable on the road.

If you plan to stay in **youth hostels,** you can avoid linen charges by making a **sleepsack** yourself. Fold a full-size sheet in half the long way and sew it closed along the open long side and one of the short sides. Sleepsacks are also sold at HI outlets.

In most European countries, electricity is 220 volts AC, enough to fry any 110V North American appliance. Visit a hardware store for an adapter (which changes the shape of the plug) as well as a converter (which changes the voltage); if you use only an adapter (unless instructions state otherwise), you'll melt your radio.

Film is just always expensive. If you will be seriously upset if the pictures are ruined, develop it at home. If you're not a serious photographer, you might want to consider bringing a **disposable camera** or two rather than an expensive permanent one. Despite disclaimers, airport security X-rays *can* fog film, so either buy a lead-lined pouch, sold at camera stores, or ask the security to hand inspect it. Always pack it in your carry-on luggage, since higher-intensity X-rays are used on checked luggage.

ONCE THERE

■ Tourist Assistance

> For **medical emergencies** in **Greece,** dial 166. In **Cyprus,** dial 190.

Two national organizations oversee tourism in Greece: the **Greek National Tourist Organization (GNTO)** and the **tourist police** *(touristiki astinomia).* The GNTO can supply general information about sights and accommodations throughout the country. Offices in the U.S. and other countries are listed under tourist offices on p. 1; the main office is at 2 Amerikis St., Athens (tel. (01) 322 4128). Note that the GNTO is known as the **EOT** in Greece. The tourist police deal with more local and immediate problems: where to find a room, what the bus schedule is, or what to do when you've lost your passport. The offices are open long hours and the staff is often quite willing to help, although their English may be limited. Tourist info for Greece is available in English 24 hours a day by calling **171**. **Nikis** and **Filellinon Streets** in Athens are lined with agencies and organizations geared towards budget and student travelers. We also list similar establishments in different cities in the **Orientation and Practical Information** section for most cities.

Tourist offices in Cyprus are extremely helpful and efficient. There are offices in Limassol, Nicosia, Larnaka, Paphos, Agia Napa, and Platres. The main office is the **Cyprus Tourism Organization,** P.O. Box 4535, 19 Limassol Ave., Nicosia CY 1390 (tel. (2) 337 715); in the **U.S.,** 13 E. 40th St., New York, NY 10016 (tel. (212) 683-5280). The CTO offices provide excellent free maps and information on buses, museums, events, and other points of interest. A particularly helpful publication available at tourist offices is *The Cyprus Traveler's Handbook* (free). Officials generally speak English, Greek, German, and French.

■ Getting Around

BY BUS

Spending time in Greece invariably means traveling by bus. Service is extensive in most areas, and fares are cheap. On major highways, buses tend to be more modern and efficient than in the mountainous areas of the Peloponnese or northern Greece. The **OSE** (see **By Train,** p. 26) offers limited bus service from a few cities. Unless you're sticking close to train routes, **KTEL** bus service should be sufficient.

Always check with an official source about scheduled departures; posted schedules are often outdated, and all services are curtailed significantly on Saturday and Sunday. The English-language weekly newspaper *Athens News* prints Athens bus schedules. Try to arrive at least 10 minutes ahead of time (Greek buses have a habit of leaving early). In major cities, KTEL bus lines have several different stations for different destinations. In villages, a cafe often serves as the bus station, and you must ask the proprietor for a schedule. Ask the conductor before entering the bus whether it's going to your destination (the signs on the front are often misleading or wrong), and make clear where you want to get off. If the bus passes your stop, stand up and yell *"Stasi!"* On the road, stand near a *Stasi* (ΣΤΑΣΗ) sign to pick up an intercity bus. KTEL buses are generally green or occasionally orange, while intercity buses are usually blue. For long-distance rides, you should buy your ticket beforehand in the office. (If you don't, you may have to stand throughout the journey.) For shorter trips, pay the conductor after you have boarded. Some lines discount round-trip fares by 20%.

In **Cyprus,** there is one island-wide **bus schedule,** which is available at tourist offices. This schedule provides all necessary information, including prices for buses and private taxi service. Most buses and service taxis run during the day; public transportation is difficult to find during the evening or late night. Buses to the **Troodos Mountains** depart once daily from both Nicosia and Limassol. You must pass through Limassol to get from Paphos to Nicosia or Larnaka. Bus service throughout Cyprus is less frequent in the winter. Shared **taxis** ("service taxis") run regularly Monday through Friday between Limassol, Paphos, Larnaka, and Nicosia (£2-3.50).

BY PLANE

In Greece, **Olympic Airways** can be found in **Athens,** 96-100 Syngrou Ave., 11741 Athens (tel. (01) 926 7251), in **Thessaloniki,** 3 Kountouritou St., 54101 Thessaloniki (tel. (26 01 21) and in many large cities and islands. While flying is quickest, it may not be the most convenient or flexible option for travel; coverage in some areas is spotty. In the U.S., contact the **New York** office, 645 Fifth Ave., NY 10022 (tel. (800) 223-1226; fax (718) 735-0215). In England, contact the **London** office, 11 Conduit St.,

London W1R OLP (tel. (0171) 409 2400; fax 493 0563). For further flight information within Greece, check regional **Practical Information** listings of airports, destinations, and prices, or get an Olympic Airways brochure at any Olympic office.

Cyprus, too, is accessible by **Olympic Airways.** Other alternatives include **Egypt Air** (U.S. tel. (800) 334-6787) and **Cyprus Airways** (U.S. tel. (212) 714-2310).

BY TRAIN

Greek train service is limited and painfully slow. Lines do not go to the west coast or to the islands. Trains are not useful for remote areas and most archaeological sites.

Though Greek rail travel may conjure up the charm and romance of a bygone era, charm and romance don't satisfy those earthly needs. Bring food and a water bottle because the on-board cafe can be pricey, and train water undrinkable. Lock your compartment door and keep your valuables on your person.

New air-conditioned intercity trains have been put into service on many lines. Although they are slightly more expensive and rare, they are worth the price. **Eurail** passes are valid on Greek trains. **Hellenic Railways Organization (OSE)** connects Athens to major Greek cities. For schedules and prices in Greece, dial 145 or 147.

BY FERRY AND HYDROFOIL

Ferries are the cheapest way to traverse the Mediterranean, but be prepared for delays and hassle (see **By Ferry,** p. 21). **Hydrofoils (Flying Dolphins)** are a tempting mode of traveling. They run relatively more frequently and reliably than ferries at twice their speed, but cost twice as much. In either case, however, you must realize that **ferry and hydrofoil travel in Greece is notoriously undependable.** Island hopping on a strictly fixed schedule is pretty much impossible. Don't bother planning an itinerary before you get to Greece or Cyprus and are able to confirm your departure times with the tourist or boat office. Although connections between major islands are frequent during summer, departure times fluctuate. To get to smaller islands, you often have to change boats several times, and some islands are accessible only a few times per week. Direct connections are less expensive than longer routes (the more stops, the higher the price), but also tend to be less frequent. The English-language weekly newspaper *Athens News* prints summer ferry schedules.

You should check in at least two hours early for a prime spot and allow plenty of time for late trains or buses and getting to the port. Avoid the astronomically priced cafeteria cuisine by bringing your own food. Also, bring toilet paper.

BY MOPED

Motorbiking is a popular way of touring the winding roads Greece and Cyprus, especially in Cyprus and the more remote and less frequented areas of Greece, where renting wheels may be the best way to assert your independence from unreliable or inconvenient public transportation systems. They don't use much gas, can be put on trains and ferries, and are a good compromise between the high cost of car travel and the limited range of bicycles. At the same time, be aware that they can be uncomfortable for long distances, dangerous in the rain, and unpredictable on rough roads.

Plenty of places offer scooters or **mopeds for rent.** Quality of bikes, speed of service in case of breakdown, and prices for longer periods vary drastically. Some agencies are open to bargaining. Expect to pay at least 2700dr per day for a 50cc scooter, the cheapest bike with the power to tackle steep mountain roads. More powerful bikes cost 20-30% more and usually require a Greek motorcycle license. Many agencies will request your passport as a deposit, but it's wiser just to settle up in advance; if they have your passport and you have an accident or mechanical failure, they may refuse to return it until you pay for repairs. Ask before renting if the price quote includes tax and insurance, or you may pay several hundred unexpected *drachmes*.

A word of **caution** about travel by moped: *the majority of tourist-related accidents each year occur on mopeds.* Regardless of your experience driving a moped, winding, often poorly maintained mountain roads and reckless drivers make driving a moped hazardous. Always wear a helmet, and never ride with a backpack.

BY CAR

Driving is a fairly luxurious way to tour Greece and Cyprus, where public transportation is almost nonexistent after 7pm. Ferries take you island hopping if you pay a transport fee for the car. Drivers must be comfortable with a standard transmission, winding mountain roads, reckless drivers (especially in Athens), and the Greek alphabet—signs in Greek appear roughly 100m before the transliterated versions.

Agencies may quote low daily rates that exclude the 20% tax and Collision Damage Waiver (CDW) insurance (2000dr per day). Without CDW, the driver is responsible for the first 15,000dr worth of damage if theft or accident is not the driver's fault, and the full amount otherwise. Some places quote lower rates but hit you with hidden charges, such as exorbitant refueling bills if you come back with less than a full tank, 1.5-2.5dr per kilometer drop-off or special charge, or 100km per day minimum mileage. Most companies won't let you drive the car outside Greece. Hertz and InterRent rent to 21-year-old drivers, but most other companies rent only to those 23 and older.

The cheaper and larger rental agencies are **Just**, **InterRent**, and **Retca**, with offices in Athens and other mainland cities, as well as on Crete and several islands. **Avis**, **Hertz**, **Europcar**, and **Budget**, rates are steeper, but service is reliable. It is often cheaper to make arrangements with these companies while still at home.

Foreign drivers are required to have an **International Driver's License** and an **International Insurance Certificate** to drive in Greece; see **Driving Permits and Car Insurance**, p. 11). The **Automobile and Touring Club of Greece** (ELPA), 2 Messogion St., Athens 11527 (tel. 779 7401), provides assistance and offers reciprocal membership to foreign auto club members. They also have 24-hour **emergency road assistance** (tel. 104) and an **information line** (tel. 174; open M-F 7am-3pm).

A reliable highway system serves much of **Cyprus**, but winding mountain roads require caution. Cars drive on the left side of the road in the south and on the right in the north. Rented cars may not cross the Green Line. The south also has several British rotaries that can be particularly intimidating for American drivers.

All Cypriot rental cars have manual transmission and standardized rental rates. The cheapest compact cars should cost no more than £17 per day, small motorbikes £5, and larger motorcycles £7-8 (most dealers rent two-seat motor bikes, but operating with two riders may result in a fine). Cypriot law requires that seatbelts be worn in front seats, and an international driver's license or a national driver's license from your home country is required. A temporary Cypriot driver's license, good for six months, can be obtained from district police stations with a photo ID and £1.

BY FOOT

Let's Go: Greece describes hikes and trails in some town and city listings; local residents and fellow travelers can suggest even more. Always make sure you have comfortable shoes and a map. Remember that hiking under the hot sun at a high altitude may be more strenuous than you expect. Good sunscreen, a hat, and water are essential. (For more information, see **Camping & the Outdoors**, p. 32.)

BY THUMB

Let's Go strongly urges you to consider seriously the risks before you choose to hitch. We cannot recommend hitching as a safe means of transportation, and none of the information presented here is intended to do so.

Consider fully the risks involved before you decide to hitchhike; not everyone can be an airplane pilot, but any bozo can drive a car. Hitching means entrusting your life to a random person who happens to stop beside you on the road and risking theft, assault, sexual harassment, and unsafe driving. Safety-minded hitchers avoid getting

in the back of a two-door car, and never let go of their backpacks. They will not get into a car that they can't get out of again in a hurry. If they ever feel threatened, they insist on being let off, regardless of where they are. They may also act as if they are going to open the car door or vomit on the upholstery to get a driver to stop. Hitch-hiking at night can be particularly dangerous; experienced hitchers stand in well-lit places, and expect drivers to be leery of nocturnal thumbers. Women should avoid hitch-hiking alone in Greece and Cyprus.

That said, it's hard to generalize about hitching in Greece and Cyprus. Greeks are not eager to pick up foreigners, and foreign cars are often full of other travelers. Sparsely populated areas have little or no traffic—you risk being stuck on the road for hours. However, favorable hitching experiences allow you to meet local people and get where you're going. Experienced hitchers pick a spot outside of built-up areas, where drivers can stop, return to the road without causing an accident, and have time to inspect potential passengers as they approach. Those who hitchhike write their destination on a sign in both Greek and English letters, and try to hitch from turn-offs rather than long stretches of road. Finally, success will depend on what one looks like. Successful hitchers travel light and stack their belongings in a visible, compact cluster. Drivers prefer neat and wholesome hitchers.

How to get to Turkey

The Greek government frowns on tourists taking advantage of cheaper fares to Greece for easy access to Turkey, and the information you receive on how to travel between the two countries may be confusing. Contrary to what tourist authorities may lead you to believe, no law prevents crossing the border. Many travelers make one-day excursions; check into regulations on longer trips.

Athens and Istanbul are connected by **Euroways Eurolines** bus and by train. If you have a railpass and are traveling from Greece to Turkey, take the train as far as Alexandroupolis, and ride the bus from there. Beware: the 38-hour ride from Athens will wear out even the most seasoned traveler. The quickest but most expensive option is an Olympic Airways **flight** to Istanbul or other points in Turkey.

Those who **hitch** between Turkey and Greece usually try to make it to Istanbul in one ride from Alexandroupolis or Thessaloniki; there isn't much traffic, and people are not permitted to walk across the border. Hitchers must make sure that their driver's license plate number is not stamped in their passports (but rather on some other, disposable piece of paper).

■ Accommodations

Relative to the U.S. and elsewhere in Europe, accommodations in Greece and Cyprus remain a bargain. Off-season prices (Oct.-May) average 20-40% cheaper than during high season. Prices may rise on weekends and are usually reduced for extended stays. Prices quoted in the guide are from summer 1998; expect a rise of 10-20% in 1999.

HOSTELS

Hostels are generally dorm-style accommodations, often in single-sex large rooms with bunk beds, although some hostels do offer private rooms for families and couples. They sometimes have kitchens and utensils for your use, bike or moped rentals, storage areas, and laundry facilities. Greek youth hostels generally have fewer restrictions than those farther north in Europe. Most are open year-round and have midnight or 1am curfews (which are strictly enforced, and may leave you in the streets if you come back too late). In summer, they usually stay open from 6-10am and 1pm-midnight (shorter hours in winter). The larger hostels offer breakfast. Some hostels have a maximum stay of five days. It's advisable to book in advance in the summer at some of the more popular hostels in Athens, Santorini, or Nauplion. Check out the **Internet Guide to Hostelling** (http://www.hostels.com), which provides a directory of hostels from around the world in addition to oodles of information about hostelling and backpacking worldwide. **Eurotrip** (http://www.eurotrip.com/accommoda-

Pack Heavy. Travel Light.

Virtual Backpack™

Access your personal email, addresses, files, bookmarks, weather, news and maps from any computer on the Web.*

exclusively at the
Student Advantage® Network
www.studentadvantage.com

*You can get access to the Web at hostels, airports, libraries and cyber cafés.

tion/accommodation.html) has information and reviews on budget hostels and several international hostel associations.

Although **Hostelling International (HI)** endorses few hostels in Greece, it has a stronger presence in Cyprus; Nicosia, Troodos, Paphos, and Larnaka all have HI youth hostels (in the U.S. call (tel. (202) 783-6161); outside call your national hostelling organization or check http://www.hiayh.org/ushostel/reserva/ibn3.htm or http://www.iyhf.org). If you arrive in Greece without an HI card, you can buy an International Guest Card (2600dr), either from the Greek Youth Hostel Association, 4 Dragatsaniou St., Fl.7, Athens (tel. (01) 323 4107; fax 323 7590), or the Athens International Hostel (HI), 16 Victor Hugo St., Athens (tel. 523 1095).

> One note on Greek **toilets**: if a trash container is within reach of the toilet, this is where used toilet paper goes. Flushing toilet paper will probably jam the toilet. Many Greek toilets are flushed by pulling a handle that hangs from the ceiling. Also, some hotels may only have pit toilets; check before accepting a room.

HOTELS

The government oversees the construction and the seemingly random classification of most hotels. Proprietors are permitted to charge 10% extra for stays of less than three nights, and 20% extra overall in high season (July-Sept. 15). In order to get more *drachmes* out of you, they may only offer their most expensive rooms, compel you to buy breakfast, squeeze three people into a hostel-like triple and charge each for a single, or quote a price for a room that includes breakfast and private shower and then charge extra for both. Most D- and E-class hotels start at 4000dr for singles and 5000dr for doubles. A hotel with no singles may still put you in a room by yourself. More information is available from the **Hellenic Chamber of Hotels,** 24 Stadiou St., Athens (tel. (01) 323 7193; fax 322 5449).

If proprietors offer a room that seems unreasonably expensive, stress that you don't want luxuries and they may tell you of a cheaper option. Late at night, in the off season, or in a large town, it's a buyer's market. You may consider bargaining. As a security deposit, hotels may ask for your passport and return it when you leave. You can often leave your luggage in the reception area during the afternoon, though check-out is at 11am or noon. Be skeptical about offers to be driven to a pension or hotel. Let the driver show you the destination on a map; it may be miles out of town.

The tourist police are on your side. If a hotel flagrantly violates the prices shown by law at the front desk or on a chart behind each room's front door, or if you think you've been exploited, threaten to report the hotel to the tourist police. The threat alone often resolves "misunderstandings."

ROOMS TO LET

Wherever there are tourists, you'll see private homes with signs offering *domatia* (rooms to let). As you arrive at more popular destinations, proprietors hustling their rooms to let will greet your boat or bus. Peddling rooms at bus stops or ports is illegal according to the tourist police. Generally, you should have a set destination in mind and head there. On occasion the rooms offered to you at the port or bus stop may be cheap. Nonetheless, it is imperative that you make owners pinpoint the exact location of their houses. "Ten minutes away, near the beach" can mean a 45-minute hike from the main town. Most rooms are cheap and dependable. There may not be locks, towels, or telephones, but there may be warm offers of coffee at night and friendly conversation. Then again, in the more touristed areas, there may be more locks than conversation. Prices here are variable, so be sure that you're paying no more than you would at a hotel. If in doubt, ask the tourist police: they'll usually set you up with a room and conduct all the negotiations themselves. Most private rooms operate only in high season, a good option for those arriving without reservations. Sleeping on hotel roofs (generally half the price of a hostel bed) is a cheap scenic option.

TRADITIONAL SETTLEMENTS

Greece has several traditional villages and buildings which have been preserved and restored by the government in an effort to maintain the country's architectural heritage. The restoration of some Greek villages promises to offer a taste of small town Greek life to visitors and to improve the regional economy. Thus far, more than ten settlements have been converted into guest houses: Makrynitsa and Vizitsa on Mt. Pelion (see p. 212), Mesta on Chios (see p. 296), Psara Island, Fiscardo on Cephalonia (see p. 254), Kapetanakos in Areopolis (see p. 169), and Papingo-Zagorohoria in Epirus (p. 229). There are 12 reconstructed towers in Vathia, Mani (see p. 166) and an expensive hotel in the Kastro in Monemvassia (see p. 170). Doubles range from 5000 to 10,000dr; tourist offices can make reservations and provide information.

■ Camping and the Outdoors

Camping is an easy way to escape the monotony of barren hotel rooms, hostel regulations, and the other limitations of conventional lodgings. More importantly, it's one of the cheapest ways to spend the night. In Greece, the **GNTO** is primarily responsible for campgrounds. Most of the official GNTO campgrounds have good facilities, including drinking water, lavatories, and electricity. The Hellenic Touring Club also runs a number of campgrounds. In addition, Greece has many campgrounds run by private organizations which may include pools, discos, and minimarkets. The prices charged at campgrounds depend on the facilities; you'll usually pay roughly 1200dr per person, plus 1000dr per tent. GNTO campgrounds tend to be ritzier and more expensive (up to 1700dr in some places).

On many islands, campers take to the beaches. Free-lance camping outside campgrounds is illegal, but during July and August, when hotels and pensions are booked solid, illegal camping becomes commonplace. Penalties run the gamut from a stern chastisement to a 50,000dr or higher fine. At peak season when camps are crowded, the police may sometimes ignore sleeping-bagged bodies sprawled in the sand. Those who decide to free-lance camp should make sure to clean up after themselves. Many beaches offer beach huts as well as designated camping sections. We urge you to consider the safety and legal risks inherent in free-lance camping and sleeping on beaches. *Let's Go: Greece* cannot recommend illegal free-lance camping.

Although **Cyprus** has few formal campgrounds, you may sleep on beaches and in forests. Choose your site discreetly and leave it as clean as you found it. Be careful if you camp unofficially; women should be especially wary and never camp alone.

CAMPING AND HIKING EQUIPMENT

Purchase equipment before you leave. This way you'll know exactly what you have and how much it weighs. Spend some time examining catalogues and talking to knowledgeable salespeople. Whether buying or renting, finding sturdy, light, and inexpensive equipment is a must.

Sleeping bags range from US$65-100 for a lightweight synthetic bag, probably what you would need for a summer visit. **Sleeping bag pads,** including foam pads (US$15 and up) and air mattresses (US$25-50) cushion your back and neck and insulate you from the ground. Another good alternative is the **Therm-A-Rest,** which is part foam and part air-mattress and inflates to full padding when you unroll it. The best **tents** are free-standing, with their own frames and suspension systems; they set up quickly and require no staking (except in high winds). Low profile dome tents are the best all-around. When pitched their internal space is almost entirely usable, which means little unnecessary bulk. Tent sizes can be somewhat misleading: two people can fit in a two-person tent, but will find life more pleasant in a four-person. Good two-person tents start at US$150, four-person tents at US$400, but you can sometimes find last year's model for half the price. Seal the seams of your tent with waterproofer, and make sure it has a rain fly. If you intend to do a lot of hiking, you should have a **frame backpack** (see **Luggage,** p. 23). **Rain gear** should come in two pieces, a top and pants, rather than a poncho. **Synthetics,** like polypropylene tops, socks, and long underwear, along with a pile jacket, will keep you warm even when wet. Large, collapsible **water sacks** will significantly improve your lot in primitive campgrounds and weigh practically nothing when empty, though they can get bulky. For those places that forbid fires or the gathering of firewood, you may need a **camp stove**—the classic Coleman starts at about US$30, or you may consider the "GAZ" butane/propane stove. Its little blue cylinders can be purchased anywhere on the continent (don't try to take them onto a plane). A **first aid kit, Swiss Army knife, insect repellent, calamine lotion,** and **waterproof matches** or a **lighter** are essential camping items. Other items include a **battery-operated lantern,** a **plastic ground-cloth,** a **nylon tarp,** a **waterproof backpack cover** (although you can also store your belongings in plastic bags inside your backpack), and a **"stuff sack"** to keep your sleeping bag dry (see p. 24). *How to Stay Alive in the Woods,* by Bradford Angier (Macmillan, US$8), is a good guide to outdoor survival.

■ Business Hours

Most **shops** close on Sundays; only restaurants, cafes, and bakeries remain open. During the week business hours vary, but most places open early (around 7am), close after 2pm for a siesta, and re-open at roughly 6pm. Most **banks** are open Monday-Friday 8am-1:30pm, and in some larger cities, open again 3:30-6pm. Banks offer the best **currency exchange** rates. **Post offices** are generally open Monday through Saturday 7:30am to 2pm. The **OTE,** the Greek phone company, is often open until 7:30pm or later in larger cities. Shops and **pharmacies** are open Monday, Wednesday, and Saturday 8am-2:30pm and Tuesday, Thursday, and Friday 8am-1pm and 5-8:30pm. There's usually a pharmacy open 24 hours on a rotating basis; its address should be posted on the doors of all other pharmacies or in the local daily newspapers. **Grocery stores** have longer hours. Government-run **museums** and **archaeological sites** close on Mondays, and have slightly shorter hours from mid-October to mid-May. On holidays, sights often have Sunday opening hours and, in many cases, do not charge admission on these days. All banks and shops close on major holidays (see **Holidays and Festivals,** p. 512). In general, travelers from punctuality-obsessed countries should be aware that many establishments in Greece have flexible and variable hours.

■ Health and Well-being on the Road

> ### Emergencies
>
> In each regional section, under **Orientation and Practical Information,** we list police telephone numbers. We also list the telephone numbers for ambulances, medical emergency centers, local hospitals, clinics, and pharmacies. Emergency phone numbers, applicable throughout most of **Greece** and operating 24 hours, include **police** (tel. 100), **first aid** (tel. 166), **fire** (tel. 199), **hospitals** on duty (tel. 106), and **tourist police** (171 in Athens, 922 7777 for the rest of Greece). For **ambulance, fire,** or **police** in **Cyprus,** dial 199. For U.S. citizens' emergency aid call (01) 722 3652 or 729 4301.

The most important part of keeping out of danger is using your **common sense.** Accidents and dangerous situations often happen when you contradict your habits or act in a way that makes you feel uncomfortable. Don't be paranoid—just don't be stupid. Below we've discussed things you should already know.

TRAVELERS' HEALTH PRECAUTIONS

Common sense is the simplest prescription for good health while you travel: eat well, drink and sleep enough, and don't overexert yourself. Travelers complain most often about their feet and their gut, so take precautionary measures. Drinking lots of **water** can often prevent dehydration and constipation, and wearing **sturdy shoes** and clean socks, and using talcum powder can help keep your feet dry and comfortable. When traveling in Greece and Cyprus, don't underestimate the dangers of sun and heat, and educate yourself about basic precautions for **heatstroke** and **sunburn.** As in all foreign countries, travelers should be wary of dubious food or water, to reduce the chances of **food poisoning** or diarrhea. Bottled water is widely available. Less of a health hazard than a nuisance are **mosquitoes,** especially in coastal towns and in campgrounds; pharmacies sell small rectangles of mosquito repellent that burn slowly on little lighted heat pads that plug into the wall (*bayvap* in Greek.)

Pharmacies in Greek and Cypriot towns stay open all night on a rotating basis; each should have a sign in the window telling which is on duty that night (the open one is known as *efimerevon*).

NASTY TRAVELERS' DISEASES

Traveler's diarrhea is the dastardly consequence of drinking or eating off dishes washed in unclean water. The illness can last from three to seven days, and symptoms include diarrhea, nausea, bloating, urgency, and malaise. The most dangerous side effect of diarrhea is dehydration; the simplest and most effective anti-dehydration formula is 8 oz. of (clean) water with a ½ tsp. of sugar or honey and a pinch of salt. Also good are soft drinks without caffeine and salted crackers. Down several of these remedies a day, make sure to eat quick-energy, non-sugary foods with protein and carbohydrates to keep your strength up, rest, and wait for the unpleasantness to run its course. Over-the-counter remedies (such as Pepto-Bismol or Immodium) may counteract the symptoms, but they can complicate serious infections. Avoid anti-diarrheals if you suspect you have been exposed to contaminated food or water, which puts you at risk for other diseases. If you develop a fever or your symptoms don't go away after four or five days, consult a doctor. Also consult a doctor if children develop traveler's diarrhea, since treatment is different.

To prevent **heat exhaustion,** relax in hot weather, drink lots of non-alcoholic fluids, and lie down inside if you feel awful. If you'll be sweating a lot, eat enough **salty food** to prevent electrolyte depletion. Wear a hat, sunglasses, and a lightweight longsleeve shirt to avoid the continuous heat stress which can lead to **heatstroke,** characterized by rising body temperature, severe headache, and cessation of sweating. Cool off victims with wet towels and take them to a doctor as soon as possible.

Less debilitating, but still dangerous, is **sunburn.** If you're prone to sunburn, bring sunscreen with you (it's often more expensive and hard to find when traveling), and apply it liberally and often to avoid burns and risk of skin cancer. Drink lots of water.

You should know that, wherever you go, **Acquired Immune Deficiency Syndrome (AIDS)** is a growing problem. The easiest mode of HIV transmission is through direct blood to blood contact with an HIV+ person; *never* share intravenous drug, tattooing, or other needles. The most common mode of transmission is sexual intercourse. Health professionals recommend the use of latex condoms; follow the instructions on the packet. Since it isn't always easy to buy condoms when traveling, take a supply with you before you depart for your trip. *Travel Safe: AIDS and International Travel* is available at all Council Travel offices.

Sexually transmitted diseases (STDs) such as gonorrhea, chlamydia, genital warts, syphilis, and herpes, are easier to catch than HIV and can result in serious health problems. If you have sex with a stranger, realize that condoms may protect you from certain STDs, but oral or even tactile contact can lead to transmission. If nothing else, you might actually *look* at your partner's genitals before you have sex. Warning signs for STDs include: swelling, sores, bumps, or blisters on sex organs, rectum, or mouth; burning and pain during urination and bowel movements; itching around sex organs; swelling or redness in the throat, flu-like symptoms with fever, chills, and aches. If these symptoms develop, see a doctor immediately.

Needless to say, **illegal drugs** are best avoided altogether. Buying or selling *any* type of drug may lead to a stiff fine and/or prison sentence—dealing drugs in Greece is regarded as a particularly serious offence, as local problems with underage use and addiction grow. Remember that you are subject to Greek laws, not to those of your home country, and it is your responsibility to familiarize yourself with these laws.

Avoid public drunkenness; it can threaten your safety and earn disdain from locals.

PERSONAL SAFETY AND MATERIAL SECURITY

When possible, keep anything you couldn't bear to lose at home. **Don't put a wallet with money in your back pocket.** Never count your money in public, carry as little as possible, and keep some separate from the rest. **Photocopies** of important documents in case they are lost or filched—carry one copy separate from the originals and leave another copy at home. Secure packs with small combination padlocks which slip through the two zippers. If you're extremely concerned, a **money belt** or **neck pouch** is a safe way to carry cash if you avoid pulling it out in public; you can buy either at most camping supply stores (or through the Forsyth Travel Library; see **Useful Publications,** p. 3). Also see **Luggage,** p. 23.

> Avoid carrying anything precious in a bulky waistpack or "fanny-pack" (even worn on your stomach): they're unfashionable, and your valuables will be highly visible and easy to steal.

When exploring a new city, extra vigilance is wise, but there is no need for panic. Find out about unsafe areas from tourist information, from the manager of your hotel or hostel, or from a local whom you trust; memorize the emergency number of the city or area. When walking at night, be your smart self: stick to busy, well-lit streets and avoid dark, scary alleyways—but don't allow fear of the unknown to turn you into a hermit. Careful, persistent exploration will build confidence and make your stay in an area that much more rewarding.

In city crowds and especially on public transportation, pick-pockets are amazingly deft at their craft. Rush hour is no excuse for strangers to press up against you on the metro. If someone stands uncomfortably close, move to another car and hold your bags tightly. Be alert in public telephone booths.

Among the more colorful aspects of large cities are **con artists.** Con artists and hustlers often work in groups, and children are among the most effective. They possess an innumerable range of ruses. Be aware of certain classics: sob stories that require money, rolls of bills "found" on the street, mustard spilled (or saliva spit) onto your shoulder distracting you for enough time to snatch your bag—do not respond or make eye contact, walk quickly away, and keep a solid grip on your belongings. Contact the police if a hustler is particularly insistent or aggressive.

Be particularly careful on **buses:** keep your eyes on your backpack, don't check baggage on trains, and don't trust anyone to "watch your bag for a second." Thieves thrive on **trains;** professionals wait for tourists to fall asleep and then carry off everything they can. When traveling in pairs, sleep in alternating shifts; when alone, use good judgment in selecting a train compartment: never stay in an empty one, and use a lock to secure your pack to the luggage rack. Keep important documents and other valuables on your person and try to sleep on top bunks with your luggage stored above you. Backpacks can make fine bedfellows.

Never leave your belongings unattended; crime occurs in even the most demure looking **hostel** or hotel. If you feel unsafe, look for places with either a curfew or a night attendant. *Let's Go: Greece* lists **locker** availability in hostels and train stations, but you'll need your own padlock. Lockers are useful if you plan on sleeping outdoors or don't want to lug everything with you, but don't store valuables in them.

Some of the most beautiful spots in Greece and Cyprus are those found on the **seaside.** While enjoying the pleasures of island life, remember to exercise caution and common sense at beaches without lifeguards. Hidden rocks and shallow depths may cause serious injury and even death. Heed warning signs about undertows or dangerous marine life. If you rent scuba diving equipment, make sure that it is up to par before taking the plunge.

Let's Go does not recommend hitchhiking under any circumstances, particularly for women—see **By Thumb,** p. 27, for more information.

■ Keeping in Touch

MAIL

> ### Receiving Mail in Greece and Cyprus
>
> Mail can be sent to internationally through **Poste Restante** (the international phrase for General Delivery) to any city or town; it's well worth using, generally without any surcharges, and much more reliable than you might think. Mark the envelope, for example, Chris <u>NICHOLS</u>, *Poste Restante*, Athens, GREECE." The last name should be capitalized and underlined. Write "Air Mail" on the side of the envelope and use a first class stamp.
>
> As a rule, in both Greece and Cyprus, it is best to use the largest post office in the area; sometimes, mail will be sent there regardless of what you write on the envelope. In Cyprus, *Poste Restante* is available **only** in Nicosia, Larnaka, Paphos, and Limassol (10¢ per piece). When possible, it is usually better to send mail express or registered. If you are expecting Poste Restante to arrive for you after you leave a town, arrange at the post office to have it forwarded to another Poste Restante address. American Express offices hold mail for up to 30 days, but often charge a small fee if you aren't a cardholder or don't use their traveler's checks.
>
> When picking up mail, bring your passport or other ID. If the clerks insist that there is nothing for you, have them check under your first name as well. In a few countries you may have to pay a minimal fee per item received. *Let's Go: Greece* lists post offices in the **Practical Information** for each city and most towns.

Most Greek **post offices** are open weekdays from 7:30am-2pm, although services (such as mailing parcels) may close early. Some larger offices keep longer hours.

For **express** mail service, ask for *katepeegon;* to **register** a letter, *sýstemeno;* for **air mail,** *aeroporikos,* and write "air mail" on the envelope. A letter or postcard to the U.S. costs 120dr to mail and takes as little as four days or as long as two weeks, sometimes longer from smaller villages.

Aerogrammes, printed sheets that fold into envelopes and travel via airmail, are available at post offices. It helps to mark "par avion," a pretty much universally understood translation, on the outside surface. Most post offices will charge exorbitant fees—or simply refuse—to send Aerogrammes with enclosures. Airmail from Europe and the U.S. averages one to two weeks; allow seven to ten days from Athens.

If regular airmail is too slow, there are a few faster, more expensive, options. **Federal Express** can get a letter from New York to Greece in two days for a whopping US$19.00; rates among non-U.S. locations are prohibitively expensive.

Surface mail is by far the cheapest and slowest way to send mail. It takes one to three months to cross the Atlantic and two to four to cross the Pacific—appropriate for sending large quantities of items you won't need to see for a while. It is vital, therefore, to distinguish your airmail from surface mail by explicitly labeling "airmail" in the appropriate language. When ordering books and materials from abroad, always include one or two International Reply Coupons (IRCs)—a way of providing the postage to cover delivery. IRCs should be available from your local post office as well as abroad (US$1.05). **American Express** travel offices will act as a mail service for cardholders if you contact them in advance. Under this free **"Client Letter Service,"** they will hold mail for no more than 30 days, forward upon request, and accept telegrams. Some offices will offer these services to non-cardholders (especially those who have purchased AmEx Travellers' Cheques). Check **Practical Information** sections; *Let's Go: Greece* lists AmEx locations for most large cities. A complete list is available free from AmEx (tel. (800) 528-4800) in the booklet *Traveler's Companion,* or online at http://www.americanexpress.com, which can connect you to world-wide sites.

TELEPHONES

In Greece, long-distance and collect **phone calls** and telegrams should be placed at the **OTE** (the Greek Telephone Organization) offices. In small villages, offices are usually open weekdays 7:30am-3pm, in towns 7:30am-10pm (shorter hours or closed on weekends), and in larger cities 24 hours. If you visit one of the latter in the middle of the night, the door may be locked, but ring and they'll let you in. Try to call early in the morning to avoid long lines later. In order to make any calls from the ubiquitous card phones *(kartotilephona)*, you must purchase a phone card *(telekarta)* for 1000dr and up, from OTE offices or kiosks. Slide the card into the phone and press "i" on the phones for English language instructions.

Cyprus has fairly reliable telephone service (administered by **CYTA**). Direct overseas calls can be made from nearly all public phones. **Telecards,** which are sold at banks and kiosks, make international calls more convenient. They can be used only in special phones and are available in denominations of £3, 5, and 10.

To call **direct,** dial the proper international access code (011 from Greece, the U.S. and Canada, 0011 from Australia, 00 from the U.K., Ireland, and New Zealand, and 09 from South Africa) followed by the country code of the country you are calling, the city code, and the local number. The country code in **Greece** is 30; the country code is **Cyprus** is 357. City codes are listed in each city's **Essentials** section. Country codes and city codes may sometimes be listed with extra zeros, but after dialing the international access code, drop successive zeros. Complete phone codes are listed in the **appendix,** p. 513. In some villages you may have to go through the operator. In others you must wait for a tone after the international access code.

Calling There, Calling Home

The country code in **Greece:** 30. The country code in **Cyprus:** 357.
The following companies may facilitate international collect or calling card calls:
   AT&T Greece: 00 800 1311. Cyprus: 080 90010.
   MCI Greece: 00 800 1211. Cyprus: 080 90000.
   Sprint Greece: 00 800 1411. Cyprus: 080 90001.

If you plan on talking for a while, ask the other party to call right back, since rates from overseas to Greece are often cheaper than rates going the other way. Some companies, seizing upon this "call-me-back" concept, have created callback services with rates about 20-60% lower than you'd pay using credit cards or pay phones—this option is most economical for loquacious travelers, as services may include a US$10-25 minimum billing per month. For information, call **America Tele-Fone** (tel. (800) 321-5817), **Globaltel** (tel. (770) 449-1295), **International Telephone** (tel. (800) 638-5558), or **Telegroup** (tel. (800) 338-0225).

A **calling card** is probably your best and cheapest bet; your local long-distance service provider will have a number for you to dial while traveling (either toll-free or charged as a local call) to connect instantly to an operator in your home country. For more information, call **AT&T** about its **USADirect** and **World Connect** services (tel. (888) 288-4685; from abroad call (810) 262-6644 collect), **Sprint** (tel. (800) 877-4646; from abroad, call (913) 624-5335 collect), or **MCI WorldPhone** and **World Reach** (tel. (800) 444-4141; from abroad dial the country's MCI access number). In Canada, contact Bell Canada **Canada Direct** (tel. (800) 565 4708); in the U.K., British Telecom **BT Direct** (tel. (800) 34 51 44); in Ireland, Telecom Éireann **Ireland Direct** (tel. (800) 250 250); in Australia, Telstra **Australia Direct** (tel. 13 22 00); in New Zealand, **Telecom New Zealand** (tel. 123); in South Africa, **Telkom South Africa** (tel. 09 03).

MCI's WorldPhone also provides access to MCI's **Traveler's Assist,** which gives legal and medical advice, exchange rate information, and translation services. Many other long distance carriers and phone companies provide such travel information; contact your phone service provider.

Remember **time differences** when you call. Greece and Cyprus are two hours ahead of GMT and seven hours ahead of Eastern Standard Time.

OTHER COMMUNICATION

Between May 2 and Octoberfest, **EurAide,** P.O. Box 2375, Naperville, IL 60567 (tel. (630) 420-2343; fax (630) 420-2369; http://www.cube.net/kmu/euraide.html), offers **Overseas Access,** a service useful to travelers without a set itinerary. The cost is US$15 per week or US$40 per month plus a US$15 registration fee. To reach you, people call, fax, or use the internet to leave a message; you receive it by calling Munich whenever you wish, which is cheaper than calling overseas. You may also leave messages for callers to pick up by phone.

If you're spending a year abroad and want to keep in touch with friends or colleagues, **electronic mail (email)** is an attractive option. With minimal computer knowledge and a little planning, you can beam messages anywhere for no per-message charges. One option is to befriend college students as you go and ask if you can use their email accounts. Or look for bureaus that offer access to email for sending individual messages. Search through http://www.cyberiacafe.net/cyberia/guide/ccafe.htm to find a list of **cybercafes** around the world from which you can drink a cup of joe and email him too. See **Internet Resources** (p. 4), for more information on global travel's newest twist.

GREECE Ελλας

When you raise your eyes to see the Mediterranean sun begin its descent over a Cretan peak, and you follow through olive groves and under rusty, barbed-wire fences to bare crags, brush, and trickling streams, shepherds guide you up to their hidden places. The slope winds into a cliff, and the shepherds unlock the door to their cave-hewn sanctuary. Their olive oil, their wine, and the light of their candles touching the blues and golds of ghost-faced frescoes on the cave's walls lend you the calm to watch the sun set behind Zeus' birthplace.

Under its many guises—Hellenic, Byzantine, or Modern—history has run its course over the Greek landscape, inspiring solitary moments of clarity and monuments of eternal genius. Monasteries and ancient cities dot islands and a mainland that still have enough open spaces for wanderers to lose themselves. Monks coexist with hedonistic revellers, and hospitality permeates the land. This has gone on for 5000 years.

ANCIENT GREECE

Origins

Humans have wandered through the land that is now Greece for more than ten millennia. Paleolithic finds from across the mainland and from Franchthi Cave in the Peloponnese indicate that indigenous populations hunted for food with small stone weapons, sailed in order to fish and gather supplies, and had begun to engage in basic agricultural activities. By 6500 BC, Thessaly, Western Anatolia, and the islands of the Aegean as far south as Crete hosted fully developed agricultural communities which produced clay pottery and were in the process of establishing regional and international trade routes. During the neolithic period, techniques of shelter progressed from circular hut dwellings to simple, compartmentalized walled towns built on high—the first forms of the **acropolis.** As primitive religious instincts began to stir, terra cotta figurines, crafted from clay in the form of females and animals, offered votive prayers for fertility when placed on peak sanctuaries and in graves. The islands and mainland coastal regions of the Aegean presented an ideal setting for human habitation. Olive trees, grape vines, forests, fertile plains, and supplies of fresh water far more ample than those available to today's inhabitants attracted immigrants and traders from the civilizations of Anatolia, the Levant, and Egypt, whose infusions would germinate the flowering of the first Greek cultures.

Aegean Civilizations of the Bronze Age

Crete received the first infusion of settlers from the east. These settlers brought knowledge of metalworking, which led to more complex and integrated ways of living. Near the end of the 3rd millennium BC, the use of fashioned bronze to develop axes and other more advanced tools and weapons had spurred the development of a palace civilization on Crete, dubbed **Minoan** after the mythical king Minos. The Minoans used seals, hieroglyphics, and later a syllabic script, Linear A, which served for legal, mercantile, and sacred purposes; scholars posit that their language was not Greek, but rather an amalgam of Anatolian languages. The major palaces at Knossos, Malia, and Phaistos, which flourished between 2200 and 1450 BC, served as centers of government and religion and as bases for colonization of the Aegean, which had been made possible by advances in ship-building. A **Cycladic** culture remarkable for its unique wall frescoes and marble figurines grew alongside the Minoans. The Minoans were in close trading contact with Egypt and the rest of the Near East, and the lack of remains of defensive walls and military artifacts have led most to believe that the internal and foreign relations of the island were peaceful. Around 1700 BC the Minoans were able to recover and rebuild after a disaster destroyed their palaces,

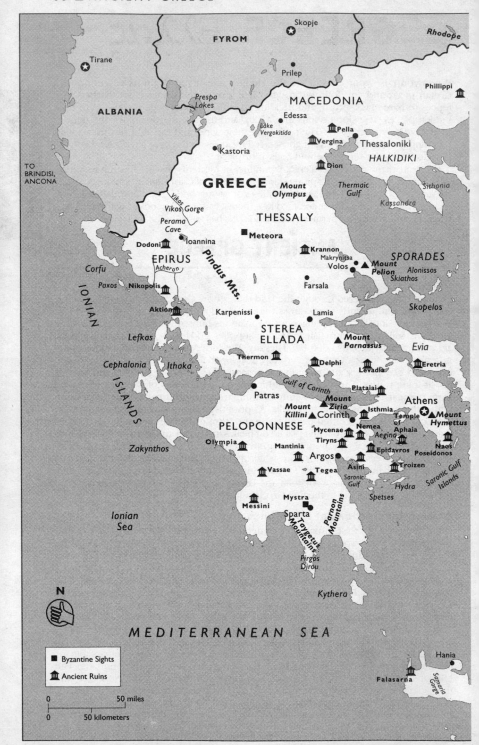

N

■ Byzantine Sights
🏛 Ancient Ruins

0   50 miles
0   50 kilometers

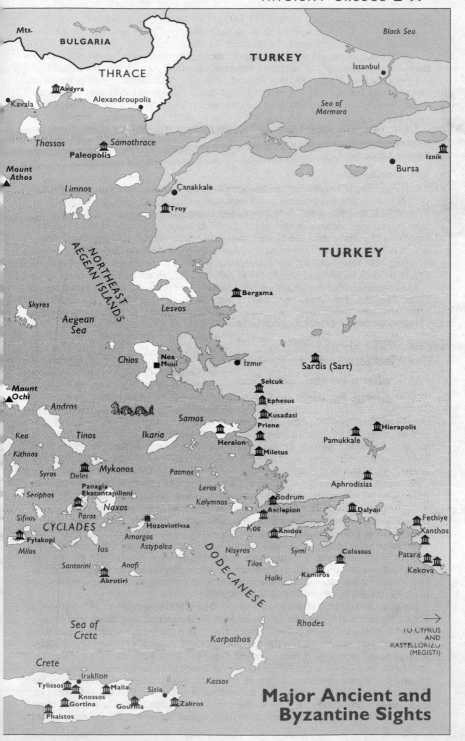

Mts.

BULGARIA

THRACE

Black Sea

TURKEY

İstanbul

Avdyra

Alexandroupolis

Kavala

Sea of Marmara

Thassos

Samothrace

Paleopolis

Bursa

Iznik

Mount Athos

Limnos

Canakkale

Troy

NORTHEAST AEGEAN ISLANDS

Skyros

Lesvos

Bergama

TURKEY

Aegean Sea

Chios

Nea Moni

İzmir

Sardis (Sart)

Mount Ochi

Andros

Selcuk

Samos

Ephesus

Kusadasi

Ikaria

Priene

Hierapolis

Heraion

Pamukkale

Kea

Tinos

Miletus

Kithnos

Patmos

Syros

Delos

Mykonos

Leros

Aphrodisias

Seriphos

Panagia Ekatontapiliani

Naxos

Kalymnos

Bodrum

Sifnos

Paros

Asclepion

Dalyan

Fethiye

CYCLADES

Hozoviotissa

Kos

Knidos

Xanthos

Fylakopi

Amorgos

Astypalea

Patara

Milos

Ios

Nisyros

Symi

Colossus

Kekova

Santorini

Anafi

Tilos

Kamiros

Akrotiri

Halki

DODECANESE

Sea of Crete

Rhodes

TO CYPRUS AND KASTELLORIZO (MEGISTI)

Karpathos

Crete

Iraklion

Kassos

Tylissos

Malia

Sitia

Knossos

Gortina

Zakros

Gournia

Phaistos

Major Ancient and Byzantine Sights

but a mysterious cataclysm around 1450 BC put an end to their dominance. An earthquake and series of tidal waves following the eruption of the Thera volcano on Santorini may have brought about the Minoans' demise.

Another possible explanation is invasion and destruction at the hands of the more martial **Mycenaeans** of the mainland. Mycenaean culture, centered in the Argolid on the Peloponnese, reaches its apex around 1250 B.C. Their citadels, now revealed at Mycenae and Tyrins, were fortified with immense boulders which formed Cyclopean walls. They held military sway over the southern mainland, Crete, the Cyclades, and even as far as Cyprus. The Mycenaeans spoke a proto-Greek language, expressed in Linear B, a script developed from the Minoan Linear A. The invasions of the **Dorians,** who swept down from Epirus and Macedonia from 1100 to 1000 BC, set back the Bronze Age advances of palaces, scripts, and widespread trade.

The Dorian Era

The coming of the Dorians has traditionally been reckoned a **Dark Age** in which the peoples of Greece were isolated and impoverished. Recent finds from a tomb on Evia, intricately constructed and richly furnished with jewels and goods from abroad, have placed such views in doubt. Although the Dorians were, upon their arrival, less advanced in culture than the Mycenaeans and Minoans who had preceded them, within a few centuries of their initial occupation in the **Archaic Period** there began to emerge the images, ideas, and designs that would generate the basic structures of Classical Greek society and forever fire the Western imagination.

The Homeric poetic tradition took form in the 9th century BC and left a permanent cultural imprint of the conflicts of the Mycenaean Era in a now thoroughly Greek language and script. To the ancient Greeks, the **Trojan War** and its poet-historian **Homer** were very real defining events of the past, but now scholars question the epics' claims to factual description of a war between Greeks and Trojans and whether they sprung from one poet's compassion or a long-standing culture of rhapsodists. In the *Iliad* and the *Odyssey*,

From these urban centers colonists spread Greek culture throughout the Mediterranean as far east as Trabzon on the Black Sea and as far west as Spain

Greeks are referred to variously as Achaeans, Danai, and Argives, but by the 8th century BC, Greeks had come to refer themselves as **Hellenes,** a term derived from the name of a tribe in southern Thessaly. They carefully distinguished themselves from foreigners by referring to non-Hellenes as *barbaroi* (barbarians), a term that connoted foreign speech (to them, anything but Greek sounded like *bar bar bar*).

Although they were able to achieve a strong sense of common language (in contrast to the peoples of the east, west, and north), tradition, and ancestry the Hellenes were far from unified. The Archaic period saw the rise of the *polis,* or **city-state,** as the predominant form of political organization. Greek city-states blossomed all over what today is Greece as well as on the Aegean coast of Asia Minor and in Cyprus. From these urban centers colonists spread Greek culture throughout the Mediterranean as far east as Trabzon on the Black Sea and as far west as Spain. The great political, commercial, and cultural diversity of these city-states both facilitated the blossoming of Greek culture in the 6th and 5th centuries BC and prevented their institutions from lasting more than a few centuries.

Religious and athletic festivals such as the **Olympic Games** (see p. 147) became a forum for interstate relations as the athletic fields, arenas, and racetracks hosted heated contests with great political ramifications. Most city-states were dominated by an oligarchy of aristocrats, but the specifics of their political organizations, military strategies, and economic dynamics varied. **Corinth** (see p. 126), in control of the isthmus between Attica and the Peloponnese, cultivated both an influential crafts industry and a seafaring commercial culture by which it maintained control over its far-flung colonies. **Sparta** (see p. 162), expanding over the south of the Peloponnese, established a firm economic base in the surrounding lands and proceeded to bring most of the rest of the Peloponnese into its sphere of influence. The Spartans would come to be known for the intense martial aspect of their culture. Male children were essentially born into the army, and their lives until the age of 60 were spent in military preparation, conquest, or defense. Despite an intense rivalry which later culminated in war, Sparta and Athens, along with the city-states under their sway, united against the Persian King **Xerxes** in the early 5th century BC. They defeated the Persians at Salamis, Marathon, and Platea and defended mainland Greece from the foreign domination suffered by several islands and the city-states on the coast of Asia Minor. Meanwhile, on the western front, the city-states of Sicily and southern Italy came together to fend off the encroaching **Carthaginians** from North Africa.

Classical Greece

From 480 to 323 BC, through decades of war, invasion, occupation, and internal conflict, **Athens** (see p. 69) produced innovations in art, literature, philosophy, and politics that have served as the touchstones of Western culture ever since. In the early 6th century the law giver **Solon** had ended the enslavement of Athenians at the hands of other Athenians and established equality for all citizens before the law. In 462 BC **Pericles** established democracy in Athens so that every male citizen took part in government as chosen by lot. In contrast to the Spartans, Athenians valued their ability to successfully wage war and augment their territories without subjecting everyone to the permanently martial lifestyles of the Spartans. Regulations of ostracism allowed for the expulsion of political figures who had accumulated too much influence and threatened the principles of democracy.

Above all, the Athenians took pride in their public monuments; the spectacular Acropolis of Athens, including the **Parthenon** (see p. 92), dates from this period. These cultural achievements were made possible by the wealth Athens had accrued from trade and its command of the **Delian League,** which had been formed as an alliance against Persia. After the defeat of Darius, the members of the Delian League became imperial subjects of Athens, and the Thirty Years Peace of 445 BC set off a cold war between Athenian and Spartan forces for 14 years.

Not satisfied with the perfection achieved in his own city, Pericles challenged the Spartans on both ideological and military terms, and the rivalry exploded into the **Peloponnesian Wars,** which lasted 27 years and ended in a nominal defeat for Athens after a hopeless attack on Syracuse. During this period the very structure of the Greek city-state began to rot from within; the Athenian historian **Thucydides,** our best source on the Peloponnesian Wars, identified the problem as a *stasis*—the cities themselves lost their internal unity, and extremist groups challenged the protonationalism of city-states.

Despite all the complications of this period, the culture and economics of Greece had ascended to levels of beauty and efficiency rarely matched before or since. Greek commercial culture realized full-scale **capitalism** with the establishment of banks and even a system of insurance to protect commercial ventures at sea. Never before had there been such ease of trade from one end of the Mediterranean to the other. In Athens, Praxiteles, Euripides, and Plato developed sculpture, drama, and philosophy into their full Classical forms.

The Macedonians and the Hellenistic Era

As the Greeks fought among themselves, the Persians and Carthaginians again began to encroach from the east and west, but in the midst of the Peloponnesian Wars a new political force was gaining strength in **Macedonia.** Between 360 and 320 BC, the Macedonians, under **King Philip II,** conquered many Greek cities. The Macedonians were labeled barbarians by their neighbors to the south. **Demosthenes** of Athens, a respected orator and statesman, staunchly resisted the Macedonians, labelling Philip a corrupt despot. **Aristotle,** a student of Plato and the last great Greek philosopher, was denied leadership of Plato's academy in Athens because he was Macedonian. Aristotle returned to Macedonia as a tutor to Philip's son, **Alexander the Great.** At first Alexander, whose allegiances may have lain with his mother **Olympias** of Epirus, stood in the shadow of his father, who after defeating Athens and Thebes had brought all Greeks into a union under his monarchical leadership to challenge Persia. In 336 BC, Philip died as a result of palace intrigues, and Alexander seized power.

After he consolidated power in Greece, razing Thebes in the process, Alexander crossed the Hellespont and tore across Anatolia, liberating Greek and Phrygian lands from the Persians. He then moved south bringing the Levant and Egypt under his control and founding **Alexandria** on the Nile. He had justified his rule to the Greeks and those he conquered by claiming to be a god himself, and in Egypt he visited the oracle of **Zeus Ammon** where he was recognized as the son of the god. In 331 BC, he launched a full-scale offensive against the Great Persian cities of Babylon, Ecbatana, and Persepolis. Upon the death of the Persian King **Darius** in 331 BC, Alexander assumed the title *Basileus* and set off on campaigns into Central Asia and India. Among the most innovative but unsuccessful of his policies at this point was to promote the intermarriage of Greeks and Macedonians with Persian aristocrats to create a new hybrid ruling class loyal only to its new king. Returning in 325 BC because his army refused to follow him past the Indus river, Alexander died of fever in the next year at age 33 and his body was delivered to Alexandria.

Alexander left no designated heir, and, after his death, violent conflicts ravaged his empire as his generals vied for control of the various territories and partitioned Greece, Egypt, and Asia. Nevertheless, Alexander's enduring legacy was the spread of Hellenic culture and the Greek language throughout the lands he conquered. During what is called the **Hellenistic Era,** the Classical literary and artistic forms that had been developed in Athens were diffused throughout the Hellenistic kingdoms and infused with local Near Eastern influences.

Under the leadership of Greek and Macedonian officers, **Antioch** in Syria, capital of the Seleucids, and Alexandria, capital of the Ptolmies, superceded the Aegean region in cultural achievement during the Hellenistic Era. Macedonia and the north of Greece came under the control of the Antigonids, who had substantial holdings across Anatolia. By 224 BC the Achaean Confederacy on the Peloponnese and the Aetolian Confederacy centered in Delphi provided for tenuous organization of the cities of Greece. In 146 BC, after 50 years of skirmishes and political intrigue, **Romans** razed Corinth and began to fill the power vacuum in Alexander's wake. While Roman legions took hold of Greek lands, Hellenic culture took hold of Roman society. The Romans adopted what they believed to be the best aspects of the Greek cultural legacy and added their own improvements and innovations to create a hybrid culture which would be enormously influential around the world.

RELIGION & MYTHOLOGY

The Use of Myth

For millennia, Greek mythology, always vivid and scandalous, has provided artists and poets with an inexhaustible repository of inspiration. The narratives of Greek mythology served two purposes, aetiological and semi-historical. **Aetiological myths** came about as divine explanations of the creation of natural phenomena or of the foundation and naming of towns and cities. Such myths involve a drama enacted by a pantheon of anthropomorphic gods and mortals. For example, the island of Ikaria is supposed to have been created when the mortal Icarus while escaping from imprisonment on Crete

For millennia, Greek mythology, always vivid and scandalous, has provided artists and poets with an inexhaustible repository of inspiration

flew too close to the sun and had his wax-wings melted by the gods. **Semi-historical myths** resulted from the embellishment of historical events. The war heroes of these myths owe their exploits to divine ancestry and divine intervention on their behalf, but it is likely that mythical heroes were based on real historical characters. The names of Homeric heroes—Achilles, Odysseus, Agamemnon, Priam, and Hector—were probably the names of real kings and military leaders of the Mycenaean Era, and the story of the Trojan War probably had some basis in a constant conflict between kingdoms of Greece and those on the Aegean coast of Anatolia. These names were memorialized in songs, poems, and places named to commemorate the deeds of great men.

Greek myths were passed from generation to generation and region to region, and gradually altered to reflect local political and religious concerns. Painting, sculpture, oral and written poetry transmitted the myths through time, and as many artists and rhapsodists tried their hand at each myth, the stories took on new, varied, and conflicting sacred details and meanings. In all these variations, Greek myths defy the simplifications imposed upon them by the modern psychoanalytic approach of archetyping; the **Oedipus** myth, as presented by Sophocles, contemplates the guilt of the ignorant and has nothing to do with any innate desire of man to knock off his father and bed his mother.

The Pantheon

The anthropomorphic gods and goddesses of the Greek **pantheon** as well as various minor divinities and heroes were the object of the worship of **mystery cults.** For civic and religious purposes the worship of gods often took on characteristics entirely alien to the character of the god as he appeared in dramatic mythical narratives. Traditionally, there were 14 major deities, most of whom resided on **Mt. Olympus,** in addition to scores of minor nymphs, satyrs, and heroes who had a share in divinity and regional devotees.

The king of the gods, **Zeus,** gained power by dethroning and killing his father **Kronos;** this changing of the guard is parallel to the invasions of the Dorians and their importation of their own deities to displace those of the Minoans and Mycenaeans. In his extramarital exploits, he was even more infamous than less powerful but equally randy minor deities. Zeus was a sexual gymnast, ready and willing to get down and dirty with just about anyone, as long as his baleful wife **Hera,** who presided over mortal child-bearing and marriage, wasn't looking. Zeus' mortal lovers, however, were not always willing or easily accessible: Danae, imprisoned in a tower by her father, was impregnated by Zeus in the form of a golden shower. Worse still for mortals, Hera, powerless to injure her husband directly, lavished her vengeance on the objects of his lust. Io was turned into a cow and chased by an enormous gadfly. Leto, pregnant with **Artemis,** goddess of the hunt, and **Apollo,** god of light and music, was forbidden to rest on solid ground until the itinerant island of Delos lent its shore for her to give birth. Callisto, who got off relatively easy, was changed into a bear. Semele, one of Zeus' voluntary cohorts, dissolved into ash. The overarching lesson of stories involving Zeus and sex, many of which come to us from Ovid's lurid accounts in the *Metamorphoses,* seems to be that **mortals never win.** Conversely, Zeus' civic and religious character, especially during the Classical period, affirmed law and morality, which he could impose with thunderbolts thrown from lofty Olympus.

Poseidon, god of the sea, attracted the veneration of sailors because he caused earthquakes, storms, and other natural disasters. Although he wasn't as promiscuous as his brother Zeus, he did score with the snake-haired gorgon Medusa, spawning Pegasus the winged horse. The odd couple of Greek mythology were **Hephaestus,** the lame god of smiths, fire, and volcanoes, worshipped by craftsmen, and **Aphrodite,** goddess of sex, love, beauty, and fertility. Their union was the source of constant frustration for the lascivious sex goddess and embarrassment for the divine smith. Often Aphrodite directed her adulterous affections toward **Ares,** god of war, who was typically worshipped by military cults.

Athena, goddess of wisdom, watched over the city of Athens and guided Odysseus on his long way home from Troy. No offspring of sexual intrigue, she popped out of Zeus' skull. **Hermes,** the messenger god and patron of thieves and tricksters, was regularly dispatched from Olympus to deliver the certified will of the gods to reluctantly obedient heroes. **Hades,** lord of the underworld, was also called *Ploutos* (wealthy one) by the mortally deferential Greeks.

Demeter, goddess of the harvest, and **Hestia,** goddess of the hearth, were the objects of particularly intense cult worship. At Eleusis, celebrants took vows to Demeter to gain her favor in making the soil fertile. As long as beachside hedonism continues in the Aegean, **Dionysis** a.k.a. Bacchus, god of the vine, remains immortal. Bacchants, often sex-crazed young women, sought divine ecstasy by deranging their senses with excess amounts of alcohol and sex.

In addition to the gods, many humans and minor deities figured prominently in Greek mythology. The three **Fates**—Atropos, Clotho, and Lachesis—spun, measured, and snipped the threads of humans' lives. The **Furies,** also optimistically called *Eumenides,* or "kindly ones," punished evildoers. The nine **Muses** brought inspiration to poets, artists, and musicians. Dryads and naiads inhabited trees and streams; nymphs cavorted in the fields; satyrs, or goat-men with long beards and tails, frolicked with maenads in the holy groves. Humans had their place in mythology as well, though not always willingly: the talented weaver Arachne, because she dared compete with Athena, was turned into a spider, lending her name to taxonomy. Tantalus was condemned to stand in a pool in Tartarus, forever tormented by hunger and thirst and surrounded by food and water just beyond his grasp. Europa was ravished by Zeus disguised as a bull.

Religion

Greek religion evolved out of these sacred stories. Unlike the denominations of most modern religions, Greek religious sects lacked any overarching unity or exclusivity, but were instead tied inextricably to localities and specific temples and rites. Some locales, such as Delphi and Eleusis, were heralded as sacred places throughout the ancient world. Practices such as **Orphism**—a widespread movement inspired by didactic verse attributed to the mythical minstrel Orpheus who had descended to Hades to retrieve his wife Eurydice—were tied, howeve,r not to places but to texts and could be celebrated anywhere in combination with other rituals. A Greek could be affiliated with any number of mysteries and, as a polytheist, could offer sacrifice and seek the favor of any number of

> *Rituals were often as scandalous as the myths that inspired them. Participants sought to achieve an ecstatic state through extreme chemical intoxication or large-scale orgies*

deities and immortal heroes. These rituals were often as scandalous as the myths that inspired them. Participants sought to achieve an ecstatic state through extreme chemical intoxication or large-scale orgies.

An always dynamic phenomenon, Greek religion took on drastically different forms from century to century. Between the Homeric age and the Classical era the idea of alienation of the soul from the body crept into the Greek religious consciousness. Alexander's conquests in Asia brought about a syncretism of Greek and Near Eastern sacred currents. Christianity emerged from this Hellenistic muddle—the Gospels were written in Greek—and, once co-opted by the Imperial seat in Byzantium, spelled the end of the diverse conglomerate of Greek paganism.

LANGUAGE & LITERATURE

> *Wherever literature consoles sorrow or assuages pain; wherever it brings gladness to eyes which fail with wakefulness and tears, and ache for the dark house and the long sleep, there is exhibited in its noblest form the immortal influence of Greece.*
>
> —Macaulay

The earliest appearances of written language in Greece are Minoan palace record tablets inscribed in duo-syllabic scripts called **Linear A and B.** These treasury records, somewhat uninspiring in content and probably dating from the end of the Bronze Age (roughly 1100 BC), were often preserved, ironically, by baking in the fires that destroyed the palaces themselves. From the 11th to the 8th centuries BC, the Greeks were generally illiterate, and it was not until the **Homeric** *Iliad* and *Odyssey* that material written in the Greek script first appeared. Scholars still question whether Homer actually composed these works. **Hesiod,** roughly Homer's contemporary, composed *Works and Days,* a farmer's-eye view of life, as well as the *Theogony,* the first systematic account in Greek of the creation of the world and the exploits of the gods. During the 7th century BC, **Archilochus** of Paros began to write anti-heroic, anti-Homeric elegies, including the often-imitated fragment in which he expresses no shame at abandoning his shield in battle to save his own life. On the island of Lesbos, during the 5th century, the gifted lyric poet **Sappho** and her contemporary **Alcaeus** sang of love, sex, and the beauty of nature; the Latin poet **Horace** would later revive their images and appropriate their meters. **Pindar** of Thebes (518-438), acclaimed by the ancients as the greatest of lyric poets, wrote Olympic odes commissioned by nobles to commemorate athletic victories.

Herodotus, the so-called "Father of History," captured the monumental battles and personalities of the Greco-Persian conflict in the *Persian Wars* while **Thucydides** immortalized the Athenian conflict with Sparta in his *Peloponnesian Wars.* **Xenophon** in the *Anabasis* detailed a march across Asia Minor, including a hallucinogenic detour along the Black Sea coast. **Callimachus** (305-240), living in Alexandria, wrote elegies in Hellenistic Greek, of which only fragments remain. His influence was felt during the Alexandrian revival in Rome, when poets like **Catullus** took his warning *mega biblion, mega kakon* (long book, big bore) to heart.

THEATER

The earliest forms of drama are said to have developed in the 5th century BC from goat songs *(tragodoi)* related to the cult of the god Dionysus. Wealthy patrons sponsored public festivals in his honor; contests were held in open-air theaters and choruses of masked men would sing and dance. According to legend, drama was born when young **Thespis,** the first Athenian thespian, stepped out of the chorus to give a brief soliloquy.

One of the great tragedians, **Aeschylus** (525-456 BC), perfected this new art form by adding a second actor and having the two actors each play several characters. His famous works include the perplexing *Prometheus Bound* and the *Oresteia,* a trilogy about Agamemnon's ill-fated return home from the Trojan war and its aftermath. **Sophocles** (496-406) created the famous *Oedipus* trilogy. **Euripides** (485-406 BC) wrote *Medea* and *The Bacchae.* "Old Comedy," a bawdy, slapstick medium, arose in the late 5th century. The greatest playwright of this genre was **Aristophanes** (450-385), who wrote *The Clouds, Lysistrata,* and *The Frogs.* Unfortunately, only 11 of his 40 plays survive. **Menander,** the father of "New Comedy," wrote more mannered comedies—love stories (usually involving lovers star-crossed through cases of mistaken identity, kidnapping, etc.) with happy endings. This set the tone for later writers (hello, Shakespeare). Greek theater did not end with the Classical era; particularly on Crete, drama continues as a vital art form.

The **Athens Festival,** held from June to September, features Classical drama at the ancient **Theater of Herod Atticus** located below the Acropolis. The festival also includes concerts, opera, choruses, ballet, and modern dance. Ancient plays are staged from July to September at the **Epidavros Festival,** 78km from Athens (see p. 138). A language barrier won't detract from the ominous choreography of the chorus, which, in Aeschylus' time, made "boys die of fright and women have miscarriages." Tickets and programs for the theater series at both festivals are available two weeks in advance at the Athens Festival Box Office, 4 Stadiou St., inside the arcade. The same office sells tickets for a number of other smaller theaters and festivals. The **Philippi, Thassos,** and **Dodoni Festivals** all feature performances of classical drama in ancient theaters. The **Lycavittos Theater,** on Lycavittos Hill in Athens, hosts a variety of artistic events from mid-June to late August.

PHILOSOPHY

The real constitution of things is accustomed to hide itself.

—Heraclitus

The Pre-Socratics

Is philosophy a process of questioning? If so, this process began in 585 BC when **Thales** of Miletus asked, "What is everything made out of?" He answered incorrectly that everything is made of water and fell into a well. His pupil **Anaximander,** going out on a limb, suggested that all springs from the "Indefinite" and comes to be "according to necessity."

Meanwhile at a Greek colony on the isle of Sicily, **Pythagoras** played guru to a cult of vegetarians who were trying to get in touch with their past lives. Once Pythagoras saw someone beating a puppy and rescued it, claiming to have recognized the soul of a deceased friend in the pooch's bark. Somehow among this crunchy set of New-Agers, he drew a few right triangles and figured that the square of the hypotenuse equals the sum of the squares of its two legs. Writing foreboding verses that earned him the moniker "dark one," **Heraclitus** of Ephesus traced the causes of all things to the *"logos."* In Greek this term usually denotes "word" or "reason," but in Heraclitus' case philologists have not yet come up with a satisfying translation. Heraclitus pointed out that you can never step twice in the same river, and rejected mystery cults and alcohol. He spoke with both political and metaphysical overtones when he said, "War is father and king of all, and some he shows as gods, others as men; some he makes slaves others free." **Parmenides** drew the line between appearance and reality by saying that what is, must be, and cannot not be, so we shouldn't even bother to think about what is not because we can't. His pupil **Zeno** blew to pieces such absurdly naive notions as motion and plurality. **Empedocles,** another Sicilian, conceived of the universe as the constant recombination of four elements—earth, air, fire, and water. The cosmological queries of these men, all of whom made significant contributions to early Greek astronomy, come down to us in fragments of papyrus and in the reports of later writers.

Socrates, Plato, & Aristotle

"Know thyself," said a poor, ugly convict who likened himself to a gadfly on the ass of the horse that was Classical Athens. **Socrates** brought philosophy down from the stars to the stalls of the Athenian *agora,* calling anyone who would converse with him to task over the minute moral aspects of their lives and facilely refuting their false beliefs. All the while he maintained an ironic facade of ignorance, maintaining that he knew more than all men only in that he was cognizant of his own lack of knowledge. His radical life-style eventually drew the ire of influential Athenians, and he was sentenced to death in 399 BC on the charge of corrupting youth.

> *"Know thyself," said a poor, ugly convict who likened himself to a gadfly on the ass of the horse that was Classical Athens*

Xenophon and Aristophanes both recorded Socrates' exploits, sometimes less than flatteringly, but most of what we know of the philosopher comes from the copious works of his allegedly corrupted pupil **Plato.** In his dialogues Plato paid tribute to Socrates' technique of refutation and later used him as a mouthpiece for his own moral and metaphysical doctrines. According to his Theory of Forms, the sensory world was the constantly changing semblance of a world of permanent immutable forms or ideas, which men can only come to know through an intense process of dialectic. He practiced an ecstatic rationalism appropriating the Greek mythological tradition and turning its gaudy and fantastic tales into urgent moral arguments. Plato was no democrat; in the *Republic,* an enlightened philosopher-king emerges from the cave of unknowing to guide society into the light of knowledge.

Aristotle, a student of Plato's, reacted critically toward his teacher's idealism. A biologist, he grounded himself in specimens at hand, appreciating the reality of the sensible world instead of relying on abstract ideas. Aristotle's empirical approach took hold of Western science and retained an influence that lasted through the Middle Ages. Politically Aristotle was grounded in the notion of civic life. Whereas Plato and Socrates had held that a man could never live a truly moral and at the same time politically active life, Aristotle's concept of the moral life was tied inextricably to the Greek *polis* and civic responsibility. When Athens came under pressure from Philip, Aristotle was forced to return to his native Macedonia, where he became tutor to Alexander the Great.

ART & ARCHITECTURE

*Such is the bloom of perpetual newness upon these works which makes
them ever to look like untouched by time, as though the unfaltering breath
of an ageless spirit had been infused in them.*

—Plutarch

It is important to remember that what we now isolate of Greek architecture and art
for its historic and aesthetic value was inseparable from its **civic context** in ancient
Greece. Although the Greeks prized beauty above all else, the idea of "art for art's
sake" was foreign to a world where form was inextricably linked to function. Greek
statues formed an integral part of temples; they were votive offerings, monuments to
the dead, commemorations of events in the life of the city. Pottery, while decorative,
was a hot export item, used for both storing wine and chugging it at dinner parties.
The mostly mythological scenes that formed the subject matter of Greek art were
vehicles for contemporary religious expression, humor, or political propaganda.

Armed with the mantra that "man was the measure of all things," ancient Greek art
focused on the human form, flirting with geometrical abstraction and stylized shapes
before developing a highly refined grammar of naturalistic representation. Emphasiz-
ing order, proportion, and symmetry,
ancient Greek architecture idealized light
and space in its purest form. It is impossible
to overestimate how much Western culture
owes to the architectural and artistic
achievements of the ancient Greeks, from
the Neo-Classical facades of Washington,
D.C., Paris, and London to the Renaissance's Michelangelo, the Victorians's Ruskin,
and the Modernists' Brancusi. The timeless spirit of Greek art as evoked by Plutarch is
as fresh today as it was under the Romans.

> *Emphasizing order, proportion, and symmetry, ancient Greek architecture idealized light and space in its purest form*

Cycladic and Minoan Period (3000-1100BC)

The most eminent artistic contribution to the culture of the Aegean Bronze Age in the
third millennium BC was the minimalist elegance of **Cycladic sculpture.** Made of Naxian or Parian marble, these figurines, with lengths varying anywhere from several
inches to several feet, owe their charm to the simplification of the human form. A typical statuette is a naked goddess with arms folded rectilinearly, her gaze a calm geometrical abstraction. Excellent examples of these enigmatic idols that captivated the
imagination of such 20th-century artists as Picasso are showcased at the **Goulandris
Museum of Cycladic and Ancient Greek Art** in Athens (see p. 97).

When it came to **architecture,** the civilizations of the Aegean Bronze Age took
their cue from the Minoans on Crete, whose monumental palaces admirably combined functionality and aesthetics. The **Minoan palaces** were cities unto themselves
whose complexity, evoked in the myth of the labyrinth, was a function of the administrative and religious role of the king in Minoan society. Under the Minoan palace's
roof were housed commodious royal apartments, domestic quarters, artisanal workshops, extensive storehouses with rows of *pithoi* storing oil, wine, and grain, shrines,
and offices for the scribes frantically trying to keep tabs on all the hoopla.

In 1899 **Sir Arthur Evans** started excavating and reconstructing a gigantic Minoan
palatial complex at **Knossos** (see p. 389) on the island of Crete. Similar palaces were
later uncovered at Phaistos (see p. 393), Malia (see p. 409), Gournia (see p. 411), and
Zakros (see p. 424) whose basic plans—a vast network of rooms sometimes rising to
three stories grouped asymmetrically around a central court—remained consistent
despite having had to be rebuilt after the periodic earthquakes which rocked the
Minoan world. These palaces featured aspects of the Near Eastern architectural aesthetic assimilated by the Minoans through commerce with ancient Egypt and Meso-
potamia: the careful chiseling of stone into large square slabs, the decorative use of
stucco, massive pillars, ceremonial stairways, and the implementation of sophisticated drainage systems.

Minoan architecture shunned exterior windows, disseminating light instead from the inside by means of light wells and wooden colonnades. Cool, well lit, and airy, the interior spaces of Minoan palaces were bedecked with bright frescoes. Known for their quasi-religious bull leaping ceremonies, magical gardens, wild goats and nubile dolphins, **Minoan frescoes** delighted in the challenge of wet plaster, responding with a vivid palette of yellow, blue, red and black pigments, a lively, impressionistic brush-stroke, and an impressive attention to naturalistic detail. Men were painted in red, women were painted white. Good examples of such frescoes were excavated on Santorini (see p. 337). Preserved by the eruption of the island's volcano around 1500 BC, these frescoes can be seen at the National Archaeological Museum in Athens (see p. 96). Similar fresco paintings, restored *in situ* by Sir Arthur Evans, can be seen at Knossos or in **Iraklion's Archaeological Museum** (see p. 387).

Minoan artisans were also renowned throughout the Aegean for their polychrome, **Kamares style pottery.** Named after the cave sanctuary in which it was first identified, the Kamares style consists of red and white ornamentation on a dark ground, the designs striking a subtle balance between curvilinear abstract patterns and stylized motifs derived from plant and marine life. Minoan craftsmen were most successful in their plastic endeavors when working on a small scale. Combining the pictorial flair displayed in the palatial frescoes with their skills in low relief they produced magnificent gold cups, ryhtons, pendants, sealstones, and signet rings with detailed engravings of animals, revelries, and cult scenes. The Minoans produced no monumental sculpture but instead churned out miniature votive statuettes such as the two *faience* **snake goddesses** (snakes were holy in the matriarchal Minoan religion), now, along with a broad range of Minoan artifacts, in Iraklion's Archaeological Museum.

Mycenaean Period (1600-1100BC)

In 1874 **Heinrich Schliemann,** fresh from his successful dig at Troy and eager to further establish a factual basis for the Homeric epics, began to excavate **Mycenae** (see p. 131), legendary home of Agamemnon. Schliemann's findings of massive walls and elaborate tombs laden with dazzling artifacts seem to fit Homer's description of Mycenae as a "well-built citadel. . . rich in gold."

The **architecture** of the mainland Mycenaean culture developed against the background of the Minoan civilization it began to supercede in 1500BC. The **palaces** at Mycenae, Tiryns, and Pylos modified the layout of their Cretan prototypes resulting in a more symmetrical design centered around a **megaron**—a Near Eastern architectural form whose palatial version consisted of a pillared porch, a vestibule, and a large throne room with a central hearth around which four wooden columns supported the roof. The **frescoes** decorating the palace adapted the Minoan model to the more martial tastes of the Mycenaean. Typical subjects include a boar hunt at Tiryns, a war scene at Pylos, and warriors preparing for battle in the *megaron* at Mycenae.

Situated on rocky promontories, the Mycenaean citadels were fortified by immense walls (dubbed **"Cyclopean"** by later Greeks convinced that only giants could have lifted such stones). As impressive as the fortifications were the concealed tunnels at sites like **Tiryns** (see p. 138), which marked the first European use of the **corbel vault** (rows of masonry placed so that each row projects slightly beyond the one below, the two opposite walls meeting at the top), a forerunner of the arch. The Mycenaeans were also the first in Europe to produce **monumental sculpture**—of which the relief work of the triangular **Lion's Gate** at Mycenae (13th century BC) and the royal Mycenaean **tombs** are the most distinctive examples.

The graves of the Mycenaean royalty, grouped together within a circular enclosure, were at first (1600-1500 BC) hewn into rock, spacious shafts covered by a slab roof. The slab roof often bore relief work, spiral designs, or charioteers. Hoards of gold and silver cups, diadems, *faience,* carved ivory, jewelry, seal stones, imported pottery, and ornate bronze weapons inlaid with niello and gold were discovered by Schliemann in the **grave shafts,** testifying not only to Mycenaean sophistication but more importantly to the tremendous influence of Minoan culture on the Mycenaean decorative arts.

By 1500 BC graves of the Mycenaean royalty had evolved into stone **tholos**, or "beehive" shapes covered with a mound of earth. These structures consisted of a narrow passageway lined with blocks of stone which opened into a circular corbelled funerary chamber; the doorway was often crowned by a massive stone lintel and elaborately decorated with sculptured friezes. The designs of the low relief work exhibit Minoan influence but the monumental masonry, closely connected to the techniques used in the Lion's Gate, is distinctly Mycenaean.

Geometric Period (1100-700BC)

Out of the Dark Ages that followed the collapse of Mycenaean civilization emerged a new Hellenic artistic style with ceramics as its primary medium and Athens as its major cultural center. Athenian pottery from 1000 BC was decorated with Mycenaean-inspired motifs—spirals, arcs, wavy lines, and concentric circles.

This **Proto-Geometric Period** (1100-900 BC) gave way to the **Geometric Period** as artists developed more expressive styles of decorating clay figurines and pottery. Large bulbous vases often used as grave markers were completely covered with decorative motifs reminiscent of basket weaving—continuous bands of meanders, zigzags, checkers, and swastikas. These rhythmic friezes of geometric shapes, separated by tight rows of thick black lines, gradually began to include identically posed stickfigure humans and grazing or reclining animals.

Increased trade with the Near East toward the end of the Geometric Period resulted in the assimilation of Syrian and Phoenician floral and animal motifs. During this **Orientalizing** phase, Corinth joined Athens as a major ceramic center, churning out pottery decorated with friezes of lions, sphinxes, griffins, lotus palmettes, and rosettes. Toward the end of the 8th century Corinthian potters invented the **black figure technique** whereby figures were still drawn in silhouette as with Geometric pottery but details were now incised revealing the white clay beneath; red, purple and white paint were also added to the figures to accentuate particular features. Although the geometric and floral patterns developed during the Geometric period would move to the periphery to make way for the increased focus on the human form they continued to play a decorative role in Greek art for centuries.

Architecture in the Geometric period concentrated its energies on developing one-room temples with columned porches. Essentially the *oikos* (house) of the god or goddess to which it was dedicated, the temple housed a representation of the cult deity. To distinguish the temple from the layout of the secular *megaron* on which it was based, the interior space of the temple was based on an elongated plan with a raised altar toward the back of the room. The rubble and mud brick exterior of the temple was sometimes embellished by a **peristyle**, an outer colonnade of pillars supporting a thatched roof.

Archaic Period (700-480BC)

The **Archaic Period** marked the transition from the Geometric Period to the ultimate sophistication of the Classical Period. The increased prosperity of Greek city-states was reflected in the innovation of the two major orders of ancient Greek architecture—the Doric and Ionic orders—while sculpture and vase painting forged a stylized portrayal of the human form.

Architecture

The urban layout of the Greek city-state was crystallized during the Archaic Period. The typical Greek city-state had evolved near a former Mycenaean stronghold strategically positioned atop a rocky outcrop (the Spartans were too cool for natural or artificial defenses and chose to stick it out in the middle of a flat plain). Known as the **acropolis**, this fortified citadel was useful for defense in times of war. As relations between city-states became cordial, the acropolis transformed into a religious center bedecked with **temples** dedicated to the city-states' patron deities. With the rise of oligarchic and democratic governments, the **agora** (marketplace) became the center of the city's commercial and social life. Flanking the agora were **stoas** (colonnaded porticos) under whose roof could be found philosophers and various market stalls. In a democracy such as Athens, the ruling council met in the **bouleuterion** (council house). Various trappings of the frequent public spectacles and athletic contests— **amphitheatres, stadia,** and **gymnasia**—were outside the city center. Unlike the hodge-podge of modern cities, the public buildings of the city-state adhered to a common aesthetic order which was derived from the architectural evolution of the temple—the iconographic embodiment of the city's wealth and soul.

The temple had been the primary focus of architects since the Geometric period. The development of the **Doric order** in the 7th century BC gave the makeshift wood and mudbrick Geometric temple, with its one-roomed *cella* and surrounding peristyle, a massive stone facelift. Huge cylindrical Doric columns with cushion capitals and wide fluted shafts, but without bases, replaced wooden columns on the outside and inside of the temple. Above the columns was placed a stone **entablature** consisting of a plain **architrave,** a Doric **frieze** of alternating grooved **triglyphs** and square **metopes,** topped by cornices framing the facade's triangular **pediments.** The early cigar-shaped Doric columns would later be slimmed slightly and stucco-covered limestone would eventually replace stone in the order. But apart from these minor alterations, the Doric order changed little throughout its history, remaining the favorite order of the Greek mainland.

Around the 6th century BC the Greek colonies along the Aegean coast of Asia Minor produced the more exotic **Ionic order.** The columns of the Ionic order, distinguished by their twin **volute** (scrolled spiral) capitals, were more slender than those of the Doric; their shafts had more flutes and they rested upon swollen, fluted bases. The Ionic order's plain, continuous frieze was simpler than that of the Doric, but the upper orders of the Ionic entablature were bedecked with elaborately decorated moldings. The temples of the Ionic order, ornate and fussy, boasted forests of columns (the **Temple of Hera** at **Samos,** built in 530 BC, had 134) that counterbalanced the more austere Doric order.

Sculpture

The **free standing sculpture** of the Archaic period took its cue from the monumental sculpture of ancient Egypt. At the end of the 7th century, large-scale sculptures of idealized youths (called **kouroi**) appeared in sanctuaries as dedications to deities or as memorials to fallen warriors. A **kouros** (singular form of *kouroi*) always depicted a naked youth in a symmetrical stance, one leg forward, hands clenched on either side, with stylized curls and a goofy smile. An early example dedicated to Poseidon at Sounion (c. 590 BC), now stands in the **National Archaeological Museum of Athens.** An increased concern with natural forms in the 6th century BC coupled with marked technical advances led to more life-like *kouroi,* such as the stunning **Anavissos kouros,** also in the National Archaeological Museum in Athens (see p. 96). Although still conforming to the traditional stylization, these statues feature more realistic facial features and musculature with softer, more beguiling Archaic smiles. Idealized proportions and stylized patterns, however, continued to hold sway over a more thorough observation of natural anatomy. The female equivalent of the *kouros* was the **kore,** which, like the *kouros,* was usually created as a votive offering. Rather than treating the female body, Archaic sculptors focused on the patterning of female drapery. Straight and bunched folds and zig-zag hemlines suggested the stylized form of the female figure.

It wasn't until the beginning of the 5th century BC that free standing sculpture took the first step toward the naturalism of the Classical period. The relaxed posture of the **Kritias Boy** (c. 490 BC), now in the **Acropolis Museum** in **Athens** (see p. 93), broke the stiff, symmetrical mold of the archaic *kouroi.* This boy had individualized features—his weight shifted onto one leg, and his hips and torso tilted slightly.

More innovative advances in the depiction of the human body were made in **architectural sculpture.** During the Archaic period mythological narratives were used in temple architecture. The rectangular **metopes** of the Doric order were decorated with scenes of two or three figures forming part of a larger sequence, like the story of Jason and the Argonauts on the **Sicyonian building** at **Delphi** (see p. 182). The triangular Doric **pediment** proved to be more challenging, as its sloping corners made the conventional layout and scale of narrative sequences difficult. The pediment was first decorated by large central figures, like the **Gorgon** of the **Temple of Artemis** at **Corfu** (now in the **Archaeological Museum** in **Corcyra**). The central figure was flanked by figures diminishing in scale—smiling, bearded, snake-tailed demons or other weirdos filled the shallow corners of the pediment. By the end of the Archaic period, sculptors had resolved all discrepancies of scale and had hit upon battle scenes, such as those of the **Temple of Aphaia** at **Aegina,** as a means of reconciling the narrative sequence to the pediment. Sculptors filled the nooks of the pediment around the central deity figure with the battles' falling bodies. The complex battle positions of the figures forced Archaic sculptors to explore the dynamics of the human body, thus laying the foundation for the Classical period's development of the human form in architectural and free standing sculpture.

Sculptural **relief** was also employed during the Archaic period—mostly to decorate grave *stelae* and the friezes of Ionic temples. The Ionic order's plain frieze posed less of a spatial challenge than the Doric entablature, allowing a greater degree of flexibility in sculptural decoration. The north frieze of the **Siphnian Treasury** at **Delphi** (525 BC) is a prime example of this shallow relief work.

Vase Painting

By 630 BC the Athenian vase painters had successfully assimilated the **black figure technique** of the Corinthian school. After a few decades of emulating the Corinthians' animal friezes and floral designs, they began to show more interest in the portrayal of the human figure and narrative sequences. By the middle of the 6th century BC, Attic pottery had recaptured the artistic and commercial lead from Corinth.

Besides Athens and Corinth, many other schools of vase painting existed in the Greek world during the Archaic period. They all adhered to the basic conventions of the black figure technique, which featured black silhouettes with incised features. **Red paint** was applied to distinguish certain items of clothing and **white paint** to depict women's faces and bodies (the patriarchy rarely allowed women to leave the house; whiteness was therefore a female virtue). Human figures were always depicted in profile, though moving figures had their chests portrayed as if in a frontal pose. The eyes were also painted as if from the front, though the head was in profile. Emotion was signified through gesticulation rather than through facial expressions—figures pulled their hair in grief or flailed their arms and legs in joy. Drapery, too, was stylized, from simple folds of flat fabric to elaborate patterns of pleats and zig-zag hemlines. Convention also dictated the subject matter of the black figure vases, with stock scenes from mythology, like the Judgment of Paris, predominating.

Sculpture and vase painting mastered naturalistic representative techniques and raised the human form to an idealized plane of immortal cool that has been both the envy and the inspiration of Western art ever since

An excellent example of black figure painting is the work of **Exekias,** whose figures radiate a spiritual refinement. A calyx-krater he painted depicting Trojans and Greeks quarreling over Patroclus' body can be seen in Athens's **Agora Museum** (see p. 93). To a certain extent, the black figure style reached a dead-end with Exekias's mastery. The introduction of the **red figure technique** of vase painting around 540 BC, however, allowed vase painters to develop their art further. The exact opposite of the black figure technique, the red figure school painted the background black and left the figure the color of the reddish clay, painting details on with a fine brush. The evocative capacity of the line and the use of the brush in the red figure technique increased the subtlety of a subject's treatment. This closer attention to the human form, along with the inspiration provided by the progress of free standing sculpture, would reach its apogee in the vase painting of the 5th century BC.

Classical Period (480-323BC)

The arts flourished during the **Classical period,** as Athens reached the pinnacle of its political and economic power under Pericles and his successors. Pushing the Doric

Order to perfection while experimenting with the Ionic format, Classical temples featured greater spaciousness, fluidity, and grace than the stocky temples of the Archaic period. Sculpture and vase painting mastered naturalistic representative techniques and raised the human form to an idealized plane of immortal cool that has been both the envy and inspiration of Western art ever since.

Architecture

Built around 460 BC, the **Temple of Zeus** at **Olympia** (see p. 148), over 27 meters long, was the largest completed temple on the Greek mainland before the Parthenon. The temple's elegant facade and columns, slimmer than their squat Doric ancestors, together with its accurately modeled pedimental sculpture, exemplified the Classical dignity that had evolved before the Persians invaded Greece.

When Athens' fortune swelled in the middle of the 5th century BC thanks to the tribute of her empire, **Pericles** set aside a portion of the city's revenue to revamp the acropolis. Some claimed that the money for the lavish Periclean building program was ill-begotten and that, as Plutarch reports, Pericles was "gilding and bedizening" the city like a "wanton woman adding precious stones to her wardrobe." Proto-marxist misogynists aside, Pericles's foresight created a peerless architectural complex that defined "classic" for the Classical world.

The architects of the new Athenian acropolis (see p. 90) displayed an admirable flair for design in their contrast of the Doric and Ionic. The architect **Mnesikles** successfully married the slender interior Ionic columns of the acropolis' entrance, the **Propylaea,** with a massive Doric exterior. The decorative **Caryatid** and Ionic porches of the complicated **Erectheion** and the Ionic **Temple of Athena Nike** expertly offset the dignified Doric of the **Parthenon,** which itself sported an Ionic frieze.

The crowning glory of the Periclean project was the **Temple of Athena Parthenos** (the Maiden), or **Parthenon,** designed by the architect **Iktinos.** Iktinos added two extra columns to the usual six in the front row of the Doric order, lending an air of stately majesty to the broadened facade. More subtle refinements that transformed the usual Doric boxiness into the elegant Parthenon were the slight tapering of the temple's base and the ever so slight swelling of its columns. The Parthenon's elegant disposition was also a direct function of the Greek obsession with **proportion**— everything from the layout to the details of the entablature respected a four to nine ratio. Inside the temple, in front of a pool of water, stood Pheidias' *chef-d'oeuvre,* a 40-foot ivory and gold statue of Athena (since lost). The reflected glow of this statue in the dimly lit interior of the temple must have been an awesome sight.

The Parthenon's sculptural decorations celebrated Athenian civilization, illustrating the victory of order over disorder in such scenes as gods fighting giants, lapiths fighting centaurs, and the parade of heroes from the **Battle of Marathon** who fought the barbarous Persians. Athenian civic pride is further reflected in the unprecedented step taken by the Parthenon's frieze of illustrating a mortal subject, the Athenian Panathenaic procession, whereby the microcosm of Athenian society is received by the gods. The Athenians thought themselves the center of the civilized world. Expertly constructed, carved, fitted, and finished, the Parthenon's radiant symmetry was the ultimate symbol of the Classical aesthetic and of Athenian imperial ideology.

Sculpture

The pedimental sculpture of the **Temple of Zeus** at **Olympia,** continuing in the tradition of the Temple of Aphaia at Aegina, was a milestone in the evolution of early Classical sculpture. The figures of the western pediments' battle scenes displayed a marked improvement in the mastery of anatomical detail. Practically sculpted in the round, the standing male figures of the eastern pediment reflected the innovation of the Kritias Boy's relaxed posture—weight shifted onto a slightly bent leg. The rendering of drapery no longer seemed like fabric simply hung on a hanger—more realistic, the folds of the cloth now evoked the contours of the body. Although the figures bore hair stylized in the Archaic manner, their individualized bodies and faces could for the first time be said to be expressing a semblance of emotion. The conveyance of mood, despite the fact that later Classical sculpture suppressed emotion in favor of an impersonal idealism, is indicative of the complete break of the early Classical style with the formulaic approach of Archaic sculpture.

Excellent examples of early Classical period sculpture can be seen in the bronze statues of the **Charioteer** (470 BC) from **Delphi** (see p. 182) and the **Poseidon** from the **Artemisium wreck** (465 BC), now in Athens' National Archaeological Museum (see p. 96). The charioteer's eyes, inlaid with glass, and his lips, covered with copper, subtly animate the delicacy of his expression. The dynamic majesty that characterizes Poseidon can be attributed to the sheer perfection of his musculature and facial features. The charioteer's grace and Poseidon's naked heroism are the twin ideals to which the predominantly male culture of ancient Greece aspired and toward which Classical sculpture strove.

By the middle of the 5th century BC, sculpture had completely eschewed the idealized style of the Archaic period in favor of a detailed naturalism. Yet it did not use its expertise to portray realistic human features and emotions. Rather, Classical sculptors raised the human form to a plane of universal perfection while suppressing the particular imperfections that make the human form unique. The disinterested virtue of Platonic philosophy and the athletic heroism of Pindar's Olympic odes met in this iconographic idealism of the Classical period, known as the **Severe Style.**

The ultimate manifestation of this new style was the architectural sculpture of the Parthenon overseen by the masterful **Pheidias** in the late 5th century BC. After the Periclean building program, sculptors went back to their usual commissions: the grave **stele.** Usually consisting of two-figure groups—a seated woman with her maid or child or a husband bidding his wife farewell—these **relief** tombstones began to exhibit the dignified calm of the mature Classical period.

Free standing Classical sculptors like **Polyclitus,** famous in antiquity for his athletes, also characterized their sculptures with the ideal human form of the Severe Style. By the 4th century BC sculptors such as **Praxiteles** had developed free standing sculpture to a virtually life-like state, abandoning the lofty monumentality of the Severe Style to express more individualized human beings. Although their sculptures were incredibly accurate models, the human body's severe and somber beauty had been softened by an extremely relaxed pose, supple contours, and a gentler expression in the eyes. The **New Museum** in Olympia houses Praxiteles' **statue of Hermes** (360 BC) holding the baby Dionysus.

Vase painting

During the Classical Period red figure vase painting completely dominated the black figure technique. Painters adapted their decorations to a wider variety of vase forms with particular studios specializing in certain types. Inspired by the new-found naturalism in sculpture, masters of the early Classical period like the **Berlin Painter** and the **Kleophrades Painter** portrayed their subjects with an unparalleled level of dignity and pyschological insight. (A few ancient potters and painters signed their works, but most vases have been attributed to particular artists through scholarly attribution based on stylistic idiosyncrasies, hence the colorful pseudonyms.)

Although they were still limited to profile views of the head and had not yet learned to tackle the frontal pose, these painters successfully experimented with foreshortening and three-quarter views in order to suggest a variety of new poses, gestures, and emotions. The representation of clothing became freer, falling loosely in folds, as opposed to the Archaic stylization of pleats and zigzag hemlines. Emboldened by this new-found freedom of expression, the Classical red figure artists increasingly included scenes from everyday life, drinking parties, women in their private quarters, and athletic contests, alongside the usual heroes and Dionysiac revels. Their lines' supple vigor, attention to musculature, and anatomical detail produced figures which would be a major inspiration for later European representational painting.

By the middle of the 5th century BC, however, vase painting was slowly being reduced to a secondary art form, replaced by a burgeoning interest in sculpture. One exception to the growing degeneracy of vase painting was the **Achilles Painter,** whose masterful portrayal of a statuesque Achilles earned him his sobriquet. The drapery of his dignified figures, reflecting the influence of the Parthenon marbles, broke up the straight folds of the fabric into interrupted lines to evoke bunched material. He and his contemporaries expanded the range of their mythological subjects to focus on Athenian-related themes, not a surprising shift in light of the concurrent rise of Athenian political might.

In the later years of the 5th century BC vase paintings were characterized by sensuality, showiness, overly florid ornamentation, and diaphanously draped, effeminate figures. By the end of the 4th century BC the figured decoration of pottery had virtually died out in Attica, though offshoots of the Athenian school based in Sicily and on the Italian mainland continued production, albeit in decadent form.

Hellenistic Period (323-46BC)

Greek craftsmen working in the Greek colonies off the coast of Asia Minor had long been instrumental to the development of new forms back on the mainland. With the spread of Greek culture under Alexander the Great's empire, Hellenic art spread through Persia to the Indus Valley (the first portrayal of the Buddha in human form in the kingdom of Gandhara in northwestern India was influenced by Hellenic forms).

Under the eastern Greeks of the Hellenistic kingdoms architecture became a flamboyant affair with monumental complexes of temples, *stoas,* and palaces. The famous **Corinthian column,** fluted with a multi-leafed **acanthus** top, was first designed during the Hellenistic Period. The Monument of Lysicrates in Athens typifies this design. Enormous **amphitheaters** were built, most notably those at Argos and **Epidavros,** where the acoustics are so precise that more than 2000 years after their construction, a coin dropped on the stage can be heard in the theater's last row.

Hellenistic **sculpture** was passionate. As technically masterful as the Classical period, the spirit of Hellenistic sculpture displayed more vivid emotions than its Classical predecessor, daring even to sculpt the grotesque. Figures like **Laocoon** (a Roman copy of a Hellenistic original) writhe and twist inviting the viewer to inspect them from different angles. The appointment of **Lysippus** as court sculptor to Alexander the Great opened the way for Hellenistic sculpture to tackle **portraiture.**

With the advent of the **Roman empire** the Hellenistic style was assimilated to suit Roman tastes. Greek artists worked for Romans in Italy and for the old Hellenistic kingdoms of the East but the innovation of the Hellenistic *geist* had ceased.

THE BYZANTINE AND OTTOMAN ERAS

Far from being another sad chapter in the Decline and Fall of the Roman Empire, the Byzantine period was witness to the cultural transformation of a renewed and prosperous polity stretching from the Balkans through Greece to the Levant and Egypt. Although the Byzantines thought themselves heirs of the classical Roman Empire, they were in fact more Greek than Roman. Another and more fundamental change had also taken place—the majority of the population had converted to Christianity.

The imperial ideology of universalism — one world, one empire, one religion — successfully forged a unified political and economic state despite the heterogeneity of the Byzantine provinces

The imperial ideology of universalism—one world, one empire, one religion—successfully forged a unified political and economic state despite the heterogeneity of the Byzantine provinces. The emperor, the church, the Greek language, and the tax system bound together a cosmopolitan Byzantine culture of Greeks, Syriacs, Egyptian Copts, Armenians, and later, Slavs. Eventually internal religious quarrels and the pressure of successive waves of Persian, Arab, and Slav raiders weakened the empire.

The East Roman Empire

As Rome spread her imperial tentacles past Greece into the Near East, her massive bureaucratic mechanisms became increasingly decentralized. In the second century AD, Rome ceased to function as the true capital of her empire. Instead the capital moved as the emperor moved. At the start of the 4th century, under Emperor **Dio-**

cletian, a notorious persecutor of Christians, the empire was divided into a two-region tetrarchy. This system of four rulers soon amounted to a frantic scramble for power. **Constantine** was able to consolidate control of the empire.

Winning a battle over his rival for the power in AD 312, Constantine had seen a cross of light in the sun with the fiery inscription, "in this sign, conquer." He then converted to Christianity. With the Edict of Milan in the following year, Christianity became officially sanctioned in the empire. In 324 Constantine founded **Constantinople** over the ancient Greek city-state of Byzantium (modern Istanbul), on the west coast of the Bosporus strait where the Black Sea meets the Aegean. In 330 the city was dedicated as the new capital of the Roman Empire, and it came to be called *"Nea Romi"* (New Rome) or simply the *"Poli"* (the City) in Greek even into the Ottoman period. To differentiate this phase of empire from Rome's Classical era, scholars call it the Byzantine Empire.

Constantine died in 338 a baptized Christian, but his Empire had not turned Christian over night. His conversion served to change Christianity's status from that of an underground, outlaw cult to that of a state-sponsored religion. Because most of Constantine's immediate successors were drawn from his house, the throne remained Christian for a long time. **Julian the Apostate,** a nephew of Constantine who had received a Classical education around the Aegean, brought paganism briefly back to power from 361-363. Thereafter all emperors were Christian, but paganism remained a common, although not state-sponsored, practice for centuries to come. Although Constantinople was founded as a Christian city, pagan monuments have been found among 4th-century ruins within the city. After the death of Emperor Theodosius in 395 an official division was established between the Greek-speaking eastern half of the empire and the Latin west.

The Founding of the Christian Church

Under the Byzantine emperors, form was given to a nascent Christian culture. Evangelical missions were scattered in all directions. Christian art flourished in liturgical elaborations, hymns, biographies of saints, theological tracts, spiritual poetry, church architecture, religious icons, and mosaics. More significantly, **Seven Ecumenical Councils** rationalized the structure of the Christian Church and clarified its doctrines in a series of state-sponsored gatherings from the 4th to the 8th centuries.

The **Council of Nicaea** in 325 and the **Council of Constantinople** in 381 articulated the organization of the Church into five **patriarchates** (diocese)—Rome, Constantinople, Alexandria, Antioch, and Jerusalem. Each had its own patriarch (pope), who functioned as a sort of local governor in addition to his religious duties. Debates at these councils over the nature of Christ's divinity led to the banning of the heretical **Arians,** who believed that although Christ was the son of God, he was a created being of a different order of existence than God. The debate spurred by such heresy prompted the promulgation of the **Nicene Creed,** which held that God was "three persons in one substance." Christ the Son was of the same divine being as God the Father and the Holy Spirit. This **Christological** controversy brought about a struggle for supremacy among the rival patriarchates of Constantinople, Alexandria, and Rome, and a political headache for the imperial bureaucracy.

At the **Council of Ephesus** in 431, Nestorius, patriarch of Constantinople, was condemned for suggesting that Mary was the Mother of Jesus, not the Mother of God *(Theotokos).* Nestorius claimed that Christ's human and divine natures were two separate entities. Supplanting **Nestorianism,** the Alexandrian patriarch **St. Cyril** emphasized the single divine nature of Christ. **Leo I,** the pope of Rome, reacted swiftly, proposing a creed wherein Christ was simultaneously "truly God and truly man." The latter view triumphed at the **Council of Chalcedon** in 451 and **Monophysitism,** the belief in the single divine nature of Christ, was labeled heresy.

Confrontation and Commonwealth

During the 6th century, Emperor Justinian I battled the Sassanians of Persia on the eastern front. At the same time he committed his resources to reclaiming Rome and

GREECE

her territories in the West, which had been sacked by the Vandals swooping down from the north in 410, its emperor finally deposed in 477. Although he was able to sustain a peace with the Sassanians and to regain territories in Italy, Justinian overextended the empire's resources with his military campaigns, payoffs, and massive building projects, including the still-standing Agia Sophia church in Constantinople. He was able to simplify and codify the copious volumes of antiquated Roman law on which the empire still relied, but even with a wife rumored to be a monophysite— **Empress Theodora,** a scandalous Athenian beauty queen who saved her husband from the Nika Revolt at the Hippodrome in 532—he couldn't heal the empire's Christological wounds. The late 5th and early 6th centuries were a dark age on the Greek mainland, as Slavs, Mongols, and Avars swept down through the Balkans as far as the Peloponnese, pressuring the empire from the northwest. Greek culture and language were wiped out in many areas of the mainland and the Peloponnese; the Greek tongue and script were returned to these areas along with Christianity by later missions out of Constantinople.

A solution to Byzantium's monophysite dilemma loomed on the horizon—Islam and the Arab conquests. The loss of southeastern territories to the Caliphate, in the short term, consolidated and unified the empire, but a long struggle with Arab forces ensued on the sea and in the Taurus Mountains of Anatolia. Byzantine forces were able to fend off an Arab seige of Constantinople in 677. Constant defeats, however, brought a cultural reaction, **Iconoclasm.** Greeks came to believe that their practice of making icons of Christ and the saints, painting them on small surfaces or on city walls, and relying on them for protection in battle was a violation of the second commandment, and that their defeats were divine punishment. By imperial order in the early 8th century, all holy images in the empire were demolished. As the tides of war turned back and forth, **Iconoclasm** was abandoned and then revived until finally scrapped in 843 to the benefit of aesthetes wandering Greece ever since.

As the borders of the empire contracted, an increasing number of Christians once united under one ruler and capital were subjected to new, non-Christian rulers. Scholars refer to this Christian diaspora as the Byzantine Commonwealth. Meanwhile, Constantinople was becoming increasingly estranged from Rome and the west culminating in the Bishop of Rome's crowning of Charlemagne as Holy Roman Emperor in 800. The Greek Orthodox and Roman Catholic Churches formally parted ways by mutual excommunication in 1054.

A dynasty of Macedonians led by Basil I came to power in Constantinople in 867, ruling until the death of **Basil II,** the **"Bulgar Slayer,"** in 1025. During this period missionaries, bringing letters and Christianity, reached out from the empire's contracted borders into Slavic kingdoms in the Balkans and Russia.

In 1071 at **Manzikert** in eastern Anatolia, the Byzantines lost a crucial battle to yet another new foe, the **Seljuk Turks** from Central Asia. For centuries the Seljuks, themselves challenged by Mongols, retained a foothold in Anatolia without threatening the capital. Greek monasteries all over the Aegean and Black Seas evolved into tightly defended fortresses constantly warding off Turkish pirates.

In 1204 Crusaders from the Latin West occupied Constantinople, imposing their Latin, Catholic culture on Greek Orthodoxy until 1260. The Crusaders, Normans and Venetians maintained control of ports on most islands in the Aegean and on Cyprus for centuries. Despite a strong line of emperors emerging from the Comnenus and Paleologus families, the empire's borders contracted until they encompassed merely Constatinople and its immediate vicinity. In the later years, Byzantium bought itself time by marrying off its daughters to Latin, Slavic, and even Turkish rulers. A new dynasty of Turks, the **Ottomans,** finally ended the Byzantine party by permanently seizing Constantinople in 1453.

Greeks in the Ottoman Empire

After 1453, Constantinople became known as **Istanbul,** a Turkish adaptation of the Greek *"steen Poli"* (to the City). Greeks formed a large itinerant merchant class in the urban centers of the Ottoman Empire. The authorities tolerated the practice of Greek Orthodox Christianity, and to some extent, Greeks preferred Ottoman subjection and tolerance to the impositions of Latin Christian Crusader rule. Greeks served as high-level conscripts in the service of the Sultanate, often as translators. Nationalist separatist ferment began with Western European and Russian intervention. The Russians conceived of Moscow—now in Constantinople's wake, the center of Orthodox Christianity—as a third Rome, the bearer of the universal Christian mission. Russia wanted a Greek Orthodox state at the Bosporus to gain strategic control of the entrance to the Black Sea. By the 19th century, movements for independence by minorities within the empire were in full swing, and a Greek state was declared on the Peloponnese in 1821.

LANGUAGE & LITERATURE

The **New Testament** of the Christian Bible was originally written in Hellenistic Greek in the first century AD. After the conversion of Constantine, most literature was written by monastery-bound theologians or court historians detailing the evolution of the empire, listing the yearly events of the empire in the annalistic style, or reviving the Classical historiographical style of Thucydides.

In the 6th century **Procopius**, one of Justinian's generals, reported on all aspects of his boss's reign. He wrote two conventional tracts for publication, *On the Wars* and *On the Buildings*, and left behind a *Secret History*—an insider's account of the deviant debauchery commonplace in the court of Justinian and Theodora. **Photios** (820-893), who was twice appointed Patriarch of Constantinople, admired the "pagan" works of Homer and encouraged their study. Photios himself wrote several important works, including the massive *Biblioteca*. Since the Hellenistic Era, Greeks had been developing the pseudo-historical romance, including *Life of Alexander*, and personal love poems, such as *Erotopaegnia* (Love Games). The epic poem of **Digenis Akritas**—the fictional borderguard—originated in eastern Anatolia where Byzantine warriors were busy fighting off marauders from the east, first Arabs and later Turks. In the 20th century, **George Grivas**, who advocated the union of Cyprus with Greece and was a leader of the militant EOKA, appropriated the borderguard tradition and took to calling himself "Digenis."

Bandits called *kleftes* composed stirring folk ballads in the 16th century when they weren't raiding Ottoman installations. These *kleftes* eventually fought to win Greece its independence.

During the Byzantine and Ottoman periods the Greek language evolved and fragmented into forms barely recognizable when compared to Ancient Greek. At various points ancient forms were revived by monastic literati, but these were increasingly alien to those spoken by the people. Only in the last 30 years has a popular dialect, *"the demotiki,"* been standardized for national usage, both oral and written. As a result of the divergence of Greek dialects over the years, much of the nation's literature has been rendered almost unreadable to speakers of modern Greek.

ART & ARCHITECTURE

The Byzantine emperor, seated on a throne surrounded by elaborately crafted mechanical animals and singing birds made of gold, administered his holy city in the image of God ruling the cosmos. The structure and decorations of the emperor's palace reflected the overwhelming concern of Byzantine art and architecture with religious expression. The artistic achievements of Byzantine culture, from mosaics to icons, were developed within rigid theological parameters rather than through creative experimentation.

First codified under the emperor Justinian (527-65), Byzantine art and architecture evolved homogeneously up to and beyond the fall of Constantinople in 1453. Byzantine artistic styles later spread to Italy, where they continued to flourish through the 13th century and served as a model for the painters of the Italian Renaissance. Because of the influence of the Eastern Orthodox Church, Byzantine artistic traditions prevailed almost intact through the 17th century in Eastern Europe, particularly in Russia. Despite having been produced over centuries of change and upheaval, the forms of Byzantine art, uniform and unchanging, evoke a timeless world of spiritual stasis.

GREECE

Architecture

The Byzantine church in its first form betrayed the influence of early Christian churches of the Roman Empire. It was based on a longitudinal **basilica** plan approached on the western side from a colonnaded outer courtyard. On the eastern side, the church's **narthex** (vestibule) was entered through two doors, often bronze and occasionally inlaid with silver, which opened onto the **naos,** or the church proper. The main body of the church consisted of a central **nave** that extended from the inner door to the choir and was separated from the two side aisles by arched colonnades. The central nave's ceiling was wooden and raised above that of the side aisles so as to incorporate a **clerestory,** a series of clear windows admitting light to the central part of the building.

The most eminent symbol of Byzantine architecture is Constantinople's **Agia Sofia,** built over the remains of a church from the era of Constantine. The Agia Sofia, like other Justinian-era churches, features a domed roof built on a square, rather than an octagonal base. In order to accomplish this, the Byzantines made revolutionary use of two architectural supports: the **squinch,** an arch in the corner of the square base, and the **pendentive,** a spherical triangle that helped support the dome by transferring weight to the ground. By the reign of **Basil I** (867-886), the domed basilicas of Justinian had evolved into a **cross-in-square** plan, featuring four equal-vaulted arms topped by a central dome. This centralized, radial plan consisted of three aisles, each ending in an apsidal chapel in the east and a transverse vestibule known as the **exonarthex** in the west. Smaller domes occasionally replaced the vaulted roofs above the four arms of the cross, producing a five-domed church known as the **quincunx.**

The floor and lower parts of the walls were usually covered in marble while the upper parts were reserved for **mosaics,** and occasionally, frescoes. After the defeat of the Iconoclasts in the 9th century, the layout of images in Byzantine churches was standardized according to a hierarchical iconographic scheme determined by Byzantine theology. The inside of the central dome was usually reserved for the **Pantocrator** (Creator of all things); in Iconoclast churches a large cross replaced the image of Christ. The central dome's image formed the physical and spiritual center around which the rest of the images in the church were organized. The base of the dome featured angels and evangelists while the walls displayed rows of saints. The **Virgin Mary** was often pictured in the half dome over the apse. Twelve scenes from the life of Christ also decorated the church, known as the **Festival Cycle** because the images corresponded to the 12 major feast days of the Byzantine calendar. Below the sacred images, the faithful assembled for the liturgy, completing the church's pictorial and architectural incarnation as the earthly microcosm of the cosmos.

Decorative Arts

Although weak on statues, the Byzantine artisanal flair ran the gamut of the plastic arts from illuminated manuscripts to carved ivory panels, embossed bronze doors, and exquisite jewel-encrusted *cloisonée* enamels. At the pinnacle of Byzantine craftsmanship were the dazzling **mosaics** and **icons** decorating Byzantine churches. Artists underwent years of spiritual and technical training before gaining permission to portray sacred subjects. Byzantine icons aimed for religious authenticity, intended to transmit—not just represent—the spiritual power of the subject. Based on the evocative capacity of the line and on swathes of color rather than form, the Byzantine pictorial style featured flat figures with idealized facial features, clothed in stylized drapery patterns. The subject's spiritual presence was accentuated by a soul-searing gaze while a determined frontal pose set against a gold background created the illusion of the figure floating between the wall and the viewer in the church's dim light.

Byzantine icons utilized many different materials: mosaic, enamel, ivory, gold, and wood. Mosaics were made of **tesserae,** small cubes of stone or ceramic covered in glass or metallic foil. The unique shimmering effect of Byzantine mosaics was achieved by setting gold and silver tesserae at sharp angles to enhance the reflection of light. Excellent examples of Byzantine mosaics can be seen in the churches of Thessaloniki (see p. 266), at the Monastery of Osios Loukas (see p. 177), on Mt. Athos (see p. 278), and at Meteora (see p. 218).

GREECE TODAY

Greek Independence and Irredentism

After 400 years of Ottoman rule and numerous false starts, Peloponnesian and Aegean rebels began battling Ottoman armies in early 1821, eventually declaring independence on March 25. From the start, foreigners took an interest in the Greek nationalist cause. First to intervene on behalf of the nationalists was the leader of Egypt, Muhammad Ali. In 1827, at the **Battle of Navarino,** European intervention in the form of the British, French, and Russian navies defeated the Ottoman fleet, ending Ottoman control of Greece.

After their intervention, the three European powers took the lead role in determining Greece's future. They drew up borders for the infant state incorporating all territories with an ethnic Greek majority, but not all of the modern Greek state. Consequently, Greek politics for the next 100 years was driven by the irridentist vision of the **Megali Idhea** (Great Idea), which called for the expansion of borders and the unification of the scattered Greek population around the Mediterranean into a unified state. Although major lands were indeed added to the Greek state (e.g., Crete), the ultimate goal of capturing Istanbul and making it the capital never came to fruition.

The assassination of Greece's first elected president thwarted the country's first attempts at modern democracy. After the assassination, European powers tried to create a constitutional monarchy in Greece by installing the German Prince Otho as King. In 1843, the military forced the reticent Otho to finally agree to a constitution, which he proceeded to ignore. Twenty years later Otho was unseated and replaced by King George I (of Denmark). George I made some half hearted attempts at land reform and tried to develop Greece's infrastructure, but the country remained predominantly agricultural throughout the 19th century, with most capital concentrated in the hands of a few large families. The country was very poor and received most of its financial support from Greeks involved in commercial enterprises in the cities of Western Europe and the Ottoman Empire.

The Twentieth Century: Catastrophe & Recovery

In 1910, the election of Eleftherios Venizelos as president inaugurated a period of economic development and geographic expansionism. The **Balkan Wars** of 1912-13 resulted in Greece acquiring Crete and parts of Thessaly and Macedonia. Due to the new king's ties with Germany, Greece remained neutral during much of WWI. Venizelos, however, saw the war as a chance to expand Greece's borders and finally realize the *Megali Idhea.* He set up his own revolutionary government, which entered the war in 1917. At Versailles, Venizelos pressed Greek claims to Smyrna (Izmir), but Allied distaste for expansion, Venizelos's defeat in the 1920 elections, and the failed Smyrna campaign against the new Turkish nation-state under **Mustafa Kemal Atatürk,** dashed Greek irredentist aspirations. Far from gaining additional territory, Greece agreed to a population exchange with Turkey, resulting in the forced resettlement of more than one million Greeks and 500,000 Turks who had been living in the other country. The efficiency of the land reforms that accompanied the resettlement of the refugee populations, and the consolidation of borders which resulted from abandoning further irredentist aspirations proved to be Greece's greatest political triumphs in the 20th century.

The next decade saw a chaotic succession of monarchies, military rule, and brief intervals of democracy. **General Metaxas,** appointed prime minister in 1936, was an autocrat and ardent Greek nationalist. On October 28, 1940, his famous "Όχι!" (No) to Mussolini's demand to occupy Greece brought the country into WWII. In 1941, Greece fell to German invaders. For the next four years, the Axis powers occupied Greece, resulting in the destruction of ancient sites, widespread starvation, large-scale executions, and the Nazi extermination of Greece's Jewish community, which had been among the largest in the Balkans. The communist-led EAM/ELAS organized resistance which received broad popular support. But Churchill's reluctance to allow a

communist movement to ascend to power made for a difficult transition to a post-lib-
eration government, and civil war broke out in 1947. Ultimately, Greece became one
of the first arenas of American Cold War military intervention. The U.S. provided vast
quantities of aid and numerous military advisers to the Greek government as part of
the **Truman Doctrine** and **Marshall Plan** in an attempt to contain the spread of communism. Consequently, the last ELAS guerillas were defeated in 1949. During the
next 15 years the U.S. continued its involvement in Greek politics.

On April 21, 1967, the army, apparently feeling threatened by increasing liberalism
and political disarray, staged a **coup** that resulted in rule by a **junta** for seven years.
The regime made extensive use of torture, censorship, and arbitrary arrest to maintain power, but it also encouraged foreign investment and therefore continued to
enjoy U.S. support. **Martial law** suppressed student demonstrations in Athens in
1973, and a year later, General Ionnidis's attempt to overthrow Cyprus's government
and unite the island with Greece provoked a **Turkish invasion of Cyprus** (see p. 480)
that ultimately led to the *junta's* downfall. Former president Karamanlis returned
from his self-imposed exile to take power. As the new prime minister, Karamanlis
orchestrated parliamentary elections and organized a referendum to determine the
fate of the government. After the monarchy was defeated by a two-thirds vote, a constitution was drawn up in 1975 that established a parliamentary government with a
ceremonial president appointed by the legislature.

The Last Twenty Years

Under Prime Minister **Andreas Papandreou,** the leftist Panhellenic Socialist Movement (PASOK) won landslide electoral victories in 1981 and 1985. Papandreou,
under whom Greece entered the European Economic
Community (EC), promised a radical break with the
past and initially oversaw the passage of women's
rights legislation and advances in civil liberties. But he
also pursued economic nationalization and economic
austerity policies in exchange for an EC loan. At the
same time, Papandreou's heated anti-NATO rhetoric
and his friendship with Qadhafi and Arafat sparked international alarm. In September
1988, Papandreou underwent major heart surgery. He attempted to run the country
while hospitalized, refusing to appoint an interim leader. After returning to work,
Papandreou discovered an embezzlement scandal involving George Koskotas, the
chair of the Bank of Crete, which threatened to implicate a number of government
officials in corruption and bribery. After Koskotas made allegations against Papandreou himself, the beleaguered prime minister managed to keep only 125 seats in the
300-seat parliament.

> *Greece became one of the first arenas of American Cold War military intervention*

In the wake of the scandals **Tzannis Tzannetakis,** who was accepted by both con-
servatives and leftists, became Prime Minister-designate through a compromise decision of the communist-right coalition. As part of the compromise, the opposing
conservative New Democracy Party (*Nea Demokratia;* ND) and the Communist
Party of Greece (*Kommunistiko Komma Ellados;* KKE) forged a short-term alliance
to oppose the incumbent socialist leadership. In 1990, after three general elections
within the space of 10 months, **Constantine Mitsotakis** of the ND became Prime
Minister. Although the ND was only able to obtain 47% of the total vote, the vagaries
of Greek electoral law left the party with a slim majority in parliament.

Mitsotakis attempted to lead Greece into the mainstream of European politics and
to solve some of the country's festering economic and diplomatic problems. In an
attempt to bring Greece's huge debt under control, he imposed an **austerity program** that limited wage increases and authorized the sale of state enterprises. The
state agencies, however, provided jobs for large numbers of Greeks who valued the
security of work in the public sector. As a result, he lost a 1993 emergency election,
and Andreas Papandreou returned to power. In January 1996, Papandreou finally
stepped down due to persisting health problems. His Socialist Party named **Costas
Simitis** as its new Prime Minister. Elections in September 1996 maintained the Social-
ists in power with Simitis remaining as prime minister.

In 1998 Simitis was pursuing aggressive economic reforms, privatizing banks and companies, but facing opposition from constantly striking labor unions. By the year 2001, he hopes to have Greece fiscally qualified to enter the **European Monetary Union,** so that by the **2004 Olympics** visitors will be shelling out euros instead of *drachmes.*

LANGUAGE

The language barrier that tourists find upon entering Greece may not crumble as easily as one might expect. Pronunciation, dialects, and vocabulary vary from region to region, and from Greece to Cyprus. Although most Greek youths under the age of 25 speak at least marginal, and often fluent English, bus destinations, many all-night pharmacies, advertisements, menus, and street signs are in Greek, at times accompanied by English transliterations. In some heavily touristed areas, those interested in picking up a bit of Greek may find their potential interlocuters more interested in speaking English than in helping out a visitor eager to learn the native tongue. In remote villages and especially in the interior of the mainland where tourism is sparse, being able to speak and understand at least a few simple Greek phrases (see **Appendix,** p. 516) is essential to getting along. It is extremely helpful to brush up on the **Greek alphabet** before you go. Learning how to read ferry schedules is more useful than being able to ask for directions to the Acropolis if you can't understand the reply. If you're at a loss for words, most tourist agencies, tourist offices, and the trusty **tourist police** speak English and are willing to help. Above all, knowing a little bit of Greek will endear you to Greeks; their language is rarely (except in Albania where Greek is now the official second language) studied outside the national borders and they appreciate the efforts of the few travelers—out of the hordes who yearly stream into their country—who attempt to learn even a little of its language.

> *Above all, knowing a little bit of Greek will endear you to Greeks*

Be conscious of Greek **body language.** To indicate a negative, Greeks lift their heads back abruptly (as if they're actually nodding "yes"), while raising their eyebrows. To indicate the affirmative, they emphatically nod once. Greeks wave a hand up and down in a gesture that seems to say "stay there" when they mean "come." Be careful when waving goodbye, keep your fingers loose because gesturing with an open palm and extended fingers may be interpreted as an insult. Also, eye contact is a key way for a Greek man to communicate with a woman. Be aware that returning the intense glare is another way of saying, "yup, I'm interested—approach me."

A note on transliteration: There is no fully satisfactory system of transliterating one alphabet to the other. Greek letters do not have an exact correspondence with English letters. Like those of the Greek government, *Let's Go*'s transliterations are different for each word; the process follows no rigid rules, but is based on historical connotation, local usage, and phonetics. Bear in mind that when we write "ch," we're trying to represent the guttural "h" sound; for a more detailed explanation, see **Greek alphabet** and **Greek-English Phrases** p. 516.

RELIGION

Today, Greek Orthodoxy is the **national religion,** although the constitution guarantees freedom of religion. The Church includes the archbishop of Athens, 85 bishops in 77 dioceses, and 7500 parishes. Like the Catholic Church, Greek Orthodoxy insists on the hierarchical structure of the church, Apostolic succession, the episcopate, and the priesthood. Rome upholds the universal jurisdiction and infallibility of the Pope, but Greek Orthodoxy stresses the infallibility of the church as a whole and does not have cardinals or a pope. Timothy Ware's *The Orthodox Church* provides a thorough description of both the history of the church and the exegesis behind Greek Orthodox beliefs. Greek Orthodox priests, who are easily recognizable by their long black robes, beards, and cylindrical hats, are closely associated with their parishes. Celebrations in churches include weddings, baptisms, and celebrations on the feast day of the patron saint.

ART

Nationalist sentiment after the Greeks attained independence from the Ottomans led the government to subsidize Greek art. The **Polytechniou,** Greece's first modern art school, was founded in 1838. Many artists have since gone abroad to study and **Modern Greek Art** has followed the European artistic trends of the 19th and 20th centuries. Theophilos, Alexis Kontoglou, George Bouzanis, Yiannis Spiropoulos, Sotiris Sorongas, and Michael Tombros are among the well known modern Greek artists.

Greek **folk art** continues to fascinate both the casual onlooker and the discerning shopper. Handicrafts include hand-painted, polychromatic terra cotta bowls and ceramics; thick, wooly woven blankets and mats; polished metalwork; intricately carved wooden furniture and gadgets; finely embroidered linens and shirts; and handmade lace.

LITERATURE

...the language I speak has no alphabet
since even the sun and the waves are a syllabic script which you decode
only in times of grief and exile...

-Odysseas Elytis

In Greece, where the ancient landscape retains its eternal, unshakable superimposition upon the modern, literature finds itself implicitly preoccupied with mythic proportions. At the pens of modern Greek writers, history becomes inextricably, necessarily entwined with the personal and the national, and past and present become equally shadowy and transformative. In expressing and inventing the constantly evolving Greek national identity, Greek authors also draw heavily upon the heritage of the Orthodox church and a very rich oral tradition of Greek folk ballads and fairy tales.

The **Ionian School** (beginning with the revolution in 1821) saw the rise of **Andreas Kalvos** (1796-1869) and **Dionysios Solomos** (1798-1857). Kalvos' lyrical poetry, known for powerful tributes to freedom, earned him high esteem among modern poets. Solomos is often called the "national poet of Greece," and his *Hymn to Liberty* became the Greek national anthem. Solomos' use of the demotic, or spoken, Greek language (as opposed to the official *katharevousa*, "purified" Greek, which borrows obsolete words from ancient Greek), marks his work as a possible starting point for modern Greek literature.

The 20th century has seen the emergence of the poets **Kostas Palamas** (1859-1943), **Angelos Sikelianos** (1884-1951), **Constantine P. Cavafy** (1863-1933), **George Seferis** (1900-63), **Yannis Ritsos** (1909-90), and **Odysseas Elytis** (1911-96). Cavafy's poetry explores tensions among the historical, the philosophical, and the hedonistic, eloquently expressing the multiple confinements of the human soul in its

Seferis is obsessed in his poetry with the haunting, fragmented nature of the ancient past, ushering in the Greek Modernist generation

attempts to span these boundaries. His poems attracted admiration worldwide, including praise from E.M. Forster and W.H. Auden. Seferis is obsessed in his poetry with the haunting, fragmented nature of the ancient past, ushering in the Greek Modernist generation. His evocative, lyrical depictions of longing, exile, and rootless suffering are expressed simultaneously on personal, national, and mythic levels, winning him a Nobel Prize in 1963. Elytis, who won Greece's second Nobel in 1979, was influenced by the liberating ideas of French Surrealism. His poetry celebrates the hope for personal and national redemption with a synthesis of the human, natural, and religious. Ritsos wrote from a Socialist, left-wing stance which brought about his arrest and exile in 1967, as well as a ban on his writings throughout the Dictatorship.

Noted Greek short story writers include **Alexandros Papadiamantis** (1951-1911), whose stories, written in *katharevousa* Greek, dwell upon life on his home island, Skiathos, and contain lyrical yet guarded commentary on the failings of mankind and his society, softened only by the ultimate redemption of God. Meanwhile, another *katharevousa* writer, **George Vizyenos** (1849-1896), who borrowed liberally from the oral folk tradition, was interested in the mysterious and supernatural as they played themselves out in local life. Perhaps the best known modern Greek author is **Nikos Kazantzakis** (1883-1957). His many novels include *Odyssey*, a modern sequel to the Homeric epic, *Report to Greco, Zorba the Greek* (1946), and *The Last Temptation of Christ* (1951). The latter two were adapted for the cinema. *Freedom or Death*, his homage to Greek revolts against Ottoman rule on his home island of Crete, can provide travelers with keen insights on the mentality of the Greek male and the depth and complexity of Greek-Turkish conflict.

The landscape and culture of Greece has also inspired some of the more inventive travel writing by English-speaking authors, such as Edward Lear's lively journals of his years in Greece, Henry Miller's classic *The Colossus of Maroussi*, and the varied works of Lawrence and Gerald Durrell, who lived in a house still visible on Corfu (see p. 240). Patricia Storace's recent (1996) colection of short essays, *Dinner With Persephone*, explores modern Greek life through an astute, subtle lens, well attuned to paradox and poetry. And let's not forget about the infamous Lord Byron.

FILM

Although most of the films shown in Greece are American or European imports with Greek subtitles, the theaters themselves have a singular atmosphere; movie houses are small, relaxed and social, and viewers regularly eat, drink, and chat throughout the film. The large, silent multiplex is practically nonexistent, so blockbuster films pass through quickly, usually about six months to a year after being released in other parts of the world. Some theaters also show sequences of film classics, but, likewise, if you're lucky enough to catch a good series, don't expect it to be around for long.

Summertime **outdoor movies** are considered an essential part of the Greek experience. Beginning at twilight, the cinemas are either screens set up in vacant lots, highrise rooftops, or daytime theaters with roofs that slide away to reveal the stars. Earlier shows are sometimes difficult to see, and later shows are often difficult to hear, as the volume is lowered to accommodate neighbors.

An entirely different story are Greek art house films. During the reign of the *junta*, prevented from political comment by government censor, Greek artists moved west to comment on the situation at home. Set in a Francophone Thessaloniki and the product of French and Greek collaboration, *Z* (1969, directed by Costas Gavras with Yves Montand) is a thrilling, humorous, and tragic account of the regime's assassination of a rising opposition candidate and its sloppy attempt to cover it up.

After suffering under the colonels' *junta*, the Greek film industry rebuilt throughout the 1980s and has recently emerged as a salient and prolific presence in the international arena, a revitalization which has significantly depended upon the re-establishment in 1982 of the **Greek Film Center,** a state-supported institute involved in the production of scores of the most highly regarded modern Greek films, including works by Nikos Perakis (*Loafing and Camouflage, Arpa-Colla*), Pantelis Vougaris (*The Engagement of Anna, Elefterios Venizelos*), Nikos Panayotopoulos (*Varieties, O Ergenis*), and Greece's most highly acclaimed Theo Angelopoulos (*Voyage to Cythera, The Beekeeper, Ulysses' Gaze*, and *Eternity and a Day*, winner of the 1998 Cannes Palme d'Or). Greece's most important film-focused event is the **Thessaloniki Film Festival,** in November.

MUSIC & DANCE

Musical instruments date from the Bronze Age on Crete, reinforcing scholars' belief that early poetry was often sung or chanted. As drama evolved, **choruses** played a major role in Greek plays. Before the 5th century BC, the Greeks had no system of musical notation, yet they managed to develop a **theory of harmonics.**

Throughout the Byzantine era, **folk music and dances** assumed regional traits: the south emphasized tragic and mourning dances, the north produced war and rural harvest dances, and religious and burial dances were performed on Crete. These

Cries from the Underground

Much of Greek lyric song is romantic and poetic, but at the end of the 19th century a new style of music began to develop on Turkey's western coast that would unsettle these classical notions. *Rembetika* was popularized in Greek cities by convicts who embraced the lustful strains of the music and lamented about smoking hashish and life on the run. During the exchange of populations with Turkey in the 1920s, the music was invigorated by the scores of refugees who lived in shantytowns on the outskirts of major Greek cities. This music that had been the voice of the underground emerged, in its mature state, as the cry of the underclass. *Rembetika*, the music of Smyrna cafes and Greek jails, is still played on the *bouzouki* and *baglama* and features lyrics such as these from the *Little Old Monk* (1929). For more information, consult Holst's *Road to Rembetika*.

> *I'll become a little old monk and wear a monkish habit*
> *And I'll carry a string of beads, sweetheart, just to please you.*
> *Your lips tell me one thing…and your friends tell me another.*
> *I'd rather be stabbed twice…than hear the words you're saying.*
> *I fixed myself up as a monk, stayed in a monastery.*
> *Then I fell into your hands, nagging bitch,*
> *And got myself defrocked.*

regional influences are still evident. For example, pontic-influenced dances like *kotsari* are danced only in the north, while the islands have their own dances called *nisiotiko*. Nonetheless, dances have become somewhat more standardized. *Tsamiko* and *kalamatiano*, for example, are now danced throughout the country.

Today it's common to see a wide circle of locals and tourists, hands joined, dancing to the tunes of clarinets and lyre (originating in Crete). The leader of the dance performs the fancy footwork, winding around a white handkerchief and twirling around in circles, sometimes throwing in a few backward somersaults. Don't hesitate to join in; the dance steps for the followers are repetitive, so you'll learn quickly. Just stamp your feet, yell *Opa*, and have fun.

Rembetika, a grittier, more urban variety of music that developed in the 1930s, uses traditional Greek instruments to sing about drugs, prison, and general alienation. *Rembetika* became popular again in the 1970s but, is played only in a few clubs today. Greek popular music continues to evolve, incorporating influences from *rembetika* as well as gypsy and traditional folk music.

FOOD & DRINK

Greek food is simple and nutritious. Recent medical studies have highlighted the Greek diet as a good model for healthy eating; its reliance upon unsaturated olive oil and vegetables has prevented heart attacks in a fairly sedentary population.

A Greek restaurant is known as a *taverna* or *estiatorio* while a grill is a *psistaria*. Before ordering, see what others are eating. If you don't know the word for what you want, point. Most places have a few fixed-price dishes available anytime; make sure they have your dish before you sit down. Waiters will ask you if you want salad, appetizers, or the works, so be careful not to wind up with mountains of food (Greek portions tend to be large). Don't be surprised if there is an extra charge for the tablecloth and bread, often listed on the menu as the *couvert*. Service is always included in the check, but it is customary to leave a few *drachmes* as an extra tip.

Breakfast can be bread, *tiropita* (cheese pie), or a pastry with *marmelada* (jam) or *meli* (honey). A particular breakfast favorite among Greeks is *patsa* (a soup made of calf or lamb tripe), served only in the early morning and particularly soothing to a travel-weary stomach. **Lunch** is eaten between noon and 3pm. The **evening meal** is a leisurely affair served late by American standards, usually after 8 or 9pm, and as late as 11pm to 1am during the summer in the larger cities. Greek restaurants divide food into two categories—*magiremeno*, meaning cooked, or *tis oras* (of the hour), indicating grilled meat. The former is generally cheaper. *Tis oras* includes grilled *moschari* (veal), *arni* (lamb), or *kotopoulo* (chicken), served with *patates* (french fries), *rizi* (rice), or *fasolia* (beans). Popular *magiremeno* dishes include *moussaka* (chopped meat and eggplant covered with a rich cream *béchamel*), *pastitsio* (a lasagna-like dish of thick noodles with *béchamel*), *yemista* (tomatoes and peppers stuffed with rice or meat), *dolmadhes* (grape leaves stuffed with rice and minced meat), and *youvarelakia* (meatballs covered with egg and lemon sauce). Fried zucchini, stuffed eggplant, *tzatziki* (spicy cucumber and yogurt salad), and/or *horta* (greens, either beet or leeks, served with oil and lemon) accompany meals at most *taverna*. Feel free to order these vegetables as the main dish **Vegetarians** might also try *spanakopita* (spinach-filled pastry) or *tiropita* (cheese pie in a similar flaky crust). *Briam*, potatoes and other vegetables cooked in oil, is another delicious possibility. **Seafood** is as readily available as you'd expect in a such an ocean-begotten nation, but it's quite expensive. Don't leave without trying fresh *chtopodi* (octopus) marinated in olive oil and oregano, and don't miss the *taramosalata* (dip made with caviar) or the *Merenda* (Greece's version of Nutella).

You can hardly avoid *souvlaki*, a large skewer of steak, generally pork or lamb. A *souvlaki pita*, consists of a pita crammed full of skewered meat and fillings (only about 300dr). *Gyros* also abound in street vendor fast-food stands. *Bifteki* are a more tender, spicy version of hamburgers; you are usually served two as well as fries. For a healthy staple at a *taverna*, try a *horiatiki*, a "Greek" salad containing olives, tomatoes, onions, cucumbers, and hefty chunks of feta cheese. (Ask for it *horees ladhi* if you don't want it swimming in olive oil.) Usually accompanied by a basket of bread and a glass of water, these salads make inexpensive and satisfying meals.

Visit an **agora** (market) to stock up on the fruit available all summer. Greek fruit has few preservatives and thus tastier than most fruits found in Western Europe or the U.S. The *seeka* (fresh figs) available in late August and September are delicious. After dinner, Greeks enjoy *karpouzi* (watermelon) or *peponi* (canteloupe). You should also try the freshly made *yiaourti* (yogurt), a thicker, fattier version of what most Americans are used to, with honey and melon mixed in. Sample indigenous cheeses like *feta* and *kaseri*, a yellow semi-soft cheese.

Greek pastries are delectable and available at **zacharoplastia,** or sweet shops. *Baklava*, a honey-rich, filo-dough pastry filled with chopped nuts, beats all the rest (usually 400dr); try *galaktobouriko*, a custard-filled dough; *kareedhopita*, a walnut cake; *melomakaron*, honey-nut cookies; *kataifi*, strands of angel hair wrapped around nuts and cinnamon; *koulouria*, shortbread cookies; or *kourabiedhes*, powdered sugar-coated almond cookies. Also try the fruit and cream laden *tartes*. Remember that *pasta*, in both Greek and Turkish, means pastry, not noodles.

Greek coffee is the most popular beverage. Like Turkish coffee, it's strong, sweet, and has a sludge-like consistency. Ask for *gliko* for sweet, *metrio* for medium, and *sketo* or *pikro* for a bitter, sugarless cup. *Elliniko* (Greek) coffee is usually served with a glass of water. American-style coffee (called *Nescafé*), usually instant, is also available. If you ask for *café frappé*, you'll get a tall glass of frothy iced coffee.

A favorite Greek snack is *ouzo* with *mezedhes*, tidbits of cheese, sausage, and octopus. *Ouzo* is a distilled spirit to which anise is added, lending it a licorice taste. *Ouzo* is drunk mostly in the islands, while potent *Raki* and *Tsipouro*, a grain-alcohol moonshine, are popular on the mainland and on Crete.

One of the great arts in Greece is **wine-making,** and every region has its own specialty. Long ago, the Greeks discovered that when wine (*krasi*) is stored in pine-pitch-sealed goatskins, it develops a fresh, sappy flavor. After much deduction, they discovered that adding pine resin in varying amounts during fermentation achieves the same result. The resulting wine became

A favorite Greek snack is ouzo with mezedhes, tidbits of cheese, sausage, and octopus

known as *retsina*. Resinated wines now come in three varieties: white, rosé, and red. White *retsina* is generally cheaper than beer. To try homemade wine ask for *doppio* (local) or *spitiko krasi* (house wine). There are also a number of non-resinated wines, including *gliko* (sweet), and *imigliko* (semi-sweet). Try the white wines of the northern Peloponnese: Rotonda, Demestika, and Santa Helena are dry. Achaïa-Clauss and Cambas Vintners are good wines. As an after-dinner aperitif, Greeks imbibe Metaxa brandy or *ouzo*.

A good place to taste various Greek wines is at a local **wine festival,** where you can drink all the wine you want for a flat admission fee. The wine festival in Alexandroupolis runs from early July to mid-August. On Crete, the festival in Rethymnon is held in July, while the one at the village of Dafnes (near Iraklion) runs in mid-July.

MEDIA

Several years ago, much of Greek media was state-owned and thus prone to expositions of government policy. More recently, private companies have bought several outlets. Many Greek language **newspapers** are still sensationalistic— akin to New York's *Newsday* or London's *Sun*. A few reputable papers are *Eleftherotipia, Kathimerini* (daily) and *Bima* (published every Sunday). Unlike most of their newsprint counterparts, glossy Greek **magazines** are worthwhile. *Diabazo* and *Anti* are more scholarly journals, *Clique* caters to the teeny-bopper crowd, and *Taxydromos* is a more sophisticated glamor magazine. American and British magazines like *Vogue* and *Cosmopolitan* also circulate (in Greek). The most noticeable change in Greek media has been in the **television** industry. Whereas ERT1 and 2 were the original stations, both state-owned and private channels like Mega Channel and ANT-1 have brought hi-tech production and, of course, wacky American sitcoms to the Greek viewing public. Greek radio plays a wide range of music in large cities, but in the remote locales you'll only be able to tune in that loud Greek-pop that bus drivers insist on playing at full blast during long trips.

SPORTS

Sports fanatics may be quick to associate Greek sports lore with the country's ancient "sound mind, sound body" principle. Although everything from handball to water polo is popular, soccer and basketball are the country's games of choice. Of the several Greek A-League **soccer** teams, three stand out in the hearts and apparel of Greek sports fans: *Olympiakos* (red), *Panathinaikos* (green), and *AEK* (yellow). Even the least devout of sports fans wear their favorite team's colors. **Basketball** is the country's newfound passion. The primary teams are the same as in soccer, but unlike the soccer league, Greek basketball among the premier European leagues. It has featured such NBA stars as Roy Tarpley, Byron Scott, Dino Radja, and Dominique Wilkens. *Olympiakos* is another basketball powerhouse. For **golfers,** there are 18-hole courses in Athens, Rhodes, Corfu, and Porto Carras on Halkidiki. **Tennis** has also gained great popularity in Greece, especially with the success of native son Pete Sampras. There are public tennis clubs throughout the country. **Watersports** are what most sports enthusiasts who visit Greece dream about. Windsurfing, water-skiing, sailing, and other sea sports are popular at most beaches. **Scuba diving** is generally forbidden in Greek waters; it is allowed only under supervised conditions in Chalkidiki, Mykonos, Santorini, Corfu, Cephalonia, and Zakynthos. Surprisingly, **skiing** has become popular among Greeks, and ski resorts can be found throughout the country.

> *Figuring prominently on the horizon of Greek sporting events is the 28th Olympiad, to be held in Athens in 2004*

Figuring prominently on the horizon of Greek sporting events is the 28th Olympiad, to be held in Athens in 2004. Scheduled for August 13-19, the Games are expected to attract unparalleled crowds. Check out the official Athens 2004 Olympics website can be found at **http://www.athens2004.gr/.**

Athens Αθηνα

In contemporary Athens, the fates have patched together a mosaic of Byzantine churches, ancient ruins, chic cafes, traditional outdoor *tavernas*, and modern shopping centers. Athens grew up around the foot of the ruggedly majestic Acropolis and is still overshadowed by the glory of its ancient inhabitants; the fame of Classical Athens can't alter the city's 2000-year term as a medieval ghost town. When power shifted first to Macedonia then to Rome and Byzantium, Athens lost its artistic dominance and shrank in upon itself as wave after wave of invaders forced its walls to contract. The 19th-century arrival of nationalist ideologies in Greece brought the royal capital and regal pomp to the forgotten city, which has been completely rebuilt over the last 200 years. During this last century, as monarchy has been shed in favor of constitutional democracy, Athens has ached with the growing pains of an adolescent metropolis. The vast majority of its neoclassical mansions and crumbling medieval architecture was gutted to make way for a concrete jungle with which to accommodate the millions of diaspora citizens who have come home to Greece and settled in the city's sprawling suburbia.

Visitors harboring mental images of togas and bearded philosophers may be surprised to find a 20th-century city in every sense of the word—Athens is crowded, noisy, and polluted. The Plaka neighborhood, which borders the Acropolis, is one of the remnants of Athens' ancient grandeur; column-bound temples stand as proud reminders of the piety of the ancient Athenians. Modernity, however, cannot stand on teetering ruins—a city needs a comprehensive subway system, a manageable communications system, and space for its citizens to live. The incessant roar and exhaust from buses, cars, and motorcycles in Syntagma and Omonia Squares can be deafening and suffocating, but the urban charm of this cosmopolitan capital's lively Kolonaki, Pangrati, and Exarhia neighborhoods makes Athens truly endearing. Digging around cisterns and the springs of lost ancient rivers, civil engineers are busier than ever preparing the city for the much-craved, long-sought athletic onslaught of the 2004 Olympic Summer Games.

⊛ HIGHLIGHTS OF ATHENS

- Float past the chic outdoor cafes of **Kolonaki** and ascend Mt. Lycavittos (p. 95) to see the sun setting over the Acropolis and sprawling Athens.
- Haggle and bargain with wily merchants at the junkshops of the flea market in **Monastiraki** (p. 95).
- Weave through the *tavernas* and *ouzeries* of medieval **Plaka** and climb rocky crags to lay an offering to Athena before the columns of the Parthenon (p. 92).
- Survey the largest collection of ancient relics from all over Greece at the National Archaeological Museum (p. 96), and then chill out sipping *frappés* among the international modeling set in the cafes of **Exarhia**.
- Check out the pom-poms on the toes of soldiers at the changing of the guard before the Parliament and the National Garden in **Syntagma Square** (p. 94).
- Don't get too squeamish looking at the raw, skinned flesh of cows, pigs, and rabbits hanging in the meat market at **Omonia Square** (p. 95).
- Wake up early to buy yourself fresh clementines and peanuts at the Thursday street market in the village-like **Pangrati** neighborhood (p. 87).

▌ History

A competition between **Poseidon** and **Athena** determined how Athens (*Athena* in Greek) would be named, when the gods of Olympus decreed that whoever gave the city the most useful gift would become its patron deity. The populace was awed when Poseidon struck the rock of the Acropolis with his trident and salt water came gushing forth, but Athena's wiser gift, an olive tree, won her the right to rule.

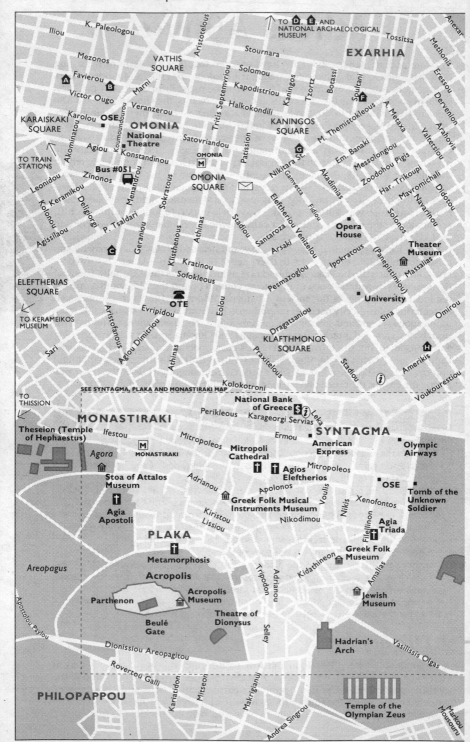

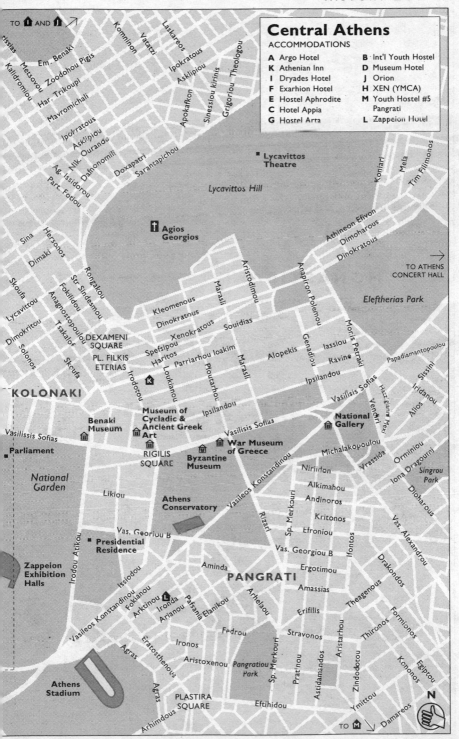

TO 🏠 AND 🏠 ↗

Central Athens

ACCOMMODATIONS

A Argo Hotel
K Athenian Inn
I Dryades Hotel
F Exarhion Hotel
E Hostel Aphrodite
C Hotel Appia
G Hostel Arta

B Int'l Youth Hostel
D Museum Hotel
J Orion
H XEN (YMCA)
M Youth Hostel #5 Pangrati
L Zappeion Hotel

Lycavittos Theatre

Lycavittos Hill

Agios Georgios

TO ATHENS CONCERT HALL

Eleftherias Park

DEXAMENI SQUARE
PL. FILKIS ETERIAS

KOLONAKI

National Gallery

Benaki Museum

Museum of Cycladic & Ancient Greek Art

RIGILIS SQUARE

War Museum of Greece

Byzantine Museum

Vasilissis Sofias

Parliament

National Garden

Athens Conservatory

Presidential Residence

Singrou Park

Zappeion Exhibition Halls

PANGRATI

Athens Stadium

PLASTIRA SQUARE

Pangratiou Park

TO 🏠

N

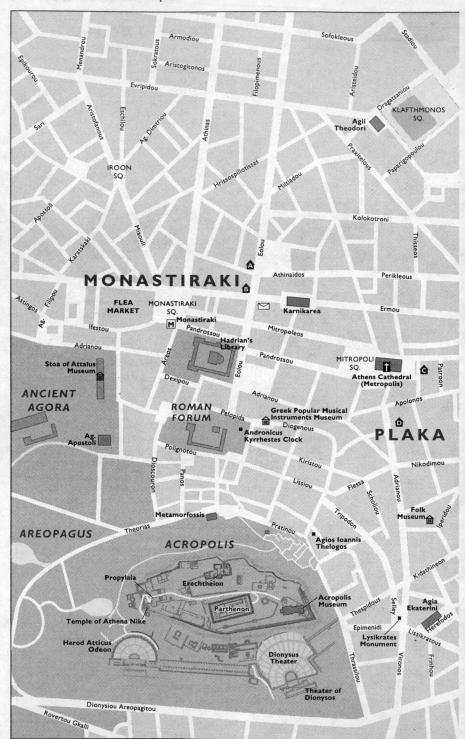

Epikourou
Sari
Astingos
Ag.
Filipou
Apostoli
Karatskaki
Aristofanous
Menandrou
Eschilou
Sokratous
Armodiou
Aristogitonos
Evripidou
Filopimenous
Athinas
Ag. Dimtriou
Hrissospiliotissas
Miliadou
Aristeidou
Sofokleous
Stadiou
Praxitelous
Dragatsaniou
Papangopoulou
Kolokotroni
Thisseos
Perikleous
Ermou

IROON SQ.
KLAFTHMONOS SQ.
Agii Theodori

MONASTIRAKI
Eolou
Ⓐ
Ⓑ
Athinaidos
✉ Karnikarea

FLEA MARKET
MONASTIRAKI SQ.
Ⓜ Monastiraki
Ifestou
Adrianou
Pandrossou
Mitropoleos
Pandrossou
Hadrian's Library
Dexipou
Areos
Eolou

Stoa of Attalus Museum 🏛

ANCIENT AGORA

MITROPOLI SQ.
✝ **Athens Cathedral (Metropolis)**
Patroon
🏛

Ag. Apostoli

ROMAN FORUM
Pelopida
Polignotou
Dioscouron
Panos
Adrianou
■ **Andronicus Kyrrhestes Clock**
Greek Popular Musical Instruments Museum
Diogenous
Kiristou
Lissiou
Flessa
Scholiou
Adrianou
Apolonos
Nikodimou
Ⓓ
PLAKA

Tripodon

Metamorfossis
AREOPAGUS
Theorias
Pratinou
■ **Agios Ioannis Thelogos**
Folk Museum 🏛
Iperidou

ACROPOLIS

Propylaia
Erechtheion
Parthenon
Acropolis Museum
Thespidous
Selley
Agia Ekaterini
Herefodos
Kidathineon

Temple of Athena Nike
Epimenidi
Lysikrates Monument
Lissikratous
Vironos
Frinihou

Herod Atticus Odeon
Dionysus Theater

Theater of Dionysos
Thrassilou

Dionysiou Areopagitou
Rovertou Gkalli

Syntagma, Plaka, and Monastiraki

ACCOMMODATIONS
E Adonis Hotel
K Dioskouros House
I Hotel Festos
D Hotel Kimon
H Hotel Kouros
J Hotel Phaedra
A Hotel Tempi
C John's Place
F George's Guesthouse
B Pella Inn
G Student's & Traveler's Inn

Koral
Athens City Museum
Eleftheriou Venizelou (Panepistimiou)
OSE
Sina
Acadimias
Omirou
Solonos
Lykavitou
Dimokritou
Voukourestiou
Lada
OTE
Amerikis
Eleftherios Venizelos Museum
National Historical Museum
Stadiou
Greek National Tourist Information Counter
Zalokosta
Akademias
Pindarou
Kanari
Merlin
Sekeri
KOLONAKI SQ.
Koumbari

SYNTAGMA

N

Karageorgi Servias
Leka
American Express
Georgiou A
Vasilis Sophias
SYNTAGMA SQ.
Parliament Building
Tomb of the Unknown Soldier
Mitropoleos
Pendelis
Voulis
Nikis
Filellinon
Olympic Airways
OSE
Agia Triada
Souri
National Gardes

National Gardens

Irodou Atikou

Presidential Residence

F
E
Nikis
Kolhrou
H
Kidathineon
G
Folk Art Museum
A. Geronta
Dedalou
Amalias
Jewish Museum
Zappeion Exhibition Halls

Tholou
K
Pitarou
Goura
J
Hadrian's Arch
Temple of Olympian Zeus
Vasilissis Olga

STADIOU SQ.

0   200 yards
0   200 meters

Ardittos Hill

Athens was an important town as early as the 16th century BC. Tradition holds that the hero Theseus, the mythical slayer of the Cretan Minotaur, united the city-state. Around the 8th century, the city became the artistic center of Greece, known especially for its geometric-style pottery; this initial fame merely foreshadowed the future. In the 6th century the law-giver and poet Solon brought Athens close to egalitarianism by ending the enslavement of native citizens. After dramatic victories over the Persians at Marathon and Salamis in the 5th century BC, Athens enjoyed a 70-year Golden Age, reaching its apogee under the patronage of Pericles. It was during this time that Iktinos and Kallikrates designed the Parthenon, Aeschylus, Sophocles, and Euripides wrote tragic masterpieces, and Aristophanes penned ribald comedies.

The bloody and drawn-out campaigns of the **Peloponnesian War** (431-404 BC) between Athens and Sparta heralded the demise of Periclean Athens. Political power in Greece then shifted north to the court of Philip of Macedon and his son **Alexander the Great.** Through the 5th and 4th centuries BC, however, Athens remained important as a cultural center, producing three of the most influential western philosophers—Socrates, Plato, and Aristotle—as well as the great orator Demosthenes. By the 2nd century AD, the Roman Empire had made the city-state democracy of 5th-century Athens obsolete. When Constantine moved the capital of the Roman Empire to Byzantium in AD 324, Athens was no more than an overtaxed backwater specializing in the Neoplatonism codified at the Academy. The city remained the center of Greek education with elaborate institutes of learning, but its status (and buildings) lapsed into ruin when Justinian banned the teaching of philosophy in 529.

Around 1000, **Basil II,** the Emperor of Byzantium, visited Athens. After praying to the Virgin Mary in the Parthenon, Basil ordered craftsmen to restore Athens to its former glory. Under successive crusading conquerors—the Franks in 1205, the Catalans in 1311, and the Accajioli merchant family in 1387—Athens underwent a renaissance. **Ottoman rule** in 1456 and Greek independence in 1821 brought further waves of renovation and restoration. Modern Athens, with its *plateias* (squares), wide boulevards, and tranquil National Garden, embodies plans drawn up by German architects under the direction of the Bavarian **King Otto,** who was awarded the newly created kingdom of Greece in the late 19th century.

In the 20th century, Athens has grown exponentially in population and industry. In 1923, Greece agreed to a population exchange with Turkey, producing a great burden on the burgeoning city. As with all industrial cities, Athens has also attracted workers from destitute regions of the country. The past century has seen the population of the city explode from 169 families to almost half the population of Greece. In an attempt to counteract noise and pollution, the transit authority now bans cars from a number of streets in the historic Plaka district and limits driver access downtown on alternate days. The **subway,** only partially completed, has eliminated much of the traffic and noise in the immediate city center, but continual construction adds to the dust. Zeus' thunderbolt now shakes down acid rain, and residents rue the infamous *nephos* (smog cloud) that settles in a sinister fashion over Athens in summer.

■ Orientation

Make use of the free **maps** available at the tourist office. The city map includes bus and trolley routes, while a more detailed street plan graces the pages of *Greece-Athens-Attica* magazine. Athenian geography mystifies newcomers and natives alike; if you lose your bearings, ask for directions back to well-lit Syntagma or look for a cab. The **Acropolis** provides a useful reference point. Be alert when crossing the street, as drivers rarely pause for pedestrians. Be aware that Athenian streets often have multiple spellings or names. Lysikrateous is also known as Lisicratous or Lissi Kratous; Aiolou St. as Eolu and Eolou; Victoriou Ougo as Victor Hugo. Panepistimiou St. is commonly called Eleftheriou Venizelou; Peiraias is Tsaldari. Many streets also change names along the way—Amerikis, for example, becomes Lykavittou.

Several publications list general information about Athens. Pick up a free copy of the tourist office's *This Week in Athens*, which gives addresses, hours, and phone numbers in English for a variety of attractions. International and local news, along with movie, restaurant, and exhibit listings appear daily in Athens' English-language newspaper, the *Athens News* (250dr). *Athenorama* lists entertainment info.

In summer, businesses are generally open Monday and Wednesday from 8:30am to 3pm, Tuesday, Thursday, and Friday from 8am to 2pm and 5:30 to 8:30pm, and Saturday from 8am to 3pm. High season officially runs from mid-June to mid-September; however, be aware that each Greek may have his or her own version of "high season" (i.e., May-Aug., July-Aug., or simply when you're there), and around August 15 most Greeks flee to the islands to celebrate the Assumption of Panagia (the Virgin Mary).

NEIGHBORHOODS

Syntagma

Coming from either airport, the bus stops at Syntagma (Constitution) Square. The center of modern Athens, this bustling plaza is packed with overpriced outdoor cafes, luxury hotels, and flashy banks. A pale yellow Neoclassical building, formerly the royal palace and now home to the Greek Parliament, gazes over the toe-nipping traffic of Syntagma. The **Greek National Tourist Office (EOT), post office, American Express office, transportation terminals,** and a number of **travel agencies** and **banks** surround the square. **Filellinon Street** and **Nikis Street,** parallel thoroughfares that head out from Syntagma toward Plaka, contain many of the city's budget travel offices, cheap hotels, and dance clubs. Unfortunately, Syntagma is currently being torn up for subway construction; cranes and dirt will detract from the square's charm for several more years.

Plaka

The center of the old city, Plaka is the temporary home of most visitors to Athens and is the busiest and safest area at night. Bounded by Athens' two largest ancient monuments—the **Temple of Olympian Zeus** and the **Acropolis**—Plaka is filled with the only medieval architecture that survived both the concrete vertical space movement of the past few decades and the double-edged shovel of zealous archaeologists. Today, on winding cobblestone footpaths, these structures house the junkshops and *tavernas* that define Greek tourism. Plaka exists in a stasis between Greece's most vivid reminders of the past and the ultra-modern, international set that comes to commune with Classical Athens.

Monastiraki

If you come by **ferry,** you can reach Athens from Peiraias (where the ferries dock) by walking left (facing inland) along the waterfront to Roosevelt St., then taking the subway to Montastiraki. Mostly known for its hodge-podge **flea market,** Monastiraki is also home to sun-tanned old Greek men making *bouzoukis,* hammering leather, and finishing furniture. Some of Athens' best budget lodgings and cheapest *gyro* stands surround the flea market, which is also the best place to test your skills in bartering with a stubborn merchant. To reach Syntagma Sq. from the subway station, turn right and walk five minutes up Ermou St.

Omonia

Northwest of Syntagma, Omonia Square is the site of the city's **central subway station,** from which trains run to Kifissia (40min.), Monastiraki (3min.), and Peiraias (20min.), among other destinations. The headquarters of the **Greek Communist Party (KKE)** towers over the square which has become the locus of Athens' drug culture. Inexpensive shops for food, clothing, and jewelry abound, but with the influx of refugees from Albania and all over the Middle East in recent years, this cosmopolitan area has become increasingly unsafe. There are, however, many cheap lodgings here. Mind your own business and try to be inconspicuous. Above all, don't travel alone at night. Two parallel avenues connect Syntagma Sq. to Omonia Sq. (Panepistimiou St. and Stadiou St.). The **university** and **library** are on Panepistimiou St., between Syntagma and Omonia. Both Larissis Station, which serves the north, and Peloponnese Station, which serves the south, are on Konstantinoupoleos St., northeast of **Karaiskaki Square** and are accessible from Deligiani St.

Exarhia

Neighboring Omonia Sq. to the east is the liberal and progressive Exarhia area. Formerly regarded as the home of Greek anarchists, in the past 10 years, the neighborhood has become safer and is now inhabited by students and international models. On Patission St., which intersects Panepistimiou St. and Stadiou St. just before Omonia, is the **National Archaeological Museum.** Thanks to the youthful population drawn from all over Greece by the **university** on Panepistimiou St., Exarhia sports some of Athens' liveliest nocturnal activities.

Kolonaki

Although Exarhia is the hang-out of professional models, Kolonaki has its fair share of local wanna-bes. On this posh, upscale foothill of Mt. Lycavittos, image-conscious Greeks shop in designer boutiques, sip *frappés,* and strut about, looking their best while they check each other out. Kolonaki is also the home of the **British Academy,** the **American School of Classical Studies,** and a small and slightly misplaced enclave of ex-patriot students. The disenfranchised Greek ex-royal family has some footholds in Kolonaki, American poets James Merrill and Charles Hartman set up shop here, and Don DeLillo put international risk analyst James Axton, the hero of his novel *The Names,* up in a Kolonaki apartment a block away from the American School.

Pangrati

Southeast of Kolonaki is Pangrati, where Athenian youth gather to chat over Fanta or coffee, monitor their mobile phones, and play backgammon. Despite its proximity to the city's center, Pangrati is remarkably successful at retaining a village-like intimacy. Visitors who settle in Pangrati even for a brief stay discover the city's secrets and are often accepted by kind-hearted locals as one of their own. With safe streets, several scattered Byzantine churches, a park, the **Olympic Stadium** and the **National Cemetery,** Pangrati invites visitors to get to know the city just by walking its streets without worry of getting lost.

■ Practical Information

TRANSPORTATION

Flights: From Athens, take the express bus #090 or 091 from either Syntagma Sq. or Stadiou St. near Omonia Sq. Buses run every 20min. from 7:30am to 9:50pm, plus 12 per night between 10:15pm and 6:45am. **East Terminal,** foreign airlines and some charters; **West Terminal,** Olympic Airways domestic and international service; **New Charter Terminal,** most charters. From the airport to Athens, look to your left after exiting customs for the blue and yellow express buses (200dr, 400dr after 11:30pm). A taxi costs 2500-3000dr (3500-4000dr after midnight), with an extra 50dr charge for each piece of luggage over 10kg, and a 300dr surcharge from the airport. Watch drivers very carefully; some rig the meters. Drivers may be unwilling to pick up travelers laden with luggage and might also make you share a taxi. Express buses and taxis are the most reliable travel option.

Trains: Call 145 or 147 for timetables. **Larissis Train Station** (tel. 524 0601) serves northern Greece and several European destinations. Trains depart for Thessaloniki (10hr., 4100dr); Belgrade, Yugoslavia (16,500dr); Sofia, Bulgaria (11,000dr); Istanbul, Turkey (16,500dr); Bradislava, Slovakia (35,500dr); Prague, Czech Republic (47,000); Bucharest, Romania (17,300dr); and Budapest, Hungary (32,000dr). Take trolley bus #1 from Panepistimiou St. in Syntagma (every 10min. 5am-midnight, 100dr). **Peloponnese Train Station** (tel. 513 1601) is in a Victorian building with a silver roof. From Larissis, exit to your right and go over the footbridge, or take blue bus #057 from Panepistimiou St. (every 15min. 5:30am-11:30pm, 100dr). Serves Patras (1580dr) and major towns in the Peloponnese. Also has OSE **buses** to Sofia, Bulgaria; Tirana, Albania; and Istanbul, Turkey. For more info, call **Hellenic Railways (OSE)** (tel. 323 6273) at 2 Sina St.

Buses: Unlike just about anything else in Greece, **KTEL** (ΚΤΕΛ) buses are punctual, so be there on time. For Athens and its suburbs, buses are blue and designated by 3-digit numbers. Fare is 100dr. Good for travel across the city, they are also ideal for daytrips to places like Daphni and Kesariani. For longer trips, take the orange or green buses. There are two main green bus terminals, **Terminal A,** 100 Kifissou St. (tel. 512 4910), and **Terminal B,** 260 Liossion St. (tel. 831 7181). You can call the terminals for general information, but each route also has an individual number. Terminal A serves most of Greece and can be reached by blue bus #051, caught at the corner of Zinonos St. and Menandrou St. near Omonia Sq. (every 10min. 5am-11:30pm, 100dr). The "information" booth at Terminal A is a privately run agency; don't get duped into buying their useless "vouchers." From Terminal A buses depart for Corinth (tel. 512 9233; 1½hr., 2 per hour 6:30am-8:30pm, 1450dr); Thessaloniki via Larissa (tel. 514 8856; 7½hr., 10 per day 7am-11pm, 7700dr); Corfu (tel. 512 9443; 11hr., 2 per day, 8400dr); Igoumenitsa (tel. 512 5954; 8½hr., 3 per day, 7750dr); and Patras (tel. 513 6185; 3hr., 19 per day 6am-9:45pm, 3350dr). Terminal B, serving some destinations in Sterea Ellada and on Evia, can be reached by blue bus #024, caught on Amalias St. outside the National Gardens on Panepistimiou St. (every 25min. 5am-midnight, 100dr). Buses depart from Terminal B for Katerini (tel. 831 7059; 6hr., 3 per day 9:45am-8pm, 6750dr); Delphi via Thebes and Livadia (tel. 831 7096; 3hr., 5 per day 7:30am-5:30pm, 4000dr); and Halkida on Evia (tel. 831 7153; 1½hr., 2 per hour 5:30am-9:30pm, 1400dr). Buses to Sounion, Marathon, and Rafina depart from **Mavromateon St.,** between the National Archaeological Museum and Areos Park in Exarhia. Take trolley #18, 11, 5, 2, or 9 to Mavromateon St. Buses to Eleusis and Daphni depart from Eleftherias Sq.; from Syntagma Sq. go west on Ermou St., turn right on Athinas St., and turn left on Evripidou St.

Ferries: Ferries bound for most of the Greek island groups dock at **Peiraias** (see p. 99). Those headed for the Sporades leave from Agios Konstantinos (see p. 189) or Volos (see p. 210). Those headed for the Ionian Islands leave from Patras (see p. 140). From Peiraias ferries go to Santorini (9hr., 5000dr); Mykonos (6hr., 4800dr); Ios (8hr., 5000dr); Aegina (1½hr., 1400dr); Paros (4hr., 4260dr); Rhodes (16hr., 8500dr); Limassol, Cyprus; and Haifa, Israel. For more info, contact the **Port Authority of Peiraias** (tel. 422 6000). From Athens to Peiraias, take the subway south to the last stop, or take green bus #40 from Filellinon and Mitropoleos St. (every 10min.). Boats also leave from **Rafina** (see p. 104), a port suburb east of Athens, and head to Andros, Tinos, and Mykonos. To Kea or Kithnos, take a ferry (1650-2300dr) from **Lavrio.** The orange bus to Lavrio (700dr) leaves from Mavromateon St. near Areos Park (take bus or taxi from Syntagma). Always check schedules prior to departure at the tourist office, in the *Athens News,* with the Port Authority of Peiraias, or at any travel agency. Ferry information is in any Greek newspaper or dial 143 for a Greek-recorded timetable.

Flying Dolphins: Hydrofoils serve the mainland and the Argosaronic, Sporades, and Cyclades islands. **Ceres' Flying Dolphins** (tel. 428 0001). Open M-Sa 8am-6.30pm, Su and holidays 8am-1pm. The hydrofoils, roughly twice as expensive and twice as fast as ferries, leave from **Zea Port** near Peiraias, Agios Konstantinos, and Volos.

Local Buses: Buy a **blue bus** ticket (100dr) at a kiosk from a station vendor and stamp it yourself at the orange machine on board. Kiosks only sell tickets for Athens and its suburbs; it is a good idea to buy several tickets at once if you intend to use the buses and trolleys frequently during your stay in Athens. If you don't stamp and hold on to your bus, trolley, or subway ticket (even when it seems nobody is there to make you pay), you may get caught by police in a check and fined 1500dr.

Trolleys: Yellow, crowded, sporting 1- or 2-digit numbers, and distinguished from buses by their electrical antennae. Tickets 100dr. Trolleys no longer accept money. Buy a ticket (same as bus ticket) ahead of time at a kiosk. Frequent service; convenient for short hops within the city. See the detailed map of Athens provided by the tourist office for trolley routes and stops.

Subway: The subway system in Athens is under construction to create branches off the current single line running from Peiraias Harbor to Kifissia in north Athens. There are 20 stops in between, including Omonia and Monastiraki, and the system is called the *elektriko.* Trains depart from either end of the line every 5min. 5am-midnight. Tickets 100dr. Buy tickets at booths or at automatic machines (which do not provide change) in the station. As with the bus system, hold on to your ticket.

Taxis: Meters start at 250dr, with an additional 62dr per km within city limits, 120dr per km in the suburbs. Rates double between midnight and 5am. If the taxi is caught in traffic, you will be charged 33dr per stationary min. 300dr surcharge for trips from the airport and 150dr charge from ports, bus, and railway terminals in addition to the 50dr for each piece of luggage. Hail your taxi by shouting your destination—not the street address, but the area (i.e., "Kolonaki"). The driver may or may not pick you up, depending on whether he is inclined to head in that direction. Get in the cab and *then* tell the driver the exact address or site. Most drivers don't speak English so have your destination written down (in Greek if possible) and include the area of the city (keep in mind that some streets in different parts of the city have the same name). Empty taxis are rare. It is common to ride with other passengers going in the same direction. For an extra 400dr, call a radio taxi (Ikaros, tel. 513 0640; Hermes, tel. 411 5200; Kosmos, tel. 801 9000). A full list of radio taxis appears in the *Athens News*. **Beware!** Pay what the meter shows, rounded up to the next 50dr, but be wary of drivers who tinker with their meters. Some drivers, especially those coming out of the airport, may not turn on the meter at all but take you somewhere and then charge an exorbitant fee; it's a good idea to say "Meter! Meter!" after you get in the taxi if you don't see the meter running right away. In addition, if you are on your way to a hotel, the taxi driver may have another one in mind for you—a hotel that has paid him off. Be firm about where you want to go and don't trust a taxi driver if he says your hotel is closed or there are no hostels in town.

Car Rental: Places abound on **Singrou St.,** all charging 10,000-15,000dr for a small car with 100km free mileage (prices include tax and insurance). Some offer discounts of up to 50% to students, and prices increase in summer. Credit cards accepted and international drivers license is not necessary. Most require drivers to have driven for at least a year.

TOURIST AND FINANCIAL SERVICES

Tourist Office: The **central office** and **information booth,** 2 Amerikis St. (tel. 331 0437, 331 0561, or 331 0562; fax 325 2815), off Stadiou St. near Syntagma Sq. Bus, train, and ferry schedules and prices; lists of museums, embassies, and banks; colorful brochures on travel throughout Greece. Ask for the detailed Athens map. Open M-F 9am-7pm, Sa 10am-2pm. There is also an office in the **East Terminal** of the airport (tel. 961 2722; fax 964 1627). After exiting baggage claim, the office is on the left before the exit. Open M-F 9am-7pm, Sa 11am-5pm.

Tourist Agencies: For **ISIC/FIYTO** purchases, see **Identification** (see p. 9). In Athens, you can buy the ISIC for 2800dr and FIYTO for 3000dr at **USIT Youth Student Travel,** 3 Filellinon St. (tel. 324 1884; fax 323 8447). Open M-F 9am-5pm, Sa 10am-2pm. **International Student and Youth Travel Service Limited,** 11 Nikis St. (tel. 322 1267; fax 322 1531), sells both ID cards and offers good student rates on ferries, trains, and planes to the rest of Europe. Open M-F 9am-5pm, Sa 9am-1pm. **Magic Travel Agency** (formerly **Magic Bus**), 20 Filellinon St. (tel. 323 7471, 323 7472, 323 7473, or 323 7474; fax 322 0219), stands out. Extremely competent, English-speaking staff. Open M-F 9am-6pm, Sa 10am-2pm. You might also visit **Consolas Travel,** 100 Aiolou St. (tel. 325 4931; fax 321 0907), next to the post office. They have a second office at 18 Filellinon St. (tel. 323 2812). Generally, it is best to shop around and look for specials at the agencies.

Accommodations: Greek Youth Hostel Association, 4 Dragatsaniou St., 7th floor (tel. 323 4107; fax 323 7590). Go up Stadiou St. and then left on Dragatsaniou St. Elevators on right as you enter the arcade. Lists hostels in Greece. Open M-F 9am-3pm. **The Hellenic Chamber of Hotels** (tel. 323 7193; fax 322 5449 or 323 6962). In the National Bank of Greece next to the tourist office. Provides information and reservations for A-, B-, C-, D-, and E-class hotels throughout Greece and some less expensive ones in Athens. All reservations require a cash deposit in trusty *drachmes*. Open M-F 8:30am-2pm, Sa 9am-12:30pm.

Embassies: Comprehensive listing of embassies available at the tourist office. **Albania,** 1 Karahristrou St. (tel. 723 4412). Open M-F 8:30am-noon. **Australia,** 37 D. Soutsou St. (tel. 721 3039). Open M-F 8:30am-12:30pm. **Brazil,** 14 Kolonaki Sq. (tel. 721 3039). Open M-F 9am-3pm. **Canada,** 4 Ioannou Genadiou St. (tel. 727 3400; fax 727 3460). Open M-F 8:30am-12:30pm. **Czech Republic,** 6 Seferi St. (tel. 671 3755 or 671 9701). Open M-F 9am-noon. **European Community,** 2 Vasilissis Sofias St. (tel. 725 1000). Open M-F 8:30am-1pm. **Germany,** 3 Karaoli Dimitriou St. (tel. 728 5111). Open M-F 9am-noon. **Hungary,** 6 Kalrou St. (tel. 672 5337 or 672

3753). Open M-F 8:30am-12:30pm. **Ireland,** 7 Vas. Konstandinou St. (tel. 723 2771). Open M-F 9am-3pm. **Romania,** 7 Em. Benaki St. (tel. 671 8020). Open M-F 8am-1pm. **South Africa,** 60 Kifissias St. (tel. 680 6645). Open M-F 8am-1pm. **Turkey,** 8 Vas. Georgiov B. St. (tel. 724 5915). Open M-F 8:30am-12:30pm. **United Kingdom,** 1 Ploutarchou St. (tel. 723 6211), at the intersection of Ypsilantou St. Open for visas M-F 8:30am-1pm. **United States,** 91 Vas. Sofias St. (tel. 721 2951; fax 645 6282). Open M-F 8:30am-5pm, for visas 8-11am. **Yugoslavia,** 106 Vas. Sofias St. (tel. 777 4344 or 777 4355). Open M-F 8:30am-1pm.

Banks: National Bank of Greece, 2 Karageorgi Servias St., Syntagma Sq. (tel. 344 0018). Open for full service M-Th 8am-2pm, F 8am-1:30pm. Open for currency exchange only M-Th 3:30-5:30pm, F 3-5:30pm, Sa 9am-3pm, Su 9am-1pm. American Express, the post office, some hotels, and other banks (list available at tourist office) offer **currency exchange.** Expect commissions of around 5%. Most banks close at 2pm on weekdays and are closed on weekends. Currency exchange at the airport is available 24hr., but the fee is high.

American Express: 2 Ermou St., P.O. Box 3325 (tel. 324 4975 or 324 4979), above McDonald's in Syntagma Sq. Air-conditioned and filled with Americans, the office cashes traveler's checks with no commission, runs a travel agency, holds mail for one month, and provides other special services for cardholders. Open M-F 8:30am-4pm, Sa 8:30am-1:30pm (only travel and mail services Sa).

LOCAL SERVICES

Luggage Storage: At the **East Terminal** of the airport, 150m outside on your right as you exit baggage claim and customs; look for the yellow "LOCKERS" sign. At the **West Terminal,** exit the baggage claim building and look for the "LOCKERS" sign on the right by a pharmacy. Keep your ticket stub to reclaim; pay when you collect. 1000dr per piece per day, 1500dr for bicycles, surfboards, or extra-large boxes. After midnight you pay for an extra day. Open 24hr. Also several offices on Nikis St. and Filellinon St., including **Pacific Ltd.,** 26 Nikis St. (tel. 324 1007; fax 323 3685). Per piece 500dr per day, 1500dr per week, 3000dr per month. Open M-Sa 8am-8pm, Su 8am-2pm. Many hotels have free or inexpensive luggage storage.

International Bookstores: Eleftheroudakis Book Store, 17 Panepistimiou St. (tel. 331 4180) and 4 Nikis St. (tel. 322 9388). A pleasure to browse through, with Greek, English, French, and German books, classical and recent literature, and many travel guides, including *Let's Go.* Open M and W 9am-4pm, Tu and Th-F 9am-8:30pm, Sa 9am-3pm. **Pantelides Books,** 11 Amerikis St. (tel. 362 3673), overflows with a variety of books; self-proclaimed best philosophy/critical theory selection in town. Open M and Sa 9am-4pm, Tu-F 9am-8:30pm. **Compendium Bookshop,** 28 Nikis St. (tel. 322 1248; fax 322 2924). Popular, new and used book selections with a full complement of *Let's Go* guides and large fiction and poetry sections. Monthly poetry readings. Also houses a **children's book room**—part bookshop, part library. Open M and W 9am-5pm, Tu and Th-F 9am-8:30pm, Sa 9am-3pm.

Libraries: In the **Hellenic American Union,** 22 Massalias St. (tel. 362 9886; fax 363 3174), behind the university, there is an **American Library** (tel. 363 8114) on the 4th floor. Open M and Th 3-7pm, Tu-W and F 11am-3pm. The union also houses a **Greek Library,** with English books on Greece, on the 7th floor. Open M-Th 9am-8pm, F 9am-5pm. The **British Council Library,** Filikis Eterias Sq. (tel. 363 3215), also has English reading material. Open M-F 9:30am-1:30pm. Closed in Aug. All also sponsor **cultural events.**

Laundromats: The Greek word for laundry is *plinitirio,* but most places have signs reading "Laundry." Expect to pay roughly 2500dr per load for wash, dry, and detergent. A kind Greek grandmother will wash, dry, and fold your laundry for 2000dr at **10 Angelou Geronta St.** in Plaka. Open M-Sa 8am-8pm, Su 9am-2pm. Near the train stations, **9 Psaron St.** (tel. 522 2856) launders one load for 2700dr. Open M-F 8am-9pm, Sa 8am-5pm, Su 8am-2pm. **41 Kolokinthous and Leonidou St.** (tel. 522 6233) does the same for 2300dr. Open M-F 9am-9pm, Su 9am-3pm. Tall, lean Giorgos at **48 Xenokratous St.,** in Kolonaki, may accept payment in Stones tapes, otherwise 2500dr per load.

Haircuts: Tasia Tania, 23 Douridos St. (tel. 721 8180), in Pangrati near Messologiou Sq. Cut 3500dr. Open Tu and Th-F 9am-6pm, W and Sa 9am-3pm. Men can get a trim and a shave for 2500dr at a traditional **barbershop** on Souidias St. in Kolonaki.

EMERGENCY AND COMMUNICATIONS

Emergencies: For **doctors** (2pm-7am), call 105, or outside Athens 101; for an **ambulance**, 166; for **poison control**, 779 3777. For the **AIDS Help Line**, 722 2222. The daily emergency hospitals are listed in the *Athens News*. Tourists can receive free emergency health care.
Police: (tel. 100).Broken English spoken.
Tourist Police: 77 Dimitrakopoulou St. (tel. 171). Great for information assistance and emergencies. English spoken. Open daily 7am-11pm.
Pharmacies: Identifiable by a green cross hanging over the street. The daily *Athens News* (250dr) lists each day's emergency pharmacies and their hours in its "Useful Information" section. One is open 24hr. (referred to as *efimerevon* in Greek). They alternate. To find out which pharmacies are open after hours, dial 107. **Syntagma:** 23 Voulis St. **Monastiraki:** 86 Ermou St. **Omonia:** 52 Pireos St. **Exarhia:** 89 Kallidromiou St. (tel. 883 5883). **Pangrati:** 7 Plastira Sq. (tel. 7211 385).
Hospitals: Geniko Kratiko Nosokomio (Public State Hospital), 154 Mesogion St. (tel. 777 8901; fax 770 5980). **Hegia,** 4 Erithrou Stavrou St. (tel. 682 7904; fax 684 5089), is a top-notch private hospital in Maroussi. Closer to the center of Athens, try the **Aeginitio** state hospital at 72 Vas. Sofias St. (tel. 722 0811 or 722 0812), and at 80 Vas. Sofias St. (tel. 777 0501; fax 777 6321). Near Kolonaki is a **public hospital** at 45-47 Evangelismou St. (tel. 722 0101; fax 729 1808). In Greek, "hospital" is *nosokomio.*
Post Offices: Omonia: 100 Aiolou St. (tel. 321 6023). **Postal Code:** 10200. **Syntagma:** (tel. 322 6253), on the corner of Mitropoleos St. **Postal Code:** 10300. **Exarhia:** at the corner of Zaimi St. and K. Deligiani St. **Postal Code:** 10691. All open M-F 7:30am-8pm, Sa 7:30am-2pm, Su 9am-1:30pm. An **Acropolis** branch offers stamps and currency exchange. Open M-F 8am-5:30pm, Sa 7:30am-2pm, Su 9am-2pm. **Postal Code:** 11702. **Parcel post** for sending packages abroad at **29 Koumoundourou St.** (tel. 524 9359). Open M-F 7:30am-8pm. Also at **4 Stadiou St.** (tel. 322 8940). Open M-F 7:30am-2pm.
OTE: 85 Patission St. (tel. 821 4449 or 823 7040) or 50 Athinas St. (tel. 321 6699). Offers overseas collect calls, recent phonebooks for most European and Anglophone countries, and currency exchange (until 3pm). Open M-F 7am-9pm, Sa 8am-3pm, Su 9am-2pm. For information on **overseas calls,** dial 161; for **directory assistance** in and outside Athens, 132. Most **phone booths** in the city operate by **telephone cards** that cost 1700dr, 7000dr, or 11,500dr at OTE offices, kiosks, and tourist shops. Push the "i" button on the phones for English instructions. For rate and general **telephone information** call 134; for **complaints,** 135; for a **domestic operator** speaking English, 151. **Telephone Code:** 01.

■ Accommodations

Concentrated within the city center, budget hotels often suffer from unwelcome background noise—ask for a room that faces away from the street. Although the noise is bearable, light sleepers might consider earplugs. Stays less than three nights may incur a 10% surcharge, but very few hotel owners take advantage of this option.

Hotel hawkers meet trains at the station. Some will distribute maps to decent places near the station; others will lure you to dumps way out of town. Unsuspecting travelers have been harmed by deceitful hawkers in the past. Call ahead to reserve a room or search on your own. Following a hawker is safest when traveling in large groups. Insist that he point the hotel suggestion out on a city map and set a firm price in writing before leaving the station. Men arriving by bus from the airport should avoid "friendly barkeepers" who may send you to brothels rather than budget hotels. Do not sleep in the city parks; camping anywhere in Athens is illegal and dangerous.

If you are in need of money and a place to stay for an extended period of time, inquire about a job at one of the city's hostels. Several hire travelers to work the lounge or the reception desk, clean rooms, or act as a runner at the port or airport bus stops. Several hotels offer breakfast for about 1000dr. For significantly less, you can buy milk or juice and fresh rolls or baked goods at any bakery.

Note that the prices quoted below are from mid-1998 and are expected to increase in the next year. In 1999, expect a 10-20% price increase. Prices are 20-40% less in the off season (Sept.-May).

SYNTAGMA

The convenient location of these hotels near the city's main square offers immediate access to transportation and business during the day as well as relative quiet and moderate safety at night. Reservations will ensure you a spot.

Hotel Festos, 18 Filellinon St. (tel. 323 2455) Come as a guest and stay as an employee! Hotel Festos hires travelers to work in the lounge and behind the desk. Although the quieter cooler rooms are slightly dimmer, and the brighter rooms are noisier and hotter, the student travelers who frequent this hotel claim to come for the friendly atmosphere. The restaurant has a rotating menu at reasonable prices. Cable TV. 24hr. hot water. Luggage storage 200dr per day. Check-out 10am. Dorms 3000dr; doubles 8000dr; triples 12,000dr; quads 14,000dr.

Hotel Kimon, 27 Apollonos St. (tel. 331 4658 or 324 8974; fax 502 0134). One block from the Mitropoli Cathedral, this friendly hotel is on a usually safe street and offers a view of the Acropolis from the roof garden. A/C 1000dr extra. 24hr. hot water. Free luggage storage. Singles 7000dr, with bath 9000dr; doubles 8000dr, with bath 10,000dr; triples 10,000dr.

Thisseos Inn, 10 Thisseos St. (tel. 324 5960). From Syntagma Sq., take Karageorgi Servias St., which becomes Perikleous St.; Thisseos St. is on the right. This home-turned-hostel is popular with students who want to stay near Syntagma's sights but far from its noise. Very quiet at night. TV in reception area, full kitchen facilities, common showers. 24hr. hot water. As always, be aware of your belongings at all times. The friendly reception staff makes up for the 2am curfew—ask and they may bend the rules. Dorms 2500dr; doubles 6500dr.

⊛YWCA (XEN), 11 Amerikis St. (tel. 362 4291). With an emphasis on female empowerment and a women-only policy, this simple guesthouse is perfect for women traveling alone. The sparkling, spacious building features laundry facilities, refrigerators on each floor, and a canteen serving breakfast (1000dr). The usually safe and central location more than compensates for the Y's strict regulations and occasionally grumpy staff. Singles 6000dr; doubles 9000dr; triples 12,000dr.

George's Guest House, 46 Nikis St. (tel. 322 6474). Nikos is the manager, and no one seems to know who George is, but there's a fair chance the man is a giant. Doorways and ceilings are consistently lofty in this no-frills hostel. The facilities, especially the bathrooms, are very well broken-in, but clean enough. The bottom line here is that you get what you pay for. Free luggage storage. 24hr. hot water. Check-out 10am. Dorms 2500dr; singles 5000dr; doubles 6000dr; triples 8000dr.

John's Place, 5 Patroou St. (tel. 322 9719). From Syntagma Sq., walk down Metropoleos St., pass Voulis St., and take a left on Patroou St. Despite their dreariness, dim hallways and quiet nights enhance this simple guest house's gothic flavor. Request hot water 10min. before use. Check-out noon. Singles 6000dr; doubles 9000dr; triples 10000dr.

PLAKA

Many of the city's cheap hotels cluster in this historic, central, and busy part of town. If you're looking for convenience, relative safety, and a good venue for sight-seeing and people-watching, this is the place to stay. During the summer months, make a reservation if possible—these qualities draw a crowd.

⊛Student's and Traveler's Inn, 16 Kidathineon St. (tel. 324 4808; fax 321 0065; email Students-inn@ath.forthnet.gr), in the heart of Plaka. With its convenient locale, friendly owner and staff, outdoor courtyard, and hardwood floors, this hotel is more than worthwhile. Internet access 1500dr per 30min., 3000dr per 100min. Travel services. 24hr. hot showers. Breakfast served 6am-noon (1000-1500dr). Singles 7000dr; doubles 9000dr; triples 12,000dr; quads 14,000dr. 10% discount with student ID or youth card.

Dioskouros House, 6 Pitakou St. (tel. 324 8165), across the street from Hadrian's Arch. The hotel is sheltered from, yet remarkably close to, the city center. Popular with weary travelers, the outdoor bar and courtyard serves breakfast (500dr), beer, and non-alcoholic beverages until 11pm. Check-out 10am. Dorms 3000dr; singles 7000dr; doubles 8000dr; triples 12,000dr; quads 14,000dr.

Hotel Phaedra, 16 Herefondos St. (tel. 322 7795). From Hadrian's Arch on Amalias, walk 1 block up Lysikrateous St. to the intersection with Herefondos St. Owned and run by 2 brothers since 1963, Phaedra has a friendly family atmosphere. In addition to the scenic park that flanks it, the hotel boasts a view of the Acropolis from almost every room. 24hr. hot water. Check-out noon. Singles 7000dr; doubles 9000dr; triples 11,000dr; quads 12,000dr. Breakfast 1300dr.

Adonis Hotel, 3 Kodrou St. (tel. 324 9737 or 324 9741; fax 323 1602). From Syntagma Sq. come down Filellinon St., turn right on Nikodimou St. and then left on Kodrou St. Adonis is very close to the intersection of Kodrou St. and Voulis St. With a bath, A/C, and telephone in every room and a marble foyer, this hotel is perfect for families traveling with children or for those with fewer budget constraints. The rooftop garden lounge offers a beautiful view of the Acropolis and Mt. Lycavittos. Singles 10,200dr; doubles 14,500dr; triples 18,270dr. Prices are cut 5-10% for stays of more than 2 days.

Hotel Kouros, 11 Kodrou St. (322 7431). From Syntagma Sq., walk down Filellinon St., turn right down the foot-path Kidathineon St., then right again on Kodrou St. This Victorian building with crown moulding provides decent accommodations in a quiet and safe neighborhood and a rooftop view of the Acropolis. Ask 10min. in advance for hot water. Luggage storage 300dr per day. Check-out 11:30am. Singles 6000dr; doubles 7000-9500dr; triples 12,000-14,000dr.

MONASTIRAKI

Near the central food and flea markets, this neighborhood has an ever-increasing, never-ceasing noise problem. However, it's also near the Acropolis and the subway, practically on top of the *Agora* site, and home to some souvenir bargains.

Hotel Tempi, 29 Aiolou St. (tel. 321 3175; fax 325 4179). From Syntagma Sq., follow Ermou St. and take a right on Aiolou St. (also spelled Eolu and Eolou). About 10 rooms have balconies and views of the flower market in Irinis (Peace) Square. 24hr. hot water. Public phone in the reception area. Free luggage storage. Laundry service 1000dr. Singles 5000dr, with bath 6500dr; doubles 8500dr, with bath 9500dr; triples 10,500dr.

◉Pella Inn, 104 Ermou St. (tel. 325 0598 or 321 2229; fax 325 0598), a 10min. walk down Ermou from Syntagma Sq., 2 blocks from the Monastiraki subway station (entrance on Karaiskaki St.). Dine in the lounge where the bright yellow and red furniture is sure to wake you up. Better yet, take your food to the exceptional terrace and enjoy the breathtaking view of the Acropolis, which is visible from 19 of the 23 rooms. No curfew; Nikos, the night watchman just out of the Greek army, will always let late night wanderers in. Continental breakfast 800dr. Free luggage storage. Dorms 3000dr; singles 7000dr; doubles 8000-10,000dr.

OMONIA

This overcrowded business and residential center is too far away from Syntagma for week-long stays, but convenient for a stop-over because of its proximity to trains, buses, and (via the Victoria or Omonia subway stop) Peiraias. Be wary of pickpockets in the subway and around the Omonia Sq. area.

Athens International Hostel (HI), 16 Victor Hugo St. (tel. 523 4170; fax 523 4015). From Omonia Sq., walk down Tritis Septembriou St. and take a left on Veranzerou St.; it will become Victor Hugo after crossing Marni St. The only HI-affiliated youth hostel in Greece. To stay here, you must either be an HI member, buy a full membership card (3600dr), or buy a temporary membership card (600dr), which becomes permanent after paying 600dr each night of a 6-night stay. Full kitchen facilities. Hot water 6-10am and 6-10pm. Free short-term luggage storage. Laundry

1500dr for guests, 2500dr for non-guests, also self-service laundry. Dorms 1500dr per night, including sheets; 2100dr per night for non-members. Make reservations in the summer.

Hostel Aphrodite, 12 Einardou St. (tel. 881 0589 or 883 9249; fax 881 6574; email hostel-aphrodite@ath.forthnet.gr). From the subway stop at Victoria Sq., follow Heiden St. for 2 blocks, then Paioniou St. for 2 more. Take a right on Michail Voda St. and a left 2 blocks later onto Einardou St. From the train station, follow Filadelfias St. until Michail Voda St. Easy access to both the train station and Victoria Sq. Friendly basement bar. Travel services; ask about the 20-day island pass for 12,000dr. Breakfast 900-1200dr. Laundry 2500dr. Dorms 2500dr; doubles 7500dr; triples 9000dr; quads 11,000dr. 10% discount with student ID.

Hotel Appia, 21 Menandrou St. (tel. 524 5155 or 524 4561; fax 524 3552). From Omonia Sq., follow Tsaldari St. to Menandrou St. Popular with international travelers, the reception staff is fluent in English, Spanish, and French. Telephones, ceiling fans, and radios in all rooms. 24hr. bar with fireplace. Breakfast 1000dr. 24hr. hot water. Check-out noon. Wheelchair accessible. Singles 4000dr, with bath 6000dr; doubles 6000dr, with bath 8000dr; triples 8000dr; quads 9500dr. Reserve July-Sept.

Hotel Arta, 12 Nikitara St. (tel. 382 7753 or 382 2881). From Syntagma or Omonia, take Stadiou St. to Benaki St., turn left, and take the 3rd left onto Nikitara St. Convenient hotel in a quiet part of the city center. Endearing non-English speaking reception. Immaculate rooms with desks and phones. Breakfast 1300dr. Free luggage storage. Reception 24hr. Singles 6000dr, with bath and A/C 8000dr; doubles 8000dr, with bath and A/C 12,000dr; triples 9000dr, with bath and A/C 15,000dr.

EXARHIA

Exarhia, the home of Athens' student population, is definitely the hippest place to stay in the city. Convenient to the National Archaeological Museum, Exarhia is within walking distance of the city's major public transportation services, but is quieter and much safer than nearby Omonia Sq.

Hotel Orion, 105 Em. Benaki St. (tel. 382 7362 or 382 0191; fax 380 51 93). From Omonia Sq., walk up Em Benaki St. or take bus #230 from Syntagma Sq. Abutting Strefi Hill, Orion has small rooms and shared baths. The hotel accommodates international models due to a deal with a modeling agency, but people of all appearances are welcome. Sun-worshippers relax on the roof-top kitchen and TV lounge Breakfast 1200dr. 24hr. hot water. Free luggage storage. Laundry 1000dr. Singles 6000dr; doubles 8000dr; triples 9000dr.

Hotel Dryades, 4 Dryadon St. (tel. 382 7116 or 330 2387). Owned by the same family as Hotel Orion, Dryades is slightly more elegant, with larger rooms and private baths. Breakfast 1200dr. 24hr. hot water. Free luggage storage. Laundry 1000dr. Singles 9000dr; doubles 11,000dr; triples 13,000dr.

Museum Hotel, 16 Bouboulinas St. (tel. 380 5611, 380 5612, or 380 5613; fax 380 0507). The hotel's location near the university and the National Archaeological Museum affords safe and quiet convenience, making it ideal for families. Breakfast 1200dr. Free luggage storage. 24hr. hot water. Credit cards accepted. Singles 6500dr; doubles 9800dr; triples 11,700dr. 10% discount for students.

The Exarcheion, 55 Themistokleous St. (tel. 380 0731, 380 1256, or 380 8684; fax 380 3296). Enjoy the stairway's stylish mural as you walk up to one of the 50 rooms equipped with telephone, TV, and colorful curtains. Breakfast 1200dr. 24hr. hot water in private bathrooms. Free luggage storage. Credit cards accepted. Call or fax to make a reservation. Singles 7000dr; doubles 9000dr; triples 11,000dr.

KOLONAKI

Rooms tend to be more luxurious and more expensive in the Kolonaki area, where Athenians parade their latest purchases from boutiques and sip over-priced *frappés*. The sights of Plaka are just down the hill and the Kolonaki area sports Athens' most unique nightspots. Exceptional views of the Acropolis and sea from the foot of Mt. Lycavittos, however, make Kolonaki the place to be if you have the money to spend.

Athenian Inn, 22 Haritos St. (tel. 723 8097, 723 9552, or 721 8756; fax 724 2268). Once inside the fully air-conditioned granite-filled hotel, you will be welcomed by exceptionally friendly, honest, and knowledgeable staff. The quiet, usually safe, and central location has kept guests coming back for 20 years. Breakfast included. Singles 18,900dr; doubles for single occupancy 21,300dr; standard doubles 28,200dr; triples 35,150dr.

PANGRATI

These rooms are in a relatively quiet, residential area. Pangrati, a 20-minute walk or speedy trolley ride east from Syntagma Sq. The village atmosphere of the street markets, cafes, and *tavernas* of Pangrati will have you searching the record stores for the old Rembetika song "Pangratissa Mou" (My Girl From Pangrati).

Youth Hostel #5 Pangrati, 75 Damareos St. (tel. 751 9530; fax 751 0616). Take trolley #2 or 11 from Syntagma Sq. to Filolaou St., or walk through the National Garden, down Eratosthenous St. to Plastira Sq., 3 blocks on Efthidiou St. to Frinis St., and down Frinis St. until Damareos St. on the right. There is no sign for the hostel on the street, just the number "75" and a green door. The cheery place features bulletin boards for hostelers to share philosophies or jokes. The owner speaks English, Spanish, Italian, French, and Portuguese. TV lounge and full kitchen facilities. Breakfast 500dr. Hot showers 500dr and 20min. wait. Sheets 100dr. Pillowcases 100dr. Blankets 50dr. Laundry 700dr. Key deposit 300dr. Check-out 10am. Quiet hours 2:30-5pm and 11pm-7am. Wheelchair accessible. Dorms 1800dr. Roof beds 1500dr.

Zappeion Hotel, 4 Ironda St. (tel. 724 1408). From Vas. Konstandinou St. turn onto Ag. Spiridonas St. and then onto Ironda St. Cheaper than most in Pangrati, this hotel is stocked with A/C, phones, a bar, and a TV lounge. Continental breakfast 1500dr. Singles 12,000dr; doubles 14,000dr.

■ Food

Athens offers a melange of stands, open-air cafes, outdoor side street *tavernas,* and intriguing dim restaurants frequented by grizzled Greek men. Athens' culinary claim to fame is cheap and plentiful *souvlaki* (250-400dr), either on a *kalamaki* (skewer) or wrapped in *pita.* Served quickly and eaten on the go if necessary, *souvlaki* is the Greek version of fast food. A *tost,* a grilled sandwich of variable ingredients (normally ham and cheese) for 300-600dr, is another option. Beer (usually Amstel and Heineken, the latter also known as "Green Beer" or the "Green Hornet" for its green bottle) runs roughly 200dr per bottle. *Tiropita* (hot cheese pie), *milopita* (hot apple pie), and *spanakopita* (hot spinach pie) go for around 300dr. Ice cream is sold at almost every kiosk. *Koulouri,* donut-shaped, sesame-coated rolls, make a good breakfast at 100dr.

The most popular place for tourists to eat is Plaka, but other neighborhoods offer less expensive, more authentic *tavernas* frequented by locals. You'll find many interesting places up and down Adrianou St. and Kidatheneon St. Once seated at the joint of your choice, relax; Greek restaurants are not known for their speedy service. Women should know that Plaka is a popular spot for *kamakia* (literally "octopus spears," or pick–up men) who enjoy making catcalls at women as they walk by. Sometimes they may follow you, but keep walking and ignore them; in most cases, harassment is only verbal. Places in Plaka serve all day, but outside touristed quarters few restaurants open before 8pm. Restaurants tend to be deserted at 6pm, near-empty before 10pm, and crowded from 11pm to 1am.

SYNTAGMA

Cheap fast food abounds in the area around Athens' central square. There are big crowds in Syntagma Sq. around the clock: young Greeks engaged in the eternal pose, tourists and executives hailing a cab or waiting for the airport bus, ex-pat students taking a break from late-night translations, mangy dogs, street musicians, gypsies, organ grinders, drug addicts, and beggars. Well lit at all hours of the night, Syntagma Sq. remains relatively safe for those craving a midnight snack.

Kentrikon, 3 Colocotroni St. (tel. 323 2482 or 323 5623), near Stadiou St. Although the fully air-conditioned dining hall has wood paneling and linen tablecloths, you can still eat a traditional Greek meal for 1800dr. International dishes like pasta *bolognaise* and pasta *carbonara* (1300-1700dr) or veal (1800dr) distinguish the restaurant from other Greek restaurants. Vegetarian options available. Open M-F 11am-6pm, Sa 11am-4pm.

Orpheas, 6 Arsakiou St. (tel. 322 7103). Coming down Stadiou St., turn right on Arsakiou St. after Pezmezoglou St. and enter the air-conditioned neoclassical arcade with the high, glass roof and surreal wallpaper featuring Orpheus and his lyre but no Eurydice. Serves a wide array of light meals and desserts, each with a special twist. Have a frothy, smoothie-like mixed juice (1500dr) or a rich baguette sandwich (1100dr). Open M-F 7:30am-10pm, Sa 7:30am-4pm.

Nikis Cafe, 3 Nikis St. (tel. 323 4971), near Ermou St. Nikis is still trying to determine which dishes are in demand. They'd like your input on the basic starch and sauce (1500dr), or the sandwiches and quiche (1000dr). Thirsty? Skip the meal and choose one of the frozen margaritas in delicious mango or strawberry flavors.

Makrigianni, 54 Nikis St. (tel. 323 3855). Syntagma staple—chicken *tost* (450dr).

Mirabelle, 34 Nikis St. (tel. 323 1612). Greek men in singlets and tourists alike enjoy cheap *souvlaki* (200dr) and *spanokopita* (350dr). Open daily 6am-midnight.

To Apollonion, 10 Nikis St. (tel. 331 2590). The masses flock here on their lunch break to buy sweets, breads, and coffee (350dr).

PLAKA

For do-it-yourself meals, various **minimarkets** on Nikis St. and in Plaka sell basic groceries. If the *taverna* isn't your style, you can bring food back to your room or make yourself a picnic at the foot of the Acropolis or in the National Garden.

Kouklis Ouzeri a.k.a. **To Gerani,** 14 Tripodon St. (tel. 324 7605). From Kidatheneon, one of Plaka's busiest strips, Tripodon is a side street. In a quiet niche with a wonderful balcony, To Gerani is cheaper than most. Its claims to be "the most traditional restaurant" are substantiated by entrees named after the owner's grandmother. The rotating menu limits your choices, but any 2 dishes make a good meal (900-1100dr each).

Eden Vegetarian Restaurant, 12 Lissiou St. (tel. 324 8858), on the corner of Minissikleous St. on the west side of Plaka. Signs will direct you to this otherwise secluded restaurant. Popular with both herbivores and omnivores. Soy-meat and organically grown vegetables in traditional dishes like *moussaka* (1500dr). The Spanish special, a combination of rice, cheese, carrots, and cream, is a filling favorite (1700dr).

T. Stamatopoulos, 26 Lissiou St. (tel. 322 8722 or 321 8549). The fenced-off, outdoor terrace keeps outsiders from peeking in, especially in the summer when live music and Greek dancing catches their attention. A family-owned restaurant since 1882, this *taverna* works on Greek time—it doesn't open for dinner until 8pm, but serves until 2am. The veal special in wine sauce (2100dr) is a popular choice.

O Platanos, 4 Diogenous St. (tel. 322 0666). Diogenous St. is parallel to Adrianou St. The restaurant is named after the *platanos* tree towering over the courtyard dining area. Lamb is the specialty—have it with eggplant, zucchini, or *fricase* for 1700dr. Open M-Sa 12:30pm-5 and 8:30pm-midnight.

Zorbas, 15 Lissiou St. (tel. 322 6188), down and across the street from Eden. Entrees 1500-3000dr. Try the lamb Zorbas (2100dr), chicken Artmenis (1950dr), or beef Stamnas (2100dr), all of which combine 2 Greek favorites, the grill and cheese. Pumpkin balls (800dr) are a good way to tease your appetite. Gum available upon request—absolutely necessary. Open M-Th 4pm-1am, F-Su 11am-1am.

Cafe Plaka, 1 Tripodon St. (tel. 322 0388). A dessert lover's haven, Cafe Plaka serves French crepes smothered in innumerable choices. Choose ham, mushrooms, chicken, or cheese for a salty meal, or sin a little and opt for the chocolate-banana option. Take-out crepes, salty or sweet, are identical to those served inside but a fraction the price (500-700dr rather than 1600-2000dr). Open daily 9am-3:30am.

MONASTIRAKI

While you're getting ripped off at the flea market junkshops, save a few coins for some *tzatziki*-smothered *gyro* goodness or grilled bananas from one of Monastiraki's street vendors. **Market Sophos,** 78 Mitropoleos St. (tel. 322 6677), near Aiolou St., is a great place to stock up on groceries before making use of your hostel's kitchen.

⊛**Savas,** 86 Mitropoleos St. (tel. 324 5048). Tucked into a corner off Ermou St., the restaurant and take-out grill are godsends to those on a budget. With vegetarian *gyros* (150dr) for less than a soda (220dr), it's an excellent pit-stop after a day exploring the Acropolis and the flea market. Open daily 7am-3am.

Kouti, 23 Adrianou St. (tel. 324 4794 or 321 2836). Located near the *Agora,* Kouti (The Box) is perfect for a slightly fancier dinner out. The menu is written in fairy tale books and features original dishes like Houkiaz Beyenti Turkish veal in red sauce (3000dr), and tartalettes with blue cheese sauce (2000dr).

Attalos Restaurant, 9 Adrianou St. (tel. 321 9520 or 321 2488), near the Thisseon area. Frequented by VIPs from the U.S. Embassy, this traditional Greek *taverna* serves meals for about 2400dr. Although the food is tasty, you're paying for the view of the *Agora.* Peak at your choices in the kitchen before ordering a wild dandelion salad or creamed meatballs in cabbage leaves. Open daily 9am-midnight.

Oasis, 82 Ermou St. For a quick bite to eat in Monastiraki, grab a cream pie with cinnamon and sugar (300dr) and a soda (190dr). Pastries baked fresh daily. Open M-F 6am-9pm, Sa-Su 6am-2pm.

OMONIA

As in Syntagma, the immediate area around Omonia Sq. is filled with fast-food joints. For those with access to a kitchen, pasta (500g, 187dr), yogurt (400g, 506dr), and other vittles are on sale at **Galaxias Discount Market,** 26 Tritis Semptembriou St.

Healthy Food Vegetarian Restaurant, 57 Panepistimiou St. (tel. 321 0966; fax 321 2043). This wholesome food store and restaurant is a rare find among Athens' *souvlaki* stands and sweetshops. Everything, including the popular potato carrot pie (400dr), the alternative breakfast meuslix (950dr), or the surprisingly delicious carrot apple juice, is made without any preservatives. After your meal, browse through the aisles of seasonings, fruit, soy milk, vitamins, and books in the adjoining shop. Open M-F 8am-10pm, Sa 8am-9pm, Su 10am-4pm.

Dafni Taverna, 65 Ionlianou St. (tel. 821 3914). From Victoria Sq., walk down Aristotelous St. and take a right on Iolianou St. The moment you enter the courtyard shaded by grape vines and enclosed on one side by barrels of *retsina* you'll know you've found a classic *taverna* and a hearty meal. Try the *moussaka* (1100dr), octopus (1400dr), or *dolmades* (1000dr), washed down by a liter of homemade *retsina* (800dr). Open daily noon-1am.

Kroskas, 88 Aristotelous St. (tel. 823 1465). Occupying 1 corner of Victoria Sq., the restaurant's interior features a 3D mural of the Parliament Building. Check out vegetarian dishes like eggplant with tomatoes and feta cheese (1100dr) or omelettes (800-1000dr). Open M-F noon-1am.

EXARHIA

The nearest refuge from the grime of Omonia, Exarhia—along with Pangrati—is the place in Athens where you're most likely to interact with Greeks on their own terms.

⊛**O Barba Giannis,** 94 Em. Benaki St. (tel. 330 0185). Athenian students, executives, and artists all seem to agree that this is the place for cheap delicious food and outstanding service. The menu includes a wide variety of fish (from 950dr), roast pork (1400dr), and vegetarian dishes (950dr), as well as cheap wine (700dr). Open M-Sa noon-1am, Su noon-7pm.

Souvlaki Kavouras, 664 Themistokleous St. (tel. 383 7981). Although the name literally means "souvlaki crabs," no seafood appears on the menu. Open almost constantly, Kavouras doles out super-cheap *souvlaki* (260dr) and beer (300dr), and invites its patrons to enjoy the courtyard to the rear. Open daily 10am-6am.

The Oasis, 44 Baltetsion St. (tel. 330 1369). Formerly a bar, Oasis has become a peaceful haven surrounded by fountains and trees for lovers of fresh fish (1300dr) and beer (500dr). Open daily 1pm-1am.

Mainas, 27 Kallidromiou St. (tel. 330 4300 or 381 2903), This pizzeria claims to start by "giving out love" and proceeds to serve spaghetti (1300d), beer (400dr), and pizza (1600dr) made fresh before your eager eyes. 10% discount for *Let's Go* users. Open daily noon-1am.

KOLONAKI

Catering primarily to a chic bourgeois crowd with *drachmes* to burn, the cafes and *tavernas* of Kolonaki tend to be a bit pricier than most. The ex-pat student crowd in the neighborhood usually finds a few affordable establishments and settles down for its time in sunny exile. The surest bargain in Kolonaki, however, is the **street market** every Friday morning on Xenokratous St., where you can grab your supply of peanuts, potatoes, fresh clementines, and underwear for the coming week.

⊛Apokentro Pizzeria and Creperie, 2 Deinokratous (tel. 725 1982 or 721 6898). Take bus #60 from Akademias St. Petros, the cook, and his wife Artemis have been known to take on ex-pat students as if they were family. Nikos the delivery man may refer you to some cool clubs. Try one of their unreal crepes with chocolate, banana, and Bailey's (1500dr). Selection of over 20 pizzas includes margarita (1150dr), garlic (1300dr), vegetarian (1300dr), and Hawaii (1450dr). Lone diners devour single-serving pizza sandwiches (1100-1600dr). Free delivery to Vas. Konstandinou St. Open M-Sa noon-12:30am, Su 6pm-12.30am.

Dexameni Taverna, Dexameni Sq. Located on the uphill side of the slope that is Dexameni Sq., this traditional *taverna* is reasonably priced for Kolonaki. Grilled cheese in lemon sauce (850dr) and fried haddock (1400dr) are popular with Kolonaki's undercover budget subculture and ex-pat students who exploit the staff for help on their Modern Greek language homework.

Jackson Hall, 4 Millioni St. (tel. 361 6098). Dominating the small footpath 2 blocks down the hill from Kolonaki Sq., this is the place for homesick Americans or those in search of the hippest Yankophiles in Athens. Mostly a place to be seen among the elite, this restaurant, bar, and nightclub serves international cuisine—chicken fillet (2900dr)—in an environment of American kitsch: carvings of Native Americans and a cheesy statue of James Dean. Their DJ spins pop rock from the 70s, 80s, and 90s. Open daily 10am-2:30am.

PANGRATI

Without the Beverly Hills wanna-be posing of Kolonaki and all the tourists of Plaka, Syntagma and Monastiraki, Pangrati resembles a Greek village only slightly removed from the city center. Get up early on Thursday mornings to find the freshest pickings at the **street market** off Plastira Sq.

Carousel, 32 Eftinidou St. (tel. 726 4085). Although it may look like a chain, this is the one and only ride in town. On your left as you enter is the traditional wood oven where regular and vegetarian pizzas (850dr) are baked. The more traditional aspects of the menu (*moussaka* 1200dr) balance the progressive influence of the Internet cafe upstairs.

Dragon Palace, 3 Andinoros St. (tel. 724 2795 or 723 5783). From Syntagma Sq. go down Vas. Sofias St., turn right onto Rizari St. at the war museum, cross the lights and take the first right onto Andinoros St. Or take bus #214 or trolley #313 or 8 to the museum stop. The large and elegant dining room is visible from the road through the carved wooden screens in the windows. The Peking duck (6700dr) with vegetarian spring rolls (1000dr) will feed several mouths. The Szechuan chicken (2100dr) packs a spicy jolt. Cover charge 250dr. Take-out and delivery available. Credit cards accepted. Open daily noon-3:30pm and 8pm-1:30am.

ATHENS

Diana Taverna, 1 Varnava Sq. (tel. 752 1014), at the intersection of Krisila St. and Mellison St. Lamb *fricase* (1400dr) and a beer (450dr) make an ideal dinner for an evening outside in the square.

Flocafe, 109 Imittou St. (tel./fax 726 5313). For a quick sandwich (750dr) and a *frappé* (800dr), join young Athenians on the go to the Flo.

Lalaggis, 29 Empedokleous St. (tel. 751 9426). The answer if your sweet tooth is yearning for confection, with *baklava* (200dr) and ice cream (1950dr per kg).

■ Entertainment

Visitors to Athens often restrict themselves to the familiar Plaka and Monastiraki neighborhoods. Don't be fooled into thinking that days in Athens consist only of T-shirt shopping or nights only of dancing the Zorba and breaking dishes.

BARS AND CAFES IN THE CITY

Athenian nightlife is diverse enough to please highbrow, chic sophisticates as well as down and dirty backpackers. Nightlife is very different in the offseason when many outdoor spots close and the clubs move back downtown, but there is still plenty to do throughout the year.

Jazz in Jazz, 10 Deinokratous St., Kolonaki. From behind the bar, Kostas, the self-proclaimed "Good Malaka," hazes his regulars with extra tasty mixed drinks (1000dr). The saxophones and trombones hanging from the walls and endless old jazz records on the box draw Athens' most faithfully mellow Bacchants. Open daily noon-3am.

The Daily, 47 Xenokratous St., Kolonaki (tel. 722 3430). A cafe by day and a bar by night, The Daily is the spot where Kolonaki chic and foreign student populations converge to imbibe, take in Latin music and reggae, and watch soccer and basketball over the tube. Pints of Heineken 1000dr. Open daily 9am-3am.

Cafe 48, 48 Karneadou St., 2 blocks up the hill from Vas. Sofias St. With U.S. and U.K. rock on the speakers, 48 is the watering hole of Kolonaki's homesick crowd of ex-pat classicists. Bring cards for a rowdy game of "Asshole." Beer 800dr. Open daily 10am-3am.

Tavern Sigalas, 2 Monastiraki Sq. (tel. 321 3036). Sells cheap cappuccino (550dr) in the heart of Monastiraki in the shadow of the Acropolis.

Cafe Floral, Exarhia Sq. (tel. 330 0938). Hang with the modeling and studying crowd and order a *fredo* cappuccino (700dr) from a menu written in the form of a newspaper, or stop in for a beer (800dr) at night when the cafe turns into a bar with DJs.

Babylon Cafe, 103 Imittou St., Pangrati (tel. 751 4024). The young and stylish idle away whole afternoons at this streetside cafe. The tables outside are filled with *frappé*-sippers (900dr) playing backgammon and scoping out the passersby. Open daily 9am-3am.

New York Bar, Makrigianni St., south of Plaka. Living up to its Yankified name, this bar draws tourists, students, and drifters to the appropriately sad and lonesome strains of John Lee Hooker. Raucous patrons have been known to repeatedly chant "USA" as they stumble home. Watch for specials of unlimited free beer after a 2000dr cover. Open daily noon-3am.

Pan Tsan, 26 Krisila St., Pangrati (tel. 701 0369). For billiards, video games, chess, and board games, Pan Tsan has it all. Beer 500dr. Billiards 50dr per game. Open daily 11am-midnight.

CLUBS OF GLYFADA

During the summer months, young and hip Athenians head to the seaside clubs on Poseidonos Ave. in **Glyfada** (past the airport). The most popular clubs are right on the beach, with cool and calming ocean views to counteract the frenzied interiors. In general, dance clubs play American or British tunes from 11pm or midnight until 2 or 3am, when either Greek music is played or a Greek singer takes the stage. Put on your best Euro-suave outfit because many of these clubs will not admit anyone in shorts. Covers range from 2000dr to 3000dr, and drinks are often ridiculously priced (cheap beers run 1000-2000dr, cocktails 1500-3000dr). Take bus A3 (200dr) from Syntagma Sq. to Glyfada (the last stop) and then catch a taxi to a particular club, or take a taxi all the way: just get in, tell them "Glyfada" and the name of the club you're going to, and they'll know where to go. As always, be careful of cabbies trying to rip you off. You'll need to take a cab back to the city (1500-2500dr). The best bars are all conveniently lined up nearby, off the water on Vouliagmenis St. For **gay clubs** (primarily male), try the northern end of Singrou St. or **Lembessi St.** off Singrou St.

King Size and **Bedside,** 5 Poseidonos Beach (tel. 894 4138 or 894 4139). From Singrou St., pass Paraliaki St. and turn left on Poseidonos St. Keeping the latest trend of splitting 1 club into 2, King Size is the big, black rave house-disco room with bikini-clad dancers shakin' their thang on stage. In the next room is polar opposite Bedside, where all the furniture and waiters wear white, and jazz and light rock fill the air. The clubs have a younger crowd and a noticeable gay contingent. Drinks 2000dr. Cover with 1st drink 4000dr. Open daily 11pm-5am.

⑩**Camel Club,** 25 Pergamon St. (tel. 965 0879). So close to the airport, you can hear the planes whiz by. A true rock club—several patrons don dog chain necklaces and float between the chill bar area outside and the bumpy warehouse indoors. Wednesday is ladies' night. Live band on weekends. Camel's sister club opens at 268 Vouliagmenis St. in the winter. Drinks 200-1500dr. Cover with first drink 2500dr. Open daily 10:30pm-5am.

Privilege, Ag. Kosmas Beach (tel. 985 2996). From Singrou St., take a left onto Poseidonos St. The club is near the Athens end of Poseidonos St. Privilege didn't get its name without reason; men must come with women, everyone must be very well-dressed (no jeans, shorts, sandals, or anything slightly casual), BMWs fill the parking lot, and the cover is a steep 3000dr. With 4 bars, a DJ, and very little dancing, the main terraced patio looks more like a pool party than a nightclub. Extremely crowed with both gay and straight folks. Open daily 10:30pm-5am.

Hook Stories, 4 Alkyonidon St. (tel. 895 2403 or 895 3973), in the Voula area near the Sounion end of Poseidonos St. With Captain Hook as the mascot and the entire ground floor decorated like a ship, the club is corny yet popular. A DJ turns soul and Greek pop tunes. A club under the same name and ownership opens in Peiraias during the winter. Martinis 3000dr. Cover 1500dr. Open Su-F midnight-4am, Sa midnight-6am.

Bo, 8-10 Alkyonidon St. (tel. 895 9645 or 895 4907). The adjoining restaurant and white cushiony couches provide a personal twist on the this otherwise average black-lit techno-pop joint. Martinis 2000dr. Cover 1000dr, free before 11:30pm. Open daily 10pm-5am.

Karting, Ag. Kosmas Beach, next to Privilege on Poseidonos Ave. The adventurous can rent go-carts at the steep rate of 3000dr per 10min. If you're more of a spectator, grab a beer (400dr) at the cafe and watch bikers in leather jackets spin out of control on the huge outdoor track. Open daily 9am-5am.

To quiet hungry stomachs, ask your taxi driver to take you to the **meat market** (no, this is not another club) on Athinas St. between Monastiraki and Omonia, where popular early-morning restaurants open while the market is closed (3-7am). Simply go into the kitchens and point away; *patsa* soup may calm a hangover, but don't order it sober—it's made with sheep entrails.

OTHER DIVERSIONS

The **Athens Festival** runs annually from June until September, featuring classical theater groups performing in the **Odeon of Herodes Atticus.** Performances are also staged in **Lycavittos Theater** on the northern flank of Mt. Lycavittos, and in Epidavros (see p. 138). The Greek Orchestra performs during this festival, as do visiting groups, which have included the Bolshoi Ballet, B.B. King, the Alvin Ailey Dance Company, theatrical companies from all over the world performing Greek dramas, Pavarotti, and the Talking Heads. The **Festival Office,** 4 Stadiou St. (tel. 322 1459 or 322 3111, ext. 240) sells affordable student tickets. *(Open M-F 8:30am-2pm and 5-7pm, Sa 8:30am-1pm, Su 10am-1pm. Tickets 3000-5000dr.)*

If you've had enough to drink, the hokey **Sound and Light Show** (tel. 322 1360 or 322 3111; ext. 350), which depicts the Parthenon over the centuries, on Pnyx Hill (opposite the Acropolis) can be quite entertaining, though you'll leave unsure whether the title refers to the program or the click and flash of cameras *(Apr.-Oct. shows daily in English 9pm; in French W-Th and Sa-M 10:10pm; in German Tu and F 10pm. Admission 1200dr, students 600dr.)*

Nearby in Dora Stratou Theatre (tel. 921 4650), on Philopappou Hill, **Greek dancers** kick and holler to live music on an open-air stage, celebrating traditions from all regions of the country. *(Shows May-Sept. nightly 10:15pm, W and Su 8:15pm. Admission 3000dr, students 1800dr.)*

During the summer months, open-air cinemas offer a peaceful respite from the fast-paced Athenian life. **Cine Paris,** 22 Kidathineon St., Plaka (tel. 322 2071; tickets 1400dr); **Cine Athenaia,** 50 Haritos St, Kolonaki (tel. 721 5717; tickets 1800dr); and **Cinema Rivera,** 46 Baltetsiou St., Exarhia (tickets 1700dr) offer the richest breeziest cinematic experiences; check *Athens News* (250dr) for show times.

■ Sights

THE ACROPOLIS

You can reach the entrance, which is on the west side of the Acropolis, from Areopagitou St. south of the Acropolis, or by walking uphill from Plaka. Follow the spray-painted signs at intervals in the narrow passageway. Tel. 321 0219. Open in summer daily 8am-7:30pm; in winter daily 8:30am-4:30pm. Admission 2000dr, students 1000dr. Not wheelchair accessible.

The **Acropolis**—and within the Acropolis, the **Parthenon**—has been Athens' highlight since the 5th century BC. Its name means "high city" and it has, with its strategic position overlooking the Aegean Sea and Attic Plains, served through the ages as both a military fortress and a religious center. The heights afford an expansive view of Athens and the Aegean. Today, the hilltop's remarkable ruins grace otherwise rubble-strewn grounds. Ongoing renovations require that steel scaffolding cling to the ancient marble columns.

To avoid massive crowds and the broiling midday sun, visit early in the morning. Warm water is available from sink-like fountains at the top of the Acropolis; bring bottled water to avoid the overpriced refreshment stand at the entrance (soda 800dr).

History

In the 13th century BC, wealthy landowners overthrew the monarchy in Athens who had ruled the city safely from their fortress in the Acropolis. The new rulers, the *Aristoi* (excellent ones), shifted the center of their government away from the Acropolis, ruling the *polis* (city-state) from the lower foothills of the city.

The Acropolis, far from being abandoned, was then used as a shrine devoted to two aspects of the goddess **Athena**—Athena Polias, goddess of crops and fertility, and Athena Pallas, military guardian of the city. The original shrine was made of wood. By the custom of entrusting money to the protection of a deity, the Acropolis also housed the city treasury.

In 507 BC, the tyrannical *Aristoi* were overthrown and Athens began its successful experiment with **democracy.** In 490 BC, Athenians began constructing a temple on the Acropolis, this time out of marble. When the Persians sacked the temple 10 years later, the Greeks threw the violated religious objects off the side of the Acropolis and buried the litter (now displayed in the Acropolis Museum).

In response to the Persian threat, Aegean rulers formed the Delian League. **Pericles** appropriated part of the taxes paid by the league to beautify Athens. Among his projects were the temples of the Acropolis, the Hephaesteion in the *Agora,* and the Temple of Poseidon at Sounion. These developments slowed during the **Peloponnesian War** (431-404 BC), but by then the Athenians were committed to Pericles' plans, and construction sputtered along during the war and after his death in 429 BC. Four of the buildings erected at that time still stand today: the Parthenon, the Propylaea, the Temple of Athena Nike, and the Erechtheion. They were designed and sculpted

ATHENS

Acropolis

1 Theater of Dionysus
2 Stoa of Eumenus
3 Odeon of Herodes
  Atticus
4 Asclepion
5 Prostyle Stoa
6 Shrine of Ageus
7 Entrance to the
  Acropolis
8 Beulé Gate
9 Avenue of Panathenaic
  Procession
10 Propylaea
11 Temple of Athena
   Nike
12 Altar of Artemis
13 Brauronion
14 Chalcotheque
15 Parthenon
16 Sanctuary of Pandion
17 Sanctuary of Zeus
   Polieus
18 Erechtheion
19 Sacred Olive Tree of
   Athena
20 Arrhephorion

N

0 ___ 30 yards
0 ___ 30 meters

by Iktinos, Kallikrates, and a slew of eager apprentices all trying to outdo each others' artistry. Their construction has had an unrivaled influence on Western architecture. Through the Hellenistic and Roman periods, the function of the Acropolis altered as often as it changed hands. The **Byzantines** converted it into a church. In a good example of Christianity appropriating older "pagan" symbols, the Parthenon became the Church of St. Sophia ("Sophia," like "Athena," means wisdom). In 1205, when Athens was taken from the Byzantines by **Frankish Crusaders,** the Acropolis once again became a fortress, serving as palace and headquarters for the Dukes de la Roche. When the political situation later settled down, the Parthenon was transformed into a Catholic church (Notre Dame d'Athènes). In the 15th century, **Ottomans** turned the Parthenon into a mosque and the Erechtheum into the Ottoman commander's harem.

Tragedy befell the Acropolis during the **Venetian siege** in 1687, when an Ottoman supply of gunpowder stored in the Parthenon was hit by a shell and the roof came tumbling down, destroying many sculptures.

Around the Acropolis

What you see before you is the reconstructed temple. The ramp that led to the Acropolis in classical times no longer exists. Today's visitors make the five-minute climb to the ticket window, enter through the crumbling **Beulé Gate** (added by the Romans and named after the French archaeologist who unearthed it), and continue through the **Propylaea,** the ancient entrance.

The Propylaea became famous for its ambitious multi-level design, although the entrance itself, begun by Mnesicles between 437 and 432 BC, was never completed. In Roman times, the structure extended as far as 80m below the Beulé Gate. At the cliff's edge, the tiny **Temple of Athena Nike** was built during a respite from the Peloponnesian War, the so-called Peace of Nikias (421-415 BC). Known as the "jewel of Greek architecture," this temple with eight miniature Ionic columns once housed a winged statue of the goddess Nike (not yet a brand-name label). One day, in a paranoid frenzy, the Athenians feared that their deity (and peace) would flee the city, so they clipped Athena's wings. Below the temple are the remains of the 5m-thick **Cyclopean wall,** which once surrounded the whole of the Acropolis.

The **Erechtheion,** to the left of the Parthenon as you face it, was completed in 406 BC, just prior to Athens' defeat by Sparta. Lighter than the Parthenon, the Erechtheion is a unique two-level structure that housed a number of cults, including those of Athena, Poseidon, and the snake-bodied hero Erechtheus. The east porch, with its six Ionic columns, was dedicated to Athena Polias and sheltered an olive wood statue of her. On the south side of the Erechtheion are the **Caryatids,** six columns sculpted in the shape of women. Their artful tunics are plaster replicas—the originals were moved to the Acropolis Museum to protect them from acid rain.

The Parthenon

Looming over the hillside, the **Parthenon,** or "Virgin's Apartment," keeps vigil over Athens and its world. Designed by the architects Iktinos and Kallikrates, the Parthenon was the first building completed under Pericles' plan to revive the city. It once housed the legendary gold and ivory statue of Athena Parthena (Virgin Athena) sculpted by Phidias. The temple intentionally features many almost imperceptible irregularities; the Doric columns bulge in the middle and the stylobate (pedestal) of the building bows slightly upward in order to compensate for the optical illusion in which straight lines, viewed from a distance, appear to bend. Originally made entirely of marble except for a long-gone wooden roof, the building's stone ruins attest to both the durability of the structure and the elegance of the Classical Age.

Metopes around the sides of the Parthenon portray victories of the forces of order over disorder. On the far right of the south side, the only side that has not been defaced, the Lapiths battle the Centaurs; on the east the Olympian gods triumph over the giants; the north depicts a faintly visible victory of the Greeks over the Trojans; and on the west, the Greeks' triumph over the Amazons. A better-preserved frieze in bas-relief around the interior walls shows the Panathenaic procession in Athena's honor. The **East Pediment,** the formerly triangular area that the columns propped up, once depicted the birth of Athena, who according to legend, sprang from the head of Zeus. The **West Pediment,** on the opposite facade, formerly documented the contest between Athena and Poseidon for Athens' eternal devotion. Various fragments of the originals are now housed in the Acropolis and British Museums.

The Museum

The **Acropolis Museum,** footsteps away from the Parthenon, contains a superb collection of sculptures, including five of the Caryatids of the Erechtheum (the sixth now resides in the British Museum). Most of the treasures housed here date from the transition period from Archaic to Classical Greek art (550-400 BC). You can trace this development in the faces of the statues, from the stylized, entranced faces and static poses of Archaic sculpture—seen in the famous *Moschophoros* (calf-bearer)—to the more familiar, naturalistic (though idealized) figures of Classical Art. Only a few pieces from the Parthenon are here—Lord Elgin helped himself to the rest, which are now in the British Museum—but the collection is nonetheless impressive. Cameras without flash are allowed, but no posing next to the objects, heathen tourist.

Below the Acropolis

*Entrance on Dionissiou Areopagitou St. Tel. 322 4625. **Open** Tu-Su 8:30am-2:30pm. **Admission** 500dr, students 250dr, children under 18 free.*

From the southwest corner of the Acropolis, you can look down on the reconstructed **Odeon of Herodes Atticus,** a still-functioning theater dating from the Roman Period (160 AD). Nearby are the ruins of the classical Greek **Theater of Dionysus,** the **Asclepion,** and the **Stoa of Eumenes II.** The Theater of Dionysus dates from the 4th century BC.

AROUND ANCIENT ATHENS

The Agora

*There are several entrances to the Agora, including 1 at the edge of Monastiraki, 1 on Thission Sq., and one on Adrianou St. Tel. 321 0185. **Open** Tu-Su 8:30am-3pm. **Admission** 1200dr, students with ID 600dr, seniors 900dr.*

The **Athenian Agora,** at the foot of the Acropolis, was the administrative center and marketplace of Athens from the 6th century BC through the late Roman Period (5th-6th centuries AD). However, prehistoric shelters and cemeteries have been unearthed here as well. The decline of the *Agora* paralleled the decline of Athens, as barbarian attacks buffeted both the city and the square from 267 BC to AD 580. It was in the *Agora* and on the **Pnyx** (the low hill and meeting place of the assembly, 1km to the south) that Athenian democracy was born and flourished. Socrates frequented the *Agora,* as did Aristotle, Demosthenes, Xenophon, and St. Paul. According to Plato, Socrates' preliminary hearing was held at the **Stoa Basileios** (Royal Promenade), which has been recently excavated and lies to the left as you cross the subway tracks upon leaving the *Agora.*

The sprawling archaeological site features three remarkable constructions. The **Hephaesteion,** on a hill in the northwest corner, is the best-preserved classical temple in Greece. Built around 440 BC, it is especially notable for its friezes, which depict the labors of Hercules and the adventures of Thisseos. The ruins of the **Odeon of Agrippa** (concert hall), built for the son-in-law of the Emperor Augustus, stand in the center of the *Agora.* In AD 150 the roof collapsed, and the Odeon was rebuilt as a lecture hall half its former size. The actors' dressing room was made into a porch supported by colossal statues (the ruins of 3 of these statues remain to guard the site). To the south, the elongated **Stoa of Attalos,** a multi-purpose building for shops, shelter, and informal gatherings, was rebuilt between 1953 and 1956 and now houses the **Agora Museum.** The original structure, built in the 2nd century BC, was given to Athens by Attalos II, King of Pergamon, in gratitude for the education he had received in the city. The museum contains a number of relics from the site and offers a cool sanctuary from the sweltering summer sun.

You can reach the Acropolis from here by exiting the south side of the *Agora* (follow the path uphill) and then turning right. The most commonly used gate is the one near the Acropolis entrance (turn right as you leave the Acropolis).

The Kerameikos

148 Ermou St. Northwest of the Agora, on the other side of the tracks at Thission Station. Tel. 346 3552. **Open** *Tu-Su 8:30am-3pm.* **Admission** *400dr, students 200dr.*

The **Kerameikos** is the site of the 40m-wide boulevard that ran from the Agora, through the Diplyon Gate, and 1.5km to the sanctuary of Akademos, where Plato founded his academy in the 4th century BC. Public tombs for state leaders, famous authors, and battle victims were constructed along this road. Worshipers began the annual Panathenaean procession to the Acropolis at the Diplyon Gate, one of the two gates excavated at this site. The Sacred Road to Eleusis, traversed during the annual Eleusian processions, ran through the Sacred Gate, the second gate on the site. Family tombs adorn either side of the Sacred Road outside the gate. A **museum** on the site exhibits finds from recent digs as well as an excellent pottery collection.

The Temple of Olympian Zeus and Hadrian's Arch

Vas. Olgas St. at Amalias St. Next to the National Garden. Tel. 922 6330. **Open** *Tu-Su 8:30am-3pm.* **Admission** *500dr, students 300dr, EU students free.*

Fifteen majestic columns are all that remain of the **Temple of Olympian Zeus**—the largest temple ever built in Greece. Started in the 6th century BC, the temple was completed 600 years later by the Roman emperor Hadrian. The Corinthian columns stand in the middle of downtown Athens, below the National Garden. The remains of a Roman bath, tiles and all, are also here. Next to the Temple is **Hadrian's Arch,** which was built in the 2nd century BC to mark the boundary between the ancient city of Theseus and the new city built by Hadrian.

AROUND MODERN ATHENS

Byzantine Churches

Byzantine sanctuaries, like their Classical counterparts, have been incorporated into the urban landscape, and it is common practice for religious Greeks to take pause in their busy days to pay respects to ubiquitous icons. Viewing hours are at the discretion of each church's priest, since he locks the door after the early evening service. Mornings are the best bet. Dress appropriately: skirts for women, long pants for men, and sleeved shirts for everyone.

Shoppers and pedestrians on Ermou St. must go around **Kapnikaria Church,** which is stranded in the middle of the street, one block beyond Aiolou St. A bas-relief and the inscription "Welcoming Virgin" decorates its west wall. It just barely escaped destruction in 1834 thanks to the clemency of Louis I of Bavaria.

Walking down Mitropoleos from Syntagma, you may also notice a tiny red church on the corner of Pentelis St., around which a modern building has been built. Another well-preserved Byzantine church in the heart of Athens is the **Agia Apostoli,** at the east edge of the *Agora.* In Plaka near Pritaniou St., **Metamorphosis,** built in the 11th century and restored in 1956, has white walls and a dome painted with Christ's face. **Agia Triada,** a few blocks from Syntagma Sq. at 21 Filellinon St., is an 11th-century Russian Orthodox church, replete with displays of priests and silver icons of angels. **Agios Eleftherios** and the **Mitropoli Cathedral** are both on Mitropoleos St.

Syntagma

The cool, pleasant **National Garden,** adjacent to Syntagma Sq., is an escape from the noise, heat, and frantic pace of Athens. *(Open sunrise to sunset.)* Walk along its tranquil paths and visit the duck pond and sad little zoo. Women should not stroll here alone.

When you're passing through Syntagma Sq., don't miss the changing of the guard in front of the **Parliament** building. Every hour on the hour, two sets of enormously tall *evzones* (guards) slowly wind up like toy soldiers, kick their heels about, and fall backward into symmetrical little guardhouses on either side of the **Tomb of the Unknown Warrior.** Unlike their British equivalents, *evzones* occasionally wink, smile, and say "I love you" to tourists. Their jovial manner matches their attire—pom-pom-laden clogs, short pleated skirts *(foustanela)*, and tasseled hats. Every Sunday at 10:45am the ceremony occurs with the full troop of guards and a band.

The Markets

Athens' two principal markets attract everyone from bargain-hunters to inveterate browsers. The **Athens Flea Market,** adjacent to Monastiraki Sq., has a festive, bazaar-like atmosphere and offers a potpourri of second-hand junk, costly antiques, and everything in between. *(Open M, W, and Sa-Su 8am-3pm, Tu and Th-F 8am-8pm.)* Although parts of it have become overtouristed, there is still the occasional treasure to be found and lots of neo-hippies to watch. If you've come to the flea market in search of a **bouzouki,** go to Bill Aevorkian, 6 Ifestou St. (tel. 321 0024; open daily 10am-3pm). On Sunday, the flea market overflows the square and Fillis Athinas St., and a huge indoor-outdoor **food market** lines the sides of Athinas St. between Evripidou and Sofokleous St. The **meat market** is huge, and certainly not for vegetarians or the faint of heart. *(Open M-Sa 8am-2pm.)* Even the smell can be overwhelming. Livers, kidneys, and skinned rabbits complete with cottontails hang throughout. There are also less visually challenging foods, such as fruits, vegetables, breads, and cheeses. It's open the same hours as regular food stores, but Athenian restauranteurs go early and purchase the choice meat and fish. Restaurants in the meat market are open late.

Mt. Lycavittos

Of Athens' eight hills, Lycavittos is the largest and most central. The best time to ascend is sunset, when you can catch a last glimpse of Athens in daylight and watch the city light up. Take the **funicular** (1000dr round-trip, children 500dr) to the top—the station is a healthy hike from the end of Ploutarchou St. The funicular leaves every 10 to 15 minutes for its dark but somewhat exciting two-minute uphill journey. Without mechanical assistance, the ostensibly daunting hike takes only 15 minutes; burn off dinner by walking up. Just bring water, watch out for slippery rocks, and don't climb alone, especially at night, when crimes, accidents, and misnavigation are most frequent. You'll know you're at the top when you see the **Chapel of St. George.** *(Open M-W, F-Su 8:45am-12:15am, Th 10:30am-12:15am.)* You can light a candle (30dr) under ornately painted ceilings, but the view is what you've come for; a leisurely stroll around the church lets you soak in Athens' endless expanse. The city's flat landscape and lack of skyscrapers facilitate your vantage of the panorama. Taking the Acropolis as a point of reference, observe on your right the Monastiraki, Omonia, and Exarhia neighborhoods. Continuing clockwise, you will see Areos Park behind a small circular patch of green—Strefi. The flashy lights and music of Lycavittos Theatre are 180° from the Acropolis. The eastern half of your view from the summit offers views of more parks, Mt. Hymettus, and back near the Acropolis, a glimpse of the Panathenaic Olympic Stadium, the National Garden, and a cluster of columns that constitute the Temple of Olympian Zeus. On a clear day you might see the Aegean to the south. Despite—or perhaps thanks to—the smog, hazy blues and reds of the sunset are pleasantly manifest.

Olympic Stadium

Vas. Konstandinou St. **Open** *daily 8am-8:30pm. Free.*

The **Panathenaic Olympic Stadium** is built into a hill between the National Gardens and Pangrati. The site of the first modern Olympic Games in 1896, the stadium was the scene of great disappointment for Greeks when 1996's hundred-year anniversary games were held in Atlanta, and the 2000 millennial games were sent to Sydney, Australia. In 1997, the stadium hosted the opening ceremonies of the World Track and Field Championships, and it will do the same for the **2004 Summer Olympics.** Today athletes ascend the stairs, and sun-bathing students dot the marble stands. Spectators used to view sporting events from the two hills that cradle the stadium before the

70,000-person capacity stands were built. The original stadium, which dated from the Classical period, was destroyed in the Byzantine era and restored in Panteli marble in 1895. Now the stadium is used for military parades, gymnastic displays, and as the finish line of the **marathon,** which begins every fall in Marathon. Marble *steles* near the front honor Greek gold and silver medalists at recent Olympic competitions. To personally experience the structure's grandeur, sprint a few laps around its black track. After your workout, cool off with a soda (300dr) at the cafe in front of the stadium.

National Cemetery

*In Pangrati. From Syntagma Sq. walk down Amalias St., turn left on Athenisiou Diakou St., and then walk down Anapavseos St. Tel. 922 1621. Open daily 8:30am-5:30pm. Free. For **guided tours** call the Cultural Center, 50 Akademias St. Tel. 361 2705 or 363 9671.*

Home to deceased Greek politicians, actors, and poets, as well as foreigners who died in Athens, the cemetery has long been a burial ground. Currently there are two kinds of graves—family graves and three-year graves (after 3 years, the bones are moved to boxes). For the sake of preserving the cemetery's cultural identity, soon no new graves will be permitted, and only three-year graves will be allowed. The three-year-old remains of VIPs will then be moved to the Mausoleum Commons.

As you enter the main gate, the well-intentioned but strictly Greek-speaking information bureau is on your left. The first graves encountered are larger and more elaborate than most since the rich and famous have first claim to these spots. On the left side of the first courtyard is a temple to the archaeologist **Heinrich Schliemann,** who excavated Troy and Mycenae. To the left of the large statue of an angel is the tomb of **Melina Mercury,** the star of *Never on Sunday,* Greece's greatest cinematic icon, and the Minister of Culture later in her life. To the right of Mercury's tomb is an austere memorial to long-time Greek political leader **Andreas Papandreou,** a simple flat white marble slab. Back on the main path, straight in from the main entrance and to the right, is a statue of a woman lying down clutching a cross. Again on the main path, there is a small church where ceremonies are held for the dead. The mayor is lobbying to turn the burial ground into a museum, so crowds and admission fees may encroach in future years.

MUSEUMS

National Archaeological Museum

44 Patission St., next to Metsovion Polytechnion St. A 20min. walk from Syntagma Sq. down Stadiou St. until Aiolou St. and right onto Patission St. Take trolley #2, 4, 5, 9, 11, 15, or 18 from the uphill side of Syntagma or trolley #3 or 13 from the north side of Vas. Sofias St. Tel. 821 7717. Open Apr.-Oct. M 12:30-7pm, Tu-F 8am-7pm, Sa-Su and holidays 8:30am-3pm; Nov.-Mar. M 11am-5pm, Tu-F 8am-5pm, Sa-Su and holidays 8:30am-3pm. Admission 2000dr, students 1000dr, seniors 1500dr, free Su and holidays. No flash photography.

The **National Archaeological Museum,** the largest collection of artifacts from all over Greece, is well worth delaying your jaunt to the islands. Pieces that would be the prizes of lesser collections seem almost unremarkable amid the general magnificence. Invest a couple of hours to explore.

After checking your bags at the cloakroom (free and mandatory) and grabbing a free map of the museum, go straight ahead into the **Mycenae exhibit** of Heinrich Schliemann's digs at Mycenae, including the golden "Mask of Agamemnon" (which is really the death mask of a king who lived at least 3 centuries earlier than the legendary Agamemnon). Also displayed are samples of Bronze Age jewelry and pottery from Mycenae, other sites in the Peloponnese, and various prehistoric sites in Greece. This primary exhibit is skirted by side rooms with artifacts from other tombs found in different parts of Greece. In the red room is the bronze statue known as **Artemisian Jockey,** from 140 BC, reassembled from fragments found in 1928.

Don't leave without viewing the **kouroi,** or standing males, in the left wing of the museum. They are displayed chronologically and in the buff, allowing you to see the evolution of this "form." Check out the enormous **amphora,** a two-handled vase for wine or water, decorated in the Geometric style, among the simple and roughly designed statues in room 7. The development and increasing detail of *kouroi* manifests itself in the ripped abs of statue 13 in room 11, a work created in 540 BC and found at Megara. Another interesting item in room 11 is a small marble disc made in memoriam of "the wise and excellent doctor Aeneas" (item 93). In room 12, a red backdrop brings out the ruddiness and vitality in the **Anavyssos Kouros** (item 3851). The inscription on his base reads, "Stop and lament at the tomb of the dead Kroisos whom furious Ares slew when he was fighting in the forefront."

For visitors planning to make a daytrip to Cape Sounion, the capitals of the columns from the town's Temple of Athena are on display in room 14 (items 4478-9). With arms outstretched and trident in hand, the larger than life statue of **Poseidon** is eerily lifelike, and epitomizes the dynamic balance of an action snapshot.

Sepulchral **steles** commemorate the deceased of the 5th century BC in room 16. Next door in room 17, the complexity of relief 2756 will floor you, once you identify the seven large gods, with medium-sized Xenokratias in the middle and the tiny little boy Xeniades. Slipped into the crowd on the right are a *satyr* and a *caryatid*. You can imagine the head of your arch rival on the body of the 2nd century AD cult statue of **Nemesis** at the far left end of room 19.

Room 34 houses a votive relief depicting nymphs, Pan, Hermes, a young boy, and a suppliant in a cave with the inscription "Agathemeros offers to the nymphs." Coincidentally, the marble *stele* was found in a cave on Mt. Panteli. In room 53, a unique terra cotta model replicates an **ekphora** (funeral procession). Four women, mourning in the typical ancient Greek style by ripping their hair out, surround the chariot carrying the covered corpse.

The **wall paintings from Akrotiri,** Santorini, (1 flight up) are intriguing. These painted architectural and artistic treasures were buried during a volcanic eruption believed to have occurred around 1500 BC and present a unique glimpse into Bronze Age life. The **mask of a slave from Diplyon** (2nd century BC), with a wide, toothless grin and crazy eyes, seems amused by the starkly stoic statues that surround it. The right wing of the museum hosts a beautifully preserved **Aphrodite-Panas-Eros** from the Hellenistic Era. Look for the statue of the **Sleeping Maenad.** Wander toward the back to view the temporary exhibits that change several times a year. Also worth viewing is the extensive **vase collection** (on the same floor as the wall paintings), with works in Red and Black Ware, Narrative, and Geometric styles.

Goulandris Museum of Cycladic and Ancient Greek Art
4 Neophytou Douka St. near Kolonaki. Accessible by trolley #3 and 13 (100dr). Tel. 722 8321. Open M and W-F 10am-4pm, Sa 10am-3pm. Admission 400dr, students 200dr.

Opened in 1986, the **Goulandris Museum of Cycladic and Ancient Greek Art** has a stunning collection in a modern building with air conditioning. Cycladic art is famous for its sleek, marble, Picassoesque figurines. Some figures have painted details, possibly representing tattoos. Many figurines were either looted from archaeological sites at the turn of the century or found buried with the dead in graves on the Cycladic Islands. Their precise use in antiquity is still an enigma, but theories range from representations of goddesses to *psychopompoi* (tour guides to the Underworld) to kept women. The bronze jewelry from Skyros, as well as the collection of Greek vases and statues from the 2nd century BC to the 4th century AD, are also impressive. The new wing of the museum, on the corner of Vas. Sofias St. and Herodotou St., is an extension of the Cycladic collection.

Byzantine Museum
22 Vas. Sofias St. Tel. 723 1570. Open Tu-Su 8:30am-2:45pm. Admission 500dr, students 300dr, EU students and classicists free.

Inside an elegant Florentine building with serene courtyards, the **Byzantine Museum** has an excellent and extensive collection of Christian art from the 4th through the 19th centuries. The collection includes early Byzantine sculptures, an icon collection containing works from the entire Byzantine period, and three reconstructed early **Christian basilicas.** Of particular interest is a room in the back left corner of the ground floor, as you enter the exhibit area. The room itself is square, but the ceiling was designed in the cut of the cross. The floor is adorned with mosaics of stones from the Acropolis and centers around an *omphalion* of an eagle and a snake. Immediately left of the ground floor entrance is an ornate replica of a 17th-century church in Cephalonia. Frescoes from Atalantis surround the hand-carved wooden altar, and the throne of the Patriarch of Constantinople from 1863 sits regally in front. On the opposite side of the reconstructed basilica lie the designer boxes used to bring the wine and bread of the holy communion to the ill. The chandelier is from Halkidiki and presents scenes from the life of Christ. For a visual history of Christian events, the altar documents the 12 most important Christian events from the birth of Christ to the Assumption of the Virgin Mary. One wing of the building features an array of well-preserved frescoes and mosaics. The exhibits are poorly labeled, however; consider buying a book (2500dr) before you visit.

War Museum
Next to Byzantine Museum. Tel. 725 2975 or 725 2976. **Open** *Tu-Su 9am-2pm. Free.*

Marked by the cannons and fighter jets outside, the **War Museum** traces the history of Greek armaments from neolithic eras, through the 5th century BC Persian invasion and expeditions of Alexander the Great, to the submachine guns of the modern era. Here you can see booty looted by the Greek Army during WWI. Read about Stephanos Saraphis, politician and leader of the Popular Liberation Army, and gaze at photos of starving Greek children during the German occupation of WWII. The primary emphasis is on the modern Greek arsenal. The museum displays not only model submarines and tanks but also bombs and booby traps from Korea and Germany.

National Gallery
50 Vas. Konstandinou St. Set back from Vas. Sofias St., next to the Hilton. Tel. 723 5857 or 723 5937. Open M and W-Sa 9am-3pm, Su 10am-2pm. Admission 1500dr, students and seniors 500dr, children under 12 free.

The **National Gallery** (Alexander Soutzos Museum) exhibits Greek artists' works supplemented by periodic international displays. The permanent collection includes some outstanding works by El Greco. The drawings, photographs, and sculpture gardens are also impressive. Consult *This Week in Athens* or call the museum for information on current exhibits.

Museums in Plaka
In Plaka, the **Greek Folk Art Museum,** 17 Kidatheneon St. (tel. 322 9031), exhibits *laiki techni* (popular art) from all over Greece, including embroidered textiles, costumes, and puppets. *(Open Tu-Su 10am-2pm. Admission 500dr, students and seniors 300dr, EU students and children free. No flash photography.)* Ornamental ecclesiastical silverwork and household pottery are also on exhibit. Don't miss the wall paintings by folk artist Theophilos Hadzimichail. The **Greek Popular Musical Instruments Museum,** 1-2 Diogenous St., Plaka (tel. 325 0198), has an interactive display of an array of musical instruments used in the 18th, 19th, and 20th centuries. *(Open Tu and Th-Su 10am-2pm, W noon-6pm. Free.)* Be sure to hear the frenetic tunes of the *kementzes* (bottle-shaped lira) on the top floor and the *tsamboura* (goatskin bagpipe) on the ground floor for a taste of the islands and the tap of metal coins jingling as dancers cavort to the beat.

On the south side of the Acropolis, just off Dionysiou Areopagiotou St., you can satiate your lust for gold at the **Ilias Lalounis Jewelry Museum,** 12 Kallisperi St. at Kariatidon St. (tel. 922 1044). *(Open M and Th-Su 9am-4pm, W 9am-9pm. Admission 800dr, students and seniors 500dr, W free after 3pm)* This private museum, formerly the home of the artist himself, houses over 3000 designs created by Lalounis over a span of 50 years. Collections display the history of jewelry in Greece from ancient to modern times, including a workshop where visitors can observe different jewelry-making techniques. Watching "Goldsmithery," the free short film on the first floor (1 flight up from entrance level), is a good place to begin. Also on the first floor, the shield of Achilles depicts scenes from Book 18 of the *Iliad*. On the second floor, to your right as you enter, is the "silver frolics" collection, jewelry designed by children who visited the museum and produced by the museum goldsmiths.

The **Jewish Museum,** 39 Nikis St. (tel. 322 5582; fax 323 1577), occupies a brand-new, air-conditioned, seven-story building. *(Open Su-F 9am-1pm. Free.)* An impressive collection of textiles, religious artifacts, and documents traces the roots of the Greek Jewish communities from the Hellenistic period. The museum also contains the reconstructed Synagogue of Patras and an exhibit on the Holocaust.

The **Children's Museum,** 14 Kidathineon St. (tel. 331 2995 or 331 2996), is a colorful, friendly, hands-on experience in the heart of Plaka. *(Open M and Th-F 9:30am-1:30pm, W 9:30am-6:30pm, Sa-Su 10am-2pm; hours can be erratic so call in advance. Free.)* The museum's philosophy is "I hear and I forget; I see and I remember; I do and I understand." Learn about the current construction of Athens' subway system or go to the attic to play dress-up in a bedroom from times past. The **Theater Museum,** 50 Akademias St. (tel. 362 9430), displays costumes, models, photographic paraphernalia, and dressing rooms. *(Open M-F 9am-2:30pm. Admission 300dr.)*

ATTICA Αττικα

The grays and whites of marble and smog in Athens quickly give way to the greens, browns, and blues that have defined the coastal landscapes of Greece for centuries. The outskirts of Athens are littered with monasteries, ancient religious centers and battlegrounds that have at different times drawn hordes out of the city. The ports of Peiraias and Rafina are gateways that act as escape valves for a constant stream of wanderers and weekending Athenians who flee Athens' urban intensity for the pace and pleasures of island living.

■ Peiraias Πειραιας

The natural harbor of Peiraias has been Athens' port since 493 BC when Themistokles began his ambitious plan to fortify Peiraias, then an island, as a base for the growing Athenian fleet. Two "Long Walls," bridging the land mass between Athens and its port, were built to keep Peiraias safe from pesky Persians; a third Long Wall was completed under Pericles, fresh for the outbreak of war with the Spartans in 431 BC. The destruction of the Long Walls according to the terms of the victorious Spartans in 405 BC signaled the end of Athenian might.

Plato set his *Republic* in Peiraias as it was at the height of Athenian power, an alluring, cosmopolitan center bustling with rich *metoikoi* (resident aliens) and exotic cults. These days Peiraias has unfortunately lost that lovin' feeling. The town's pollution rivals Athens. A mere block away from the congested port, neighborhoods are run-down and dirty. The waterfront is lined with junkshops and aged pastries glistening with grease. A far cry from the classical charm of Plato's discourse or Kazantzakis's more recent portrayal of a quiet port town in *Zorba the Greek*, Peiraias can *only* be appreciated as a useful point of departure to the Greek isles.

ORIENTATION

To get to Peiraias from Athens take the subway to the last stop in the Peiraias direction, or take blue bus #049 on Athinas St. just off Omonia Sq. From Syntagma Sq., take green bus #040 on Filellinon St. and get off at the Public Theater (Demotikon Theatron) and head down the hill toward the port. The subway takes roughly 20 minutes, while the bus is a 40 minute ride. There is a small but invaluable map of Peiraias on the back of the Athens map (available at the tourist office in Syntagma Sq.).

The subway deposits you at the top of Akti Poseidonos; facing the water, head left. It merges with Akti Miaouli St. at **Themistokleous Square,** where you arrive if you walk down **Vas. Georgiou St.** (from the bus stop at **Korai Square**). Themistokleos Sq. is also the departure point for boats to the Saronic Gulf Islands and **hydrofoils** to Aegina. The larger ferries dock at Akti Miaouli; international ferries are at the end toward the Customs House. Small ferries depart from Akti Poseidonos. Long-distance

trains for Patras and the Peloponnese leave daily from the train station on **Akti Kali-massioti**. Long-distance **trains** for northern Greece (Larissis) leave daily from the station on **Ag. Dimitriou** across the harbor.

On the opposite side of the peninsula is the port of **Zea**, a 10-minute walk away from the water on any of the roads off Akti Miaouli. Private boats dock in the harbor on the left; hydrofoils depart from the right to the other Saronic islands.

PRACTICAL INFORMATION

Transportation

Ferries: Most of the boats and ticket agencies are on two streets, **Akti Poseidonos St.** and **Akti Miaoul St.** Ferries ply the waters from Peiraias to nearly all Greek islands except the Sporades and Ionians: Iraklion on Crete (10hr., 2 per day, 5500dr), Hania on Crete (10hr., 1 per day, 5500dr), and Rethymnon on Crete (10hr., 1 per day, 5500dr). Other destinations include Rhodes (16hr., 2 per day 7000dr); Mykonos, Naxos and Paros (6hr., 6 per day, 5000dr); Chios and Lesbos (9-11hr., 1 per day, 5500dr); Aegina, Poros, Spetses, and Hydra (1-4hr., 1 per hour 8am-7pm, 2000-3000dr); and Sifnos, Kythnos, Serifos, and Milos (3-5½hr., 3 per week, 3000-4000dr).

Tourist and Financial Services

Tourist Office: Kentriko (tel. 412 1181 or 412 1172; fax 413 3193), in the subway station, flagged by a large blue-lettered sign. Offers extremely helpful advice on where to find your boat in the port's glut of vessels. Open daily 6am-8pm. Inquire about their special 20-day unlimited island-hopping package, available after June 15 (9500dr). The tourist office at Zea (tel. 452 2586 or 452 2591) is above the Zea post office. Look for the EOT sign.Open M-F 8am-2:30pm.

Banks: It is harder to avoid banks than to find them in this town—most are located on the waterfront. **National Bank of Greece,** 3 Antistasseos St. (tel. 417 4101), is one block up from Themistokleous Sq. Open M-Th 8am-2pm, F 8am-1:30pm. **Citibank,** 47-49 Akti Miaouli (tel. 417 2153), sports **ATMs**. Open M-Th 8am-2pm, F 8am-1:30pm. All banks offer **currency exchange** services.

Bookstore: Telstar Booksellers, 57 Akti Miaouli St. (tel. 429 3618), offers an impressive array of magazines in English and French. Open M-F 7am-8pm, Sa 8am-4pm.

Emergency and Communications

Port Police: (tel. 422 6000). The Zea **port police** office (tel. 459 3145, 428 2900 or 459 3144) is along the water and under the sidewalk.

Post Office: (tel. 412 4202), on Tsamadou St., on the right off Antistasseos St., one block inland from Themistokleous Sq. Open M-F 7:30am-8pm, Sa-Su 8am-2pm. The subway station offers travelers a smaller post office, to the right of the Akti Poseidonos doors. Open M-F 7:30am-2pm. A **post office** at Zea (tel. 418 3380) can be found near the Zea port police. Open M-F 7:30am-2pm. **Postal code:** 18503.

OTE: 19 Karaoli Dimitriou St. This office is for all telephone services including telegram, fax, telex, and long-distance overseas collect calls. Open M-F 7am-2:40pm. **Telephone Code:** 01.

ACCOMMODATIONS

You'll have better luck finding inexpensive, quality accommodations in Athens, but if you must stay in Peiraias, head away from the water, where the hotels will at least be safe. Don't sleep in the dirty and dangerous park at Themistokleos Sq.

Hotel Phidias, 189 Koundouriotou St. (tel. 429 6160), near Zea on a side street off Boumboulinas, which is itself off Akti Miaouli St. Take trolley #20 to the stop near Grigoriou Lambraki St. or a blue bus to Korai Sq. Rooms all have A/C, baths, and TVs. Singles 13,000dr; doubles 17,250dr; triples 20,700dr.

Hotel Glaros, 4 Char. Trikoupi St. (tel. 451 5421 or 453 7887; fax 453 7889), on a street which runs away from the lower part of Akti Miaouli, offers cheaper rates than Hotel Phidias. Singles 7000dr; doubles 9000dr; triples 11,400dr.

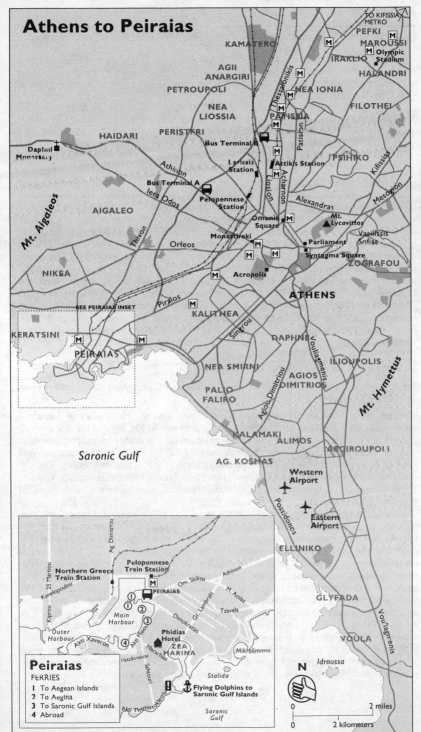

Athens to Peiraias

TO KIFISSIA
METRO

PEFKI

MAROUSSI

M Olympic
Stadium

IRAKLIO

HALANDRI

KAMATERO

AGII
ANARGIRI

PETROUPOLI

NEA IONIA

M

FILOTHEI

NEA
LIOSSIA

PATISSIA

Thessalonikis

Patision

PERISTERI

Bus Terminal B

PSIHIKO

Kifissias

HAIDARI

Athinon

Larissa
Station

Attikis Station

Daphni
Monastery

Ira Odos

Bus Terminal A

Acharnion

Liosion

Alexandras

Mesogion

Peloponnese
Station

AIGALEO

Thivon

Omonia
Square

M

Mt.
Lycavittos

Vasilissis
Sofias

Orfeos

Monastiraki

Parliament

M

NIKEA

M

Syntagma Square

ZOGRAFOU

Pirzios

Acropolis

M

ATHENS

SEE PEIRAIAS INSET

KERATSINI

M

KALITHEA

Sinarou

DAPHNE

Vouliagmenis

ILIOUPOLIS

PEIRAIAS

M

NEA SMIRNI

AGIOS
DIMITRIOS

Mt. Hymettus

PALIO
FALIRO

Agiou Dimitriou

KALAMAKI

ALIMOS

ARGIROUPOLI

Saronic Gulf

AG. KOSMAS

Western
Airport

Possidonos

Eastern
Airport

ELLINIKO

GLYFADA

VOULA

Vouliagmenis

Peiraias Inset

Ag. Dimitriou

25 Martiou

Kanelopoulou

Kiprou

Northern Greece
Train Station

Peloponnese
Train Station

M PEIRAIAS

Om. Skilitsi

Athinon

M. Assias

① ①

Main
Harbour

②

Dimokratias

Gr. Lambraki

Tzavela

Outer
Harbour

③

Akti Xaveron

④

Akti Miaouli

Phidias
Hotel

ΣEA
MARINA

Mikrolimano

Hatzikiriakou

Navarhou

Saltouri

Stalida

N

Idroussa

Akti Themistokleous

Flying Dolphins to
Saronic Gulf Islands

Saronic
Gulf

Peiraias

FERRIES

1 To Aegean Islands
2 To Aegina
3 To Saronic Gulf Islands
4 Abroad

0   2 miles

0   2 kilometers

FOOD

Inexpensive fast food joints line the dock, offering mediocre fare at uniform prices.

Peiraikon Supermarket (tel. 417 6495). The best approach to a good, cheap meal is to do it yourself. Go one block up Antistasseos St., and turn left onto Makras Stoas St. at the National Bank of Greece; the supermarket is at the end of that block. Open M-F 8am-9pm, Sa 8am-4pm.

Drosopigi, 24 Akti Moustopoulou (tel. 452 0585 or 428 0645), proffers tasty and inexpensive pita roll-ups. Although the menu is extensive, the rolled *souvlaki* gyros (400dr) are the most popular choices. Sit outside and eat along the Zea boardwalk.

Europa Bakery, 166-168 Koundouriotou (tel. 412 2577), near Hotel Phidias, offers cheap, mouth-watering treats (*baklava* 300dr).

SIGHTS

The prize possession of the **Archaeological Museum,** 31 Char. Trikoupi St. (tel. 452 1598), is the ancient "Peiraias Kouros," a large, hollow, bronze statue with outstretched arms. (*Museum open Tu-Su 8:30am-2:30pm. Admission 1500dr, students 300dr, EU students free, seniors 300dr. No charge for video, no flash allowed.*) Three other bronze statues found by the port in 1959 are in the likeness of Athena and Artemis. Near the museum is the 2nd-century BC **Hellenistic theater.** Farther south at Zea, facing the harbor and underneath the sidewalk on Akti Themistokleous, is the **Maritime Museum** (tel. 451 6822), which traces the history of the Greek navy using detailed ship models. (*Museum open Tu-F 8:30am-2pm, Sa-Su 9am-1pm. Admission 500dr.*) Of particular note in Room 3 is a model of the Athenian trireme "Olympias," used in the Persian Wars (490-480 BC). The courtyard is home port to torpedo tubes, naval weapons, and the top part of *Papanikolis*, a submarine from World War II.

■ Kesariani Μονη Καισσαριανης

Tel. 723 6619. **Open** *Tu-Su 8:30am-2:30pm.* **Admission** *800dr, seniors 400dr, students with ID 400dr, EU students free.*

If you're worn down by Athens' insane congestion, visit the **Monastery of Kesariani** for serenity and salvation. Located near the top of scenic **Mt. Hymettus** and providing a bird's eye view of Athens, the site was originally a temple to Demeter, goddess of agriculture and nature. In the Roman period (AD 100-300), another temple was erected in its place whose stones were used to build the existing monastery. The layers of sacred atmosphere, complemented by 17th-century frescos by Ioannis Ypatios, are arresting; come alone or with a spiritual friend, as tour buses are likely to whirl you through too quickly.

To reach Kesariani take blue bus #224 from the KTEL stop two blocks up Vas. Sofias St. from Syntagma Sq. (20min., every 15min., 100dr). Get off at the last stop, follow the left-hand road uphill and, when you reach the overpass, bear right under it, staying to the right through two forks. A bit farther up, the road splits, with the right section going up the mountain, the left coming down from it. Once again, stick to the right. Roughly a five-minute jaunt farther uphill, just as the road bends left, two branches spring from the right side. Ignore the barred one on the right, and take the stone path left up to the monastery. The entire walk takes 40-50 minutes, so be sure to bring lots of water. Avoid the temptation to accept a ride from one of the speeding motorists that fly by next to the all-too-narrow pedestrian path. If you drain your water bottles, a 15-minute walk up the main road leads to a small store and a drinkable fountain. For a fabulous view overlooking Athens all the way to the sea, keep walking for 15 more minutes past the store. Many hiking trails meander away from the road throughout the area, making the monastery a wonderful spot for a picnic.

■ Daphni Μονη Δαφνι

*Tel. 581 1558. **Open** daily 8:30am-2:45pm. **Admission** 800dr, students and seniors 400dr, EU students free. No flash photography.*

The **Monastery of Daphni,** surrounded by a high fortified wall, is a peaceful retreat blessed with the caress of cool breezes, it stands 10km west of Athens along the Ancient Sacred Way at the corner of Iera St. and Athinon Ave. Built on the site of the ancient Temple of Daphnios Apollo, the monastery owes its name to the laurels, *(daphnai)* that were sacred to Apollo and once graced this ancient sanctuary. The yellow-orange 11th-century structure with flower shaped windows is pock-marked with birds' nests and populated by a dozen cats. Inside are celestial mosaics of Jesus' life. Immediately to your right as you enter the octagonal room is a depiction of the *anastasis* (resurrection of Christ). The four corners of the ceiling portray (counter-clockwise from near right) the angel's announcement of Mary's pregnancy, Christ's birth, his baptism in the Jordan River, and the *apotheosis* or transfiguration of Christ. Mosaics in the narthex depict the betrayal of Judas, the Last Supper, the birth of Mary, and her blessing as a young girl. There is a pronounced scowl on Christ's face as he stares down from the masterful mosaic dome; depicting Christ as displeased with man's misdeeds was a common theme in 11th-century Christian art. The expression was perhaps prophetic as the sanctity of the site was twice violated in the last millen-nium when the monastery was used as an army camp and then an insane asylum.

To reach Daphni from Athens, take bus #A16, B16, or C16 from **Eleftherias Sq.** (from Omonia Sq., go up Peiraias St./Tsaldari St.; about 10min. on foot). A bus leaves every 30 minutes and the trip should take 20 minutes. From Peiraias Port, take #804 or #845 (35min., every 15min., 6am-11:30pm). From the *psychiatrio* stop, go to the highway, cross it, and walk to your right to get to the monastery.

■ Cape Sounion Ακρωτηριο Σουνιο

> Place me on Sunium's marbled steep,
> Where nothing, save the waves and I,
> May hear our mutual murmurs sweep;
> There, swan-like, let me sing and die:
> A land of slaves shall ne'er be mine —
> Dash down yon cup of Samian wine!
>
> —Lord Byron, *Don Juan*

A formidable rocky promontory rising 60m out of the Aegean, Cape Sounion affords some of the most invigorating views of the Aegean. Lord Byron was so taken that he mentioned the experience in his paean to Greek Independence, the "Isles of Greece" in his *Don Juan*.

Check the schedule at the bus station upon arrival. Two orange-striped KTEL buses travel the 65km road to Cape Sounion. One goes along the coast and stops at all points on the Apollo Coast (2hr., 6:30am-6:30pm, 1200dr), leaving Athens every hour on the half hour from the 14 Mavromateon St. stop near Areos Park—catch a seat on the right side of the bus to enjoy a view of crystal blue water for the entire ride. The other bus leaves from Areos Park (2¼hr., 1 per hr. 6am-6pm, 1200dr), and follows a slightly less scenic inland route.

Every hour on the half hour, buses head from Cape Sounion to the port of **Lavrio** (20min., 200dr). Buses depart from 14 Mavromateon St. in Athens to Lavrio to catch the ferries (1½hr., every 30min. 5:50am-7pm, 8:15pm, 9:30pm, 900dr). **Ferries** (tel. 26 177) go from Lavrio to Kea (1¼hr., 1750dr) and Kithnos (2½hr., 2300dr).

If you want to spend the night to see the temples, or if you miss the last bus to the ferry at Lavrio, you can find pricey accommodations at the **Aegaeon Hotel** (tel. 39 200; fax 39 234), located five minutes from the bus stop toward the temples (if you plan to stay, get off the bus at the main stop rather than up at the temples). Look for the large yellow building down by the beach on the right (singles 15,000dr; doubles 18,000dr, all with bath). The **Belle Epoque Hotel**, 33 Klioni St. at Lavrio (tel. 27 130 or 26 059), has reasonably priced rooms (doubles 14,000dr; triples 18,000dr; full breakfast included). To find it, walk a very short distance from the bus stop away from the port and the center of town. **Telephone code:** 0292.

Temple of Poseidon

Tel. 39 363. Site open daily 9am-sunset. Admission 800dr, students 400dr, EU students free. Pack a lunch and bypass the pricey cafeteria. Sunrise and sunset are the ideal time to view the temples; try to avoid visiting in the early afternoon, when the tour buses funnel in. The last bus to Athens departs according to the hour of the sunset, usually 8:30-9pm in summer.

The **Temple of Poseidon**, gracing the highest point on the Cape, has for centuries been a dazzling white landmark for sailors out at sea. The original temple was constructed around 600 BC, destroyed by the Persians in 480 BC, and rebuilt by Pericles in 440 BC. The 16 remaining Doric columns rise majestically above the coast, suggesting the graceful symmetry of the original temple and inspiring awe in seafarers and tourists alike. Look closely at the graffiti on the columns for the name of the vandalous Lord Byron. Scattered remains of the **Temple of Athena Sounias**, the patron goddess of Athens, litter the lower hill.

Around Cape Sounion

To reach the ocean, follow one of the many paths from the inland side of the temple. The agile and adventurous can negotiate the cliff on the ocean side. Swarmed with vacationing families, the **beaches** along the 70km **Apollo Coast** between Peiraias and Cape Sounion have a crowded carnival atmosphere, especially on summer weekends. Some are owned by hotels, which charge a 150dr admission fee, but towns usually have free public beaches as well and some seaside stretches along the bus route remain almost empty. The driver will let you off almost anywhere.

■ Rafina Ραφηνα

Rafina might as well be named "Little Peiraias," situated, as it is, opposite its counterpart on the Attic Peninsula. However, the smaller rendition is more pleasant on the eyes, ears, and lungs than its bigger, badder counterpart. Uphill from the port, life centers on the white-paved town square.

The ramp up from the waterfront leads to Plastira Sq. The **Commercial Bank** (tel. 25 182) is located on the far left corner of the square (open M-Th 8am-2pm, F 8am-1:30pm) and the **Ionian Bank** (tel. 24 152) is two blocks farther inland (open M-Th 8am-2pm, F 8am-1:30pm). Both banks offer **currency exchange** and **ATM** machines. English-speaking offices along the waterfront offer information and ferry tickets. **Strintzis Lines, Goutos Lines, Agoudimos Lines,** and **Ventouris Ferries** operate various ferries, while **Ilios Lines** and **Hermes Lines** operate hydrofoils. **Taxis** line up right in front of the square. There is a **pharmacy,** 6 Kyprion St. (tel. 25 625), one block down off the left side of the square. Look for the green cross (open M, W 8:30am-2pm, Tu, Th 8:30am-2pm and 5:30-9pm). With the water at your back, the **post office** (tel. 23 777) stands two streets to the right on El. Venizelou St. (open M-F 7:30am-2pm); the **OTE** (tel. 25 182) is across from the post office on the far side of the square (open M-F 7:30am-3pm). **Postal code:** 19009. **Telephone code:** 0294.

Rafina is accessible by frequent **buses** from 29 Mavromateon St., two blocks up along Areos Park in Athens (1hr., every 30min. 5:45am-10:30pm, 440dr). **Ferries** sail to Karystos in Evia (1¾hr., 2-3 per day, 1250dr); Marmari in Evia (1¼hr., 4-6 per day, 1800dr); Andros (2hr., 5-6 per day, 2500dr); Tinos (4hr., 5-6 per day, 3500dr); Mykonos (4¾hr., 5-6 per day, 4000dr); Paros (5hr., 1-2 per day, 4100dr); and Naxos (6hr., 1-2 per day, 4200dr). **Hydrofoils** sail to Andros (1hr., 1 per day, 5000dr); Tinos (2hr., 1 per day, 7000dr); Amorgos (10hr., 4700dr); and Mykonos (2½hr., 1 per day, 8000dr). A **super-catamaran** also sails to the Cyclades in summer: Tinos (1½hr., 1-2 per day) and Mykonos (2hr., 1-2 per day). **Nel Lines,** a domestic company, goes to Agios Efstratios, Limnos, and Kavala (3 times per week) and Lesbos (1 per week). The **port authority** (tel. 22 300, 22 487, 28 888, or 22 300) has more info.

Be prepared to pay a good deal for the dubious pleasure of spending a night in Rafina. **Hotel Korali,** 11 Plastira Sq. (tel. 22 477), offers cramped but clean rooms with shared baths (singles 5000dr; doubles 8000dr; triples 12,000dr). **Hotel Avra's** (tel. 22 780 or 22 782; fax 23 320) similar rooms are immeasurably enhanced by ocean views. Visible from the port, this enormous brown concrete building can be reached by heading left at the top of the ramp leading away from the boats (singles 13,500dr; doubles 21,000dr; triples 25,000dr). Those who wish to camp can head to the beach of **Kokkino Limanaki** (tel. 31 604 or 78 780; fax 31 603), 1½km from the port; there is a blue and white sign at the top of the ramp (1500dr per person; 1300dr per small tent; 1450dr per large tent; 24hr. hot water shower included).

Of interest to those catching early ferries may be the **Arktopeio,** a quick and inexpensive bakery; facing away from the water, it's located on the left side of the square. (fresh bread 150dr, filled croissants from 200dr, yogurt 210dr; open daily 6:30am-11pm). The pier is lined with innumerable *psarotavernas* (fish restaurants), all of which display their catch in storefront, ice filled counters. If you can't stand the smell of octopus, the grill next to the bakery can fill you with *souvlaki* and pita bread.

■ Marathon Μαραθώνας

In 490 BC, when the Athenians defeated the Persians at the bloody battle of Marathon, the messenger Pheidippides ran 42km to Athens to announce the victory and then collapsed dead from exhaustion. Today, international marathons (*sans* fatal collapse) relive the glory of this act. Runners trace Pheidippides' route twice annually, beginning at the commemorative plaque.

Beautiful **Lake Marathon,** with its huge marble dam, rests 8km past the otherwise uninspiring town. Until WWII, the lake was Athens' sole water source. At **Ramnous,** 15km to the northeast, lie the ruins of the Temple of Nemesis, goddess of retribution, and Themtis, goddess of law and justice. On the coast near Marathon, **Schinias** to the north and **Timvos Marathonas** to the south are popular beaches. Many people camp at Schinias since the trees offer protection, but the mosquitoes are thirsty and mean, and free-lance camping is illegal.

The **bus** for Marathon leaves from 29 Mavromateon St. by Areos Park in Athens (1hr., roughly every hr. 5:30am-10:30pm, 700dr). To get to the **Archaeological Museum of Marathonas** (tel. 55 155), ask the driver to let you off at the sign for the museum, "Mouseion and Marathonas." *(Open Tu-Su 8am-2:30pm. Admission 500dr, students 250dr, EU students, children under 18, and students of the classics or archaeology free.)* Follow the signs and don't despair, the museum is 2km farther at the end of the paved Plateion road at #114. After your scenic trek through farmlands, bear right when there is a fork in the road and, for the first time, no sign to direct you.

The small museum consists of five rooms packed with exciting archaeological finds. Objects from Neolithic (4000-2500 BC) graves fill **room 1** and Geometric period (from 2500 BC) sepulchers and Cycladic grave offerings occupy **room 2.** The highlight of **room 3** is the 10-meter high Athenian trophy commemorating the battle with the Persians (found in nearby Schinias). In **room 4,** you'll find the tombs of Athenians and their allies, the Plateians, who died in Marathon, along with body ashes and remnants of bones. For those interested in ancient grooming, a mirror cover and comb rest on the bottom shelf of case #12 in room 4. Your visit will end with a bang in **room 5.** Marble heads of Marathon native and patron of the arts Herodes Atticus and his star pupil Polydenkion line one wall; Egyptian statues, perhaps from the temple of Isis, line the other. Also displayed is a poem of Herodes Atticus and the skeleton of a baby surrounded by two beehives (1st century BC). Since the museum is very near the ancient site of the estate of Herodes Atticus and his wife Regilla, the museum courtyard houses an arched gate which reads, "This estate is dedicated to Regilla" and bears marble statues of the couple's heads on either side.

ATHENS

The bus heads back to Athens from the Marathon Museum stop twice per hour. To reach the Marathon Tomb or the nearby beach, walk 1.5km back toward Athens. Lake Marathon, Amphiareion, and Ramnous are accessible by automobile only.

No Strings Attached

The origins of the Greek folk **shadow puppet theater** can supposedly be traced to the 14th-century Ottoman Empire, in present-day Turkey. Two workmen, the stonemason Karagöz and his foreman, Hacivat, engaged in conversations so ribald and witty that the entire crew stopped work on Sultan Orhan's new mosque to listen. Orhan, enraged, rashly commanded the execution of the two jokesters, but soon found himself bored and dejected without their humor. An inventive dervish attempted to entertain the melancholic sultan with figures of the late twosome made from transparent camel skin. He manipulated these puppets behind a screen lit with candles or oil lamps. Passed on orally from one anonymous puppet-master to the next over the following centuries, these "Karagöz" shadow shows evolved into bewitching spectacles of color, music, bawdy comedy, clever word play, slapstick, and political satire, migrating west in the early 19th century to usher in the development of the distinctly Greek **"Karaghiózis"** shadow theater. Expert shadow puppet players, a mostly illiterate, itinerant artistic group, traveled the countryside, sailed around the islands, and performed before cafe crowds sipping *ouzo* or coffee under the night sky. After the show, owner and puppet master split the proceeds from the food and drink. Today shadow puppets can be seen occasionally on children's TV programs, or live at one remaining permanent theater, in the suburb of **Nea Smirni** in Athens. Ask at the Syntagma Square tourist info window for details .

Saronic Gulf Islands
Τα Νησια του Σαρωνικου

Their captivating landscapes and proximity to Athens have made the Saronic Gulf Islands enduringly popular destinations. Ever since King Saron of Troezen drowned while hunting a swimming doe in the gulf that now bears his name, sojourners have been enticed by the islands' mountainous interiors dotted with ancient temples and tranquil monasteries. Pebbly beaches surrounded by green hills make a swim in the Saronic one of Greece's most scenic.

Despite geographic proximity, each island retains a distinct character. Poros' magnificent lemon grove, Aegina's Temple of Aphaia, Spetses' pine-filled forests, and Hydra's seductive port attract countless Athenians seeking weekend getaways. Unfortunately, the Saronic Gulf Islands' popularity does not come cheap so travelers should budget accordingly.

👉 HIGHLIGHTS OF THE SARONIC GULF ISLANDS

- Hike up to the 5th-century BC Temple of Aphaia on **Aegina** (p. 111) and soak in a view of the island's entire coastline.
- Rinse off in the curative waters of a sacred spring at the 18th-century Monastery of Zoodochos Pigis on **Poros** (p. 115).
- Experience the quietude of a city without motor vehicles on **Hydra** (p. 115).

AEGINA Αιγινα

Who does not know the renowned Aegina who went to bed with Zeus?
—Bacchylides

Aegina's whitewashed buildings, narrow streets, horses decorated with brightly colored tassels, and aqua-hued water recall the work of a Disney production studio; behind the waterfront, you'll discover a gritty little town that can be fun to explore.

Aegina is an easy daytrip for pistachio-lovin' Athenians and, unsurprisingly, summer weekends find the island saddled with the bustle of Greece's capital. Many tourists visit not simply for the beaches and Agia Marina's nightlife, but also to see the island's famous Temple of Aphaia and Temple of Apollo.

In ancient times, relations between Aegina and Athens were far less chummy. The little island made up for its size with spunk and initiative, consistently resisting Athenian political and military encroachment. The island produced the first Greek coins—the silver "tortoises" that gained great financial leverage throughout the Greek world—and Aegina's sprinters (who practiced with jugs of water on their shoulders) zoomed past the competition at the pan-Hellenic games. With the onset of the Persian War in 491 BC, the citizens of Aegina sided at first with Xerxes' army, angering the besieged Athenians. In 480 BC they

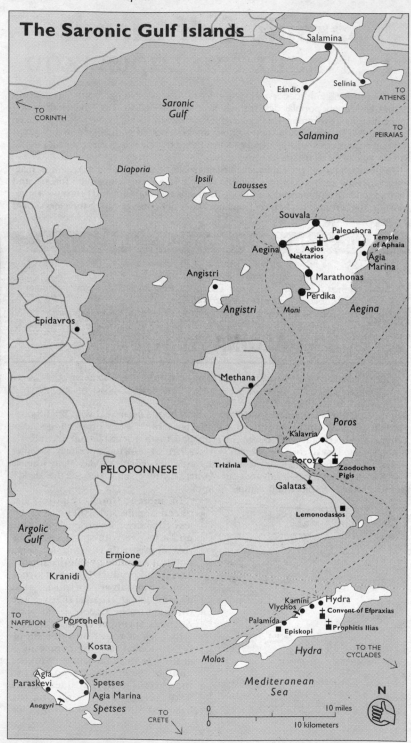

The Saronic Gulf Islands

Salamina

Eándio   Selinia

TO
ATHENS

*Saronic
Gulf*

TO
CORINTH

TO
PEIRAIAS

Salamina

Diaporia   *Ipsili*

Laousses

Souvala

Paleochora

**Temple
of Aphaia**

Aegina   **Agios
Nektarios**

**Ágia
Marina**

Angistri   Marathonas

Perdika

Moni

Angistri   *Aegina*

Epidavros

Methana

Poros

Kalavria

PELOPONNESE   **Trizinia**   Poros

**Zoodochos
Pigis**

Galatas

Lemonodassos

*Argolic
Gulf*

Ermione

Kranidi

Kamíni   **Hydra**

Vlychos   **Convent of Efpraxias**

Palamída

TO
NAFPLION   Portoheli   **Episkopi**   **Prophitis Ilias**

Kosta

Molos   *Hydra*

TO THE
CYCLADES

Agia
Paraskevi   Spetses
Agia Marina

Anagyri   *Spetses*

*Mediteranean
Sea*

N

TO
CRETE

0   10 miles

0   10 kilometers

SARONIC GULF

returned to the Greek side and won the praise of the Delphic Oracle as the swiftest navy on the seas thanks to their performance at Salamis, the mother of all sea battles. In the peaceful inter-regnum that followed Persian defeat, island life flourished and Aegina's inhabitants built the magnificent Temple of Aphaia. With the eventual return of war, this time between Athens and Sparta, Aegina suffered the misfortune of siding against Athens. This time the island didn't have time to switch sides and it was thoroughly trounced by Athens in 459 BC. By 431, Athens had displaced Aegina's population with Athenian colonists. The island sank into geopolitical obscurity but did make a brief reappearance on the international stage as the temporary capital of partially liberated Greece in 1827.

To get to Aegina from Athens, take green bus #40 from almost anywhere in Athens and get off at the Public Theater (*Demotikon Theatron*) in Peiraias (30min., 100dr). From there, you can see the pier where ferries leave for Aegina. Alternatively, take the subway (100dr) to the stop at Peiraias and walk the few blocks to the ferry. From the Athens airport, take bus #19 directly to Peiraias.

■ Aegina Town

As soon as your ferry docks in Aegina Town, you'll quickly realize that you are in the "Pistachio Capital of the World." Kiosks with nuts by the kilo, pistachio preserves, candies, and free samples certainly differentiate this port from the rest in Greece. Even if you don't buy any, you're sure to try some before you leave; Aeginic chefs sprinkle everything from pastries to entrees with the green flakes.

ORIENTATION AND PRACTICAL INFORMATION

The waterfront in front of and to the right of the quay is lined with overpriced cafes. To find more practical amenities, including cheap hotels, *tavernas,* and the bus station, turn left at the quay and follow the waterfront street.

Transportation

Ferries: Service to Peiraias (1½hr., 11 per day, 1400dr); Methana (45min., 11 per day, 800dr); Poros (1hr., 11 per day, 800dr); Hydra (2hr., 4 per day, 1600dr); and Spetses (3hr., 2 per day, 2400dr). Request discounts for students and seniors. Ticket stands are near the boat landing, but each stand represents only one ferry company. Check with the port police for overall schedules.

Flying Dolphins: Ticket stand (tel. 27 462) is next to the port police. Sells hydrofoil tickets to Kythera, Nafplion, and Peiraias (35min., 16 per day, 1995dr); Poros (40min., 3 per day, 2230dr); Methana (25min., 1 per day, 1895dr); Hydra (1hr., 2 per day, 2840dr); Spetses (2hr., 2 per day, 4240dr); and Porto Heli (2hr., 2 per day, 4470dr). **Catamaran** tickets to Poros, Hydra, and Porto Heli also available.

Buses: (tel. 22 787). The bus station is in Ethnegarcias Park, at the corner of the waterfront left of the ferry quay. Buses run 6:30am-8:30pm to Agia Marina and the Temple of Aphaia (30min., every 45min., 400dr). If you are going to the temple, buy a round-trip ticket in Aegina Town.

Tourist and Financial Services

Tourist Office: 1 Cr. Lada (tel. 25 588; email Aegina@aigina.hellasnet.gr; http://www.aigina.hellasnet.gr/aegina), in the big, yellow town hall to the far right of the ferry quay. Officers help find lodgings and hand out maps of Aegina. Open M-F 8am-2:30pm and 7-9pm, Sa-Su 10am-1pm and 7-9pm.

Bank: National Bank (tel. 25 697), on the waterfront to the right of the quay past all the cafes. 24hr. **ATM.** Bank open M-Th 8am-2pm, F 8am-1:30pm.

Bookstore: Giotis (tel 23 874), #25 along the waterfront, just right of the cafes. International books and magazines; small selection of used books in English. Open daily 7am-11pm.

Emergency Services and Communications

Police: (tel. 22 100). For emergencies or other problems.

Tourist Police: (tel. 27 777), 2 blocks up Leonardou Lada St. at #11, left of the quay. English spoken. Helpful in locating rooms. Open daily 7:30am-10pm.

Port Police: (tel. 22 328), on the pier. Provides updated ferry schedules. English spoken. Open 24hr.

Pharmacy: 11 Aiakou St. (tel. 22 404). Open M and W 7:30am-1:30pm, Tu and Th-F 7:30am-1:30pm and 5-8:30pm.

Medical Center: (tel. 22 222), 2km along the waterfront to the right of the ferry quay. If you have a problem call the tourist police and they will arrange transport.

Post Office: 6 Kanari St. (tel. 22 398), to the left of the ferry landing. Cashes traveler's checks. Open M-F 7:30am-2pm. **Postal Code:** 18010.

OTE: 6 Paleas Choras St. (tel. 22 399; dial 161 for assistance costs 300dr), up Aiakou St. to the right. Keep trudging up Aiakou St. when the street narrows into a walkway; the building has a monstrous rooftop satellite dish. Open M-F 7:30am-3:10pm. **Telephone Code:** 0297.

ACCOMMODATIONS

Rooms here are cheaper than on any of the other Saronic Gulf Islands. Even in the high season expect to find a double for around 4000dr. *Domatia* owners often meet the ferries, but as always bargain and discuss location before you follow them away.

Hotel Plaza, 4 Kazatzaki St. (tel. 25 600 or 28 404), on the waterfront left of the ferries and around the bend. A trifle expensive, but the owner runs two other pensions, Christina and Ulrica, from the desk of Hotel Plaza. All rooms have private bathrooms. Free luggage storage. Doubles 13,500dr.

Hotel Artemis, 20 Kanari St. (tel. 25 195; fax 28 466), on Leonardou Lada St. up from the tourist police. Friendly management offers simple, spotless rooms decorated in pink and red. Rents motorbikes and mopeds. Breakfast 1200dr. Singles 8000dr; doubles 12,000dr; large triples or quads 10,000dr.

Hotel Xenon Pavlou, 21 Aeginitou St. (tel. 22 795), behind the church on the far right of the quay. Owned by the same kind-hearted man for 27 years. Offers comfortable rooms with balconies and psychedelic curtains. Breakfast 1500dr. Singles 9000dr; doubles 12,000dr.

Hotel Areti (tel. 23 593), to the left of the ferries, before Hotel Plaza. Offers 25 rooms with private granite baths. Singles 11,000dr; doubles 13,000dr; triples 15,000dr. Credit cards accepted.

FOOD AND ENTERTAINMENT

There are many no-frills *tavernas* along P. Irioti St., which runs parallel to the waterfront one block inland along the right side of the harbor. For make-your-own meals, try **George Sarris Supermarket,** 13 Irioti (tel. 25 944).

To Steki, 47 Irioti St. (tel. 23 910). To get here, turn up from the water after the movie advertisements and walk through the fish market. A salty atmosphere that includes an outdoor barbecue and a small TV tuned permanently to Greek music videos (grilled octopus 1000dr; garlic-potato salad 400dr).

Bessis, 13 Dinokratias St. (tel. 25 700), on the waterfront, offers a delightful array of sweets and pastries (*kataifi* 400dr; Bessis chocolate cake 400dr). Don't be tempted by the sit-down service or 500dr will be tacked on to your bill.

Avli, 17 P. Irioti St. (tel. 26 438), is a stylish and fully air-conditioned restaurant/bar. International menu at reasonable prices (Greek salad 900dr; spaghetti Neapolitan 900dr). 10% discount with student ID. Open 9am-3am.

Anissis, 2 Aiantos St. (tel. 24 757). This outdoor **cinema** at the intersection with Aiakou St. often shows American films (summers only; admission 1700dr). In the winter, you can see a film at **Titina.** Check the signs on the waterfront after the National Bank.

Perdikiotika, 38 Afeas St., is the highlight of Aegina town's nightlife. The seller's window and safe near the DJ's turntable attest to the building's history as the first private bank. The ceiling, adorned by a painting of winged Hermes and his *caduceus,* complements the traditionally decorated courtyard, where clubbers can get a drink (1500-1800dr) and a breath of fresh air. Be on the lookout for the occasional hip-hop or full moon party. Open nightly 10:30pm-4am.

SIGHTS

Aegina Town's archaeological fame rests tenuously on the last half-column of the **Temple of Apollo.** The 8m-tall Doric column dates to 460 BC and stands on Kolona hill, a short walk out of town to the north. A new **archaeological museum** has opened at the site. *(Site and museum open Tu-Su 8am-2:15pm. Admission 500dr, students 300dr, EU students free, free Su.)* The underground church of **Faneromeni,** a 15-minute walk inland just south of the town, houses a rare icon of the Virgin Mary. *(No regular hours. Contact tourist office to arrange a visit.)* Locals say that the night before construction was to begin on a site above Faneromeni, the architect had a vision in which he was instructed to dig instead. The man discovered the church and unearthed the icon.

■ Around Aegina

Temple of Aphaia

*Tel. 32 398. **Open** Tu-F 8am-8pm and Sa-Su 8am-2:30pm. **Admission** including museum 800dr, students with ISIC 400dr, children and EU students free.*

The magnificent 5th-century BC remains of the **Temple of Aphaia** rest 2km from **Agia Marina.** Aphaia, daughter of Zeus, was a hunting nymph worshipped (solely on Aegina) as a protector of women. Her temple, which is built on the foundation of an earlier 6th-century BC temple, boasts a rare and spectacular set of standing double-tiered columns. The Agia Marina bus from Aegina Town stops right in front. Determined and fit classicists can bicycle uphill to the temple from Aegina Town (11km, 14km via Souvala). The coastal route is much gentler and proffers gorgeous views of rocky shores and other islands. To get to the temple from Agia Marina, walk to the end of town with the water on your right and then straight up Kolokotroni St. until it becomes a wooded trail. This is the footpath to the Temple of Aphaia. At night, peacocks roam the quiet hills by the temple. A small **museum** opens for 15 minutes at 9am, 11am, noon, and 1pm.

Agia Marina

According to the residents of Agia Marina, the town's fortuitous location to the east of Aegina affords it lush greenery and clean waters. The small town is built around the main avenue, Afeas Rd., which is parallel with the sea. Here you will find an **OTE,** a **pharmacy** (tel. 32 416), and a handful of little shops. Several hotels surround the port. Of note is **Hotel Myrmidon,** off Afeas St. (tel. 32 691 or 71 337; fax 32 558), where *Let's Go* users enjoy a considerable 40% discount (singles normally 10,560dr; doubles 13,200dr; triples 15,840dr). The courtyard sports a swimming pool and footbridge adorned with dolphins.

The **Galavis Supermarket,** 230 Afeas St. (tel. 32 208), and the **Dimitris Garis** bakery also on Afeas (tel. 32 525) offer alternatives to restaurant meals. The proprietors of **Kiwi Cafe,** across from the bus stop (tel. 32 138), are Greek New Zealanders; though their main focus is on Greek dishes, the milkshakes (from 750dr) really hit the spot. Known for its pita gyros and *souvlaki* (each 350dr), **Tomas' place** (tel. 32 787) doesn't need an official name although he's been searching for an appropriate one for some years now. You can guess when **24 Hours** (tel. 32 602) is open, but choosing from the extensive menu of snacks is a more challenging feat (sandwiches 900dr; ice cream floats 1000dr; Greek coffee 300dr). By night, it's one of Agia Marina's most popular bars, playing jazz, rock, and reggae music.

Paleochora

On the road between Aegina and Agia Marina is the village of **Paleochora,** where the islanders used to take refuge from pirate invasions. Paleochora was once "the town of 300 churches." Only 15 remain, some with inspiring frescoes. The bus between Aegina Town and Agia Marina stops at the foot of the new church of **Agios Nektarios,** the largest place of worship in the Balkans. The octagonal main chamber draws attention to the mosaic of a two-headed bird on the floor. Zigzagging steps lead up the hill from the church, through blackberry bushes and to the monastery of Agios Nektarios. Originally Nektarios's personal residence, the series of courtyards displays the saint's bedroom, along with his bed and books. Modest dress is required.

Marathonas

The beach town of **Marathonas** is the locals' well-kept secret, only a 10-minute ride from Aegina town on the bus to Perdika (approximately 1 per hr. 6:30am-8:30pm). Young by Greek standards (only 150 years old), the town boasts clear, shallow waters and a sandy shore. There aren't many dining options, but **Tassos** (tel. 24 040), right on the beach, serves tasty dishes with a smile (veal 1450dr; *ouzo* 350dr). **Tavern Paris** is the place to kick back with a beer (450-500dr) and **Ostria Cafeteria** (tel. 26 738) doles out yummy breakfasts, sandwiches (400-600dr), and beachside snacks (pizza from 1300dr; ice cream from 450dr; milkshakes 600dr).

POROS Πορος

Only a sliver of water separates the sinewy hills of the mainland from this tiny island. A mere three hours from Peiraias, Poros is actually two small, juicy islands—Kalavria and Sphaeria—cut by a canal. Its name, meaning "passage," refers to the channel that forms its border with the Peloponnese.

The Kalavrian League, a seven-city council, met in Poros to ward off hostile naval powers and order the building of the Temple of Poseidon in the 6th century BC. Three hundred years later, the great orator Demosthenes, who improved his diction by speaking with marbles in his mouth, killed himself beside its columns. Poros was sparsely populated until Greeks arrived from Turkey in the 1920s.

▓ Poros Town

Poros Town occupies most of tiny Sphaeria, while woods extend over rugged Kalavria. Less crowded than Aegina, Poros still overflows on the weekends. You can find serenity and spectacular views by climbing the narrow passageways that lead to the top of Poros Town and the hills beyond. The waterfront, especially near the ferry dock, seems consumed by tourism, but a walk left along the water takes you to a calmer area and establishments with slightly higher standards.

ORIENTATION AND PRACTICAL INFORMATION

In Poros Town, the hydrofoil quay is the center of activity, with tourist agencies to the left, restaurants and souvenir shops in the center, and discos and bars to the right.

Transportation

Ferries: Car ferries tie up on the northwest side of town. To Peiraias (2½hr., 6 per day, 2000dr), stopping in Methana (30min., 800dr) and Aegina (1hr., 1200dr). Ferries also run once daily to Spetses (2hr., 1600dr), stopping in Hydra (45min., 1000dr). Small boat ferries to the far right of the quay go to Galatas on the mainland 24hr. (every 10min., 80dr).

Flying Dolphins: (tel. 22 297). Hydrofoils dock at the main landing in the center of town. To: Peiraias (1-1¼hr., 9-10 per day, 4100dr); Aegina (40min., 2 per day, 2460dr); Hydra (30min., 5-7 per day, 2050dr); Spetses (1hr., 4-5 per day, 3300dr); and Monemvassia (3hr., 2 per week, 6100dr). Office open daily 6am-9:30pm.

Moped Rental: Stelio's (tel. 23 026) is on the waterfront to the left of main landing, near Lela Tour. Rents bikes (1000dr) and mopeds (2000-5000dr). Open daily 8:30am-8:30pm.

Tourist and Financial Services

Tourist Agencies: Family Travel, on the waterfront, opposite the ferry docks (tel. 23 743). English-speaking staff. Provides general info, ferry tickets, **currency**

exchange, and rooms. Open M-F 9am-10pm. **Lela Tour** (tel. 24 439 and 24 780) offers showers (1000dr) and organizes excursions. Open daily 9am-10pm.
Bank: The **National Bank** (tel. 22 236) is on the waterfront, right of the ferry landing. Open M-Th 8am-2pm, F 8am-1:30pm.
Bookstore: Mastropetros (tel. 25 205), up a flight of stairs on the waterfront near George's Cafe. Sells books and magazines in English and Spanish and does photocopying (25dr per page). Open daily 8am-11pm. **Skipper & Trout International Bookshop** (tel. 26 245) is in the arcade behind Diana Cinema to the left of the main landing. Buys, sells, and exchanges new and used books in English, Swedish, Norwegian, German, Dutch, Italian, French, and Greek. Offers telephone, fax, and translation services.
Laundromats: Suzi's Launderette Service, to the right of the OTE. Wash and dry 2000dr, drop-off only. 2hr. service. Open M-Sa 9am-2pm.

Emergency and Communications

Tourist Police: (tel. 22 256). Same office and telephone number as the **regular police.** Open 24hr. From Iroon Sq., the central square, walk inland and turn right after the post office. Then turn left at Igloo ice cream shop, go up the steps past the Church of St. George and keep walking down the path. A Greek flag marks the office, which helps find rooms. Open daily 8am-9pm.
Pharmacy: (tel. 25 523), by ferry docks. Open daily 8:30am-2:30pm and 5:30-11pm.
Post Office: (tel. 22 275). Occupies the first square to the right along the water. Open M-F 7:30am-2pm. **Postal Code:** 18020.
OTE: (tel. 22 199), on the waterfront, left of the main landing. Open M-F 7:30am-3:10pm. **Telephone Code:** 0298.

ACCOMMODATIONS

During high season the cheapest double is listed at 7000dr, but try to bargain, especially on weekdays. Prices go way down in the off season. Less touristy **Galatas,** just a two-minute boat ride across the strait (every 10min., 80dr), offers cheaper, quieter rooms.

KTM Pension (tel. 25 125), a 500m walk left from the ferries, turning inland just before signs for the Agricultural Bank. Their signs say "Best Price," and for once it is partly true. The pension has 10 neat rooms, all with private baths. Singles 6000dr; doubles 10,000dr; triples 15,000dr.
George Douros (tel. 24 780) has a block of rooms to the left of the ferries, beyond the Agricultural Bank, all with private baths. If you want a kitchen, ask for a room downstairs. If you don't want air-conditioning (1500dr extra), ask for a free fan. Inquire at **Lela Tours,** where George works, for more information. Singles 6000dr; doubles 8500dr; triples 12,000dr.
Manos Pension (tel. 22 000 or 23 456), in Galatas. Walk left when you disembark the small boat from Poros Town. Rooms and apartments are all equipped with private baths and balconies. In winter central heating kicks in as prices decrease. Rooftop lounge and kitchen available for breakfast. Bike (1200dr) and moped (3000dr) rental service. Singles 4000dr; doubles 6000dr; triples 8000dr; quads with kitchen 12,000dr.
Seven Brother Hotel (tel. 23 412; fax 23 413; http://www.all-hotels.gr), in the middle of the waterfront, 100m right of the ferry landing. Each large room comes with private bath and balcony. A/C 2000dr. Singles 10,000dr; doubles 13,000dr. Prices negotiable, with 15% discount for students and seniors.

FOOD

Poros Town has many of the best restaurants in the Saronic Gulf. Restaurants line the harbor, and "charming" waiters try to convince tourists to sit down. Little distinguishes one from another, so you might choose between views or waiters. For a cheap make-your-own meal, stop in the **grocery stores** near the ferry landing or **To Stachy** (tel. 25 271), a bakery to the right of the National Bank (fresh bread 160dr).

Karavolos (tel. 26 158), behind the cinema arcade to the left of the ferry landing. Try their namesake escargot dish (1000dr) while you enjoy the warm cottage atmosphere with dried flowers, a fireplace, gingham tablecloths, and an owner who speaks only Greek.

Alkyone Restaurant, in Galatas, is where boats from Poros deposit you. New management has turned this former bar into a cheerful restaurant with a fountain and a view of Poros Town across the water (*moussaka* 950dr, grilled *calamari* 1000dr, shrimp *saganaki* 1300dr). Open daily 7am-2am.

Seven Brothers (tel. 22 446 or 23 336; http://www.galaxynet.gr) is just back from the water in the center of the waterfront. The oldest *taverna* in Poros has large portions of well-prepared food (from 900dr), and lively Greek dancing by three of the brothers every night—the other four are cooking—and by professionals at 9pm on Monday nights. Try their lamb chops (1700dr). 10-15% student discount

Lagoudera & Caravella (tel. 23 666), on the wharf, right of the ferry landing. Offers mussels *saganaki* (2000dr) and stuffed tomatoes (1200dr). Open daily 10am-2am.

George's Cafe (tel. 22 508), with its cute blue and white nautical decor, is located in the center of the quay. It offers a breakfast special of coffee, pastry, and orange juice (1150dr) along with an a la carte menu. Open daily at 6:30am.

Vessala (tel. 25 890), a little farther away from town to the left of the port, has homemade *galactobureko* (300dr) that melts in your mouth. Open daily 9am-10pm.

ENTERTAINMENT AND SIGHTS

Diana open-air cinema (tel. 25 204), to the left of Lela Tours, lets you experience a unique aspect of Greek movie culture. Sprawled out in a lawn chair on a roof and under the stars, cigarette and beverage in hand, you can view the American movies (subtitled in Greek) you missed six months ago (1500dr, children 1000dr).

The key difference between bars and discos in Poros is that the former are required to shut off their music at 3am while the latter keep up the beat into the wee hours. The majority of these establishments are located about 1km to the right of the ferry landing on the waterfront. Two of the most popular are **Korali** and **Sirocco.** Cover charges of 1000dr may pop up on weekends; expect drinks to cost 1000-1500dr. The **Posidonion** (tel. 22 435) is a hotel, resort, bar, and disco located 2km above the other clubs. Hop in a taxi to get there.

In Poros Town itself, the **archaeological museum** (tel. 23 276) in the middle of the waterfront has some interesting inscriptions and photographs of the ruins at Troizen in the Peloponnese. *(Open Tu-Su 8:30am-3pm. Free.)* A highlight in the tiny building is the enormous marble foot originally from a Roman period statue, now situated at the bottom of the stairs.

■ Galatas Γαλατας

From Poros you can see **Galatas** just across a thin strait. The town on the Peloponnese mainland resembles Poros Town and is less touristy. The farming land surrounding Galatas is beautiful, and the flat, well-paved roads are perfect for bike riding. Boats run between Galatas and Poros every 10 minutes all day (2 min., 80dr). See Poros Town (p. 112), for food and accommodations. When you arrive, turn left (facing inland) to find the pleasant sand beaches of **Plaka** and **Aliki.** Plaka is just off the main road about 2km from Galatas, and is marked by a wall that reads "Poros Marine." A small taverna is the only business near the deep-water beach geared toward families. Aliki is another kilometer down the main road (follow the signs), and is the more lively of the two beaches. Young people play volleyball or paddleball or rent jet skis (3000dr per 30min.) on this narrow strip of sand. Only the water on the ocean side is safe for swimming. A gravel path 1km past the turn-off for Aliki is on the right of the road and leads up through the enormous lemon grove of Lemonodassos. If you are riding a bike, leave it here before going up the dirt road. It is a pleasant but dusty 20-minute walk up to **Kardasi Taverna** (tel. 23 100), where you can find a cool glass of fresh lemonade (350dr), a view of windmills, and 30,000 lemon trees peering onto the sea.

■ Around Poros

The island's main sight is the 18th-century **Monastery of Zoodochos Pigis** (Virgin of the Life-Giving Spring), secreted away in an overgrown glade 6km from Poros Town. *(Open daily 8am-4pm. Guidebook sold at the entrance, 500dr. Modest dress required.)* Monks have been quaffing the monastery's blessed, curative waters since as early as 200 BC. Inside you'll find a spectacular gold-inlaid altarpiece depicting scenes from the lives of Jesus and the Apostles, as well as St. Barbara and St. Nikolas. The monastery, ensured as a safe zone from Turkish disturbance, was the ideal meeting place for Greek naval leaders Miaoulis, Jobazis, and Apostolis, who strategized the uprising of 1821. To get there, take the green bus for a scenic ride from the stop next to the main port in town (20min., every 30min. 7am-11pm, 150dr). Along the route to the monastery is the secluded but popular beach of **Askeli**.

Unless you're a true Greek history aficionado, the main incentive to visit the knee-deep rubble of the 6th-century BC **Temple of Poseidon** is the panoramic view of the gulf. The Athenian statesman Demosthenes took sanctuary from his Macedonian enemies here in 322 BC. Ignoring the temple's tradition of sanctuary, the Macedonians gave him only a few moments reprieve to write a farewell letter to his family. His captors mocked his cowardice as he sat chewing his pen, but the crafty orator died as they waited, having dipped the end of his quill in poison.

HYDRA Υδρα

At first blush, Hydra appears to be a snazzy version of the typical Greek port town. Eighteenth-century stone mansions and red-tiled, whitewashed houses ascend the steep limestone hills surrounding the half-moon harbor. The uneasy knowledge that Hydra is unlike almost anywhere else you've been may come gradually, as the absence of rumbling cars, mopeds, or even bicycles sinks in. On the island you'll find donkeys, wild horses, boats bearing the sign "taxi," and sharply inclined roads and steps. The only automobiles are three garbage trucks. A favorite backdrop for filmmakers, Hydra was a hip artists' colony in the 60s; today, most foreigners to the island today are well-heeled tourists looking for a beautiful spot not to create but to recreate. Nonetheless, the island still has an artsy feel with a relatively large expatriate artist community and a famous art school that sends young palette-laden students into the streets. Follow their lead to the peaceful back alleys where the only disturbance is the occasional bray of a donkey. For wind and waves, set off from Hydra's port in the inexpensive boats that regularly sputter to far-off peaceful beaches.

ORIENTATION AND PRACTICAL INFORMATION

Most tourist agencies and accommodations on Hydra are centered around the pleasant but chic waterfront area accentuated by the clock tower. The crescent-shaped main street wraps around the harbor.

Transportation

Ferries: The **Hydraioniki Ticket Office** (tel. 54 007; fax 52 157) is the first door on the left in the alley to the left of the National Bank. Ferries run to Peiraias (3¼hr., 2 per day, 2300dr), stopping in Poros (1hr., 1000dr), Methana (1½hr., 1000dr), and Aegina (2¼hr., 1600dr). There's also a ferry to Spetses (1hr., 1100dr). From Spetses you can go to Portoheli. Ask about student and child discounts.

Flying Dolphins: Ticket office (tel. 54 053) in front of the landing. Poros (30min., 7 per day, 2050dr); Ermione (30min., 5 per day, 1750dr); Portoheli (45min., 8 per day, 2350dr); Spestes (30min., 7 per day, 2350dr); and Piraeus (1½hr., 13 per day, 4450dr). Open M-F 6:30am-8:20pm, Sa-Su 6:30am-10pm.

Tourist and Financial Services

Tourist Agency: Saitis Tours (tel. 52 184), on the main waterfront. Very friendly staff offers information, **currency exchange,** and a free *Holidays in Hydra* guide. Open daily 9am-9:30pm.

Bank: National Bank (tel. 53 233), on the waterfront. Open M-Thu 8am-2pm and F 8am-1:30pm.

Emergency Services and Communication

Tourist Police: (tel. 52 205), along the main waterfront and left after the clock tower. Open 24hr.

Port Police: (tel. 52 279; fax 53 912), in the big gray building adorned by the Greek flag, left from the dock and up a flight of stairs. Open 24hr.

Pharmacy: (tel. 52 059), inland from tourist police and to the left. Open M-F 8:30am-1:30pm and 5-8:30pm.

Hospital: (tel. 53 150), inland and across the street from the OTE. Ask for the *hoskomio.* Open 24hr. for emergency care.

Post Office: (tel. 52 262), in the alley to the left of the Bank of Greece. There are signs along the quay. Open M-F 7:30am-2pm. **Postal Code:** 18040.

Internet Access: HydraNet (tel. 54 150), left of the pharmacy, then take first right. Call for hours. 500dr to send an email message.

OTE: (tel. 52 199), opposite the tourist police. Open M-F 7:30am-3:10pm. **Telephone Code:** 0298.

ACCOMMODATIONS

Hydra has the most expensive accommodations in the Saronic Gulf. Singles are practically nonexistent and doubles cost at least 7000dr. Finding a place without reservation on summer weekends can be trying.

⊛Sophia Hotel (tel. 52 313), located smack in the center of the wharf. The green iron-railed balconies give the place away. In business for 64 years, and one of the cheaper places in town. Rooms overlook the busy waterfront. Sophia has only 6 rooms, so reservations are recommended. Doubles 7700dr; triples 9900dr.

Pension Elena (tel. 52 464 or 53 290; mobile tel. 094 80 8062), a small hike up the street to the right of the clock tower. A lovely courtyard covered by an ivy-entwined veranda welcomes visitors to 7 rooms, all with private baths, although the baths might not be directly joined to the room. Full kitchen facilities as well as coffee and tea are free to guests. Singles 7000dr; doubles 10,000-12,000dr.

Rooms to Let Glaros (tel. 53 679 or 53 336), in a back alley at the left corner of the waterfront, but get directions at Theano's Tourist Shop by turning left when you get off the ferry. Large and airy rooms, each with private bath and balcony. Doubles 9000dr, 10,000dr on weekends.

To Corali (tel. 52 997; mobile tel. 094 130 182), in the street to the left of the clock tower. Large rooms and new-looking furniture. All rooms have private baths. Singles 7000dr; doubles 10,000dr; triples 12,000dr.

FOOD AND ENTERTAINMENT

Although the food in Hydra tends to be more expensive than elsewhere in Greece, it is possible to find cheap, scrumptious food. Wander in Kamini Square, west of the port, for more affordable meals. The **supermarket** (tel. 52 283) on Miaouli Rd. and **Chioti Bakery** near Glaros (Hydra's signature dessert, *anidthalota,* 100dr per piece) can also help protect your pocketbook.

⊛Christina's Taverna (tel. 53 615), in a corner, 2 blocks from the water, displays no nameplate, and is hard to find. Your best bet is to ask directions, remembering that "Christina" is with a phlegmy "ch," not a "k." Has a seasonal menu, but always serves vegetables (900dr) and pork rolls (1400dr), not to mention both cheese and spinach pies (700dr). Open noon-3pm and 7pm-12:30am.

Restaurant Lulu (tel. 52 018), straight up from the dock on the same road as Sophia's Hotel, is a bargain. Food is served in small but tasty portions. Salads 500dr, *moussaka* 1200dr, veal dishes 1300dr. Open daily 11am-midnight.

Anemoni (tel. 53 136). Bear left up from the OTE. A dream for an after-dinner treat of Greek pastries (300-350dr) and portions are large. Try the fresh homemade ice cream (300dr). Open daily 8am-midnight.

Art Cafe (tel. 52 236), near the ferry landing, is relatively affordable. They offer ice cream (300dr), sandwiches (500dr), and *tyropita* (300dr). Open daily 7am-1am.

To Steki (tel. 53 517). Follow the road to the right of the National Bank and the restaurant will be on your right. Hydra's traditional *taverna* with straight-up dishes like *moussaka* (1200dr) and beef *giouvetsi* (1300dr).

Captain George (tel. 53 660). Despite occasionally rowdy patrons, the restaurant is worthwhile, with warm service and hearty food (lamb chops 1750dr; fried vegetables 600dr). Open daily 6am-1pm and 11pm-3am.

Hydra's clubs all have overpriced cocktails (1500dr), but die-hard vampires won't want to miss the scene. Most clubs are open nightly 8:30pm-6am, but don't bother showing up before 1am. Check out **Karos Music Club** (tel. 52 416) on the way to Kamini or **Disco Heaven** (tel. 52 716)—up the whitewashed stairs—above the right end of the harbor for a more modern disco/dance club atmosphere. Quieter souls sit outside at the **Pirate Bar** (tel. 52 711) on the water and watch the world go by clad in sequined bra tops. Greek music fans head to **Saronicos** (tel. 52 589), underneath Disco Heaven. It stays open late into the night and boasts crazed Greek dancing on tables and the bar (open daily 9pm-6am).

"Like a Bird on a Wire

Like a drunk in a Midnight Choir I have tried in my way to be free..." Leonard Cohen, often called Canada's answer to Bob Dylan, spent several of his most inspired years in the late 60s living on Hydra in a house he bought for $1500. Writing "Bird on a Wire" as he sat contemplating the construction of telephone poles and wires on the technologically primitive island, he reflected on his inability to escape the oppressive weight of modernity. For Cohen, Hydra, an island that even today bans automobiles, was an oasis of pacific beauty, unencumbered by the material and religious weight he associated with life in his native Montréal. Cohen was fascinated by the Aegean—its waters, its colors, and the light reflected from its surface—and attributed to that shifting, magical body the depth and meaning of his poetry. As he said in 1963, "there's something in the light that's honest and philosophical..." Cohen's inspiration cannot be attributed to natural beauty alone, however, and when he described his life on the island, he did not forget the proper acknowledgments, "Thank god for hashish, cognac, and neurotic women who pay their debts with flesh." This combination of isolation and decadence led him to reflect, "I chose a lonely country/broke from love/scorned the fraternity of war/I polished my tongue against the pumice moon." Despite his isolation, Cohen was captivated by Hydra, and explained that he found his muse there, because in Greece, he "just felt good, strong, ready for the task" of writing.

SIGHTS

Despite its name, Hydra's land has always been too arid for lucrative agriculture. With few natural resources and refugee populations from the Peloponnese, Balkans, and Turkey, Hydra's inhabitants turned to managing the exports of others. Hydriots grew prosperous by dodging pirates and naval blockades during the late 18th and early 19th centuries, emerging in 1821 as financial and naval leaders of the revolt against the Ottomans. Without the significant contribution of Hydriot ships and commanders, the Greek fleet might not have been as effective in the War of Independence. The mansions of these merchants turned naval heroes dot the hills behind the harbor. Built by Venetian architects, they are definitely worth a gander. If you're in Hydra

SARONIC GULF

town during the **Miaoulia** (second or third week of June), celebrate the feats of **Admiral Andreas Miaoulis** while watching a bang-up mock battle held in the harbor.

George Koundouriotis was one of the many Hydriot leaders in the Greek War of Independence, and his grandson, **Pavlos Koundouriotis,** became the President of Greece in the 1920s. The Koundouriotis house will soon become a public museum. To get to the house, which is on a hill to the west of the harbor, walk up the narrow alley to the right of the Pirate Bar, which becomes Lignou St. Take the second alley on your right, turn right and go straight and up following the scenic path until you reach a small church in a shady pine grove. Koundouriotis' home is opposite the church. The view of the harbor is superb and explains Hydra's spot in the hearts of artists from around the world. The houses of **Votsis** and **Economou,** two Hydriots who also contributed to the island's naval fame, are closer to the crest of the hill, right on Voulgari St. East of the harbor, in the **Tsamados** mansion, is the **Pilot School** of the Greek Merchant Marine. *(Open variably 8am-10pm. Free.)* Set off by winding, anchor-flanked stairs it features maritime paintings and models.

The **Historical Archives Museum of Hydra** (tel. 52 355 or 54 142) is left of the ferry landing. *(Open Tu-Su 9am-4:30pm. Admission 500dr.)* This newly opened museum houses naval treasures such as tools, wood-carved ship decorations, and guns, as well as a large collection of watercolors of Hydriot sailing ships. Don't miss the heart of Admiral Andreas Miaoulis, embalmed and preserved in a silver and gold urn.

The **Orthodox Church** bears the clock tower that dominates the wharf. *(150dr donation requested, free postcard in return.)* Before serving as a monastery, the structure was a convent, housing 18 nuns from 1648 to 1770. The church is now dedicated to the *kemesis*, or ascension of Mary. Its peaceful courtyard, completely removed from the activity of the waterfront, houses the tomb of Koundouriotis, his statue, and a statue of Miaoulis. Monks who lived in the monastery are also buried here, and their monument, around the corner from the chapel's entrance, is covered with recent mosaics depicting St. Constantine of Hydra, his mother, the monastery of Athos, and the head monks Neophytus and Ienthytus presenting the monastery to Maria. Inside the calming chapel, the beauty of gold and silver icons framed by marble altars matches that of the chandeliers which hang from the ceiling. Smyrnian in origin, the big silver chandelier is over 200 years old and weighs 60kg. Under the ceiling decorated with paintings of Christ *Pantokrator* and the heavenly firmament, you will also find a bishop's throne, a deacon's stand, and a special icon adorned with small charms representing God's miracles. Also interesting are the frescoes at the **Church of St. John** in the Kamina Sq. Modest dress is required at both of these churches.

An arduous 90-minute hike up A. Miaouli St. from the waterfront will take you to the **Monastery of Prophitis Ilias** and, on a lower peak overlooking the harbor, the **Convent of Efpraxia.** *(Both open daily 9am-5pm. Modest dress required.)* While the nuns at Efpraxia do beautiful embroidery work, Ilias is the prettier of the two and the monk may be willing to show you around.

On the right of the harbor are three levels of flat rock perfect for sunbathing; leave your top at home to fit in with the other sunbathers. The beaches on Hydra are rocky ledges a short walk west from town. When the water is calm, small *kaikia* run regularly to pretty **Palamida** and neighboring beaches on the west side. You should take food and drink with you; there's no place to buy it nearby. Another option is to bypass the boats and foot it to **Vlychos,** a small beach village just beyond Kamini. Walking there along the coast and taking the inland path back to the main port will allow you to enjoy the ocean view and get a glimpse of the old country's hills, goats, and stone bridges. **Mandraki** is easier to reach, either by a beautiful 30-minute walk along the water from the east end of town or by a 15-minute boat ride (300dr). While convenient, Mandraki is dirtier and less attractive than the other beaches, and is dominated by a new watersports center.

SPETSES Σπετσες

Ancient *Pitiusa* (Pinetree Island), Spetses is a floating pine forest bordered by white and blue houses. With picturesque villages and rocky beaches, the island has become a playground for wealthy Greeks. A favorite among British tourists, Spetses offers a variety of moods. Cafes, discos, and the waterfront supply excitement, while the quieter interior provides the serenity that prompted John Fowles to write *The Magus* within Spetses' tranquil embrace. An important maritime center throughout the 19th century, Spetses was the first island to take part in the revolution. This distinction is commemorated annually by ceremonies held near Agia Marina.

■ Spetses Town

The vast majority of Spetsiots live in Spetses Town, which is concentrated along the waterfront. Cafes and bars are strung along 4km of water, and little pebble beaches pop up about every 50m. All of this makes the town feel like a round-the-clock beach club. Jet-setters dock their yachts in Spetses's Old Harbor to the left (facing inland) of the ferry quay. You should bear in mind the delicate state of legal affairs: although topless sunbathing is illegal on Spetses, the law is about as well-heeded as the one requiring helmets on mopeds.

ORIENTATION AND PRACTICAL INFORMATION

Restaurants and shops form a 2km line on either side of the port. Facing inland, the old harbor is a 20-minute walk left of the boat landing.

Transportation

Ferries: Depart every afternoon for Peiraias (4½hr., 3200dr); Poros (2hr., 1600dr); Methana (2¼hr., 1900dr); Aegina (3hr., 2400dr), and Hydra (1hr., 1200dr). **Alasia Travel** sells tickets and posts the exact schedule. Small ferries leave for **Kosta** (15min., 4 per day, 130dr); look for signs on the dock.

Flying Dolphin: Ticket office (tel. 73 141), inland from the dock. **Hydrofoils** and **catamarans** to Peiraias (2hr., 5-7 per day, 6200dr); Hydra (30min., 7 per day, 2350dr); Poros (1hr., 5 per day, 3300dr); Aegina (1½hr., 2 per day, 4850dr); Nafplion (1hr., 2 per day, 3160dr); and Monemvassia (2½hr., 2 per day, 4400dr).

Moped and Bike Rental: Nameless shop (tel. 73 074), 50m to the right of the post office. Bikes 2000dr per day, motorbikes 4000dr per day. Open Easter-Nov. daily 9:30am-2pm and 4:30-6pm.

Tourist and Financial Services

Tourist Agencies: Several around the corner on the left side of the boat landing. **Meledon Tourist and Travel Agency** (tel. 74 497 or 74 498; fax 0298 74 167) is open daily 9am-9pm. **Alasia Tours** (tel. 74 098, 74 130, or 74 903; telex 226 087; fax 0298 74 053), next door to Meledon, is the only agency that sells ferry tickets. Open Mar.-Oct. daily 8am-9pm.

Banks: National Bank (tel. 72 286), left of the OTE. Open M-Th 8am-2pm, F 8am-1:30pm. 24hr. **ATM**.

Emergency and Communications

Police: (tel. 73 100). Follow signs to the Spetses Museum; 150m before museum. Also houses **tourist police** (73 744) in basement. Open 24hr.

Port Police: (tel. 72 245), on waterfront 50m left of ferry quay on 2nd floor. Posts ferry and hydrofoil schedules. Open 24hr.

First Aid Station: (tel. 72 472). Open M-F 8:30am-1:30pm; 24hr. for emergencies. Call police for doctor.

Pharmacy: Kapelaki (tel. 72 256), in the square at the end of the street parallel to the waterfront. Behind the port police. Open M-Sa 8:30am-1:30pm and 5:30-10pm, Su 10am-1:30pm and 5:30-9:30pm.
Post Office: (tel. 72 228), left of the ferry dock on the road parallel to waterfront behind Stelios Restaurant. Open M-F 7:30am-2pm. **Postal Code:** 18050.
OTE: (tel. 72 199), on the water to the right side of the Star Hotel. Open M-F 7:30am-10pm. **Telephone Code:** 0298.

ACCOMMODATIONS

Traditionally a weekend playground of wealthy Athenians, Spetses is a relatively expensive island. Hotels are plentiful and very visible, but the larger ones overflow with tour groups. Look for something smaller, like the rooms offered by travel agencies in town. Both **Meledon Tours** and **Alasia Travel** have their own rooms starting at 6000dr for singles and 8000dr for doubles. They can also put you in contact with other *domatia*. Keep in mind that agencies take a percentage from *domatia* owners; you may do better bargaining at the ferry quay. Also consult the tourist police. Bear in mind that prices are as much as 30% higher on weekends, when the island receives most of its tourism.

Hotel Star (tel. 72 214; fax 72 872), about 100m from the ferry dock walking with the water on the right. The cheapest of the high-profile waterfront hotels, rooms have balconies and private baths. Singles 6500dr; doubles 11,000dr.
Hotel Dapia (tel. 72 295), 30m up the narrow road running inland from the kiosk at the quay. Private baths and fridges in airy rooms. Singles 7000dr; doubles 12,000dr.
Villa Christina (tel. 72 218). Comfortable rooms off a flower-filled courtyard. Follow the signs up from the street inland from the OTE, or the manager will pick you up from the ferry if you call ahead. All rooms have private bath with shower. Open Apr.-Oct. In Aug., call ahead. Singles 8000dr; doubles 10000dr. Breakfast 1000dr.
Villa Helena (tel. 73 194). A 20min. walk to the old harbor. Turn inland at the plaza, follow the mosaic path, and climb the winding stairs. Look for a blue door. Has simple rooms with private bath. Doubles 8000dr.

FOOD AND ENTERTAINMENT

On Spetses, food tends to be more expensive than on the mainland, and only at certain places is it worth the price.

Patralis Tavern. Turn right, facing inland, at the ferry quay and follow the sea for about 500m. A favorite restaurant among Athenian visitors to Spetses, the original seafood recipes are scrumptious with unusually subtle flavors. Be sure to try the grilled squid stuffed with seafood rice (2000dr), and the fresh tuna salad. Their home-made *retsina* is a must (800dr per liter). Open M-F 10:30am-4pm and 6:30pm-1am.
Stelios (tel. 73 748), on the waterfront in the opposite direction, has traditional fare. Specialties include veal with pasta cooked in a ceramic pot (1600dr). Entrees and fruit desserts (2000dr). Open daily from noon until late, with a break for siesta.
Politis (tel. 72 248), a coffee and pastry shop on the waterfront before the National Bank, serves full English breakfasts, which include coffee, fruit salad, eggs, bacon, toast, butter and jam (1300dr), outside by the water. Homemade pastries and biscuits baked by the same family for 36 years are a perfect mid-afternoon snack. Delicious *amigdaloto* (3400dr per kg). Open daily 7am-midnight.
Spanos (tel. 22 516), on the walk toward Patralis, is a small bakery that sells fresh loaves (170dr) and crispies (like biscotti, 800dr per kg) to locals. Come early—they sell out fast. Open daily 6am-2pm.

Sports-watching Spetsiots gather for drinks at the **Socrates** bar (beers 500dr, drinks 1000dr). A younger crowd heads to **Mama's,** on the way to the Old Harbour, where drinks are more expensive, but way cooler. Trendy Athenians can be found in bars along the Old Harbor *(Palio Limani)*. Try **Mouraio, Bracera,** or **Naos.** Pulsating **Club**

Fever (tel. 73 718), past the old harbor, hosts popular all-you-can-drink bacchanals (3000dr at the door) every Wednesday, Friday, and Sunday night beginning at 11pm; fill up on unlimited beer, wine, *ouzo,* and Metaxa. Halfway between the old and new harbors, **Spetsa Bar and Cafe** plays an excellent selection of classic rock without catering exclusively to tourists.

For a mellow evening, try one of Spetses's two open-air cinemas. **Ciné Marina,** near the mansion of Laskarina Bouboulina, often shows English language films (1500dr), as does **Ciné Titania** (tel. 72 858). Marina is covered when it rains; Titania is always covered. Both have showings nightly at 9 and 11pm.

SIGHTS

The **Anargyrios and Korgialenios College** is a 25-minute walk from town, with the water on the right, past the Poseidonian Hotel. John Fowles taught here and immortalized the high school and the island in his novel *The Magus.*

In the heart of the town is the **Spetses Museum** (tel. 72 994), housed in the crumbling, late-19th-century mansion of Hadjiyanni Mexi, Spetses' first governor. *(Open Tu-Su 8:30am-2:30pm. Admission 500dr; students 300dr.)* The imposing structure affords a great view of the island and houses coins, costumes, mastheads, folk art, religious artifacts, and a casket containing the remains of Bouboulina. The building itself is worth seeing, with an old island fireplace, stained glass windows, and carved wooden doors. Follow signs to get there. The **House of Laskarina Bouboulina** (tel. 72416) is next to the park near the Dapia. *(Open 10am-1pm and 5-7:30pm. Admission 1000dr; children 300dr. English tours every 30min.)* Mme. Bouboulina was a ship's captain in the Greek War of Independence—this rare woman's heroic exploits are celebrated on Spetses with a mock naval battle, in which a small boat is blown up on the first Saturday after September 8th. The **Monastery of Agios Nikolaos** stands opposite a square of traditional Spetsiot mosaics, just above the old harbor. A memorial plaque commemorates Napoleon's nephew, who was pickled in a barrel of rum which was stored in a monastic cell at Agios Nikolaos from 1827-32. The nuns give free samples of their homemade yogurt. Modest dress is required.

The water in Spetses is clean and clear, and visitors seem eager to jump in at the drop of a hat, despite pesky sea urchins. There are a couple of crowded but pleasant rocky beaches right in town and on the way to the Old Harbor. **Kaiki Beach,** a 1.5km walk from the quay with the water on your right, is just down from the Anargyrios and Korgialenios College. Also close is **Paradise Beach,** past the old harbor. Sand, water sports, and plenty of refreshments make this beach live up to its name. The island's prettiest beach, **Anagyri,** is a bus ride away. Catch the bus in front of Mama's Cafe (3 per day, 750dr round-trip). **Motorboats** leave the harbor for Anagyri as soon as they are full (10am-noon, returning from the beaches at about 4pm, 1500dr). **Sea taxis** cost a fortune and only help save money for groups of eight or more (7500dr for Anagyri). Since only registered cars are allowed on the island, land transportation is provided by horse-drawn carriages, which usually will not go past Kastelli Beach or Agia Marina. Ask at travel agencies for details about **Blueberry Hill Cove** and **Ligoneri.** The bus to these destinations leaves from in front of the Poseidonian Hotel, to the right of the quay.

Peloponnese
Πελοποννησος

We let the features gather, the low skies and mists, the hilltops edged with miles of old walls, fallen battlements, that particular brooding woe of the Peloponnese.

—Don DeLillo

Connected to the mainland only by the narrow isthmus of Corinth, the Peloponnese is a broad, hand-shaped peninsula that unites human achievement and diverse natural beauty. The Peloponnese contains the majority of Greece's best archaeological sites, including Olympia, Mycenae, Messene, Mystra, and Epidavros. It also offers some of Greece's most stunning landscapes, from the barren crags of the Mani to the forested peaks and flower-blanketed pastures of Arcadia. By heavenly happenstance, this rich, beautiful land is sparsely populated and relatively untouristed; a different world from the islands, the Peloponnese is a harbor for true Greek village life.

HIGHLIGHTS OF THE PELOPONNESE

- **Mycenae** (p. 130), with its Lion's Gate, Cyclopean walls, and *tholos* tombs, set the scene for the first dysfunctions of the Western family.
- The theater of **Epidavros** (p. 138) retains perfect acoustics after two millennia of drama.
- Orthodoxy's last resort as the Turks encroached upon Constantinople, **Mystra** (p. 165) is Greece's most vivid Byzantine ghost town.
- The imaginative medievalist will be rewarded at the top of **Corinth's** Acrocorinth (p. 111) with a window into the site's past as a "temple of love."
- Greek city-states across the Mediterranean sent their athletes to **Olympia** (p. 148) to square off in chariots and body oil at the Olympic Games.

CORINTHIA AND ARGOLIS
Κορινθια και Αργολιδα

In the good old days, Argos, a grotesque beast covered with 100 unblinking eyes, stalked vast stretches of the north Peloponnese, subduing unruly satyrs and burly bulls. Today's Corinthia and Argolis hold a lion's share of impressive archaeological sites, but, alas, no roving beasts. Nafplion is an excellent base from which to explore the region, with access to the major dig sites at Mycenae, Corinth, Tiryns, and Epidavros, as well as the smaller sites of Nemea, Isthmia, and Argos's Heraion.

■ New Corinth Κορινθος

New Corinth sits on the Gulf of Corinth just west of the canal that separates the Peloponnese from the Greek mainland. Like its ancient predecessor (7km southwest of the city), New Corinth has been a victim of several recent earthquakes. As a result, the city issues building permits for only the most shake-proof structures, and New Corinth sits low and secure. Since most tourists merely pass through en route to the surrounding ancient sites, the city proper caters primarily to its own citizens. The waterfront is surrounded by open-air restaurants, where Corinthians of all ages gather by evening to stroll and play; the harbor improves the city's appearance considerably.

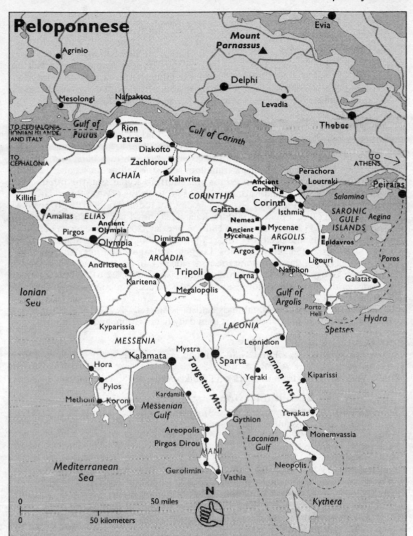

Peloponnese

Evia
Mount Parnassus ▲
Agrinio
Delphi
Mesolongi   Nafpaktos
Levadia
Gulf of Corinth
TO CEPHALONIA
IONIAN ISLANDS
AND ITALY
Gulf of Patras   Rion
Patras
Thebes
TO CEPHALONIA
Diakofto
Zachlorou
TO ATHENS →
ACHAÏA   Kalavrita
Perachora
Loutraki
Peiraias
Killini
CORINTHIA
Ancient Corinth
Salamina
Galatas   Corinth
Amalias   ELIAS
Pirgos   Ancient Olympia
Nemea ■
Isthmia
SARONIC GULF ISLANDS   Aegina
Ancient Mycenae ■   Mycenae ■
Olympia   Dimitsana
ARGOLIS
Epidavros
Tiryns
Argos
ARCADIA
Andritsena
Ligouri
Poros
Karitena   Tripoli
Lerna
Nafplion
Galatas
Megalopolis
Ionian Sea
Kyparissia
Gulf of Argolis
Porto Heli
Hydra
LACONIA
Spetses
MESSENIA
Leonidion
Mystra
Kalamata   Sparta
Kiparissi
Hora   Yeraki
Pylos
Kardamili
Taygetus Mts.
Parnon Mts.
Methoni   Koroni
Messenian Gulf
Yerakas
Areopolis   Gythion
Monemvassia
Pirgos Dirou   MANI
Laconian Gulf
Mediterranean Sea
Gerolimin
Neopolis
Vathia
Kythera

0 ___ 50 miles
0 ___ 50 kilometers
N

ORIENTATION AND PRACTICAL INFORMATION

The easiest way to navigate New Corinth is to find the harbor, turn your back to the sea, and look inland at the perfect grid of the downtown streets. **Ethnikis Antistasis St.** is the main drag running perpendicular to the waterfront. Both **Ermou St.** (to the east) and **Kolokotroni St.** (to the west) are parallel to Ethnikis Antistasis St. All three streets intersect **Damaskinou St.,** the street bordering the harbor. Two blocks inland, between Ethnikis Antistasis St. and Ermou St., is the central park of the city. **Buses** drop off passengers here. The **train station** is a few blocks east of the center of town. To find the waterfront from the station, turn right out of the building onto **Demokratias St.** and then right again onto Damaskinou St.

Transportation

Buses: Ermou and Koliatsou Station (tel. 24 481), on corner of Ermou St. and Koliatsou St. Buses run until 10:10pm, to Athens (1¼hr., 32 per day, 5:30am-9:30pm, 1500dr); Loutraki (20min., 2 per hr., 6am-10pm, 280dr), Isthmia (10min., 5 per day, 220dr); and Nemea (1hr., 7 per day, 800dr). **Ethnikis Antistasis and Aratou Station** (tel. 24 403) is located at the corner of Ethnikis Antistasis St. and Aratou St. inside the cafe Zacharoplasteio with a blue and white striped awning. Buses to Mycenae (40min., 700dr), Argos (1hr., 900dr), and Nafplion (1¼hr., 1100dr) leave at 7am and every hr. 8:30am-9:30pm. Note that the bus to Mycenae drops passengers at Fichtia, a 1.5km walk from the site. To catch a bus to Sparta and other Peloponnesian points south, take the Loutraki bus to the Corinth Canal and pick up buses from Athens to Sparta, Kalamata, Koroni, and Tripoli.

Trains: Station (tel. 22 523) on Demokratias St. Trains run to Athens (2hr., 15 per day, 800dr) via Isthmia. Two major train lines serve the Peloponnese: one along the northern coast from Corinth to Pirgos and south to Kyparissia; the other south from Corinth to Tripoli and Kalamata. Trains go to Patras (2½hr., 8 per day, 8am-midnight, 1000dr); Pirgos (4½hr., 8 per day, 1440dr); Argos (1hr., 6 per day, 510dr); Tripoli (2hr., 4 per day, 900dr); Kalamata (5hr., 4 per day, 1640dr); Lefktro (3hr., 1 per day, 1120dr); Kyparissia (5hr., 5 per day, 2050dr); Kalavryta (1½hr., 5 per day, 1200dr); and Diakofto (1hr., 13 per day, 600dr). Express trains can cost 400-1000dr extra. 25% off round-trips. **Luggage storage** 270dr per piece per day.

Taxis: (tel. 22 361 or 24 844), along the park side of Ethnikis Antistasis St.

Car Rental: Gregoris Lagos, 42 Ethnikis Antistasis St. (tel. 22 617). Prices start at 6500dr per day plus 2000dr for insurance and 18% tax. Minimum age 21. Open M-Sa 8am-1:30pm and 4-9pm.

Moped Rental: Liberopoulos, Ethnikis Antistasis St. (tel. 72 937), across the street from the car rental. 5000dr per day. Open daily 8am-1:30pm and 5-8:30pm.

Tourist and Financial Services

Banks: National Bank, 7 Ethnikis St., 1 block up from the water, offers **currency exchange** and a 24hr. **ATM.**

Public Toilets: Across from the park on Ethnikis Antistasis St. Free. Open 24hr.

Emergency and Communications

Tourist Police: 51 Ermou St. (tel. 23 282), upstairs, who can supply maps and brochures as well as assistance. English-speaking. Open M-Sa 8am-3pm and 5-8pm.

Police: 51 Ermou St. (tel. 100), facing the park. Open 24hr.

Pharmacy: 23 Ethnikis Anastasis St. (tel. 22 515). Open M-F 8am-1:30pm. Many others on Koliatsou St.

Hospital: (tel. 25 711), on Athinaion St. Cross the train tracks and turn left. It's quite a walk, so use a cab or call for an ambulance in an emergency. Open 24hr.

Post Office: (tel. 22 015), 35 Adimantou St., borders the park on the end farthest from the water. Open M-F 7:30am-2pm. **Postal Code:** 20100.

OTE: 32 Kolokotroni St. (tel. 22 111). Open daily 7am-10pm, collect calls M-F 7am-10pm. **Telephone Code:** 0741.

ACCOMMODATIONS

Corinth's hotels are either on Ethnikis Antistasis St. or along the waterfront on Damaskinou St. Prices may rise 15% in the summer.

🏅**Hotel Acti,** 3 Ethnikis Antistasis St. (tel. 23 337), near the waterfront. The best deal in town, this hotel is friendlier than it may seem at first. Rooms are tiny but virtually spotless. A shared balcony at the end of the hall has a beautiful view of the water. Singles 3500dr; doubles 7000dr.

Hotel Apollon, 18 Pirinis St. (tel. 225 87), off Damaskimou St. near the train station, has clean, wood-paneled rooms with private bath. Some also have TV and A/C for an extra price. Singles 4000dr; doubles 8000dr; triples 9000dr.

Ephira Hotel, 52 Ethnikis Antistasis St. (tel. 24 021; fax 24 514), two blocks inland from the park. Spacious rooms, A/C, TVs, private baths, and daily maid service. It's the biggest hotel (45 rooms), and one of the more posh. Continental breakfast 1000dr. Singles 8000dr; doubles 11,000dr; triples 13,000dr.

Corinth's two beachfront **campgrounds** are pleasant and inexpensive alternatives to the city's hotels. To get to them, catch a bus (every 30min., 210dr) on Kollatsou St. near Kolokotroni. Ask to be let out when you see the campground signs. **Camping Korinth Beach** (tel. 27 920; 1100dr per person, 600dr per tent) is just out of town and **Blue Dolphin** (tel. 25 766) is 3km farther, with campsites on the beach (1300dr per person; 850dr per small tent; 1000dr per large tent; 700dr per car; electricity 800dr; tents rented for 2000dr). Catching a bus back to New Corinth is tricky.

FOOD

Restaurants and cafes come alive in downtown Corinth, especially after 9pm. Most either aim for atmosphere or good food—few can manage both. Speed also seems to be a culinary virtue in Corinth; fast food joints are *de rigeur,* and waiters scurry even at the sit-down *tavernas.*

24 Oro, 19 Agios Nicholou St. (tel. 71 912), on the waterfront, is a traditional Greek *taverna* of uncommon quality and service. They serve the classic staples, prepared with unusually fresh ingredients, less fat, and more attention to detail. Cucumber and tomato salad (700dr), *pastitsio* (300dr), *orso* in clay bowl (1600dr).

Aspetto di Pasta, 34 Damaskinou St. (tel. 804 45), on the waterfront square, serves a greater selection of pizzas and pastas than most Italian restaurants. It is an excellent break from *taverna* food. Spaghetti 1100-1800dr, pizza 1700-2500dr.

Kanita (tel. 28 834) is one of the best of the harbor eateries. Its indoor *taverna* on Damaskinou is charming, and across the street is additional outdoor seating under a tent—be sure to sit under the right one, as all of the restaurants claim waterfront space and the tables look the same. The tasty *tzatziki* (600dr) and fresh fish (1300dr) are both excellent. Open 24hr.

Fast Food (tel. 85 335), on Ethnikis Antistasis St., features fries, *gyros* (1500dr), *souvlaki* (200dr), and fluorescent lights. Open 24hr.

ENTERTAINMENT

During the day New Corinth is a serious, bustling place with little to offer the traveler except a bus to its neighboring ruins. By 10pm, however, the city has let down its hair. Motorcycle-mounted teens pop up out of nowhere and head immediately west of the city to **Kalami Beach.** A curious visitor can reach Kalami even without a motorcycle: walk four blocks past the park along Ethnikis Anistasis St., and any right turn will take you there (about ten blocks). Instead of walking the 1.5km alone at night, women may prefer to get a taxi from the park (300dr). Just tell the driver *"Thalisa"* (the sea). There may not be any taxis waiting to take you back to town, but you can ask any restaurant owner to call you one (about 500dr).

Kalami's strip has something for everyone. Behind the street and looking out at the dark water and sparkling lights of Loutraki are a line of happening cafes and clubs. Each tries to outdo the others with the volume of its bass beat and the span of its palm umbrellas. **La Plaza's** decor is based on green stained wood and **Montezuma's** on totem poles and cave paintings. Both offer beer (700dr), a spot to watch the motorcycles whiz by, and a DJ to mix your favorite 80s hits into techno dance songs.

On the beach side of the main drag humbler cafes like the **Kafeteria** draw family crowds. Children foozle around as adults looking out on the ocean sip coffee (300dr) and beer (450dr). **Pizza Ami** is also out of earshot of the raucous bars; families share pizza, couples share silent gazes and stroll down to the pebbly beach.

If you'd rather stay downtown, an alternative to the beach is car-free **Theotke St.** Walking away from the harbor on Ethnikis Antistasis St., turn right half way down the second block. Past the intersection with Kolokotroni St., the street becomes filled with outdoor tables from the numerous cafes, pubs, and small restaurants that line this lively block. The trendy **Aenaon Club** (tel. 21 773), where beer costs 700dr and you can sit and talk all night, is typical of these establishments. **Le Creperie** stands apart amidst the uniformity, serving cooked-to-order crepes with your choice of filling (600dr for chocolate filling, 700dr for meat; open daily 9am-early morning).

■ Ancient Corinth Αρχαια Κορινθος

History

Strategically based on the isthmus between the Corinthian and Saronic Gulfs, Corinth was a powerful commercial center and one of the most influential cities in ancient Greece. Corinth reached the apex of its power in the 5th century BC and allied with Sparta, its neighbor to the south, against the naval strength of Athens. This power struggle resulted in the Peloponnesian Wars. Ancient Corinth was greatly weakened in the fighting, but Sparta became the leading city in Greece. Eventually Corinth was conquered by the Romans, who sacked the city in 146 BC, destroying buildings and ferreting art and other precious objects back to Rome. Corinth remained deserted until Julius Caesar rebuilt it in 44 BC.

Museum

Tel. 31 207. Museum and site open daily 8am-8pm; in winter 8am-5pm. Admission to both 1200dr; students 600dr; free on Sunday.

The remains of the ancient city stand at the base of the **Acrocorinth,** where the **Ministry of Culture Archaeological Museum** and **archaeological site** are located. Columns, metopes, and pediments lie in fascinating chaos in the museum's courtyard. Facing the entrance of the museum, the Corinthian columns on your left are the facade of a Roman shrine. If you want a good guide, pick up Nikos Papahatzis' *Ancient Corinth* at the museum entrance (2200dr). The museum houses a wonderful collection of statues, well-preserved mosaics, tiny clay figurines, and pottery that traces Corinth's history through Greek, Roman, and Byzantine rule. The Roman frescoes and mosaics are from the same period as Pompeii, and the collection of pottery follows the evolution of Greece from neolithic to Byzantine times. The museum's collections of sarcophagi (one with a skeleton under glass) and headless statues in the green, open-air courtyard are morbidly impressive. Especially odd are the votive offerings from the sick to the god of medicine, which include misshapen phalluses, sore ears, and wart-afflicted hands.

Touring Corinth

As you exit the museum, down the stairs to your left is the archaeological site most notable for the few reconstructed columns of the 6th century BC **Temple of Apollo.** Behind the museum is the **Fountain of Glauke,** named after Jason's second wife, who drowned while trying to douse the flames that sprouted from an enchanted shirt given to her by Jason's first wife, Medea. If you stand at the Temple of Apollo and face the mountainous Acrocorinth, the remains of the forum—the center of Roman civil life—lie in front of you. Walk down the middle of the row of central shops and you'll see the **Julian Basilica.** To the left, near the exit at the edge of the site farthest from the museum, a broad stone stairway descends into the **Peirene Fountain,** perhaps the most impressive structure on the site. Although smoothed and patinated by the water that still flows today, the columns and fresco-covered tunnels inside the fountain have survived the centuries unharmed by human hands. The ancients believed that winged Pegasus was drinking here when he was captured by Bellerophon. Just past the fountain is the **Perivolos of Apollo,** an open-air court surrounded by columns. Near the Perivolos is the **public latrine.** On the uphill edge of the site on the side farthest from the museum, what look like shabby toolsheds actually cover the mosaic floors of a Roman villa. You will have to peer at them through rusted chain link fence, as entry is not permitted.

Getting to the **fortress** at the top of Acrocorinth is a tough 90-minute walk. Alternatively, you can call a taxi (tel. 31 464), which will drive you to the site and wait for an hour (2500dr). The summit originally held a **Temple to Aphrodite,** which was served by "sacred courtesans" who initiated free-wheeling disciples into the "mysteries of love." The surprisingly intact remains are a medievalist's fantasy. Relatively empty, the fortress contains acres of towers, mosques, gates, and walls.

■ Near Corinth

Isthmia

Take the bus from Corinth heading toward Isthmia, and ask to be let out at the museum, a green building up and on the right of the road from the bus stop. Open Tu-Sa 8:45am-7pm; Su and off-season 9:30am-2:30pm. Admission 500dr, students 300dr, EU students free.

Like Olympia, Isthmia was the site of prestigious tetra-annual athletic contests. The remains of the ancient complex are complemented by an excellent museum. The carefully diagrammed exhibits display finds from the Temple of Poseidon and the sites of the Isthmian games. Of particular interest are the glass *opus sectile* (mosaic panels), discovered at nearby Kenchreai that managed to survive the earthquake of 375. The entrance to the **ruins** lies to the right of the museum. All that remains of the **Temple of Poseidon** is its despoiled foundation. The **theater** is below and farther to the right of the temple. **Cult caves,** where many people enjoyed dinner and entertainment during the Archaic Period, lie above the theater.

Nemea

The ruins of Ancient Nemea are 4km from Modern Nemea; coming by bus from Corinth, ask to be let off at the ancient site (1hr., 800dr). Museum open Tu-Su 8:30am-7pm; off season Tu-Sa 8:30am-3pm. Admission 500dr, students 300dr, EU students free.

Pausanias wrote in his accounts of his second-century travels: "Here is a temple of Nemean Zeus worth seeing although the roof has fallen in and the cult statue is missing." Although still worth a gander, the temple has dwindled to three columns. The walkway takes you past a wall built around a glass-encased grave, complete with skeleton. Try not to miss the well-preserved **baths.** The **stadium** is 500m down the road to Corinth. The **museum** on the site (tel. (0746) 22 739) has excellent explanatory notes in English, some artifacts, and several reconstructions of the site.

■ Loutraki Λουτρακι

The name may seem familiar, as much of the bottled water (half liter 100dr) you will be clutching during your travels gushes from Loutraki's sweet wells; however, Loutraki hardly springs to mind as an ideal Mediterranean vacation spot. A clean little city of uniform architecture, Loutraki rests a short bus ride across the crescent-shaped bay from Corinth (20min. bus ride, 240dr). Stroll along the stone boardwalk that flanks the body-blanketed beach, shadowed by the **Yerania Mountains.** The main street is El. Venizelou St., which runs parallel to the water, curves at the port, and becomes Georgiou Lekka St.

ORIENTATION AND PRACTICAL INFORMATION To get to Loutraki from Isthmia, cross the canal bridge; the bus stop is next to a railroad station sign. Stay on the bus until the last stop, a triangular road island where **El. Venizelou St.** meets Periandou St. and Eth. Antistasis St. English-speaking **tourist police** (tel. 65 678) respond to the needs of travelers (open daily 9am-9pm). Day boat excursions are available at the dock past the park. **Albona Cruises** sail to Lake Vouliagmeni, the "Blue Lake" (Tu-Th, 3000dr). Cruises down the Corinth Canal leave Sundays at 10am and Thursdays at 5pm (4500dr). To get to the **National Bank,** 25 Martiou Sq. (tel./fax 219 37), bear left where the road forks (open M-Th 8:30am-2pm, F 8:30am-1:30pm). At 10 El. Venizelou St., you'll find the **OTE** (open M-F 7:30am-3:10pm). **Buses** (tel. 22 262) from Loutraki go to Athens (8 per day, 6am-7:30pm, 1500dr, round-trip 2600dr), Corinth (20min., 2 per hr. 5:30am-10:30pm, 280dr); Perachora (20min., 9 per day 6am-8pm, 220dr); and Vouliagmeni (45min., July-Aug. departs 10am, returns 1pm, 700dr).

For **moped rentals,** make a right at the post office and turn at the second corner on the left to reach **Andreas** (tel. 23 812; Vespas 4000-5200dr, bikes 1000dr). Follow E. Venizelou St. (which changes to G. Lekka St.) toward the mountains. Periandrou St., the first side street on the right across from the bus station's road island, is home to

Laundry Self-Service (tel. 63 854), which provides wash (1200dr), wash and dry (1600dr), and ironing (open M-Tu 8:30am-1:30pm, W-Sa 8:30am-1pm and 6-9pm). On the left, the densely congregated trees guard a **public fountain** that spouts Loutraki water. For the **health center**, dial 63 444. The center itself is roughly 5km from the center of town. To reach it, walk five blocks up from El. Venizelou St., turn right, and continue along that road. There is a **pharmacy** at 21 El. Venizelou St. (tel. 21 787), and an outdoor movie theater opposite the tennis courts (summer only). From the bus station, walk down El. Venizelou Street with the water to your left, and you'll reach the **post office** at #4 28th Octovriou St., one block down to the right (open M-F 7:30am-2pm). **Police** (tel. 63 000 or 22 258) keep the peace across the street from the OTE. The **Postal code** is 20300. The **Telephone code** is 0744.

ACCOMMODATIONS There are only a few budget hotels in Loutraki. **Hotel Brettagne**, 28 G. Lekka St. (tel. 22 349), has a kindly, manager who speaks some English. Rooms and baths sparkle, and every floor has a refrigerator (singles 5000dr; doubles 8500dr; triples 11,000dr). To find **Pension Marko** (tel. 63 542), go left from the bus station (facing the water) and take your second right onto L. Kalsoni St. Marko. All rooms have balcony and bath (singles 6000dr; doubles 8000dr). **Camping** is available at Lake Vouliagmeni, accessible by bus.

FOOD AND ENTERTAINMENT The best food is what's closest at hand—what's closest in Loutraki is fish, and that's what you will find strung along the 2km of white-tiled waterfront walkway. (Vegetarians may have to work the back streets and markets for flesh-free options.) **Horiatiki Taverna**, 70 El. Venizelou St. (tel. 22 228), has been serving fruits and stellar fish dishes for over 30 years. This *taverna's* staff (as its card suggests) are "specialists in fish." An elegant garden seating area and the freshest seafood draw large French and German crowds. **Kazino's** (tel. 22 332), on the waterfront, has an English menu and inexpensive fare including Greek salads (700dr) and stuffed tomatoes (1000dr; open daily 7am-2am). **Canadian Steak House** (tel. 23 993) is on the waterfront next to Kazino's—cute place, inaccurate name. From schnitzel (2000dr) to *souvlaki* (1900dr), carnivores of all stripes make the trek to the Steak House for atmosphere and copious protein (open 10am-4pm and 6pm-late).

Nightlife consists of a ritual vascillation between eating and dancing. Waterfront restaurants swell in summer until midnight and beyond. Taxis lorry anxious feet to the discos on the fringe of the city. The flagship disco in Loutraki is undoubtedly **Baby-O**. Precariously placed between a vast and lonely looking bottling company and a shrub-covered wasteland, Baby-O caters to a weekend crowd of 1000 to 1500 people, and is the only disco open year-round in the Corinth-Loutraki area. **Biblos** and **Club Bazaar** are both in town and near the waterfront.

SIGHTS The majority of Greek tourists go to Loutraki for the healing waters. Whirlpool baths and hydromassage are offered at the **Hydrotherapy Thermal Spa**, 26-G. Lekka St. (tel. 22 215). *(Open M-Sa 8am-1pm.)* The spa will cure "rheumoatoarthritic, spondycarthritic" and "chronic gynecological diseases," or so the bilingual sign printed on the door promises. The waterfalls, on the edge of town away from Corinth, merit a visit. *(Open daily 10am-3am.)* They are theme-park-like in construction but less impressive, although as pleasant to listen to as their cousins in nature. Hike around the waterfalls to the top, where the water funnels out from a series of fountains at the base of the cliff. You will see rows of tables along the terraced sides of the falls belonging to the **cafe** that sits below.

■ Mycenae Μυκηνες

Mycenae's hazy origins, its interactions with other Near Eastern civilizations, and its subsequent decline have long puzzled historians. The site was settled as early as 2700 BC by tribes from the Cyclades who were colonizing the mainland; for centuries in the second millennium BC, major Greek cities such as Mycenae and Pylos were under the domination of the Minoan capital Knossos. Yet after the abrupt collapse of

Minoan civilization in the mid-15th century BC due to a sudden cataclysm—perhaps an earthquake or another natural disaster—Mycenae surged to the head of the Greek world, giving its name to an entire period of prosperous Greek civilization. Under its most powerful city, Mycenae, Greek culture flourished for the next several hundred years until a warlike and barbarian Indo-European population called the Dorians swept down from the north, burning and looting as they went. The so-called Mycenaean period came to an end as Greece slipped into a dark age under the Dorians; the old site of Mycenae was inhabited into the Roman period but in Byzantine times was swallowed up by earth and forgotten. Mycenae's history resumes with its discovery by European antiquarians and treasure hunters in the 18th and 19th centuries.

Having been uncovered by successive excavations that began with the notorious Schliemann and continue today, Mycenae is now one of the most touristed archaeological sites in Greece. In summer, mobs stampede to the famed Lion's Gate and Tomb of Agamemnon. Visit early in the morning or late in the afternoon to avoid the rush. Most travelers make Mycenae a daytrip from Athens, Argos, or Nafplion. Perhaps the best plan is to make it a daytrip from Nafplion, a pleasant and historical city that gives convenient access to the sights of the Argolid, including Argos, Epidavros, and Mycenae; however, it is possible to spend the night in the charming modern village, which is surprisingly peaceful since most bus tours drive straight through it.

Married with Children

Anyone who thinks that his or hers is a dysfunctional family should thank the gods that their problems are not of the epic proportions that bloodied the mythology of Mycenae. Atreus, Mycenae's first chosen ruler, brought the fabled curse upon himself and his progeny when he cooked his nieces and nephews for dinner and served them to his hated brother, Theytes. This culinary atrocity provoked the wrath of the gods, and out of sympathy for Theytes, who had just digested his own children, the Olympians put a curse on the House of Atreus. A leader of the Greek army in the Trojan War, Agamemnon decided to sacrifice his daughter Iphagenia to speed their journey across the Aegean. Years later when he returned to Mycenae a war hero, his wife Clytemnestra had not forgiven his murdering their daughter and killed him in his bath. Agamemnon's son Orestes later plotted with his sister Elektra to avenge the murder of their father by slaying their mother, and was haunted by the Furies, who torment those who kill their own family. Athena finally pardoned Orestes and lifted the curse from the House of Atreus.

ORIENTATION AND PRACTICAL INFORMATION The only direct **buses** to Mycenae are from Nafplion (40min., 4 per day, 550dr) and Argos (30min., 4 per day, 260dr). A bus from Athens (2½hr., 15 per day, 1750dr) stops at Fihtia, 1.5km away. From Fihtia, the site is located on the Corinth-Argos road; simply follow the sign to Mycenae. Four buses make the return trip to Nafplion. They stop in the town of Mycenae (in front of the Hotel Belle Hellene) and at the site (a 20-minute walk from the town). **Trains** (3 per day) run from Athens via Corinth to Fihtia. Although Mycenae has no banks, the **post office** has **currency exchange** (open Apr.-Oct. M-F 9am-3:15pm). **Postal code:** 21200. **Telephone code:** 0751.

ACCOMMODATIONS Mycenae has few cheap accommodations; if campgrounds aren't your thing, seek out private rooms. You may want to browse the signs off the main road, because prices vary considerably. The **Belle Helene Hotel** (tel. 76 225) serves as a bus stop on the main road. This quiet hotel opened its doors in 1862, and hosted Heinrich Schliemann and his excavating team for two years in the 1870s. If it is available, ask for room #3, Schliemann's room, with an iron bed and period furniture. Other rooms are modern, clean, and carpeted. In the lobby you can read framed photocopies of the Belle Helene's guest book, which features the signatures of Virginia Woolf, Claude Debussy, and Alan Ginsberg (singles 6000dr; doubles 7000dr; triples 10,000dr). **Camping Mykines** (tel. 76 121; fax 76 247), is shaded by pine trees in the middle of town. Popular because of the owner's reputation for hospitality, it is an ideal camping spot. The campsites are close to an inexpensive outdoor restaurant where the owners prepare homemade food for campers (Greek salad 800dr). A washing machine is available, and hot showers are included (1300dr per person; car 900dr; small tent 1000dr; large tent 1200dr).

FOOD A few good restaurants exist among the multitude built solely to feed the bus-borne masses. **Point Restaurant and Bar** (tel. 76 096), 50m down the street from the Belle Helene, is unrivaled in the quality of its food. Chicken *souvlaki* (1500dr) and oven-baked spaghetti (1350dr) are not uncommon dishes, but here they are raised to the level of exceptional. **Spiros Restaurant and Taverna** (tel. 76 115), just across the street from Point, is the least expensive option, yet quality and serving size are hardly compromised (Greek salad 880dr, omelettes 650-950dr, grilled meats from 1300dr). **Restaurant/Taverna Micinaiko** (tel. 76 245), farther down the hill, has nice folks and tasty food (Greek salad 900dr, chicken 1300dr, squid 1400dr).

■ Ancient Mycenae

Mycenae, after one turns the last bend, suddenly folds up into a menacing crouch, grim, defiant, impenetrable.

—Henry Miller

History

The excavated site of ancient Mycenae (see p. 50) sits atop a rocky knoll between Mt. Agios Elias to the north and Mt. Zara to the south, surrounded by tremendous 13m-high, 10m thick walls, called "Cyclopean" by the ancients. (They believed that the city's founders, Perseus and his descendants, could have lifted the stones only with the help of the Cyclopes, one-eyed giants with superhuman strength. Moderns still marvel at what it must have taken to move the stones into place.) The fortified city is the centerpiece of the ruins. Several *tholos* (beehive tombs), most notably the so-called treasury of Atreus, are just outside the walls. The bulk of the ruins standing today date from 1280 BC, when the city was the center of the far-flung Mycenaean civilization. The remarkable artifacts that the site yielded, among the most celebrated archaeological discoveries in modern history, are on display at the national museum in Athens. A large museum that will show more of what has been found is being built at the site but is still several years from completion.

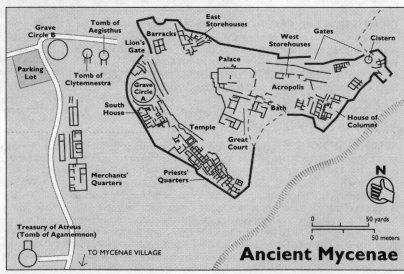

Ancient Mycenae

German businessman, classicist, and amateur archaeologist **Heinrich Schliemann** uncovered Mycenae in 1874, having located the site by following clues in the writings of Homer and later Greek dramatists. Schliemann began digging just inside the citadel walls at the spot where several ancient authors indicated the royal graves should be located. Discovering 15 skeletons "literally covered with gold and jewels," Schliemann bedecked his new 17-year-old Greek wife with the baubles and had her pose for photographs. Schliemann believed he had unearthed the skeletons of Agamemnon and his followers. He sent a telegram to the Greek king that read, "Have gazed on face of Agamemnon." Moments after he removed its mask, the "face" underneath disintegrated. Modern archaeologists shudder at the thought of such high-spirited, incautious excavations, and with modern precision have dated the tombs to four centuries before the Trojan War.

Touring Mycenae

Open *Apr.-Sept. 8am-10pm; Oct.-Mar. 8am-5pm.* **Admission** *1500dr, students 800dr; EU students free. Keep your ticket for entry into Agamemnon's Tomb after the main site or you will pay twice. Bring a flashlight. Many* **guidebooks** *are available at the entrance to the site in Greek, English, German, and French: the book by S. E. Iakovidis, covering both Mycenae and Epidavros, includes a map and is well worth 2500dr; the book by George E. Mylonas, director of the excavation, takes a more scholarly approach (1700dr). If you want information on other ruins, buy the larger guide, The Peloponnese, by E. Karpodini-Dimitriadi (3000dr).*

The bus will take you to the end of the asphalt road; the ruins are on your right. The gate and the **Cyclopean Walls** of the upper citadel date from the 13th century BC. The imposing **Lion's Gate,** with two lions carved in relief above the lintel, is the portal into the ancient city. These lions were symbols of the house of Atreus and their heads (now missing) had eyes of precious gems. Schliemann found most of his artifacts (now on display in Athens) in **Grave Circle A.** These 16th-century BC shaft graves were originally located outside the city walls. The **barracks** are up the stairs to your left immediately after the gate.

The ruins on the hillside are the remnants of various homes, businesses, and shrines. The **palace** and the **royal apartments** are at the highest part of the citadel on the right. The open spaces here include guard rooms, private areas, and more extensive public rooms. Look for the **megaron,** or royal chamber; it has a round hearth surrounded by the bases of four pillars. To the left of the citadel sit the remaining stones of a Hellenistic **Temple of Athena.** At the far end of the city, between the palace and the **postern gate,** is the underground **cistern,** which offers solitude and complete darkness. Be careful, as the steps are worn and slippery.

Follow the asphalt road 150m back toward the town of Mycenae to the **Treasury of Atreus** (also called the Tomb of Agamemnon; tel. 76 585), the largest and most impressive *tholos* (beehive tomb). The tomb of Agamemnon can be reached through a 40m passage cut into the hillside. As you walk into the *tholos,* look up at the 120-ton lintel stones above you. The famous tomb was found empty, but is believed to have held valuables that were spirited away by thieves. To the left on the walk down to the tomb from the main site are pathways to two often overlooked *tholoi,* the **tomb of Aegistheus** and the more interesting **tomb of Clytemnestra.** Hold tight to that flashlight; these *tholoi* are especially dark inside.

■ Argos Αργος

According to Homer, Argos was the kingdom of the hero Diomedes and claimed the allegiance of Mycenae's powerful King Agamemnon. Invading Dorians captured Argos in the 12th century BC, as they did all the other Mycenaean centers in Greece, and then used it as their base for controlling the Argolid Peninsula. Through the 7th century BC, Argos remained the most powerful state in the Peloponnese, defeating even its rival Sparta: in the famous 494 BC battle, Kleomenes and the Spartans nearly defeated Argos but failed to penetrate the city walls.

Argos claims to be the oldest continuously inhabited city in Europe, and archaeology reveals that, indeed, the city dates back to prehistoric times. However, like many other ancient cities in Greece, each period largely obliterated or buried the remains of the previous era. The modern city is no exception, as it is built almost entirely on top of every previous layer of inhabitation; it has grown rapidly, despite a healthy dose of archaeological red tape. Urban and dusty, and too far from the shore to catch any sea breezes, modern Argos has little to offer beyond what remains of its ancient incarnation. The museum is excellent and the ruins of the ancient theater, *agora*, and Roman baths on the edge of town are worth seeing. Every Wednesday and Saturday the city hosts the largest **open-air market** in the Peloponnese in an empty square across from the museum. Evening festivals punctuate the summer months in the city's **theater,** drawing crowds from Athens and beyond (call 62 143 for details).

ORIENTATION AND PRACTICAL INFORMATION

Most amenities, hotels, and restaurants can be found in or around Argos's main square. The large church of **St. Peter** marks the square, and behind the church, a small shady park extends towards the train station. Downtown Argos has few landmarks and navigation can be difficult beyond the square. Your best bet is to pick up one of the laminated maps that the archaeological museum provides for free.

Transportation

Buses: There are two stations. The **Argolida** station (tel. 66 300) is on Kapodistriou St. very near the square. From here buses go to Athens (2½hr., 1 per hr., 2210dr); Nafplion (20min., 2 per hr., 250dr); Nemea (1hr., 2 per day, 550dr); Mycenae (30min., 4 per day, 280dr); and Prosimni (30min., 2 per day, 280dr). There is also the **Arcadia-Laconia Station,** 24 Feidonos St. (tel. 67 157). From the square, follow Vas. Olgas St. two blocks past the museum, turn left, and walk past the Agricultural Bank. Buses leave for Tripoli (1hr., 5 per day, 1050dr). From Tripoli you can make connections to Sparta, Olympia, Andritsena, Gythion, and Monemvassia.

Trains: The **station** (tel. 67 212) is 1km from the main square. To get there from the main square, head down Nikitara St. past the OTE and follow the signs to Nafplion from the five-point intersection. At the next big intersection follow the sign to Athens and you'll see it at the end of the street. Five trains per day go to Athens (3hr., 1040dr) and Corinth (1hr., 510dr). Trains also go to Tripoli (1hr., 600dr); Kalamata (4hr., 4 per day, 1280dr); Mycenae (10min., 105dr); and Nemea (20min., 210dr).

Tourist and Financial Services

Bank: National Bank (tel. 29 911), on Nikitara St., off the square behind the church. **Currency exchange** and **ATM.** Open M-Th 8am-2pm and F 8am-1:30pm.

Emergency and Communications

Hospital: (tel. 24 455) North of town on Corinth St., opposite St. Nicholas Church. Open 24hr.

Police: (tel. 67 222) On the corner of Inaxou and Papaoikonomou St. Head out from Vas. Sofias St. English spoken. Open 24hr.

Post Office: (tel. 68 066) Follow the signs from Hotel Telesilla. Open M-F 7:30am-2pm. **Postal Code:** 21200.

OTE: 8 Nikitara St. (tel. 67 599). Facing the park from the main square, take the street running on the park's left side past the National Bank and around the bend to the right—it's on the right. Open daily 7am-9pm. **Telephone Code:** 0751.

ACCOMMODATIONS

Argos has few accommodations. Since the sights can be seen in half a day, it's advisable to make Argos a daytrip from Nafplion or, if you want to camp, from Mycenae.

Hotel Apollon, 13 Papaflessa St. (tel. 68 065). Take Nikitara St. off the square, then take the road running by Mickey's. It's on the left; follow the signs. Sweet yellow

and white rooms with balconies. Some with TV and private bath. Singles 4300dr, with bath and TV 5500; doubles 6800dr, 7500dr with bath; triples 8000-9000dr.
Hotel Palladion, 5 Vas. Sophias St., on the side of the square opposite the museum, has clean modern rooms with private baths, A/C, and TV. Singles 6000dr; doubles 8000dr; triples 10,000dr.

FOOD AND ENTERTAINMENT

The food is discouragingly bad in Argos, so you might want to eat something quickly and get it over with. If, however, you're willing to shell out for overpriced cafe fare, you can sit in the air-conditioning indefinitely.

Restaurant Egli (tel. 67 266), in the corner of the square facing the church next to the Hotel Mycenae, has the most *taverna*-like menu of any establishment in the area. Pizza 1500dr, spaghetti 1000dr, calamari 1000dr.
Retro Pub and Restaurant, next to the Hotel Mycenae, has the shockingly discordant decorating theme of chrome on the inside and wicker outside. They serve spaghetti (1300dr), Greek salads (1000dr), and pizzas (1600dr).
York Cafe, next to the Telesilla Hotel on the corner of Danaou St. and the square, is by far the newest and best decorated of the town's cafes. Wood paneling and exposed red brick give a turn-of-the-century feel. Tables inside and out. Espresso 500dr, *frappé* 550dr, cappuccino 650dr.
Cafe Croissant (tel. 63 013), past the archaeological museum, is the place for dessert or an afternoon snack. Ice cream 180dr, pastries 250dr.

SIGHTS

Argos' superb **Archaeological Museum** (tel. 68 819) is off the main square on Vas. Olgas St. *(Open Tu-Su 8:30am-7pm, in off season 8:30am-3pm. Admission 500dr, students 300dr, EU students free.)* In light of the city's early alliances, the collection is heavily Mycenaean, including pottery, jewelry, and weaponry; the Roman sculpture in the upper two rooms and the Roman period mosaics outside under the coverings are also notable. In the most striking of the mosaics, a series of figures represents the 12 months of the year, each matching the character of his or her respective month in dress, expression, and accoutrement. The well-preserved helmet and curass of the Geometric period in the museum's first room also deserves a careful look.

Archaeologists hope to uncover a large part of the ancient city of Argos, but unfortunately, most of it still lies under the modern town. The principal **excavations** to date have taken place on the city's western fringe on the site of the ancient *agora*, though archaeologists dig elsewhere in the city as chance building or demolition permits. To reach the theater, *agora*, bath complex, and small odeon, walk past the post office, turn right, and walk to the end of Theatrou St.

With a seating capacity of 20,000, the ancient **theater** was the largest in the Greek world when it was built in the 4th century BC. Although not as well-preserved as its famous counterpart in Epidavros, it is nonetheless striking. Across from the theater are the remains of the extensive **Roman bath complex.** What remains of the walls gives a good impression of the magnitude of the structure. Many of the original floor mosaics are intact, intricate, and colorful from wall to wall. The **Roman Odeum,** 30 meters from the baths to the left facing the theater, survives mostly in outline, as the rows dissolve into the hillside. Across the street from the theater, baths, and odeon are the scattered remains of the **agora,** built in the 5th century BC and destroyed by Alaric's Visigoths in AD 395. Toppled columns and crumbling foundations demonstrate the destructive effects of nature and barbarians.

In medieval times, Franks, Venetians, and Ottomans in turn captured and ruled Argos. Each had a hand in creating the **Fortress of Larissa,** an architectural hodgepodge that includes Classical and Byzantine elements. Getting to the fortress is a hike. You can walk along Vas. Konstantinou St. for roughly an hour, or climb the foot path from the ruins of the ancient theater. The ruins, which lie among overgrown weeds, are mainly of interest to scholars.

Hera was the patron deity of the Argives, and the temple of her cult, the **Argive Heraion,** is a short bus ride north of Argos (take the Prosimni bus, 220dr). The complex flourished in the 5th century BC but continued to prosper into the second century AD, when Pausanias visited it. Besides being the site of annual festivals, the sanctuary was also used to celebrate the official ending of the Heraia Games, archery contests held at Argos in the second year after each Olympiad. At **Prosimni,** several kilometers northeast of Argos and past the Heraion, lie a series of prehistoric graves. A few kilometers east of Agias Trias are the remains of the city of **Dendra,** where tombs yielded the completely preserved suit of bronze armor now on exhibit in the Nafplion museum.

■ Nafplion Ναυπλιο

Boasting a beautiful old town, Nafplion is the perfect base for exploring the archaeological treasures of the Argolid. Indeed, its Venetian architecture, two fortresses, shady squares, pebble beach, and hillside stairways that foil noisy mopeds may entice you to spend a few days away from the ruins. In contrast to the old town, New Nafplion is about as attractive as an ongoing construction site.

Nafplion's history has been both dramatic and unstable. Before the Venetians built it on swamp land in the 15th century, the city (named for Poseidon's son Nauplius) consisted entirely of the hilltop fortresses. It passed from the Venetians to the Ottomans and back again, then, in 1821, served as headquarters for the Greek revolutionary government, and as the first capital of Greece (1829-1834). John Kapodistrias, the former president of Greece, was assassinated here in St. Spyridon Church. The bullet hole is still visible in the church walls; the assassins hid behind the fountain visible across the street. Other remnants of Nafplion's turbulent past include Palamidi, a Venetian fortress in which Ottomans imprisoned the Greek nationalist Kolokotronis before the Revolutionary War of 1821, and the Bourtzi, a small island fortress that once housed retired executioners.

ORIENTATION AND PRACTICAL INFORMATION

The bus terminal, on **Singrou St.,** sits near the base of the Palamidi fortress. To reach **Bouboulinas St.,** the waterfront promenade, just walk left out of the bus station down Singrou St. to the harbor. Everything to your left as you walk towards the water from the bus station is the old town. If you arrive by ferry, Bouboulinas St. will be directly in front of you, across the parking lot and parallel to the dock.

Besides Bouboulinas, there are three other principal streets in the old town, all of which run off Singrou St., parallel to Bouboulinas St. Moving inland, the first is **Amalias St.,** the shopping street. The second, **Vasileos Konstandinou St.,** ends in **Syntagma Square,** which has *tavernas*, a bookstore, bank, museum, and at night, scores of aspiring soccer stars. The third street is **Plapouta St.,** which becomes **Staikopoulou St.** in the vicinity of Syntagma Square. Here you will find good restaurants.

Across Singrou St., Plapouta St. becomes **25th Martiou St.,** the largest avenue in town. This side of Singrou St.—everything behind the statue of Kapodistrias—is the new part of town. It radiates outward from the 5-way intersection split by the road to Argos and the road to Tolo. While ugly, the new town is where you'll find many of the city's inexpensive hotels.

Transportation

Buses: Station (tel. 28 555), on Singrou St. off Kapodistrias Sq. Daily buses go to Athens (3hr., 15 per day, 2450dr); Argos (30min., 2 per hr., 240dr); Corinth (2hr. 1100dr); Mycenae (45min., 4 per day, 550dr); Epidavros (1hr., 5 per day, 550dr); Tolo (20min., 1 per hr., 240dr); Kranidi (2hr., 3 per day, 1450dr); Galatas (2hr., 2 per day, 1550dr); and Ligouri (30min., 7 per day, 480dr).

Flying Dolphins: Staikos Travel, 50 Bouboulinas St. (tel. 27 950). Open daily 8:30am-3:30pm and 6-10pm. Purchase tickets two days before departure date. A Dolphin leaves Tu-Su for Peiraias (4hr., 8800dr) stopping at Spetses (1hr., 3150dr); for Hydra (2hr., 4850dr); Poros (3hr., 5910dr); and Aegina (3hr., 8300dr).

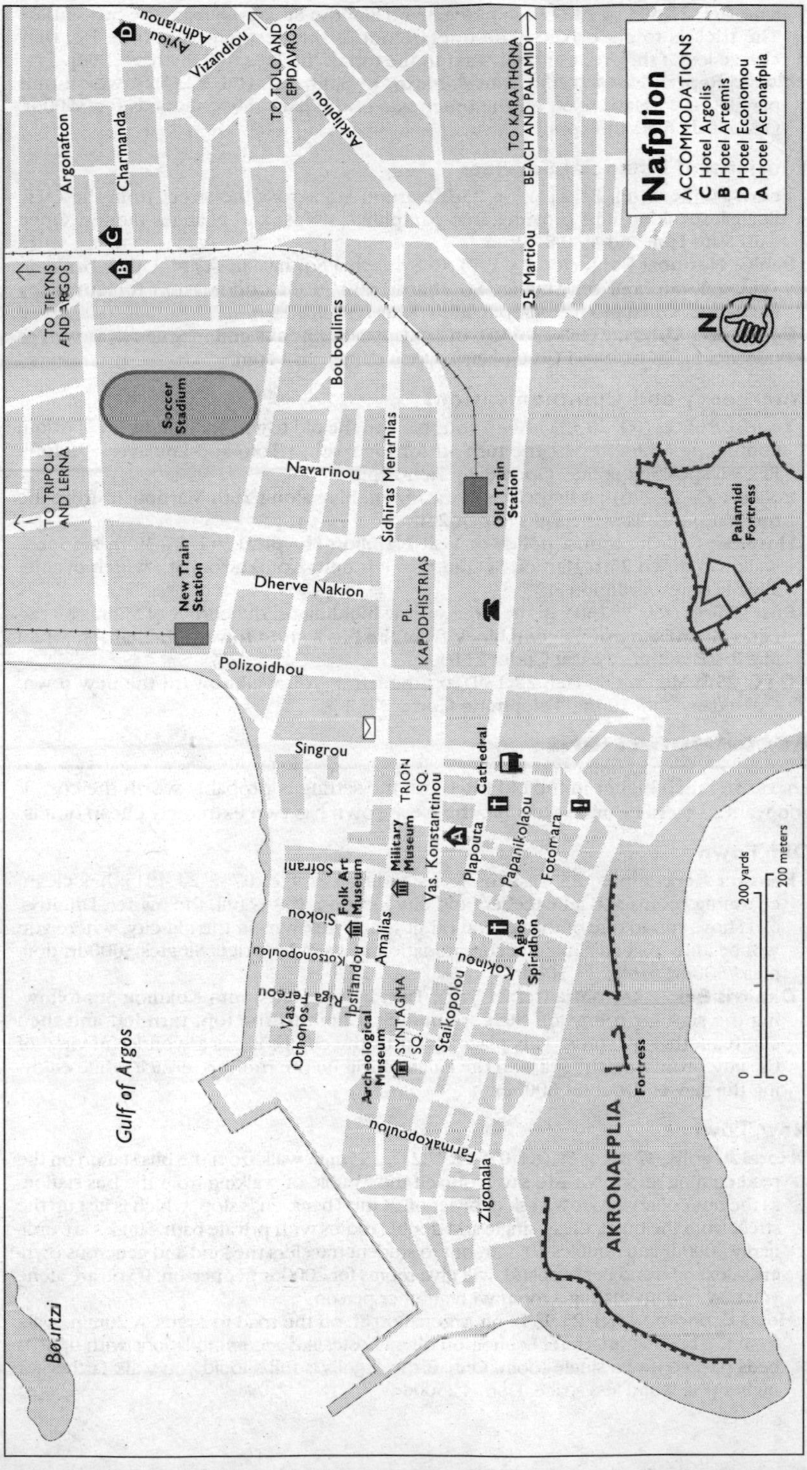

Nafplion

ACCOMMODATIONS
C Hotel Argolis
B Hotel Artemis
D Hotel Economou
A Hotel Acronafplia

Ayion Adhrianou
Vizandiou
TO TOLO AND EPIDAVROS
Askitjiou
TO KARATHONA BEACH AND PALAMIDI
Argonafton
Charmanda

TO TIRYNS AND ARGOS

25 Martiou

Bot.boulinis

Soccer Stadium

TO TRIPOLI AND LERNA

Navarinou
Sidhiras Merarhias
Old Train Station

New Train Station
Dherve Nakion
PL. KAPODHISTRIAS

Polizoidhou

Singrou

TRION SQ.
Vas. Konstantinou
Military Museum
Cathedral
Plapouta
Papanikolaou
Fotor ara

Sofrani
Folk Art Museum
Siokou
Kotsonopoulou
Amalias
Ipsilandou
Agios Spiridhon
Kokinou
Staikopolou
Riga Fereou
Vas Othonos
SYNTAGMA SQ.
Archeological Museum

Palamidi Fortress

N

Farmakopoulou
Zigomala

AKRONAFPLIA Fortress

Gulf of Argos

Bourtzi

200 yards
200 meters
0
0

Taxis: (tel. 27 393 or 23 600) congregate on Singrou St. across from the bus station. The trick is to get drivers who operate out of the destination you desire; they charge less if they're returning. Taxi to the top of the Palamidi fortress 700dr.

Moped Rental: Motortraffic Rent-A-Moto, 15 Sidiras St. (tel. 22 702), which runs parallel to 25 Martiou St. on the other side of the park. 50cc mopeds for 3500dr. Open daily 8:30am-11pm.

Tourist and Financial Services

Tourist Office: (tel. 24 444), on 25th Martiou St., across the street from the OTE. English-speaking staff provides free pamphlets, maps, and changes money. Open daily 9am-1pm and 4:30-8:30pm.

Banks: National Bank (tel. 23 497), in Syntagma Sq, has an **ATM**. Other banks in Syntagma Sq. and on Amalias St. charge 500-700dr commission for **currency exchange**. Open M-Th 8am-2pm and F 8am-1:30pm.

Bookstore: Odyssey (tel. 23 430), in Syntagma Sq. Books and magazines as well as translations of Classical Greek plays. Open daily 8am-11pm.

Emergency and Communications

Tourist Police: (tel. 28 131). With your back to the old town, walk along 25 Martiou, continuing 6 blocks past the turn-off for the road to Tolo and Epidavros. Helpful English-speaking police. Open daily 7am-10pm.

Police: (tel. 27 776) on Praitelous St., a 15min. hike along 25th Martiou St. from the bus station. Follow the signs. Open 24hr.

Hospital: Call the tourist police or visit **Nafplion Hospital** (tel. 27 309), a 15min. walk. Go down 25th Martiou St. and turn left onto Kolokotroni St., which eventually becomes Asklipiou St.

Post Office: (tel. 24 230), in the large yellow building on the corner of Sidiras Merarchias St. and Singrou St., one block from the bus station toward the harbor. Open M-F 7:30am-2pm. **Postal Code:** 21100.

OTE: 25th Martiou St. (tel. 22 139), on the left as you walk toward the new town. Open daily 7am-10pm. **Telephone Code:** 0752.

ACCOMMODATIONS

Prices are much higher in the old town but the setting is probably worth the cost. If you want to sacrifice and save a bit, the New Town has two extremely cheap hotels.

Old Town

Pension Acronafplia, 23 Vasileos Konstandinou St. (tel 0752 24 481), has clean, charming rooms and an excellent old city location. If it is full, the owner, Dimitris, can show you to one of the several other hotels he owns in the old city, where you will be able to get a similar accommodation at a similar price. Singles 5000dr; doubles 7500dr; triples 13,500dr.

Dimitris Bekas' Domatia (tel 24 594). Turn up the stairs onto Kokinou St., following the sign for rooms off Staikopoulou St. Climb to the top, turn left and then climb another 50 steps. This place is worth the climb; it has a wonderful view of the city's rooftops, the sea, and the Palamidi. Sit on the rooftop terrace while enjoying the sunset. Doubles 6000dr.

New Town

●**Hotel Argolis,** 32 Argos St. (tel. 0752 27 721), a 15min. walk from the bus station on the road coming into town—to save yourself the trouble of walking from the bus station, as the bus comes into town ask to be let off at the Thanasenas stop, which is just up the street from the hotel. Clean single and double rooms with private bath. Singles are ordinarily 4000dr and doubles 6000dr, but to student travelers the kind and generous owners, Alexandra and her husband, will give rooms for 2000dr per person. If you are alone you may end up sharing a room with another person.

Hotel Economou (tel. 23 955), on Argonafton St. off the road to Argos. A 20min. walk from the bus station, Hotel Economou offers hostel-like accommodations with up to 4 beds packed into a single room. Only if the Argolis is full should you walk farther for higher prices and less space. Dorms 2500dr.

Hotel Artemis (tel. 27 862), across the street from the Argolis in the noisy New Town, has large clean rooms with balconies and private bath. Singles 4000dr; doubles 6000dr; triples 8000dr.

Hotel IRA, 9 Vas. Georgiou B St. (tel. 28 184), off Bouboulinas St. in the new part of town. Clean, airy rooms. Singles 4000dr; doubles 6000dr; triples 8000dr.

FOOD AND ENTERTAINMENT

The food in Nafplion is excellent, though not often cheap. At times the city may seem one *taverna*-packed back alley after another, lit by soft flood lights and strewn with plants, balconies, and people. The waterfront is lined with fish restaurants, which charge as much as 7000dr per entree. Better dining options occupy the street above Syntagma Sq., behind the National Bank, where proprietors will lure you with calls of "Good food, good food here."

⊛Taverna O Vasiles (tel. 25 334), on Staikopoulou St. one street above the square, serves wonderful fresh fish, and a rabbit in onions (1500dr) that will delight even the most avid Beatrix Potter fan.

Zorba's Tavern (tel. 25 319), to the left of O Vasiles, caters to local tastes (*moussaka* 1100dr) and offers some cheap starters (stuffed tomatoes 900dr).

Ellas (tel. 27 278), in Syntagma Sq., is the cheapest restaurant around (chicken and fish entrees 950-1300dr), and boasts an international clientele including Marcello Mastroianni. It closes early though, and you may be asked to leave by 11pm.

The Agora Music Cafe, 17 Vas. Konstandinou St. This is the best place for an evening cocktail or ice cream—plus, it's decorated with traditional household and farm implements. R&B plays on a good sound system inside. Drinks 1100dr, beer 700dr, ice creams 800-1200dr.

There is a string of average cafes along the waterfront. Nafplion's discos have all relocated to **Tolo** (15min., 1400dr by taxi). At the far end of the waterfront is **Luna Park,** a carnival where you can relive your childhood under the neon lights. Or take a **minicruise** of the harbor (which run until 7pm), and toodle around the Bourtzi. Small *caiques* leave from the end of the dock (500dr round-trip).

SIGHTS

In its impressive architectural diversity, the Old Town itself constitutes an important historical sight; on Syntagma Square alone a Venetian mansion, a Turkish mosque and a Byzantine Church all share space. One particularly amazing specimen is the 18th-century **Palamidi fortress** (tel. 28 036). *(Open M-F 7:45am-7pm, Sa-Su and off season daily 8:30am-3pm. Admission 800dr, students 400dr, EU students free. On-site snackbar opens at 9:30am.)* The grueling 999 steps that once provided the only access to the fort have been supplemented by a 3km road; taxis cost 700dr each way, or you can attack the road by foot. If you opt for the steps, they begin on Arvanitias St., across the park from the bus station; bring water and climb in the morning. However you reach the top, you'll be rewarded with spectacular views of the town, gulf, and much of the Argolid. Note the Venetian lion *stelae* that adorn some of the lower citadel's walls. Years ago there were eight working cisterns at the site; today you can still tour the cool interiors of the two remaining underground reservoirs.

The fortress walls of the **Acronafplia** were fortified by three successive generations of conquerors—Byzantines, Franks, and Venetians. Approach the fortress by the tunnel that runs into the hill from Zigomala St., where you can take the Xenia Hotel elevator. The views of the Palimidi, the Gulf, and Old Nafplion are fantastic. Ludwig I, King of Bavaria, had the huge Bavarian Lion carved out of a monstrous rock as a memorial after seeing many of his men die in an epidemic in 1833-34. Today, a small park sits in front of it. To get there, make a left onto Mikh. Iatrou St. and walk 200m.

Nafplion's **Folk Art Museum,** winner of the 1981 European Museum of the Year Award will reopen after years of renovation in 1999. The **Military Museum,** toward the new town from Syntagma, has artifacts and high-quality black and white photographs from the burning of Smyrna (Izmir), the population exchanges of the 1920s, and WWII. *(Open Tu-Su 9am-2pm. Free.)* The **archaeological museum** (tel. 27 502), in a Venetian mansion on Syntagma Sq., has a small but esteemed collection of pottery and idols from Tiryns, Mycenae, and other Mycenaean sites nearby, plus a Mycenaean suit of bronze armor. *(Open Tu-Su 8:30am-3pm. Admission 500dr, students 300dr.)*

Karathona Beach in Nafplion is accessible by foot; follow the road that curves around the left-hand side of Palamidi. There's also a footpath from the parking lot between the Palamidi and the end of Polizoidou St. It runs along the water from the left. The 45-minute walk will reveal three quiet, rocky coves. The beach is nothing special, but is quite convenient.

■ Near Nafplion

Tiryns

The site is easily reached by the Argos bus from Nafplion (every 30min., 220dr). Tel. 22 657. Open 8am-10pm. Admission 500dr, students 300dr.

About 4km northwest of Nafplion on the road to Argos lie the Mycenaean ruins of **Tiryns,** or Tirintha, birthplace of Hercules. Schliemann began excavation of the site in 1875 and it has been continued since by the German Archaeological Institute; the site is now one of the finer prehistoric sites outside of Mycenae. Perched atop a 25m-high hill, Tiryns was impregnable during ancient times until it was captured by the Argives and destroyed in the 5th century BC. Parts of the stronghold date as far back as 2600 BC, but most of what remains was built 1000 years later, in the Mycenaean era. Standing 8m in both height and width, the massive walls surrounding the site are evidence of the immensity of the original fortifications. They reach a width of 20m on the eastern and southern slopes of the ancient acropolis. Inside these structures lurk vaulted galleries. The palace's frescoes are in the National Archaeological Museum in Athens (see p. 96). One huge limestone block remains—the floor of the bathroom.

Tolo

If you're staying in Nafplion and are desperate for a long, sandy beach, Tolo is the place to go. Buses leave Nafplion frequently, and on summer days, scads of pre-teens head for the water. You can rent jet skis (5000dr per 15min), umbrellas (2000dr per day), paddle boats (1500dr per hour) or wind surf (2000dr per hour) on the beach. In addition, there is a fast developing strip of cafes (mediocre) and hotels (crowded).

■ Epidavros Επιδαυρος

> At Epidaurus, in the stillness, in the great peace that came over me, I heard the heart of the world beat.
>
> —Henry Miller

History

Like Olympia and Delphi, Epidavros was not merely a town but a sanctuary—first to an ancient chthonic deity Maleatas, then to Apollo, and finally to Apollo's son by Coronis, Asclepius, under whom Epidavros became famous across the ancient world as a center of healing, reaching the peak of its fame in the early fourth century BC. The sick traveled miles for cures that were both medical and mystical. Treatment was determined by visits of the god in dreams. Over the centuries, the complex grew and became more and more grand with the benefactions of former patients, continuing to operate until AD 426, when the Byzantine emperor Theodosius II closed it and all other pagan sanctuaries.

Built in the early second century BC to accommodate 6000 people, the theater is undisputably the grandest structure at the site. In the second century BC its capacity was expanded to 14,000. Despite severe earthquakes in AD 522 and 551, the theater has survived the centuries almost perfectly intact and is now perhaps the most famous ancient theater. After centuries of silence the theater comes alive again on Friday and Saturday nights in July and August for the popular Epidavros Theater Festival.

Touring Epidavros

*Theater, site, and museum **open** in high season Tu-Su 8am-7pm and M noon-7pm, off-season Tu-Su 8am-5pm, M noon-5pm. **Admission** 1500dr, students 800dr, EU students free; hold on to your site admission ticket to get into the museum. Try to visit Epidavros during the **Epidavros Festival**, Friday and Saturday nights from late June to mid-August, when the **National Theater of Greece** and visiting companies perform plays from the classical Greek canon translated into modern Greek (Euripides, Sophocles, Aristophanes, etc.). Performances are at 9pm and tickets can be purchased at the site (open M-Sa 9am-5pm and F-Sa 5-9pm). You can also buy tickets in advance in Athens at the **Athens Festival Box Office** (tel. (01) 322 14 59; see p. 89) or at the bus station in Nafplion. Tickets cost 6000dr, 4000dr, and 2000dr for students. Children under six are strictly prohibited. Performances are in modern Greek, so bring your favorite translation.*

*Unless you're going to Epidavros for a performance, make the small town a daytrip from Nafplion, Athens, Corinth, or a Saronic Gulf Island. Buses travel to and from Nafplion (1hr., 6 per day, 550dr) and Galatas (2 per day). On performance nights, **KTEL** buses make the round-trip circuit from the Nafplion station, departing at 7:30pm (1500dr). There is no town near the sight of Epidavros, so bring a picnic lunch and eat at the site, or shell out for bad cafeteria food at **Xenias,** the only place at the site.*

Theater

In rolling flaxen foothills, the ancient theater of Epidavros combines natural splendor and architectural majesty. The theater's acoustics are miraculous; the slightest sound onstage is perfectly audible from the back row of Epidavros's graceful 55 tiers of superbly preserved seats. Even as the theater reverberates with the din of annoying tourists shouting and dropping coins, Epidavros harbors a marked peace, for just as it can magnify the noise of obnoxious tourists, it can amplify the subtle, serene sound of nature.

Museum

The **museum** (tel. 22 009) is on the way from the theater to the ruins. Most of the museum's finest pieces, most notably the exquisite architectural carvings of the site's maze, *tholos,* have been under restoration for years, sequestered and hidden from visitors. The three rooms remaining open, however, contain more than a few interesting pieces. Intricately carved entablature from the temple of Asclepius and the *tholos* line the first room. Also in the first room are a marble pillar inscribed with a hymn to Apollo and an array of ancient medical implements. The second room is filled with elaborately decorated architectural reconstructions and randomly placed statuary. In the third room most of the beautiful decorative elements from the *tholos* have been removed and replaced temporarily with plaster copies. Authentic and impressive, however, is the perfectly preserved Corinthian capital thought to be the architect's prototype for all of the capitals of the temple of Asclepius. Archaeologists found it buried in the ground a ways from the site, apparently unconnected with any ruin.

Sanctuary of Asclepius

The ruins of the Sanctuary of Asclepius are extensive and can be confusing. Walking from the museum, you will first pass the **Xenon** or hostel, which remains only as a maze of foundations. The gymnasium that contains the remains of a Roman Odeon, is the first structure of the more concentrated complex of ruins. To the left is a stadium, of which the starting blocks and a few tiers of seats have survived. In front and to the left are the temple of Asclepius and the famous *tholos,* two of the most important structures of the ancient sanctuary. The *tholos* in particular, thought to have been built by Polycleitos the Younger in the mid-fourth century BC, is an architectural masterpiece, richly decorated with carvings and other ornamentation. Although certainly a place of worship, its exact function is unknown. Beside the *tholos* are the remains of the **abaton,** or sleeping ward, where the sick would lie down hoping that the form of their therapy would be revealed to them by the god in dreams. Farther from the *tholos* along the path on the eastern edge of the site lie the ruins of the extensive Roman baths of the second century AD.

PELOPONNESE

ELIAS AND ACHAÏA
·Ηλειας και Αχαια

In the rural provinces of Elias and Achaïa, tomatoes ripen beneath the blazing sun as beachgoers redden to a similar hue. The area between Pyrgos and Patras, the capitals of Elias and Achaïa, is a vegetable farmer's dream. Corn fields rimmed with golden-sand beaches are studded with ancient, Frankish, and Venetian ruins. The locals call these regions of the Peloponnese "tame" as opposed to the "wild" landscape in other parts of Greece. The current tranquility of the northwest Peloponnese hides centuries of diverse influence. The Achaïans from the Argolid were the first settlers of Achaïa, and in 280 BC the Achaïan Confederacy was created. In 146 BC the region fell to the Romans, in 1205 it was captured by the Franks, in 1460 it became Ottoman property, and from 1687 to 1715 it was a Venetian colony. Ruins from each of these periods stand to this day. In 1828 Achaïa joined the Greek state.

■ Patras Πατρας

Greece's third-largest city, Patras sprawls noisy and dusty along its harbor. Menacing semi-trailers crowd the pot-holed harbor roads of this transportation hub, threatening hapless pedestrians who rarely have the safety of a sidewalk. Most treat Patras as a stopover and leave the city having seen nothing but tour agencies, bars, and sleazy hotels; if you hope to enjoy Patras, buy your ferry ticket, store your luggage, and head for the hills. The upper city is peaceful and perfect for an afternoon stroll. Ruins from the city's long history dot the streets, and in places, the city approaches picturesque.

Patras provides a base to reach much of the Peloponnese, including **Olympia,** the northern coast, and a resort-free beach in Kalogria. It also has the second largest number of bars and pubs of any European city. From mid-January to Ash Wednesday, Patras hosts Carnival, featuring music, food, and an all-night fête. Hotels are booked solid and the port becomes one vast dance floor on which, for once, people stand a chance against massive speeding vehicles.

ORIENTATION AND PRACTICAL INFORMATION

If you're coming from Athens by car, choose between the **New National Road,** an expressway running inland along the Gulf of Corinth, and the slower, scenic **Old National Road,** which hugs the coast. Those coming from the north can take a ferry from **Antirio** across to **Rion** on the Peloponnese (30min., every 15min. 7am-11pm, 300dr per person, 1800dr per car) and hop on bus #6 from Rio to the stop four blocks uphill from the main station, at **Kanakari St.** and **Aratou St.** (30min., 270dr).

If you're arriving by boat from Italy or any of the Ionian Islands, turn right as you leave customs onto **Iroon Polytechniou St.** to get to the center of town. Just before the train station the road curves and its name changes to **Othonos Amalias St.** Past the train station is the large **Trion Simahon Square,** with palm trees, cafes, and kiosks. **Agios Nikolaou St.** runs inland from the square and intersects the major east-west streets of the city. From the corner of Agios Nikolaou St. and Mezanos St., three blocks from the water, turn right. You will see **Georgiou Square.**

Between Georgiou Sq. and Olgas Sq., 3 blocks to the west, is the heart of new Patras. However, you'll probably want to skip the lower city's squares in favor of the upper's parks. Walk inland on Agios Nikolaou St., climb the daunting steps, and you will be rewarded.

Transportation

Ferries: From Patras, boats reach Cephalonia, Ithaka, and Corfu in Greece, and Brindisi, Bari, Ancona, and Venice in Italy. From Italy, ferries to **Sami** on Cephalonia depart daily (3hr., 3220dr); the same boat goes to **Vathi** on Ithaka (3¾hr., 3526dr). To **Corfu,** ferries leave every night at varying hours (deck passage 6-8hr., 5800dr). To **Italy,** most ferries also leave in the late evening or night, but prices vary according to the season. **Deck passage** ranges from about 10,000dr in the off-season to

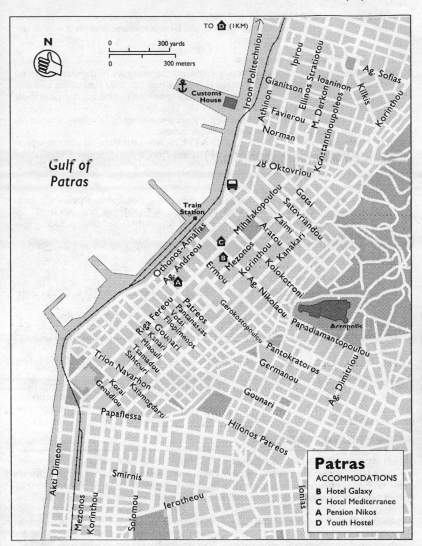

about 15,000dr in the high season. Several different ferry lines make the trip so you should check in the travel offices along Iroon Polytechniou St. and Othonas Amplias St. for the particulars of price, departure times, check-in, and boarding. Ask about student discounts. If you have a railpass, go to **HML** (tel 45 25 21), on Iroon Polytechniou St., near the customs complex. **Strintzis Tours,** the main office for Strinzis Lines at 14 Othonas Amalias St. (tel. 622 602), is professional, helpful, and almost always available (open daily 9am-11pm).

Buses: KTEL (tel. 623 886 or 623 887), on Othonos Amalias St. between Aratou St. and Zaïmi St. Buses depart for Athens (3hr., 26 per day, 3350dr); Kalamata (1hr., 2 per day, 4000dr); Pyrgos (11 per day, 1780dr); Tripoli (4hr., 2 per day, 3000dr); Ioannina (4 per day, 4250dr); Thessaloniki (3 per day, 8000dr); Kalavrita (4 per day, 1450dr); and Egion (15 per day, 680dr).

Trains: (tel. 273 694), on Othonos Amalias St. Trains go to Athens (8 per day, 1600dr, express 2600dr); Kalamata (4½hr., 2 per day, 1500dr); and Pyrgos, from which you can transfer to Olympia (2hr., 8 per day until 10pm, 820dr, express

1220dr); and Egio (320dr, express 720dr). Expect delays and a shortage of seats, especially on the trains to Athens. Even if you have a railpass, reserve a seat at the ticket window before taking a train.

Tourist and Financial Services

Tourist Office: (tel. 622 249), on the waterfront at the entrance to the customs complex. Multi-lingual staff gives free maps as well as bus and boat timetables and can help with accommodations. Open M-F 7am-10pm. Go to the tourist police on weekends when the office is closed.

Consulates: British, 2 Votsi St. (tel. 277 329), on the corner of Othonos Amalias St. Variable hours, often M-F 9:30am until late morning.

Banks: National Bank (tel. 221 643), with **ATM.** In Trion Simahon Sq., on the waterfront, just past the train station. Open M-Th 8am-2pm, F 8am-1:30pm. Other banks with **ATMs** are also on the square.

Local Services

Luggage Storage: In the pink building near the customs complex. Open daily 7am-9:30pm; 200dr per item per day. Also at train station (300dr per item per day).

International Bookstore: Biblia Clio, 27 Patreos. Scholarly collection, including several university presses.

Laundromat: (tel. 620 119), on Zaïmi St. near Korinthou St. Wash and dry 2000dr. Open M-Sa 9am-9pm.

Emergency and Communications

Tourist Police: (tel. 451 833 or 451 893), inside the customs complex. Offers same services as tourist office. Open 7:30am-11pm.

Hospital: The **Red Cross Emergency Station** (tel. 227 386) dispenses first aid. It is on the corner of 28 Oktoviou St. and Agios Dionysiou St. Open daily 8am-8pm. **Rio Hospital** of Patras University (tel. 999 111) is a large, modern hospital 5km away, accessible by taxi or bus #6.

Post Office: (tel. 223 864), on Mezonos St. at the corner of Zaïmi St. Open M-F 7:30am-8pm, Sa 7:30am-2pm. **Postal Code:** 26001.

OTE: (tel. 421 998) at customs complex, across from the tourist office. Open daily 7:30am-10pm. For collect international calls, go to the OTE at Trion Simahon Sq. Open M-F 7am-2:30pm, Sa-Su 7:20am-1pm. Also at the corner of Kanakari St. and Gounari St., up from the waterfront. **Telephone Code:** 061.

ACCOMMODATIONS

Hotels are threaded through the tangle of buildings on Agios Andreas St., one block up and parallel to the waterfront. Most of them aren't as cheap as they might appear; many of Patras' cheap hotels—some of which were bordellos—have closed down in recent years, leaving behind vacant buildings with brightly colored plastic signs.

Pension Nikos, 3 Patreos St. (tel. 221 643), 2 blocks off the waterfront, is probably your best bet in Patras. The rooms are clean and the location convenient. Go up to the third floor when you arrive. Singles 4000dr; doubles 6500dr, with bath 7000dr.

Youth Hostel, 68 Iroon Polytechniou St. (tel. 427 278). From the ferry docks walk away from town with the water on your left for about 1½km. The hostel is housed in a creaky turn-of-the-century mansion that sat empty for 40 years after being used as a German headquarters in WWII. Unfortunately, its high ceilings do not compensate for its spotty walls and dirty bathrooms. If you stay here, you may consider leaving anything of value at the reception desk; as a port town with a large itinerant population Patras is home to more than its share of thieves. Sheets 150dr. Breakfast 600dr. Dorms 1700dr.

Hotel Mediterranee, 18 Agios Nikolaou St. (tel. 279 602). Expensive for the budget traveler, but if you can't find anyplace else, treat yourself to a TV and a very hot shower. Singles 8500dr; doubles 13,500dr.

Hotel Galaxy, 9 Agios Nikolaou St. (tel. 275 981) also has TV and private bathrooms, but is slightly cheaper for pairs. Singles 9000dr, doubles 12,500dr.

Rio Camping (tel. 991 585), 8km east of Patras. To get there, catch bus #6 at the corner of Aratou and Kamakari, get off at Rion, and follow the signs. 1100dr per tent; 600dr per car. Electricity 800dr. 1200dr per person, children 600dr.

Rio Mare Camping (tel. 992 263), near Rio Camping. 800dr per small tent; 1100dr per large tent; 750dr per car. 1200dr per person.

FOOD

Patras's waterfront restaurants are aimed at tourists, overpriced, and virtually indistinguishable from one another. While Patras has more than its fair share of pubs and cafes, the city has surprisingly few *tavernas* and restaurants.

Taverna Nikolaras (tel. 225 253), three blocks inland on Agios Nikolarou, is a traditional *taverna*. It isn't flashy, but the food is delicious and the variety wider than usual. Among other dishes, you can choose between beans (800dr), *dolmades* (950dr), and salmon (1300dr). Great for vegetarians.

Kosmiki Taverna, at the top of the stairs ascending from the end of Agios Nikolaou St., just outside the castle walls, also serves traditional fare (*souvlaki* 1400dr, *moussaka* 1300dr). From its outside tables you can see most of the city below.

Gusto, on Agios Nikolaou two blocks up from the square, is the best place for fast food (*gyros* 330dr, *souvlaki* 250dr). It is new and spotlessly clean, which is seldom true of Greek fast food restaurants.

Artopoisio Bakery (tel. 274 139) is a good place for a snack or for a quick breakfast. It is located at the foot of the stairs to the upper city, making it a perfect place to break and restore your energy after a hike around the castle (bread 170-250dr per loaf, ginger cookies 28dr).

ENTERTAINMENT

It's not the city of lights, but Patras may be the city of light beer; the city's tiny side streets hide many small bars and cafes.

Caffé Luz, off Olgas Sq. on Aratou St., has more backgammon tables in use at any one time than the rest of the city's cafes combined. As elsewhere, beer, coffee, and *frappés* are the primary choices.

Blue Monday, along Radinou St., one street east of Olgas Sq., serves ordinary cafe fare, but plays more Elvis Presley than any other bar on the Peloponnese. It takes its name from an old rock song, and silver-screen idols provide labels for each chair—try Charlie Chaplin, Cary Grant, or Katherine Hepburn, all beside each other. Look for its red Coke-bottle cap sign.

Rion

Although Patras has a lot to offer in the way of bars and cafes, the wildest party-goers head out of town at night. As with many large coastal cities, a beach town satellite is only minutes away. **Rion** is a small city, roughly 8km to the northeast of Patras. This stretch of beach bars, clubs, restaurants, and discos is where Patras's nightlife transports itself in the summer months. Decor is taken seriously at the beach bars; the most exciting bars resemble theme parks minus the rides, and the majority have a vaguely Caribbean theme, with elaborate lighting.

In **Mioiouia 105,** a bright yellow WWII plane hangs above the dance floor and plastic soldiers engage in desert combat under plexiglass at the bar. A beer will set you back 600dr, a *frappé* 500dr. **Soka Bay** goes for the jungle motif: green atmosphere lighting illuminates rope-wrapped trees and fake ruins. Play on the giant tree swing as you sip your beer (500dr). **Mojo Club** has cacti and southwestern geometric patterns on its walls. **Ku** goes father than most, occupying a pyramidal stone structure built, presumably, to resemble the Venetian fortress 800m down the street at the port.

There are some more serious restaurants at Rion Beach, frequented by families. **La Piscina,** at the end of the strip, has a fountain, pizza (1600-2200dr), and a variety of fish (600-5500dr).

To get to Rion, take bus #6 from the Kamakari and Araton St. (30min., 230dr), and ride it all the way to the port. From the port walk along the beach-side road with the water on your right. Within 100m you'll be at the start of the strip. Be aware that buses to Rion run only until 11pm; you may have to take a cab home (1000dr).

SIGHTS

A 13th-century **Venetian castle** crowns the city. *(Open until 8pm. Free.)* It is built on the ruins of the ancient acropolis that was once the site of the temple of Panachaïan Athena. From up here, you can see downtown Patras for the beehive that it is. At the center of the castle is a verdant courtyard with chirping birds, bright flowers, and olive and orange trees, lending the site a medieval feel. If the entrance near the steps from the lower city is closed, walk around to the main entrance at the opposite corner of the castle. In the summertime look for concerts and theater at the park.

Also in the upper city, west of the castle, is the **Ancient Odeum.** *(Open Tu-Su 8:30am-3pm. Free.)* This ancient Roman theater was built sometime before AD 160 and used until the 3rd century AD. The ancient traveler Pausanias described it as the second most impressive in Greece, after the Theater of Herodus Atticus in Athens. The theater was excavated in 1889 and restored with brick and marble after WWII. The mosaic floors of a Roman house can be seen nearby. From June 15 until October 15, the theatre hosts the **Patras Festival,** where Greek music groups perform every evening starting at 9pm (tickets average 1500dr).

The **Archaeological Museum,** 42 Mezonos St. (tel. 220 829), next to Olgas Sq. at the corner of Mezonos St. and Aratou St., has a small but interesting collection from excavations in and around the city. *(Open Tu-Su 8:30am-3pm. Free.)* The most striking pieces are from the Roman period, including statuary, mosaics, and fascinating household items such as glassware and oil lamps. In all, the museum collection would probably furnish an entire Roman villa.

The largest Orthodox cathedral in Greece, **Agios Andreas** is dedicated to St. Andrew, who lived and died in Patras. *(Open daily 9am-dusk.)* As he felt himself unworthy to die on the same kind of cross as Jesus, St. Andrew was martyred by crucifixion on an X-shaped version. A little more than 10 years ago, the Catholic Church presented the Bishop of Patras with the saint's relic—his head. To the right of the cathedral is the old church of St. Andrew, which houses a small **well,** said to have been built by the saint himself. It can be reached by a doorway to the right of the church, and legend has it that whoever drinks from this well will return to Patras again. Photography and videotaping are prohibited and modest dress is appropriate. To get here, follow the water to the west end of town, roughly 1.5km from the port (20min.).

Achaïa Clauss Winery, probably the most famous winery in the country, is in the hills 9km southeast of town. *(Tours daily 11:30am-7:30pm. Free.)* Its founder, Baron von Clauss, moved to Greece from Bavaria and planted the vineyard in the 1870s. He fell in love with a local Greek woman named Daphne, and upon her death, in her honor, he made a wine with his darkest grapes, called *Mavrodaphne* ("Black Daphne," for her eyes). If you don't go for the free wine, go for the view and the peaceful wooded setting. Take bus #7 (30min., 230dr) from the local station at the intersection of Kolokotroni St. and Kanakari St.

The **carnival season** in Patras begins in mid-January every year and lasts until Ash Wednesday. The locals describe *karnavali* as an undefinable energy that sweeps through town. Carnival's last night is capped by a ritual burning of King Carnival, and an open, boozy party on the harbor that lasts all night. The last Sunday of Carnival is topped off with a 12-hour marathon parade that takes over the streets. Call the youth hostel (tel. 427 278); they provide program details. Hotel rooms are booked for much of Carnival in a 100km radius; advance reservations are a necessity.

■ Diakofto Διακοφτο

Lying halfway between Corinth and Patras at the base of precipitous rocky mountains, Diakofto attracts tourists primarily with its famous rack-railway train through the mountains to Kalavrita. Yet, with its fruit tree-lined streets and modest beach, Diakofto is a town whose tourist potential has hardly been exploited in full. Houses are hidden by orange and lemon trees, while magenta bougainvillea shield their facades. Accommodations are a little better in Kalavrita, but if you plan to catch an early train toward Athens or Patras, Diakofto is an agreeable place to spend the night.

ORIENTATION AND PRACTICAL INFORMATION The train station intersects Diakofto's main road about 200m from the beach. If you walk inland on the winding main road toward the spectacular mountains that frame the town you will see the **post office** (tel. 41 343) on the left side of the road (open M-F 7:30am-2pm), as well as the **National Bank of Greece,** which offers **currency exchange** (open M-F 8:45am-12:45pm). Walking down the main road toward the sea you will pass through a picturesque residential area and end up at the harbor and public beach. The **train station** (tel. 43 206), flanked by cafes and restaurants, is the social center of Diakofto. Tiny rack-railway trains to Kalavrita make for an exhilarating ride (90min., 6 per day, 1000dr, 1700dr round-trip). **Postal code:** 25003. **Telephone code:** 0691.

ACCOMMODATIONS, FOOD, AND ENTERTAINMENT Hotel Helmos (tel. 41 236) is on the main road on the inland side of the tracks. Convenient to everything in Dia kofto, the rooms are small but spotless. Showers and toilets are shared, but heat and water pressure here is second to none. There are also private sinks in each room (singles 4000dr; doubles 6000dr; triples 8000dr). **Hotel Lemonides** (tel. 41 820) is halfway between the train station and the beach on the main road. It offers very clean, bright white, and spacious rooms with private baths. Downstairs is a pleasant *taverna*, and the surrounding neighborhood is lovely (singles 5500dr; doubles 8800dr; triples 9600dr). Several cafes and bars line the train station and the main street inland from the station. The service is quick and the outdoor dining pleasant at **Festaria Taverna** (tel. 43 228), which offers delicious *souvlaki* (200dr), grilled meats (1300dr), and quick salads (900dr). Surprisingly, despite its small size and lack of tourists, Diakofto has its own outdoor **cinema,** playing slightly out-of-date American movies. Find it on the winding main road 100m up from the train station next to the bank.

■ Great Canyon Monastery Μονη Μεγαλου Σπηλαιου

Located 9km inland from Diakofto, the famous monastery is accessible only by a combination of 19th-century rack-railway and hiking. Getting there is actually half the fun: the 40-minute railway ride, which has the same "will-we-make-it?" excitement as a rollercoaster's uphill climb, winds through spectacular canyons and gorges created by the Vouraikos River, passing through smoke-blackened tunnels and over old bridges (1000dr round-trip). To get to the monastery, get off at the **Zahlorou,** the first stop on the line. Be sure to bring a water bottle, long-sleeved shirt, and sturdy shoes.

Zahlorou is a small mountain village reminiscent of a mining or timber town in the old American West. A few well-shaded rustic buildings cluster around the tracks where they pass over the river. The path that leads to the monastery is marked in English. Frequent water stops are a must and will give you a chance to admire the panoramic views with the occasional donkey or goat. You should reach a paved road after about 45 minutes of walking. Turn left and follow the road to the sign for Mega Spilaeou on your right. Stairs in front of the monastery lead to the main entrance. Modest dress (no shorts, long sleeves if possible) is appropriate inside. A monk will lead you to the upstairs museum containing gold-encased relics and beautiful icons (some say one was painted by St. Luke). Photographs describe the destruction of the centuries-old monastery by an explosion of stored gunpowder in 1934. The new monastery is built up against the cliff wall, and one of the cliff's caves is accessible from the second floor of the building. Let the cool darkness of the cave envelop you as you peer into the darkness and look for the cave's miraculous icon. On your way back down the mountain, be careful of loose rocks and keep an eye out for the occasional snake.

▓ Kalavrita Καλαβρυτα

In a small valley at the end of the rack-railway line, Kalavrita is a charming mountain that offers more to winter skiers than to summer visitors. The town is quiet, picturesque, and has a few budget accommodations. Although the town has only one quite humble sight, if you wish to make the rack-railway a two-day event, Kalavrita is a more pleasant stay than Diakofto.

ORIENTATION AND PRACTICAL INFORMATION Two roads perpendicular to the train station lead to the main square, **Konstantinou St.** (later called **Agios Alexiou St.**) to the left and **Syngrou St.** (later called **25 Martiou St.**) to the right. The **National Bank of Greece** at #4 25 Martiou (tel 22 212) offers **currency exchange**, but no ATM (open M-Th 8am-2pm, F 8am-1:30pm). The **post office**, 25 Martiou St. (tel. 22 225), is to the right of the town hall at the lower right corner of the square coming up from the train station (open M-F 7:30am-2pm). The **police** (tel. 23 333) are 3 blocks beyond the OTE, off Agios Alexiou St., at 7 Fotina St. (open 24hr.). The **OTE** is at 10 Agios Alexiou St. (open daily 7:30am-3:10pm). **Postal code: 25001. Telephone code: 0692.**

ACCOMMODATIONS AND FOOD Hotels in Kalavrita are pleasant but expensive (prices quoted here are higher during ski season). **Karabelas Rooms to Let** (tel. 22 189) are a little hard to find, but are spacious and recently renovated, each with private bath and TV. Everything is bright and new (singles 5000dr; doubles 7000dr). To find the building, turn right on the street fronting the train station. Turn right again at the first intersecting road you come to after about 100m. Fifty meters down this street, which has a row of trees dividing it down the center, take yet another right on the first cross street. The home is 50m down on the left. Look for the sign. **Hotel Megas Alexandros** (tel. 22 221), on Agios Alexiou St. two blocks before the square, has spacious rooms with wood floors. The private bathrooms' showers are tiny. To find the hotel, turn right on B. Kapota St. from 25 Martiou St. (singles 5000dr; doubles 6000dr; triples 8000dr). Across the street, **Hotel Maria** (tel 22 296; fax 22 686) is luxurious with TVs, telephones, and lavender furniture (singles 8000dr; doubles 16,000dr; triples 21,000dr).

Agios Alexiou St. and 25 Martiou St. have many *tavernas* which are all more or less the same. **Taverna Stani** (tel. 23 000) has entrances on both streets and offers traditional fare (*tzaziki* 500dr, salads 500-1000dr, seafood 1500dr), while **Ekplixi** on 13 Dekembriou is less expensive, with pizza (450dr), *gyros* (350dr), and beer (450dr).

SIGHTS The town's only sight is morbidly depressing. On December 13, 1943, Nazi soldiers gunned down the town's entire male population, over a thousand in total, in retaliation for the murder of one of their troopers. They gathered the men and boys on a hill outside of town under the pretext of giving a stern lecture about the soldier's murder by an unconfessed villager. Troopers with machine guns lurked in trees above the hill and opened fire on command. Today the clock of the town's church is set permanently to 2:34, and an extensive memorial commemorating the excursus is located on the site of the massacre.

■ Killini Κυλληνη

For a port town that handles almost all of the tourist traffic to Zakynthos, Killini is surprisingly underdeveloped; the town has almost no bus service and only one hotel. There is nothing to keep you busy should you find yourself at loose ends here.

The path to town from the dock leads to the **police** (tel. 92 202; no English spoken). The **port police** (tel. 92 211) are on the dock (open 24hr.). The **post office** is a few blocks farther down, on a side street leading inland (open daily 10am-noon). Three **buses** a day go from Killini to Pyrgos, the last at 4:30pm (½hr., 450dr). Assuming you are coming from Zakynthos—there is no other reason you should be in Killini looking for a bus—you can take the Zakynthos buses if you are planning to go to Patras or Athens. These buses leave from Zakynthos Town and have a ferry ticket included in their price (see p. 242). For all other bus connections you will have to spend 2000dr on a **taxi** (tel. 71 764) to Lehena, the nearest town on the main Patras-Pirgos highway, or take one of the buses to Pirgos. Killini has no bus station proper. Buses leave from the kiosk near the gate to the port. **Ferries** sail from Killini to Zakynthos (1hr., 5 per day, 1450dr) and to Argostoli (2½hr, 1 per day at noon, 2700dr) and Poros (90min., 1 per day at 6:30pm, 2000dr) on Cephalonia. Buy tickets on the dock. **Postal code: 27068. Telephone code: 0623.**

Should you find it necessary to stay the night, turn right from the dock, cross the train tracks, and walk along the beach. **Hotel Ionion** (tel. 92 318) offers large rooms

(go down in history)

and use **AT&T Direct**^{SM} Service
to tell everyone about it.

It's all within **AT&T** your reach.

Before you go exploring lost cultures, get an

AT&T Direct[SM] Service wallet guide.

It's a list of access numbers you need to call home fast and clear from

around the world, using an AT&T Calling Card or credit card.

What an amazing culture we live in.

For a list of **AT&T Access Numbers,**
take the attached wallet guide.

It's all within  **AT&T** your reach.

www.att.com/traveler

For your calling convenience tear off and take with you!

AT&T Direct℠ Service

WALLET GUIDE

Inside you'll find simple instructions on how to use AT&T Direct Service to place calling card or collect calls from outside the U.S.

All you need are the AT&T Access Numbers when you travel outside the U.S., because you can access us quickly and easily from virtually anywhere in the world. And if you need any further help, there's always an AT&T English-speaking Operator available to assist you.

www.att.com/traveler

Special Features

Just dial the AT&T Access Number for the country you are in and follow the instructions listed below.

● To call U.S. 800 numbers: Enter the 800 number you are calling. (Note: Based upon the 800 number dialed, calls may be toll-free or AT&T Direct℠ Service charges may apply for the duration of the call; some numbers may be restricted.)

● To set up conference calls: Dial AT&T TeleConference Services at 800 232-1234. (Note: One conferee must be in the U.S.)

● To access language interpreters: Dial AT&T Language Line℠ Services at 408 648-5671.

● To record and deliver messages: Dial #123 if you get a busy signal or no answer, or dial AT&T True Messages℠ Service at 800 562-6275.

Here's a time-saving tip for placing additional calls: When you finish your conversation, or if there is a busy signal or no answer, don't hang up – press # and wait for the voice prompt or an AT&T Operator.

To Call the U.S. and Other Countries Using Your AT&T Calling Card* or credit card∞, Follow These Steps:

1. Make sure you have an outside line. (From a hotel room, follow the hotel's instructions to get an outside line, as if you were placing a local call.)

2. If you want to call a country other than the U.S., make sure the country you are in is highlighted in blue on the chart like this: ▭

3. Enter the AT&T Access Number listed in the chart for the country you are in.

4. When prompted, enter the telephone number you are calling as follows:
   ● For calls to the U.S., dial the Area Code (no need to dial 1 before the Area Code) + 7-digit number.
   ● For calls to other countries,† enter 01 + the Country Code, City Code, and Local Number.

5. After the tone, enter your AT&T Calling Card* or credit card number (not the international number). If you need help or wish to call the U.S. collect, hold for an AT&T Operator.

* You may also use your AT&T Corporate Card, AT&T Universal Card, or most U.S. local phone company cards.
† The cost of calls to countries other than the U.S. consists of basic connection rates plus an additional charge based on the country you are calling.
∞ Credit card billing subject to availability.

Calling From Specially Marked Telephones

Throughout the world, there are specially marked phones that connect you to AT&T Direct℠ Service. Simply look for the AT&T logo. In the following countries, access to AT&T Direct Service is only available from these phones: Ethiopia, Mongolia, Nigeria, Seychelles Islands.

Public phones in Europe displaying the red 3C symbol also give you quick and easy access to AT&T Direct Service. Just lift the handset and dial ✱60 (in France dial M60) and you'll be connected to AT&T.

Pay phones in the United Kingdom displaying the New World symbol provide easy access to AT&T. Simply lift the handset and press the pre-programmed button marked AT&T.

NEW WORLD

Customer Care

If you have any questions, call 800 331-1140, Ext. 707.

When outside the U.S., dial the AT&T Access Number for the country you are in and ask the AT&T Operator for Customer Care.

106-25   © AT&T 6/98

Printed in the U.S.A. on recycled paper.

AT&T

AT&T Access Numbers

(Refer to footnotes before dialing.) From the countries highlighted in blue below, like this ☐, you can make calls to the U.S. location in the world; and from *all* the countries listed, you can make calls to virtually any

It's all within your reach.

Albania ●	00-800-0010
American Samoa	633-2-USA
Angola	0199
Anguilla +	1-800-872-2881
Antigua +	1-800-872-2881
(Public Card Phones)	#1
Argentina	0-800-54-288
Armenia ▲ ●	8◆10111
Aruba	800-8000
Australia	1-800-881-011
Austria ○	022-903-011
Bahamas	1-800-872-2881
Bahrain	800-001
Bahrain →	800-000
Barbados +	1-800-872-2881
Belarus ✕ ⟶	8◆800101
Belgium ●	0-800-100-10
Belize	811
(From Hotels Only)	555
Benin ●	102
Bermuda +	1-800-872-2881
Bolivia	0-800-1112

Bosnia ▲	00-800-0010
Brazil	000-8010
British V.I. +	1-800-872-2881
Brunei	800-1111
Bulgaria ■ ▲	00-800-0010
Cambodia ✱	1-800-881-001
Canada	1 800 CALL ATT
Cape Verde Islands	112
Cayman Islands +	1-800-872-2881
Chile	800-800-311
or	800-800-288
(Easter Island)	800-800-311
China, PRC ▲	10811
Colombia	980-11-0010
Cook Island	09-111
Costa Rica	0-800-0-114-114
Croatia ▲	99-385-0111
Cyprus ●	080-90010
Czech Rep. ●	00-42-000-101
Denmark	8001-0010
Dominica +	1-800-872-2881

Dom. Rep. ✱ □	1-800-872-2881
Ecuador ▲	999-119
Egypt ● (Cairo)	510-0200
(Outside Cairo)	02-510-0200
El Salvador ○	800-1785
Estonia	8-00-8001001
Fiji	004-890-1001
Finland ●	9800-100-10
France	0800 99 00 11
French Antilles	0800 99 00 11
French Guiana	0800 99 00 11
Gabon ●	00◆001
Gambia ●	00111
Georgia ▲	8◆0288
Germany	0130-0010
Ghana	0191
Gibraltar	8800
Greece ●	00-800-1311
Grenada +	1-800-872-2881
Guadeloupe + ✱ (Marie-Galante)	0800 99 00 11

Guam	1 800 CALL ATT
Guantanamo Bay ↑ (Cuba)	935
Guatemala ○ ☀	99-99-190
Guyana ★	165
Haiti	183
Honduras	800-0-123
Hong Kong	800-96-1111
Hungary ●	00◆800-01111
Iceland	800 9001
India ★ ▲	000-117
Indonesia →	001-801-10
Ireland ✓	1-800-550-000
Israel	1-800-94-94-949
Italy ●	172-1011
Ivory Coast ●	00-111-11
Jamaica □	872
Jamaica ●	1-800-872-2881
Japan KDD ●	005-39-111
Japan IDC ▲	0066-55-111
Kazakhstan ●	8◆800-121-4321
Korea →	550-HOME or 550-2USA
Korea ▲²	0072-911 or 0030-911

Kuwait	800-288
Latvia (Riga)	700/7007
(Outside Riga)	8◆2700/7007
Lebanon ○ (Beirut)	426-801
(Outside Beirut)	01-426-801
Liechtenstein ●	0-800-89-0011
Lithuania ✕ ⟶	8◆196
Luxembourg †	0-800-0111
Macao	0800-111
Macedonia, F.Y.R. of ● ○	99-800-4288
Malaysia ○	1-800-80-0011
Malta	0800-890-110
Marshall Isl.	1 800 CALL ATT
Mauritius	01-111
Mexico ▽¹	01-800-288-2872
Micronesia	288
Monaco ●	800-90-288
Montserrat +	1-800-872-2881
Morocco	002-11-0011
Netherlands ●	0800-022-9111
Netherlands Antilles ◈	001-800-872-2881

New Zealand ●	000-911
Nicaragua	174
Norway	800-190-11
Pakistan ▲	00-800-01001
Palau	02288
Panama	109
(Canal Zone)	281-0109
Papua New Guinea	0507-12880
Paraguay ▲ (Asunción City)	008-11-800
Peru ●	0-800-50000
Philippines ●	105-11
Poland ●	0◆0-800-111-1111
Portugal ▲	05017-1-288
Qatar	0800-011-77
Reunion Isl.	0800 99 0011
Romania ●	01-800-4288
Romania →	01-801-0151
Russia ● ▲ (Moscow)	755-5042
(Outside Moscow)	8-095-755-5042

Russia ● ▲ (St. Petersburg)	325-5042
(Outside St. Petersburg)	8-812-325-5042
Saipan ▲	1 800 CALL ATT
San Marino ●	172-1011
Saudi Arabia ◇	1-800-10
Senegal	3072
Sierra Leone	1100
Singapore ■	800-0111-111
Slovakia ▲	00-42-100-101
Solomon Isl.	0811
So. Africa	0-800-99-0123
Spain	900-99-00-11
Sri Lanka ■	430-430
Sudan	800-001
Suriname △	156

Sweden	020-795-611
Switzerland ●	0-800-89-0011
Syria	0-801
Taiwan	0080-10288-0
Thailand ◁	001-999-111-11
Trinidad/Tob.	0800-872-2881
Turkey ●	00-800-12277
Turks & Caicos + ↑	01-800-872-2881
U. Arab Emirates	800-121
Uganda	800-001
Ukraine ▲	8◆100-11
U.K. ▲ ✦	0800-89-0011 or 0500-89-0011
U.S. ▼	1 800 CALL ATT
Uruguay	000-410
Uzbekistan 8◆	641-7440010
Venezuela ▲	800-11-120
Vietnam ●	1-201-0288
Yemen	00 800 101
Zambia	00-899
Zimbabwe ▲	110-98990

● Public phones require coin or card deposit. ✂ Press red button ↑ Additional charges apply when calling outside of Moscow. ■ AT&T Direct℠ calls cannot be placed to this country from outside the U.S. ✱ Available from pay phones in Phnom Penh and Siem Reap only. ✕ Not available from public phones.
⊕ From St. Maarten or phones at Bobby's Marina, use 1-800-872-2881.

◇ From this country, AT&T Direct℠ calls terminate to designated countries only.
→ From U.S. Military Bases only. ⟶ Not yet available from all areas. ☀ Select hotels.
▲ May not be available from every phone/public phone. † Collect calling from public phones. ▽ Available from phones with international calling capabilities or from most Public Calling Centers. ✓ From Northern Ireland use U.K. access code.

★ Collect calling only. ○ Public phones require local coin payment through the call duration. ◆ Await second dial tone. ▽ When calling from public phones, use phones marked "Ladatel." ¹ If call does not complete, use 001-800-462-4240. △ Available from public phones, and select hotels. ◈ Public phones only. ✦ Public phones and select hotels. ◁ When calling from public phones use phones marked Lenso.

□ Calling Card calls available from select hotels. ✂ Use phones allowing international access. ▼ Including Puerto Rico and the U.S. Virgin Islands.
▼ AT&T Direct℠ Service only from telephone calling centers in Hanoi and post offices in Da Nang, Ho Chi Minh City and Quang Ninh. ✦ If call does not complete, use 0800-013-0011.

WE GIVE YOU THE WORLD...AT A DISCOUNT

LET'S GO®

TRAVEL

MERCHANDISE CATALOG FOR 1999

LET'S GO Travel Gear

World Journey

Equipped with Eagle Creek Comfort Zone Carry System which includes Hydrofil nylon knit on backpanel and lumbar pads. Parallel internal frame. Easy packing panel load design with internal cinch straps. Lockable zippers. Detachable daypack. Converts into suitcase. 26x15x9", 5100 cu. in., 6 lbs. 12 oz. Black, Evergreen, or Blue. $30 discount with railpass. **$225.00**

Security Items

Undercover Neckpouch Ripstop nylon with a soft Cambrelle back. Three pockets. 5 1/2" x 8 1/2". Lifetime guarantee. Black or Tan. **$10.50**

Undercover Waistpouch Ripstop nylon with a soft Cambrelle back. Two pockets. 12" x 5" with adjustable waistband. Lifetime guarantee. Black or Tan. **$10.50**

Continental Journey

Carry-on size pack with internal frame suspension. Comfort Zone padded shoulder straps and hip belt. Leather hand grip. Easy packing panel load design with internal cinch straps. Lockable zippers. Detachable daypack. Converts into suitcase. 21x15x9", 3900 cu. in., 4 lbs. 5 oz. Black, Evergreen, or Blue. $20 discount with railpass. **$175.00**

Travel Lock Great for locking up your World or Continental Journey. Two-dial combination lock. **$5.25**

Hostelling Essentials

Hostelling International Membership

Cardholders receive priority, discounts, and reservation privileges at most domestic and international hostels.

Youth (under 18)....................	free
Adult (ages 18-55)................	**$25.00**
Senior (over 55)....................	**$15.00**

European Hostelling Guide

Offers essential information concerning over 2500 European hostels. **$10.95**

Sleepsack

Required at many hostels. Washable polyester/cotton. Durable and compact. **$14.95**

International ID Cards 1999

Provide discounts on airfares, tourist attractions and more. Includes basic accident and medical insurance. **$20.00**

International Student ID Card (ISIC)
International Teacher ID Card (ITIC)
International Youth ID Card (GO25)

1-800-5LETSGO

http://www.hsa.net/travel

— Prices are in US dollars and subject to change.—

Eurailpass Unlimited travel in and among all 17 countries: **Austria, Belgium, Denmark, Finland, France, Germany, Greece, Holland, Hungary, Italy, Luxembourg, Norway, Portugal, Republic of Ireland, Spain, Sweden, and Switzerland.**

	15 days	21 days	1 month	2 months	3 months	10 days	15 days
First Class	*consecutive days*					*in two months*	
1 Passenger	$554	$718	$890	$1260	$1558	$654	$862
2 or More Passengers	$470	$610	$756	$1072	$1324	$556	$732
Youthpass (Second Class)							
Passengers under 26	$388	$499	$623	$882	$1089	$458	$599

Europass Travel in the five Europass countries: **France, Germany, Italy, Spain, and Switzerland.** Up to two of the four associate regions (Austria and Hungary; Benelux (Belgium, Netherlands, and Luxembourg); Greece; Portugal) may be added.

	5 days	6 days	8 days	10 days	15 days	first	second
First Class	*in two months*					*associate country*	
1 Passenger	$348	$368	$448	$528	$728	+$60	+$40
2 to 5 Passengers traveling together	$296	$314	$382	$450	$620	+$52	+$34
Youthpass (Second Class)							
Passengers under 26	$233	$253	$313	$363	$513	+$45	+$33

Pass Protection For an additional **$10**, insure any railpass against theft or loss.

Discounts *with the purchase of a railpass*
- $30 off a World Journey backpack
- $20 off a Continental Journey backpack
- Any *Let's Go* Guide for 1/2 Price
- Free 2-3 Week Domestic Shipping

Call about Eurostar–the Channel Tunnel Train–and other country-specific passes.

Airfares & Special Promotions

Call for information on and availability of standard airline tickets, student, teacher, and youth discounted airfares, as well as other special promotions.

Publications & More

Let's Go Travel Guides— *The Bible of the Budget Traveler*

USA • India and Nepal • Southeast Asia............**22.99**
Australia • Eastern Europe • Europe...................**21.99**
Britain & Ireland • Central America • France •
Germany • Israel & Egypt • Italy • Mexico •
Spain & Portugal.......................................**19.99**
Alaska & The Pacific Northwest • Austria &
Switzerland • California & Hawaii • Ecuador
& The Galapagos Islands • Greece • Ireland.....**18.99**
South Africa • Turkey.................................**17.99**
New York City • New Zealand • London •
Paris • Rome • Washington D.C. **15.99**

Let's Go Map Guides
Know your destination inside and out! Great to accompany your Eurailpass.

Amsterdam, Berlin, Boston, Chicago, Florence, London, Los Angeles, Madrid, New Orleans, New York, Paris, Rome, San Francisco, Washington D.C. **8.95**

Michelin Maps

Czech/Slovak Republics • Europe • France • Germany • Germany/Austria /Benelux • Great Britain & Ireland • Greece • Italy • Poland • Scandinavia & Finland • Spain & Portugal **10.95**

LET'S GO Order Form

Last Name*	First Name*	Home and Day Phone Number* (very important)

Street*   (Sorry, we cannot ship to Post Office Boxes)

City*	State*	Zip Code*

Citizenship‡§□ (Country)	School/College§	Date of Birth‡§	Date of Travel*

Qty	Description	Color	Unit Price	Total Price

Shipping and Handling

2-3 Week Domestic Shipping	
Merchandise value under $30	$4
Merchandise value $30-$100	$6
Merchandise value over $100	$8
2-3 Day Domestic Shipping	
Merchandise value under $30	$14
Merchandise value $30-$100	$16
Merchandise value over $100	$18
Overnight Domestic Shipping	
Merchandise value under $30	$24
Merchandise value $30-$100	$26
Merchandise value over $100	$28
All International Shipping	$30

Total Purchase Price	
Shipping and Handling	+
MA Residents add 5% sales tax on gear and books	+
TOTAL	

☐ Mastercard   ☐ Visa

Cardholder name:

Card number:

Expiration date:

When ordering an International ID Card, please include:
1. Proof of birthdate (copy of passport, birth certificate, or driver's license).
2. One picture (1.5" x 2") signed on the reverse side.
3. (ISIC/ITIC only) Proof of current student/teacher status (letter from registrar or administrator, proof of tuition, or copy of student/faculty ID card. FULL-TIME only).

* Required for all orders
‡ Required in addition for each Hostelling Membership
§ Required in addition for each International ID Card
□ Required in addition for each railpass

Prices are in US dollars and subject to change.

Make check or money order payable to:
Let's Go Travel
17 Holyoke Street
Cambridge, MA 02138
(617) 495-9649

1-800-5LETSGO

Hours: Mon.-Fri., 10am-6pm ET

decorated in various shades of gray. Some have private baths (singles 8000dr; doubles 11,000dr; triples 13,000dr). On a side street just before the Ionion is **Voultses Domatia** (tel. 92 161), which offers a tiny room with a shared bath for 5000dr and a larger room with a private bath for 10,000dr.

■ Near Killini

The Frankish **Chlemoutsi Castle** and the mineral springs of **Loutra Killinis**, a well-manicured resort with a long beach, are 20km from Killini; getting to either is difficult unless you have your own transportation or are willing to pay for a taxi (1200dr to the castle, 3000dr to Loutra). Near Loutra is **Camping Killinis** (tel. 96 259). The campgrounds are close to the sea and include a market and hot showers (1200dr per person; 700dr per small tent; 1200dr per large tent, 700dr per car). Three buses per day leave Loutra for the castle. Nearby is **Karitena**, the village pictured on the 5000dr bill. The birthplace of Kolokotronis (a famous Greek nationalist of the revolutionary period), Karitena has ruins of a Frankish castle and a 13th-century church dedicated to St. Nicholas. Its beauty may entice you to stay. **Stamata Kondopoulos** (tel. 31 206) has rooms near the post office (singles 5000dr; doubles 7000dr).

■ Olympia Ολυμπια

Shaded by lush trees and sprinkled with potted flowers, modern Olympia is a friendly and attractive town in its own right. However, one cannot but feel that the town exists only as a place to sleep and eat near that gold mine of a tourist attraction, the ruins of the site of the ancient Olympic games. Generally, modern Olympia handles its intense tourism with commendable taste; its tourist shops do not spill out onto the sidewalks, and no one lurks outside of restaurants to harass passers-by. Modern Olympia knows its place and serves its supportive role well in the shadow of the magnificent archaeological site and museum.

ORIENTATION AND PRACTICAL INFORMATION

Modern Olympia consists primarily of a 1km main street, **Kondili St.** The bus will drop you off across from the tourist office. Head out of town on the main road for a five-minute walk to the ruins and the archaeological museum.

Transportation
Buses: bus stop is directly across from the tourist information shack, which has an up-to-date schedule posted. Buses go to Pirgos (40min., 16 per day between 6:30am-10pm, 380dr); Tripoli (3½hr., 3 per day, 2300dr); Dimitsana (M and F, 1500dr), and Lala (30 min., 1 per day, 300dr). Reduced service on weekends.

Tourist and Financial Services
Tourist Office: (tel. 23 100), Kondili St., on the east side of town, towards the ruins. July and Aug open daily 9am-9pm, Sept.-June open daily 11am-5pm. Has a photocopy machine, stamps, and provides maps.
Bank: National Bank, on Kondili St., has an **ATM,** and offers **currency exchange.** Open M-Th 8am-2pm, F 8am-1:30pm.
Bookstore: Athanasia Bookshop, Kondili St., on the east end of town. Carries a selection of guidebooks, novels, and books on Greece. Open daily 8am-11pm.

Emergency and Communications
Police: 1 Em. Kountsa Ave., 1 block up from Kondili St. (tel. 22 100). Open 9am-9pm, but someone is there 24hr. **Tourist police** may be around in the morning.
Hospital: (tel. (0621) 22 222) in Pirgos, (tel. 22 222) in Olympia. Olympia uses Pirgos' hospital, but has a **health center** of its own. Walk from the ruins down Kondili St. Before the church (on your left), turn left. Continue straight, and after the road winds right and then left; take a left. Open M-F 8am-2pm.
Post Office: (tel. 22 578), on a nameless, uphill side street just past the tourist information center. Open M-F 7:30am-2pm. **Postal Code:** 27065.
OTE: Kondili St., by the post office. Open M-F 7:30am-2pm. **Telephone Code:** 0624.

ACCOMMODATIONS

If all you want is a cheap place to crash, head for the youth hostel. Otherwise, choose from dozens of hotels, most of which offer private baths and balconies. Prices vary but hover around 8000dr per double. They are 20-40% less in the off season.

Youth Hostel, 18 Kondili St. (tel. 22 580). Convenient location. Membership not needed. No curfew. Check-out 10am. Breakfast 600dr. 1600dr per day.

Pension Possidon (tel. 22 567), turn uphill at the National Bank and go 2 blocks. Offers clean rooms, some with bath. Singles 4000dr; doubles 6000dr.

Pension Achilleus (tel. 22 567), across the street and one block down from Pension Possidon. Clean rooms with private bathrooms. Doubles 6000dr, triples 9000dr.

Rooms to let, ask at **O Thraka Restaurant** (tel. 22575), on Kondili closer to Pirgos than the site. Large rooms with bath and balcony. Singles 5000dr; doubles 8000dr.

Camping Diana (tel. 22 314), uphill from the Sports Museum. Offers a clean pool, hot water, and breakfast (900dr). Electricity 900dr. 10-20% student discounts. 1400dr per person; 890dr per car; 900dr per small tent; 1300dr per large tent.

Camping Olympia (tel. 22 745), 1km west on the road to Pirgos, has a baby pool and larger pool. Electricity 850dr. 1100dr per person; 750dr per car; 900dr per small tent; 1050dr per large tent.

FOOD

Along Kondili St. there are numerous markets where you can pick up the makings for a picnic lunch. Most restaurants on Kondili Ave. are cramped and overpriced, but a walk toward the railroad station or up the hill and away from the busloads of tourists reveals some charming and inexpensive *tavernas.* Since the town caters mainly to tourists, most restaurants open at 8am and close after 1am.

O Kladeus, behind Olympia's train station (its sign is obvious), is that perfect *taverna* you've been seeking. The menu features fish (1200dr) and Greek salad (700dr). The dirt floor, ramshackle canopy, ragged table settings, and the mysterious, potent "house wine" set the mood. Be sure to bring bug repellant.

Ambrosia (tel. 23 414), in a white building just before O Kladeus, has the same peaceful location in the woods but is slightly more refined. Excellent quality. Drigan lamb with potatoes (1850dr), rabbit with lemon sauce (1800dr).

Pension Possidon's small taverna (tel. 22 567), under vine-covered lattices just outside the pension, has a small selection but unbeatable prices. George, the owner, makes the wine and his mother cooks the fare. When he recommends the dishes, one feels he is naming childhood favorites. Chicken from the grill 1200dr; home made *retsina* 800dr per liter.

SIGHTS

On the other side of town, towards Pirgos, sports enthusiasts will appreciate the **Museum of the Olympic Games** (tel. 22 544), with paraphernalia from each of the modern Olympic games. Located on Angerinou St., it's two blocks uphill from Kondili St. *(Open M-Sa 8am-3:30pm, S 9am-4:30pm. Admission 500dr.)*

■ Ancient Olympia

> Let us not proclaim any contest greater than Olympia. From there glorious
> song enfolds the wisdom of poets, so that they loudly sing.
> —Pindar, *Olympian Odes 1.5*

History

This legendary site between the Kladeo and Alphios Rivers was never a city, but an event. Here, the leaders of rival city-states shed their armor and congregated in peace to enjoy the games and make offerings to the gods. A green and tranquil tract between the two rivers, Olympia was, for over a millennium, one of the most important cultural centers of the Greek world. Here, Greeks convened from across the Hel-

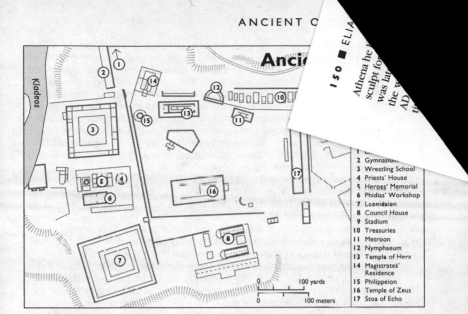

Athena he...
sculpt fo...
was la...
the w...
AD...

2 Gymnasium
3 Wrestling School
4 Priests' House
5 Heroes' Memorial
6 Phidias' Workshop
7 Leonidaion
8 Council House
9 Stadium
10 Treasuries
11 Metroon
12 Nymphaeum
13 Temple of Hera
14 Magistrates'
   Residence
15 Philippeion
16 Temple of Zeus
17 Stoa of Echo

0   100 yards
0   100 meters

lenic world, from Sicily to Asia Minor, from North Africa to Macedonia, and set aside their hostilities to worship, compete, and most of all—listening to poetry and musicians, surrounded by architectural and artistic masterpieces—appreciate Greek culture. At that time Greeks were organized into hundreds of small states often at war with one another, but when heralds arrived every four years to call a truce and announce the games, all shed their armor to travel with reverence to Olympia and participate in the most splendid Panhellenic assembly of the ancient world.

The ancient Greeks dated the inception of the games to mythical times. The first recorded Olympiad was in 776 BC, when Koroibos of Elis was victor, and every four years thereafter another champion added his name to the illustrious list, representing the first certain and accurate chronology of Greek history. The central sanctuary of the Olympic complex, which was eventually walled and dedicated to Zeus, was called the *Altis;* over the centuries, temples, treasuries, and numerous monuments to the gods were erected in the sanctuary. Surrounding the *Altis,* were various facilities for participants and administrators, including the stadium on the far east side

Touring Olympia

*Tel. 22 517. **Open** daily 8am-7pm. **Admission** 1200dr; students 600dr, EU students free. A guide and map are vital, as the ruins are poorly marked. Two thorough **guides** are available at the site—the red Olympia by Spiros Photinos (2000dr) and the Blue Guide to the Museum and Sanctuary by A. and N. Yalouris (2500dr).*

Pausanias, a traveler writing in the 2nd century AD, mentions a whopping 69 separate monuments built by victors in offering to the gods, yet it is probable that he did not include all of them in his account. Although the ruins are not especially well preserved, the site's colossal dimensions remain impressive. Few sections are corded off; you can climb up the steps of the Temple of Zeus and wander through Phidias' workshop as you please.

As you enter the site, the thigh-high remains of the **Gymnasium,** dating from the 2nd century BC, lie to your right. To the left is the **Prytaneion,** with its sacred hearth. Past the Gymnasium stand the re-erected columns of the **Palaestra,** the wrestling school. Always more than just an athletic facility, the *Palaestra* served an educational role as philosophic as it was athletic. Here young men trained their minds as well as their bodies, wrestling at one moment and studying Homer the next.

The next group of buildings includes the **Workshop of Phidias,** who came to Olympia after he was banished from Athens in a scandal connected to the statue of had created for the Parthenon. While in Olympia he was commissioned to the Temple of Zeus; he produced a statue of the god so magnificent that it r called one of the **seven wonders of the ancient world.** As you will notice, orkshop was converted to a Christian church sometime after the 4th century The walls were changed but the foundation remains the same. For years the identity of the site was debated, as some doubted the traditional sources that claimed it as the workshop of the famous sculptor; however, recent excavations of the building yielded moulds, various sculpting tools and, most amazing of all, shards of a plain wine jug that, when they were cleaned and mended, had the inscription, ΦΕΙΔΙΟ EIMI, "I belong to Phidias." All of these finds are on display in the museum. Farther on is the huge **Leonidaion,** the lodgings of game officials.

To the left and slightly raised are the ruins of the once gigantic **Temple of Zeus,** the centerpiece of the *Altis* after its construction in 457 BC. The tremendous columns lie toppled in segments as they fell in an earthquake in the sixth century AD. Parts of the original mosaic floor can still be seen on the temple base. The nave of the temple once housed Phidias' magnificent gold and ivory statue of Zeus. The Emperor Theodosius had the statue removed to Constantinople after he banned the pagan Olympic games at the end of the 4th century AD, where it was destroyed by fire in 475.

Continuing east past the temple, you will reach the remains of the **Stoa of Echo,** said to have had a seven-fold echo. At the northern edge of the *Stoa* is the **Krypte,** the official entrance to the stadium, used by both the athletes and the judges. This domed passageway (only one arch survives of the domed roof) and the stadium seen today are the work of the Hellenistic period, built over the remains of the earlier stadium, which was roughly in the same position.

Because earthquakes cannot topple it and because men must go to considerable effort to destroy it, the stadium appears today very much as it did 2300 years ago. **The Judges' Stand** is still in place, as are the start and finish lines, and the stadium's grassy banks can still seat nearly 40,000 spectators.

In a row on the bank to your right as you leave the passageway to the stadium are the remains of the numerous treasuries erected primarily by distant states to house their ever-accumulating votive offerings. Eastward, beyond the treasuries, lie the remains of the **nymphaeum** and the **metroon,** an elegant temple in the Doric style, built to honor the gods in the 4th century BC.

Westward, past the metroon and the nymphaeum lie the dignified remains of the **Temple of Hera.** Although it is the oldest building at Olympia as well as the oldest Doric temple in Greece—erected in the 7th century BC—the temple of Hera is the best-preserved structure at the site. Originally built for both Zeus and Hera, it was devoted solely to the goddess when Zeus moved to separate and grander quarters in 457BC. This temple figured prominently in the **Heraia,** a women's foot race held every four years. The **Olympic flame** is still lit here, then borne to the site of the modern games by the necessary vehicles, runners, school children, Hell's Angels, classicists, mangy dogs, and anyone else wishing to join the Coca-Cola-sponsored panoply.

On your way out of the complex you will pass the remains of the **Phillipeion,** a *tholos*-style structure built by King Phillip of Macedonia in the late 4th century BC.

Museum

The museum is through the parking lot opposite the ancient site. Tel. 22 742. **Open** *Tu-F 8am-8pm, Sa-M noon-8pm.* **Admission** *1200dr, students 600dr, EU students and children under 18 free. Cameras with flash prohibited.*

The gleaming **New Museum** and its countless treasures is, for many, a greater attraction than the ancient site. A team of French archaeologists began unearthing the site from 1400 years of silt in 1829; systematic excavations commenced in 1875 and have continued to this day. Most of what has been extracted from the ground in these 124 years, from the mundane to the wildly spectacular, resides in the museum.

Since military victors across the Greek world sent spoils and pieces of their own equipment to Olympia in offering to the gods, the new museum, not surprisingly, could also be a museum of Greek military history. Helmets, cuirasses, greaves, swords, spear points, and other military paraphernalia fill entire rooms. Easily the most spectacular of all of the military offerings is a helmet of the common Corinthian type, partially destroyed by oxidation. Seemingly inferior to the richer and better preserved examples to be found elsewhere in the museum, the helmet's lodestone lies in a faint inscription on the chin guard, ΜΙΛΤΙΑΔΕΣ ΑΝΕΘΕΚΕΝ ΤΟΙ ΔΙΙ, "Miltiades dedicated this to Zeus." Miltiades was the victor of what is perhaps the most famous battle of antiquity, at Marathon in 479 BC, when his outnumbered Greek army defeated the Persians. Educated speculation suggests that Miltiases wore this helmet during the battle. In an unbelievable convergence of history and archaeology, displayed beside the Miltiades helmet is another headpiece whose inscription reveals that it was taken from the Persians in the same battle.

The museum also has an awesome array of sculpture. Most notable of these are the **Nike of Paionios,** the **Hermes of Praxiteles,** and the **podimental sculptures** from the Temple of Zeus. The last two fill their own rooms, as their fame fills the world. Upon confronting them in the museum, any visitor will almost certainly have the sensation of having seen them before. However, even the lesser known objects will not fail to impress—because of the magnitude of the museum's collection, every case contains objects that would be the centerpieces of smaller collections.

ARCADIA Αρκαδια

Poets since Theocritus have fancied Arcadia to be the archetypal pastoral setting. Gods, too, appreciated the area—Pan and Dionysus chose this lush, mountain-ringed land as the site of their gleeful dances. Rural serenity still fills hidden bays, deep green vegetation, dramatic mountains, and vast fir forests. Elsewhere, as in the bustling metropolis of Tripoli, the modern era has brought a rumble of buses and cargo to the fields where satyrs once cavorted.

▓ Tripoli Τριπολη

Tripoli is the transportation hub of Arcadia. Its crowded streets and sidewalks, both dominated by motorists who demonstrate their driving prowess by narrowly missing pedestrians, can be initially dismaying. Buses to the wonderful mountain villages are infrequent, and travelers may have to spend the night. If you stay, don't despair; Tripoli has pleasant squares with cafes, churches, trees, and a tourist-free atmosphere. Nightlife may feel a bit adolescent, but Tripoli's integrity rests in its unspoiled, albeit modern, charm.

ORIENTATION AND PRACTICAL INFORMATION

Think of Tripoli as a cross. At the joint is **Agios Vasiliou Square,** a large square marked, unsurprisingly, by the Church of Agios Vasiliou. The square is the geographical center of the city. Four other squares form the ends of the cross along the four roads that radiate out from Agios Vasiliou. Most buses arrive at Arcadia station in **Kolokotronis Square,** the square to the east of the center. Georgiou St. will take you from here to Agios Vasiliou Sq. Facing the Church of Agios Vasiliou, take a left on Ethnikis Antistasis St. to reach **Petrinou Square,** home to the police and recognizable by the large, neoclassical Maliaropouli Theater. This is the north part of the cross and, along with Kolokotronis Sq., sees most of the city's activity. Continue along Ethnikis Antistasis St., the main shopping boulevard, looking to your right to find the **park,** occupying about eight city blocks, and a vast open square with a 5m-high statue of Kolokotronis, a hero of the War of Independence. The blocks around the park house boutiques, cafes, clubs, and hotels, and provide the best outpost for people-watching. The park is in **Areus Square.**

Transportation
Buses: Arcadias Station (tel. 22 25 60) in Kolokotronis Sq. has buses to Athens (2hr., 13 per day, 3000dr); Dimitsana (1hr., 2 per day on weekdays, 1 per day on weekends, 1200dr); Pirgos (3½hr., 2 per day, 2500dr); Andritsena (2hr., 1 per day,

1450dr); and Megalopolis (45min., 9 per day, 600dr). Buses go from the **KTEL Messinia and Laconia** bus depot (tel. 24 20 86), across from the train station, to: Kalamata (2hr., 12per day, 1500dr); Pylos (3hr., 5 per day, 2400dr); Sparta (1hr., 8 per day, 1000dr); and Patras (3hr., 2 per day, 3000dr). **Blue buses** leave from the kiosk at Areus Sq. for Tegea and Mantinea (15min., every hr., 200dr).

Trains: The station (tel. 24 12 13) is 1km west of Kolokotronis Sq. Go through the bus station and turn right—the station is at the end of the street. 4 trains per day to: Athens (4hr., 1500dr); Corinth (2½hr., 900dr); Argos (1½hr., 590dr); and Kalamata (2½hr., 840dr).

Tourist and Financial Services

Tourist Office: (tel. 23 18 44) In the town hall past Petrinou Sq. on Ethnikis Antistasis St. Look for the flag and colored windows. Open M-F 8am-12:30pm.

Bank: National Bank (tel. 22 54 89 or 24 29 53), on Ethnikis Antistasis St., is one block from Agios Vasiliou Square. It offers **currency exchange** (open M-Th 8am-2pm, F 8am-1:30pm). A 24hr. **ATM** is located 10m from the bank's entrance—look for the metal door on Ethnikis Antistasis St.

Emergency and Communications

Police: (tel. 22 24 11), on Ethnikis Antistasis St., next to the theater at the center of Petrinou Sq. Open 24hr.

Hospital: (tel. 23 85 42), located on Panargadon Rd. (on the far western ring of the city). Walk due west from Agios Vasiliou St. The road becomes E. Stavrou, which intersects with Panargadon St. after 500m. At the intersection, turn left. After another 300m, look right.

Post Office: on Plapouta St. (tel. 22 2565). With your back to the church in Agios Vasiliou Sq., go straight on V. Pavlou St. (away from the church). Take the first right on Nikitara St. and, after one block, the post office is across the street (open M-F 7:30am-2pm). **Postal Code:** 22100.

OTE: #29 Octovriou 28th St. (tel. 22 63 99). From Agios Vasiliou Sq., take Eth. Antistasis St. and bear left immediately on 28th Octovriou St.—you'll see its tower (open M-F 7am-10pm). **Telephone Code:** 071.

ACCOMMODATIONS

Tripoli is better suited to business conventions than to budget travelers with numerous bloated and middle-range hotels with spotty lighting. Camping near Tripoli is non-existent, and impromptu camping, as ever, is illegal.

Hotel Anactoricon (tel. 22 25 45; fax 22 20 21), on Ethnikis Antistasis St. two blocks before the park. This is usually your best bet—with a magnificent main hall and high ceilings in the rooms, this place borders on elegant. However, you may not want to stay here on a weekend, as the hotel is directly above a cafe with a good sound system. Singles 4000dr, with bath and TV 8000dr; doubles 8000dr, with bath and TV 10,000dr; triples 12,000dr with bath and TV.

Hotel Alex, 26 Vas. Georgios St. (tel. 22 34 65), between Kolokotronis Sq. and Agios Vasiliou Sq., offers standard rooms in varying shades of puce. Ask for a room at the back, because the noise from the nearby bus station can make Tripoli seem like the city that never sleeps. Singles 6000dr, with bath 7000dr; doubles 10,000dr, with bath 12,500dr.

Hotel Artemis (tel. 22 52 21), right on the park, is a little pricey, but it offers large rooms with TVs and double beds. Singles 6000dr; doubles 11,000dr.

Galaxy Hotel (tel. 22 51 95; fax 22 51 97), across the square from the church of Agios Visiliou, another expensive but well-furnished option. All rooms with private bath and television. Singles 9000dr; doubles 13,500dr; triples 16,000dr.

FOOD

The best food in Tripoli borders the park; elsewhere in the city, trendy cafes and fast food dominate. Overall, Tripoli lacks culinary inspiration, but if you subscribe to the quick-fix theory of dining out, a number of sandwich shops serve up tasty baguettes stuffed with meat and cheese (300-500dr). Just walk up and down Ethnikis Antistasis St. and Georgiou St.

Menalon Restaurant, on the bottom floor of the hotel with the same name along the south edge of the park, serves well-prepared traditional dishes at prices much lower than its elegant table settings might suggest. Their seating stretches out into the main square of the park, called Areus Sq. Greek salad 850dr; veal with tomato sauce 1600dr. Open daily 8:30pm-late.

Restaurant Lido, on the far west side of the park's square, serves large portions of mostly Italian fare among roses (900-1100dr). It is open for lunch as well as dinner. Spaghetti 900dr; tuna salad 950dr.

Park Chalet, also on the south side of the park's square, includes some seafood on its menu. Ocean perch 1300dr, chicken with lemon 1400dr, Greek salad 850dr,

Kipos Sosoli Restaurant, a more traditional Greek restaurant located in a garden-like backyard one block off Ethnikis Antistasis St. on Pavlou St., offers entrees under 1500dr. The menu is in Greek, but the staff will gladly translate for you.

ENTERTAINMENT

At night you can rub shoulders with Tripoli's high school students at the bars along Ethnikis Antistasis St. past Petrinou Sq. Especially popular is the **Cinema Classic Billiards Club** on the pedestrian street off Ethnikis Antistasis St., just before the park. Air-conditioned and with a big screen TV, this place fills up every night (beer 400dr; 1hr. of pool 1600dr). Numerous other cafes crowd this same pedestrian street, competing to play the loudest music. **The American Music Bar,** about 20m down the street, is always in the running, if not the victor.

In the summer, posters advertise dance groups, choirs, and plays that can be seen in the city's main squares and in nearby villages. The **Lera Panigyris** is a 10-day cultural festival that starts August 15. Traveling companies and local performance groups also stage Greek-language shows in the attractive **Maliaropoulio Theater,** which dominates Petrinou Sq. If you're interested, ask at the tourist office (tickets 1000-2000dr). During Easter, the town's bishop roasts a lamb in one of the squares, and all in attendance eat for free.

SIGHTS

The **Archaeological Museum** (tel. 24 21 48) is on Evangelistrias St., in a yellow flower-bedecked building. From Kolokotronis Sq. to Agios Vasiliou Sq., take the first left, and turn left again. The museum has an especially large prehistoric collection, with room after room displaying predominantly pottery—but also jewelry and weaponry—from the neolithic to the Mycenaean periods. Among the later pieces is an Hellenistic relief showing one of its figures with a scroll in hand, making it one of the few surviving artistic depictions of the ancient form of book. The large **Church of Agios Vasiliou** is in the square of the same name. Check out the shops under the church—they're great for religious art.

■ Near Tripoli

About 60km west of Tripoli on the high ridges of the Erimanthos, Menalo, and Oligirtos mountain ranges, lie the small villages of **Dimitsana** and **Stemnitsa.** Both villages offer a quintessentially Arcadian setting, clinging to steep, rocky mountainsides covered variously with pine trees, olive trees, grass, and goats. In places, the landscape seems so steep and barren as to defy inhabitation, but in others—beside a mossy fountain in Stemnitsa, or up a narrow, cobbled street in Dimitsana—you might swear that this was the only place people were meant to live. Fortunately, because buses run infrequently to and from Dimitsana, if you make it here, you will not likely have anyone with whom to share the fountain, nor anyone to sell you a picture of it afterwards. At most, the towns receive Greek weekenders and determined foreign tourists with their own transportation.

■ Dimitsana Δημητσανα

Built on the ruins of ancient Teuthis, with a magnificent view of the plain of Megalop-olis and the Lousios river, Dimitsana has been a center of Greek learning and revolu-tionary activity since the 16th century. The Dimitsana School and the nearby Monastery of the Philosopher, where there was a secret school during the Turkish occupation, produced several notable church fathers of Roumeli and the Morea dur-ing the War of Independence.

The bus deposits you on Labardopoulou St. across from a cafe that doubles as a **taxi stand. Pesonton Square,** the heart of the town, is 30m up the road and around a bend. Walking up the town, you will first pass the **OTE** on your right (open M-F 7am-2:30pm). Walk through the square and just around the second bend, and the **National Bank** (tel. 31 503) will be on your left (open M-Th 8am-2pm, F 8am-1:30pm). Be sure to bring money with you, because the bank has no ATM. Just past the bank is the **post office** (tel. 22 007; open M-F 7am-2pm). **Telephone code:** 0795.

Transportation can be tricky in the mountains, and you'll find locals in the towns frustratingly indifferent to the passage of time. When planning connections, keep in mind that the two taxis in some towns might *siesta* all afternoon. To Dimitsana, **buses** run from Tripoli (1½hr., 2 per day, 1200dr), and from Olympia (1hr., 2 per week M and F, 1500dr). From Dimitsana, buses leave for Tripoli (2 per day M-F, 7:30am and noon, weekends 7:30am only, 1200dr). From Karkalou, a 20-minute (1000dr) taxi ride away, buses to Tripoli, Pirgos, and Olympia make frequent stops.

There's one hotel in Dimitsana, the pretty but pricey **Hotel Dimitsana** (tel. 37 578), 1km down the road to Stemnitsa. To find the hotel, keep walking on the main road away from the bus station. Where the road splits, about 500m past the National Bank and the post office, take the left fork. The hotel is a few meters ahead (singles 10,000dr; doubles 13,500dr; breakfast included).

A better option is to let a room in town. The rooms above the grocery store in the main square are newly remodeled, with bathrooms, balconies, and televisions (sin-gles 5000dr, with balconies 8000). More rooms can also be found off the square: turn right on Grigoriou St. off the main square and follow the signs to a house in which a family lets more newly remodeled rooms with bathrooms, balconies, and excellent views (singles 6000dr; doubles 8000dr).

Two small museums commemorate the town's ecclesiastic, scholarly, and revolu-tionary heritage. The **historical museum** within the library (tel. 31 219), halfway up the main road, displays an eclectic collection of objects, including war of indepen-dence-vintage pistols, two 15th-century illuminated psalters from a nearby monas-tery, and a handful of Italian edition Greek-Latin *incunabula* of various church fathers and ancient authors. *(Open M-F 9am-1:30pm, Su 8am-noon.)* To find the museum and library, climb the steps wither at the bus stop or at the main square. Look for a church across from an elementary school in a small gravel courtyard. The entrance to the museum and library is at the far end of the elementary school, facing the plain of Megalopolis in the distance. Walking away from the bus station, the second of these, the **Icon Museum** (tel. 31 465), is off the main square up the second alley on the right. *(Open Sa-Tu and Th 10am-1:30pm and 5-7pm.)*

■ Stemnitsa Στεμνιτσα

From Dimitsana, walk 11km along the road (or pay 1000dr for a taxi) past thick for-ests on the slopes above and remote monasteries built against the cliffs below, to **Stemnitsa,** a gorgeous town whose narrow, irregular cobbled streets betray medi-eval construction. Many consider the town to be one of the most beautiful in Greece. Adding to this claim is the splendid **Hotel Triokolonion** (tel. 81 297, fax 81 483) on the left side of the main road (singles 7500dr; doubles 9000dr; triples 11,500dr). The **post office** (tel. 81 280) is behind the church in the square (open M-F 8:30am-11:25am). **Postal code:** 22024. **Telephone code:** 0795.

From among the square's numerous cafes and tavernas, consider the tiny **Taverna Klinitsa** (tel. 81 438) for an inexpensive treat. Here Mama Roilos serves up original dishes, specializing in creative vegetarian fare (*fasolacia* 600dr, *briam* 500dr). If you're lucky, you may get to try Mama's special fried bread on the house. **Katholikon,** a cafe with tables on a grassy lawn, occupies an excellent vantage above the main square. Walk past the main square in the direction of the hotel (away from Dimitsana) and the stone stairs leading up to the cafe will be on your left (beer 400-500dr, orange juice 300dr).

Off the road from Dimitsana to Stemnitsa are several monasteries, some built right into the mountain face. One of these is the **Monastery of Agios Ioannis Prodromos,** 12km from Dimitsana, (*Open dawn-dusk to modestly dressed visitors. Free, though a small donation is expected.*) The road goes from asphalt to dirt, and finally becomes a footpath on the mountain. Here you can see the icons painted on the bare stone walls and monastic cells almost defying gravity as they hang off the mountain. It is now inhabited by only 12 monks.

MESSENIA Μεσσηνια

An oasis in the arid Peloponnese, Messenia is a refreshing stop for travelers. Olives, figs, and grapes spring from the rich soil on the region's rocky coastline, which remains largely tourist-free. Most Messenians live at the head of the gulf, around sprawling Kalamata, a convenient town from which to tour Mani's west coast. More alluring is the port town of Pylos, strategically located for bus, moped, and car travel to Koroni, Methoni, and the beaches of the south.

■ Kalamata Καλαματα

Kalamata, the second largest city on the Peloponnese, flourishes as a port and beach resort. On March 23, two days before the official start of the war, a group of Kalamatans, impatient to end Ottoman rule, massacred the enemy while they slept. The event is commemorated each year with a reenactment of the Greek victory, parades, and dancing. Today fast-growing Kalamata has all of the characteristics of a large Greek city—excessive noise, confusing transportation networks, and traffic problems—and though the city can be pleasant in places, there is little to merit a long stay.

ORIENTATION

Kalamata sprawls inland from its long beachfront lined with hotels, restaurants, and tourist shops. Behind the beach, the city can be divided into three sections. Closest to the water is a residential section distinguished by the municipal park. Next is the central square, with the train station and most amenities. Finally, the old town, with its castle, market, and bus station, is 3km from the beach. Navigation from one end to the other can be very confusing, and you should get a map from the tourist police.

Kalamata recently won an EU award for city planning, but it is difficult to see why; the bus station is so far separated from the main hotel area on the beachfront that walking is impossible on a hot day. The city's bus system is extremely limited in its network, and overpriced, at 200dr for distances that would cost less in a taxi. To get to the waterfront from the bus station, take a taxi (400-500dr).

After you have checked into a hotel and relieved yourself of your luggage, it is possible to travel the city on foot or, if you wish, by the city bus. **Navarinov St.** runs along the water. Perpendicular to it, but never actually intersecting it, is **Aristomenous St.,** running along the park and then through **Georgiou Square,** the heart of downtown. Bus stops are scattered throughout the city. The main stop/upper terminus is in 25 Martinou Sq., at the base of the upper city.

PRACTICAL INFORMATION

Transportation

Buses: Station (tel. 28 581 or 22 851) provides info daily 7am-10pm. Buses go to Athens (4hr., 11 per day, 4100dr) via Megalopolis (1hr., 1000dr); Tripoli (2hr., 1500dr); the Corinth Isthmus (3hr., 2900dr); Patras (4hr., 2 per day, 4000dr) via Pirgos (2hr., 2250dr); Sparta (2hr., 2 per day, 1040dr) via Artemisia (30min., 440dr); Mavromati and ancient Messene (1hr., 2 per day, 550dr); Koroni (1½hr., 8 per day, 900dr); and Kalamata and Pilos (9 per day, 900dr). Five per day continue to Methoni (3 on Sunday; 2hr., 1050dr) and two per day to Finikountas (2½hr., 1050dr). For Areopolis and Gythion, go via Itilo (2hr., 4 per day, 1300dr) and change buses for Areopolis (15min., 220dr) or Gythion (1½hr., 400dr). The bus passes Kardamili (650dr) and Stoura (750dr) before it reaches Itilo.

Flights: To Athens daily at 9:25pm (30min., tickets 13,500dr, under 24 11,500dr). **Olympic Airways,** 17 Sideromikou Stathmou St. (tel. 22 376), just before train station. Open daily 8am-3:30pm. Taxis to the airport (6km from town, near Messini) cost about 1500dr. From the KTEL station, catch a bus to Messini.

Trains: Station (tel. 95 056) at the end of Sideromikou Stathmou St. Turn right on Frantzi St. at the end of Georgiou Sq. and walk a few blocks. Cheap but slow. To: Athens (7hr., 4 per day 5:30am-3:40pm, 2400dr) via Tripoli (2½hr., 840dr); Argos (4hr., 1300dr); Corinth (5¼hr., 1700dr); Kyparissia (2hr., 600dr); Pirgos (3¼hr., 860dr); Patras (5½hr., 1500dr); and Olympia (3hr., 900dr).

City Bus: Depart from the bus depot near 25 Martiou Sq. Take the #1, which goes down Aristomenous Sq., then turns to run along the water, winding up at the waterfront or camping areas (200dr). Runs daily 8am-10pm.

Taxi Service: (tel. 22 522). A ride to the campsites from the city costs 500dr.

Moped Rental: Alpha Rental (tel. 93 423), on Vironos St. Mopeds 3500dr per day. Near waterfront and open daily 8am-8pm. Also **Verga Rent-A-Car,** 202 Faron St. (tel. 95 190). Mopeds 3000dr per day. Open 10:30am-2pm and 6:30-10pm.

Financial Services

Bank: National Bank (tel. 28 047), on Aristomenous St. off the north end of Georgiou Sq., and on Akrita St. at the waterfront. Both offer **currency exchange.** Open M-Th 8am-2pm, F 8am-1:30pm. 24hr. **ATMs** at both locations.

Emergency and Communications

Medical Emergency: Call 25 555.

Tourist Police: (tel. 95 555) Located in the port on Miaouli St., on the 2nd floor of a yellow building. They distribute an invaluable map. Open daily 7:30am-9:30pm.

Port police (tel. 22 218), on the harbor near the tourist police in a blue building.

Police: (tel. 22 622) located in Georgiou Sq. on Aristomenous St. (open 24hr.).

Hospital: Athinou St. (tel. 85 203).

Post Office: 4 Iatropolou St. (tel. 22 810). Follow this street from the south end of Georgiou Sq. Another branch on the waterfront at the port next to the tourist police. Both open M-F 7:30am-2pm. **Postal Code:** 24100.

OTE: Georgiou Sq., opposite National Bank. Open daily 7am-9:30pm. **Telephone Code:** 0721.

ACCOMMODATIONS

Most of Kalamata's hotels are on the waterfront. Accommodations abound, but rooms to let are uncommon here.

Hotel Nevada, 9 Santa Rosa, which runs off Faron St. one block up from the water (tel. 82 429). Take bus #1 and get off as soon as it turns left along the water. Tons of potted plants inside and outside, on tables and posters. Shared bathrooms. Singles 4000dr; doubles 5000dr; triples 7000dr.

Pension Avra, 10 Santa Rosa (tel. 82 759). Hard wood floors, shared bath, and kitchen. Singles 5000dr; doubles 7000dr; triples 10,000dr.

Hotel George (tel. 27 225), right near the train station. Clean, convenient, and charming. Private bathrooms. Singles 6000dr; doubles 7000dr.

Camping Maria's Sea and Sun (tel. 41 060) is luxurious for a campsite. Take bus #1 east past the other campsites. Hot showers included. 850dr per small tent; 1000dr per large tent. 800dr per car. Electricity 800dr. 1300dr per person;

FOOD AND ENTERTAINMENT

Before leaving town, sample the famous Kalamata olives and figs. The immense **New Market,** just across the bridge from the bus station, is a collection of meat, cheese, and fruit shops, as well as a daily farmer's market. It's a perfect place to assemble an inexpensive picnic. Great sit-down meals can be found along the waterfront.

Taverna Tzamaika (tel. 24 940) is the best of the waterfront *tavernas,* but also the farthest from town (2km down the road away from the port, with the water on your right). It has its own outdoor oven, a large collection of farm implements that appear to have lingered since the Agricultural Revolution, and even a horse. Grilled lamb (1500dr) and stuffed tomatoes (1000dr) get rave reviews.

Tampaki Restaurant (tel. 23 225) is closer to town than Tzamaika, and serves good food at reasonable prices (*moussaka* 1200dr, stuffed vine leaves 1300dr). Open daily for dinner around 7pm.

Exociko Kentro (tel. 22 016), with a seating area over the beach, serves a mean lamb and potatoes (1400dr), veal (1500dr), and Greek salad (1000dr).

The Park Cafe and Restaurant serves ice cream (800-1200dr), pizza (1050-1450dr), and countless beverages, from lemonade (300dr) to floats (600dr), out of the old train station at the center of the train park, where the vintage steamers, shined and polished, find their final resting place on the tracks now used only for display.

Nightlife in Kalamata revolves around the beach scene—unfortunately the beach bar strip (1km east of the port) lacks some of the over-the-top fun that other cities boast. Expect lots of umbrellas and subdued techno music. Kalamata's newest disco, **Palladium,** costs a small fortune (cover 1200dr, including one drink), and is not to be confused with **The Million Dollars Club,** housed in the same building (it hosts strippers). Palladium attracts great crowds, but more moderately priced clubs surround it.

SIGHTS

Only a few sights remain in Kalamata. The **Castle of the Villehardouins,** which crowns a hill above the old city, has survived despite a violent history. Built by the Franks in 1208, it was blown up by the Ottomans in 1685 and restored by the Venetians a decade later. It was damaged in the 1986 earthquake and is still being repaired today. The castle houses an open-air theater which hosts "Cultural Summer of Kalamata" in July and August, with everything from jazz and rock to classical Greek drama (ticket prices average 2000dr). To get to the gates from 23 Martiou Sq., walk up Ipapandis St. past the church on the right side and take your first left. At the foot of the castle is the **Convent of Agios Konstantinos and Agia Elena,** where nuns sell their linen and lacework at bargain prices. At the far end of the site is the 14th-century **Church of the Agioi Apostoli** (Holy Apostles), where the first Greeks to rise in revolt swore their loyalty on March 23, 1821. *(Open daily 8am-dusk. Free.)* In addition, it is the church in which was found the doe-eyed Virgin Mary icon that gives the city its name—Kalamata translates to "good eyes." Also in the old city is the **Benaki Museum,** which presents its small but interesting collection with an artfulness and professionalism far beyond the vast majority of Greek museums. *(Open Tu-Su 8am-2:30pm.)* Lengthy and informative placards in flawless English explain unusual objects, enlivening pieces that might otherwise seem dull and common. Especially admirable is the large and exceptionally well-preserved mosaic floor taken from the remains of a nearby Roman villa. At the far edge of the site, there are remains of a Byzantine church—scramble up for a sublime view. *(Open daily 8am-dusk.)* At 221 Faron St., off the waterfront, Kalamata's **School of Fine Arts** exhibits work by Greek artists.

(Open daily 9am-1pm and 6-10pm.) Kalamata also supports two professional theaters and cinemas; ask the **tourist police** for information on events in the **Pantazopoulion Cultural Center** on Aristomenon St.

Kalamata has had considerable success cleaning up its beaches. They are increasingly less crowded as you go eastward. With large shady trees, cafes, a performance area, and a duck pond, the **Train Park** (at the end of Aristomenous St., closer to the waterfront) extends several blocks toward Georgiou Sq. The main attractions are an old train station which has been converted into a restaurant and ice cream parlor, and antique trains on the tracks.

■ Mavromati Μαυροματη

For more antiquities, travel to **Mavromati** (1hr., 2 buses per day, M-Sa, 400dr) to see the well-preserved remains of **Ancient Messene** on Mt. Ithomi, one of the most impressive ancient archaeological sites in Greece. *(Open daily 8:30am-3pm. Admission 500dr, students 300dr, EU students free.)* After the battle of Leuctra in 371 BC, which marked the end of Spartan domination of the Peloponnese, the Theban general and statesman built the town of Messene, naming it after the first queen of the region. Excavations within the last 15 years have exposed more of the extensive site. The remains of a theater, stadium, gymnasium, public baths, and nine different temples survive, but it is the city's defensive walls that usually receive the most attention. Three meters wide, stretching in a 9km circuit, they are the finest example of military architecture in the 3rd and 4th centuries BC. Massive gates reinforced with the two-story towers and battlements interrupted the circuit, each taking its name from the direction of the road that it barricaded. Of the four gates that survive, the Arcadian gate is the best preserved and the most impressive; the road that proceeds from it is paved with large slabs of stone that still bear the traces of chariot wheels. A museum at the site houses the statuary and other objects that excavations have yielded.

Nearby is the 17th-century **Monastery of the Vourkano,** which was a starting point for fighters in the war of independence and whose library contains several priceless manuscripts. Getting to Mavromati by public transportation is a feat of dedication: two buses leave Kalamata, the first at 5:40am and the second at 2:30pm (550dr). One bus runs from Mavromati to Kalamata at 2:30, meaning that the early bus there and the 2:30 bus back are the only possible combination, unless you choose to spend 4000-5000dr on a taxi. If you decide to rent a moped, be sure to get one with at least 50cc's, because the mountains on the way to the site are extremely steep.

■ Taygetus Mountains

South of Kalamata, the bus to Areopolis winds through the Taygetus Mountains, which soar to 2630m at their highest point. These alluring gray peaks of Mani loom behind olive-covered hillsides. The first major bus stop comes at the coastal village of **Kardamili.** With its distinctive stone houses and long white pebble beaches, Kardamili is attracting more and more visitors. It doesn't feel like a tourist trap yet, however, and it's still possible to enjoy the charming town on a budget. The bus drops passengers off on the main road in front of the square. At the Kalamata end there is a well-stocked **supermarket** and **bakery.** The road past the church leads to the main square. Beyond is the **post office** (open M-F 7:30am-2:30pm). Kardamili's **police station** (tel. 73 209) is on the main road farther toward Itilo (open 24hr.). **Telephone Code:** 0721.

"Rooms to Let" signs are everywhere, but such *domatia* can be expensive, especially the newly remodeled rooms above the restaurant **Skardamouvlas** (tel. 73 516 or 73 259). on the edge of the square. Further from Kalamata are the cheapest in town. They have high ceilings and private bathrooms. Some have balconies with excellent views of the sea and mountains (singles 5000dr; doubles 8000dr). Another option is the **rooms to let** (tel. 73 623) which are across from the police station on the right hand side of the road coming from Kalamata (singles 6000dr; doubles 9000dr).

For good food with a beautiful waterfront view try the family-run **Taverna Kiki,** downhill from the **O Kypos Rooms** in the main square (veal and potatoes 1600dr, rabbit 1500dr). Assorted fast food can be found at the restaurant across from the yellow Pelops Car Rental sign, about 100m from the square down the road towards Areopolis (*gyros* 300dr, *souvlaki* 200dr). **Oi Eileis** restaurant and snack bar serves an exceptionally good Greek salad (1000dr) as well as numerous other traditional dishes and cold refreshments, under olive trees along the beach.

If you've a yearning to slip yourself into crystal clear waters or massage your hot bare feet with a stroll along a small white pebbled beach, walk toward Kalamata from the main square and turn left at the signs for **Camping Melitsana,** 1.5km down the beach (tel. 73 461; 1200dr per person; 1000dr per small tent; 1100dr per large tent; 700dr per car; 750dr for electricity). Buses go to Kalamata from Kardamili (1½hr., 5 per day, 650dr) and to Itilo (3 per day at 8am, 2pm, and 6pm, 650dr), where you can switch buses for Areopolis (250dr from Itilo).

The frescoed **Monastery of Dekoulo** and the 17th-century Ottoman **fortress** are poised on a nearby hill. The entertainment consists of two cafes off the small square and a reasonably priced restaurant. The bus continues 3km down to the magnificent **Neo Itilo.** At the heart of an enormous natural bay encircled by monumental barren mountains, the white pebble beach is ideal for swimming. From Neo Itilo, the road winds uphill, affording a view of **Limani,** the old harbor of Areopolis. The tiny port is home to the Mavromichaeli **Castle of Potrombei.** From here, buses continue to Areopolis. Bad roads make this ride about as much fun for your gut as a trip through the spin cycle, but the views are rewarding.

▓ Pylos Πυλος

Despite its beaches, its castle, its two museums, and its considerable charm, Pylos is not presently a major tourist destination—the town's beauty alone is enough to make this surprising. Flower-laden buildings line the narrow streets and steep stairways lead up from the waterfront square to the residential town, saddling the surrounding hills. Pylos' harbor cuts a unique silhouette, marked by the perpendicular cliffs of Sfakteria Island.

In addition to its striking setting, Pylos prides itself on the 1827 Battle of Navarino. As Ottoman forces battered the coast, English, French, and Russian fleets arrived and sunk the invaders' battalions.

ORIENTATION AND PRACTICAL INFORMATION The **police** (tel. 22 316) are located on the second floor of a building on the left side of the waterfront (English spoken; open 24hr.). The **tourist police** (tel. 23 733) are in the same building (open daily 8am-2pm). Continue around the curve of the waterfront road to reach the **port police** (tel. 22 225). The **post office** (tel. 22 247) is on Nileos St., uphill to the left (facing the water) from the bus station (open M-F 7:30am-2pm). A **National Bank,** with an **ATM,** is on the main square (open M-Th 8am-2pm, F 8am-1:30pm). To get to the **hospital** (tel. 22 315), take the road right of the square (open 24hr.). **Buses** (tel. 22 230) go to Kalamata (1½hr., 9 per day, 900dr); Athens (6½hr., 2 per day, 5000dr); and Finikountas (1hr., 4 per day, 420dr) via Methoni (15min., 5 per day, 220dr). No buses travel directly to Koroni, but you can go to Finikountas and take a bus from there to Horokorio, the nearest stop to Koroni. Buses also leave for Kyparissia (1½hr., 5 per day, 1080dr), all stopping at Nestor's Palace (40min., 300dr) and Hora (45min., 300dr). **Rent-A-Bike,** 100m off the main square on the road that runs in front of the police station away from the water, has a monopoly on moped rentals, and their prices are steep (5000dr per day; open daily 9am-2pm and 5-9pm). To get to the **OTE** (tel. 22 399), pass the post office and take your first left; then turn right (open M-F 7:30am-3:10pm). **Postal code:** 24001. **Telephone code:** 0723.

ACCOMMODATIONS There are several "Rooms to Let" signs as the bus descends the hill, coming into town from Kalamata. In general, expect to pay 4000-6000dr for singles, 8000-10,000dr for doubles, and 5000-8000dr for triples. Try the **rooms** advertised by **The 1930 Restaurant** and the large, fancy hotel next door—they do not have good views but are clean and cheap (singles 4000dr, doubles 6000dr). Another option is the **Pension** (tel. 22 748), just before the OTE, offering high-ceilinged rooms with private baths (singles 5000dr; doubles 6000dr). **Hotel Nilefs,** 4 Rene Pyot St. (tel. 22 518), on the road running along the water out of the right side (facing inland) of the waterfront square, has large, clean rooms, bathrooms, and balconies with views of the sea, (singles 5500dr; doubles 7500dr; triples 9500dr). **Navarino Beach Camping** (tel. 22 761) lies 6km north at Yialova Beach (1100dr per person; 800dr per small tent; 1000dr per large tent; electricity 600dr).

FOOD Many restaurants along the waterfront offer *taverna* staples and a beautiful view of the sunset over the water. While a little on the expensive side, **The 1930 Restaurant,** on the road that leads into town from Kalamata, is easily the most charming of them. Beautiful wood paneling and antique fishing paraphernalia set the mood. The menu is mostly seafood, including octopus on the grill (2000dr) and fish soup (1000dr). **Ta Adelpha** (tel. 22 564), around the bend past the police station, is also a little removed from the rest of the pack, offering a traditional menu and an especially striking view (*tzatziki* 550dr, *pastizzio* 1030dr). Uphill from the main square, on the same road as Rent-a-Bike, **La Piazza** is a haven for those seeking a non-*taverna* menu. Both pasta (700-1000dr) and pizza (1450dr) are delicious (open daily 6:30pm-1am).

SIGHTS **Fortresses** guard both sides of Pylos' harbor. **Neokastro,** (tel. 22 448) to the south, is easily accessible from the town; walk up the road to Methoni and turn right at the sign. *(Open Tu-Su 8:30am-3pm. Admission 800dr, senior citizens 400dr, students free.)* The well-preserved walls enclose a church (originally a mosque), a citadel, and a collection of European philhellene paintings. The hexagonal courtyard up the hill to your right after entering the castle was restored in the last decade and has a small room of photographs detailing the undertaking. The **Archaeological Museum** (tel. 22 448), located just before the castle on the road to Methoni, houses finds from Mycenaean and Hellenistic tombs. *(Open Tu-Su 8:30am-3pm. Admission 500dr, students free.)* Of the Mycenaean material located in the first of the two rooms, the partial remains of a battle helmet made of boar's tusks are most impressive, and of the Hellenistic material in the second room, three richly colored glass vessels in a case along the far wall.

The **Paleokastro,** north of Pylos, is harder to reach. The tourist police say making the dangerous trip is not worth the badly preserved remains. If you are undaunted, however, check with them for instructions (you must have transportation). To see **Sfakteria** up close, you can take a **boat tour** from the port. The hour jaunt around the island stops at various monuments to the allied sailors of the Battle of Navarino and shows off a sunken Ottoman ship. Boat captains try to organize groups for tours (roughly 10 people). Inquire at the small booth on the waterfront or at the neighboring coffee bar under the police station, where the captains often rest. The cost is 10,000dr for four people. The ride takes 90 minutes.

■ Nestor's Palace

Tel. (0763) 31 437 or 31 358. Open Tu-Su 8:30am-3pm. Admission 500dr, students free.

In the Mycenaean world, Pylos was second only to Mycenae in economic prosperity and cultural breadth. The **palace** at Pylos, where Nestor met Telemachus in Homer's *Odyssey,* was built in the 13th century BC. The site is still being excavated and consists of three buildings. The main building, possibly the king's residence, originally had a second floor (and walls) with official and residential quarters and storerooms. To the southwest, archaeologists think that an older, smaller palace stood. To the northeast lie the ruins of a complex of isolated workshops and more storerooms. Important finds from Nestor's Palace are pottery, jewelry, various bronze and ivory objects, and a cache of **Linear B tablets** explaining some of its administrative operations. Most tablets are on display in the National Archaeological Museum (see p. 96).

To get here by bus see Pylos bus information; the last bus back to Pylos stops at Nestor's Palace at 5:30pm. Touring it does not fill all of the time between buses. Luckily, the site is covered by a broad metal protective roof that provides ample shade; bring your own water and bring a book, or read the University of Cincinnati's scholarly *Guide to Nestor's Palace* (500dr), available at the entrance.

■ Methoni Μεθώνη

With its hibiscus-lined streets and relaxed small-town atmosphere, Methoni is a restorative reprieve for the traveler arriving from the noisy bustle of Kalamata or Tripoli. The town's 15th-century castle, projecting itself, by means of narrow stone walkways, onto rocky outcroppings in the bay, is among the most spectacular in Greece. Forever the "Camelot of Greece," Methoni was once offered by Agamemnon to the sulking Achilles to cheer the warrior and bring him back to the fight. Much later, Cervantes was so taken with the place that he churned out romances even while imprisoned under Ottoman guard.

ORIENTATION AND PRACTICAL INFORMATION The town's two main streets form a "Y" where the Pylos-Finikountas buses stop. The beach is at the end of the lower street, and a little beachfront square is to the left. To get to the castle follow the upper street to its termination. The **police** (tel. 31 203) are near the bus station on the upper street, just past the bank (open 24hr.). The **National Bank** (tel. 31 570) is 40m down the right fork (open M-Th 8am-2pm, F 8am-1:30pm). The **post office** (tel. 31 266) is two blocks down the lower street on the left side (open M-F 7:30am-2pm). The **OTE** (open M-F 7:30am-3:10pm) is difficult to find. It's a cream colored building with blue shutters. Go down the lower fork and turn left going toward the beachside square. **Postal code:** 24006. **Telephone code:** 0723.

Buses leave from the same place they drop off. There is no station but you can ask in the market with magazine stands out front, 20m down the road back to Pylos, in whose window the minimal bus schedule hangs. **Buses** go to Pylos (15min., 7 per day, 220dr) and Finikountas (30min., 4 per day, 200dr). For all other connections you will have to go to Pylos or Kalamata.

ACCOMMODATIONS Since Methoni receives a fair amount of tourism in the month of August, hotels are abundant and reasonably priced. **Hotel Galini,** just off the beachfront square, is the cheapest. Like every other hotel in town, the rooms have balconies and modern private bathrooms (singles 5000dr; doubles·7000dr, triples 8000dr; in August, prices rise 5000dr or more). On the left side of the beach, **Hotel Achilles** (tel. 31 819), built last year, is the newest hotel in town. Everything is spotlessly new and the prices are lower than one might expect (singles 6000dr, doubles 8000dr, triples 9000dr). **Hotel Giota** (tel. 31 290 or 31 291) offers clean, air-conditioned rooms for similar prices (singles 7000dr; doubles 10,000dr; triples 12,000dr). There are dozens of "Rooms to Let" signs along both forks of the road, but their prices—especially in the high season—are generally the same as the hotels while their accommodations are much worse. **Camping Methoni** (tel. 31 228), several kilometers from Methoni, is crowded but on the sea (1100dr per person; 650dr per car; 750dr per small tent; 950dr per large tent).

FOOD There are several excellent *tavernas* and restaurants in Methoni. **Oraia Methoni** is a small, humble establishment, but what it might lack in swanky atmosphere it more than makes up for in quality and economy (tomato and cucumber salad 400dr, *moussaka* 900dr, *souvlaki* 200dr). Turn left one block down the lower road and walk for 30m, the restaurant will be on your right. **Kali Karthia,** four blocks down the upper street, has been serving traditional cuisine in the town for over 50 years. Their prices are higher than Oraia but their atmosphere and reputation are second to none. **Restaurant Venetiko** (tel. 31 120), two blocks down the lower street on the left, serves a selection of pizzas (1300-2000dr) as well as traditional fare, under leafy banana trees.

SIGHTS No visitor to the southwest Peloponnese should miss Methoni's **Venetian fortress,** a 13th-century mini-city. *(Open M-Sa 8am-8pm, Su 9am-8pm. Free.)* Venture behind the fortified gate onto a windswept field of low shrubs dotted with crumbling walls. Frankish foundations, Venetian battlements, and Turkish steam baths testify to the castle's varied history. At the tip of the peninsula a narrow bridge connects an islet and its fortified tower to the main structure with all of the invention and playfulness of medieval defensive architecture.

■ Finikountas Φοινικουντας

Halfway between Methoni and Koroni, Finikountas, a colorful fishing village, coaxes visitors to bask in sunshine and watch colorful *kaïkia* glide across the surface. For swimming, take the time to go to **Paradise Beach,** the cove beyond the rock jetty to the east. If you stay, change money in advance: Finikountas has neither a bank nor a post office. The **Supermarket Phoenix** sells stamps and houses an **OTE** (open daily 7am-1pm and 5-9pm). **Bus transportation** from Finikountas to anywhere but Kalamata is tricky to figure out. The bus stops across from the Hotel Finikounta, but there is no station, so check out times. Buses go to Kalamata (2hr., 3 per day, 210dr). Some Kalamata buses go west via Methoni, but most go east stopping at Horokorio (30min.), the closest stop to Koroni. Check with drivers about routes. Look for signs for **rooms to let** on the waterfront or on the road from Koroni as you enter town. Most restaurateurs either rent rooms or know who does. For a large room with a private bath, try asking at **Taverna Vasso** (tel. 0793 71 242), where singles are 5000dr and doubles 7000dr. **Telephone code:** 0793.

LACONIA Λακωνια

In the 12th century BC, an Indo-European population known as the Dorians swept down into Greece from the north, driving out the Mycenaean inhabitants with a brutality unforgotten after 3000 years. Only Attica escaped the Dorian extermination, as Mycenaean centers on the Peloponnese became Dorian strongholds. Into the Archaic and Classical periods, when Greece had recovered from the cultural dark age brought on by the barbaric, destructive, palace-burning Dorians, people from Doric areas—especially in the eyes of the sophisticated Athenians—retained certain traits of their pillaging ancestors.

Laconia was one such area. Laconians never lost their penchant for aggression, and ever disdained the frivolities of rhetoric and poetry, limiting their speech to bare syllabic necessities. In time, this economical reticence became "Laconic." Today the barren Laconian landscape maintains this ancient severity. Although Laconia boasts one of the Peloponnese's most popular sites—Byzantine Mystra—the region remains lowkey. Laconia's friendly villages are a welcome break from the urban atmosphere of other over-touristed areas.

■ Sparta Σπαρτη

As the capital of bellicose Laconia, Sparta dominated the Peloponnese for centuries after the Peloponnesian war in the middle and late 5th century BC, with its invincible, highly disciplined armies. Spartans traced the austere regimentation of their daily life back to Lycurgus the law giver, who lived in the 8th century BC. Among other things, he prescribed that the Spartan citizen must dress plainly, eat unextravagant food, and undergo a strict gender-specific program of training from an early age. Despite difference in the character of this training for men and that for women, there was scarcely a disparity in severity. Sparta's first conquest was the neighboring Messenians, whom they held as slaves—Helots—beginning shortly after the Mycenaean breakdown. This particular conquest would prove troublesome even centuries after its completion; at times, especially after wars, Messenian Helots outnumbered their own Spartan masters seven to one, making it almost impossible for the Spartans to cope with the continual Helot uprisings. Even as Spartan armies marched over the Peloponnese, devastating the opposition with ease, their most dangerous enemy remained at home, toiling in the fields and quarries.

Because Sparta produced almost no memorable literature, art, or architecture, the city's history is remembered almost exclusively by military actions. Perhaps the most significant of these is the Peloponnese War, waged between Sparta and Athens and their respective allies in the middle and the late 5th century BC. After glorious victories and bloody defeats for both sides, Sparta ended the war in 404 BC by capturing Athens. Spartan domination did not last long in Athens, yet the brief tyranny over such a mighty power as that Classical capital testifies to Sparta's unparalleled military skill and discipline. Even in victory, Sparta never grew soft, as the Romans did in the autumn of their empire. Only the effects of earthquakes, depopulation (through war), and Messenian resistance broke Sparta's hegemony in the end.

In their quiet city, today's Spartans prefer to make olive oil, not war. In a landscape in which few buildings challenge a delicate balance between asphalt and orange trees, modern Sparta makes little effort to win over the occasional tourist. The city's surviving ruins are meager, resulting, for the most part, from the fact that modern Sparta is built directly on top of the ancient city. Still, Sparta is the best and most convenient base for exploring the more significant ruins of Byzantine Mystra, 6km away.

ORIENTATION AND PRACTICAL INFORMATION

Sparta is laid out in an appropriately spartan grid. Sparta's two main streets, **Paleologou** and **Lykourgou St.** (named after Lycurgus the law giver), intersect in the center of town. To get to the center from the bus station, walk west on Lykourgou St. for about 10 blocks. The town square is one block up from the intersection of Lykourgou St. and Paleologou St. All necessary amenities are on these two streets.

Transportation
Buses: (tel. 26 441). Walk downhill on Lykourgou St. away from the square, continue past the fire station until the road peters out, and the station will be on your right, 1500m from the center of town. Buses go to Athens (3hr., 9 per day, 3600dr.), via Corinth (2hr., 2250dr.) and Tripoli (1hr., 1000dr.). Buses also head to Neapolis (2½hr., 2-4 per day, 2350dr.); Monemvassia (2hr., 2-3 per day, 1750dr.); Pirgos Dirou and the caves (1½hr., 1 per day, 1750dr.) via Areopolis (1½hr., 2 per day, 1200dr.); Kalamata (2 per day, 2hr., 1040dr.); Gerolimenas (2 per day, 3hr., 1800dr.); and Gythion (1hr., 5 per day, 750dr.). For buses to Mystra, the station is at the corner of Lykourgou St. and Kythonigou St. on the left, 2 blocks past the town square away from the main bus station (every 1½hr., 6:50am-8:20pm, 220dr). The schedule varies; call the tourist office to check.

Tourist and Financial Services
Tourist Office: (tel. 24 852), to the left of the town hall in the square. English spoken and very helpful. Bus schedules, hotels, and information. Map 400dr. Open daily 8am-2pm.
Banks: National Bank (tel. 26 200), on the corner of Dioskouron St. and Paleologou St., 3 blocks down from the intersection, offers **currency exchange.** Open M-Th 8am-2pm, F 8am-1:30pm. Banks line Paleologou St. **ATM** on Dioskouron St.

Emergency and Communications
Police: 8 Hilonos St. (tel. 26 229). From the intersection, turn left on Lykourgou St. away from the square. The police are on a side street to the right, a block past the museum. Open 24hr. Helpful, earnest, English-speaking **tourist police** (tel. 20 492) are housed in the same building. Open daily 8am-3pm and 7-9pm.
Emergency: Dial 100.
Hospital: (tel. 28 671 or 28 675), Nosokomeio St. (Hospital St.), 1km to the north of Sparta. Open 24hr.

Post Office: (tel. 26 565), on Arhidamou off Lykourgou St., 5 blocks before the intersection. Open M-F 7:30am-2pm. **Postal Code:** 23100.
OTE: 11 Kleombrotou St., (tel. 23 799), off Lykourgou across from the museum. Open M-F 7am-9:40pm. **Telephone Code:** 0731.

ACCOMMODATIONS

Among the numerous mid-range hotels on Paleologou St., a bargain is hard to find, but TVs and a private bath are not.

Hotel Panellinion (tel. 28 031), just past the Lykourgou intersection. The cheapest place to stay, with minimalist but high-ceilinged rooms, balconies, and shared bathrooms, but without air conditioning. Singles 4000dr; doubles 6000dr.

Hotel Cecil (tel. 24 980), five blocks north on the corner of Paleologou St. and Thermopilion St. Lemon yellow inside and out, you'll spot this trim, pretty hotel from down the block. Everything has been renovated in the last two years. Private baths, televisions, and direct phone lines. Singles 5000dr; doubles 8000dr.

Hotel Laconia (tel. 28 952), also on Paleologou St. Offers attractive dark wood furniture, TVs, and even shower curtains. Singles 5000dr; doubles 8000dr; prices rise 20% in high season.

Camping Castle View (tel. 83 303), near Mystra. Take the regular Mystra bus and ask the driver to let you off at the signs. New, with pool, modern showers and toilets, and a mini-market. 1200dr per person; 700dr per car; 700dr per small tent; 1000dr per large tent; electricity 700dr.

FOOD AND ENTERTAINMENT

Sparta's restaurants serve expensive fast food. There are a few exceptions.

⊛Dias Restaurant (tel. 22 665), on the first floor of the luxurious Maniatis Hotel on the corner of Lykourgou and Paleologou St. Probably the best restaurant—surprisingly reasonably priced—in town. The decor is a little hotelish but the food is traditional and delicious (Greek salad 850dr; lamb in oil and oregano sauce, 1350dr).

Dhiethenes (tel. 28 636), a.k.a. **Restaurant in the Garden,** on Paleologou St. 150m from the main intersection, serves traditional fare in a garden behind the restaurant (*moussaka* 1300dr; tomato salad 600dr).

Parthenon Restaurant (tel. 23 767), off the right side of Paleologou on Vrasidou St. not too far from Dhiethenes, has the best fast food in town, specializing in *gyros* (350) and *souvlaki* (200dr). A reasonably priced meal under fluorescent lights.

Elyssa Restaurant, up the street from Dhiethenes, has identical prices but greater selection. Look for the pink tablecloths (lamb 1600dr; *tzatziki* 500dr).

At night, bop 2.5km down the road toward Gythion to the **Aithrio Disco.** The **Imago,** a hip, artsy bar, is in the alley behind the town hall (open daily 10pm-3am).

SIGHTS

What little remains of ancient Sparta lies in an olive grove 1km north of the town square down Paleologou St. At the north end of Paleologou St. stands an enormous **statue of Leonidas,** the famous warrior king of the Spartans. The Spartans built a large pseudo-tomb for their leader, who fell at the Battle of Thermopylae in 480 BC, in hopeful anticipation of his remains, which were never found. The tomb is in an especially green section of the grove which was converted to a public park, on the left of the road heading up to the ruins. The ruins consist of the lower rows and the outlines of one of the larger theatres in antiquity and a few fragments of the acropolis. To find the tomb and the ruins, walk to the northern end of Paleologou St., to the right from the bus station, to the statue of Leonidas. At the statue turn left and then right at the signs for the ruins about 50m from the statue. From the sign the ruins are about 400m up the road.

A Hard-Knock Life

A young Spartan's training for a life of war began early, even before conception. Lycurgus believed two fit parents produced stronger offspring, so he ordered all Spartan women to undergo the same rigorous training endured by men. Furthermore, newlyweds were permitted only an occasional tryst on the theory that the heightened desire of the parents would produce more robust children. If they weren't winnowed out as weak or deformed, boys began a severe regimen of training under an adult Spartan. The young were forced to walk barefoot to toughen their feet and wore only a simple piece of clothing in both summer and winter to expose them to drastic weather changes. The Spartan creed dictated that young men be guarded against temptations of any kind—strict laws forbidding everything from drinking to pederasty governed Spartans' actions. Moreover, young Spartans were given the plainest and simplest foods for fear that rich delicacies would stunt their growth. One visitor to Sparta, upon sampling the fare, allegedly quipped, "Now I know why they do not fear death."

Finding the various surrounding ruins may be a bit of a challenge. Before you set out, ask the tourist police for a hand-drawn map. Five kilometers away are three remaining platforms of the **shrine to Menelaus and Helen,** history's most sought-after beauty. The remains of the Spartans' **shrine to Apollo** are on the road to Gythion. A short walk east on the banks of the Eurotas River leads to the **sanctuary of Artemis Orthia.** Spartan youths had to prove their courage here by unflinchingly enduring public floggings.

Sparta's **archaeological museum** (tel. 28 575) stands along the edge of a beautiful, well-kept park with a fountain and assorted ancient statuary, just down Lykourgou St. on the right side, heading from the intersection toward the bus station. *(Open Tu-Su 8:30am-2:30pm. Admission 500dr, students 300dr.)* The collection includes spooky votive masks used in ritual dances at the sanctuary of Artemis Orthia, and a large marble statue of a warrior thought to be Leonidas. An entire room is devoted to the prehistoric era, displaying pottery, weaponry, and jewelry from the Neolithic and Mycenaean periods. Especially impressive are the "unpublished" mosaics from the Roman period. For modern art, visit the **National Art Gallery,** 123 Paleologou St. (tel. 81 557). *(Open Tu-Sa 9am-3pm, Su 10am-2pm. Free. English not spoken.)* The permanent collection of 19th-century French and Dutch paintings is unusual for this part of the world. On the second floor are exhibits of watercolors by modern Greek artists.

For an evening excursion from Sparta, share a cab to the village of **Paroli,** 2km from Mystra. There you can sit in a *taverna* and watch the nearby waterfalls. Two kilometers farther is the village of **Tripi,** which has larger waterfalls, some of which run right under the excellent grill-restaurant **Exochiko Kentro** (tel. 98 314).

■ Mystra Μυστράς

*6km west of Sparta. Tel. (0731) 83 377. **Open** daily 8am-8pm in summer, 8:30am-3pm in winter. **Admission** 1200dr; students 600dr. **Guidebook** Mystra, 2000dr. Water taps inside the main gate, at the Metropolis, and at the Pantanassa, but bring your own bottle in addition. Tough shoes are needed on many of the rocky paths. Even a cursory look at the site requires at least 3hr., including the long climb to the top. Public bathrooms not in working condition. In summer, the sun's heat can become unbearable as early as 10am.*

Overflowing with Byzantine churches and fortifications, the extraordinary Medieval ruins of Mystra reveal the splendor of Byzantium's final flourish. During the 14th and 15th centuries, this small town was the center of Constantinople's rule over the entire Peloponnese. The **castle** crowning the hill, built by Frankish crusader Guillaume de Villehardouin in 1249, was Mystra's first building. Ceded to the Greeks in 1262 after Villehardouin's defeat, Mystra grew from a small village to a city, draining the site of ancient Sparta of all its inhabitants, and becoming the seat of Byzantine rule on the Peloponnese. During the next two centuries, churches, monasteries, a palace, and many luxurious homes sprang up behind Mystra's projectile walls. In the early 15th century, Mystra, prospering from a lucrative silk industry, became an intellectual center. Many free thinkers, unhappy under the control of repressive feudal lords and clergy, surged into town and set up schools, tying Mystra to the Florentine humanist movement. As was happening elsewhere in Greece around the same time, Mystra fell to the invading Turks in 1460. By the early 19th century travelers found more houses in ruins than standing. The year 1831 marked the final demise of the town, when King Otto founded modern Sparta, which drained Mystra of its inhabitants, just as Mystra had of Sparta 500 years before.

At various times, crusaders, monks, philosophers and Byzantine governors wandered the intricate network of paths that weaves the city together and today renders sightseeing a complex affair. Try tracing a path around several key sites on the three tiers that correspond to the sectors for the commoners, the nobility, and the royalty (in ascending order, naturally). Mystra is one of the better-labeled sites in Greece; nevertheless, you will enjoy Mystra more with a good guidebook and map. Manolis Chatzidakis' *Mystras,* which you can buy at either of the entrances, is the best.

Don't miss the beautiful **Metropolis of St. Demetrios** in the lower tier, with its flowery courtyard and museum of architectural fragments. Wander on to the two churches of the monastery of **Brontochion, St. Theodori,** and the **Aphentiko** (Hodegetria) with its magnificent two-story frescoes. On the same tier is the **Pantanassa,** a convent with an elaborately ornamented facade and a multitude of frescoes, not to mention a miracle-working Virgin Mary icon. Finally, at the extreme left of the lower tier, the **Church of Peribleptos** is perhaps Mystra's most stunning relic; every centimeter of the church is bathed in exquisitely detailed religious paintings, still fascinating, though most were vandalized by invading Ottomans.

Getting there

Two different buses go to Mystra. The bus that leaves from the Mystra stop at the corner of Lykourgou and Kythonigou on the left, two blocks up from the town square (ask the tourist police if you have trouble finding it), drops off 50m down the road from the main gate (every 1½hr., 220dr) at the base of the city. The bus that departs from the bus station (1 per hr., 220dr) drops at the **Kastro** entrance, near the top of the city, allowing one to walk downhill rather than uphill most of the time. If you start at the Kastro entrance, you still want to catch the bus back to Sparta from the lower city bus stop. Aside from campsites, accommodations at the town of Mystra, another 1½km down the road from the bus stop, are pricey.

MANI Μανη

The province of Mani derives its name from the Greek word *manis* meaning wrath or fury, an etymology that history has proven apt time and again. In the Roman period, Mani broke free of Spartan domination and founded the league of Laconians. Since then, Maniotes have ferociously resisted foreign rule, boasting even today that not a single Ottoman set foot on Maniot soil. Not always, however, did Maniot wrath take an external direction; European travelers of the early 19th century noted the savage feuds that developed between neighboring families. Generations after some seemingly trivial offense, a feud would still be raging; sons of rival families were known to brutally gun each other down in the streets in the name of revenge.

Today, Maniot culture has softened. Although they revel in their historical ferocity, the Maniots make excellent hosts to visitors seeking beautiful beaches and views. The sparsely settled territory stoically circles the cinnamon-brown Taygetus Mountains, (see p. 158), which border the sea. Traditional tower houses of grey stone complement the stark, mountainous landscape with muted greys and greens.

■ Gythion Γνθειο

The "Gateway to the Mani," Gythion, in the Northeast corner of the territory, has a more colorful and lively feel than the dramatic but bleak land to the south. Bright fishing boats bustle in and out of the port, and dockside restaurants hang strings of octopuses out to dry. A causeway connects Gythion to the tiny island of **Marathonisi,** where Paris and Helen consummated their ill-fated love, and beautiful sand and stone beaches are within easy walking distance. In addition, Gythion is the only city in the area where you can rent a motorbike to explore the hard-to-reach Mani on your own.

ORIENTATION AND PRACTICAL INFORMATION

The bus stop is on the north side of the waterfront. Small **Mavromichali Square** is in the middle of the waterfront near the quay. The harbor road continues to the right, where it eventually meets the causeway to Marathonisi.

Transportation

Bus station (tel. 22 228), on the north end of the waterfront. Buses head to Athens (4hr., 6 per day, 4350dr), via Sparta (1hr., 750dr); Tripoli (2¼hr., 1750dr); Corinth (3hr., 3000dr); Kalamata (2 per day, 1950dr) via Itilo (1hr., 650dr); Gerolimenas (2hr., 4 per day, 1000dr), via Areopolis (1hr., 460dr); and Pirgos Dirou (1¼hr., 1 per day, 600dr). Buses also go to the **campgrounds** (including Meltemi, Gythion Beach, and Mani) south of town (4 per day, 220dr).

Ferries: to Kythera (2hr., Su-Tu, Th-F, 1535dr) and Crete (7½hr., 2 per week, 4560dr).

Taxis: (tel. 23 423). Open 24hr.

Rent-A-Moped (tel. 22 901), on the waterfront near the causeway, rents mopeds for 4000dr per day.

Tourist and Financial Services

Travel Agency: Theodore V. Rozakis (tel. 22 650) sells tickets for the two ferry lines depart out of Gytheio.

Banks: National Bank (tel. 22 313), just beyond the bus stop toward the water, has a 24hr. **ATM** and offers **currency exchange.** Open M-Th 8am-2pm, F 8am-1:30pm.

Emergency and Communication

Police (tel. 22 100), on the waterfront, halfway between the bus station and Mavromichali Sq. (English spoken; open 24hr).

Port Police (tel. 22 262), before the causeway, past the square. The post office and the OTE are both inland from the bus station.

Health clinic: (tel. 22 001, 22 002 or 22 003), on the water near the causeway.

Post Office: (tel. 22 285), on Ermou St. Open M-F 7:30am-2pm. **Postal Code:** 23200.

OTE: (tel. 22 799), at the corner of Herakles and Kapsali St. Open M-F 7:30am-3:10pm. **Telephone Code:** 0733.

ACCOMMODATIONS

Many hotels and *domatia* that look out at the sea are prohibitively expensive, but there are some inexpensive and charming ones inland. Gythion's **campgrounds** are an alternative to city lodging—all are about 3km south of town, toward Areopolis. The bus is infrequent, and a taxi costs about 900dr.

⊛**Xenia Karlafti's Rooms** (tel. 22 719), on the water just 20m from the causeway. Rooms are spacious and the manager provides a breakfast area and washing machine for her guests. Singles 4000dr; doubles 6000dr; triples 7000dr.

Koutsouri Rooms (tel. 22 321). From Mavromichali Sq., go up Tzanaki Gregoraki, turn right at the clock tower, and look for a sign past the bakery on your left. At the gate, go past the (chained-up) dogs, and you're there. Singles 4000dr; doubles 6000dr. Show your *Let's Go* book to get these prices.

Domatia Leoridas (tel. 22 389), a beautiful pink building in the heart of the waterfront, has large rooms with TVs and balconies. May look too rich for the blood of budget travelers, but for groups of three it offers a great deal. Triples 12,000dr.

Meltemi Camping (tel. 22 833), 3km south on the road toward Areopolis. 1200dr per person; 700dr per car; 1000dr per tent; electricity 800dr.

Gytheio Bay Campgrounds (tel. 22 522), 3km south on the road toward Areopolis. 1200dr per person; 700dr per car; tent 800dr; electricity 700dr.

Mani Beach (tel. 23 450). 1000dr per person; 600dr per car; small tent 750dr; large tent 950dr; electricity 700dr.

FOOD AND ENTERTAINMENT

The fish *tavernas* along the water are not cheap, but they also are not a great deal more expensive than the typical *tavernas;* you may decide a view of Moratorisi at sunset is worth the price. Mavromichali Sq. is perfect for lunch or a cheap dinner.

Saga (tel. 23 220), on the water between the causeway and the square, has deliciously prepared food and tables pulled right up to the water. You can watch the fish swim by after it gets dark. Crispy grilled and seasoned bread replaces the usual staple, and vegetarian salads are cheap. Boiled zucchini 500dr, eggplant salad 500dr, fresh kalamari 1800dr.

Taverna To Nisi is a charming outdoor *taverna* on Mavothonisi islet just across from the church. A great view of Gythion's unique architecture. *Tzaziki* 400dr, grilled chicken 1000dr, minnows 1000dr.

The Cork Room, past the square coming from the bus station on the corner as the road straightens and heads towards the causeway, has more octopus hanging out to dry than any other restaurant in town. Their specialty, not surprisingly, is octopus (1500dr). They also have squid (1500) and a range of fish dishes (2000dr).

Masouleri Kokkalis (tel. 22 832), at the center of the square behind the plastic chairs, is the place for fast food. Generously proportioned *gyros* (300dr) and *souvlaki* without too much fat (200dr). Across the street are a **fruit store** and **bakery.**

SIGHTS

The compact and masterfully built **ancient theater** of Gythion, by the military base on the north edge of town, has endured the centuries remarkably well. Note the differences between the seats for dignitaries in front and the simpler seats farther back. Next to the theater and scattered up the hill in the grass are crumbling Roman walls. To get there, walk down Herakles St. from the bus station, go to Ermou St., and then right onto Archaiou Theatrou St. to its end. If you arrive in the early evening, you can join the soldiers getting their nightly pep talk here. **Paliatzoures Antique Shop** (tel. 22 944), #25 on the waterfront, is as good as a museum. *(Open daily 10am-2pm and 5-10pm.)* Indeed, as the owner Costas will tell you, many museums have been created from his shop. The majority of his collection, consisting of household items, artwork, furniture, coins, and hundreds of assorted trinkets, is from the 19th century, but he claims to have a few medieval and even ancient items interspersed throughout. By Greek law, only items made after the fall of Constantinople in 1453 are exportable by foreigners, but unless you are prepared to spend a great deal of money on souvenirs, this probably won't be a concern. This store is the last of its kind in the Peloponnese.

The Museum of the Mani (tel. 22 676), in a Maniot tower and hidden by pines on Mavothonisi Island, presents the Mani through the eyes of European travelers, archaeologists, and cartographers from the Venetians in the 17th century to the French and British in the 19th. *(Open daily 9:30am-9pm. Admission 300dr.)* Despite the numerous prints, maps, and lengthy quotations, the exhibit is a little disappointing because the primary sources are presented in such small, tantalizing portions, making the museum come off as a glorified list of European visitors to the Mani. Yet the collection itself is not without its bright spots. An English traveler early in the 19th century proves that the nuisances of travel are timeless when he complains of "squadrons of fleas and bugs that marched zealously to battle."

There is a **public beach** just north of the bus station, but the best beaches are farther north and south of town. Three kilometers to the south is the long, sandy beach of **Mavrovouni**, with a high surf and a number of surfer bars (mixed drinks 900-1000dr, beer 500dr). Three kilometers north is rocky **Selinitsa,** which has earned accolades from the European Union for its clean water. Neither beach is accessible by bus—ride a moped, take a taxi (700dr), or walk. Farther north than Selinitsa is a sandy beach with the remains of an ex-drug-runner's abandoned ship.

When traveling from Gython to Areopolis, look for the Frankish **Castle of Pasava** on the right (roughly 10km down the road; tours available). Farther along, the **Castle of Kelefa** looks out to sea.

■ **Areopolis** Αρεοπολη

The sun feels too close in Areopolis' blindingly bright main square, but shade in the labyrinth of tower houses and tiny chapels in the old section of town is just a few hundred meters toward the sea. In the old town, streets are cobbled and buildings constructed from the same sand-colored rock, lending a unique monochromatic dignity to town life. Although its restaurants are superb and its tower houses provide romantic and inexpensive accommodations, Areopolis remains under-touristed, visited mainly by artists seeking inspiration from the stark landscape. You will understand why after an evening walk through the rocky olive groves framed against the purple Taygetus Mountains at the western edge of the town, against the sea.

ORIENTATION AND PRACTICAL INFORMATION The bus stops in front of **Nicola's Corner** in the main square. The bus points toward the main street of the old town, **Kapetan Matapam Street**. All amenities can be found off this street or in the main square. The **police** (tel. 51 209) are in the square at the end of a little street that starts behind the statue (open 24hr.). The **post office** is just off the square on Kapetan Matapan St. (open M-F 7:30am-2pm). For all of your pressing financial needs, walk down Kapetan Matapan St., turn right at the first small church, and continue up the street—before you pass the Hotel Mani you'll find the **National Bank** (open M-F 9am-noon). The bus station and the post office with **exchange currency** and traveler's checks for a hefty fee. The **OTE** (tel. 51 399) is 50m down a street. that starts in the main square; the statue's right hand points down the street with its sword. Opposite the OTE is a **health center** (tel. 51 242) that is open 24hr.

The **bus station** (tel. 51 229) is in the cafe on the eastern edge of the square, across the street from Hotel Kouris. Buses from Areopolis go to Kalamata (3 per day, 1600dr) via Itilo (30min., 250dr); Sparta (1½hr., 4 per day, 1200dr), via Gythion (30min., 460dr); and Athens (6hr., 4 per day, 4800dr). A bus goes from Areopolis to the Glyfatha Lake Caves (220dr) three times per day (returns 1¾ hours later). A bus goes deep into the Mani from Areopolis, stopping in Gerolimenas (30min., 500dr) and Vatheia (1hr., 3 per week, 700dr). **Postal code:** 23062. **Telephone code:** 0733.

ACCOMMODATIONS If you spend the night here, try to find a room in the old town, which best evokes Mani's intriguing, turbulent past. You may become a player in a feud if you decide to stay at either **Tsimovas Rooms** or the **Pension** just opposite, whose respective proprietors are balding men who stare menacingly at the other's door. Both are delightful, but choose at your own risk. To find them, turn left at the end of Kapetan Matapan St. **Tsimova** (tel. 51 301), in a traditional tower-house, has narrow rooms with tiny doors and windows typical of the architectural style. The owner has a small military museum downstairs in his living room with rifles, swords, and uniforms dating back to the War of Independence. Everything has been passed down through his family, making the collection all the more impressive. In addition, Kolokotronis supposedly slept here (singles 5000dr; doubles 8000dr). **Pierros Bozagregos** (tel. 51 354), just across the street, has spotless doubles with private baths. Pierros and his family are extremely friendly (rooms 10,000-12,000dr). **Hotel Mani** (tel. 51 190; fax 51 269) is spacious and new; to find it, walk down Kapetan Matapan

St. for 50m from the bus station. Turn right at the first small church you come to on your right and walk another 200m; the hotel will be on your left. All rooms have private bath and balcony (singles 5000dr, doubles 8000dr, triples 10,000dr). **O Barba Petros** (tel. 51 205), off Kapetan Matapan St. above the restaurant, has the cheapest rooms in town. The small rooms all share two bathrooms and may feel a bit tight (singles 3000dr; doubles 4000dr; triples 6000dr; quads 8000dr).

FOOD Nicola's Corner (tel. 51 366), in the square, is easily the best restaurant in town, serving excellent traditional dishes, including Greek salads (1000dr), a delicious vegetarian ratatouille (1000dr), and trademark grilled and seasoned bread (300dr). **Tsimova** (tel. 51 219) serves veal with tomato sauce (1500dr) and *moussaka* (1300dr) with smiles, and is a good place to sip Greek coffee (150dr). **Pistaria O Alepis** (tel. 51 436), is on the main road. For something cheap and easy, try the souvlaki (200dr), chicken (2000dr per kilo), or other grill items.

■ Pyrgos Dirou Πυργος Διργου

The caves are 4km from town, accessible by bus from Areopolis. **Open** *June-Sept. 8am-5pm, Oct.-May 8am-2:45pm.* **Admission** *3500dr. Some guides speak only Greek, so you may need the* **guidebook,** *Caverns of Mani (1500dr), at the ticket booth uphill from the cave entrance.*

With its subterranean river, the **Glyfatha Cave** (also known as Spilia Dirou or Pyrgos Dirou) is one of Greece's most splendid natural attractions. The boat ride through the cave is 1200m and lasts about 30 minutes. Originally discovered at the end of the 19th century and opened to the public in 1971 (a new section was found in 1983), to this day the cave has not been fully explored. The cave is believed to be 70km long and may extend all the way to Sparta. Vermilion stalagmites slice through the water, which is 30m deep in places and squiggling with eels. The cavernous echo of dripping water contributes to a clammy coolness that is a little spooky but a welcome relief from summer heat. Lights floating in styrofoam rings illuminate the course of the tour but unlighted recesses of the cave branch off into the depths on the left and right. Don't miss **Poseidon's Foot,** a striking formation resembling a giant foot hanging in the air.

After the boat trip, you must walk five minutes through more of the caves to reach the exit (the entrance and exits are different). In a booth just outside of the exit, back in the stinging daylight, you can purchase your own picture as a souvenir; that fellow taking photographs of your boat as you set off on the tour 30 minutes ago was not doing it for promotional reasons (pictures 1000dr each.) The small pebble beach next to the caves is beautiful from afar, but the pebbles are slimy and the water is suspiciously cloudy. A small **museum** (tel. 52 222 or 52 223) houses neolithic artifacts from the cave's early inhabitants, who were trapped when an earthquake sealed the entrance. *(Open Tu-Su 8:30am-3pm. Admission 500dr, students 300dr.)*

■ Monemvassia Μονεμβασια

Travelers who have seen countless postcards of the Byzantine city of Monemvassia may be puzzled when the bus drops them off in the unabashedly modern—albeit pleasant—town of **Gefyra.** Just beyond the breaking waves of Gefyra's shore lies an impressive island, dominated by spectacular vertical cliffs. "The rock," as it is known, looks uninhabited from the mainland; only after crossing the causeway and walking along the main road for 20 minutes does the gate to Monemvassia appear.

ORIENTATION AND PRACTICAL INFORMATION While saving as much time as possible for wandering around the old city, take care of most of your needs on the mainland in the much cheaper Gefyra. An orange bus runs between the causeway and Monemvassia gate all day long (every 10min., free). In Gefyra, **23rd Iouliou St.,** the principal thoroughfare, runs along the waterfront to the causeway leading to the island. Across from the bus station is the **National Bank** (tel. 61 201; open M and W

9am-1:30pm and F 9am-1pm; no ATM), and next door, the **post office** (tel. 61 231; open M-F 7:30am-2pm). The **police station** (tel. 61 210) is on the same side of the street, toward the causeway (open 24hr.). The **tourist police** (tel. 61 941) are in the same building. Room listings are available. The **OTE** (tel. 61 399) is 200m uphill bearing left from the bus station. Look for it on the left in a second-floor balcony (open M-F 7:30am-3pm). Helpful **Malvasia Travel** (tel. 61 752; fax 61 432) houses the bus station and is opposite the post office and National Bank (open daily 7:15am-2:15pm and 6-9pm). Ask the manager about **currency exchange** and **moped rental** (3500dr per day). English language **books** ranging from romances to *Zorba the Greek* are sold at **Bibliopoleio Polilpono** (tel. 61 021; open daily 9:30am-1:30pm and 6-9pm).

The **bus station** (tel. 61 752) is on 23rd Iouliou St., in the Malvasia travel agency opposite the post office. Buses for all destinations either connect or stop in Molai. The only exception is the 4:10am direct express to Athens (6hr., 5350dr). Buses leave (2 per day) for Sparta (2½hr., 1750dr); Tripoli (4hr., 2750dr); Corinth (5hr., 3950dr); and Athens (6hr., 5350dr), via Molai (20min., 460dr). Daily buses connect Molai to Gythion, leaving Monemvassia (1½hr., 1400dr). In the summer, **Flying Dolphins** go to Kythera (1¼hr., 4910dr) and Neapolis (1½hr., 3300dr) four times a week. One or two hydrofoils per day leave for Piraeus (3½hr., 8952dr) stopping at Spestes (2½hr., 4200dr) and Hydra (3hr., 5200dr). Check at the **ticket office** (tel. 61 219), next to the Mobil station on the island for schedules. **Postal code: 23070. Telephone code: 0732.**

ACCOMMODATIONS There are numerous hotels in Gefyra, but most are on the expensive side. Alternatively, *domatia* dot the waterfront. Off-season prices are 20-40% lower in some cases. **Hotel Sophos** (tel. 61 360), across the street from the post office in the direction of the sea, has clean, recently renovated rooms for decent prices (singles 5000dr; doubles 7000dr). **Kritikos Domatia** (tel. 61 439), about 200m away from the bus stop, offers a suite of rooms with a kitchen and bathroom, for 6000dr. **Malavasia Hotel** (tel. 61 160) is a treat in the island's old city; rooms are expensive, but the great location and spectacular stone floors, fireplaces, beamed ceilings, and woven decorations may be worth it (doubles 11,000-15,000dr; triples 17,000-19,000dr). **Camping Paradise** (tel. 61 123), 3.5km along the water on the mainland, is more affordable (1100dr per person; 750dr per car; 800dr per small tent; 1100dr per large tent; 20% discount for longer stays).

FOOD Restaurants are plentiful in both Gefyra and Monemvassia, although most of those in medieval Monemvassia are a better quality. There is not much to keep you from taking a meal in medieval Monemvassia; there are plenty of affordable options, and the restaurants in Gefyra are nothing special in terms of quality. **Matoula** (tel. 61 660) is somewhat expensive, but its old city location boasts fig trees and a pleasant stone terrace with a view to the sea (*moussaka* 1300dr, stuffed tomatoes 1300dr). On the mainland, follow the water past the causeway to the harbor and to: **To Limanaki** (tel. 61 619; stuffed eggplant 1200dr, kalamari 1300dr). Try **Pipinellis Taverna** (tel. 61 004), located 2km from Monemvassia on the road to Camping Paradise. It has featured home-grown produce for the past 25 years (stuffed tomatoes 1100dr, veal 1400dr). **Basilis Kamarinos** (tel. 61 134) is a cheap, quick grill on the waterfront behind the sea of other restaurants' tables (*gyros* 300dr, *souvlaki* 200dr).

SIGHTS For good reason the old city of Monemvassia is one of the major tourist sights on the Peloponnese. Most striking about the old city is a pervasive quality of other-worldliness; passing through the single gateway (hence the town's name, which means "one way") into old Monemvassia, one may get an eerie feeling of having crossed into another time. No cars or bikes are allowed through the gate, so pack horses bearing groceries and cases of beer are led back and forth to restaurants; narrow streets invite the explorer to discover stairways, child-sized doorways, flowered courtyards, and even the occasional cactus. The winding cobbled main street that passes the town's tourist shops and restaurants is visible immediately upon entering the gate; it continues past the strip of tourist shops to reach the **town square.** Facing the ocean, the **Christos Elkomenos** (Christ in Chains) church is on the left. To get to

PELOPONNESE

the oft photographed **Agia Sofia,** perched on the edge of the rock cliffs, find your way through the maze of narrow streets to the edge of town farthest from the sea at the base of the mountain. There a path climbs the side of the cliff to the tip of the rock, and you'll find the church on the far side of the rock. The Agia Sofia is modeled after the monastery at Daphni and had some of its frescoes restored 30 years ago. From the top of the rock, which is scattered with crumbling castle ruins, the views of the town and sea below are splendid.

KYTHERA Κυθηρα

According to ancient myth, the island of Kythera rose from the waters where Zeus cast his father Chronus' severed member into the sea; simultaneously, Aphrodite sprang from Chronus' sea-born misfortune and washed up onto Kythera's shores, making the island her homeland. In antiquity, the island supported a large cult to the goddess, just as Olympia did to Zeus and Delphi to Apollo. Although one might not associate the island's barren, mountainous landscape with the fertility for which Aphrodite is known and worshipped, its flowering shrubs, sandy beaches, and secluded villages hold a potent beauty.

Improved ferry schedules have recently made Kythera a more convenient destination for budget travelers. Travel by bus is still difficult, but mopeds are plentiful and cheap and allow travelers to expand their choices of inexpensive *domatia* and charming villages. If you stay, be mindful of the fact that there is currently no ATM anywhere on the island. Kythera's major sites can easily be seen in a day if you have transportation, but if you enjoy clean beaches and the relaxed pace of an uncrowded island, you will probably want to stay longer.

■ Agia Pelagia Αγια Πελαγια

Ferries dock in Kythera at the west port of **Agia Pelagia,** and Flying Dolphins dock at the newer port of **Diakofti.** The island's main road runs between Agia Pelagia and **Kapsali,** a lively port town with small villages connected by subsidiary roads. Besides the port towns, this road passes through **Potamos, Livadi,** and **Kythera** (Hora). Although Agia Pelagia is very small, it does offer almost everything a tourist could want, including accommodation, food, moped rental, and clean beaches on both sides of the quay.

If you plan a short stay on the island, and especially if you're catching a ferry, Agia Pelagia is a good place to stay. The town is smaller and less picturesque than Hora or Kapsali in the south, but accommodation and moped rental are considerably cheaper here. You also do not have to pay for a cab to get to the ferry docks.

Ferries leave Agia Pelagia daily for the mainland, stopping at both **Neapolis** (1hr., 1500dr) and **Gythios** (2½hr., 1530dr). Ferries also travel to Kastili on Crete (5hr., M and Th., 3750dr). A daily **bus** in late July and August runs between Agia Pelagia and Kapsali; it leaves Agia Pelagia at 8am and returns from Kapsali at noon (300dr). Ask at the tourist office for details.

In a little cottage to the left of the quay is a very helpful **Volunteer Tourist Office** (tel. 33 815). The friendly staffers can provide information about accommodations and sights around the island (open daily July-Sept., 9am-1pm and 5-9pm). Across the road is **Conomos Travel** (tel. 33 490), an agency that sells tickets for ferries and Flying Dolphins (open June-Sept. 9am-1pm and 4-8:30pm, reduced hours in winter). The **port police** (tel. 33 280) also provide schedules. **Telephone code:** 0735.

If you decide to spend the night in Agia Pelagia, all of your creaturely needs can be taken care of in one building. Across from the quay, a little to the right, is **Taverna Faros** (tel. 33 343). This delicious *taverna* offers a great ocean view (breakfast 900dr, baby goat and potatoes 1300dr, Greek salad 1000dr). Simple rooms with balconies and private baths are available above the restaurant (doubles 6000dr, 5000dr if you are alone). The tourist office has lists of other *domatia* owners and will put you in contact with them. Just to the right of the taverna is **Easy Rider** moped rental (50cc mopeds 3000dr per day; a passport is required for rental).

■ Potomas Ποταμας

The pleasant inland town of **Potomas** is on a hill 9km south of Agai Pelagia on the main road. Its square is home to many of the island's amenities. The **National Bank** (tel. 33 350) marks the main square (open M-Th 8am-2pm, F 8am-1:30pm). The **post office** (tel. 33 225) is uphill from the square (open M-F 7:30 am). The **police station** (tel. 33 222) is behind the National Bank, tucked in a lemon-tree lined corner (no English spoken). The **hospital** (tel. 33 325) is on the road to Hora (many doctors speak English). **Postal code: 80200. Telephone code: 0735.**

The **Olympic Airlines** office (tel. 33 362) is in Potomas's square, but the airport is a taxi ride away on the eastern half of the island. Olympic runs three flights a day into Kythera (14,500dr to Athens, 12,300dr for people under 24 or over 60; office open M-F 8am-3pm). **Taxis** park in Potomas' square, or call 33 676.

For a treat, try **Chrisafiti Bakery** (tel. 33 244), in the main square. Their *focaccio* (350dr) is divine, and you can sit in the main square for a picnic.

■ Hora Χωρα

Hora, also called Kythera, is the capital of the island. Its whitewashed plaster houses will make you wonder whether there is a city ordinance requiring everyone to paint their shutters blue. The effect is powerful under the bright sun, especially along the narrow main street that starts in the town's square and leads to the castle. You can see the azure sea and the small island called **Hydra,** which looks just like the Pruden-tial rock from many vantage points.

Hora's **post office** (tel. 31 274) is in the main square (open 7:30am-2pm), as is the **National Bank** (tel. 31 713; open M-Th 8am-2pm, F 8am-1:30pm). To get to the **OTE** (tel. 31 299), go up the stairs next to Kithira Travel and turn left at the top (open 7:30am-2pm). Facing the water, Hora's main street starts from the square's lower left-hand corner. About 500m down this street are the **police** (tel. 31 206), where the **tourist police** can be found in the morning.

In the square, **Kithira Travel** (tel. 31 390) has lots of information, including **Flying Dolphin** schedules (open daily 9am-2pm and 6:30-10pm). Flying Dolphins leave Dia-kofti (M, W, Sa-Su at 5pm) and go to Peiraias (4hr., 10,400dr) via Monemvassia (1hr., 5000dr); and Spestes (2hr., 6700dr). **Taxis** (tel. 31 320) from Hora to Diakofti cost about 4500dr. **Telephone code: 0735.**

Among Hora's sparkling white buildings are numerous "Rooms to Let" signs, but many are quite expensive. **Pension Pises** (tel. 31 070) has rooms with great views, shared baths, and creative decor (doubles 6000dr). From the main road through town, turn left at the "pension" sign onto Ag. Elesis St.

At the end of Hora's main road are the remains of the town's **castle.** Wildflowers have sprouted around the old battlements, and the wind-swept plateau offers intoxi-cating views of Kapsali's double harbor. The **Archaeological Museum** is on Kythera's highway just before the turn-off for Hora. *(Open Tu-Sa 8:45am-3pm, Su 9:30am-2:30pm. Free.)* This small and under-funded Piraeus museum houses pottery, sculpture, and coins from the classical to the Byzantine periods and in another room, gravestones from the English military base that was on the island in the 19th century.

Sterea Ellada
Στερεα Ελλαδα

By the time Sterea Ellada became one of the original parts of the Greek state in 1832, it had seen its share of tragedy. During the struggle for independence the renowned British poet and philhellene Lord Byron landed at the swampy outpost of Messolongi to lend his hand to the cause. Byron came down with a fever a few months after his arrival and died before Greece shed the Ottoman yoke. His death drew international attention and support to the eventually successful Greek national struggle.

East of Messolongi, the region is littered with the holy and tragic centers of the Classical and Byzantine eras. In antiquity the Delphic Oracle drew pilgrims from all over the Mediterranean; they sought answers to profound questions and came home with perplexing replies. Just a bus ride away from Delphi, the Monastery of Osios Loukas, which dates from the 10th century, is one of the best examples of Byzantine monastic architecture in all Greece. Below the monastery are the crossroads where unknowing Oedipus met and slayed his own father, so, as the blind prophet Tiresias would say while he throbbed between two lives, be kind to strangers you meet on the road.

🖐 HIGHLIGHTS OF STEREA ELLADA

- Observe the nuanced squinches and glittering gold mosaics of the **Monastery of Osios Loukas** (p. 177), a true Byzantine oasis.
- Bring the whole family to **Thebes** (p. 174) for days and nights of Oedipal delights.
- Forget the psychic hotline! Collect and decode cryptic advice at **Delphi** (p. 181) from Apollo's oracle.

■ Thebes Θηβα

Thebes sits on top of an illustrious past—literally. Set on a hill and surrounded by agricultural fields, the modern city rests upon layers of ancient habitation, reaching back to the Bronze Age (3000-2000 BC). Above the ground, Thebes pays homage to its history with streets named after Cadmus (the legendary first king of Thebes), Oedipus (the most infamous of the Theban kings), Antigone (daughter of Oedipus), and Pindar (the famous Theban lyric poet of the 5th century BC). In the heyday of the *polis*, from the 6th to the 4th centuries BC, Thebes was among the most prominent city-states in Greece; its fertile plain gave it material prosperity and a strategically advantageous position in control of the passage from northern Greece into the Peloponnese. This didn't stop Alexander the Great from sweeping down from Macedonia and razing the city to the ground. He spared only the temples and the ancestral home of Pindar, who, in a street, a park, and a public bust, remains the pride of Thebes even after 25 centuries. These days, peaceful Thebes is not powerful, or even very big, but its fields still support a great deal of agriculture, and its streets still retain a feeling of ancient gravity.

ORIENTATION AND PRACTICAL INFORMATION Buses for Thebes leave Athens from Terminal B, 260 Lission St. (tel. (01) 831 7096; 1½hr., every hr. 6am-9pm, 1500dr) which is a considerable distance from the city center. To get to the Athens station take blue local bus #024 (100dr), which passes regularly by the bus stop in front of the National Gardens. Allow 45 minutes for the ride to the terminal, and get off at the motorcycle repair shop at 260 Lission St. Buses leave from a small road to the right of the shop.

In Thebes, buses arrive at a new station on Estias St. (tel. 27 512), down the hill from the center of town. Find the bottom of Eteokleous St. and follow it up the hill to

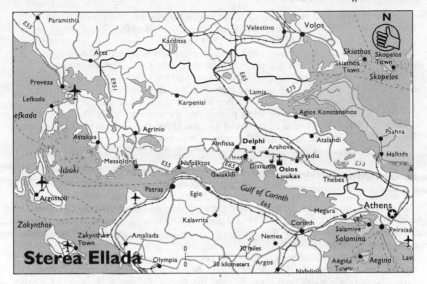

a grassy area where the road splits. To the left is Epaminon St., to the right Pindarou St., the two main roads in Thebes. Buses depart regularly for Levadia and points west (45min., every hr. 6:30am-8:30pm, 800dr) from the fountain at the base of the wooded knoll, just down the hill from the museum, and for Athens (1½hr., every hr. 6am-9pm, 1500dr) from the main station on Estias St. To travel to Halkida, take the Athens bus to the Skimatari stop (30min., 500dr). Across the street, catch the Athens-Halkida (10min., every 30min., 300dr). Tickets for both routes are available from the main station on Estias St. For a **taxi**, call 27 077.

An abundance of **banks** and **pharmacies** line Pindarou St. The **National Bank,** 94 Pindarou St. (tel. 23 331), has an **ATM** (bank open M-Th 8am-2pm, F 8am-1:30pm). The town's **hospital,** 2 Tseva St. (tel. 27 733), is located directly across the street from the museum while the **post office,** 17 Drakou St. (tel. 27 810), is near the top of Epaminon St. (open M-F 7:30am-2pm). The **OTE** at 2 Vousouba St. (tel. 80 099) is in the center of town between Epaminon St. and Pindarou St. (open M-F 7:30am-3pm). **Postal code:** 32200. **Telephone code:** 0262.

ACCOMMODATIONS AND FOOD If you plan to spend the night in Thebes, the **Hotel Niobi,** 63 Epaminon St. (tel. 29 888), is definitely your best bet. Everything from the tiles to the furniture is spotless and brand new, and each room has its own bath (singles 8000dr; doubles 10,000dr). By evening, the many *tavernas* lining Epaminon St. provide live music and drink for the field workers. The **Dionysos,** 88 Epaminon St. (tel. 24 445), is a local favorite with dinners of beef or lamb with bread, potatoes and assorted vegetables for 1500dr.

SIGHTS Thebes' main attractions are its antiquities. Open **excavation pits** are sprinkled haphazardly between buildings throughout the central city, revealing tantalizing segments of the extensive **Mycenaean** (1350 BC) palace and acropolis that lie beneath the city. Historians and archaeologists begrudge Thebes' every new building, fearing construction may endanger what little remains of the Mycenaean civilization. A five-minute walk down any street running perpendicular to Epaminon St. will bring you to the outskirts of town, where more **ancient walls** protrude from the soil.

Toward the top of Epaminon St. you will find the well-preserved **Fountain of Dirki Stream.** Long since run dry, the fountain is made inconspicuous by tall grass and thistle. Only a small sign marks the spot. You are not likely to have the company of other tourists as you step down into the stone-paved pool and take a seat to ponder which great ancient personages might have tread the same path.

The **Archaeological Museum** (tel. 27 913) is at the end of Pindarou St. *(Open Tu-Su 8am-3pm. Admission 500dr, students 300dr, seniors 400dr, children free.)* On the way to the museum, on the left side of Pindarou St., is a particularly impressive excavation pit dubbed the **House of Cadmus**, after Thebes' legendary founder and first king. It is part of a Mycenaean palace dated to the 14th century BC. Not surprisingly, the museum itself is especially strong in Mycenaean and pre-Classical antiquities. Be sure to see the Mycenaean **larnakes**, elaborate clay urns richly adorned with paintings, mosaics, and reliefs of funerary rites. Keep in mind as you examine the jewelry, pottery, and weapons of the Mycenaean period that these were the implements of the culture described by Homer in the *Iliad* and the *Odyssey*. Some of the swords and spear points graced the hands of warriors contemporary with fierce Achilles and mighty Agammemnon.

■ Levadia Λεβαδια

For oracle enthusiasts who want a second opinion, the **Oracle of Trophonius** is on a cliff overlooking Levadia. At the base of the cliff, the river **Herkina** bubbles up from springs and traces its way over rocks and under shady trees all the way through town. To the ancients these were the springs of *Lethe* (forgetfulness) and *Mnemosyne* (remembrance), where pilgrims had to bathe before consulting Trophonius, in order to forget everything before their arrival in Levadia and remember the answer of the oracle. Niches carved into the cliff for votive offerings are still visible. In the 14th century, Frankish crusaders built a **castle** over the site of the oracle. It is the best-preserved castle in the area, and only a 15-minute walk from town. From the bus station, turn right, walk uphill to the square, go right again onto Venizelou St., turn right at the end of the street, and then left at the church. The oracle and castle are about 200m up the river, through the park. If you feel like a hike you can continue past the oracle on the path that leads up into the canyon. About 300m up a beautiful **theater** has been built in the ancient style into the mountainside. Visible high up on the cliff ahead is the lonely whitewashed cell of a **monk**.

To ponder the oracle's inspiration, make your way to **Xenia**, a trendy bar and restaurant built directly over the Herkina right next to the springs. Sip refreshing fruit *granitas* (950dr) or a variety of iced coffees (500dr) to the peaceful sound of rushing water (open daily 9am-3am).

Levadia is good as a daytrip from Athens or as a stop on the way to Delphi or Osios Loukas. **Buses** from Athens through Thebes to Levadia leave Terminal B at 260 Lission St. (2hr., every hr. 6:30am-8:30pm, 2250dr). From Levadia, buses depart for Athens via Thebes (2hr., every hr. 6am-8pm, 2250dr). Buses also go to Delphi (7 per day, 750dr) and to Osios Loukas, (45min., 1:40pm, 480dr). If you miss the bus to Osios Loukas, catch one to Distomo (9 per day, 460dr) and then get a cab from Distomo to Osios Loukas. Levadia is accessible by **train**, but the station is 5km from town.

■ Distomo Διστομο

Distomo is an almost unavoidable stop on a trip to Osios Loukas by public transportation. It is a quiet town with a tragic history; in 1944 the Nazis shot most of the townspeople (about 200), in retaliation for a surprise guerilla attack. On the outskirts of town, a large marble monument commemorates the terrible day; follow the signs to the mausoleum. Despite the town's bleak history, its setting is picturesque with mountains rising up on all sides.

The **bus station** in Distomo is a joke; buses, when they come, only go to Levadia (9 per day 6:30am-8:00pm, 460dr). One bus leaves Distomo for Arahova at 4pm (15min., 280dr). If you don't want to wait for the bus, walk 2km down 10th Ioniou 1944 St. to the main road running to Arahova and and then the remaining 13km to Arahova, or else take a taxi (tel. 22 322) for 2000dr. Osios Loukas is only 9km away from Distomo. There is no bus and not much traffic, so a taxi is the only option (1500dr). All of the taxis in Distomo run out of the main intersection. The owner of the cabs speaks good English and can be found in the cafe next to where all the taxis are parked. To make your own meal, choose one of several mini-supermarkets on

10th Ioniou 1944 St. for cheese or sweet hazelnut-chocolate spreads, then head to **Matina Bakery,** next to the bank, for fresh bread (60-130dr). Right next door, **Cafeteria In & Out** (tel. 22 420, open daily 9am-2:30pm and 5pm-2am) will make you a sandwich for 500dr. **Telephone code:** 0267.

■ Osios Loukas Οσιος Λουκας

Tel. (0267) 22 797. **Open** *May 3-Sept. 15 8am-2pm and 4-7pm; Sept. 16-May 2 8am-5pm.* **Admission** *800dr, students 400dr, seniors 600dr.*

Although it is toilsome to reach, the **Osios Loukas** monastery is worth the trouble for those who seek a combination of spiritual and natural divinity. This pastoral and inspiring spot may give you pangs of longing for the monastic life. More than 1700m above sea level, the stone monastery complex contains magnificent mosaics and affords tremendous views. Perched on the verdant slopes of Mt. Elikon between Boeotia and Phokis, Osios Loukas is the best known and perhaps the most beautiful of the Byzantine monasteries in Greece. Although the monastery is neither cheap nor easy to reach, usually requiring at least one taxi ride, its splendor is worth the effort; such beauty and spirituality does not and perhaps should not come without a price. Remember to dress appropriately: no shorts or bare shoulders, long skirts instead of pants for women; makeshift coverings are available at the gate.

History

St. Osios Loukas, the founder of the monastery, was born in AD 896, ironically, at the former religious center of the pagan world—Delphi. From an early age he displayed an inclination to the ascetic life and became a monk at the age of 14. In 946, at the age of 49, Osios Loukas settled at the lush and enchanting site where his monastery stands today. There he built a cell, a small church and a garden. With other hermits who had been attracted by his reputation and the economic assistance of his many admirers, he undertook construction of **Agia Barbara,** the smaller of the two churches at the monastery, which today is dedicated to **Panagia,** the Virgin Mary. He died February 7, 953 at the age of 56, before the church was completed. After his death, not only was the church of Agia Barbara completed but a second, larger church, the **katholikon,** was built in 1011 and dedicated to Osios Loukas, becoming the site of his reliquary. Osios Loukas is said to have worked countless miracles in his lifetime. Even after his death, thousands came as suppliants and were cured at his tomb, from which a myrrh tree had sprouted.

Over the years the monastery suffered many pitfalls. During the Frankish occupation in the early 13th century, it was damaged and many of its precious vessels were lost. Today the monastery consists of the two churches, the crypt, a refectory, a bell-tower, and cells with ancillary rooms. Also on the grounds are an archaeology museum and, unfortunately, several tourist shops. A handful of monks live in the monastery and tend its gardens, cheerfully putting up with irreverent tourists.

Around the Monastery

Compared to the splendor of the churches and the grounds, the **Archaeology Museum,** to the right after the entrance to the monastery, seems meager, but is worth seeing. *(Open M-F 8am-6pm, Sa-Su 9:30am-3pm. Admission 400dr.)* Its collection comprises fragments—from moldings to murals—of long-since-destroyed sections of the monastery.

Past the Archaeology Museum in the main courtyard, you will enter the *katholikon.* Its northeast corner is attached to the smaller and slightly older Church of Panagia. The **crypt** is accessible by an entrance on the exterior of the *katholikon,* on the west side between the church and the museum. Although not as famous as the ones in the upper church, the 11th-century **frescoes** that cover most of the crypt's interior are every bit as gorgeous. The darkness has preserved their color, which gives an idea of how vivid the frescoes in the upper church once were.

The mosaics encrusted on the walls and ceilings of the **narthex** of the *katholikon* immediately overwhelm the visitor with their visual splendor. In three pictures they enact the drama at the center of the Christian faith: the crucifixion, Christ suffering and dying on the cross; the *anastasis,* Christ descending to hell to retrieve blessed souls; and *Christ Pantokrater,* the savior ruling in heaven. The mosaics are composed in miraculously vivid colors with glittering gold backgrounds.

Inside the church take note of the mosaics in the squinches (the areas above the pillars that connect to the dome); the three surviving squinch mosaics are the most impressive..In the large dome a fresco of Christ is displayed where there was once another mosaic. The original was destroyed in an earthquake in 1659, but from the new fresco, which itself is impressive, we can imagine how stunning the original must have been. The interior of the adjoining Church of Panagia is less ornate, but its exterior brickwork is finer than that of any other structure at the monastery.

Getting There and Away

To allow for transportation difficulties, give Osios Loukas a full afternoon preceded by a morning jaunt in Levadia. One daily **bus** goes from Levadia to Osios Loukas (45min., 1:40pm, 480dr); be sure to tell the driver you are going to the monastery or he might skip the mountain route altogether and go directly to Distomo. Six buses a day leave from Delphi (730dr). If you miss the sole direct bus to Osios Loukas, head over to Distomo by taking an afternoon bus from Levadia to Distomo (30min.; 2pm, 3:45pm, and 5pm; 460dr), and then take a taxi (tel. 22 322) to the monastery.

Getting out of Osios Loukas is a bit more tricky. Travelers used to mooch lifts from commercial tour buses, but because drivers have become increasingly wary of police and because there may not be a tour bus there in the evening, you should not plan on doing this. If you have come by **taxi** from Distomo, all you need to do is tell the driver to pick you up at a certain time to bring you back to Distomo. If you have come by bus from Levadia, you can ask someone at the monastery to call the taxi service in Distomo. You can have a taxi deposit you on the main road to Athens; here you might be able to catch a late bus going in either direction between Athens and Delphi.

■ Arahova Αραχοβα

Stacked onto the slopes below Mt. Parnassos 10km east of Delphi, the village of Arahova revels in its own relaxed atmosphere in summer and caters to skiers in winter. This is a perfect place to collapse after you've spent the day fighting the crowds at Delphi. It's a charming mountain town with narrow streets and little shops. Even though Arahova has the intensity of a ski resort in winter, a breezy summer afternoon spent wandering and enjoying the mountain view can be a delight. The area's culinary distinctions are its amber honey and tasty *saganaki* (fried cheese). The main street oozes with *souvlaki* and souvenirs. The sweaters, woven rugs, and coonskin-type hats hint at the town's popularity in winter.

ORIENTATION AND PRACTICAL INFORMATION Roughly five **buses** per day run between Athens and Delphi, stopping in Arahova, while an additional eight make the run from Arahova to Delphi (20min., 220dr). All buses to Delphi go to Itea (1hr., 540dr) and two make connections from Itea to Galaxidi (15min., 150dr). A brown and yellow "Celena" sign identifies the **bus station** (tel. 31 790), which doubles as a cafe and restaurant. The owner can usually be found sipping coffee in the square directly across the street.

The **Cooperative Office Kiparissos** (tel. 31 519) serves as a **tourist office** with information on the town and accommodations. To find it, continue on the main road in the direction of Athens. You'll soon see the school, a stone building with a red painted entrance. The cooperative office is right across the street (look for the red and yellow sign). In the first of the town's three squares you'll find the **post office** (open M-F 7:30am-2pm), which **exchanges money.** Stay on the main road and head farther into town to find the **National Bank** on your left (open M-Th 8:30am-2pm, F 8:30am-1pm). If it's closed, don't pout—it has a 24hr. **ATM.** The **police** (tel. 31 133) are across from the bus station, on the second floor. Farther east, past the third square, is a **pharmacy** (tel. 31 186). **Postal code:** 32004. **Telephone code:** 0267.

ACCOMMODATIONS AND FOOD Near the first square (coming from Delphi) are several hotels, pensions, and rooms to let. The **Apollon Inn,** on the first left off the main road coming from Delphi (appropriately called Delphi St.), has singles (5000dr, 7000dr in ski season) and doubles (7000dr, 9000dr in ski season) with bath. **Pension Nostas** (tel. 31 385; email nostos@otenet.gr), off the main road from Delphi in between the first and second squares (follow conspicuous signs), has beautiful rooms and a friendly owner. Every room has a bath, TV, fridge, and touch-tone phone (singles 7000dr, 11,000dr in ski season; doubles 12,000dr, 18,000dr in ski season). The closest **campground** is west of (see p. 180).

Moderately priced *tavernas* include **Liakoura** (tel. 31 783), across from the post office on the first square (*saganaki* 900dr, *souvlaki* 1400dr), and **Lakka** below the police station (salad 700 1000dr, *saganaki* 500dr) More daring non-vegetarians can head over to **Dasargiri** (tel. 31 291) for *kokoretsi* (1500dr) and *kontosouvli* (1800dr)—both delightfully cooked animal viscera.

ENTERTAINMENT Apollo and the Muses now share their abode with ski buffs on **Mt. Parnassos** (2700m). If you're interested in hiking up in summer, take a taxi to the **Mt. Parnassos Ski Center,** 27km northwest of Arahova. From the ski center, it's a steep 2km climb up to the summit, where vultures glower overhead. The ski season on Mt. Parnassos runs from November to May. There are 14 lifts and tickets average 6000dr per day; rentals are 4000dr per day. Renting in Arahova can save you about 2000dr if you have a means of transporting equipment to the slopes.

Founded in 1996, the **Hellenic Center of Mountain Sports in Arahova** (tel. 31 846) organizes mountain biking, skiing, trekking, and snowboarding excursions to Mt. Parnassos. There's a small information booth next to Cafe Neo on the main road. To stay in the area, try Delphi or Arahova, but you'll have to pay 7000-8000dr for the round-trip cab, since the taxi lobby won't allow public buses to run to the ski center (taxi tel. 31 566). Alternately, make a daytrip from Athens (3hr., 6am, 2500dr round-trip). For information on skiing, find Mr. Kostas Koutras at his **ski shop** (tel. 31 841 or 31 767) on the first left coming from Delphi. In addition to information, Mr. Koutras rents skis for 2500dr and snowboards for 5000dr per day. He also sells new equipment at decent prices. In the summer, when his shop is closed, Mr. Koutras is a good source of tourist information—find him in the main square drinking coffee with the bus manager.

■ **Delphi** Δελφοι

As any Delphinian will proudly attest, this town of 2500 marks the *omphalos* (navel) of the earth. An ancient myth holds that, to determine the world's *omphalos,* Zeus simultaneously released two eagles, one from the east and one from the west. The birds collided, impaled each other with their beaks over Delphi and fell to the ground. A sacred stone still marks the spot. First the oracle of Gaia, Mother Earth, was built here in the 2nd millennium BC; then in the 8th century BC, when the Olympian gods of Homer succeeded the chthonic gods of remote antiquity, the oracle became Apollo's. This transfer of power required struggle: Apollo had to slay the Python, a snake-like beast of the underworld who presided over the site. With the oracle under Apollo's control, troubled pilgrims from across the world sought the guidance of the Pythia—a priestess who presided over the oracle directly. She would inhale vapors emitted from a chasm in the temple floor, enter a state of ecstasy, and mumble incoherent words then interpreted by a group of priests and pronounced in cryptic verse to the waiting public. Dubious as it sounds, Pausanias, a traveller who visited Delphi in the 2nd century AD, attested that of all the oracles in the world, the one at Delphi was the most often true.

ORIENTATION AND PRACTICAL INFORMATION Buses leave Athens from Terminal B at 260 Liossion St. for Delphi (3½hr., 5 per day, 2800dr). Buy your ticket at the booth labeled Δελφοι (Delphi). Arrive early to avoid long lines. With a railpass, take a train to Levadia; from there, buses head to Delphi (750dr). From Delphi, buses leave for: Thessaloniki via Volos, Larissa, and Katerini (5½hr., 7 per week, 6200dr); Patras (3hr., 1-2 per day, 2200dr); Lamia (2hr., 3 per day, 1600dr); Nafpaktos (2½hr., 4 per day, 2040dr); Amphissa (30min., 7 per day, 340dr); Itea (30min., 7 per day, 340dr); and Galaxidi (50min., 4 per day with a switch in Itea, 660dr).

The municipal **tourist office** (tel. 82 900), housed in the town hall with entrances on both Pavlou St. and Apollonos St., is run by friendly and tetra-lingual Mrs. Efi. Come here to get tips on just about anything under the Delphic sun, including bus schedules, hotels, and camping rates (office open M-F 7:30am-2:30pm). If the office is closed, head to the bus station, 14 Frangou St., where English-speaking staff can help decipher complicated bus schedules and provide directions (open daily 8am-10pm). The **tourist police** (tel. 82 220) and the general **police station** (tel. 82 222) are located at 3 Angelos Syngrou St., directly behind the church at the peak of Apollonos St. (open daily 9am-2pm, but staffed 24hr.). The **National Bank** (tel. 82 622) is at 16 Pavlou St. (open M-Th 8am-2pm, F 8am-1:30pm) and has a 24hr. **ATM.** At the foot of Pavlou St. across from Hotel Pythia are free **public toilets** and the **taxi stand** (tel. 82 000). The **post office** (tel. 82 376; open M-F 7:30am-2pm) is at 25 Pavlou St. The **OTE** is at 10 Pavlou St. (open M-Sa 7:30am-3:10pm, Su 9am-2pm). **Postal code:** 33054. **Telephone code:** 0265.

ACCOMMODATIONS Delphi is full of hotels, but most of them are expensive. Fortunately for the budget traveller, differences in quality do not separate the pricey from the affordable; just about every room in town has its own bathroom and a balcony with a breathtaking view of the mountains and the Gulf of Corinth. **Hotel Sybylla,** 9 Pavlou St. (tel. 82 335; fax 83 024), with baths and excellent views from every room, is no exception, and compensates for the closure of the youth hostel several years ago (singles 4000dr; doubles 6000dr). Down the same street toward the bus station, **Hotel Pan,** 53 Pavlou St. (tel. 82 294; fax 82 320) has private bathrooms and similar views (singles 5500dr; doubles 7500dr; triples 10,000dr). The nearest campsite is **Apollo Camping** (tel. 82 762, 82 750; fax 82 639), 1.5km down from the bus station (1300dr per person; 700dr per tent; 750dr per car). **Delphi Camping** (tel. 82 363) is 4km down the road (1300dr per person; 900dr per tent; 750dr per car), and **Chrissa Camping** (tel. 82 050) is 10km out of town (1300dr per person; 900dr per tent). The bus can drop you at any of these campsites.

FOOD Delphi's *tavernas* have terraces that overlook the mountains and the Gulf of Corinth. **Taverna-Restaurant Sunflower,** 33 Pavlou St. (tel. 82 442 or 82 686), offers a filling assortment of *mezedes* that allow you to taste several Greek specialties at once. Entrees, including their specialty, *yiouvetsi* (meat and *kritharaki* cooked in a ceramic pot), range from 1000 to 3000dr.For great fresh breads and pastries, take a left at the whitewashed church on the peak of the hillside on Apollonos St. and follow the signs to the **Artotechniki Bakery** (tel. 82 042). Your small effort will be rewarded with *voutimata* (dipping cookies for coffee or milk) and the regional specialty, *kourabiethes* (almond cookies covered in icing; open daily 5am-10pm).

ENTERTAINMENT The only places to shake a leg after dark are **Club No Name,** 33 Pavlou St. (tel. 82 600), and **Katoi** (tel. 82 053), across the street from the bus station, where you can mingle with Delphi's youth for a 500dr cover, sipping 500dr beers or 1000dr cocktails. Both open at 10pm and stay open until sunrise if customers are enjoying themselves. If your timing is lucky, there is also a **Festival of Ancient Greek Drama** put on in July and August by the **European Cultural Center of Delphi** (tel. 82 731 or 82 792; fax 82 733). The center, open daily from 9am to 2pm, also has temporary international art exhibitions. To find it, walk down the Amphissa/Itea road and follow the signs back uphill. Delphi is home to several other summer festivals, so ask around and keep a sharp eye out for posters when you arrive. Also, from April to October **Villa Symposio** offers nightly food, drink, and Greek folk dances. Call **Delphi Consultants** (tel. 82 086) for information on prices and transportation.

On the north coast of the Gulf of Corinth, **Itea** is a quiet escape from Delphi and offers a rocky beach and a long waterfront boardwalk lined with cafes and *tavernas*.

The beach east of town is equipped with outdoor showers. Cleaner and more solitary is **Kira Beach,** 2km from town. Frequent **buses** run from Delphi to Itea (1hr., 11 per day 6:30am-8:20pm, 340dr). The last bus back to Delphi from Itea is at 5:45pm; a **taxi** (tel. 32 200) is a good option for late returns (1200-2500dr according to the number of passengers). It takes six hours to walk uphill to Delphi.

■ The Oracle of Delphi

> *The god whose oracle is at Delphi neither utters nor hides his meaning but shows it by a sign.*
>
> —Heraclitus

The Oracle of Delphi was the most important and famous source of sacred wisdom in the ancient world. It marked the *omphalos* (navel) of the pagan religious world from at least the 7th century BC until the advent of Christianity. Pilgrims came from around the globe, from Greece and all the Hellenistic lands in the Near East, where Alexander the Great had brought Greek culture, and later from Rome and all her far-flung provinces. The oracle's authority extended beyond religious matters and personal fortune-telling; Delphic approval sanctioned many political decisions, including the reforms that would lead to the implementation of pure democracy in Athens. The oracle's pronouncements altered nations and set off or extinguished military conflicts. Realizing this power, city-states from all over the Greek world erected treasuries and donated immense tributes at the site of the oracle, propitiating the divine powers and staking their own claim to the glory the oracle could grant.

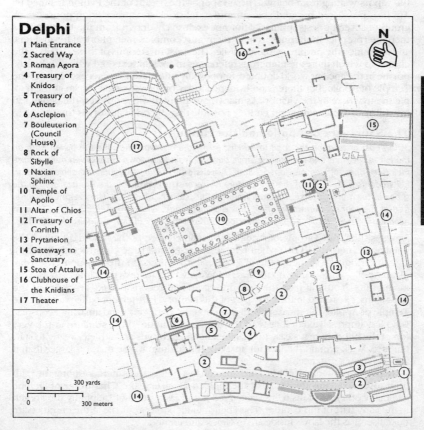

Delphi

1 Main Entrance
2 Sacred Way
3 Roman Agora
4 Treasury of Knidos
5 Treasury of Athens
6 Asclepion
7 Bouleuterion (Council House)
8 Rock of Sibylle
9 Naxian Sphinx
10 Temple of Apollo
11 Altar of Chios
12 Treasury of Corinth
13 Prytaneion
14 Gateways to Sanctuary
15 Stoa of Attalus
16 Clubhouse of the Knidians
17 Theater

STEREA ELLADA

The Irony of Oracles

The Delphic Oracle was renowned for giving obscure, deceptively metaphorical answers. Many a suppliant went home more confused than he came, having failed to draw meaning from the answer, or—worse still—having drawn the wrong meaning from it. King Croessus of Sardis, who ruled a vast territory encompassing most of Asia Minor and was known in antiquity as the richest man in the world, came to the oracle in the 6th century BC to ask about the threat the Persians were posing to his kingdom. The oracle's answer: "A great Empire will be destroyed." The king returned to Sardis thinking that he would conquer the Persian Empire, which even at that time was as large as his own. Of course the empire the oracle had meant was his own, which he realized as he watched his empire and his capital fall to the Persians. Later, Themistocles, leader of Athens during the first Persian War, asked the oracle how to prepare for approaching war. He was told to "build wooden walls." Naturally, most interpreted this to mean that wooden walls should be built around the city. Themistocles, however, set to work building a fleet of ships. Only after Athens' decisive victory over the Persians at the great naval battle of Salamis did the Athenians realize Themistocles' great wisdom. Such stories demonstrate that the nature of the oracle was not simply to answer questions. This was part of the meaning of the exhortation once inscribed on the Temple of Apollo: "Know thyself."

The details of the operation of the oracle are unclear. We know that the Pythia, an older woman chosen from the residents of Delphi, would sit over a chasm and inhale the vapors wafting from below. These vapors—the breath of the Python maimed by Apollo—possessed her and she entered a delirious state, muttering nonsense. A group of several priests, primarily but not exclusively drawn from the town, would then interpret her mutterings, render them into complex metaphorical hexameters, and announce the prophecy to the public. The most mysterious of these details is the chasm, to which there are numerous references in ancient texts and whose existence no one in the ancient world doubted. Supposedly, the chasm was accessible from the Temple of Apollo, but there is no evidence today of there being a chasm at the temple or anywhere in the vicinity. As many have pointed out, however, the geological instability of the area makes it entirely possible that the original story is true.

The Sanctuary of Apollo and the Museum

300m east of town on the road to Athens; follow the highway and take the paved path on the left to the ruins and museum, a 5min. downhill walk from town. **Site: Open** *daily in summer 8am-8pm; off-season 8am-5:15pm.* **Admission** *1200dr, students and seniors 600dr, EU students free.* **Maps** *of the first century BC reconstruction of the site are available in the shops in town or at the kiosk across from the bus station for 300dr. The Delphi brochure, free at the tourist information office, has a smaller map.* **Museum: Tel.** *82 312.* **Open** *M noon-6:30, Tu-Su 7:30am-8pm.* **Admission** *1200dr, students 600dr.* **Guidebooks** *2000dr.*

Now, as then, the **Temple of Apollo** is the centerpiece of the sanctuary ruins. The building burned in 548 BC (when temples were by and large constructed of wood), and an earthquake shattered the 373 BC reconstruction. On the way up to the Temple of Apollo, visitors hike up the **Sacred Way,** which follows the same path as it did in antiquity. You will pass the well-preserved and reconstructed **Treasury of the Athenians,** excavated in the early part of this century. Farther along the path past the Temple of Apollo, the **theater,** with its geometric perfection and amazing acoustics, is no less impressive. For a taste of the Roman, continue to the **stadium** at the very top of the hill, where it's easy to imagine cheering crowds and athletes ready to start the race. Walk around the interior space of the stadium to see that it is larger than it appears from a distance.

Delphi's **Archaeological Museum,** located just before the sanctuary along the path from town, contains the frieze of the **Siphian Treasury,** the **Charioteer of Delphi,** and many other precious relics uncovered in the excavation of Delphi by the French in the early part of this century. The English guidebooks available at the entrance are quite useful as the labels inside are in Greek and French.

The Temple of Pronaia Athena

The second set of ruins is roughly 300m farther down the path heading away from town. Around the corner, pass the **Castelian Spring,** where pilgrims cleansed themselves both physically and spiritually before calling upon the oracle. The remains of the original spring are up the steps and about 20m into the small gorge. This area was covered by rocks until the beginning of this century, when a clever archaeologist cleared them away. Today you can see the niches carved into the rock for votive offerings. Drinking from the spring is said to confer the gift of eloquence.

Among the second group of ruins is the **Temple of Pronaia Athena** (open 24hr., free). This area served as a welcoming lounge for pilgrims before they entered the sanctuary. Also find the **Tholos,** an architectural masterpiece of the early 4th century BC. Its three remaining Doric columns are probably the most photographed of the Delphic ruins. Nearby is the **gymnasium,** ever a central component of ancient Greek culture. Of all the Delphic ruins, these have been damaged the most by falling rocks; 15 columns of the Temple of Pronaia Athena survived when first excavated almost 100 years ago, but further rockfalls in 1905 left standing only the three we see today.

■ Galaxidi Γαλαξίδι

Asking the origin of Galaxidi's name can pit neighbor against neighbor. Men are likely to claim that the mermaid Galaxa rose from the sea to establish the seaside town—hence the name in her honor. Women tell a different story. A combination of *gala* (milk) and *xithi* (vinegar), the town's name, they say, reflects the bittersweet existence of a seaman's wife. Stemming from Galaxidi's history as a prominent naval base, this story is now out of date. Navy wives no longer sit impatiently for news of a safe voyage—instead, they await a speedy return from the local *taverna.*

ORIENTATION AND PRACTICAL INFORMATION The bus station is in the town square at one end of **Nik. Mama St.,** the main street in the town center leading down to the waterfront and harbor. Buses run from Galaxidi to Nafpaktos (1½hr., 5 per day 6:15am-9:20pm, 1350dr). For indigestion and other post-party traumas, head to the **pharmacy** (tel. 41 122), one block to the right of the bus station on Nik. Mama St. A new branch of the **National Bank,** with a 24hr. **ATM,** is right next door (open M-Th 8:45am-1:30pm, F 8:15am-1pm). Galaxidi's **post office** is at the end of Nik. Mama St. (open M-F 7:30am-2pm). **Postal code:** 33052. **Telephone code:** 0265.

ACCOMMODATIONS From the bus stop, turn right and head down Nik. Mama St. to find **Hotel Poseidon** (tel. 41 246 or 41 1271), a breezy old home-turned-hotel blessed with a friendly manager, Costas, who just may break open a bottle of *ouzo* on the evening of your arrival (singles 5000dr; doubles 9900dr). **Pension Votsalo** (tel. 41 788 or 41 542) is pricier but near the waterfront. Cross the square from the bus stop and go down Novorhou Ageli St. on the right side of the square until you see the *pension* on your left. Don't be put off by the twists and turns of the street; you'll see the place soon enough (doubles 12,000dr; longer stays get better deals). On a summer weekend, expect the prices to be 20% higher. There are also a few **rooms to let;** keep your eyes peeled for signs, or ask at the bus station.

FOOD In the strip of moderately priced *tavernas* along the water, **Omilos** (tel. 42 111 or 42 110), a restaurant whose tables extend onto a pier, has the best atmosphere. In keeping with the surroundings, fresh fish is the entree of choice, but stretch your imagination and sample grilled sardines and the secret-recipe mussels (2500dr). Prices may require a bit of a splurge, but view and quality make it well worth the strain on your daily budget. For a quick, cheap meal or snack, **To Megkali,** right next to the bus station, is the local favorite (*souvlaki* 400dr, *gyros* 350dr). But perhaps the best deal is a trip to either of the bakeries on Nik. Mama St., followed by a swing through **To Konaki** (tel. 42 258), an excellent **sweet shop** next to the supermarket closest to the bus stop (ice cream 200dr, special soupy almond concoction 1900dr per kg).

ENTERTAINMENT AND SIGHTS For wonderful swimming, head to the forest side of the harbor, over the "bridge" as you walk down Nik. Mama St. past Restaurant Steki. Small islands sit offshore and flooded caves hang over scant beaches. The **Church of St. Nicholas,** near the museum, houses many fine mosaics. The 13th-century **Monastery of Transfiguration,** with sublime centuries-old wood carvings and a great view of town, is 6km from Galaxidi on the uphill road outside of town. It is over an hour by foot up a steep road with no protection from the sun. If it is a cool day and you have the time, the views themselves make it an excellent hike. Follow K. Papapetrou St. out of town past the school and into the terraced orange orchards. Otherwise, you might consider hiring one of the taxis waiting in the square out in front of the bus station.

Although Galaxidi is pretty sleepy most of the year, things get more lively in winter; around Carnival time in February, the town holds a **festival** bordering on the Bacchic. *Ouzo* bottles are emptied by the hundreds; food fights have been known to break out. The town's children dancing in traditional garb offer more sedate entertainment.

■ Nafpaktos Ναυπακτος

From the towering battlements of the Venetian castle on the hill above the city you can see all of Nafpaktos. Its expansive beaches, pastel buildings set beside Venetian walls, and veil of pine, palm, orange, and elm, make it one of the most beautiful cities on the Gulf of Corinth. Nafpaktos, whose name derives from its ancient role as a ship-building naval colony—*"nats"* (ship) + *"pignymi"* (to manufacture)—is a rewarding place to spend some time before crossing into the land of the Pelops at Antirrio.

ORIENTATION AND PRACTICAL INFORMATION Buses drop off at **Athinon St.** at the base of the main town square. The **bus station** itself is across from the church 10m down the street that intersects Athinon St. at the bus stop. From Nafpaktos buses to the **ferry** crossing at **Antirrio** which serves the Peloponnese (15min., 2 per hr. 6am-10pm, 250dr). Inquire at the bus station for more information. In addition, buses leave for Athens (6hr., 10 per day, 3500dr) and Messolongi (4 per day, 850dr) and from there on to Agrinio (1550dr).

Nafpaktos Travel Agency, 29 Athinon St. (tel. 22 290 or 25 979; fax 28 745), 20m up Athinon St., serves as a tourist office, providing information of all kinds (open M-F 8am-2pm and 5-9pm, Sa 8am-2:30pm). If the travel agency is closed, find Chris Zographos in his **kiosk,** the first on the square next to the bus stop; he went to college in Iowa and speaks excellent English—with a Midwestern American accent—and is happy to help in any way he can. In the square there are **taxis** (tel. 27 792 or 27 678) and a phone for calling them, if there aren't several already waiting there. Out of the square, at the end opposite the bus stop, is the **National Bank** (tel. 27 682) with a 24hr. **ATM** (bank open M-Th 8am-2pm, F 8am-1:30pm). Down Dem. Psarou St., which intersects Athinon St. in front of the bank, is the **OTE** (open 7am-2:40pm). The **post office** (tel. 27 232) is farther down Athinon St. from the bank on the right side of the street (open M-F 7:30am-2pm). There are a number of **pharmacies** around the square, all with varying hours; if the one you choose is closed, there should be a sign on the door telling you which other pharmacies are open, or else ask at the travel agency or Chris' kiosk. In case of emergency, call the **police** (tel. 27 258). **Postal code:** 30300. **Telephone code:** 0634.

ACCOMMODATIONS AND FOOD The two comparable budget hotels in town are **Hotel Aigli** (tel. 27 271 or 27 323) just down from the bank on Athinon St., and **Hotel Niki** (tel. 28 901), a block further down. Both have singles for 5000dr and doubles for 7000dr, all with private bathrooms. If you must be on the beach and care to spend the money, there are several large resort hotels right on the sea; walk along the beaches and you cannot miss them. Expect to pay at least 15,000dr a night.

Tavernas and cafes are plentiful in Nafpaktos. A restaurant with no name on the footpath next to the church is the cheapest, with salads for around 500dr and entrees in the 1000-1300dr range. However, for only slightly higher prices, you can dine on the waterfront at **O Stavros**. Walk to the sea on the road that passes the bus station and turn left onto the road that runs along the beach. With the water on your right, follow the road past a playground; O Stavros is under a row of trees on the left side of the road. For those feeling less frugal, there are dozens of trendy cafes surrounding the small port protected by the castle walls.

SIGHTS AND ENTERTAINMENT The 15th century **Venetian castle** dominates the picturesque setting of the town with five zones of fortification from port to crest. Many footpaths wind around the walls past fountains and through century-old gates; one of these paths begins off Athinon St. just past the post office, on the right. A leisurely but direct walk to the main fortifications on the hill takes about 25 minutes. For a longer and more circuitous route, stop at fountains and detour through the original castle buildings. On the paved road that leads to the castle is **Cafe Kastro** (tel. 25 121), a perfect place for refreshment. Pristine white tables shaded by small trees and set on narrow grassy terraces carved into the steep hillside command an unparalleled view of the town and turquoise gulf below (coffees 400-700dr, beer 700-800dr, assorted *frappés* and fruit juices 800-1200dr; open 3pm-midnight).

The Death of Byron

Messolongi (a stop on the Athens-Delphi-Astakos bus route) has the tragic distinction of being the place where **Lord Byron** caught a fever and met his end in 1824, while he was leading the local troops in the War of Independence. In Byron's time the town was mostly wet, stagnant marshes, and although many buildings have appeared since, the town remains a gloomy, depressing place. Though you may be drawn to the port to pay tribute to the poet, you probably won't want to spend the night. In Messolongi there is a small **War of Independence Museum** in the old town hall at the center of the square; exhibits include an unexceptional collection of Byron memorabilia. Another stop on the Byron pilgrim's trail is the large statue of the poet dressed in Greek garb out in front of the Hotel Liberty and just before the entrance to the **Garden of Heroes.** The park consists mainly of crumbling busts and other poorly maintained monuments to various national war heroes. **Byron's heart** is buried beneath the statue; the noise and unsightly view of dirty, modern Messolongi around the park, however, is tragically unromantic.

■ Astakos Αστακος

The word itself—*astakos*—means lobster, but these days, the livelihood of this small coastal village is more closely tied to its ferry service to the Ionian islands. The town is charming, but not amazingly pretty; it has just enough to keep one satisfied until the ferry comes the next day. While waiting for the ferry, enjoy Astakos' **beaches,** which are sandier and wider than most you will find on the Ionian islands.

Ferries stop once and sometimes twice a day at Astakos; the first at midday, departing around 1pm. Unless the winds are too high to allow the trip, the ferry departs at 1pm for Cephalonia (1½hr., 1300dr) and Ithaka (2½hr., 1850dr); buy your tickets shortly before the ferry departs at a booth next to the bus station. The **post office** (tel. 41 254; open M-F 8am-3pm) and the **National Bank** with 24hr. **ATM** (open M-Th 8am-2pm, F 8am-1:30pm) are on the next parallel street down. To find the **OTE** (tel. 41 399), make the first right after the post office and follow the street 30m up the hill (open daily 7:30am-3:10pm). **Postal code:** 30006. **Telephone code:** 0646.

Because the erratic buses cannot be relied upon to take you away and bring you back the next day, if you miss the ferry you should probably stay the night in Astakos. The only hotel is about 200m down the waterfront from the bus station, past the row of restaurants. The **Stratos** (tel. 41 911 or 41 906; fax 41 227) is a clean establishment offering rooms with private bath and spacious balconies looking out to the sea (singles 6000dr; doubles 12,000dr). For two people, letting a room would be considerably cheaper. Coming from the bus station, just before the Stratos there are **rooms to let** above the **Florida Bar** (tel. 41 135 or 41 375); inquire at the bar (doubles 5000dr; triples 7000dr). Farther from the sea, at the bus station end of the third road running up parallel to the coastline, George Foundas (tel. 41 097 or 41 984)lets doubles and triples with private bathrooms for the same prices above the **Enalax Bar.**

All of the town's restaurants are along the sea between the Stratos and the bus station and have nearly identical menus; the varied colors of their respective patio chairs are the distinguishing features among them. **Cafe Stou Baklava,** at about the middle of the strip, has an "English Breakfast," including two eggs, bacon, bread, and jam (700dr). For dinner, **Ntina,** near the bus station end of the strip, may be the best choice, because of its slightly newer chairs and decor.

■ Karpenisi Καρπενησι

Evritania, a land of evergreen forests, roaring rivers, and jagged mountains, is the Switzerland of Greece; it was recently ranked the fifth-cleanest place on earth. Summer adventurers in Evritania enjoy some of the best hiking, climbing, and rafting that Greece has to offer; trails through the firs amid maple forests of the Timfristos Mountains abound, as do opportunities for aquatic sports in the Achelos and Tavropos Rivers. Thanks to the recent development of a ski resort at Mt. Velouchi, winter visitors can now share in the panoramic vistas and relax in one of the region's many villages.

The goats that first fashioned a path to Karpenisi, capital of Evritania, never rode teetering buses through a never-ending series of switchback runs, but the town is well worth the hair-rising ride. A relaxed town located at the foothills of the towering Timfristos Mountains, Karpenisi brims with natural beauty though there is not much left that is worth seeing in the town itself. The Germans razed Karpenisi to the ground in 1941, as did the Communists in Greece's 1949 Civil War. Nevertheless, its friendly atmosphere makes Karpenisi a comfortable base for stunning outdoor excursions through the surrounding countryside and nearby traditional villages.

ORIENTATION AND PRACTICAL INFORMATION Everything of importance is within a five-minute walk from the bus station. The main road leading down from the bus station forks at the square. The OTE and the police station are in close succession along **Evritanon St.,** the street that forks to the right. On **Zinopoulou St.,** the street forking to the left, you'll find most of the town's shops. Parallel to Zinopoulou runs **Karpenisioti St.** Just about everything else in Karpenisi is across the street from or on the main square. The **bus station** is uphill from the square on the main road. **Buses** run to Athens (5hr., 3 per day, 4850dr); Lamia (1¾hr., 4 per day, 1350dr); Agrinio (3½hr., 1 or 2 per day, 2000dr); Proussou village (45min., 2 per week, 600dr); and Mikro Horio and Megalo Horio villages (20min., 2 per day, 250dr). Ask at the bus station about bus service to smaller villages, which runs 1-2 times per week. Taxis (tel. 22 666) line the south side of the square. A **tourist office** across the street from the square's east side offers maps, brochures, and ideas for excursions into the Evritanian countryside (open M-Sa 10am-2pm and 5-9pm, Su 10am-2pm). The **Greek Mountaineering Club (EOS),** 2 Georgiou Tsitsara St. (tel. 23 051), near the Agricultural Bank, provides invaluable information about hiking, rafting, camping, and even parachuting in Evritania. The **National Bank** is on the south side of the square (open M-Th 8am-2pm, F 8:30am-1:30pm). The **police station** (tel. 25 100) is on Evritanon Rd. (open 24hr.). In case of emergency call the **hospital** (tel. 22 315). The **post office** is on Karpenisoti St. (open M-F 7:30am-2pm) and the **OTE** is on Evritanon Rd. (open daily 7am-10pm). **Postal code:** 36100. **Telephone code:** 0237.

ACCOMMODATIONS Rates at Karpenisi's hotels are higher from December to March when Greeks flock to the hotels of Karpenisi to ski at the **Velouchi Ski Center** (12km away), and from July to August, when Evritania draws visitors trying to escape Greece's summer heat. Both in summer and winter, hotel prices are raised for the weekend warriors. In addition to hotels, the region around Karpenisi brims with **Rooms to Let,** a far better taste of Greek life than the rather bland hotels. Rates start around 10,000dr in Karpenisi and 7000dr nearby. Call the tourist office for more information. To reach **Hotel Galini,** 3 Riga Ferraiou St. (tel. 22 914), go downhill from the square past the Agricultural Bank and take the first right. Galini offers clean, comfortable rooms with phones, baths, and TVs (singles 6000dr; doubles 12,000dr). **Hotel Lecadin** (tel. 22 131; fax 22 133) is a 15-minute walk from the square along Evritanon St. Perched high above the town, this is Karpenisi's very own castle in the clouds. The views of the countryside are to die for. Rooms come with phone, bath, and TV (singles 8000dr; doubles 12,000dr). **Hotel Elvetia,** 7 Zinopoulou St. (tel. 80 111; fax 80 112), takes its name from the Greek for Switzerland and tries charmingly to live up to Evritania's reputation (singles 6500dr; doubles 8000dr; triples 9500dr).

FOOD AND ENTERTAINMENT Karpenisi's dining options begin with inexpensive meals from the many supermarkets or fruit stores. If you have transportation or are willing to take a taxi, you can get fresh local trout, traditional sausages, and *katiki,* a cheese, at the village *tavernas.* At **Yevsi Taste,** 10 Zinopoulou (tel. 23 777), sit down, grab one of the 2½ booths, try a *gyro* (280dr), and chat with the Australian owner. **I Klimataria** (tel. 22 230), just below the Hotel Galini, is a wonderful dining experience if you have more than a couple of minutes on your hands. The owner, Fotis, speaks English or Greek to visitors. He has meticulously designed his restaurant in the style of a traditional Byzantine church and lavishes the same care on his dishes. Try the *kokoretsi* or *chirino krasato* (entrees 1600-1800dr). **I Folia** (tel. 24 405) is on a small pedestrian walkway parallel to Zinopoulou St. The *kotopoulo lemonato* (lemon chicken) is delicious. **Pizza Il Gusto** (tel. 25 901), located in the same walkway as I Folia, lives up to its name (pizzas 1300-1800dr). **Esi Oti Pis** a.k.a. Whatever You Say (tel. 24 080), farther up the street from I Folia, serves savory lamb in a stone dining room (entrees 1400-1800dr). **I Plateia,** located directly under the town hall, is the square's most popular spot for a *frappé;* be sure to try the mouth-watering chocolate *sokolatina.* A pink and white sign advertises the sweet shop **Georgos Kitsios and Co.,** 13 Zinopoulou St. (tel. 24 082), just opposite the square, which sells *kourabiedes* and some of the best *baklava* you may ever taste. Head to the main square for dessert and a relaxing *frappé* (400dr). If there's still life in your legs after dinner, go to one of the many bars near the square or to one of Karpenisi's two discos, **O Labirinthus,** across the street from Esi Oti Pis, or **Club Nemisis,** about 1.5km south of town at the Kephalovriso. Both of these nightclubs are only open Friday and Saturday nights.

SIGHTS There's not much to see in Karpenisi itself, though throughout the summer the town celebrates saints' days with religious services in the mornings and traditional cooking, music, and dances at night. In the surrounding villages, however, a wide range of sights and activities beckons.

A few kilometers from Karpenisi is **Korishades,** a traditional village whose well-preserved stone mansions sport elaborate wooden balconies characteristic of the area. If you're in the mood for more alpine glory, catch the daily bus to **Mikro Horio** ("Big Village") and **Megalo Horio** ("Little Village"), a pair of secluded mountain hamlets on the slopes of **Kaliakouda.** About 15km past Megalo Horio—and accessible only by dirt road—is **Prousos.** Here you'll find the renowned **Monastery of the Virgin of Proussiotissa,** which holds a miracle-working icon of the Madonna said to have been painted by St. Luke the Evangelist himself. Also in Prousos are the **castles** of the great war hero Karaiskakis and the eerie **Black Cave,** alleged to be the site of an oracle in ancient times. Other scenic villages near Karpenisi include **Klafsion** (8km away), a village whose name—derived from the Greek verb "to cry"—is a tribute to the hardships endured by the townspeople. Beyond lies **Frangista,** home of a fresco-covered church well worth visiting.

Evritania also has plenty to offer to those seeking athletic diversions. The **Achelous** and the **Tavropos,** the province's two main rivers, are ideal for beginner and intermediate rafting and kayaking. **Lake Kremaston,** literally the "hanging lake," offers visitors a setting of unrivaled natural beauty for water sports and Evritania's great forested mountains are perfect for hikers and mountain climbers. For details on specific activities or excursions consult Karpenisi's tourist office and tour agencies.

■ Lamia Λαμια

Lamia is no coastal resort. It has no sun-drenched beaches, hordes of backpack-toting tourists, sly hotel owners trying to rip visitors off, or rows of kiosks selling cheap gifts. By day in this transportation hub, old men gather and talk in the *kafeneia* clustered in the leafy **Laou Square;** by night, the entire town hits the streets around the larger **Eleftherias Square** for drinks, *souvlaki,* and Lamia's renowned *gyros.* The lack of tourism doesn't make Lamia a bore; the town has plenty of attractions for the adventurous traveler, including the recently opened Architectural Museum within the ancient castle's walls, and, on the other side of town, the exquisitely tended gardens of **Agios Loukas,** ideal for a sunset stroll or a tender kiss under the stars.

ORIENTATION AND PRACTICAL INFORMATION Four large, leafy squares define Lamia's roughly rectangular downtown district: **Eleftherias Square,** the largest square and the center of Lamia's nightlife, occupies the northwest corner; the much smaller **Laou Square** is in the northeast corner; **Diakou Square** is in the southwest; and **Parkou Square** (also known as Dimokratias Square), where most of Lamia's banks and shops are located, is in the southeast. The **local train station** (tel. 61 061) is on Konstantinoupoleos St. Walk south 10 minutes from Parkou Sq. along Satobriandou St. The **main train station** is at **Leiakokladiou,** a 6km trip from Lamia. Trains go to Athens from Leiakokladiou (3hr., 15 per day, 1790dr); Thessaloniki (4¼hr., 15 per day, 2450dr); and Larissa (2¼hr., 12 per day, 1070dr). **KTEL** (tel. 24 895) in Lamia has three **bus stations,** all clustered together south of the town center. The station serving Evritania and Karpenisi (2hr., 5 per day, 1350dr) is on Botsari St. The station serving the local area is at the end of Satobriandou St. on the right; the station serving Athens (2½hr., 15 per day, 3000dr) and Thessaloniki (4hr., 2 per day, 4000dr) is on Papakirazi St., a side street off Satobriandou St. A **tourist office** is on the south side of Laou Sq. (tel. 30 065). Ask here or at the town hall, on the east side of Eleftherias Sq., for tourist information (open M-F 7am-3pm). There are several **banks** with 24-hour **ATMs** on Parkou Sq. The **police** (tel. 22 331) are on Patroklou St., one street below Parkou Sq. (open 24hr.) A **hospital** (tel. 30 126 or 30 121) is on Karaiskaki Rd., 20 minutes from the town center (open 24hr.). The **post office** is on the south side of Diakou Sq. (open M-F 7:30am-8pm). The **OTE** is on the west side of Eleftherias Sq. (open 24hr.). **Postal code:** 35100. **Telephone code:** 0231.

FOOD AND ACCOMMODATIONS Since Lamia is not a tourist town, it has few hotels. They are also expensive and blandly furnished. Choose your accommodation with care, or simply get on your way before dark. **Hotel Neon Astron** (tel. 22 645), on Laou Sq., is well situated and offers clean, airy rooms (with ceiling fans) for the best rates in town (singles 4500dr, with bathroom 5500dr; doubles 7800dr).

No traveler will go hungry in Lamia for lack of options; at night, all four squares are encircled by a seemingly endless array of *tavernas* and *kafeneia.* None have strict hours; they open in the morning, close late, and will sometimes take a few hours off in the afternoon. **Allo Schedio** (tel. 42 711; email allosxedio@lamianet.gr; http://www.lamianet.gr/allo-sxedio) is set in a secluded corner between Eleftherias Sq. and Laou Sq. Attentive staff and a charming accordion player make this a wonderful eating experience (entrees 1200-2000dr). **Detpa** (tel. 22 322), on top of Agios Loukas hill, has beautiful, sweeping views of Lamia. Be sure to try the chef's specialty *moshari filoxenia* (1870dr), a potato stuffed with beef, topped with melted cheese and sprinkled with the restaurant's signature red sauce. **Lucky Time Grill** (tel. 62 750) on Eleftherias Sq. is quick and satisfying, with inexpensive but delicious *souvlaki* and *gyros.*

ENTERTAINMENT After a day of touring or traveling, Lamia is an ideal party town, boasting a wide array of bars and clubs where you can drink and dance the night away. Most revelers flock to Eleftherias Sq. and its surrounding streets, where almost all of Lamia's bars are found. The **Sportline Club** and **Cafe Remazzo,** both on the east side of Eleftherias Sq., are particularly crowded at night. More intrepid party-goers often head to the large outdoor discos in the countryside. **Yazz,** about 3km south of the town center, is the best of these. It plays a melange of Greek and American music. The crowds arrive around 1:30am (2000dr admission includes first drink, additional drinks 2000dr). The other discos—notably **Trombley's**—are out of the way and less crowded, but still worth the trip for dance demons.

SIGHTS The most attractive—but surprisingly under-visited—sights in Lamia are the **castle** and its enclosed **Architectural Museum.** *(Open Tu-Su 8:30am-3pm. Admission 500dr, students free.)* The castle, which is still in use by the military, was built in the Classical period and refurbished by the first Greek king, King Otto, in the early 1800s. The spacious and well-organized museum covers the history of Lamia and the surrounding area from the Paleolithic period (600,000 BC) through the Hellenistic era. The museum's artifacts include primitive stone tools, arrowheads, bronze figurines, and ceramic pottery; most were found in burial tombs outside Lamia. Some of the museum's highlights are the earliest preserved vase depicting a naval battle, a large engraving showing a pregnant mother's sacrifice to Artemis, and a collection of ring-like bronze coins used for currency in the Archaic period.

■ Thermopylae Θερμοπυλες

> *Honor to those who in the life they lead*
> *Define and guard a Thermopylae.*
> — C.P. Cavafy

Set against jagged, deep green mountain peaks and the windswept waters of the Aegean is the small, sleepy village of Thermopylae. Often called the gateway to southern Greece, Thermopylae's strategic location has made it a prime target for invading armies over the years. Both the Ottomans and the Nazis launched fierce attacks at the straits. In 480 BC, Leonidas and his 300 Spartans heroically held off the vast Persian army of Xerxes (a force estimated at five million by the ancient historian Herodotus, and more conservatively numbered at 300,000 by modern scholars). A fifteen-foot bronze statue of Leonidas, inscribed with the words *molon lave* (the one who stayed fast), commemorates the site of the battle. About 500m farther north along the highway are the famed **hot springs** of Thermopylae. The springs' 44°C waters originate in the mountains that loom overhead. Infused with sulphur, the waters exude the aroma of rotten eggs; the stench, however, does not prevent visitors (mostly elder or ailing Greeks) from bathing in the pools and enjoying supposedly therapeutic effects.

The village of Thermopylae and the nearby springs are organized around the Athens-Lamia highway. The village itself has a **post-office** and an **ATM** just off the highway. The statue of Leonidas is located about 1km north of the town's border, and the springs are just a bit farther.

There is no lodging available in Thermopylae itself; there's no need for any in such a small town. By the hot springs are **Hotel Asklipios** (tel. 93 303) and **Hotel Aigli** (tel. 93 304), under a common management; each offers clean, if rather bare, rooms at very good prices (singles 3300dr, doubles 6100dr). The one restaurant in the area, the **Cafe-Restaurant Thermopyles** (tel. 93 589) has a limited selection of dishes (basically beef and chicken) for between 1000dr and 1300dr. The restaurant's talkative owners will regale you with historical facts and anecdotes.

■ Agios Konstantinos Αγιος Κωνσταντινος

Although in peak season tourists flood the streets of Agios Konstantinos, few visitors are lured by the delights of the town itself; most are in town because it is the closest port to Athens with ferries to the lovely Sporades. However, the rare visitor who resists the Sporades' siren song (or misses the ferry) and spends a night in Agios Konstantinos has little to regret. The town is a study in Greek charm, from the central *plateia* filled with swaying palms and effervescent fountains, to the town's namesake, the recently renovated Church of Agios Konstantinos, capped by a red tile roof and a bell tower whose clock displays a time all its own.

ORIENTATION AND PRACTICAL INFORMATION Almost all the action in Agios Konstantinos is in the town's main square. If you face the square with your back to the water, the **bus station** (tel. 32 223) is about 200m to the left. Buses leave for Athens (2½hr., every hour, 2950dr); Lamia (1hr, every hour, 900dr); and Thessaloniki (5hr, 2 per day, 6950dr). The ferry terminal, located across the street from the town square, serves both **ferries** (tel. 31 920) and **Flying Dolphins** (tel. 31 874). Ferries leave once or twice a day, depending on the season, for Skiathos (3½hr., 3319dr); Skopelos (4½hr., 4085dr); and Alonissos (6hr., 4394dr). Hydrofoils leave two to five times a day for Skiathos (1½hr., 6000dr), Skopelos (2½hr., 7900dr), and Alonissos (3hr., 7400dr). For more information, contact the **port police** (tel. 31 920) or visit one of the many **travel agencies** dotting the square. You'll find a **National Bank** (open M-Th 8am-2pm, F 8am-1:30pm), which exchanges currency and has an adjacent 24hr. **ATM,** between the bus stop and the town square along Euboikou St., the principal coastal avenue. Farther along Euboikou St. is the **OTE** (open 8am-2pm). Perpendicular to Euboikou St. are Karaiskaki St. and Thermopylon St., where the **Town Hall** (*dimarhio*) is located; these two streets contain most of Agios Konstantinos' shops and restaurants. **Postal code**: 35006. **Telephone code**: 0235.

ACCOMMODATIONS AND FOOD Since most visitors choose not to spend the night, the options for lodging in Agios Konstantinos are rather limited. **Hotel Poulia** (tel. 31 663) offers small, clean rooms at affordable prices (singles 4500dr; doubles 6500dr). **Hotel Olga,** 6 Euboikou St. (tel. 32 266), located on the main road next to two other hotels, has larger rooms (and a friendly owner) for slightly higher prices (singles 5000dr; doubles 7500dr; triples 8500dr). A more luxurious alternative is the **Hotel Astir** (tel. 31 625) located next door, whose spotless rooms offer picturesque views of the sea (singles 6000dr; doubles 8500dr).

The dining scene in Agios Konstantinos is centered around the main *plateia,* which is lined on each side by the standard array of cafes, *kafeneia,* and *pagotatzithika.* **O Alekos,** on the far side of the square, serves a mouth-watering *loukaniko* (1100dr) and *katsiki* (1300dr). The ample shade provided by the over-hanging roof and the old backgammon-playing clientele make this a great place to relax as you wait for your ferry or bus to arrive. **Restaurant Ostria** (tel. 31 987), located on Thermopylon Rd., is a slightly more expensive (and more delicious) choice. If you're lucky, the owner's adorable little girl will help you decide what to order; take her advice and try the stuffed hamburger (1500dr) and house specialty red wine.

The Sporades and Evia
Σποραδες και Ευβοια

The jagged coasts and thickly forested interiors of the Sporades (Scattered Ones) and Evia were first colonized by Cretans who cultivated olives and grapes on the scattered islands until Athenians took over in the 5th century BC. The residue of ancient structures on these islands attests to the 2nd century BC Roman presence, the Venetians' 13th century rule, and Ottoman rule until 1821, when they joined the new Greek state. Lush islands of fragrant pines, luxurious beaches, and abundant fruit orchards, the Sporades of today offer travelers—mostly Germans, Scandinavians, and Brits—a smorgasbord of earthly delights—while Evia remains a refuge for Athenians fleeing the city. Luckily, although word has gotten out about the Sporades, and the islands' fledgling tourist facilities are quickly maturing, there are spots on this small archipelago that remain relatively quiet, inexpensive, and attractive to the traveler seeking back roads, hidden churches, and exploratory adventuring.

🖐 HIGHLIGHTS OF THE SPORADES AND EVIA

- Get your mojo Bacchanized cruising the rowdy bars and pulsating clubs of **Skiathos Town** (p. 194).
- Rent a moped and tear across the untouched island of **Alonissos** (p. 198).
- On **Skyros** (p. 201), climb up over the old town to the Monastery of St. George and the Castle of Licomidus to watch the setting sun.

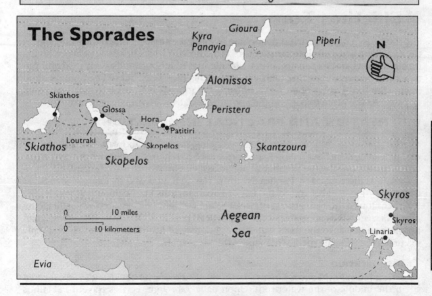

The Sporades

SPORADES & EVIA

SKIATHOS Σκιαθος

Foliage aside, a brief glance at Skiathos' glorious sand beaches, glitzy gold jewelry shops, and growing social scene brings to mind a slightly less idyllic and experienced island racing to catch up to its distant Cycladic cousin, Mykonos. The incredible nightlife attracts more tourists each year. While the number of nightclubs increases,

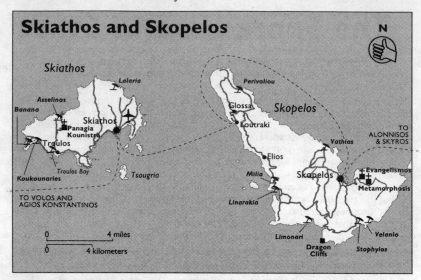

Skiathos and Skopelos

however, much of the older culture of the island is being lost. Your only recourse may be to read of the bygone era. Skiathos is one of the only places where you can find the writings of **Alexandros Papadiamantis** (1815-1911) in English translation. So either take a night away from the disco, or pack a book to the beach.

■ Skiathos Town

Skiathos Town has weathered the deluge of foreign tourists in much the same way as the coastline. The cobblestone streets of the commercial section are packed with loitering tourists and expensive stores. Residential neighborhoods with peaceful terraces and balconies bursting with white gardenia blossoms and red geraniums stand in contrast to the rows of *domatia* housing the tourists who flock to Skiathos Town to party. As *the* place to party in the Sporades, Skiathos Town never sleeps.

ORIENTATION AND PRACTICAL INFORMATION

The long waterfront, lined with travel agencies, *tavernas,* and various bike and car rental dealers, is intersected by **Papadiamantis St.,** where the number of travel agencies is beaten only by the number of high-class jewelry stores. Traveling inland, Papadiamantis is intersected by **Pandra St.** at the National Bank and by **Evangelistra St.** at the post office. Parallel and to the left of Papadiamantis St., beginning at Pandra St., **Politechniou St.** houses a string of bars. On the far right of the waterfront, still facing inland, a road winds up to the airport and several beaches. On the far left, along a harbor perpendicular to the main waterfront, is a row of fishing boats that charter daily excursions. The same mediocre map (500dr) is available everywhere.

Transportation

Ferries: Nomikos/Goutos Lines (tel. 22 209, 22 276, or 22 029; fax 22 750), located in the middle of the waterfront. Open daily 7am-9pm. Ferries travel to Skiathos most frequently from Agios Konstantinos, Volos, Skopelos, and Alonissos. From Athens, take the daily bus from the station at 260 Liossion St. (2½hr., 16 per day, 2650dr) to Agios Konstantinos, and then the ferry (3½hr., 2-3 per day, 3300dr). From Volos, ferries run from Skiathos to Skopelos (1½hr., 3-4 per day, 1400dr), Alonissos (2hr., 3-4 per day, 1900dr), and Volos (2700dr).

Flying Dolphins: (tel. 22 018). Look for the yellow signs at the center of the waterfront. Open daily 7:30am-9:30pm. Hydrofoils travel to Agios Konstantinos (75min., 3-4 per day, 6650dr); Skopelos (35min., 9-11 per day, 2800dr); Volos (75min., 3-4 per day, 5500dr); Alonissos (1hr., 8-9 per day, 3610dr); Thessaloniki 3¼hr., 1 per day, 9500dr); and Glossa (15min., 1-3 per day, 1850dr).

Flights: Olympic Airways Office (tel. 22 200 or 22 049), at the airport. Call 24hr. prior to take-off to confirm flight. Open M-F 8am-4pm. Taxis from the harbor to the airport cost about 1000dr. Three flights per day to Athens (50min., 16,800dr).

Buses: Depart from the **bus stop** at the far right end of the wharf (facing inland), travel along the main road and make 24 stops, ending at Koukounaries beach (19 per day, 280dr). Schedule posted at wharf bus stop and at Koukounaries.

Taxis: (tel. 21 460). Queue along the waterfront next to the "rooms to let" kiosk; prices are posted on the shack. Open 24hr.

Moped Rental: Places to rent litter the waterfront. The ones at **Avis** (tel. 21 458) are expensive (4000dr, helmets 250dr), so try **Alamo** (tel. 23 025), farther along the street (3500dr including helmet).

Tourist and Financial Services

Tourist Police: (tel. 23 172) A small white building on the right side of Papadiamantis St., inland past the OTE. *Summer in Skiathos* brochure. Open daily 8am-9pm.

Police (tel. 21 111), across the street and upstairs, are open 24hr. Although they speak very little English, they can help arrange *domatia*.

Banks: National Bank (tel. 22 400), midway up Papadiamantis St. on the left side, offers **currency exchange** and an **ATM**. Open M and W 8am-2pm, Tu and Th 8am-2pm and 7-9pm, F 8am-1:30pm, Su 9am-noon.

American Express: 21 Papadiamantis St. (tel. 21 463 or 21 464; fax 21 793), on the left before the post office, in the travel agency of Mare Nostrum Holidays. Provides all tourist services, including **currency exchange** and long lines. Open M-Sa 8am-2pm and 5-11:30pm, Su 9:30am-1pm and 2-10:30pm.

Bookstore: Skyline (tel. 23 647) on Evangelistra St. Carries translations of Papadiamantis' and Kazantzakis' books. Open daily 8:30am-midnight.

Laundromat: Miele Laundry, about 200m up Papadiamantis St. on a side street on the right. The owner is in the grocery store across the street, from which you buy tokens and soap. Wash 1400dr, soap 600dr, dry 1000dr. Open daily 9am-11:30pm.

Emergency and Communications

Medical Emergency and Hospital: (tel. 22 222) on the "Acropolis" hill behind Skiathos Town. Open 24hr., but emergencies only after 1pm.

Pharmacy: (tel. 22 988 or 22 666) Look for the three green cross signs, first by the National Bank, second by the post office, and third past the school. All pharmacies open daily 8:30am-2pm and 4:30-11:30pm.

Post Office: (tel. 22 011), at the intersection of Papadiamantis and Evangelistra St. Open M-F 7:30am-2pm. **Postal Code:** 37002.

OTE: (tel. 22 135), on Papadiamantis St., 1 block from the post office. Open in summer M-F 7:30am-10pm; in winter M-F 7:30am 3pm. **Telephone Code:** 0427.

ACCOMMODATIONS

Most tourists make reservations for July and August before they arrive, and tour groups often book most of the hotel rooms for summer almost a year in advance. Never fear, for although most hotel rooms and *domatia* are simply whitewashed doubles, it is not impossible to find somewhat clean, safe accommodations. Be sure to bargain in the off season, especially if you are met with an offer at the port. Typical rooms run 6000-8000dr in winter, 8000-10,000dr in spring and fall, and 10,000-14,000dr in summer. Signs abound, particularly on Evangelistra and the streets parallel to it, but if you are stuck or tired of carrying your pack, pop over to the tourist police or the **Rooms to Let Office** (tel. 22 990 or 24 260; fax 23 852) in the wooden kiosk by the port (open daily 8:30am-midnight).

Pension Angela (tel. 22 962), to your left at the end of Papadiamantis St., offers typical, clean rooms with baths. Doubles 7000 10,000dr depending on the season.

Australia Hotel (tel. 22 488), just left off Evangelistra St., needs sweeping and perhaps a couple panoramic views, but the simple rooms with baths are pretty cheap. Lovers beware, the doors and walls are thin! Doubles 5000-12,000dr.

Lena's House (tel. 22 009; fax 22 241), on a left-side street past Evangelistra off Papadiamantis St. by the second pharmacy. All rooms have fridge and fan, with a common kitchen. Breakfast 1000dr. Doubles 8000-15,000dr; triples 12,000dr.

Camping Koukounaries (tel. 49 250), on the bus route between stops 19 and 20. Has restaurant, minimarket, and campground 1km from the beach. 1700dr per person; 1000dr per tent; pay extra for the usual amenities.

FOOD

The cheapest dining options in Skiathos are to hit the *gyro/souvlaki* (350dr) stands which line Papadiamantis and the waterfront or to forage in any of the numerous **supermarkets.** Any *taverna* away from Papadiamantis will cost you less than those which are right on the main drag.

Ellinikon Taverna. Walk down Politechniou toward the harbor, until it turns slightly to the right, and look for the blue sign. Features five or six different specialties each night for only 1000dr. While their vegetarian plate may be uninspiring, it nonetheless offers an alternative to the omnipresent Greek salad.

Desperado Restaurant (tel. 24 624), on the far right of the waterfront (facing inland) serves up gigantic portions of Mexican food in a setting designed to look like a Western joint ready for a bar-room brawl. Try the chicken *fajitas* (2800dr) or one of the many vegetarian plates. Open daily 7:30pm-12:30am.

ENTERTAINMENT

Although a quiet evening with a Papadiamantis translation in a waterfront cafe may strike your fancy, most visitors either dance the night away in one of the clubs lining the far right side of the coast, or drink at one of the innumerable bars and pubs on Politechniou St., Evangelistra St., or on Papadiamantis Sq. If you venture along the coast, choose whose blaring music you like best and shake your booty there with your 1500dr cocktail in hand. Most of these clubs close in the off season.

⊛**Kentavros** (tel 22 980), on Papadiamantis Sq. in town, decorated with a poster from *Casablanca.* 700dr will buy you a beer and 1500dr a cocktail while everything from rock to jazz carries the night along in Skiathos's oldest bar.

Kalypso (tel. 23 051), one of the classier places in town, is on the water above the restaurant of the same name; the door is on the street parallel to the waterfront road. The owner, who works at an Athens radio station, will guide you on a journey through classical, traditional, ethnic, and jazz music in the relaxed (and gay-friendly) atmosphere. Beer 600dr, cocktails 1500dr.

BBC (tel. 21 190), beyond Desperado Restaurant, spins British tunes as well as outrageous acid jazz and trip-hop in a sprawling white-stucco pad (don't worry, it somehow works). Later, move inside to the dance floor with your 1500dr. Open nightly 10:30pm-4am.

Banana Bar (tel. 21 232), on the left side of a small street parallel to Papadiamantis St. Take Evangelistra St. to get over, then veer right. The rowdy crowd gathers early. Beer is 600dr, and laughs and pick-up lines are free. Open daily 9:30pm-4am.

Lalaria Bar (tel. 22 913), up Papadiamantis St., strewn with hanging plants and an ethereal spa-like interior, plays soul, reggae, and has a Greek night 2-3 times per week with live classical guitar. Beer 700dr, cocktails 1300dr. Open daily 7pm-7am.

Scorpion Club, just off Papadiamantis St., about halfway along on the left and upstairs; there are signs. Bathed in an eerie red glow, the huge dance floor is there to move on—a more typical European techno club.

For more sedate entertainment, the open-air **Cinema Paradiso** (tel. 23 975) screens recent Hollywood hits in English with Greek subtitles (1600dr). Inquire at the American Express office for schedules as well as information regarding summer cultural and artistic events at the **Bourtzi,** on the far left of the harbor.

SIGHTS

Excursions around the island and to neighboring islands can be arranged through any of the local travel agencies (3000-6000dr per person). As you walk inland, Papadiamantis Sq. lies to your right off Papadiamantis St. Follow the signs to author Alexandros Papadiamantis' 140-year-old house, which now serves as the **Papadiamantis Museum,** housing his few possessions. *(Open Tu-Su 9:30am-1pm and 5-8pm. Admission 250dr.)* The museum honors the 19th-century realist who was one of Greece's most eminent prose writers. In the museum, information and translations of short stories are available in English.

■ Around Skiathos

The island's main paved road runs along the south coast from Skiathos Town to Koukounaries. Resort hotels dominate the beaches. A **bus** travels this route leaving the harbor in Skiathos Town (2 per hr. 7:15am-1am, 280dr), with stops at many beaches, including **Megali Ammos, Nostos, Vromolimnos, Platanias,** and **Troulos.** The bus route and the road end at the pine grove beach of **Koukounaries,** where swaying branches shelter clear turquoise water and fine white sand. A short walk away is the curved yellow **Banana Beach,** slightly less populated than the others. From Koukounaries, take the paved road to the left of the bus stop, follow it to the bend, and make a right on the uphill dirt road. At the top, take the worn path through the gate on the left. The hike over the next hill leads to the **Little Banana Beach,** the island's **nude** beach which, popular with gay men, is the refreshing beach it claims to be if you are willing and wanting to bare all.

Just east of Troulos, a road turns off for **Asselinos,** a beach on the north edge of Skiathos. For a calmer afternoon, take the high road that forks after 2km—the right branch leads uphill to **Panagia Kounistra,** a small monastery with a grape arbor and *taverna* within its walls. West along the coast past **Lalaria Beach** are the ruins of the medieval walled **castle** (a 2hr. walk on a path from Skiathos Town). The Greeks built the castle during the 16th century to take refuge from marauding pirates. With independence in the 19th century, they abandoned this headland and began work on what has blossomed into present-day Skiathos Town. Two churches are all that remains of the ancient community, but the **Church of the Nativity** boasts fine icons and frescoes. For details on **boat excursions** around Skiathos and to neighboring islands, call the AmEx office or any other major tourist office along the waterfront, or ask at the "rooms to let" kiosk. Most trips cost 3000-4500dr per person.

SKOPELOS Σκοπελος

Looming cliffs rising above the ocean gave this island the name "Steep Rock From the Sea." Tempering the mountains' starkness, acres of pine, olive, and plum trees blanket the hills. Originally a Cretan colony ruled by King Staphylos, strategic Skopelos has been occupied by Persians, Spartans, Athenians, Romans, Franks, Venetians, and Ottomans. It was conquered in 1538 by the illustrious Ottoman admiral Khayr El-Din Barbarossa (Red Beard), who killed the entire population. Unfortunately for old Red Beard, that didn't leave the island *sans* humans forever. Today, women wearing the distinctive Skopelan *morko*—a silk shirt, short velvet jacket with flowing sleeves, and kerchief—practice traditional occupations of weaving and embroidery.

■ Skopelos Town

Except for the front line of tourist offices and *tavernas* curving around the horseshoe waterfront, Skopelos Town is a delightful cobblestone maze stacked against the hillside. The tightly packed town is a jumble of Venetian, Byzantine, Macedonian, and Neoclassical architecture. Climb to the top of the castle walls on the left side of the harbor for a lovely view of the town.

ORIENTATION AND PRACTICAL INFORMATION

Boats dock at the concrete jetty on the left tip of the horseshoe as you look seaward. Behind you rises the old town. Tourist agencies, *tavernas,* and cafes line the water-

front. Behind the crowded eateries, **Galatsaniou St.,** a fashionable path rich with trinkets and goodies, darts upward. Buses and taxis depart from the right edge of town.
Directly inland from the stop is a shady square (actually a triangle) affectionately
known as **Platanos.**

Transportation

Ferries: Nomicos/Goutos Lines (tel. 22 363, 23 056, or 22 055) runs to Ag. Konstantinos (4½hr., 2 per day, 4085dr); Volos (4½hr., 3 per day, 3380dr); Skiathos (1½hr.,
4-5 per day, 1400dr); Alonissos (30min., 2 per day, 1100dr); and Thessaloniki (6hr.,
3 per week, 4800dr).

Flying Dolphins: Tickets sold by **Madro Travel** (tel. 22 145 or 22 133; fax 22 941).
Open daily 6:30am-9:30pm. To Ag. Konstantinos (2¼hr., 3 per day, 8200dr); Volos
(2hr., 4-6 per day, 6800dr); Skiathos (45min., 8-12 per day, 2800dr); Alonissos
(20min., 8-12 per day, 2200dr); and Thessaloniki (4hr., 1-2 per day, 8500dr). You
must arrive 1hr. before departure to check in and receive your boarding pass,
without which you will not be allowed to board.

Buses: Stop located on the right of the waterfront. Bus service vary weekly. Buses
serve Panormos (30min., 360dr); Milia (35min., 460dr); Elios (45min., 460dr);
Glossa (55min., 600dr); Stafilos (5min., 220dr); and Agnotas (15min., 220dr).

Taxis: (tel. 094 843 738 for Kostas) Available at the waterfront, particularly near the
bus stop, daily 7am-2am.

Moped and Car Rental: Shop around, as most travel agencies arrange rentals.
Mopeds start at 3500dr per day, cars 12,000dr per day. Prices vary by season.

Tourist and Financial Services

Tourist Agencies: Most **exchange currency,** rent mopeds and cars, sell ferry and
hydrofoil tickets, and arrange expensive excursions to neighboring islands. **Thalpos** (tel. 22 947 or 23 466; fax 23 057; email thalpos@otenet.gr), behind Restaurant
Akteon, on the 2nd floor. Owners Alekos and Mikhos are virtual lexicons of information on everything from Flying Dolphin information or renting a villa, to the best
place to catch a squid. Open daily 9am-2pm and 6-8pm; longer in July and August.

Banks: National Bank (tel. 22 691), on the right side of the waterfront. Has 24hr.
currency changer. The **Commercial Bank** (tel. 22 015) at the right of the waterfront has a 24hr. **ATM.** Both banks open M-Th 8am-2pm and F 8am-1:30pm, with
additional hours in the summer.

Laundromat: Several around town. Wash 1800-2400dr; dry 1100dr, ironing available. Open M-Sa 9am-1:30pm and 6-8:30pm.

Emergency and Communications

Medical Center: (tel. 22 222) Follow the left-hand road inland from Souvlaki Sq.
until it dead-ends, then turn right and you'll see it shortly on the right. Open M-F
9am-2pm for free walk-ins; open 24hr. M-F for emergencies.

Pharmacy: (tel. 22 252) Across from OTE. Open M-F 9am-2pm and 5:30-11pm.

Police: (tel. 22 235) Behind the National Bank. Open 24hr.

Post Office: Follow the signs along the circuitous route to the office. Open M-F
7:30am-2pm. **Postal Code:** 37003.

OTE: (tel. 22 399) walk 100m uphill from the waterfront on Galatsaniou St. from the
waterfront. Open in summer M-Sa 7:30am-10pm, Su 9am-2pm and 5-10pm; in winter M-F 7:30am-3:10pm. **Telephone Code:** 0424.

ACCOMMODATIONS

If your pack's feeling heavy, bargain with the dock hawks for rooms—some yield
pleasant surprises, but if you arrive and do not like the accommodations, don't feel
obligated to stay. However, the cheapest accommodations can be found by wandering through the narrow labyrinthine streets behind the waterfront, looking for
"rooms to let" signs and the EOT seal. There are no campgrounds on Skopelos.

Rooms and Apartments Association of Skopelos (tel. 24 567), an office in the
small white building near the left edge of the waterfront. Open daily 9:30am-

1:30pm and 5:30-8:30pm. Singles and doubles 5000-6000dr in June, 8000-10,000dr in July, and 10,000-12,000dr in Aug.

◉Pension Sotos (tel. 22 519; fax 23 668), 10m to the left of Thalpos travel, is a gem, both for its setting and relative affordability. A renovated old Skopelan house, each room is different, clean, with glowing wood A-frame ceilings. All rooms have bath and fan, and there is a common kitchen, fridge, quiet courtyard, and book exchange. Reserve in advance for Aug. Doubles 6500-10,000dr; triples 9000-15,000dr; quads 11,000-16,500dr.

Hotel Eleni (tel. 22 393; fax 22 936), on the far right side of the waterfront, past the bus station, has adequate rooms available by reservation. Singles 6500-8500dr; doubles 8500-13,500dr.

FOOD

Platanos Sq. is home to many 350dr *gyros*. Cafes lining the waterfront offer exotic ice cream sundaes in the afternoons and evenings.

Greca's Crêperie, 20m right of the Folk Art Museum, earns local praise. A Parisienne artist, Greca came to Skopelos decades ago on a UNESCO project to help children. Ever since, she has run her crêperie for the love of it, offering delicious crepes with all fresh ingredients (600-1400dr), her rare *joie de vivre,* and now internationally recognized prints. Open daily 10am-3pm and 7pm-12:30am.

Molos, on the left side of the waterfront, gains fame for its delicious vegetarian entrees (500-1000dr), Greek fare (starting at 1300dr), and friendly service.

ENTERTAINMENT

On the far left near the pier, the **Platanos Jazz Club** serves coffee and cocktails in the shade of a beautiful plane tree. Enjoy your drink (beer 600dr, cocktails 1500dr) or dessert to blues or new jazz music. More traditional jazz is served up in the **Blue Bar,** housed in a traditional Skopelan home. A wilder scene fills the streets behind Platanos Sq. to the far right side of the harbor. **Club Kirki,** on the far left of the harbor, is the place to jive at a late-night party. Just follow the glare of the huge neon sign.

SIGHTS

On a slightly more cultured note, Skopelos is gradually developing into a European center for the study of photography, drawing international students and recognition. Stop by the **Folk Art Museum** (tel. 23 494), 200m to the left of the OTE for special exhibits. *(Open 11am-4pm and 6-10:30pm. Admission 500dr.)* You can also visit the **Photographic Center of Skopelos** (tel. 24 121; fax 24 231).

■ Around Skopelos

Monasteries

Mt. Palouki, facing the town across the harbor, conceals three **monasteries.** Two paved roads leave the town from the bus depot on the right end of the waterfront. To reach the monasteries, follow the left road, which circles the harbor, ascends the mountain, and becomes a dirt road 600m past the Hotel Aegean. At the next fork, 30 minutes by foot from town, two signs point the way to the monasteries. **Evangelismos** hails from the 18th century, but its enormous altar screen from Constantinople is 400 years older. Take the left-hand fork up the hot and winding mountain road for 45 minutes and start early in the morning before the heat and bugs intensify. If you are a dedicated monastophile or a masochistic hiker, descend back to the fork and climb an hour and a half to the **Monastery of Metamorphosis,** standing amid pines on a breezy knoll. The chapel, set in a flowery courtyard, dates from the 16th century. **Prodromou,** visible from Metamorphosis, sits on the next ridge. Once a monastery, this refuge is now a cloister dedicated to St. John the Baptist and inhabited by nuns. It's about a two-hour walk from the original fork. A path described in *The Soto's Walking Guide* would shorten your trip (buy it at bookstores and shops; 2500dr).

Skopelos is a rich island whose beauty and beaches are best seen with the freedom of car or moped. The hills are lined with plum trees, olive groves, and beehives, and the land itself is rich with folklore. On the road to Glossa, turn off at signs pointing to the monastery, constructed in 375 in honor of **St. Rigine.** According to local tradition, a fierce dragon rampaged and ate almost everyone, until St. Rigine appeared on the scene, killed the dragon, and became protector of the island. The dragon cliffs, where the hungry, scaled creature was tossed to his death, offer a secluded picnicking spot with a view of the sea and an altar portraying the dragon's grisly demise.

At the end of the road, the hilltop town of **Glossa** overlooks Skopelos' second port. Glossa remains a quiet Greek town. For a superb hike from the village, walk the dirt track across the island to the **Monastery of Agios Ioannis,** which clings to a boulder above the ocean. Take the main road east from Glossa and turn left on the first dirt road to Steki Taverna, after which it's clear sailing. At the road's end a path drops to the sea, and stone steps, cut in the escarpment, lead up to the monastery. Allow four hours for a round-trip visit to Agios Ioannis, and bring a liter of water per person. All of the road is navigable by motorbike. Another hike takes you to the eastern side of Skopelos, to Agia Anna, a beautiful, secluded monastery. Leave Skopelos Town and head towards Mt. Palouki on the road past Moni Vararas and Agia Triada. The road will end shortly after—watch for the old sign pointing the way to the church.

Beaches

If dragon chasing isn't your style, Skopelos has amazing beaches lining the southern coast up to Loutraki. Archaeologists discovered the tomb of the ancient Cretan general **Staphylos** on a nearby hillside, as well as a gold-plated sword dating from the 15th century BC, now displayed in the Volos museum. A large rock separates Staphylos from the quieter **Velanio.** Advertised as the only **nude beach** on Skopelos, it remains uncrowded. Take the bus to the small fishing village of **Agnondas,** and take a water taxi to the pristine beach of Limnonari. Past the sleepy fishing village of Agnostas, the bus stops at the beach of **Panormos.** From here a five-minute walk leads to the isolated **Adrina** beaches, named for the female pirate who once terrorized the islands (and leapt to her death in this cove when cornered by island residents)—noteworthy among these are **Mili,** offering watersports, and **Hovolo** farther up the coast.

ALONISSOS Αλοννησος

On the quietest and least populated island of the Sporades, Alonissos' 2000 inhabitants enjoy magnificent beaches and pristine mountains. Archaeological discoveries attest to Alonissos's ancient prosperity, but its story remains one of the more painful in Greece's tumultuous post-war history. In 1950, disease annihilated its once lucrative vineyards, and most men were forced into construction work in Athens. An earthquake in 1965 then destroyed the Old Town, and Patitiri developed as the island's new center as a result of government-directed housing projects. Because of this devastation, Alonissos lacks polished beauty but remains one of the friendlier and less-touristed islands in the Sporades—an escapist can find respite here from hordes of fellow travelers without missing the conveniences of ticket agents and cash machines. The **National Marine Park** of Alonissos and the Northern Sporades protects the island's landscapes and helps to preserve the sedate, unruffled atmosphere.

▓ Patitiri Πατητηρι

All boats dock at Patitiri; it is, for all intents and purposes, the only town on the island. Above, the whitewashed Old Town clutches the slopes of the hill. As a city of concrete, Patitiri is no subtle introduction to Alonissos, but it does provide a ferrying stopover and a base from which to explore the island and surrounding Marine Park.

ORIENTATION AND PRACTICAL INFORMATION From the docks, two main parallel streets run inland, **Pelasgon** on the left, and **Ikion Dolophon** on the right. In the center of the waterfront, **Alonissos Travel** (tel./fax 65 511) offers currency

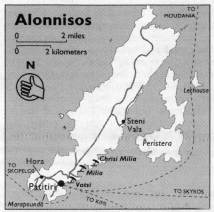

exchange, finds rooms, books excursions, and sells ferry tickets (open daily 9am-midnight). To the right, amiable, English-speaking Mr. and Mrs. Athanassiou at **Ikos Travel** (tel. 65 320 or 65 648; fax 65 321) provide similar services as well as excellent information about **ecological excursions, Flying Dolphin** ticketing, and **book exchange** (open daily 6:15-7:15am, 9am-2:30pm, and 3-10pm). **Ferries** travel daily to Agios Konstantinos (5½hr, 4300dr); Volos (5¼hr., 2 per day, 3700dr); Skiathos (2hr., 3 per day, 1800dr); Skopelos (30min., 3 per day, 1100dr); and Glossa (2 per day, 1500dr). Ferries run once per week to Thessaloniki (6hr., 5630dr). **Flying Dolphins** leave for Agios Konstantinos (2¾hr., 3 per day, 8800dr); Skiathos (1¼hr., 10 per day, 3610dr); Thessaloniki (4hr., 1 per day, 8500dr); Volos (2½hr, 3-5 per day, 7500dr); Skyros (3 per week, 8050dr); and less frequently to Skopelos (2200dr) and Kimi (8650dr). **Taxis** (tel. 65 425) wait just to the right of the travel agencies until 2am; they can be called anytime. Look for the red sign of the **laundromat,** farther inland on the left (open daily 9:30am-2pm and 6-9:30pm).

Up Ikion Dolophon St., the **National Bank** (tel. 65 777) lies on the left (open M-Th 8am-2pm, F 8am-1:30pm). The **post office** (tel. 65 560) is farther inland on the right (open M-F 7:30am-2pm). Uphill, on the left, **Rent-A-Bike** (tel. 65 140) has rentals starting around 4000dr per day. The English-speaking owner can direct you to the gas station (purchase your own gas). The **police** (tel. 65 205) and the **hospital** (tel. 65 208) sit at the top of the hill. **Postal code:** 37005. **Telephone code:** 0424.

ACCOMMODATIONS Domatia provide the best accommodations on Alonissos. You may be met with offers at the harbor, so remember to bargain. Reservations are recommended for high season (July-Aug.). Although the **Rooms to Let Office** (tel./fax 65 577), next to Ikos Travel, offers its services daily 9:30am-3pm and 6-10pm, you may find a less expensive room by negotiating with locals and looking for signs with EOT seals on inland streets. Prices should range from 4000 to 6000dr per person. Inquire at **Boutique Mary,** on the right side of Pelasgon, for rooms with private baths at the **Dimakis Pension** (tel. 65 294; singles 5000-7000dr; doubles 6000-7500dr). A right turn up the alley just before the boutique leads to **Pleiades** (tel. 65 235) if you follow the cheery blue signs. Studios with bath, kitchen, fridge, and verandas overlook a spacious, if somewhat rundown courtyard facing the sea (studios 10,000dr; doubles with common bath 8000dr). Off Pelasgon St., follow signs uphill 1km to **Camping Rocks** (tel. 65 410; 1000dr per person, 500dr per tent). Their **disco** rocks *bouzouki* music late into the evening (cover 1500dr; open daily until 6am).

FOOD AND ENTERTAINMENT On the left side of the waterfront, **Dolphin Restaurant** serves a traditional Alonissos cheese pie (1100dr). Locals hold the small *ouzerie* **To Kamaki** (tel. 65 245), on the left side of Ikion Dolophon, especially close to their hearts. All of their traditional Greek food is delectable—especially the warm octopus salad (1500dr) and the swordfish kebab (1500dr; open daily noon-3pm and 7pm-2am). Down the road towards the waterfront, **La Bricola** has a great atmosphere and cheap food with lots of vegetarian options (sandwiches 100-300dr). Try the spinach salad with Roquefort cheese, peppers, and onions (1200dr). Alternatively, follow the downward branch of the footpath with some bread and feta, and the romance of moonlight, seascape, and Greek music will cost you far less.

On the left end of the waterfront, Dennis and his sons entertain at the island's oldest bar, **Pub Dennis.** Exotic tropical cocktails cost at least 1500dr. Just up Pelasgon St. is **Club Enigma,** the only place to boogie.

■ The Old Town—Hora Χωρα

Set high on a hill to ward off pirate attacks, the Old Town is now being rebuilt, mostly by Northern European vacationers. The town maintains its tradition through the **Christ Church.** Run by Papa Gregorias, village priest and local legend, the tiny chapel dates from the 12th century AD. The island's only **bus** runs between Hora and Patitiri (10min., one per hr. 9am-3pm and 7-11pm, 270dr). A schedule is posted at the stop across from Ikos Travel. **Taxis** are available (about 2000dr round-trip), but a walk, though parching, affords as glorious a view as from the town itself—start uphill on Pelasgon and continue on the main uphill road for an hour (map 400dr). The parching walk from Patitiri takes about an hour and requires a liter of water per person. At the top, enjoy the **sunset** over the Aegean and **Kaphereas'** traditional almond sweets, which take a month to prepare and are not to be missed.

■ Around Alonissos

Only the south end of the island is inhabited, leaving the mountainous central and northern sections cloaked in pristine pine forests. A motorbike can traverse the length of the island, from Patitiri to Gerakas, at the northern tip, in about two hours. Many roads remain unpaved, so a map is useful. With little public transportation, your feet remain the best means of exploring Alonissos. Ikos Travel provides information about ecological hiking trails on the island.

Walk over the hill to the left of the village to **Votsi** beach, where you can cliff-dive. A word to the wise: do as the local boys do! A 30-minute walk downhill leads to the beaches of **Vrissita, Megalo Mourtia,** and **Mikro Mourtia.** Steep, pine-clad slopes shelter these beaches on the southern tip of the island. Inquire at the port and in travel agencies about boats traveling up the eastern coast to the sandy **Chrissi Milia,** where you can walk over 300m out into the clear water. Just north, at **Kokkinokastro,** swimmers occasionally find old coins. Here, the sea has inundated the ancient acropolis of Alonissos. Pot shards from Ikos, as it was then named, are among the significant archaeological discoveries. Farther north, the fishing villages of **Steni Vala** and **Kalamakia** remain only lightly touristed, although there are several *tavernas* and *domatia* available at Steni Vala.

■ National Marine Park

Either a 9500dr full-day tour or a 3000-4000dr charter boat will allow you to visit some of the various islands neighboring Alonissos.

The 25 islets surrounding Alonissos constitute Greece's **National Marine Park**— small, ecologically protected areas that play host to unique wildlife and virgin forests. The largest and most important are **Peristera, Skantzoura, Piperi, Kyra Panagia, Jura,** and **Psatnoura,** the former five of which are held under strict regulations and visited only by organized tour boats in summer. Psatnoura, Kyra Panagia, and Skantzoura are owned by nearby Mt. Athos and used in part for grazing goats. Any sort of visit to Jura and Piperi is strictly forbidden to protect many such species once described by Homer, including the **Mediterranean Monk Seal.** Numbering 800 total in the Mediterranean, a colony of 45-50 is now carefully monitored by MOM, a sea patrol unit based on Alonissos (and constantly at odds with Marine Park officials concerned with the bigger ecological picture). Unless you are a stowaway aboard a MOM boat, forget about seeing these two islands or the monk seals—it's no SeaWorld.

A shipwreck off Peristera significantly changed archaeologists' understanding of ancient shipping. **Cyclops Polyphemous** lived in a cave on Gioura until Odysseus and his crew came across him. Although many islands claim this distinction, Gioura's cavern and endangered brown goats with black crosses covering their spines and shoulderblades best fit the Homeric description.

SKYROS Σκυρος

Rolling purple hills nibbled by goats, groves of fragrant pines, sandy beaches, and gnarled cliffs form the spectacular backdrop for daily life on Skyros. The island's culture remains strong; throughout the entanglement of side streets, women embroider and weave rugs while men fashion sandals, ceramics, and intricately hand-carved wooden furniture. By far the quietest island of the Sporades, Skyros is also the largest, most isolated, and perhaps most intriguing for the traveler seeking quasi-immersion in traditional Greek life.

■ Skyros Town

Crowned by a Venetian castle, Skyros Town spills down from a rocky summit away from the sea. It was built on an inland cliffside as protection from pirate invasions. Today, its stark white cubist architecture remains unique among the Sporades. Its steep, narrow paths bear no resemblance to streets, so watch your step on the slick cobblestones and remember that what confounded pirates in the past will confuse you now. Being lost here, however, is a pleasant experience—toothless old men smile from shop doorways, children shriek and play in the even narrower side streets, and the heavenly onion smells of cooking waft into lanes that suddenly reveal shaded courtyards or views of nearby slopes.

ORIENTATION AND PRACTICAL INFORMATION Boats to Skyros dock at quiet **Linaria,** where they are met by a bus to Skyros Town (250dr). Still, ask drivers their destinations, as buses may be marked somewhat counterintuitively (e.g., "Topikon" for the town and "Skyros" for the beach). The bus stops right outside the maze of Skyros Town, but at least the main street, **Agoras St.,** runs straight uphill to the **central square** and taxi stand. From here it winds through *tavernas,* cafes, and tourist agencies before forking at Kalypso Bar and a kiosk. Turning left here and walking up what could never be a main street, you will arrive at another fork where a small sign points right "to Brooke and museums." To find **Rupert Brooke Square,** continue "straight" on this cobbled path. The square, overlooking Molos and the sea, received its name from the famed English poet Rupert Brooke (1887-1915), who died here en route to Gallipoli during the disastrous Dardanelles campaign of WWI. He is depicted here in an uncharacteristically nude, bronze **statue.** The stairs to Brooke's left pass the archaeological museum on their way to Molos. After a 15-minute walk downhill, the beach and many *domatia* will lie to the right.

 Skyros Travel (tel. 91 123, 91 600, or 094 884 588), past the central square on Agoras St., is the agent for **Flying Dolphins** and **Olympic Airways.** Skyros organizes one boat trip per week to the south (6000dr), arranges bus trips (300dr per person), helps with accommodations, rents mopeds (3500dr per day) and sells island maps (500dr) loaded with information (open daily 9:15am-2:15pm and 6:30-10pm). Their port office is open in accordance with the Dolphin schedule.

 A **military airport** (tel. 91 625) 20km from Skyros Town on the northern tip of the island can only be accessed by taxi (2500dr). There are regular flights to Athens (35min., 2-5 per week, 14,300dr). **Buses** run from Skyros Town to Linaria (20min., 3-5 per day, 270dr) and Molos (10min., 3-4 per day, 270dr). Check Skyros Travel

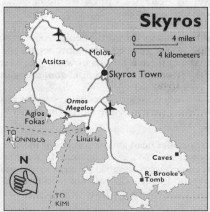

Skyros

0   4 miles
0   4 kilometers

Atsitsa
Molos
Skyros Town
Ormos Megalos
Agios Fokas
TO ALONNISOS
Linaria
Caves
R. Brooke's Tomb
N
TO KIMI

for a posted schedule, which roughly corresponds to the ferry and Dolphin schedule. **Likomidis Lines** (tel. 91 790), on the right past the bank, arranges **ferry** tickets. To get to Skyros, travel by bus from Athens to Kimi on Evia (3½hr., 2 per day, 2600dr). Ferries from Kimi's port area travel to Skyros (2hr., 2 per day, 2300dr). There is no ferry service to the other Sporades. Flying Dolphins serve Alonissos (1¼hr., 3 per week, 7250dr); Skopelos (1¾hr., 2 per week, 6850dr); Skiathos (2¼hr., 2 per week, 7150dr); Volos (4½hr., 4 per week, 11,300dr); Kimi (45min., 1 per week, 4650dr); Moudania (2 per week, 8500dr); and Thessaloniki (6hr., 1 per week in high season, 13,400dr). **Taxis** (tel. 91 666) queue at the central square (not to be confused with Rupert's Sq., at the far edge of town). Cabs not available late night or siesta hours. The house below the National Bank rents **mopeds** (tel. 91 223 or 91 459) for 3500dr.

To reach the **tourist office** (tel./fax 92 789), take the first right after the street with the post office. They offer information in English and help arrange accommodations (open daily July-Aug. 9am-3pm and 6:30-11pm, in winter daily 7:30am-2:30pm). With 24hr. **ATM**, the **National Bank** (tel. 91 802 or 91 803) is up from the bus stop, on the left before the central square (open M-Th 8am-2pm and F 8am-1:30pm). A **clinic** (tel. 92 222) with two doctors is located at the edge of the village, 400m from the bus stop. There are **pharmacies** on the right near the central square (tel. 91 617; open daily 8:30am-1pm and 6:30-11pm), and on the right past Skyros Travel (tel. 91 111; open daily 9am-2pm and 6pm-1am). To find the **police** (tel. 91 274), turn right just past Skyros Travel, and at the end of the road, take another right. It's the white building with light blue gates and trim. For the **post office** (tel. 91 208), take the first right as you walk from the bus stop to the central square. There you can **exchange currency** and cash traveler's checks (open M-F 7:30am-2pm). The **OTE** (tel. 91 399; fax 91 599) is just across the street from the police (open M-F 7:30am-1pm and 1:30-2:30pm). **Postal code:** 34007. **Telephone code:** 0222.

ACCOMMODATIONS Although there are rooms to let in tiny Linaria, to experience the Skyrian culture you should search the winding streets of Skyros Town. Wandering along the narrow stairs while carrying any sort of luggage will surely bring the simple question, *"Domatia?"* Even if you have a room, accept the offer just to see a Skyrian house. The stark white architecture of the Skyrian home hides rooms cluttered by treasures, where even the bamboo ceilings are artwork. The Skyrians embellish their homes with family heirlooms of copperware, crockery, embroidery, icons, and hand-carved furniture. Initially, aristocratic families bought these prizes from pirates around the world. By the late 19th century, however, as the aristocracy moved to Athens, these possessions were being sold to the lower classes. If you stay in a Skyrian house, remember to bargain for the price and look carefully for landmarks and house numbers, as the streets may be extremely confusing. You will probably miss the entire experience and pay much more if you are snatched up at the bus station or head to a travel agency. However, be aware that if you arrive during siesta, the town is deader than a doornail, and your calls for a domatia may be answered only with snores from within.

For something simpler and closer to the bus stop, try the marble-floored rooms (tel. 91 459) below the National Bank. A simple double runs 6000dr in low season and 8000dr in high season. Showers are shared, but there is no lack of water pressure. Next to the post office, **Hotel Elena** (tel. 91 738 or 91 070) offers plain *domatia* with baths (singles 5000dr; doubles 8000dr; triples 10,000dr).

Near the beach, a **campground** (tel. 92 458) offers the amenities of a restaurant and a mini-market, along with the opportunity to get back to nature with some horses in the same field (2500dr for two people with tent).

FOOD As always, small, half-hidden *tavernas* offer deals and food superior to those of their better-situated counterparts. **Sisyfos** (tel. 91 505), 250m up from the bus stop past the National Bank on Agoras St., serves delectable vegetarian entrees (950dr) and a great variety of traditional Greek dishes (1100-1300dr). Choose your meal from the day's selection and ask the English-speaking owner about the myth of Sisyfos.

Tucked away in the maze of Skyros Town, **Kabanera** (tel. 91 240) features *rollo* (ground meat, cheese, and tomato wrapped in phyllo pastry, 1200dr). To find it, walk up Agoras to the first "fish taverna" sign and follow it and its successors. To grab a quick, cheap dinner, nothing beats the **souvlaki/pita/gyros stand** in the central square (250-300dr). Dessert comes from the unnamed **sweet shop** (tel. 91 005) along Agoras St. where the Skyrian specialty, *amigdolata* (sweet almond taffy covered in powdered sugar) costs about 300dr.

SIGHTS Perched above Skyros Town, the 1000-year-old **Monastery of St. George** and the **Castle of Licomidus** command magnificent, free views of Skyrian sunsets. *(Open daily Mar.-Aug. 7am-10pm, Sept.-Feb. 7:30am-6pm.)* Remember to dress modestly if you want to peek at the monastery's 11th-century fresco of St. George as you climb to the *Kastro.* Generally believed to be Venetian, the castle may be a stellar repair of an earlier Byzantine fortification. The reclining marble lion set in the stone above the gate dates from the 4th century BC, when Athenians taunted Skyrians with this symbol of Attic ascendancy. The steep hike uphill from anywhere on Agoras St. is much nicer in the evening and with water.

In July and August, house #995 is open as a **Traditional Skyrian House,** which you may be able to tour in the mornings or evenings for a few hundred *drachmes.* Farther downhill, to the naked Brooke's left, the **Faltaits Museum** (tel. 91 232) also boasts a model of a Skyrian home. *(Open daily 10am-1pm and 6-9pm. Free.)* The private collection of a Skyrian ethnologist, the museum displays embroidery, carved furniture, pottery, costumes, copperware, rare books, and relics from the island's annual carnival, and is an excellent introduction to the island's traditional culture. Guided tours in English are provided, and you can inquire here or at the affiliated shop on Agoras St. about the **theater and music festival** in late July and August. To Brooke's left, the **Archaeological Museum** (tel. 91 327) holds significant artifacts found on the island, but may be a letdown after the richness of the Faltaits Museum. *(Open Tu-Su 8:30am-2:30pm. Admission 500dr, students 300dr.)* English brochure is available.

Among Hellenes the island is best known for the **Skyrian Carnival.** In February, forty days before Easter, an old man dressed in a goat mask and costume covered with clanging sheep bells, leads a young man dressed as a Skyrian bride, and a man mockingly dressed as a 17th-century European man, with one large bell hanging from his waist, on a wild, raucous dance through town to the monastery. The festival commemorates a legendary land dispute between shepherds and farmers, drawing upon many myths and religious customs. One hypothesis is that the transvestism refers to the warrior Achilles, who dodged the Trojan War draft on Skyros by dressing as a girl. When Achilles couldn't resist buying a sword from Odysseus, the well-worn traveler called his bluff. These days the only warriors you'll see are in the Greek military, as they sun themselves on their tanks.

The pleasant beach below the town stretches along the coast through the villages of Magazia and Molos, and continues around the point. Crowded and crawling with children in July and August, it's undeniably convenient. Ten minutes south of the town beach the local **nude beach,** ironically named *Tou papa to homa* (The Sands of the Priest), remains clean and uncrowded. In addition, the regular public bus, which runs from Linaria to Skyros Town, stops at the crowded **Ormos Megalos** beach.

■ Around Skyros

Just 35km long and 5km wide at its narrowest point, most of Skyros is inaccessible. You can explore by car, motorbike, or one of the weekly bus or boat trips. Once home to nymphs, the natural spring at **Nifi Beach,** on the south side of Skyros, remains beautiful and deserted. Scenically barren beaches and **Rupert Brooke's grave** on the south portion of the island are accessible only by dirt paths and boat. Boats can also explore the sea caves at **Spilliés,** which once served as a pirate grotto, and **Sarakino Island,** once Despot's Island and one of the largest pirate centers in the Aegean. During Ottoman rule, merchant and war ships sought refuge in this natural harbor. As you travel, look for the endangered **Skyrian horses.**

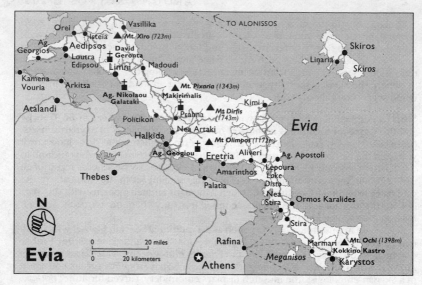

EVIA Ευβοια

Wrenched from the mainland by an ancient earthquake (or perhaps by Poseidon's trident), Evia grazes the coastline north of Athens. The second largest island in Greece (after Crete), Evia was, in ancient times, a major trading center and maritime power. Chestnuts and pines choke its central mountain range—paradise for hikers. At present, Evia is a weekend getaway for Athenians and a stopping-off point for those heading to the Sporades. As a result, it can be difficult to find accommodations on weekends or English-speakers willing to help sweaty backpackers.

■ Halkida Χαλκιδα

To travelers, Halkida may appear either as a throbbing town full of heat and sensations, or as Athens' evil little sister. Relish the few tree-lined avenues that dart up from the harbor. Aristotle was desperate because of his inability to comprehend what still may be the most interesting thing about Halkida: the bizarre tidal flow through the straits between Evia and the mainland. Aristotle threw himself into the nearby Evia strait in a fit of anguish; *Let's Go: Greece* does not recommend following in his footsplashes. Scientists still can't explain why the water changes direction at the narrowest point between the land masses—up to six times daily around full moons, one to four times per day during the rest of the month.

ORIENTATION AND PRACTICAL INFORMATION The English-speaking **tourist police**, 32 El. Venizelou St. (tel. 22 100), are located two flights above the police station and can help with **bus schedules** (open M-F 7am-2:30pm; for emergencies 24hr.). You can **change money** and find a 24-hour **ATM** closer to the water at the **National Bank** (open M-Th 8am-2pm, F 8am-1:30pm). The **bus station** is at 28 Favrierou St. in the center of town. A **bus** from Liossion Station in Athens goes to Halkida (1½hr., 2 per hr., 1600dr). The **train** runs nearly as frequently from the Larissa station (18 per day, 2hr., 900dr). Arrival by train leaves you on the mainland; just cross the bridge to the island and the busier section of Halkida. El. Venizelou St. runs uphill about five blocks to the left of the bridge. If you get off at the bus depot, look for Papanastasiou and turn right; walk down one block to El.

Venizelou St. **Flying Dolphins** leave from the dock to the right of the bridge. Purchase **tickets** to Limni, Aedipsos, and the Sporades at the shack on the waterfront just in line with the dock (tel. 21 521 or 21 621). If you have questions, try your luck with **Port Authority** across the bridge in the huge building.

Taxis (tel. 24 411) are available 24 hours. For a **pharmacy** (tel. 24 646), go down El. Venizelou and turn left on A. Gobiou St. just before the waterfront. The **post office** is on Karamourzouni St., the second left off El. Venizelou St., uphill from the water (open M-F 7:30am-0pm). Go early to avoid ridiculously long lines. The **OTE** (tel. 22 599) is located on Papiadaiou St.; walk up El. Venizelou St. four blocks from the water, two blocks after the park with the fountain, make a left on Papiadaiou St. and walk one block (open M-F 7am-10pm). **Postal code:** 34100. **Telephone code:** 0221.

ACCOMMODATIONS If you *must* spend the night, try **Hotel Kentriko** (tel. 22 375 or 27 260), the pink building at 5 Ageli Gobiou St., the last left off El. Venizelou just before the waterfront (singles 7000dr; doubles 8000dr, with bath 9500-12,000dr). Prices vary depending on season and amenities; ask for a discount with a student ID. A couple of doors down on Aggeli Gobiou St., **John's Hotel** (tel. 24 996, 24 997, or 22 998) is a bit more expensive, but offers TV, CNN, A/C, and baths in all rooms (singles 9500; doubles 13,000).

FOOD Baltas Bakery, 49 El. Venizelou St. (tel. 22 228), will overwhelm you with baked goods appropriate for breakfast on a bus. *Tsoureki,* a Greek specialty sweet bread baked in braid form (220dr), will leave you craving a second loaf (open daily 6am-4pm and 5:30-9pm). The waterfront is lined with trendy cafes, outdoor tables and colorful umbrellas that shade die-hard people-watchers. Order a *frappé* (600dr) and join in the fun, but eat elsewhere—the prices will give you heartburn. Instead, make a right onto Ermou St. at the far right end of the pier, and join the local Halkidians for traditional Greek foods at **O Thanasis** (tel. 24 241). Salted codfish with garlic paste and sauteed *okra* and green beans in tomato sauce display the sign of a good home-cooked meal—you'll need a thick piece of bread to wipe your plate. Several vegetarian options are available (open daily 7:30am-10pm).

SIGHTS The **Archaeological Museum** (tel. 25 131 or 76 431), on El. Venizelou St. across from the police station, is a roomful of findings from the Classical and Roman eras. *(Open Tu-Su 8:30am-3pm. Admission 500dr, students 300dr, senior citizens 400dr.)* Facing the big pink building, head down the street and turn right on the little downhill road. Look for the **Folklore Museum** (tel. 21 817) on your left at 4 Skalkola St. *(Open W 10am-1pm and 6-8pm, Th-Su 10am-1pm. Free).*

■ Aedipsos Springs Λουτρα Αιδηψου

The village of Aedipsos, northwest of Halkida on the coast of Evia, was praised by Herodotus, Aristotle, and Aristophanes for its healing sulphurous waters. Aedipsos is worth a daytrip for anyone who wishes to enjoy the hot springs' relaxing vibes. Locals advise that you swim no longer than 30 minutes, as hours of bathing will leave you in a therapeutic stupor. The bus drops off in a small square at Ermou St., where you will be able to see the waterfront. The **hot springs** are in a large complex on a road heading inland from the left end of the waterfront (facing the water) 200m past the post office. For more information call the **tourist information office** (tel. 23 500). They are open all year but extend their hours in summer. *(Open daily 7:30am-1pm and 5-7pm.)* A variety of specialized pools and equipment is available. To hang with a younger crowd, experience the relaxing effect of the hot springs at the beach on the far left end of Poseidonos St. (the waterfront strip). Here, the hot springs' water mixes with the sea water as it cascades down a small waterfall, cooling the temperature slightly while retaining the hot-tub quality (adults 300dr, children 150dr). **Buses** run from Halkida via Limni to Aedipsos (2½hr., 4 per day, 2000dr).

■ Eretria Ερετρια

First inhabited between the 15th and 17th centuries BC, permanent occupation of Eretria began in the 8th or 9th century BC. The town rivaled ancient Chalkis as the most important city on the island, its importance stemming from its convenient location for trade between Greece (and later Italy) and the Near East. In the 3rd century BC, Menedimos, the town's most famous son and a disciple of Plato, founded a school of philosophy here. The Roman era saw a decline in Eretria's fortunes and the town was only sporadically occupied from the first century AD onward. More recently, the town's easy access from Halkida (30min. by bus) and from Oropos on the mainland (30min. by ferry) has led to a resurgence in this now modest town. The streets brim with Athenian tourists in summer, who flock to Eretria for several fascinating archaeological and historical sights, as well as to a long sandy stretch of beach.

ORIENTATION AND PRACTICAL INFORMATION Boats from Oropos (roughly every 30min., 310dr) dock on the mid-left side of the town's harbor, where the two stretches of waterfront meet at a potted palm intersection. Cut up the street to the right of Cafe Antique and walk the 3 blocks to the **National Bank** on Menedimos St. to **change money** or use the **ATM** (open M-Th 8am-1:45pm, F 8am-1:30pm). The bus stop, about 20m to the left, has a complete bus schedule for the entire island. Check inside, as some destinations require you to buy your ticket before you board the bus. The large intersection of town is a right turn from the dock. Turning left leads eventually to the **Archaeological Museum** and a few *tavernas;* turning right leads to the square where locals chat at night, the few night-scene bars, pensions, and the town beach. Eretria is accessible by **bus** from Halkida, because everything heading south to Karystos, Kimi, or Amarinthos swings through (2 per hr., 420dr). **Taxis** (tel. 62 500) wait by the water. Two blocks up from the ferry dock near the National Bank is the **post office** (open M-F 7:30am-8pm, Sa 8:30am-2pm), which also changes money. A right at the main intersection leads to the **OTE** (open M-F 7:30am-3:10pm), a few blocks down on the right. **Postal code: 34008. Telephone code: 0229.**

ACCOMMODATIONS Athena runs a tight and wonderful ship at **Pension Diamanto** (tel. 62 214). Turn right at the potted palm intersection onto Archaiou Theatrou St.; it lies about 300m down the road to your left above La Crepe Cafe. All rooms have bath, fridge, TV, and the comfort of A/C (doubles 10,000dr; triples 13,000dr). A full breakfast including freshly squeezed orange juice is available for 1000dr. Before La Crepe, turn left at the sign and walk 200m inland for the modern apartments (all with kitchen, fridge, A/C, and bath) of the **Eretria Sun Rise Hotel** (tel. 63 263; fax 60 648). Sadly enough for the budget traveler, this hotel is one of the better deals in town (doubles 12,000dr; triples 14,000dr; quads 16,000dr). Ask at *tavernas* for rooms.

FOOD AND ENTERTAINMENT If the fresh air whets your appetite, look for **La Cubana** (tel. 61 665) on Archaiou Theatrou St. near the waterfront and try the *dolmadakia* (900dr) or a plate of *moussaka* (1100dr). Next door, **Ethrio** (tel. 6311) serves gigantic proportions of wonderful Greek food and seafood pastas. The marinara with fresh seafood feeds at least two (1450dr). On the other waterfront stretch across from the dock is **Dionysos** (tel. 61 728), which boasts *kolokythakia* (fried zucchini 700dr) and fresh fried squid (1400dr). **Volkanos,** near the potted palm intersection, serves what the locals declare are the best *gyros* and *souvlaki* in town (300dr). For dessert, **Stamatoukos** (tel. 60 909), the large sweet shop on Archaiou Theatrou, serves homemade ice cream in 24 delicious flavors (200-250dr per scoop). Nightlife hotspots serve beer for 500dr and cocktails for 1500dr. **Cafe Antique,** just up the street from Dionysos, is a fabulous place to relax with a drink. Two solemn life-size statues in yoga positions peer out the window, and inside lie treasures from all over the world (fodder for wishful thinking while you sip your drink, 1500dr). They play blues, jazz, and eccentric mellow music until late in the night (open daily 9am-3am).

SIGHTS The **Archaeological Museum** (tel. 62 206) is at the inland end of Archaiou Theatrou St. *(Open Tu-Su 8am-2:30pm. Admission·500dr, students and senior citizens 300dr, EU students free.)* It's not the biggest collection around, but there are some quality pieces, such as a gorgeous terra cotta Gorgon's head from the 4th century BC, and the mysteriously six-fingered Centaur of Lefkandi, which dates from 750-900 BC. Exhibits are in Greek and French, but you can get the red guidebook in English (2000dr). Beyond the museum is a large excavated area of the old city. You also might explore the creatively named **House with the Mosaics.** You must find some-one at the museum to bring you to the site (300m away) and unlock it, but it's defi-nitely worth the effort. The four works in two separate rooms are among the best preserved and oldest (4th century BC) of all Greek mosaics. Because of their age and importance, they are enclosed in a room which visitors can't enter without special permission, but the glass walls afford a good view. The Swiss School of Archaeology in Greece has put out a brochure (in Greek, English, French, and German) explaining the house's history (available from the museum for 1000dr).

▓ **Karystos** Κάρυστος

Surrounded by mountains and flanked by two long sandy beaches, Karystos, which takes its name from the son of the centaur Chiron, retains a relaxed atmosphere despite being the largest town in South Evia. Pointed round straw umbrellas, like the mushrooms in *Fantasia,* dot the sands that extend in either direction from the port.

ORIENTATION AND PRACTICAL INFORMATION The bus stops one block above the main square, next to the **National Bank** (open M-Th 8am-2pm, F 8am-1:30pm); look for the KTEL sign above a restaurant roasting chickens in the window. The **OTE** is on Amerikis St., the next cross-street beyond the square, across from the Church of St. Nicholas (tel. 22 399; open daily 7:30am-3pm). **Buses** from Karystos travel twice daily to Chalkis (4hr., 2 per day, 2100dr); Stira (1¼hr., 2 per day, 600dr); Marmari (30min., 3 per day, 300dr). Three to four **ferries** per day head to Rafina (2hr., 1950dr) and Marmari (1½hr., 1340dr). In Karystos, ferry tickets are sold across from where the boat docks. **South Evia Tours** (tel. 25 700; fax 22 461; open daily 8am-10pm), on the left of the square as you face the water, sells tickets for **Flying Dolphins,** which go three times weekly to Andros (2870dr), Tinos (5350dr), and Mykonos (6510dr). **Taxis** (tel. 22 200) queue in the square. To find the **police station** (tel. 22 252), turn into the small alley past the bank and climb the stairs. To reach the **post office** from the OTE, turn left on Amerikis St. and then take the first right past the playgrounds; you'll see the round yellow sign (open M-F 7:30am-2pm). **Postal code:** 34001. **Tele-phone code:** 0224.

ACCOMMODATIONS The tourist kiosk, at the center of the waterfront, is stocked with colorful pamphlets and tour suggestions. English-speaking staff are helpful with cryptic bus schedules. **George and Bill Kolobaris,** 42 Sachtouri St. (tel. 22 071), offer cozy rooms and boundless hospitality. George may pick you up on his motorbike and sing to you on the way to his pension. Rooms include hot water and use of a fully equipped kitchen (doubles 8000dr; triples 8000dr). Carry on along the waterfront (200m) to the more luxurious rooms of **Hotel Karystion** (tel. 22 391; fax 22 727). The proprietor, the amiable Charis Mitros, is the president of the local Tourist Associ-ation and a good source of information about the area; he also speaks fluent English. Rooms all have bath, TV, A/C, and free breakfast (singles 7000-8000dr; doubles 10,1000-11,000dr; triples 12,900-14,940dr).

FOOD AND ENTERTAINMENT The yummy octopi *(oktopodia)* lined up and dry-ing in the sun give fair warning of the town's favorite food. Find incomparable food and prices at **Kabontoros,** one block inland on Parodos Sachtouri St., in the alleyway half a block right of the main square (sauteed green beans in olive oil with a pureed garlic sauce 800dr), or walk to the very end of the strip (on the far right facing the water) until you come to the all-Greek crowd at **Kalamia** (tel. 22 223; stuffed toma-toes 650dr). If you're not stuffed after your meal, skip down the alleyway off Parodos Sachtouri St. to the water and find **Tsimis' sweet shop.** The regional specialty, almond cookies covered in icing, are about 200dr each.

Various seaside pubs and cafes are popular day and night. **Archipelagos,** on the beach at the right edge of town, offers beer for 500dr. The view and heady sea air here may tempt you to linger. For serious dancing, head to the **Barbados Disco** (tel. 24 119), 3km from town toward the mountains. The 1300dr cover includes your first drink. A cab will run 500dr, probably more after midnight.

SIGHTS Peek into one of the holes at the back of the **Fort of Bourtzi,** the impossible-to-miss structure on the waterfront. In the 11th century, your peep-hole was used to pour boiling oil on attackers. Today, the fort opens to host summer student theatrical productions. The **Archaeological Museum** (tel. 22 472) provides another glimpse of the area's military prestige. *(Open daily 9am-3pm. Admission 500dr, students 300dr.)* Located on the waterfront past the fort, it shares a building with the local library.

■ Near Karystos

If you have a free morning, you may wish to explore the villages north of Karystos. Follow Aiolou St., one block east of the square, out of town; continue straight at the crossroads toward **Palio Hora,** a village bounded by lemon and olive groves. For a more strenuous walk, turn right at the crossroads outside Karystos and head toward the village of **Mili.** The road ascends sharply, following a stream to the village, where water flows from the mouths of three lions in a small roadside fountain. From Mili, a 20-minute hike up the hill on the left and across the stone bridge leads to **Kokkino Kastro** (the Red Castle). This 13th-century Venetian castle is named for the blood spilled there during the war between the Greeks and the Ottomans. The village of **Agia Triada** is also worth a trek; take a left when you come to a crossroads and walk to this shady valley, where two small, rustic churches sit under gnarled trees.

For more extensive hiking, climb Evia's second-highest mountain, **Mt. Ochi** (1398m), where Zeus and Hera fell in love. The refuge hut on the mountain is a three-to four-hour hike from Karystos. Some claim that the refuge, made of unmortared stone blocks during the Pelasgian Period, was a temple to Hera; others believe it was a signal tower. The ruin, now known as the "dragon's house," is allegedly haunted.

Thessaly and Epirus
Θεσσαλια και Ηπειρος

A bastion of Greek culture under 19th-century Ottoman rule, Greece's forgotten regions are graced with mountain goat paths leading to some of the country's most precious Byzantine treasures, freshest springs, and windswept mountain-top vistas. Silvery olive groves, fruit-laden trees, and intricate patchworks of cultivated farmland form the subtle beauty of this varied landscape.

🖐 HIGHLIGHTS OF THESSALY AND EPIRUS

- Levitate like the great Byzantine saints up to the cloud-swept monasteries of **Meteora** (p. 218).
- Relive the mayhem, intrigue, and buggery of Albanian "Lion of Epirus" Ali Pasha amid the fortresses and mosques of **Ioannina** (p. 224).
- Divine your fortune like Homer's barefoot priests from the rustling leaves of the oracular oak at **Dodoni** (p. 227).
- Trek through the super-steep Vikos Gorge into the time-warped villages of the **Zagorohoria** (p. 229).

THESSALY Θεσσαλια

Thessaly is a land of contrast; while claiming some of Greece's largest and least appealing cities—Larissa, Trikala, and Volos—it is also home to some of Greece's most impressive natural and spiritual phenomena. In the north, the rocky crags of Mount Olympus, throne of the pantheon of Greek gods, watch over the wine-colored Aegean with stark majesty. In the west, just beyond the cultivated Thessalian plain, the monasteries of the Meteora cling to other-worldly black spires in a transcendental balancing act. To the southeast, traditional mountain hamlets on Mt. Pelion lie scattered among forests, apple orchards, and grapevines stretching out to the sea.

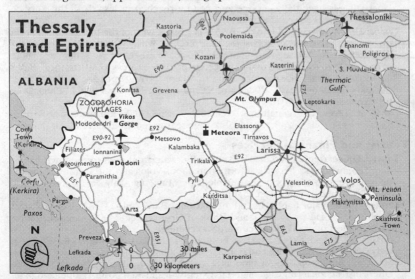

■ Volos Βολος

In ancient times, Jason and the Argonauts set sail from Volos on their quest for the Golden Fleece. The city, which has two important streets and half a dozen hotels named after the Argonauts' famous voyage, will not let you forget this mythological tidbit. Over a century ago, Volos was a small, sleepy town on the Pagasitic Gulf. However, after the 1922 population exchange (see p. 61), refugees from Turkey asserted their influence on the atmosphere of the port town in a bang-up-fun-loving way; Volos quickly became famous throughout the land for its prodigious *ouzeris*. Today, Volos has exploded into a fast-growing industrial center and transportation hub, connecting mainland Greece with the Sporades. Unfortunately, modernity has taken its toll. The port is filled with cranes and ugly oil tankers, the streets are packed with honking cars, and an oppressive haze pervades the air above the city. Only on the less developed eastern part of the waterfront or inland, where pleasant pedestrian arcades abound, is Volos more than a congested example of poor urban planning.

ORIENTATION AND PRACTICAL INFORMATION

The **bus station** lies at the end of **Lambraki St.**, an easy 15-minute walk from town and the waterfront. The **main road**, leading from the bus station to town, runs past the train station and the tourist office and splits to become **Dimitriados St., Iasonos St.,** and **Argonafton St.,** all parallel to the waterfront. The intersecting roads lead to various hotels and other services including banks, pharmacies, and the post office.

Transportation

Ferries: Daily service to Skiathos (3hr., 3000dr); Skopelos (4½hr., 3400dr); and Alonissos (6hr., 3750dr). More on Sundays, fewer in the off season. Tickets (tel. 35 846) are sold at agencies on the waterfront (tel. 35 846) and on the pier itself.

Flying Dolphins: Daily service to Skiathos (1¼hr., 4-6 per day, 5500dr); Skopelos (2¼hr., 3-5 per day, 6700dr); Alonissos (2¾hr., 3-5 per day, 7300dr); and Glossa (1¾hr., 2-3 per day, 6250dr). Inquire at the waterfront (tel. 21 626; fax 25 688).

Buses: (tel. 33 254), at the end of Lambraki St. In summer M-F, buses travel to Athens (5hr., 10 per day, 5100dr); Thessaloniki (3¼hr., 5 per day, 3350dr); Larissa (1¼hr., 14 per day, 1050dr); and Kalambaka (3½hr., 4 per day, 2900dr). Inquire at the bus station or tourist office about bus service to the Pelion villages, including Portaria, Makrynitsa, Zagoria, Horefto, Afissos, Platania, Drakia, Kala, Nera, and Ag. Ioannis. Most villages have daily service and can be reached in less than 3hr. Service reduced on weekends and in winter.

Trains: The station (tel. 24 056 or 28 555) is 1 block west of the tourist office. From town, turn right at the kiosk past the tourist office. Walk 2-3min. down the parking lot parallel to the tracks in the train yard. To get to Athens or Thessaloniki, change in Larissa (1hr., 10 per day, 600dr) or catch the daily express to Athens (5hr., 4 per day, 5820dr). Otherwise regular service to Athens (6-7hr., 4 per day, 3120dr); Thessaloniki (4hr., 4 per day, 1980dr); and Kalambaka (3½hr., 4 per day, 1140dr). Only the express train has A/C.

Car Rental: Avis, 41 Argonafton St. (tel. 20 849; fax 32 360). **European Car Rental,** 83 Iasonos St. (tel. 36 238; fax 24 192). High-season rentals from 16,000dr per day.

Tourist and Financial Services

Tourist Office: (tel. 23 500 or 36 233), on the waterfront next to the town hall in Riga Fereou Sq. Ask here for information about Volos and the Pelion Peninsula. Informative map of the city is available. Open July-Aug. daily 7am-2:30pm and 5-7pm, Sept.-June daily M-F 7am-2:30pm.

Banks: All the major banks, including **National Bank** (tel. 23 382), **Agricultural Bank** (tel. 23 411 or 54 030), and **Bank of Greece** (tel. 23 442) are located on Iason St. Most offer **ATM** and **currency exchange.**

Consulates: Belgium (tel. 23 318); **France** (tel. 25 870); **Germany** (tel. 25 379); **Italy** (tel. 38 565); and **Holland** (tel. 24 356).

Bookstore: Bookstop, 163 Alexandras St. (tel. 22 924), behind Ag. Nikolaos church. Offers instructional language material. Open W-F and Su 8:30am-1:30pm and 5:30-

9pm, M-Tu and Sa 8:30am-2pm. **International Press** (tel. 27 054), on Venizelou, just off the waterfront road, offers magazines and newspapers.

Emergency and Communications

Police: (tel. 72 400). Open 24hr.
Tourist Police: #179 28th Octovriou St. (tel. 72 421). Locals still call the street by its former name, "Alexandras St." Help in English provided when the tourist office is closed. Open daily 7am-2:30pm, but available 24hr.
Hospital. (tel. 27 531), next to the museum on the eastern waterfront. Open 24hr.
Post Office: On P. Mela St., off 28th Octovriou St. Open M-F 7:30am-8pm. **Postal Code:** 38001.
OTE: On the corner of El. Venizelou St. and Sokratous St., across from the fruit market. Open 24hr. **Information:** 131. **Telephone Code:** 0421.

ACCOMMODATIONS

Volos doesn't make its money from tourism; shipping and manufacturing are its big revenue earners. Volos's hotels vary tremendously in size, location, appeal, and amenities, but are almost all quite expensive for the financially constrained traveler. Wave a student ID in the air and ask for a simple room (*aplo domatio*) for a small discount.

Hotel Iolkas, 37 Dimitriados St. (tel. 23 416 or 24 509). On the corner of Dimitriados St. and 54th Sintagma Elas St., next to the Conservatory. Bright green tendrils fill every inch of the hotel's lobby, but fortunately not its spacious, high-ceilinged rooms, which come with phone and TV. Singles 4500dr; doubles 6000dr.
Hotel Roussa, 1 Iatrou Tzanou St. (tel. 21 732; fax 22 987). On the corner of Plastira St. and Iatrou Tzanou St., across from Anavros Park. If you don't like what you see through your window, take a look at the pastoral image hanging above your bed and you'll instantly be transported into the lush forests of Thessaly. Rooms come with bath, phone, TV, and A/C. Singles 5500dr; doubles 7500dr; triples 9000dr.
Hotel Iasson, 1 P. Melo St. (tel. 26 075). Right on the waterfront across from the harbor. Gleaming white rooms with phones, baths, and TVs. Singles 7000dr; doubles 10,000dr; triples 12,000dr.

FOOD AND ENTERTAINMENT

Cafes, *tavernas,* and *ouzeris* ooze across the waterfront like oil on a Greek salad. *Ouzeris* in Volos are a way of life. Sip *tsipouro* and gorge yourself on a cornucopia of *mezedbes* such as *spetzofai,* spicy sausages, and seafood. In late July and August, Volos hosts a **festival** in Riga Fereou Park featuring concerts, dances, and theater.

⑩Rotonda, 15 Plastira St. (tel. 34 973), on eastern edge of waterfront near Hotel Roussas. Serves delicious *calamari psito* and offers a wine list sufficient for even the most discriminating connoisseur (entrees 1600-2500dr).
Enidrio, on Plastira St. across from the beach. One of the most consistently popular restaurants in the city, Enidrio specializes in fish (entrees 1500-2200dr).
Plaza Pizza, on Argonafton St. a little east of Kartali. Serves tasty pizza in the traditional Greek style: with the cheese over the toppings, not the toppings over the cheese (pizzas 1400-2000dr).
Cafe Memories, in the middle of the pedestrian walkway on Argonafton St. Sure, the drinks here are expensive (a Coke is 500dr; cocktails are up to four times more) but, engulfed in the cafe's sumptuous seats, you probably won't even notice.

SIGHTS

Volos' Archaeological Museum, 1 Athonassaki St. (tel. 25 285), displays finds from the latter part of the Paleolithic era to the Roman period. (*Open Tu-Su 8:30am-3pm. Admission 500dr, students 300dr.*) The museum is set in a floral garden in the east part of town and merits the 40-minute walk from the waterfront. For the most recent archaeological finds, check out the central display room; also notable are the treasures found in ancient burial tombs across Thessaly, located in rooms 5 and 6. Inquire here or at the tourist office for information on the nearby archaeological sites at **Dimini** and **Sesklo.** On the opposite end of Volos, on the corner of Lambraki St. and Metamorphoseos St., is the city's **art gallery** (tel. 39 644). *(Open Tu-Su 8:30am-3pm.)* Here you'll find works by popular *laiki* painters, including **Theophilos,** the decorator of Pilion's most beautiful mansions, and **Giorgio de Chirico,** that most enigmatic of metaphysical painters.

■ Mount Pelion Peninsula Ορος Πηλιο

In the misty mythological past, the rugged Pelion Peninsula was home to centaurs—half-man, half-horse creatures with enormous sex drives. Chiron, a legendary healer and tutor to the hero Achilles, was the most civilized of the centaurs carousing in the peninsula's thick forests. He chose Pelion for his stomping ground because of its profuse medicinal herbs—the region is said to possess more than 1700 different types. The diversity of plant life in the region stems from the peninsula's cool, moist climate, much appreciated today by tourists weary of the scorching sun.

Over the years, the mountains of Pelion have helped protect the area from invasion. While the rest of Greece was under Ottoman rule, the peninsula was a virtually autonomous center of Greek nationalism. These days, Pelion's steep slopes help protect it from intrusive tourists. As a result, many of Pelion's villages, especially the ones inland, look much as they did centuries ago—idylls tucked away among lush woods of beech, chestnut, and oak.

■ Makrynitsa Μακρυνιτσα

The winding mountain road from Volos transcends noise and smog to bring you to tranquil Makrynitsa. The wooden balconies and shuttered windows of this traditional settlement command such impressive views of the city of Volos and the nearby Pagasitic Gulf that Makrynitsa is nicknamed the Balcony of Pelion. Making the views from the village even more appealing is the lack of traffic; thanks to its designation by the European Community as a protected architectural site, the town's roads are closed to cars. In Makrynitsa luxurious mansions (*arhondika*) mingle with charming 18th-century churches, hiking trails weave past mountain springs, and, in the central square itself, a massive, gnarled plane tree—seven centuries older than most of Makrynitsa's churches—shades the square's shops and cafes from the sun.

Makrynitsa is organized in a hub-and-spoke pattern: at the center lies the town square, from which various streets extend outward. Most important of the spokes are **17 Martiou 1978 St.** and **Agiou Gerasimou St.** The former leads to the central parking spot and the road to Volos, while the latter extends northward past some of the village's more important churches. Makrynitsa's mailbox is behind the fountain in the central square; stamps can be bought with postcards. The village of **Portaria,** about 5km south, has a **post office** which also offers **currency exchange.** Ten buses per day run from Volos to Makrynitsa (round-trip ticket 600dr). Inquire at the bus station or the tourist office in Volos for info about other villages on the Pelion Peninsula. **Telephone code:** 0428.

Makrynitsa has been designated a traditional settlement by the Greek National Tourist Organization, so staying here will cost an arm and a leg. Budgeteers should either splurge on one of the town's posh pensions, or make the town a daytrip. For the cost of one night's stay, you could easily buy bus tickets to several other villages on Pelion. Uphill from the Galini Restaurant, **Pension Archontiko Diomides** (tel. 99 430) features aged rooms, with cozy communal living rooms and an outdoor terrace (singles 8000dr; doubles 10,000dr; triples 12,000dr; all prices higher in winter).

A handful of dining options are clustered in the main square. On the south side of the square overlooking the sea is **Pantheon** (tel. 99 143), which serves delicious *moshari kokkinisto* and *spedzofai* (a casserole of pepper and sausage). Also in the square is **O Theophilos,** named after the artist by the same name. Don't leave without looking at the Theophilos painting on the right wall of the cafe.

While in Makrynitsa, be sure to visit the **Museum of Folk Art and the History of Pelion** (tel. 99 505), located about 200m southeast of the square along a winding cobbled path. *(Open Tu-Su 10am-2pm and 6-9pm. Free.)* The curator gives tours of the authentic clothes, scabbards, and folk art contained in this converted mansion. The museum's highlights include its collection of *feggides* (adornments placed over windows and doors in Makrynitsa's mansions), and its paintings by **Christopoulos,** all of which depict ships, gorgons, and sundry sea-related subjects. The **Metamorphosi,** built in 1797 and located directly below the museum, is one of the village's smallest—but prettiest—churches. In the town square is another tiny church, the one-room chapel of **Agios Yiannis the Beheaded,** decorated in a unique style of curved stone. As you face Agios Yiannis, climb uphill to the clock tower to your right. Here you'll find the austere **Xamiseos Theotokou,** the still-functioning church of Makrynitsa that once housed the *krifto sholio,* a secret school that taught the forbidden Greek language during the Ottoman era. The town's churches remain open at the whim of their caretakers; early to mid-morning and evenings are your most likely opportunities for a visit. All of the churches require modest dress (skirts for women and pants for men). If you get hot, cool off at one of Makrynitsa's more than 50 fountains, decorated with stone *lithanaglifa.*

■ Larissa Λαρισα

Larissa throbs amidst the vast agricultural plains of Thessaly, not only a thriving commercial center and transportation hub but also Greece's hottest city (temperature-wise). Tourists rarely see more of Larissa than its bus and train stations; if you get stranded, stroll down the town's elegant tree-lined squares (site of the evening *volta*) and check out the recently excavated ancient theater. Vibrant cafes and packed discos just outside of town can salvage your stay.

ORIENTATION AND PRACTICAL INFORMATION

Larissa is located directly southeast of the **Pinios River. Tahydromiou Sq.,** is the heart of the town, anchoring the city's cafe, shopping, and financial districts. To the northwest and northeast of Tahydromiou Sq. are Larissa's two other main squares, **Mihail Sapka Sq.** and **Laou Sq.** Around all three squares, and Tahydromiou in particular, are pedestrian shopping arcades. The **bus station** is located about 150m north of Laou St. on **Olympou St.;** the **train station** is on the south side of town on **Paleologou St.**

Transportation

Buses: (tel. 53 77 77). The main station is on the north end of Olympou St., 150m north of Laou St. Service to Athens (4¾hr., 6 per day, 5800dr); Thessaloniki (2hr., 14 per day, 2800dr), Volos (1¼hr., 12 per day, 1050dr); and Ioannina (4¼hr., 3 per day, 3400dr). Buses for Trikala (1hr., 21 per day, 1150dr) leave from a station on Iroon Polytechnion St.; to get there, head south on Panagouli St. and turn right at the 5-way intersection.

Trains: The station (tel. 23 62 50) is at the end of Paleologou St. Head south on Panagouli St. and turn left (but not a sharp left) at the 5-way intersection. Trains go to Athens (5hr., 14 per day, 2800dr); Thessaloniki (2¾hr., 17 per day, 1400dr); and Volos (1hr., 14 per day, 650dr).

Tourist and Financial Services

Tourist Office: 18 Koumoundourou St. (tel. 25 09 19). From Tahydromiou Sq., go west on Papkyriazi St., turn left on Papanasiasiou St., and then take your second right to find Koumoundourou St. At the tourist office you'll find helpful maps and brochures of the city. Open M-Sa 8am-2:30pm.

Emergency and Communication

Police: (tel. 62 31 68 or 62 31 64), on Papanastasiou St., south of Ipeirou crossing.
Hospital: (tel. 23 00 31), on Georgiadou St., east of the bus station. Open 24hr.

Internet Access: Planet Cafe (email cafe@planet-cafe.com; http://www.planet-cafe.com), founded in 1996, is Greece's first cybercafe (1200dr per hr).
Post Office: (tel. 53 23 12), on corner of Papanastasiou St. and Diakou St. Open M-F 7:30am-8:30pm. **Postal Code:** 41000.
OTE: (tel. 134), on Filellinion St. To get there, head west on Kyprou and make a right at Sapka Sq. **Telephone Code:** 041.

ACCOMMODATIONS

Larissa is not a tourist town, so chances are you'll be able to find a room without any problem. Lodging quality varies widely—from palatial comfort to dingy and cramped.

Hotel Pantheon (tel. 23 48 10 or 23 67 26), on west side of O.S.E. St. Clean, sparsely decorated rooms with a view of the square and shared bathrooms. Singles 5000dr; doubles 6600dr.
Hotel Diethnes (tel. 23 42 10), next door to Hotel Pantheon. Small traditional rooms with shared bathroom. Singles 5500dr; doubles 6600dr.
Hotel Adonis, 8 Panagouli St. (tel. 53 46 48 or 53 46 51; fax 53 66 28), near Tahydromiou Sq. Offers clean pleasant rooms with bath, phone, and TV. Singles 8000dr; doubles 12,000dr.

FOOD AND ENTERTAINMENT

Most of Larissa's cafes, bars, and *tavernas* are centered around Tahydromiou Sq. and its adjacent streets, where the disparate eating establishments blend into one never-ending series of chairs, tables, and blaring TVs. **Restaurant Philoxenia** (tel. 25 86 60) and **To Sidrivani** (tel. 53 59 33 or 53 14 00), both on the south side of Tahydromiou Sq., offer old favorites like *pastitsio* and *mosheri* for good prices (entrees 1000-1600dr). On the opposite side of the square, you can find good food (and occasional free glasses of wine) at **Ta Dio Fengaria.**

For after-dinner entertainment, the lively bars of Larissa will not disappoint; they are always packed at night. Some of the best are **Cafe del Mar,** on the corner of Roosevelt St. and Mandilara St., a hip joint in tune with the current scene, and the **Jazz and Funk Cafe,** which, tucked away behind the bus station, is another local hangout for the safe and sound. After drinking at the bars, check out some of Larissa's dynamic discos. **Mezzo Mezzo** (tel. 28 88 45) a 600dr taxi ride from downtown, is an absolutely enormous open-air nightclub boasting a row of towering fountains and a mini club-within-a-club called **Planet Babe.** Slightly smaller but still impressive are **Kameni** and **Monopolio** (which is only open in winter).

SIGHTS

The important monument in Larissa is the recently discovered—and still not completely excavated—**ancient theater,** located in the northwest part of town. Near the ancient theater is the town's **fortress** (now converted into a restaurant); this *frourio* is built on the site of an ancient temple to Pallas Athena. To the northeast of the fortress are the **Pinios River,** a rather pitiful yellow trickle, and the shady **Alcazar Park,** always a nice place to escape the heat. In the center of town at Laou Sq. is the small **architectural museum,** an Ottoman-style building containing objects such as farming tools and weavings found in the area around Larissa. *(Open Tu-Su 8am-2:30pm. Free.)*

■ Trikala Τρικαλα

Tell a Greek you're vacationing in Larissa and he'll snicker—and Greeks tend to think of Trikala as a smaller, less cosmopolitan replica of Larissa. Despite its apparent lack of potential, however, Trikala does hold some points of interest for the determined traveler of northern Greece. Chances are, of course, that you're in Trikala because it's a transportation hub, not because of the sights it holds. But if you do miss the last bus out of town, wipe the frown off your face: Trikala's Varousi district, with its over-hanging balconies and meandering labyrinthine streets, some ancient ruins said to be the birthplace of the ancient physician Asclepius, and the fascinating Katsikoyianni Museum are more than enough to keep you busy for a day.

ORIENTATION AND PRACTICAL INFORMATION Trikala is bisected diagonally from northwest to southeast by the **Litheos River.** Lying directly across the river from each other are the town's two main squares, **Riga Feraiou Sq.** on the south side and the larger **Iroon Polytechniou Sq.** on the north side. The most important road is **Asklipiou St.,** which runs north-south through the two main squares. The status of Trikala's bus and train connections is in question for 1999. Call ahead. The **bus station** (tel. 73 130) is on the west bank of the river on **Othonos,** about 150m south of Riga Feraiou St. Buses depart for Athens (5hr., 8 per day, 5200dr); Thessaloniki (3hr., 6 per day, 3500dr); Volos (2½hr., 4 per day, 2550dr); Ioannina (3hr., 4 per day, 2650dr); Kalambaka (30min., 22 per day, 400dr); and Larissa (1hr., 21 per day, 1050dr). The **train station** (tel. 27 214) is located at the far southern end of Asklipiou, about 700m south of Riga Feraiou Sq. Trikala's **police station** (tel. 27 301) is on the corner of Kapodistriou and Asklipiou St. Its **post office** (tel. 32 983) is on 13 Sarafi; go west on Sarafi from Iroon Polytechniou Sq. (open M-F 7:30am-2pm). A **National Bank** with **ATM** is located right on the north side of Polytechniou Sq. (open M-Th 8am-2pm, F 8am-1:30pm). The local **OTE** (tel. 95 511) is on 25 Martiou St., which runs parallel to Sarafi St.; again, go west from Polytechniou Sq. **Postal code:** 42100. **Telephone code:** 0431.

ACCOMMODATIONS The most affordable hotel in a town that caters to business travelers is the **Hotel Palladion,** on 4 Vyronos, one street behind Riga Feraiou Sq. (tel. 28 091 or 37 260). Spacious rooms offer comfort and TVs that receive more than 20 channels (singles 6000dr; doubles 8000dr). The newly renovated **Dinas Hotel,** 1 Koranasiou (tel. 74 777, 74 778, or 74 779), with its gleaming modern lobby and clean carpeted rooms, is another good bet (singles 9000dr; doubles 12,000dr).

FOOD AND ENTERTAINMENT Trikala's cafes and restaurants are particularly concentrated in the pedestrian area around Plateia Riga Feraiou. Fast food *souvlatzithika* and pizzerias such as **Roma Pizza,** on the corner of Asklipiou and Kapodistriou, and **Trikki,** on 35 Asklipiou St., abound in Trikala. Try the well-priced Special Pizza at Trikki (only 800dr). A more conventional Greek dining experience can be found at **Taverna O Babis,** located next to the Dinas Hotel. The *pastitsio* and *moussaka* here are particularly good. For after-dinner drinks and merriment head to the ominously titled but always packed **Black Door Cafe** or the **Rolling Under Cafe;** both offer lively settings near Riga Feraiou Sq., ear-splitting music, and relatively affordable drinks. The biggest disco in the area is **Lemon** (tel. 72 131), located about five minutes from town by taxi. With its exuberant beach decor and good blend of Greek and American music, Lemon is always packed with rowdy revelers (cover 1000dr).

SIGHTS The most rewarding area in Trikala is the oldest district, in the northwest part of town. Here you'll find **Varousi,** the old Ottoman quarter, whose quiet meandering streets seem worlds apart from the bustling commercial area that lies only a few meters away. Looming above Varousi are the grand stone walls and bell tower of **Fort Trikkis,** which was first constructed in the 4th century BC and is currently being excavated. At the base of the fortress is the **Katsikoyianni Museum,** which houses all of the paintings and sculptures of the local artist (and ardent communist) Legos Katsikoyiannis. His surrealist work—characterized by his busts from which other hands and faces spring—often glorifies the Greek resistance against the Nazis and the simple pastoral life of the Greek farmer. *(Open Tu-W, F-Su 9am-1:30pm, M, Th 5:30-8:30pm. Free.)* On the south side of Trikala, about 250m south of the bus station along Othonos, is the **Koursoun Tzami,** a well-preserved 400-year-old Turkish mosque (unfortunately missing the top half of its minaret). The Koursoun Tzami, built by the same architect who designed Istanbul's Blue Mosque, is currently being restored.

■ Pyli Πυλη

Although they seem to stretch endlessly, the vast plains of Thessaly do eventually come to a halt—in Pyli. A gateway (as its name suggests) to the area's mountains, Pyli is itself unremarkable. The splendid Byzantine church of Porta Panagia, however, superbly set at the beginning of a pine-covered gorge, is worth the detour.

Ermou St. and **Trikalonortis St.**, which goes toward Trikala, are Pyli's two main streets. The **bus station** is at the intersection of the two; buses go only to nearby Trikala (30min., 13 per day, 340dr). The **town hall** is on Ermou; to get there, turn right, past the Hotel Babanara, at the bus station. Clustered together south of the bus station on Trikalonartis St. are a **National Bank** (open M-Th 8am-2pm, F 8am-11:30pm); a 24-hour **ATM;** the **OTE** (open M-Th 8am-1pm, F 8am-12:30pm); the **post office** (open M-F 8am-7:30pm); and **Agios Visarionas,** Pyli's functioning church. **Postal code:** 42100. **Telephone code:** 0434.

Pyli has only one hotel, the comfortable **Hotel Babanara** (tel. 22 325 or 23 261; fax 22 242), across the street from the bus station. Babanara's rooms come with bath, TV, phone, and air conditioning (singles 7500dr; doubles 12,000dr; triples 14,500dr). The area around the Hotel Babanara, particularly along Ermou, is packed with cafes and taverns. If you can, try to return to Trikala for dinner; if you're stuck, eat at the pleasant **Restaurant Pyli,** next to the historic bridge about 1.5km from the town center or sample one of the *tavernas* just above the Porta Panagia.

The two sights of any significance in Pyli are the often photographed **stone footbridge,** built in Roman times, that crosses the river about 1.5km upstream from the village, and the well-preserved Byzantine church, the **Porta Panagia,** which is about 1km from the center of town. To enter the Porta Panagia, request the key at the squat green-trimmed building adjacent to it; someone will be glad to open the church and discuss its storied past with you. *(Admission 300dr.)* The Panagia Porta was built in 1283 by **Ioannis Dukas,** Despot of Epirus, on the site of an ancient Greek temple. The *narthex* of the church sports a domed *Pantocrator* still in good condition. The church's main area, the *naos*, is built in a *trikliti stavrepisteli* style, meaning that it is divided into three vertical regions and one horizontal region, which intersect to form a sort of cross. In the *naos* are the church's treasures: a pair of 700-year-old mosaic icons, one of the Panagia and one of Christ. The Porta Panagia's *iconostasis* is unusual in that the icon of the Virgin (Panagia) is located to the right of Christ—not the standard left. On the walls of both the *narthex* and the *naos* are beautiful frescoes, painted with dyes extracted from flowers. Some of the frescoes have been damaged by fire, earthquake, and Nazi bullets, but most remain unscathed.

■ Kalambaka Καλαμπακα

Once famous for its architecture, Kalambaka lost most of its important buildings to the occupying Nazis' theories of urban renewal. Kalambaka's proximity to the monasteries of Meteora—its Turkish name means "the rock with the cowls of monks"—makes it a convenient base for international tourists and their ubiquitous tour buses. If traveling in the more remote parts of central Greece has made you miss backpacker banter, Kalambaka is the place to be.

ORIENTATION AND PRACTICAL INFORMATION

Kalambaka has two main squares. The upper square, two blocks east of the **main bus station** along **Ioanninon St.,** is the town's central transit hub, from which all major thoroughfares radiate. **Riga Fereou Square,** complete with shops, restaurants and leafy trees, is a few blocks southeast along **Trikalon St.** Beyond the square, Trikalon St. becomes an all-out nightlife scene.

Transportation

Buses: From the **smaller bus station** (tel. 22 432) on the upper square, buses go from Kalambaka to Meteora (20min., 2 per day, 220dr) and Kastraki (10min., 25 per day, 150dr). The early bus to Meteora (9am) allows you time to hike around the monasteries, which are open 9am-1pm and 3:30-5pm. Most people walk back to Kalambaka (6km downhill), visiting monasteries along the way. From the **main station** on Ikonomou St. and Averof St. buses also go to Volos (4 per day, 2900dr); Thessaloniki (6 per day, 3500dr); Athens (8 per day, 5200dr); Metsovo (2 per day, 1300dr); and Ioannina (2 per day, 2300dr).

Trains: Station (tel. 22 451), on the corner of Pindou St. and Kondyli St. Take Kondylifrou St. to Triga Fereou Square. Unfortunately, rail service to Kalambaka will not exist through 1999 because the line is being expanded to handle larger trains. Call ahead for details; buses may replace train routes through Kalambaka.

Taxis: (tel. 22 310) congregate at a small kiosk on Ioanninon St. near the bus station. Open daily 6:30am-midnight.

Tourist and Financial Services

Town Hall: (tel. 22 339), in Ioanninon Sq. Open M-F 8am-2pm.
Banks: National Bank, facing Riga Fereou Sq., on the west side. **ATM** and automatic exchange machine. Open M-Th 8am-2pm, F 8am-1:30pm. **Ionian Bank,** facing the northern square (the one by the town hall) has a 24hr. **ATM.** Open M-Th 8am-2pm and F 8am-1:30pm.

Emergency and Communications

Police: 11 Hagipetrou St. (tel. 22 109). From the main bus station, walk up the hill on Ikonomou St. and take your first right. Non-English-speaking but amiable, they will help travelers find rooms. Open daily 9am-9pm, but officer on duty 24hr.
Tourist Police: 10 Hagi Petrou St. (tel. 22 109). Next door to the police.
Pharmacy: at the top of Riga Fereou Sq.
Health Center: (tel. 24 111), 1km from town, on the road to Trikala. Open 24hr.
Post Office: (tel. 22 466), diagonally across from the OTE. Open M-F 7:30am-2pm. **Postal Code:** 42200.
OTE: (tel. 22 121). From the bus station, down Ioanninon St. (look for signs for Ioannina and Grevena, at the top of the street). **Telephone Code:** 0432.

ACCOMMODATIONS

Chances are that as soon as you step out of your bus or train into Kalambaka, you will be approached by someone—usually from a member of the ubiquitous Totis family—offering you a room for the night. Think carefully before you accept; Kalambaka's room-peddlers are known to lure travelers with promises of good prices only to change their rates or add surcharges when the time comes to pay. A far better bet than rented rooms is one of Kalambaka's many hotels and campgrounds.

Koka Roka (tel. 24 554), a 15min. walk up from the upper square along Vlachava St. and then Kanari St. Koka Roka offers large, airy, comfortable rooms, fantastic food in the *taverna* below, and awe-inspiring views of the Meteora. Singles 3000dr, with bath 4000dr; doubles 6000dr, with bath 7000dr; triples 7500dr.
Hotel Meteora (tel. 22 367; fax 75 550). From the upper square go west on Patriarchou Dimitriou and turn right onto Ploutarchou St. Superb views of the rocks. Singles 6000dr; doubles 7000dr; triples 9000dr; breakfast included.
Hotel Astoria (tel. 22 213 or 23 557) is a bit farther from the rocks and the views, (follow Kondyli St. south from Riga Fereou Sq. almost until the railway station) but some rooms have electric fans. Singles 5000dr; doubles 6000dr, with bath 8000dr; triples 9000dr.
Camping: Kalambaka (tel. 22 309) has the best location. **Philoxonia** (tel. 24 466), **Theopetra** (tel. 81 406), and **International** (tel. 22 239), are all on the national road between Trikala and Kalambaka.

FOOD AND ENTERTAINMENT

Most of the town's restaurants and almost all of its bars are located on Trikalon St., the town's central north-south thoroughfare. Kalambaka has several **markets,** the largest of which is uphill past Hotel Astoria (open daily 7am-2:30pm and 5-9pm).

Koka Roka Taverna (tel. 24 554). One of the few *tavernas* not on Trikalon St., Koka Roka is inside its namesake hotel, off Vlachava St. Wayfarers from the monasteries are rewarded with delicious homemade specialties (entrees 1000dr).

Restaurant Panellinio, in the central square, is always packed. Tasty and satisfying vegetarian entrees including *papoutsakia* and *briam* (900dr).

O Zikos (tel. 75 051), east of the upper square along Vlachava. In addition to standard Greek fare, O Zikos offers Mexican dishes such as *fajitas* and *burritos* and Middle Eastern specialties like *kofta* and *falafel* (entrees 700-1400dr).

Restaurant Diethnes (tel. 22 449 or 23 349), right on the upper square, is a friendly family-owned restaurant known to give free *ouzo* to bearers of *Let's Go: Greece.*

SIGHTS

In the land of monasteries, it is no surprise that Kalambaka's foremost sight is the Byzantine **Church of the Dormition of the Virgin,** once the seat of the bishop of Kalambaka and Trikala. *(Open daily 9am-2pm. Admission 400dr. Modest dress is preferred.)* Follow the signs in the central square and after several blocks you'll spy the graceful bell tower of the old church, crowned by a stork's nest. Built in the 11th century on the ruins of a 5th-century basilica, the main structure was remodeled in 1573. Unfortunately, the interior frescoes, painted by the Cretan monks **Neophytos** and **Kiriazis,** have been badly blackened by centuries of candles and incense. Of particular interest is the church's marble pulpit, located in the center of the nave. George Dailianas, the church tour guide, is fond of practicing his English with visitors. In late July the town honors its patron saint with Glendi (celebration). Kalambaka also holds a three-day **wine festival** with traditional dancing and free wine in late August.

■ Monasteries of Meteora Μετεωρα

The monasteries have staggered their closing days, but all are open Saturday, Sunday, and Wednesday from April until the end of September, 9am-6pm. Admission 500dr to each. Modest dress (pants for men, skirts for women) is strictly enforced and visitors should cover their shoulders. Men with long hair may be asked to wrap it in a bun (as the monks do). Photography and filming inside the monasteries are forbidden; illicit attempts have been known to provoke the ire of monks, not to mention the Holy Ghost.

The enigmatic iron-gray pinnacles of the Meteora formations rise in cryptic majesty above the surrounding Thessalian plain; no one really knows how these stone pillars were formed, though one theory claims that the rocks are large salt deposits from a primordial sea. Whatever their origin, the Meteora formations would be a must-see even if they didn't hold atop their summits 24 gravity-defying Byzantine monasteries complete with beautiful frescoes and astonishing views. Of the 24 monasteries, six are still inhabited by religious orders and open to the public. Although the site is one of the most visited in northern Greece, the monasteries themselves offer a calming and invigorating experience; take a full day to see the monasteries properly. Grand Meteoron and Varlaam are the largest and cater to tourists; the others are more intimate but offer less spectacular displays.

Stairway to Heaven

The first ascetics scaled the sheer cliff faces by wedging timbers into the rock crevices, thereby constructing small platforms, traces of which can still be seen. After the monasteries were completed, visitors usually arrived by means of extremely long rope ladders, but when these were pulled up, the summit became virtually inaccessible. Visitors who were either too weak or too timid to climb the ladders were hoisted up in free-swinging rope nets. The half-hour ascent, during which the rope could be heard slowly unwinding, no doubt made even atheists pray to God for their safety. Motorized winches have since replaced monk-powered rope-spool cranes, and today only provisions, not pilgrims, are elevated. In 1922, steps were carved into the rocks and bridges built between the pillars, so even the vertigo-prone could feel secure.

Orientation

Buses travel from the main square in Kalambaka to the Grand Meteoron (20min., 2 per day, 220dr). Flag down the bus at any of the blue stasis signs along its route or go to the central square with the large Meteora bus stop sign. The bus may stop at the different monasteries along the way to the Grand Meteoron, but it is best to begin your walking tour from the Grand Meteoron, the uppermost monastery, and then to visit the others on your way down. From Grand Meteoron, a road leads down to Varlaam. After Varlaam, the road splits in two. The right fork leads to Roussanou, Agios Nikolaos, and, eventually, the village of Kastraki. The left fork, after about 1km, splits again. The new path to the right (a dead end) leads to Agia Triada and Agios Stefanos; the new left path to the right ends up at the town of Kalambaka.

History

In the 11th century, hermits and ascetics began to occupy the wind-beaten pinnacles and crevices of the Meteora, building a church dedicated to the **Theotokos**. As religious persecution at the hands of Serbian marauders increased in the 12th century, devout Christians flocked to take refuge on the summits of these impregnable columns of rock. In 1344, the region's first monastic community was founded when Athanasios and 14 fellow mountain-climbing monks began to build the first of the monasteries. In the late Byzantine period, when the Ottomans ruled most of Greece, Meteora became a bastion of Christian faith rivaled only by Mount Athos, eventually growing into a powerful community of 24 monasteries, each embellished by the age's finest artists. Unfortunately, the communities' wealth turned out to be their downfall. Quarrels over power and riches led to neglect and deterioration during the 16th century—where most of the monasteries once stood, there remain today only echoes and memories. All was not lost, however—some of the monasteries (**Grand Meteoron, Varlaam, Agia Triada,** and **Agios Nikolaos**) are still active, while others (**Agios Stephanos** and **Roussanou**) now serve as convents.

Grand Meteoron

The Monastery of the Transfiguration, known as **Grand Meteoron** *(Megalou Meteorou)*, is the oldest, largest, and most important in the area. *(Open W-M 9am-1pm and 3-6pm.)* Built on Platys Lithos, the most imposing of the occupied stone columns, the complex looms 613m above the Thessalian plain. Founded by Athanasios, a monk who fled from Mt. Athos to avoid the Turkish threat, the monastery rose in prominence when John Uros, grandson of the Serbian prince Stephen, retired here in 1388. Grand Meteoron's importance reached its peak in the 16th century, when it was visited by the reigning patriarch and accorded the same privileges as the autonomous Mount Athos. The monastery's central feature is the 16th-century **Church of the Transfiguration,** which sports an exalted dome with the standard *Pantocrator* and in the narthex, gruesome frescoes of Christians being stoned, skinned, tickled, beheaded, and boiled alive by Romans.

Varlaam Monastery

Some 800m from the Grand Meteoron stands the **Varlaam Monastery,** the second-largest monastery on Meteora. *(Open Sa-Th 9am-1pm and 3:30-6pm.)* Varlaam was founded in the 14th century by a contemporary of Athanasios who humbly gave his own name to the monastery—but was not really developed until two brothers, Theophanis and Nektarios, built the Church of All Saints in 1541. The *katholikon* is replete with 16th-century frescoes depicting desert hermits, martyrs, the Apocalypse, and Saint Sissois chilling with Alexander the Great's skeleton. Varlaam has an extensive net and pulley system, now used for supplies, which shows how earlier visitors were hoisted up, as well as a museum housing a collection of monastic manuscripts.

Roussanou

If you choose to visit more of the monasteries, bear right at the fork in the road to reach **Roussanou.** *(Open in summer daily 9am-6pm; in winter Th-Tu only.)* Visible from most of the valley, it is spectacularly situated and frequently photographed. To a greater extent than its peers in the Meteora, the monastery of Roussanou seems more of a continuation of the boulders than a creation of man. Even with continued renovation, the interior—which includes paintings of the criminal in paradise and the Virgin Mary flanked by angels—cannot compare to the exterior. Founded in the mid-16th century, Roussanou's greatest moments came when it housed refugees during wars with the Turks in 1757 and 1897.

Agios Nikolaos

Farther down the road lies the Monastery of **Agios Nikolaos,** only 2.5km before Kastraki. *(Open daily 9am-1pm and 3-6pm.)* Built in 1388 and expanded in 1628, its highlight is the incomparable fresco work painted by the 16th-century Cretan master **Theophanes.** Visitors are admitted only in small groups. Wait at the top of the steps for the door to open. Because of the narrowness of the boulder on which it is situated, Agios Nikolaos was forced to grow vertically rather than horizontally; as a result, it is now the second-tallest of the monasteries, next to Grand Meteoron.

Agia Triada

Walking back to Roussanou, a footpath across from the monastery leads to the road above, which is the left fork at the main intersection. Follow the road and keep bearing right to find **Agia Triada.** *(Open daily 9am-6pm.)* Movie buffs will recognize it from the James Bond flick *For Your Eyes Only.* Looming above Kalambaka, the peak of Agia Triada gives a soul-searing view of Kalambaka and the distant, snow-capped **Pindos Mountains.** The monk Dometius built the monastery in 1476, but the wall paintings were added 200 years later. A 3km footpath near the entrance leads to Kalambaka.

Agios Stephanos

At the end of the road, past Agia Triada, is **Agios Stephanos.** *(Open Tu-Su 8am-noon and 3-6pm.)* Founded as a hermitage by Antonius Katakouzinos and Philotheos, it became a monastery in the early 15th century and is now a large and bustling convent (beware the gift-selling nuns). Stephanos is cleaner, lighter, and more spacious than Grand Meteoron and Varlaam. It is also the most accessible of the monasteries, thanks to an 8m-long bridge that links it to Koukoula Hill. Of its two churches, only the more modern **Agios Charalambos,** built in 1798, is open to the public. The museum displays well-preserved icons, manuscripts, liturgical vestments, and crosses.

EPIRUS Ηπειρος

Stark mountains, verdant forests, and fragrant wildflowers place under-touristed Epirus among the more beautiful regions in Greece. Black-clad women haunt the streets, and staff-holding shepherds stalk the fields. The Romans stationed their forces here, and the Vlach people, who speak a Romance dialect, are a living relic of those outposts. After breaking off from Byzantium to form its own state, the region spent about 500 years under Ottoman rule. Ancient ruins, Roman artifacts, and Ottoman mosques co-exist in close proximity to one another. Epirus is a playground for mountain-climbers, hunters, and hikers. The picturesque town and resplendent beaches of Parga see their share of visitors, but the mountains and timeless villages of Zagorohoria near the Vikos Gorge remain undisturbed.

■ Igoumenitsa Ηγουμενιτσα

Passengers tread in the footsteps of the illustrious Lord Byron as they disembark the many boats from both Italy and Greece that drop anchor in Igoumenitsa; the city is, for many, the first, disappointing glimpse of the Greek mainland, just as it was for the distinguished poet. Igoumenitsa is Greece's third largest port and consummate transportation hub, linking Central and Northern Greece, the Ionian islands, and Italy. Tourist agencies line the streets, harried backpackers scurry about in search of their ship, and the stench of the port fills the air. Try to avoid staying the night in Igoumenits. Since many ferries depart in the early morning, doing so is not as easy as it sounds—if you do find yourself stuck, head for the waterfront.

ORIENTATION AND PRACTICAL INFORMATION

On the north edge of the waterfront, cafes abound; to the south, across from the ports, are the myriad travel agencies and a couple of kiosks selling foreign papers. Igoumenitsa's main shopping area is on the first two streets parallel to the waterfront. The uninspiring central square is four blocks inland; to reach it, head inland from the waterfront on the street with an Ionian bank at its corner.

You'll reach Igoumenitsa's three main ports in rapid succession. The **Old Port,** on the north edge of the waterfront, mostly sends boats to Italy. **Corfu Port** is in the middle of the three ports. Beyond the Corfu Port is the **New Port,** which sends boats to Italy and Corfu.

Transportation

Ferries: Tickets to Corfu (1¾hr., 22 per day, 1500dr) can be purchased at the Corfu Port, in the yellow kiosk in the parking lot, 100m farther to the left as you face the harbor. For tickets to **Italy,** shop around at the waterfront agencies. Budget carriers vary from year to year, some have student rates, and some (including **Adriatica** and **HML**) accept Eurail and Inter-Rail passes. Destinations include Brindisi (8hr., 6 per day, 8600dr); Ancona (20hr., 2 per day, 18,000dr); Venice (25hr., 1-2 per day, 18,800dr); and Bari (12hr., 3 per day, 10,000dr). Prices do not include port dues (at least 1500dr in Greece, L4000 in Italy) and are lower in the off season. Most boats depart before noon or late in the evening.

Buses: (tel. 22 309). Depart to Ioannina (2hr., 10 per day, 1750dr); Thessaloniki (7hr., 1 per day, 7550dr); Athens (8hr., 4 per day, 8050dr); Parga (1hr., 4 per day, 1100dr); and Preveza (2hr., 2 per day, 2050dr). To reach the **bus station** from the ports, walk up the street past the Ionian Bank. When you reach the town square, turn left and walk two blocks to the **ticket office,** behind a cafe on the left.

Tourist and Financial Services

Tourist Office: (tel. 22 227), in the old port. Has timetables and brochures, a list of hotels and their prices, and a helpful **map.** Multilingual. Open daily 7am-2pm and 5-10pm. A second **tourist office** is in the New Port.

Banks: National Bank (tel. 22 415), across the road from the Old Port in a string of banks with 24hr. **ATM** and automatic **currency changer.**

American Express: (tel. 22 406 or 24 333), near the National Bank, across from the old port. Will **change money,** issue traveler's checks, and give you cash from an AmEx card. Open M-Sa 7:30am-2pm and 4-11pm, Su 7:30-11am and 5:30-10pm.

Bookstore: Bibliorama (tel. 28 313), on the south edge of the waterfront.

Emergency and Communications

Police: (tel. 22 100), across from Corfu Port. Available 24hr.

Tourist Police: (tel. 22 222), across from Corfu Port with police, speak little English.

Port Police: (tel. 23 094, 22 240 or 22 235), have a booth in Corfu port, next to the yellow ticket kiosk.

Medical Center: (tel. 24 420). Handles most health problems. If you need to go to a hospital, they will help you get to the one 15 minutes away. Open 24hr.

Internet Access: Time Out Must (tel. 25 596), in the town square. Internet use 1000dr per hr.

Post Office: (tel. 22 209), go left from the bus station, and turn left at the first corner; it's in the same building as the OTE (open M-F 7:30am-2pm). **Postal Code:** 46100.

OTE: (tel. 22 399), in the same building as the post office. Open daily 7am-10pm. The new port also houses an **OTE** (tel. 27 757), which **exchanges currency,** sells telephone cards, and provides fax and telephone services. Open daily 7am-10pm. **Telephone Code:** 0665.

ACCOMMODATIONS

Most people try to arrange their transportation so that they avoid spending a night in Igoumenitsa. Suspiciously inconvenient ferry schedules may force you to stay.

Staurodromi (tel. 22 343). Follow the large signs uphill from the main square. Your best bet in Igoumenitsa, rooms are cheap and squeaky clean. Singles 4000dr; doubles 7000dr; triples 10,000dr.

Hotel Rex (tel. 22 255). From the port, walk up the street with the Ionian Bank on the corner, and turn left at the first corner. Look for the small sign on the white building with green shutters on your right, in the middle of the block. Inexpensive but rather uncomfortable, offering cramped rooms with shared baths. Singles 4000dr; doubles 6000dr; triples 7000dr.

Hotel Egnatia (tel. 23 648). Find the sign at the central square's far right corner. Large, airy rooms with bath, TV, and phone. Singles 8800dr; doubles 12,600dr;

Hotel Oscar (tel. 22 675 or 23 338; fax 23 557), strategically situated across from the New Port. Pretty, carpeted rooms offer modern amenities such as bath, TV, and phone. Singles 8000dr; doubles 13,000dr.

FOOD

Food isn't so amazing in Igoumenitsa. The better restaurants (and those most popular with locals) are on the north edge of the waterfront past the ports and junkshops.

Mykonos (tel. 27 567), at the beginning of the waterfront strip. Boasts a varied menu (entrees 1400-2300dr) and a hallucinogenic polka-dot floor.

Alekos (tel. 23 708), next door to Mykonos, specializes in fish dishes, caught in the pristine harbor waters. Entrees are 1400-2000dr.

Meeting Cafe, across the street from the bus station, has dim lights, cold drinks (*frappé* or beer 400dr), clean bathrooms, and, most importantly, air conditioning.

⊛**Bakery Alexiou Spiridon** (tel. 24 617), just off the waterfront at 7 El. Venizelou St. If you're not in the mood for the cafe or restaurant scene, look for the Ionian Bank at the waterfront corner and try to catch the subtle white "Bakery" placard hanging a few storefronts inland. Offers an array of baked goods and sweets. Stop by early morning to get a piece of their delicious *spanakopita*. Open daily 6am-6pm.

■ Parga Παργα

Snug within an arc of green mountains and a row of rocky islets, there is perhaps no place in mainland Greece that feels more like an island than Parga. Like much of the nearby Ionians, Parga has the long luxuriant beaches and bustling waterfront that draw the fun- and sun-loving crowd—as well as the over-priced jewelry shops, "effervescent nightlife," and stone alleys lined with t-shirt vendors that unfailingly spring up around the shore. Parga today has been swamped by tourism, drawing enough people to make its summer population (30,000) more than fifteen times greater than its full-time population. Yet despite the tourists, Parga's narrow streets, neo-classical houses, and harbor views create a pleasant romantic mood that seems to have infected even the pink pastel supermarket.

Parga's quirky history also sets it apart from the rest of Epirus. While most of Greece languished under Ottoman rule, Parga was controlled by the Venetians for close to four centuries. The town's castle, set high on a hill overlooking the water, still bears the Venetian coat of arms in mute testimony to the early occupation. Parga was later occupied by the French, the British, and, after the British sold the seaside town to Ali Pasha, the Ottomans.

ORIENTATION AND PRACTICAL INFORMATION Parga is organized primarily around its waterfront. The main waterfront road, which brims with *tavernas*, bars, and tourist agencies, has four different names: from west to east, **Lambraki, Anexartissias, Fereou,** and **Athanassiou. Baga St.,** which runs perpendicular to the waterfront, contains most of Parga's municipal buildings. The **Venetian castle** is at the far southwest corner of town. To the north of the castle lies **Valtos Beach**.

To reach the bus stop from the port, head to the corner of the waterfront (to the left, facing inland), and walk uphill along Baga St. and inland. You'll find the **National Bank** (tel. 31 719) one block inland on Vassila St., which feeds into Baga St. (open M-F 7-9pm). Continue uphill to pass the **OTE** (tel. 31 699) sporting a maroon facade (open M-F 7am-3pm). Farther up, the **bus stop** sits at the intersection with the church on the corner, while the **post office** (tel. 31 295; open M-F 7:30am-2pm), **police station**, and **tourist police** (tel. 31 222) are next door (open 24hr.). For emergencies you can also call the **port police** (tel. 31 227) or a private **doctor** (tel. 31 100). On the waterfront you'll find a **pharmacy** (tel. 31 635; open M-Sa 8am-2pm). Next door, a **bookstore** sells English books and papers.

Tourist agencies pack the streets around the waterfront. They will help find rooms, rent mopeds, and arrange daytrips (open M-Sa 9am-2pm and 5:30-10pm). They also sell **ferry tickets** to Paxos (one per day, 4000dr round-trip) and Antipaxos (one per day, 5000dr round-trip) and Corfu Town (2 per week, 7900dr), as well as providing information about **buses** connecting Parga with Igoumenitsa (1½hr., 4 per day, 1150dr); Preveza (1¾hr., 5 per day, 1350dr); Athens (8½hr., 3 per day, 7500dr); and Thessaloniki (8½hr., 1 per day, 8800dr). Of all the agencies, the charming staff of **Parga Tours** (tel. 31 580; fax 31 116), on the waterfront, caters least to northern European package tours (open daily 8:30am-2:30pm and 5:30-10:30pm). **Postal code:** 48060. **Telephone code:** 0684.

ACCOMMODATIONS As the number of vacationers in Parga increases, the summer rooms keep up the pace. However, hotels in Parga are expensive; for a cheaper stay, look off the beaten track, at the south end of the town and the top of the hill. The rented rooms of **Andreou Nausika** (tel. 31 306), located about 10 steps below the castle on Gaki Zeri St., are probably the best deal in this overpriced town (singles 5000dr; doubles 8000dr; triples 9000dr). **Kotsis** (tel. 31 567) and **Agios Nektarios** (tel. 31 150), are both on side streets off Baga St. (singles 10,000dr; doubles 12,000dr). The budget traveler may wish to skip Parga's high-priced lodging altogether and camp instead on the nearby beaches. Campsites include **Elia Camping** (tel. 31 130), **Valtos Camping** (tel. 31 287), and **Lihnos Beach Camping** (tel. 31 161).

FOOD Parga's dining options are, for the most part, limited to the waterfront. Some of the establishments, especially near the harbor, are outright tourist traps; several, however, offer memorable food and lively atmosphere. Perhaps the best food is at the always packed **O Psaras** (tel. 31 711), located just below the town hall along the waterfront. The cook here, Christos Glakis, freely innovates with the standard repertoire of Greek dishes; for instance, he makes his *pastitsio* (1200dr) with a mix of cheeses instead of pasta. On the far side of the waterfront, by the town beach, are **Restaurant Ionio** (tel. 31 402) and **Balthazar Restaurant** (tel. 31 888), a pair of establishments with good atmosphere, varied menus, and affordable prices (entrees 1400-1900dr). On the opposite side of the waterfront is the more posh **Rudis** (tel. 31 693), which serves creative Greek and Italian cuisine (entrees 1600-2700dr).

ENTERTAINMENT Bars and cafes, usually noisy and crowded with inebriated northern Europeans, line the waterfront and surrounding streets of Parga. The **Blue Bar** (tel. 32 067), located on the road leading to the castle, offers stunning views of the sea and attractive decor. Try the Happy Company cocktail; served in a massive ceramic jug, it packs enough potent punch to knock out you and three of your friends. **Caravel** (tel. 31 359), in the center of the waterfront, is one of the town's most popular bars and offers more than 30 cocktails (1800-2000dr). Parga also has an array of kickin' discos, all of which are packed by 2:30am. **Factory** (tel. 32 625) and **Camares** (tel. 32 000) are located on adjacent side streets off the waterfront road (admission at both 1000dr). High up on the castle hill is **Island** (tel. 32 446), which is slightly less packed.

SIGHTS Looming ominously above Parga is the massive **Venetian fortress.** *(Open daily 7am-10pm. Free.)* Although built by the Normans, the castle was controlled by the Venetians from 1401 to 1797. Today the fortress is a luscious spot for a picnic or snooze under the shade of the high walls and majestic pines. Follow the steps from the harbor up the hill, only five minutes from the water. A three-minute walk down and behind the castle lies **Valtos Beach,** a voluptuous crescent of fine pebbles, clear water, and endless hordes of sun-worshipping tourists. **Golfo Beach,** five minutes to the left of the town beach, is more secluded but has rocks the size of golfo balls. The town beach pales in comparison to Valtos, but it's clean. A short swim or pedal boat ride will bring you to the islet 100m offshore, home to a small **church.** Boats sometimes travel to the smaller beaches.

Parga's ubiquitous travel agencies book a variety of excursions; visit the **River Styx,** the mythical pathway to the underworld, or the **Necromonteion,** the Oracle of the Dead, which was excavated in 1958. *(Open M-F 8:30am-4:30pm, Sa-Su 8:30am-3pm. Admission 500dr, students 300dr.)*

■ Ioannina Ιωαννινα

Belying its present concrete superficies, Ioannina has a rather colorful past. Over the centuries, Ioannina has been a favorite target of invaders, a consequence of its position on the shores of the murky Lake Pamvotidas. The city was founded in AD 527 by Emperor Justinian, who ordered the citizens of nearby Evroia to relocate to the peninsula where the city's castle now lies. Norman and Serb rulers ensued before the Ottomans took the city in 1431. Now Epirus' largest city and capital, Ioannina displays the most marked Turkish influence of all of the cities in Greece, an Eastern flavor reflected in the city's distinctive museums, architecture, and way of life.

The town's most intriguing and charismatic historical figure was undoubtedly Ali Pasha, the Ottoman governor of Epirus just before the Greek War of Independence. Although nominally subject to the Sultan in Istanbul, the Albanian born Ali Pasha did pretty much whatever he wanted during his 34-year rule. Famed for his cunning and debauchery, the "Lion of Ioannina" would regularly cavort with his harem of hundreds of men and women, carouse with the legendary Lord Byron, and engage in endless vindictive skirmishes. Having always dreamed of ruling his own independent fiefdom, Ali Pasha alternately fought and served the Sultan, flirting with Napoleon, the British, and the Venetians, until the Sultan tired of him and had him beheaded for high treason in 1822.

ORIENTATION AND PRACTICAL INFORMATION

The names of the main thoroughfares in Ioannina change often, and many posted street signs are obsolete. The main bus station is between **Sina St.** and **Zossimadon St.** Zossimadon St. continues south, changing its name twice, to merge with **28 Octovriou St.** in front of the post office. The merged street crosses **Averof St.** at the town's largest intersection, and changes to **Bizaniou St.** as it continues behind the central park area to the town's second bus station. Averof St., running northeast, heads toward the Old Town, the castle, and the harbor before it narrows, then turns left, and becomes **Anexartissis St.,** which merges with Zossimadon St. going north from the main bus station. The city of Ioannina is built around **Lake Pamvotidas,** which has an island in the middle. To reach the waterfront, walk straight down Averof St. and keep the castle walls on your right.

Transportation

Buses: From **main terminal** (tel. 26 404) service to Athens (7hr., 10 per day, 7000dr); Igoumenitsa (2hr., 10 per day, 1750dr); Metsovo (1½hr., 4 per day, 1050dr); Thessaloniki (6½hr., 6 per day, 5850dr); Konitsa (1½hr., 1 per day, 1100dr); Parga (2¾hr., 1 per day, 2200dr); and Larissa (4hr., 6 per day, 3350dr). Check the schedule; changes are common and buses may run more frequently at times. Buses leave from the **lesser station** (tel. 25 014) for Preveza (2hr., 10 per day, 1900dr); Arta (1¼hr., 10 per day, 1350dr); Agrinio (3hr., 6 per day, 2800dr); and Dodoni (30min., 2 per day except Th, 360dr).

Flights: To Athens (50min., 1-2 per day, 18,000dr) and Thessaloniki (40min., 1-2 per day, 12,000dr). The **Olympic Airways** office (tel. 26 218) sits across from the M-Sa. An **airport branch** (tel. 26 218) is available for tickets and information (open 10am-5pm).

Tourist and Financial Services

Tourist Office: EOT office (tel. 25 086, fax 72 148). Turn right onto Dodonis St. (an extension of Averof St.) from 28 Octovriou St., with the central park on your left. Open daily in summer 7:30am-2:30pm and 5:30-8:30pm; in winter 7:30am-2:30pm.

Hellenic Mountaineering Club: 2 Despotatou Ipirou St. (tel. 22 138), a little west of the stadium. Information on mountain trips through the outlying region every weekend Sept.-June. Open M-Sa 7:30-9pm.

Banks: National Bank, on Averof St., on the right toward the waterfront from the central square. 24hr. **ATM**. Open M-Th 8am-2pm, F 8am-1:30pm.

Laundromat: Express Wash, 86 Napoleon Zerva St. (tel. 66 493). Wash 900dr; dry 700dr. Open M-F 8:30am-3pm and 5-9pm, Sa 8:30am-2:30pm.

Emergency and Communication

Tourist Police: (tel. 25 673) from the main bus station, follow Zassimadon St. to the post office and double back on 28 Octovriou St. until you reach the police station. Police and EOT have a brochure including a very helpful map. Open daily 8am-10pm. The tourist police also has a kiosk on the waterfront on Filosoffou St.

Police: (tel. 22 660 or 26 226) with the tourist police. Open 24hr.

Hospital: There are two hospitals, each about 5km from the center of town, that handle emergencies on alternating days of the month, one for even dates (tel. 80 111), another for odd dates (tel. 99 111).

Post Office: (tel. 25 498) at the intersection of 28 Octovriou St. and Zossimadon St. Open M-F 7:30am-8pm. **Postal Code:** 45221.

OTE: (tel. 22 350 or 42 777), opposite the police behind the post office. Open daily 7am-11pm. **Telephone Code:** 0651.

ACCOMMODATIONS

Staying in Ioannina unfortunately carries a pretty hefty price, as hotels here generally cater to deep-pocketed business travelers. If you avoid peak season, however, you can usually wring a better price from the hotel owner.

Hotel Paris, 6 Tsirigoti St. (tel. 20 541), on a side street by the main bus terminal. Offers large traditional Greek (not Parisian) rooms. Singles 5000dr, with bath 7000dr; doubles 8000dr, with bath 9000dr.

Hotel Tourist, 18 Koletti St. (tel. 26 443, 25 070). The virtually spotless rooms have TVs. Singles 10,000dr; doubles 14,000dr.

FOOD AND ENTERTAINMENT

Little *souvlaki* stands can be found throughout Ioannina. The dining scene centers on the waterfront and old town areas of the city. Because Ioannina has so far been spared the ravages of tourism, food is generally tasty and well-priced. The bars and nightlife of the city are also clustered along the waterfront.

To Kourmanio, 16 Georgiou Sq. (tel. 38 044), in the old city, directly across from the main entrance to the castle. Comfortable shady atmosphere under the castle walls, with great food and better prices (entrees 800-1500dr).

I Kira Vasiliki (tel. 81 253; fax 81 726), on the island next to the dock. For a convenient escape from the city's bustle, head to the island for delicious specialties from the lake including frogs, eels, and trout. Entrees 900-1400dr.

Propodes (tel. 81 214), on an island near the Ali Pasha Museum. For seclusion from the world, head here. Check out the aquarium filled with trout and other fish. Entrees 800-1200dr.

Monopolio (tel. 35 985), on the waterfront 200m past the square. A massive disco with two large pools. Entrance and a beer are 1000dr, cocktails 2000dr.

SIGHTS

The Frourio

The city's **castle** makes a logical point to begin your excursions. Rising ominously from the surrounding waters, the castle's massive stone walls contain the old city, complete with museums, shops, a **mosque** and a **synagogue,** mutely attesting to the former prominence of the city's Jewish population.

Within the **Its Kale,** the inner sanctum of the castle, lie the **tomb of Ali Pasha** and the **Inner Acropolis** with eerie stone tunnels just waiting to be explored. *(Open Tu-Su 7am-10pm.)* Also within the Its Kale are the **Byzantine Museum** (tel. 25 989) and adjacent **Silverworks Gallery.** *(Both museums open M 12:30-7pm, Tu-F 8am-7pm, Sa-Su 8am-2:30pm. Admission 500dr, seniors 300dr, students free.)* The Byzantine Museum houses an array of mosaics, Epirot icons, and other Byzantine relics, all chronologically arranged and described in detail in English. The Silverworks Gallery contains a dazzling collection of local silverwork; Ioannina is the silver and gold capital of Greece. During the summer on nights of the full moon, the museum holds free Byzantine music concerts within the walls of the Its Kale. At the northern corner of the castle is the **Municipal Museum** (tel. 26 356), exhibiting Epirot costumes, furniture, clothing, and tapestries from the past two centuries. *(Open daily 8am-8pm. Admission 700dr, students 300dr.)* More interesting than the museum's contents, however, is its architecture; it resides in the splendid **Aslan Pasha Mosque,** built by Aslan Pasha in 1618 to celebrate the failed 1611 Greek insurrection led by the fanatical Bishop of Trikala, Dionysos Skilosofos. Skilosofos was flayed alive on the cliff near his namesake esplanade, which runs lakeside beneath the castle walls.

Around Town

Outside of the castle, behind the clock tower in a park south of Averof St., you'll find the **Archaeological Museum** (tel. 33 357), whose collection is a must-see for those visiting Dodoni. *(Open M noon-6pm, Tu-F 8am-6pm, Sa-Su 8:30am-3pm. Admission 500dr, students 300dr.)* Besides Paleolothic tools and some well-preserved ancient funerary artifacts, the museum features lead tablets etched with political, romantic, and cosmological questions asked of the oracle at Dodoni between the 6th and the 3rd century BC. The translated tablets lead one to wonder how the oracle answered when asked, "Has Pistos stolen the wool from my mattress?"

Also on Averof St. is the **Athanasios Vrellis' Wax-Works Museum** (tel. 22 414), featuring famous historical and mythological scenes such as Socrates drinking hemlock, Diogenes telling Alexander the Great to step aside so he could enjoy the sun's warmth, and Prometheus being tortured by vultures for giving the gift of fire to man. *(Open daily 9am-4pm. Free.)* Unfortunately for wax figure buffs, the Vrellis brothers had something of a falling out, and Pavlos' larger museum (tel. 92 128) is 13km from Ioannina towards the village of **Bizani.**

The Island (To Nesi)

On the island, chickens wander among whitewashed *tavernas,* cheap **silver shops,** and the five curiously silent **monasteries** all adorned with vivid 16th-century frescoes in various states of decay. If his tomb in the Its Kale wasn't enough, you can get more of the renegade Ali Pasha at the **Ali Pasha Museum** located in the **Pantelimonos Monastery** on the north end of the island. *(Open daily 8am-8pm. Admission 150dr.)* The monastery, in whose upper floors Ali Pasha had sought refuge from the Sultan's forces, witnessed his assassination in 1822. He was shot from below (you can still see the bullets in the floorboard) and his head was sent to the Sultan in Istanbul. The museum displays Ali Pasha's bong, among other things. The nearby **Filanthrapinon Monastery,** built in 1222 and once site of the *Krifto sholio* (secret school) during the Ottoman occupation, is the largest and best preserved of the island monasteries. Particularly impressive are its frescoes, painted by Katelanou in 1542. A few hundred yards away is the **Stratigopolou Monastery.** The oldest monastery on the island, Stratigopolou's *katholikon* houses a fine fresco of Judas returning the pieces of silver.

Boats (tel. 25 885) leave for the island from the dock directly northwest of the castle. *(10min. In summer, every 30min. 8am-11pm; in winter every hr. 7am-9pm. Fare 200dr.)* A sign in the central square will direct you to any of the island's sights.

Perama Cave

Four kilometers northeast of Ioannina, the 17°C **Cave of Perama** (tel. 81 521) provides respite from Greece's summer heat. *(Open daily in summer 8am-8pm; in winter 8am-5pm. Admission 1500dr, students 700dr. The local bus #16—catch it behind the park across from 28 Octovriou St—travels there every 20min., 300dr round-trip.)* Discovered in 1941 by villagers seeking shelter from Italian bombings, the caverns are now accessed by a 163-step staircase. A 45-minute guided tour passes by the almost two-million-year-old stalagmite and stalactite formations, in which bear teeth have been found.

■ Dodoni Δωδώνη

For a site that has attracted gods, priests, gladiators, and rock stars, Dodoni is surprisingly difficult to visit. Groups can reach the oracle by hiring a car or **taxi** *(at least 5000dr roundtrip). In the summer, two* **buses** *a day come from Ioannina—but at very inconvenient times (25min., F-W 6:30am and 4pm, 4pm on Su.; 360dr). The buses depart for Ioannina from Dodoni about 45 minutes after they leave Ioannina. Site* **open** *daily 8am-7pm.* **Admission** *500dr, students 400dr.*

Ancient Dodoni, the site of Greece's oldest oracle, is located at the base of a mountain 22km southeast of Ioannina. According to myth, Zeus resided in Dodoni as the roots of a giant oak while courting a nearby cypress tree (Zeus was an omnivore). Years later a dove perched on the tree and told the inhabitants that there should be a oracle to Zeus on the spot. "Build it and they will come." Countless heroes, mortal and immortal, have since come to Dodoni to seek guidance on everything from the meaning of life to the intricacies of sex. Although little remains of the oracle itself, stop by this ancient sanctuary for one of Greece's most impressive amphitheaters, and see whether you can hear the answers to your questions rustling in the past.

The site

The name Dodoni is a relic of the primitive Linear B language and may mean "great mother of civilization"—an early clue to the site's significance. Excavations show evidence of settlements in the area around Dodoni as early as the 18th century BC, though cult activities can only be dated to the 8th century BC. The cult of Zeus at Dodoni was already well established by Homer's time. Odysseus came to the oracle at "wintry Dodona" for advice on how to rid his house of Penelope's suitors.

At the center, both physically and spiritually, of Dodoni's cult of Zeus was a great oak tree from whose branches hung large bronze cauldrons. For centuries a clan of priests with "unwashed feet" known as the **selloi** made prophecies based on rustlings in the oak tree's leaves, the flight of doves, and the ringing of votive bronze tripods. The male *selloi* were later supplanted by wild priestesses prone to divine frenzies. The oracle itself was eventually supplemented by a series of additional buildings: a temple in 500 BC, the *bouleuterion* and *prytaneion* in 350 BC, and a larger temple to Zeus and the great amphitheater in the early third century BC. At its height, Dodoni was one of the ancient world's greatest oracles and home of the **Naia festival,** a series of athletic and dramatic contests held every four years in honor of Zeus. Unfortunately, the area was sacked by the Aetolians in 219 BC, by the Romans in 168 BC— and was ruined for good by the ascendance of Christianity in the fourth century AD.

With the oracle long-gone, the chief attraction at Dodoni today is the well-preserved **amphitheater,** which in its heyday was grander than that of Epidauros. The amphitheater, originally designed to seat 18,000 but expanded in Roman times to accommodate their penchant for bloodsports, still dominates the landscape around it. You can walk in the footsteps of wily Odysseus or weep with the audience of a Sophoclean tragedy. In late July and August, the **theater** (tel. 82 287) recreates the glory of antiquity by hosting a festival of Classical drama.

THESSALY & EPIRUS

The one hotel in the area, **Hotel Andromache** (tel. 82 296), offers fairly generic rooms for a rather hefty price (doubles 14,000dr) so you'd be better off making Dodoni a day trip. The only restaurant in the immediate vicinity is also at the Hotel Andromache. Its beef stuffed with *feta* (1600dr) is particularly good.

■ Metsovo Μετσοβο

Snuggled in the Pindos mountains below the 1690m Katara Pass, Metsovo is a picturesque hamlet complete with old stone houses, red-tile roofs, and winding cobbled roads. Thanks to Metsovo's official designation as a "traditional" settlement, junkshop owners enjoy a booming trade in postcards and handmade wooden trinkets (most of which are made across the border in Albania). Although tourism has profitably romanticized the central square, genuine charm prevails in the rest of the town. Native Metsovans descend from the **Vlachi,** a people descended from Latin-speaking Roman legions stationed in the Balkans. An Ottoman vizier who had fallen out of favor in Istanbul sought refuge here in 1659. Later reentering the sultan's good books, the vizier repaid the village for its hospitality by granting it virtual independence. As a result many wealthy Christian families sought refuge at Metsovo, which has since developed a reputation for philanthropy. Metsovo's current wealth and charm can mostly be attributed to Mihail Tositsas, a Swiss baron with Metsovite roots, who donated most of his vast fortune to his hometown. You really can't escape the influence of Tositsas and his friend, Evangelos Averoff-Tositsas; half the buildings and roads in town are named after them.

ORIENTATION AND PRACTICAL INFORMATION On the wall of an outdoor cafe's patio in the square, a faded (albeit large) English-language town map lists hotels, sights, monasteries, restaurants, discos, and a 24hr. "sanitary station" (tel. 41 111) for **medical emergencies.** Everything of import in Metsovo is clustered in the sprawling, confusing main square. There is only one named road in town, **Tositsas St.,** which extends eastward from the main square. There is a **National Bank** (tel. 41 203) in the square (open M-Th 8am-2pm, F 8am-1:30pm) and a 24hr. **ATM** at the intersection of the main road entering the square. The municipal **police** (tel. 41 233) are on the right, downhill past the bus stop, with an English-speaking police chief (office open daily 8am-2pm and 4-6pm, but available 24hr.). **Buses** depart from the stop in the square to Ioannina (1¼hr., 4 per day, 1050dr) and Trikala via Kalambaka (2hr., 2 per day, 1800dr). Buses to Thessaloniki stop at the main highway above town (about 5 times per day). For **schedule information,** check the cafe opposite the bus stop; tickets, however, must be purchased on the bus. The **post office** (tel. 41 245) is uphill on the main road leaving the square (open M-F 7:30am-2pm). The **OTE** (tel. 42 199) is across the street from the police (open daily 7:30am-3:10pm). The **town hall** (tel. 41 207), where you can obtain helpful brochures on the area, is on the left of Tositsas St. on the way from the square. **Postal code:** 44200. **Telephone code:** 0656.

ACCOMMODATIONS Rooms in Metsovo usually offer a range of amenities as well as astounding views of the surrounding mountains. Prices are usually highest from mid-July to early September and from December to March during the ski season. The **Hotel Athens** (tel. 41 725), just below the main square, offers traditional rooms with private baths for the best prices in town. Hikers and campers are welcome to store their gear here free of charge during visits to Pindos Mountain. The owners can also suggest good routes, and may in fact be your best source of information in Metsovo (singles 3500dr; doubles 5000dr). If Hotel Athens is full, talk to the owners about staying in their slightly fancier **Hotel Filoxenia** (tel. 41 725), which boasts TVs, radios, phones, and beautiful mountain views (singles 5000dr; doubles 8000dr). The **Duros family** (tel. 42 415) offers appealing rooms on the path away from the square, downhill from the post office (singles 5000dr; doubles 7000dr). For a bit more of a pampering, try the **Hotel Bitouni** (tel. 41 217 or 41 700; fax 41 545), complete with sauna and massages. Check out the traditional fireplace and vintage 19th-century sofas in the lobby (singles 8500dr; doubles 10,000dr).

FOOD AND ENTERTAINMENT Metsovo brims with restaurants, cafes, and bars. The **parkside restaurant** (tel. 41 725) in Hotel Athens, founded in 1925, serves delicious Greek specialties in a serene shady environment. The bean soup (700dr), a regional specialty, stuffed vegetables (900dr), and *Katogi*, the local wine (500dr), are of a price and quality generally superior to restaurants in the square. While in the square, locals favor the **Kriti Folia** (tel. 41 628) for its grilled meats, which include *kokoretsi* (1600dr) and *kontosoufli* (1400dr). Two other good choices on the central square are **Kria Vrisi** (tel. 41 723), which specializes in *hilopittes fournou* (a type of pasta), and the always packed **Galaxias** (tel. 41 202), which has Metsovo's largest selection of dishes. If you need a drink or three after dinner, head to **Tositsas St.** There's little difference between the various establishments that line the street. All have similar decor and music, and charge 500dr for beer and 1500dr for cocktails.

SIGHTS Thanks to the largesse of Baron Tositsas, and Averoff-Tositsas, Metsovo has far more sights than you'd expect in a 3500-person village with one main road. Off the main square, the **Museum of Modern Greek Art of the 19th and 20th Centuries** (tel. 41 210) alone merits a trip to Metsovo. *(Open W-M 10am-7pm. Admission 500dr, students 300dr.)* The spacious, well-lit gallery houses the private collection of Evangelos Averoff-Tositsas, Metsovo's local benefactor, politician, and writer. It is the second-largest museum of its kind in Greece, surpassed only by the National Gallery in Athens (see p. 98). The fantastic display has information in English. Some highlights from the museum's 250 paintings include Lytras' "Burning of the Turkish Flagship," Pantazis's pseudo-impressionist landscapes, Gyzis' portraits of Averoff-Tositsas, and Moralis' post-modern "Erotic." A museum shop sells postcards and gallery publications, and in the summer a terrace cafe reveals beautiful views of the Pindos Mountains. Inquire here about exhibits and events.

The **Tositsas Museum,** housed in a stone and timber *arhontiko* (mansion) up the main road on the left (look for the sign opposite the Shell station), shows how the wealthy Tositsas family lived. *(Open F-W 8:30am-1pm and 4-6pm. Admission 500dr.)* In the museum's rooms you'll find beds, sofas, rugs, jewelry, clothing, and kitchen utensils used by the Tositsas family from 1661 up until 1950, when Mihail, the family's last scion, died. Keep in mind that this is a museum about the good life in Metsovo; ordinary *Vlach* families' living standards was of a somewhat simpler nature. The museum's upper floor served as Averoff-Tositsas's apartment until his death in 1990. Visitors wait at the museum's door until the guide appears (every 30 minutes).

Signs near the square point to the **Agios Nikolaos Monastery,** which has a 14th-century chapel with period frescoes and icons. A family now lives in the monastery, so knock to be admitted. For information about skiing, hiking, and rafting opportunities near Metsovo, contact the town hall or the family that owns Hotel Athens.

■ The Zagorohoria Τα Ζαγοροχωρια

The Zagorohoria is a cluster of 46 traditional villages north of Ioannina. Perhaps the most striking feature of the villages is their lack of whitewashed concrete *polikatikies*; the strictures of Zagori custom—and, more recently, Greek law—require that all homes be crafted out of gray slate from the surrounding mountains. Bridging streams between villages are the famous two- and three-arched stone bridges of Epirus.

Unfortunately, the beautiful setting has failed to convince Zagorians to remain in their native villages; with the exception of Monodendri, the Papingo villages, and Tsepelovo, most of the Zagorohoria is now tragically depopulated. In addition, despite the dramatic setting and unique architecture, the Zagorohoria (at least away from the vicinity of Vikos Gorge) fails to attract more than a handful of adventurous travelers each year.

THESSALY & EPIRUS

Although the villages themselves are well worth a day or two, most tourists come to this rugged region for what lies in the hinterlands—wild untamed rivers, stark mountain peaks, and the renowned Vikos Gorge. Outdoor enthusiasts of every skill level will find more than enough to satisfy them in the Zagorohoria. For more information, contact the **GNTO** in Ioannina (tel. (0651) 22 138), or the **Center for Visitor Information** in Megalo Papingo (tel. (0653) 41 931), which has maps and refuge information on the area. Because of the Zagorohoria's proximity to politically unstable Albania, exercise extra caution while hiking here, especially if traveling alone.

■ Monodendri Μυνοδενδρι

This mountainside village of traditional stone houses would be remarkable even if it were not for its superb location at the entrance to the Vikos Gorge; many an enchanted traveler has lost himself walking by twilight through Monodendri's cobbled maze of paths. There is only one paved road in Monodendri, at the upper end of the village; this is where the **bus stop,** all of the hotels, and most of the restaurants are located. The town square is accessible only by a footpath descending to the right as you leave the bus stop. Follow the path downhill and eventually turn left when you hit a fork in the road to find the square. There is a **card-phone** on the paved road after Zarkada. **Buses** go to Ioannina (1½hr., 2 per day, 700dr). **Telephone code:** 0653.

Lodging in Monodendri is plentiful and generally extremely well-priced given its quality. The **Xenonas Ladias**, a castle-like structure at the entrance to the village, offers resplendent modern rooms (singles 5000dr; doubles 10,000dr). A bit farther down the road are **Zarkada** (tel. 71 305 or 71 405; fax 71 505) and **Pension Monodendri** (tel. 71 300), which both have cozy rooms for good prices (singles 6000dr; doubles 8000dr).

Interspersed among these pensions on the main road are a few *tavernas*. The best and always the most crowded is the one on the porch of the Pension Monodendri (tel. 71 300). The owner and his wife both speak fluent German and prepare a lamb *kleftiko* or *lemonato* that absolutely melts in your mouth.

There's not much to see or do in Monodendri beyond looking at the distinctive architecture, breathing the fresh mountain air, and stocking up for a foray into Vikos Gorge. However, for those unwilling to tackle the gorge—or perhaps just anxious for a preview of what is to come—the **Monastery of Agia Paraskevi**, about 600m from the square, offers majestic views of the gaping canyon below.

■ Vikos Gorge Βικος

Although few speak of Vikos Gorge in the same breath as the Grand Canyon, Vikos surpasses its famous peer in at least one respect; according to the Guinness Book of World Records, the Vikos Gorge, whose walls are 900m deep but only 1100m apart, is the steepest canyon on earth. The canyon was formed over millions of years by the Vikos River, which still trickles along the 15km stretch of canyon floor. It is most often entered from Monodendri, but can also be accessed from the Papingo villages.

A note about the Vikos Gorge: if possible, do not hike alone. Most maps of the gorge are fairly inaccurate, and illegal Albanian immigrants can, on occasion, pose a threat to solitary travelers. Bring water and wear serious hiking boots.

To reach the gorge from Monodendri, take the marked path from the square. After about 40 minutes along the steep descending trail, you'll reach a fork in the path. Go left to enter the canyon (to the right, about an hour away, lies the little village of Kypi with its trademark stone bridges). The hike along the gorge is a rather long four-and-a-half hours, but is impressive enough to keep you going; the nearly vertical canyon-sides, onto which throngs of stubborn trees cling, tower hundreds of meters over your head. The trail is in good shape and is easy to follow; red circles and red diamonds on white square backgrounds with the term "O3" stenciled on them consistently mark the path. After your hours in the gorge (5½ hours from Monodendri), water suddenly begins to gush from the previously bone-dry river-bed. These Void-homatis Springs, the place to replenish your water supply, mark a major crossroads.

About an hour's hike past the springs, you'll reach the little hamlet of **Vikos,** which has only one rather expensive spot for lodging: rooms rented by **Sotiris Karpouzis** (tel. 41 176; 12,000dr). To reach more affordable lodging, turn right at the intersection, and after an arduous 90-minute ascent you'll find the twin villages of **Megalo Papingo** and **Mikro Papingo.** On the hike up, check out the eerie pillars of stone on the mountainside, which resemble miniature replicas of the rocks of the Meteora.

■ Megalo Papingo Μεγαλο Παπινγο

The two Papingo villages are the most developed of the Zagorohoria. Their position at the end of the Vikos Gorge ensures their popularity with backpackers and independent travelers. In recent years, Megalo Papingo, the larger of the two, has also become a favorite spot for vacationing Greek families—so much so that the village boasts seventeen separate lodging choices, while most of the 46 Zagorohoria don't have seventeen full-time residents. Luckily, commercialization hasn't stolen the Papingo villages' charm. The gray stone houses are a visual treat, as are the rock pools located about 300m away from Megalo Papingo.

Megalo Papingo is basically organized around one long north-south street, on which most of the pensions and restaurants are located, as well as a functioning church and a helpful **tourist office** (tel. 41 931). **Buses** go to Ioannina (2hr., 6 per week, 1050dr). Megalo Papingo has a phone and a mailbox, both on its main street.

Because of its popularity with rich Greeks, lodging in Papingo is extremely expensive. The best deal is the 120-year-old **Astraka** (tel. 41 693), whose rooms have a bath, fireplace, and thick crimson carpets (singles 6000dr; doubles 12,000dr). The rest of the hotels in town all have prices starting at 10,000dr a night, though a better deal may be reached by bargaining with one of many proprietors of rented rooms. Food in Papingo, like lodging, is pretty expensive. **Restaurant Papingo** (tel. 41 121), at the south end of the main road, is the most popular place in town.

If you wish to do more in the outdoors of Epirus than hike the Vikos Gorge, the Center for Visitor Information can provide you with more information. About three hours from Papingo is a **refuge** (tel. 41 115), open from May 20 to October 30, for tired hikers (2500dr). From there, hike to the nearby Dracolimni (dragon-lake), or climb Mount Astraka (20min. away) or Mount Gamila (three hours from refuge).

Ionian Islands
Νησια Του Ιονιου

Somewhere between Calabria and Corfu the blue really begins.
—Lawrence Durrell

The Ionian islands have shared an historic fate distinct from mainland Greece. Situated on the country's western edge, the islands escaped Ottoman occupation, and were instead conquered at various times by Venetians, British, French, and Russians. Each of the Ionians' uninvited visitors left a lasting cultural, commercial, and architectural imprint. Because of their status as a British protectorate until 1864 and an Italian occupation during WWII, the islands are comparatively wealthy. Historical ties make the islands a favorite among Brits and Italians, as well as with ferry-hopping backpackers who make the short trip from Italy.

🖐 HIGHLIGHTS OF THE IONIAN ISLANDS

- Weave your way through the British and Italian churches, fortresses and palaces of the old town on **Corfu** (p. 238).
- Dionysus and Eros wrestle for the souls of hedonistic revelers at **Kavos** (p. 239) and on **Corfu's north coast** (p. 241).
- Trace the footsteps of archaeologists trying to determine the true home of Odysseus on the islands of **Ithaka** (p. 248) and **Lefkada** (p. 245).
- Investigate the caves, lakes and myriad natural anomalies of earthquake-ridden **Cephalonia** (p. 251).

CORFU Κερκυρα

Corfu's luscious beauty has delighted visitors and enchanted writers for millennia. Homer was the first to sing Corfu's praises, when in the *Odyssey,* Odysseus commented on the fertility and beauty of the land. Over the centuries, writers such as Goethe, Wilde, and the Durrell brothers and artists such as Sisley and Lear immortalized the island in their prose and paintings. Cultural luminaries were not the only ones attracted to Corfu; imperialist Franks, Venetians, and British also coveted the island for its natural charms and strategic location. Each occupying power left a distinct mark on the culture and architecture of the island.

Today, visitors to Corfu Town amble throughout the shuttered alleyways of a Neoclassical Venice, stroll along a Parisian esplanade, and sip tea while watching cricket on the grounds of a British imperial palace. Outside of Corfu Town, the emphasis is not so much on tradition or history as on debauchery—beaches, drinking, and nighttime revelry. Resort towns in the north—Dassia, Gouvia, Sidari, and Kassiopi—as well as Benitses and the infamous Kavos in the south are thronged with young, tanned, mostly inebriated Brits and Italians. Fortunately, the hedonistic mayhem has declined a bit in recent years, and Corfu's fine sandy beaches, sparkling blue waters, and verdant flower-strewn hillsides are now more accessible than ever.

◼ Corfu Town

Corfu Town is the logical base for touring the island, as all ferries and most buses originate here. At the new port, a barrage of tourist agents proffering scooters, ferry tickets, and rooms greets every arrival. Beyond the frenzy of the harbor is an old-fashioned town brimming with tradition and elegance. A pair of Venetian fortresses

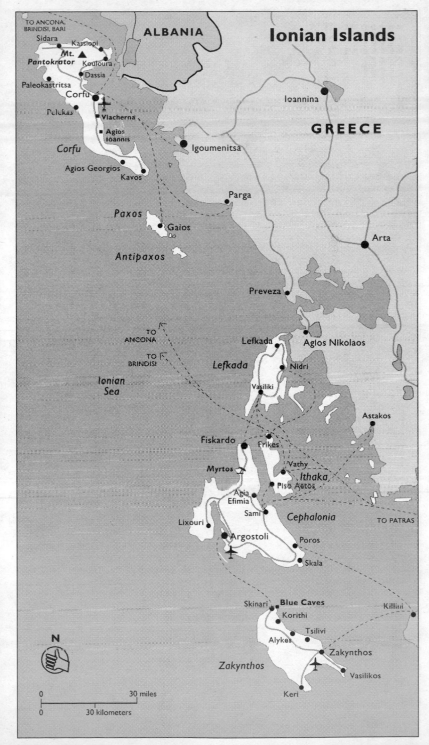

TO ANCONA,
BRINDISI, BARI

ALBANIA

Ionian Islands

Sidara

Kassiopi

Mt.
Pantokrator

Kouloura

Dassia

Ioannina

Paleokastritsa

Corfu

GREECE

Pelekas

Vlacherna

Agios
Ioannis

Corfu

Igoumenitsa

Agios Georgios

Kavos

Parga

Paxos

Gaios

Arta

Antipaxos

Preveza

TO
ANCONA

Lefkada

Agios Nikolaos

TO
BRINDISI

Lefkada

Nidri

Ionian
Sea

Vasiliki

Astakos

Fiskardo

Frikes

Myrtos

Vathy

Ithaka

Agia
Efimia

Piso Aetos

Sami

Cephalonia

TO PATRAS

Lixouri

Argostoli

Poros

Skala

Skinari

Blue Caves

Killini

Korithi

Tsilivi

Alykes

Zakynthos

Zakynthos

Vasilikos

Keri

N

0   30 miles

0   30 kilometers

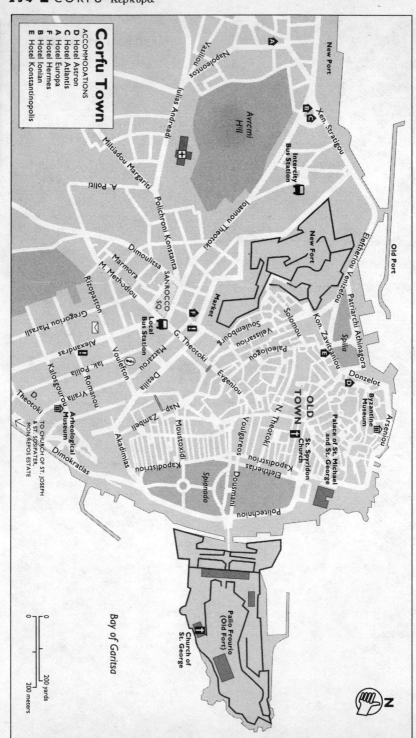

Corfu Town

ACCOMMODATIONS
D Hotel Astron
C Hotel Atlantis
A Hotel Europa
F Hotel Hermes
B Hotel Ionian
E Hotel Konstantinopolis

New Port

Old Port

Avemi Hill

New Fort

Intercity Bus Station

Napoleontos Vasiliou

Iulias Andreadi

Miltiadou Margariti

A. Politi

Polichroni Konstanta

Ioannou Theotoki

Dimoulitsa

SAN ROCCO SQ.

Marmora

M. Methodiou

Rizopaston

Gregoriou Marasli

Alexandras

Voulefton

Iak. Polila

Vralia Romanou

Kalosgourou

Arheologikal Museum

D. Theotoki

Dimokratias

Akadimias

Kapodistrion

Moustoxidi

N. Zambeli

Desila

Mavzarou

G. Theotoki

Local Bus Station

Market

Souleimbourti

Velissariou

Paleologou

Eugeniou

Solomou

Kon. Zavitsianou

Spilia

Donzelot

Byzantine Museum

Arseniou

Palace of St. Michael and St. George

St. Spyridon Church

N. Theotoki

Voulgareos

Eleftherias Kapodistrion

Dousmani

Spianda

Politechniou

OLD TOWN

Eleftheriou Venizelou

Patriarchi Athinagora

Xen. Stratgou

TO CHURCH OF ST. JOSEPH & ST. SOSIPATER, MON. KEPOS ESTATE

Bay of Garitsa

Palio Frourio (Old Fort)

Church of St. George

N

0 200 yards

0 200 meters

loom over Corfu Town, giving it a dramatic medieval feel. Narrow winding lanes and century-old houses near the Spianada and Sanrocco Square present a mesmerizing mix of Byzantine, Venetian, and Greek architecture. The numerous junkshops and their magnetically attracted tourists have done away with any pretense of innocence, but have not destroyed the charm of Corfu Town's narrow streets, pastel and white neoclassical buildings, brilliant pink flowers, stray cats, and errant classicists.

ORIENTATION AND PRACTICAL INFORMATION

Prepare to familiarize yourself with the Theotokos family. Four of Corfu's main streets are named after members of this clan; you may pass from **N.** to **M.** to **G.** to **I.** Theotoki Street without even realizing it. Corfu Town is built on a peninsula that juts northeast into the Ionian Sea. On the north coast of town find both the **new and old ports.** The **New Fortress,** behind which sits Corfu's intercity **bus station,** separates the two. The old town, at the center of historic Corfu, is a beautiful and befuddling tangle of alleyways whose western edge is marked by the **Spianada,** an esplanade dotted with chic and expensive cafes. To the east of the Spianada are the massive stone walls and fortifications of the **Old Fortress.** To reach the Spianada from the old port, simply follow the waterfront road right, walk through the arch of the British palace, and you will see the long set of cafes straight ahead and the park to the left. From there, any right will lead into the maze. From the new port, follow the same strategy, or turn inland onto Avraniou St., which becomes I. Theotoki St. This leads you past **Sanrocco Square,** site of the city bus terminal. Turn left along G. Theotoki St., and head into old town. Any reasonably straight walk will bring you to the Spianada, the old fortress, and eventually the water.

Transportation

Ferries: Get your tickets a day early in high season, especially to Italy—even deck-class sells out. Find out if the port tax is included in the price of your ticket when traveling to foreign ports. **Corfu Mare** (tel. 32 467), at the new port beneath the Ionian Hotel, sells tickets. For updates on ferry schedules, contact the **port police** (tel. 38 425), in the customs house along the port, or the **port authority** (tel. 32 655 or 40 002). Agents for the various shipping companies line Xen. Stratigou St., opposite the new port, so shop here for the lowest fares. Try **Fragline** and **Minoan** to Brindisi (8hr., 4 per day, 5600-11,500dr) and Patras (9hr., 2 per day, 5800dr). **Adriatica** and **Hellenic Mediterranean** recognize Eurail and Inter rail passes. Ferries sail for Ancona (23hr., 3 per day, 15,800dr); Bari (10hr., 1 per day, 12,000dr); and Venice (26hr., 1-2 per day, 15,800-19,800dr).

Flights: Tickets at 20 Kapodistriou St. (tel. 39 910; airport 32 468), on the Spianada. A taxi ride takes only 5min. and is the only way to get to the airport unless your hotel or tour group has buses (before getting in, agree on a fare of roughly 1500dr). Planes go to Athens (50min., 3 per day, 20,400dr) and Thessaloniki (2 per week, 20,800dr). Almost 50 charter flights a day in summer also fly through Corfu's crowded airport. In summer, book 2-3 days ahead.

Buses: KTEL, behind the New Port on Avraniou St. (tel. 30 627 or 39 985). Pick up a handy timetable available at the station or from tourist agencies. Schedules for the main KTEL line are also posted on a billboard outside the new office behind Corfu Town's new fortress, from which the green KTEL buses leave. **Blue buses** (city buses) leave from Sanrocco Sq., where schedules are printed on the signs, to Paleokastritsa (10 per day, 420dr); Glyfada Beach (10 per day, 300dr); Kavos (11 per day, 800dr); Kassiopi (4 per day, 500dr), Sidari (11 per day, 600dr); Athens (3 per day, 7900dr); and Thessaloniki (1-2 per day, 7700dr). Buy tickets for Corfu destinations on the bus; all others in the bus station. Open daily 5:30am-8pm.

City Buses: #10 to Achilleon from Sanrocco Sq. (6 per day), #6 to Benitses (13 per day), #7 to Dassia (7 per day), #11 to Pelekas (7 per day). Fares for city buses range from 140dr to 200dr. Less Sunday service. For information call 31 595 or ask at the booths in Sanrocco Sq. Schedules are seldom posted, so ask for one.

Taxis: (tel. 33 811). At the old port, the Spianada, Sanrocco Sq., and G. Theotoki St. Available by telephone 24hr.

Car Rental: A Fiat Panda should cost 12,000-13,000dr per day. Make sure quoted prices include the 20% tax. Third-party insurance is also usually included. International license required. Agencies along Xen. Stratigou St. all rent for roughly

10,000dr per day. International car rental at **Greek Skies,** 20 Kapodistriou St. (tel. 33 410), has good prices, but requires you be 23 or older. Full payment in advance or major credit card required. Open M-F 8:30am-1:30pm and 5:30-8:30pm, Sa-Su 8:30am-1:30pm.

Moped Rental: A popular way to see the island—rental places abound. Don't pay more than 3000-4000dr per day. Make sure the brakes work and get a helmet. Rental fee should include third-party liability and property damage insurance.

Tourist and Financial Services

National Tourist Office: (tel. 37 520) At the corner of Rizospaston Voulefton St. and Iak. Folila St. The building is marked, and a sign directs you to the first floor (which is really the second floor). Note that the information office has moved since the publication of even their own maps. Open May-Sept. M-F 7:30am-2:30pm.

British Consul: 1 Menekratous St. (tel. 30 055; fax 37 995), a few blocks down the street from the post office. Open M-F 8am-1pm. Call 39 211 in an emergency.

Banks: Banks with 24hr. **ATMs** line the larger streets and the waterfront by the ports, including **National Bank** on G. Theotoki St., near where it narrows and becomes Voulgareos. Open M-Th 8am-2pm and F 8am-1:30pm; for **currency exchange** July-Aug. M-F 4-6pm or 5:30-7:30pm, Sa 8:30am-1pm.

American Express: Greek Skies Travel, 20A Kapodistriou St., P.O. Box 24 (tel. 30 883 or 32 469), at the south end of the Spianada. Holds mail and cashes AmEx traveler's checks. Open M-F 8am-noon and 5:30-8:30pm, Sa 8am-noon.

Room-Finding Services: Tourist agencies along Arseniou St. and Stratigou St., by the new port, find rooms in pensions. Many operate without commission and have information on cheap lodgings. Most open daily 8:30am-1:30pm and 5:30-9pm. Singles from 4000dr; doubles from 5000dr; triples from 6000dr; add 1000-1500dr for private bath. Prices negotiable for longer stays. Ask at the tourist police for rooms or call the **Association of Owners of Private Rooms and Apartments in Corfu** (tel. 26 133; fax 23 403), in the heart of the old town.

Luggage Storage: on Avrami St., directly across from the new port and above the bank on your right (400dr per day). Open 9am-10pm.

Laundromat: 42 I. Theotoki St. (tel. 35 304), just past Sanrocco Sq. Wash and dry 2500dr per basket. Open M-Sa 9am-2pm, and Tu and Th-F 5:30-8pm.

Public Toilets: on the Spianada near the pavilion, and in Sanrocco Sq. Those on the Spianada are clean and wheelchair accessible.

Emergency and Communications

Tourist Police: (tel. 30 265). Walk along G. Theotaki St. in the direction of Sanrocco Sq., with the old town at your back. Turn right on I. Theotaki and take the first right; they're on the 4th floor. Open daily 7am-2:30pm.

Police: (tel. 39 509)**,** in same building as tourist police.

Hospital: Corfu General Hospital (tel. 45 811, 45 812, or 45 813; 24hr. emergency room 25 400). Walk down G. Theotoki St., turn right at I. Theotoki St., and when the road splits into 3 after one block, choose the middle course, Poluchroniou Koustanta St. After 3 blocks this road forks. Bear right onto Iulias Andreadi St. and look right. For a list of English-speaking doctors, call the Medical Association of Corfu (tel. 39 615) or the tourist office. For an **ambulance,** call 166.

Post Office: (tel. 25 544), on the corner of Alexandras St. and Voulefton St. Walk down G. Theotaki and turn left at Sanrocco Sq. The post office is in the yellow buildings, 2 blocks down on your right. Open M-F 8am-8pm for stamps and Poste Restante, M-F 7:30am-2:30pm for all else. **Postal Code:** 49100.

OTE: Main office at 9 Mantzarou St., off A. Theotoki St. Open daily 9am-midnight. Card phones on the Spianada and in white mobile buildings at the old and new ports. **Telephone Codes:** Corfu Town 0661; south Corfu 0662; north Corfu 0663.

ACCOMMODATIONS

Accommodations in Corfu Town are scarce, expensive, and scattered throughout the town. Hotels near the water fill up first, especially in high season, and the effectiveness of bargaining diminishes later in the day. Prices drop in the off season, and pension owners discount longer stays. Consider finding a room in a base town and taking advantage of Corfu's bus service for daytrips around the island. A good starting point is any one of the **room finding services** along the port. Although rooms to let will provide the best accommodations at the best prices, it is easier to reserve a hotel room.

🖑**Hotel Europa,** 10 Giantsilio (tel. 39 304). Head west along the coast toward the Igoumenitsa port, bear left on Xenofonto Stratigou St. right after Hotel Atlantis, and then take your fourth left. The rooms here are clean and comfortable (though hot), very well located (next to the New Port), and the best-priced in Corfu Town. Singles 4000dr, with bath 7000dr; doubles 7000dr, triples 9000dr.

Hotel Ionian, 46 Xen. Sratigou St. (tel. 39 915 or 30 628), at the new port, offers inexpensive rooms with green turf-carpet suited for mini-golf and life-saving fans. Singles 7000dr; doubles 10,000dr, triples 12,000dr.

Hotel Hermes, 14 Rue G. Markora (tel. 39 268; fax 31 747). Clean, spacious rooms with bath by the daily market. Singles 8500dr; doubles 10,500dr; triples 12,500dr.

Hotel Astron, 15 Donzelot St. (tel. 39 505), on the waterfront to the left (facing inland) from the new port. Has clean traditional rooms with TV, phone, fan, and bath. Singles 10,000dr; doubles 18,000dr.

Hotel Atlantis, 48 Xen. Stratigou St. (tel. 35 560), at the new port. Large carpeted rooms have A/C, baths, and satellite TV. Singles 12,000dr; doubles 17,000dr.

Hotel Konstantinoupolis, 1 Zavitsianou St. (tel. 48 716 or 48 717), on the waterfront. A beautiful neoclassical building with recently renovated blue-hued rooms with TV, phone, bath. Singles 12,000dr; doubles 19,000dr; triples 23,000dr.

FOOD

The premier restaurant areas are at the two ends of N. Theotoki St., near the Spianada and by the old port. Most places serve lunch outdoors until 3pm and dinner until 11pm. Tourist police strictly regulate all restaurants in town, so the prices are fair and the cuisine monotonous. While in Corfu, try the local meat specialties: *sofrito* and *pastitsiada*. For a visual treat and fresh, inexpensive produce, head to the daily **open-air market** on Dessila St., near the base of the New Fortress (open 6am-2pm). *Gyro* stands abound (350dr), but you might try the delicious tomato and feta sandwiches (500dr) at the **Art Cafe,** in a garden behind the Palace of St. Michael and St. George. Below the palace on a small pier, a yellow building has been converted to the **En Plo Cafe** and **Faliraki Restaurant,** where you can enjoy a cup of coffee or dinner by the sea. They are in old town, one block off the Spianada.

🖑**Restaurant Bellissimo,** 2 Kyriaki St. (tel. 41 112), off N. Theotoki St. Coming from the Spianada, look for their sign and turn right on the alleyway to Kyriaki St. In a quiet square of its own. Nicely priced: stuffed vegetables 900dr, *sofrita* 1400dr.

Faliraki Restaurant, on the corner of Kapodistriou and Arseniou St. Offers innovative entrees (1800-2200dr) and beautiful views of the sunset over the Ionian Sea, while the waves virtually lap at your feet. Open daily.

Restaurant Rex, 66 Kapodistriou St. (tel. 39 649), one block back from the Spianada. A bit pricey, but long famed as one of Corfu's best restaurants. Try the stuffed rabbit or savory *stifado* (both 2200dr). Open daily.

🖑**Restaurant Andronik,** 21 Arseniou St. (tel. 38 858), on the northern waterfront. Established in 1920 by Armenian refugees, Andronik continues today to draw in large multi-ethnic crowds (entrees 1500-2200dr). Open daily.

Nautikon, 150 N. Theotoki St. (tel. 30 009), near the old port. A large place with appetizing food, some English-speaking staff, and 50 years of experience. Entrees 1400-1900dr. Open daily Apr.-Oct. noon-midnight.

Restaurant Skouna (tel. 36 949), on Mitropoleos Sq., just off Donzelot St. on the waterfront. Has friendly staff who like to talk politics and a wide variety of dishes.

ENTERTAINMENT

The undisputed focus of Corfu Town's nightlife is the so-called **Disco Strip,** on the waterfront on Ethnikis Antistaseos St., about 2km west of the new port. The many bars and clubs on the strip bustle with Greeks and a multicultural crowd of tourists. British general don't frequent the strip, going instead to Anglicized hangouts elsewhere on the island. The **Coca Club** (tel. 34 477), built into the hillside, begins the mayhem of the strip. After Coca Club are the two biggest bars: the good ol' **Hard**

Rock Cafe (tel. 23 736) and the more popular **Electron** (tel. 26 793), located side by side on adjacent rooftops. Nearby, the sleazily named **Sodoma Club** plays mostly Greek tunes. At the end of the Disco Strip are the three most popular discos of Corfu: the massive two-in-one **Hippodrome** (tel. 43 150), where U.S. dance music is played outside and Greek music inside; the elaborately decorated and ominously named **Apocalypsis** (tel. 40 345), which boasts an array of pools; and the slightly smaller **Embargo Club** (tel. 31 153) at the very end of the strip. Cover at those clubs averages 2000dr with one drink. Inside, beers cost 1000-1500dr and cocktails 1500-2000dr.

For a more mellow night, head to the Spianada and its adjacent park; they stay alive until early morning. The demographics of a weekend evening lean heavily toward young girls and middle-aged tourists. Being seen in this posh hangout has its price—cafes charge double what those in less popular locales do. Wander off the main catwalk into the streets of the old town for less touristy alternatives. Several **open-air cinemas** screen English language films (1500dr). If you visit during Easter week, you'll witness the local tradition of smashing pottery to celebrate the Resurrection.

SIGHTS

Churches and Fortresses

Corfu's two most famous churches are the **Church of St. Jason and Sosipater** and the **Church of St. Spyridon.** *(Both churches open until 7pm.)* The former is a 12th-century Byzantine stone structure located in a fishing neighborhood on the way to Mon Repos Beach; to get there, continue past the archaeological museum along the waterfront. Dazzling silver and gold ornaments, medieval paintings, an impressive ceiling mural, and exquisite Byzantine icons are displayed. The church was once covered entirely by murals of saints, but the islanders painted over them to prevent their destruction by the Ottomans.

The Church of St. Spyridon, named for the island's patron saint, was built in 1590. Following plague outbreaks in the 17th century, residents of Corfu began parading the silver reliquary containing the remains of the saint around town every Palm Sunday and on the first Sunday of November. Each year St. Spyridon is given a new pair of slippers to replace the old pair he wears out wandering the island doing good deeds. In the right light, if you lift the gold cover, you can still see his oddly disconcerting grin beneath a black shroud behind the glass. St. Spyridon holds a **traditional festival,** with music and dancing on August 11. To find the church, take Ag. Spyridon off the Spianada; it's on your left.

Finished by the Venetians in the late 14th century, the **Palio Frourio** (tel. 48 311), just east of the Spianada, was thought to be impregnable. *(Open daily 8am-8pm. Admission 800dr, students 400dr.)* In 1864, however, the British blew it up before leaving Corfu to the Greeks. Along with much of Corfu Town, the castle's imposing fortifications were restored to some semblance of their one-time glory for the 1994 EU summit. On the grounds are the **Church of St. George,** now a museum and a **Byzantine Gallery** which possesses early mosaics and wall paintings.

The 375-year-old **New Fortress** (tel. 27 477), above the ferry ports, affords panoramic views of Corfu Town ideal for sun-drenched picnics. *(Open daily 9am-9pm. Admission 400dr.)* The fort houses a small gallery of etchings, maps, and watercolors with nautical motifs, as well as an additional gallery with contemporary exhibits.

Museums and Archaeological Sites

At the north end of the Spianada stands the **Palace of St. Michael and St. George** (tel. 30 443). *(Open Tu-Sa 8:30am-3pm, Su 9:30am-2:30pm. Admission 500dr.)* Unmistakably British, the palace was built as the residence of the Lord High Commissioner but now houses a pair of museums. The more interesting one is the unique (at least in Greece) **Sino-Japanese Museum,** which houses a range of Oriental artifacts collected by diplomat Gregorios Manos. The second museum is the recently opened **Modern Art Museum,** which contains a small but steadily expanding collection of Corfuit painting. *(Open daily 9am-9pm. Admission 300dr, students 100dr.)* The **Archaeological Museum,** 1 Vraila St. (tel. 30 680), on the waterfront south of the Spianada, contains relics of the island's Mycenaean and classical past. *(Open Tu-Su 8am-2:30pm. Admission 800dr, students and seniors 400dr, children and EU students free.)* The collection's highlight is the magnificent **Gorgon Pediment,** taken from a temple to Artemis. The pediment, which is housed in its own room, shows the Gorgon giving birth to the **Centaur** and **Chrysaor** at the moment when her head is cut off.

Down N. Theotoki from the Spianada lies the Ionian Bank Building, which houses a **museum of paper currency** (tel. 41 552). *(Open M-Sa 9am-1pm. Free.)* Advertising itself as "one of the most interesting museums of its kind in the world," it is home to the first bank note printed in Greece and is recommended by *Let's Go: Greece* for fanatical finance capitalists. Behind the old port lies the **Jewish Quarter.** The **synagogue,** on Velissariou St., served the Jewish community from its construction in 1537 until 1940, when 5000 Jews were gathered on the Spianada and sent to Auschwitz.

Corfu's most recently opened sight is the **Mon Repos Estate,** given by the British government to the Greek royal family in 1864. Since the royals' exile in 1967, the lovely neoclassical palace has fallen into disrepair, and large gardens filled with rare trees are overgrown. The grounds are now open to the public, largely because they contain two Doric temples: the rather decrepit **Temple to Hera** and the more impressive **Temple to Artemis.** Just before the gated entrance to the estate is the entrance to the **Monastery of Agios Efthimeaos.** *(Open daily 8am-1pm and 5-8pm.)* On the opposite side of the road is the **Archaeological Site of Paleopolis Roman Baths,** closed to the public but visible through the fence. The **Byzantine Museum** houses a vast collection of icons by Cretan school painters in the converted church of Kyra Antivouniotissa along the waterfront between the Spianada and the New Port. *(Open Tu-Su 8am-2:30pm. Admission 500dr, students and seniors 300dr, EU students free.)* Look for the sign or the steps leading up to the building.

■ Eastern Corfu

The east coast of Corfu is by far the most developed and least aesthetically pleasing part of the island. The first 20km north of Corfu Town in particular have become thoroughly Anglicized by throngs of rowdy British expats. **Gouvia** and **Dassia** are the first two resorts north of town; both thrive off package tourism despite meager beaches. A bit farther north is the notorious little town of **Ipsos.** Come here to drink your nights (and days) away in any of the countless bars and discos.

In the village of **Gastouri,** 9km south of Corfu Town, is the gaudy **Achillion Palace.** *(Open daily 9am-4pm. Admission 1000dr, students 500dr.)* Eccentric, ostentatious, and lovely, it was commissioned by Empress Elizabeth of Austria as a summer residence in honor of Achilles and Thetis. The Empress was obsessed with Achilles, probably due to the death of her favorite son, whom she felt resembled the god. Kaiser Wilhelm II of Germany spent his summers here until WWI diverted his attention. The gardens and view are especially cinematic; the 1981 James Bond flick *For Your Eyes Only* was filmed here. Take bus #10 from Sanrocco Sq. (30min., 6 per day, 200dr).

■ Southern Corfu

Southern Corfu is home to some of the island's most serene beaches, as well as much of its most inebriated revelry. It was the first part of Corfu to develop mass tourism and still holds crowds of drunken British tourists, primarily in **Benitses** and **Kavos.** Benitses was once much wilder than it is today; new ordinances against noise, public intoxication, and pollution have reduced the town's once legendary excesses and restored a touch of traditional Greek charm. Further south is **Messongi,** another British-dominated place devoted to tanning, drinking, and dancing. The massive **Messongi Beach Hotel** (tel. 38 684), Corfu's largest, dominates the town.

Kavos

At the far southern tip of Corfu is Kavos, the one resort that has not experienced a decline in tourism in recent years. Kavos enjoys legendary status in Corfu for its unrestrained hedonistic mayhem; bars, discos, and pool halls line its one long main street. If you want decent beaches, drunken cavorting all night long, and not a hint of Greek culture, tradition, or language, crazy Kavos is *the* place to go to on Corfu.

Kavos has one main road located just inland from the beach; everything in town is on this manic mile-long stretch of gaudy neon. A **doctor** (tel. 61 497) can be reached 24 hours a day across from Chaplin's Bar. **Pandis Travel Agency** (tel. 61 400 or 61 001) and others handle excursions, accommodations, and rental cars (open daily 9am-11pm). Because Kavos' population shrinks to 500 in winter, there is no National Bank, OTE, or post office in town. **Postal code:** 49080. **Telephone code:** 0662.

Lodging in Kavos is a hit-or-miss affair. Most hotels are booked by package tour operators and are often completely full in high season. Rented rooms, on the other hand, are ubiquitous and fairly cheap. **Lefkimi Hotel** (tel. 61 188) has clean rooms (7000dr). Nearby, the more luxurious **Kavos Hotel** (tel. 61 514 or 61 107) tantalizes visitors with a lovely pool and large clean rooms (singles 9500dr; doubles 12,000dr). For rented rooms, ask around and expect to pay 3000-5000dr for a single, 5000-8000dr for a double, and 7000-11,000dr for a triple.

Food in Kavos is far more British than Greek; restaurants with names such as The British Restaurant and Her Majesty's Grill vie to be the most Anglo-Saxon spot in town. For fare at least a little Greek, try the *yiouvetsi* at the **Knife and Fork Restaurant** (tel. 61 183) or the standard Greek repertoire at **Taverna O Pavlos.**

Nightlife in Kavos has to be seen to be believed. Enormous crowds of young Brit revelers absolutely flood the entire main street, bars and clubs—especially those broadcasting UK Football—are so packed that you can't lift an elbow, and the shouts and songs of partiers fill the air. From east to west the most popular bars in Kavos are **Empire, Rolling Stone** (which doubles as a disco), **Memphis,** the karaoke-playing **Sammy's Bar,** the lushly decorated **Jungle,** and the enormous **The Barn.** The town's four discos, none of which charge cover, are **Rolling Stone, Time, Whiskers,** and **Limelight,** the biggest and most popular of the group.

Corfu's British Son

Lawrence Durrell was born the child of British colonialism in India in 1912. He was sent to England to be educated but recoiled from his motherland, dubbing it the "Pudding Isle." When the rest of his family moved back from the East, he suggested they ditch their stuffy homeland for the sun and sand of Corfu, until recently a British colony itself. In 1935, at age 23, Durrell landed on Corfu with his wife, mother, sister and two brothers. Durrell came of age on the island and called it a rebirth from the "English Death." He and his brother Gerald paid tribute to the island in books—Lawrence's poetic, Shakespeare-entwined *Prospero's Cell* and Gerald's jovial *My Family and Other Animals.* Among their friends and visitors were the Greek Nobel Laureate George Seferis and Henry Miller, who abandoned his habitual obscenities to write what some reckon to be the greatest travelogue of our time, *The Colossus of Maroussi.* Durrell was exiled from Greece by Hitler's invasion to Egypt, which inspired his most renowned work, *The Alexandria Quartet.* After the war, Durrell returned to the Greek isles, writing about Rhodes in *Reflections on a Marine Venus* and Cyprus (where he served in the colonial government) in *Bitter Lemons.* Durrell's writings glow with a spiritual bond to the landscape, people, and history of Greece.

■ Western Corfu

Swimming on Corfu's west coast is like being trapped inside an all-blue kaleidoscope. The **Paleokastritsa beach,** next to the coast's premier resort, rests among some of the lovelier scenery in Greece, with six small coves and sea caves casting shadows over shades of blue. Renting a pedal boat is the best way to visit the caves where Odysseus supposedly washed ashore. The 13th-century fort of **Angelokastro** sits above the town, while a natural balcony, **Bella Vista,** rests halfway up. Jutting out over the sea is the bright white **Panagia Theotokos Monastery** with a collection of Byzantine icons, spectacular views, and the skeleton of a sea monster. Come as early as possible because by mid-morning it is a mess of tour buses. **Buses** run to Paleokastritsa from behind the new fortress (45min., 10 per day, 420dr).

Pelekas is ideal for watching sunsets over whitewashed villages in the hillsides. **Pelekas Beach,** a 30-minute downhill walk from town, attracts a large number of backpackers. Don't attempt to make the harrowing journey by moped. Bus #11 runs to Pelekas Town from Sanrocco Sq. (7 per day, 190dr). **Glyfada Beach,** 5km up the coast from Pelekas Town, is served directly by the Glyfada bus from behind the new fortress (8 per day, 300dr). It is far more touristed than Pelekas, but still picturesque. Both beaches, bracketed by scrubby cliffs, are remarkably shallow.

A little north of Glyfada, accessible via dirt path off the main Pelekas road, lie the isolated beaches of **Moni Myrtidon** and **Myrtiotissa,** extolled by Lawrence Durrell as the most beautiful beaches in the world. A section of sand at Myrtiotissa is the island's unofficial nude beach. Everything here is very casual, although once in a while the local monks from the **Monastery of Our Lady of the Myrtles** complain to the police, who reluctantly bring offending nudists to court.

Accessible by bus (45min., 7 per day, 280dr), **Agios Gordios,** offers steep cliffs, impressive rock formations, and the immensely popular **Pink Palace** (tel. (0661) 53 024; fax 53 025). The pink-hued "palace" has the feel of a particularly cozy American frat party—no surprise, since most visitors are college-aged Americans and Canadians. Try to get to the Pink Palace on a weekend, when wild toga parties and the smashing of plates conjure scenes from *Animal House.* Rooms vary significantly in quality (6000dr per person includes breakfast, dinner, and nightclub entrance).

■ Northern Corfu

The Kassiopi bus serves the northern coast. It leaves from the bus station and stops at every hamlet along the way (1¼hr., 8 per day, 600dr). Past Pirgi, the road begins to wind below steep cliffs. **Mt. Pantokrator,** on your left, towers 1000m above, while dramatic vistas of Albania come into view across the straits. After passing through Nis-

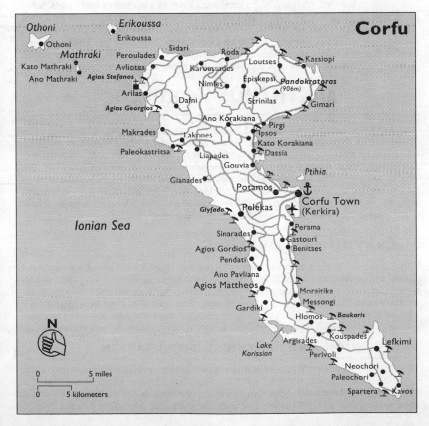

Travel Advisory: Albania

On June 10, 1997, the U.S. State Department issued a **travel warning** advising against all unnecessary travel to Albania, and a **state of emergency** existed throughout that country at the time this book went to press. Violent turmoil infects much of the southern half of Albania, where several of the best archaeological sites are located. While improved relations between Greece and Albania have made Albania's Ionian coast accessible to tourists from Corfu, *Let's Go: Greece* discourages people from traveling to Albania until the political situation improves.

---

saki and Gimari you will reach **Kouloura,** 28km north of Corfu, with its Venetian manor-house, pebbled beach, marina, and matchless *taverna.* The right fork to **Kalami** meanders down to a sandier beach where, in the 1930s, author Lawrence Durrell lived with his family, including his wacky brother Gerald. His small white house can still be seen, from the outside at least. Buy the brothers' Corfu-inspired books—Lawrence's *Prospero's Cell* and Gerald's *My Family and Other Animals*—in **Lychoudis Bookstore.** Rooms are available for rent in both towns. The walk to Kalami or Kouloura from the main road takes 15 minutes.

Although Emperors Tiberius and Nero of Rome once vacationed here, all traces of ancient Greece and Rome have been erased by the development of tourism on the north coast. Kassiopi is one of the north coast's premier party resorts—**Kalamionas, Pipitos,** and **Kanoni** beaches and bustling nightclubs draw hordes each summer.

Even more busy is **Sidari,** on the far northwestern corner of the island. Sidari's sprawling golden beach and picture-perfect sandstone coves—called the **Canal d'Amour**—are among the most breathtaking sights in Corfu. Unfortunately for the independent traveler, package tour companies such as Thomson's and First Choice book almost all of Sidari's hotels and rooms; this may be the one place on Corfu where if you don't call ahead, you *really* won't find a room. Sidari's heavy tourism makes it a rowdy place at night; try **Oh La La** or **Caesar's** for dancing. The large numbers of families here and less than uniformly British population, however, make Sidari's late-night antics a bit less scandalous than those of towns like Kavos.

ZAKYNTHOS Ζακυνθος

A tour of Zakynthos's varied land and seascapes reveals an exceptional palette of colors—white cliffs rising from turquoise water, sun-bleached wheat waving in the shadows of evergreens, and magenta flowers framing the twisting streets. If you remain in Zakynthos Town or on its neighboring beaches, however, all you'll see are the sweaty backs of other tourists. Zakynthos's best natural sights, including the famous blue caves, are in the north of the island; anyone who ventures there will understand why the discriminating Lord Byron so loved the island, and why the Venetians christened Zakynthos "Fior di Levante," the flower of the east.

■ Zakynthos Town

Tidy Zakynthos Town welcomes visitors to the east coast of the island with arcaded streets and whitewashed buildings. After an earthquake destroyed it in 1953, locals restored the city to its former state, making an effort to maintain the Venetian architecture in areas like the spacious Solomou Square, to the right of the boat landing. It's a pretty town, but not without its share of unsightly tourist shops. With all the other opportunities available, you may want to head for more remote beaches in the north.

ORIENTATION AND PRACTICAL INFORMATION

The waterfront runs between **Solomou Square** at the right end (facing inland) and Agios Dionysios Church at the left end. Each end has a port at which boats from the mainland dock. **Lombardou St.** runs along the water between the two ports and is lined with restaurants, gift shops, and ferry agencies. The first street parallel to Lombardou away from the water is **Filita St.**, home to the bus station. Behind it are, in order, **Foskolou St., Alexandrou Roma St.** (the main shopping street), and **Tertseti St.** Three blocks inland from stately Solomou Sq. is **Agiou Markou Square,** a gathering spot with outdoor restaurants and cafes.

Transportation

Ferries: arrive at Zakynthos Town port from Killini (1½hr., 4-6 per day, 1400dr) and also from Ag. Nikolaos on their way to Pesado in Cephalonia (1½hr., 2 per day, 950dr). Tickets available at the **boat agencies** along the waterfront. For more information, call the **port police** (tel. 28 117).

Buses: 42 Filita St. (tel. 22 255), on the corner of Eleftheriou St., 6 blocks along the water from Solomou Sq., then 1 block inland. 4 buses per day go to Patras (3hr., 2850dr) and on to Athens (6hr., 4500dr); they piggyback on the ferry to Killini (ferry ticket is included in the price). Schedules for local service posted outside the bus station; a complete list is available at the information window. Buses run to Vasiliko and Porto Roma (4 per day, 280dr); Alykes (5per day, 280dr); Argasi (9 per day, 220dr); Tsilivi (11 per day, 220dr); Laganas (15 per day, 220dr); Kalamaki (8 per day, 220dr); Schinari and Korithi, a.k.a. Agios Nikolaos (2 per day, 650dr); and Keri Lake (2 per day, 280dr). Full bus excursions around the island are 2500dr. Buses run less frequently on weekends and the schedule changes often, so ask for the updated schedule at the station information window.

Flights: The **airport** (tel. 28 322) is 6km south near Laganas. Flights to Athens (45min., 2 per day, 17,500dr, under 24 14,700dr). **Olympic Airways,** 16 Alex. Roma St. (tel. 28 611), is open M-F 8am-3:30pm.

Taxis: line the side streets off the waterfront (tel. 48 400; 24hr.).

Car Rental: Hertz, 38 Lombardou St. (tel. 45 706). Cars from 15,000dr per day. Many moped places also rent cars. Must be over 21 to rent cars. Open daily 8am-2pm and 5:30-9:30pm.

Moped Rental: Your best bet is **EuroSky Rentals** (tel. 26 278), one block inland from the water on A. Makri. They are the cheapest (2000dr per day) and may not hassle you with formalities. Open daily 8am-10pm.

Tourist and Financial Services

Banks: National Bank (tel. 44 113), on Solomou Sq., has **currency exchange** and an MC/Cirrus **24hr. ATM.** Open M-Th 8am-2pm, F 8am-1:30pm, Sa-Su 9am-1pm. Other ATMs on Alex Roma St. and Lombardou St.

Emergency and Communications

Police: (tel. 22 200), Lombardou St. and Fra. Tzoulati St., 5 blocks along the waterfront from Solomou Sq. Open 24hr.

Tourist police: (tel. 27 367). Speak English, answer questions, and can help find rooms. Open daily 9am-10pm.

Hospital: (tel. 42 514 or 42 515), above the city center. Walk down Lombardou St. until Ag. Eleftheriou. Follow this road inland until Kokkini St., where the road jogs right and becomes Ag. Spiridona. The hospital is at the end of this road (roughly 1km from the water). Open 24hr.

Post Office: (tel. 42 418), on an unnamed side street between Alex. Roma and Tertseti near Damiri St., but hard to find. Offers **currency exchange.** Open M-F 7:30am-8pm. **Postal Code:** 29100.

OTE: 2 Dimokratias, between the 2 squares. Open daily 7am-2:30pm. Offers **currency exchange** until 8pm. **Telephone Code:** 0695.

ACCOMMODATIONS

Rooms in Zakynthos Town tend to be expensive and scarce in July and August. Look for the signs that advertise *domatia,* and bargain in the off-season.

Hotel Egli, on Lombardou St., is two blocks from Solomou Sq. and has large, clean rooms. Singles 5000dr; doubles 8000dr.

Rooms for Rent on St. Lucas Sq. (tel 26 809) are on the waterfront, 2 blocks toward Agios Dionysios from the tourist police. Rooms are large and clean with private baths. Prices are negotiable. Singles 5000dr; doubles 8000dr.

FOOD

Finding food in Zakynthos is easy. Restaurants line the waterfront and Ag. Markou Sq., and every other establishment on Alexandrou Roma is a cafe or candy shop. Zakinthian specialities include *melissaki*, a nougat candy available at gift shops, and veal in tomato sauce. Fast food is ubiquitous, and a *gyro* will only cost you 400dr.

The Village Lion, on the waterfront, is a little pricey, but has unbeatable indoor and garden seating (with live music). Most servings are big enough to share (mixed grill dishes 2000-2800dr, salads 1400dr).

Molos Restaurant (tel. 27 309) is another popular waterfront joint (*moussaka* 1300dr, stuffed tomatoes 1200dr).

House of Latas (tel. 41 585) is 2km above the city (follow the signs to Bohalis) near the Venetian castle. Spectacular views of Zakynthos and live local music are available every evening. Try the grilled swordfish (1900dr) and you won't be disappointed. Open daily 9am-midnight.

Artos and Ugea Bakery (tel. 23 134), on the corner of Alex. Roma and D. Stefaniou, is the perfect place to stock up for a picnic. They sell drinks, ice cream, and a delicious selection of cookies (1400dr per kg) and breads (200dr per loaf).

Coop Supermarket (tel 22 262), on Lombardou near the police station, is well stocked. Open daily 8am-9pm.

SIGHTS

Zakynthos is famous for its **Church of Agios Dionysios,** named in honor of the island's patron saint. The church displays a silver chest which holds the saint's relics. The modest dress code is strictly enforced; a monk has long skirts to wrap around visitors clad in shorts. In Solomou Sq., the **Byzantine Museum** (tel. 42 714) houses two floors of icons from the "Ionian School," a distinctive local hybrid of Byzantine and Renaissance artistic styles, as well as elaborately carved iconostases, chalices, and miscellaneous church items. *(Open Tu-Su 8am-2:30pm. Admission 800dr; students free.)* If you enjoy a good hike, climb 2km above town to the **Venetian Castle** in which the 19th-century poet Dionysios Solomos wrote the words to the Greek national anthem. *(Open Tu-Su 8am-2:30pm.)* To get there, follow Tertseti St., later N. Koluva St., to the edge of town and then the signs uphill to Bohalis St. Turn left after 1km, and follow the signs for the Kastro. The hike affords panoramic views of the island.

■ Around Zakynthos

The terrain and beaches on Zakynthos will easily lure you away from the pleasant port town. It's possible to see the entire island, including the otherwise inaccessible **western cliffs,** by boat. Shop around for a cruise on Lombardou St. Most tours leave in the morning, but require a reservation the night before (about 6000dr). KTEL also offers a **bus tour** of the island every Wednesday and Saturday at 10:15am for 2500dr. **Boats** make excursions to the blue caves, turtle beach, and "Smuggler's Wreck." Inquire at the tourist police or agencies. To explore independently, tour the island by **moped**—there's at least one rental place at each beach—or by bus. Because the island is developing rapidly, many new roads won't appear on maps, so rely on a combination of road maps (400dr at gift shops) and asking directions.

Beaches

The beaches at **Laganas,** 10km south, have been mangled by large hotels, souvenir stands, and hordes of tourists. If you must stay, try **Laganas Camping** (tel. 51 708), which has a pool (1500dr per person; 900dr per car; 800dr per small tent; 1100dr per large tent). Unscathed beaches carpet the peninsula extending out to the town of **Vasilikos,** 16km from Zakynthos Town, and are most plentiful near **Porto Roma.** Signs for rooms to let coat the road to Vasilikos, especially near **Agios Nikolaos Beach.** On the other side of Vasilikos, facing Laganas Bay, lies **Gerakas Beach.** Daily buses leave Zakynthos Town for Vasilikos (4 per day on weekdays, 2 per day on Saturday and Sunday, 280dr).

The closest beach to Zakithnos Town is **Tsilivi** beach, 6km up the waterfront road with the water on your right. **Planos,** just inland, has plenty of rooms. Buses run from Zakynthos Town to the beach (30min., 11 per day, 220dr). **Zante Camping** (tel. 44 754), 3km farther up the road from Planos, is Zakynthos' only campsite located on a beach. It has a cafeteria and minimarket (1300dr per person; 720dr per car; 870dr per small tent; 1020dr per large tent; 10% discount for *Let's Go* users).

Alykes, 16km from Zakynthos Town, is more pleasant and less crowded than its counterparts in the south. Filled with romantic restaurants and fringed with soft, clean, sand beaches, Alykes mysteriously escapes the fate of Lagana beach. **Montes** (tel. 83 101) is a vacation complex that lets large rooms with beautiful balconies and kitchens (low season 8000dr, high season 13,000dr). Ask for an attic room. Downstairs a restaurant serves excellent budget fare (*tzatziki* 400dr, *moussaka* 1100dr, soup 400dr). Next door is a bakery and supermarket. Many other signs along the main drag advertise rooms to let. The **Apollo Restaurant,** on the edge of town, has fantastic chicken *souvlaki* (1200dr). Buses run to Alykes five times per day; the last bus returns at 7pm (280dr).

Volimes

To get to Volimes, a small old village where the resident women specialize in needle-point and crochet, take the twice-daily bus to Schinari (650dr), which passes through Volimes, or take the bus tour around the island, which stops in Volimes before returning to Zakynthos Town (W and Sa 10:15, 2500dr). Bring cash because this is the perfect opportunity to get a cheap, colorful rug, or other non-tacky present (no credit cards accepted). One kilometer east, up the hill in the upper part of the village (Ano Volimes), signs advertise rooms to let. Crumbling medieval bell towers and abandoned windmills dot the villages.

Korithi

At the extreme northern tip of Zakynthos is the tiny village of **Korithi,** locally known as **Agios Nikolaos,** where the ferry to Cephalonia departs. Two buses a day travel between Zakynthos Town and Schinari, which is the beach a short distance from Korithi. The evening bus returns to Zakynthos town at 7pm. From the beach, you can hire a fishing boat to take you on a tour of the eerie **blue caves,** accessible only from the water. A one-hour excursion costs roughly 1500dr per person. You can also rent canoes and other small craft on the tiny beach. A drive between Korithi and Volimes through the northern farmlands of Zakynthos, either by rented car, moped, or bus, is breathtaking, and should not be missed by any visitor to the islands.

LEFKADA Λευκαδα

According to Thucydides, Lefkada (white rock) was part of the mainland until 427 BC, when inhabitants dug a canal. The modern bridge connecting Lefkada to the mainland just 50m away has only recently replaced an archaic chain-operated ferry built by Emperor Augustus. Despite their ancestors' attempts to keep people away, modern Lefkadians are passionate devotees of tourism. Souvenir shops and over-priced tourist restaurants abound, especially in Nidri, which boasts little besides these traps and a profusion of liquor stores. However, it is possible—and even worth-while—to skirt these patches of tacky tourism and discover unspoiled beaches and towns. Lefkada itself remains a beautiful island.

■ Lefkada Town

Lefkada Town, directly across from the mainland, is a thinly touristed city next to a section of sea that looks like a vast swamp. It may be a poor copy of upscale Greek resort towns, but for that reason it offers a break from the commodities of heavy tour-ism—here, you'll find no gaudy signs, endless leather and jewelry stores, or fields of buses. Downtown consists of narrow pedestrian-only streets that weave through brightly painted walls.

ORIENTATION AND PRACTICAL INFORMATION Lefkada was identified as Homer's Ithaka by the archaeologist William Dörpfield. Today, Dörpfield is the main street in Lefkada Town and runs right down the middle of the peninsula that comprises the city's downtown area. Dörpfield St. and all the little winding streets that branch off it are for pedestrians and bikes only. Cars may drive along the waterfront and inland from the peninsula. There is no tourist office, but the **tourist police,** 30 Iroon Politechniou St. (tel. 26 450), a few blocks to the right of Lefkada Town's bus station (facing the water), offer handy brochures and will help locate rooms (open daily 8am-10pm). In the same building is the **police station** (tel. 22 100; open 24hr.). For more detailed information about ferries, tours, or sights, try **Travel Mate** (tel. 23 581) at the tip of the peninsula (open daily 9am-2pm and 6-9pm), or one of the numerous travel agencies clustered around the bus station. There is a **National Bank** with a 24-hour **ATM** along Dörpfield St. (open daily 8am-2pm). Dörpfield St. also leads to the main square, with its cafes and occasional traveling music acts.

From the **bus station** (tel. 22 364), on the waterfront with a gray and yellow striped awning, buses cross the canal to Athens (5½hr., 4 per day, 6000dr) and Aktion (4 per day, 360dr). The local island buses run to Nidri (30min., 13 per day, 280dr); Agios Nikitas (20min., 3 per day, 240dr); Poros (45min., 2 per day, 440dr); and Vasiliki (1hr., 4 per day, 650dr). Be sure to pick up a bus schedule at the station (or from tour offices) detailing additional transit routes and return times. **Ferries** leaving from **Nidri** and **Vasiliki** link Lefkada with Ithaka and Cephalonia to the south. From Nidri (tel. 92 427), ferries sail to Frikes on Ithaka (1 per day, 935dr), and then to Fiskardo (1 per day, 1220dr). Travel offices provide times and sell tickets.

Excursion boats run daily day-long cruises to Cephalonia, Ithaka, and Skorpios (every morning, roughly 4000dr). Boats also shuttle beach zealots to Lefkada's numerous cloistered beaches. Some also stop at the cave of **Papanikoli.** Inquire at waterfront kiosks or travel offices, or read the hard-to-miss signs aboard the little boats.

The **post office** is on Dörfield St. (open M-F 7:30am-2pm). For the **OTE,** turn right off St. Melas St. to Pantaneromenis St., head toward the waterfront, and look for the satellite tower (open daily 7am-10pm). **Postal code:** 31100. **Telephone code:** 0645.

ACCOMMODATIONS Prices listed are for low season; in high season, when hotels are booked up, they may increase by about 20%. **Hotel Byzantion** (tel. 22 629), at the waterfront end of Dörpfield St., is more pleasant than other hotels in its price range. There are sinks in the rooms and bathrooms down the hall (singles 4000dr; doubles 8000dr). **Hotel Patras** (tel. 22 359), just up the street on the square, has bathrooms in every room and similar prices (singles 5000dr; doubles 10,000dr). **Santa Maura,** off Dörpfield St. about three blocks from the water, offers large, bright rooms with sparkling private baths (singles 8000dr; doubles 12,000dr). For more budget options call the **Union of Pension Owners** (tel. 21 266). Expect private rooms to cost between 4000dr and 8000dr, depending on the season.

FOOD AND ENTERTAINMENT Taverna Regentos, off the main square on Verrioti St.—coming from the water, turn right at the old stone building on the square—has a delightful decor that matches the excellent quality of the traditional food (*moussaka* 900dr, grilled meats 1200dr; open daily 7:30pm-2am). **Taverna of the Nine Islands** is off Dörpfield St. before the square. Roses bloom over tables lining a charming narrow street (*aubergines* 1000-1200dr, salads 600dr; open 6:30pm-late).

The **folklore museum** is off the main square; turn right and follow the signs. *(Open M-F 10am-2pm and 8-10pm. Admission 500dr.)* The small museum offers a taste of old Lefkada and its Italian legacy. Although it occupies only a single room, the unusual **Phonograph Museum** is in many ways more impressive. *(Open M-F 9am-1pm and 6-11pm. Free.)* It has not only old phonographs, but also antique trinkets, from matchboxes to swords and muskets. To find it, take the second left after the square coming from the water. The **Archaeological Museum** (tel. 23 678), 1km down the road to Agios Nikitas, is tiny and worthwhile for only the most dedicated, since the majority of Lefkada's treasures are in Athens or Ioannina. *(Open daily 9am-1:30pm. Admission 500dr.)* Every year Lefkada hosts its famous **Folklore Festival,** now in its 34th year, in the second half of August.

SIGHTS While Lefkada Town has no sandy beaches, the northern half of the west coast offers miles of white pebbles and clear water. Rent a moped (3000dr per day for *Let's Go* users) at **Travel Mate/Eurocar** on the tip of the peninsula. The best stretch lies north of **Agios Nikitas**. The road leads to the **Faneromenis Monastery** (tel. 22 275), with a sweeping view of the sea and one resident monk. *(Open daily 7am-10pm. Free.)*

■ Nidri Νιδρι

Nidri ensnares unwary travelers solely because it's the last stop of the otherwise delightful Frikes-Nidri ferry. The waterfront, crowded with pleasure boats, boasts a handsome view of the dappled coves of the numerous small islands just offshore, but the town itself is little more than a strip of garish tourist shops and tacky cafes. The **post office** (open M-F 9am-1pm) is on the main street, parallel to and one block inland from the waterfront. **Buses** from Nidri go to Lefkada (30min., 17 per day, 280dr) and Vasiliki (8 per day, 360dr). "Rooms to Let" signs are scattered along the main street. In July and August, when the island sags under the burgeoning weight of tourism, rooms are always full and prices are inevitably high (doubles from 10,000dr). In the off season prices drop as low as 4000dr. **Camping Episkopos** (tel. 71 388) is 8km north of Nidri, toward Lefkada (1200dr per person; 900dr per small tent; 1100dr per large tent; 600dr per car). To escape the glitz but not the mosquitoes of Nidri, climb the 3km to **Neochori** at dusk. The tiny village of **Vliho** is 3km south, accessible by bus from Lefkada (13 per day, 300dr); here there's a striking church in an idyllic setting of wildflowers and cypress trees.

■ **Vasiliki** Βασιλικη

Vasiliki, at the southern tip of Lefkada, bears charms both tranquil and invigorating. Smaller and currently less touristed than Nidri, Vasiliki is becoming increasingly popular with the young international watersports crowd. Rated among the world's finest windsurfing resorts, Vasiliki is usually graced with consistent gentle winds in the morning, which rise to steady force-five gales in the afternoon.

ORIENTATION AND PRACTICAL INFORMATION **Buses** run five times per day from Lefkada (640dr) and Nidri (360dr). Almost everything in Vasiliki lines the main road running inland. Up the street from the waterfront, **Star Travel** (tel. 31 833; fax 31 834) will be on your right, with information about ferries, buses, accommodations, and boat excursions around the islands (open daily 9am-11pm). The office offers daily round-trips to Lefkada's best beach, **Porto Kastiki** (40-50 min., 2500dr). From Vasiliki **ferries** (tel. 31 555) make the run to Fiskardo on Cephalonia (1hr., 3 per day, 1220dr), then to Frikes on Ithaka (1¾hr., 1220dr), and Sami, Cephalonia (2½hr., 1700dr). Inquire at the kiosk next to the pier. For emergencies, contact the **health center** (tel. 31 065). The **police** (tel. 31 218) are a short distance inland along the main road (open 24hr.). Farther up from Star Travel, just after the crossroad, is the **post office** (open M-F 7:30am-2pm). **Postal code:** 31082. **Telephone code:** 0645.

ACCOMMODATIONS Rooms are plentiful and signs easy to spot, particularly along the road leading uphill from the bus stop, on the waterfront, and along the main post road. Prices may as much as double in the high season. The popular **Vasiliki Beach Camping** (tel. 31 308 or 31 457; fax 31 458) boasts superlative amenities and rests a hop, skip, and jump away from the beach. Head for the beach and make a right on the road running inland just before the Windsurfing Club (1550dr per person; 1000dr per child; free for kids under 4 years of age; 1100dr per small tent; 1100dr per car). The **Galaxy Market** (tel. 31 221), around the corner at the back side of the ferry dock, lets tidy, simple rooms (singles 3000dr, doubles 7000dr).

FOOD AND ENTERTAINMENT Full meals can be inexpensive and well-prepared in Vasiliki, even in the waterfront cafes and eateries. The **Penguin Restaurant,** on the waterfront at the corner of the main road running inland, has the most extensive menu; for reasonable prices (entrees 1500-2000dr), you can choose between dozens of seafood, pasta, and traditional Greek dishes. The **Miramare Restaurant,** a local favorite on the main road toward the water, specializes in pizza (around 2000dr), but has a good selection of seafood as well. **Zeus' Bar** serves up drinks to soothe the salt- and sun-weary. The orange juice with soda water (300dr) is particularly refreshing. For a morning treat or for bus journey snack provisions, try the **bakery** above the bus stop. Scoop into their barrels of sweet rolls (molasses and a taste of caraway 50dr).

SIGHTS A **lighthouse** built on the site of the **Temple of Lefkas Apollo** sits at the southernmost tip of the island. Worshippers exorcised evil with an annual sacrifice at the temple. The victim, usually a criminal or a mentally ill person thought to be possessed, was thrown into the sea from the cliffs. Live birds were tied to the victim's arms and legs for amusement as well as aerodynamic advantages. It was from these 70m cliffs that the ancient poet **Sappho** leapt to her death when Phaon rejected her. The cliff, called **Sappho's Leap,** is known in Lefkada as *Kavos tis Kiras* (Cape of the Lady). A number of different **boat excursions** round the point, providing a better view than can be had by driving to the site.

ITHAKA Ιθάκη

The least touristed and quite possibly the most beautiful of the Ionian islands, Ithaka is all too often passed over for the tourist havens of Lefkada and Cephalonia. Even in the Ionian high season, Ithaka has fewer tourists to crowd its beaches, drive its restaurant prices up, and finance its junkshops, than any other Ionian island. Those who discover Ithaka find the island's pebbled, rocky hillsides and terraced olive groves quiet, docile, and at their disposal.

According to Homer, Ithaka was once the kingdom that **Odysseus** left behind for his legendary journey, where **Penelope** faithfully waited 20 years for his return from the Trojan war. Although crowds of suitors pressed for her hand—and Odysseus' kingdom—she told them that she would not choose between them and remarry until she finished the cloth which she was weaving by day (and secretly unwinding the day's progress each night)! However fair Penelope may have been, it is easy to see why Odysseus' kingdom attracted so many would-be successors; Ithaka is an island fit for the gods themselves.

■ Vathy Βαθυ

Ithaka's largest town and capital wraps around a circular bay skirted by precipitous green hillsides. Colorful fishing boats bob on the water, and in the evening, the dying sun deepens the tint of the pastel-painted houses and their red-shingled roofs, making Vathy one of the island's most beautiful towns. Vathy becomes even more striking as you climb higher; from the surrounding hillsides, Vathy's rich, crisp hues and small boat-filled harbor gain an air of miniature, unworldly perfection.

ORIENTATION AND PRACTICAL INFORMATION Facing inland, Vathy's ferry docks are to the right of the town square; depending on where you have come from, you may have to take a taxi from the ferry docks at Piso Aetos (10min., 2000dr) or Frikes (30min., 4000dr). All directions—left and right—are given relative to someone facing inland. Keep in mind that most establishments have longer hours and higher prices in the high season (late July-Aug.).

The web of **ferries** around the Ionian Islands enmeshes Ithaka. Schedules vary drastically depending on the season. Check with the helpful staff at **Delas Tours** (tel. 32 104; fax 33 031), located in the main square right off the water, but even they might only know the schedule for the current month (open daily 9am-2pm and 5-9:30pm). Ferries connect Frikes (nearby, on northern Ithaka) to Nidri on Lefkada (2hr., 2 per day, 935dr). From Vathy proper, ferries run to Sami on Cephalonia (1hr.,

950dr). There are also boats from Piso Aetos to Sami (3 per day, 500dr) and to Astakos on the mainland (2½hr., 1 per day, 1850dr). Be sure to check boat schedules at your port of departure.

Some form of transportation around the island is essential to making the most out of a visit. **Taxis** (tel. 33 033) are overly expensive to fill this need; a moped is an excellent way to explore the island. **Rent-A-Bike** (tel. 33 243), behind the new cultural museum, near the center of the waterfront, has the cheapest prices (4500dr per day). Run by Spiros and Nikos, two friendly brothers from South Africa, the shop is open daily from 9am to 8pm. An EU or International Drivers license is usually required. To reach the **hospital** (tel. 32 222), turn left and walk out of the square 1km until you see a sign reading "Hospital." Along the way, you will see the **police station** (tel. 32 205), where English is spoken (open 24hr.). There is a **pharmacy** right next to Delas Tours along the waterfront on the right side of the harbor. A new chapter of the **National Bank** with a 24hr. **ATM** is at the right corner of the waterfront, about 20m out of the main square (open M-Th 8am-2:30pm, F 8am-1:30pm). The **post office** (tel. 32 386) is in the main square, on the left side of the waterfront (open M-F 7:30am-2pm). The **OTE** sits on the water, left of the square (open M-F 7:30am-2:30pm). **Postal code:** 28300. **Telephone code:** 0674.

ACCOMMODATIONS Your best bet is to find a private *domatia*. Sometimes proprietors will meet the ferry. It is possible to get a very good deal (3000-4000dr per night in low season, at least twice as much in high season), but be sure to discuss price and distance before you follow them away from town. If you need help finding a room call Delas Tours (tel. 32 104) in the square or **Polyctor Tours** (tel. 28 300; open daily 7am-11pm). The **Hotel Mentor** (tel. 32 433) lies on the water, left of the square and next to the OTE (singles 11,400dr; doubles 15,500dr; triples 19,350dr; breakfast included). Farther down the road, **Captain Yiannis Villas** (tel. 33 173; fax 32 849) has luxurious rooms with air-conditioning, television, and access to a tennis court and pool (doubles 14,000dr). **Camping** on the beach under the eucalyptus trees or any place else outside is generally tolerated, provided campers clean up after themselves

FOOD The food is generally good in Ithaka, and prices are average for Greece. **Taverna To Trexantiri** (tel. 33 066) dishes out huge portions and is the hands-down favorite among locals (entrees 1400dr, salads 500dr.) **O Nikos** (tel. 33 039), just down the street on the corner across from the National Bank, is not far behind in local popularity, offering a variety of traditional foods (meals around 2000-2500dr). On the other side of the bay past the OTE is Gregory's **Taverna Paliocaravo** (tel. 32 573 or 33 159), which, in addition to traditional food, also serves excellent seafood. Gregory is the former chef to Aristotle Onasis; expect to pay higher prices (3000-4000dr) and make a reservation in the high season. Outside of Vathy in Perichora, the town directly up the hill, the **Cypress Tree Restaurant,** owned by a Swiss chef, serves traditional foods as well as a few French dishes for similar prices. The restaurant is near the grave yard.

SIGHTS The **Vathy Archaeological Museum** displays, among other things, finds from ongoing excavations at a site on the island that some believe is Odysseus' palace. *(Open Tu-Su 8am-2:30pm. Free.)* Follow the signs from the waterfront street to get to the museum. The brand new **Folklore and Cultural Museum** (tel. 33 398) is a beautiful airy building that houses fully assembled bedrooms, kitchen, and sitting room from Ithaka's colonial period as well as photographs of the 1953 earthquake devastation. *(Open M-F 9:30am-2pm and 6-10pm. Admission 250dr.)* Those with poetic imaginations may want to make the 45-minute, 4km climb up to the **Cave of the Nymphs,** where Odysseus hid the treasure that the Phoenicians bestowed upon him. *(Admission 200dr.)* The cave has been under archaeological excavation in recent years, so if you visit, you may have the pleasure of chatting with a few archaeologists. To get there, walk around the harbor with the water on your right and follow the signs. The hike provides stunning views of Vathy. Bring a flashlight. A two-hour hike southeast up a well-marked but rocky road leads to the Homeric **Arethousa Fountain,** along a

A Good Pose Is Hard to Find.

Penelope's curse was one that only seems to have happened back in the good old ancient days: the curse of an absentee husband who leaves you with too much treasure, rich land, and time on your hands, and too many suitors begging for your hand on all sides. A tough position, to be sure, but her unending lamenting of Odysseus' obsence—all those fits of moaning about a sorrow greater than all others—does seem to wear thin after a while. Did she really have so little relish for her role in life? Or did Homer lend her some inkling of the exquisite melodrama of it all? Late in the epic, she sighs in the pitiful words a woman who's lost her chance at life, "The immortals did away with my qualities of form and body...if Odysseus could to return...greater would be my reputation, and fairer..."(XIX, 124-128). Perhaps, Penelope— but we suspect that your reputation as history's most faithful (though not its fairest) woman could be quite as much reputation as one woman deserves...and perhaps you felt a just small thrill every time you emerged to the suitors "divine among women, and stood by the pillar of the solidly built roof,"(1, 332-334) and just *had* to slip into one more noble pose.

steep mountain path through orchards. In summer, the fountain is dry. To find the path to the fountain, follow Evmeou St. up hill until it turns dirt and look for the signs.

Also in the vicinity of Vathy is the small village of **Perichora,** set on the steep mountainside 5km above Vathy. The town is largely devoted to the vine, producing the island's best wine and hosting a **wine festival** on the last Sunday of July. If you make it up to Perichora, visit the ruins of **Paleochora,** the capital city of the island until abandoned in the early 16th century. The crumbling stone walls are clustered on the hillside next to Perichora; follow signs in Perichora to the beginning of a footpath that leads through olive groves to the ruins. The ruins of the town church are the first you will encounter; although the roof is gone and the walls are crumbling, frescoed icons still cling to the interior walls. The views of Vathy from here are unbeatable.

After a day of hiking, relax on the beach at **Loutsa's Bay,** at the terminus of the road on the left side of the harbor. The beach is small but fully equipped with a bar. Just up the hill are the remains of a **Venetian fortress** whose **two cannons** are still in place.

■ Around Ithaka

An excursion from Vathy to the secluded villages scattered along Ithaka's rocky coast is essential to any trip to Ithaka; a moped is not cheap, but mobility is decidedly worth the price. The island's one **bus** runs north from Vathy, passing through the villages of Lefki, Stavros, Platrithiai, Frikes, and Kioni. The bus doubles as a school bus, and schedules are erratic. Check in town, but in the high season, the bus usually runs three times per day (1hr., 350dr to Frikes). The bus route skirts both sides of the isthmus and offers superlative views of the strait of Ithaka and Cephalonia on the west and of the coastline on the east. Check the times of return buses before setting out; **taxis** from Kioni to Vathy cost roughly 4500dr. **Frikes** and **Koni,** both with small, crystal-blue harbors on the northern coast of the island, are exceptionally beautiful.

Stavros is high in the mountains on the way to Frikes and Kioni. Follow signs in town to a small museum at the alleged site of Odysseus' palace, filled with items from excavations of the site. *(Hours vary. Free, but a small tip is expected.)* Homer described the palace site as a place from which three different waters could be seen; still visible from this point are the bays of Frikes, Aphales, and Polis, although several other sites of similar description on Ithaka and in Cephalonia compete for the same distinction. Also worthy of a visit is the **Monastery of Panagia Katharon,** on the highest mountain in Ithaka. To get there, take a taxi or moped to Anogi and follow the signs.

Ithaka's **beaches** are beautiful, if a trifle hard to reach. **Daxa** is the closest to Vathy. According to legend, this is where Odysseus landed when he returned to Ithaka. From Vathy, follow the main road out of town with the water on your right. On the other side of Vathy, **Filiatro** is also a gorgeous beach. **Gidaki,** the island's best beach, is only accessible by boat.

CEPHALONIA Κεφαλονια

Scientists and explorers have dubbed Cephalonia the "Island of Peculiarities." Surprisingly diverse environments—sandy beaches, subterranean caves, rugged mountains, and shady forests—can be found around the island and are the legacy of powerful earthquakes. Colonialism has also left its varied mark. Over the years, Cephalonia has been part of the Byzantine, Frankish, Ottoman, Venetian, Napoleonic, and British Empires. In this century, Cephalonia has endured a troubled history. When the Germans invaded in 1943, 9000 Italian soldiers occupying the island mutinied and resisted their Nazi "allies" for seven days. Only 33 Italians survived. Ten years later, a disastrous earthquake forced the island to rebuild. Because of this, only Fiskardo, which was relatively undamaged, retains the pastel Neoclassical look associated with the Ionian Islands. Cephalonia is ideal for a week-long vacation that allows time to explore all the island's beauty. Because of the island's multiple ports and inconvenient bus network, however, a trip to Cephalonia requires careful planning on the part of the budget traveler.

■ Argostoli Αργοστολι

The capital of Cephalonia and Ithaka, Argostoli is a busy, noisy town whose palm tree-lined streets are regularly jammed with traffic. Although there is no shortage of hotels, restaurants, and souvenir shops, Argostoli is unique among Ionian islands in that it is not easy to forget that people actually live here. Argostoli is hardly the most beautiful town in which to spend your time on Cephalonia, but, as it is the hub of the island's bus network, you may find it convenient to use the city as a base from which to explore the rest of the island.

ORIENTATION AND PRACTICAL INFORMATION

The town's main square is one block up from the water on Rokou Vergoti St.

Transportation

Ferries: Unlike most islands, Cephalonia has several ports for different destinations. Buses connect Argostoli to other ports, including **Sami,** where international ferries leave for Italy (see p. 253). Prices and times vary with the season; inquire at one of the many travel agencies in town. From **Argostoli** boats go to Killini on the mainland (1 per day 2:30pm, 2820dr), and Lixouri (1 per hour, 300dr).

Buses: The bus station (tel. 22 281) is on the south end of the waterfront. Open 7am-8pm. Buses head to Skala (2 per day, 600dr); Poros (3 per day, 800dr); Fiskardo (1½hr., 2 per day, 900dr); Sami (3 per day, 500dr); Agios Gerasimos (3 per day, 550dr); and Kourkoumelata (3 per day, 300dr). There are also buses that piggyback on the ferry to Athens (7:45am and 1:30pm). Buses to Argostoli meet the ferry arriving in Sami (1 per day, 500dr). Service reduced on Sa. No service Su.

Flights: Olympic Airways 7 R. Vergoti St. (tel. 28 808 or 28 881). Flights to Athens at least once per day (14,100dr). Open M-F 8am-3:30pm. Their airport office (tel. 41 511) is open daily, but hours vary.

Car Rental: Myrtos Rent-a-Car (tel. 24 230 or 25 023), on the waterfront. Must be over 23 to rent. Starts at 13,000dr per day. Open daily 9am-1:30pm and 6-9pm.

Moped Rental: Sunbird (tel. 23 723), near the port authority on the water, rents mopeds at 3500dr per day and bicycles at 1500dr per day. Gas is not included, but it costs 1000dr at most. Open daily 8:30am-2:30pm and 5:30-9:30pm.

Tourist and Financial Services

Tourist Office: (tel. 22 248 or 22 466) At the port. Provides free maps and candid advice on accommodations, restaurants, and beaches in the area and has a list of rooms to let. Open in high season, M-F 7:30am-2:30pm and 4-10pm, Sa 9am-1pm and 5pm-9pm; in off-season, M-F 7:30am-2pm.

/

Banks: National Bank on Sitemporon St., which runs parallel to and two blocks up from the water. Has a Visa/MC/Cirrus **ATM** and offers currency exchange. Open M-Th 8am-2pm, F 8am-1:30pm.

International Bookstore: Petratos Bookstore (tel. 22 546), on Lithostrotou St. at the intersection of Ithakis St., two blocks up from the water. English newspapers. Foreign newspapers and magazines. Open daily 8am-8pm.

Emergency and Communications

Tourist Police: Check inside the regular **police station** (tel. 22 815 or 22 200) on I. Metaxa St. across from the port authority and the tourist office. The tourist police provide service but have irregular hours.

Post Office: (tel. 23 173), two blocks up from the water on Lithostrotou St. at the intersection of Kerkyras St. Open M-F 7:30am-2pm. **Postal Code: 28100.**

OTE: At the corner of Rokou Vergoti St. and Georgiou Vergoti St. Open M-Sa 7:30am-3:10pm, Su 8:30am-1:30pm. **Telephone Code: 0671.**

ACCOMMODATIONS

Probably the best budget option is to let a private room. Signs advertising **rooms to let** are ubiquitous in Argostoli, but if you seek guidance, you can go to any of the travel agencies or the tourist offices. The prices of such rooms are rarely set so you should bargain as much as possible. In the high season, do not expect to find them for much less than 9000dr.

Villa Aspasiana Rooms To Let (tel. 23 511), 300m up the hill from the town square on the road running behind the park, has clean, recently remodeled rooms for decent prices but is by no means the only game in town. Doubles 6000dr.

Hotel Allegro (tel. 28 684), up from the waterfront on Andrea Choïda St., has double beds, private baths, and a cute little boy who speaks English. Singles 5000dr; doubles 7000dr.

Hotel Tourist (tel. 23 034) has sparkling rooms with balconies and TVs. Coming from the bus station, it is located on the waterfront before the port authority. Breakfast included. Singles 12,200dr; doubles 16,000dr.

Hotel Cephalonia (tel. 23 180; fax 23 180), farther down the street on the waterfront, has slightly cheaper prices. Singles 6000dr; doubles 8000dr.

FOOD

The restaurants in the square are good but decidedly on the expensive side. Those that line the water fall into roughly the same category, though they serve mostly Greek dishes and seafood. Another inexpensive option is to visit the exciting and well-organized **farmers' market** that takes over the waterfront near the bus station on Saturday mornings. Permanent **fruit shops** line the waterfront, 100m toward town from the bus station.

⊛**Kalafatis Restaurant,** one of the first restaurants on the waterfront coming from the bus station, may be the best of them. Their Cephalonian meat pie (1600dr) is said to be the best on the island.

Igloo Cafe, just off the waterfront on Andrea Choïda St., serves economical sandwiches (500dr) and croissants (300dr).

Mister Grillo (tel. 23 702), near the port authority, offers plenty of vegetarian options including black beans in oil (600dr) and stuffed peppers (800dr).

SIGHTS

Argostoli's **Archaeological Museum** (tel. 28 300) is housed in the squat yellow building in the main square. *(Open Tu-Su 8:30am-3pm. Admission 400dr.)* To reach Corgialenios Library, which houses the **Historical and Folk Museum** (tel. 28 835), from the museum, turn right onto R. Vergoti St. and continue two blocks. *(Open M-Sa 9am-2pm. Admission 500dr.)* The museum is crammed with 19th-century objects of all kinds, from household items to military medals. Argostoli's French coffee cups, English top hats, and antique dolls suggest a luxurious colonial past. Particularly interesting are the photographs of Argostoli during the last century, including shots of the damage from the devastating 1953 earthquake and ensuing reconstruction.

■ Near Argostoli

There are several options for exploring more of the island. A **moped rental** in Argostoli or elsewhere accords one a lot of freedom. To swim at **Lassi,** one of the island's best sandy beaches, follow the road leading from the town to the airport.

The Venetian **Castle of St. George,** 9km southeast of Argostoli, rests on a hill overlooking the village of Travliata; chug along the road to Skala and turn right when the road splits. (*Open M-Sa 8:00am-8pm, Su 8am-3pm. Free.*) **Buses** travel to the site (10min., 2 per day, 200dr). From the battlements, admire the panorama that once inspired the celebrated Lord Byron.

Additionally, boats leave regularly for **Lixouri,** in the center of the west peninsula (30min., every hour, 300dr). Once home to the satiric poet Andreas Laskaratos, Lixouri offers miles of practically tourist-free coastline. You can rent **mopeds** at several places in Lixouri; **buses** run to several smaller villages in the area.

A few beaches and interesting towns dot the island south of Argostoli. One of the best beaches is at **Ormos Lourda,** in the middle of the south coast; closer to Argostoli is **Platis Gialos** (30min., 7 buses per day, 150dr). Here, visit one of the eminent Lord Byron's adopted towns (though his house no longer exists) at **Metaxata,** or see **Kourkoumelata,** a village completely restored by a Greek tycoon after the 1953 earthquake. Check out the comfortable **Hotel Kourkoumi** (tel. 41 645) if you decide to stay (doubles with bath and breakfast 6000dr). Outside the city in the village of **Dargoti,** a multi-layered **Mycenaean tholos tomb** is taken as evidence that modern-day Cephalonia was, centuries ago, the site of Homer's Ithaka, as some believe that the tomb belongs to Odysseus himself. **Poros,** on the southeast coast, is a modern coastal town with a beach; rooms to let are everywhere. Buses run from Argostoli to Poros (1½hr., 3 per day, 800dr).

East of Argostoli is the **Monastery of Agios Gerasimos,** home of its canonized founder's preserved corpse. On the night of August 15, the nearby village of **Omala** hosts a festival and a vigil in the saint's church. The town goes wild on the saint's name days (Oct. 20 and Aug. 16); inquire at the tourist office. Omala also has an excellent **Archaeological Museum** (tel. 28 300) (*Open daily 8:30am-3:30pm.*)

By far the best beach on the island is the pebble and sand beach at **Skala.** The town itself is prohibitively expensive (9000dr for plain singles), but the beach to the right of the rocks is heavenly. Also in Skala are the remains of a second-century **Roman villa.** Almost all of the structure is gone but the exquisite mosaic floors are remarkably well-preserved. (*Open daily 9am-3pm. Free.*) Look for a sign when you enter Skala or ask someone for directions. Three buses per day arrive from Argostoli; the latest returns at 5pm. If you must stay, ask at **Skalini Tours** for rooms, and catch a bite at the **Sun Rise Restaurant** (beef stew 1000dr).

■ Sami Σαμη

A small town on a harbor surrounded by precipitous, lush green hills, Sami offers a mignon white pebble beach, proximity to the natural wonders of Melissani Lake and Drograti cave, and a break from the bustle of Argostoli. Ferries leave Sami for Patras fairly early in the morning, making Sami a good place to spend the afternoon and night before cruising back to the mainland.

ORIENTATION AND PRACTICAL INFORMATION The blue and white Hotel Kyma, two blocks from the ferry landing, points the way to Sami's main square, which you will hit if you follow the street from the hotel as it turns inland. There is no official tourist office, but the **police** (tel. 22 100) may be able to answer your questions (open 24hr.). **Sami Travel** (tel. 23 050) offers rooms, tickets to Italy, excursion tickets, and general information. It is located near the port authority building, off the far end of Akti Posidonos St., which runs along the water. The **Marketou Travel/Strintzis Line Office** (tel. 22 055 or 23 021), on the waterfront just to the left of the ferry landing in Sami, is also very helpful. From Sami, **ferries** sail to Ithaka (1hr., 3 per day in the high season, 1 in low season, 480dr), Patras (8:30am, 3200dr), and Astakos (1 per day 8:45am, 1850dr). Sami is also the place to catch **international ferries** to Brindisi and Ancona in Italy. You can exchange money at the **Commercial Bank of Greece** on Sami's waterfront (open M-Th 8am-2pm, F 8am-1:30pm) or at most of the travel agencies, but make sure to bring cash, as the closest ATM is in Argostoli. The **OTE** is in the main square (open M-F 7:30am-3:10pm), as is the **post office** (open M-F 7:30am-2:30pm). **Postal code:** 28080. **Telephone code:** 0674.

ACCOMMODATIONS Lodging in Sami can be relatively cheap, especially in the low season; prices rise 20-40% in July and August. Try the **Hotel Kyma** (tel. 22 064) in the town square. Many of the clean rooms offer spectacular views and cool breezes (singles 4500dr; doubles 6000dr). The **Hotel Melissani** (tel. 22 464; fax 22 464), several blocks back from the water on the left side of town as you face inland, offers lovely views of the harbor and surrounding hills (singles 7,000dr; doubles 8000dr; breakfast included). By far the most hospitable accommodation you will find is the **Hotel Kastro** (tel. 23 001; fax 23 004), on the waterfront near the ferry docks, where the owner of the hotel will treat you like one of her own (singles 4000dr; doubles 8000dr). If the Kastro is full, she will direct you to her overflow rooms above the **Riviera Restaurant** (tel. 22 777), which are just as nice and come at the same or even cheaper rates. **Karavomilos Beach Camping** (tel. 22 480) is indeed right on the beach; walk along the beach from the town with the water on your right for about five minutes. With a snack bar, a mini-market, a small restaurant, and laundry services, Karavomilos is clean and popular, (1100dr per person; 700dr per small tent; 1000dr per large tent; person with a sleeping bag 1500dr).

SIGHTS The underground caves of **Melissani** and **Drograti,** two sites near Sami, impress both troglodytes and surface-dwellers. Melissani, perhaps the more stunning of the two, can be reached by foot from Sami in about 30 minutes. *(Open daily 8am-8pm. Admission 1100dr.)* Walk along the beach with the water to your right until you come to a small lake with a water wheel on your right. Turn left after the restaurant by the lake, walk inland about 30m, and turn right at the first cross street. A bit down this street you will see signs to the cave, which is only a few hundred meters away. At the lake, guides will show you around the two large caverns flooded with sparkling water, studded with stalactites, and squirming with eels. For best viewing, go when the sun is high. To reach Drograti, 4km from Sami, head inland on the road to Argostoli and follow the signs. *(Open daily until nightfall. Admission 864dr.)* Just 10km north of Sami at the other end of the bay is the pretty harbor town of Agia Efimia.

■ Fiskardo Φισκαρδο

The road north ends at **Fiskardo,** the only town left undamaged by the 1953 earthquake and thus the only remaining example of 18th- and 19th-century Cephalonian architecture. Once called Panoramos, Fiskardo was magnanimously renamed after Robert Guiscard, a Norman who died here in 1085 while attempting to conquer the town. On the wooded neck of land across the harbor stands the lighthouse and ruins of a 15th-century Venetian fortress. It is a splendid walk through the woods and a splendid swim from the rocks along the water. Staying the night in Fiskardo is exceedingly expensive; some, to escape the high prices of letting a room in town, camp here on the sly. Of course, *Let's Go: Greece* cannot recommend this tactic.

In general, Fiskardo is a bit intimidating for the budget traveler. Rooms are expensive (doubles 8000-10,000dr), but the cheapest are on the road back to Argostoli. Here you may find singles as low as 5000dr. Try **Regina Rooms To Rent** near the bus stop. The **Panoramos** is Fiskardo's most accessible hotel (tel. 51 340; singles with bath 9000dr). An open excavation of a second century Roman graveyard is right next door, along the water. Restaurants line the harbor and are fairly expensive. Fiskardo's beach is unbeatable, lying 500m out of town on the road back to Argostoli and offering flat rocks for sunbathing. One **bus** per day arrives from Sami (1hr., 700dr). Two buses arrive daily from Argostoli (1½hr., 900dr). Buses leave for Argostoli at 6:30am and 4:30 pm from the bus stop in the parking lot next to the church.

■ Around Cephalonia

Cliffs plunge into the sea along the coastal road north from Argostoli or Sami to Fiskardo. The pleasant beaches of **Agia Kyriaki** and **Myrtos** lie on this road. Signposts on the main road after the hamlet of Divarata advertise Myrtos, but swim cautiously there—the undertow can be powerful and sudden. Roughly 4km up the road from Myrtos is the fantastic Venetian castle of **Assos**, on a steep, wooded peninsula joined to the island by a narrow isthmus. Completed in the early part of the 17th century, much of the castle and the houses inside are well preserved. Unfortunately, most of the peninsula inside the walls is privately owned and fenced; the owner's goats and chickens are penned in the crumbling shells of original castle buildings, which can add or detract from the medieval romance of the place, depending on your sensibilities. A daily bus from Argostoli departs at 2pm, returning the next day at 6:45am (600dr). The 30min. walk from the main road is challenging.

On August 15, an unusual and spooky festival in the village of **Markopoulo** in the southeast corner of the island celebrates the Assumption of the Virgin Mary. Celebrants hold an all-night church liturgy. According to local belief, hundreds of small harmless snakes with black crosses on their heads appear during the service and slither over the icons.

Macedonia and Thrace
Μακεδονια και Θρακη

In ancient times cosmopolitan Athenians labeled Macedonians and Thracians primitive barbarians. Orpheus—the mythical Pied Piper who could tame wild animals with his song—was born a Thracian and cults of his devotees filled the hills of Macedonia and Thrace. He had traveled to the underworld and back vainly seeking to recover his wife Eurydice; his accounts of the underworld were retold in Orphic poems, guidebooks to the underworld. Commentary on such a poem was found on a papyrus at Derveni outside Thessaloniki. Late-comers to the artistry and commerce developed at Athens, the peoples of northern Greece always centered their lives around the profound. When the Romans paved the Via Egnatia across the Balkans, they encountered Thracian tribes still uncivilized and without cities. Now, even as Athenian sophistication takes hold of Thessaloniki, ascetic hermits on Mt. Athos shun modern luxury, take to caves, and contemplate the next world.

🖐 HIGHLIGHTS OF MACEDONIA AND THRACE

- **Thessaloniki** (p. 257), Greece's second city, possesses 2000 years worth of Byzantine and Ottoman monuments.
- Explore the tombs and palaces at **Pella** (p. 267) and **Vergina** (p. 267), seat of Phillip II and Alexander the Great, who left home to conquer the East.
- Climb **Mt. Olympus** (p. 268) to reach the divine heights where Zeus gazes down, tossing thunderbolts at mortals below.
- Trek from monastery to monastery on **Mt. Athos** (p. 277), home of Byzantine monks who live as they did in the 10th century.
- In the hills of Thrace near the Turkish border, **Xanthi** (see p. 285) and **Komotini** (p. 286) retain Muslim populations and skylines punctuated by minarets.

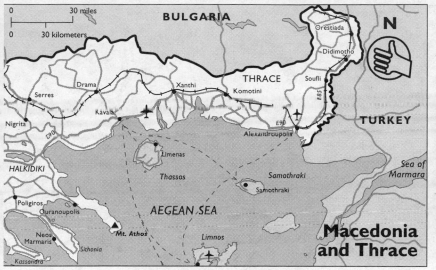

Macedonia and Thrace

MACEDONIA Μακεδονια

The ancestral home of Philip II, conqueror of Greece, and Alexander the Great, self-titled conqueror of world, Macedonia is Greece's largest province. Look for symbols of Macedonian pride such as the 16-pointed star of Vergina. Thessaloniki, the focal point of all northern Greece, rivals Athens. In the northwestern reaches of Macedonia is the natural splendor of the Lakes District. Within an hour of Thessaloniki are some of Greece's foremost archaeological sites: Vergina, Pella, Dion, and Philippi. In the southeast is the three-pronged peninsula of Halkidiki, two-thirds hedonistic delight and one-third—on Mount Athos—monastic austerity. Fun-loving beach bums, archaeology buffs, and reclusive religious devotees can find amusement here.

■ **Thessaloniki** Θεσσαλονικη

Thessaloniki has a western European feel unlike that of any other Greek city. Its broad tree-lined avenues, and spacious squares make it seem more Parisian than Athenian. But despite its many fashionable shops and cafes, its rows of modern high-rises, and its glamorous waterfront, Thessaloniki retains the spirit of the Old World. This side of Thessaloniki comes to life throughout the city—but particularly in the quiet winding streets of the old town, in the seemingly infinite stone Byzantine churches, and in the thick-walled ruins of the Romans. Visit these relics of past civilizations and you will find that the bustle of the modern city slowly fades away and is replaced by images of Macedonian glory, sights of resplendent Roman legions, and the sounds of Byzantine chanting. Few foreigners manage to see this side of Thessaloniki, but those who do discover a deeply gratifying anomaly—a Greek urban center that succeeds in showing off its history without being overshadowed by it.

HISTORY

The capital of Macedonia and second city of Greece, Thessaloniki, known historically as **Salonica,** has had a long and rich past replete with its share of triumph, humiliation, and tragedy—much of which is captured in the city's excellent archaeological

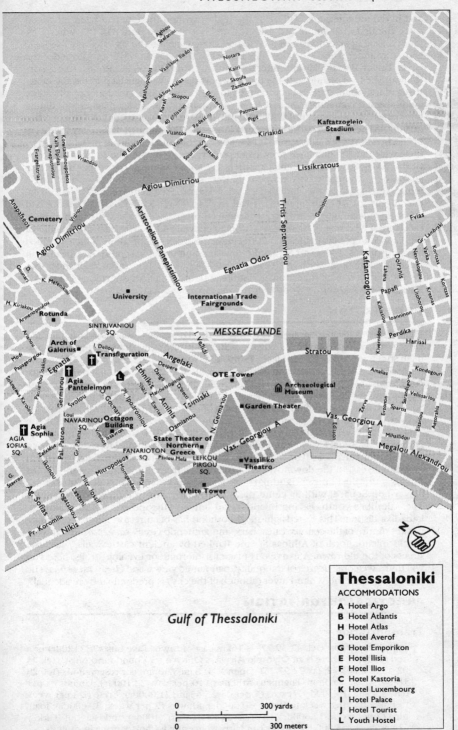

Gulf of Thessaloníki

Thessaloniki

ACCOMMODATIONS

A Hotel Argo
B Hotel Atlantis
H Hotel Atlas
D Hotel Averof
G Hotel Emporikon
E Hotel Ilisia
F Hotel Ilios
C Hotel Kastoria
K Hotel Luxembourg
I Hotel Palace
J Hotel Tourist
L Youth Hostel

0   300 yards
0   300 meters

and Byzantine museums. Although the region around the city had been inhabited since the first millennium BC, Salonica was not founded until 315 BC, when Cassander, King of Macedonia, decided to build a new city on the shore of the Thermaic Gulf. Cassander named the city after his beloved wife—the sister of Alexander the Great. Under Macedonian and, after the Battle of Pydna in 168 BC, Roman rule, Salonica flourished; its unique status as the only port on the Via Egnatia put it at the crossroads of important trade routes and transformed Cassander's creation into a bustling cultural and commercial center. Salonica's prominence made it a magnet for cultural luminaries: in the first century AD, the Apostle Paul wrote two epistles in churches he founded here (I and II Thessalonians). After the 10th century, missionary followers of the brothers **Methodius** and **Cyril**—inventors of the Cyrillic alphabet—exerted their wide-ranging influence from headquarters here. Despite the frequent raids by Goths, Avars, Slavs, Bulgars, and Crusaders, Salonica continued to prosper under Byzantine rule, eventually becoming the Empire's second city behind Constantinople while Athens was in the throes of cultural decline. Five centuries of Ottoman rule ended only in 1912 during the First Balkan War, 90 years after most of Greece had achieved independence. In 1881, while still Ottoman, Salonica saw the birth of **Mustafa Kemal** who would become an Ottoman general and later, as Atatürk, founder of the Turkish Republic. In the early 20th century, the city's population, which included Slavs, Albanians, and a vast Sephardic Jewish community, was more European than Hellenic. More homogeneously Greek today—because of population exchanges during the partitioning of the Ottoman Empire and the tragic extermination of the city's Jews by the Nazis during World War II—the city retains a cultural vigor.

ORIENTATION

Thessaloniki is located on the north shore of the Thermaic Gulf. It is a fairly thin and elongated town stretched out along the waterfront. Running parallel to the water, the main streets are **Nikis, Mitropoleos, Tsimiski, Ermou, Egnatia,** and **Agiou Dimitriou.** Intersecting all these streets and leading from the water into town are **Aristotelous, Agia Sophias,** and **Ethnikis Aminis.** The main shopping streets are Tsimiski, Mitropoleos, and Ag. Sophias. As it reaches the waterfront, Aristotelous forms Aristotelous Sq., which is lined by the tourist office, train office, airport bus terminal, and a string of overpriced cafes. The cheaper hotels are on Egnatia St., banks and post office on Tsimiski, and waterfront bars and cafes on Nikis St. The train station is west of **Dimokratias Square** (also known as **Vardaris Square**) along Monastiriou St., an extension of Egnatia St. The main park, fairgrounds, university, and Archeological Museum lie east of the downtown area, just inland from the **White Tower**—*Lefkos Pirgos*—the best-known landmark of Thessaloniki. Inland from Tsimiski St., **Navarinou Square,** with its centerpiece of Roman ruins, is a meeting ground for Thessaloniki's youth. Facing inland, head left on Mitropoleos St., to reach the **Ladadika** district. This ex-red-light neighborhood has been restored into a charming pocket of turn-of-the-century cafes, bars, and authentic Greek *tavernas*. Roughly 15 blocks inland, north of Athinas St. and flanked by ancient castle walls, wind the streets of the **old town.** A marvelous place for morning or evening strolls, here you will find a welcome degree of tranquility, panoramic views, and cheap *tavernas*. The large area east of the White Tower (about half the city) is predominantly residential.

PRACTICAL INFORMATION

Transportation

Flights: The airport (tel. 47 39 77) is 16km east of town. Take bus #78 (120dr) or a taxi (2200dr). There is an **Olympic Airways Office** on 3 Koundouriotou St. (tel. 23 02 40 or 26 01 22; fax 22 97 25). Open M-Sa 8am-3:30pm. For reservations (tel. 28 18 80) M-Sa 7am-9pm. Flights to Athens (9-10 per day, 22,100dr); Limnos (1 per day, 5:45am, 15,300dr); Lesvos (1 per day, 5:45am, 21,000dr); Crete (2-3 per week to Iraklion, 2 per week to Hania, 30,000dr); Rhodes (2 per week, 32,000dr); Ioannina (2 per week, 12,300dr); Cyprus (2 per week, 67,100dr); and Istanbul, Turkey (2 per week, 55,000dr). Flights run fairly frequently to most European capitals.

Trains: Main terminal (tel. 51 75 17) is on Monastiriou St., in the western part of the city. Take any bus down Egnatia St. (80dr). Trains to Athens (8hr., 10 per day, 4100dr); Volos (4½hr., 8 per day, 2020dr); Larissa (4½hr., 11 per day, 1370dr); Edessa (2½hr., 8 per day, 840dr); Xanthi (4hr., 5 per day, 2160dr); Alexandroupolis (7hr., 3 per day, 3000dr); Istanbul, Turkey (12hr., 1 per day, 12,730dr); and Sofia, Bulgaria (7hr., 1 per day, 6310dr). A **ticketing office** (tel. 27 63 82) is at the corner of Aristotelous St. and Ermou St. Open Tu-F 8am-8pm, Sa and M 8am-3pm.

Buses: The privately run **KTEL** bus company operates out of dozens of stations scattered throughout the city, each servicing a district of Greece named for its largest city. Although printed timetables and price lists are almost nonexistent, departure times are posted above ticket counters. In addition, the **EOT** has virtually complete information, in Greek, regarding bus schedules, fares, trip duration, station locations, and telephone numbers. There are buses to Athens (7hr., 17 per day, 8000dr); Katerini (1hr., 25 per day about every 30min. 6:30am-10pm, 1200dr); Kozoni (2½hr., 13 per day about every hr. 6am-9pm, 2250dr); Veria (1½hr., 21 per day about every 45min. 6am-8pm, 1300dr); Larissa (4hr., 14 per day, 2800dr); Volos (3½hr., 6 per day, 3450dr); Alexandroupolis (6hr., 6 per day, 5400dr); and Kavala (3hr., 16 per day every hr. 6am-10pm, 2800dr). Call 141 for Greek language information on the telephone numbers and street addresses of all depots.

Public Transportation: An extensive network of local buses services Thessaloniki and suburbs up to 1hr. away. An office across from the train station and the EOT provides limited scheduling information. #8, 10, 11, and 31 run up and down Egnatia St. Buy your ticket on the bus (price depends on distance 80-220dr).

Ferries: Ticketing at **Karacharisis Travel and Shipping Agency,** 8 Koundouriotou St. (tel. 52 45 44; fax 53 22 89). Open M-F 9am-9pm, Sa 9am-3pm. Ferries travel to: Crete (24hr., 11,900dr); Paros (14hr., 9300dr); Naxos (14hr., 8700dr); Syros (12hr., 8400dr); Santorini (17hr., 9900dr); Tinos (13hr., 9100dr); and Mykonos (13hr., 9200dr). Ferries travel twice a week to Limnos (7hr., 5300dr); Lesvos (9hr., 8000dr) and Chios (12hr., 8300dr). Ferries go once a week to Rhodes (20hr., 14500dr) and Kos (18hr., 12300dr). Private cabins without bath generally cost an additional 50% of quoted fare, and cabins with bath average twice the deck fare. In July and Aug., it is best to reserve a seat 2-3 days in advance. Ferry service is reduced significantly in the winter.

Flying Dolphins: Hydrofoils travel daily (June-Sept. only) to Skiathos (3hr.), Skopelos (4hr.), and Alonissos (5hr.). Fares average 10,000dr. **Crete Air Travel,** 1 Dragoumi St. (tel. 54 74 07 or 53 43 76), directly across from the main port, sells tickets. Open M-F 9am-9pm, Sa 9am-3pm.

Tourist and Financial Services

Tourist Offices: EOT (tel. 27 18 88, 22 29 35, or 26 55 07; fax 26 55 04), on Aristotelous Sq. at #8, one block from the water. Take any bus on Egnatia St. to Aristotelous Sq. The office has free city maps, hotel listings, transportation schedules, and information about the **International Trade Fair, Song Festival,** the **Thessaloniki Festival of Film,** and the **Dimitria Cultural Festival,** all held between Sept. and Nov. Open M-F 8am-8pm, Sa 8:30am-2pm. **United Travel System,** 28 Mitropoleos St. (tel. 28 67 56; fax 28 31 56), near Aristotelous Sq. There is no sign on the street, so ring the bell to be let in and go to the 7th floor. Ask for English-speaking Liza and make sure you're carrying Let's Go. Open M-F 9:30am-5pm. Other offices at the **port** (tel. 59 35 78) and the **airport** (tel. 42 50 11, ext. 215).

Banks: National Bank, 11 Tsimiski St. (tel. 53 86 21). Open for **currency exchange** M-F 8am-2pm and 6-8pm, Sa 9am-1pm, Su 9:30am-12:15pm. Smaller banks charge slightly higher commissions. Many line Tsimiski St., including **Citibank,** 21 Tsimiski St. (tel. 26 60 21), which handles sophisticated international banking needs and has a 24hr. **ATM.** Most banks open M-Th 8am-2pm, F 8am-1:30pm.

American Express: 19 Tsimiski St. (tel. 26 15 21). Open M-F 10am-4pm, Sa 9am-2pm. Also at **Memphis Travel,** 23 Nikis St. (tel. 22 27 96), on the waterfront.

Consulates: Bulgaria, 12 N. Manou (tel. 82 92 10). **Cyprus,** 37 L. Nikis (tel. 26 06 11). **Italy,** 63 Vas. Olgas (tel. 83 00 55). **Turkey,** 151 Ag. Dimitriou (tel. 24 84 52). Consulates generally open M-F 9am-6pm. **U.S.,** 59 Nikis St. (tel. 24 29 00), on the waterfront west of the White Tower. Open M, W, F 9am-noon, but will assist Mt. Athos pilgrims even when officially shut. **United Kingdom,** 8 Venizelou St. (tel. 27 80 06). Open M-F 8am-3pm.

MACEDONIA & THRACE

Ministry of Northern Greece: (tel. 25 70 10), on the corner of Ag. Dimitriou St. and Venizelou. After obtaining letters from their consulate, men wishing to visit Mt. Athos must obtain permits here in room 222 (see **Mt. Athos** p. 277). Open M-F 8am-2pm (10am-2pm for Mt. Athos permits).

International Bookstore: Many of the kiosks in Thessaloniki sell foreign newspapers and magazines. **Molcho Books,** 10 Tsimiski St. (tel. 27 52 71), across from the National Bank, has an excellent selection of English and other foreign language books, as well as many international daily newspapers. Open M, W, and Sa 8:40am-2:50pm, Tu and Th-F 8:40am-2:20pm and 5-8pm. **Mitakas** (tel. 28 68 06), right next to the branch post office on Ethnikis Aminis St., also has a large selection. Open M-F 8:30am-2pm and 5-8:30pm, Sa-Su 8:30am-3pm.

Laundromats: Bianca, 3 L. Antoniadou St. (tel. 20 96 02). Behind the church to your right as you face the Arch of Galerius. 1400dr per load includes wash, dry, and soap. Open M-F 8am-8:30pm, Sa 8am-3pm.

Emergency and Communications

Tourist Police: 4 Dodekanissou St., 5th floor (tel. 55 48 70, 55 48 71). Offers free maps and brochures. Some English spoken. Open daily 8am-11pm.

Hospital: Ippokration Public Hospital, 50 A. Papanastasiou (tel. 83 79 20). Some doctors speak English. **Red Cross First Aid Hospital,** 6 Koundouriotou St. (tel. 53 05 30), located at the entrance to the main port. Free minor medical care.

Post Office: The main post office is on Aristotelous St. right before Egnatia. Open M-F 7:30am-8pm, Sa 7:30am-2pm, Su 9am-1:30pm. A major branch office is on Ethnikis Aminis close to the White Tower. Open M-F 7:30am-8pm. **Postal Code:** 54101.

Internet Access: The flashy **Globus Internet Cafe,** 12 Amynta St. (tel. 23 29 01; http://www.globus.gr; email globus@amynta.globus.gr) offers web access, email, and telnet. Take Egnatia St. toward the ancient *agora,* turn right on Platonos St., then diagonally left on Amynta. Internet access is 1300dr per hr.

OTE: 27 Karolou Diehl St., at the corner of Ermou St., 1 block east of Aristotelous St. Open 24hr. **Telephone Code:** 031.

ACCOMMODATIONS

Fortunately for the budget traveler, most of Thessaloniki's less expensive hotels are clustered together along the western end of Egnatia St., between Vardaris Sq. (500m east of the train station) and Dikastirion Sq. Be aware that Egnatia, one of the city's most important thoroughfares, is loud at all hours. Prices rise about 25% between September and November during the international fair and festivals. Single women should avoid offers for cheap rooms touted by English-speaking tourist information impersonators at the train station.

Youth Hostel, 44 Alex. Svolou St. (tel. 22 59 46; fax 26 22 08). Take tram #8, 10, 11, or 31 on Egnatia St. and get off at the Arch of Galerius. Walk toward the water and turn left 2 blocks later onto Svolou St. Cheap and committed to cleanliness. Hot showers available 9-11am and 6-10pm. 1-night max stay without Hostel Membership, 3 nights with it. 10% discount for HI card. 2000dr per person. No curfew, but 11am-6:30pm lockout during which only the lobby stays open.

Hotel Argo, 11 Egnatia St. (tel. 51 97 70). Clean, green-hued rooms (sometimes with fridges), good bargains, and classical music. Singles 5000dr, with bath 6000dr; doubles 6000dr, with bath 8000dr.

Hotel Atlantis, 14 Egnatia St. (tel. 54 01 31). Old-fashioned pink pastel exterior and patriotically decorated blue and white rooms with shared baths. Singles 6000dr; doubles 8000dr; triples 11,000dr.

Hotel Emporikon, 14 Singrou (tel. 52 55 60, 51 44 31), at Egnatia. Offers clean, comfortable rooms with shared bath. Singles 6000dr; doubles 9000dr; triples 12,000dr.

Hotel Averof, 24 L. Sofou St. (tel. 53 88 40; fax 54 31 94), at Egnatia St. New furniture, friendly staff, and clean rooms with bath and balcony. Communal living room with TV. Singles 6000dr, with bath 8000dr; doubles 8000dr, with bath 10,000dr.

Hotel Kastoria (tel. 53 62 80; fax 53 62 50), at the intersection of Egnatia St. and L. Sofou St. 17. Clean, somewhat claustrophobic rooms arranged in a ring around a large common space. Singles 6500dr; doubles 7500dr; triples 9000dr.

Hotel Luxembourg, 6 Komninon St. (tel. 27 84 49 or 27 57 25), on intersection with Tsimiski St. Turn-of-the-century facade and clean nondescript rooms. Singles 6000dr, with bath 9000dr; doubles 9000dr, with bath 12,000dr.

Hotel Ilisia, 24 Egnatia (tel. 528 492). Small but clean rooms with bath. Singles 8000dr; doubles 10000dr; triples 12000dr.

Hotel Ilios, 27 Egnatia St. (tel. 51 26 20 or 51 26 21). Loudly patriotic—at least to Americans and French—red, white, and blue floors. Rooms with bath. Singles 9000dr; doubles 13000dr; triples 15000dr.

Hotel Tourist, 21 Mitropoleos (tel. 27 63 35; fax 22 68 65), 1 block from Aristotelous Sq., on a pleasant, tree-lined street near the waterfront. Has 4.5m-high ceilings, cavernous hallways, and an old-fashioned salon and elevator. Singles 8000dr, with bath 10,000dr; doubles with bath 11,000dr; triples with bath 18,000dr.

Hotel Palace, 12 Tsimiski (tel. 25 74 00, 25 65 88, or 24 21 88; fax 25 65 89). This is the place to go if you want luxurious lodging without paying the high rates charged by Thessaloniki's more pretentious hotels. Rooms here are large, softly carpeted, very elegant, and come with phone, bath, and TV. Singles 14,000dr; doubles 18,000dr; breakfast included.

Hotel Atlas, 40 Egnatia St. (tel. 53 70 46 or 51 00 38; fax 54 35 07). Overpriced; worth staying in only if all the nearby budget hotels are full. Rooms with shared bath. Singles 7000dr; doubles 10000dr; triples 13000dr.

FOOD

Don't go to Thessaloniki for the standard *moussaka* and Greek salad—this town is known and loved throughout Greece for its excellent *mezedes*. Prepared for locals, the food is almost sure to be cooked well and priced fairly. Thessaloniki's downtown is dotted with inexpensive self-service food outlets and shops. Lively and full of bargains, the marketplace *(agora)* is bounded on four sides by Irakliou St., Egnatia St., Aristotelous St., and Venizelou St. To stock up on fruits, vegetables, bread, and groceries, visit the **open-air markets** of Vati Kioutou St. just off Aristotelous. The Aretsou Area, along the bay about 4km toward the airport, boasts excellent seafood. Explore the old town and Ladadika district for inexpensive, family-oriented *tavernas*.

The Brothers (tel. 26 64 32), in Navarino Sq., offers traditional Greek meals, at good prices (full meal 1500dr). They are popular, delicious, but very busy. Open daily noon-midnight.

Ouzeri Tavernaki, 3 Aristotelous Sq. (tel. 23 77 15). One of the many establishments in Thessaloniki owned by the powerful Tottis company. Offers tasty food with elegant atmosphere (entrees 1500-2500dr).

Ta Spata, 28 Aristotelous St. (tel. 27 74 12), offers a wide selection of tasty, inexpensive, moderately sized entrees (1500dr). Open daily 11am-midnight.

To Chriso Pagoni, 42 Alex. Svolou St. (tel. 26 53 38 or 22 30 14), next to the hostel. Has a variety of traditional dishes for low prices.

Tsampouro, 2 Bagdamali St. (tel. 28 14 35), in the maze of streets between Egnatia St.and Tsimiski St. around Emboriou Sq. Tasty, inexpensive chicken and fish.

Rogoti, 8 Venizelou St. (tel. 22 77 66 or 27 76 94). Established in 1928, this restaurant has a delicious secret recipe for *soutzoukakia* (1650dr).

Dell Arco (tel. 206 423), on Egnatia St. right next to Arch of Galerius. Specializes in pizza, pasta, and calzones (entrees 1350-2250dr).

Mesogeios, 38 Balanou St. (tel. 28 84 60), about 50 yards from Tsampouro. The largest *ouzeri* in the area. One of the few places around with English-speaking staff.

New Ilyssia, 17 Leontos Sofou St. (tel. 53 69 96), a neighborhood restaurant and grill located off Egnatia St. Serves large helpings of traditional Greek food in an unpretentious setting (entrees from 1250dr). Open daily 8:30am-2am.

Amaltheia, 26 Vas. Irakliou St. (tel. 27 82 76). Head up Aristotelous St. and turn left. A variety of salads (700-1000dr) and a selection of chicken dishes (1200-1800dr).

Cafe Extrablatt, 46 Alex Svolou (tel. 25 69 00), next to hostel. Expensive but delicious meals and a choice of every beer you've ever heard of and many you haven't.

Streetsmart in Northern Greece

If you travel through Northern Greece for long enough, you will start to notice something very odd about the street and square names—they're all the same. Here's a guide for all travelers in Greece who have ever wondered what it *really* means to stand at the corner of **25 Martiou** and **Pavlou Melas**.

25 Martiou: March 25, 1821—Greece's national holiday, celebrating Greece's declaration of independence from the Ottoman Empire.

3 Septemvriou: September 3, 1863—Greeks riot against monarchical rule and demand a constitution.

11 Noemvriou: November 11, 1912—Thessaloniki liberated from the Ottomans.

28 Octovriou: October 28, 1940—"Ohi Day!" President Metaxas refused to surrender to Mussolini's Italians.

Athanassiou Diakou: A hero of the Greek Revolution roasted on a spit after being captured by the Turks.

Pavlou Melas: Guerilla leader who freed Macedonian villages from Bulgarians.

Iroon Polytehniou: The heroes of the Polytechnio—students who rioted against the military *junta* in 1974 and contributed to its downfall.

Riga Ferreou: The great Greek poet before the Revolution who wrote "Better one day of freedom than 40 years of slavery and oppression."

Averof: The name of one of Greece's oldest, richest, and most munificent families. The primary recipient of their generosity is the mountain village of Metsovo.

ENTERTAINMENT

Thessaloniki's varied and dynamic nightlife booms at all hours of the night—and is often considered to rival that of Athens. There are three main hubs for late-night *glendi* in Thessaloniki: the **Ladadika** district (once the city's red-light strip), the bustling waterfront, and the area around the exit for the airport. Bars and cafes are in the Ladadika area across from the central port and on the waterfront, while all the big open-air discos throbbing to the beats of techno (and sometimes of Greek music) are on the road toward the airport, about a 2000-2500dr taxi ride from the center. A more grunge crowd mellows out with a cup of coffee in the park and at **Navarinou Square,** one block west of D. Gounari St.

Mylos, 56 Andreou Georgiou St. (tel. 52 59 68), in the far west of the city, accessible by bus #31 or by taxi. A converted old mill, Mylos is now a massive entertainment center, containing art exhibits, a restaurant, bars, and an area for live shows.

Ipnovates (tel. 47 21 59), 11km east of the city along the main highway. An enormous open-air disco-bar that is absolutely packed every Friday and Saturday night. U.S. music lovers beware though—only Greek beats are played here. Cover Su-Th 1500dr, F-Sa 3000dr; includes one drink.

✪Tataboo Disco (tel. 47 17 31), right on the exit for the airport, about 13km outside of town. Disco fever may have died in America with the 80s, but it lives on at Tataboo. Cover 2000dr.

Theatron (tel. 47 11 60), next to Ipnovates club. Arguably the most sophisticated club in Thessaloniki—a sophistication apparent in the 4000dr cover. Check out the Greek colonnade here as you rub elbows with the city's richest and hippest.

Soho (tel. 47 17 68), next to Tataboo. A booming U.S.-style nightclub with deafening house music. Cover 2500dr.

Iguana, 45 L. Nikis St. (tel. 26 37 30). One of the largest bars on the waterfront, named after the life-size stuffed lizard that hangs from the ceiling. Beer 1000dr; cocktails 1600-1800dr.

Isalos Cafe, 43 L. Nikis St. (tel. 28 81 58). A pleasant mid-sized cafe crowded day and night. Friendly staff and inexpensive drinks, at least by waterfront standards.

Steven's, 57 L. Nikis St. (tel. 26 37 30). Join locals gazing at the Thermaic Gulf's dark waters at this mellow bar. Beer 1000dr; cocktails 1600dr.

Villa 11, 11 Katouni St. (tel. 55 16 00). Head west down Niki's past Eleftherias Square and turn right on Katouni. A smallish two-story bar in the heart of the Ladadika district. Good if you're feeling nostalgic for U.S. or British tunes.

Rodon, 3 Aigiptou St. (tel. 54 20 93), one block west from Katouni St. One of the largest bars in the Ladadika, replete with loud music and hyperactive strobe lights. Beer 1000dr; cocktails 2000dr.

Taboo, on Kastritsiou St., one block from Egnatia St. One of the few places in Thessaloniki that caters to gay and lesbian parties.

Natali Cinema, 3 Vas. Olgas St. (tel. 82 94 57), on the waterfront, 5 minutes past the White Tower. Shows open-air movies in summer.

SIGHTS

Archaeological Museum

To get to the museum, take bus #3 from the railway station to Han Sq. Tel. 83 05 38 or 83 10 37. Open M 12:30-8pm, Tu-Sa 8am-8pm, Su 8am-7pm; in winter M 10:30am-5pm, Tu-F 8am-5pm, Sa-Su 8:30am-3pm. Admission 1500dr, non-EU students and seniors 800dr, EU students and under 18 free.

If you have time for only one stop in the city, the superlative **Archaeological Museum** is your destination. The treasures of the Macedonian tombs in Vergina used to be the highlight of the Archaeological Museum but have now been returned to their site of origin (see p. 267). In place of the Vergina artifacts is an impressive exhibition on gold in Macedonia. Many of the golden works display exceptional artistic skill and attention to detail. Particularly impressive are the elaborate gold myrtle wreaths, found in Derveni and the cemetery at Pydna. The rest of the museum houses a large collection of Roman-era statues, grand mosaics from homes in Thessaloniki, and other artifacts from nearby burial sites such as Lembet, Sedes, and Gona. Also notable is the **Derveni papyrus,** the only surviving papyrus in Greece. Greece's relatively moist climate—compared to the arid crags of North Africa, where most papyri are found—prevents scrolls from surviving; the Derveni papyrus, an interpretation of an eschatological poem by Orpheus, survived only because it was half-burnt.

More Museums

The **Museum of Byzantine Culture** (tel. 86 85 70 or 86 85 71) is a massive brick structure right next to the Archaeological Museum. *(Open M noon-8pm, Tu-Su 8am-8pm. Admission 1500dr, non-EU students and seniors 800dr, EU students and under-18 free.)* The three galleries focus respectively on the evolution of Byzantine churches, the nature of everyday Byzantine life, and the attitudes of the Byzantines towards death and burial. The well-preserved fresco-covered tombs in the third room—containing a mixture of Christian and pagan elements—are especially interesting.

The **International Fairgrounds,** across from the Archaeological and Byzantine Museums, hold a variety of festivals in the fall, including the International Trade Fair in September (for info call 23 92 21). The fairgrounds also house the **Macedonian Museum of Contemporary Art** (tel. 24 00 02; fax 28 15 67). *(Open Tu-Sa 10am-2pm and 6-9pm, Su 11am-2pm. Admission 500dr, students 300dr, artists and groups free.)* The new museum frequently hosts displays of internationally renowned modern artists.

On the other side of the park looms Thessaloniki's best-known landmark, *Lefkos Pirgos*—**White Tower** (tel. 26 78 32), all that remains of a 16th-century Venetian seawall. *(Open Tu-Su 8am-2:30pm. Free.)* Formerly known as the Bloody Tower because an elite corps of soldiers was massacred within it, it was painted white to obliterate the gruesome memories. The tower now houses a **Museum of Early Christian Art** and a cafe in the turret. Follow the spiral staircase up and peruse a vast collection of iconography. Views of the city and its waterfront from the top are spectacular.

Greek history buffs will want to visit the interesting **Museum of the Macedonian Struggle,** 23 Koromila St. (tel. 22 97 78; fax 23 31 08), one block in from the water, about halfway between the White Tower and Aristotelous Square. *(Open Tu-Su 8am-2:30pm. Admission 200dr.)* Brimming with images and models of warriors and battles, it depicts the story of Thessaloniki's struggle for independence—a struggle not completed until October 26, 1912, toward the end of the First Balkan War.

Classicists should check out the ruins of the **Eptapirgion Walls,** erected during the reign of Theodosius the Great, which stretch along the north edge of the old city. Take bus #22 from Eleftherias Sq. on the waterfront. Eleftherias Sq. is also where buses #5, 33, and 39 leave for the **Ethnology and Popular Art (Folklore) Museum,** 68 Vas. Olgas St. (tel. 83 05 91), which contains a wide range of traditional costumes, embroidery, and farm tools. *(Open F-W 9:30am-2pm. Admission 200dr.)* Note the display of photographs by Fred Boissonas.

A very different experience from the usual Greek folklore and archaeological museums can be found at the recently opened **Museum of Cinematography** (tel. 25 70 50) on Aristotelous St. *(Open M-F 9am-3pm. Free.)* The small museum has massive old movie cameras and pictures of famous American stars, as well as ground-breaking Greek artists and directors such as the Mannakis brothers.

Roman and Byzantine Salonica

The celebrated **Arch of Galerius** stands at the end of Egnatia St. at the corner of Gounari St., but remains under renovation and covered with scaffolding. Next to it and also closed for reconstruction, the **Rotunda** was designed as an emperor's mausoleum, but renamed **Agios Georgios** by Theodosius the Great for use as a church. For further historical pursuits, head north of Dikastirion Sq. to the **Roman Market** between Filippou and Olibou St. The ruins, which include a somewhat hyper-restored theater, continue to be excavated. The centerpiece of the remains of the **Palace of Galerius,** near Navarino Sq., is the well-preserved octagonal hall.

Because Salonica was for many years the second most important city in the Byzantine Empire, Thessaloniki boasts a large number of churches. Walk down the city's streets (especially Egnatia) and it seems as if small stone Byzantine churches reside in every corner. Over the centuries, earthquakes, fire, and conversions into mosques by the Ottomans have severely damaged most of Salonica's churches. Many, nonetheless, are still worth a visit. Located well inland on Agiou Dimitriou St., the city's oldest and most famous church is **Agios Dimitrius,** built in the basilica style in the 5th century AD and named for Dimitrius, a famous early Christian martyr and the patron saint of Salonica. *(Open Su 10:30am-8pm, M 12:30-7pm, Tu-Sa 8am-8pm. Free.)* The **catacombs** beneath the church conjure memories of a time when Christians were persecuted and had to gather in secret underground tunnels to practice their religion.

Another famous Salonica church is the domed 7th-century **Agia Sophia,** modeled on the Agia Sophia in Constantinople. *(Open daily 9am-1pm. Free.)* Most of the church is painted in drab colors. Atop the dome, however, is a splendid 9th-century mosaic of the Ascension—the only image to survive the church's conversion to a mosque in 1585. The church is just below the intersection of Prassanaki St. and Egnatia St.

On Egnatia St., almost directly north of Agia Sophia is the large **Panagia Ahiropoeitos,** one of the first known basilica-style churches. The church's name, Ahiropoeitos, means "created without hands" in Greek and stems from a 12th-century legend that an icon miraculously appeared one day in the church.

If Agios Dimitrios was not enough to sate your appetite for catacombs, head to **Agios Yiannis Prodromos,** next to Agia Sophia. *(Open daily 7:30am-12:30pm and 6-9pm. Free.)* In the crypts are an underground church and winding paths with beautiful silver-plated icons.

Some of Thessaloniki's smaller, lesser known—but still fascinating—churches include **Ossios David,** an early domed church in the steep streets of the old town; **Panagia Halkeon,** a red brick edifice named for the copper-selling industry it used to center; and the **Church of the Holy Apostles,** which boasts skillful architecture and excellent wall paintings. You can also visit the beautiful **Old Synagogue** at 35 Singrou St. Although it is not in use, the caretaker at the **Jewish Community Center,** 24 Tsimiski St., will let you in.

■ Pella Πελλα

Along the main highway, just 38km west of Thessaloniki. Buses to Pella depart from the 22 Anagenniseos St. depot near the train station in Thessaloniki (every 30-45min., 800dr). Walk down Octovriou St. past the courthouse and turn right onto Anagenniseos St. The KTEL is on the corner of Damonos St. Buses to Thessaloniki (2-3 per hr.) pass the site, which is right on the main highway. Tel. (0382) 31 160. Open Apr.-Oct. M noon-8pm, Tu-Su 8am-8pm. Admission to site and museum requires separate tickets. Each site is 500dr, students and seniors 300dr, EU students free.

History

The ruins at Pella, discovered in 1957 by a farmer with an archaeological bent, date back to a time when the Aegean covered the surrounding fields, and Pella served as a port on the Thermaic Gulf. The area around Pella was heavily inhabited in prehistoric times, as the remains of 26 neolithic settlements indicate. According to legend, Pella's earliest inhabitants were Cretan in origin; they were, however, rapidly replaced by Macedonians sweeping in from the north. Around 400 BC, King Archelaus opted to build his palace here, and Pella became the largest city in Macedonia, and home of such cultural luminaries as Zeuxis, one of the greatest artists in antiquity. Pella, the birthplace of King Philip II, prospered under the king's reign. The erection of a splendid new palace attracted great minds and talents from the entire Hellenic world to his court, as Pella became the new capital of Macedonia, and the first ever capital of a Greece united under Macedonian conquerors. Pella's halcyon days continued with the rule of Phillip's son Alexander the Great and his Hellenistic successors, then came to an abrupt end when it was ransacked by the Roman general Aemilius Paulus in 168 BC after his victory over the Macedonians at the battle of Pydna.

Museum

Pella only takes an hour to see, but the museum alone makes the trip worthwhile. The museum houses various objects found in the ruins of Pella, including bronze statuettes, many terra-cotta figurines, and glazed and unglazed Macedonian pottery. Its most important objects, however, are the exquisite mosaics "Dionysus Riding a Panther," "The Lion Hunt," and "Griffin Devouring a Deer." These skillful works are the earliest-known mosaics to attempt three-dimensionality.

Touring Pella

Directly across the highway from the museum is Pella's vast archaeological site, much of it still being excavated by budding young Schleimanns from the University of Thessaloniki. At the site are the remains of the **Agora,** the commercial center of the city in ancient times, and a few grand houses. The **House of Dionysos** and the **House of the Abduction of Helen** both have expansive, well-preserved mosaic floors; the **House of Plaster** has no mosaics but a splendid rectangular Ionic colonnade. North of the houses and the *Agora* are the Acropolis and palace (off limits to visitors). The palace, built in ten stages, is a makeshift amalgam of architectural styles. It was expanded by Philip, but its effulgence ended with the rest of Pella at the hands of Aemilius Paulus.

■ Vergina Βεργινα

Buses run from Thessaloniki (2hr., every 30min., 1300dr) and Edessa (6 per day, 900dr) to Veria, from which you can take the "Alexandria" bus and get off in Vergina (20min., 8 per day, 280dr); the bus stop is next to the complex housing the Royal Tombs. Tombs and palace open Tu-Su 8am-8pm. Admission to the tombs is 1200dr, students 600dr, EU students free. Admission to the palace is 500dr, students free. Guidebooks to Vergina's ruins are available at the cafe/souvenir stand across from the tombs; the site office at the entrance to the palace ruins has a smaller selection.

History

The discovery of the ancient ruins of Vergina, 13km southeast of Veria, was an archaeological watershed. That Vergina contained ancient Macedonian remains had been known since the French archaeologist L. Heusey discovered portions of a palace in 1861. The extent and significance of the ruins, however, were not revealed until 1977, when Manolis Andronikos began excavating the remains of **royal tombs** and a large **palace** dating from 350 BC. The tombs display such superb artistry (and skeletal remains) that scholars believe that they could only have belonged only to the royal Macedonian family of **King Philip II,** father of Alexander the Great. Ancient sources report that one of the Philip's legs was longer than the other, and the discovery of shin guards of different length in a tomb has confirmed that it was Philip's. The remains suggest that Vergina was the site of the ancient Macedonian capital of **Aigai.**

Museum

Housed until recently in Thessaloniki's Architectural Museum, most of the remains of the Vergina tombs are now located in an impressive subterranean museum in Vergina itself; the **museum** will without a doubt be the highlight of any visit to Vergina. Perhaps the most unusual aspect of the museum is that it lies completely underground, beneath the Great Tumulus, a massive burial mound more than 12m high and 110m in diameter. In the museum are artifacts found in the tombs such as marble funerary *steles,* pottery, and gold jewelry. Also exhibited, in their original locations, are four of the majestic royal tombs. Two of the tombs belong to unknown members of Macedon's royal family. One, the Tomb of the Prince, belongs to Alexander IV, who was the son of Alexander the Great and grandson of Philip II; the last is the grand tomb of Philip II himself. The designs of all four tombs are similar: in each one there is an anterior Ionic (or Doric) colonnade, usually decorated with scenes from mythology; the large room behind the colonnade contains the remains of the deceased, and various items meant to accompany him into the afterlife.

Touring Vergina

Uphill and to the south of the museum are the open ruins of the 3rd-century BC **Palace of Palatitsa,** which can be reached by a 30-minute walk. On the walk up is another tomb, the **Rhomaios Tomb,** containing a stately marble throne. The palace and the adjoining theater are now little more than a large spread-out collection of toppled columns and ancient rubble; in 336 BC, however, it was here that Philip II was assassinated while celebrating the marriage of his daughter, Kleopatra.

Food and Accommodations

The best restaurant is **Filippion** (tel. (0331) 92 892; fax 92 891), on the same road as the tombs. You'll find a wide variety of creative dishes and a wine list which the proprietors humbly claim is the third largest of its kind. On the road up to the intersection for the tombs is the more traditional **Olymbiada Restaurant** (tel. (0331) 92 432). If all you want is a *frappé* or a cocktail, head to **Cafe Kastro** (tel. (0331) 92 421), a large castle-like structure located across from Olymbiada.

There are two choices for lodging, both on the same road as the tombs. The larger **Pension Vergina** (tel. (0331) 92 510; fax 92 511) has beautiful modern rooms and a lovely veranda (singles 8000dr; doubles 12,000dr; triples 14,000dr; prices include breakfast). The technicolor **Oikos Rented Rooms** (tel. (0331) 92 366 or 24 975) offers clean, comfortable rooms (singles 7000dr; doubles 11,000dr).

■ Mount Olympus Ολυμπος

> The charm of Olympus does not lie in its natural beauty; nor its physical magnitude; the beauty of Olympus is spiritual, it is divine...
>
> —Boissonade

Rising from the coastal plain 90km southwest of Thessaloniki, Mt. Olympus so awed the seafaring ancient Greeks that they believed it to be the home of their pantheon of gods. The mountain's rocky summit brims with divine intrigue, the fire of Zeus' thun-

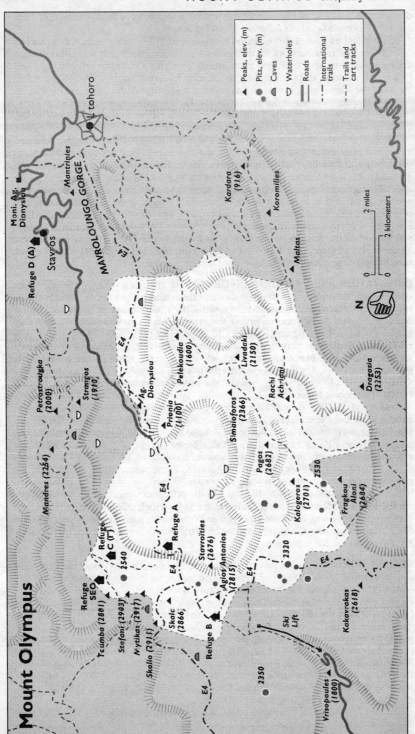

Mount Olympus

Legend
- ▲ Peaks, elev. (m)
- ● Pits, elev. (m)
- ◖ Caves
- ◖ Waterholes
- ▬ Roads
- ┄ International trails
- --- Trails and cart tracks

N

Litohoro

Moni. Ag. Dionysiou

Mantriqies

MAVROLOUNGO GORGE

Refuge D (Δ) ▲
Stavros ●

Kardara (916) ▲

Koromilies ▲

E4

Maltas ▲

D

Petrostrouvga (2000) ▲

Strangos (1961) ▲ D

D

Ag. Dionysiou

Pelekoudia (1600) ▲

Livadaki (2150) ▲

Dragasia (2353) ▲

Mandres (2254) ▲

D

◖

Prionia (1100) ▲

Simaloforos (2366) ▲

Rachi Achriou ▲

Pagos (2682) ▲

D

D

2530 ●

Refuge SEO

Refuge C (Γ) ▲ 2540 ●

Refuge A ▲

Stavroities (2676) ▲

Agios Antonios (2815) ▲

Kalogeros (2701) ▲

Fragkou Aloni (2684) ▲

● ●

2320 ●

Tcumba (2801) ▲
Stefani (2909) ▲
Nyctikas (2917) ▲

Skolio (2911) ▲

Skala (2866) ▲

E4

Refuge B ▲

E4

2350 ●

Ski Lift

Kakavrakas (2618) ▲

Vrisopoules (1800) ▲

2 miles

2 kilometers

0

0

derbolt, the lusty cup of Ganymede, the jealous grumblings of Hera, the heat of Hephaestus' forge, and glints of Athena's gleaming armor.

Mortals first ascended this celestial mountain in 1913. Since then, Olympus has been harnessed by a network of well-maintained hiking trails that make the summit accessible to just about anyone with sturdy legs and a taste for adventure. Even before the summit, the path up the mountain rewards visitors with incomparable views of the surrounding towns and mountains and ethereal blue skies, particularly in June and September, when the air is clearest. Each winter, six or more feet of snow bury Mt. Olympus—even in late July there are glacier dregs in shady corners—so the climbing season lasts only from May to October.

The gateway to Olympus is the small town of **Litohoro.** Surprisingly, Litohoro caters not only to fearless mountain-climbers but also to beach-loving hedonists, as the sands and bars of nearby **Plaka** beach draw crowds from as far as Larissa and Thessaloniki. If you make the ascent between May and September, you'll need no special equipment besides sturdy shoes (hiking in sandals is insane), sunglasses, sunscreen, a hat, and at least two liters of water. If you plan on climbing the upper regions, you may need a waterproof windbreaker, an extra shirt, and gloves. To fully enjoy the wilderness, you may want to plan a two- or three-day trip with an overnight stay in one of the refuges or campsites on the mountain. Be prepared with warm clothes and cushy recovery supplies but leave your pack in Litohoro; as you hike ever upward, you'll regret every extra pound on your shoulders.

ORIENTATION AND PRACTICAL INFORMATION The main street in Litohoro runs east to west. To the east lies the highway to Athens and the sea; to the west is Olympus. About 500m after the entrance to town is the **main square** of Litohoro. On the main street, near the **bus station** before the main square, is an information booth that acts as the town's **tourist office** (tel. 83 100), providing free maps of the area (open mid-June to Sept. daily 9am-8pm). The **health center** (tel. 22 222) has **emergency facilities.** Litohoro's **National Bank** (tel. 81 025) is in the main square (open M-Th 8am-2pm and F 8am-1:30pm) along with the **post office** (open M-F 7:30am-2pm). The **OTE** sits on the main street across from the tourist information booth. **Postal code:** 60200. **Telephone code:** 0352.

Trains (tel. 22 522) stop at Litohoro on the Thessaloniki-Volos and Thessaloniki-Athens lines, but the station is 1km from the bus stop near the beach (by the BP station, left facing the water). The Katerini-Litohoro bus will take travelers the remaining 5km into town (20min., 13 per day, 220dr). **Buses** (tel. 81 271) from the KTEL station, opposite the church in the main square, travel from Litohoro to Thessaloniki (1½hr., 12 per day, 1650dr) via Katerini (20min, 17 per day, 420dr); Larissa (2hr., 8 per day, 1400dr); and Athens (6½hr., 3 per day, 7000dr).

From the main square, follow the signs to the offices of Greece's two alpine clubs: the **EOS Greek Mountaineering Club** (tel. 84 544), which offers a free map and brochure (open June-Aug. M-F 9am-12:30pm and 6:30-8:30pm, Sa-Su 9am-noon), and the **SEO Mountaineering Club** (tel. (031) 224 710). The EOS offers several refuges on Mt. Olympus; the SEO runs one.

ACCOMMODATIONS Litohoro's youth hostel has recently been closed; the best rates in town (about 3000-4000dr per person) can be found in rented rooms around the square. The most affordable hotel is the **Hotel Park** (tel. 81 252), located just after the entrance to town on the main road on the right. Its rooms have TV, phone, and bath (singles 6000dr; doubles 7000dr; triples 8000dr). The pleasant **Hotel Aphroditi** (tel. 81 415; fax 22 123) is located on the uphill road from the main square. Many of the comfortable rooms offer stunning views of the mountain, and the friendly management can offer suggestions about other places to stay. They will hold baggage for 500dr (singles 7500dr; doubles 9500dr; triples 12000dr). Another appealing place is the pink pastel **Hotel Markesia,** 5 Dionysiou St. (tel. 81 831 or 81 832), on a little side street to the left of the square. Rooms here come with bath, fridge, and kitchen (singles 7000dr; doubles 8000dr; triples 10000dr).

The beach area, about 5km from town, is full of **campgrounds,** of which **Olympus Zeus** (tel. 22 115, 22 116, and 22 117) and **Olympus Beach** (tel. 22 112 or 22 113) are the largest and best situated. **Do not free-lance camp** on the north side of the road connecting the town and the highway; it's a training ground for the Greek army.

FOOD Restaurants abound in Litohoro. **To Vareladikon** (tel. 83 917), on the main road at the bottom of town, has a large varied menu and friendly English-speaking staff (entrees 1200-1600dr). **Taverna Pazari** (tel. 82 540), about 15m from the Hotel Markesia, specializes in fish dishes such as red snapper and octopus (entrees 1200-1300dr). In the central square itself is the **Olympus Cafe** (tel. 84 282), a favorite with locals. The traditional food and wine here are the least expensive in the square (entrees 800-1300dr). If partying before the climb interests you, there are bars clustered both at the entry to Litohoro and at the beach. The most popular bars in town are **Garage** (tel. 84 427)—said to be frequented by the prettiest girls in Greece—and **Monopolio** (tel. 83 710). The most kickin' disco/bar on the beach is the **Michele Club** (tel. 22 215), located right on the beautiful clear water in the Plaka area.

THE PEAKS Mt. Olympus has eight peaks: **Kalogeros** (2701m), **Toumba** (2785m), **Profitis Ilias** (2803m), and **Antonius** (2817m) are dwarfed by the summits of **Skala** (2866m), **Skollo** (2911m), **Stefani** (also called the *Throne of Zeus*, 2909m), and **Mytikas** (or the *Pantheon,* 2917m). Two approaches to the peaks begin from Litohoro. To reach the trailheads, walk, hitch, or drive the asphalt road to **Prionia** (eventually a dusty unpaved path) that winds upward just before the square in Litohoro. There is no bus service between the trails and the village, so it's best to find a group to share a taxi (6000dr to Prionia). Those who hitch usually start early, since most climbers drive up in the morning.

If you'd rather turn your first approach into a scenic event, hiking alongside the Enipeas River from Litohoro to Prionia is an option; the 18km trail is wonderful but difficult. It begins past the town cemetery and Restaurant Mili, in the upper part of Litohoro. At the fork in the trail, follow the yellow diamond markers up the left side of the **Mavrolungo Gorge.** The four-hour path traverses astonishing scenery, including the charred shell of a **monastery** that gave refuge to Greek partisans during WWII until the Nazis burned it. When you reach Prionia you'll find a diminutive tavern, the last opportunity for food before the refuges.

The most popular route up the mountain begins at Prioria. A three-hour walk uphill takes you to the EOS's **Refuge A** (tel. 81 800), which has 90 beds and serves hot meals from 6am to 9pm. Lights out is at 10pm (2500dr per person, 2000dr for any alpine club members). The refuge fills up Friday and Saturday nights. Try to make reservations three to four days in advance through the club offices. EOS also owns three other refuges on Mt. Olympus. Both it and SEO provide maps and information about the mountain, maintain the trails, and organize emergency rescues.

At 2917m above sea level, **Mytikas,** the most climbed peak, has the highest elevation of the Mt. Olympus summits. Follow the red marks up the rocky mountainside and turn right at either of two successive forks. The first right (the harder way up) takes you to the base of the rockslide-prone **Locki,** a nearly vertical, hour-long ascent to the top. The second right takes you first to **Skala** (2860m) and then, after a series of sinuous ups and downs, to Mytikas. The trails to Mytikas are considered dangerous, as they are prone to rock slides and avalanches; it's not a good idea to lug a large pack along the route. The Locki path in particular should only be tackled by the enthusiastic, fit, and experienced mountain hiker.

If you decide not to tempt the gods by ascending Mytikas, a quick 30-minute hike from Skala takes you to **Skolio,** the second highest peak (2911m) and best point for viewing the sheer western face of Olympus.

The second approach to the peaks is at **Diastavrosi,** just 14km from Litohoro. This longer but more picturesque route offers views of the Aegean, the Macedonian plain, and the smog layer over Thessaloniki far below. You can find water in two places along this trail: at the turn-off between Barba and Spilia (1½hr. from the trail head, marked on the map), and at the spring at Strangos. It's a long haul (5-6hr.) from the start of the trail to the **SEO refuge** (keep following the red marks), where you can seek shelter (2000dr). Ample blankets are provided and hot meals are served throughout the day. At 2760m (only 157m from the summit of Olympus), this shelter is less frequented than its counterpart Refuge A below, and offers a magnificent view of the Stefani peak at sunrise. Just as exhilarating is the lunar landscape overlooking the **Plateau of the Muses,** named after the mythical Muses who inspire poetry. From here, the summit is only 90 minutes away, including a difficult ascent up Locki.

■ Edessa Εδεσσα

Edessa was named "the waters" by an occupying Bulgarian army. Perched on top of a steep butte in the foothills of Mt. Vermion, the town ends on the brink of a ravine, where numerous streams channelled through stone waterways and under Edessa's arched bridges cascade 32m to the valley floor, the country's only notable falls. It's not quite as magnificent as it sounds; concrete viewing balconies, overgrown weeds, litter, and danger signs along the water's edge detract from the experience. Although Edessa's main attraction is slightly sullied, the town's temperate climate, aromatic flowers, petite parks, and water-bound walkways are beautiful in their own right.

ORIENTATION AND PRACTICAL INFORMATION Edessa's bus station is at the corner of **Filippou St.** and **Pavlou Mela St.** Go north on Pavlou Mela St. to reach **Dimokratias St.** (also called **Egnatia St.**), one of the town's main thoroughfares and the site of most of Edessa's hotels. A little while after **Megalou Alexandrou Square** (on your right if your back is to the bus station), Dimokratias St. turns into **25 Martiou St.** and passes a large, leafy park full of bars and cafes. **Filippou St.,** another major commercial street, runs parallel to Dimokratias, then merges with it at **Timendon Sq.**

To find the **police station** (tel. 23 333), follow Dimokratias St. toward the waterfalls and turn left on Iroon Polytechniou St. The station is at the intersection with Arhelaou St. (open 24hr.). The **tourist information office** (tel. 20 300), located just to the right of the waterfalls, provides information about sights, hotels, and transportation (open daily 9am-10pm). The **National Bank,** 1 Dimokratias St., is surrounded by a fence on the corner of 2 Arch. Penteleiminos St. and has an **ATM** (open M-Th 8am-2pm and F 8am-1:30pm).

The main **bus station** (tel. 23 511) is at the corner of Pavlou Mela and Filippou St. **Buses** run to Athens (8hr., 3 per day, 8600dr); Thessaloniki (2hr., 5 per day, 11 on Sundays, 1550dr); and Veria (1hr., 6 per day, 900dr). A **second depot,** marked by a bus sign, is located at a family-run sandwich shop and grill just up the block at Pavlou Mela and Egnatia (look for "KTEL" painted on the window). Buses go to Kastoria (2½hr., 4 per day, 2050dr) and Florina (1½hr., 6 per day, 1400dr). The **train station** (tel. 23 510) is at the end of 18 Octovriou St., a 10-minute walk from the post office. **Trains** run to Florina (2hr., 4 per day, 720dr); Thessaloniki via Veria and Naoussa (2hr., 7 per day, 840dr); Kozani (2½hr., 6 per day, 820dr); and Athens, either directly (7hr., 1 per day, 8100dr) or via Plati (9hr., 3 per day, 4310dr). **Taxis** (tel. 23 392 or 22 904) congregate on 18th Octovriou St., near the bank. Edessa's **post office** (tel. 23 332), on Dimokratias St., one block from the *agora*, exchanges money for a commission (open M-F 7:30am-2pm). The **OTE** is a blue and white building facing the Byzantine clock tower on Ag. Dimitriou. **Postal Code: 58200. Telephone Code:** 0381.

ACCOMMODATIONS There are only a handful of hotels in Edessa. Fortunately, there are a few good deals among them. The best value is **Olympia Rented Rooms** (tel. 23 544), on 18 Octovriou near the train station (singles 5000dr; doubles 7000dr). The more centrally located **Hotel Pella** (tel. 23 541), on the intersection of Pavlou Mela St. and Egnatia St., offers large but rather drab rooms with phone, TV, and bath (singles 7000dr; doubles 12,000dr). Next door to Hotel Pella is the slightly fancier **Hotel Alfa** (tel. 22 221 or 22 231; fax 24 777), which boasts an astounding two (2!) elevators. Rooms come with phone, TV, and bath (singles 8000dr; doubles 12,000dr). Closer to the waterfalls and across from the Timendon Sq. is the very modern **Hotel Elena** (tel. 23 218; fax 23 951), whose gleaming rooms come with phone, TV and bath (singles 8000dr; doubles 12,000dr; triples 13,000dr).

FOOD Edessa has no shortage of the lethal twin-food demons known as cheese pies and rotisserie chicken, but restaurants are rather scarce except in the immediate vicinity of the waterfalls. The center of the town's nightlife is in a shady park off Dimokratias right before the post office. The fish *taverna* **Boulgouri,** near 18 Octovriou on the way to the train station, provides a pleasant atmosphere for a fish dinner (1200dr). The largest, most popular, and best situated restaurant in town is the **Public Waterfall Center Restaurant** (tel. 26 718), right at the top of the falls. It has three separate terraces for seating, and serves a variety of dishes. Try the *tseblekkebab,* a combination of beef, eggplant, pepper, and cheese (1700dr). Also near the falls, on the side street off Dimokratias St. that leads to the falls, is **Mam** (tel. 27 02), a cozy traditional *taverna* with a thatch roof to protect you from the elements. In the center of town, right next to Hotel Pella, is the less touristy **Restaurant Omonoia** (tel. 25 459), which serves tasty fare, point-and-choose style (entrees 1000-1200dr). The most unusual and picturesque of Edessa's cafes is the **Cafe High Rock** (tel. 26 793), located in the southwest corner of town on 2 M. Alexandrou St. on a (surprise, surprise) high rock reminiscent of the Meteora (coffee 700dr; cocktails 1200dr). A pair of bars popular with the young and fashionable are **Saloon** (tel. 25 004) and **River** (tel 20 033), both off Dimokratias St.

SIGHTS A good way to appreciate the town is to walk west up Monasteriou St., behind Egnatia St. and to the right of the **Byzantine Clock Tower,** to the **Byzantine Bridge,** under which flows the main rivulet that eventually splits off to form the many streams flowing through town. In the direction of the waterfalls, a few restaurants offer seats with a magnificent view of the mountains and the valley below, including the ruins of the ancient city, whose marble columns are visible in the distance.

Below the town about 3km to the southwest lie the 4th-century BC ruins of the ancient city which were unearthed in 1968. Until the discovery of the ruins at Vergina, Edessa was thought to be ancient Aigai, the capital of Macedonia; Edessans were perhaps the only Greeks not thrilled about the unearthing of Vergina's tombs. One of the more interesting sights in Edessa itself is the **Varossi district,** the old church-dotted town that remained a Christian enclave during the Ottoman occupation. A **folklore and architectural museum** is set to open in the heart of Varossi in 1999; inquire at the tourist information office for details.

Although Edessa's churches and ancient ruins are interesting, the town is famous for its waterfall. To reach Edessa's tremendous **Katarrakton** (Greek for waterfall), walk down Dimokratias St. and watch for the large and clear waterfall signs, which will tell you when to turn left; the roar of surging cascades and bustling souvenir stands will herald your arrival. A series of steps descend next to the waterfall—almost all of the cliffside terraces spanning the east rim offer beautiful panoramic vistas of the agricultural plain below. You'll be able to spot a convent and the ruins of the ancient town. On one of the larger terraces, there is a photographer eager to catch you, your friends, and the falls. A none-too-impressive **cave** also beckons (admission 50dr). Waterfall enthusiasts should continue down the path at the bottom of Katarrakton into the valley to see the three larger falls near the hydroelectric plant.

■ Kastoria Καστορια

Kastoria and Florina, tucked against the borders of Albania and the former Yugoslav Republic of Macedonia, are rarely visited by tourists. The natural setting is stunning, the villages are attractive and unassuming, and the absence of sputtering buses is as refreshing as a glimpse of the glimmering lake.

The city of Kastoria (named after Kastor, one of Zeus's sons) originally rested securely on an island in Lake Kastoria. Around the 10th century AD, the townspeople began dumping garbage into the lake in an attempt to build a causeway to the shore. Today, the bulk of the city is squeezed onto this narrow isthmus, and the island proper is nearly deserted. Savor the beauty of the lake from a distance, but don't even think about taking a dip; the town only recently stopped dumping raw sewage into the water, and the biological clean-up process is still years from completion.

Despite the unsavory waters that encircle Kastoria, the town itself is beautiful. Byzantine churches, centuries-old *arhontika* (mansions), and modern apartment buildings come together in a surprisingly comfortable blend of old and new. Kastoria is the fur capital of Greece; fur made the town rich hundreds of years ago, and the presence of more than 3000 local furriers shows that it continues to be the mainstay of the local economy.

ORIENTATION AND PRACTICAL INFORMATION

Kastoria is on a peninsula that juts into Lake Kastoria. The town has two lakefronts formed by **Nikis St.** on the north and by **Megalou Alexandrou St.** on the south. There are also two important squares in the town. **Davaki Sq.**, in the northwest part of Kastoria, is close to the **bus station;** the other, **Omonoia Square,** is in the southeast part of town at the base of the old acropolis. **Mitropolis St.**, Kastoria's most important commercial street, links the two squares.

Transportation

Buses: KTEL, 3 Septemvriou (tel. 83 455), 1 block from the lake. Take 7 Septemvriou away from Davaki Sq. Buses run to Thessaloniki (3½hr., 7 per day, 3600dr); Edessa (2hr., 4 per day, 2050dr); Athens (9hr., 3 per day, 9400dr); Kozani (1¾hr., 5 per day, 1700dr); and Veria (2½hr., 3 per day, 2350dr). Multiple bus connections are required to reach Florina or Kalambaka.

Flights: Olympic Airways (tel. 22 275 or 23 125) office is on the southern waterfront on Megalou Alexandrou St., just above a big parking lot. Open M-F 8:30am-4pm. A taxi travels to the **airport** (12km away) in Argos for 1500dr. Flights depart in the morning for Athens (6 per week, 19,300dr).

Taxis: (tel. 82 100 or 82 200) converge near the bus station. Available 24hr.

Tourist and Financial Services

Tourist services: (tel. 22 777 or 23 068) available on the first floor of the town hall in room #3; from the bus station, face the water and go left on Diakou St., which turns into 3 Septemvriou St. When you hit Davaki Sq, bear left onto Ioustinianou St. Open M-F 7am-5pm, Sa 10am-3pm.

Banks: National Bank (tel. 22 350), on 11 Novemvriou St., which bears left off Gramou St. as you head northeast uphill. 24hr. **ATM.** Open M-Th 8am-2pm, F 8am-1:30pm.

Emergency and Communications

Police: Gramou St. (tel. 83 333), behind the bus station. English spoken. Open 24hr.

Hospital: (tel. 28 341, 28 342, or 28 343).

Post Office: (tel. 22 991), on the southern lakefront road, Megalou Alexandrou Ave., around the bend from the bus station. **Exchanges currency.** Open daily 7:30am-2pm. **Postal Code:** 52100.

OTE: 33 Ag. Athanasiou St. (tel. 22 599 or 22 135), uphill midway between Davaki Sq. and Dexamenis Sq. Open daily 7am-10pm. **Telephone Code:** 0467.

ACCOMMODATIONS

There are more hotels than you might expect in Kastoria. Wherever you find yourself sleeping, insist on an upper level room; so you'll have a view of the lake.

Hotel Keletron, #52 11 Novemvriou St. Follow Grammou St. from behind the bus station until it turns into 11 Novemvriou. Offers large, carpeted rooms with phone, personal bath, TV. Singles 5800dr; doubles 8250dr; triples 9900dr.

Hotel Acropolis, 14 Gramou St. (tel. 83 737), one block behind the bus station. One of the better bargains in Kastoria. Singles 6325dr, singles with bath 7590dr; doubles with bath 8200dr.

Hotel Anesis, 10 Gramou St. (tel. 83 908; fax 83 768), next to Acropolis, but fancier. Spacious, airy rooms with bath and TV. Singles 9000dr; doubles 12,500dr; triples 12,600dr.

Camping (tel. 22 714) is available at Mavriotissa Church. Get permission from the priest. 1000dr per person.

FOOD AND ENTERTAINMENT

Choices for dining are scattered throughout the city. A few *tavernas* and a lot of trendy bars and cafes are on the north waterfront by Ioustinianou St. More cafes are on Mitropoleos St. A couple of good restaurants are at Omonia Sq. *Ouzeries* and *mezedopoleia* dot the southern waterfront.

Restaurant Omonia, on Omonia Sq., a favorite with locals. The food, the atmosphere, and the prices are all excellent. Entrees 1100-1400dr.

To Krontiri, 13 Oresteiados (tel. 28 358), on the far eastern part of the southern waterfront. Serves traditional Kastorian *mezedes,* including snails, mushrooms, and tomato-meatballs.

Swan Restaurant (tel. 27 994), at Ioustinianou St. and Nikis St., on the north waterfront. Limited variety but tasty selection of dishes (1200-1900dr).

Mantziaris Restaurant (tel. 29 492 or 25 066), on Omonia Sq. Try the *lahanos-mardes* (a combination of lettuce, rice, and meat; 1500dr).

Cafe Domus, 7 Ermou (tel. 26 422), on a pedestrian arcade between 11 Novemvriou St. and Ioustinianou St. Friendly, vivacious staff and well-priced drinks (by Kastorian standards) make this a happening place.

Cafe Boubuillon, 35 Mitropoleos (tel. 29 072), close to Davaki Sq. on Mitropoleous St. One of the trendiest nightspots in town. Cocktails 1300dr.

SIGHTS

Kastoria is renowned first for its voluminous fur garment industry (some 5000 garments produced per day), and second for its churches. There are 40 Byzantine and 36 post-Byzantine edifices scattered throughout the city, many with elaborate masonry and exquisite decoration. The tiny Byzantine **Panagia Koumblelidhiki,** in the center of town, and the **Agii Anargiri,** on Vitsiou St. off Athanasiou, house particularly spectacular frescoes; unfortunately, some of the paintings—rare exterior frescoes—have recently been marred by graffiti. The walls of 11th-century **Mavrotissas Monastery,** located about 3km from the southeast corner of town along the waterfront, are also laden with frescoes. *(Open daily 9am-10pm.)* The priest who lives in the church conducts tours in Greek or German. If you want to be certain of gaining access to any of the town's churches, stop first at the **Byzantine Museum** (tel. 26 781), off Mitropoleos St. in Dexamenis Sq., and arrange for a guide to open the churches for you. *(Open Tu-Su 8am-6pm. Free.)* In the museum is a wonderful collection of Byzantine iconography, whose oldest icon dates back to 1180. Icons from the Byzantine museum were recently loaned to New York City's Metropolitan Museum of Art for exhibition.

One kilometer outside of town stands **Mt. Psalida,** where Alexander the Average resolved to become Alexander the Great by conquering the world. About 9km from Kastoria, in the village of Nostimo, is a bizarre petrified forest. *(Call 84 588 for details.)*

■ The Lake District

To the north of Kastoria, bounded by Albania and the former Yugoslav Republic of Macedonia, is the **Lake District** proper, a tranquil area of dense wilderness and, you guessed it, lakes. The largest and most beautiful lakes in the area are **Mikri Prespa** and **Megali Prespa;** custody of the second is shared by Greece, Albania, and the Former Yugoslav Republic of Macedonia. **Florina,** accessible from Edessa and Thessaloniki, makes a good base from which to explore the area. **Trains** run to the Florina **train station** (tel. (0385) 36 239) from Thessaloniki (4hr., 7 per day, 1500dr) and Edessa (2hr., 7 per day, 800dr). **Buses** run from Thessaloniki (3½hr., 6 per day, 2800dr) and to Edessa (2hr., 6 per day, 1500dr). For the Florina **bus station,** call (0385) 22 430. Florina has little to offer tourists apart from its location, a fragrant market area, and the **Hotel Ellenis** (tel. (0385) 22 671) in the town center (singles 8000dr; doubles 11,000dr; triples 14,000dr). The **Alpine Club** runs a large refuge near the village of **Pissoderi** on Mt. Verna.

■ Halkidiki Χαλκιδικη

The fingers of the Halkidiki peninsula project southward into the Aegean like a shadow of Poseidon's three-pronged trident, yielding spectacular scenery and some of the finer sandy beaches in Greece. Tourists with money and tanning lotion swarm to the middle and western prongs, **Sithonia** and **Kassandra.** Although natural beauty tempers tourist gloss, the peninsulas are devoid of monuments to any period of Greece's past. In contrast, the eastern prong, **Mt. Athos,** is open to male tourists by permit and completely off limits to women—a living link to the traditions of the Byzantine Empire. Visitation to Mt. Athos is strictly regulated, and reservations for serious male pilgrims should be made a month in advance (see p. 277). There are no hoops to jump through to reach Kassandra or Sithonia; just crack the codes of the Halkidiki public transportation system. Frequent **buses** run between the 68 Karakassi St. station in Thessaloniki (tel. (031) 92 44 44) and the three peninsulas, but bus service does not accommodate travelers wishing to hop from prong to prong. You will have to return to Thessaloniki in order to catch a bus to another prong. Moped rental is a visually rewarding option for cruising Halkidiki's quiet, beautiful roads.

■ Sithonia Σιθωνια

Although it held out longer than its western neighbor, Sithonia has recently been ravished and seduced by visitors sporting BMWs and fistfuls of *drachmes.* The area has since plunged into the sordid world of beachside villas, tour buses, and plastic souvenirs. On the more isolated beaches on the south and southwest coasts, a measure of tranquility persists. Sithonia is popular as a beach and nature retreat from Thessaloniki and is still quieter, less expensive, and more relaxed than Kassandra to the west.

There are two back road routes through Sithonia: west via **Neos Marmaras** and east via **Vourvourou.** Neos Marmaras was a quiet fishing village not long ago but has been transformed into a bustling tourist hub. Greeks and foreigners swim at the town's long, sandy beaches, walk the seaside streets, and party in bars and discos.

Neos Marmaras enjoys its existence largely due to the **Porto Carras** (tel. 72 500) hotel complex situated just across the bay. This enormous 900-room complex is among Greece's largest and most up-scale hotels. It boasts restaurants, boutiques, beaches, a cinema, a nightclub, phenomenal athletic facilities, including tennis courts one of four 18-hole golf courses in Greece, and **Casino Porto Carras** (tel. 70 500). Although doubles start at 25,000dr in high season, all rooms are fully booked in summer. Ferries shuttle between the second square and Propondis in Marmaras to Porto Carras (15min., 2 per hr., 500dr). The coast is a 20-minute walk.

Most of the action in Neos Marmaras centers on the main waterfront road. The Neos Marmaras **police** (tel. 71 111) are on a side street left of the main street, away from the church. The town **post office** (tel. 71 334; open M-F 8am-2pm) is in the second square, near the **Cafe Metro** (open M-F 7:30am-2pm). To reach the **OTE** from the bus stop, walk to the bottom left corner of the square, then hike up the street (open daily 7:30am-midnight). The **National Bank** (tel. 72 793) is on the main street (open M-Th 8am-2pm; F 8am-1:30pm; **currency exchange** also on Sa 9am-1pm). **Postal code: 61381. Telephone code: 0375.**

The English-speaking staff at **Doucas Tours** (tel. 71 959), near the bus stop, recommends rooms, **exchanges currency,** and books excursions (open M 3-11pm, Tu-Sa 9am-3pm and 6-11pm, Su 9am-3pm). **Moudania Tours** (tel. 72 090) is one street behind Doucas Tours, behind Roma Pizza, and sells **Flying Dolphin** tickets for Volos (2hr., 1 per week, 6100dr) and the various islands of the Sporades (1 per week, 11,000dr round-trip). Daily service to the Sporades exists from the town of **Nea Moudania** in Kassandra (open M-Sa 9am-2pm and 5-11pm, Su 10am-2pm and 6-11pm). **Bus timetables** are posted next door, outside of Dionysios'. They run to Thessaloniki (2½hr., 7 per day, 2450dr) and nearby small towns.

Rooms in Neos Marmaras are generally extremely expensive. There are 76 proprietors of rented rooms in town, but vacancies are still tough to come by on midsummer weekends. **Albatros Rooms To Let** (tel. 71 738), on Themistokli St., has clean, spacious, modern rooms with kitchenettes and large balconies. Inquire at Rigalo Jewelers, near the bus stop (doubles with bath and kitchen 6000-8000dr; triples 10,000dr). On the beach, **Camping Marmaras** (tel. 71 901) is 1km back and clearly marked by road signs (open June to early Oct.; 1400dr per person; 1300dr per tent).

The most unusual restaurant in town is the pagoda-like **Zoe's Little China** (tel. 72 004; open daily 4pm-1:30am), which serves a variety of Chinese dishes. For more traditional Greek fare, head to one of the many waterfront *tavernas* such as **Poseidon** (tel. 71 189), on the western edge of town, or **Pelagos** (tel. 71 638), on the main square, whose specialty is schnitsel. The most popular place in town with locals is the smallish **Ta Kimata** (tel. 71 371), which makes savory fish dishes.

Nightlife in Neos Marmaras centers on the coastal strip of bars and a pair of discos about 4km away. The most happening bar in town is the centrally located seaside **Prestige Bar** (tel. 72 330; 1500dr cover includes one drink), where Greeks and foreigners rub elbows as they drink and watch the waves. West of Prestige Bar the strip is essentially one long bar divided in three—**Cool Bar, Sugar Bar,** and **Smile Bar** (open daily 9pm-2:30am). The two big discos are **Argo** (tel. 71 971) and **Vareladiko** (tel. 72 900), both about 4km away. On weekend nights, a van goes back and forth between the discos and the main street in Neos Marmaras. Another choice for nightlife is **Asteria Club** (tel. 72 500), at the Porto Carras complex.

To see more of Sithonia than Neos Marmaras, take the **bus** around the peninsula to Sarti (1hr., 4 per day, 650dr), which passes by the most deserted, desirable turf on the peninsula. After climbing the road 5km south of Porto Carras, you'll see a beach near **Agia Kiriaki,** with a small reef and an outlying island. It's a long, hard climb down, but well worth the effort.

■ Mount Athos Αγιον Ορος

The monasteries on Mt. Athos have been the standard bearers of Christian asceticism for more than a millennium. Today, the easternmost peninsula of Halkidiki is an autonomous state comprised of 20 Orthodox monasteries and countless hamlets *(skites),* with some 1400 monks. The absence of development has helped to preserve the peninsula's luxuriant foliage. Only the jagged marble peak of Mt. Athos itself, soaring 2033m above the encircling waves of the Aegean, is exposed. Against the background of this lush turf, the monks of Mt. Athos isolate themselves from the outside world in an attempt to transcend material pleasures and live a truly spiritual life. The community on Mt. Athos has existed since 883 AD, when Basil I issued an

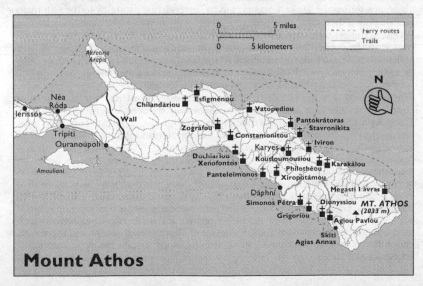

Mount Athos

imperial charter to Athos preventing local military officials from interfering with the monks. A 1060 edict of Emperor Constantine, enforced to this day, forbids women and even female animals from setting foot on the peninsula. Men who wish to see Mt. Athos first-hand should secure a permit (see below). Those without a permit can view the monasteries by boat. A **day cruise** from Thessaloniki costs 10,500dr. From Ouranoupolis, tours (roughly 3½hr.) cost 3000dr. Contact Doucas Travel, 8 Venizelou St., Thessaloniki (tel. (031) 26 99 84), or try Avdimiotis Theophilos in Ouranoupolis (tel. (0377) 51 207 or (377) 51 244).

History

According to tradition, the Christian history of Mt. Athos began when the **Virgin Mary,** on a sea trip from Ephesus to visit Lazarus in Kitium on Cyprus, was thrown off course and led by divine sign to the Athonite coast. The peninsula, then known as **Akte,** was a notorious center of paganism, but the moment Mary's foot graced its soil, the false idols all disintegrated in realization of their own worthlessness. Mary then declared the third leg of Halkidiki her **holy garden,** forbidden to all other women for eternity, and blessed the land before continuing with her voyage. The name "Athos" predates both Christianity and Hellenism and is derived from the name of a Thracian giant of myth buried beneath the mountain by Poseidon. According to Plutarch, among other sources, in the 4th century BC, **Alexander the Great** humbly rejected a plan by his architect Deinokrates to carve the young king's image into the mountain, a sort of monomaniacal Hellenistic Mt. Rushmore. By rejecting Deinokrates' advice, Alexander avoided becoming the second great king of antiquity to dig up Athos; during his invasion of Greece in 481 BC, the Persian King Xerxes dug a massive canal through the peninsula to facilitate the transport of his ships and avoid the fearsome storms of the northern Aegean.

Although legend claims that the first monastic settlements were founded by Constantine the Great and his wife, Helen, the first record of monkish habitation does not come until the 7th century AD. The first monastery, **Megistis Lavras,** was built in 963 by **Saint Athanasios** with the support of the Byzantine emperor, Nikephoras Phokas. Over the centuries that followed, Athos alternately flourished—at one point containing 40 monasteries and 40,000 monks—and declined—buffeted by natural disasters, invasions by pirates, and internal squabbling. The edict banning women from the area was enacted in 1060, officially out of respect for the Virgin Mary, but possibly because of reports of scandalous frolicking between the monks and Vlach shepherdesses who had settled on the mountain. Unlike most of Greece, Mt. Athos retained its autonomy during the Turkish occupation by surrendering promptly to the Ottomans and accepting their rule.

During the centuries preceding the Greek liberation of 1821, Mt. Athos was supported and populated by Serbs, Bulgarians, Romanians, and Russians, who still have affiliations with particular monasteries. At the height of imperial Russia's expansionist dynastic policies, some 3000 Russian monks inhabited **St. Panteleiomon,** supplied weekly by cargo-laden ships arriving straight from Odessa.

After World War II, the Treaty of Lausanne made Mt. Athos officially a port of Greece while allowing it to retain an **autonomous theocratic agreement** (the so-called **Agia Epistasia**—a body of monks elected from the 20 monasteries who legislate and govern the peninsula). Due to gradual attrition and the diminishing influx of young novices, Mt. Athos's eminence slowly declined through the 1950s, when it became a prime target for greedy real estate developers. In recent decades, however, Athos has been rejuvenated and hundreds of young men, inspired to take their vows, have donned the black robes and cap of Orthodox monasticism. Now more than 1700 predominantly Greek monks live alone in *skites* or communally inhabit the 20 monasteries. Most of the new monks are extremely zealous and doctrinaire; Athos is stricter and harder to visit now than ever before, and while the monasteries which used to be divided into more lax, less-regulated idiorhythmic groups and more rigid cenobitic groups are now uniformly cenobitic, with strictly enforced communal schedules and duties.

Athos retains unsurpassed wealth in Paleologian and Late Byzantine art, manuscripts, treasure, and architecture. Each monastery houses *lipsana*, remains of dead saints which only Orthodox Christian men are allowed to see and venerate. Especially impressive are the **hand of Mary Magdalene,** who bathed Jesus, which remains (skin intact) in **Simonos Petra** as warm as a living hand, and the **belt of the Theotokos** in **Vatopediou,** the only extant relic of the Virgin Mary. Several monasteries possess fragments of the **True Cross.** The **Gifts of the Magi**—gold, frankincense, and myrrh—presented to Christ at his birth, are housed in **St. Paul's;** 5 of the 28 pieces are displayed for veneration every night.

Permits

A special entrance pass, issued **only to adult males,** is required to visit Mt. Athos. These passes are issued at **Ouranoupolis,** the main gateway to Athos, upon presentation of a special permit. To get this permit, call at least 15 days (in winter) or one month (in summer) in advance to make a reservation with the Ministry of Northern Greece in Thessaloniki (tel. (031) 26 4321; ask for Mrs. Plessa). This office will offer you no special favors and may even discourage you from visiting Mt Athos. Because only 10 visitors per day are admitted to Mt. Athos, visits are always booked well in advance. Arrive in Thessaloniki at least two days before you plan to visit. Stressing (or fabricating) your Greek ancestry, devout Orthodox faith, or scholarly interest in Mt. Athos can make a lucky procrastinator the day's eleventh visitor. Once in Thessaloniki, obtain a letter of recommendation from your country's embassy or consulate (tell them you are a student interested in theology, history, architecture, or Byzantine art); a letter from your university stating your academic interest in Mt. Athos could also be helpful. Deliver the letter from the consulate to the **Ministry of Northern Greece,** room 222 Dikitirou Sq., Thessaloniki (open daily 10am-2pm). In Ouranoupolis, bring your permit and your passport to the **Athos office,** just uphill from the bus stop by the gas station, by at least 9am of the day your visit begins. Passes cost 5000dr for foreigners and 3000dr for students with ISIC. You must strictly observe the **date of arrival** on your permit. If you arrive a day late, you will be turned away. Without your **passport,** you will not be admitted. The **tourist office** in Thessaloniki has more information. A **separate permit** is required if you wish to photograph the monasteries' exquisite iconography. The procedure for obtaining this permit is the same as for the regular one; get a form letter from your consulate and take it to the Ministry of Northern Greece. The regular permit is valid for a **four-day stay.** To get your stay extended, you must go to the peninsula's capital, Karies; unless you have an extremely compelling reason for extending your sojourn (i.e. you now want to become a monk), your request will almost certainly be denied. Unofficial extensions are easier to come by; especially during low season, kind monks often allow considerate, genuinely interested visitors to stay longer.

Getting There via Ouranoupolis

Permit in hand, arrive in Halkidiki the night before your entry date into Athos, or catch the 6am bus leaving Thessaloniki for **Ouranoupolis** the day of your visit. Ouranoupolis, the last settlement in secular Athos, functions dually as the gateway to monastic Athos and as a hedonistic beach resort popular among Germans.

Those staying overnight have several reasonably affordable choices. **Hotel Athos** (tel. 71 368), located above a supermarket one street back from the waterfront, offers elegant rooms with bath (singles 5500dr; doubles 8000dr). **Hotel Acrogiali** (tel. 71 201; fax 71 395), at the corner of the main waterfront road, has airy rooms overlooking the sea (singles 6000dr; doubles 8000dr).

Those looking for a last non-fasting meal before their entrance into Mt. Athos or a triumphal reward after experiencing the monks' spartan cuisine should head to the row of similar-looking taverns on the waterfront. **Restaurant Pyrgos** (tel. 71 236) and **Restaurant Karydas** (tel. 71 280 or 71 180) are two of the more popular establishments in this strip. The standard approach to Athos is via Ouranoupolis, by boat to Daphni, then by bus to the capital city of Karies. **Buses** for Ouranoupolis leave from

Thessaloniki's Halkidiki station (tel. 92 44 44), located at 68 Karakassi St. (4 per day, 3hr., 3000dr). A bus for Thessaloniki will be waiting immediately after your return from Mt. Athos. There is one boat a day to Daphni from Ouranoupolis at 9:45am (2hr., 1000dr). The boat returns to Ouranoupolis at 12:10pm. From Daphni you can take Athos's one **bus line** (1 per day, free) to the capital, Karies (30min.), or to several of the monasteries. There is also limited (and extremely expensive) **taxi service** (tel. 23 266) between monasteries. **Boats** also travel throughout the peninsula. The main boat leaves Daphni for Agia Anna at 12:30pm; other more sporadic routes also exist.

Karies has an **OTE** next to the Athonite Holy Council Building, a **post office** (open M-F 8am-2pm), and two inexpensive hotels (1500dr per person). **Postal code:** 63086. **Telephone code:** 0377.

Being a Pilgrim

Life in Mt. Athos is dedicated to building faith and devotion to God—and, as such, is likely to be a complete culture shock. The monks operate on a schedule twice removed from our own: they use the **Julian** (not Gregorian) calendar, which is 13 days behind our own, and mark the hours of the day according to the sunset, which is midnight. At most monasteries, the morning liturgy begins at 4am (our time) and stretches until 8am. Although only the most devout pilgrims attend the beginning of the service, the periodic ringing of bells and tapping of wooden planks help keep less zealous visitors turning in their beds until they too get up and go to church. Breakfast is served immediately after service in fresco-covered *trapezaries* to the sound of Byzantine chanting. Only the chanter, talks during meals and everyone ceases eating the moment the chanter stops. Non-Orthodox pilgrims must sit at a separate table in the refectory from the monks and Orthodox visitors. Breakfast generally consists of homegrown squash or zucchini, somewhat sour bread, water, and fruit. Since visitors can stay only one night in each monastery, it is a good idea to start hiking to your next destination right after breakfast. Hikes through Mt. Athos's winding mountain paths, filled with fluorescent butterflies and chirping crickets, rival any nature experience in Greece. Because the hikes, though beautiful and brightened by fluorescent butterflies, can be long and arduous, it is a good idea to pick up a copy of the brown **Mount Athos Tourist Map** or buy a guidebook (1200-3000dr) with pull-out map in Ouranoupolis or Karies. And by all means, leave your pack in Ouranoupolis; a heavy load can make you wish you had never heard of monks or Mt. Athos. Always leave plenty of time for hiking. Paths are narrow, overgrown, and poorly marked; furthermore, the ones on the map might unexpectedly fork in four different directions or not exist at all. If possible, keep to the roads and seaside paths and travel in groups.

Always reach the monastery where you plan to stay the night before sunset, when the gates close (and earlier if you want anything besides leftovers to eat). The evening *esperino* church service starts at 5pm and goes until 6:30 or so, with dinner served immediately afterward. Relics are presented for veneration either before or after dinner, depending on the monastery. Both food and lodging are free at every monastery. Talk to the *arbondari* (guestmaster) for specific schedule information and to obtain beds (generally quite comfortable) for the night.

While at the monasteries, be as courteous and cooperative as possible. Always address monks by their title, *Patera*, and instead of hello and good-bye, say *evlogite* (bless us, father). Avoid talking loudly at all times (this disturbs monks trying to meditate), and especially during siesta and after nightfall.

Monasteries of Mount Athos

Athos' 20 monasteries ring the peninsula's northern and southern coasts. Despite their similar architecture (most monasteries consist of a large rectangular wall with lodging and churches within), each monastery has its own distinctive character. **Megistis Lavras** is the oldest, largest, and richest of the monasteries—and also the only one to escape destruction by fire at some point in its history. Its monks tend to be old, stern, and conservative. **Iuiron** is delightfully dilapidated, full of relics and icons such as the **Panagia Portaitissa,** the most renowned of Athos' miracle-working

Fast Times at Mount Athos

Mount Athos used to be a land outside time. Beyond its borders, the frenetic pace of the outside world accelerated through the centuries, but within the monasteries of the Holy Mountain, monks chanted the same hymns and pursued the same austere life-styles as their devout predecessors from centuries before. Today, however, Mount Athos is starting to change ever so slowly. Construction work at many monasteries takes place around the clock; newly paved roads are beginning to make hiking obsolete after it was for centuries the only means of travel for monks and their visitors; and computers—the ultimate symbol of modern times—are sprouting throughout Athos. Lately, politically correct Europeans have even attempted to force Mount Athos to let in female visitors for the first time in a millennium. Although most monks embrace the changes taking place, a few of their more conservative peers are not thrilled to have the outside world knocking on their door. "The outside world is a living hell," thundered one monk at Karakallou Monastery. "Every little change we make—every little break with tradition—severs another one of our ties to God." A monk at Grigoriou had similar complaints, "When I look at the world beyond Mount Athos, I see people scurrying around blindly without any thought to where their final destination might be. Do we want the same kind of blindness to infect us too?" But despite the grumblings of a few, modernity on Mount Athos is no longer a contradiction in terms.

icons. According to legend, Athos will never fall as long as the Panagia Portaitissa remains within its borders. Moated and turreted **Vatopedi** is, along with Iuiron, the most popular of the monasteries. Its treasures are the **belt** of the Virgin Mary and the largest known **fragment** of the True Cross. Although beautiful and well worth visiting, these three are called the "museum monasteries"; for a grittier, more accurate view of monastic life, try to visit some of the smaller, more remote spots on Athos.

The medieval fortress-like **Simonopetra,** perched on the edge of a sheer cliff, is one of the most dramatically located of Mt. Athos's monasteries. Simonopetra's death-defying architecture and splendid frescoes would attract more visitors if it were not for its limited 10-room capacity for lodging. Close to Simonopetra is the more popular **Gregoriou.** In this relatively liberal seaside place, the meals are a little tastier, the beds a little cushier, the monks a little friendlier, and the sunset views a little more poignant. On the opposite side of the peninsula are **Philotheou,** the proud possessor of the arm of St. John Chrystostom, and **Karakalou,** ravaged three times by fire but still a pleasant picturesque place.

In addition to these predominantly Greek monasteries, there exist several abbeys inhabited mostly by Slavs. At one time, there were nearly equal numbers of Greek and Slavic monks on the mountain. However, political turmoil (notably the 1917 Russian Revolution) cut off the supply of funds and novices at its source and today only three Slavic monasteries remain. The onion-domed Russian **St. Panteleimon,** the Bulgarian **Zagrafou,** and the Serbian **Hilandariou** contrast (at least linguistically) with the rest of the monasteries on the peninsula. The recent collapse of Communism has reopened Russian souls and wallets to the favorite opiate of the masses, and swelling church coffers have financed an ongoing restoration of Panteleimon. Five thousand Russians seek entry to this large monastery, but its population is forbidden to outnumber that of its nearest Greek neighbor, which is home to a booming community of about 50.

Just a little more rugged than monastic life is the hike to the top of Mt. Athos itself. The approach is by path from the skitic community of **Agia Anna,** accessible by boat daily from Daphni. A five-hour climb will take you to the **Church of the Panagia,** which has beds for an overnight stay and is only one hour from the summit.

▓ Kavala Καβαλα

Kavala rests upon the ruins of ancient Neapolis (later Christoupolis), where the Apostle Paul once preached. Kavala's most notable local character is Mehmet Ali, a 19th-century Ottoman ruler who eventually became the Pasha of Egypt. Like much of Greece, Kavala saw its size dramatically increase during the population exchange following WWI. Kavala reversed both its preferred commodity and political orientation after the end of WWII; it was a tobacco town and a bastion of Communism in the 1930s, and is now a modern commercial port. The bustling city with tree-lined avenues stretching from the seaside up the slopes of Mt. Simvolo is well organized and relatively smog-free—although modernized, Kavala retains a traditional appeal, as congested avenues give way to fruit vendors and flower markets, particularly around Kavala's old section, the Panagia District (District of the Virgin Mary).

ORIENTATION AND PRACTICAL INFORMATION

The city's main attraction, the **Panagia District,** sits southeast of the port on its own peninsula, hemmed in by ancient walls under the shadow of the **Byzantine fortress.** The entrance is near **Doxas Square.** Just outside the walls to the west is **Eleftherias Square,** the main square from which Kavala's two major commercial streets, **Eleftheriou Venizelou St.** and **Erithrou Stavrou St.,** extend westward. **Ethnikis Andistassis** runs along the waterfront near the Thassos ferry dock. Parallel to it, one block inland, is Erithrou Stavrou St. Two blocks inland is Eleftheriou Venizelou St.

Transportation

Buses: (tel. 22 35 93), at the corner of Eterias St. and Kavalas St., a block from Vas. Pavlou St. and the waterfront, around the corner from the OTE. Service to Thessaloniki (3hr., 20 per day, 2800dr); Drama (1hr., 32 per day, 700dr); beaches to the west (take bus to Iraklitsa; 20min., every 20-30min., 350dr); and Athens (10hr., 3 per day, 11,000dr). Contact the **KTEL Office** (tel. 22 22 94) near the post office (open daily 6am-8pm). For service to Alexandroupolis (3hr., 6 per day; 2900dr), go to the **Dore Cafe,** 35 Erithrou Stavrou St. (tel. 22 76 01), beyond the Oceanis Hotel, which sells tickets, posts departure times, and maintains the bus stop.

Ferries: Nikos Milades (tel. 22 00 67 or 22 34 21), on the corner of the main port, provides ferry information for islands other than Thassos. Open daily 8:30am-1:30pm and 6-8:30pm. Ferries go to Limnos (4½hr., 3 per week, 3670dr); Lesvos (11½hr., 3 per week, 6320dr); Chios (14hr., 1 per week; 7300dr); and Peiraias. **Arsinoi Travel,** on 16 K. Dimitriou (tel. 83 56 71), has other information. Open daily 8am-9pm. Ferries to Samothrace (4hr., 5 per week, 2900dr) and Thassos (2hr., 11 per day, 850dr).

Flying Dolphins: Hydrofoils connect Kavala with nearby Thassos and Samothrace. For tickets and schedule information, head for the booths near the hydrofoil dock, opposite the OTE. Schedules are posted there.

Flights: Olympic Airways (tel. 22 36 22), across from Thassos ferry dock on the corner of Ethnikis Andistassis and Kavalas St. Open M-F 8am-2:30pm. Tickets to Athens (1hr., 2 per day, 20,000dr). Public buses to the airport leave 2 hours before scheduled airplane departures (30min., 850dr), and from the airport to Kavala center immediately following flight arrivals.

Taxis: (tel. 23 20 01) congregate in 28 Octovriou Sq. Available 24hr.

Tourist and Financial Services

Tourist Office: (tel. 22 24 25, 22 87 62, or 23 16 53), on its own little traffic island at the corner of El. Venizelou St. and Dragoumi St., a block inland from the main port. Has city maps and a list of hotels. Open M-F 8am-2pm.

Tourist Police: (tel. 22 29 05), on the ground floor of the police station. Open daily 7:30am-2:30pm.

Bank: The **National Bank** (tel. 22 21 63), on the corner of Omonias St. and Pavlou Mela St., 1 block north of the GNTO. Has a 24hr. **ATM** and **currency exchange.** Open M-Th 8am-2pm, F 8am-1:30pm.

International Bookstore: Thodoros Theodoridis, 46 Omonias St., sells English publications. Open M W 8am-2pm, Tu, Th-F 8am-3pm and 5:30-9:30pm.

Emergency and Communications

Hospital: 113 Stavrou St. (tel. 22 85 17). Open 24hr. Call 166 in case of **emergency.**
Police Station: 119 Omonias St., 4 blocks north of the port. Open 24hr. **Emergency** tel. 100. **Port police** (tel. 22 44 72) are in the OTE building. Open 24hr.
Post Office: Main branch at Kavalas St. and Stavrou St. 1 block north of the bus station. **Exchanges currency.** Open M-F 7:30am 8pm. **Postal Code:** 65110.
OTE: (tel. 22 26 99). West of the port at the corner of Eth. Andistassis St. and Averof St. Open daily in summer 8am-midnight. **Telephone Code:** 051

ACCOMMODATIONS

Kavala is not a wonderful place for the budget traveler to spend the night; rented rooms are scarce and hotels fairly expensive. In addition to being expensive, many of Kavala's rooms overlook the port; if you are a light sleeper, remember that the shipping industry does not shut down when you go to bed.

George Alvanos Rented Rooms, 35 Anthemiou St. (tel. 22 17 81 or 22 84 12). Enter the Panagia district on Poulidou St., bear left on Mehmet Ali St., and make a sharp left on Anthemiou St. Without a doubt your best bet in Kavala. Large lovely rooms with fans in the heart of the scenic Panagia district for the lowest prices in town. Rooms have shared bath. Singles 4000dr; doubles 6000dr;
Hotel Akropolis, 29 El. Venizelou St. (tel. 22 35 43; fax 83 07 52). Clean, high-ceilinged, traditional rooms with a view of the bay. The 75-year-old hotel has charm, and you can bargain with the gregarious owner for a much better price. Singles 7500dr; doubles 8000-10,000dr, with bath 14,000dr.
Hotel Esperia, 44 Stavrou St. (tel. 22 96 21, 22 96 25, or 22 32 24; fax 22 06 21). One of the city's largest and most popular hotels. Soundproof doors and windows keep out the city's din. Singles 9000dr; doubles 11,000dr; triples 13,000dr.

FOOD AND ENTERTAINMENT

Dining in Kavala may not compare to savoring a crepe on the French Riviera (or in Athens for that matter), but it offers quality Greek food at reasonable prices. Taverns are located along the long waterfront and on Poulidou St. in the Panagia district.

Cafe-Restaurant Imaret, 32 Poulidou St. (tel. 23 33 25 or 83 62 86), is the most surreal eating experience in Kavala—Ottoman-era towers surround you as you eat and watch the waves below.
Antonia Restaurant, a little downhill from Imaret on Poulidou St., is popular and always packed with locals.
O Vangelis (tel. 83 88 85), on the waterfront near the entrance to Panagia, is a bustling fish *taverna* that greets visitors with a giant neon dolphin.

Nightlife in Kavala is surprisingly limited for such a large city. There are a few cafes and bars on the waterfront, but most of the action takes place in the lively village of **Pallio,** a few kilometers outside of Kavala. If you can't make it to Pallio, try **I Kriti** (tel. 22 30 97) or one of the other homogeneous waterfront cafe-bars.

SIGHTS

The sprawling 13th-century **Byzantine Castle's** turreted walls dominate the city. *(Open daily 10am-7pm.)* Saunter atop them for a great view of the city; the guard often gives tours and would appreciate your tip. A small **amphitheater** occasionally hosts musical and cultural performances here—ask the guard or the people at the refreshment stand. During the **Eleftheria Festival** in late August, students celebrate Kavala's liberation from the Ottomans by performing dances at the castle. Visitors are welcome.

The 400-year-long Ottoman domination of Northern Greece left its mark on the city. The **Imaret** (an Ottoman soup kitchen for the poor), the largest Muslim-built building in western Europe, is now a trendy cafe-bar. On the corner of Pavlidou St. and Mehmet Ali St. stands the **House of Muhammad Ali.** Born here in 1769, Ali was the self-appointed ruler of Egypt and an important—though disruptive—force in Ottoman politics in the 19th century. *(Tip 100dr.)*

Also be sure to check out the colossal 16th-century **Kamares Aqueduct** at the north edge of the old town near Nikotsara Sq. Süleyman the Magnificent had the graceful, double-tiered structure built in 1556 to transport water from mountain springs above the city. On the other side of town, overlooking the water, the **archaeological museum** (tel. 22 23 35) on Stavrou St. contains such treasures as polychrome busts of goddesses from Amphipolis and a Hellenistic mosaic of the rape of Europa from Abdera. *(Open Tu-F 8am-6pm, Sa-Su 8am-2:30pm. Admission 500dr, students 300dr, EU students free.)* Also check out the massive Ionian columns, all that remain of a Temple of Parthenos in Neapolis, and the ruins of a Macedonian tomb found near Kavala. Kavala has a small **municipal museum** (tel. 22 27 06) with folk art displays and a gallery of work by the famed Thassian artist Polygnotos Vagis, whose works include odd images of one-eyed giants riding centaurs and many busts and animal sculptures. *(Open Su-F 8am-2pm, Sa 9am-1pm. Donation requested.)* Patriotic Americans will want to check out "The Military Forces of the USA," a sculpture in which the profiles of four American soldiers blend into the proud eagle.

■ Near Kavala

Several sandy **beaches** west of Kavala are accessible by intercity bus. The closest is just outside the city of **Kalamitsa.** There's a **GNTO campground** (tel. 24 30 51) in **Batis,** 3km outside of Kavala, which you might mistake for a parking lot (1200dr per person; 1500dr per large tent; 900dr per small tent; 750dr per child; 500dr to swim). They've got a supermarket. Blue bus #8 treks to Batis from Kavala every 30 minutes.

Philippi, roughly 15km north of Kavala, lies in ruins. Philip of Macedon founded the city to protect Thassian gold miners from Thracian attacks, and modestly named the city after himself. Philippi is most famous as the site of the Roman Civil War battle in 42 BC, in which the combined forces of Octavian and Antony defeated the armies of Cassius and Brutus, the assassins of Julius Caesar. In AD 50, missionaries Paul and Silas arrived from Anatolia to preach Christianity, and the first European Christian, **Lydia,** was baptized here. The **Cell of Paul** is the apostle's own budget accommodation. *(Open daily 8am-7pm. Admission 800dr.)* Shut the door and peek at the Roman **latrines;** most of the 42 marble seats are intact, but the lids have all been left up. Call 51 64 70 for more information.

The entrance on the other side of the highway leads up to the **acropolis.** Classical drama is performed here on summer weekends. *(Open daily sunrise-sunset. Admission 200dr; students 100dr.)* Ask at the theater or the Kavala GNTO for details. There's an **archeological museum** nearby (tel. 51 62 51). *(Open Tu-Su 9am-3pm. Admission 800dr; students 400dr.)* A **bus** to Philippi leaves every 20 minutes. Tell the driver you're going to the archaeological site, not the village—otherwise, you'll end up in the boonies. The bus back to Kavala stops down the road from the site.

THRACE Θρακη

Thrace, separated into the Greek west and Turkish east by the Evros River, remains the political and cultural frontier of both countries. Ruled by the Ottomans until 1913, the region fell under Allied control during WWI, and joined the Greek state in 1919. Continued Western influence resulted in the 1923 Lausanne Treaty, which divided Thrace and ceded the eastern region to Turkey. The division, however, left Greek communities in Turkey and Turkish communities in Greece. Most Greek Orthodox communities moved to Greece, but some Muslims have remained in Greek

Thrace. The treatment of this minority group in Greece remains a significant question 75 years later. Unfortunately, if your travels include only modern Alexandroupolis, you will miss this tangle of cultures, mirrored in a chaotic landscape of rivers, swamps, and lonely rolling hills. However, you will get up close and personal with the region's military forces centered at a base in Alexandroupolis.

The border between Thrace and **Turkey** is one of the most tense in Europe. Forces on both sides are on alert at all times, and minor aggressive incidents occur more often than you'd like to imagine. This political tension between Greece and Turkey makes crossing the border a little bit more of a hassle than it should be. **Trains** and **buses**, departing from Thessaloniki and all major Thracian cities, cross the border several times a day, though often at very inconvenient times. Buses and trains all make sometimes lengthy stops (1-2hr.) at the border.

■ Xanthi Ξανθη

Xanthi, the seat of Greek's tobacco industry, is probably the most charismatic city in Thrace. Muslims (who make up 10% of Xanthi's population) and Christians mingle amiably in the streets of this bustling modern city without the awkwardness that pervades relationships between Christians and Muslims in other Thracian towns. The bustle of modernity doesn't penetrate the Old Town of Xanthi, and narrow cobbled streets meander aimlessly through neighborhoods of well-preserved Ottoman houses. Wandering the Old Town's labyrinthine hills without a map is a good way to get lost, but also the best way to capture the atmosphere of Thrace as it once was.

ORIENTATION AND PRACTICAL INFORMATION Xanthi's most important square is the aptly titled **Kentriki Square,** also known as **Dimokratias Square.** To get here from the bus stop, turn left on Iroon, right on Isidorou, and left again on 28 Octovriou. **28 Octovriou St.,** which runs south from the central square to **Eleftherias Square,** is Xanthi's main street. **Karaoli St.,** another important thoroughfare, leads southeast from the central square to the smaller **Baltatzi Square.** Running north from the central square into the heart of the old town is **Vas. Konstantinou St.**

Xanthi's **train station** (tel. 22 581) is about 2km southeast of the central square; to get there, head down Karaoli St. (which eventually turns into Dimokritou St.) and turn right when you hit the train tracks. You can buy tickets at the station or at the **OSE Office** (tel. 22 277 or 27 840) in the Agora Nousi shopping area on Tsaldari St. just east of the central square. Trains go to Athens (11hr., 5 per day, 6260dr); Thessaloniki (4hr., 5 per day, 2100dr); and Komotini (1½hr., 5 per day, 420dr). The **bus station** (tel. 22 684) is on Iroon, which runs parallel to 28 Octovriou. Buses go to Thessaloniki (3½hr., 7 per day, 3450dr), Athens (10hr., 2 per day, 11600dr); Komotini (1hr., 16 per day, 1000dr); and Kavala (7 per day, 1050dr). Xanthi has no tourist office, but the **town hall** (tel. 24 444), on the upper end of Vas. Konstantinou St., provides a helpful city map. The **National Bank,** which has an **ATM,** is located above the main square on Kunitsis St., a pedestrian walkway. A **foreign bookstore** (tel. 73 911) at Eleftherias Sq. has a wide selection of newspapers and magazines. Two blocks southeast of Baltatzi Sq. is the **hospital** (tel. 72 131; open 24hr.). The **police** (tel. 22 654) are at #223 28 Octovriou St. The **post office** (tel. 22 511; open M-F 7:30am-2pm) and the **OTE** (open M-F 7:20am-10pm, Sa 8am-3pm, Su 8am-10pm) are on parallel side streets west of the central square. **Postal code:** 67100. **Telephone code:** 0541.

ACCOMMODATIONS Despite its charms, tourists have not yet discovered Xanthi—unfortunately, neither have budget hotels, and staying in Xanthi is expensive just about everywhere. If you have good bargaining skills, this is the time to use them; if you don't, this is the time to learn them. The simple rooms of **Hotel Dimokritos** (tel. 25 111, 25 112, or 25 113; fax 25 537) are the cheapest in town (singles 8100dr; doubles 12,100dr). To get here follow 28 Octovriou St. south from the main square. Quite a bit nicer—but more expensive—is the modern comfortable **Hotel Orfeas,** 40 Karaoli St. (tel. 20 121 or 20 122; fax 20 998). Rooms here come with bath, TV, phone, and dramatic pictures of seaside sunsets (singles 11000dr; doubles 14000dr; triples 16000dr). Another luxurious option is the gleaming black glass **Hotel Vanthippion, #**212 28 Octovriou St. (tel. 77 061, 77 062, 77 063, 77 064, or 77 065; fax 77 076), located below Eleftherias Sq. The spacious, well-furnished rooms come with TV, phone, bath, A/C, and minibar (singles 12,000dr; doubles 15,000dr; triples 18,000dr).

FOOD AND ENTERTAINMENT Many of Xanthi's culinary specialties, including its syrupy *kariokes* and the *soutzouk-lookoum*, reflect the town's marked Turkish influence. Restaurants are clustered around the central square and on Vas. Konstantinou St., which leads into the Old Town. Cafes and bars ring the main square and Vas. Sofias St., a side street off Vas. Konstantinou St. **I Klimataria** (tel. 22 408 or 28 140), located under the shadow of the clock tower on the main square, serves a large selection of tasty inexpensive dishes and is a favorite with locals (entrees 900-1600dr). **I Gonia,** 28 Konitsis St. (tel. 25 654), located across from the National Bank, is a packed *ouzeri* that specializes in fish dishes (entrees 980-1480dr). Of the six or seven *tavernas* on Vas. Konstantinou St., the most pleasant are **To Palio Meraki,** a traditional Greek establishment, and **To Haleri,** which specializes in Arabic cuisine.

Of Xanthi's many overpriced cafes, the best situated and most lively are **Cafe Central,** right on the central square, and the **Jolly Caffé** (tel. 77 577), on Vas. Sofias St., which is *the* strip for people-watching in Xanthi.

SIGHTS The most interesting sight in Xanthi is the traditional **Old Town** neighborhood. Home to several mansions, most built with tobacco money, the area betrays a strong Turkish influence; the deeper you venture into the Old Town, the less Greek you will hear and the more shawl-covered women you will see. Both of Xanthi's museums are in the Old Town. The **folklore museum** is on Antikas St. *(Set to reopen in 1999 after renovations are completed.)* Directly across from the folklore museum is the **Christos Pavlidis Painting Gallery** (tel. 76 363), which houses a collection of 20 paintings by local luminary Christos Pavlides.

In the hills to the northeast of town are a pair of functioning convents. **Panagia Archangeliotissa** has an array of vivid frescoes; the more run-down **Panagia Kalamou** is more notable for its views of the town below than for its inner artistic merits. To get to the convents, follow Vas. Sofias St. for about 1km, cross the river, and eventually turn left onto Evrou St. *(Proper dress required.)*

▨ Komotini Κομοτηνη

Like nearby Xanthi, Komotini is a large and busy city notable for its significant Turkish population (or Greek Muslim, as the authorities like to say). But there the similarities stop; Komotini's grid of modern whitewashed apartment buildings lack the charm of Xanthi's Old Town, and the city as a whole is a bit more cramped, more prosaic, and less cosmopolitan. Nevertheless, Komotini's unappreciated but excellent architectural museum and its marked Turkish flavor make it an interesting spot to stop for a day or so. Walking the minaret-laden Turkish parts of town is a unique and memorable experience.

ORIENTATION AND PRACTICAL INFORMATION Komotini's main square is **Eirinis Square,** located in the very center of town. **Orfeos St.** runs east-west directly above Eirinis Sq. To the north of Orfeos St. is the Turkish part of town and the smaller **Ifestou Square.** Following Orfeos east from Eirinis Sq. takes you to **Viziinou Sq.** Running east-west through Viziinou Square and roughly parallel to Orfeos St. is **Zoidi St.,** Komotini's other major commercial thoroughfare. The **bus station** (tel. 22 912 or 26 111) is on **Tsounta St.:** walk west on Zoidi St. with your back to Viziinou Sq. and turn left on Tsounta. Buses go to Thessaloniki (4hr., 5 per day, 4300dr); Athens (11hr., 2 per day, 12400dr); Xanthi (1hr., 17 per day, 850 or 1000dr depending on route); Kavala (2hr., 7 per day, 1850dr); and Alexandroupolis (1hr., 12 per day, 1150dr).

Komotini's **train station** (tel. 22 650) is located at the far southwest corner of the city. To get here, walk west down Orfeos St. with your back to Eirinis Sq. At a large five-way intersection, turn left onto Vironos St., which turns into Kiriakidi St. then

Tsaldari St., and eventually reaches the station. There is an **OSE office** in town on Zoidou St. (tel. 26 804; open M-F 8am-3pm). Trains go to Athens (11hr., 4 per day, 6600dr); Thessaloniki (4½hr., 5 per day, 2500dr); Xanthi (30min., 5 per day, 420dr); and Istanbul, Turkey (7hr., 1 per day, 6330dr). Some routes are intercity express routes, on which tickets cost about 30% more, but trains go about 30% more quickly.

The **tourist office** for all of Thrace is in Komotini on 14 Apostolou Souzou St. (tel. 70 995 or 70 996; open M-F 8am-2pm). The office has information on hotels and sights in the area. To get here, walk down Zoidi St. towards Viziinou Sq.; the EOT office is on the left, on the third floor of a building adorned with Greek flags. On 1 Thisaius St. is the **National Bank** (open M-Th 8am-2pm, F 8am-1:30pm) and **ATM**. Follow Orfeos St. east with your back to Eirinis Sq.; a little after Orfeos turns into Vas. Georgiou, the bank is on the left at the intersection with Thisaius St. The local **hospital** (tel. 22 222 or 24 601) is on Sismanoglou St. in the southeast corner of town. The **police** (tel. 34 444) are on Zoidi St. and available 24-hours. The **post office** (tel. 23 195; open M-F 7:30am-2pm) and **OTE** (tel. 139; open M-F 7am-10pm, Sa-Su 7am-3pm) are located one after the other on Parasiou St., a side street off Eirinis Sq. **Postal code:** 69100. **Telephone code:** 0531.

ACCOMMODATIONS The weary but choosy traveler should be advised that Komotini's hotels are fairly scattered throughout the city; it takes some ambling around to find a decently priced hotel. The best deal in the area is **Hotel Hellas,** 31 Dimokritou St. (tel. 22 055), on a large intersection just north of the Archaeological Museum. Its rooms are clean though minimally furnished (singles 5000dr; doubles 7000dr; triples 8000dr; rooms have shared bath). The small **Adrianoupolis Hotel,** 25 Ifestou St. (tel. 24 563), is another inexpensive choice, ideal if you want to see the Turkish part of the city. Rooms here are old-fashioned, high-ceilinged, and share baths (singles 4500dr; doubles 7000dr). A bit more luxurious but reasonably priced is the recently built **Hotel Orpheus** (tel. 37 180 or 37 185; fax 28 271), on Eirinis Sq., which has rooms with bath, phone, and TV (singles 8500dr; doubles 12000dr; triples 16000dr).

FOOD AND ENTERTAINMENT Komotini has the standard array of cafes and bars, but not too many restaurants. The center for both dining and nightlife is the area around Eirinis Sq. **Restaurant Dimokritos** (tel. 24 445) is a bright and classy place located directly under the hotel of the same name at Vizinou Sq. Sit in pink-walled splendor as you dine on shrimp or *spetzofai* (two of the specialties here). Entrees run 1600-2500dr (open daily noon-midnight). If Greek food has you longing for some crunchy pizza, try the popular **Roma Pizza** (tel. 37 742 or 37 743)—both the pizza and the garlic bread are delicious. For *frappés* (or headier brews), Eirinis Square's rows of lively cafes and bars are the place to be. **Cafe Nemesis,** 69 Eirinis Sq. (tel. 33 493), is a lively place usually packed from morning through the night. On the opposite side of the square, under the red and green facade of the Hotel Astoria is the **Cafe Astoria** (tel. 35 054 or 35 055). This quieter cafe offers a central location without cacophony. Prices in Komotini average 800-1000dr per beer and 1500dr per cocktail.

SIGHTS The **Archaeological Museum** (tel. 22 411) is superb, at least by Thracian standards, and easily the foremost sight in Komotini. *(Open daily in summer, 9am-6pm; in winter 9am-3pm. Free.)* To get here, follow Zoidi St. westward and bear right at the big five-way intersection onto Simeonidi St.; the museum will be on your right. Arranged in meticulous chronological order, the museum's artifacts are gleaned from archaeological sites in nearby Dikaia, Mesemuria, and Meroneia, the site of Homer's Ismaros, where Odysseus found the wine he later used to intoxicate the fearsome Cyclops, Polyphemus. Some of the highlights of the museum are its archaic funerary statues of lions and men, a painted terra cotta sarcophagus, and a golden bust of the Roman Emperor Septimius. If you find yourself with time on your hands, have a look at the **Museum of Folk Life and History** (tel. 27 344 or 25 975). *(Open M-Sa 10am-1pm.)* In the converted old mansion you'll find household utensils, costumes, and manuscripts that depict Greek life in the good old days. To get here, turn onto Tsounta St. from Zoidi and then turn right before the bus stop on Mameli. About half an hour by taxi from Komotini are several lovely **beaches,** and the somewhat tourist-ridden town of **Maroneia,** whose ruins, though little known, are quite impressive.

■ Alexandroupolis Αλεξανδρουπολη

Alexandroupolis is pretty much the end of the road in Greece; it is farther north, farther east, and closer to Turkey than any other mainland Greek city. Yet Alexandroupolis' bustle and sophistication belie its border post status. Tourists—mostly Greek—flock to its streets in summer because of its location on the main east-west highway, rail line, and its proximity to the islands of the northern Aegean. Rows of fashionable stores (e.g. Benetton) and a lovely wooded waterfront make Alexandroupolis a pleasant stop for a night—accommodations in high season are scarce and expensive, so either call ahead or consider whether sleeping on the beach is a palatable option.

Alexandroupolis is named not for the legendary Macedonian Alexander the Great but for an obscure 19th-century Greek king. Russian occupation during Crimean War in 1877 gave the city its gridlike street plan, which greatly simplifies transit.

Alexandroupolis is a less than ideal departure point for Turkey, especially in the summer. Trains are hot, slow, and crowded. Most buses originate in Thessaloniki and overflow by the time they reach Alexandroupolis. People who hitch across the border make a trilingual sign asking for a ride, but *Let's Go: Greece* cannot recommend hitchhiking. It is illegal to cross on foot. Expect at least an hour delay at the border.

ORIENTATION AND PRACTICAL INFORMATION

Walking inland from the **ferry** and **hydrofoil dock,** the active waterfront and Alexandrou Ave. stretch to your left, while the **train station** lies a few meters to your right in front of **Eleftherias Square.** The three main streets running parallel to Alexandrou lie about three blocks inland: L. Dimokratias Ave., El. Venizelou St., and Paleologou St. The **bus station** sits at the corner of El Venizelou St. and 14th Maiou St., almost directly inland from the docks.

Transportation

Buses: (tel. 26 479). Service to Thessaloniki (5hr., 8 per day, 5400dr); Xanthi (2hr., 7 per day, 2000dr); Komotini (1hr., 14 per day, 1150dr); Kavala (2hr., 8 per day, 2800dr); and Kipi (30min., 5 per day, 700dr). The bus to Istanbul leaves from the train station and tickets can be bought there (7hr., 1 per day, 4500dr).

Ferries: Arsinoi and Saos (tel. 22 215), at the corner of Kyprou St. and the waterfront, sends ferries to Samothrace (2hr., 2-3 per day, 2300dr) and Limnos (6hr., 1 per week, 2900dr). Open daily 7am-2pm and 5-10pm. **Kikon Tours,** 68 Venizelou St. (tel. 25 455), has one ferry per week to Limnos (6hr., 3280dr); Lesvos (10hr., 4980dr); Chios (14hr., 6710dr); Samos (17hr., 8280dr); Kos (26hr., 10,760dr); and Rhodes (30hr., 11,540dr). Open M-Sa 9am-2pm and 6-9pm, Su 9am-2pm.

Flying Dolphins: Arsinoi and Saos send hydrofoils to Samothrace (1hr., 2-3 per day, 4700dr) and Limnos (1 per week, 6500dr). Tickets may be bought on board.

Flights: Olympic Airways, 4 Ellis St. (tel. 26 361), offers flights to Athens (2 per day, 45min., 17,400dr). No buses run to the airport, but taxis only cost about 500dr. Office open M-F 9am-3pm.

Trains: Station (tel. 26 398). Open daily 6:30am-11:30pm. Service to Thessaloniki (7½hr., 5 per day, 4800dr); Komotini (2½hr., 3 per day, 2160dr); Xanthi (3½hr., 3 per day, 2500dr); and Istanbul (10hr., 1 per day, 6500dr).

Taxis: (tel. 22 000 or 27 700). Available 24hr.

Tourist and Financial Services

Tourist Office: (tel. 24 998), on the corner of L. Dimokratias St. and Mitropolitou Kaviri St. Offers maps and info on lodging and transportation. Open M-F 8am-2pm.

Banks: L. Dimokratias St. is one long string of banks, so if the **National Bank's** 24hr. **ATM** rejects your card, try another. Open M-Th 8am-2pm and F 8am-1:30pm.

Emergency and Communications

Tourist Police: 6 Karaiskaki St. (tel. 37 411), 2 blocks inland from the waterfront, just before the lighthouse. Provides city maps with transportation, accommodations, and sights marked. Open M-F 7am-2:30pm and 5-11pm, Sa-Su 7am-2:30pm.

Police: (tel. 37 424). With the **tourist police,** open 24hr.

Hospital: 19 Dimitras St. (tel. 25 772). Open 24hr. **Post Office:** on the waterfront, past Karaiskaki St. Open M-F 7:30am-2pm. **Postal Code:** 68100.

OTE: Located on I. Kaviri St. in the block between L. Dimokratias Ave. and El. Venizelou St. Open M-Sa 7am-10pm, Su 7am-6pm. **Telephone Code:** 0551.

ACCOMMODATIONS

With only a few exceptions, hotels in Alexandroupolis are crowded and expensive. Lodging choices are clustered on the east edge of the waterfront and inland between Kaviri St. and 14 Maiou St.

⊛**Hotel Lido,** 15 Paleologou St. (tel. 28 808). Large modern rooms, congenial staff, and a classy lobby make you wonder how prices are kept so low. Singles 4000dr, with bath 5500dr; doubles 5000dr, with bath 6500dr; triples 6500dr, with bath 7500dr.
Hotel Majestic (tel. 26 444), on 7 Eleftherias Sq., visible from the train station. Old—but clean—rooms. Shared baths. Singles 4500dr; doubles 6000dr; triples 9500dr.
Hotel Mitropolis, 11 Athan. Diakou St. (tel. 26 443 or 33 808), on the corner of Emporiou St. and Athan. Diakou St. From Eleftherias Sq., turn left onto Emporiou and walk down several blocks (to the left facing inland). Immaculate rooms include bath, radio, and phone. Singles 10,000dr; doubles 14,000dr; triples 15,000dr.
Hotel Oceanis, 20 Paleologou St. (tel. 28 830 or 25 156; fax 34 118). One of the most modern and popular hotels in town. Rooms with TV, A/C, phone, bath. Singles 12,500dr; doubles 17,000dr.
Camping Alexandroupolis (tel. 28 735), located 2km west of the center on the water. 1180dr per person.

FOOD AND ENTERTAINMENT

Dining in Alexandroupolis is basically limited to two areas: a small cluster of restaurants where Kyprou widens into Polytehniou Sq., and the many choices on the long, sweeping, seemingly endless waterfront. The first restaurants of note are the cluster of fish *tavernas* (frequented mostly by old Greek men) across from the docks and next to the train station. If you're not in the mood to dine, get a *gyro* (400dr) to go on the waterfront or on one of the side streets off Dimokratias St.

I Klimataria (tel. 26 288), on Polytehniou Sq. Hoppin' casual local hang-out.
⊛**Neraida** (tel. 22 867), located diagonally across from I Klimataria on Polytehniou Sq. Point-and-choose menu, popular with locals.
Ouzerie Mynos, opposite the post office at the intersection with Kyprou St., is in a cluster of *ouzeries* west on the waterfront. Unmistakable Dutch windmill and unforgettably sweet, permeating scent of olive oil and freshly baked bread.

Nightlife in Alexandroupolis centers almost exclusively around the waterfront, which blends into one loud, lively, mile-long cafe. **Cafe Akrotiri,** on the western edge, is one of the largest cafe-bars, and an ideal spot from which to watch the sun set into the shimmering Aegean waters. Farther east, the most popular places are **Cafe Aeolus** and **Cafe del Mar.** Because Alexandroupolis is not much of a tourist town, these cafes are filled almost exclusively with hip natives. If you'd rather watch a movie than sip *ouzo*, try the **Municipal Theater** (tel. 28 735), located at the campground 2km west of the town center.

SIGHTS

Alexandroupolis' most important site is probably the **Ecclesiastic Art Museum** housed within the Cathedral of Agios Nikolaos, two blocks inland from the National Bank. *(Open M-Sa 8am-1pm. 200dr donation.)* An 18th-century icon of a limber Christ, its best piece, portrays Jesus with his legs forming a heart. The museum is worth a visit but due to a lack of funding does not hold regular hours. Try if you can to get an English-speaking priest to give you a tour; often he will relate some Thracian history and important distinctions between icon styles.

Alexandroupolis' other museum is the brand-new **Historical and Folklore Museum** (tel. 28 926), on the corner of Dimokratias St. and Kanari St. *(Open Tu-Sa 10:30am-1:30pm and 6:30-9:30pm.)* Its contents—typical folklore museum fare such as farm tools, costumes, and embroidery—depict the evolution of the Thracian lifestyle.

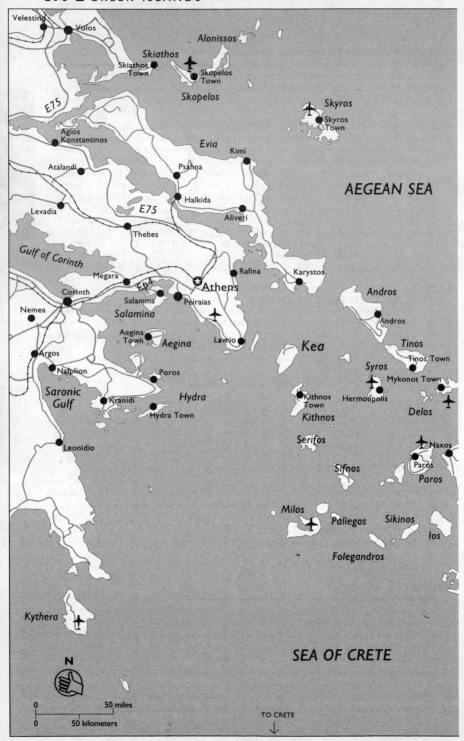

Greek Islands

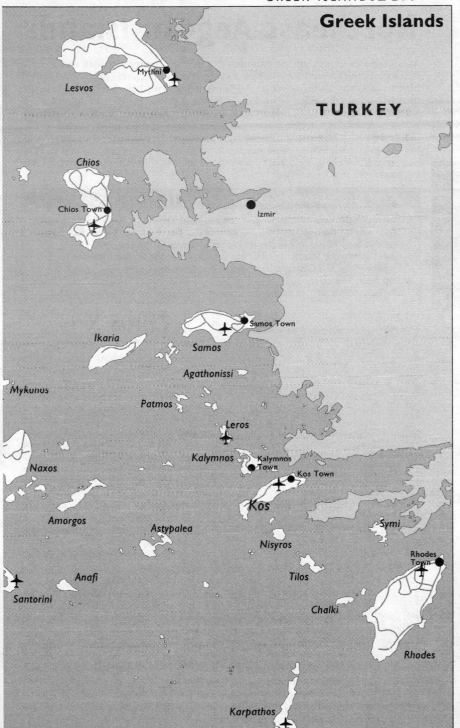

Northeast Aegean Islands

After centuries of resisting the Ottoman Empire, the northeast Aegean islands have developed a finely-tuned sense of how to keep themselves closely guarded. Although pirates and Ottomans no longer pose a threat, many of the islands continue to isolate themselves from the influx of tourism in hopes of preserving their traditional atmosphere. Intricate, rocky coastlines and unassuming port towns enclose the thickly wooded mountains that give way to unspoiled villages and secluded beaches. A few miles off the Turkish coast, the islands have a sizable military presence; the large numbers of Greek soldiers may cause women traveling alone to feel uncomfortable. However, travelers seeking undiluted Greek culture without the intrusion of foreign influence may well find it here.

🗺️ HIGHLIGHTS OF THE NORTHEAST AEGEAN

- For more than two millennia the volcanoes of **Lesvos** (p. 297), Greece's premier lesbian destination, have inspired native poets—from the ancient sensual lyricist Sappho to the Modernist Nobel Laureate Odysseus Elytis.
- Kneel before the Sanctuary of Great Gods of Anatolia on **Samothrace** (p. 313), where Philip and Olympia conceived Alexander the Great.
- Skip from **Samos** (p. 303), the birth place of math-guru Pythagoras, to Ephesus in Turkey, the largest excavated ancient metropolis in the Mediterranean.

Chios

CHIOS Χιος

When the mythical hunter Orion drove all the wild beasts from Chios, grand pine, cypress, and mastic trees sprouted on the vast mountainsides. Since antiquity, Chios has cultivated and exported masticha, a bittersweet, gummy resin used in varnishes, cosmetic creams, chewing gum, floor waxes, and color television sets. Long both a military base and a center of Greek shipping, Chios has only recently been opened to the tourist industry. As its striking volcanic beaches and medieval villages become more accessible, the island is slowly becoming another hotspot for northern European package tours and for vacationers hopping between Greece and Turkey.

Chios lies across a narrow strait from Çeşme, Turkey. Before Ottoman rule, this reputed birthplace of both Homer and Christopher Columbus hosted Venetian and Geonoese Crusaders. The island tragically gained modern fame in 1822, when a Greek nationalist rebellion failed and resulted in over 25,000 deaths.

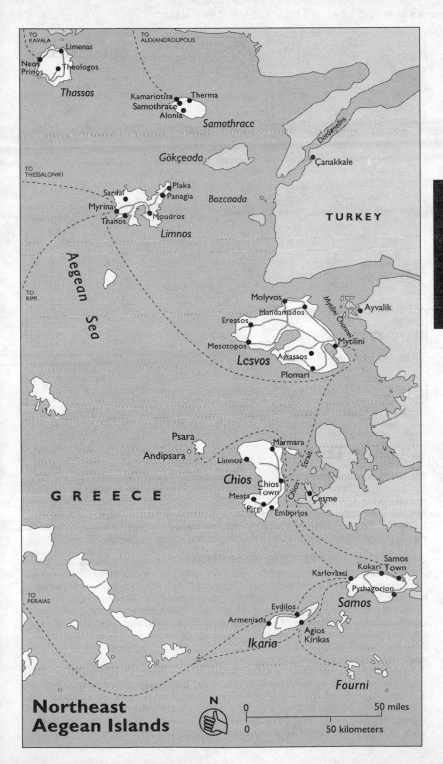

TO
KAVALA

Limenas

Neos
Prinos
Theologos

Thassos

TO
ALEXANDROUPOLIS

Kamariotisa   Therma
Samothrace
Alonia

Samothrace

Gökçeada

Dardanelles

Çanakkale

TO
THESSALONIKI

Plaka
Sardai   Panagia
Myrina
Thanos   Moudros

Limnos

Bozcaada

TURKEY

*Aegean
Sea*

TO
KIMI

Molyvos
Mandamados
Eressos

Ayvalik

Mesotopos

Mytilini
Agiassos
Plomari

Lesvos

Myrina Channel

Psara

Marmara

Andipsara

Limnos

Chios   Chios
Town
Mesta   Cesme
Pirgi   Emborios

Chios Strait

Strait

G R E E C E

Samos
Kokari   Town
Karlovassi
Pythagorion

Samos

TO
PEIRAIAS

Evdilos
Armenistis
Agios
Kirikas

Ikaria

Fourni

Northeast
Aegean Islands

N

0   50 miles

0   50 kilometers

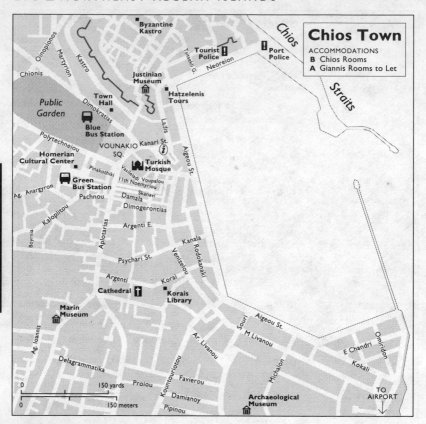

Chios Town

ACCOMMODATIONS
B Chios Rooms
A Giannis Rooms to Let

■ Chios Town

Chios Town is home to many sailors—identifiable by their red license plates—and several wealthy ship owners—identifiable by their luxury cars. Ravaged by German troops during WWII, the unadorned waterfront, with its modern Athenian-style skyline, turns a rather indifferent face to the newcomer. The groups of young men who lounge in the streets and coffee shops may intimidate the lone female traveler, but the busy streets beyond the waterfront are fun and safe to explore.

ORIENTATION AND PRACTICAL INFORMATION Most services, buses, and taxis gather around **Vounakio Square,** the social center of town located two blocks inland from the right side of the waterfront (facing inland). Left from Vounakio lies the **market street,** pleasantly bustling and shaded in the morning. Most points of interest around the island are accessible only from Chios Town, the source from which all transit routes radiate. Every night the waterfront closes to traffic, cafes fill up, and the Greeks begin their *volta* (promenade), bringing an atmosphere of pleasant respite from the clamor that roared through the streets after midday shutdown. This is the place to be from late evening to early in the morning.

To reach the **tourist office,** 11 Kanari St. (tel. 44 344), turn off the waterfront onto Kanari St., walk toward the square, and look for the "i" sign. They provide lists of accommodations and reservation assistance (open May-Sept. M-F 7am-2:30pm and 6:30-9:30pm, Sa-Su 9am-1pm, Oct.-Apr. M-F 7am-2:30pm). **Hatzelenis Tourist Agency** (tel. 26 743 or 27 295; fax 26 531), is immediately to the left of the ferries dock, at the far right end of the waterfront. The agency provides ferry info and ticketing for all lines except NEL, which has its own exclusive agency in the center of the waterfront; they arrange **car rentals** (from 12,000dr in the high season, 6000dr per day in the off season, unlimited mileage, full insurance, and all taxes included); they also offer help in finding accommodation, trips to Turkey, excursions, **weekend currency exchange,** and bus schedules (open M-Sa 7am-1:30pm and 6-9pm, Su 10am-1pm and 6-9pm, and often open when boats arrive late at night). The **Ionian Bank,** 16 Kanari St. (tel. 23 522 or 23 434), is by the tourist office and offers an **ATM** and **currency exchange** (open M-Th 8am-2pm, F 8am-1:30pm, Sa 9am-1pm).

Olympic Airways (tel. 23 998), on the waterfront near the corner of Psychari St., sells plane tickets to Athens (3 per day, 15,900dr; open M-F 8am-4pm). From Chios **ferries** go to Samos (4½hr., 3 per week, 2800dr), Lesvos (3hr., daily, 3200dr), Piraeus (overnight, daily, 5760dr), and Çeşme on the Turkish coast (45min., 2 per day, 8000-9000dr plus 5000dr port tax). A Greek and a Turkish line each serve this last route once per day. American, European, and other non-Greek citizens will have to purchase a visa if staying more than one day (by date) in Turkey. Ferries also sometimes travel to Alexandroupolis, Limnos, Lesvos, Samos, Patmos, Laros, Kos, Rhodes, and Crete. **KTEL buses** (tel. 27 507 or 24 257) leave from both sides of Vounakio Sq., right off the public gardens. Hatzelenis offers schedules and fare information. All one-way trips are less than 1000dr. **Blue buses** (tel. 23 086), on the right side of the square on Dimokratias St., are for travel within the immediate vicinity of Chios Town (9km), making 5 to 6 trips per day to Karfas, Vrondados, and Karies. **Taxis** (tel. 41 111) cluster in the main square around the clock.

A **hospital** (tel. 44 306) is 2km north of Chios (open 24hr.). Chios Town has more than 20 **pharmacies**. Notices on pharmacy doors indicate which are open on weekends. To find the **post office** (tel. 443 50), follow Omirou St. one block inland past the Olympic Airways waterfront office (open M-F 7:30am-2pm). The **OTE** is across from the tourist office, and there are phones on the waterfront. **Postal code:** 82100. **Telephone code:** 0271.

ACCOMMODATIONS

Most of Chios Town's accommodations are converted neoclassical mansions with creaky wooden staircases and high ceilings. In high season, when rooms become scarce, it's best to let a tourist agency call around for you. Ask at **Hatzelenis Tourist Agency** about the clean **Chios Rooms** on the opposite side of the waterfront (singles 3000dr; doubles 5000dr, with bath 6000dr). If they are full, Hatzelenis can help you find another inexpensive pension. Most of these cluster at the south end of the waterfront. You should be able to find single rooms to let for 4000dr and doubles for 5000dr. Prices remain relatively constant through both high and low seasons, with private bath an additional 1000dr. One block behind Aigeou St. on the waterfront, **Giannis Rooms to Let,** 48 Livanou St. (tel. 27 433), has rooms with baths, a common kitchen, and a lovely backyard garden shaded by drooping grape vines heavy with fruit (doubles from 7000-9000dr). A right off Aigeou St. onto Korai St. and up two blocks leads you to **Artemis Rooms to Let** (tel. 25 011 or 093 756 612). The rooms are noisy due to traffic but convenient (doubles from 7000dr with common bath and kitchen). Look for the "Welcome, Rooms to Let" sign outside. Tourist agencies also have info on **Chios Camping.**

FOOD AND ENTERTAINMENT

Myriad vendors hawk all kinds of food on the market street near Vounakio Square. Although locals praise the small *taverna* next door to Hatzelenis Tourist Agency, they warn that most waterfront *tavernas* cater to the undiscerning tastebuds of sunburnt tourists. Your best bet may be to lunch on the fresh *spanakopita* (spinach pie) or *tyropita* (cheese pie) available in **bakeries**. For full meals, ask the locals where they eat, and you're destined to find better fare.

Cafes and **bars** line the waterfront. Of these, locals flock particularly to **Remezzo** and **Metropolis.** A taxi ride (1500dr) will take you to a cluster of bars outside of town in **Karfas.** Of these, **Stasi** is the hottest and has the cheapest beer.

> ### Craftsmen with a Fork and a Dream
> Although it is built in the twisting alleyways of a medieval castle, Pirgi is most recognizable for its *ksista*, the unique geometric patterns that coat walls of every house in the village. Instead of whitewashing homes, as is common in the Cyclades, Pirgian craftsmen first coat each house with a paint made from the gray stone at Emborio. The houses are then whitewashed and, while the paint is still wet, the craftsmen form geometric patterns with a fork, creating the village's trademark design. After both coats have dried, artists add splendidly colorful designs to the otherwise black-and-white geometry.

SIGHTS Relics of the town's past encircle Vounakio Sq. The walls of the **Byzantine Kastro** (tel. 26 866), a castle reconstructed by the Genoese, enclose the narrow streets of the **old town.** *(Open Tu-Su 10am-1pm. Admission 500dr.)* The castle houses a tiny **Byzantine Exhibition.** The **Ottoman mosque** on Vournakio Sq. is actually a museum. *(Open Tu-Sa 8am-1pm and Su 10am-3pm. Free.)* The **Folklore Museum,** on the first floor of the **Korais Library,** is next to the **Mitropolis,** Chios Town's cathedral. *(Open M-Th 8am-2pm, F 8am-2pm and 5-7:30pm, Sa 8am-12:30pm.)* Don't bother to follow the yellow signs leading to an archeological museum closed for renovation. Only 6km south of Chios Town lies the popular sandy beach **Karfas,** victim of Chios' latest burst of development. Nine kilometers north, beachgoers will find the rocky shores of **Vrondados** and **Daskalopetra.** Blue buses from Vournakio Sq. service all three.

■ Around Chios

Pine-covered mountains 16km west of Chios Town cradle the impressive **Nea Moni** (New Monastery), built in the 11th century. *(Open daily 9am-1pm and 4-8pm. Free.)* An icon of the Virgin Mary miraculously appeared to three hermits who promptly founded the monastery with the aid of an exiled emperor. Over the centuries, the monastery complex has been rebuilt and enlarged, and today remains one of the world's most important Byzantine monuments. An earthquake in 1881 destroyed much of the complex itself, but most of its structures have been carefully restored. Don't miss the 11th-century mosaics in the inner narthex. Even their state of partial decrepitude can't hide the original artistry. **Anavatos,** 15km west of Nea Moni, is a staggeringly beautiful village with a tragic past. The women and children of the village threw themselves off these cliffs after their failed attempt to withstand an 1822 Ottoman invasion. Check with the bus station for excursions to both sites (2 per week). Taxi drivers may agree to drive you to the site, wait 30 minutes, and bring you back. From Chios, a **taxi-tour** of Nea Moni and Anavatos costs 8000dr (agree on a fare before leaving for the monastery). The road is hilly but well paved until Nea Moni, where it deteriorates into an uneven, rocky path, passable by car and motorcycle, but murderous on mopeds.

The villages in the southern half of the island, called *Mastichochoria,* are home to Chios's famous resin, produced by squat mastic or lentisk trees. **Pirgi** is called "mastic village" and is high in the hills 25km from Chios. The big attraction in Pirgi is not the mastic, but rather the unique black and white geometrical designs covering traditional buildings. Here you will find the **Women's Agricultural Tourist Collective** (tel. (0271) 72 496), which arranges rooms in private farmhouses in Armolia, Pirgi, Olymbi, and Mesta. The female farmers, symbolized by the *melissa* (bee), will show you around their farms, but it's best to make reservations a few weeks in advance, especially in July and August. You can also make arrangements with village proprietors by asking at places with "rooms to let" signs.

Pirgi is also home to the 14th-century **Agioi Apostoloi** church, a replica of the Nea Moni. Sixteenth-century frescoes and paintings by a Cretan iconography school cover almost every inch of the interior. The caretaker must unlock the front gate for you;

ask for Michalis Vassilis at 27 Mix. Kolika St., directly across from the OTE (open M-F 9am-3pm; 100dr donation is expected).

On the southern end of Chios lies the beach of **Emborio**. Its light brown volcanic cliffs contrast strikingly with the black stones and deep blue water below. The bus from Chios Town or Pirgi drops passengers off at the harbor. The first beach is up the only road to the right (facing the water). There's a smaller, less crowded shore up the stairs to your right. Good shoes are a must.

The poorer and less visited northern half of Chios is the silent partner of the *Masti-chochoria*. Roughly 5km outside Chios Town, just past Vrondados, Homer held classes at the beach of **Daskalopetra**. After Daskalopetra, the main roads wind northwest along the coast past Marmaron to **Nagos** (30km away), which features a gray stone beach (perhaps a popular spot for cutting Homer's classes in antiquity). **Volissos** (40km west), Homer's legendary birthplace, is crowned by a Byzantine fort.

LESVOS Λεσβος

Ironically, Lesvos' seemingly barren volcanic landscape has nurtured one of the richest cultural legacies in the Aegean. Once home to the musician Terpander, the poet Arion, the writer Aesop, and the 7th-century BC poet Sappho, Lesvos (often called Mytilini) now supports tourist haunts, indicating that its greatness remains in the fabled past. Yet even in this century, Lesvos has given rise to the Nobel Prize winning poet Odysseus Elytis, the neoprimitive artist Theophilos, art publisher Tériade, and the family of 1988 U.S. Presidential candidate Michael Dukakis.

According to legend, the population of Lesvos, Greece's third largest island, was once entirely female. This notion may owe its origin to the Athenian assembly's 428 BC decision to punish the recalcitrant residents of Mytilini by executing all adult males on the island. In reality, the assembly repealed the decision after some debate. Mytilini flourished as a cultural center for hundreds of years. Its long-gone inhabitants would be astonished to learn that the West has come to consider 5th-century Athens, not Mytilini, to be the zenith of Greek civilization. In particular, the Philosophical Academy, where Epicurus and Aristotle taught, brought Lesvos well-deserved fame.

Until recently, the island remained relatively remote and cultivated its own offbeat character—a blend of horse breeding, serious *ouzo* drinking, and leftist politics. Although Lesvos's major towns now host a growing number of foreign visitors, tour-

Lesvos

ism has not reached Cycladean proportions. The island remains something of a mecca for lesbians and attracts long-term visitors taking weeks to explore the many historical sites and discovering the island's tall pines, olive groves, corn fields, long sandy beaches, and barren hillsides eerily reminiscent of the moon.

■ Mytilini Μυτιληνη

This central port city and capital of Lesvos is picturesque from a distance. Yachts and colorful fishing boats adorn the yawning harbor, while modern high-rises and neo-classical mansions stand shoulder to shoulder on the ascent to the Amali mountains. Yet the decaying Gattelusi castle is only one indication that the city is crowded and crumbling. Her once grand mansions are in a state of decay—it is too expensive to restore them, yet illegal to tear them down.

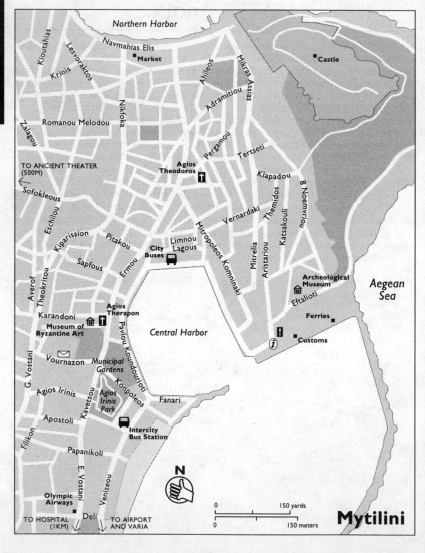

ORIENTATION AND PRACTICAL INFORMATION Boats dock at the far right of the waterfront, while inter-island buses leave at the left end. The town beach lies to the right of the boats. The city spreads chaotically along the waterfront on **Pavlou Koudoutrioti St.**, with **Ermou St.** running parallel one block inland. In the most interesting quadrant of town, the **old market** advances inland from the waterfront, below the castle and to the right of the church. Get lost among the market's knotted streets and cobbled ways and shop in the aromatic fish market nearby. To reach the **tourist office,** 6 James Aristarchou (tel. 42 511; fax 42 512), with your back to the tourist police, walk uphill one block; the office will be on your right. They offer information, free brochures, and maps (open M-F 8:30am-3pm). For the **Tourist Police** (tel. 22 776), from the ferry, head left towards the interior harbor and main waterfront road. The official passport control building, at the corner of the pier, houses the tourist police (open in summer daily 8am-1pm and 5-9pm; in winter 8am-2pm). The **Rooms to Let Office,** one block inland from the center of the waterfront, helps find accommodations (open M-Sa 9am-10pm). The **National Bank,** with a 24-hour **ATM,** is in the center of the waterfront (open M-Th 8am-2pm, F 8am-1:30pm).

Olympic Airways, 44 Kavetsou Ave. (tel. 28 659), or any ticketing agent can book flights to Athens (4-5 per day, 17,200dr), Thessaloniki (1 per day, 21,000dr), Limnos (1 per day, 13,500dr), and Chios (1 per week, 7500dr). Buy your ticket a week in advance. To catch your flight head to the nearby **airport** (tel. 61 490 or 61 590). **Green buses** leave from the intercity bus station (tel. 28 873) and service all destinations on the island. The station is behind Ag. Irinis Park, diagonally one-and-a-half blocks from the south edge of the harbor. In summer, buses from Mytilini go to Molyvos (1½hr., 4 per day, 1300dr), Sigri (2½hr., 2 per week, 1900dr); Skala Eressou (2½hr., 1 per day, 1900dr); Plomari (1¼hr., 3 per day, 800dr); and Petra (1¼hr., 4 per day, 1200dr). Fewer buses chug along on weekends. **Blue buses** (tel. 28 725), based on the waterfront, service local routes around Mytilini. **Ferries** connect Lesvos to the northeast Aegean and beyond. **NEL Lines,** 67 Pavlou Koudoutrioti St. (tel. 22 220 or 28 480; fax 28 601), along the waterfront three blocks from the pier, is open daily from 6am to 9pm. In summer their ferries travel to Peiraias (12hr., 1 per day, 7030dr); Limnos (5hr., 4 per week, 3600dr); Thessaloniki (12hr., 2 per week, 8300dr); Kavala (12hr., 2 per week, 6360dr); Chios (3hr., 1 per week, 3250dr); Syros (8hr., 1 per week, 5600dr); Andros (9hr., 1 per week, 5200dr); and Volos (12hr., 1 per week, 6000dr). Inquire about other lines which may connect to different islands. Ferries also run to Çesme, Turkey (45min., at least 3 per week, 9000dr, plus 5000dr Greek port tax, and 3000dr Turkish port tax). The **hospital** (tel. 43 777) is southwest of the city on E. Vostani St. (open 24hr.). Dial 166 for an **ambulance.** The **post office** (tel. 28 836), is on Vourhazon St. near the intercity bus station (open M-F 7:30am-3pm). Signs pointing the way to the post office are behind the park (which has free **public toilets**), near the taxi stand. Look for the **OTE** (tel. 28 199) two doors up from the post office. **Postal code:** 81100. **Telephone code:** 0251.

ACCOMMODATIONS AND FOOD If you must stay in Mytilini, it is easiest to head to the Rooms to Let office, one block inland and well marked by information signs. Singles should run you 5000-6000dr and doubles 7000-8000dr. **New Life Rooms** (tel. 093 279 057, 46 100, or 42 650) is a stately brown building on the corner of Ermou and Olimpou St., with a range of high-ceilinged rooms (all rooms 9000-13,000dr).

Cafes and *tavernas* abound along the waterfront, and while locals dine in the north, tourists congregate in the south. On the cobbled streets, cheese pies, charmless croissants, and gyros abound. **Averof,** in the center of the waterfront, has traditional food and low prices. Remember that charm, too, has its price. For breakfast with the locals, saunter behind the local bus station onto Limnou St. and take the first right onto Thasou St. You will see them, they will see you. Expect a few stares, and real Greek coffee. The cafe adjacent to the Rooms to Let Office is another place to sip coffee (delicious), play *tavli*, and be conspicuous—if you like that sort of thing.

NORTHEAST AEGEAN

SIGHTS The ubiquitous signs in Mytilini helpfully point tourists to the various sights. The **Archaeological Museum,** 7 Argiri Eftalioti St. (tel. 28 032), houses a collection of the island's artifacts. *(Open Tu-Su 8:30am-3pm. Admission 500dr, students and seniors 300dr, EU students free, all free Sundays.)* Accompanied by thorough descriptions of their respective roles in Lesvian history, the artifacts include Mycenaean, Protogeometric, and Archaic pottery, Classical and Hellenistic vases and sculpture, and remnants from the Temple at Fressos. Don't miss the smaller building hiding behind the main museum quarters, which contains rare Aeolian tablets. If you have a spare hour in Mytilini, visit the enormous late 19th-century **Church of St. Therapon,** on Ermou St., whose dome betrays Western influence. *(Open daily 9am-7pm.)* The church towers over the fish market's daily catch—sardines, octopi, and occasionally, small sharks. Near the tall clock tower at the south end of the harbor is the impressive **Church of Agios Theodoros,** containing the bones and skull of its patron saint.

From the ferry dock, all roads leading uphill will take you to the **Gattelusi Castle** (tel. 27 970). *(Open Tu-Su 8:30am-3pm. Admission 500dr, students 300dr.)* Surrounded by redolent pines above the town, the fortress protects its panoramic view over Mytilini and across to Turkey. It was originally constructed by Emperor Justinian on the site of a Byzantine castle, and bears the name of Francesco Gattelusi, who received Lesvos as dowry in 1355 after he married Justinian's daughter. The castle walls contain evidence of successive epochs in a losing battle to keep them in repair: Genoese, Ottomans, and Greeks. They are now capped them with telephone cable, the 20th century's contribution.

The highest point on the north side of Mytilini is the 3rd-century BC **ancient theater,** built during Hellenistic times. *(Open Tu-Su 8:30am-3pm.)* Here, 15,000 spectators attended performances with near perfect acoustics—the effect was so impressive that it inspired Pompeii to build Rome's first stone theater.

■ Varia Βαρια

Only 4km south of Mytilini along El. Venizelou St., the tiny, unassuming village of **Varia** surprises wayfarers with the **Theophilos Museum** (tel. 41 644), featuring the work of the famous neoprimitivist Greek painter Theophilos Hadzimichali. *(Open Tu-Su 9am-2pm and 5:30-8pm. Admission 500dr.)* Next door, the **Musée Tériade** displays an excellent collection of Picasso, Miró, Leger, Chagall, and Matisse lithographs. *(Open Tu-Su 9am-2pm and 5-8pm. Admission 500dr.)* Tériade, a native of Lesvos born Stratis Eleftheriadis, rose to fame as a leading publisher of graphic art in Paris during much of the 20th century. **Buses** to Varia depart from the Mytilini waterfront depot every hour (230dr). Or, head northwest 6km to a well-preserved Roman aquaduct at **Moria.** Buses to Moria also run about every 30 minutes from the waterfront.

■ Petra and Molyvos Πετρα και Μολυβος

With only 5km between them, the artists' colonies of Petra and Molyvos (Mithimna) lie at the northern tip of Lesvos. Both situated on long, lovely stretches of beach, the towns are Lesvos's most visited spots after Mytilini, yet prices remain quite reasonable. Molyvos conveys almost picture-perfect charm. Cobbled alleyways and stone houses topped with red tile roofs are all intricately stacked into a hill. Petra stretches along a sand beach and presses into the fertile plain behind it.

Just up from the Molyvos **bus stop**—bear left at the fork—a small building on the left houses the **tourist office** (tel. 71 347), which provides maps, schedules, and help finding rooms (open M-F 9am-3pm and 6-9pm). Next door, a **National Bank** has a 24-hour **currency exchange** (open M-Th 8am-2pm, F 8am-1:30pm). Nearby **Akti Rentals** (tel. 71 997), rents **mopeds** (3000dr per day), **cars** (10,000dr per day), and **jeeps** (18,000dr per day). They are open daily 8am-1:30pm and 5:30-10pm. Across the street, a stand sells **international newspapers.** Continuing uphill, a mobile **post office** is on the main traffic route (open June-Aug. M-F 8am-2pm). Ascending the hill in a switchback, this steep, cobbled road winds through the town's center. Here you can find the local **laundry** (wash 1100dr, dry 600dr; open M-Sa 9:30am-2pm and 6-11pm) and **pharmacy** (tel. 71 427; open daily 9:30am-2pm and 6:30-11pm). On the next switchback, across from the main post office (open M-F 8am-2pm), a thickly shaded cafe serves as the local haunt for morning coffee. Signs direct you to the **police station** (tel. 71 222). **Postal code: 81108. Telephone code:** 0253.

The bus stops in **Petra** at the central square opening onto the water. As you face inland, one street stretches in front of you. The **post office** is on this street, as is **OTE** (open M-Sa 7:30am-3:10pm). The **National Bank** lies on the street to the right (open M Th 8am-2pm, F 8am-1:30pm). The **Women's Cooperative of Petra** is on the same street as the National Bank. The balconies of their restaurant overlook the square, and they provide rooms to let throughout the community. **Postal code:** 81009.

The best accommodations in both Molyvos and Petra are **rooms to let.** Your stay will be much simpler if you let the **tourist office** or **Women's Cooperative** help with arrangements. If these offices are closed, or if you seek the adventure of finding your own rooms, take heart. Nearly every corner in both towns displays at least one "room to let" sign. Rooms with private baths start at 4000dr for singles, 6000dr for doubles, and 7000dr for triples. Remember to bargain.

Beachfront **cafes** exist in both towns. On an inviting terrace shaded by large plane trees overlooking Molyvos and the Aegean, **Taverna Sansibala** serves traditional Greek entrees (1300-2000dr), as well as breakfast and lunch. In Petra, the **Women's Cooperative Restaurant** prepares delicious, home-cooked meals (1500dr).

Although Molyvos has an **archaeological museum** and regular **exhibitions by local artists** in its town hall, and Petra boasts a **folk art museum,** the real attractions are the **beaches** around which these towns lie. If these beaches get too crowded, do not hesitate to take the rugged road north out of Molyvos toward **Eftalou.** Here secluded beaches hide beneath towering cliffs (5km northeast).

■ Plomari Πλομαρι

After arson destroyed the village of Megalochori in 1841, people resettled in the Turkish inhabited region 12km south, now modern **Plomari.** From its earliest days, this southern coastal town has manifested a split personality—it is at once a no-holds-barred resort town (with discos, cheery *tavernas,* and all the other package tour trappings) as well as a fishing village, full of fishermen nailing octopi to telephone poles to dry in the sun. The overall effect, aided and abetted by Plomari's large *ouzo* industry, is cheerful and relaxing. The local product is far better than the bottled industrial variety. Try a sample at the **Barbayanni Ouzo Factory** (tel. 32 741; fax 32 231), roughly 2km east toward Agios Isodoros on the way to Plomari, which has its own **Ouzo Museum** (open M-F 9am-7pm and Sa 9am-2pm). An annual week-long **Ouzo Festival** is held in late August and features song, dance, drunken tourists, and, of course, free *ouzo.* Large groups may receive a free tour. Throughout the summer, Plomari also hosts several religious celebrations and cultural events. The one-week **Festival of Benjamin** in late June commemorates the leader of the 1821 war with dancing and theatrical presentations. **Postal code:** 81200. **Telephone code:** 0252.

Beaches appear intermittently around Plomari. To reach rocky **Arnovdeli Beach,** turn onto Agios Nikolaou Rd. and follow the signs; it's a 15-minute walk south of town. If you continue straight on Agios Nikolaou you will come to **Agios Nikolaos,** a church sparkling with icons spanning 400 years. If you aren't into rocky coasts, the best beaches are at **Agios Isodoros,** 3km east of town along the main road.

Agiassos, a village 15km north of Plomari on the slopes of Lesvos's Mt. Olympus, remains a center for ceramic crafts. An **Orthodox church** here contains an icon of the Virgin Mary made by St. Lucas, originally destined for Constantinople in 330. When the priest transporting it heard rumors of war, he feared for the icon's safety and deposited it in the church. On August 15 Agiassos hosts **Panagia,** a grand annual celebration in honor of the Virgin Mary. The village also boasts an **Ecclesiastical Museum** with Byzantine religious works (ask church officials and priests in town), a **Folk Museum** featuring traditional costumes, and a **library** with some English books.

■ Skala Eressou Σκαλα Ερεσου

Skala Eressou's seemingly endless beach stretches across the opposite end of Lesvos from Mytilini. Awarded the EU's Blue Banner award for cleanliness, its western half remains one of the few legal nude beaches on the island. The birthplace of the poet Sappho has become a lesbian mecca as well as an extremely beautiful and laid-back beach town for all travelers.

ORIENTATION AND PRACTICAL INFORMATION Skala Eressou is a coastal getaway a short distance from the inland village of Eressos. **Eressos Travel** (tel. 53 076; fax 53 576), one block inland from the waterfront, provides **currency exchange,** a kiosk for calls, excursion and accommodations information, book exchange, and **car rentals** (from 14,000dr per day; open M-Sa 8:30am-10pm, Su 8:30am-2pm). The friendlier **Rinellos Travel and Tourist Agency** (tel. 53 246; fax 53 982) close to the water offers similar services at similar hours. A stand sells **newspapers** across the street. There is no bank, so bring either cash or traveler's checks. As you face the sea, signs point to the **mail box** and **card phone** three blocks to the right. Further services, including the **police** (tel. 53 222), can be found in Eressos. **Postal code:** 81105. **Telephone code:** 0253.

ACCOMMODATIONS Ask at **Eressos Travel** about the **Eressos House,** which has sparkling rooms with private bathrooms and shared refrigerators (doubles 6000dr). Otherwise, they may be able to point you to other rooms to let. Of course, you can always count on the hotel hawkers at the bus station, or inquire at one of the many signs on Skala's wide streets. **Motel Sappho** (tel. 641 388 55), on the waterfront, is a women's only hotel with immaculate, airy rooms and activities almost every night—from belly dancing to salsa—(doubles with bath from 7000dr). There is unofficial **camping** at the far end of the beach, by the nude section farthest from town, with primitive facilities (women's only). While tolerated, this is not legal, so camp at your own risk, and lather on repellent—the bugs are vicious.

FOOD AND ENTERTAINMENT Outdoor cafes and the serene Aegean Sea surround the stone-layered **Square of Anthis and Evristhenous.** Across the bridge, **Yamas** offers cozy tables and couches shaded by huge umbrellas, killer milkshakes (800dr), and damn good North American food. You can't go wrong with the veggie chili cheeseburger (1400dr), the veggie deep dish pizza, or the to-die-for homemade chocolate cake with ice cream. Restaurants with bamboo-covered wooden piers sit on the beach and serve elegant sunset views of **Sappho's Profile,** formed by the ridge of the western mountains. At the end of the walkway is the **Bennetts' Restaurant** (tel. 53 624). Run by the Brits Max and Jackie Bennett, the restaurant has quite a few vegetarian options. Prices are reasonable, and you'll lick the platter clean (open daily 9:30am-3pm and 6-11pm). **The Tenth Muse,** in the main square, is Skala Eressou's most popular lesbian bar.

SIGHTS The early Christian basilica of **Agios Andreas,** three blocks north of the beach, once housed 5th-century mosaics, which are now located in Mytilini's Archaeological Museum. Behind the church, the **Skala Museum** displays 5th- and 6th-century vases, sculptured tombstones, Aeolian inscriptions, and an anchor from an Ottoman frigate used in the 1821 Greek War of Independence. In the museum yard rests the **tomb of St. Andrew.** Along the uphill road leading east lies the pilgrimage route for travelers visiting the remains of **Sappho's home** in Eressos. At dusk, the view from the hill is transcendent. The river, just west of Skala's center, serves as a habitat for many rare and exotic birds. Peak **birdwatching** season is April to May. Farther inland at **Antissa** are the **petrified trees** of Lesvos, preserved by volcanic activity at least 700,000 years ago in one of only two such forests in the world—the other is on the Arizona-New Mexico border in the U.S. Roughly 200 plant and animal fossils constitute the "forest," which requires a 90-minute walk to be properly appreciated. From Mytilini, take the bus to Sigri and walk or ride the 8km to the forest. From Skala, rent a moped or car, or check at Eressos Travel about tours.

SAMOS Σαμος

With its sultry landscape and engrossing archeological remains, Samos is perhaps the most beautiful and certainly the most touristed island in the northeast Aegean. The island draws an older, more sedate crowd, and is quieter than many of the popular spots in the Cyclades and the Dodecanese. The wealthiest of the Aegean islands, Samos was home to many notable Greek architects, sculptors, poets, philosophers, and scientists. Among Samos's most famous residents were Epicurus, the moral philosopher, Aesop, the fable writer, and Aristarchus, the astronomer who argued that the sun was the center of the universe 1800 years before Copernicus. The island's most beloved native son is the philosopher Pythagoras.

Many people come to Samos simply to make the short hop to Kuşadası and ruins of Ephesus on the Turkish coast. The archaeological site is the most extensive and possibly the most evocative remnant of ancient Hellenic civilization. Founded around 1100 BC, Ephesus rapidly bloomed into the largest metropolis in Asia Minor. Alternately, those who are archaeologically impaired teeter to Samos to partake of the sumptuous local red wine (*kokkino krasi*) that oozes from village-made barrels and gives the island its 15 minutes of lush-ous fame.

■ Samos Town

With its wide white sidewalks, colorific fishing boats, and red-roofed houses on the mountainside, Samos Town, commonly referred to as Vathy, is among the northeast Aegean's more attractive ports. While the waterfront is a snarl of junkshops and cafes, the residential lanes farther inland offer a collage of local lifestyles.

ORIENTATION AND PRACTICAL INFORMATION

Samos Town unfurls around a crescent-shaped waterfront. **Pythagoras Square,** easily identifiable by its four large palm trees, hosts cafes, taxis, and a giant statue of a lion.

Transportation

Ferries: Service to Peiraias via Ikaria (12hr., 1 per day, 6700dr); Naxos and Paros (6hr., 5 per week, 4370dr); Chios (5½hr., 4 per week, 2940dr); Fourni (2hr., 4 per week, 1800dr); Lesvos (8hr., 1 per week, 4090dr); Patmos (2½hr., 5 per week, 4280dr); Syros (6hr., 1 per week, 3990dr) and Mykonos (6hr., 1 per week, 4400dr). Ferries to Kuşadası, Turkey, leave from Samos Town (2hr., daily at 8am and 5pm). Boats to Kuşadası cost 8000dr in addition to a 5000dr Greek port tax and a 3000dr Turkish port tax. Turkish entrance visas must be purchased at the Turkish port by Americans ($45), British (£10), Irish (£15), and other assorted non-Greeks, and can be paid in Greek, Turkish, or your native currency, which will probably be the best option. If you stay overnight in Turkey and leave from Kuşadası, you will have to pay the tax again.

Flying Dolphins: Zip from Samos Town to Patmos in half the time and twice the *drachmes* as a ferry (1hr., 1 per day, 5500dr). Consult waterfront agencies for recent schedules and high-season service. Flying dolphins are coordinated so that connections between Eastern Cyclades and other popular Cycladic destinations are minimal, ensuring that the beeline from Ephesus to Ios and Santorini moves quickly and efficiently.

Flights: Olympic Airways (tel. 27 237), near the post office, has daily flights to Athens (1hr., 4 per day, 14,000dr) and two flights weekly to Thessaloniki (22,000dr). Open M-F 8am-4pm. Samos's **airport** (tel. 61 219) is 4km out of Pythagorion and can be reached only by taxi from Samos Town (2500dr).

Taxis: (tel. 28 404). In Pythagoras Sq.

Bike Rental: Rent A Motor Bike Bicycle (tel. 23 756), left side of the waterfront.

Buses: To get to the **station,** follow the waterfront past Pythagoras Sq., turn left at Europe Rent A Car onto Lekati St., and continue one block. Schedule posted.

Tourist and Financial Services

Tourist Office: (tel. 28 530 or 28 582), on a side street one block before Pythagoras Sq.; follow signs from the waterfront. Open July-Aug. M-Sa 8:30am-2pm.

Tourist Agencies: ITSA Travel (tel. 23 605; fax 27 955), next door. Open daily 6am-midnight. Offers comprehensive ferry and Flying Dolphin services, as well as boats to Turkey, free luggage storage, help with accommodations, and other travel services. Calling here for boat schedules is more accurate than the port police, particularly during the winter. **Samos Tours** (tel. 27 715), next door, provides similar services and info on everything from museum hours to accommodations. Free luggage storage. Open daily 6am-midnight and when boats arrive.

Laundromat: (tel. 28 833), near Georgiou's Taverna, one block to the left side of the waterfront. Wash 1000dr; dry 800dr; soap 200dr. Open daily 8am-11pm.

Emergency and Communications

Police: (tel. 27 100), on the far right of the waterfront (facing inland), doubles as the **tourist police.** Some English spoken.

Hospital: (tel. 27 426), to the left of the ferry dock (facing inland).

Post Office: (tel. 27 304), 1 block up from the waterfront behind the Hotel Xenia; turn at the immense palm tree and walk through the municipal gardens. Open M-F 7:30am-2pm. **Postal Code:** 83100.

OTE: Next to the post office. Open daily 7am-10pm. **Telephone Code:** 0273.

ACCOMMODATIONS

On Samos, there aren't nearly enough rooms to go around, so finding one can be a chore. If the following are full, try the pensions around the Ionia.

Pension Ionia, 5 Manoli Kalomiri St. (tel. 28 782). Turn right at the end of the ferry dock, left onto E. Stamatiadou St. before the Hotel Aiolis on the waterfront, and then take the second left onto Manoli Kalomiri St. Be skeptical of port-side room-hawkers who tell you it is full—the Ionia is 3 buildings of inexpensive, attractive rooms. Hot showers. Singles 4000-5000dr; doubles 5000-7000dr.

Pension Trova, 26 Kalomiris St. (tel. 27 759), up the road just to the left of Pension Ionia. Singles 4000dr; doubles with bath 5500-7000dr.

Pension Avli, 2 Areos St. (tel. 22 939), the reddish, mansionesque building near Ionia. Pleasant rooms around an elegant courtyard. Doubles 5000-8000dr.

Pythagoras Hotel (tel. 28 601; fax 28 893), a 10min. walk along the waterfront away from town. Clean, well-maintained rooms and a restaurant downstairs. 24hr. hot water. Singles 4000-5000dr; doubles with bath 5000-7000dr.

FOOD AND ENTERTAINMENT

"Gourmet" magazine won't be visiting Samos Town anytime soon—meals here seldom exceed lackluster touristy fare.

Gregory's, just past the post office, is a worthy local favorite. The menu is the same as everywhere else in town, but it tastes better here.

Christos (tel. 24 792), two blocks inland from the library, serves above-average *taverna* food with dishes hovering around 1000dr.

The most popular bar at night is **Escape,** a five-minute walk on the way to the Pythagoras Hotel. A patio stretches out over the bay below. By 3am, the party is underway at the discotheque **Totem,** a 250dr taxi ride from town.

SIGHTS

The island's phenomenal **archaeological museum** (tel. 27 469) sits behind the lovely Lilliputian municipal gardens, two blocks inland and four blocks from Pythagoras Sq. *(Open Tu-Su 8am-2:30pm. Admission 800dr, students 400dr.)* Finds from ancient Heraion and other local digs have found their way into the two recently renovated buildings here. Intricate Laconian ivory carvings depicting, among other mythological notables, Perseus and Medusa, vie for attention next to more awesome statues like the colossal 5m **Kouros,** from 575 BC. The stunning votive offering, dubbed "the Geneleas Group," once graced ancient Heraion's "ancient way." In the second building, bronze objects from Ancient Egypt, Cyprus, and the Near East are testament to the island's extensive early trade, as are nightmare-inducing griffin *protomes.*

■ Pythagorion Πυθαγορειο

The ancient city of Pythagorion, once the island's capital, thrived during the second half of the 6th century BC under the reign of **Polykrates the Tyrant.** According to Herodotus, Polykrates undertook the three most daring engineering projects in the Hellenic world, all of them in and around Pythagorion. One of the more impressive is the **Tunnel of Eupalinos** (tel. 61 400), 1500m up the hill to the north of town, which diverted water from a natural spring to the city below. *(Open Tu-Su 9am-2pm. Admission 500dr, students 300dr.)* About 1.3km long, it is in remarkably good condition, although only about 200m are open to visitors. Polykrates' second feat was the 40m deep **harbor mole** (rock pier), on which the modern pier now rests. Polykrates' *magnum opus* stood 5km west of Pythagorion, toward Ireon. The goddess Hera had been worshipped on Samos for seven centuries when Polykrates decided to enlarge her temple. Supported by 134 columns, the 530 BC **Temple of Hera** (tel. 95 277) was 118m long, and 58m wide. *(Open T-Su 8:30am-3pm. Admission 800dr, students 400dr.)* It has only minimally been reconstructed since damage by fire in 525 BC.

A walk along the beach will bring you to the temple at your own pace; there is a back gate leading directly onto the beach. If you can not enter through the gate, a path brings you inland to the main road and main entrance farther along the beach, past two houses. This inland path runs close to the route of the ancient **Iera Odos** (Sacred Way) from Pythagorion to the temple. For full effect, consider donning a toga and bear libations in jugs, as was once local custom.

On the south side of town rest the ruins of the **Castle of Lycurgus,** built during the beginning of the last century by Lycurgus himself, a native of Samos and leader in the Greek War of Independence. The **Church of the Transfiguration** is a pale blue variation on the classic Orthodox architecture and interior decoration theme.

Blocks of columns, walls, and entablatures are strewn throughout Pythagorion like Lincoln Logs after a floorquake, and the presentation in the small **archaeological museum** (tel. 61 400) is no different. *(Open Tu-Su 9am-2:30pm. Free.)* In fact, only a little over half of the collection fits into the building; many of the ruins are haphazardly scattered on the sidewalk in front. Fourteen kilometers south of Samos Town, Pythagorion is served by hourly buses (20min., 280dr).

■ Northern and Western Samos

Built on a peninsula 10km west of Samos Town, the northern village of **Kokkari** deserves a spot on your Samos itinerary. White pebble beaches and clear waters encompass the village. The northern coast of Samos has a few deserted pebble beaches tucked away in little coves and a number of sandy crowded ones. Most of the coast is easily accessible from the road to Karlovassi.

Lemonakia Beach, 1km west of Kokkari next to Tsamadou, and the wide white beach just west of **Avlakia** are both alluring. You can trek into the mountains from the village of **Platanakia,** near **Agios Konstandinos,** in the "valley of the nightingales." The valley is famous for its effluvient greenery, tall trees, and the thousands of birds that wake up to sing in the mountain valley after midnight. The birds will lull you to sleep (or wake you up) at 3am. Hiking is best from May through June and especially during September, when the grapes from nearby vineyards are harvested and sweeten the air. The 16th-century monastery **Moni Vrontianis** rests near the village of **Vourliotes,** 5km south of Avlakia. **Vourliates** gained notoriety after Greek Minister of Culture and celebrated actress Melina Mercury visited the village and publicly exalted it for years afterwards. But the star of *Never on Sunday* has not been the only one charmed by the village square and surrounding houses. Cheap, delicious *tavernas* on the square are well patronized. A monument in the village commemorates the lives of children who died in a 1975 school bus accident, tragically killing almost an entire generation of Vourliotes's population. **Marathokampos,** 7km southwest of Platanos, is uncrowded and probably the easiest place on the island to find rooms. A couple of kilometers west of this peaceful coastal hamlet stretches the spacious beach at **Votsalakia;** a bit farther is an even better beach at **Psili Ammos.** Two kilometers west of **Paleo,** an obstacle course of a path (involving wading through a pond and climbing sets of ropes) leads to three successive waterfalls in the island's northwest corner.

NORTHEAST AEGEAN

■ Kuşadası

A gateway to the ancient city of Ephesus, Kuşadası has something to offer almost every traveler. Its extensive daily **bazaar** overflows with leather goods, Turkish carpets, and other wares. Overcrowded but clean **beaches** are a short distance away by *dolmuş,* as is the gorgeous **Dilek National Park,** a great place for canyon climbing, picnicking, and swimming (the park has 4 beautiful beaches). By night, this former fishing village comes alive with cafes, bars, and dance clubs. The nearby towns of Selçuk, Priene, Miletus, and Didyma are also convenient daytrips.

You must pay a US$10 port tax upon entering (generally best paid in US$ to avoid commissions and weak exchange rates). **Ferries** run to Samos, Greece daily in summer (2 per week off-season). Contact **Ekol Travel** (tel. (256) 614 92 55 or 614 55 91), and flash *Let's Go* for a discount. The main **bus station** is about 2km east of the port area, but frequent *dolmuş* connect it with the city center. Buses run to Ankara (10hr., US$16.70), Bodrum (2½hr., US$6), and Istanbul (11hr., US$15). The **tourist office,** No. 13 Liman Cad. (tel. (256) 614 11 03), is on the corner of Liman Cad. and Güvercin Ada Sok (open daily in summer 8am-6pm; in winter M-F 8am-noon and 1:30-5:30pm). To get there from the bus station, take a taxi.

Use discretion when dealing with the hustlers who meet buses and ferries and offer "bargain accommodations." You'll find many cheap pensions along **Aslanlar Cad.** and **Aydinlik Cad. Hotel Rose,** 7 Aslanlar Cad. (tel. (256) 612 25 88; fax 614 11 11), has a bar, **Internet access,** laundry service, free luggage storage, and transport to Ephesus. (Dorms US$4; rooms US$5-8; roof accommodations US$2.50. 10% off for students; 15% *Let's Go* discount.) Down the street from Hotel Rose, **Park Pension,** 17 Aslanlar Cad. (tel. (256) 614 39 17 or 612 69 12), offers comfort in colorful rooms (rooms US$6-8; breakfast included; reserve ahead). **Kaylon Hotel,** Kibris Cad. No. 7 (tel. (256) 614 33 46), offers comfortable rooms (US$5) and pick-up service from the bus station. Bring your sleeping bag and tent to **Onder** (tel. (256) 614 24 13) or **Yat Camping** (tel. (256) 614 13 33), 2km north of town on Atatürk Blv. (US$2.40 per person, US$1.60 per tent, caravans US$1.60). There are many cheap restaurants along **Kahramanlar Cad.** and its alley tributaries. The madness of the nightclubs on **Barlar Sok,** parallel to Kahramanlar Cad., spills into the streets (many open until 4am).

■ Ephesus Εφεσος

For an archaeological fix, search no farther than **Ephesus** (Efes), where ruins from the Roman and early Christian era are extensive and well preserved. If you see Ephesus on your own, you'll approach the ruins from the road between Kuşadası and Selçuk; your first glimpse of the site will be the outskirts of the ancient city. The most important of these remains is the **Vedius Gymnasium,** to the left as you proceed down the road to the main entrance. Farther along lies an enormous **stadium** (the seats were removed to build the Byzantine city walls). Once you pass through the main entrance, marvel at the **Arcadian Street,** a magnificent, colonnaded marble avenue. Uphill, the imposing ruins of the **Temple of Hadrian** dominate the right side of the road. Farther up the hill are the ruins of the exquisite **Fountain of Trajan.** To get to Ephesus from the Kuşadası bus station, take a *dolmuş* to Selçuk, and tell the driver you want to get off at Ephesus. Guided tours of the ruins are expensive (about US$15-25); instead, get a good guidebook at the entrance (US$5) and tour the site on your own (open daily 8am-6pm; US$4, free with ISIC).

IKARIA Ικαρια

Ikaria is associated with one of the better-known Greek myths. While in prison, Daedalus fashioned wings for his son Icarus to use in order to escape from Crete. Intoxicated with his newly acquired power, Icarus soared too close to the sun, melted his waxen wings, and plunged to his death near Ikaria's coast. Today, Ikaria is rife with idiosyncrasies—the stuff of modern legend. Villages adhere to a daily schedule by which stores and restaurants close most of the day and open much of the night.

Ikaria has long been a stronghold (and during certain periods, a sequester) for left-wing politics. In 1912, the island enjoyed a four-month stint as an independent state, with its own constitution, currency, and stamps. Today, the most tangible signs of the island's political bent are an abundance of communist graffiti, a resistance to development, and a relatively low-profile tourism industry.

While the lack of a focus on tourism may be a blessing for travelers who feel overwhelmed by such attention on other islands, it invites a series of logistical problems. Bus service is minimal and utterly unreliable. Bank services are hard to come by outside **Agios Kirykos,** which is separated by over 40 treacherous kilometers from **Evdilos** (the island's other main port) and the more populated villages of the **north coast.** At one time, Ikaria was known for its thriving apricots; however, locals got tired of "shaking the trees" to harvest the fruits. Now Turkey has the Ikarian apricot trees and Ikaria has only memories. Visitors today (mostly Greek) arrive hoping to be healed by Ikaria's famous chemically complex radioactive medicinal springs.

Split by a rocky mountain chain, the deceptively rugged landscape boasts up to 2500 species of plants, mostly herbs, lending the island subtle color and fragrance. Large patches of Ikarian forest, devastated by a 1993 fire, are slowly returning. Most villages cling to the winding coastline.

■ Agios Kirykos Αγιος Κηρυκος

Unassuming and congenial, Agios Kirykos is Ikaria's capital and is visited mostly for its nearby thermal springs. As Ikaria's main port, Agios Kirykos is the most convenient place from which to coordinate your tour of the island.

ORIENTATION AND PRACTICAL INFORMATION The town's pier is marked by a large sculpture of Icarus plummeting to the ground, but getting here has become considerably easier and safer since Icarus's time; coming off the ferry, walk up the pier onto the main waterfront road, then turn right to reach the town square. On the way to the town square from the ferry dock you will pass the **Sine Rex,** formerly the town's movie theater, and **Ikariada Travel** (tel. 23 322; fax 23 708), which offers friendly, English-speaking service and can arrange room or vehicle rental (open daily 8am-9:30pm). The **port police** (tel. 22 207) and **tourist police** (tel. 22 207) share a building; climb the steps to the left of Dolihi Tours and continue up the road (both open 8am-2pm). The island's only two **banks,** including the **National Bank** (tel. 22 894), are in Agios Kirykos, in the square near the ferry offices (open M-Th 8am-2pm, F 8am-1:30pm). After hours, tourist offices and big hotels offer **currency exchange.** Credit cards are not accepted on the island. About 100m up the street are the **post office** (tel. 22 413), to the right of the National Bank (open M-F 8am-2pm), and the **OTE** (tel. 22 399; open M-F 7:30am-3pm).

Ikaria's new **airport** offers service to Athens and is located on the northeastern tip of the island, near Fanari Beach (7 flights per week to Athens, 7200dr, under 25 4500dr). **Ferries** run to Peiraias (10hr., 1-2 per day, 5500dr); Samos Town (3hr., 2-3 per day, 2200dr); Patmos (1½hr., 4 per day, 2800dr); Paros (4hr., 3 per week, 3300dr); Fourni (1hr., 2-3 per day, 1300dr); and Mykonos (4hr., 3 per week, 3200dr). Boats alternate stops at Evdilos in the north and Agios Kirykos, where taxis await to shuttle passengers to the other port (2000-2500dr). Finding a hotel can be difficult on your first night, so make sure you know your port of arrival and call ahead for reservations. **Flying Dolphins** leave for Samos (1½hr., 4 per week); Patmos (1hr., 4 per week); and Fourni (30min., 4 per week), and cost roughly twice as much. Three caïques leave for Fourni every week (1100dr). **Buses** cannot be relied upon, but, in theory, run twice daily between Agios Kirykos and Armenistis via Evdilos. **Postal code:** 83300. **Telephone code:** 0275.

NORTHEAST AEGEAN

ACCOMMODATIONS, FOOD, & ENTERTAINMENT Climb the stairs to the left of Dolihi and take your first left, just before the police station, to reach the new **Hotel Kastro** (tel. 23 480). Comfortable, modern rooms overlook the harbor (12,000dr with bath and TV). To reach **Hotel Akti** (tel. 22 694), climb the same stairs to the left of Dolihi, but take your first right into a tiny, seemingly private alley and climb the steps; follow the new signs. Hotel Akti has a decidedly Greek appeal, enhanced by a plant-filled courtyard overlooking the Aegean Sea (singles 7000dr; doubles with bath 9500dr; triples 10,500dr). On the way to Hotel Akti you'll pass the **Hotel O'Karras** (tel. 22 494), offering pink rooms and spacious baths (singles 3000dr, with bath 4000dr; doubles 5000dr, with bath 6000dr).

The **T'Adelfia Taverna,** the town's most established full-scale restaurant, offers summer "Greek nights," which include popular music (entrees from 700dr; open daily 9am-2am). At **Flik-Flak,** 1km out of town, get down to popular radio tunes. Nearby **Aquarius** plays Greek music and hits from the age of *Hair*. There are some rocky **beaches** west of the ferry dock. To the east of town, you can clamber down to the sandy beaches and crystal blue water of the coves past the tourist police office.

■ Evdilos Ευδηλος

Heading north from Agios Kirykos, the tiny road to Evdilos offers breathtaking views of the coast as it snakes along sheer cliffs through florid hill country. From the island's eastern heights you can see Samos, Patmos, and the Fourni Archipelago. On the way to Evdilos, the road passes a few tiny villages and beaches, many of which offer limited services and accommodations. **Buses** are supposed to run twice daily between Agios Kirykos and Armenistis via Evdilos, but service is unreliable and operates only in July and August. The schedule reported by the tourist police is often inaccurate. **Taxis** may be your best bet; sharing a cab will cut costs (Agios Kirykos to Evdilos 6000dr; Agios Kirykos to Armenistis 8000dr; Armenistis to Evdilos 2000dr). Hitchhiking is another option, but *Let's Go: Greece* cannot recommend it.

Evdilos, the island's minor port town, sports red-tiled roofs against its steeply sloping hill. The **post office** (tel. 31 225) sits at the top of a set of white stairs that lead to the right of the square (open M-F 7:30am-2:30pm). The **OTE** (tel. 31 559) is past the post office, across from the church. The **pharmacy** (tel. 41 352) is between the town and ferries arrival dock. In case of emergency call for **first aid** (tel. 31 228). The **Port Police** (tel. 31 007) is directly inland from the square. **Blue Nice Holidays** (tel. 31 990 or 31 991; fax 31 572) **exchanges currency,** handles **ferries, Flying Dolphins, excursions, flights,** and **car rentals,** and posts a weekly schedule for ferries serving both Evdilos and Agios Kirykos, as well as Flying Dolphins serving Agios Kirykos (open daily 11am-2:30pm and 7-10pm). There is no bank in town.

Quality of lodging in Evdilos is a direct reflection of the price. **Ioannis Spanos** (tel. 31 220) offers basic rooms with shared bath near the square at the base of the hill along the road leading to the Agios Kirykos-Armenistis road (doubles 5000dr). **Cavos Rooms** (tel. 31 518) has large, well-maintained rooms with private bath along the water, opposite the ferry dock (singles 5000-6000dr; doubles 6000-7000dr). **Atheras Hotel** (tel. 31 434 or 31 426), along the small street next to Ioannis Spanos, has modern rooms and a small pool and gym (singles 9000dr; doubles 10,000dr).

Restaurant tables fill the square, offering similar fare in the same setting. **Cuckoo** (tel. 31 540), whose tables strategically surround the square's central monument, infuses a Smyrnese influence on some dishes. Try the spicy squid in wine (1400dr) or *saginaki* with three cheeses (1300dr).

■ Kampos Καμπος

A picturesque 3km west of Evdilos, the quiet village of Kampos sits where Ikaria's ancient capital once stood. Discernible signs of the legacy of **Ancient Oinoe,** including clay statuettes and neolithic tools, can be found in the **Kampos museum. Agia Irini,** the island's oldest church, sits adjacent to the museum. Contact Vassilis Dionysos at the village general store or at **Dionysos Rooms** (tel. 31 300 or 31 688) for the key to the museum or church. Vassilis, a walking history book, rents rooms in a cheery and friendly atmosphere (doubles 6000-8000dr). His bright blue and white building is 400m down the dirt road across from the village restaurant. Kampos, as with much of Ikaria's north coast, just might boast a stellar beach.

■ Armenistis Αρμενιστης

Ikaria's tourist haven, Armenistis' streets, characterized by postcard and knick-knack shops, seem anathema to the rest of the island. Nevertheless, excellent nearby beaches are plentiful (though often crowded). East of Armenistis, **Livadi** and **Mesachti** are large sandy beaches highly conducive to napping the day away underneath umbrellas and waking up periodically to hit the beachside *tavernas*.

Pashalia Taverna (tel. 71 302) has well-maintained rooms (doubles 6000-7000dr). **Ikaros Rooms** (tel. 71 238) offers comfy rooms, up the steps from the waterfront road, or by the church from the Evdilos-Nas road (doubles 5000-6000dr).

■ Nas Νας

West of Armenistis, asphalt cuts out, leaving a dirt road running to Nas, one of the Aegean's undiscovered gems. The inspiring beach, flanked by huge rock walls, separates an aggressive sea from a seductively serene river.

Bordered by the beach, a freshwater pool forms the final destination for a shallow meandering river, which begins a 25-minute hike south at a small waterfall. Inland of the pool, past a flat field, trees envelop the river, lending cool sanctuary from the unrelenting sun. Within this shady den, the incantatory cadence of chirping cicadas replaces the roar of crashing waves. Tents dot the alternately sandy and rocky banks most of the way to the waterfall.

With no set path, the hike is best accomplished by staying close to the river and following partial trails and chains of large rocks. At certain points, feet will get wet. Approaching the final leg of the hike, at a rocky clearing, notice the remarkable cavernous rock enclosure perched atop the eastern ledge. However, think twice about trying to claim it for a nap; this is a favorite haunt for local goats. The smallish waterfall lies a few minutes beyond this point.

Camping along the river transpires regularly, despite being technically illegal. Inhabitants are a mix of short-term visitors in search of free lodging and an attractive setting in which to pitch a tent, and long-term Ikarians keen on perpetuating the summer of love with a commune-esque atmosphere and propensity for nudity.

More conventional lodgings sit above the beach and river. **Artemis Pension** (tel. 71 485) offers small but tasteful rooms with balconies (doubles with shared bath 4500dr, with private bath 5500dr). Artemis also runs mind/body exercise classes, has a relaxing *taverna*, and spins tunes from a record collection resembling a *Rolling Stone* greatest rock albums of all time retrospective. A path to the river descends from the steps next to the *taverna*. Gastratory desires can also be satiated at **Nas Taverna** (tel. 71 486) which serves some of the island's best *taverna* fare and offers rooms to let.

THASSOS Θασος

According to legend, when Zeus abducted Europa, the captee's devoted brother Thassos wandered the earth in search of her. During his journey, he discovered Greece's northernmost island and named it after himself. However, Thassos' imposing, dark green mountainsides and villages, archaeological sites, and beaches engulfed in lush foliage, strikingly different from the chalky dry cliffs of many Greek islands, have earned Thassos a nickname: "the Green Island."

Even in antiquity, Thassos was renowned for its natural wealth. The island produced gold, silver, wine, and white marble in abundance, and exported its goods throughout the Mediterranean world. Thassos' prosperity attracted unwelcome attention from successive waves of conquerors: Phoenicians, Athenians, and Romans all held sway over the island at some point in ancient times. Thassos was also the birthplace of Timoxenos, an athlete credited with some 1400 victories, and, for a few years, the home of the good doctor Hippocrates. During medieval times, marauding pirates and Ottoman invaders drove the inhabitants to the interior of the island. Along with most of far northern Greece, Thassos returned to Greek rule in 1912 at the conclusion of the First Balkan War. Massive forest fires in recent years threatened to turn the island's verdant nickname into a mockery, but Thassos' forests are now slowly reviving. Thassos today thrives both on tourism and on traditional activities such as bee-keeping and jam-keeping.

■ Limenas Λιμενας

Built atop the foundations of the ancient city, Limenas' streets wind around ruins. In this century, it has become the island's capital and tourist center. Accordingly, this lively port is more crowded and more expensive than the rest of the island.

ORIENTATION AND PRACTICAL INFORMATION

A central crossroad near the ferry landing connects the waterfront road and 18 Octovriou St., a bustling walkway running parallel to the water one block inland. The small central square lies about two blocks farther inland. A large blue sign at the dock lists the names and phone numbers of area hotels, pensions, and campgrounds.

Transportation

Ferries: Run from Limenas to Keramoti (35min., 12 per day, 400dr), and from **Prinos**, another port on Thassos, to Kavala (2hr., 9 per day, 850dr) and N. Peramus (1½hr., 4 per day, 850dr). Be sure to note from which port, Limenas or Prinos, your boat leaves. Bus schedules between Prinos and Leminas are synchronized with the ferries. You must return to Kavala for ferry connections to other islands. The gray port police building posts schedules.

Flying Dolphins: Hydrofoils zip between Thassos's main port of Limenas and nearby Kavala (45min., 6 per day, 2000dr) and Samothrace (1½hr., 3 per week, 4500dr). Hydrofoils also travel between Limenaria on Thassos's south coast and Kavala (1¼hr., 2 per day, 3000dr). Schedules are posted near the pier at the port police, and docked boats indicate upcoming departure times with signs on board. Tickets are bought on board or at Thassos Tours.

Buses: The **station** (tel. 22 162) is across from the ferry landing, on the waterfront. Open daily 7:30am-8:15pm. Buses head west across the island to Limenaria (1½hr., 12 per day, 850dr), stopping at Skala Prinos (30min., 12 per day, 360dr); Panayia (15min., 13 per day, 220dr); and Skala Potamia (15min., 13 per day, 300dr). Others trek to Potos and Pefkari (1½hr., 12 per day, 900dr); Aliki Beach (1hr., 4 per day, 700dr); Theologos (1½hr., 5 per day, 1100dr); and all the way around the island and back to Limenas (2½hr., 8 per day, 1950dr). Ask at the tourist police or the bus office for schedules.

Car Rental: Budget (tel. 23 050), on the main street perpendicular to the waterfront. Prices start at 12,000dr.

Motorbike Rental: Billy's Bikes (tel. 23 253, 22 490, or 23 295), next to Budget, has bikes starting at 4000dr.

Tourist and Financial Services

Tourist Agency: Thassos Tours (tel. 22 546 or 23 225; fax 23 005), under the blue awning. Continue left (facing inland) on the waterfront road from the port police toward the old port. They rent motorbikes (from 2000dr per day), suggest accommodations, and sell Dolphin and ferry tickets. Open daily 9am-11pm.

Bank: National Bank, at the main crossroad on the waterfront, has an automated 24hr. **currency exchange** and **ATM.** Open M-Th 8am-2pm, F 8am-1:30pm.

International Bookstore: Leather Plus (tel. 23 411), on the far right corner of the central square, has an eclectic selection of English, German, and Dutch novels available "for rent." Open more or less daily 9am-1:30pm and 5:30-11:30pm.

Emergency and Communications

First Aid Hospital: (tel. 71 100), in Prinos. Open 24hr. Nearest hospital is in Kavala.
Tourist Police: (tel. 23 111 or 23 580), on the waterfront. Open daily 8am-2pm and 6-10pm. **Police:** (tel. 22 500), in the same building as the tourist police.
Port Police (tel. 22 106), in a gray building at the waterfront's center. Open 24hr.
Post Office: head inland from Thassos Tours and turn right at the fourth corner. Open M-F 7:30am-2pm. **Postal Code:** 64004.
OTE: Heading inland from Thassos Tours, turn right at the first corner, and it's on the left. Open M-Sa 7:30am-10pm. **Telephone Code:** 0593.

ACCOMMODATIONS

The sign in front of the bus stop includes some accommodation options but focuses on pricier hotels. Its worthwhile to hunt on inland streets for substantially cheaper pensions. Ask at Thassos Tours for suggestions.

Giorgos Raxos (tel. 22 778), on the right side of the waterfront if you're facing inland; look for the green-tiled house next to the barber shop. Rooms are spacious and clean. Doubles 6000dr; triples 8000dr.
Hotel Lido (tel. 22 929), on same street as post office, about 100m towards the center. Clean rooms with fridge, phone, and bath. Singles 7000dr; doubles 9000dr.
Eleni Chrisatis-Mitroglou (tel. 22 032), on the street running at a 45-degree angle to the one with the post office; the doorway is surrounded with flowers. Clean, airy rooms all with bath. Doubles 7000-8000dr.

FOOD AND ENTERTAINMENT

Like most island towns, Limenas has a wide array of restaurants catering mostly to tourists. *Bougatsa* and gyros abound just off the waterfront.

Selinos Taverna, some 800m in from the port past the overgrown "Sanctuary of Hercules," serves delicious grilled octopus appetizers (1200dr) and *kolikomezedhes* (zucchini burgers 700dr.) Open daily 6pm to midnight.
Restaurant Syrtaki (tel. 23 353) has a fairly innovative menu and a pleasant view of the little boats in the old port.
Simi Restaurant (tel. 22 517), close to Syrtaki on the waterfront, is one of the best located and most popular spots in Limenas.
I Stoa (tel. 23 785), on the other edge of town and one street inland, is the best of a row of *tsipouradika,* where food is eaten with the potent liquor *tsipouro.*

Nocturnal hotspots are scattered throughout Limenas. The **Island Cafe** (tel. 22 895), next to the beach on Limenas's eastern edge, is popular early in the night. Later in the night, head to **Marina's Bar** or **Vertigo Bar** (tel. 22 753), located side by side one street inland. Both places have a mixed crowd of Greeks and foreigners and offer beer for 700dr and cocktails for 1500dr. The two pounding discos in town are the barnyard-like **The Barrels** (tel. 23 741 or 23 090; 1000dr cover) and the more hi-tech **Chaos Club** (tel. 23 685; 1000dr cover). Both clubs are just off the main square and have a different promotional event (e.g. Pirates Party, Bikini Party, Ladies' Night) every day. A little outside of town (800dr taxi) is **La Scala,** voted the best club in northern Greece three years ago.

SIGHTS

In addition to impressive remains of an **agora** and **acropolis** from the 6th and 5th centuries BC, the island retains a 4th-century BC Greek **theater** still used for theatrical productions. *(Open during daylight hours. Free.)* Tucked away in a pine forest, the theater boasts wooden seats, some of which have shrubs and baby pine trees growing out of them. Ringing the hills around Limenas are the well-preserved marble **city walls,** much of whose length is inscribed with Archaic reliefs. The **ruins** are easy to find: turn right behind the old port and continue to a fork in the road, just beyond the ruins of the **Temple of Dionysus.** The middle of the three paths leads to the theater. Also under renovation, the **Thassos Museum** near the old port displays mosaic floors and sculptures found on the site, including a colossal 6th-century BC marble statue of Apollo with a ram draped around his shoulders.

The **Vagis Museum,** in the village of Potamia, displays sculptures of the famous Thessian artist, Polygnotos Vagis. *(Open Tu-F 10am-noon and 6-7:30, Sa-Su 10am-1pm. Free.)* After emigrating to America, Vagis (1894-1965) gained fame for his sculpture, which varies from classically influenced to abstract.

Beachgoers may have difficulty choosing between Thassos' many beautiful sands. Between the ports of Panagia and Potamia, the popular golden beach of **Chrisi Ammoudia** stretches endlessly. On the southern edge of the island, the twin coves of **Aliki** hide more tranquil beaches. The northern one, surrounded by foliage, often remains isolated. The south beach cove, formed as sand shifted over a Roman marble quarry, shelters slabs of bleached white rock and crevices ideal for snorkeling.

▓ Limenaria Λιμεναρια

Limenaria, Thassos's thriving second city, is located on the southern tip of the island almost exactly opposite Limenas. The town's streets are packed with English and Germans during peak season; during the rest of the year, Greek tourists hold sway.

ORIENTATION AND PRACTICAL INFORMATION Limenaria's two main streets run parallel to the waterfront. One main crossroad, **Ethnikis Antistasis St.,** has the town's **OTE** (open M-F 7:30am-3pm) and **Speedy Rent-a-Car** (tel. 52 700). The **post office** (open M-F 7:30am-2pm) and **National Bank** (open M-Th 8am-2pm, F 8am-1:30pm) are both on the far right edge of the waterfront if facing inland. The **police** (tel. 51 111) are on the first street inland in the center of town. **Internet access** is available at **Larry's Internet Cafe** on the waterfront (tel. 53 215; email sakis@larrys.gr; http://www.larrys.gr) for 1500dr per hr. **Postal code:** 64002. **Telephone code:** 0593.

ACCOMMODATIONS Hotels and rented rooms abound throughout Limenaria, especially on the left part of the waterfront if facing inland. **Hotel George** (tel. 51 413), at the base of Ethnikis Antistasis St., has clean rooms with private baths (singles 6000dr; doubles 8500dr; triples 10,000dr). **Hotel Asterias** (tel. 52 497), on the waterfront, offers rooms with bath and balcony (singles 5000dr; doubles 7000dr; triples 8000dr). Close to Asterias is **Hotel Molos** (tel. 51 389), whose pleasant rooms have bath and balcony (singles 7500dr; doubles 8500dr).

FOOD AND ENTERTAINMENT The entire waterfront in Limenaria swarms with restaurants and *tavernas.* **Restaurant Maranos** (tel. 51 239), on the right edge of the waterfront if facing inland, offers a pleasant shady environment, soothing classical tunes, and many fish choices. **O Vasilis** (tel. 51 390 or 51 198), on the opposite edge of the waterfront, is a large popular restaurant with its own effervescent fountain. In the middle of the waterfront, **Palataki Restaurant** (tel. 53 253) has a varied menu and is always crowded. Nightlife in Limenaria is loud and booming. **Istos Cafe-Bar** (tel. 52 188) is the noisiest and most popular place on the waterfront and plays blaring American music. Two streets inland (follow the ubiquitous signs) and tucked into the hillside is the mellow **Rock Cave Bar** (tel. 52 107), which plays great music but is quiet enough that you can actually hold a conversation (beer 500dr; cocktails 1000dr). The most popular disco is the massive **Bolero** (tel. 52 180), which booms at all hours every night (cover 1500dr).

SAMOTHRACE Σαμοθρακη

Arriving in Samothrace by boat is quite a surreal experience. The main port, **Kamariotissa**, is built upon an odd peninsula bereft of vegetation and surrounded by modern minimalist windmills; in the distance looms massive 1670m **Fengari** (mountain of the moon), the tallest peak in the Aegean, whose slopes are blanketed with majestic forests of pine and oak and countless clear mountain springs.

Samothrace first welcomed Thracian colonists in the 10th century BC. Soon after, the island achieved fame as a religious center. The deities worshipped were not the familiar Olympian pantheon but the **Great Gods**—a group of gods of Anatolian origin. Chief among the Great Gods was the **Cybele,** the Great Mother; other notables included her companion, **Kadmilos,** god of virility, and the **Kabeiroi twins,** protectors of sailors. Following the settlement of colonists from Lesbos around 700 BC, the cult of the Anatolian gods was subsumed into the worship of the Olympian gods. Samothrace nevertheless continued to be a site of prime religious importance. Here at the Sanctuary of the Great Gods, **Philip II** of Macedon met his wife Olympia. After the requisite nine months, **Alexander** (soon to be "Great") was born. Other figures of note initiated into the cult included Sparta's **Lysander** and Julius Caesar's father-in-law, **Piso.** The cult remained active until Christianity became predominant in the 4th century AD and polytheistic pagan practices were banned.

▓ Kamariotissa Καμαροτισσα

Located on a peninsula more reminiscent of the Great Plains' amber waves of grain than the greenery of the rest of Samothrace, Kamariotissa is the island's transportation hub and largest town. Don't come to Kamariotissa in search of crowds of tourists or nightlife; the town is so small that only the coastal street has lights.

ORIENTATION AND PRACTICAL INFORMATION Everything in Kamariotissa is right on the waterfront. Facing inland, on the left of the waterfront, a Greek flag marks the **port police** (tel. 41 305; open 24hr.). On the road running inland, next to the **National Bank** (open M-Th 8am-2pm and F 8am-1:30pm), sits the **pharmacy** (tel. 41 581; open M-F 9am-2pm and 6-10pm, Sa 9:30am-1:30pm and 7-9:30pm, Su 10:30am-12:30pm). Uphill on the left, a mini-market displays the **OTE** sign. The **post office** and another **OTE** are located in Hora.

Ferries connect Samothrace with Alexandroupolis (2½hr., 2-3 per day, 2300dr) and Kavala (4hr., 5 per week, 2900dr). **Flying Dolphins** travel to Alexandroupolis (1hr., 2-4 per day, 4700dr); Kavala (2hr., 2 per week, 5800dr) via Thassos (1½hr., 3 per week, 4500dr); and Limnos (1½hr., 1 per week, 4900dr). For tickets and full schedule information inquire at the port police or at one of the two waterfront travel agencies: **Saos Tours** (tel. 41 505; open daily 9am-2pm and 6-10pm) and **Nikis Tours** (tel. 41 465; open daily 8am-2pm and 5-9pm). Nikis also rents cars and organizes excursions.

Saos Tours doubles as the island's main **bus station.** In summer, **buses** run five to twelve times per day around the island, leaving from the ferry dock to Profitos Ilias (320dr); Therma (320dr); Psira Potomos (420dr); Paleopolis (220dr); Alonia and Hora (220dr); Lacoma and Kariotis (280dr); and the campsites (650dr). **Taxis** wait on the waterfront between 8am and 1am. **Moped rentals** are available at **Niki Rent Motor Bike's** colorful, flag-adorned lot across from the pharmacy (tel. 41 035). Rentals at both start at 4000dr per day. Niki also rents non-motorbikes (2000dr per day). Either way, don't forget a helmet. **Postal code: 68002. Telephone code:** 0551.

ACCOMMODATIONS Although foreigners generally skirt Samothrace, Greeks come here in droves during midsummer. As a result, all accommodations (especially hotels but also rented rooms) are expensive and tough to come by. English-speaking **Saos** and **Niki Tours,** your all-purpose tourist agencies, can brief you on the current room situation in town and often help to find accommodations. Doubles average 6000dr, or 8000dr with bath, although in high season they can run much higher. Singles are almost nonexistent; if traveling alone, expect to have to pay for a double. Friendly, family-run **Vasiliki Karoyiannis** (tel. 41 165) has clean rooms with shared bath. (6000dr). Turn inland next to Niki Tours and the pension and *taverna* lie on your left. For other cheap rooms with private baths, continue uphill and turn right at the road's end. On your left next to the **supermarket,** a family (tel. 41 536) rents rooms with private bath (singles 6000dr; doubles 8000dr). Do be certain that your room has windows, as some have only skylights, allowing no breeze as respite from the greenhouse effect. If you insist on staying in a hotel, try the **Hotel Kyma** (tel. 41 263), Kamariotissa's best-located and cheapest hotel. Large clean rooms come with lovely views of the sea. The hotel is on the left edge of the waterfront if facing inland (doubles 8500dr, with bath 10,000dr; triples 11,000dr). Inquire at any of the many "rent rooms" or *"domatia"* signs. Remember to bargain.

FOOD AND ENTERTAINMENT The restaurant beneath **Vasiliki Karoyiannis** (tel. 41 165) serves delicious Greek meals (Greek salad 800dr). To order, ask to see the kitchen and the daily creations which Mrs. Karoyiannis identifies for you in the international language of "Baa-aa" and "Moo" (1200dr). In the mornings try the delicious, fresh *loukoumades* (Greek honey doughnuts, 500dr).

On the waterfront, close to Hotel Kyma, is the very popular **I Klimataria** (tel. 41 535), which makes the regular assortment of Greek dishes as well as more innovative ones such as *yiannotiko* (a tasty concoction of pork and various vegetables and cheeses). Another spot packed with locals is **To Kehayiadiko,** across from the port, which specializes in goat dishes.

Nightlife in Kamariotissa is tame, especially by Greek island standards. **Cafe Aktaion,** almost directly across from the port, and the nameless (but very popular) vine-covered **bar** right next to it constitute the most happening spot in town. A 10-minute walk towards the windmills takes you to the large **Mylos Disco,** Samothrace's biggest. Those with a car can go to **Club Saoki** (tel. 41 256), located in nearby Therma, which plays music ranging from traditional Greek *rembetika* to hard rock.

SIGHTS Just 6km east of Kamariotisa lie **Paleopolis** and the **Sanctuary of the Great Gods,** Samothrace's premier attraction. *(Open Tu-Su 8:30am-8:30pm. Admission 500dr, students 300dr, Su free.)* The sanctuary was the focal point of an ancient cult worshipping the Great Gods, deities so old they antedate the Olympian bunch. Disclosure of the cult's initiation secrets was punishable by death, but as always, sources leaked information to the press. It appears that initiation into the cult consisted of two stages, the first of purification in the sanctuary and the second of rites in the **Hieron,** where five reconstructed columns now form the central visual attraction of the site.

Various buildings imbued with religious importance dot the archaeological site. The **sacristy,** at the southern end, was the place where inductees into the cult put on their vestments and prepared for initiation. The large cylindrical **arsinoein,** given to Samothrace by Queen Arsinoe of Egypt, was the site of sacrifice. Near the arsinoein is the **Sacred Rock,** the original center of the cult's practices. In the center of the area are the oft-photographed **Doric Hieron,** the remains of an ancient **theater,** and the spot upon which the famed **Nike of Samothrace** once stood.

The **Paleopolis Museum** (tel. 41 474), next to the ruins, houses artifacts including gargantuan entablatures from the Rotunda Arsinoe and the Hieron and a cast of the **Nike of Samothrace.** *(Open Tu-Su 8:30am-3pm. Admission 500dr, students 300dr.)* Also known as "Winged Victory," the statue was discovered in Edirne, Turkey and then looted in 1863 by a French consul. It now resides in the Louvre. Sign the book if you believe that it should be returned to Samothrace.

A short bus ride farther along the island brings you to the therapeutic waters of **Therma.** *(Open daily 6-11am and 4-7pm. Private tubs 600dr, common swimming pool-like baths 400dr.)* Although the plain, white building housing the baths can't compare with those of the Romans, it does provide facilities for both men and women. All bathing must be done nude, and facilities for men and women are separate. After your bath, sip coffee at the nearby shaded terrace cafe.

LIMNOS Λημνος

It is said of Limnos that when one insensitive clod made a dirty joke about Aphrodite, the goddess put a curse on the island that caused the women to kill all the men. Only the king, helped by his daughter, escaped. The Argonauts, upon arrival, found only grieving widows on the island, but, aiming to please, the sailors got down to business and shortly thereafter repopulation of the island was well on the way. As one of the Aegean's well-kept secrets, Limnos is still a traveler's dream: its scruffy, bleating-goat-filled hills shoulder vast expanses of golden wheat fields, and its knuckled ridges of volcanic handiwork and fantastic rock formations fall away to long smooth beaches.

▓ Myrina Μυρινα

The island's capital and primary port, Myrina is a well-proportioned fishing village keenly aware of its own beauty. The skyline, made strange by volcanic configurations, is dominated by an impressive Byzantine fortress that is illuminated each night. Against the star-studded sky, its turreted tower achieves an almost ethereal silhouette.

ORIENTATION AND PRACTICAL INFORMATION Myrina has two main **waterfronts** that run perpendicular to one another. **Romeikos,** the Greek coast, is the longer, prettier, and more popular waterfront lined with rundown but once-regal neoclassical mansions, cafes, and *tavernas* perfect for spectacular sunsets behind Mt. Athos. **Turkikos,** the Turkish coast, is the active port, where ferries and hydrofoils dock. This harborfront fashions a plaza around which lie *tavernas,* ferry and tour agencies, and a few old hotels. The **bus station** (tel. 22 464) is located in El Venizelou Sq., the second square along Kyda St. Although buses serve all of the island's villages, you may get somewhere and find yourself unable to return; the soldiers who gather in El Venizelou Sq. to catch the night bus to the barracks get the best service. You may be better off seeing Limnos by renting a **bicycle** (1500dr), **moped** (3500dr), or **car** (10,000dr). Inquire on the harborfront at one of the many agencies. For a more colorful tour, find Tassos Zographos the taxidriver – if he's not at the taxi stand in downtown Myrina, the other taxi drivers will generally know where to find him. Tassos' local knowledge and stories can't be beat. He speaks English and will drive you anywhere on the island for a negotiable fee, but even if you aren't in immediate need of a taxi ride, stop by and ask a question. Not surprisingly, on a small island it's the locals – especially the taxi drivers, who go everywhere and know everybody – who are often a good source of knowledge of local events, or of other locals who are renting out cheap rooms for the tourist season.

    Ferries depart from the side of the port opposite the castle. Ferries run to Kavala (6hr., 4 per week, 3600dr); Lesvos (6hr., 5 per week, 4245dr); Thessaloniki (8hr., 2 per week, 5540dr); Chios (10hr., 3 per week, 5230dr); Rafina (10hr., 3 per week, 5540dr); Peiraias (22hr., 3 per week, 7020dr); Alexandropolis (6hr., 1 per week, 3000dr); Samothrace (4hr., 1 per week, 2500dr); and Agios Efstratios (2hr., 2 per week, 1620dr). Visit **Nicos Vayakos' Tourist and Travel Agency** (tel. 22 900 or 22 460; fax 23 560) in Myrina's port square for tickets and information on ferries (open 8:30am-1:30pm and 6:30-9pm). **Flying Dolphins** speed to Alexandropolis (3hr., 3 per week, 6500dr) and Samothrace (1½hr., 2 per week, 5000dr).

    Kyda St. leads inland past a variety of shops and into the town's **central square,** recognizable by its many **taxi stands** (tel. 23 820). The **OTE** (tel. 22 299; open M-Sa 7:30am-3:10pm) and the **National Bank** (tel. 22 414) with a 24-hour **ATM** (open M-Th 8am-2pm, F 8am-1:30pm) are both in the square. One block farther on Kyda St., Garofalidi St. runs to the right. Here you will find the **post office** (tel. 22 462; open M-F 7:30am-2pm) and a **laundromat** (tel. 24 392; 1600dr per kg; open M-F 8:30am-2pm and 6-11:30pm, Sa 8:30am-11:30pm, Su 11am-11:30pm). The **police** (tel. 22 201) are a few blocks past the post office. The **hospital** (tel. 22 222 or 22 345) is to the left of Garofalidi St., on the street farthest from the waterfront (open 24hr.). In the middle of the main port square, a shop sells **international newspapers and books** daily from 7am to 3pm and 5 to 11pm. **Postal code:** 84100. **Telephone code:** 0254.

NORTHEAST AEGEAN

ACCOMMODATIONS In high season, waterfront hotel rooms will cost at least 8000dr, so a better choice is to follow one of the many "Rooms to let" signs or ask at the tourist booth by the port. You'll find clean rooms at **Hotel Akteon** (tel. 22 258), on the port near Nicos Vayakos' Agency (singles 5000-6000dr; doubles 6000-7000dr; triples 7000-8000dr). **Dionisia Rooms to Let** (tel. 23 966 or 24 741) has apartment-like setups with A/C, kitchen, and bath. Walk down the Romeikos waterfront with the Kastro at your back, and take the last right before the large apartment building (doubles 12,000dr; triples 14,000dr).

FOOD AND ENTERTAINMENT Typically, the waterfront *tavernas* are uniform in their prices and identical in their offerings. Try **Kosmos Pizzeria's** prime seating for the sunset behind Mt. Athos and delicious steamed mussels (1100dr). **To Limani** (tel. 23 809), near Hotel Akteon, dishes out cheap *gyros* and *souvlaki* (450dr; open daily 6pm-3am). Later at night, stroll along the Romeikos among many cafe-bars, of which **Karagiozis Bar** is particularly popular.

SIGHTS The **Kastro** which dominates the skyline and divides the waterfronts also houses several dozen deer. If you climb up and don't catch sight of them, you can at least enjoy the stunning view and ruins from the 7th-century BC fortress, reworked in the 13th century by the Venetians. The network of dungeons and tunnels underlying the castle should be avoided by the less-than-intrepid; bring a flashlight. Work up an appetite climbing, then stop by any of the local pastry shops for bougatsa. This cream-filled pastry, a Mediterranean specialty, is not to be missed – stop by early and buy some fresh out of the island oven. The **Romeikos Yialos** beach stretches across the opposite end of the waterfront. Directly across from the scads of sun worshippers, the **archaeological museum** offers both air-conditioned relief and a fascinating and extensive collection from the many archaeological sites on Limnos, namely Poliochini, along with long gauze panels decorated with informative labels in Greek, English, and Italian. *(Open Tu-Su 9am-3pm.)*

The excavations at **Poliochini** are of particular importance, as the first of the seven levels is thought to date from almost 6000 years ago. *(Open Tu-Su 9am-3pm.)* On this half of the island, you can also see Aliki Lake, which dries in the summer to become a huge salt lick. Limnos holds an annual **festival** with concerts, traditional dancing, and exhibitions of local cheeses, honey, and wines, during the first ten days of August.

■ Plati Πλατη

No Greek forgets the *horio*. It translates simply as "village," but the *horio* is your homeland, the place your parents or grandparents came from, where three hundred of your closest relatives have hated and loved each other for as many years, and to which your loyalties ultimately belong. Like all things intensely familial, it's for some a source of strength and for others a nightmare-in-law. All the adolescent angst and deep loyalties of this ouzo-drinking, fiercely political people come out in visits to The Village. Any traveler seeking to understand Greece should spend a day in the ancestors' land.

All towns, especially island towns, have a peculiar character; in particular, Plati's accessibility has not compromised its candor and quirks. Plati translates roughly as "wide," and at first, the 400-person village seems like little more than a wide place in the road. Two kilometers from Myrina, Plati edges against the rock of the Malliaris Hills, spilling around their edges towards the sea. But if you end up in Myrina—if you are at all tired with the budding capitalist and cosmopolitan of the island ports—make the half hour's walk and see this, the purely untouristed.

The road from the capital ends in Agios Anastasios Malliaris, the tiny town promenade, named doubly for the illustrious founder and for his grandson, the noted American economist. At block's end, it splits immediately into an intricate network of tiny, winding footpaths, crossing and recrossing mazelike around the haphazardly spaced Greek village houses. Every meter here is accounted for; on the islands land is the most precious of inheritances, and misunderstandings spark centuries of ill will. Villagers—especially those in a town of four hundred—do not forget.

If you arrive during the day, ask for directions to the springs, where the town gets its water. The road to the source winds through the village and emerges on the seaward side of the hill. The source is about five minutes' walk further on the left—look for the women carrying large containers of water. The water is clean and fresh for drinking, it's tapped straight from the mountain. Make sure you've found the drinking water—farther up the mountain are various other springs, each with their designated use: animals' water, washing water, bathing water. The drinking source is the most easily accessible, and don't forget to turn around for a spectacular view of the sudden valley, stretching fifteen minutes' walk to the sea.

At night, the village comes alive—follow your ears to the tiny village square, home to a church, two eateries, and a memorial building. Old people pull their chairs out onto the streets to sit and gossip, and children play on the church steps while their parents talk philosophy and local politics at the *taverna*. Treat yourself to the perpetually overpriced (actual price depends entirely on how good business has been that day) *kaidaifi* dessert with *kaimaiki* ice cream on top—ask at the *gyros* shop next to the *taverna*. Look, listen, and above all talk to the locals. Their stories and complaints are timeless. All of Greece began in a village.

The Multifaceted Pomegranate

Pomegranates, or ροδια (rodhia), can be seen growing everywhere in Greece in summer and fall, usually on small shrubs in the shade of olive and fig trees. The fruits may seem small compared to the type you might be accustomed to plucking from supermarket shelves, but they play a large role, weighted in much symbolic resonance, in Greek culture. The burgeoning, juicy, blood-red seeds that burst from under the leathery skin of the well-ripened fruit have granted it a timeless dual association with both fertility and death. For the ancient Greeks, red food was thought to be suitable only for the dead. In the pomegranate's most famous tale, Hades, lord of the dead, raped and abducted Persephone, daughter of the fertility goddess, Demeter, holding her captive in his netherworldly kingdom. An infuriated Demeter wandered the earth, spreading famine and barrenness in her wake, until a worried Zeus negotiated a deal with his deathsome brother: Persephone would be returned to the living, on the condition that she had tasted none of the food from Hades' orchards. When the gardener of Hell attested that she had, indeed, sampled seven pomegranate seeds there, Zeus struck another deal on the behalf of the distraught Demeter. For seven months of the year Persephone presided as Queen of the Underworld, during which time Demeter's sadness was felt on earth as the cold, infertile winter. For the remaining five summery months, the fields sprung to life again as Demeter was re-united with her daughter on Mt. Olympus. The seven seeds may also represent the seven moon phases in which farmers awaited the sprouting of their corn.

For modern Greeks, the pomegranate continues to appear as a bridge between life and death, or old and new. Κολλυβα (kolliva), a standard dish to eat at Greek funerals, is made with wheat seeds, almonds, and pomegranate. On New Year's Eve, tossing a pomegranate out the door to smash it on the pavement will bring good luck and prosperity for the coming year. Meanwhile, Orthodox priests hold that the fruit is a sign of spiritual fertility.

And such a sumptious, decadent fruit must also have its sexy side. Ancient Greeks believed the blood of the pomegranate tree to be that of Dionysus, god of wine and debauchery. Today, the fruit is often associated with erotic desire, especially an extremely ripe one that has begun to split its own rind.

Cyclades Κυκλαδες

Happy is the man, I thought, who, before dying, has the good fortune to sail the Aegean Sea.

—Nikos Kazantzakis

When people speak longingly of the Greek islands, they are probably talking about the Cyclades. Whatever your idea of the Aegean—peaceful cobblestone streets and whitewashed houses, *ouzo* sipped seaside during breathtaking sunsets, inebriated revelry—you can find it here. In classical antiquity, the islands received their name from the shape of their layout. The ancient Greeks saw the Cyclades forming a *kyklos* or "cyclical" pattern, spiraling around the sacred island of Delos. Today, somewhat less metaphysically, the islands can be grouped into three broad categories. Although each has quiet villages and untouched spots, Santorini, Mykonos, and Ios are known to all as the party islands and are the most heavily touristed. Of these three, Santorini, the most chic and the most expensive, offers an impressive history and some of the most spectacular views in Greece. Mykonos is a close second in sophistication (and price), but also provides some of Greece's most sizzling nightlife. Ios can be summed up in four words: American frat party run amok (all right, that was five words, but after a week on Ios you won't be able to count either). Paros, Naxos, and Amorgos are also popular but less frantic and more pristine, frequented more by families and hikers. Syros, Tinos, Andros, Folegandros, Kithnos, Serifos, Sifnos, and Milos get few foreign visitors and are dependent primarily on Greeks. This group of islands are, for the most part, blissfully unexploited by the ritzy international tourist scene, and their beaches, mountains, and villages are as clean and welcoming as they were years ago. If visiting in the winter, you may be the lone foreigner on these islands.

Note that many tourist amenities on many of these islands, especially accommodations, are only open April through October.

HIGHLIGHTS OF THE CYCLADES

- Lose your pants. Lose your shirt. Lose your mind. Party naked on **Ios** (p. 327).
- The sun sets over the volcano-formed cliffs of the west coast of **Santorini** (p. 331) to the sounds of symphonies.
- The Classical Greek *symposium* survives in the bars and cafes of **Mykonos** (p. 320), the Aegean's premier gay destination, and the ruins of the Cyclades' ancient religious capital linger at nearby **Delos** (p. 325).
- The bleached Byzantine Hozoviotissa Monastery juts out of a sheer cliff on **Amorgos** (p. 356), an island full of pristine hikes and dives as seen in the French film *The Great Blue*.
- Whitewashed **Andros Town** (p. 370) preserves pure Greek island living—the type of place fit for raising children.

MYKONOS Μυκονος

Go Bacchae, go! With the luxury of Tmolus that flows of gold, sing of Dionysus beneath the heavy beat of drums! Celebrate with shouts and cries the god of delight when the sweet sounding sacred pipe plays a playful tune suited to the wanderers.

—Euripides, *The Bacchae*

Mykonos has been the object of envy and desire since ancient times when merchants vied for the lucrative trade of supplying pilgrims *en route* to the holy island of Delos. By Byzantine and Ottoman times, the pilgrim trade had given way to marauding

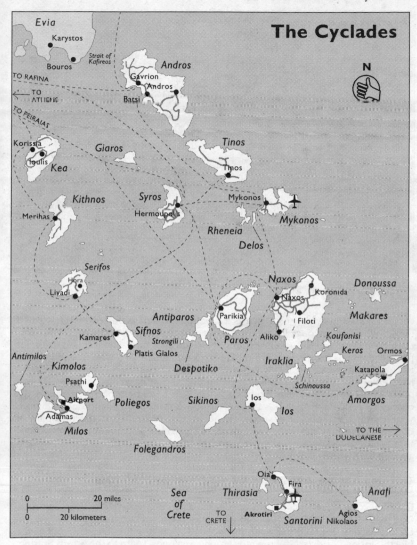

The Cyclades

N

CYCLADES

pirates eager for the rich plunder to be found in the waters around Mykonos. In the '70s Mykonos' gay scene and wild nightlife secured the island's place among the premiere resorts of the Mediterranean. Today, the island is the plaything of the sleek and chic—*kosmopolitikos*. Though Mykonos' gay scene has lost the preeminence it once enjoyed among other Mediterranean hotspots, its continued vibrance still helps the Mykonosian nightlife command international Bacchic awe. Sophisticated revelers flock to this St. Tropez of the Aegean, lounging all day on the island's long, blonde beaches and clubbing until dawn in the frenzied alleys of Mykonos Town.

The honor of frolicking with the hordes of the European jetset levies a hefty tax on the budget traveler's purse, but Mykonos makes up for being crowded and expensive with some of the Cycladic islands' finest beaches, an undulating interior of lunar beauty, and one of the most picturesque towns.

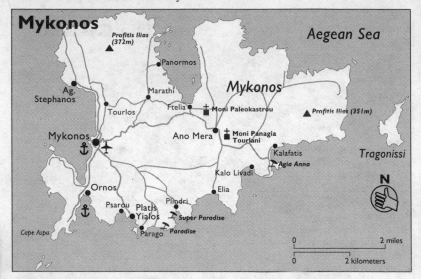

Mykonos

Profitis Ilias (372m)

Aegean Sea

Panormos

Ag. Stephanos

Marathi

Mykonos

Tourlos

Ftelia — Moni Paleokastrou

Profitis Ilias (351m)

Mykonos

Ano Mera — Moni Panagia Touriani

Kalafatis

Agia Anna

Tragonissi

Kalo Livadi

Ornos

Elia

Plindri

Psarou Platis
Yialos — Super Paradise

Cape Aspa

Parago — Paradise

N

0 — 2 miles

0 — 2 kilometers

CYCLADES

■ Mykonos Town

On an arid island, Mykonos Town is a dazzling oasis of geometric whitewashed houses whose charm once inspired the modernist architect Le Corbusier. These labyrinthine streets, closed to motor traffic, were created to disconcert and disorient pirates—perhaps islanders never bothered to straighten them out because they seem to work just as well for tourists. Despite the influx of visitors, the town has resisted large hotel complexes, and fishing boats in the harbor, basket-laden donkeys, drag queens, high-fashion models, and Petros the Pelican all help preserve the town's charm. Nevertheless, Mykonos is unmistakably a tourist town, and depending on your degree of homesickness, you will either exult in or grieve over the availability of cheeseburgers, milkshakes, fish and chips, Chinese food, and continental breakfasts. Don't come to Mykonos to experience unadulterated Greek culture; come to witness a world of Dionysiac delight.

ORIENTATION AND PRACTICAL INFORMATION

If you're facing inland, incoming boats dock at a pier on the far left of the waterfront. One road leads to the right along the water past the town beach to **Taxi Square** and the center of town. Another road, parallel and above the first, heads uphill to the **North Station** bus depot, then wraps around Mykonos Town to the **South Station.** Everything you need or want is near the waterfront—banks, travel agencies, shops, cafes, *tavernas,* bars, and discos—but much of the real shopping, fine dining, and partying go on in the infamous narrow, winding back streets (especially **Matogianni St., Kalogera St., Mitropoleas St.,** and **Enoplon Dinameon St.**). On the right side of the waterfront is another pier for excursion boats headed primarily for nearby Delos. Past the pier is a series of churches, the lovely part of town called **Little Venice,** and a small hill with a line of windmills.

Transportation

Ferries: Boats sail to Tinos (45min., 3-5 per day, 1200dr); Paros (2hr., 2-3 per day, 1800dr); Naxos (3hr., 1-2 per day, 1850dr); Syros (2½hr., 1-3 per day, 1610dr); Andros (3½hr., 1-3 per day, 2640dr); Santorini (6½hr., 1-3 per day, 3500dr); Ios (4hr., 1-2 per day, 3200dr); Peiraias (6hr., 1-4 per day, 5100dr); Iraklion (3 per week, 5550dr); Thessaloniki (3 per week, 9280dr); Samos (2 per week, 4700dr); Ikaria (2 per week, 3070dr); and Rafina (1-3 per day, 4150dr).

Flying Dolphins: Hydrofoils are faster but more expensive and have less reliable schedules due to weather conditions. Daily boats go to Paros (3400dr); Santorini (6800dr); Naxos (3600dr); Ios (6350dr); Amorgos (2 per week, 6130dr); and Sikinos (1 per week, 6640dr); Tinos (2 per day, 2480dr); Syros (3025dr); Andros (2 per day, 5300dr); and Rafina (1-2 per day, 8250dr).

Buses: KTEL (tel. 23 360) has two stations in town. **North Station,** uphill from the ferry dock, serves Agios Stefanos beach (every 30min., 210dr); Ano Mera and Kalafatis (every 2hr., 320dr); Elia Beach (6 per day, 290dr); and Kalo Livadi beach (2 per day, high season only, 290dr). **South Station,** uphill from the windmills at the opposite edge of town, serves Plati Yalos beach (every 30min., 240dr); Paradise Beach (every 30min., 220dr); Ornos Beach (every 30min., 220dr); and Agios Ioannis (every hr., 220dr). Schedules are posted at the stations.

Flights: Olympic Airways (tel. 22 490 or 22 495 in town, 22 327 at airport). Flights to Athens (40min., 6-7 per day, 18,900dr); Thessaloniki (3 per week, 27,700dr); Santorini (30min., W-M, 19,200dr); Iraklion (1hr., 2 per week, 22,500dr); and Rhodes (1hr., 3 per week, 22,700dr). There are no buses to the airport; a taxi from Mykonos Town costs 1300dr.

Taxi: (tel. 22 400 or 22 700). Available at Taxi Sq., along the waterfront.

Moped Rentals: Agencies surround both bus stops. Be ready to bargain. 2000-5000dr per day. Some rent jeeps as well (10,000-16,000dr per day).

Tourist and Financial Services

Tourist Police: (tel. 22 482), in an office at the ferry landing. Very helpful English speakers. Open daily 8am-9pm.

Banks: National Bank of Greece (tel. 22 234), in the center of the waterfront, offers **currency exchange** and **ATM.** Open June-Sept. M-Th 8am-2pm and 6-8pm (evening hours for currency exchange only), F 8am-1:30pm, Sa-Su 10am-1pm; Oct.-May, M-Th 8am-2pm, F 8am-1:30pm.

American Express: (tel. 22 322), left of the bank inside **Delia Travel Ltd.** Full travel services for cardholders. Open M-F 9am-9pm, Sa-Su 9am-3pm and 6-9pm.

International Bookstore: International Press (tel. 23 316), in a small square opposite Pierro's, follow signs from the waterfront. Eclectic books, magazines, and newspapers in several languages, including English. Open daily 8am-midnight.

Laundry: on Psarou road heading towards the windmills from the bus terminal (tel. 27 600). A full load costs 2500dr. Open daily 8:30am-10pm.

Emergency and Communications

Hospital: (tel. 23 994 or 23 996), 1km east of Mykonos Town. Take the bus or taxi (600dr) to Ano Mera (8 per day, 190dr). **Emergency:** call an **ambulance** at 166.

Medical Center: (tel. 24 211, 27 464, or 27 407), on the higher road leading from the port to South Station, just beyond the turnoff for the hospital. Doctors on hand include general practitioner, microbiologist, cardiologist, X-ray guru, and gynecologist. Open daily May-Oct. 8:30am-midnight; Nov.-Mar 8:30am-9pm. **24-hour emergency** call 094 35 12 53 or 094 33 82 92.

Police: (tel. 22 716 or 22 215). In Laka past the South Station. Open 24hr.

Post Office: (tel. 22 238), around the corner from the police in Laka, behind South Station. **Exchanges currency.** Open M-F 7:30am-2pm. **Postal Code:** 84600.

Internet Access: Mykonos Cyber Café (tel.27 684; fax 27 685; email info@mykonos-cyber-cafe.com), by the South Station bus terminal. Offers email (750dr), faxes, and net-surfing (100dr per min.). Open daily 8:30am-11pm.

OTE: (tel. 22 699). Left end of waterfront in big white building, uphill to the right of the dock. Open M-F 8am-3pm. **Telephone Code:** 0289.

ACCOMMODATIONS

Contrary to popular belief, reasonable accommodations are available, especially if you are willing to stay outside the immediate town area. The information offices located on the dock are numbered according to accommodation type and are helpful: 1 for hotels (tel. 24 540; open 9am-midnight), 2 for rooms to let (tel. 24 860; open daily 9am-11pm), and 3 for camping (tel. 23 567; open daily 9am-midnight). Follow one of the hawkers at your own risk. Many claim to have rooms "on the beach," but they are often miles from town. Remember free-lance camping is illegal. Prices are 20-40% less in the off season and in nearby towns such as Ornos.

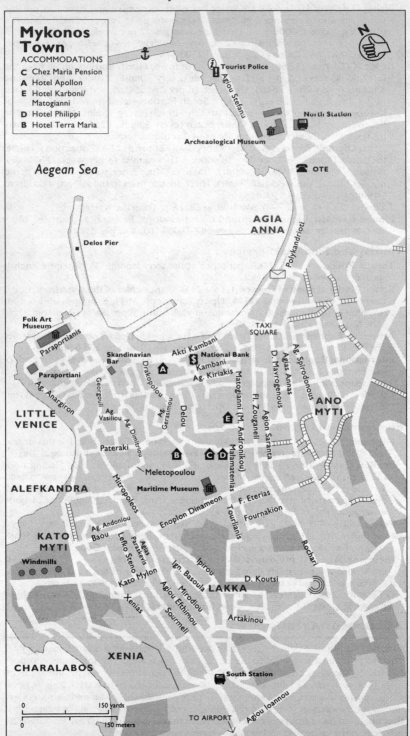

Mykonos Town
ACCOMMODATIONS
C Chez Maria Pension
A Hotel Apollon
E Hotel Karboni/
Matogianni
D Hotel Philippi
B Hotel Terra Maria

CYCLADES

Aegean Sea

⚓

ℹ Tourist Police

Agiou Stefanu

North Station

Archeological Museum

☎ OTE

AGIA ANNA

Polykandrioti

Delos Pier

✉

TAXI SQUARE

Folk Art Museum

Paraportianis

Paraportiani

Skandinavian Bar

Drakopolou

Akti Kambani

National Bank

Kambani

Ag. Kiriakis

Ag. Spirodonous

Agias Annas

D. Mavrogenous

Ag. Anargiron

LITTLE VENICE

Georgouli

Ag. Vasiliou

Ag. Dimitriou

Ag. Gerasimou

Delou

Matogianni (M. Andronikou)

Fl. Zouganeli

Agion Saranta

ANO MYTI

Pateraki

Malamatenias

ALEFKANDRA

Mitropoleos

Meletopoulou

Maritime Museum

Enoplon Dinameon

F. Eterias

Fournakion

Tourlianis

KATO MYTI

Ag. Andoniou

Baou

Lefko Steno

Agios Paraskevis

Kato Mylon

Mirodiou

Agiou Efthimiou

Ipirou

Ign. Basoula

LAKKA

D. Koutsi

Rochari

Windmills

Xenias

Sourmeli

Artakinou

XENIA

CHARALABOS

South Station

| 0 | | 150 yards |
| 0 | | 150 meters |

TO AIRPORT

Agiou Ioannou

Hotel Terra Maria, 33 Kalogera St. (tel. 24 212; fax 27 112), in an alley off Kalogera St. Don't confuse it with Chez Maria or the nearby Marios Hotel. A/C, private baths, TVs, and mini-bars. Despite central location, surrounding city park makes it very peaceful. Run by Petros, a former soccer star. Breakfast 1800dr. Doubles 15,000-21,000dr; triples 18,000-24,000dr.

Hotel Apollon (tel. 22 223), on the waterfront. Oldest hotel in town—an antique-laden house with many rooms overlooking the harbor. Common baths. Singles 8500-10,000dr; doubles 12000-14,000dr; triples 13,000-17,000dr.

Hotel Karboni/Matogianni (tel. 22 217), on Matogianni St., inland from the water-front. Pleasant and spotless. Ask about cheaper rear rooms. Breakfast included. Doubles 22,000dr, triples 24,000dr.

Hotel Philippi, 25 N. Kalogera St. (tel. 22 294; fax 24 680), next to Chez Maria. Friendly owners, gorgeous gardens, and clean rooms with phones. Rooms with common bath cost as much as those with private bath. Singles 7000-9000dr; doubles 11,000-15,000dr; triples 18,000-20,000dr.

Chez Maria Pension, 27 N. Kalogera St. (tel. 22 480; 27 565). From the waterfront, turn inland next to Sea & Sky Travel Agency onto Matogianni St., turn right onto Kalogera at the yellow building across from the Credit Bank. There are signs to help. Above Chez Maria Restaurant—conveniently located meals, but perhaps a lit-tle noisy when others feast while you try to sleep. Doubles 10,000-15,000dr; triples 12,000-18,000dr.

Paradise Beach Camping (tel. 22 852, 22 129; fax 24 350), on beach 6km from the village. You can take a bus here (round-trip 380dr). Situated directly on one of island's more popular beaches. Even though it's quite large, it often feels crowded. Because of its location, nude bathers on Paradise Beach are a common sight. Free shuttle service from port and airport. 1700dr per person; 1000dr per small tent; 1300dr per large tent.

Mykonos Camping (tel. 25 915, 22 916; fax 24 578), near Paradise Beach. Smaller, quieter, and cleaner. 1500dr per person; 1000dr per tent; 1500dr per tent rental.

Greek Chic

So you've just spent a long day visiting ancient temples, Roman ruins, and Byzan-tine churches, or cavorting on beaches. Now it's nighttime and you're wondering what to wear. Here's the Let's Go guide to looking cool in Greece. **Men,** Greek fashion doesn't allow you much room for creativity. You *must* wear asphyxiat-ingly tight jeans and an equally skin-tight short-sleeved shirt (preferably V-necked) tucked in all the way beneath a big black belt. Your pants should be white, blue, or black and your shirt white, grey, or black. And remember to keep your hair oiled back! **Women** in Greece have a little more room for improvisation. Pretty much anything goes—as long as it's at least a little risqué and tight enough that breathing is difficult. Tight black pants with tighter shirts and short, skimpy, somewhat scandalous dresses are currently *de mode*. So whether you're male or female, if you want to look hip, stuff your baggy attire in the bottom of your pack and put on your most body-revealing outfit. And if you still find yourself unsure what to wear, think back not to ancient Greece but to the fashion of John Tra-volta's *Grease* and you'll start enjoying your summer nights.

FOOD

Klimataria (tel. 24 051), on Florou Zouganeli St., the first street to your right as you face inland with Taxis Sq. right in front of you—look for blue tables. Good prices and a 5-language menu, including English. Draws a tourist crowd, but serves authentic Greek cuisine. Try *moussaka* (1100dr), rabbit stew (1700dr), or rooster in red sauce with pasta (1800dr). Open daily 9am-1am.

Alexi's (tel. 26 906), back of Taxi Sq. The oldest greasy spoon in Mykonos. Alexi puts on a show as he cooks up your *gyro*-pita (350dr), hamburger (450-650dr), or bar-beque chicken with fries (1100dr). Also serves a complete breakfast including a fried tomato for 1350dr. Open daily 10am-7am.

Niko's Taverna (tel. 24 320), in a cluster of restaurants inland from excursion boat docks. A hoppin' place for traditional Greek cuisine. Taste the baked *kalamari* and cheese (2500dr), mussels with tomato and cheese (1500dr), lamb *kleftiko* (baked with cheese in aluminum foil 2000dr). Open daily noon-2am.

La Mexicana (tel. 27 602), at the end of Kalogera St. Chicken enchiladas 1900dr; chicken, beef, or shrimp fajitas 2500dr. A good choice for homesick Mexican food lovers. Happy Hour daily 6:30-8:00pm—discount on sangria, frozen margaritas, and tequila shots. Open daily 6:30pm-late.

Philippi Restaurant and Bar (tel. 22 295), off Kalogera St. by the Hotel Philippi. Beautiful garden atmosphere where the waitstaff pays you scrupulous attention. it is worth the higher prices (curry chicken 3200dr, salmon salad 2600dr). Excellent wines and smooth drinks. Open daily 7pm-late.

The Donut Factory (tel. 22 672), at the intersection of Mitropoleos, Ipirou, and Enoplon Dinameon St., roughly 3 blocks down from South Station. Delightful donuts (300-450dr) and fresh fruit juices (500-700dr). Open 24hr.

Euthymios Euthymiou (tel. 22 281), off of Taxi Sq. The divine smells of this store will draw you in where you can snack on the island's delights like *amigthalota* (almond cookies) and *kalathakia* (pastry tarts filled with walnuts). Open daily 8am-11pm.

ENTERTAINMENT

◉**Skandinavian Bar,** near Niko's Taverna and the waterfront (follow the pumping bass). This perennially packed party complex sprawls over 2 buildings and a patio. Evening mellowness becomes madness 'round midnight. *Everyone* passes through this place. Beer 800dr; shots 900dr; cocktails 1500dr. Open Su-F 10:30pm-3am, Sa 10:30pm-4am.

◉**Caprice Bar,** on the water in Little Venice. Popular and crowded, with a fruit motif befitting a waterfront bar. A perfect après beach place complete with breathtaking sunsets, feel-good music, and a friendly crowd always ready for a good time. Open daily 4:30pm-4am.

◉**Mad Club,** off Taxi Sq., up a flight of stairs. Serves up pounding techno in an intimate bar meets jungle gym setting. Refreshing balcony overlooking the sea. Cover 1000dr. Cocktails 2000dr.

Pierro's, on Matogianni St., reputedly the most happening place on Mykonos. Pierro's was the first gay bar in Greece. Free lovin' in the corners. Best dancing on the island—the crowd spills out into the square. Beer 1000dr, cocktails 2000dr.

Nepheli-Blue Bar, upstairs from Pierro's. A popular gay hangout, but like most gay bars on Mykonos, all are welcome. Beer 1000dr, cocktails 1400-1600dr. Next door, **Icaros** has a similar atmosphere and a nightly drag show at 2am. Work it cover girl!

Montparnasse, 24 Agion Anargyron St. (tel. 23 719). Step into a Toulouse-Lautrec at this piano bar in Little Venice. Have a cocktail by the bay window overlooking the water while being serenaded by cabaret tunes from a live piano. Groovy and sophisticated. Wine 800dr, cocktails 900-2000dr. Open daily 7pm-3am.

Mykonos Bar, in Little Venice, next to the Caprice Bar. Watch Greek dancers perform the *zebekiko* and *zorba*, then join them until sunrise. They are here to teach you! Cover 800dr. Beer 700dr, cocktails 1500dr. Open daily 10pm-4am.

Veranda, the place for high brow drink sippin'. Up the stairs off Venetias St., in Little Venice. Big veranda (funny that) and slow movin' fans. Cool, cool, cool. Cocktails 2200-2500dr. Open daily 5:30pm-late.

Cine Mant (tel. 27 109), by **Astra**, plays films in English twice daily (1500dr).

SIGHTS

Losing yourself in the flagged, colorful alleyways of Mykonos Town at dusk or dawn is one of the most exhilarating experiences the island can offer. At every corner you're bound to stumble upon a miniature church or quiet corner of beauty glowing in the ethereal Cycladic light. Walk to the **Kastro** area behind the pier servicing ferries to Delos (at the far left of the port if you're facing the sea). Next to the Folklore Museum is the **Paraportiani,** a cluster of white churches, probably the most famous of Mykonos' sights and on every other Greek postcard. From there walk through **Little Venice,** grab a seat at **Caprice** to watch the sun set and the tide roll in. If you feel like your energy hasn't been fully tapped after a night of clubbing take the winding road leading from the North Bus Station up the hill overlooking the port to catch a magnificent view of the Aegean at sunrise.

Beaches

The prime daytime activities on Mykonos are shopping and tanning. You will inevitably find yourself on the unexceptional town beach in Mykonos. Very accessible by bus is the unspectacular **St. Stefanos Beach** (10min., every 30min. from North Station 8:15am-2am, 210dr). **Ornos Beach's** clear shallow water is also a short bus ride away (10min., 30min. from South Station 8:15am-2am, 220dr), as is crowded **Psarou Beach** (15min., every half hour, from South Station 8:15am-2am, 210dr).

Although all the beaches on Mykonos are **nudist,** the degree of nudity depends on where you go. The more daring beaches, **Plati Yialos, Paradise Beach, Super Paradise Beach,** and **Elia** are reputedly the best. Reach the latter three by catching a bus from South Station to Plati Yialos (every 30min., 220dr), then take a *kaiki* across the water. From Plati Yialos, *kaikia* go to Paradise Beach (300dr), officially called Kalamopodi and packed with beach towels, and to Super Paradise Beach (380dr), the most popular and craziest beach on the island. Paradise can also be reached by the 7km strip of road connecting it to town. For a more quiet sun-bathing experience with an excellent taverna to boot choose **Elia Beach,** the last stop on the *kaikia's* trajectory. Climb the footpath across the promontory behind Elia to be greeted on the other side by the majestic and even more remote **Kalo Livadi Beach.** Another beach perfect for escaping the crowds complete with hip *taverna* and a great lunar view is **Panormos,** on the northern coast, accessible by bus from North Station (290–320dr).

Museums

Although cultural enrichment may not be a primary activity on Mykonos, several museums exist. The **Archaeological Museum** (tel. 22 325), on the paved road between the ferry dock and the center of town, has a 7th-century BC *pithos* (large terra cotta storage jar) with relief scenes from the Trojan War, and a bronze *kouros*. *(Open Tu-Su 8:30am-2:30pm. Admission 500dr, students 300dr, EU students free, seniors 300dr.)* The **Aegean Maritime Museum** (tel. 22 325), around the corner from the inland end of Matogiannis St., contains ship models, rare ancient coins with nautical subjects, and navigational instruments. *(Open daily Apr.-Oct. 9am-3pm. Admission 200dr, students 100dr.)* The **Folklore Museum** (tel. 22 591) is in the 300-year-old house of a former sea captain, at the south edge of town, near the bus station, inland from the excursion boat docks. *(Open Apr.-Oct. M-Sa 5:30-8:30pm, Su 6:30-8:30pm. Free.)* The collection is open at convenient hours for beach-goers. **Lena's House** is a 300-year-old home with traditional 19th-century furniture. *(Open M-Sa 6-9pm, Su 7-9pm. Free.)* The home is part of the folklore museum and remains exactly as its owner left it.

Excursions

If you stay long enough in Mykonos head to Panormos beach and take a walk to the nearby town of Ano Mera. The convent of **Panagia Tourliani's** icons merit a peek. Not too far away by foot, just north of Ano Mera, is the 13th-century monastery of **Paleokastrou.** Climb the arid moon-like slope near the monastery to the medieval fortification known as *Durga* for some spectacular views of the island's windswept hills.

DELOS Δηλος

> Apollo wher'er thou strayest, far or near,
> Delos is still of all thy haunts most dear,
> Thither the robed Ionians take their way,
> With wife and children to keep thy holiday,
> Invoke thy favor on each manly game,
> And dance and sing in honor of thy name...
>
> —Homer, *Hymn to Apollo*

While the beaches of Mykonos are tantalizing in their sensuality, an excursion to Delos, the sacred navel around which the Cyclades whorl, is not to be missed. Even those little interested in mythology or history will be captivated by the powerful spell of the Delian ruins' wrinkle in time. The most famous sanctuary in the Cycladic islands, Delos claims *the* **Temple of Apollo,** built to commemorate the birthplace of Apollo and his twin sister, Artemis. After Zeus impregnated Leto, he cast her out, fearing his wife Hera's wrath. Leto drifted about the Aegean desperately searching for a place to give birth. All the islands fearing the vindictive Hera refused Leto shelter. At last he came across a rocky island clouded in mist that she had never seen before. Every time Leto approached the frightened island it would bob about furtively. She swore by the river Styx that the island would come to no harm and that the child she would bear would stay forever at his birthplace, casting light upon the surrounding riches. At her word, the island, reassured, stopped drifting, and Leto, exhausted, collapsed by the sacred lake. Upon her son's birth, the island was bathed in radiance; its name, A-delos (invisible) was changed to Delos because it could now be clearly seen. Immensely grateful, Leto promised to make the island the seat of Apollo's worship. The presence of the sanctuary and Delos' central location in the Aegean transformed the once invisible island into a major commercial and religious center.

History

Although first settled in the 3rd millennium BC, it was during the Mycenaean Period (1580-1200 BC) that Delos began to flourish. Mycenaean rule ended around 1100 BC, and one century later the Ionians dedicated the island to the **cult of Leto.** By the 7th century BC, Delos had become the political and mercantile center of the Aegean League of Islands. Three centuries of struggle for power between the Delians and the Athenians ensued. During these years, the Athenians ordered at least two "purifications" of the island, the latter, in 426 BC, decreeing that no one should give birth or die on its sacred grounds. Delians who violated the edict were banished to nearby Rheneia. The Athenians later instituted the quadrennial **Delian Games,** which they always dominated.

After Sparta's defeat of Athens in the Peloponnesian War (403 BC), Delos enjoyed independence and wealth. Sweet prosperity soured, however, during the Roman occupation in the 2nd century BC. Once the treasure house of the Greek world, Delos' commercial prestige was reduced to being the slave-trading center of Greece, where the transfer of as many as 10,000 slaves occurred daily. By the 2nd century AD, after successive sackings, the island was left virtually uninhabited apart from a few odd pirates. Today, its only residents are legions of leaping lizards, huge spider webs, and members of the French School of Archaeology. The latter have been excavating here since 1873.

Touring Delos

*Open Tu-Su 9am-2:30pm. **Admission,** including museum, 1200dr, students 600dr, EU students free. **Map** of the site free with ticket. **Guidebook** by Photini Zaphiropoulou which includes map is available at the entrance, museum, or tourist shops in Mykonos (1700dr).*

Occupying almost an entire square mile of this very small island, the archaeological site is neatly sectioned off into the central part of the ancient city, including the Temple of Apollo and the *Agora,* and the outlying parts of the city, Mt. Kythnos, and the theater quarter. While it takes several days to explore the ruins completely, you can see the highlights in three hours or less. A map of the site is recommended, whether you choose to follow the tour detailed below, tag along with a guided tour, or improvise. Most of your fellow ferry passengers will follow a similar route when they disembark; reverse the route if you want some privacy. Bring a hat, good shoes, and a water bottle as the cafeteria on site is expensive (soda 600dr).

From the dock, head straight to the **Agora of the Competaliasts,** where Roman guilds built their shrines. Nearby are several parallel **stoas,** the most impressive of which were built by Philip of Macedon. This line of altars, pillars, and statue bases (you can still see the statues' prints) forms the western border of the **Sacred Way.** Follow this road to the **Temple of Apollo,** with its immense, partly hollow hexagonal pedestal that once sustained the weight of the 8m-tall marble statue of the god of light. The famous **Delian Lions,** a gift from the people of Naxos to the holy island, lie

50m to the north. In the 7th century BC, nine marble lions were placed in a row on a terrace facing the sacred lake; only five remain here—a sixth, pirated by the Venetians, guards the entrance to the arsenal in Venice. Proceed up the small crest left of the lions to the **House of the Hill.** Because the building was dug deep into the earth, this archetypal Roman house is still substantially intact. Downhill lies the **House of the Lake,** with a well preserved mosaic decorating its atrium and the desecrated **Sacred Lake.** A lone palm tree keeps watch over the surrounding shrubbery and the *Agora* of the Romans. Next to the cafeteria, the museum contains an assortment of archaeological finds from the island; unfortunately, the best sculpture from the site is in Athens. From there, you can hike up the path to the summit of **Mt. Kythnos** (where Zeus watched the birth of Apollo). Along the way, you will pass several temples dedicated to the Egyptian gods. The elegant bust in the **Temple of Isis** depicts the sun, while the 120m hill affords a marvelous view of the ruins and islands. Although the climb is not difficult, wear comfortable yet sturdy shoes—some of the rocks that comprise the makeshift stairs dislodge easily. The **Grotto of Herakles** is on the way down. Its immense building blocks seem to date it to Mycenaean times, though some experts suggest it is a Hellenic imitation of Mycenaean architecture.

At the base of the hill, go towards the water to the **House of the Dolphins** and the **House of the Masks,** which contains the mosaic *Dionysus Riding a Panther.* These mosaics are beautifully preserved and soothing in their detailed intricacy. Continue on to the **ancient theater,** which has a rather sophisticated cistern (as cisterns go), **Dexamene,** with nine arched compartments. Also try to explore the **House of the Trident,** graced by a mosaic of a dolphin twisted around a trident; the **House of Dionysus,** containing another mosaic of Dionysus and a panther; and the **House of Cleopatra.** The famous statue of Cleopatra and Dioscourides is sequestered in the museum; a plaster copy takes its place on the site.

Getting There

Delos is most accessible as a daytrip from Mykonos. **Boats** leave from the dock near town, not the dock for large ferries (25min., Tu-Su departing every 30-45 minutes 8:30am-11:30am, returning 11am-3pm, 1700dr round-trip). Most will let you explore the site for three hours. Guided tours, offered in several languages by each excursion boat company, are expensive (7500dr, including admission to the ruins). Take the free map that accompanies your admission ticket and eavesdrop on the groups at each site. Each boat line has several return trips in the afternoon, so you have some flexibility about how much time you spend exploring. Tickets can be bought at the dock. Other islands (especially Tinos, Naxos, and Paros) offer joint trips to Mykonos and Delos, but allow less time to explore the ruins.

IOS Ιος

If you're not drunk by the time you get here, you will be by the time you leave. On Ios, beers go down and clothes come off faster than you can say *"Opa!"* It has everything your mother warned you about—people swilling wine from the bottle at 3pm, wishing you slobbery "good evenings," drinking games all day along the beach, condoms scattered on dirt roads, men and women dancing naked in bars (of which Ios had 113 at last count), and oh so much more. Drinks here are cheap and plentiful; Ios imports one and a half mega-truckloads of beer a day—and exports the same number of empty bottles each morning. Though the island has settled down a bit in the past few years, it's still about ready to sink under the weight of well-built, suntanned 20-year-olds. There is little to do in Ios but sleep late, sunbathe in the afternoon, and join the drunken cavorting by night. Make the pilgrimage to this mecca of the young and the restless only if you're prepared for hangovers, the occasional groping hand, and the lustful stares of the inebriated.

CYCLADES

The island quiets down in the off season. University students flee the scene, leaving locals behind to prepare for the next attack. September is an ideal time to experience this beautiful yet slightly misbehaved Cycladic island.

■ Yialos and Hora Γιαλος και Χορα

ORIENTATION AND PRACTICAL INFORMATION

The good life centers around three locations, each 20 minutes apart along the island's paved road. The **port** (Yialos) is at one end of the road. The **village** (Hora), the focus of nocturnal activity, sits above the port on a hill. Miraculously, Hora has not become as trashed as its visitors. As you approach the density of bars with storefront advertising gimmicks, the occasional dried sidewalk vomit, and the odd comatose carouser will be enough assurance that you're in the right place. You can do most of your "serious" business by foot within five minutes of the village bus stop on the paved road opposite the large, blue domed church. Crowded **Mylopotas beach** rests over the hill on the other side of the village. Frequent buses shuttle from port to village to beach and back (8am-2am, every 10-20 minutes, 220dr).

Transportation

Ferries: From Ios to Peiraias (7-8hr., 4-6 per day, 5200dr); Naxos (1½hr., 6-8 per day, 2100dr); Santorini (1¼hr., 4-6 per day, 1500dr); Paros (2½hr., 6-8 per day, 2400dr); Mykonos (4-5hr., 4-6 per day, 3040dr); Syros (5hr., 2-4 per day, 3700dr); and Crete (5hr., 3 per week, 4300dr).

Flying Dolphins: serve Rafina (4-5hr., 1 per day, 8240dr); Santorini (35min., 3 per day, 3000dr); Paros (1¼hr, 3 per day, 4800dr); Naxos (45min., 2 per day, 4200dr); Mykonos (2hr., 2 per day, 6280dr); Syros (2½hr., 1 per day, 7280dr); Andros (3½hr., 1 per day, 8640dr); Tinos (2½hr., 1 per day, 7050dr); and Amorgos (2hr., 3-4 per week day, 4325dr). There are also four round-trip excursions per week to Sikinos (2200dr) and Folegandros (3000dr).

Car rental: Trohokinisi (tel. 91 166), past the parking lot between the church and the main road (cars 10,000-22,000dr per day). A license is absolutely necessary.

Tourist and Financial Services

Travel Agencies: Tourist Information Center (tel. 91 135), a private travel agency immediately adjacent to the bus stop. Sells ferry and hydrofoil tickets, provides currency exchange, helps with accommodations, and offers free luggage storage, maps, and safety deposit boxes. Open daily 7:30am-midnight. **Acteon Travel** (tel. 91 343, 91 318, or 91 002; fax 91 088) has offices all over the island, an English-speaking staff, free luggage storage, excursions around the island, stamps, maps, travel services, a full-service **American Express** office, and a **Western Union.** It is also the place to make or confirm airline reservations. The main office is by the bus stop in the port while the **village branch** (tel. 91 004 or 91 005) is just up the road from the bus stop. Both open daily 7:30am-midnight.

Banks: National Bank (tel. 91 354), next to the main church. **ATM** and will handle all your MasterCard needs. Open M-Th 7:45am-2pm, F 7:45am-1:30pm.

Emergency and Communications

Emergencies: (tel. 91 727, 91 827, 093 40 04 23, or 093 42 32 07). Open 24hr.

Police: (tel. 92 222), on the road to Kolitsani Beach, just past the OTE. Open 24hr.

Port authority: (tel. 91 264), at the far end of the harbor next to Camping Ios. Open 24hr.

Medical Center: (tel. 91 227), next to the bus stop at the back of the big yellow building. Specializes in drunken mishaps. Open daily 10am-1pm and 6-7pm.

Postal Code: 84001.

OTE: (tel. 91 399). A few minutes out of the village along a path starting from the main paved road after Sweet Irish Dream, by the large antenna atop the hill. Look for signs. Open M-F 7:30am-3:10pm. **Telephone Code:** 0286.

ACCOMMODATIONS

Make sure you are in a bargaining mood when you disembark. Staying in the port is a good idea if you want to avoid the late-night chaos of the village.

Francesco's (tel./fax 91 223; email fragesco@tenet.gr). From the top of the "donkey steps," walk up the path to the square next to the church, take the uphill steps in the left corner of the square, then the first left. Rooms with a spectacular view of the harbor sit atop the hotel's terrace bar, where you'll be downing your welcome shot two minutes into your stay. Exceptionally fun staff. Reservations encouraged. Doubles 5000dr, with bath 8000dr; triples 6000dr, with bath 9000dr.

Pension Irene (tel./fax 91 023), on the waterfront offers clean, quiet rooms with bath and a view of the water. Doubles 8000dr; triples 10,000dr.

Petros Place Hotel (tel. 91 421; fax 91 866). Head up the side street that faces you as you disembark from the ferry to find the hotel. Complete with bath in every room, breakfast, an outdoor swimming pool, poolside bar, and tennis courts, Ideal for those seeking a peaceful stay. Doubles 10,000dr; triples 12,000dr.

Pension Markos (tel. 91 059; fax 91 060). From the bus stop, take the right (uphill) just before the supermarket. It's on another side street to the left, with a sign visible from the street. Friendly, clean, popular, with a happening pool and cheap cocktails. Bar serves breakfast all day (600dr). Reserve your room a few days in advance. All rooms with bath. Doubles 8000dr, with A/C 9000dr; triples 9,000dr, with A/C 10,000dr.

Hotel Petradi (tel./fax 91 510), equidistant from the village and the beach on the main road. Every room has a balcony with a romantic ocean view. Large, pleasant patio. Quiet at night. Bar downstairs. Doubles 8000dr; triples 9000dr.

Kolitsani View (tel. 91 061; fax 92 261). Follow the path past the OTE and look for the white archway. Approximately 10min. from the village action, it offers a quiet collection of spotless rooms with a family atmosphere. Expansive view of beaches and even Santorini. Free pick-up from the port. Doubles 7000dr, with bath 9000dr; triples 9000dr, with bath 13,000dr.

Pension Panorama (tel. 91 592 or 91 186), a bit of an uphill hike on a path below the village, next door to Francesco's. The view makes up for the hike. Doubles 9000dr; triples 12,000dr. Continental breakfast 700dr.

Far Out Camping (tel. 92 301 or 92 302; fax 92 303), at the far end of Mylopotas beach, is the hippest, most luxurious camping choice. Club Med at 1000dr per night, with a restaurant, bar, minimarket, basketball, volleyball, swimming pool, water slides, nightly movie, scuba diving (lessons open to public), showers, laundry, live music, and "happenings" with live bands and parties during summer. Open Apr.-Sept. 1400dr per person; 500dr tent rental.

Camping Stars (tel./fax 91 612, or 91 611), on Mylopotas beach. Quieter and less crowded than Far Out, with many of the same services, including a swimming pool. Open June-Sept. 2000dr per person; 500dr tent rental.

Camping Ios (tel. 91 329), at the port, is ideal for late-night arrivals. 1700dr per person; tent rental 500dr. Open June-Sept.

FOOD

Eating is definitely a secondary concern for the hard-core Bacchants. You can always refuel for a pittance (400dr) at the cheap *gyro* joints, eager to serve starving revellers. For more discerning palates, there are several good, reasonably priced restaurants interspersed among the ubiquitous bars and discos in Ios village.

Enigma (tel. 91 847; fax 91 407), on the waterfront. This is one of the few places in all of Greece that serves a dozen different baked potatoes (900-1000dr) and good onion rings (600dr). Gulp draft beer (600-700dr) while playing pool.

Pithari, near the National Bank, is hard to surpass when it comes to Greek specialties. *Exohiko* (lamb wrapped in pastry) 2000dr; chicken *methismeno* (drunk chicken) 1400dr.

CYCLADES

⊛**Lordos Byron** (tel. 92 125), uphill from the National Bank on the tiny street below the main drag, features exquisite Greek cuisine and forgotten Greek recipes. *Strapatsada* (special Greek omelette) 1200dr, *fava* dip 1000dr. Choose freely from the menu—everything is divine. Open daily 7pm-midnight.

Delfini, at the bottom of the footpath leading to Mylopotas beach from the village, serves up an enormous menu of Thai food (stir-fried vegetables with basil and garlic 1600dr).

Polydoros (tel. 91 132), 2km north of the port on Koubara Beach. True gourmands can be found here delecting in snails (1200dr) and shrimp with tomato sauce and mouth-watering feta (2400dr).

ENTERTAINMENT

Of Ios's alleged 113 bars, the majority are packed into the old village area. The larger and louder hang-outs can be found along the main paved road. To find serious drinking, climb the infamous "donkey steps" to the right of the paved road. Smaller bars line the main pedestrian street in the village. Some bars offer Happy Hours early in the evening, but the real drinking doesn't begin until at least 11pm.

⊛**Blue Note,** popular with Americans, Scandinavians, and those staying at Francesco's. Follow the main pedestrian path as it curves to the left. You will most likely have to ask for directions. Beer 600dr; cocktails 1000dr.

Sweet Irish Dream (tel. 91 141), a large building near the "donkey steps." Almost everyone ends up here, but most save it as the night's last stop. Come here after 2am to dance on tables. No cover before 2am. Beer 500-600dr; cocktails 1000dr.

The Slammer Bar (tel. 92 119), just uphill from the main square in the Village. Pain before pleasure; have the bartender whack your helmeted head with a hammer before you down the tequila slammer (shot glass filled with tequila, Tia Maria, and Sprite, slammed on the bar 900dr). Always packed.

Kalimera, lower down off the main strip. Perhaps the classiest bar, playing jazz and reggae. Beer 500-800dr; cocktails 1000-1200dr.

Dubliner (tel. 92 072), next to the bus stop. Proximity to Sweet Irish Dream makes it a great warm up—and the only place to enjoy Guinness on tap. The large outdoor terrace is the main attraction before midnight, sometimes featuring live bands. Beer 500dr; cocktails 1000dr.

Red Bull (tel. 91 019), in the main village square, is another good place to fire up your mojo (shots 800dr) before you head out for the mother of all battles.

Scorpion Disco, on the perimeter of town, on the way to the beach. Techno techno a go go. Shake your electric tailfeather at this crazy dance emporium. 1000dr cover after 2am includes your first drink.

Shooters (tel. 91 131), next to the main square, features erotic pics on the walls and Dionysiacs dancing on the bar. Cocktails 1000dr; shots 800dr.

Fun Pub (tel. 92 022), on the main road just beyond the supermarket. Restaurant and bar playing the latest movies to entertain or rescue you from unwanted conversation while you drink. Beer 600dr; cocktails 800dr.

Lemon Club (tel. 91 036), by the square, sports a small stage with mirrors, poles, and A/C. Cheap beer (500dr), White Russians (1000dr), and different music every night panders to the fickle tastes of the rabble.

Other clubs worth checking out are **Disco 69,** as well as **The Parachute** and for those seeking more of a ravish feel **Upside Down** and **Anjuna.**

SIGHTS

With the exceptions of a solitary monastery, some castle ruins, a modest pile of rubble at the north tip of the island reputed to be **Homer's tomb,** and the ancient town on the hill to the left of Hora, the **beaches** are the place to be on Ios. If you feel like repenting the night's excess at the monastery go to the windmills above the village and find the path near the top of the hill (take water if you're already dehydrated).

CYCLADES

Most head for **Mylopotas Beach** on foot (roughly 20min. downhill from Ios town) or by bus service from the port or village (daily 8am-1am, 220dr). The beach, like the town, has loudspeakers blasting everywhere. The outer reaches offer a modicum of privacy. The farther you go, the fewer clothes you will see (or wear). **Watersports** are available at the shack on the beach—look for the yellow *Body Glove* flags; windsurf (2000dr per hr.), water-ski (3000dr per hr.), or snorkel (800dr per hour).

Of course, there are prettier and less crowded beaches on Ios. If you continue uphill from the OTE, look for the path that leads down to the secluded beach and crystal pool of water at the little **Kolitsani** bay (a 15-min. walk from Hora). Excursions leave daily for the **nude** beach at beautiful **Manganari Bay,** stopping—appropriately enough—at the monastery (11am, return 6pm, 2000dr). **Nudist,** secluded **Psathi** on the eastern coast is a 7km walk along donkey trails. An excursion goes to Psathi several times per week, stopping at the castle ruins (11am, return 6pm, 2000dr). Other **nude** beaches include **Koubara** (2km walk north from the port) and **Ag. Theodoti** near Psathi.

SANTORINI Σαντορινη

Plunging cliffs, burning black sand beaches, and deeply scarred hills make Santorini's landscape as dramatic as the cataclysm that created it. Even those with no interest in Santorini's intriguing past will find ample delights in its present—long stretches of beach, whitewashed towns strewn against cliffs rising sharply out of the Aegean, and spectacular landscapes forged by centuries of volcanic activity. Blessed with a soil enriched with volcanic minerals, Santorini is the greenest of the otherwise barren Cyclades; endless vineyards attest to the island's love of winemaking, a passion second only to the island's biggest industry—tourism. The black beaches, stark against cobalt waters, and the searing-hot fields of pumice are unique in their beauty among the Greek islands, as is the sheer power of the technicolor sunsets over the island's western caldera.

According to Greek mythology, Santorini arose from a clod of earth given by the sea god Triton to the Argonauts. First inhabited by the Phoenicians, by 2000 BC the island was a prodigious outpost of the Minoan society, then called Thira. Around 1450 BC, a massive volcanic eruption buried every sign of civilization beneath tons of lava and pumice. In the centuries since, fact and fiction have mingled, leading some to believe that Santorini is Plato's lost continent of Atlantis. More serious historical speculation has convinced many scholars that the eruption on Santorini triggered a tidal wave large enough to account for the destruction of several Minoan sites in Crete. Another erup-

tion in 1956 caused serious damage to much of the island; the skeletons of many buildings destroyed by this blast are still visible within the presently thriving community.

Modern Santorini is only the eastern crescent of what was once a circular island, originally called Strongili (round). The ancient eruption left a crust of volcanic ash stretching over the hollow center of the island. When the crust caved in, water filled the resulting caldera (basin) that is now Santorini's harbor. The two islands to the west, **Thirasia** and **Aspronisi,** separated by water, are in fact a continuation of the original island's rim.

■ The Ports

Santorini is easily accessible and incredibly crowded. Boats dock at one of three ports: Athinios, Fira, or Oia. **Athinios** is the most important and has frequent buses (30min., at least 20 per day, 340dr) to Fira and Perissa Beach. Hostel-bound travelers can board the free shuttle bus to Thira Youth Hostel, Perissa Youth Hostel, or Youth Hostel Perissa-Anna. It is also possible to get free rides from the pension proprietors at the port. The port of **Fira** is down a 587-step footpath from the town, where cruise boats stay for the afternoon and boats leave on caldera tours. The cable car departs every 20 minutes, from 6:40am to 10pm, and costs 800dr. You can also hire a mule for the same price.

Ferries depart for Anafi (2hr., 5 per week, 1900dr); Ios (1½hr., 4-8 per day, 1700dr); Mykonos (7hr., 4 per day, 3600dr); Naxos (4hr., 4-8 per day, 3000dr); Paros (4hr., 4-8 per day, 3200dr); Peiraias (9hr., 4-8 per day, 6100dr); Sikinos (6 per week, 1900dr); Syros (8hr., 4 per week, 4300dr). Three ferries per week go to: Folegandros (1½hr., 1900dr); Milos (4hr., 3900dr); Serifos (3335dr); Sifnos (4hr., 3200dr); and Thessaloniki (15hr., 10100dr). Two per week go to: Iraklion (4hr., 3390dr); Kithos (5hr., 4000dr); and Rhodes (16hr., 6200dr). One per week goes to: Karpathos (11hr., 4800dr); Kassos (10-12hr., 4000dr); and Skiathos (12hr., 7790dr). **Flying Dolphins** serve Amorgos (4493dr); Ios (3227dr); Mykonos (6756dr); Naxos (5765dr); Paros (6210dr); Rafina (9403dr); Syros (8017dr); and Tinos (7852dr). Olympic Airways has daily flights to: Athens (21,600dr); Mykonos (15,400dr); Iraklion (15,000dr); Rhodes (21,900dr); and Thessaloniki (29,100dr). All prices—especially those for Dolphins and Olympic Airways—vary greatly with port, company, discount packages, class, wind, weather, etc.

Renting a moped may be the ideal way to travel around the island. During the summer, however, Santorini becomes densely crowded and moped dealers rent bikes to just about anyone. Inexperienced riders, poor bikes, and carefree drivers create a dangerous combination. If you choose to ride, make sure you are satisfied with the bike's quality, and be cautious. Travel by foot or bus (Santorini's service is excellent) may be a better option. The least painful choice is a half- (3000dr) or full-day (4500dr) bus tour. **Kamari Tours** (tel. 31 390 or 31 455), with offices all over the island, is reputable. Other agencies may offer student discounts. There is a severe **water shortage** on Santorini; fresh water accounts for the high cost of rooms on the island.

■ Fira Φηρα

The center of activity on the island is the capital city, **Fira**, pronounced Fee-rah by Greeks. Some say that the harbor below the town plunges into a bottomless abyss leading to the door between heaven and hell; stepping off the bus from the port into the mess of glitzy shops, whizzing mopeds, and scads of tourists, first-time visitors have been known to wonder aloud whether hell has begun to leak through that portal. Fortunately, the ugly roadside strip and mopeds screaming into the night constitute only one aspect of this multi-faceted town. Although tourism has made it almost too easy to find a hamburger or wiener schnitzel, Fira's simple pristine beauty and honest Greek food still prevail. Fira is perched on a cliff, and the short walk to the *caldera* (the town's western edge) reveals a stunning view of the harbor. Santorini's coastline, the neighboring islands, and its volcano make it a popular site for weddings and honeymoons. For all the kitsch and over-crowding, nothing can destroy the pleasure of wandering among the narrow cobbled streets, inspecting the craft shops, and arriving at the western edge of town in time to watch the sunset.

ORIENTATION

Facing the street with the bus station behind you, walk right and uphill (north) to **Theotokopoulou Square,** full of travel agencies, banks, and restaurants. At the fork in the road, the street on the right is **25th Martiou St.,** the main paved road leading from the square north towards Oia, on which can be found Fira's youth hostel as well as

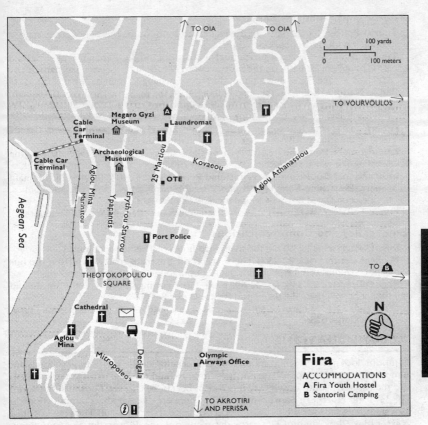

TO OIA   TO OIA

0 ____ 100 yards
0 ____ 100 meters

TO VOURVOULOS

Cable Car Terminal

Megaro Gyzi Museum
Laundromat

Cable Car Terminal

Archaeological Museum

25 Martiou
Kovaeou
OTE

Agiou Athanassiou

Aegean Sea

Agiou Mina
Marinatou
Erythrou Stavrou
Ypapantis

Port Police

THEOTOKOPOULOU SQUARE

TO B

Cathedral

Agiou Mina

Micropoleos
Decigala

N

Olympic Airways Office

Fira
ACCOMMODATIONS
A Fira Youth Hostel
B Santorini Camping

TO AKROTIRI AND PERISSA

CYCLADES

other accommodations. Head from the left branch north of the bus stop to 25th Martiou and turn on to any westbound street to find back streets with many of the best bars, stores, and discos. Farther west is the caldera, where expensive restaurants and art galleries are overshadowed only by the spectacular view.

PRACTICAL INFORMATION

Transportation

Airplanes: Olympic Airways (tel. 22 660). From the bus depot, go downhill (south) on the main road, across from the post office. Reserve tickets 1-2 weeks in advance. Standby tickets are possible (arrive 2hr. before take-off), but book as soon as you know you're flying. Office open daily 7:30am-11pm.

Buses: To Akrotiri (30min.; every hr. 9am-8pm; 360dr); Athinios (15min.; 6:45, 8am, noon, 3, 6, 8pm; 350dr); Kamari (20min.; 40 per day; 240dr); Oia (30min.; about 18 per day; 260dr); Perissa (30min.; 7:15am, then every 2hr. 8am-11pm; 380dr); and to the airport (30min.; 7:15am, then every 2hr. 10am-6pm; 240dr).

Taxis: (tel. 22 555) in Theotokopoulou Sq.

Moped and Car Rental: Universal Car Rental (tel. 24 411), south of the main square. 11,000dr per day. Unlimited mileage. Insurance included. For mopeds, try **Marcos Rental** (tel. 23 877), 50m north of the square. 3000dr per day; 2500dr per day for extended rentals. Helmets included. Open daily 8am-7pm.

Tourist and Financial Services

Tourist Police: (tel. 22 649) On the main road south of the bus depot. They share a building with the **police.** Open 24hr.

Tourist Agencies: Dozens surround Theotokopoulou Sq. **Pelican Travel** (tel. 22 220, 23 667, or 22 940), on the northwestern corner of the square, has particularly efficient service. Ticketing on-line. Currency exchange. Open daily 8am-10pm.

Banks: National Bank, on the road branching off the main road south of the square, offers currency exchange. Open M-F 8am-2pm. **Agricultural Bank** and **Commercial Bank** also exchange currency. Both open M Th 8am-2pm, F 8am-1.30pm.

American Express: In the office of **X-Ray Kilo Travel and Shipping Agency** (tel. 22 624) in the square. All AmEx services. Open daily 8am-11pm.

Laundromats: Penguine (tel. 22 168), on the main street, north of the square on the left. For 5kg, wash 1050dr, dry 950dr, soap 200dr. Open daily 7:30am-midnight.

International Bookstore: International Press (tel. 25 301), located in the main square. Everything from *Vogue, Men's Health* in multiple languages, and comics, to books on David Bowie. Open daily 8:30am-midnight.

Public Toilets: 25th Martiou St., down and across the street from the bus depot.

Emergency and Communications

Port Police: (tel. 22 239) On the main road north of Theotokopoulou Sq.

Medical Center: (tel. 22 237) The first left off the main road down from the bus depot. Handles routine problems 9am-2:30pm; open for **emergencies** 24hr.

Post Office: (tel. 22 238; fax 22 698). On 25th Martiou St. between the square and the bus stop. Open M-F 8am-3pm. **Postal Code:** 84700.

OTE: (tel. 22 135) north of square on the main road. Open daily 8am-3pm. **Telephone Code:** 0286.

ACCOMMODATIONS

Santorini does not lack accommodations, but in summer the pensions and hotels are almost all booked by noon. The cheapest options, and the best bet if you arrive late, are the (non-HI) youth hostels in Fira, Perissa Beach, or Oia; see **Southern Santorini** (p. 337) and **Northern Santorini** (p. 339). There are also good accommodations in private homes all over the island, so don't hesitate to branch out. The settlement of **Karterados,** 2km south of Fira, provides many options. Private doubles in outlying towns run as low as 2500dr. Head for **Karterados, Messaria, Pyrgos, Emborio,** or any of the small inland towns along the main bus routes. Some hawkers at the port misrepresent their rooms, so be clear about where you are going and what you are getting. In Fira, doubles run roughly 11,000-13,000dr from May through September, except from late July through August, when rates may increase by as much as 50%.

Thira Youth Hostel (tel. 22 387 or 23 864), on the left roughly 300m north of the square, set back 25m from the road to Oia. Clean, quiet dorm rooms, a few even quieter "small dormitories," and pension-quality private rooms with baths. Large courtyard for lounging. Good views. Hot showers 24hr., but bring your own toilet paper. Dorms 1500dr; doubles 5000-8000dr. Sheets 200dr; pillowcase 100dr. Reception open 24hr. Owner enforces quiet after 11pm. No smoking in dorm rooms. Check-out noon. Open Apr.-Oct.

Pension Petros (tel. 22 573; fax 22 615), one of a line of new, clean, and nearly identical pensions lining the road to Santorini Camping, 1 block east of the main square. The owner of the pension, Petros, has five adorable daughters, and often shares stories and bottles of his homemade wine with travelers, lending a family atmosphere to the place. All rooms with bath. Fridges in most rooms. Free transportation to and from the port. Doubles and triples 7000-8000dr. If this is full, check out **Villa Anemone,** also owned by Petros, 400m east.

Hotel Leta (tel. 22 540 or 23 903). Walking toward Oia, follow the signs and arrows off to the right. If you hit the Backpacker's Bar, you've gone too far. Doubles and triples upstairs are all clean, with bath and fridge. Doubles 7000dr; triples 9000dr. The rooms downstairs are simpler but just as nice, with bath (2500dr per person).

Santorini Camping (tel. 22 944 or 25 062; fax 25 065). Follow the blue signs leading east of the square. Lively atmosphere and shady campsites make this a great option for those who don't mind sleeping on the ground, with swimming pool free for campers, and a cafe, bar, and minimarket on the premises. In June, 1000dr per person; 650dr per tent. 200dr per tent rental. 600dr per car; 400dr per motorbike. Hot showers 5-9pm. Washing machine 1200dr (soap included). Reception open 24hr. Quiet hours midnight-8am. Open Apr.-Oct.

FOOD

⊛Nikolas Taverna (tel. 24 550). Head uphill on the side street on the northwestern corner of the square (next to Pelican Travel), then take the first right at the Hotel Tataki. The *taverna* will be bustling with pleased diners on your right. Decipher the Greek-only menu, or choose blindly—you can't go wrong. Try the excellent beef stew with noodles (1500dr), stuffed tomatoes (900dr), or stuffed *kalamari* (2200dr), and top it off with a small glass of *raki,* a traditional Greek dessert wine guaranteed to knock your socks off (300dr).

Restaurant Poseidon (tel. 25 480), down the stairs next to the taxi stand in the main square. Rumored to have the best *tzatziki* on the island, Poseidon serves enormous portions of excellent Greek food, and all entrees come with 2 side dish helpings. *Moussaka* (1200dr), *soutsoukakia* (Greek meatballs served with tomato sauce, 1300dr). 200dr cover for dinner. Open daily 7am-1am.

Taverna Simos (tel. 23 815), a 5min. walk uphill from the OTE. An overwhelmingly varied list of inexpensive appetizers may keep you from ordering a main course. Grilled red peppers (400dr), *dolmades,* stuffed vine leaves (500dr), and the local speciality *fava* (500dr). Live Greek music daily. Open daily noon-1am.

Mama's Breakfast Cafe (tel. 24 211). Head north on the road to Oia, on the left side. Legitimately advertised as the best American breakfast, perhaps in all of Greece. Mama is a character, a one-in-a-million bundle of energy you must witness to believe. Homesick American travelers will find comfort in the down-home fare and the warm atmosphere. Stuff yourself on Mama's special: 2 pancakes, 2 eggs, bacon, toast, and coffee (1100dr, free coffee refills). Maple syrup smothers the stack. Open daily 8am-1pm.

To Limanakitou Vourvoulou. Follow the signs to Vourvoulou Beach. A diamond in the rough—it takes effort and an adventurous spirit to find, but is worth the U-turns and dead-end streets. This fish *taverna* is authentic and inexpensive, an excellent combination of great food and warm hospitality. Not too many tourists make it out here—don't make the same mistake. Open daily noon-midnight.

Popou (tel. 24 184), overlooking the caldera across the path from the Tropical Club. A seemingly out-of-place, dream-like candy store decorated with huge tubes of every kind of sugary concoction imaginable. Take a plastic bag and start scooping (420dr per 100g). 14 varieties of licorice. Open daily 10am-midnight.

Poldo, up the street from the banks. Excellent, cheap vegetarian entrees such as falafel (700dr), *tabouli* (700dr), and hummus (800dr). Large and small (400dr) gyros for all starving carnivores. Open 24hr.

Sphynx (tel. 23 823). If you feel the gentle pull towards cloth napkins, water in a wine glass, and a prime view of the orange-gelati-colored sunset, gravitate towards this caldera-side restaurant just north of Hotel Atlantis. Don't miss the large and succulent artichoke and feta cheese in dill cream sauce (200dr); move on to the spaghetti *putanesca* (2900dr) or the fresh swordfish (5200dr). Savor a fine wine as the caldera grows dark and the glass lanterns come out. Reserve a table in high season. Credit cards accepted. Open daily noon-3pm and 6pm-12:30am.

Kastro's Cafeteria & Bar. Take in a cappucino with the view and order an omelet, or a filling club sandwich (1400dr). The menu offers lighter, less pricey fare than that of its sister restaurant, which is also available for perusal. Open daily 8am-2am.

ENTERTAINMENT

The bars are for early birds; after 2am, discos take over for some of the most intense, chic scenes in Greece.

CYCLADES

Kira Thira Jazz Club (tel. 22 770), across from Nikolas Taverna, on a side street parallel to the main road out of town. Mellow out to jazz while sipping a gin fizz or a piña colada (both 2000dr). The Jazz Club has been around since 1975, and not much has happened to change the place except an improvement of the sound system. The brass hangs from the ceiling and the regulars kiss the DJ goodnight. Open daily 9pm-late.

Tithora Club (tel. 23 519), practically in the center of the main square, is the place for hard rock and headbanging beats. Buy a beer (800dr) or a cocktail (1500dr) and you may get free shots for the rest of the night in the setting of ancient Fira. Exceptionally friendly and jovial management and staff. Outdoor bar to serve those waiting in line. 1500dr cover includes your first drink. Open daily 10pm-4am.

Backpacker's Bar (mobile tel. 0941-39323). This is where most budget travelers begin their evening, pin their hometown on the map, and sing along to the best of the '70s and '80s. Dirt-cheap drinks (pint beer 600dr, cocktails 800dr) ensure you'll be weaving to the next stop of your evening. Located near Thira Youth Hostel. Open daily 8pm-late.

Tropical Club (tel. 23 089). High up on the caldera, a native Californian mixes signature cocktails that are as tasty as they are creative (1800dr). "Sunset coffees" like the Bob Marley *frappé*—dark rum, Kahlua, iced coffee, and cream—go well with the breathtaking sunset views over the caldera. Arrive by 8pm for prime seating on the balcony (open daily noon-4am).

Blue Note (tel. 24 211), across the street from the Backpacker's Bar. A place to sit at the bar with a beer (700dr) and watch tipsy tourists bust a move to "Walk This Way" and other American rock favorites. Outdoor seating, low lighting indoors, clientele of all ages. (Shots 800dr, nightly special cocktail 800dr.) 2 for 1 cocktails during Happy Hour 9:30-11pm.

Koo Club (tel. 22 025) and **Enigma** (tel. 22 466). Catering to a young local crowd, these are the clubs at which to be seen and be European chic. The clubs face each other across the street; each crank into the wee hours and charge high covers (1000-3000dr depending on the season), with drinks priced to match. Even so, the outdoor decks are cool places to watch the steam rise on the dance floors inside.

Trip into the Music (tel. 23 623), next door to Kira Thira Jazz Club. Plays a variety of tunes (including new British rock) that keep its dance floor crowded. Beers 800dr, cocktails 1700dr. First beer included in 1000dr cover. Open daily 10pm-late.

Two Brothers Bar (tel. 23 060), next to Poldo up the street from the banks. Serves a more personal, relaxed crowd of both locals and tourists of all ages. Be sure to try a watermelon shot when you receive your one-shot-free card at the door, but don't miss the great deal on beer (700dr). Open daily 9pm-late.

Lava Club (tel. 22 248), next to Enigma. An intimate environment that pulsates with techno and earnest, tightly-clad dancers. Cover 1000dr gets you a first drink for 500dr. Beer 1500dr.

Town Club (tel. 22 820), next to Lava Club. Small room with a castle motif and pumping techno. Shots 1000, beer 1000dr, cocktails 1500dr.

SIGHTS

Just steps away from the **cable cars** you'll find Fira's **archaeological museum** (tel. 22 217) *(Open T-Su 8am-3pm. Admission 800dr, students 400dr.)* It holds an impressive array of vases, figurines, and statues, mostly from the site of Ancient Thira. The private **Megaro Gyzi Museum** (tel. 23 077) is housed in a restored Santorinian mansion just northwest of Thira Youth Hostel. *(Open May-Oct. M-Sa 10:30am-1:30pm and 5-8pm, Su 10:30am-4:30pm. Admission 500dr, students 200dr.)* It has an engrossing collection of old maps, engravings, and Greek island photographs; a few steps away is the **icon workshop,** where Catherine Ioannidou recreates religious imagery painted on wood. The museum hosts several classical music concerts and temporary art exhibitions in July and August. As you head south on the main road, you'll find **The Greek Cultural/ Conference Center and Library** (tel. 24 960), on the side street before the post office. *(Open daily 9am-2pm and 6-9pm; in winter 9am-2pm and 5-9pm.)* Recently opened to provide free public lectures, concerts, and exhibitions, it is the island's only library.

CYCLADES

■ Southern Santorini

Akrotiri

The archaeological site of **Akrotiri** is a powerful experience cloaked in heavy silence. *(Open daily 8:30am-2:30pm. Admission 1200dr, students 600dr. Guidebook 1200dr.)* In 1967, Professor Marinatos uncovered the paved streets of Akrotiri, lined with houses connected by a sophisticated central drainage system. Each house had at least one room decorated with wall paintings, some of which are among the most magnificent in Greece. Since no valuables were found in the city, a common theory is that everyone escaped before the eruption of the island's volcano in 1450. The less adventurous folks tag along with the guided tours, but this once-bustling town hits hardest when seen at a more pensive pace. Signs keep the visitor well-informed, though the guidebook is helpful and comprehensive. One emerges from the tin-roofed site (excavations are still underway) blinking in the sun and pleasantly disoriented. Fifteen buses per day run here from Fira (350dr). Bus tours (4000-4500dr) are available through a travel agency which couple this site with a visit to Profitis Ilias Monastery in Pyrgos and a local wine-tasting.

Pyrgos and Ancient Thira

Buses to Perissa stop in lofty **Pyrgos,** a town surrounded by medieval walls. *(Open Tu-Su 8am-3:30pm. Free.)* Once a Venetian fortress, the town was conquered by the Ottomans, who remained here until 1828. The village's 25 blue- and green-domed churches dot the horizon. The **Profitis Ilias Monastery,** a 20-minute hike up the mountain from Pyrgos, graciously shares its site with a radar station. On July 20, the monastery hosts the **Festival of Profitis Ilias.** From Profitias Ilias, it is approximately a one-hour hike to the ruins of **Ancient Thira.** The ancient theater, church, and forum of the island's old capital are still visible, though less spectacular than the Akrotiri excavations. Cheerful, whitewashed **Emborio,** some 3km inland from Perissa, has frequent bus connections to the beach and to Fira.

Perissa

One of the two most frequented black sand beaches of Santorini's southeast coast, Perissa is farther from Fira than Kamari, it's counterpart; of the two, the beach town is also the more popular of the two with students, offering a youth hostel, nearby camping, and a casual nightlife. The black sand sizzles in the sun—a straw mat and sandals are welcome accessories. It is easily accessible by bus.

 Youth Hostel Perissa-Anna (tel. 82 182; fax 81 943), 500m along the road leading out of town, provides clean women's and mixed dorms, private rooms, cooking facilities, proximity to the market, solar-heated fresh spring water showers, use of a nearby pool, and free safety deposit boxes. (Dorms 1000dr, 2000dr in high season; private rooms 2000dr per person, 4000dr in high season. Hot showers 9am-9pm. Luggage storage 200dr. Linen 200dr; 24hr. reception. Checkout 11:30am.) **Stelio's Place** is a four-minute walk from the square: from the road leading out of town, turn left just before two side-by-side travel agencies, and find it 50m down on your left. Just recently opened, Stelio's offers 15 spic-and-span rooms, all with private bath, fridge, and access to common kitchen and a welcoming pool. Transportation to and from the airport and port are provided. (May-July and Sept. 2000dr per person; Aug. 4000dr per person. Reservations recommended.)

 Enormous **Perissa Camping** (tel. 81 343 or 81 686; fax 81 604) is right off the main hub, adjacent to the beach, in one of the few tree-covered spots on the island, and offers a beach bar, minimarket, kitchen facilities, very clean restrooms, discounts on nearby scuba package deals, and a restaurant serving traditional Cretan meals (snails 1400dr). Some sites are overused. (1300dr per person; 800dr per tent.) Check-out is at 1pm. **Rooms-to-let** in private homes (you'll meet the proprietors at the dock) offer more privacy (doubles 6000-8000dr).

 The delicious calzones, pizza, and pasta at **Bella Italiana** (tel. 82 671), near the end of the main road will make your taste buds hot for more. Over 10 varieties of each are prepared by an Italian chef who knows what he's doing. Try the house speciality pizza—the Bella Italiana—for ham, bacon, mushrooms, green peppers, and cheese piled on a thin crust (1650dr; open daily 11am-1am). Across the street, the **Full Moon Bar** (tel. 81 177) is the only spot on the island that serves Guinness on tap (1000dr). From 11am to 4am, you can listen to the Stones and the Doors, watch MTV, Euro-sport, or CNN, while sipping on 1500dr cocktails, 1000dr mixed drinks, or a 500dr Amstel. Half-price drinks are served during Happy Hour (all day until 11pm). DJs slam a funky beat every night; jazz bands sometimes play during high season (open daily 8am-4am). Next door, **Santo Food** (tel 82 983), crams french fries, tzatziki, and onions into its *souvlaki* (450dr); breakfast and vegetarian sandwiches are also served (open 24hr.).

A path at the base of the mountain between Perissa and Kamari leads to a small church built into the rock several hundred feet up. Huff and puff your way up to a wonderful view and light a candle, or continue up to Ancient Thira.

Kamari

Although referred to as a black sand beach, Kamari beach is actually covered in black pebbles, and the slippery seaweed-covered rock bottom makes wading especially dif-ficult. Upscale shops line the waterfront; the long beach is covered in umbrellas and lined with pricey hotels, cafes, and travel agencies. Forty buses per day travel from Fira (240dr), and a rocky **shuttle boat** scoots between Kamari and Perissa (every 30min. or whenever a boatload has gathered, 9am-5pm, 1000dr). The boat is conve-nient because the towns are separated by a mountain.

All over town, doubles range from 10,000-24,000dr. Contact **Kamari Tours** (tel. 31 390) or stop in the office on the waterfront if you have any questions or need assis-tance. The **Pension Golden Star** is on the road that goes inland from the beach at the Yellow Donkey Disco. It has clean double rooms with balconies (8000dr). Take the next side street inland to reach **Hotel Preka Maria** (tel. 31 266; fax 31 266), where you can rent spotless doubles (9000-12,000dr), or furnished apartments (16,000dr). All rooms include a refrigerator, music, a bath, and a cooking sink. Check-out is at noon. **Kamari Camping** (tel. 31 453), 1km inland along the main road out of town, is open June through September (1200dr per person; 1000dr per tent).

To pick up an inexpensive snack along the waterfront, head to **Ariston** (tel. 32 603). Betwixt the touristy restaurants and *souvlaki* shops, this bakery and small gro-cery sells fresh loaves of bread (50dr) and raisin bread twists (250dr; open daily 6:30am-11pm). The winery **Canava Roussos** (tel. 31 954 or 31 278), 1km from Kamari Camping, will both wine and dine you with red, white, and rose *bougan-villa*. Try the house favorite *mavrathiko*, a sweet wine with a port-like taste, made with red grapes instead of the traditional white, for a lovely afternoon break (100dr per glass; open daily 10am-8pm). The **Yellow Donkey Disco** (tel. 31 462) is one of the busier clubs along the waterfront of Kamari Beach. It's often crowded with people who come from all over the island to enjoy the 1500dr cocktails that come with a free shot. The owner Theo offers to teach Greek dances to all those eager (or inebriated) enough to learn (open daily 9pm-late).

Monolithos

Those who prefer sandier beaches might want to check out **Monolithos Beach.** More popular with locals than with tourists, this small beach is easily accessible due to its proximity to the airport (15 buses per day, 230dr). If you want a bite to eat, the fish *taverna* **Skaramagas** (tel. 31 750) is the least expensive on the strip. The owners catch the fresh seafood, keep what they need for the restaurant and sell the rest to other establishments. Many locals come here for lunch several times a week to enjoy the famed fish soup *kakavia* (1500dr), *kalamari* (1200dr), and great Greek salads (800dr; open daily May-Oct. 11am-midnight).

■ Oia Οια

Oia (pronounced EE-ah), is an intricate cliffside town on the northwestern tip of the island, famous for its dazzling sunsets and a fascinating mixture of devastation and renewal. The 1956 earthquake leveled this small town on the island's rocky north point. Its present 600 inhabitants have carved new dwellings into the cliffside among the shattered ruins of the old. The narrow cobblestone streets are peaceful and free of cars and mopeds. Although the budget traveler will not thrive long in Oia, an afternoon visit affords enough time to wander the cobbled streets, window-shop at exquisite jewelry, craft, and embroidery shops, and glance at the menus of elegant restaurants before taking in the riveting sunset. A 20-minute climb down 252 stone stairs at the end of the main road leads down to rocky **Ammoudi** beach, where a few boats are moored in a startlingly deep swimming lagoon. A few relaxing hours spent lying on the rocks, and another few swimming in the beautiful blue water, are well worth the climb back up the cliff; the sun-drenched visitor may choose to re-energize before the climb with a meal of fresh fish at one of the three *tavernas* at the bottom of the stairs, where the fish is hauled straight from the net to the table; others may choose to hire a donkey (800-1000dr per person) for a ride to the top. **Buses** run from Fira to Oia (20min., 25 per day, 260dr), and a few **ferries** dock at Oia before continuing to Fira or Athinios—check when you buy your ticket.

In Oia, the Karvounis family can help meet all your tourist needs. **Karvounis Tours** (tel. 71 290, 71 291 or 71 292; fax 71 291) answers questions about Oia and Santorini as a whole, in addition to selling both ferry and airline tickets. The family's **Youth Hotel Oia** (tel. 71 465; fax 71 291) is the classiest of Santorini's youth hostels. Built as a hostel in 1989, the rooms and courtyard are spacious, with clean bathrooms and large mirrors for each room. The location boasts a superb view from its roof terrace and a bar that is open for both breakfast and evening drinks. (Dorms 3000-3500dr, full breakfast included. Rooms single-sex or mixed. Free safety deposit boxes. Hot water 24hr. Check-out 10am. Wheelchair accessible. Reservations recommended in the high season.) It is possible to find rooms and houses to let, but short-term arrangements are difficult to come by; most proprietors expect a stay of at least five days.

Likewise, dining will cost you a bit more than in Fira, but some restaurants serve exceptional food. At the end of the main road in Oia, overlooking the caldera, is **Petros** (tel. 71 263), the oldest restaurant in Oia. Ask for the fresh fish soup, or try any of the outstanding seafood (including *stifado* octopus with onions, tomato, and garlic); the Santorinian tomato balls are especially delicious in June and July, when Santorini's fresh cherry tomatoes are available (900dr). Fresh, savory seafood is always grilled to perfection (*kalamari* 1200dr), while old Greek recipes provide a pleasant alternative to the common *moussaka,* and Petros Jr. continues the family tradition of making homemade wines. If you are traveling in the winter months, stop by **Thalami Taverna** (tel. 71 009), also operated by Petros Jr. Just up the street, it serves up live music with fare similar in price to **Petros.** The Karvounis' **Neptune** (tel. 71 294), located in the main square near the church, serves traditional Greek specialities, including a lamb lemon special (1600dr; "good enough to kill for," raves one patron), rich *dolmades* served piping hot, and veal in *risolto* (1700dr; open daily 1-3pm and 6pm-12:30am). **Restaurant Lotza** (tel. 71 357) has been serving lunch with a view since 1982. Time-tested favorites include curried chicken (1700dr), shish-kebab (1600dr), yogurt with walnuts and fruit (1800dr), and a drink of ouzo (700dr), all perfect to ease you into an afternoon slumber. (Open daily 9am-late.) **Cafe Greco** (tel. 71 014) has *gyros* in pita for 500dr (open daily 11am-1am). There is a small **grocery/bakery** (tel. 71 121) close to the square in which the buses stop. Follow the signs to the bakery for fresh loaves (250dr), and croissants and pies (170-350dr; open M-Sa 7am-9pm, Su 7am-2pm). On your way out of town, stop by **Santorini Mou I Love You,** a restaurant where the owner strums his guitar along with other music acts, 1km along the road back to Fira.

CYCLADES

■ Thirasia and Surrounding Islands

When the sweet hum of mopeds becomes a grating roar, grab your sunscreen and take an afternoon hiatus to Santorini's unspoiled junior partner, Thirasia. Built along the island's upper ridge, the villages of **Manolas** and **Potamos** have spine-tingling views of Santorini's western coast. Organized tour groups dock at one of two ports—Korfos or Reeva. From Korfos, the villages can only be reached by climbing a steep flight of 300 steps, though donkey rides (800dr) are available if the walk looks unbearable. Reeva, however, provides a paved road leading up to both villages. Reward yourself at the top with a large Greek salad and wonderful homemade bread at **Taverna Cadouni** (tel. 29 083).

If you desire an extended stay of quiet, visit the island's one hotel, **Hotel Cavo Mare** (tel. 29 121; fax 29 176). It offers a restaurant, pool, and doubles with bath for 10,000dr, and a bite at the restaurant includes a dip in the pool.

Excursions to Thirasia are often coupled with trips to the **volcanic crater** and **hot springs,** where one can billy-goat up hills of sharp lava rock and then bathe in a sea reputed to have the healing qualities of sulphur. Be warned that to get to the hot sulphur springs you'll have to swim through cold water first; to get to the volcano's crater you'll have to hike uphill for 30 minutes. Tours can be booked at travel agencies on Santorini (1500-5000dr). **Theoskepasti Agency,** in the main square in Fira, offers daily trips to the volcano for 2000dr. As with most trips, reservations should be made a day in advance.

FOLEGANDROS Φολεγανδρος

Although its name is more than a mouthful, the island of Folegandros offers a quiet alternative to some of the more hectic, touristy Cyclades. Named after the son of King Minos—who made the first footprints on the island's shores—and secluded from outside influence for many centuries due to its high rocky cliffs and inaccessible ports, Folegandros is a rich study of traditional Greek life. The island's steep hills are terraced with low, snaking stone walls worn by centuries of fierce wind, marking the strong link between land and man. There is a sense of calm to this nearly treeless island, in the silence of the jagged cliffs at sunset, the narrow cobbled streets, and the warmth of its inhabitants.

■ Hora Χωρα

ORIENTATION AND PRACTICAL INFORMATION After disembarking from the ferry, you and your luggage can board the only bus that runs up from the port **Kararostassi** to the main town in Folegandros, **Hora** (220dr). On your way up, the **post office** (open M-F 8:30am-2pm) will be on your left as you enter the village. If you get off the bus with your back to the road you just came up, most of the village, including the **Medical Center** (tel. 41 222), will be down to your left. To your right lie a few hotels and apartments and the path up to **Church of Panagia.** If you leave Pounta Square and head into town, on your left will be **Mataki Travel** (tel. 41 273 or 41 221) which sells ferry tickets to Ios, Mykonos, Naxos, and Paros, Santorini, and Sikinos, and also exchanges money.

Straight past the next two squares filled with trees, cut across right, and then down left again. A sharp right before the **market** leads to the **police** (tel. 41 249). If you continue on to the left you will come to a widening in the road where buses leave for Ano Meria (6km, 250dr). Check the posted listings for the bus, or call the one taxi on the island (tel. 41 048 or 41 094). Located by this bus stop are a few bars, and the **tourist office** (tel. 41 444; fax 41 430). As there is no bank, American Express office, or OTE office, this excellent tourist resource can take care of many of your needs including lost luggage, money exchange, boat tours, and telephone. (Open daily 10am-2pm and 5:30pm-midnight.)

Near the tourist office is one of two motor rental offices: **Venetia Motorent** (open daily 10am-2pm and 8-9pm, 5000dr per day). However, the only road dwindles away after 12km, so it may be in your best interest to traverse the island by bus or by foot. **Telephone code: 0286. Postal code: 84011.**

ACCOMMODATIONS Although it is fairly easy to find accommodations in early summer, by high season (July-Aug.) it is nearly impossible. If you wish to stay in the port Kararostassi, you can bargain with a dock hawk for rooms to let. **The Hotel Poseidon** (tel. 41 272; fax 41 008), 10m from the beach, offers terraced rooms (double 16,000 in high season, breakfast included). Up in Hora, there are many places with "Room to Let" signs. Most run about 12,000-14,000dr per night for a double in high season. **Maria's Rooms** (tel. 41 265) has a lovely view of the island and the sea (double 12,000dr, triple with kitchen 16,000dr). Down toward the port about 300m from the post office is **Pavlo's Rooms** (tel. 41232), which boasts roof sleeping with common bath for 3000dr per person, and doubles without private bath for 10,000dr. The recently finished **Meltemi Hotel** (tel. 41 328 or 41 068) has lovely rooms with private terraces, refrigerators, and tiled baths so pristine you could eat *tzatziki* off them. Take the road leading to Panagia, and Meltemi will be on your right 30m from Pounta Square (doubles 15,000dr; triples 17,000dr).

FOOD *Tavernas* abound and it is easy to keep yourself nourished and hydrated. Several fresh fruit and bread markets line the road up from Kararostassi. **Meltemi Restaurant,** by the port bus station, has good fresh fish. In Hora, taste the *fava,* a dip of ground beans (500dr) or the roast chicken (800dr) at **Nikos Cafe Restaurant** (tel. 41 179; open daily 5pm-late). The **Folegandros Snack Bar** (tel. 41 226), across from Makari Travel, serves excellent dishes speedily; here Nikolas the bionic proprietor provides vegetarian options, milk shakes, games, books, maps, and information on the island. Top off your meal with a special shot of Metaxa, *raki,* or *ouzo*—which Nikolas pours down patrons' throats as crowds cheer (open daily 6:30am-late). When the craving for rabbit or octopus becomes too strong to ignore head to **Melissa's Restaurant** (tel. 41 067), between the snack bar and the tourist office. Also try the lamb with lemon sauce (1600dr) or, if you're feeling adventurous, *kokoretsi*—sheep bowels on a skewer.

ENTERTAINMENT In the summer, when the island's permanent population of 650 swells to three times that size, Hora gets rocking and a few of its bars merit a knocking. **Greco,** next to the tourist office, serves up 1500dr cocktails along with techno music and backgammon. **Astaki** plays traditional Greek music, and **Aniochto** caters to a livelier crowd with rock and funk. A calm place to chat, **Kellari Wine Bar,** in Pounta Sq. next to the medical center, boasts an amazing selection of Greek wines in a small cozy stone-walled room reminiscent of a castle wine cellar. Try the dry and fruity Limnos white (700dr a glass) or rely on hostess Isabel's expertise (open 7:30am-late; live music in July and August). *Tavernas* and bars also line **Agali** and **Agios Nikolaos beaches.**

■ Around Folegandros

Folegandros may exist solely for the development of its visitors' calves; beyond Hora, the island is best explored on foot. The **Church of Panagia** (open only for religious festivals), above the town on Paliokastro hill, is an excellent place to watch the sunset. Nearby is a monastery from the 17th century. For a superb glance in to Greek life in the Ottoman period, check out the **Folklore Museum.** *(Open daily June-Aug. 5-8pm. Guidebook 2000dr.)* On an island whose history is empty of epoch-defining events, the olive presses, looms, and fishing nets reveal the secret history of a self-sufficient island whose infertile soils and tempestuous harbors never allowed for a surplus. To get to the museum, take the bus to Ano Meria and ask the driver to let you off at the folklore museum on the way.

Those who continue on to **Ano Meria** will find many footpaths to secluded beaches, including **Ampli** and **Ligaria.** The steep, winding trails—the only access to these beaches—take at least an hour each. A better option for families may be **Agali Beach,** accessible by motor and by foot. To get to the lovely (though shade-less) **Kartego Beach,** go to the port and head right as you face the water. The Folegandros tourist office offers full-day boat tours around the island stop at several beaches; inquire upon arrival. High on Paliokastro Hill is Chryssospilia ("Golden") Cave. During pirate invasions it was used as an hidden refuge, and local lore insists that there is a secret tunnel entrance connecting the cave to Panagia. The caves make a good hike destination, but entering them is dangerous.

Those planning an extended stay in Folegandros who desire a deeper understanding of the intricate workings of the island's way of life may wish to look into **The Cycladic School** (tel. 41 137; fax 41 472), run by Anne and Fotis Papadopoulous. The courses, which last from six to twelve days, focus on drawing and painting instruction, as well as theater, music, sailing, diving, history, and philosophy. Days include a lecture, practice, and excursions about the island. For more information, contact Anne and Fotis GR-840-11, Folegandros, Cyclades, Greece.

PAROS Πάρος

That hue more dazzling than Parian stone!

—Horace, *Odes 1.19.6*

Paros was famed throughout antiquity for its pure white marble, slabs of which have been sculpted into the renowned Venus de Milo and parts of Napoleon's mausoleum in Paris. Unlike their unclouded marble, the Parians didn't enjoy such a rosy reputation. When Heracles stopped over in Paros on his quest for Hippolyte's belt, two of his sailors were murdered by the sons of the local big shot, Minos of Crete. Enraged, Heracles roared loudly, slew Minos' sons, and promptly left. In the 7th century BC Greeks feared to set foot on Paros lest Archilochus, one of the earliest lyric poets and inventor of the iambic verse, lambast them with his biting satire. So intense was his mockery that a father and daughter reputedly committed suicide.

Today, Paros, the geographical center of the Greek islands and third largest of the Cyclades, gracefully absorbs the masses that arrive each summer. Paros's golden beaches and tangled whitewashed villages make the island a favorite tourist destination. More importantly, Paros has the necessary means to accommodate tourists without fully relinquishing its idyllic Cycladic atmosphere; it has struck a careful balance between new world nightlife and old world dignity.

■ Paroikia Παροικια

Behind Paroikia's commercial facade, flower-filled streets wind beneath archways, past two-story whitewashed houses, a historic basilica, and windmills. Wander through the traditional *agora* (marketplace) to find trendy clothing, dazzling jewelry, local arts and crafts, and cozy coffee houses with outdoor terraces.

ORIENTATION AND PRACTICAL INFORMATION

From the ferry, most restaurants, hotels, and offices lie to the left, as well as the town beach. Straight ahead, past the windmill and the tourist offices, is the main square, behind which a whitewashed labyrinth brims with shops and cafes. To the far right around the bend, a host of bars awaits—the island's party district.

Transportation

Buses: (tel. 21 395 or 21 133). Complete schedule posted in the shack a few blocks to the left of the windmill (facing inland). Buses run to Naoussa (15min., 20-30 per day, 240dr); Lefkes (25min., 8 per day, 250dr); Pounda (15min., 9 per day, 220dr); Aliki and the **airport** (30min., 10 per day, 290dr); Piso Livadi (40min., 8 per day, 550dr); Chrisi Akti (50min., 8 per day, 550dr); Drios (1hr., 8 per day, 550dr); Marp-

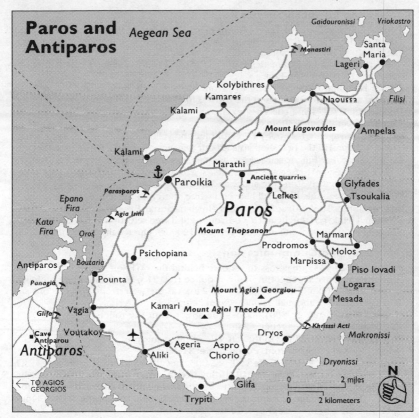

Paros and Antiparos

Aegean Sea

Gaidouronissi
Vriokastro
Monastiri
Santa Maria
Lageri
Kolybithres
Kamares
Naoussa
Filisi
Kalami
Mount Lagovardas
Ampelas
Kalami
Marathi
Ancient quarries
Paroikia
Glyfades
Parasporos
Lefkes
Tsoukalia
Epano Fira
Paros
Agia Irini
Kato Fira
Oros
Mount Thapsanon
Marmara
Prodromos
Molos
Antiparos
Boutaria
Psichopiana
Marpissa
Piso lovadi
Panagia
Pounta
Mount Agioi Georgiou
Logaras
Mesada
Glifa
Vagia
Kamari
Mount Agioi Theodoron
Cave Antiparou
Voutakov
Khrisssi Acti
Makronissi
Antiparos
Ageria
Dryos
Aliki
Aspro Chorio
Dryonissi
TO AGIOS GEORGIOS
Glifa
Trypiti

0   2 miles
0   2 kilometers

N

CYCLADES

issa (35min., 8 per day, 420dr); Kamares (20min., 2 per day, 220dr); and the Valley of the Butterflies (10min., 8 per day, 220dr).

Ferries: Sail to Peiraias (5-6hr., 6-8 per day, 4900dr); Naxos (1hr., 15 per day, 1370dr); Ios (2½hr., 8-10 per day, 2480dr); Santorini (3½hr., 10-11 per day, 3080dr); Mykonos (6-8 per day, 2hr., 1710dr); Syros (1½hr., 3-7 per day, 1620dr); Amorgos (3hr., 2-3 per day, 2740dr); Rhodes (16hr., 6 per week, 6820dr); Crete (8hr., 8 per week, 4800dr); Samos (6hr., 6 per week, 4050dr); Ikaria (4hr., 6 per week, 3050dr); Tinos (4 per day, 1800dr); Kos (4 per week, 4070dr); Sikinos (7 per week, 1940dr); Astypalea (3 per week, 4370dr); Koufonisi (3 per week, 2830dr); Folegandros (6 per week, 1920dr); and Rafina (3-4 per week, 4150dr).

Flying Dolphins: Catamarans and hydrofoils speed to Santorini (2-3 per day, 6100dr); Mykonos (3-5 per day, 3400dr); Ios (2-3 per day, 4900dr); Naxos (2-3 per day, 2700dr); Syros (4 per week, 3100dr); Rafina (9 per week, 8200dr); Tinos (2-4 per day, 3500dr); Amorgos (1 per week, 5500dr); Koufonisi (2 per week, 5423dr); and Sifnos (variable, 1920dr); Anafi (variable, 6950dr); Milos (variable, 5730dr); Folegandros (variable, 3800dr), Sikinos (variable, 3500dr), Crete (variable, 9900dr), and Andros (variable, 5500dr). **Minoan Lines** go to Peiraias (3hr., 9700dr).

Flights: Olympic Airways (tel. 22 092, 22 333), housed in the **General Travel Agency,** next to the OTE. Flights to Athens cost 18,700dr but schedules fluctuate. Taxi to the airport 2200dr; bus to Aliki (290dr).

Taxis: (tel. 22 620) Look inland and to the right of the windmill.

Tourist and Financial Services

Tourist Agency: General Travel Agency (tel. 22 092 or 22 093; fax 21 983) is next door to the OTE. Has up-to-the-minute ferry, hydrofoil, and airplane schedules. Information on buses, sights, and beaches, and free maps of the island can be obtained here or for that matter at any of the other tourist agencies which litter the streets. Open daily 8am-1am.

Banks: National Bank (tel. 21 298), from the windmill, head inland to the main square and to the right—it's in the fortress-like building at the far corner, past the playground. **ATM** and **currency exchange** machine available 24hr. Bank open M-Th 8am-2pm, F 8am-1:30pm.

Luggage Storage: (tel. 21 096). Look for blue and yellow "Left Luggage" signs across from windmill in the first shop area (200dr per piece per day). Open 8am-1am.

Laundromat: For full- or self-service, go past bus station and look for **Top** (tel. 23 424), on right just after ancient ruins. Wash, dry, soap, and folding (optional) 2000dr. Open daily 9am-2pm and 2:45-11pm.

Public Toilets: Beside the small blue and white church to the left of the windmill.

International Bookstore: M.K. Bizas (International Press; tel. 21 247) is past National Bank; go straight and it's on your right. Large selection of English-language books (1500-4000dr) and newspapers (250-1200dr). Open daily 9am-midnight.

Emergency and Communications

Police: (tel. 23 333) are across the square behind the OTE, on the 2nd floor above the photo shops. Open 24hr. **Tourist police** (tel. 21 673), in the same building. Open 9am-3:30pm. **Port Police** (tel. 21 240), off the waterfront, past the bus station. Information about all sailings. Open 24hr.

Medical Clinic: (tel. 22 500). Across the street from the toilets. Open M-F 7am-2:30pm. Open for emergencies 24hr.

Post Office: (tel. 21 236). On the left side of the waterfront, 2 blocks past the bus stop. Open M-F 7:30am-2pm. **Postal Code:** 84400.

Internet Access: Wired Cafe (tel. 22 003; fax 21 453; email Stnicolas@BIG-FOOT.com), on Market St. Virtual surfing over a cup of html java 2500dr per hr. or 12min. for 500dr. Open M-Sa 9am-11:30pm, Su 10:30am-2pm and 6-11:30pm.

OTE: (tel. 21 299) One block to the right of the windmill (facing the water). Open M-F 7:30am-2:30pm. **Telephone Code:** 0284.

ACCOMMODATIONS

There are many hotels and rooms to let near the waterfront and in the old town, but a slew of new, inexpensive pensions have opened behind the town beach. Dock hawks often offer good deals and many represent better options in Naoussa, Piso Livadi, and Antiparos. Just make sure it's not too far from where you want to be. In the off season, rooms are 30-50% less than the prices listed. The **Room Association** (tel. 24 528) by the dock offers excellent deals.

Festos Pension (tel. 21 635; fax 24 193). From the dock, walk left and diagonally back towards the church. Head for the far right corner of the main square (the church will be to your left). Look for the side street marked with an arrow and sign for "the Festos." 2500 per person. Breakfast 500dr. Friendly staff. Laundry 1000dr. Luggage storage 300dr. Check-out 10am. Reserve early.

Pelagos Studios (tel. 22 725 or 22 726; fax 22 708). Fully furnished, clean rooms with kitchen and private bath. Vasili will send you off to your next destination with a barbecue feast complete with dancing and dish breaking—that is, if you ever decide to leave. Accommodations are peaceful, despite proximity to nightlife, but solo travelers may want to know this haven lies at the end of a long, dark dirt road. Doubles 7000dr; triples 9000dr, high season 16,000-20,000dr.

Parasporos Camping (tel. 22 268 or 21 100), 1500m south of the port with shuttle service. Showers, laundry, and kitchen. 1000dr per person; 500dr per tent, 1200dr with tent.

Koula Camping (tel. 22 081, 22 082; fax 22 740), 400m north of town on the beach. Market, laundry, and kitchen. 1400dr per person; 1000dr per tent.

Rena Rooms (tel./fax 22 220 or 21 427). Turn left from the dock and take the right that leads you to Top laundromat, then take your first right and follow the signs. Bright, clean rooms, all with private bath and balcony, some with sea view. Doubles 6000dr; triples 9000dr. Reserve a few days in advance. 20% discount for *Let's Go* readers.

Nautilus Rooms (tel 21 529). Turn left from the dock walking towards the town beach and make a right at Scouna Restaurant. Nautilus is all the way down on the left side. 16 clean, quiet, cheap rooms. Doubles 5000dr; triples 7500dr. 20% discount for *Let's Go* readers.

Hotel Argonaftis (tel 21 440, 22 278 or 22 090; fax 23 442). Next to the National Bank in the old part of town. Small, clean, air conditioned rooms with bath. Reservations recommended. Doubles 10,000dr; triples 12,000dr.

FOOD

Apollo Garden Restaurant (tel. 21 875), by Hotel Dina on Market St. Savor mouth watering traditional Greek dining in an enthralling garden. Try the *panakota* dessert (sweet cheese and milk; 1500dr) or the *papon-suki* (half an eggplant smothered in beef). Open daily 5pm-1am.

Happy Green Cow (tel. 24 691), a block farther inland off the main square behind the National Bank. Delicious vegetarian food in a psychedelic setting. Stuffed potato rolls with cheese and walnuts are 2000dr. For an inexpensive, yet mouthwatering meal, the *falafels* are a great choice for 1000dr. Open daily 6pm-midnight.

To Tamarisko, near Mimikos Rooms— follow the signs. Lush flower garden, romantic setting. Traditional Greek cuisine—everything is homemade, including the menus! Excellent shrimp risotto with tomatoes and capers for 1450dr.

Levantes (tel. 23 613), near Hotel Dina on the "Market" street beyond the National Bank. Try roasted pepper rolls stuffed with feta, pine nuts, and capers (1200 dr). Open daily 6:30pm-midnight.

Nick's Hamburgers (tel. 21 434), next to Corfo Leon. Paros' first hamburger joint, established in 1977. 100% beef Nikburger 450dr; Nikfeast (2 burgers, chips, and salad) 890dr. Only place to get fish and chips (950 dr). Open daily 5-10pm.

ENTERTAINMENT

Almost all of Paros' nightspots are along the waterfront, left of the windmill. On any given night, throngs of foreigners congregate on the strip, sit in circles around *ouzo* bottles, and sing songs. There are hangouts for English-speakers on the far end of the ferry dock, just before the small white bridge. **Saloon D'Or** and **Black Bart's Cafe Bar** are especially popular—the number of travelers in these bars gives them the aura of a foreign convention gone especially rowdy. **The Slammer Bar** joined to **7 Muses Disco**, specializes in tequila slammers for 600dr—there are posted instructions for the uninitiated. The 'Parian Experience' consists of two mind-boggling party complexes which round out any night out on Paros. The larger of the two, at the far end of the strip of bars, contains under one roof **The Dubliner, Down Under, Cactus Shots Bar,** and the **Paros Rock Cafe.** Sit around or dance to any of the four tunes blaring simultaneously (beer 600-700dr; cocktails 1200dr). A little closer to town is the other boozing megaplex containing **Tequila Bar** and **Sodoma Dance Club** (beer 600-700dr; cocktails 1200dr). If you're sick of drinking, **Cine Rex** shows movies in its outdoor theater which is a fun, fun treat. Walk right along the waterfront and turn left up the diagonally slashed road. Two showings daily in English (1700dr).

SIGHTS

Panagia Ekatontapiliani
Open daily 8am-9pm. Dress appropriately: no shorts.

Anyone with a fondness for Byzantine architecture will be thrilled by the **Panagia Ekatontapiliani.** The Church of Our Lady of 100 Gates is an imposing edifice in the shape of an imperfect Greek cross that houses three separate churches, cloisters, and a large peaceful courtyard. Tradition holds that only 99 of the church's 100 doors can be counted. When the 100th door appears, Constantinople will once again belong to the Greeks. If you can't count more than 12 you probably haven't had enough *ouzo*.

The Ekatontapiliani was supposedly conceived in the 4th century when St. Helen, the mother of Constantine, stopped to pray here on her way to the Holy Land. Helen saw the True Cross in her prayers and vowed to build a church befitting the site of her vision but died before she could fulfill her promise. In the 6th century the Emperor Justinian, a devout legomaniac, commissioned a student of Isidorus of Miletus called Ignatius to build the church Helen had envisioned. Upon seeing the beauty of the completed church, Isidorus was seized by a fit of jealousy and lunged violently at his pupil, Ignatius. In the ensuing scuffle both fell to their deaths near the entrance to the narthex. The repentant architects can be seen bemoaning their fate on the sculpted bases of the columns across the courtyard. Why Isidorus, the architect of the immensely more wondrous Agia Sophia in Constantinople, would bother being jealous has no doubt never factored into this local legend's penchant for hyperbole.

The main structure of the complex is the mammoth **Church of the Assumption,** sporting three tremendous chandeliers in its interior. The **Church of Agios Nikolaos** (the oldest of the three) flanks this central structure to the north as does the **baptistry** (tel. 21 243), to the south. There are two tiny museums in the courtyard. The **Church Museum** is on the right. *(Open daily except Tu and Th 9am-1pm and 5:30-9pm. Admission 500dr.)* The **Byzantine Museum** is next to the entrance. *(Open daily 9am-1pm and 5-9pm. Admission 500dr.)*

In Paroikia

Behind the church next to the schoolyard, is the **Archaeological Museum** (tel. 21 231), which includes a 5th-century BC statue of wingless Nike and a piece of the Parian Chronicle, a history of Greece up to 264 BC engraved in marble. *(Open Tu-Su 8:30am-2:30pm. Admission 500dr, students 300dr, Su free.)* Wandering through the old town is one of the best sights Paroikia has to offer. Take a walk in the vicinity of the **Frankish Castle,** whose walls were built with marble removed from the ancient **Temple of Athena.** You can actually spot the temple's columns in the Venetian structure. To get there, turn right after the bookstore and look for it near the top of the hill. At the top of the same hill is the charming, yet eerie, Byzantine **Church of Agios Konstantinos.** If you have time for another rewarding excursion take the unpaved road behind the Archaeological Museum up to the **Agii Anargyri Monastery** for some excellent vistas. Once there be sure to sigh dramatically among the cypress groves and compose Homeric odes to the tune of the babbling fountain.

Around Paroikia

Boats run from Paroikia's harbor to **Krios, Martselo,** and **Kaminia** beaches (15min., 4 per hr., 9:30am-7pm, 360dr), all of which are relatively adequate for a bathe. The beaches south of Paroikia, **Parasporos** and **Agia Irini,** while about an hour away by bus, are calmer and more secluded.

Just 10km south of town is the cool, spring-fed **Valley of the Butterflies** *(Petaloudes),* home to an enormous swarm of brown-and-white-striped butterflies who cover the foliage, blending into their surroundings until they expose their bright red underwings in flight. *(Open M-Sa 9am-8pm, Su 9am-1pm and 4-8pm. Admission 230dr.)* In June, the butterflies converge on this lepidopterous metropolis to mate. You can visit by taking the bus from Paroikia that goes to Aliki (10min., 8 per day, 200dr). Ask to be let off at the *petaloudes.* From there, follow the signs up the steep winding road 2km to the entrance. Alternatively you could opt for a more expensive tour of the valley by donkey with the General Travel Agency (3000dr).

▓ Naoussa Ναουσσα

Naoussa is Paros' second port after Paroikia. It is a natural harbor, cradled on both sides by long, sandy arms in the shape of crab claws. Persian, Greek, Roman, Venetian, Ottoman, and Russian fleets have all anchored in the harbor. The tradition continues today as visitors from all over the world converge on Naoussa's beaches.

Although much of the town's once unspoiled Cycladic charm has been overwhelmed by this influx, a stroll along the harbor proves that beneath its touristy exterior, Naoussa remains a traditional Greek fishing village at heart.

ORIENTATION AND PRACTICAL INFORMATION Naoussa's layout is not very complicated. From the bus stop facing the water, the road heading left past the little bridge leads to the beaches of **Kolibithres** and the partly **nudist** beach of **Monastiri.** Naoussa's commercial strip flanks the town on the right. To find the police (tel. 51 202), walk left (facing the water) up the hill; turn left on the curving road before Mike's Moto Rent; at the top of the hill, turn left and it will be shortly on your left (open 24hr.). The **medical center** (tel. 24 410; open M-F 10am-2pm and 5-10pm) is on the commercial strip, directly across from the Zorbas restaurant. In an emergency, call the doctor at home (tel. 093 53 06 88 or 24 410). Farther down on the left is the **General Bookstore** (tel. 51 532), which sells English books (open daily 9:30am-11:30pm). You will find the **post office** (tel. 21 236) 400m down the same road, just past the Santa Maria turn-off (open M-F 7:30am-2pm). The **pharmacy** (tel. 51 550, for emergencies 51 004) is on the main street inland (open M-Sa 8:30am-2:30pm and 5:30-11pm, Su 10am-2:30pm and 5:30-11pm). Polyglot pharmaceutical junkies rejoice! The staff speaks French, English, German, and Italian. The **National Bank** is along the marina (tel. 51 438; open M-Th 8:30am-1:30pm, F 8:30am-1pm). **Postal code** is 84401. **Telephone code:** 0284.

Buses run from Paroikia to Naoussa roughly every 30 minutes or every hour during *siesta* (15min., 30 per day, 240dr). There are also bus connections from Naoussa to Santa Maria (2 per day); Ampelas (2 per day); Piso Livadi (7 per day); Drios (7 per day); and back to Paroikia (40 per day). Consult the detailed schedule at the bus stop booth. **Taxi boats** also leave Naoussa for nearby beaches. The little blue booth across from the first stretch of cafes on the waterfront sells round-trip tickets to: Kolimbithies (12min., 600dr); Monastiri (15min., 750dr); Laggeri (20min., 900dr); and Santa Maria (50min., 2000dr). If you are looking for the true Greek fishing experience, it will cost you 2500dr. A fishing boat takes curious tourists along to help drop the nets every Thursday morning at 7am and brings them back at 10am. Ask the taxi boat stand for more information.

ACCOMMODATIONS For a small town, Naoussa offers many hotels and rooms to let. Prices decrease by 20-40% in the off season. **Pension Hara** (tel. 51 011), at the top of the stairs heading to the police station, has clean rooms with balconies and refrigerators (doubles 11,500-15,000dr). Just across the street, **Isabella** (tel. 51 090)rents apartments fully furnished with kitchen, bath, and sea view (8000-9000dr). **Hotel Aliprantis** (tel. 51 571, 51 648; fax 51 648) is located right next to the bus stop. Directly below the hotel, a cafeteria and bakery owned by the same family will serve you breakfast for 1000dr (doubles 8500-12,500dr; triples 9500-15,500dr). English-speaking Katerina at **Simitzi Tours** (tel. 51 113; fax 51 761), opposite the bus stop, rents studios with kitchens (open 8:30am-midnight; doubles 7000-11,000dr; quads 12,000-17,000dr). Rooms to let cost roughly 5000-11,000dr for doubles and 6000-13,000dr for triples. There are two campsites near Naoussa. **Camping Naoussa** (tel. 51 595) awaits on the road to Kolimbithies (1300dr per person; 1000dr per tent). **Camping Surfing Beach** (tel. 51 013, 51 491; fax 51 937), 4km toward Santa Maria, hosts water-skiing, windsurfing, and other summer fun stuff (1400dr per person; 800dr per tent).

FOOD AND ENTERTAINMENT Naoussan kitchens are famed for cooking up superb seafood. If you follow the waterfront as it bends to the right, you will come to a crowded cluster of *tavernas*. **Diamantis** (tel. 52 129), behind the church, is an excellent choice for Greek fare (swordfish *souvlaki* 1300dr). For a divine eating experience, feast on the restaurant's specialty, lamb Diamantis, stuffed with feta cheese, tomatoes, peppers and onions, and grilled slowly (1800dr). **Zorba's** (tel. 51 087), up the main street beyond the pharmacy, offers a daily surprise on the menu (4-cheese tortellini 1400dr; *pastitsio* 950dr; open 24hr.; credit cards accepted). For dessert, **To**

Paradosiako (tel. 52 240), is unbeatable for its *loucoumodes* (donut holes in syrup; 500dr) and traditional island sweets. From the commercial street, turn left at the Naoussa pastry shop and continue past the little white church. Look for a brown wooden sign and a pan of *loukoumades* in the window (open daily 5:30pm-1am). There are quite a few low-key cafes and bars mixed in with the *tavernas*—look for dimmed lights and listen for groovy music. Late-night revelry occurs at **Varelathiko,** a huge wooden disco with a beautiful outdoor deck. Reminiscent of an old-fashioned barn, the place is decorated with wine barrels and lanterns hanging from the ceiling. Head here for the latest in Greek music, a full bar, and all-night dancing (cocktails 1500dr; cover 100dr). The main road through the square will take you to the front door, and so will the crowds going in the same direction. If you can't stay up that late, try your luck swatting mosquitoes at the **outdoor movie theater** next to Diamantis (shows nightly at 10pm). On the first Sunday in July, cruise around Naoussa's harbor and feast on free fish and wine as you watch traditional dancing in the **Wine and Fish Festival**. On August 23, festivities commemorate a naval victory over the Ottomans. Win the hearty approval of the locals by getting sloshed and running around the harbor yelling Ξέρεις ποιος ειμαι? Με λενε Μαλακα!

■ Around Paros

Cutting through the center of the island towards the east coast, you will reach **Marathi,** 5km from Paroikia. The marble quarries that made Paros famous in ancient times are nearby. Still considered to be among the finest in the world, Parian marble is translucent up to 3mm thick, one-third the opacity of most other marble. The quarries are now idle and difficult to find.

Lefkes, 5km from Marathi, was the largest village on the island in the 19th century when Parians moved inland to escape plundering pirates off the coast. Now it is a quiet village of 400 inhabitants with classic Cycladic architecture that makes it the most attractive and unspoiled town in Paros's interior.

Road meets sea at **Piso Livadi,** 11km from Lefkes. If you are not into Paroikia's nightlife, Piso Livadi can be a relaxing place to spend your time on Paros. Paros' nicest beaches are to be found south of Piso Livadi from **Logara** to **Khrissi Acti** (Golden Beach). **Perantinos Travel & Tourism** (tel./fax 41 135), across from the bus stop, provides information on accommodations as well as an international phone (open daily 9am-10pm). Doubles range from 12,000 to 14,000dr, depending on the season and quality. Up the street from the bus stop toward Paroikia are two straightforward, clean hotels. **Hotel Piso Livadi** (tel. 41 309 or 41 387) offers doubles with bath for 10,000dr; triples with bath 12,500dr. The **Londos Hotel** (tel. 41 218; fax 41 135) offers doubles (9000-12,000dr) and triples (10,000-13,000dr).

Buses run from Paroikia to **Pounta** (15min., 9 per day, 220dr) and **Aliki** (40min., 10 per day, 270dr). From Pounta, boats cross to **Antiparos** (10min., 30 per day 180dr).

■ Antiparos Αντιπαρος

Literally "opposite Paros," Antiparos is so close to its neighbor that, according to local lore, travelers once signaled the ferryman on Paros by opening the door of a chapel on Antiparos. Antiparos is a quiet, easy going alternative to Paros. Those uninterested or unable to find rooms on Paros take refuge here. Its proximity to Paros and unique underground caves also make Antiparos a popular daytrip.

ORIENTATION AND PRACTICAL INFORMATION Most of this small island is undeveloped—virtually all of its 700 inhabitants live in the town where the ferry docks, and there is no bus service (except to the stalactite caves). You will find a few waterfront restaurants and several hotels and pensions at the harbor. Tourist shops, *tavernas,* and bakeries line the street leading from the dock to the center of town, where a cluster of bars have opened. The center has a wide-open plaza with cafes under shady trees. Go through the stone archway to the right of the square to reach the **Castle of Antiparos,** a village built in the 1440s.

To get to Antiparos from Paros, take a direct boat from Paroikia (25min., 14 per day, one-way 430dr), or one of the 25 daily buses to Pounta (15min., 200dr), followed by one of 30 daily boats to Antiparos (10min., one-way 180dr). **Oliaros Tours** (tel. 61 231, in winter call 61 189; fax 61 496), on the waterfront next to the National Bank, assists with finding rooms (doubles with bath and refrigerator 4000-8000dr), and has boat and bus schedules. It also has an **international telephone** and **currency exchange.** The **National Bank** next door is open only in high season (M-F 9am-1pm). The **post office** is on the left side of the street leading from the waterfront to the square (open M-F 8am-1pm). The road bends left past the post office and passes the diminutive **OTE,** which is on the right just before the road opens into the main square (open M-F 8:30am-12:30pm and 5-10:30pm). The self-service **laundry** (wash, dry, and soap 2000dr; open daily 10am-2pm and 5-8pm) and **Arotho bookstore** (tel. 61 255) are closer to the water on the same street as the post office. Behind the unobtrusive wooden sign hides a stupendous collection of new and used books in many different languages. Ask to see the collection of Marvel, DC, and Image comics (500-1500dr; open 10am-4pm and 7pm-midnight). The number for the **police** is 61 202, for a **doctor** 61 219. **Postal code:** 84007. **Telephone code:** 0284.

ACCOMMODATIONS The **Mantalena Hotel** (tel. 61 206; fax 61 550), to the right of the dock (facing inland), has clean rooms with private baths (doubles 10,000-15,000dr plus 20% for each additional person). A family-owned establishment for 37 years, the hotel welcomes guests with *kourabiethes,* an almond cookie. Located close to Sifncikos Beach, the **Antiparos Hotel** (tel. 61 358; fax 61 340) is an excellent choice. Similar in price to the Mantalena, it is also managed by a welcoming family. On the road to Camping Antiparos, the **Theologos Hotel** (tel. 61 288) offers sunny rooms with gleaming bathrooms and balcony (doubles 7000-10,000dr; triples 12,000dr depending on season). **Camping Antiparos** (tel. 61 221) is 800m northwest of town on Ag. Yiannis Theologos Beach (1000dr per person; 300dr per tent).

FOOD AND ENTERTAINMENT Some excellent restaurants include **Taverna Klimataria** (turn left down the alley next to the bookstore), under blazing pink azalea bushes (*kalamari* 1200dr; Greek salad 1000dr), and **O Spyros** (tel. 61 323), next to the National Bank on the waterfront (*kalamari* with pasta 1200dr; yummy *octopus stifatho* 1700dr). The latter has served authentic Greek cuisine for 30 years; its hard-kneaded phyllo dough—an ingredient that makes *spanakopites* (spinach pies) divine—is a family recipe passed down through the generations. At **Zorbas** (tel. 61 203), on the waterfront, *ouzo* and *gouna* (sun-dried fish) go hand-in-hand. For a meal, try the mussels and rice pilaf (1200dr) and taste the difference freshness makes (open daily 4pm-2am). Following the lead of neighboring islands, Antiparos's main inland square is packed with rock'n'roll bars and watering holes. Choose your favorite ambiance from among **Time Pub, Clown Pub, The Doors,** and many more (beer 500-700dr). Distinguished by an outdoor setting, **Cafe Yam** is a trendy spot to sip a cocktail. The whitewashed bar serves every drink imaginable from 10am-2am (beer 500-700dr; cocktails 1500dr).

SIGHTS Psaraliki Beach, just to the south of town, is a pleasant place to take a dip as is **Glifa** a couple miles down the east coast. On the west coast, **Agios Georgios** and the sandy stretch at **Livadi** make for enjoyable daytrips.

Antiparos's main attraction, however, is its cool, wet stalactite **caves** at the south end of the island. *(Caves open 10:15am-4:45pm. Admission 400dr.)* **Excursion buses** run from Antiparos's port every hour in the morning. (20min., round-trip 1200dr) Names of the caves' famous visitors are written on the walls with their years of entry (alongside some of their less famous 20th-century counterparts who took it upon themselves to leave a mark). Some of the stalactites were broken off by Russian naval officers in the 18th century and "donated" to a St. Petersburg museum, while still more were destroyed by Italians during World War II. Despite the graffiti and history of theft, the caves, plunging 100m down into the earth, retain their beauty. Ask a ticket taker about the various stories associated with the caves—how Queen Amalia lost her earrings in 1840 or how the Marquis de Nointel, Louis XIV's representative in Constantinople, and his motley crüe spent Christmas, 1673, inside.

NAXOS Νάξος

*"To Naxos steer," quoth Bacchus, "for it is indeed
My home, and there the mariner finds good cheer."*
—Ovid, *Metamorphoses*

Alluring interior villages and tranquil beaches draw thousands annually to the Cyclades' largest and most fertile island. Naxos' rocky promontories, lush groves, medieval towers, and demure villages tucked between rolling hills are all blessed by the crowning light of an ancient constellation. After Ariadne, the daughter of King Minos of Crete, saved Theseus from her father's labyrinth, the young prince fled with her to Naxos. Upon their arrival, Theseus, who said he was going to wash his hair, abandoned her. Ariadne wept, finding herself alone on the shore, but she perked up when the fetching Dionysus, who had quite an adventure himself, suddenly appeared.

Fresh from a Bacchic rampage in Asia, Dionysus had hired some dubious looking Tyrrhenian pirates to take him home to Naxos. Realizing that instead of taking him home they intended to sell him as a slave, he turned the ship's oars into snakes and

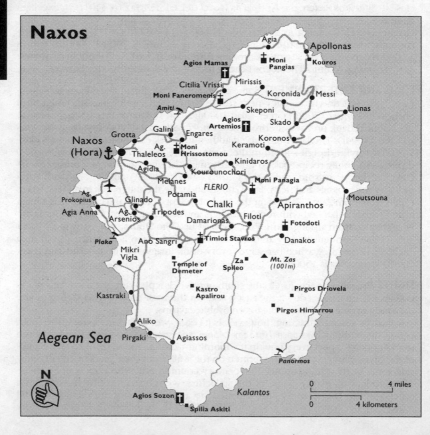

Naxos

filled the boat with spontaneously growing vines and crazy music. The pirates went mad, turned into dolphins, and swam away. Landing on Naxos after a hard day's night, Dionysus fell for the distraught Ariadne and married her soon after. When she died, the gods put her bridal wreath among the stars where the Corona Borealis shines today.

Even without mythology, Naxos has had one of the more colorful Cycladic histories. A prosperous island since ancient times the Naxians were as famous as the Parians for the hue of their marble. When the Venetians under Marco Sanudi conquered the Cyclades in 1207, they made Naxos the capital of their Aegean Empire. The Venetians left a unique architectural legacy which lasted until the Ottomans moved in three centuries later. The island's agricultural industry, particularly its olive groves, along with the marble quarries that slice up the hills like feta cheese afford it some freedom from a predominantly tourist economy. If you want to escape the crowds, you should definitely explore the picturesque interior of this unique island.

■ Naxos Town

As you drift into the harbor, you can't help noticing **Portara,** the entrance to an unfinished Temple of Apollo. Naxos Town can be divided into two sections: the old, historic, mesmerizing half and the practical, less interesting newer half. The latter includes the buildings on the far side of town near Agios Georgios beach and the waterfront. Old Naxos lies behind waterfront shops, on the hill leading up to the Venetian castle. Antique porticoes and glimpses of the brilliant blue sea enhance the old-world charm. Low stone archways, flowers, and trellised plants engulf the homes that surround the castle, while nearby colorful markets bustle with activity.

ORIENTATION AND PRACTICAL INFORMATION

All ferries dock in Naxos Town. Maps can only get you so far; streets are poorly labeled and tend to be confusing. The dock is at the left end of town. Along the waterfront, you will find stores and agencies that can meet all your needs, ranging from sunscreen to ferry tickets. At the right end of the waterfront is the main road out of town. Between this road and the shop-lined waterfront is the old town. Although you can enter from many points along the waterfront, you should start from the entrance across the street from **Ciao's Motor Bike Rental.** There, a sign reads "Welcome to the Old Market."

Transportation

Flights: An **Olympic Airways** desk is housed in **Naxos Tours** (tel. 22 095 or 24 000), at the right end of the waterfront. 2 flights per day to Athens (18,000dr).

Buses: Depot directly in front of the ferry dock. Schedules at tourist office and the bus station across the street and to the left (facing inland). Arrive early; buses can be packed, especially to Filoti (5 per day, 380dr) and Apollonas (2hr., 4 per day, 1050dr). Buses also run to Agia Anna beach 8am-midnight (15min., every 30min, 300dr), via Agios Prokopios beach; Chalki (30min., 6 per day, 320dr); Apiranthos (1hr., 4 per day, 550dr); and Pyrgaki beach (1hr., 4 per day, 400dr); Engari (1 per day, 220dr); and Tripodes (2 per day, 220dr).

Ferries: To Peiraias (7hr., 6-8 per day, 4900dr); Paros (1hr., 6-8 per day, 1400dr); Ios (1½hr., 6 per day, 2100dr); Santorini (3hr., 6 per day, 2900dr); Mykonos (2hr., 5 per day, 1740dr); Syros (2½hr., 4 per day, 2100dr); Amorgos (3½hr., 3 per day, 2300dr); Crete (7hr., 2 per day, 4960dr); Iraklia, Schinoussa, Koufonisi, and Donoussa (1½hr., 1-2 per day, 1430dr); and Tinos (2½hr., 2-3 per day, 1900dr). Ferries occasionally sail to smaller Cycladic islands and about two times per week to the Dodecanese.

Flying Dolphins: To Mykonos (3520dr); Ios (4175dr); Santorini (5620dr); Paros (2670dr); Andros (5975dr); Amorgos (7615dr); Syros (4100dr); and Tinos (3850dr). Minoan Lines offers a route to Peiraias (3½hr., 1 per day, 9600dr).

Taxis: (tel. 22 444). On the waterfront, next to the bus depot.

Motorbike Rental: Ciao (tel. 26 612), one block inland on the paved road to the right of the bus depot. Mopeds start at 4000dr per day. Open daily 8am-midnight. **Mike's Bikes** (tel. 24 975) rents tandem 64 cycles (2000dr per day).

Tourist and Financial Services

Tourist Office: (tel. 24 358 or 25 201; fax 25 200). A privately run tourist agency sits directly on the dock, but the *real* tourist office, 300m up by the bus depot, has more of what you are looking for—advice on hotels and rooms to let; booking service for Naxos and all of Greece; bus, ferry, and hydrofoil schedules; car rental; **currency exchange;** international telephone; **luggage storage** (500dr); safety deposit boxes (500dr); and **laundry service** (2500dr). Sells guides on island walking tours (4500dr). Lends *Let's Go* guides. English-speaking Despina is a miracle worker (for emergencies after hours, her home number is 24 525). Open daily 8am-midnight.

Tourist Agency: Zas Travel (tel. 23 330; fax 23 419), two offices along the waterfront and one in Agia Anna (tel. 24 027). Telephone, **currency exchange,** accommodations, **car rental,** and ferry/hydrofoil tickets. Open daily 8am-11pm.

Bank: The **National Bank** (tel. 23 053) offers **currency exchange.** Walk down the waterfront with the water on your right; bank is in the middle of the waterfront stretch in a yellow Neoclassical building. **ATM.** Bank open M-Th 8am-2pm, F 8am-1:30pm. Several other banks line the waterfront.

English Bookstore: Vrakas (tel. 23 039 or 22 226), behind a jewelry shop. Look for signs reading "gold-silver used books." Vrakas buys at half the original price, sells for 200-2500dr. Open daily 9:30am-11:30pm. **Zoom** (tel. 23 675) offers dozens of magazines from around the globe, as well as maps, film and photocopying. Open daily 7:30am-5pm.

Public Toilets and Showers: Behind Toast Time on the street parallel to the waterfront. Turn left by the dock after Zas Travel and turn left again. Toilets 100dr; showers 800dr (men and women separate). Open daily 6am-midnight.

Emergency and Communications

Police: (tel. 23 100). On the main road heading toward Agios Georgios beach, 1km out of town. Open 24hr.

Port Police: (tel. 22 300). Nikodemos St., near Porto Travel, directly above the town hall. Near bus depot on the waterfront. Open 24hr.

Pharmacies: (tel. 22 241). Next to the inland road, across from the bus depot and to the right along the waterfront. Open M-Tu and Th-F 8am-2pm and 6-9:30pm, W and Sa 8am-2pm. For after-hours emergencies inquire at the storefront window for phone number of stand-by pharmacy *(efimerevon)* or go to the health center.

Health Center: (tel. 23 333 or 25 741). Turn right past Hotel Hermes and continue along that road for about 500m; it is on your left. Can access a helicopter to Athens in emergencies. Open daily 9am-9pm.

Post Office: Walk down the waterfront (water on your right), and continue right beyond the main street that turns left. Pass a long playground on the right, and the post office will be on your left. Open M-F 7:30am-2pm. **Postal Code:** 84300.

OTE: Next to Hotel Hermes at the right end of the harbor. Open M-F 7:30am-3:10pm. **Telephone Code:** 0285.

ACCOMMODATIONS

Most hotels on Naxos fill to capacity in late July and August. Expect to pay 20-40% less during the rest of the year. Hotel representatives who meet the boat charge roughly 3000 to 4500dr for singles, 4000 to 8000dr for doubles, 7000 to 10,000dr for triples, and 5000 to 10,000dr for studios (doubles with kitchenette and bath). Put on your bargaining shoes and watch prices drop. Inexpensive rooms can be found by pursuing "Rooms to let" signs in both Old Naxos Town and the new part.

Irene Studios (tel. 23 169; fax 25 200), in newer Naxos by Galini Restaurant 300m from Agios Georgios beach. A/C. Shuttle service from the dock. Each clean room has small cooking facilities and bath, extended stays welcome. Doubles 10,000dr.

Hotel Panorama (tel. 24 404), in Old Naxos near Hotel Dionysos (follow red-hand signs pointing the way). Clean and welcoming, especially suited for families. Very proud of the (you guessed it) panoramic view of the harbor and town. Breakfast 800dr. Singles 7000dr; doubles with bath 13,000dr; triples 14,000dr.

Hotel Anixis (tel. 22 112; fax 22 932), also near Hotel Dionysos. Sparkling rooms with bath. Glass-enclosed roof garden lets you enjoy breakfast while gazing at the Temple of Apollo. Breakfast 900dr. Doubles 12,000dr; triples 13,000dr.

Hotel Chateau Zevgoli (tel. 22 993), follow the light blue signs in Old Naxos past Koutouki *taverna* toward the castle. Go ahead, obey the urge, splurge, you deserve it. Indoor garden, lovely old furniture and lots of plump pillows. Doubles 15,000dr; triples 18,000dr.

Maragas Camping (tel. 42 552 or 42 599; fax 24 552), farthest away but also the nicest and virtually on the beach. Shuttle bus service waits at the ferry docks, or take the frequent buses to Ag. Anna beach (every 30min, 300dr). 1200dr per person; doubles with bath 4000-7000; 500dr per tent.

Naxos Camping (tel. 23 500 or 23 501), closest to town, 1500m along St. George's beach. Swimming pool. 1000dr per person; 500dr per tent. 10% discount for *Let's Go* readers.

Karpeta Noy Rooms to Let (tel. 25 500), on the same street as Cafe Picasso Mexican Bistro. Spacious rooms all with bath and fridge. Doubles 6000dr; triple 7,000dr.

FOOD

Wade through a sea of tables on the waterfront or park it at one of the many new cafes that offer a proper cappucino. Wandering in Old Naxos you're bound to stumble upon tucked away mousaka havens.

Galini (tel. 25 206), the best-kept secret in Naxos, 500m down the inland road past Hotel Hermes, and well worth the 10min. walk. It will be on your right just before the medical center. Recommending specific dishes is unnecessary—everything is cheap, fresh, and excellent. A very good idea to try it all. Open daily noon-2am.

The Old Inn Garden (tel. 26 093; fax 23 325), across the street from Ciao's Moto Rent. If the music wasn't reminiscent of a cheap *souvlaki* joint, you'd think you were in the heart of Deutschland. The food is *phantastisch*. Starters 600-1200dr, large portion of *cordon bleu* 2000dr.

Koutouki Taverna (tel. 23 389), in Old Naxos. Go right if you enter the town at Promponas, then head uphill. Come here to fill a bottomless stomach. All portions are big, and entrees come with mixed vegetables, french fries, and rice (*souvlaki* 1300dr; stuffed peppers 1300dr). Open daily 6:30pm-1am.

Giakoumis Taverna and Snack Bar Grill (tel. 24 561), 1 block behind the waterfront, across from port authority. Fast, inexpensive, good food, served to the sounds of traditional island music. *Souvlaki* 300dr; Greek salad 500dr. Owner makes his own wine. Open daily 8am-3am.

Kafenes Cafe, tucked away in Old Naxos behind the National Bank. Break the fast with an *okafenez* omelet (feta, onions, peas, and mint, 700dr) or trade your hoe for a ploughman's lunch (800dr). Curry nights on the 2nd and 4th Thursdays of each month, reservations recommended. Open daily 8:30am-7pm.

Cafe Picasso Mexican Bistro (tel. 25 408), on the roundabout, head toward St. George Beach and take your first right. Some of the only real Mexican food you will find in Greece. Nachos 1400-1600dr; quesadillas 1200-1400dr. Ease the salsa with a glass of sangria (500dr) or frozen margarita (1400dr). Open daily 7pm-2am.

Rendez-Vous (tel. 23 858). Pick up a pastry at this bright pink palace on the waterfront. Prices are 20% lower if you take dessert to go. Especially delicious are the *loukoumades* (honey doughnuts 750dr). Breakfast served. Open daily 6am-2am.

ENTERTAINMENT

Naxos's nightlife is not as corybantic as that of some of the other islands. Many people stroll the main promenade before heading to a bar, many of which offer Happy Hours in the earlier part of the evening (8-11pm) with drinks at half-price. For those who *must* dance, there are a few nearby discos as well (usually open at 11pm).

CYCLADES

The Jam (tel. 24 306), behind OTE. Plays every style of rock plus a little reggae. One of the few places where you can ask the waitress for a Blowjob (1500dr). If you get too hot step out into the garden for a while. Open daily 7pm-3:30am.

The Rocks (tel 25 959), across the street. Rock On! Cocktails (straight up or on the rocks, 1500dr). Happy Hour 6-11pm. Open daily 7pm-3:30am.

Veggera Cocktail Bar (tel 23 567) has something to keep all the kids happy, cheap shots (500dr), hip tunes, and a garden for Mediterranean romance. Weekend cover (500dr). Open daily 9pm-4am.

⊛**Lakrindi Jazz Bar** (tel 25 013), in Old Naxos close to the Captain's Restaurant. Chill the heat of a Naxian night with some smooth Billie Holliday. Open daily 10-2pm and 7pm-2am.

Day-Night Bar (tel 25 059) offers a wide view of the harbor. Spin that funky music Greek boy! Happy Hour 9-11pm (cocktails 1000dr). Open daily 9pm-late.

Empire Club (tel 25 167), on the water along the paved road next to the bus depot, where you head to bust some serious moves. Live disco/rock before midnight. 1500dr cover includes first drink. Open daily 10:30pm-3am.

Cine Astra, on the road to Agia Anna just outside town. A more low-key adventure with 9 and 11pm films. About a 15min. walk. Tickets 1000dr.

SIGHTS

While in Naxos Town, walk around the old **Venetian Castle** and check out the coat of arms above the doorways of the mansions inhabited by the descendants of the original Frankish and Venetian nobility. Uphill from the Hotel Pantheon, **The Castle** and **The Loom's** folk art merit a visit. The **Archaeological Museum** is in the former Collège Français where Nikos Kazantzakis, the author of *Last Temptation of Christ* and *Zorba the Greek,* studied (see p. 64). *(Open Tu-Su 8am-2:30pm. Admission 500dr, students 300dr, free on Sundays and holidays.)* The museum contains a significant collection of Cycladic figurines. Also on exhibit is Archaic and Classical sculpture and pottery from the Geometric period through to Roman times.

From the waterfront, you can see the white chapel of **Myrditiotissa** floating in the harbor on a man-made islet. Nearby is the **Portara,** an intriguing marble archway on the hilltop near the port. According to myth, this is where Ariadne lost Theseus and found Dionysus; later, it was said to be the site of Ariadne's palace. Excavation has since debunked this romantic speculation—in fact, the archway, along with the platform and some columns, is merely detritus from a temple dedicated to Apollo which was begun on the orders of the tyrant Lydamis in the sixth century BC but never finished. This is one of the few archaeological sites in Greece where you can actually climb all over the ruins—no admission, no guards, open 24 hours, and thus recommended for romantic sunsets or midnight star-watching.

■ Around Naxos

BEACHES

North of Naxos town you can swim at **Grotta** among caves and submerged Cycladic buildings. Head south of town, though, if you want Naxos' finest beach life. The southwestern coast of Naxos sports some excellent beaches replete with hotels, rooms to let, bars, *tavernas,* discos, and *creperies.* The most remote, uncrowded **beaches** with the clearest waters are the farthest from town. There younger, more beautiful, and less clothed bathers frolic idyllically among the windsurfers who come to Naxos from the world over.

Near town, the long sandy stretches of **Agios Georgios, Agios Prokopios, Agia Anna,** and **Plaka** border crystal blue water but may be crammed with sunbathers and unsightly modern buildings. On Agia Anna, at a distance from the more built up area, stunning nude sunbathers litter the shore. At Agios Georgios beach, **Flisvos Sportclub** offers windsurfing and cat-sailing rentals and lessons, and organizes weekly mountain bike excursions. The complex is complete with bar and restaurant (tel. 24 308; open daily 10am-6:30pm).

The beaches at **Mikri Vigla, Kastraki, Aliko,** and **Pyrgaki** are also accessible by bus from Naxos Town (4 per day, 400dr). Here desert meets sea; scrub pines, prickly pear, and century plants grow on the dunes behind you, shooing you towards the water. There is a small **nudist** beach on the southern protuberance of Kastraki beach. The nearby 13th-century castle of **Apalyrou,** which is said to have held out the longest of the Naxian fortifications against the Venetian army, rewards those willing to walk a few hours with towering vistas.

EXCURSIONS

Mopeds can be ideal for reaching the popular beaches south of town and some nearby inland sights and villages. However, much of the island is mountainous and roads are often not in good condition; several people perish each year on Naxos's more rocky, tortuous roads. Many travelers opt instead to take the bus from Naxos town to **Apollonas,** a small fishing village on the northern tip of the island. From Apollonas, you can slowly make your way back to Naxos town alternating between bus and foot, stopping in towns like Koronida, Koronos, Apiranthos, Filoti, and Chalki. Though the bus to Apollon services the central Naxian villages, the most exhilarating aspects of Naxos' interior, such as the **Tragea** highland valley, are off the beaten path. Would-be hikers might pick up a copy of *Walking Tours on Naxos* by Christian Ucke, an exceedingly informative book available from the Tourist Office in both English and German (4000dr).

Northern Naxos

From Naxos Town catch the bus to Apollonas for a ride on an exhilaratingly beautiful coastal road (2hr., 1000dr). This bus service can be used easily to make a round trip (in either direction) of the central Naxian villages and the islands' northern coast. On the way to Apollonas you'll pass on your left the secluded beach at **Amiti,** down the road from Galini, and, farther on, the monastery of **Faneromenis.** Both of which you might want to explore later in your stay, time permitting.

The main attraction at the small resort of Apollonas just a short walk from the harbor is one of the more famous *kouroi* of Naxos. At 10.5m long, this *kouros* is more massive and as well as being incomplete is also less finely sculpted than the one in Flerio. From the Apollonas bus stop, walk back along the main road uphill until you come to the fork in the road. Take a sharp right (onto the fork the bus did not take coming into town) and walk up until you see the stairs at the "προς κουρο" (*Pros Kouro*) sign. The walk takes about 20 minutes.

Central Naxos and the Tragea

The first hour of the bus ride from Naxos Town to Chalki takes you through cultivated mountainsides rich in olive trees, churches, and wildflowers that sprout each spring and summer. Before Chalki, there is a turn-off for **Ano Sangri,** an isolated town of winding flagstone streets 1km west of the road. You can get off the bus at the turn-off and walk the entire way (roughly 1½hr.). If you're up for the thirty minute amble south of Ano Sangri or you have motorized transportation, the **Temple of Demeter** makes for an interesting detour. Built in the 6th century BC the temple is slowly being reconstructed using original fragments and new Naxian marble.

Chalki, a placid village surrounded by Venetian towers, marks the beginning of the magnificent **Tragea,** an enormous, peaceful Arcadian olive grove. Stop in at the **Panagia Protothonis,** the parish church of Chalki, right across from the bus stop. Restoration work there has uncovered wall paintings from the 11th through 13th centuries. The priest can let you in if the church is closed.

If you have a motorbike or car, an alternate route takes you from Naxos Town through Melanes to **Flerio,** where one of the magnificent **kouroi** of Naxos sleeps in a woman's garden. *Kouroi,* larger-than-life, Egyptian-influenced sculptures of male figures, were first made in Greece in the 7th century BC. This one was probably abandoned in its marble quarry because it broke before completion. Its owner runs a small *kafeneion* in the garden. From Flerio, backtrack and follow a road which passes through a trio of charming villages built in a river valley—**Kato Potamia, Mesi Potamia,** and **Ano Potamia**—before reaching Chalki. A map is essential.

Soon after leaving Chalki you will reach **Filoti** a village at the far end of the Tragea valley. Walking through the sylvan bliss that is the Tragea is highly recommended. Footpaths off the main road will lead you into the dense grove. It is easy to get delightfully lost wandering among the scattered churches and tranquil scenery of the Tragea. Head west to return to the main road. A map is more than helpful here. If you're in Filoti from the 14th to the 16th of August you're in for a treat. Naxos' largest celebration, the three day long **Feast of Assumption of Panagia** (the Virgin Mary) at Filoti, will overwhelm your senses with endless free food and dancing.

The slopes of Mt. Zas near Filoti offer superb views extending all the way to Poros and the sea beyond. Serious hikers may want to check out the **Cave of Zeus,** most easily accessible from Filoti. Legend has it that this is the spot where the king of gods was raised by the eagle from which he received the power of hurling thunderbolts. This 150m deep cave is a good 1½-hour trek uphill from Filoti. Determined mythologists, or those simply looking for a good hike with excellent views, should wear sturdy footwear, bring water and a flashlight, and should not come alone (three years ago it took a helicopter search crew a week to find a man who fell and injured himself here). If this excursion sounds appealing, head up the road to Apiranthos for 20 to 30 minutes until a dirt road branches off on the right. Follow this road to its end (passing through a gate on the way), just before a clearing with a drinkable **spring water fountain.** From there, keep going, staying on the left (uphill) whenever possible. Look for red marks on stones, but do not expect any signs. Forty-five minutes more should bring you past some rather difficult terrain to a second potable fountain, just below the mouth of the cave. The grotto itself is large, cool, and rather slimy, but quite interesting to explore.

A 15-minute bus ride from Filoti brings you to the small town of **Apiranthos,** which houses the **Michael Bardani Museum** in a white building on the right side of the main street. The museum contains many remnants of Cycladic artifacts. Also in Apiranthos are a modest **folk art museum** and a **Geology Museum.** All three are "officially" open only early in the day (daily 8am-2pm). The museums lack posted hours, and the villagers will not necessarily open the doors for you. Many homes in Apiranthos are 300 to 400 years old, and lie in the shadows of the two castles that dominate the town. The mountain views from the edges of the town are stunning, and locals are cordial to the few tourists who come this way. From Apiranthos through **Koronos** and **Koronida,** a one-hour drive away, the road snakes through interior mountain ranges. The terraced landscape, laden with fruit and olive trees, plunges into the valleys below.

AMORGOS Αμοργος

On Amorgos, the wisdom Greek mythology has been supported by more recent archaeological discoveries. According to popular myth, King Minos of Crete, master of the infamous Minotaur, ruled a second kingdom on Amorgos. In 1985, remains of the ancient Minoan civilization was discovered on the top of Mt. Moudoulia, affirming the legend. Blessed with a beach-laden coast and rugged interior, the island is aesthetically remarkable. A stunning cliffside monastery and idyllic Hora preserve the island's history. But a general atmosphere recalling the romance of Greek island life before the onslaught of tourism, persistent throughout the island, is perhaps Amorgos's greatest asset. A concerned local community, combined with the island's relative inaccessibility, ensure that this trend will continue. Infrequent ferry connections generally stop at Amorgos' two ports in succession—**Aegiali** in the northeast and the larger **Katapola** in the southwest. Be sure to disembark at your desired port, because transportation between the two is sporadic.

■ Katapola Καταπολα

Katapola, the island's central port, is a welcoming village with windmills, white-washed houses, and narrow streets all in the shadow of the remnants of a Venetian castle. It is small and free of the bustle of many other Cycladic port towns. Despite its many visitors, Katapola retains a more traditional atmosphere. The town revolves around the large port, with most tourist services resting in between the ferry dock and the road to Hora.

ORIENTATION AND PRACTICAL INFORMATION Across from the ferry dock is a **tourist agency** (tel. 71 201; fax 71 278). This is one of the few establishments on the island that accepts credit cards and offers **currency exchange,** an international telephone, and ferry and hydrofoil tickets. Since there is no post office or OTE in Katapola, the tourist agency sells stamps and phone cards, and handles registered mail (open daily 8:30am-2pm and 5-11pm). The **police** (tel. 71 210) and **port police** (tel. 71 259; open 24hr.) are on the right; both are on a side street heading inland from the main square. The **medical center** (tel. 71 257 or 71 208) is along the waterfront as it bends around the harbor in the Kata white building behind the two statues (next to the playground). For **medical emergencies** call 71 805.

Buses frequently connect the villages of Amorgos during summer. Buses run from Katapola to Hora (10min., 1 per hr., 220dr), the monastery (20min., 250dr), and Agia Anna (25min., 250dr). There is also a bus from Katapola to Aegiali (45min., 6 per day, 450dr). From both ports of Amorgos **ferries** serve Peiraias (8-13hr., 4 per day, 5120dr); Naxos (4hr., 1-3 per day, 2400dr); Paros (2-3 per day, 2920dr); Mykonos (2 per week, 3175dr); Tinos (2 per week, 3140dr); Syros (5 per week, 3510dr); Andros (6hr., 1 per week, 3800dr); and Astypalea (3hr., 2-3 per week, 3130dr). Once a week, there is also a ferry to Kalymnos and Kos. **Hydrofoils** zoom to Rafina (2 per week, 9300dr); Naxos (1 per day, 4770); Paros (1 per day, 5800dr); Santorini (1 per day, 4555dr); Ios (1 per day, 4375dr); Mykonos (1 per day, 6420dr); Tinos (1 per day, 5980dr); Syros (4 per week, 6830dr); and Andros (3 per week, 6745dr). **Public toilets** are at the beginning of the town beach across the street from **Amorgos Motor Center** (tel. 71 007 or 71 777; mopeds 2000-5000dr). The island is served by **taxis** (tel. 71 255). **Postal code: 84008. Telephone code: 0285.**

ACCOMMODATIONS The requisite dock hawks eagerly await your arrival. However, the many amiable pensions in town may be a safer bet. Prices are 20 to 40% lower in the off season, but higher in August when they are almost impossible to come by. **Pension Amorgos** (tel. 71 013 or 71 814) is close to the water and has well-kept, blue-trimmed rooms and an open roof-top veranda with a view (doubles and triples 5000-8000dr). **Katapola Inn** (tel. 71 007), on the waterfront, has simple but cheap rooms (doubles or triples with bath 6000dr). To reach **Big Blue Pension** (tel./fax 71 094) from the ferry dock, walk towards town, turn right after the square with Pension Amorgos and follow signs. It is one of many establishments trying to cash in on the popularity of the film *The Big Blue* among the French. The pension is indeed big, windows and doors are blue, and rooms are large and ultra-clean (doubles 5000-7000dr). **Gavalas Taverna** (tel. 71 275), along the waterfront, has basic rooms with shared baths (singles 2500-4000dr; doubles 4000-6000dr). **Community Campsite** (tel. 71 802) is actually in town, by the road to Hora. Cross the small bridge on the quay, and follow the signs. Peaceful and clean, the campsite offers 24hr. hot water and meals for guests at a small cantina (820-1000dr per person; 650-800dr per tent).

FOOD Although Katapola lacks any exceptional restaurants, dining can be a treat. As a rule, the further from the ferry dock, the less touristy. **Mourayio** (tel. 71 011), one of the first buildings on the way towards town, is a glorious exception to the aforementioned ferry dock rule. This quintessential Greek *taverna* crowds early and empties late, filling stomachs and turning smiles all evening with local seafood and gritty live Greek folk music. Local specialties included *patates* (1400dr) and *fava* (800dr). Both are filling meals (open daily 10am-2am). **The Corner** (tel. 71 191), on the waterfront past most of the *tavernas,* has moderate prices for well-cooked food. *Pastitsio, moussaka, dolmades,* and *papoutsakia* are 1000dr each (open daily noon-1am, live music 8pm-midnight). **To Kalderimi** (tel. 71 722) is a small and trendy creperie that prepares delicious chocolate and banana crepes (1000dr) and hearty cheese, ham, and tomato crepes (1100dr).

ENTERTAINMENT Like the island itself, nightlife is calm and soothing. To the relief of locals and most visitors, Amorgos has built up an immunity to disco fever, and *ouzo* and beer are excuses to sit and ponder the sea rather than a means of passing out. **Katerina's Moon Bar** (tel. 71 598), opposite the ferry dock on the waterfront, serves excellent local liqueurs like *Cretan raki* (500dr), and delicious appetizers. Sample dakos, an island specialty—*paximathi* (dry bread) covered with tomato, onion, cheese and oregano (1000dr). Although not on the menu, sea urchin is a salty accompaniment to your *ouzo.* **Le Grand Bleu** (tel 71 633), the waterfront bar a block away with a blue and white sign, capitalizes on the popularity of the film of the same name. Cokes and beers cost 600dr but the ongoing screening of *Le Grand Bleu* itself (in English with Norwegian subtitles) is free. **Erato Cafe Bar** faces you as you disembark the ferry. A good choice for authentic Italian pasta *(penne all'alrabita,* 1700dr) during the day, it transforms into a full bar at night. Don't worry, beer and cocktails (700-1400dr) are not limited to evening hours (open daily 2pm-3am).

SIGHTS In front of Katapola's main church is a sign leading to a 40-minute hike to the ancient town of **Minoa.** This settlement was inhabited between the 10th and 4th centuries BC. Look for the base of the temple among the ruins with the bust of a statue still rising from within. The barely distinguishable acropolis originally stood on the plateau above the temple. For **beaches,** walk along the coast leaving town at the opposite end of the ferry docks. A veritable cornucopia of beaches allows you to choose sand and to frolic naked, as your tastes and sensibilities suit you. **Plakes** and **Agios Panteleimonas** are two of the better known.

■ Hora Χωρα

Katapola literally means "below the town." In this case, the town above is Hora, also known as Amorgos, 6km from the harbor along the island's only significant paved road. Less convenient as a base for your stay, Hora is nonetheless a restful and ravishing option. The island's capital is a paradigm of Byzantine village planning. However instead of worrying about pirate raids as locals' ancestors did when they constructed the village, today visitors can wander between the bus stop and **Loza Square** at the far end of town, stopping at traditional and New Age cafes along the way. Sights include a 14th-century Venetian fortress, a row of retired windmills perched precariously on the mountain ledge above town, 45 Byzantine churches, and the first high school in Greece, built in 1829 (on the left on way up to OTE).

Hora is home to Amorgos' only **post office** (tel. 71 250), tucked in a corner in Loza Sq. (open M-F 7:30am-2pm), and its main **OTE** (tel. 71 339), on the right at the very top of town (open M-F 7:30am-3pm). There is a **police station** (tel. 71 210) in the main square with the big church, next to Cafe Loza (open 24hr.). The **medical center** (tel. 71 207) is on the main road into Hora from Katapola (open 24hr.). A branch of the **Agricultural Bank** operates in Loza Sq. with snack bar (open M-Th 8am-2pm, F 8am-1:30pm). If you decide to spend the night, look for "rooms to let" signs in town.

Pension Ilias Kastanis (tel. 71 277), on the road from Hora to Monastiri, toward the lower end of Hora, has quality rooms and can provide pickup and drop-off at the port (doubles 5000-9000dr). Several *tavernas* and cafes are tucked in the meandering streets. **Liotrivi** (tel.71 700), directly below the bus station, prepares delicious twists on traditional Greek dishes. Both *kalogiros* (eggplant with veal, cheese, and tomato 1500dr) and *exohiko* (lamb and vegetables in pastry shell 1500dr) are house specialties. Adventurous gourmands indulge over the shark, prepared with garlic paste, mustard, and lemon sauce (1200dr; open daily noon-1am). Enhanced by an outdoor balcony and beautiful view, **The Sunset** is the only place for *soya moussaka*

(1000dr). Another worthwhile choice is the palatable grilled octopus and *patato* (1500dr). Head to **Vegara** (tel. 74 017) for an omelette (650-1100dr), every type of coffee imaginable, and sweet desserts. The cafe chills out with eclectic art and music (open 9am-3am). **Zygos** (tel. 71 350) serves peerless apple cake (450dr), among other tasty treats and on certain nights, and has live music and dancing till 5am.

■ Hozoviotissa Monastery Μονη Χωζοβιοτισας

From Katapola, you can catch a bus that goes through Hora. If you are in Hora, you may choose to go down the steps that begin at the top of Hora, past the OTE antenna. Both routes take you to the beginning of the 350-step staircase that climbs to the monastery. Tel. 71 274. Open 8am-1pm and 5-7pm. Modest dress required.

A trip to Amorgos is incomplete without a visit to the **Hozoviotissa Monastery.** The 11th-century whitewashed edifice is built so flawlessly into the sheer face of a cliff that it appears like an organism growing out of the rock. Legend has it that attempts to build the monastery on the shore were twice thwarted by divine intervention before the workers discovered their bag of tools mysteriously hanging from the cliff, which they interpreted as an omen advising them on where to recommence construction. The monastery is positively otherworldly, undoubtedly one of the more exhilarating visual spectacles in all of Greece. If you complete the hike, the monks may reward you with cold water, *raki,* and *loukoumi* (Greek sweets). Before leaving, visit the downstairs exhibit, which includes writings, relics, and church items dating to the founding of the monastery. Wander through the chambers farther below to get a sense of the hamlet's serenity and solitude.

■ Near Hora

South

The road from the turnoff for the monastery takes you to the lone and crystal waters of **Agia Anna** with its two enchanting beaches; from the bus stop, one is at the end of the path through the clearing, the other at the bottom of the central steps. Although the villages in southern Amorgos are less memorable, several beaches grace the coast. **Paradisia** at the island's southern tip may be the best on the island. The serene beach rests next to the remains of a Byzantine church. Ask locals to direct you to the **Olympia shipwreck** *(navagio),* remains of a boat that sank roughly 60 years ago.

North

Rugged mountains and placid coast mark the road connecting Hora with Aegiali. The intrepid hiker, however, can brave the 4-hour walking path beginning behind Hora and stretching up the mountains to the village of **Potamos.** forty minutes into the hike, the Byzantine church **Christasomas** stands abandoned and crumbling. Cut out of the rock above, the church is hewn out of small cave, thought to have been a hermit dwelling. The trail ascends past a series of monasteries, before descending to views of miniature **Nikouria Island,** which swimmers can reach from the beach by the main road. Lonely and deserted, **Agios Mammas Church** is the last significant marker before Potamos appears. Large and touristy Aegiali lies directly below.

▓ Aegiali Αιγιαλη

The island's other port, Aegiali is as close as Amorgos comes to feeling tourism-saturated. With a town beach and numerous rooming and camping opportunities, Aegiali can be a good base for the north portion of the island. Nearby villages make for interesting excursions, but you may go stir crazy staying in one. The beach past the port, surrounding villages, and leisurely pace are Aegiali's main draws.

PRACTICAL INFORMATION Nautilus Travel (tel. 73 217; fax 72 231) handles ferries, **currency exchange,** and other travel services (open daily 10am-1pm and 6-

10pm). **Aegialis Tours** (tel. 73 393 or 73 107; fax 73 395) handles Flying Dolphins and boat excursions. Both are just inland from the waterfront. **Ferry and Flying Dolphin** schedules are virtually the same as Katapola. Buses run to Katapola via Hora (6 per day, 250dr). The bus stop is on the waterfront. The **post office** (tel. 73 037) also has **currency exchange.** Follow signs from the waterfront (open M-F 7:30am-2pm). A **first aid station** (tel. 73 222) is above the town, by the road to Potamos (open daily 9am-1:30pm, available 24hr. for emergencies). **Amorgos Motor Center** (tel. 73 444) on the waterfront, rents new bikes (4000dr per day). If mopeds, ferries, and buses are too tame for moving about, ask **Amorgos Dive Ventures** (tel./fax 73 611) about beginner and PADI certified courses in **SCUBA** diving.

ACCOMMODATIONS Look for "rooms for rent" signs going up the stairpaths in the middle of town. **Popi Chalari Rooms for Rent** (tel. 73 207), by the post office, has clean rooms with balconies overlooking Nikouria Island (singles 4000dr; doubles 6000-7000dr). To reach **Adonis Similidas Rooms to Let** (tel. 73 225), follow the middle stairpath and signs for the bakery. They offer simple rooms above the bakery (doubles 4000dr). **Amorgos Camping** (tel. 73 500; fax 73 388), just outside town, by the road to Tholaria, is a 10-minute walk from the port and beach but provides free port pickup and dropoff. The site boasts laundry and cooking facilities, safety deposits, showers, a restaurant, and a bar (2 people with tent 1500dr. Tent rental 600dr).

FOOD AND ENTERTAINMENT To Limani (tel. 73 269) is just inland from the waterfront near the travel agencies. Paintings of Greek island life adorn the walls of this spacious and welcoming town favorite which spins delicious twists on standard *taverna* fare: Amorgian fish soup (1600dr), octopus salad (1400dr). **Celini Cafe Bar** (tel. 73 066), across from the beach, satiates beachside patrons day and night with breakfasts, dinners, and a bar (calamari 1200dr; pasta with pesto 1000dr). **Seventies** (tel. 73 016) is Celini's beachside neighbor. The bar revolves around the patio outside and the pool tables inside, where "loser pays" is the house rule. **Paspartou** (tel. 73 277), next to the post office, is 50s Americana meets Greek nautica with serene views of Nikouria Island (open 10am-2:30am).

■ Near Aegiali

The thoroughly traditional villages of **Tholaria** and **Langada** have been left unscathed by Aegiali's brisk tourism. Both are 45 minutes by footpaths from behind Aegiali or 10 minutes by car along main roads. A 5-minute footpath connects Tholaria and Langada. Tholaria is noted for its vaulted passageways, constructed out of stone and wood, which lend a peculiar feel to the villages.

What little remains of ancient **Vigla's** acropolis lies on the hill opposite Tholaria. Minimal statue bases and wall remains necessitate a good deal of visualization. Behind the acropolis, a steep 25-minute path descends to **Mikri Vlichadiou**—remember it's a steep ascent on the return—where you'll probably be alone on the small congregation of pebbles that constitute the beach. Any visit to Langada should begin or end at **Nikos Taverna** (tel. 73 310), where Greek cuisine is raised to an art. Nikos' gorgeous rooms next door are probably not for budget travelers' wallets. Both are at the lower end of the quiet walking-friendly village.

TINOS Τηνος

Tinos has been a place of religious significance for Greeks since the War of Independence, when a nun named Pelagia, guided by a vision, found a miracle-working icon of Christ and the Virgin buried in an underground church. This **Icon of the Annunciation,** also known as the *Megalochari* (Great Joy) or *Panagia Evangelistria*, is one of the most sacred relics of the Greek Orthodox Church. Each year on the Feasts of the Annunciation (Mar. 25) and the Assumption (Aug. 15), thousands of pilgrims seeking

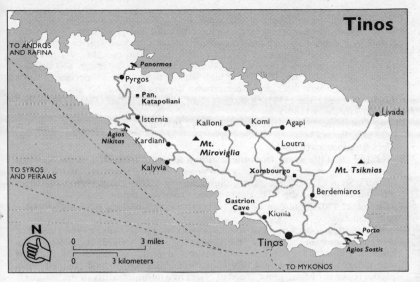

the icon converge, and the port town's ordinarily quiet streets leading up to the massive church are lined with carpet for those who wish to crawl on their knees.

Approaching the island from the south, the sudden appearance of trees will delight you as gentle hills cascade tier by tier to the clear sea. Wildflowers line the road in summer, and a bit of exploration yields quiet, secluded beaches. Inland lie opportunities for hiking, and chances to discover a rich cache of ruins, as well as the flock of doves which colonize the island's 2000 beautifully latticed dovecotes. Not only on feast days, Tinos is a popular destination for Greek travelers, but its growing nightlife has been mistakenly overlooked by international travelers; as a result, the breathtaking beauty, wealth of historical artifacts, and burgeoning social scene on Tinos remain virtually undiscovered.

▒ Tinos Town

This bustling port town garners special recognition for historical and religious reasons, as well as its approachability, its open market, and the increasing number of bars and discos: the Panagia Evangelistria church and miraculous icon of the Virgin Mary make the town a spiritual center, and, on August 15, 1940, the port rose to prominence when an Italian submarine torpedoed the Greek cruiser *Elli*, which was docked in the harbor for the observance of a religious holiday. Mussolini declared war two months later.

Today, Tinos Town is the most visited part of the island, although exploration of the rest rewards visitors if their schedule allows. The plethora of souvenirs, hotels, restaurants and tourist-oriented services attracts domestic and international visitors, particularly during July and August. To avoid throngs of other backpackers as well as the island's famous high winds, visit in May, June, or September.

ORIENTATION AND PRACTICAL INFORMATION

From the main dock next to the bus depot, walk left to the center of town to the sprawling **Megalochares St.** This wide avenue leads uphill to the Neoclassical facade of the **Panayia Evangelistria Church.** Parallel to Megalochares St., **Evangelistrias St.** (nicknamed Bazaar St. by the locals) overflows with religious goods such as six-foot long candles and other shopping delights.

Transportation

Ferries: Tinos can be reached by frequent ferries and hydrofoils from Peiraias and Rafina near Athens, as well as Mykonos, Syros, and Andros. Ferries from Tinos travel to Mykonos (30min., 4-5 per day, 1140dr); Andros (2hr., 2-4 per day, 1750dr); Syros (40min., 2 per day, 1195dr); Peiraias (5½hr., 2 per day, 4700dr); and Rafina (4hr., 2-4 per day, 3610dr). In high season, there is weekly service to Paros (1730dr) and Naxos (1920dr). A **catamaran** departs daily for: Mykonos (30min., 2275dr); Paros (1¼hr., 3385dr); Naxos (1¾hr., 3750dr); Rafina (3hr., 7225dr); and Amorgos (6¼hr., 6115dr).

Flying Dolphins: Leave daily for Mykonos (2270dr); Andros (3500dr); Rafina (7225dr); Paros (3460dr); Naxos (3850dr); Santorini (7970dr); and 2 times per week for Amorgos (6200dr).

Buses: (tel. 22 440). Leave from the station a few storefronts left of the National Bank. They depart 2 to 7 times daily for Pyrgos (700dr); Panormos (750dr); Kalloni (550dr); Steni (320dr); Skalados (400dr); Kionia (200dr); and Porto (200dr). A schedule is posted in the KTEL ticket agency across the depot.

Taxis: (tel. 22 470), Inquire at the blue booth to the right of the waterfront. Available daily 6am-2am.

Mopeds: Getting your own set of wheels is probably the best way to see Tinos, but take special care on the narrow gravel mountain roads. Try **Vidalis,** 16 Zanaki Alavanou St. (tel. 23 400), which is on the main road leading out of town off the right side of the waterfront. Ask for Christina. Cars rent for 6000-10,000dr, mopeds from 2500dr (open daily 8am-9pm). The staff offers free information about the island. Or try **Jason's** (tel. 24 583 or 24 283), just before Alavanou St., on the waterfront (open daily 8am-10pm). Prices are 2500-3000dr per day for a moped and 6000-15,000dr per day for a car.

Tourist and Financial Services

National Bank: (tel. 22 328 or 23 590). On the waterfront across from the bus depot. Has an **ATM.** Open M-Th 8am-2pm, F 8am-1:30pm.

Tourist Agencies: Mariner (tel. 23 193), next to the pharmacy, and **KTEL Travel,** on the waterfront, handle **Flying Dolphins** and an **excursion boat** to Mykonos and Delos (Tu-Su 9am, returning 6pm, 4000dr).

Bookstores: International News and Magazines (tel. 22 581). On the left of the waterfront, sells international newspapers and magazines. Open daily 8am-11pm.

Public toilets: At the left end of the waterfront near Dolphin Sq., behind Hotel Lito.

Emergency and Communications

Police station: (tel. 22 100 or 22 255). Also houses the **tourist police,** is located 5min. out of town on the road to Kionia.

Post Office: (tel. 22 247). Facing inland, on the far right end of the waterfront, behind the small square. Open M-F 7:30am-2pm. **Postal Code:** 84200.

OTE: (tel. 22 499). A few blocks up Megalochares St. on the right. Open M-F 7:30am-3:10pm. **Telephone Code:** 0283.

ACCOMMODATIONS

Tinos has plenty of accommodations, except at festival time (Eastern Orthodox Easter week) and occasionally weekends in July and August, when vacationing Athenians descend. Most hotels are expensive, so try your bargaining skills with the crowd of smiling faces holding "Rooms to Let" signs when you disembark.

Giannis (tel. 22 515), at the far right end of the waterfront (facing inland), offers peaceful, lovely, airy rooms in a 75-year-old home with blue shutters. Giannis himself will give you Greek lessons with a cup of Greek coffee in the garden sitting area. Common baths, kitchen and laundry facilities. Doubles 7000dr; triples with private bath and kitchen 8000-12,000dr.

Loukas Apergis' Rooms (tel. 23 964, mobile tel. 093 66 8888) are a good choice if you can't face the hustlers. Take a left onto Zanaki Alavanou St. just before the post office, then the second left onto 25 Martiou St. at the 2nd park (the one with the fountain in the shape of a little boy) and look for signs on that street. All rooms with bath. Doubles 6000dr; triples 8000dr. Ask about rooms in the countryside.

Mrs. Plyte (tel. 23 228) also has rooms in the same neighborhood with common baths and kitchens. Take the second left onto 25 Martiou St. at the second little park (the one with the little boy fountain), then look on your right for a white house with blue shutters above a woodshop. Inquire about rooms in the woodshop. Doubles 5000-7000dr; triples 7000-10,000dr.

Tinos Camping (tel. 22 344 or 22 548), a clearly marked 10min. walk to the right-hand side of town. Well-kept, has kitchen and laundry facilities, showers, bungalows, and a restaurant and bar. 1000-1200dr per person; 700-800dr per tent.

FOOD

Pigada (tel. 24 240). Take the first right off Evangelistrias St., past a few other restaurants. If you can stand bright lights and incessant TV, don't shy away—the food is excellent. Try *moussaka* (1200dr) or *dolmades* (1200dr). Open daily 8am-11:30pm.

Pallatha (tel. 83 516, 23 516), on the left side of the waterfront and inland by the bar street. Open year-round; serves authentic Greek cuisine and local specialities. Big portions, and food so good you might want to bring bread from next door to wipe your plate. Try fava beans and spinach (900dr), or local sausage and potatoes (1000dr). Open daily 9am-4pm and 6pm-1am.

Old-fashioned Wood-Burning Bakery (tel. 25 727) is next door to Pallatha. Head to the new port, next to the only one on the island. Try amazing fresh bread (80-200dr). Open daily 7am-3pm and 5-11pm.

☙**Mesklies** (tel. 22 151 or 22 373), on the left side of the waterfront, look for the Mesklies sign. Both the best pastry shop in town and the last word in pizza, if you want variety and crispy crust. Two doors farther to the left, the same owner makes excellent pizza in a wood oven at his pizzeria, also called Mesklies. After having pizza (1900-3000dr), spaghetti (1000-1900dr), or a calzone, top off your meal with the island's dessert specialty, *tyropitakia. Tyropitakia* of Tinos are made with sugar instead of salty feta cheese. The product is denser than cheese cake but just as good (open daily 7am-3am).

Giannis Snack Bar. Turn left up Alavanou St.; it will be on the right. Try a surprisingly non-greasy *gyro* pita for only 250dr. Open 10am-3:30pm and 6pm-midnight.

ENTERTAINMENT

Most of the town's bars are on the water to the left of the harbor, behind Hotel Lito. **Metropolis Club** plays the latest Greek tunes for an often wall-to-wall crowd, while **Kaktos Club,** located inside a windmill behind the Panagia Evangelistria church, caters to American music lovers while providing them with an incredible hilltop view, and special nights with live bands (look for posters around town). **Kovros Bar** (tel. 24 028), on Bazaar St. across from Vinaki Pizzeria, is perfect for people-watching, as its balconies overlook the open market (wine from the bottle 4500dr, 1600dr cocktails; open 11am-3am). Also a snazzy coffee bar in the day.

There are a series of **bars** in the Palada St. neighborhood, each with its own theme, including an "underwater" one. **Gyrsos** on the far left of the waterfront, has a large dancefloor and huge pillow-bedecked benches over which patrons drape themselves while sipping drinks (cocktails 1500-1800dr; beer 1000dr). Along the waterfront, **Fevgotas** has billiard tables and a TV tuned to MTV all night long. Prices at these nightspots are similar (beer 800-900dr; cocktails 1500dr).

SIGHTS

In 1822, Sister Pelagia, a Tiniote nun, had a vision in which the Virgin Mary instructed her to find an icon buried at the site of an ancient church, destroyed in the 10th century by pirates. A year later, the icon was housed, amid great rejoicing, in the **Panagia Evangelistria** (tel. 22 256), where it still resides. *(Open daily 7am-8pm. Free. Modest dress required.)* To the faithful, the find is evidence of the power and presence of the Holy Virgin. The relic reputedly has curing powers and is almost entirely covered with gold, diamonds, and jewels left at the church by people wishing to thank the Holy Mother for their good health. Countless *tamata*—beautifully crafted plaques praising the Virgin's healing powers—have won the Panagia the title "Lourdes of the Aegean." Even on non-Feast days the church is bustling with activity, lines to see the icon, and heaps of the devout resting in the church's square. Visitors of any denomination light offertory candles (100-1000dr donation depending on candle size).

The **Well of Sanctification** flows below the marble entrance stairs in a chapel. It is a natural spring discovered during excavations, whose waters visitors bottle and drink or carrying as talismans. The spring is said to have been dry until the icon was unearthed; since then, it has flowed continuously. To the right of the well is the mausoleum of the Greek warship *Elli*, sunk by an Italian torpedo in 1940. To the left of the well, in an adjoining chamber, the spot where the icon was found is marked by a marble plaque and wooden icon.

There are lodgings and facilities in Tinos Town, but it so crowded on August 15 that the nearly 30,000 visitors sleep elsewhere, *everywhere*—along the dock, on the sidewalks, and even in the church itself. The next day, after making the 10km walk to the convent of Kechrovouni in a procession led by the icon, the masses depart on dozens of specially chartered ferries.

Don't miss the oil painting of a weeping Mary Magdalene contemplating the crown of thorns in the gallery opposite the church entrance. A free English information booklet full of history, colorful reports of miracles, and explanations of holidays is available at the second floor to the right of the sanctum. Tinos is also famed for its art, particularly its marble sculptures; after you visit the Panagia, drop by the church complex's **art and archaeological museums,** which features works by native Tiniotes. *(Open 8:30am-3pm; hours variably extended in summer. Free.)*

Tinos' **Archaeological Museum,** on Megalochares St. across and uphill from the OTE, contains artifacts from Poseidon's sanctuary at Kionia, a first-century BC sundial, and a few vases from Xombourgo. *(Open Tu-Su 8:30am-3pm. Admission 500dr, students 300dr, European students free.)* Don't miss the large *pitnoi* (relief pottery) that portrays Athena rushing out of Zeus's head, from the end of the geometric period (early 7th century BC). The museum is small but clearly marked.

At **Kionia,** explore the ruins of the 4th-century BC temple of Poseidon and Amphitrite, then sit by the sea at the steadily touristed **Tinos** or **Stavros Beaches,** both near town. If you stay late at Stavros, enjoy the locally acclaimed **Chroma Bar/Homa Club.** A closer and equally crowded beach, **Agios Fokas,** is a short walk east (on the opposite side) of Tinos Town.

■ Around Tinos

Rustic Tinos will reward adventurers with secluded beaches and wonderful views of a verdant countryside. The best beaches on the island are outside of Tinos Town, a short bus ride away. **Agios Sostis, Porto, Panormos,** and **Kolimbithra** top the list. Walking left around the hills from Panormos Beach reveals some beautiful, lonely stretches of beach. To get to spectacular **Kardianis** beach, take the Pyrgos bus to Kardiani and travel down the winding street from the main road. The 2000 **dovecotes** dotting the landscape have become the island's symbol. Built in medieval times, these small white buildings have intricate lattice-work, complete with nesting birds. No longer used to breed birds, abandoned *peristonies* are being transformed into striking summer homes. Stop by the picturesque town of **Pyrgos,** 33km northwest of Tinos Town (1hr., 3-5 times per day, 700dr).

With a marble quarry, Pyrgos has always been home to Tinos' artists and sculptors, including Giannouli Chalepas, whose *Sleeping Daughter* graces Athens's central graveyard; today, it is also home to the only marble sculpting school in all of Greece. If you want a lovely souvenir and don't mind dragging it around for the rest of your trip, there are some exquisite marble statues to be found. If your budget restricts you, find terra-cotta statues with marble bases that are just as nice and not as expensive. **The Blue Trunk** (tel. 31 870), on Sardela St. in Pyrgos, sells them and other gifts.

Nearby are 3 *tavernas* which the locals frequent. Two kilometers northeast of Pyrgos, **Panormos Bay** has a small beach and three *tavernas*. Be careful not to get stranded in the village; there are no night buses on Tinos, and taxis are hard to find.

If you have wheels, investigate the delightful villages that encircle **Mt. Exobourgo,** 14km north of Tinos Town, and the precipitous site of the Venetian Fortress, **Xombourgo.** After withstanding 11 assaults, the 13th-century island capital fell to the Ottomans in 1715. It was the very last territorial gain of the Ottoman Empire. Climb the mountain from the east foothill (near the village of Xinara or Loutra), and indulge in the resplendent panorama.

SYROS Συρος

Syros's rise as a commercial power began with the Phoenicians who used the island as a sea port. Venetian control of the island, which began in the 13th century, solidified Syros's title as the trading capital of the Cyclades. The large Catholic population here is a vestige of this era. Many of the buildings in Hermoupolis date from this period, when rich merchants built mansions and erected monuments. But all good things must come to an end, and the advent of steam-powered ships coupled with the rise of Peiraias sent Syros into decline. During the last 20 years Syros has managed to recover, due primarily to a shipbuilding industry which now keeps the island afloat year-round. This source of income has allowed the island not to concentrate on attracting large numbers of tourists. The port town, Hermoupolis, is hot and noisy; it is best to seek idyllic Greek island charm beyond the port. Particularly in Ano Syros, one of the two peaks on the island, diligent hikers can find uncharted terrain.

Syros

■ Hermoupolis
Ερμουπολις

With a Greek Orthodox church on one hill and a Catholic church on the other, Hermoupolis, the spiritual city of Hermes (god of commerce), rests serenely on its natural harbor. Despite its decline as a major port, the city remains the shipping center and capital of the Cyclades. Elegant Miaouli Square and the 19th-century mansions in Dellagrazia let us peek at Hermoupolis's opulent past and explain its former nicknames—the "Manchester of Greece" and "little Milan."

ORIENTATION AND PRACTICAL INFORMATION

The center of activity in Hermoupolis is **Miaouli Sq.,** two blocks up El. Venizelou St. from the winged statue at the center of the harbor. You can't miss the palatial town hall and large marble plaza.

CYCLADES

Transportation

Ferries: Depart from the right of the harbor to Peiraias (4½hr., 1-4 per day, 4450dr); Tinos (40min., 2-3 per day, 1240dr); Mykonos (1½hr., 2-3 per day, 1525dr); Paros (1½hr., 1-2 per day, 1580dr); Naxos (2½hr., 1-2 per day, 2100dr); Ios (4hr., 4 per week, 3120dr); Santorini (5hr., 1 per day, 4190dr); Rhodes (2 per week, 8450dr); Kos (2 per week, 5250dr); Crete (5450dr); and several of the smaller Cycladic islands. Some boats, however, leave from the left of the harbor by the winged statue, so be sure to ask when you buy your ticket.

Flying Dolphins: Departing from across the ferry docks on the left, speed daily to Tinos (2150dr); Mykonos (3000dr), Paros (3150dr); Naxos (4150dr); Santorini (8230dr); and Ios (7350dr). **Sea Jets** run daily to Rafina (1½hr., 6930dr); Tinos (15min., 2150dr); Mykonos (35min., 3000dr); and once weekly to Andros (3715dr). **Minoan Lines** carry cars and passengers daily to Peiraias (2hr., 8650dr).

Buses: (tel. 82 575). Leave from the depot near the ferry dock and travel regularly to Galissas (18 per day, 270dr); nearby beach Kini (6 per day, 250dr); and Ano Syros (3 per day, 220dr). Service is less frequent on Sunday, and an excellent schedule is posted next to the buses.

Flights: There are two-three daily **flights** to Athens (15,000dr).

Taxis: (tel. 86 222). Wait in front of the town hall.

Tourist and Financial Services

Tourist Agencies: Gaviotis Tours (tel. 86 606; fax 83 445), near the ferry dock and across from the bus depot, provides schedules and prices and sells **tickets** for ferries, hydrofoils, and flights for Syros. Open daily 9am-10pm.

Banks: National Bank (tel. 82 451), on Kosti Kalomenopoulou St., in an elegant building at the end of the street the post office is on, offers **currency exchange.** Open M-Th 8am-2pm, F 8am-1:30pm. **Credit Bank,** just off Venizelou St. near the post office, has an **ATM.**

Emergency and Communications

Police: (tel. 82 620), behind the theater off the upper right corner of Miaouli Sq. A **tourist police officer** is on duty in the mornings.

Port authority: can be reached at 88 888.

Hospital: (tel. 86 666), at the left end of the waterfront (facing inland) at Iroon Sq., a 20min. walk from Miaculi St.

Post Office: (tel. 82 596) is 40m down the 2nd right off El. Venizelou St. Open M-F 7:30am-2pm. **Postal Code:** 84100.

OTE: (tel. 82 799), on the square. Open daily 7am-11pm. **Telephone Code:** 0281.

ACCOMMODATIONS

Hermoupolis has plenty of cheap rooms, and off-season prices are generally about 20 to 40% cheaper. There is a large map with names and phone numbers of hotels at the ferry dock. When staffed, the kiosk directly in front of you as you step off the ferry provides information on accommodations; someone is likely to be there when boats arrive during the day in the summer.

Villa Nefeli, 21 Parou St. (tel. 87 076), along the waterfront and left on Hiou St., just before Venizelou St. Parou St. is the first left off Hiou St. The traditional house turned brand new hotel has clean rooms with high ceilings. Have a drink with the extra-friendly owner and his extra-passive dog on the roof garden bar, which has a full view of the harbor. Doubles 8000-10,000dr; triples 9,000-13,000dr.

Hotel Esperance (tel. 81 671, 81 434 or 87 053), to the left of the ferry dock, will win you over with its gleaming rooms with bath, TV, A/C, and the wonderful giggling mother of the owner who helps out at the top of the marble stairs. Doubles 8000-13,000dr; triples 10,000-15,000dr.

Ariadni Rooms to Let (tel. 81 307 or 80 245), on Nik. Fylini St. near the ferry dock (look for signs), provides a dose of luxury. The hotel prides itself on a class "A" rating, and deservedly so—the rooms are spotless and radiant. Some rooms have a kitchen for the same price as the rooms without this perk, so call ahead if you plan on cooking. Doubles 8000-13,000dr; triples 10,000-15,000dr. Show your *Let's Go* for a discount.

FOOD AND ENTERTAINMENT

◉**Folia** (tel. 83 715). Head up the main road leading from the top right corner of the main square. Stay to the left of St. Nicholas and keep going up, even after the road turns to stairs. Look for the sign on the left and turn onto Xenofontos St.—after roughly 50m, take a right and head uphill to the restaurant. At the top of a seemingly endless flight of stairs; excellent cuisine and friendly service await. Three main dishes are particularly divine—the *kouneli stifado* (rabbit stew 1250dr), the *arni rigonatto* (lamb cooked with oregano 1300dr), and the only pigeon dish on the island (grilled and served with potatoes 1100dr). Open daily 5pm-1am.

Elysee (tel. 81 741 or 88 245), on the far right-hand edge of the harbor next to the port authority. Elysee is perfect if your ferry arrives in Syros late at night and you're famished. The joint offers good pizza (1700-1900dr) and a hearty portion of spaghetti *carbonara* (1200dr), served until 4am. Show your *Let's Go* for a discount.

Amix Italian Restaurant (tel. 83 989) serves up huge portions of amazing Italian food, almost directly across from the ferry dock. Try the *tagliatelli carbonara* (1800dr). They have an extensive gourmet pizza list (1700-2400dr).

Kechayia Sweet Shop (tel. 88 076), on the waterfront corner of El. Venizelou St., will floor you with amazing renditions of traditional local specialties, like delicious *loukoumi* (450dr) and *chalvathopita* (a sweet concoction of almond paste mixed with nuts and chocolate 350dr).

The waterfront and Miaouli Sq. buzz with activity at night. On the right-hand strip of the waterfront, **Seasons** serves 35 varieties of beer and the necessary *mezethes* (finger food to whet your alcohol appetite). Don't bother asking what goes into the specialty cocktail *epoches;* it's a secret recipe (open daily 8am-3pm and 7pm-3am). The **Cotton Club,** a block farther left along the waterfront, offers similar drinks at similar prices. For the latest Greek music, hit the waterfront at **Odyssea** or **Skiés.** Both bars spin the Greek Top 40 and serve beer and cocktails until the wee hours.

Kazino Eyéou, the only casino on any of the surrounding islands, mimics those in big gambling towns. If you have a surplus of *drachmes* and want to blow it all for the sake of highbrow luxury, this is the place to be. Men must wear pants and foreign visitors must leave their passport and 5000dr at the door. Gambling starts at 12:30pm.

SIGHTS

Sights and sounds swarm Syros's small **open market,** between the lower left of Miaouli Sq. and the waterfront. From there, visitors make the ascent to **Ano Syros,** a medieval Venetian settlement that is still home to Syros's Catholics. To get there, climb the steps behind Miaouli Sq. or take the bus from the waterfront. The **Archaeological Museum,** the entrance to which is at the upper left corner of the Town Hall, has a small collection of Cycladic Art. *(Open Tu-Su 8:30am-3pm. Free.)* At the **Church of the Assumption** *(Kimisis Theotokou)* on St. Proiou St., view a painting created in 1562 at age 20 by **El Greco.** The discovery of this painting on Syros helped confirm the painter's Greek origin.

■ Around Syros

The main beach at **Galissas,** a village to the west of Hermoupolis, is beyond crowded; every inch—down to the last sand grain—is alive and writhing. From Hermoupolis, 18 buses per day travel to Galissas, alternating between a direct 15-minute route and a 45-minute route that stops in other villages first (270dr). In Hermoupolis, buses leave from the depot near the ferry dock, where an up-to-date schedule is posted. Climb past the chapel of Agia Pakou on the left side (facing the water) to discover **Armeos Beach**—tiny, beautiful, and **nudist.** Clothing is definitely an option.

Farther south along the coast are the beaches at **Poseidonia, Finikas, Angathopes,** and **Komito,** all connected by bus to Hermoupolis. The beach resort of **Vari** is most popular with families and package tour groups because of its shallow waters and relaxed atmosphere. North of Galissas is the tiny fishing village of **Kini**—if you happen to be in this picturesque hamlet on June 29th, the Church of St. Peter invites you and every other living thing within earshot to an all-night festival. The *kakavia* (fish soup) is plentiful and accompanied by the sounds of *baizoukia*.

ANDROS Ανδρος

Winding above splendid scattered beaches, the hour drive from the ferry landing at **Gavrio** to **Andros Town** is magnificent, and both the latter and **Batsi** have gorgeous town beaches as well as blossoming nocturnal activities. Tiers of straw fields and stretches of green and purple growth are partitioned by a network of streams and stone walls, lying like a spider's web fallen on the face of Andros' hillside, while ruins sprinkled across the Andrian hills memorialize the island's checkered history of occupation. Andros is not a sleeping island, but rather a place where tourism has been gracefully integrated into the easy-going life-style of its inhabitants. On an island with 300 beaches the intrepid visitor can leave the village behind, find a solitary stretch of sand and stare for hours into the lonely Aegean. It is the perfect place for families on holidays, or the visitor who delights in exceptional food, swimming, and sunsets.

■ Gavrio Γαωριο

Crowned by the three-domed Church of Agios Nikolaos, the dusty port town of Gavrio has little else to offer tourists. Most visitors stay overnight to catch an early ferry; one could also use Gavrio as a base to explore some of the best stretches of smooth sand between the port and the popular tourist beach town of Batsi.

ORIENTATION AND PRACTICAL INFORMATION Good **maps** are available at tourist shops (500dr). The **police** (tel. 71 220) are to the right on a road parallel to the waterfront, up the steps opposite the bus stop. The building is unmarked, so look for the Greek flag (open 24hr.). The **OTE** stands one block to the left of Hotel Galaxy, on a side street in a building with green shutters (open M-F 7:30am-3pm). The **post office** (tel. 71 254) is two blocks farther on the waterfront (open M-F 7:30am-2pm). The **Agricultural Bank** (tel. 71 478 or 71 308) is on the corner at the right-hand end

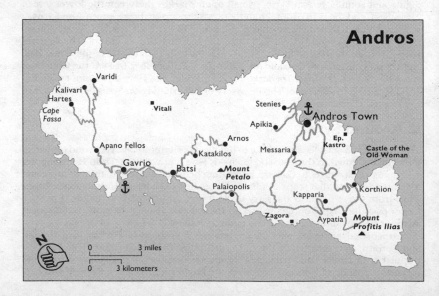

Andros

Varidi
Kalivari
Hartes
Cape Fassa
Vitali
Stenies
Andros Town
Apikia
Apano Fellos
Arnos
Ep. Kastro
Messaria
Castle of the Old Woman
Gavrio
Katakilos
Batsi
Mount Petalo
Palaiopolis
Kapparia
Korthion
Zagora
Aypatia
Mount Profitis Ilias

0   3 miles
0   3 kilometers

of the waterfront facade (open for **currency exchange** M-Th 9am-2pm, F 9am-1:30pm). For medical emergencies call the **hospital** (tel. 71 210). **Postal code:** 84501. **Telephone code:** 0282.

To get to Andros Town, take one of the **buses** from the depot next to the ferry dock (1hr., 5-7 per day, 700dr). The same bus passes through Batsi (from Gavrio 15min., 270dr). Check the schedules as early as possible. They tend to be erratic and structured around ferry arrivals and departures. From Andros, **ferries** sail to Athens's minor port, Rafina (2hr., 2-5 per day, 2330dr). They also head to Tinos (2hr., 2-3 per day, 1810dr); Mykonos (2½hr., 2-3 per day, 2600dr); Syros (2-3hr., 2 per week, 1815dr); Paros (1 per week, 2645dr); and Naxos (3½hr., 2 per week, 2870dr). There is daily **Sea Jet** service to Rafina (1hr., 4750dr); Tinos (50min., 3500dr); Syros (1½hr, 3595dr); Mykonos (15min., 5330dr); Naxos (2hr, 6000dr); and Paros (1¾hr, 5475dr). **Flying Dolphins** from Batsi zip to Tinos (1 per day, 3600dr); Mykonos (1 per day, 5220dr); Paros (4 per week, 5475dr); Naxos (4 per week, 5935dr); Ios (one per day, 8455dr); Santorini (1 per day, 9560dr); Kea (3000dr); and Peiraias (7500dr). A **taxi** to Batsi costs 1200-1500dr and to Andros Town costs 3500-4000dr. You can rent a **moped** at **Andros Moto Rental** (tel. 71 605), behind the port authority (from 3500dr per day; open daily 8am-9pm).

ACCOMMODATIONS AND FOOD Most accommodations are designed for longer visits and family groups, but simple rooming arrangements and camping are available. At the center of the waterfront, **Hotel Galaxias** (tel. 71 005, 71 228) has standard, simple rooms (singles 6000dr; doubles 10,000dr; triples 11,000dr).

Fix your own meals with goodies from the **Andrios Supermarket** (tel. 71 341), on the right end of the waterfront (open daily 6:30am-11pm). **Galaxias** (tel. 71 005), adjoining the hotel, has traditional Greek dishes (stuffed tomatoes 900-1000dr); less traditionally Greek—but mighty tasty—is a pizza from **San Remo** (tel. 71 150), next to the post office (1100-1700dr). For breakfast, try the bakery **Gavrio** (tel. 71 126), next to the pharmacy (chocolate croissant 350dr; ham and cheese pita 350dr).

■ Batsi Μπατσι

With its long stretch of golden sand and crystal-blue water, Batsi is the tourist capital of Andros. The town beach is glorious and the food is unexpectedly tasty everywhere you go. If you take a bus from the port, sit on the right side to enjoy the scenery. Between Gavrio and Batsi, there are coves with very swimmable pools, as well as beaches at **Agios Petros, Psili Ammos,** and **Kipri.**

ORIENTATION AND PRACTICAL INFORMATION If you stay on the bus until Batsi, the main bus stop is at the end of the beach in a small square. The **taxi** stand is also there. There is a branch of the **National Bank** (tel. 22 400), to the right, continuing on the road to Andros Town (open M-F 8am-1:30pm). If you need an **ATM,** go to the **Ionian Bank** on the waterfront (tel. 41 880; open M-F 8am-1:30pm). Beware, though, the ATM closes at night. The conveniently located **mobile post office** is down the road along the beach, inland from the Hotel Karanassos sign; the **post office** is across a dirt road from the hotel (open M-F 7:30am-2pm). Also on the waterfront is a **kiosk** (tel. 41 432), which sells all **international papers** and magazines. On a street parallel to the main road, accessible from the stairs past the National Bank, is **Dolphin Hellas Travel** (tel. 41 185 or 41 064; fax 41 719) which offers **currency exchange,** information, and excursions. There are **taxi boats** that leave Batsi for other beaches on the island (round-trip 1500dr; open 9:30am-1:30pm and 6-9pm). Renting a moped costs 3000dr on average; the cheapest rental car is 11,500dr for 24 hr. **Buses** run to Andros Town (2-3 times per day, 600dr), and to Gavrio (2 per day, 270dr).

ACCOMMODATIONS It is easier to find accommodations here than in either Gavrio or Andros Town, but they tend to be more expensive. Expect to pay 8000 to 10,000dr for a double at one of the beachfront hotels. Look for "Rooms to Let" signs or inquire at souvenir or tourist shops (6000-10,000dr). **Meltemi Studios** (tel. 41 016 or 41 702; fax 41 564), is worth the significant walk up the hill—take the first set of stairs going up as you leave the beach with the water on your right. The studios offer beautiful ocean views with kitchen, private bath, TV, fridge, and balcony (doubles 12,000dr; triples 14,000dr). There are also larger suites (quads 18,000dr) with full kitchen and private entrance. To get to the office of **Villa Maroni** (tel. 41 706), take the stairs past Dolphin Hellas Travel, then your first right. Some rooms a great but expensive view (doubles 16,000dr); you may opt for ones without to save money (doubles without bath 10,000-11,000dr). All have TV, phone, kitchen, and bath. **Hotel Karanassos** (tel. 41 480 or 41 481), one block from the beachfront, has breezy rooms with balcony and bath (doubles 7000-14,000dr; triples 9000-15,000dr; quads 10,000-17,000dr; breakfast 1500dr).

FOOD Eating in Batsi is not simply refueling. It's a delight. **Restaurant Sirocco** (tel. 41 023) is at the top of the first set of steps on your left leaving the beach. Head for the string of lights and you will not be disappointed; the owner Louie was born under the bar years ago and serves delicious food, like homemade garlic bread (300dr) and hummus and vegetables (1100dr). For main dishes, the curried taste of chicken biryani (1700dr) with yogurt and the Shrimp Sirocco grilled in a spicy red sauce (3000dr) are out of sight (open daily 6pm-midnight). **Oti Kalo** (tel. 41975), on the right side of the waterfront (facing inland) offers traditional Greek food far better than its *taverna* counterparts. The *moussaka* has a delicious dose of nutmeg and the chicken *souvlaki* is tender and delicately seasoned (1200dr), and both go well with the cheap wines (open daily noon-4pm and 6pm-1am).

ENTERTAINMENT AND SIGHTS To the left of the square, in a vine-covered setting along the waterfront, is **Skala** (tel. 41 656). Listen to trendy music and choose from a vast variety of beers (600-3000dr). If you want music with a faster beat, head to **Placebo** (tel. 71 800), half-way to Gavrio on the main road. The night club has a 1500dr cover including the first drink, but you can skip the cover and go into the bar (beer 800dr; cocktails 1200-1500dr). **On the Rocks,** smack dab on the waterfront and up the stairs, is a good place to watch the sunset and then begin to drink cocktails for 1500dr to rock and dance music. **Capriccio Music Bar** offers big, fun, fruity drinks like a Bing Bamboo, a gin fizz, or the popular piña colada (all 1500dr). Put the fun drink decorations in your hair and dance to rock music with the ocean meters away and a breeze blowing in. **The Music Cafe,** between On the Rocks and Capriccio on the waterfront, is a more mellow scene playing all those hits we love to love, including Madonna.

For daytime partying, take a taxi boat to the **Ammo beach,** where there is water polo, canoeing, windsurfing, and other beach fun around a bar (beer 500dr). Be sure to ask Argiris when he's planning his next beach party. On a quieter and more sophisticated note, check out the ruins of the ancient capital **Paleopolis** on the road to Andros Town, where remains of a theater and a stadium still stand. 2km southeast of Palaeokastro is the **Bay of Korthion,** with some of the finest swimming spots on Andros. The remnants of the **Castle of the Old Woman** are north of **Korthion.**

■ Andros Town

A sophisticated village with striking neoclassical architecture, **Andros Town** is on a spit of land that juts out deep into the Aegean. Behind the town, the land rises in green-hued tiers and is cut only by the road leading to Batsi. The wide-laned cobbled streets quietly lead to the tip of the peninsula, past hotels, shops, and the more residential part of town, to where furious blue waves pound the black rocks below.

ORIENTATION AND PRACTICAL INFORMATION The **post office** (tel. 22 260), where you can **exchange currency** (open M-F 7:30am-2pm), resides next to an open, airy square where **taxis** (tel. 22 171) queue. The **OTE** (tel. 22 199) is across from the central square on the left (open M-F 7:30am-3pm). The **National Bank** (tel. 22 400) is on the left farther down, on the way to the water (open M-Th 8am-2pm, F 8am-

MCI Spoken Here

Worldwide Calling Made Simple

For more information or to apply for a Card call: **1-800-955-0925**

Outside the U.S., call MCI collect (reverse charge) at: **1-916-567-5151**

International Calling As Easy As Possible.

Calling Card

MCI

123 456 7890 1234
J.D. SMITH

WorldPhone

The MCI Card
with WorldPhone
Service is designed
specifically to keep
you in touch with the
people that matter
the most to you.

The MCI Card with WorldPhone Service....

- Provides access to the US and other countries worldwide.

- Gives you customer service 24 hours a day

- Connects you to operators who speak your language

- Provides you with MCI's low rates and no sign-up fees

**For more information or
to apply for a Card call:**
1-800-955-0925

**Outside the U.S., call MCI
collect (reverse charge) at:**
1-916-567-5151

Pick Up the Phone, Pick Up the Miles.

Please cut out and save this reference guide for convenient U.S. and worldwide calling with the MCI Card with WorldPhone Service.

You earn frequent flyer miles when you travel internationally, why not when you call internationally? Callers can earn frequent flyer miles if they sign up with one of MCI's airline partners:

- American Airlines
- Continental Airlines
- Delta Airlines
- Hawaiian Airlines
- Midwest Express Airlines
- Northwest Airlines
- Southwest Airlines
- United Airlines
- USAirways

Your MCI Worldphone Access Numbers

COUNTRY	WORLDPHONE: TOLL-FREE ACCESS #
#Singapore	8000-112-112
#Slovak Republic (CC)	00421-00112
#Slovenia	080-8808
#South Africa (CC)	0800-99-0011
#Spain (CC)	900-99-0014
#Sri Lanka	440100
St. Lucia ÷	1-800-888-8000
#St. Vincent	1-800-888-8000
#Sweden (CC) ♦	020-795-922
#Switzerland (CC) ♦	0800-89-0222
#Syria	0800
#Taiwan (CC) ♦	0080-13-4567
#Thailand (CC) ♦	001-999-1-2001
#Trinidad & Tobago ÷	1-800-888-8000
#Turkey (CC) ♦	00-8001-1177
#Turks and Caicos ÷	1-800-888-8000
#Ukraine (CC) ♦	8♦10-013
#United Arab Emirates ♦	800-111
#United Kingdom (CC: To call using BT ■	0800-89-0222
To call using C&W ■	0500-89-0222
#United States (CC)	1-800-888-8000
#Uruguay	000-412
#U.S. Virgin Islands (CC)	1-800-888-8000
#Vatican City (CC)	172-1022
#Venezuela (CC) ‡ ♦	800-1114-0
Vietnam ●	1201-1022
Yemen ●	008-00-102

(Outside of Colombo, dial 01 first)

- # At connection available from most locations.
- (CC) Country-to-country calling available to/from most international locations.
- ‡ Limited availability.
- ÷ Wait for second dial tone.
- ▶ When calling from public phones, use phones marked LADATEL
- ▲ International communications carrier.
- ■ Not available from public pay phones.
- ● Public phones may require deposit of coin or phone card for call tone.
- ♦ Local service fee in U.S. currency required to complete call.
- ▲ Regulation does not permit Intra-Japan calls.
- Available from most major cities

And, it's simple to call home.

1. Dial the WorldPhone toll-free access number of the country you're calling from (listed inside).

2. Follow the voice instructions in your language of choice or hold for a WorldPhone operator.
   - Enter or give the operator your MCI Card number or call collect.

3. Enter or give the WorldPhone operator your home number.

4. Share your adventures with your family!

The MCI Card with WorldPhone Service... The easy way to call when traveling worldwide.

For more information or to apply for a Card call:
1-800-955-0925

Outside the U.S., call MCI collect (reverse charge) at:
1-916-567-5151

Please cut out and save this reference guide for convenient U.S. and worldwide calling with the MCI Card with WorldPhone Service.

COUNTRY	WORLDPHONE TOLL-FREE ACCESS #
American Samoa	633-2MCI (633-2624)
# Antigua	1-800-888-8000
(available from public card phones only)	#2
# Argentina (CC)	0800-5-1002
# Aruba ÷	800-888-8
# Australia (CC) ◆ To call using OPTUS ■	1-800-551-111
To call using TELSTRA ■	1-800-881-100
# Austria (CC) ◆	022-903-012
# Bahamas	1-800-389-8000
# Bahrain	800-002
# Barbados	1-800-888-8000
# Belarus (CC) From Brest, Vitebsk, Grodno, Minsk	8-10-800-103
From Gomel and Mogilev	8-10-800-103
# Belgium (CC) ◆	0800-10012
# Belize From Hotels	815
From Payphones	557
# Bermuda ÷	1-800-888-8000
# Bolivia (CC) ◆	0-800-2222
# Brazil (CC)	000-8012
# British Virgin Islands ÷	1-800-888-8000
# Brunei	800-011
# Bulgaria	00800-0001
# Canada (CC)	1-800-888-8000
# Cayman Islands	1-800-888-8000
# Chile (CC) To call using CTC ■	800-207-300
To call using ENTEL ■	800-360-180
# China ✦ For a Mandarin-speaking Operator	108-12
# Colombia (CC) ✦	980-16-0001
Collect Access in Spanish	980-16-1000
# Costa Rica ◆	0800-012-2222
# Cote D'Ivoire	1001
# Croatia (CC) ★	0800-22-0112
# Cyprus ◆	080-90000
# Czech Republic (CC) ◆	00-42000112
# Denmark (CC) ◆	8001-0022
# Dominica	1-800-888-8000
# Dominican Republic Collect Access in Spanish	1-800-888-8000
	1121
# Ecuador (CC) ÷	999-170
# Egypt (CC) ◆	355-5770
(Outside of Cairo, dial 02 first)	
El Salvador	800-1767

FOLD

COUNTRY	WORLDPHONE TOLL-FREE ACCESS #
# Federated States of Micronesia	624
# Fiji	004-890-1002
# Finland (CC) ◆	08001-102-80
# France (CC) ◆	0800-99-0019
# French Antilles (CC) (includes Martinique, Guadeloupe)	0800-99-0019
French Guiana (CC)	0-800-99-0019
# Gabon	00-005
# Gambia	00-1-99
# Germany (CC)	0-800-888-8000
# Greece (CC) ◆	00-800-1211
# Grenada ÷	1-800-888-8000
# Guam (CC)	1-800-888-8000
# Guatemala (CC) ◆	99-99-189
Guyana	177
# Haiti ÷	193
Collect Access in French/Creole	190
# Honduras ÷	8000-122
# Hong Kong (CC)	800-96-1121
# Hungary (CC) ◆	00▼800-01411
# Iceland (CC) ◆	800-9002
# India (CC) ✦	000-127
Collect Access	000-126
# Indonesia (CC)	001-801-11
# Iran ÷	(SPECIAL PHONES ONLY)
# Ireland (CC)	1-800-55-1001
# Israel (CC)	1-800-940-2727
# Italy (CC) ◆	172-1022
# Jamaica ÷	1-800-888-8000
Collect Access (from public phones)	873
# Japan (CC) ◆ (from Special Hotels only)	*2
To call using KDD ■	00539-121 ▼
To call using IDC ■	0066-55-121
To call using ITJ ■	0044-11-121
# Jordan	18-800-001
# Kazakhstan (CC)	8-800-131-4321
# Kenya ◆ Collect Access	080011
# Korea (CC) To call using KT ■	009-14
To call using DACOM ■	00309-14
To call using ONSE ■	00369-14
Phone Booths ÷ Press red button, 03, then ✱	
Military Bases	550-2255
# Kuwait	800-MCI (800-624)

FOLD

COUNTRY	WORLDPHONE TOLL-FREE ACCESS #
# Lebanon Collect Access	600-MCI (600-624)
# Liechtenstein (CC) ◆	0800-89-0222
# Luxembourg (CC)	0800-0112
# Macao	0800-131
# Macedonia (CC)	99800-4266
# Malaysia (CC) ◆	1-800-80-0012
# Malta	0800-89-0120
# Marshall Islands	1-800-888-8000
# Mexico (CC) Avantel	01-800-021-8000
Telmex ▲	001-800-674-7000
Collect Access in Spanish	01-800-021-1000
# Monaco (CC) ◆	800-90-019
# Montserrat ÷	1-800-888-8000
# Morocco	00-211-0012
# Netherlands (CC) ◆	0800-022-9122
# Netherlands Antilles (CC) ÷	001-800-888-8000
# New Zealand (CC) ◆	000-912
# Nicaragua (CC) Collect Access in Spanish	166
(Outside of Managua, dial 02 first)	
From any public payphone	*2
# Norway (CC) ◆	800-19912
# Pakistan	00-800-12-001
# Panama	108
Military Bases	2810-108
# Papua New Guinea (CC) ◆	05-07-19140
# Paraguay ÷	00-812-800
# Peru	0-800-500-10
# Philippines (CC) ◆ To call using PLDT ■	105-14
To call using PHILCOM ■	1026-14
Collect Access via PLDT in Filipino	105-15
Collect Access via ICC in Filipino	1237-77
# Poland (CC) ÷	00-800-111-21-22
# Portugal (CC) ÷	05-017-1234
# Puerto Rico (CC)	1-800-888-8000
# Qatar ◆	0800-012-77
# Romania (CC) ÷	01-800-1800
# Russia (CC) ÷ ◆ To call using ROSTELCOM ■	747-3322
(For Russian speaking operator)	960-2222
To call using SOVINTEL ■	747-3320
# Saipan (CC) ÷	950-1022
# San Marino (CC) ◆	172-1022
# Saudi Arabia (CC) ÷	1-800-11

If you're stuck for cash on your travels, don't panic. Millions of people trust Western Union to transfer money in minutes to 153 countries and over 45,000 locations worldwide. Our record of safety and reliability is second to none. So when you need money in a hurry, call Western Union.

WESTERN UNION | MONEY TRANSFER®

The fastest way to send money worldwide.®

1:30pm). Call 23 991 for emergencies. On the same road, a store sells **International Papers and Books** (tel. 24 234; open daily 8am-10pm). Look for the racks outside. The **bus station** is coupled with a friendly restaurant, just to the right of the section of the town's main street which is closed to traffic. A full schedule is posted in the outdoor waiting area. Walk down the stairs next to the high blue domes of the church to find the town's center. The **police station** (tel. 22 300; open 24hr.) is at the far inland end of the main street. **Postal code:** 84500. **Telephone code:** 0282.

ACCOMMODATIONS Rooms tend to be hard to find and expensive. **Hotel Egli** (tel. 22 303) fills up quickly; reservations are a good idea (singles 5000-8000dr; doubles 8500-10,000; triples 9000-12,000; breakfast 2000dr). From the water, the expensive **Hotel Xenia** (tel. 22 270) lurks downhill to the left of the main street, where the beach meets the upward slope (singles 6700-7500dr; doubles 9700-12,700dr; triples 12,500-15,500dr). The numerous places on the beach get cheaper farther from the main strip. In high season, doubles go for 5000 to 10,000dr.

SIGHTS Following the main street downhill leads to a small square with outdoor cafes and a marble fountain. On the left is the **Archaeological Museum** (tel. 23 664), which has an excellent display on the Geometric village of Zagora and many later (through post-Byzantine) marble relics and Kouros, including a deservedly famous 2m-high statue of the messenger god Hermes. *(Open Tu-Su 8:30am-3pm. Admission 500dr, students 300dr.)* Down the steps to the left of the square is the **Museum of Modern Art** (tel. 22 650), which prominently displays works by 20th-century Greek sculptor Michael Tombros. *(Open M and Th-Sa 10am-2pm and 6pm-8pm, Su 10am-2pm. Admission 1000dr, students 500dr.)* The weird noises from downstairs are not a mechanical failure but the clatter of the electromagnetic "pieces" of the artist Takis. Don't miss the enormous temporary exhibition space across the street a little farther downhill. Visiting exhibitions arrive every summer. One ticket is good for admission to both. Continuing straight through the square, through the white archway, you will find the **Maritime Museum of Andros.** *(Open M and W-Sa 10am-1pm and 6-8pm, Su 10am-1pm. Free.)* It pales somewhat in the splendor of the first two museums, but if you've got the time, stop by. If it happens to be closed during open hours, the guard next door will give you a key. Otherwise, proceed onward for a view of the walls of an off-island Venetian turret.

After all your trucking about, head down the steps to the right of the square to a sandy beach. At the end of the peninsula, down the rocky face, the cove offers an excellent swimming hole beneath old Venetian arch ruins. Watch out for sea urchins.

MILOS Μηλος

Much of Milos's claim to fame has been its association with celebrated artistic achievements—the Venus de Milo, Thucydides' Melian Dialogue, and the film *Bête Milo and Otis* are perhaps the most well-known. Today, Milos is recognized for the breathtaking beauty of its natural landscapes. Visitors immerse themselves in the blue water of Paliochori, swim among the rock formations at Papatragas, wander the narrow alleys of Plaka, and embrace the warm hospitality of the Milians, to fully appreciate the splendor of the Cycladic island.

■ Adamas Αδαμας

This bustling port town is not the island's most attractive locale, but it can be a convenient base. Most of the island's nightlife and amenities are on Adamas' waterfront, and frequent buses can carry you to other parts of Milos.

CYCLADES

ORIENTATION AND PRACTICAL INFORMATION

Transportation

Ferries: From Milos, ferries follow a twisted and complex—yet well posted—schedule. The destinations are Peiraias (8hr., 2 per day, 5000dr); Sifnos (1½hr., 2 per day, 1500dr); Serifos (3hr., 2 per day, 1700dr); Kithnos (1-3 per day, 2540dr); Kimolos (3 per week, 1290dr, and from Pollonia daily 700dr); Folegandros (3 per week, 1660dr); Sikinos (3 per week, 2820dr); Santorini (4 per week, 3630dr); Kassos (9hr., 1 per week, 5850dr); and Karpathos (10hr., 7150dr). Ferries also head to the Cretan ports of Agios Nikolaos (6hr., 3 per week, 4845dr) and Sitia (6½hr., 3 per week, 5100dr).

Buses: (tel. 22 219). Buses stop in the busy area on the waterfront. Schedules posted.

Flights: Olympic Airways, 25th Martiou St. (tel. 22 380, at the airport 22 381). 2-3 daily Olympic Airways **flights** between Milos and Athens (12,700dr). Open M-F 8am-3pm.

Taxis: (tel. 22 219), stand along the waterfront. Taxis are available 24hr. A list of fixed taxi fares is posted.

Tourist and Financial Services

Tourist Office: (tel. 22 445), across from the dock. Multilingual staff. Ask for brochures, maps, ferry and bus timetables, and a complete list of the island's rooms and hotels. Open daily 10am-midnight.

Tourist Agencies: Milos Travel (tel. 22 000 or 22 200; fax 22 688), on the waterfront, sells most ferry tickets (open daily 9am-1:30am). However, John at **Vichos Tours** (tel. 22 120 or 22 286; fax 22 396) is fluent in English and is knowledgeable about the island. They deal with tourist information and rent mopeds (3500-4000dr) and cars (8000dr). By the dock next to Puerto.

Banks: National Bank (tel. 22 077), near the post office along the waterfront. Open M-Th 8am-2pm, F 8am-1:30pm.

Bookstore: (tel. 22 060), by the bus stop. Sells **International News**. Open daily 8:30am-2:30pm and 5pm-midnight.

Emergency and Communications

Port authority: (tel. 22 100). Open 24hr.

Post office: (tel. 22 288). Along the waterfront, 2 doors down and on the 2nd floor of the port authority. Open M-F 7:30am-2pm. **Postal code:** 84801 in Adamas, 84800 elsewhere on the island.

Telephone Code: 0287.

ACCOMMODATIONS

Although high-season prices may discourage the budget traveler, a little persistence in the side streets of Adamas will unearth more affordable private rooms; few tourists look beyond the port for accommodations.

⊛Semirami's Hotel (tel./fax 22 118 or 22 117). Head along the main waterfront road and turn left after the supermarket on the left side of the fork in the road, the hotel is straight ahead. Sit in the vine-covered garden and reach up to help yourself to grapes. Breakfast 1000dr. Doubles 13,000dr; triples 15,000dr; there are also cheaper downstairs rooms with common bath 5000dr.

Manovsos Rooms to Let (tel. 21 956), just before Semirami's, has gorgeous, clean rooms, and if you're lucky, you might score an honest-to-goodness bathtub. All rooms are doubles with fridge and TV. A/C 1500dr. Doubles 7000-14,000dr;

Hotel Chronis (tel. 22 226 or 21 900; fax 22 900) is, indubitably, a splurge—doubles 15,000dr in low season—but the bungalow-style rooms with A/C and TV and verdant gardens will have you feeling positively tropical as you dig into your free American-style buffet breakfast. Reserve a few months in advance.

FOOD

While the two restaurants on the corner of the waterfront may not welcome English-speakers with open arms, the superb food makes up for it: even the *souvlaki* shop by the bus station wraps a mean vegetarian *souvlaki* pita for 200dr.

Kinigos (tel. 22 349) pops up around the first bend on the waterfront. Try the lamb cooked in lemon sauce (1350dr) or the fava beans (800dr).

Floisvos (tel. 22 275), before the bend in the waterfront, offers superb, cheap food. Chicken and potatoes 1000dr.

Trapatseli's Restaurant is a five-minute walk on the road to Achivadolimni Beach. For an elegant dinner, ask for a table on the water. Scrumptious octopus in vinegar and olive oil 1250dr.

ENTERTAINMENT

There isn't a huge bar or disco scene in Adamas, but there are a few places to be-bop the night away. **Notos Club,** to the left of the ferry dock facing inland, spins folk, house, Greek, and disco for your dancing pleasure—hydrate yourself with 2000dr cocktails and 1500dr beer, or just dance, you crazy thang, under the strobe lights. If a dark, wood paneled, slightly seedy but fun bar strikes your fancy, head to **Vipera Lebetina** (tel. 22 501) for slightly cheaper cocktails (1500dr) and whatever the DJ feels like spinning—it can get crazy—until the wee hours of the night.

■ Around Milos

Plaka

Six winding kilometers from Adamas, the town of **Plaka** rests upon the mountain tops. A **post office** (tel. 21 214; fax 21 155) sits at the bus stop—follow the path leading left (open M-F 7:30am-2pm). On the main road going through Plaka are an **OTE** (tel. 21 199; open 7:30am-3pm M-F), and farther down is the **medical center** (tel. 22 700 or 22 701); ask the bus driver to let you off there. The Milos **police** (tel. 21 378) are at the top of the hill at the end of the road where it runs into a "T."

The terrace of the **Church of Panagia the Korfiatissa** leans into a view of lush countryside and blue sea only an arm's length away. Next door, the town's **Folk Museum** (tel. 21 292) has an eerie, but otherwise not particularly worthwhile, display of mannequins in household settings; the few existing signs are only in Greek and there is no guidebook. *(Open Tu-Sa 10am-2pm and 6-8pm, Su 10am-2pm. Admission 400dr, students and children 200dr.)* Near the bus stop on the road to Tripiti, the **Archaeological Museum** (tel. 21 620) houses artifacts unearthed at Fylakopi, including the mesmerizing "Lady of Fylakopi" *(Open Tu-Su 8:30am-3:30pm. Admission 500dr, students 300dr, EU students free, seniors 300dr.)* For a truly spectacular view, head upward until you reach the **Panagia Thalassitra Monastery** at the top of the old castle. The 15-minute walk from the bus stop is more than worth it.

Accommodations in Plaka are predominantly rooms rented out by friendly families. Mr. and Mrs. Moraitis rent rooms in **Machi's House** (tel. 41 353), the hiding spot of the Venus de Milo after she was found in 1820 by farmer Theodnos Kentrotas. You can stay under the same roof for 8000 to 10,000dr.

Several *tavernas* line Plaka's main square near the police station. Walk away from this spot along the road to the catacombs and prepare instead to feast at the *taverna-ouzeri* **Plakiani Gonia** (tel. 21 024). The tomato balls are everything a vegetarian could desire (750dr). Add a serving of *pitarakia* (small cheese pies 200dr) to complete an inexpensive meal. **Achodulah,** near the Church of Panagia the Korfiatissa, let's you check off what you'd like from the menu; try the baked potato (800dr). The **Blue Cafe Bar** (tel. 094 948 819), at the far end of the Plaka, is an excellent place to watch the sunset or, later on, dance the night away.

Tripiti

South of Plaka, outside the small town of **Tripiti,** the **catacombs** (tel. 21 625), hewn into the cliff face, are the oldest site of Christian worship in Greece. *(Open M-Tu and Th-Sa 8:45am-2pm. Free.)* The ruins are small and there is no information available at the site, but deep inside it's cool enough to make the walk worthwhile. Archaeological finds in the ancient city on the hillside above the catacombs represent three periods of Greek history. You can still see part of the Dorian stone wall built between 1100 and 800 BC. A plaque marks the spot where the **Venus de Milo** was buried around 320 BC; she now resides in the Louvre. A well-preserved theater dating from the Roman occupation offers a riveting ocean view; ask at the tourist office about performances there. A 20-minute walk downhill from Plaka on the road that goes through Tripiti will get you to the seaside village of **Klima.** This tiny fishing village, with its whitewashed houses looming over the waves, remains a beautiful representation of the Greek fishing community. **Pollonia** is a quiet fishing town with a pleasant beach. Boats run between Pollonia and the tiny island of **Kimolos** (2-3 per day). Kimolos Town and the port of Psathi are perfect places to unwind; few tourists venture there. Archaeology buffs will want to scramble among the ruins of **Filakopi,** 3km from Pollonia toward Adamas, where British excavations unearthed 3500-year-old frescoes (now displayed in the National Museum in Athens). There is a bus from Pollonia to **Papafragas** (15min., every 45min., 220dr), where gangling rock formations surround a pool of clear blue water. Take the bus from Adamas and ask the driver to stop at Papafragas. Buses run frequently from Adamas to Plaka and Tripiti (15min., every 30min., 230dr) and Pollonia (20min., every 45min., 230dr).

Beaches

There are several **beaches** with exceptional seascapes on Milos. Most are on the eastern half of the island, inaccessible by bus, but accessible by the intrepid moped rider. Beaches of renown cling to the southeastern coast **Paleochori** (25min., 6 buses per day, 350dr) and, northwest of Plaka, secluded **Plathiena.** Seven daily buses from Adamas journey to the more densely populated **Achivadolimni Beach** (15min., 350dr). On the southern coast, **Provatas** (8km from Adamas) is an ideal spot for a swim. Ask about the **excursion boat** at **Milos Travel**—it's an excellent way to see the beaches, fishing villages, lava formations of **Glaronissia,** and the enchanting blue waters of **Kleftiko** (tel. 22 000). For an amazing swimming hole, pull off the road towards Pollonia at Filakopi, park in the dirt, and look for a steep trail that leads to a small, protected cove with clear blue ocean water.

SIFNOS Σίφνος

In ancient times, Sifnos was renowned for the abundant gold, silver, and copper in its mines. Each year the islanders, in order to placate Apollo, would send a solid-gold dancer to Delphi. One year, the locals decided to substitute a gold-plated egg. As a result of this insult, Apollo sank the Sifnian mines under the sea and cursed the land with infertility. Today, barrenness claims most of Sifnos' western half, where boats arrive. A short bus ride brings you to the whitewashed villages of Sifnos' eastern half. This side of Sifnos is affluent; hillsides smothered in olive groves plunge down to rock caves and calm beaches. Tourism is more restrained and respectful than on most islands, which lends Sifnos a peaceful, relaxed air, yet not a deserted one. During high season, accommodations are limited, so your best bets are private rooms, camping, or reservations made several months in advance.

■ Kamares Καμαρες

Boats dock at Kamares, a magnificent harbor filled with sailboats and yachts surrounded by formidable brown cliffs which stand in fierce contrast to the gentle emerald sea. The excellent town beach sweeps the harbor rim and a few *tavernas* line its

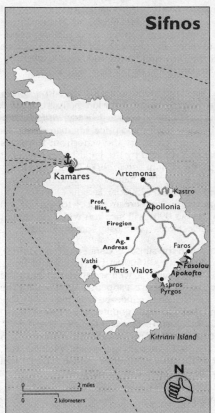

Sifnos

Kamares
Artemonas
Kastro
Prof. Ilias
Apollonia
Firogion
Ag. Andreas
Faros
Vathi
Platis Vialos
Fasolou Apokofto
Aspros Pyrgos
Kitriani Island

N

0   2 miles
0   2 kilometers

shallow perimeters. Kamares is a gentle town pleasing to the senses and easy on the days. Here you can secure a room, swim, dine, and meander into the shops featuring local ornate **pottery;** look for *keramiko* (ceramic) signs throughout the village.

ORIENTATION AND PRACTICAL INFORMATION Just opposite the ferry dock, Sofia at the **Community Information Office** (tel. 31 977) helps find rooms and decipher boat and bus schedules (hours depend on ferry schedule). The **port authority** (tel. 33 617) located next door has sea travel information (open 24hr.). A visit to the **Aegean Thesaurus Travel Agency** (tel. 33 151; fax 32 190), located along the waterfront as you walk from the dock to town, almost always pays off. The friendly, English-speaking staff **exchanges currency,** finds accommodations, stores luggage, and organizes excursions around the island (open daily 9:30am-10pm, or until the last ferry arrives). There is an **International Press** (tel. 33 521) on the main strip (open daily 9am-midnight). In case of emergency call the **police** (tel. 31 210).

From Sifnos, **ferries** head to Peiraias (6hr., 1-2 per day, 4500dr); Milos (1½hr., 1-2 per day, 1500dr); Kimolos (1½hr., 1 per day M-Sa, 1450dr); Serifos (1hr., 1-2 per day Sa-Th, 1500dr); Kithnos (2½hr., 1-2 per day Sa-Th, 2000dr); Folegandros (45min., 1-3 per week, 1620dr); Sikinos (2½hr., 1-3 per week, 1930dr); Santorini (4hr., 1-3 per week, 3050dr); Syros (4½hr., 2 per week, 2100dr); and Ios (3hr., 1-3 per week, 2610dr). There is weekly **hydrofoil** service to Paros (1hr., 1900dr); Mykonos (1½hr., 6200dr); Tinos (2hr., 6245dr); Rafina (6hr, 7350dr); Milos (3000dr); and Peiraias (8900dr). Prices rise during high season. From Kamares, **buses** go to Apollonia and then to Vatni (420dr) at least every hour from 7:30am-10:30pm (190dr).

ACCOMMODATIONS During high season, you are unlikely to find a budget hotel room; try private rooms, either by following "Room to Let" signs or by asking at one of the many waterfront *tavernas*. Off-season prices are roughly 1000 to 2000dr lower (Doubles 6500-8500dr; triples 8000-11,000dr).

In Kamares, **Hotel Stavros** (tel. 33 383 or 31 641; fax 31 709) has clean, pleasant rooms with baths, many with panoramic views of the harbor's beach. Stavros and his English wife also offer travel services, car rental, and a book exchange (doubles with bath 6000-11,000dr, without bath 5000-9000dr; triples with bath 7000-13,000dr in high season). For tighter budgets, there are also rear rooms with shared baths (3000dr). **Hotel Kiki** (tel. 32 329, mobile tel. 01 69211971; fax 31 453) farther along the waterfront road toward Apollonia, offers spotless rooms, each with a bath, television, TV, and balcony overlooking the harbor. (Doubles 7500dr; triples 9000dr; prices roughly 40% higher in July and August. Breakfast 800dr.) Ask about the owner's brother's rooms just below for spacious two-bedroom apartments with full kitchen (10,000-16,000dr). Free-lance camping on Sifnos is illegal, but **Maki's Camping** (tel./fax 32 366) lies across the road from the beach in Kamares (1250dr per person, 1500 with tent). Other campsites in more secluded parts of the island include calm, clean **Platis Yialos Camping** (tel. 31 786), amid trees and stone walls, a 10-minute walk inland from the Yialos Sq. bus stop (1000dr per person).

FOOD On Sifnos, chick-peas are a local specialty found in a soup called *revithada* (700dr; served only Su). It gets polished off early, so try it for lunch. There are also several **groceries** and **bakeries** selling the local almond cookie delicacy, *amigdaloto*.

Each *taverna* offers food of roughly the same quality and price, but many have seaside seating. For Greek food with a charming twist, try the waterfront **Kamares Ouzeri** (tel. 32 398). Among the specialties prepared by the English-speaking chef and staff are the stuffed chicken (1400dr), the shrimp *saganaki* (1700dr), and *tzatziki* (500dr). **Ristorante Italiano** (tel. 31 671), up the main street heading towards Apollonia, serves up a mighty fine grilled swordfish (2500dr), lasagna (1500dr), and *rigatoni delicati* (pasta with chicken, asparagus, and cream sauce; 1600dr). If you need a sweet snack, **Pipi's Pastisseries** (tel. 33 090) will lure you with heaven-sent scents of apple pastry (400dr) and other delectables (open daily 7am-midnight).

ENTERTAINMENT An excellent way to watch the sunset is **Cafe Folie** (tel. 31 183), at the far end of the beach. It's a bit pricey (beer 1000-1500dr), but the colorful, funky decor, great beats, and proximity to the water make it well worth it. Closer to the dock, **Collage** (tel. 32 351) is on the second floor above a supermarket. Look for the sign hanging over an outdoor terrace. Enjoy freshly squeezed fruit juices (800dr), non-alcoholic cocktails (800-1000dr), and their alcoholic counterparts (1300-1500dr) while gazing over the water (open daily 11am-3am). The **Old Captain Bar** (tel. 31 990), just across the street, has cheap beer (600dr), plays string music at sunset, then swings to everything from country to calypso. Farther along the road, **Mobilize** (tel. 32 357) attracts a later crowd and keeps them dancing until sunrise. The DJ will accommodate requests while you enjoy the bar (open daily 10pm-6am).

■ Apollonia Απολλωνια

Apollonia, the island's capital, meanders about the hill in a somewhat haphazard manner—pick a landmark to get your bearings by the road. It lacks Kamares's seaside charm, but its winding roads, hilltop views, and rare quietude offer a different type of island respite; the city also serves as Sifnos' central travel hub.

ORIENTATION AND PRACTICAL INFORMATION Just about everything you need to conduct your important business stands in a row along the main square. **Aegean Thesaurus** (tel. 31 727, 33 151; open 9:30am-10pm), near the post office, is your source for **currency exchange,** accommodation assistance, bus and ferry schedules, and island information packs (600dr). The neighboring **National Bank** (tel. 31 237) has an **ATM** (open M-Th 8am-2pm, F 8am-1:30pm). There is an **OTE** (tel. 31 215 or 33 399) a few doors down on the road back to Kamares (open 7:30am-3:10pm). From the other bus stop near Hotel Anthousa, head up the road to Artemonas to find the **medical center** (tel. 31 315) on your left and the **police station** (tel. 31 210) in a small white building on your right. The bus from Kamares drops you off at the main square. Next door is the **post office** (tel. 31 329; open M-F 7:30am-2pm). Buses to **Kamares** (10min., 190dr) stop in the square in front of the post office, while those to villages and beaches like **Kastro** (190dr) and **Plati Yialos** (370dr) stop around the corner near the Hotel Anthousa. Buses run to all three at least once every hour. **Postal code: 84003. Telephone code: 0284.**

ACCOMMODATIONS Summer vacancies are rare in Apollonia. Prices increase 3000-4000dr in high season. The **Hotel Sofia** (tel. 31 238) is just off the square; head up the wide paved road from the main square until you see it on your left above supermarket Sofia. Reservations should be made a month in advance (singles 6500dr; doubles 7000dr; triples 8000dr). **Hotel Anthoussa** (tel. 32 220), framed by trees and located above the pastry shop, has luxurious accommodations with daily cleaning service. Make Reservations n several months in advance (doubles 10,000dr; triples 12,000dr).

FOOD, ENTERTAINMENT, AND SIGHTS Restaurants are excellent and not as expensive as their beautiful exteriors might suggest. The better *tavernas* are along the path across from the police. The restaurant at the **Sifnos Hotel** serves the island specialty—chick-peas served with olive oil and lemon, cooked all night in special ovens in another town. This delicacy is gone by dinner, so try it for Sunday's lunch. The fricasé is also a delicious choice   goat and rice covered with greens and baked in a ceramic pot (1800dr).

For Apollonia's nightlife, stroll along the street behind the museum. **Bodgi** (tel. 32 358), a bar and coffee house, is likely to catch your eye or ear. Lit by candles that fill both levels and the outside terrace, this bar moves from folk music to jazz, then funk, as the night progresses. Drink slowly—the bar closes at 6am.

The **Museum of Popular Art** in the square features hand-woven laces, traditional dress, local pottery (still an important industry), and several unusual paintings. *(Tel. 31 341 for an appointment with the museum guide; otherwise, the museum has sporadic hours. Admission 200dr.)*

■ Around Sifnos

Travel in Sifnos is easy with the assistance of the map available at any kiosk (250dr). Pack some picnic treats to nibble as you go through Apollonia's adjacent hillside villages. The quiet but expansive village of **Artemonas,** a 10-minute walk from Apollonia, has a magnificent view and several fine mansions built by refugees from Alexandria. The enchanting village of **Kastro** is 3km east of Apollonia and can be reached by bus (15min., 190dr). This cluster of beautiful whitewashed houses and narrow streets rests on a mountain top overlooking the sea. You may find the tiny **archaeological museum** while walking through the former capital's streets. *(Open Tu-Su 11am-2:30pm. Free.)* There are no hotels, but ask around for rooms. Walk left at the base of the hill for the monastery of **Panagia Poulati.** The smooth alcove below reputedly offers the best swimming on the island.

To the south, **Faros** has several popular beaches. **Fasolou,** the island's only **nude beach,** is tucked away beneath promontories farther east. Continue west along the rocky hillside path past a dilapidated mine to reach a better beach at **Apokofto.** You can also reach Apokofto by getting off the bus to Yialos Sq. at the Chrysopigi stop. At the far end of this bay, you will see the striking **Panagia Chrysopigi Monastery.** A bridge connects this 17th-century monastery's rocky islet to the mainland. The monastery (tel. 31 482) has rooms to let; make reservations about two months in advance (doubles 4000dr). Forty days after Easter, the two-day festival of Analipsos is celebrated at Chrysopigi. If the walk to Chrysopigi works up an appetite, the restaurant on the beach to the left of the monastery (tel. 71 295) serves authentic Sifnian cuisine. Mr. Lebesi prepares *mastelo* (lamb cooked in wine and spices 1270dr), and *kaparosalata* (750dr), a salad of caper greens, (open daily noon-11pm). To go to Chrysopigi, take the bus to Platis Yialos and ask the driver to let you off at the monastery, then walk along the descending dirt path and cement stairs for 10 minutes. Allot twice as much time to get back to the main road.

SERIFOS Σεριφος

Serifos, acquiring its name from the ancient Greek word for "stony," owes its existence to the Gorgon Medusa. According to Greek mythology, it was here that Perseus, the son of Zeus and Danae, accomplished the impossible task of slaying the Gorgon monster, assigned to him by King Polydictes, who sought to occupy Perseus while he occupied himself with Danae. Upon returning to Serifos and learning of the King's forceful advances, Perseus turned King Polydictes and his royal court into stone by showing them the severed head of Medusa—the very prize he had been sent to retrieve. Ravaged by a once thriving mining industry, the barren terrain contrasts sharply with the whitewashed houses of Hora that spill over the slopes of the island's highest mountain peak. Due to poor roads and a lack of knowledge on the tourists' part, most of Serifos lays blissfully undiscovered, while the port town is annually inundated with Greek tourists fleeing Athens.

■ Livadi Λιβαδι

Boats dock only in Livadi. It's easy to get the feeling the town is trying too hard with its creperies and strings of *tavernas* (maybe it is), but there persists nonetheless a feeling of ease and escape. Just make sure not to make the same mistake as the boats.

ORIENTATION AND PRACTICAL INFORMATION An island map which lists useful telephone numbers is available at kiosks (300dr). The **Apiliotis Travel** (tel. 51 155), located in the center of the waterfront strip next to a supermarket, offers hydrofoil and ferry tickets and schedules in English (open daily 9am-2pm and 6-8:30pm). The **police** (tel. 51 470) are up the narrow steps marked with a large Greek flag, less than 100m from the arrival dock. The **Ionian Bank** (tel. 51 780), equipped with an **ATM**, is hard to miss along the waterfront (open M-Th 8am-2pm, F 8am-1:30pm). The emergency tel. is 0936 058 59. For **taxis,** call 51 245 or 51 435. **Telephone code:** 0281. **Postal code:** 84005.

Serifos can be reached by regular **ferries** from Peiraias and other Western Cyclades, as well as occasional boats from Paros, Syros, Ios, and Santorini. From Serifos, ferries travel to Peiraias (4½hr., 1-3 per day, 3900dr); Kithnos (1½hr., 4 per week, 1800dr); Sifnos (45min., 1-3 per day, 1450dr); Milos (2hr., 1-3 per day, 1700dr); Kimolos (2hr., 3 per week, 1740dr); Folegrandros (3hr., 3 per week, 1570dr); Sikinos (5hr., 3 per week, 2500dr); Ios (5½hr., 2 per week, 2800dr); and Santorini (6½hr., 1 per week, 2600dr). High-speed **flying dolphins** connect daily to: Peiraias (7470dr); Kithnos (3500dr); and Milos (3300dr); and once weekly to Kimolos (3550dr). For schedules and more information, contact **Krinas Travel** (tel. 51 488; fax 51 073).

ACCOMMODATIONS Don't go to Serifos expecting people to aggressively offer rooms at the port. Instead, look for pensions on the waterfront, on the street parallel to the waterfront road, and on the road that bears left from the Milos Express office heading toward the campgrounds (doubles 5000-9000dr, depending on season and amenities). Arrive early or call the tourist police for information about reservations. Prices are 2000 to 4000dr less in winter. **Hotel Serifos Beach** (tel. 51 209 or 51 468) is a block back from the beach, but easy to find by virtue of its large blue sign on the main waterfront road. Away from the main strip, rooms are comfortable and quiet (doubles 10,000-12,000dr; triples 12,000-14,400dr; breakfast 1000dr). **Hotel Areti** (tel. 51 479 or 51 107; fax 51 547), on the first left as you step off the ferry, is a whitewashed building with blue shutters. With a backyard terrace and private balconies for each room, the hotel offers a beautiful view of the harbor. (Open Apr.-Oct. Singles 6500-10,000dr; doubles 8000-14,000dr; triples 9500-16,500dr.)

FOOD AND ENTERTAINMENT One of the islanders' favorites for a delicious, well-prepared meal is **Mokkas** (tel. 51 242), one of the first *tavernas* along the waterfront. Come here for locally grown ingredients and deliciously prepared fresh seafood. Try the *fasolakia* (green beans with tomato sauce and olive oil; 1200dr), or the chicken Antonio (tender meat wrapped in bacon with ultra-divine cream sauce; 1600dr). Another option for an inexpensive and filling meal, is **Stamadis.** You can get fresh fruit at the **Marinos** market (tel. 51 279), on the waterfront past the main stretch of *tavernas* and shops (open daily 7:30am-2pm and 4:30pm-midnight). If you feel like unwinding after a hard day at the beach, the places to be are **Praxis,** a sound bar and dance club scene, in the middle of the waterfront, and **Metalio,** on the road to Hora (beer 1000dr). **Mytnos,** near Praxis but set back in a small shop complex, has a pool table and games and a more mellow scene. Beer is 600dr. Next door, **Alter Ego Music Club** is the place to bump and grind, (cover 1500dr; open daily after 11pm).

■ Around Serifos

Not surprisingly, Serifos beaches are a prime attraction. Closest to Livadi is the relatively crowded **Livadakia** beach. It's a 10-minute walk on the inland road to the right of the dock; there's a sign. A two hour walk past Livadakia Beach leads to the adjoining sandy havens of **Koutalas, Ganema,** and **Vaya Beach. Psili Ammos,** perhaps the island's best beach, is a 45-minute walk past Livadakia Beach in the other direction. **Karavi,** over the hill from Livadakia Beach, away from Livadi Harbor, is a popular **nude beach,** although many enjoy it clothed.

The northern part of the island offers small traditional villages, scattered churches, several monasteries, and traces of ruins. The rest of the island is fairly inaccessible without a car or moped, a map, and excellent driving skills. For **moped rental,** call **Blue Bird** (tel. 51 511; 3000dr per day). By car or moped, visit the **Monastery of the Taxiarchs,** 10km beyond Hora towards the village of Galini. Built in 1400 AD on a site where a Cypriot icon mysteriously appeared (and to which it returns whenever removed), the monastery houses an Egyptian lantern and several Russian relics, in addition to the enigmatic icon. Try to visit close to sunset in order to meet the lone monk, who has lived there for 20 years. Lucky visitors may be treated to coffee and cherries. Call in advance (tel. 51 027) in the morning or afternoon to arrange a visit.

KYTHNOS Κυθνος

Upon entering **Merichas,** the main port of Kythnos, you will either embrace its barren rocky hills and lack of foreigners and conventional touristic pleasures, or you will go to bed early, sleep late, and leave. Hikers may find austere pleasure in the island's quiet landscape, as do pockets of Athenians seeking its scarcely populated beaches. Mainly unmauled by tourism's soft and glitzy paw, this simple Cycladic island will disappoint travelers seeking nightlife, museums, or luxury comforts.

■ Merichas Μεριχας

The port town is littered with "Rooms to Let," a few *tavernas,* and a few places to conduct business. The **tourist office** (tel. 32 250), right by the dock, offers information on the island, maps, and boat schedules, but is open erratically. The **port police** can also help out with ferry information. Past the dock heading into town and up a short flight of stairs is the **Milos Express** travel agency (tel. 32 104; fax 32 291) which has information on ferries, rooms, island maps, and rents mopeds (4500dr all summer) and cars (12,000dr). Open daily 8am-midnight in the high season. Farther along the waterfront which houses a grocery store, a representative of the **National Bank** to exchange currency, and **Flying Dolphin** information and tickets (tel. 32 345; open daily 8am-2pm and 5-10pm).

If you need a **taxi** or **bus,** search the streets to find one parked, or call 31 272 or 31 280. There are no bus schedules posted around, so ask the bus driver when, where, nd how much (buses run to **Loutra, Driopis,** and **Kithnos**—also known as Hora). **Ferries** sail to Peiraias (1-2 per day, 3100dr); Serifos (1-3 per day, 1800dr); Sifnos (once daily, 1950dr); Kimolos (once daily, 2400dr); Milos (once daily, 2600dr); twice weekly to Santorini (3800dr) and Sikinos (3200dr), and once weekly to Folegandros (2900dr). **Hydrofoils** speed to Peiraias (once daily, 6050dr). There is no **OTE** or **post office. Telephone code:** 0281. **Postal code:** 84006.

The abandoned hulk Hotel Posidonion leers over the small town beach, but the surrounding area has several nice pensions and Rooms To Let that won't break your budget. Walking with the sea on your right, turn left just before the children's playground to find **Panaciota Rooms To Let** (tel. 32 268). All rooms are equipped with 3 beds, kitchen, bath, fridge, and are clean and roomy (6000-12,000dr, depending on the season). Continue walking with the sea to your right past the old hotel and up the slight hill for **Anna Gouma** (tel. 32 105), a big white building on the left side with curved archways and brown wooden railings. These rooms also have kitchen, bath, and fridge as well as a sea view (doubles 8000-11,000dr; triples 9000-12,000dr). If you desire air conditioning, you're out of luck in the port town.

Several **supermarkets** line the waterfront with huge displays of fresh fruit for a cheap meal. **Sailors Restaurant** on the waterfront has scrumptious pork *souvlaki* (2000dr) and fried balls of Kithnos goat cheese (1000dr). After dinner, bring the crew to the **Byzantio Sailors Pub** for a Güsser beer on tap (600dr), or ask Yiannis for a heavenly thick chocolate drink—if it's almost your turn to man the helm—while he grooves behind the bar.

■ Around Kythnos

Loutra, the village inlet resting down winding roads from Hora, is named for its hot springs, which reputedly can cure rheumatism, dermatitis, and gynecological problems. King Othon and Queen Amalia had a castle there, where Queen Amalia soaked in the warm waters, helping her to conceive.

Hora boasts the only **post office** and **OTE,** and hikers can leave the town and follow a beautiful trail for about one-and-a-half hours—bring water—to the town of **Driopis,** once the island's capital. The best **beaches** are situated near Merichas, including **Episkopi,** 30 minutes north by foot.

Crete Κρητη

In middle of the sable sea there lies
An isle call'd Crete, a ravisher of eyes,
Fruitful, and mann'd with many an infinite store;
Where ninety cities crown the famous shore,
Mix'd with all-languag'd men.

—Homer, *Odyssey*

There is a Greek saying that a Cretan's first loyalty is to the island and second to the country. Indeed, some of Crete's rugged individualism, which treats even Greeks as foreigners, persists; simply look to the long-mustached men who sit by the harbor polishing their high black boots. Like the island, they are hospitable, but prefer to keep their distance, staid and stoic.

As far back as 6000 BC, the neolithic Cretans dwelled in open settlements and worshipped their deities by placing terra cotta statuettes on the tops of mountains, now referred to as peak sanctuaries. Crete's glory days, however, began when settlers arrived from Asia Minor around 3000 BC.

Since the third millennium BC, Crete has held a distinct cultural identity, expressed in the unique language, script, and architecture of the ancient Minoans through to the novels of Nikos Kazantzakis, several of which play out Crete's heroic struggle for freedom from foreign rule. In many ways Greek mythology had its beginnings on Crete's Mt. Ida, the mythical birthplace of Zeus. The myth of the man-eating Minotaur was enacted in the shadow of Mt. Ida, and the hybrid beast's slaying at the hands of Theseus, King of Athens, metaphorically transferred power from the Minoans of Crete to the Achaeans of mainland Greece.

⊛ HIGHLIGHTS OF CRETE

- The Minoan civilization—flower of Bronze Age Crete—endures in palaces at **Knossos** (p. 389), **Phaistos** (p. 393), and **Malia** (p. 409).
- **Samaria Gorge** (p. 404)—6 hours all the way down—is Europe's longest.
- At **Matala** (p. 394), cliffs full of caves overhang the waves of the Libyan Sea.
- Arab, Venetian, and Ottoman architecture mingle around the harbors of **Rethymnon** (p. 396) and **Hania** (p. 400).
- Remains of Europe's last leper colony, **Spinalonga** (p. 414), linger off the coast of **Agios Nikolaos** (p. 411), Crete's most sophisticated resort town.

Throughout the span of a few thousand years, these inhabitants created sophisticated palaces. Among the artifacts found from this time are gracefully flared pottery shards, frescoes, jewelry, ceremonial horns, stone libation vessels, Linear A and B tablets, and figurines. This period lasted from 2800 to 1100 BC and was the height of the Minoan Civilization. The extensive ruins of this unique civilization, all unearthed during this century, offer visitors an impressive spectacle.

The Minoans not only survived three waves of destruction—an earthquake, a series of tidal waves following the eruption of the volcano on Santorini, and (probably) a Mycenaean invasion—but also rebuilt their civilization after each setback. These periods are now referred to as the Early, Middle, and Late Minoan Periods, based on pottery styles. Iconography of enthroned females suggest that the Early Period may have been a matriarchy. This period is also famous because it was believed to have been the one and only time in human history when men and women lived together in pure peace, harmony, and equality. However, archaeological discoveries in recent years (weaponry and evidence of human sacrifice) suggest that the state of Minoan affairs may not have been so socially advanced after all. Crete's most glorious days were during the Middle Minoan Period, when the Palace at Knossos functioned as the center

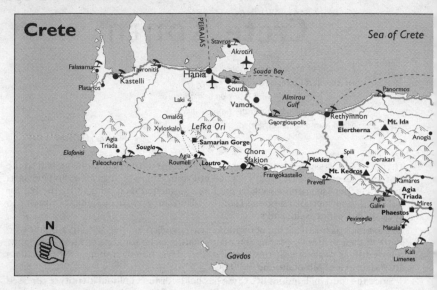

of an Aegean marine empire. Newly established trade routes fostered prosperity and sophistication, and Minoan artistry reached its climax.

In the 8th century BC, Dorians occupied the island; they introduced the Greek language, as jewelry-making, sculpture, and pottery thrived. The Roman conquest in 67 BC found the island increasingly unstable, with dominant aristocratic families and frequent intercity warfare. In later years, Crete was wrested from Byzantine rule at various points by Arabs, Crusaders, and Ottomans. In 1898, the island became an English protectorate. After the Balkan War of 1913, Crete entered the Greek state. This peace was interrupted by a WWII German occupation, which the islanders bitterly resisted.

Getting There

Olympic Airways has cheap, fast, domestic **flights** from Athens to Sitia on the east, Iraklion in the center, and Hania on the west. Air Greece also has flights to points Cretan, sometimes for cheaper prices. Most flights take less than an hour. Consult the **Orientation and Practical Information** of your destination city for more information.

Most travelers arrive in Crete by **ferry.** The island has frequent connections during summer, but boats often fall behind schedule. The larger the boat, the more frequently it runs, and the more dependable its schedule. All prices listed here are for deck-class accommodations. Boats run to Iraklion, Rethymnon, Hania, Agios Nikolaos, and Sitia. There are **international ferry** connections to Ancona in Italy, Çeşme in Turkey, Limassol on Cyprus, and Haifa in Israel. For Egypt, change boats in Cyprus. From April to October, the *Vergina* leaves Haifa on Sundays and travels to Cyprus, Rhodes, Iraklion, and Peiraias; deck-class costs roughly 20,000dr between any two ports. Those heading to Italy must go to Peiraias and change boats.

CENTRAL CRETE

■ Iraklion Ηρακλειο

Greece's fifth-largest city, Iraklion is both Crete's capital and its primary port. The city's chic native population lives a fast-paced life, and the urbanite brusqueness will make you appreciate the hospitality that comes so naturally in Iraklion's surrounding mountain villages. Still, sophisticated Iraklionites support a nightlife more diverse than

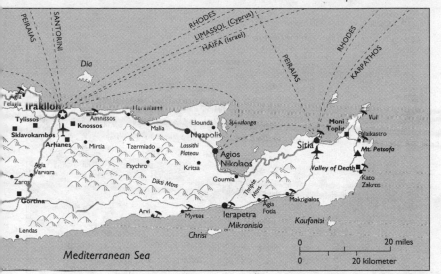

that in nearby beach resorts Malia and Hersonissos. While architectural aesthetics find the city's unplanned jumble of Venetian monuments sandwiched between Turkish houses and two-story concrete flats utterly offensive, many others consider the mosaic of buildings a ubiquitous reminder of Iraklion's impressive history. Regardless, with its rich museums and daytrip proximity to the Minoan palaces of Knossos, Phoistos, and Malia, Iraklion is an ideal base for a cultural tour of Crete.

ORIENTATION AND PRACTICAL INFORMATION

Although Iraklion spreads telescopically, the area bordered by **Dikeosinis Ave., Doukos Bofor St., Handakos St.,** and the waterfront, contains most necessities. The city centers are **Venizelou Square,** (also known to tourists as **Lion Fountain Square** or **Four Lion Square**), home to Morosini Fountain, where Handakos St. meets Dikeosinis Ave. and 25th Augustou Ave. in the center of town, and **Eleftherias Square,** at the intersection of Doukos Bofor St. and Dikeosinis Ave. on the east side of the old city.

Transportation

Ferries: Boat offices on 25th Augustou Ave. Most open daily 9am-9pm. Boats leave for Athens (12hr., 2 per day, 700dr); Santorini (4hr., 6 per week, 5185dr); Paros (8½hr., 6 per week, 5185dr); Naxos (7hr., 5 per week, 5185dr); Mykonos (9hr., 6 per week, 5964dr); Rhodes (12hr., 1 per week, 6442dr); and Thessaloniki (11hr., 3 per week, 11,965dr). International ferries to Limassol, Cyprus (25hr., 1 per week, 15,500dr); Haifa, Israel (44hr., 1 per week, 23,500dr); Brindisi, Italy (23hr., 1 per week, 18,000-21,600dr).

Buses: There are several **KTEL** bus terminals, so match the station to your destination. **Terminal A** (tel. 24 50 17 or 24 50 20), between the old city walls and the harbor near the waterfront, serves Agios Nikolaos (1½hr., 24 per day, 1350dr); Lassithi (2hr., 1-2 per day, 1350dr); Hersonissos (45min., 31 per day, 600dr); Malia (1hr., 31 per day, 750dr); Sitia (3¼hr., 5 per day, 2750dr); Ierapetra (2½hr., 9-10 per day, 2050dr); Archanes (30min., 6-15 per day, 340dr); and Agios Pelagia (45min., 7 per day, 650dr). For **Terminal B** (tel. 25 59 65), outside the Hania Gate of the old city walls, take local bus #135 from Terminal A (340dr). Runs buses to Phaistos (1½hr., 10 per day, 1250dr) via Gortyn (900dr); Agia Galini (2¼hr., 6-8 per day, 1500dr); Matala (2hr., 6-8 per day, 1500dr); Lentas (3hr., 1 per day, 1550dr); Anogia (1hr., 2-5 per day., 700dr); and Fodele (1hr., 2 per day, 600dr). The **Hania/Rethymnon Terminal** (tel. 22 17 65) is near the waterfront. Walk down 25th Augustou Ave. to the waterfront, turn right, and walk another 500m. The station

N

Sea of Crete

Koules Fortress

Venizelou

Historical Museum

TO FERRY

Agios Andreas

Venizelou

Skordilon

Westbound

Hania/ Rethymnon

Eastbound

Vistaki

Handakos

Choraslou

Priouli Fountain

Minostavrou

Grevenon

National Bank

25th Augustou

Idomeneos

Agios Sabbionera

Dikus

Kissamou

Delimarkou

Giamalak

El Greco Park

St. Titus

Ag. Titou

Town Hall

Androgeou

Archaeological Museum

D. Beaufourt

Ikarou

TO AIRPORT

Makariou

Nea Odos

Kalokerinou

Kariotissas

VENIZELOU SQ.

Morosini Fountain

San Marco

N. FOKAS SQ.

Dikeosinis

Daedolou

Agios Tou Pantokratou

Machis Kritis

South/ West Martiron

KORAKA SQ.

Chanion Gate

Cathedral of Agios Minas

St. Catherine's

Giannari

ELEFTHERIAS SQ.

Venizelou Monument

Iherissou

Nikolaou Plastira

Kourmoulidon

Vikela

1821

1866

Evans

Trifitsou

Olympic Airways

Tombazi

KORNAROU SQ.

Agios Bethlehem

Piranthou

Romanou

Pediados

Evans

Agios Vitouri

Trikoupi

Athinas

Dimokratias

Kondilaki

Kenouria Gate

Plastira

Agios Jesus

Kazantzakis Open Air Theater

Charilaou

Tomb of Kazantzakis

Agios Tou Martinengou

Kikladon

G. Georgadi

Akadimias

Knossou

Chrisostomou

Georgiou A

Iraklion

ACCOMMODATIONS

D Hotel Paladion
C Hotel Rea
A Rent Rooms Hellas
B Rent Rooms Vergina
E Youth Hostel

0 — 300 yards
0 — 300 meters

CRETE

will be on your right 200m before the ferry landing. Buy tickets in the cafe building. Service to Hania (56 per day, 2800dr); Plakias (2400dr); Paleochora (via Hania, 4250dr); Samaria (via Hania, 4150dr); Hora Sfakion (via Vrises, 2900dr); Akrotiri (14 per day, 3650dr); and Rethymnon (1½hr., 28 per day, 1500dr).

Flights: Inquire at **Travel Hall Travel Agency,** 13 Hatzimihali Yiannari St. (tel. 34 18 62 or 28 21 12; fax 28 33 09), one block southwest of Eleftherias Sq. Sells tickets for Olympic Airways to Athens (1hr., 4 per day, 22,000dr); Mykonos (1hr., 2 per week, 19,300dr); Rhodes (45min., 4 per week, 18,500dr); Thessaloniki (2hr., 10 per week, 26,500dr); and Santorini (1hr., 3 per week, 12,000dr). Flights on **Air Greece,** which are less expensive, are also available. Discounted fares for those under 24. Open daily 9am-9pm. Bus #1 departs for the airport from Eleftherias Sq. every 10min. (240dr). Cabs to the airport cost 2000-2500dr.

Taxis: Tariff Taxi of Iraklion (tel. 21 01 02 or 21 01 68). Open 24hr. When taking a taxi from the airport or port, beware of drivers drawing commission from a local hotel who may claim that the rival hotel you name is closed or full.

Car Rental: Rental car companies are scattered along 25th Augustou Ave. Shop around. Make the owners compete for your business by quoting prices from their neighbors. **Caravel** at #39 25th Augustou Ave. (tel. 24 53 45 or 24 53 50; fax 22 03 62) will rent cars to anyone over 19. Prices average 9000dr per day in the low season. A copy of *Let's Go* will get you free personal insurance (1000dr) or a 40% discount on a car rented for more than 1 week. Open daily 6:30am-10pm.

Moped Rental: Cheap rentals line Handakos St., El Greco Park, and 25th Augustou Ave. Check if the quoted price includes the 20% tax and insurance (50cc bikes 4500dr per day when you rent for a week, tax and third-party liability insurance included). **Motor Club,** #1 18 Agglon Sq. (tel. 22 24 08, 22 60 12, or 28 60 31; fax 22 28 62), by the port, has a huge selection of new bikes. Open daily 7am-9pm.

Tourist and Financial Services

Tourist Office: 1 Xanthoudidou St. (tel. 22 82 03 or 24 44 62), opposite the Archaeological Museum in Eleftherias Sq. Free city maps, lists of hotels, message board for travelers, bus schedules, and some boat schedules. Staff is helpful but busy. Info on cultural events and museums. Open M-F 8am-2:30pm.

Tourist Agencies: Several agencies on 25th Augustou Ave. **Arabatzoglou Bros. Shipping Agents Travel Bureau,** #54 25th Augustou Ave. (tel. 28 86 08, 22 66 97, or 22 66 98; fax 22 21 84) has a friendly staff. Helpful with air and boat tickets. Open daily 8am-9pm. Many agencies **exchange currency** at bank rates.

Banks: The banks on 25th Augustou Ave. are open M-Th 8am-2pm and F 8am-1:30pm. **National Bank,** #35 25th Augustou Ave. (tel. 22 67 45 or 22 67 46). Shops in Venizelou Sq. **exchange currency** after hours at lower rates.

Laundromat: Washsalon, 18 Handakos St. (tel. 28 08 58; fax 28 44 42). 2000dr for wash and dry, soap included. Also provides **luggage storage** (300dr, with locker 450dr). Be very clear with care instructions here. Open daily 8:30am-9pm.

Public Toilets: In El Greco Park, look for the blue cage-like entrance near the swings; more in public gardens near Eleftherias Sq. 150dr per use. Open daily 6am-9pm.

Library: Vikelaia Municipal Library (tel. 39 92 37 or 39 92 49), in Venizelou Sq. Limited number of books in English, French, Italian, Russian, and Chinese. Most of the international books are on philosophy, literature, classics, and history. Has a luxurious A/C reading room on the second floor. Open M-F 8am-3pm.

Bookstores: Newsstands in Eleftherias Sq. sell foreign newspapers like the *International Herald Tribune* (300dr) as well as paperbacks. Open daily 8am-10pm. **Planet Bookstore,** 23 Kidonias (tel. 28 15 58; fax 28 71 42), a 5-floor megastore on the corner of Hortatson and Kidonias St. Open M-F 8:30am-2pm and 5:30-8:30pm, Sa 8:30am-noon.

Emergency and Communications

Police: 29 Venizelou Sq., a yellow building among the cafes. Open 24hr. One station for the east side of town (tel. 28 45 89, 28 22 43, or 28 26 77); another station in the building serves the west (tel. 29 34 66). **Port Police** (tel. 22 60 73), in the harbor.

Tourist Police: 10 Dikeosinis St. (tel. 28 31 90 or 28 96 14), one block from intersection of 25th Augustou Ave. and Dikeosinis St. Open daily 7am-11pm.

Pharmacy: 1 Androgeou St. (tel. 34 63 77), at the intersection of Androgeou St., Agio Titou St., and 25th Augustou Ave. Open M, W 8:30am-2pm, Tu and Th-F 8:30am-2pm and 5-9pm. One open 24hr. by rotation—its name and address is posted on the door of every pharmacy. All are marked by a red cross.

Hospital: Venizelou Hospital (tel. 23 19 31 or 23 75 24) on Knossou Ave. Take bus #2 (20min.). Also **Panepistimiako Hospital** (tel. 31 36 00, 31 36 01, or 26 15 55; appointments 39 11 11 or 54 21 07).

Post Office: Main office (tel. 28 99 95), in Daskalogianni Sq. off Giannari St. Open M-F 7:30am-8pm. **Branch office** (tel. 22 04 17), in El Greco Park. Open M-F 8:30am-3pm. **Postal Code:** 71001.

Internet Access: Polykentro (tel. 39 92 12), on Androgeou St., just off 25th Augustou. Computers 400dr per hour. Open Su-Th 9am-1am, F-Sa 10am-2am.

OTE: 10 Minotavrou St. (tel. 39 52 76 or 39 52 75); follow signs on Minotavrou near El Greco Park. Open daily 7:30am-1pm. **Telephone Code:** 081.

ACCOMMODATIONS

Iraklion has a bunch of cheap hotels and hostels, most near Handakos St. at the center of town. Others are on Evans St. and 1866 St. near the market.

🌐**Youth Hostel,** 5 Vyronos St. (tel. 28 62 81 or 22 29 47). From the bus station, walk with the water on your right, take a left on 25th Augustou Ave., and turn right on Vyronos St. Standard hostel rooms. Midnight curfew. Luggage storage 300dr.

Check-out 10am. Larger rooms for families and couples. Breakfast 500dr, beer 350dr. 1500dr per person; singles 3000dr; doubles 4000dr; triples 6000dr.

◉**Rent a Room Hellas,** 24 Handakos St. (tel. 28 88 51), 2 blocks from El Greco Park. Formerly the HI Youth Hostel. Offers sheets, verandas, book exchange, and garden bar. Hot water available 6-10pm. Dorms 1700dr; singles 4000dr; doubles 5500dr; triples 7000dr. Breakfast 600-850dr. Extra bed 1000dr.

Hotel Rea, Kalimeraki St. (tel. 22 36 38; fax 24 21 89). Walking toward the harbor, turn right off Handakos St., 2 blocks from the waterfront. Clean, airy rooms and jasmine-scented reception. Hot showers. Luggage storage free. Full kitchen facilities. Breakfast downstairs or in your room 900dr. Also runs **Ritz Rent a Car** (13,000dr per day, 49,000dr per week) 30% off for hotel guests. Singles 5000dr, with bath 6500dr; doubles 6300dr, with bath 7300dr; triples 7700dr, with bath 9000dr.

Rent a Room Vergina, 32 Chortason St. (tel. 24 27 39). Walking toward the harbor, turn right off Handakos St. onto Kidonias St., take your first left on Hortason St., and walk down 2 blocks—it's on the right. Clean, homey rooms surround a palm-tree-filled courtyard. High ceilings, new furniture, and shared baths that resemble outhouses with their red wooden doors but have sparkling floral-tiled interiors. Free luggage storage. Check-out noon. Doubles 6000dr; triples 8000dr.

Hotel Paladion, 16 Handakos St. (tel. 28 25 63). A walk through a white stucco-walled courtyard lined with potted plants takes you to neat rooms with colorful tile floors. Singles 3900dr; doubles 6000dr; triples 8100dr; quads 9800dr.

FOOD

Around the Morosini Fountain, near El Greco Park and in Eleftherias Sq., are ritzy cafes perfect for lounging. Take a left off 1866 St., one block from Venizelou Sq., to reach tiny Theodosaki St. Although not the most upscale place in town to dine, it's certainly colorful, with 10 *tavernas* jammed side by side serving Greek fare. The cheaper dishes go for roughly 800dr and the portions are impressive. If there's no menu, fix the price before you sit. For more elegant dining, try any of the *tavernas* on boutique-lined Daedolou St. *Souvlaki* joints abound on 25th Augustou Ave.

◉**Thraka,** 14 Platokallergon St. (4 Lions Square), is the most fun, thanks to its 30-year tradition of serving only grilled ham gyros and *souvlaki.* No electricity here, only charcoal. Try the *souvlaki* with *thraka* bread crust (450dr). Open M-Sa 10am-5am.

Minos Restaurant, 10 Daedalou St. (tel. 34 48 27 or 24 64 66). The manager will guide you in the kitchen to choose the dish that looks best. The owner has served a velvety special of lamb with yogurt for 26 years. *Elvasan* 2500dr, stuffed tomatoes and peppers 1000dr, *stifado* 1800dr. Open daily 11am-3pm and 6-10pm.

◉**Tierra del Fuego,** 26 Theotokopoulou St. (tel. 34 15 15). Next door to the OTE, down the street behind Xalkiadaki market in El Greco Park. Feast on a wide range of Mexican food (Iraklion's latest trend) in the cactus courtyard. Salads 700-950dr, generous mixed plates 1600dr, vegetarian tacos 1200dr. Open daily 8:30pm-2am.

Tou Terzaki, 17 Loch. Marineli St. (tel. 22 14 44). Marineli St. is off of Vyronos St., 1 block from 25th Augustou Ave., and the *ouzeri* is across from the Agios Dimitrios chapel. The friendly staff serve excellent *mezedes,* including the owner's grandmother's special *dolmades,* in a pleasant setting. Open M-Sa for lunch and dinner.

Lychnostatis, 8 Ioannou Chronaki St. (tel. 24 21 17). This romantic *mezedopoleio* plays soft Greek music and serves candle-lit dinners of goat with tomatoes (1100dr) or potatoes in the oven (600dr). Open daily noon-1am.

Ippokampos, 3 Venizelou St. (tel. 28 02 40). Seafood on the waterfront. Calamari 950dr, horta greens 450dr, shrimp 1000dr. Open daily 12:30pm-3:30pm and 7-11pm.

Antonios Nerantzoulis, 16 Agios Titou St. (tel. 34 62 36), behind the St. Titus Church. The bakery has been run by the same family since 1900. They're famous for *oktasporo* and *kalitsounia* (little cheese biscuits; 2000dr per kg). Open M-Sa 7am-3pm, Tu and Th-F 5-8pm.

During the day, the best show in town is the **open-air market** on 1866 St., which starts near Venizelou Sq. Both sides of the boisterous, aromatic, narrow street are lined with stalls piled high with sweets, spices, fresh fruits, vegetables, cheeses, and meat in glass cases. **Kirkor,** 29 Venizelou Sq. (tel. 24 27 05), sells *bougatsa,* a cheese or cream-filled *phyllo* pastry (450dr; open daily 5:30am-midnight). **Amalthia** (tel. 28 50 84) has cauldrons of yogurt that far eclipse the filtered, pasteurized brands found elsewhere. Named after Zeus' goat, the store serves traditional sheep's milk yogurt (700dr per kg), as well as local cheeses like the special Cretan *gruyere* (market open M, W, Sa 8am-3pm, Tu, Th-F, 8am-2pm and 5-9pm). Visit Koutoulakis (tel. 34 16 19) for mouth-watering raisins (700dr per kg) and walnuts (2350dr per kg) as well as olive oil with less than 0.1% acidity (1000dr per 500mL; open M-Sa 7am-7pm).

ENTERTAINMENT

Iraklion natives are the first to point out that the "in" places change rapidly, so ask around. Try **Aktarika Cafe** (tel. 34 12 25), across from the Lion Fountain Square. All day and all night this huge atrium-like cafe teems with hip black-clad twenty- and thirty-something Iraklionites and the people who watch them (*frappés* 700dr, cocktails 1700dr. Open daily 9am-2:30am. DJ on duty 11am-4pm and 8pm-2:30am). For a quieter, more intimate drink, check out **Ontas,** 25 Ellis St. (tel. 24 44 49). The beautiful cafe is on a quiet, untrodden alley behind St. Titus Church in the city center (open M-Sa 10am-2:30am, Su 1pm-2:30am).

Trading tourist kitsch for genuine urban energy, Iraklion outdoes the resort towns with its pulsing nightlife. Cretans mingle with travelers and everybody gets it on. Most clubbers head west 3-4km outside the city center during the summer. **Yacht, Limenico,** and **Bahalo** mix Greek pop music with techno house by the half hour.

Schedules for Iraklion's **movie theaters** are posted near the tourist police office. For an evening of free sociological entertainment, join Greeks and tourists at Venizelou Sq., where Iraklion's annual **summer festival** combines cultural events such as concerts, theater, ballet, and folk dancing. Most shows begin at 9:30pm and cost up to 2000dr. Students under 25 pay half price. Pick up a schedule of events from the tourist police or tourist information office (tel. 24 29 77, 39 92 11, 39 92 12, or 24 19 50; fax 22 71 80 or 22 92 07; email heolaia@heraklion-city.gr).

SIGHTS

Archaeology Museum

Off Eleftherias Sq. Tel. 22 60 92. **Open** *in summer M 12:30-8pm and Tu-Su 8am-8pm; winter M 12:30-8pm and Tu-Su 8am-5pm.* **Admission** *1500dr, students and EU seniors 800dr, under 18 free and EU students. An illustrated* **guide** *is available at the museum's gift stand and is worth the 1500dr.*

Iraklion's capital attraction is its superb **Archaeological Museum.** While most museums in Cretan cities offer merely a hodgepodge of local finds strung across millennia, the Iraklion museum, which has appropriated major finds from all regions of the island, presents a comprehensive record of neolithic, Minoan, Hellenistic, and Roman stages of the island's history. Exhibits are organized chronologically. The museum houses the famed **Phaistos disc,** a day circle engraved with heiroglyphics of possible ritual significance, in room 3.

Two pieces fight for your attention in room 4. The **snake goddess** is a small sculpture of a priestess or goddess who, although topless, sports a layered skirt, a cat on her head, and a flailing serpent in each of her outstretched arms. A **bull head libation vase** occupies the room's central glass case. Made of steatite, the vessel is a stunning combination of fiery red eyes, a white mustache, and tight curls of hair.

If you take a close look at the gold jewelry in room 7, you will discover an intricate **bee pendant** composed of two bees joined delicately at their stingers. The insects form a cage with their antennae to enclose a golden ball, and a honeycomb lies at the center of this luxurious creation from Chryssolakkos at Malia. The large, frightened eyes of the octopus on the **vase from Palaikastro** in room 9 seem to cry out for help. The jumble of tentacles, suction cups, seaweed, shells, and ink has a presence greater than the two-handled amphora would suggest.

CRETE

> ### It's El Greco to Me
>
> Although he made his name at the Spanish court, Domenikos Theotocopoulos (1541-1614) clung to his Greek heritage throughout his artistic career. Born in Iraklion (then under Venetian rule), the Cretan artist melded his early Byzantine training with the teachings of the Venetian and Roman schools, where he trained with masters like Titian, Raphael, and Michelangelo. El Greco, as he came to be known, was a master of Mannerism, a style of painting that places internal emotions above nature and the ancients. His reputation was built on portraits and religious imagery that featured rigid figures filled with emotion. His best-known work, *The Burial of the Count Orgaz*, staged a historical event in the contemporary world, a strong tradition in Western art. Although El Greco moved to Toledo, Spain, in 1576, the Spanish subjects and contexts of his work never eclipsed his feeling that he was a stranger in that land. Throughout his career, El Greco would continue to sign his paintings in Greek.

The clay *larnakes* or coffins in room 13 are uncannily short, but a peek at the sarcophagus' skeletal contents reveals that the corpses were snugly put to rest with their knees bent to their chests.

The museum's most outstanding feature is the **Hall of the Minoan Frescoes.** An illustrated guide available at the museum's gift stand is well worth the 1500dr. The frescoes depict ancient Minoan life: ladies in blue offering libations, blue monkeys frolicking in palatial gardens, and Minoans in procession.

Historical Museum

Tel. 28 32 19. **Open** *M-F 9am-5pm and Sa 9am-2pm.* **Admission** *1000dr, students 750dr, children under 12 free.*

Iraklion also has a **Historical Museum** on the corner of Grevenon St. and Kalokerianou St., across the street from the Xenia Hotel. Unlike the crowded Archaeological Museum, it is undervisited. Its collection includes Byzantine and medieval works, a folk collection, finely woven tapestries, photographs from the WWII Nazi invasion, and **View of Mt. Sinai and the Monastery of St. Catherine** (1578), the only work of **El Greco** on Crete.

Kazantzakis Remembered

The austere **Tomb of Kazantzakis** has views of Iraklion, the sea, and Mt. Ida to the west, and offers a peaceful and green respite from the crowded city of Iraklion. To get there, either walk along the top of the Venetian walls to Martinengo Bastion at the south corner of the city, or go down Evans St. until you reach the walls and the bastion. Because of his heterodox beliefs, Kazantzakis, the author of *The Last Temptation of Christ*, was denied a place in a Christian cemetery and was buried here. True devotees can visit the **Kazantzakis Museum** (tel. 74 16 89) in nearby Varvari. *(Open Mar. 1-Oct. 31 M, W and Sa-Su 9am-1pm and 4-8pm, Tu and F 9am-1pm. Admission 1000dr, students and children 300dr.)* The carefully presented exhibit includes many of the author's original manuscripts, as well as photographs of his theatrical productions. A slide show (in English) provides historical background. A bus from Station A takes you to Mirtia (15km from Iraklion), only a short walk from the museum. For schedules, inquire at the station (tel. 24 50 17 or 24 50 19).

Churches

Several interesting churches hide in the modern maze of Iraklion's city streets. Built in 1735, the **Cathedral of Agios Minas** (tel. 28 24 02) piously graces Agia Ekaternis Sq. *(Open daily 7am-8pm.)* **St. Catherine's Church of Sinai** (tel. 28 88 25), also in the square, served as the first Greek university after the fall of Constantinople in 1453. The church has six icons by the Cretan master Damaskinos as well as other icons from monasteries and churches around Crete. *(Open M-Sa 9am-1:30pm, Tu and Th-F open additionally 5-8pm. Admission 500dr.)* The magnificent edifice of **St. Titus Church,**

25th Augustou Ave., is a mosque converted into a church, and is lit every night. Note the *tamata*, or charm-like votives, that depict the target of churchgoers' prayers. The **Armenian Church** (tel. 24 43 37) can be reached by heading away from the town center on Kalokerianou St. Take a right on Lasthenous St. after Yianni's store and *oriste*—the church is left of the bend. A priest gives tours of the grounds.

Venetian Iraklion

As you scamper around, take note of the various monuments built during the Venetian occupation of Iraklion: **Moroshi Fountain,** centerpiece of Lion Fountain Sq., and the nearby reconstructed **Venetian Loggia** turned town hall. The 17th-century **Venetian Arsenal,** off Kountouriotou Sq. near the waterfront and the **Koules Fortress** (tel. 24 62 11), guard the old harbor. *(Open M-F 8am-6pm, Sa-Su 10am-5pm. Admission 500dr, students 300dr.)* For a dose of peace and beauty which will surprise you in Iraklion's urban context, climb up and walk along the southeast section of the **Venetian walls,** an olive tree-lined refuge. Also accessible from Iraklion is **Fodele,** a village full of orange trees and famous as the home of **El Greco** (see p. 388).

■ Knossos Κνωσσος

History

Knossos is undoubtedly the most famous archaeological site in Crete, partially because of an ancient myth (see p. 391). During the first millennium BC, Cretans were ridiculed for imagining that they sprang from such illustrious forebears as the

CRETE

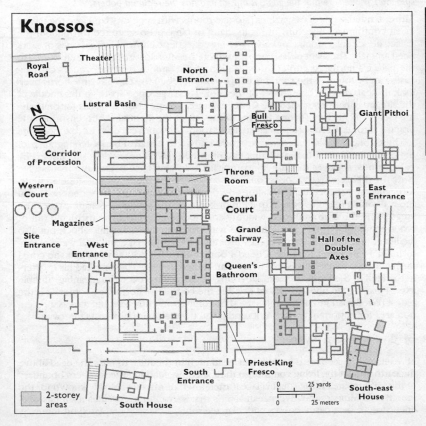

Knossos

Royal Road

Theater

North Entrance

Lustral Basin

Bull Fresco

Giant Pithoi

N

Corridor of Procession

Throne Room

East Entrance

Western Court

Central Court

Magazines

Site Entrance

West Entrance

Grand Stairway

Hall of the Double Axes

Queen's Bathroom

Priest-King Fresco

South Entrance

0   25 yards

0   25 meters

South-east House

2-storey areas

South House

Minoans. Time, however, has proven the Cretans right. **Sir Arthur Evans,** one of Heinrich "Troy" Schliemann's British cronies, purchased the hill and spent his fortune and the next 43 years excavating it. His work showed that from 1700-1400 BC Knossos was indeed either a temple complex or distribution center that stood at the center of the first great European civilization.

Dr. Evans creatively, though in many instances inaccurately, restored large portions of the palace to what he believed were their original configurations based on evidence unearthed during the excavations. Walls, window casements, stairways, and columns were reconstructed in reinforced concrete, and copies of the magnificent frescoes were mounted in place of their original counterparts (which are now in Iraklion's Archaeological Museum). In some cases, restorations prevented the walls from falling down as the excavations continued, but Evans' reconstruction crossed the boundaries of preservation and reflected his own interpretation. While purists feel that the complex at Knossos is an outrage, it is nonetheless impressive.

Touring Knossos

*From Iraklion take bus #2 (every 20min., 230dr), which stops along 25th Augustou Ave., and look for signposts on the street. Tel. 23 19 40. **Open** in summer daily 8am-8pm; in winter daily 8am-5pm. **Admission** 1500dr, students 800dr, in winter free on Su. For a general reference **guide**, check out Knossos and the Iraklion Museum, by Costis Davaris (1500dr), Knossos: The Minoan Civilization, by Sosso Logadiou-Platonos (1500dr), and the new Knossos: A Complete Guide to the Palace of Minos, by Anna Michailidou (2200dr), all on sale at the site. Even more helpful and enlightening is a **tour** in English (1000-2000dr for 1hr. tour; less for students). Make sure that the guide is official and has the required papers.*

The extended series of **magazines** (storage rooms with large clay jars) give the palace its labyrinthine architecture and is its claim to fame. Also scattered throughout the palace are circular storage pits that were used as depositories for the bones of sacrificed animals. The giant **pithoi** (jars) for which the Minoans are famous were stored in the palace's northeast corner. A replication of the famous fresco of youths carrying vases can be found in the **corridor of procession. A bull fresco** with large horns overlook the palace from one corner of the roof. The large open space in the middle of the site, imaginatively named the **Central Court,** was probably an arena for bull-leaping (see p. 417). The **Throne Room,** to the left of the Central Court, enshrines the original throne. A replica sits in an adjacent room for your very own Kodak moment.

The throne faces an enigmatic structure known as a **lustral basin.** Iconography of the first palatial era, often depicting an enthroned queen or goddess surrounded by palm fronds, suggests that the Minoan civilization may have begun as a matriarchy. Note the drainage system, occasional mason's marks on the shiny, cut-stone architecture, and the I-shaped cement bumps on the ground marking where doors slid into the walls in an ingenius system to let in or keep out the sunlight, as appropriate. The areas painted red around each window and door were actually constructed out of wood in antiquity; they cushioned the walls from frequent seismic shock but also facilitated the palace's destruction by fires after the earthquake and tidal wave of Santorini in 1450. Don't miss the **Queen's Bathroom**—over 3000 years ago she could flush her own toilet. This is also where she bathed in milk. The king had his quarters in the **Hall of the Double Axes;** "labyrinth" is derived from a word meaning "double axe." Finally, gaze upon the **Royal Road** in the complex's northwest corner. It is the oldest paved road in Europe and served not only as an entryway, but also as a reception area for important guests. At its end is the **theater,** with box seats for royalty.

■ Arhanes Αρχανες

Minoans and Mycenaeans buried their dead high in the hills, to raise the dead above the earth and let the living continue in their shadow. Marking the southern boundary of the Iraklion area is the small village-turned-town of Arhanes. Mostly known for the remarkable Minoan and Mycenaean tombs that surround it, Arhanes itself has tree-lined streets, neat pastel houses with clay tile roofs, a thriving grape export industry,

Half-breeds, High Taxes, and Wax Wings

One of the most complex and resonant myths in all Greek mythology, that of **King Minos,** begins with a simple crime of ingratitude. When Minos withheld the sacrifice of a fine white bull which Poseidon had granted him for that exclusive purpose, Aphrodite was dispatched to exact a twisted retribution: an unconquerable lust in Minos' queen **Pasiphaë** for the bull itself. To woo the bull she hired master engineer **Daedalus** to build a sexy cow costume that might rouse the bull's affections. After a lusty roll in the hay, Pasiphaë bore—to King Minos' disgust and dismay—the **Minotaur,** a fearsome beast which had the head of a bull and a human body, and a taste for human flesh. The Minotaur was kept in the inescapable **labyrinth** designed by Daedalus, and to feed his queen's child Minos imposed an annual tax of seven maidens and seven youths upon mainland Greece. **Theseus,** an Athenian prince, volunteered for the sacrifice and, once within its labyrinth, slew the minotaur. With a ball of string given him by **Ariadne,** Minos' daughter (who had conspired with Daedalus to save her Athenian squeeze), Theseus retraced his path out of the labyrinth and escaped with Ariadne by ship. Although he had promised her marriage, he later left Ariadne on the beach of Naxos to be swept off by Dionysus. Meanwhile, Minos imprisoned Daedalus and his son **Icarus** as conspirators. Always resourceful, Daedalus constructed wings of wax for the two of them, with which they took flight into the ultimate jailbreak. With freedom in sight, Icarus, in a fit of hubris, flew straight at the sun, melting his wings and sending him plummeting to his death.

and a reputation for friendly community. Arhanes' wine factory, set back from Kapetanaki St. behind the clock tower, is open seasonally for visiting.

A visit to the **Arhanes Archaeological Museum** provides an adequate understanding of the area's sites. (Open M and W-Su 8am-2:30pm. Free.) Head away from the main square on Kapetanaki and look for the sign directing you left to the museum. The cool and sleek one-room museum houses fascinating finds from Phourni, Anemospilia, Vathypetro, and the Minoan Palace at Arhanes as well as photos of the finds which now reside in Iraklion's archaeological museum.

The **Minoan Cemetery at Phourni** lies on a hill northwest of Arhanes. (Open Tu–Su 8am-2:30pm. Free.) To get there, follow Kapetanaki St. out of town and follow signs to the site. Used from the Pre-Palace Period until the Post-Palace Period (2400-1200 BC), the burial ground is remarkable for its diverse array of funerary buildings including the large mound-like *tholos* graves and well-preserved burial offerings. Most of these funerary objects have been moved to Iraklion, but some remain in Arhanes: terra cotta *pithoi*, child and adult sarcophagi, and baby burial jars, as well as skeletons from Phourni. Tholos A was the first unlooted royal burial ground to be found on Crete. A wealthy woman sporting fancy clothes and jewelry was buried in *tholos* D with a mirror now kept in the town's museum. Phourni Building 4 housed a wine press and a vat for treading grapes, as well as an *amphora* for the wine itself, which can be found in the archaeological museum.

On Mt. Iouktas is the 17th-century BC **shrine of Anemosppilia,** in which astonished archaeologists found the remains of a human sacrifice. The shrine was apparently destroyed by an earthquake, and the sacrifice is believed to have been a futile attempt to appease the gods and prevent the inevitable. The bronze dagger found on the body of the sacrificial victim can be viewed at the Arhanes Archaeological Museum.

■ Gortyn Γορτυνα

*To get to Gortyn from Iraklion, take one of the **buses** that go to Matala or Phaistos, and ask the bus driver to stop at Gortyna (900dr). Tel. (0892) 31 1144. **Open** daily in summer 8am-8pm, Sept.-Apr. 8am-7pm. **Admission** 800dr, students and EU seniors 400dr, children under 18, classicists, and EU students free.*

The first stop of historical interest on the road south, **Gortyna** contains the ruins of the Greco-Roman city **Gortyn.** In 67 BC, when it fell to the Romans, Gortyn was made the island's capital. Now the site is conveniently divided by the paved road that leads to Iraklion in the east and Matala in the west. The most famous part of the site of ancient Gortyn, en route to Phaistos, is on your right as you come from Iraklion. The first thing you'll see is the 7th-century **Basilica of Saint Titus,** where the Ten Saints were martyred in AD 250. This was the first Christian church on Crete, and its *berma* (half dome with windows) still stands grandly above a courtyard full of fallen columns. Behind the church is the area in which the town's earliest *agora* is believed to have been located. Behind this location is the **Roman odeon** (music hall). One of the few remains from the Hellenic city, the **Law Code tablets** are the most important extant source of information regarding pre-Hellenistic Greek law. They are written in a Dorian dialect of Greek and date from 450 BC. The tablets were so well-cut that the Romans used them as building materials for the odeon.

Across a small wooden bridge from the odeon is the **Platanos tree,** from which it is said that the brothers Minos, Sarpidon, and Rodaman were born. Mysteriously, the tree is perpetually green. The 7th-century BC **acropolis** lies on the hill to the west of the odeon, and can be reached by continuing 50m down the main road toward Matala. Take a right after the river, walk 200m, and when you reach the corner of the fence, hike up a country road for 30 minutes. Here you will discover the ruins of a temple as well as pottery dedicated to Athena Poliouchos.

Near the cafe (orange juice 600dr) and entrance booth is a small museum with 14 sculpted figures. To the left of the caged-in hall is a larger-than-life statue of the Roman emperor Antonious Pius. A resourceful people, the Romans changed the head of the statue every time a new emperor came into power.

On the southern side of the main road is the **Sanctuary and Sacrificial Altar of Pythian Apollo.** Also in this area is the 4th-century Roman **Praetorium,** which even at that time was fully equipped with a water heating system. The nearby **Nymphaion** was the terminus for an aqueduct that brought spring water from Zaros.

■ Zaros Ζαρος

Decidedly agricultural, Zaros is by all counts a village, yet it stands out as a leader among villages and will soon become the capital and political center of a newly formed union of villages including the neighboring Vorisia, Kamares, and Moroni. Although the members of the 3000-person community may at first be unaccustomed to newcomers, as soon as you learn and use the words for good morning *(kalimera),* good afternoon *(kalispera),* and good night *(kalinikta),* the warm and hospitable locals will be quickly won over. Visitors tend to agree that Zaros, like its famed spring water, is wholesome, pure, and refreshingly unadulterated.

ORIENTATION AND PRACTICAL INFORMATION According to locals, Zaros has everything a tourist could possibly need—except a **bank,** for which you will have to visit the nearby town of Mires. Two buses run from Zaros to **Mires** every day (40min., 340dr). Two buses also run to Iraklion every day. Zaros has one main road, along which you will find most essentials. Coming from Mires and walking uphill, the **police station** (tel. 31 210) is on your left in the square before you reach the village center. The **pharmacy** (tel. 31 386) is in the center of the village (open M-F 8:30am-2pm and 5-8pm). The **post office** and **OTE** share one building and one phone number (tel. 31 170; open M-F 7:30-3pm). **Taxis** are available by the Shell gas station (taxis from Zaros to Mires 2000dr). Zaros is served by a **medical center** in Mires (tel. (0892) 23 312). **Postal code:** 70002. **Telephone code:** 0894.

ACCOMMODATIONS *Drachma* for *drachma,* **Keramos Rent Studios** (tel. 31 352) is the best deal in the village. Turn left immediately before the post office and OTE as you walk uphill through the village and the studios will be on your left. An incredibly warm family maintains the lovely lobby, mini-folk museum, and immaculate rooms of this new establishment. Each tasteful wood furnishing was handmade by the father, and the responsible son manages the daily needs of guests. The dedicated mother rises at 4am every morning to prepare amazing traditional breakfasts of Cretan delights like *pitaraki* (Christmas pastry), yogurt curded from the family goats' milk, tea from mountain leaves collected by the son, and eggs of the family hens. Most studios have kitchenettes, and all have private baths, central heating in the winter (singles 6000dr; doubles 8000dr; triples 11,000dr; breakfast included.). **Charikleia Rent Rooms** (tel. 31 787), near the police station, offers clean rooms with shared baths and a common courtyard. Look across the street for the owner if no one is around (singles 4000dr; doubles 5000dr).

FOOD Incidentally, there are two *tavernas* named **Votomos** in the village. Both are good, but the one further uphill about 200m beyond the Idi Hotel, run by Petrogiannakis and Ieronimakis, is known across Crete for outstanding fish raised from eggs on the premises (tel. 31 071 or 31 454). After touring the *taverna's* fish farm, savor delicious trout (1500dr per kg) and salmon (8000dr per kg) cooked by the owner's mother (open in summer daily 9am-midnight and in winter on weekends and special occasions). **Papadaki Rena** (tel. 31 055), a pastry and sweet shop behind Keramos Studios, doubles as a gift shop. Try their special *tulta* cream cake or the *baklava* standby (each 250dr; open daily 8am-10pm).

SIGHTS Zaros has been Crete's most salubrious source of **water** from the time of ancient Gortyna until now. Natural springs can be spotted throughout the village, and the Zaros water company just outside is open for visiting. Every July and August, the village celebrates its aquatic bounty in an annual **water festival**. At the end of the road beyond the Idi Hotel and both Votomos *tavernas* is the **lake** of Zaros, which is the most popular attraction for Greeks from the surrounding areas.

A hike through the nearby gorge, uphill beyond the Agios Nikolaos Church, makes a scenic and pleasant daytrip. Another path up the mountains leads to the **Monastery of Vrondisi,** where you will find impressive frescoes said to be painted by El Greco himself. Every May, the annual **Paniel festival and bazaar** takes place here to commemorate the ascent of Thomas. Trails and streams up through the hills around the monastery lead to a cliffside sanctuary dedicated to Agios Euthymios, a Cretan saint. Shepherds keep large bottles of olive oil in the sanctuary and bring hikers into the shrines three cave chambers to meditate before frescoes of the saint.

Yet another mountain road leads to the **Kamares Cave,** in which, according to ancient mythology, the earth mother Gaea hid her infant son Zeus from Kronos, her husband, who had a voracious appetite for his own offspring. Here, archaeologists discovered important finds of ceramics and skeletons, which have been moved to the Iraklion museum. Zaros also holds an annual **summer festival** near the town library every August. *(Festival admission 2000dr.)*

■ Phaistos Φαιστος

Buses from Phaistos go to Iraklion (1½hr., 12-13 per day, 1250dr) via Mires (250dr); Matala (20min., 6-7 per day, 260dr); and Agia Galini (25min., 6 per day, 340dr). Tel. (0892) 42 315. **Open** daily Apr.-Aug. 8am-8pm, Sept. 8am-7pm, Oct.-Mar. 8am-5pm. **Admission** 1200dr, students and all EU seniors 600dr, students of classics or fine arts, children under 18, and EU students free.

Imperiously situated on a plateau with a magnificent view of the mountains, the palace at Phaistos housed Minoan royalty. At the turn of the century, Halbherr began excavations here and unearthed two palaces. The first was destroyed by the earthquake that decimated Crete around 1700 BC; the second was leveled in a mysterious catastrophe in 1450 BC. A final excavation in 1952 came upon traces of two even older palaces. Since the excavations, minor reconstruction work has been done on the walls, chambers, and cisterns. Built according to the standard Minoan blueprint, the complex included a great central court from which extended the private royal

CRETE

quarters, servants' quarters, storerooms, and chambers for state occasions. Today, visitors enter Phaistos and immediately see the **West Courtyard** and **theater area** on their right. On the left, the grand staircase is intact. At its top is the **propylaea**, which consists of a landing, a portico, a central column, and a light well. Cut through the hypostyle **main hall** to reach the central court, from which there is a magnificent view of the Messara Plain. Off the **central court** to the west is the main hall with a central and fenced-off **storeroom** where you can view various goodies like *pithoi* similar to those at Knossos.

As you exit the main court with your back to the plain, note the columns and boxes where sentries used to guard the palace. Beyond this area, plastic-roof-covered **royal apartments** with a queen's **magaron** are similar to the famous queen's bathroom at Knossos, and a lustral basin (covered pool) is analogous to that of the Knossos throne room. Nearby in the **peristyle hall**, the remains of columns lining the walls can be seen. Explore the area northeast of the central court and you will find the narrow halls of the palace **workshops** as well as the 7-compartmented room where the renowned **Phaistos disc** was discovered. Phaistos may be disappointing to those unversed in Minoan archaeology, as it is difficult to visualize what the palace looked like in its former glory days. However, enthusiastic classicists may find the large palace, with fewer tourists and less interpretive renovations than Knossos, truer to its history and very rewarding. Combined with a day at the Matala beach, Phaistos makes for an ideal daytrip from Iraklion for all.

■ Matala Ματαλα

Along the beach with the best waves in Crete are cliffs with tiers of caves that have been inhabited since neolithic times. Anyone who visited Matala 20 years ago is likely to muster only intoxicated memories of a more hallucinogenic trip—LSD, psychedelic colors, and groovy music once filled the caves strewn along Matala's seaside cliffs. However, before you pack your rolling papers, be aware that hardly a trace of these hedonistic fiestas remains; Matala is now a resort town for families.

ORIENTATION AND PRACTICAL INFORMATION Matala has three main streets: one on the water, one behind it, and one that intersects both. On the first you'll find cafes, restaurants, souvenir stands, and a covered market; on the second, the bus station, motorbike rental agencies, and stores. At Matala's square, these two join the hotel- and pension-lined road to Phaistos. Several motorbike rental places, all in the main square, handle **currency exchange. Monza Travel** (tel. 45 732, 45 359, or 45 586) serves as an informal tourist office and provides information on hotels and beaches. Monza rents **mopeds** for 3500-9000dr per day, with reduced prices for longer rentals (open daily 9am-11pm). The **laundromat,** across from the campground and up a small road in a marked white building, charges 2800dr per wash and dry (open M-Sa 9am-5pm). The **post office** (tel. 42 034) is near the entrance to the beach parking lot (open M-F 8:30am-2pm). In summer, **buses** go to Iraklion (1¾hr., 5-8 per day, 1500dr); Phaistos (20min., 6-7 per day, 260dr); and Agia Galini (45min., 5-6 per day, 600dr). The **police, hospital,** and **pharmacy** are in Mires, 17km northeast. In an **emergency,** call (tel. 22 222) for police or for a doctor (tel. 22 225 or 23 312). **Public toilets** are located in the main square next to Monza Travel. **Postal code:** 70200. **Telephone code:** 0892.

ACCOMMODATIONS Matala has more than a dozen hotels and pensions, but bargains are scarce. Singles cost as much as doubles and rarely drop below 3000dr in summer. Germans and Brits often pack the town in tour groups, but there are lots of **rooms to let** on the road forking off the main road 750m out of town. It may be a good idea to make Matala a daytrip. Cheaper accommodations are available in nearby villages. Don't try to sleep on the main beach or in the caves; it's illegal and police raid them. Your best bet in town is **Dimitri's Villa** (tel./fax 45 002 or 45 003; fax 45 740; mobile (0933) 20 737; http://www.c-v.net/crete/hotels/matala/dimitris_villa).

From the town center, walk out of town 200m, turn right onto the winding road at the blue "Dimitri's Villa" sign, then follow the path around; call from the bus stop and one of the owners may come pick you up by motorbike. Dimitri has gleaming rooms with private bath, balconies, refrigerators, safes, and hot water. He also offers *Let's Go* users myriad advantages including **currency exchange** without commission, 800dr breakfasts, a 25% discount on bike rentals, and a free ride from Mires to Matala to stay in his rooms (singles 3200dr; doubles 4200dr; triples 5000dr). Another fine option is **Pension Matala View** (tel. 45 114), on the pension-lined road to Red Beach running inland near the main square. They have tidy bedrooms with baths and balconies (singles 3500dr; doubles 5000dr; triples 6000dr). Also on the road to Red Beach is **Hotel Fantastic** (tel. 45 362). Despite fantastically head-turning pink door frames and curtains, this place is a worthy choice with clean beds and private baths (for *Let's Go* readers: singles 4000-5000dr; doubles 5000-5500dr; apartments 7000dr). **Matala Camping** (tel. 45 720), on your right in the town center, has showers (1050dr per person; 700dr per small tent; 600dr per car; 1200dr per RV).

FOOD As usual, better food is farther from the mainstream hangouts. **Nasos** (tel. 45 215), near the waterfront, offers good *souvlaki* (300dr) and gyros (500dr; open daily 9am-1am). Tucked away near the end of the stream of bars that face the caves is **Skala** (tel. 45 489; http://www.c-v.net/matala/tavern/skala), a family-run restaurant known by its nickname, the "Fish Taverna." Try the Cretan salad, a sampler of all the *tzatziki*-related dishes Crete has to offer (2000dr; open 9am-midnight). **Antonio's Taverna** (tel. 45 552), near the turn-off for Dimitri's Rooms, has tasty charcoal-roasted chicken (1400dr; open in summer daily 10am-1am, in winter Sa-Su 5pm-1am). The **bakery** (tel. 45 450) in front of the police station sells a large array of standard Greek pastries, biscuits, and loaves of fresh bread (*baklava* (300dr); *kalitsounia* (2000dr per kg.); open daily 6:30am-midnight).

ENTERTAINMENT Nightlife in Matala means drinking, dancing, and gazing at the ocean until dawn in bars built into the caves on the Easter ridge. At the **Seahorse Bar** (tel. 45 724), dig the reggae, hear the waves, sip the Metaxa, and gaze across to the caves from this porch-turned-bar with tropical plants and a water wall (open just about all day). **Kahlua** (tel. 45 253) is a more mellow nightspot. Sip coffee or brandy among patrons who are out to converse rather than carouse (open daily 5pm-late). **Yorgos** (tel. 45 722), the energetic bartender and owner of this lively bar, is bound to win you with his spunky dancing, chit-chat, and ice-cold beers (open daily 6pm-late).

SIGHTS Matala's main attraction is its three tiers of **caves** next to the beach. (*Open daily 8am-7pm. Free.*) Sit in their cool, dim interiors and spy on the beach action while reflecting on the cave's possible previous occupants—singer-songwriter Joni Mitchell, Nazis searching for British submarines, and, long ago, Roman corpses.

Matala also has more than its share of great **beaches.** Past the crashing waves rises the dim outline of Paximadia Island; check in with vacationing environmentalists who run a stand providing information about local **sea turtles,** endangered by the bright lights of big development. If you're running low on clothes, pick up a turtle t-shirt (profits to benefit turtles, 3500dr). For an equally good shore and more secluded caves, bikini and Speedo-clad sun worshipers join nude bathers on **Red Beach,** 20 minutes down the path behind the church. Comparatively shut off, with a small community of free-lance summer residents and a lone *taverna*, **Kommos Beach** is a 5km walk from Matala. Archaeologists are currently excavating a Minoan site that overlooks the sea, arguably the bluest patch of water in Crete. The bus from Iraklion will let you off roughly 500m from the beach (bus schedule posted by the station in Matala). Bring water; the hike down is long and dusty.

WESTERN CRETE

While many of the resort towns of eastern Crete seem to have sprung from the brains of British booking agents, the vacation spots of western Crete have grown naturally around towns with rich histories and Cretan characters. The meld of Ottoman, Venetian, and Greek architecture in Rethymnon and Hania complements the blue waters of the southwest coast and the sheer cliffs of the Samaria Gorge.

■ Rethymnon Ρεθυμνο

The mix of Ottoman and Venetian influences pervading the cities of northern Crete is best appreciated in Rethymnon's harbor. Arabic inscriptions lace the walls of its narrow arched streets, minarets highlight the old city's skyline, and a Venetian fortress guards the harbor's west end. On any given day, even the most energetic travelers may inexplicably find themselves waking up just in time for the afternoon *siesta* and lounging until the wee hours of the next morning in a cafe by the sea.

ORIENTATION AND PRACTICAL INFORMATION

You'll find everything you need in the rough triangle formed by **Arkadiou St.**, **Antistassios St.**, and **Gerakari St.** To get to Arkadiou St. and the waterfront from the bus station, follow Igoum Garrill St. from behind the station until it becomes **Kountouriotou St.**, and make a left onto **Varda Kallergi St.**

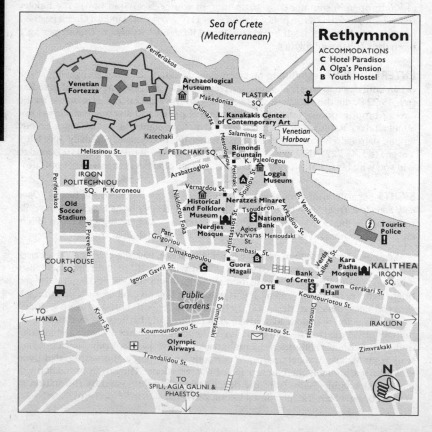

Sea of Crete (Mediterranean)

Rethymnon

ACCOMMODATIONS
C Hotel Paradisos
A Olga's Pension
B Youth Hostel

Periferiakos

Venetian Fortezza

Archaeological Museum

PLASTIRA SQ.

Makedonias

Chimaras

L. Kanakakis Center of Contemporary Art

Katechaki

Salaminus St.

Venetian Harbour

Melissinou St.

T. PETICHAKI SQ.

Messologiou

Rimondi Fountain

K. Paleologou

Arabatzoglou

Petichaki St.

Loggia Museum

IROON POLITECHNIOU SQ. P. Koroneou

Vernardou St.

Soúliou St.

El. Venizelou

Periferiakos

Nikiforou Foka

Historical and Folklore Museum

Neratzes Minaret

Tsouderon

Tourist Police

Old Soccer Stadium

Nerdjes Mosque

Antistasios St.

Agios Varvaras St.

National Bank

Menioudaki St.

Verda Kallergi St.

Kara Pasha Mosque

KALITHEA IROON SQ.

COURTHOUSE SQ.

P. Prevelaki

Patr. Grigoriou

I Dimakopoulou

Tombasi St.

Guora Magali

Bank of Crete

Town Hall

Gerakari St.

Igoum Gavril St.

Kountouriotou St.

Dimokratias

OTE

TO HANIA

Krian St.

S. Dimitrakaki

Public Gardens

Koumoundourou St.

Moatsou St.

TO IRAKLION

Olympic Airways

Trandalidou St.

Zimvrakaki

TO SPILI, AGIA GALINI & PHAESTOS

N

Transportation

Buses: Reythymnon-Hania station (tel. 22 212 or 22 659), south of the fortress on the water at Igoum Gavril St. Service to Iraklion (1½hr., 28 per day, 1500dr); Hania (1hr., 28 per day, 1450dr); Agia Galini (2hr., 4-5 per day, 1150dr); Plakias (1hr., 5 per day, 900dr); and Arkadi Monastery (45min., 3-4 per day, 460dr).

Flights: Olympic Airways, 5 Koumoundorou St. (tel. 24 333 or 22 257), opposite the public gardens. Open M-F 8am-8pm and Sa 8am-4pm.

Taxis: (tel. 25 000, 22 316, 24 316, or 28 316). Available 24hr. in 4 Matrion Sq.

Bike Rental: Fahrrad, 17 Kountouriotou St. (tel. 29 331 or 28 617), near the OTE, Mountain bikes 2000dr per day. Open M-F 9am-2pm and 5:30-9pm, Sa 9am-2pm.

Tourist and Financial Services

Tourist Office: (tel. 29 148), down by the waterfront on El. Venizelou St., east of the old city. Staff provides free maps, bus and ferry schedules, museum hours, and information on rooms and restaurants. They also suggest daytrips and local events. Open M-F 8am-4:30pm and Sa 9:30am-3pm.

Banks: Bank of Crete (tel. 24 716, 29 843, or 27 637), at the intersection of Kountouriotou and Varda Kallergi St., has **currency exchange.** The **National Bank** (tel. 29 271) is at 18 Tsouderon St. Both open M-Th 8am-2pm and F 8am-1:30pm.

Bookstore: International Press, 15 Petichaki St. (tel. 24 111), near the water. Sells books, newspapers, and magazines. Open daily 9am-11pm. **Spontidaki Toula,** 43 Souliou St. (tel. 54 307), buys and sells new and used books. Open daily 9am-11pm.

Laundromat: 45 Tombasi St. (tel. 56 196), next to the youth hostel. Wash and dry 2500dr, 2000dr for students and soldiers. Open M-F 8am-2pm and 5-8pm, Sa 8am-2pm and 5-7pm. Drop-off service available.

Emergency and Communications

Police: Located in Iroon Sq. (tel. 25 246 or 25 247). Open 24hr.

Tourist Police: 5 Venizelou St. (tel. 28 156; fax 53 450), next to the tourist office. Provides services similar to the tourist office. Open M-F 7am-10pm.

Hospital: 18 Trantalidou St. (tel. 27 814), in the southwest corner of town. From Igoum Gavril St. at the bus station take Kriari St. to G. Trantalidou St. and bear left; it's on the left. Open 24hr.

Pharmacy: 2 Koumoundourou St. (tel. 25 123). Open M-F 8am-2:30pm, Tu Th 5:30-9pm.

Post Office: Main branch, 19 Moatsou St. (tel. 22 303), near the public gardens. Open M-F 7:30am-8pm, Sa 7:30am-2pm. **Caravan office,** on the beach by the second dock. Open M-Sa 8am-2pm. **Postal Code:** 74100.

OTE: Kountouriotou St. (tel. 59 500). Open M-Sa 7am-3pm. **Telephone Code:** 0831.

ACCOMMODATIONS

Near the fortress and Venetian port, Arkadiou St. and the harbor are lined with spacious and expensive hotels and rooms to let. The **Association of Rooms to Let,** 2 Petichaki St. (tel. 29 503), a block from the harbor, finds rooms. Off-season is 20-40% less.

✺**Youth Hostel,** 41-45 Tombazi St. (tel. 22 848). From the bus station, walk down Igoum Gavril, take left at the park traffic light, walk through the Guora Megali gate, and Tombazi is the first right. Rooms and outside bunk beds on the veranda or roof are available. Teeming in the summer with young people enjoying the pleasant garden areas and bar. Spontaneous parties and communal meals sometimes form. Hot showers in summer 8-10am and 5-8pm. Reception open in summer daily 8am-noon and 5-9pm. 1500dr per person. Sheets 150dr. Breakfast 400dr.

✺**Olga's Pension,** 57 Souliou St. (tel. 53 206, 28 665 or 54 896; fax 29 851), on a restored street off Antistassios. Cheery decor in comfortable rooms, all with bath. Note the coin mosaic on your way up the front stairs. Coffee and meals can be brought up from Stella's. Friendly owners. Singles 4500dr, with bath 5000dr; doubles 6000dr, with bath 7000dr; triples with bath 10,000dr.

Hotel Paradisos, 37 Igoum Gavril St. (tel. 22 419). From the bus station, walk down Igoum Gavril; the hotel is on the left, across from the public garden. Clean, quiet rooms. Singles 3000dr; doubles 4000dr; triples 5000dr. Hot showers 500dr.

Elizabeth Camping (tel. 28 694), 3km east of town at the beginning of the old road to Iraklion. Tent pitches on shaded grass. Free parking next to reception. The staff lends supplies, guitars, and books. Self-service *taverna* open 8:30am-1am. "Texas" BBQ every Thursday. Bus service to Rethymnon station (3 per hr., 170dr). Open mid-Apr.-Oct. 1300dr per person, 1000dr per tent, single person and tent 1800dr.

FOOD AND ENTERTAINMENT

Rethymnon has plenty of *souvlaki* (350dr) stands scattered throughout the city. There's also an **open-air market** on Thursdays next to the park, between Moatsou St. and Kountouriotou St. The market opens early (6 or 7am) and closes by midday (1 or 2pm). By 9 or 10am the selection is drastically diminished. For a thriving night-time dining scene, tourists and locals head to Petichaki Sq. and fill the *tavernas*.

Dimitris, 35 Agios Varvaras St. (tel. 28 933). There is no menu in this *raki* bar, but the food is tasty. If you order alcohol made by the owner (150dr), you'll receive a plate of snacks, usually olives, cheese, and meat. Their specialty (besides *raki*) is oven-roasted potatoes (500dr). Open daily 8am-2pm and 5-11pm.

Taverna Kyria Maria, 20 Moskovitou St. (tel. 29 078). Rabbit (1600dr), lamb with potatoes (1300dr), and octopus (woo-hoo!) in wine sauce (1100dr). Free hot cheese pies drenched in honey after dinner. Pleasant atmosphere among chirping birds. Open mid-Mar. to Oct. daily 10am-11pm.

Pontios, 34 Melissinou St. (tel. 57 024). Homemade Greek specialties: fresh, delicious stuffed *kalamari* (1300dr), Greek salad (700dr), and *souvlaki* with pita (350dr). The street closes every day at 3pm, making these outdoor tables beneath the Fortezza a pleasant place to dine. Open daily 8am-midnight.

Akri, 27 Kornarou St. (tel. 50 719), just off Souliou St. in the old town. Enjoy Greek music and feast on house specialties, like sausages (1200dr), fried mussels (1200dr), zucchini balls (800dr), and baked haricot beans (900dr). 15% student discount, 10% senior discount. Open daily 11am-4pm and 6pm-1am.

⊛**Stella's Kitchen,** 55 Souliou St. (tel. 28 665 or 54 896). Family-run coffee shop below Olga's Pension serving homemade cakes (250-350dr), snacks (300-1000dr), and full meals (1500dr). Open daily 7am-midnight.

The bar scene at Rethymnon centers around Petichaki St. and Nearchou St. near the west end of the harbor. The happening **Rockafé Bar,** 8 Petichaki St., and the **Fortezza Disco Bar,** 14 Nearchou St. (tel. 21 493), bookend several Greek *bouzouki* places. Both have pricey beers (1000dr). **Baja** on Salaminos St. packs crowds in with its air-conditioned dance floor and techno house tunes.

SIGHTS

Rethymnon has been occupied nearly continuously since the late Minoan period. At its apex in the 14th century BC it was overrun by Mycenaeans. During the Fourth Crusade, the Franks sold the island to the Venetians for 520 pounds of silver. The Venetians fortified Rethymnon, which was crucial to their chain of trading outposts. The Ottomans then took the city in 1646, enlarging it and incorporating their designs into the buildings. At some point during your visit you should make a pilgrimage to the 1580 **Venetian Fortezza** (tel. 28 101). *(Open Tu-Su 8am-7pm. Admission 700dr.)* The walls of the citadel are in excellent condition, but most of the buildings inside the fortress were destroyed by Ottomans in the 17th century, and even more bit the dust three centuries later during WWII. The city's **Renaissance Festival,** featuring theater, concerts, and exhibitions, is held in the fortress in July and August.

Rethymnon's **Archaeological Museum** (tel. 54 668) is in a former Ottoman prison adjacent to the fortress. *(Open Tu-Su 8:30am-3pm. Admission 500dr, students and seniors 300dr, EU students free.)* Once inside, you'll feel like you've wandered into the storeroom of an absent-minded archaeologist—headless statues lean on walls behind rows of figurines, and Minoan sarcophagi lie next to Roman coins. The **Historical and Folklore Museum,** 28-30 Vernardou St. (tel. 23 398; fax 23 667), showcases traditional arts and farming tools. *(Open M-Sa 10am-2:30pm. Admission 500dr, students 200dr.)*

The **L. Kanakakis Center of Contemporary Art,** 5 Himaras St., at the corner of Salaminus St. (tel. 52 530, 52 689, or 55 847; fax 52 689; email rca@ret.forthnet.gr),

Winnie the Pooh: Through the Looking Glass

In the 5th century BC, Cyrus of Persia recruited a ragtag troop of jack-booted Greek thugs to pillage various villages in Asia Minor. Among the 10,000 Greeks was the perennial gangsta Xenophon, who recorded their wacky misadventures in the *Anabasis*. On the march home they happened upon a swarm of bees whose hives brimmed with wild honey. Ironically, the taste of honey proved more hazardous than the bees' stings: of soldiers who sampled the nectar, some ended up unconscious, and others very ill. However, those who consumed the ambrosia in moderation reported fantastical visions. The morning after, the entire legion woke up with a wicked hangover, but, like Phrygians roughed up by a few Cimmerian nomads, or Assyrians battered at the hands of the much-disputed Mushki warlords, they cut their losses. After enduring a few days of rehab and detox from the deleterious effects of too many psychedelics, the iron-hearted Hellenes were marching west to Trabzon.

houses a large collection of modern Greek paintings. The center also hosts temporary exhibitions. *(Open Tu-Sa 10am-2pm and 6-9pm, Su 10am-3pm. Admission 500dr.)*

Tattooed with graffiti and untamed by museum keepers, Rethymnos' Ottoman monuments blend uncelebrated into its scenery: the **Neratzes Minaret** on Antistassios St.; the **Nerdjes Mosque**, 1 Fragkiskou St., a block farther, formerly a Franciscan church; the **Kara Pasha Mosque** on Arkadiou St. near Iroon Sq.; and the **Valides Minaret,** which presides over **Porta Megali** gate at 3 Martiou Sq.

Rethymnon's own **craft shops** cluster around Arkadiou, Antistassios, and Gerakari St. The **Herb Shop**, 58 Souliou St. (tel. 29 664), stocks folk remedies and herbs exclusive to Crete. For 50 years this shop has sold dried Cretan herbs for cooking and healing. *Senes* is said to help heal stomach ailments (300dr for a small bag), and oregano (500dr per bag) tastes good on salad. *(Open M-Sa 10am-2pm and 6-11pm, Su 6-11pm.)* Rethymnon's **Wine Festival** (in July or August) is a crowded all-you-can-drink fest. *(First-night admission 1000dr, descending 100dr per night. Required souvenir glass 150dr.)* A local dance troupe performs early in the evening.

■ Arkadi Monastery Μονη Αρκαδη

23km from Rethymnon. 3-4 buses per day from Rethymnon with return trips leaving an hour later. 460dr each way. Admission 500dr.

As Greeks all over the empire fought to throw off the Ottoman yoke, Crete was the scene of the fiercest struggles defined by the mentality of "Freedom or Death"—Ελευθερια η θανατος. In November 1866, in the midst of one of Crete's several revolts against the Ottomans, Greeks and Turks engaged in a two-day stand-off at the monastery. When their defenses finally gave way, the monks and *kleftes* holding out in the monastery set off their own ammunitions supplies, and hundreds were killed on both sides. The story of Arkadi inspired much support for Cretan independence among the intelligentsia of western Europe, and the monastery's remains continued to serve as a strategic outpost even into World War II. Today you will recognize Arkadi's Venetian chapel from 1587 for its prominent place on 100-*drachma* notes. A few monks still maintain the monastery; its chapel, the roofless chamber where the ammunition was detonated, and a small museum are open for reflective touring.

■ Plakias Πλακιας

Sunny and secluded, Plakias has remained pleasantly underdeveloped and inexpensive compared to most other Cretan beach towns. The crystal clear waters of the south coast, as well as mountain villages and remote monasteries within hiking distance, make Plakias an ideal budget escape from Crete's cosmopolitan north coast.

ORIENTATION AND PRACTICAL INFORMATION Everything in Plakias lies either on the beach road or on the roads and foot paths that recede into the hills. **Buses** drop off and pick up visitors right on the beach. They run to Rethymnon (4-5 per day,

CRETE

900dr); Agia Galini (2 per day, 1200dr); Preveli (3 per day, 340dr); and Hora Sfakia (1 per day, 900dr). **Monza Travel** (tel. 31 882 or 31 433; fax 31 883), on the beach road, has both British and Greek staff, rents cars (12,000dr) and mopeds (5000dr), arranges for scuba instruction and other watersports, and runs excursions to all parts of Crete (7000-11,000dr). A **doctor** and **pharmacy** (tel. 31 770; mobile (094) 859 983), are behind Monza (open M-Sa 9:30am-1:15pm and 5:15-9pm, Su 5:30-9pm), but call the **hospital** in Rethymnon in an emergency (tel. (0831) 27 814). A **post office** trailer sets up on the beach for the summer (open M-F 8:30am-2pm), but a larger, year-round post office and the **police** (tel. 31 338) are 1km north in Mirthios. **Postal code:** 74060. **Telephone code:** 0832.

ACCOMMODATIONS Follow several signs pointing inland to reach the **Plakias Youth Hostel** (tel. 32 118). The bungalows have dorm beds (1300dr) where a funky international set of backpackers spends quiet *siestas* between swims and hikes. The common refrigerator, bathroom, and lounge (with jukebox) are kept clean by a friendly staff. The roof provides a somewhat private getaway for couples. Reception is open 9am-noon and 5-9pm, but if you arrive during off-hours, grab an open bed and settle up in the morning. For private doubles (4000dr), ask at the Youth Hostel about **Fethra Rent Rooms.** At **Pension Kyriakos** (tel. 31 307), the rooms are decked out with kitchenettes and comfy couches, the bathrooms are private, and the motto is "no *raki,* no rooms." Kyriakos insists on treating all his guests to *raki* (doubles 5000-6000dr, apartments for 3-4 people 10,000dr). To get there, walk down the street with the doctor and pharmacy. The pension is above the leather store at the end of the road. **Camping Apollonia** (tel. 31 318), with its two pools, snack bar, and bike rental, looks more like a country club than a campsite. To reach the site, with your back to the beach, walk towards the right down the road to the right of Old Alianthos Taverna (open May-Oct; reception open 8:30am-9:30pm; showers free for campers, 250dr for outsiders, laundry 1000dr for wash only; bicycles 1500dr per day, motorbikes 3500-4500dr per day; 1200dr per person; 600dr per tent; 600dr per car; 700dr per child 4-10 years old; 300dr per bike; 1200dr per caravan; 700dr per trailer).

FOOD AND ENTERTAINMENT Locals highly recommend the **Old Alianthos Taverna** (tel. 31 851) at the eastern end of the beach road. Go for their special *stifado* (1300dr) or butter beans (900dr; open daily 11:30am-10:30pm). Or head past the doctor's office and pharmacy to have a family-style meal at **Medousa** (tel. 31 321) under a vine-covered veranda (*moussaka* 1000dr, beef with lemon sauce 1500dr, homemade wine 1000dr per kilo). Over the tiny bridge to the west, **Lysseos** serves inexpensive traditional village meals (*moussaka* 1150dr; open daily 7-10pm). For those in search of **nightlife,** even far from the city lights, **Hexagon** and **Meltemi** dance clubs grind nightly from midnight to 6am.

SIGHTS You may be too tired for such nocturnal activities after **hikes** through the surrounding hills. Follow posted signs or ask around town for a one-hour climb past the village of Mirthios to **Preveli Monastery.** *(Open daylight hours. Admission 500dr. Modest dress required.)* Return the same way or climb down the cliff road to **Preveli Beach,** where you can hitch a ride back to Plakias on a passing ferry (1000dr).

■ Hania Χανια

Crete's second largest city, Hania is a curious combination of Cretan natives, Scandinavian tourists, and American military officers. Although no longer Crete's official capital, Hania is still regarded by many islanders as the spiritual capital. Visitors meander through winding streets, absorb folk music from streetside cafes, or spend the day gazing at the old Venetian Harbor. No matter how tourist-oriented the waterfront cafes become, they don't mar the harbor's beauty, glowing at sunset behind silhouettes of Arab and Ottoman domes.

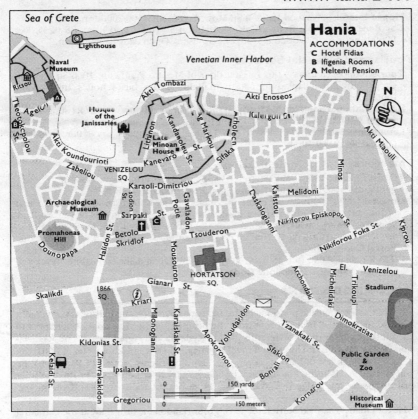

Hania
ACCOMMODATIONS
C Hotel Fidias
B Ifigenia Rooms
A Meltemi Pension

ORIENTATION AND PRACTICAL INFORMATION

From the bus station, walk right on Kidonias St. for two blocks and turn left onto 1866 Sq.; going north, the road becomes Halidon St. and leads to the old **harbor,** the setting for much of Hania's nightlife. To lighten the load while looking for a room, **leave your bags** at the bus station (storage open 6am-9pm; 300dr per bag). Ferries dock in **Souda,** the nearby port. A bus from Souda drops you off at Hania's Municipal Market (15min., 230dr). Facing the market, turn left and walk two blocks on Gianari St., then turn right onto Halidon St. Even with maps from the tourist office, finding your way around is challenging. Luckily, Hania is small, so you can't stay lost for long. Hania's business district is mostly contained within the area across from the market, around the intersection of **Gianari St.** and **Tzanakaki St.**

Transportation

Buses: Central bus station (tel. 93 052 or 93 306), on the corner of Kidonias and Kelaidi St. Schedules change often so check before you go. Service to Paleochora (5 per day, 1450dr); Hora Sfakion (3 per day, 1400dr); Kastelli (14 per day, 850dr); Samaria Gorge (1 per day, 1300dr); Elafonissi (1 per day, 1900dr); Sougia (2 per day, 1350dr); Rethymnon (16 per day, 1450dr); and Iraklion (16 per day, 2800dr).

Ferries: ANEK Office (tel. 27 500), in Venizelou Sq., near National Bank. *Lato* and *Lissos* go to Peiraias (11hr., once nightly, tourist-class 8600dr, deck-class 5900dr). Open daily 7:30am-8:30pm.

Flights: Olympic Airways, 88 Tzanakaki St. (tel. 57 701, 57 702, or 57 703), near the public garden. Tickets sold M-F 8am-3pm. Phone reservations M-F 7am-10pm, Sa 8am-3pm. Flights to Athens (3 per day, 20,000dr).

Moped Rental: Several on Halidon St. Mopeds rent for 4500-7000dr per day.
Car Rental: Olympic Rent-a-Car, 74 Halidon St. (tel. 94 915; fax 88 025). Fiat 9000dr per day. 25% discount for *Let's Go* users. Open daily 8am-9:30pm.

Tourist and Financial Services

Tourist Office: (tel./fax 92 624). First floor of Megaro Pantheon, 1866 Sq., behind Greek Agricultural Bank. Information on flights, ferries, buses, hotels, and package tours; free maps. Open M-F 7:30am-2:30pm.
Banks: National Bank (tel. 28 810), on the corner of Nikiforou St., Foka St., and Tzanakaki St. Open M-Th 8am-2pm, F 8am-1:30pm.
Laundromat: (tel. 52 494), next to Hotel Fidias. Wash 1000dr; dry 800dr. Soap free. Open daily 8am-9:30pm.

Emergency and Communications

Tourist Police: 60 Karaiskaki St. (tel. 73 333), by the central bus station. In an **emergency,** call 100. Open daily 7:30am-8pm. **Port Police:** tel. 98 888.
Hospital: (tel. 27 000), on the corner of Dragoumi and Kapodistriou St., 5 blocks east of the harbor center. Outpatient clinic open M-Sa 12:30-2pm and 6-9pm, Su 8am-9pm. For **emergencies,** call 22 222; for an **ambulance,** call 166. Available 24hr.
Post Office: 3 Tzanakaki St. (tel. 28 445). Open M-F 7:30am-8pm, Sa 7:30am-2pm. **Postal Code:** 73100.
OTE: 5 Tzanakaki St. (tel. 35 519). Very efficient. Open daily 7am–10pm. Telex and telegram M-F only. **Telephone Code:** 0821.

ACCOMMODATIONS

Most of the inexpensive pensions in the old town overlook the harbor, a convenient but noisy area. Small hotels sprout from the beaches on the west coast, but expect to lay out the cash for the brown sands of **Nea Kydonia** and **Agia Marina.** The **Association of Rooms to Let: Unikreta Travel Agency,** 20 Dor. Episkopou (tel. 43 601; fax 46 277), a block left of harbor center, can help find rooms (open M-F 9am-2pm). Be wary of the locals at the bus station who *illegally* try to entice visitors to stay in their private rooms. It is dangerous, as they may be dishonest about prices and intentions.

◉**Hotel Fidias,** 6 Sarpaki St. (tel. 52 494). From Halidon St. turn right at the cathedral on Athinagora St., which becomes Sarpaki St. With poster-coated walls and linoleum floors, it looks like a clean college dorm. TV and free coffee breakfast. Reception open daily 7am-10pm. Dorms 1500-2000dr; singles 2000-4000dr; doubles 3000-4500dr; triples 4500-6000dr, depending on season. 15% senior discount.

Meltemi Pension, 2 Agelou St. (tel. 92 802), at end of west side of harbor, next to the Naval Museum. Rooms have wooden floors, marble-topped desks, high ceilings, and some harbor views. The Meltemi Cafe downstairs serves *frappés* (600dr), breakfast, and drinks. Doubles 4000-6000dr, with bath 7000-8000dr; triples 6000dr, with private shower 9000-10,000dr.

Ifigenia Rooms (tel. 99 184, 94 033; mobile phone (094) 501 319; fax 94 357). Head to Hotel Capt. Vassilis to find the manager. To get there, walk up Angelou St. from the Naval Museum and left on Theotokopolou St. Several buildings in the old town close to the harbor, with many rooms available. Most with private bath, some with kitchens. The cafe and pension are on the right. Doubles 8000-12,000dr.

FOOD AND ENTERTAINMENT

The **public market,** at the south end of the old town at the intersection of Tzanakaki St. and Hatzi Michali Gianari St., is in a beautiful building built in about 1912. Produce, cheese, herb, and meat shops mix with leather shops and tiny seafood restaurants (open M, W, Th, Sa 8am-2pm, Tu, F 8am-2pm and 6-9pm). Small restaurants serve fresh fried seafood and delicious stews for good prices.

◉**Tamam,** Zabeliou 49 (tel. 96 080). Intimate dinners of super veal with mushrooms (1300dr), as well as *hounkiar beyiendi* (chicken in aubergine puree, 1600dr) and vegetarian alternatives. Open daily 7-12:30pm.

Anaplous (tel. 41 320), Sifaka St.and E. Mexisedek St. The romantic open-air bistro serves brilliant chicken kebab (1600dr), garlic pie (280dr), and a variety of savory baked potatoes (780dr). Open 7pm-midnight.

Akrogiali, 19 Akti Papanikoli, Nea Hora (tel. 73 110). Keep walking to the west along the water beyond the end of the harbor to the nearby beach of Nea Hora. This is where all the locals and savvy tourists come for sea urchin eggs (1300dr) and shrimp (1700dr). Open M-Sa 7pm-1am, Su 11am-1am.

Hania's lively nightlife has a distinct dichotomy—the American music young Greeks groove to on the west side of the harbor, and the Rembetika beats old men drink to is on the east side. Tiny **Fagotto Bar,** 16 Agelou (tel. 71 877), plays hot jazz and rhythm and blues from its huge collection (cocktails 1200dr; open daily 10pm-5am). For a hard-core Cretan experience head east to **Cafe Kriti,** 22 Kalergon St., which offers traditional music and dancing among old men with long mustaches and big black boots. (Beer 500dr. Open nightly 6pm-3am. Not for women traveling alone.)

SIGHTS

The **Venetian Inner Harbor** is a thriving social scene and an architectural relic that has retained its original breakwater and Venetian arsenal. Egyptians restored the Venetian **lighthouse** during their occupation of Crete in the late 1830s (enter at the east end of the harbor). On the opposite side of the main harbor, the **Naval Museum** (tel. 91 875), exhibits nautical pictures and pieces of boats. *(Open in summer daily 10am-4pm. Admission 500dr, students 300dr.)*

Kastelli Hill, the area north of Kanevaro St., is studded with reminders of Hania's past. Remnants of Ancient Kydonia's Bronze Age prosperity are evident at the **Late Minoan House** (circa 1450 BC), on the corner of Kandanoleu and Kanevaro St. Unfortunately, the site is fenced off. In the Middle Ages, Venetian occupiers enriched the city's architecture, but WWII destroyed much of their artistry. The waterfront alleys, with a melange of Ottoman and Venetian architecture, reflect the city's past. Pass through several archways on Moshon St. to reach the **Venetian Chapel,** decorated with Latin and Turkish inscriptions. Young Greeks mellow out in the **Municipal Gardens,** *Dimotikos Kypos,* once the property of a *muezzin* (Islamic prayer caller). The garden also harbors a small zoo and an open-air movie theater that shows international films. UNICEF sets up an annual **International Fair** in the gardens—consult the tourist office for details. **Sfakianaki,** a 19th-century neighborhood with tree-lined streets, is beyond the gardens to the east, as is the **Historical Museum and Archives,** 20 Sfakianaki St. (tel. 52 606), which contains Cretan weaponry, photos of 19th-century generals, old clothing, and a tattered Cretan flag. *(Open M-F 8am-1:30pm. Free.)*

The **Archaeological Museum** (tel. 90 334), on Halidon St. opposite the cathedral, displays Cretan artifacts. *(Open Tu-Su 8:30am-3pm. Admission 500dr, students 300dr.)* Once a Venetian monastery, it also served as the mosque of Yusuf Pasha. In the **Venetian Shiphouse** (tel. 28 435) at the east end of the harbor, a temporary museum is set up with a new theme each summer, so stop by the shiphouse or consult the tourist office for current information.

■ Balos Βαλος

On the northwestern tip of Crete is the beautiful and secluded lagoon of Balos. Chartered boats reach this shore; driving there is a slight hassle, but more rewarding. From Hania, drive about ninety minutes on the main road past Platanias and through Kissamos until you reach a dirt road. On this dirt road you'll find a small white **chapel,** notable for its spring of healing water. Watch out for the wasps that swarm around the spring or you might really need those healing powers. After driving (about 30min.) on the country road until it ends, a 45-minute hike downhill will take you to the lagoon. But before rushing down, take a moment to enjoy the view of Balos' brilliant blues, greens, and whites, and the surrounding islands.

■ Samaria Gorge Φαραγγι της Σαμαριας

Open May 1-Oct. 15 6am-4pm. **Admission** 1200dr, children under 15, organized student groups free. For gorge information, call the **Hania Forest Service** (tel. (0821) 92 287), or pick up information at the tourist offices in Hania, Rethymnon, or Iraklion.

The most popular excursion from Hania, Rethymnon, or Iraklion is the four- to six-hour hike down Europe's longest gorge—the formidable 16km **Samaria Gorge.** Worn away by millions of years of river runoff, this pass through the White Mountains, **Lefka Ori,** retains its allure despite being mobbed by visitors of every nationality. Bird watchers can glimpse the rare bearded vulture, horticulturists can admire the wildflowers and shrubs that peek out from sheer rock walls, and goat lovers can spot the nimble *agrimi,* a wild Cretan species in one of its few remaining natural habitats. The towering beauty of the gorge is visible at all points, but only to those who stop long enough to take their eyes from their feet. Please observe Hania Forest Protection Service's rules concerning litter to preserve the trail's natural beauty.

The 44-kilometer, one-and-a-half-hour bus ride from Hania to **Xyloskalo,** at the start of the trail, offers spectacular scenery. Passing between cliff walls up to 300m high, the downhill path, only 3m wide at some points, winds down along a riverbed that runs nearly dry in the summer. Parts of the hike are shaded by clumps of pine trees, goats, and the towering walls of the gorge itself. The hike ends in Agia Roumeli on the south coast. From there a boat sails to Loutro and Hora Sfakion, where buses run back to Hania. Experienced hikers can hike from Agia Roumeli to Hora Sfakion (10hr.) along one of the more outstanding coastlines in the country. The downhill hike favored by most people (from Xyloskalo in the Omalos Plain to Agia Roumeli) takes four to six hours. A less traveled path ascends Mt. Gingilos to the west.

Whichever route you choose, bring plenty of water and trail snacks, and wear good walking shoes. The gorge is dry and dusty in summer, and the stones on the path become slippery. Furthermore, the altitude often makes the top of the gorge cold and rainy. If you get tired on the hike, do not worry; you can always take the donkey taxis that patrol the trail. If all you want to see is the dramatic tail of the gorge, Agia Roumeli is the place to start the journey. The path to the trail begins just behind Rooms Livikon. From the quay, walk straight to the rear of the village. Known as "Samaria the Lazy Way," the two-hour climb to the north takes you to the gorge's dramatic and narrow pass, the "Iron Gates." During the winter and spring, the river goes back to work cutting its trail through the rock—flash floods have claimed many lives.

A hot and dusty hike beyond the official exit of the gorge leads to **Agia Roumeli,** a seedy oasis for tired and thirsty hikers. Beyond Agia Roumeli proper is a town with little but its beach to offer. The black pebbles are unbearably hot, but the water is refreshing. The town itself exists mainly to sell food, souvenirs, and lodgings to tired and weak-willed hikers. If you do stay, you can sleep at **Hotel Livikon** (tel. 91 363), on the inland end of town (doubles 5000dr; triples 6000dr).

Getting There and Away

Buses for Omalos and Xyloskalo leave Hania (4 per day, 1200dr). The 6:15, 7:30, and 8:30am buses will place you in Xyloskalo for a day's hike while the 4:30pm bus will put you in Omalos for a hike the next day. From Rethymnon, take the 6:15 or 7am buses through Hania to Omalos (2450dr). Intrepid early risers can take the 5:30am bus from Iraklion through Rethymnon and Hania (3750dr) to Omalos. Since Agia Roumeli is served by **ferries** leaving at 90min. intervals to Hora Sfakion, you can make the complete round-trip from Hania, Rethymnon, or Iraklion in one day, leaving on a morning bus. Taking the earliest bus will ensure cooler weather and less company for the hike. The last buses out of Hora Sfakion leave at 7:15pm for Hania (1400dr) and Iraklion (2900dr) via Rethymnon (1400dr). You can also plan a leisurely hike and spend the night in a coastal town.

■ Hora Sfakion Χωρα Σφακιων

The scenic town of Hora Sfakion lacks the intimacy of Plakias to the east or Loutro and Paleochora to the west, but serves as the transportation hub of the south coast. The town's pebbly cove and fishing fleet look tempting from afar, but up close you will see that the beach is littered. Since Hora Sfakion lacks the dusty heat that pervades Agia Roumeli, it is an adequate resting spot after a Samaria Gorge hike.

The town centers around a main square just 50m uphill from the ferry dock. With your back to the water and facing the square, the post office (tel. 91 244) is on your left next to Sfakia Tours near the waterfront (open M-Sa 7:30am-2pm). The **OTE** (tel. 91 299) is to your right on the road leading uphill from town, near where buses leave (open M-F 7:30am-3:15pm). The **supermarket** is also on the street behind the harbor—a good place to stock up for a tour of remote beaches. The 24-hour **police station** (tel. 91 205) and **port police** (tel. 91 292) are inland from the square. Walk uphill and look for the flag-marked building on your right behind the bus stop. **Sfakia Tours** (tel./fax 91 130) sells bus tickets and rents cars (9000dr per day; open daily 8am-9:30pm). **Telephone code:** 0825.

Buses from Hora Sfakion go to Plakias (1¼hr., 2 per day, 1000dr) and then to Rethymnon (1½hr., 4 per day, 1400dr) to meet the ferry. At the same time, a bus leaves for Agia Galini (2hr., 1 per day, 2100dr) or Anapolis (30min., 1 per day, 400dr). Change buses at Vrises for Iraklion (2650dr). Four buses per day go to Hania (2hr., 1400dr), the last at 7:15pm. If your ferry is late, don't worry—the buses wait for the boats to arrive. **Boats** from Hora Sfakion travel to Agia Roumeli (1¼hr., 5 per day, 1500dr). Most routes stop in Loutro. These run from April to October; in winter, travelers go to Loutro by foot or fishing boat. It is a good idea to check schedules with the **ticket office** (tel. 91 221). Boats run from Hora Sfakion to Gavdos, an uninhabited island which is the southernmost point in Europe, three times a day. **Caïques** to Sweetwater Beach run twice daily.

There are plenty of cheap accommodations in Hora Sfakion. The cool, grotto-like **Hotel Xenia** (tel. 91 490; fax 91 491) has spacious, immaculate rooms (singles 7000dr; doubles 8000-9000dr; triples 9000dr). **Lefka Ori** (tel. 91 209), on the waterfront, rents rooms with views of the harbor (singles 3500-4000dr; doubles with bath 5000-6500dr; triples 7000-8500dr). **Rooms Samaria** (tel. 91 261), on the east end of the back street, is large and cool, with wrought-iron balconies (open Mar.-Nov.; doubles with terrace and bath 6000dr; triples 8000dr). The town's restaurants are basically limited to those downstairs from the hotels, where meals run from 1500-4000dr. The town's only disco, **Underground,** rocks nightly to, in the words of the owner, "whatever the people want" (open nightly 10pm-morning, no cover).

▓ Paleochora Παλεοχορα

Once a refuge for the embattled rear guard of the 1960s counterculture, Paleochora is the stop for diehard devotees. Just 77km from Hania, Paleochora is a pleasant retreat with a sandy beach and a stunning backdrop of Cretan mountains. *Tavernas* and necessities line one main street and reasonably priced pensions dot the harbor.

ORIENTATION AND PRACTICAL INFORMATION Paleochora is on a small peninsula. Running north-south through the town center is **Venizelou Street,** the main thoroughfare. It crosses **Kentekaki Street** which leads west to the beach and east to the harbor. **Buses** to Hania (2hr., 5 per day, 1450dr) stop at this intersection.

The **tourist office** (tel. 41 507) is on Venizelou St. (open W-M 10am-1pm and 6-9pm), as is the **National Bank** (tel. 41 430) with 24-hour **ATM** (open M-Th 8am-2pm, F 8am-1:30pm) and the **OTE** (tel. 41 299; open June-Sept. M-Sa 7:30am-10pm; Oct.-May M-F 7:30am-3pm). The **police station** (tel. 41 111) is on Kentekaki, near the quay; **port police** can be reached at 41 214. **Syria Travel** (tel. 41 198; fax 41 535) is a general tourist office which is helpful for ferry information and tickets, as well as basic information about the region. From Paleochora, one to two **ferries** per day

CRETE

leave for Sougia (1hr., 950dr); Agios Roumeli (2hr., 2100dr); Hora Sfakion (3hr., 2900dr); and Loutro (2¾hr., 2600dr). One boat a day departs Paleochora at 10am and leaves from Elafonisi at 4pm (1hr., one-way 1300dr). A post boat goes to **Gavdos** twice per week (3½hr., 3100dr), and a regular ferry goes to Gavdos once per week (3½hr., 3100dr). A bus departs for Samaria daily at 6am (one way 1300dr) and returns to Paleochora by boat from Agia Roumeli at 4pm (3150dr round-trip). Entrance to Samaria costs 1200dr. For a taxi, call **Paleochora Taxi Office** (tel. 41 128 or 41 061). The **medical center** sits down the road from Interkreta Travel (from the office, make a right onto the cross street). Look for the sign with the blue cross (open M-F mornings until 2pm). The **pharmacy** (tel. 41 498) is on Venizelou St. (open daily 8am-2:30pm and 4:50-11:50pm). The **post office** (tel. 41 206) is on the beach near Sfaki Tours (open M-F 7:30am-2pm). **Postal code:** 73001. **Telephone code:** 0823.

ACCOMMODATIONS A walk along the road closest to the harbor will bring you to the small hotels. At the end of the harbor stands a tall white building marked "Dream Rooms" which is run by **Nikos Bubalis** and his wife (tel. 41 112). The kindly older couple has clean doubles and triples off a staircased area. All rooms have access to balconies that look out onto the picturesque harbor and the gorgeous mountains that descend to the sea (doubles 5000-7000dr; triples 6000-8000dr). The **Cafe Alaloom,** adjacent to the OTE, books rooms at **Savas Rooms** (tel. 41 075) for reasonable prices (singles 4000dr; doubles 6000dr). Another good option, **Rooms Oriental Bay** (tel. 41 322), is right on Rocky Beach as you enter town (doubles 7000-8000dr; triples 8000dr). **Christos Restaurant** (tel. 41 359), along the harbor, has clean rooms with private baths (doubles 6000dr; triples 7500dr). **Camping Paleochora** (tel. 41 120) rests 1500m east of town, convenient to Paleochora Club, the town's popular disco that hosts some pretty wild parties. To reach the campground, walk north on Venizelou (away from the harbor), turn right opposite the gas station, take the second left on the last paved road before the beach, and walk 1km to the site (open Apr.-Oct.; 1000dr per person; 600dr per tent; 400dr per car; 600dr per child; children under 4 free).

FOOD AND ENTERTAINMENT Several markets stand in the center of the town and on Venizelou St. The waterfront sports a row of restaurants serving traditional Greek food from standard tourist menus at the usual mid-range prices (*tzatziki* 400-600dr, *moussaka* 1000-1200dr, *baklava* 500-700dr). More *tavernas* line Venizelou St. and have similar menus. Vegetarians and carnivores alike should appreciate the fresh homemade Greek, Asian, and European vegetarian dishes prepared by the family at the **Third Eye Vegetarian Restaurant** (tel. 41 234). Everything is delicious, but you might hope to catch the vegetarian *paella* (850dr) or the vegetable curry (950dr). Nothing on the menu costs more than 950dr, unless, of course, you order something from the grill, which they've kept open for meat lovers who just can't live without their *souvlaki* (open Apr.-Oct. daily 8am-3pm and 6pm-midnight).

For inexpensive Greek baked goods, **George Vakakis's** bakery (tel. 41 069), close to the ferry dock (follow the signs), sells generously sized cheese, spinach, or sausage pies (200-250dr), chocolate croissants (150-250dr), and traditional biscuits (1500dr per kg). Cretan *kalitsounia* are fresh and tasty (2000dr per kg). They also bake fresh Cretan sweet bread to serve on special occasions like weddings and christenings (600dr per kg.; open in summer daily 7:30am-3pm and 4-11pm). **Paleochora Club** (tel. 42 230), across from Camping Paleochora, is the town's open-air disco; a minibus transports clients from Skala bar by the port to the disco every 30 minutes (cover F-Sa 1000dr; beer 600-700dr; open M-Sa 11pm-5am, Su 11pm-6am).

■ Around Paleochora

Nine kilometers above Paleochora the peaceful town of **Azogizes** affords a lovely view of the promontory and the sea. Here you'll find the 13th-century caves of the 99 Holy Fathers and a museum with relics of the Turkish occupation dating from 1770. Farther inland, the frescoed churches of **Kakodiki** date back to the 14th century. To reach these villages, take the bus toward Hania. Boats (2½-4hr., 5 per week, 2900dr) run to the nearly deserted island of **Gavdos,** the southernmost point of Europe.

The residents of nearby **Moni Chrisoskalitissis** can provide water and lodgings. **Buses** run daily from Kastelli as far as Chrisoskalitissis (9:30am and 2:30pm, 900dr). From there, a 5km hike leads to a pinkish-white beach. You also can hook up with excursions leaving from Paleochora or Hania. Boats go from Paleochora to the beach across from Elafonisi daily (1hr., 1270dr one-way). The boat ride along the coast is astounding, and the cliffs diving into the deep sapphire blue sea at the extreme south-western tip of Crete are inspiring. Even closer to Paleochora is beautiful **Anidri Beach.** A one-hour walk west brings you to one of the lovelier beaches in Crete.

■ Elafonisi Ελαφονησι

The satisfying journey to miraculous **Elafonisi,** a small uninhabited island at the south-west corner of Crete, must be made on foot. Boats can't make the crossing, but the sea is so shallow that you can wade out to the island. The island's perfectly clear waters allow you to admire the fish, which can be spotted despite their camel camou-flage. Explore the island to escape the crowds of beachgoers and discover why the shore appears pink. A recent influx of tourists has left this retreat strewn with litter, but the authorities are increasing their efforts to keep it clean. Several small cantinas serve snacks and drinks, but packing a picnic will bypass high prices. A bus from Hania (7:30am, returning 4pm, 1350dr) runs to the opposite beach.

EASTERN CRETE

The road east from Iraklion along the north coast passes first through overcrowded, overpriced beach resort towns. All traces of traditional culture have been wiped clean from these towns, but the road becomes gradually quieter and more scenic as it passes through smaller villages sustained not by tourism, but by thriving local agricul-ture. The endlessly winding main highway joining Malia and Hersonissos to Agios Nikolaos, Ierapetra, and Sitia is spectacular. It grips the side of the mountains, ascend-ing and descending deep valleys. Seemingly psychotic bus drivers dart through these hills, passing mopeds and even other buses amid treacherous curves. Miraculously, perhaps due to the prayers of elderly village women in traditional dress who franti-cally make the sign of the cross at every swerve, the buses actually arrive on time and charge reasonable prices. The locally favored destinations east of Agios Nikolaos are entirely worthwhile—white villages with small green gardens, olive plains, and an astonishingly blue sea.

▓ Hersonissos Χερσονησος

This resort town, 26km east of Iraklion, is free of ancient sites and monasteries, but maintains some Cretan culture in Koutolofari and Piskopinao, its mountain villages to the south. More than 150 bars, discos, and nightclubs cluster in a 500m radius, and the beach is never far away. If you're bored with Iraklion's nightlife, just hop on the bus; you probably don't have to know the Greek words for vodka and orange juice here because your bartender won't know them either.

ORIENTATION AND PRACTICAL INFORMATION

There is one main road in Hersonissos, **Eleftheriou Venizelou St.,** with offices, mar-kets, and discos. Perpendicular streets lead either to the beach or to the hills.

Transportation

Buses: Several bus stops in Hersonissos, but there's no central bus station, just an information booth near the Hard Rock Cafe. Bus service to Iraklion (45min., 4 per hr., 600dr); Malia (20min., 4 per hr., 220dr); Agios Nikolaos (55min., 2 per hr., 800dr); Sitia (2½hr., 2200dr); and Ierapetra (2hr., 1500dr).

Taxi: Station (tel. 23 723, 23 722, 23 193, or 22 098) on the west end of El. Venizelou St. near the Hard Rock Cafe. Available 24hr.

Car and Motorbike Rental: Several agencies on El. Venizelou. **Eurorent,** 31 El. Venizelou St. (tel. 24 370, 23 122, or 24 958; fax 24 371; email euro@her.forthnet.gr), rents cars (7500dr per day with free kilometers, full insurance, and tax included) and motorbikes (3000-4000dr per day).

Tourist and Financial Services

Tourist Police: 8 Minoas St. (tel. 21 000), toward the beach in the police station. Offers **currency exchange.** Open M-F 7am-11pm, Sa-Su variably.

Tourist Agencies: Mareland Travel has four branches, one conveniently located at 13 Minoas St. (tel. 24 424, 25 046, or 25 047), across from the police station. Open daily 9am-11pm. **Zakros Tours,** 46 El. Venizelou St. (tel./fax 24 715). Open Apr.-Oct. daily 8am-10pm. Central office at 12 Dimokratias St. (tel. 25 064 or 25 065; fax 21 312) open all year. Both rent cars, sell boat and plane tickets, exchange currency, find rooms, and have maps.

Banks: Several on El. Venizelou exchange currency. **National Bank** is on the east end of the road. Open M-Th 8am-2pm, F 8am-1:30pm.

Laundromat: Wash Saloon Ilios, 3 Margaraki St. (tel.22 749, 21 921), just up the street from Selena Pension and restaurant. Does laundry in 3hr. 1500dr per 6kg, includes soap price. Open daily 9am-9pm.

Public Toilets: Across from Zakros tour office on El. Venizelou St. Free.

Emergency and Communications

Medical Services: Medical Emergency of Kriti (tel. 22 063, 22 600, or 22 111; fax 21 987; mobile 51 71 70) is at the corner of Venizelou St. and Kassaveti St., near the Hard Rock Cafe. Open 24hr. **Hersonissos Health Center,** 19 El. Venizelou (tel. 25 141), near the Hard Rock Cafe. Open 24hr.

Pharmacies: Several on El. Venizelou. Get off the bus at the first stop in Hersonissos from Iraklion, cross the street, and after 2 or 3 blocks (or 30m), **Lambraki's Pharmacy** (tel. 22 473) will be on your left. Open M-F 9am-11pm. Consult the signs on the doors to find one open after hours and on Sundays.

Post Office: 122 El. Venizelou. See signs. Open M-F 8am-2pm. **Postal Code:** 70014.

OTE: Behind the town hall at 11 Eleftherias St., down El. Venizelou from PTT. Open M-Sa 7:30am-10pm, Su 9am-2pm and 5-10pm. **Telephone Code:** 0897.

ACCOMMODATIONS

Hersonissos's digs can be pricey and hard to come by. Tour companies book a majority of the rooms for the entire season. Before arriving, consult Iraklion's **"Rooms to Let Association"** (see p. 382).

Selena Pension, 13 Marogaki St. (tel. 25 180), just off Main St. toward the waterfront. All immaculate rooms have private bath and balcony. Doubles 8000dr.

Camping Hersonissos (tel. 22 902), in Anisara. Take a bus or walk 3km toward Iraklion—it's on the right. Restaurant, supermarket, bar, and hot water. 1000dr per person; 690dr per tent.

Camping Caravan (tel. 22 025); in Limenas. Walk or take the bus 2km east toward Agios Nikolaos until Nora Hotel, then another 300m next to the Lychnostatis Museum. English spoken. Bike rental and restaurant. Open May-Oct. 1200dr per person; 900dr per tent.

FOOD

The Hersonissos waterfront sports the usual assortment of restaurants serving "traditional Greek food"—pre-packaged facsimiles, often inferior to the equally common western imitations.

⊛**Taverna Kavouri,** 9 Archeou Theatrou St. (tel. 21 161), is a thoroughly enjoyable escape from the commercialized waterfront. Walk toward Iraklion, turn right onto

Irinis Kai Filias St. near the Hard Rock Cafe, and walk around the bend. Fifteen tables rest under grapevines and among hanging fishing equipment. The lamb special costs 2400dr, but classic *moussaka* or chicken with lemon is 900dr. Delicious fried *tiganites* are served with ice cream (900dr) Open daily noon-midnight.

Krete Taverna, 4 Kanyadaki St. (tel. 24 138), near the Black Cactus Bar, just off the main road. Genuine real-live locals eat here. Try the chicken and potatoes (1000dr) or goat in its own juices (1250dr). Open daily noon-11pm.

Elli Taverna, 2 Sanoudaki St. (tel. 24 758), is where tour guides come to eat after dropping off their group at a glitzier, more expensive restaurant. Walk up the main road towards Iraklion, take a right after the Cretan Medicare center, and the modest *taverna* will be on your left. There's no menu, so peek inside the pots which clutter the counter and choose from broccoli (800dr), lamb fricassee (1500dr), or beans (600dr), all cooked fresh in olive oil produced by the owner. Open 7am-2am.

Selena Restaurant (tel. 22 412), beneath Selena Pension. A good place to escape the commotion of town, Selena serves house wine from their own vineyard and fresh rabbit (2000dr) from their farm (not on the menu—ask for it grilled or stewed in wine). Greek salad 700dr, *tzatziki* 550dr. Open daily 10am-12:30am.

ENTERTAINMENT

Nightlife is the only reason to come to Hersonissos because the beach is mediocre relative to those south and east. The bars and dance clubs on El. Venizelou St. offer an essentially homogeneous facsimile of any species of atmosphere. Tourist patrons are rowdy and ready for hot action. Nightlife in Heronissos is "jammin'," as Greeks like to say. The bars and discos that line Main St. and the Paraliakos offer every kind of atmosphere, music, and drink imaginable. Try the **Black Cactus Bar,** 72 El. Venizulou (tel. 21 123), on Main St. Happy hour is before 11pm so buy a drink (beer 600-1200dr, cocktails 1500dr) and get one free. As the night progresses, hit the bars on Paraliakos and on the waterfront (beer 600dr). The dance floors of **Disco 99** or **Veronica** (tel. 21 029) are large and crowded by English tourists. The hottest club in town is the **Camelot Dancing Club** (tel. 22 734), where both locals and tourists crowd in to dance to international rave and house. Most of the clubs open at dusk and close at dawn, soaked in beer and lust. The **Hard Rock Cafe** (tel. 24 255) offers live music from British rockers most nights (open 9am-3:30am). The **Cine Creta Maris,** around the corner from the Hard Rock Cafe, is an outdoor summer cinema showing English-language (usually American) films nightly (1500dr).

SIGHTS

The open-air museum **Lychnostatis** (tel. 23 660) is located roughly 1km toward Agios Nikolaos. (*Open Tu-Su 9:30am-2pm. Admission including tour 1250dr, students 800dr, under 12 600dr. 3 daily guided tours at 10:30, 11:30am, and 12:30pm.*) It exhibits Cretan houses and offers a windmill, and ceramics and weaving workshops, as well as the opportunity, during the harvest season, to tread grapes or bake pumpkin pie. The museum cafe serves a refreshing cinnamon beverage (400dr).

■ Malia Μαλια

Its Mediterranean climate and nearby Minoan palace aside, Malia, with its pubs and Guinness taps, comes closer to evoking the pages of Dickens or Joyce than those of Homer or Kazantzakis. Young British tourists, booked months in advance on pre-packaged holidays, descend on Malia's beach like salmon in the midst of a mating frenzy. The number of advertisements in languages other than Greek is matched only by the number of sandwich boards displaying kitschy photographs of food. Nevertheless, the palatial Minoan site at Malia merits a visit. Malia is best as a daytrip or, if you must stay, the old village is cheaper than the glitzed-out, pre-sold waterfront. Bring lots of *drachmes,* a jersey from your favorite football (a.k.a. soccer) team, condoms, and a canonical knowledge of Irish drinking songs.

CRETE

ORIENTATION AND PRACTICAL INFORMATION The main road from Iraklion, El. Venizelou St., should satisfy most practical needs, while the path to the beach, with the discos and watering holes, panders to the primal. The old village between the main road and the inland hills has no discos, but just as many bars and cheaper rooms. **Stallion Travel and Tourism** (tel. 33 690; fax 32 031), next to the old church on the main road, offers extensive, personalized services. Sarah, the British proprietor, secures 100% insurance on every **car** or **motorbike rental.** This is the best source for **travel information** and **currency exchange.** The **National Bank** (tel. 31 833 or 31 152) is just off the main road. Bear left at the first street past the road to the beach (open M-Th 8am-2pm, F 8am-1:30pm). Work off those beer calories at the **Malia Gym** (tel. 32 567). Turn right off Beach Rd. at Hellenic Cafe; the gym is #28. (2000dr per session; open M, W, F 9:30am-3pm and 5-9:30pm, Tu, Th 9:30am-3pm and 6-9:30pm, Sa 9:30am-3pm.)

Buses connect Malia with Iraklion (1hr., 750dr) via Hersonissos (20min., 2-4 per hour, 220dr); Agios Nikolaos (1½hr., 25 per day, 1350dr); and Lassithi (1½hr., 8:30am, returning at 2pm, 1150dr). **Taxis** (tel. 31 777 or 33 900) idle at the intersection of the main road and the National Bank road. **Limpo Laundry** (tel. 31 709) is down the road to Iraklion next to the Galaxy and Skyline bars (wash and dry 2300dr; open daily 9am-8pm). A free **medical center** (tel. 31 594) is open daily from 9am to 1:30pm near the church on the main road. Also, **Medical Emergency of Kriti** (tel. 32 227 or 33 100) is on your right as you head toward the beach on the road across from the old church and is open 24-hours. The **pharmacy** (tel. 32 132) is across from the free medical center at 91 El. Venizelou St. (open M-Sa 9am-10pm, Su on rotation). The **post office** (tel. 31 688) is off the main street toward Iraklion (look for the sign), behind the old church (open M-F 7:30am-2pm). The **OTE** (tel. 31 299) is in the old village—follow signs from 25th Martiou St. at the Bimbo Cafe (open M-F 7:30am-2:30pm). **Postal code:** 70007. **Telephone code:** 0897.

ACCOMMODATIONS Finding reasonably priced rooms in Malia is a challenge. If you can't find them, look for the cluster of pensions and rooms to let in the old village. You can wander off into 25th Martiou St. and look around for a place that suits your fancy. Walking east toward Agios Nikolaos and away from town, after the point where the bus drops you off on the main road, make a right onto 25th Martiou St. then a left on Konstantinou St. to reach **Pension Aspasia** (tel. 31 290), with large, balconied rooms and common baths. There's sunbathing on the roof and prices are negotiable (singles 2000-3000dr; doubles 4000-5000dr; triples 6000dr). Or, try **Pension Menios,** #2 25th Martiou St. (tel. 31 361), near the corner of the main road. It has new, immaculate rooms, wood furnishings, small balconies, and private baths (singles 5000dr; doubles 6000dr; doubles with bath 7000dr). You can also consult **Stallion Travel** for rooms.

FOOD The most popular dishes in Malia are the "English" breakfast (600dr), pizza (1500dr), and the "steak" dinner (1900dr). **Cafe Mylos** (tel. 33 150), on the road to the OTE in the old village, recalls Malia's more traditional days. Turtles amid cactus plants and *bouzoukis* next to keyboards—the decor is eclectic and the staff is warm. Catch up on the hippest modern Greek music as you order *mezedes* (500-700dr) or a huge Greek salad (700dr) from the leather-bound, wooden menu (open daily 9am-3pm and 5pm-3am). Ironically (perhaps appropriately), the best-known authentic Greek fare in Malia is prepared by the Dutch chef at **Petros** (tel. 31 887) in the old village. An excellent Greek salad (1100dr) complements a plate of *stifado* (2300dr; open daily 5pm-1am). On the main road, **banana vendors** sell bunches for 400-500dr.

ENTERTAINMENT The waterfront road is home to many of Malia's (and Crete's) more popular dance clubs. On Beach Rd., house, international, rave, and dance music blare at **Zoo, Zig Zag,** and **Corkers,** while **Terma's** is the place for Greek tunes. Clubs open around 9pm, get really packed by 1am, and stay that way until 3:30 or 4am during the week. Most of them rock all night (until 6am), Thursday through Saturday. For a quieter but still Dionysiac night, head for the narrow, cobbled streets of the old town. Due to the presence of many Irish, English, and Scottish vacationers, plenty of pubs exist for your greater imbibalogical pleasure. Ireland meets the Mediterranean at **The Temple Bar** (tel. 31 272), where huge tropical plants grow out of the bar tables, and Greeks and Celts lap up pints of Guinness on tap (1100dr per pint). Every hour is happy hour at this open-air pub, and cocktails are always 700dr. (Next to St. Dimitrios Sq., it's open daily 9am-3 or 4am.) At the end of the beach road, current videos from Hollywood and old British comedies play all day and most of the night at **Charlie Chaplin's** and **Union Jack's**. Movies are free, and drinks and snacks are cheap (800dr or less; open daily 11am-1am).

SIGHTS The **Minoan Palace** (tel. 31 597) at Malia, one of the three great cities of Minoan Crete, lacks the labyrinthine architecture and magnificent interior decoration of Knossos and Phaistos, but is still imposing. *(Open daily 8am-2:30pm. Admission 800dr, seniors 400dr, students with ID free.)* First built around 1900 BC, the palace was destroyed in 1650 BC, rebuilt on an even more impressive scale, but then destroyed again around 1450 BC. Notice the **Hall of Columns** on the north side of the large central courtyard, named for the six columns supporting the roof. The *loggia,* the raised chamber on the west side, was used for state ceremonics. West of the *loggia* are the palace's living quarters and archives. Northwest of the *loggia* and main site slumbers the **Hypostyle Crypt** that may have been a social center for Malia's intelligentsia. Follow the road to Agios Nikolaos 3km to the east and turn left toward the sea, or walk along the beach and then 1km through the fields.

▓ Agios Nikolaos Αγος Νικολαος

Agios Nikolaos has moved closer to the naughty mood of a nouveau chic resort town, but retains some nice facets of a low-key fishing village. The town's visitors include beach-obsessed patrons, one-stop holiday-makers, and hikers on their way to more obscure destinations. There are few bargains in Agios Nikolaos or in its satellite beach towns, but the town's intense nightlife, its diverse selection of intriguingly glamourous tourists, and its remnants of indigenous Cretan culture make Agios Nikolaos a lively concoction—a town that moves, yet lacks the sense of having been chewed up and spit out by tourists.

ORIENTATION AND PRACTICAL INFORMATION

It's easy to get around Agios Nikolaos—the center of town is actually a small peninsula, with beaches on three sides and most services, hotels, restaurants, and discos in the center. If you've just gotten off the bus, walk to the end of the block (with the terminal on your right), and take the first right. Follow **Venizelou St.** to the monument, where it leads into **R. Koundourou St.,** which heads downhill to the harbor. The tourist office is to the left, across the bridge. Don't confuse the nepotistic street names: R. Koundourou, I. Koundourou, and S. Koundourou St.

Transportation

Flights: Olympic Airways Office (tel. 22 033), on Plastira St. overlooking the lake. Open M-F 8am-3:30pm. The closest airport is in Iraklion.

Buses: (tel. 22 234), Atlandithos Sq., on the opposite side of town from the harbor. To Iraklion via Malia (1½hr., 25 per day, 1350dr); Lassithi (1½hr., 3 per week, 1100dr); Ierapetra (1hr., 9 per day, 700dr); Sitia (1½hr., 6 per day, 1450dr); and Kritsa (15min., 11 per day, 220dr). Buses to Elounda (20min., 20-26 per day, 220dr) and Plaka (40min., 6-7 per day, 340dr) leave opposite the tourist office.

Ferries: Nostos Tours, 30 Koundourou St. (tel. 22 819), open daily 8am-1:30pm and 5-9pm. Ferry tickets for departures from Agios Nikolaos and other Cretan ports. To Peiraias (12hr., 7500dr), via Milos (7hr., 4700dr); to Rhodes (12hr., 6250dr), via Sitia (1hr., 1500dr); Kassos (6hr., 3150dr); and Karpathos (7hr., 3800dr). Ferries leaving for Cyprus and Israel are also available.

Car and Motorbike Rental: Shop around on Akti Koundourou St. **Ross Rentals,** 10 Akti Koundourou (tel. 23 407), will match any price, but their own are already as reasonable as 18,000dr for 3 days with a Fiat Panda. Open daily 8am-8:30pm.

Tourist and Financial Services

Tourist Office: 21A S. Koundourou St. (tel. 22 357 or 24 165; fax 82 534), at the bridge between the lake and the port. Assists with accommodations, **exchanges currency,** sells phone cards and stamps, and provides bus and boat schedules and a brochure with a map and practical info. Open Apr.-Oct. daily 8:30am 9:45pm.

Banks: National Bank (tel. 28 735), at the top of R. Koundourou St., near Venizelou Sq. Open for **currency exchange** M-Th 8am-2pm, F 8am-1:30pm.

Bookstore: Anna Karteri, 5 R. Koundourou St. (tel. 22 272). Books in English, German, Russian, Dutch, and French. Open M-Sa 8:30am-10pm.

Emergency and Communications

Police: (tel. 22 321) share the tourist police building. Open 24hr.

Tourist Police (tel. 26 900), 34 Kontoghianni St. Follow 28th Octovriou St. past Venizelou Sq. until it becomes G. Kontoghianni St. After a 10min. walk, it will be on the right. Regulates hotels, registers complaints, gives general info. Open 24hr.

Hospital: (tel. 25 224), on Paleologou St., at the north end of town. From the lake, walk up Paleologou St., 1 block past the archaeological museum.

Pharmacies: Dr. Theodore Furakis (tel. 24 011), at the top of R. Koundourou St. at 23 El. Venizelou. Open M-Tu, Th-F 8am-2pm and 5:30-9pm, W 8am-2pm.

Internet Access: Multiplace "Peripou," #25 28th October St. (tel. 24 876; email peripou@agn.forthnet.gr). Two computers available, 600dr per hour. Also sells international CDs and books.

Post Office: Main branch, #9 28th Octovriou St. (tel. 22 062). Open M-Sa 7:30am-2pm. Branch at 8 Metamorphosis St. (tel. 22 276) for packages only. Open M-F 7:30am-2pm. **Postal Code:** 72100.

OTE: (tel. 82 880), on the corner of 25th Martiou and K. Sfakianaki St. Open M-Sa 7am-midnight, Su 7am-10pm. **Telephone Code:** 0841.

ACCOMMODATIONS

As a result of Agios Nikolaos's popularity, many of the better hotels are booked months in advance by European tour groups. There are many pensions in town that offer clean, cheap rooms. They do fill up quickly, so it may be wise to call ahead and make a reservation. The tourist office has a bulletin board with many of Agios Nikolaos's pensions and their prices. Prices listed are 20-40% less in the off season.

Argiro Pension, 1 Solonos St. (tel. 28 707). From the tourist office, walk up 25th Martiou and turn left onto Manousogianaki. After 4 blocks uphill, go right onto Solonos. Unsullied, cool rooms (with common or private baths) in a huge, stately old house with a serene, jasmine-scented garden. Quiet, yet close to a town. Doubles 4800-5500dr; triples 7000dr.

Christodoulakis Pension, 7 Stratigou Koraka St. (tel. 22 525), one block south of the lake. Spotless rooms, kitchen facilities, and friendly proprietors. Singles 4000-5000dr; doubles 5000-6000dr.

Pension Perla, 4 Salaminos St. (tel. 23 379). Big clean rooms, some with balconies and ocean views. Comfortable TV lounge and fridge space. All but 2 rooms have private bath. Singles 4000dr; doubles 5000dr; triples 6000dr.

The Green House, 15 Modatsou St. (tel. 22 025). From the tourist office, turn left onto R. Koundourou St., left again onto Iroon Polytechniou St., and right onto Modatsou. Relax in the shady, tangled garden. If you're lucky, you'll get homemade Italian ice from the multilingual proprietors. Clean rooms and common baths. Laundry 1500dr per load. Singles 3000dr; doubles 4000dr.

Victoria Hotel (tel. 22 731, 22 266), about 1km from the harbor on Akti Koundourou St., near Amoudi Beach. This bona fide hotel has white stucco walls and rooms equipped with private baths, balconies, and phones. Singles 4000dr; doubles 5000dr; cheaper for longer stays.

FOOD

Agios Nikolaos is overrun by overpriced, touristy, mediocre restaurants claiming to serve "traditional Greek food." Many of these places are recognizable by their brightly colored menus with photographs of their food in front, along with pushy waiters who try to pull you in. Generally, the restaurants that are open all year (rather than just in the summer tourist season) cater to the native Greek clientele and serve more indigenous flavors.

Itanos (tel. 25 340), off the main square, serves large fresh Greek salads (700dr), homemade barreled wine (1500dr per 1L), vegetarian entrees (plate of stuffed vegetables 900-1500dr), and meat entrees (600-1400dr). Open daily 10am-10pm.

Stelio's (tel. 22 773), at the bridge. If you don't mind relaxed service, sit down for a dazzling harborside view and excellent *tzatziki* (600dr) and octopus salad (1100dr). Open Apr.-Oct. daily 8am-midnight.

New Kow Loon Chinese Restaurant, 1 Pasifais St. (tel. 23 891). Walk from the harbor down Kitroplateia, and take a left on Pasifais St., across from the cinema. Serves surprisingly tasty Chinese cuisine. Egg rolls (950dr), mixed veggies (1100dr), and lemon chicken (1700dr) are an interesting surprise in Greece. Take-out menu 10% cheaper. Open daily 6pm-1am.

Xenakis Family Bakery, 9 M. Sfakianaki St. (tel. 23 051), several blocks from the port on the street leading to Kitroplatia Beach, sells delicious loaves of freshly baked bread (150-300dr). Try their *tyropitas* (220dr) or delicious raisin rolls (130dr). Open M-F 7am-3:30pm and 6-8pm, Sa 7am-4pm.

Loukakis Taverna, 24 Akti Koundourou St. (tel. 28 022). It seems as if prices haven't changed since this family-run *taverna* opened in 1952. Veal *stifado* (1200dr), chicken *okra* (800dr), and plenty of vegetarian dishes (400-800dr). Open Apr.-Oct. daily 1-4pm and 7:30-11pm.

Elena, 26 K. Palaiologou St. (tel. 23 450), for the sweet-starved traveler. Uniquely delicious *gantotika* costs 300dr and ice cream is 250dr.

Multiplace Peripou, #25 28 Octovriou (tel. 24 876). At around 9:30pm, Greek youths stream into to sip *frappés* (500dr) and play or watch their friends play *tavli*. As its name suggests, this establishment has many functions—cafe, international bookstore, internet access site (600dr per hr.), and music store. With a view of the lake and seashells preserved under glass tabletops, this is the perfect spot for one-stop entertainment. Open daily 9am-2am.

ENTERTAINMENT

For nocturnal pursuits, stroll around the harbor on I. Koundourou St., or walk up 25th Martiou St. Each summer from mid-July to mid-September, the town celebrates with the **Lato Festival.** Visit the tourist office for details.

Cafe Candia, 12 Akti Koundourou St. (tel. 26 355), is "the place to be" for local sophisticates and travelers who know how to blend. Well-dressed twenty- and thirty-somethings overflow from the candle-lit cafe into tables that line the harbor, and the scene is chic relaxed mingling. Open daily until 4am.

Roxy, 25 Martiou St. (tel. 22 984). A cocktail bar providing more breathing room and louder, Greek music. The bird-nest chandelier hovers above an almost empty dance floor as most people talk and smoke while the DJ spins the latest in Greek and European tunes. Open daily 10:30pm-4am.

Yanni's, Akti Koundourou St. (tel. 23 581). Another local favorite, catering to the more hardcore rockers. Black and white photos line the walls and Greeks in black jeans circle the bar. Open daily 10pm-4am.

Rififi (tel. 23 140). Provides a meeting place for backpackers and other tourists who sip coffee (600dr) and alcohol (cocktails 1500dr, beer 600dr) on the harborside terrace. Open daily 11am-3am.

Sorrento Bar on the waterfront is a good place to warm up before hitting the dance floors, with insane dancing bartenders and free shots of the house special "fluffy" when you walk in the door. Cocktails 1500dr, beer 700dr.

CRETE

Lipstick Night Club (tel. 22 377), on the waterfront, close to the Mediterranean restaurant. Attracts the fun-seeking tourist action. Free shooters with every drink on Fridays, free tequila shot at the door every night. Open daily 10:30pm-late.

SIGHTS

According to legend, Artemis and Athena bathed at the "bottomless" lake, **Voulismeni**, near the present-day tourist office. Even though the lake is actually 64m deep, locals insist that there is a hole in the floor of the lake which is somehow connected to the volcano of Santorini. As evidence of the hole's infinite depth, they offer Dutch weapons which were lost and never found during the war. In 1867, the regional governor dug a canal linking the lake with the sea, creating a perpetual flushing mechanism. To shop for inexpensive clothes, visit the weekly **market** on Eth. Antistassios St., next to the lake. *(Open W 7am-1pm.)* Here you'll find sundry items from perfume to paintings to knock-off Prada bags. In case you forgot the essentials, swimming trunks go for 300dr and underwear is sold 4 pairs for 1000dr. At the top of the hill are food stands with watermelon (100dr per kg), tomatoes (50dr per kg), *kefalotiri* (2300dr per kg), and Cretan honey (1000dr per 500g).

The archaeological site of **Gournia** is located 2km from Agios Nikolaos. *(Open Tu-Su 8am-2:30pm. Admission 500dr, students 300dr, EC students free.)* The Minoan settlement's spectacular view of the sea more than makes up for the rubble, which can be difficult to distinguish. Take the bus heading to Ierapetra or Sitia—ask the driver to stop. One kilometer before Kritsa on the road from Agios Nikolaos, Crete's Byzantine treasure, the **Panagia Kera** (tel. 51 525), honors the Dormition of the Virgin. *(Open M–Sa 9am-3pm, Su 9am-2pm. Admission 800dr, seniors 400dr, students free.)* The interior is adorned with a patchwork of smoky 14th-century paintings in the central nave and 15th-century Byzantine frescoes in the wings.

Beaches

Three **beaches** are within walking distance of the main harbor. With minimal effort, you can sunbathe on the concrete piers that jut out from S. Koundourou St. Also in the immediate area are **Ammos Beach** by the National Stadium, **Kitroplatia Beach** between Akti Panagou St. and the marina, and **Ammoudi Beach** farther up Akti Koundourou away from town. To reach a better spot, catch the bus, which departs every hour headed to Ierapetra or Sitia, and get off at **Almiros Beach,** 2km east of Agios Nikolaos. The sandy beach at **Kalo Chorio,** 10km farther along the same road, is less crowded. Get off the bus headed for either Sitia or Ierapetra at the Kavos Taverna (tell the driver to stop). Another beautiful, clean, and secluded beach on the road to Elounda is the **Harania Beach,** which can be reached by taking the bus toward Elounda and alighting at Harania. Residents of Agios Nikolaos will proudly inform you that all of their beaches are winners of the European Blue Flag award.

Museums

For more cerebral pursuits, see if anything is playing at the theaters on M. Sfakianaki St. or Antistasseos St. (1500dr), or visit one of Agios Nikolaos's two museums. The **Archaeological Museum** (tel. 24 943), just outside the center of town, a few blocks down the road from Iraklion, houses a modest collection of Minoan artifacts. *(Open Tu-Su 8am-2:30pm. Admission 500dr, students 300dr, EC students and children under 18 free.)* The **Folk Art Museum,** (tel. 25 093), next door to the tourist office, displays tapestries, embroidered clothes, furniture, icons, 16th-century manuscripts of contracts, and stamps for the holy bread at church. *(Open Su-F 10am-3pm. Admission 300dr, children under 12 free. No flash photography.)*

■ Spinalonga Σπιναλογκα

Across stunningly clear waters from the stylish town of Plaka lies Spinalonga Island. Small but striking, the island as we see it today seems to have been created in a dichromatic scheme: robust green brush softens the harsh linearity of the orange stone fortifications. Yet Spinalonga's visual simplicity is no indicator of the island's complex and evocative past.

Several private boats and travel agencies offer guided daytrips to this shop- and *taverna*-free island. Don't forget your bathing suit, as most boats make swim stops. Like the quality of their boats and their tour guides, the prices of these excursions vary greatly. Trips on smaller fishing boats (on the left side of the harbor near the tourist office) can be as cheap as 1000dr, while an excursion on the souped-up **Nostos Travel** cruiser with a detail-oriented tour guide or a trip with KTEL will cost you three times as much. In general, the trip takes approximately four hours, leaving Agios Nikolaos around noon and returning around 4pm.

History

In 1204, the Venetians literally bought Crete. After the destruction of the fortresses on Barba Rossa and Agios Nikolaos, the Venetians invested 75 years building a third fortress on Spinalonga. When the Turks, along with some Greeks, regained possession of Spinalonga in 1745, and Crete regained independence in 1898, the Greeks were determined to rid the island of all non-Greeks, the Turks in particular. In a kill-two-birds-with-one-island fashion, the Cretans innovatively decided to establish a leper colony, thereby sequestering the infected who had been inhabiting mountain caves until then, and frightening away the Turks. On October 22, 1904, the first lepers arrived at their new home. Despite German efforts to capture the island during World War II, the leper community existed until 1957, making Spinalonga the last leper colony in Europe. During that 53-year span, 1100 lepers lived on the island and sixty children were born to leper families. The island was reopened in 1970, leaving a good thirteen years to ensure the absence of bacteria and the safety of visitors. Today, there is probably no need to worry about catching leprosy on your daytrip to the island. Although its mechanism of transmission is still uncertain, scientists believe the disease is passed through bacteria in the blood and even in these instances of blood-to-blood contact, the chances of infection are one in a million.

Touring Spinalonga

When you arrive at the island, you will enter just as the lepers did—through **Dante's Gate,** a chillingly dark and grim procession through an iron-barred tunnel. When lepers passed through this "gate to hell," they knew they would never emerge.

Once inside the island complex, you will see reconstructed Venetian houses and then reconstructed Turkish houses as you walk down **Market Street**. For the first nine years of the colony's existence, the lepers were not only poor, but also exploited by their corrupt governor, who sold them food at exorbitant prices rather than giving it to them. It was only in 1913 that the lepers began receiving social security payments of one *drachma* per day, which was a large allowance at the time. The island was then perceived by opportunistic Cretans as having the potential to be extremely lucrative. They subsequently came to Spinalonga just long enough to set up shops and *tavernas* along Market Street and capitalize on the lepers' new wealth.

At the end of Market Street is the **Church of Agios Pandelemonis**, founded and dedicated to the Roman doctor Pandelemon by the Venetians in 1709. Appropriately, the lepers later used this church to pray for miraculous cures from the heavens and maintained an ardent faith in the power of Pandelemon, protector of the ill. Stairs in front of the church lead to the **laundry area,** where water from the roof was collected into tubs, heated over fire, and used to rinse used bandages for reuse. Spinalonga's **hospital** stands halfway up the hill and is identifiable by its eight-window facade. Although patients went to Santa Barbara Hospital in Athens for major operations such as amputations, this hospital oversaw non-invasive surgery and general care for the lepers. The reasoning behind the hospital's lofty location is that a higher altitude allows for more wind which can mitigate the unpleasant odor of rotting flesh. In addition, the windows are barred to prevent self-defenestration by patients who sought permanent escape from leprosy's pain and from life on Spinalonga.

Beyond the laundry area, on your left, are steps that lead to the sea and the original arched entrance to the Venetian fortress. Across the water from here is the town of Plaka. When, in 1941, German troops withheld provisions from the island in order to starve its inhabitants, several lepers attempted to swim the distance to Plaka in order to survive. Unfortunately, the stronger of the afflicted survived the swim only to meet the gunfire of German troops which awaited them in Plaka.

In front of the arched entryway is the **disinfecting room,** where everything from bedsheets to clothing to coins were sterilized.

Back up at the top of the steps and to the left are modern concrete houses with balconies and electrical wiring. These buildings contained apartments for couples and families, as well as those for lepers who had no relatives.

Continuing on the path around the rest of the island, you will find the orange-roofed **Church of St. George.** Built in 1661 by the Venetians, this is where the lepers took their final communion. The church is smaller than that of Ag. Pandelemon and is usually locked. Past this church, at the top of the ramp leading back to Dante's Gate, is the cemetery, which houses forty-four unmarked graves. In 1954 the government determined that a combination of the medicines Dopsin and Promil were effective in treating leprosy. Three years later, the colony was closed. A day on Spinalonga will inevitably be a solemn and highly personal one, especially compared to the rest of your vacation. Travelers may find their visit edifying, disturbing, and perhaps even uplifting, as they visit a place of reflection and alienation.

■ Lassithi Plateau Οροπεδιου Λασιθου

Bypassing much of the jagged northern coastline, the inland route to Agios Nikolaos traverses the Lassithi Plateau, ringed by steep mountains. The plain is a rural area, encircled by twelve small villages and laden with white-washed buildings, exhausted donkeys, and yeomen husbanding their fields. The residents of the region have harnessed the plain's persistent breezes with thousands of wind-powered water pumps. In recent years, electric pumps have superseded this form of irrigation, but mills still bristle on the horizon.

ORIENTATION AND PRACTICAL INFORMATION Lassithi is a good choice for a daytrip if you have access to wheels, or plan to visit only one town. Due to the infrequency of bus service, you may find yourself stranded for hours in a town, or limited to the few towns which are accessible by foot.

If you're coming from Iraklion, take the coastal road 8km past Gournes, and then turn right on the road to Kastelli (not the one on the west coast). After about 6km the road forks right to Kastelli; stay left, heading toward **Potamies.** Stand akimbo and ogle the giant plane tree in the center of Potamies. It takes 12 men to wrap their arms around the trunk, but you have to get the villagers really drunk to do it. Bypassing Krassi, the main road winds around mountain ridges with tibia-fracturing panoramas. The road continues to climb among the abandoned stone windmills of the Seli Ambelou pass, finally descending into the Lassithi Plateau. No matter which route you take, bring a jacket—it's nippy in this land of undulation.

Buses run directly from Agio Nikolaos to Lassithi Plateau and from Lassithi Plateau to Agios Nikolaos 3 times per week (1½hr., 1100dr). On other days, one can take a bus to Hersonissos and catch a bus to Lassithi Plateau from there.

All the basics can be found in **Tzermiado,** the capital of the subprovince of Lassithi and the first and only large village you pass through upon entering the plain. The bus stops at the center of the town's main square in front of the Kronio Restaurant. A few doors down from Kronio is the **police station** (tel. 22 208; open 24hr.). The tourist police for Lassithi Plateau is located in Agios Nikolaos. Further down the road from the police is the **OTE** (tel. 22 299, open M-F 7:30am-3:10pm). The **Agricultural Bank** (tel. 22 390; fax 22 560) is across the street from the Kronio and **exchanges currency** (open M-F 7:45am-3:30pm). The **pharmacy** (tel. 22 310) is 100m from the Tzermiado bus stop along the road to Marmaketo and Agios Nikolaos (open M-F 8:30am-2:30pm and 5:30-9pm, Sa 9am-2pm and 6-9pm, Su 10am-1pm and 6-9pm). A **medical center** (tel. 22 602) is open 24 hours for emergencies and basic primary care. Walk down the road to the right of the Agricultural Bank, turn left at the church, and follow this road for 300m. The **post office** (tel. 22 248) is next door to Kronio (open M-F 7:30am-2pm). There is also a small **OTE** (tel. 31 228) in Agios Georgios down the hill from the museum (open daily 7am-11pm). **Postal code: 72052. Telephone code: 0844.**

Bull Leaping, Minoan-style

For those who might wonder what the Minoans did for kicks, the constantly recurring images of bulls and their horns in all of Crete's archeological museums conjure visions of a great bull kicking up dust and preparing to charge. Unlike modern bull-fighting in Spain, scholars now think that Minoan bulls' opponents had more in common with young Olympic gymnasts than with wily middle-aged moustached *toreudors*. The bull games of the Minoans probably occupied the large central court of a palace and followed a boxing match. For the main event, the court's ground-level exits were blocked and fans crowded the upper windows and balconies. Well-trained and scantily clad boys and girls then engaged the bull in chases about the court. As things heated up, a youth might lure the bull to a platform, climb up, and then leap the bull as he clumsily attempted to follow. Other, more treacherous flips occurred at mid-court where the athlete grabbed the horns of the bull and used head rearing to launch a spectacular flip.

ACCOMMODATIONS Dias Hotel (tel. 31 207), in Agios Georgios, has a sunny court yard that separates the rooms from the Dias *taverna* on the main street next to the OTE. Potpourri freshens up these tidy rooms with sinks and 24-hour hot water, (singles 2500dr; doubles 4000dr; breakfast 600dr; 500dr student discount). **Hotel Kourites** (tel. 22 054, 22 254 or 22 194) is at the edge of Tzermiado on the road to Marketo and Agios Nikolaos. Bear left at the fork in the road and the hotel will be beyond the Texaco gas station. If no one is at reception, keep walking down the road to the other building of the hotel and the adjoining *taverna*. Rooms are large and bright with private baths, balconies, and free breakfast (singles 6000dr; doubles 9000dr; group rates available). **Hotel Rea,** in Agios Georgios, is near the village's bus stop and school. Dried flowers line the stairs which lead from the Rea Restaurant to firm beds and neat shared baths (doubles 4000dr). The same owner runs the stylish **Hotel Maria** on the opposite side of town (singles 3000-4000dr; doubles 5000-6000dr). **Maria Vlassi Rent Rooms** (tel. 31 048), in Agios Konstandinos, is on your left behind Maria's embroidery shop as you pass through the town on the road from Tzermiado. Basic but clean, these are the only rooms in Agios Konstandinos (singles 2000dr; doubles 3000dr).

FOOD Most restaurants in Lassithi Plateau are a joint venture with hotels. **Kronio Restaurant** (tel. 22 375, 22 006), at the center of Tzermiado, is an exception. This is the oldest *taverna* in Lassithi, and people don't just come for the food (roasted *fisti* 1000dr, season's vegetables 900dr, lamb with spinach 1500dr). Its central location has made the restaurant a meeting place for villagers to settle utilities bills and a favorite coffeeshop of village priests. Although the **Kri Kri Taverna** (tel. 22 170) used to double as a hotel, recently the hotel has closed and all efforts have concentrated on the food. Go down the road to the right of the Agricultural Bank in Tzermiado, turn left at the church and the restaurant is on the left. Ivy-covered walls and a homey fireplace add to the ambience and make the food seem even tastier (*moussaka* 850dr, Greek salad 500dr). The **Dikti Taverna** in Agios Konstandinos (tel. 31 225) is the best in the Plateau, according to regulars. *Moussaka* costs 1000dr and Greek coffee a mere 150dr (open Apr.-Oct. daily 7am-10pm). In Agios Georgios the only restaurants are attached to hotels. The menu at **Taverna Dias** includes pizzas (large, 1200dr) and **Rea Taverna** serves traditional dishes (*souvlaki* 1200dr, Greek salad 500dr, vegetables 800dr) and free wine to Hotel Rea or Maria guests.

SIGHTS **Agios Georgios** is home to a **folklore museum,** whose human models and stuffed fowl are more amusing than edifying. Next door is the **El. Venizelou Museum,** a hall completely dedicated to honoring the former prime minister of Crete and president of Greece. *(Open Apr.-Oct. 10am-5pm. Admission to both museums 700dr, students 500dr, children under 12 free.)*

Caves

Insignificant compared to the spelunker behemoth called Dikteon Cave at Psychro, the **Kronion Cave** merits a quick side trip. Clear signs in Tzermiado will direct you to the grotto (2km away), the mythical home of Kronos and Rhea, parents of Zeus. The last kilometer is badly marked and manageable only by foot. Stay on the people path—don't stray onto the numerous goat paths. Don't forget a flashlight.

The village of **Psychro** caters to afternoon tourists but retains its rural charm. One kilometer past Psychro is the **Dikteon Cave.** *(Open daily 8am-6pm. Admission 200dr, students 100dr. Guided tour 600dr.)* Legend has it that Zeus' father, Kronos, ate his newborn children here after hearing a prophecy that one of them would dethrone him. By the time Rhea gave birth to Zeus, she was stuck in a cave, and she handed Kronos a tasty, swaddled stone to eat in his place, and hid the baby. Zeus emerged to kill his father and free his five older brothers and sisters, who had luckily survived Kronos' digestive juices. When archaeologists excavated the cave at the beginning of this century, they found hundreds of Minoan artifacts crammed into its ribbed stalactites. Many of these are displayed at Iraklion's Archaeological Museum.

Arthur Evans (of Knossos fame) excavated this spot and, in a wave of misguided enthusiasm, blew apart the entrance. If you get to the cave by 9:30am or after 3pm you should be able to explore it without the distraction of tour groups. The guides who hover around the base of the path seldom justify their fees.

■ Ierapetra Ιεραπετρα

Although German tourists have made inroads, Ierapetra hosts more Greeks than foreigners. The city sits in tourism's rare *purgatorio*—it teeters between the cosmopolitan and the rural. Touted as Europe's southernmost town, this city betrays its station on Crete's south side, which is usually considered more scenic and less corrupted by tourism than the north.

ORIENTATION AND PRACTICAL INFORMATION Most of Ierapetra's services are on the streets parallel to the waterfront. From north to south, Plastira Square is connected by Lasthenous Rd. to E. Venizelou Sq., which is joined with Kanoupaki Sq. by Koraka St. and Koundouriotou Rd. Eleftherias Sq. is the nebulous region east of Koraka St. and north of Kanoupaki Sq. The old town district is to the south by the port. The **police station** (tel. 22 560) is on the waterfront at 35 Eleftherias Sq. Ierapetra is under the jurisdiction of the Agios Nikolaos **tourist police** (tel. 0841 26 900). The **port police,** 29 Kyvra St. (tel. 22 294), are near the excursion boat port. The **National Bank,** in Eleftherias Sq., is across the street from Ierapetra Express (open M-Th 8am-2pm, F 8am-1:30pm). In Kanoupaki Sq., five blocks south of the bus station toward the port, is the **post office,** 3 Stilianou Houta St. (tel. 22 271; open M-F 7:30am-2pm). **Tourist agencies** on the street parallel to the water distribute free city maps. The **Ierapetra Express office,** at 24 Eleftherias Sq. (tel. 28 673 or 22 411), is helpful (open daily 8am-1:30pm and 4-9pm). **Olympic Airways,** 26 Losthenous St. (tel. 22 444), has flight information and sells tickets (open M-F 9am-2pm and 6-9pm, Sa 9am-2pm). Across the street is the **bus station,** 41 Lasthenous St. (tel. 28 237). To get to the waterfront from there, head past the palm tree and you'll see signs for the beach. **Radio Taxi** (tel. 26 600 or 27 350) lines up cars in Kanoupaki Sq. **Free Rider** (tel. 22 571; fax 25 810), south of the bus station at 5 Plastira Sq., rents motorbikes (6000dr) and cars (13500dr). The **hospital** (tel. 22 488 or 22 766) is north of the bus station, left off Lasthenous St. at 6 Kalimerake St. (open daily 8:30am-1:30pm, open 24hr. for emergencies). The town has several **pharmacies,** including one (tel. 23 363) in Eleftherias Sq. (open M, W 8am-2pm, Tu, Th-F 8am-2pm and 5:30-9pm). The **OTE** is at 25 Koraka St., three blocks from the water (open M-F 7:30am-1pm). **Postal code:** 72200. **Telephone code:** 0842.

ACCOMMODATIONS A sign at the bus station leads visitors to the charming **Cretan Villa,** 16 Lakerda St. (tel. 28 522). The 205-year-old building hides a garden surrounded by beautiful, white stucco-walled, brick-floored, high-ceilinged rooms. The owner, a University of Missouri alum, speaks fluent English. All rooms have private bath (singles 7000dr; doubles 8000dr; triples 10,000-12,000dr). **Hotel Coral** is at 18 Ioanidou St. (tel. 22 846 or 28 743). From Kanoupaki Sq., walk down Kyrva St. and take a right after passing the port police, to find large, pristine rooms with private baths including the rare Greek shower tub. Free luggage storage (singles 3000dr; doubles 5000dr; triples 7000dr; 500dr discount to students and seniors; 1000dr cheaper in the low season). For your camping pleasure, **Ierapetra** (tel. 61 351) and, 7km from Ierapetra, the new **Koutsounari** (tel. 61 213), 9km away on the coastal road to Sitia, each provide the ground, a restaurant, a bar, and a beach. Take the bus to Sitia via Makri Gialo (10min., 1 per hr., 220dr) and ask to be let off at the campgrounds (1300dr per person; 900dr per tent).

FOOD AND ENTERTAINMENT Nearly all of Ierapetra's restaurants lie on the waterfront and feature identical prices (*moussaka* 1200-1400dr). Among the touristy *tavernas,* **Notos** (tel. 0943 40 551), with panoramic views of the harbor, near the Venetian Fortress, offers traditional Greek fare (*moussaka* 1200dr, *tzatziki* 550dr), as well as delicious grilled fresh seafood (octopus, delectable, 1500dr). Friendly service complements the scenic vista (open Apr.-Oct. daily 9am-midnight). **Gorgona Taverna,** 12 Stratigou Samouil St. (tel. 26 619), offers fresh fish and large portions of traditional meals like *giovetsi* (1600dr). *Let's Go* readers get a 20% discount, and the owner may be able to arrange discounts on trips to Chrisi. For a unique change, try the array of Asian dishes at **Panda Kala,** 14 Stratigou Samouil (tel. 24 078). Vegetarian dishes start at 1250dr, *nasi goreng* 950dr, curry chicken 1550dr; open Tu-Su. At **Veterano** (tel. 23 175), in Eleftherias Venizelou Sq., you can peek in the gigantic kitchen where you may see old men alongside young boys shelling almonds, mixing frostings, and layering cakes. Sit in the shade with a large piece of fresh *baklava* (500dr) or Ierapetra's own *kalitsounia,* an individual-sized sweet cheese tart-like pie (150dr each; open daily 7:30am-midnight). On Saturdays there is a **street fruit market** on the corner of Panagou St. and Kalimerake St. (open 7am-1:30 or 2pm).

Nightlife in Ierapetra is low key. The bars at the south end of the waterfront (closer to the Fortress) are frequented by locals and play mostly Greek music. **Bar Alexander,** 2 Kyrva (tel. 26 271), is packed with locals who come to groove to the DJ'd Greek tunes (cocktails 1200dr; open daily 9pm-3:30am). The bars on the other end of the harbor are busy with primarily German tourists. **Acropolis,** 51 Markopoulou (tel. 25 561), has a beautiful view from the center of the waterfront; inside, tourists enjoy oldies and jazz mixed by the DJ with rock, rave, and even Greek music (open Mar.-Oct. 9am-4am).

SIGHTS There are loads of historical sights in Ierapetra; unfortunately, most are closed. Locals laud **Napoleon's House,** in the old town, where the French commander supposedly spent the night on June 26, 1798, en route to Egypt to battle the Mamluks. Also in the old town are a **mosque** and an **Ottoman fountain** (*Krini*), decaying and covered with Greek graffiti, built near the end of the 19th century. The restored **Venetian fortress** (*Kales*), at the extreme south end of the old harbor, was started in the early 13th century. (*Open Tu-Su 8:30am-3pm.*) The **Kervea festival** each summer in July and August sometimes holds some of its music, dance, and theater performances at the fortress. Call the **town hall** (tel. 24 115) for information. (*Open M-F 7:30am-2:30pm.*) Ierapetra's **Archaeological Museum,** at the beginning of Adrianou St. at Kanoupaki Sq. on the waterfront, has a small collection of Minoan and classical artifacts from the south coast. (*Open Tu-Sa 9am-3pm. Admission 500dr.*) The large, perfectly preserved Hellenistic sculpture, a double representation of the Greek **Persephone** (Queen of Hades) and the Egyptian **Isis,** proves Aphrodite wasn't the only beauty in the Greek pantheon.

Chrisi

Ierapetra's star attraction is its remote island, **Chrisi,** eight nautical miles from the mainland. *(Ferries 1hr., departing daily 10:30am or 12:30pm, returning 5pm, round-trip 5000dr; 1500dr beach chair charge.)* Free from stores and crowds, Chrisi is completely flat, adorned by green pines and surrounded by transparent green sea. Pack a lunch and bring water; there's nothing but two *tavernas* near the dock are open all day.

■ Sitia Σητεια

A windy drive on coastal and mountain roads from Agios Nikolaos leads to Sitia, a fishing and port town. The wave of tourism that has engulfed the coast from Iraklion to Agios Nikolaos slows to a trickle before Sitia, and pelicans walk the streets at dawn. Use Sitia as your base for exploring Crete's east coast.

ORIENTATION AND PRACTICAL INFORMATION

To get to the center of the waterfront from the bus station, head for the sign for Vai and Kato Zakros, then bear left. **Kapetan Sifi** and **Venizelou Street** intersect with the waterfront at the square, where you will find a small palm-treed traffic island, a strip of cafes and restaurants, and several kiosks.

Transportation

Ferries: Port Office (tel. 22 310). The *Kornaros* travels twice per week to Rhodes (12hr., 5950dr), Kassos (4hr., 2600dr), and Karpathos (5hr., 3400dr) and thrice weekly to Peiraias (16-17hr., 7550dr) via Agios Nikolaos (1½hr., 1600dr) and Milos (9hr., 5200dr). The *Romilda* goes once per week to Rhodes (12hr., 5950dr), Kassos (4hr., 2600dr), and Karpathos (5hr., 3400dr). **Porto-Belis Travel,** 34 Karamanli St. (tel. 22 370; fax 23 830; email pbelis@sit.forthnet.gr), near the bus station, provides ferry information, rents rooms, sells airplane tickets, rents cars and mopeds, and exchanges currency. Open daily 9am-9pm.

Buses: (tel. 22 272), **station** on Pisokefalo St. on the east end of the waterfront. To Agios Nikolaos (1½hr., 6 per day, 1450dr); Iraklion (3¼hr., 6 per day, 2750dr); Ierapetra (1½hr., 4-6 per day, 1200dr); Vai (1hr., 4-6 per day, 560dr); and Kato Zakros (1hr., 1-2 per day, 1000dr). Buy round-trip tickets at the bus station, where 25% discounts are available to students and 50% discounts to seniors.

Flights: Airport (tel. 24 666) connects to Athens (3 per week in summer, 2 per week in winter, 23,200dr). No buses to airport. Taxis cost 1000dr for the ride 1km uphill.

Taxis: (tel. 28 321, 23 810, 23 298, 22 455, or 28 591) lounge in Venizelou Sq. Sometimes do, sometimes don't run all night, usually cabs are ready 24hr. on weekends.

Moped Rental: Knossos (tel. 22 057) at 10 Papandreou St. up the block from Sitia Rent-a-Car. Knossos rents cars and bikes and can help you find a room. Vespas 4000dr per day. Open M-Sa 8:30am-8pm, Su 9am-8pm.

Tourist and Financial Services

Banks: National Bank (tel. 22 250 or 22 218), in Venizelou Sq., offers **currency exchange.** Open M-Th 8am-2pm, F 8am-1:30pm. Main branch (tel. 24 990 or 22 675) at 11 Papanastasiou St. Open M-Th 8am-2pm, F 8am-1:30pm.

Emergency and Communications

Tourist Police: 31 Therissou St. (tel. 24 200). From the square walk up Kapetan Sifi St. 2 blocks to Mysonos St. Take a left on Mysonos and continue until it turns into Therissou St.; it's marked by the Greek flag. Open daily 7:30am-9pm.

Police: (tel. 22 266 or 22 259), in the same building as the tourist police. Open 24hr.

Pharmacies: Many on streets behind the waterfront. One is straight from the square up 3 blocks, at 6 Kapetan Sifi. Open M, W 7:30am-1:30pm, Tu, Th–F 8am-1:30pm and 5:30-8:30pm.

Hospital: (tel. 24 311), off Therissou St. just past the youth hostel, away from town. Follow the signs from the main square. Open 24hr.

Post Office: Main branch, 8 Dimokritou (tel. 22 283; fax 25 350). From the main square, walk toward the bus station on Venizelou St., take your first left on Dimokritou, and the post office will be on your right. Sells telephone cards in addition to standard services. Open M-F 7:30am-2pm. **Postal Code:** 72300.

OTE: 22 Cap. Sifis St. (tel. 28 099). From the main square, turn inland at the National Bank, and go uphill 2 blocks. Open M-Sa 7:30am-10pm. **Telephone Code:** 0843.

ACCOMMODATIONS

It is difficult to find rooms in July and August, and during mid-August, when the Sultana Festival is held, it is nearly impossible. Off-season prices are 20-40% less. The youth hostel is friendly and informal, but for more privacy, head to the main road which leads up to the hostel, and to the back streets at the west end of the waterfront, especially Kornarou St. and Kondilaki St.

✪Youth Hostel, 4 Therissou St. (tel. 22 693). From the bus station, take a left on Pisokefalo, another left on Papanastasiou, follow until the BP gas station, where the road becomes Therissou, and head uphill another 100m on the left. Reception open daily 9am-noon and 6-9pm; but if no one is around, feel free to find a bed and register later. Call ahead and you may be picked up at the bus station for free. Common kitchen and book exchange. Hot water 24hr. Dorms 1300dr per person; singles 2500dr; doubles 3000dr; triples 4500dr.

Nora Hotel, 31 Rouselaki St. (tel. 23 017). To the far right of the harbor (facing inland) near the second pier. A goldfish will greet you at reception in this hotel by the sea. All rooms with telephone, hot water during the day, balcony heating during the winter, and private bath. TV lounge. Free luggage storage. Continental breakfast 1000dr. Singles 5000dr; doubles 7000dr; triples 9000dr. Tell management that you're a student in advance and receive a 1000dr discount.

Pension Maria Hamilachi, 35 Kondilaki St. (tel. 22 768). 20m down, on the opposite side of the street from Venus. The friendly owner opens her home to provide travelers with presentable rooms and well-maintained shared baths. 24hr. hot water. Doubles 4000dr; triples 4300dr.

Rooms to Let Apostolis, 27 Kazantzakis St. (tel. 22 993 or 28 172). A walk up bright granite stairs leads you to pleasant rooms with private baths. Wash basin and linens. Doubles 7000dr; triples 9000dr. 1000dr less in winter.

Porto-Belis, 34 Karamanli Ave. (tel. 22 370). Apartments, studios, and rooms above the Porto-Belis Travel Agency. The bright, sunny rooms in this new building are spacious and clean. All have large private baths, balconies, and refrigerators. Hot water 8am-11pm. Doubles 7500dr; triples 8500dr; studio for 2-3 people with kitchenette 8500-9800dr; 2-room apartment with kitchenette for 3-4 people 12,800dr. 20% cheaper in the low season.

Venus Rooms to Let, 60 Kondilaki St. (tel. 24 307). Walk uphill from the OTE and take your first right. Green courtyard, sunny rooms with balconies, and kitchen facilities. Clean shared baths. Doubles upstairs have private bath, couch, and sea view balcony for 7000dr. Singles 4000dr; doubles 5000dr; triples 8400dr.

FOOD

Sitia's restaurants specialize in fresh fish and lobster. The waterfront spots offer typical tourist fare, and more authentic cuisine is served a few blocks inland at the *tavernas* frequented by the native population. The lightly strummed tones of the bazouki, however draw the visitor to the harbor to be serenaded.

✪Cretan House, 10 K. Karamanli (tel. 25 133), sits to the left of the harbor. Tables inside allow you to appreciate Cretan objects like an old-school threshing plow and a traditional brick oven, while outdoor seating provides a view of the sea. Friendly staff serves a huge variety of dishes, but Cretan recipes are their specialties. *Mezethra* cheese pies 700dr, *Kouloukopsomo* (crunchy bread topped with tomatoes, cheese, and spices) 700dr, *Xigalo* (the "Cretan Viagra") 850dr. Open daily 9am-1:30am.

Kali Kardia, 22 Fountalidou St. (tel. 22 249). Two blocks up from the central square, this modest taverna offers a wide variety of cheap dishes in generous portions (Greek salad 700dr, rabbit 1000dr) in a friendly, informal atmosphere.

Taverna Michos, 117 V. Kornarou (tel. 22 416), is, according to locals, Sitia's best restaurant. Swordfish-prawn *souvlaki* is served with rice and delicious Cretan vegetables (1600dr), lamb stew is served in wine sauce with rice (1600dr). For an appetizer try *dolmades,* grape leaves overstuffed with spicy goo (800dr). 15% discount for seniors. In winter, live music on Fridays and Saturdays. Open M-Sa noon-3pm and 6:30pm-1am, Su 6:30pm-1am.

Mike's Creperie 162 El. Venizelou (tel. 25 207), belongs to the waterfront restaurant strip. The Belgian owners serve up sweet and salty crepes (bacon and mushroom 750dr, chocolate 500dr).

Taverna Panorama (tel. 25 160), in neighboring Agia Fotia on the road to Palaikastro and Vai, serves home-cooked traditional Cretan dishes. The menu varies daily, but specialties include yummy octopus cooked in red wine and tomato sauce, fresh fish, and grape leaves. It is usually only open for dinner, but call ahead, just in case.

Paradosiaka Glyka, 71 Viksendzoukornarou St. (tel. 28 466), one block from the main square. This is a "real" Cretan bakery, specializing in traditional Cretan biscuits and pastries. *Kserotigano* are special wedding pastries (they're round, sticky, and covered with sesame seeds, 2650dr per kg). *Kalitsounia* come in two varieties—an open tart-like pie and a small, soft roll-like biscuits and both are filled with cinnamon-spiced delicious Cretan cheese (2150dr per kg). Open daily 8am-9pm.

ENTERTAINMENT

People-watching is a mainstay of Sitian nightlife, especially along the row of restaurants and cafes near the main square. **Scala** at 193 El. Venizelou St. (tel. 23 010) is a popular bar, favored by a younger crowd for its DJs and free popcorn (cocktails 1500dr; open daily 9am-2am). For a relaxed evening, take a stroll by the harbor, where moonlight removes ruggedness from the boats and adds romance to conversations.

After midnight everyone who's anyone heads to **Hot Summer** (tel. 26 476), way down the road to Palaikastro by the beach. Here, the main attraction is the swimming pool, which is the foundation of the club's tropical theme. The high-society, the young, and the talkative self-segregate at the three fully-stocked bars, and half the fun is figuring out which crowd is where (cover 1000dr, cocktails 1800dr). **Planetarium Disco,** 2km west of the second pier on a sweeping balcony, is the largest nightclub in Crete. The 1500dr cover includes a first drink (open daily 1am-sunrise). **di Settia Peris** (tel. 25 521) is a "garden bar" in Sitia, past all of the *tavernas* on the harbor, near the end (no cover; beer 700-1000dr, cocktails 1700dr; open Su-Th 9pm-3:30am, F-Su 9pm-dawn).

SIGHTS

The **fortress** on the hilltop provides a view of the town and the city's bay. Watch for signs for a performance of a classical Greek tragedy in the fortress. They are put on in Modern Greek, but if you learn the words for kill *(skotoso),* mother *(mitera),* and father *(pateras),* you'll be able to follow the action. The town's **beach** extends 3km east of Sitia toward Petra; the distant end is usually empty. The **Archaeological Museum** (tel. 23 917) houses a small collection from nearby sights, although most artifacts have been shipped off to Iraklion. *(Open Tu-Su 8am-2:30pm. Admission 500dr, students and seniors 300dr, EU students and children under 18 free.)* The museum is across a dusty road, 100m from the bus station. Be sure to note the Late Minoan **Palaikastro Kouros** statuette, one of the very first representations of Zeus. Sitia's **Folk Art Museum** has moved to a newly renovated building with green gates and white washed walls. *(Open Tu 10am-2:30pm and 5-8pm, W-Sa 10am-2:30pm.)* From the main square, walk up Kapetan Siphi and the museum is on the right.

Stop by **Sitian Arts** at 145 Vitsentzou Kornarou (tel./fax 22 600) to see local arts, including ceramics and watercolors. Ask and the knowledgable shop owner can arrange a visit to his pottery workshop by the sea in nearby Agia Fotia.

During the middle of August, just before the grape harvest, Sitia hosts the **Sultanina Festival,** a four-day celebration of Sultanina golden raisins. The festival takes place near the second pier, in a triangular park on Rouselaki St. beyond the ferry harbor and features unlimited wine, dancing, and music for roughly 2000dr.

■ Palaikastro Παλαικαστρο

The village's name literally means "old castle," but Palaikastro is new, by Greek standards. Here, the pace is slow and the faces are familiar, yet several points of interest dot the lazy village's periphery, making Palaikastro an ideal spot for travelers seeking a balance of tranquility and diversion.

ORIENTATION AND PRACTICAL INFORMATION The village has the bare necessities in its main square. Palaikastro is a stop on two bus routes, one running between Sitia and Vai and the other between Sitia and Kato Zakros. **Buses** leave from the main square for Sitia (45min., 4-7 per day, 600dr); Vai (15min., 4-6 per day, 200dr); and Kato Zakros (30min., 1-4 per day, 550dr). You may buy tickets at the kiosk in the square or the small shop by the church. Walk from the central square 100m down the road toward Sitia and you will find the **tourist information office** on your right (tel. 61 456). The office **exchanges currency** and distributes free brochures on rooms and restaurants, as well as maps and general information (open daily 9am-10pm). The **police station** (tel. 61 222) is a few doors away from the tourist office, toward the bus stop. The office is one flight upstairs in a building marked by Greek flags and provides help with emergencies as well as general information. **Taxis** are available by phone (tel. 61 380, 61 271, or 61 224). **Lion Car Rental** (tel. 61 482 or 61 511; mobile tel. 094 58 1665; fax 61 482), in the square, across from the church, is on your left when you bear right going downhill from the bus stop. A small car is 8000dr per day in the high season, and cars can be delivered to Iraklion upon request. They exchange currency with 2% commission (open daily 8am-1pm and 5-9:30pm). A **doctor** (tel. 61 204) calls on the village twice per week and sees patients in the mayor's building. To get there, walk down the road immediately to the left of the tourist information office. The **OTE** (tel. 61 225) is in the same building as the tourist office. **Telephone code:** 0843.

ACCOMMODATIONS You can find rooms and warm atmosphere in the home of **Yiannis Perrakis** (tel. 61 310). When you get off the bus, follow the road that forks to the right. Look for Pegassos Taverna on your right; the pension is up the gravel path on the left. Lemon trees and magenta flowers invite you to bright rooms (singles 2500dr; doubles 4500dr; triples 5000dr; prices lower in the off season). **Pegassos Rooms** (tel. 61 479), above Pegassos Taverna on Forschiona Rd., offers clean rooms with balconies and private baths and the convenience of restaurant downstairs where the owner's wife prepares full breakfasts (600dr) and meals (*moussaka* 800dr) at discounts to guests (singles 6000dr; doubles 8000dr; triples 9000dr; apartments for 5 people 12,000dr).

FOOD, ENTERTAINMENT, AND SIGHTS To stock up on basics, visit one of the village's **mini markets:** opposite the church entrance, 20m down the road to Vai (including a **bakery,** tel. 61 255), or opposite the tourist office (tel. 61 080). The **Hotel Hellas** (tel. 61 455) serves standard Greek food (Greek salad 750dr; stuffed eggplant 950dr; open daily 8:15am-1am). **Restaurant Mythos** (tel. 61 243), across from Hellas in the square, is a local favorite with friendly management and good prices (*moussaka* 1100dr, *pastitsio* 1000dr, boiled vegetables 600dr; open daily 6am-1am).

The hip and energetic of Palaikastro break it down on the dance floor of **Club Design.** From the square, bear left along the road to Vai and the club will be on your right (cocktails 1200dr, *cappuccino* 450dr).

If you're looking for activities outside of Palaikastro, take the bus headed for Kato Zakros and ask the driver to let you off at **Chochlakes**. From this village, you can walk through the valley to the secluded beach and bay of **Karoumes**. Several kilometers of some of Crete's most scenic beaches stretch south to the **Minoan Palace** at **Roussolakos**. The tiny village of **Agathias** provides a change of scenery on the otherwise unremarkable walk to the clear waters of pleasant **Chiona Beach**.

■ Zakros Ζακρος

A natural gorge called the Valley of Death connects the quiet village of Zakros or Ano Zakros, "Up Zakros," and the beautiful beach town of Kato Zakros, (lower Zakros). This region has something to offer everyone, from nature lovers to classicists to beach bums. Even the wildlife throughout the area suggests its diversity. Goats graze by the mountain road between the two Zakroi, snakes and scorpions make themselves visible in the valley, and elegant geese strut the streets of Kato Zakros.

Buses travel from Sitia to Kato Zakros, stopping in Palaikastro and Zakros (1hr., 2 per day, 1000dr). The 11am bus from Sitia provides just enough time to hike the gorge, visit the Minoan Palace and take a quick swim at Kato Zakros. The bus stop of Zakros is in the main square, where one can find three **taxis** and an **OTE**. You'll want to buy your phonecards here, as there are none for sale in Kato Zakros. A **police station** (tel. 93 323) is on the left side of the square as you come from Sitia. A **nurse** (tel. 93 265) comes to Zakros twice per week and can be found in an office by the town's cemetery, outside the square on the way to Sitia. One of the three entrances to the Valley of Death is located down the road from Zakros' main square. At the end of the gorge, turn left on the dirt path and bear right at the gate. This path leads to the *taverna*-lined main street which parallels the beach of Kato Zakros. At the far end of the road is the bus stop. Even on the bus ride to Zakros, there are notable places of interest. The **Sorg Spring,** one of Zakros' famous sources of curative waters, is visible on your right as you approach the town from Sitia.

■ Valley of Death

Those seeking an active excursion and physical challenge should hike the **Valley of Death,** which leads from Zakros to Kato Zakros. Ask the bus driver to let you off at the gorge's entrance, just outside the center of Zakros. Look for signs and maps of the Valley of Death. The walk is fairly untrodden, smaller and less crowded but equal in scenery to Samaria in the west. Because rainfall alters the location of pebbles and rock in the gorge each year, you may have to rely on your wits to navigate through the gorge. Although it's impossible to wander too far astray in a gorge, a compass, long pants (to shield your legs from prickly and possibly allergy-stimulating vegetation), and plenty of water and snacks may come in handy. Snakes and scorpions aside, you may also hear the frantic cry of billy goats. The gorge is filled with beautiful trees and bushes—look for *phaskomilo,* a tea plant with small and fuzzy green leaves. Its scent is naturally refreshing, a marked change from the odor of the onion plants (identified by their small purple flowers) which also inhabit the valley. Although the variable path obscures estimates, the entire walk, excluding breaks, should take less than ninety minutes.

At the end of the gorge, turn left on the dirt path and bear right when you see a fenced gate. This leads you to the coast and the modest ruins of the **Minoan Palace of Kato Zakros,** (tel. 93 338), destroyed in 1450 BC. *(Open daily 8am-7:30pm. Admission 500dr, students and seniors 300dr, with student ID free. Guidebook 800dr, available at entrance.)* The royal rubble extends up a hill, and even though adrenaline might still be flowing from the hike through the gorge, resist the temptation to climb around on the archaeological site. Note the baths of the king, pools near the bottom of the hill, and a little farther uphill, the fenced-in, long ditches where copper was melted.

Keep walking along the path away from the palace and you will arrive at the **beach** of Kato Zakros. Supplied with a ramp, connecting the main street with the water, this beach is uniquely wheelchair accessible. To your left as you face the water is a mountain, on the opposite side of which is **Pelitika cave,** about a 1½hr. walk from the beach. The path to the cave is marked with clusters of red-painted stones and the entrance of the cave with a large tree.

■ Vai Βαι

Not long ago, tourists headed east to the sylvan palm beach at Vai for refuge from Sitia's crowds. Today, several buses roll into this outpost every day, depositing tourists eager to ponder Europe's only indigenous palm tree forest. According to local tradition, the forest is the legacy of the Arabs who conquered Crete in the 9th century. In the 60s Vai was a haven of British rock stars including drummer Ginger Baker of Cream—now the park is closed to the public and Vai is primarily a beach.

The bus from Sitia will deposit you in Vai's parking lot. You'll be able to see palm trees and sand from there. **Buses** leave Sitia and stop at Palaikastro en route to Vai (1hr., 4-6 per day, Sitia-Vai 600dr, Palaikastro-Vai 220dr). A **tourist information booth,** located in the parking lot, offers **currency exchange. First aid** is offered in the parking lot near the W.C. For emergencies call the **police** (tel. 61 222).

Camping is forbidden in the park itself; nonetheless, many unfurl sleeping bags in the cove to the south of the palm beach. If sandy pajamas and the possibility of arrest don't appeal to you, rent a room in quiet Palaikastro, a town 8km back toward Sitia. Although there is one restaurant and a snack bar (sandwiches 500-550dr) in Vai, you're better off packing a picnic or eating in Palaikastro or Sitia. When those places where the sun don't usually shine start burning, slap on some more cocoa butter (and clothes) and check out the **watersports center** on the far end of the beach. Rent a jet ski (6000dr for 15min.) or a pedal boat (2000dr for 1hr.), or go scuba diving (10,000dr per session; open daily 10am-6pm).

At the Vai tourist shop, inquire about the nearby **Open Air Banana Plantations and Sub-Tropical Cultivations** (tel. (0843) 61 353). *(Open Apr.-Oct. daily 8am-7pm, though hours vary depending on the season's weather. Admission 800dr.)* A retired sea captain gives tours in German, English, French, and Greek. A free banana awaits you at the tour's end. Although island winds may have deleterious effects on open-air banana plantations, they facilitate and improve **windsurfing** conditions at **Kouremenos beach** on the way from Palaikastro to Vai. Also near Vai (6km into the mountains) is the **Monastery of Toplou.** The monks have kept the 14th-century structure and castle like complex in mint condition; along with its museum, the site merits a visit. Beyond Vai sprawls the mellow **Itanos Beach,** with beachside archeological sites.

CRETE

Dodecanese
Δωδεκανησα

The Dodecanese are lean wolves and hunt in packs; waterless, eroded by the sun. They branch off every side as you coast along the shores of Anatolia. Then towards afternoon the shaggy green of Cos comes up; and then slithering out of the wintry blue the moist green flanks of Rhodes.

—Lawrence Durrell

Littering the coast of Turkey, the Dodecanese (Twelve Islands) are the farthest group of Greek islands from the mainland. Named after the 12 islands that united in 1908 to protest their loss of special status within the Ottoman empire, the archipelago has, thanks to its proximity to Asia Minor and distance from Athens, both enjoyed greater privileges and suffered more invasions than the rest of Greece.

In ancient times the Dodecanese flourished independent of the imperial Athenian yoke before losing their sovereignty to the Hellenistic empire of Alexander the Great. A favorite evangelical target of such biblical luminaries as St. Paul and St. John, the inhabitants of the Dodecanese were some of the first Greeks to convert to Christianity. Though they prospered in the early years of the Byzantine empire, the islands suffered greatly from the Persian, Arab, and then Turkish raids that racked the Byzantine empire from the 7th to the 13th centuries. The Dodecanese earned a brief respite under the rule of the Crusaders at the beginning of the 14th century. The Crusaders, dubbed the Knights of St. John, built a series of heavily fortified castles on the islands from which to conduct their holy war. They were ousted in 1522 by the Ottomans who granted the "Twelve Islands" special concessions within their empire. The Dodecanese had no such luck with the fascist imprint of Italian occupation from 1912 to 1943 and endured fierce fighting in WWII before joining Greece in 1948.

The varied history of the islands has left a unique legacy of architectural styles—Classical ruins, Crusader castles, Ottoman mosques, and Mussolini-style public buildings. Travelers will also be well rewarded by a diverse topography ranging from the fertile island of Rhodes to the paradoxical landscape of the volcanic Nisyros. A rare display of heterogeneity there is something here for everyone: Kos' hopping nightlife, Rhodes' medieval city, the apocalyptic beauty of Patmos, and the secluded beaches and traditional life of northern Karpathos. The islands' proximity to the Turkish coast (a scary thought for most Greeks) makes them popular points of departure for tourists visiting Turkey.

🏛 HIGHLIGHTS OF THE DODECANESE

- As apocalyptic millennial hysteria sets in, visit the Monastery of St. John the Revelator on **Patmos** (p. 453)...before it's too late.
- Climb through the cobwebbed pall of lace tablecloths to the acropolis at **Lindos** (p. 438), on Rhodes; the sunset is, in a word, nice.
- Get your commemorative taxonomic sponge memento, while getting acquainted with the history of the world's least complex animals and the turn-of-the-century sponge barons who loved them on **Kalymnos** (p. 449).
- Discover the sublime sound of millions of beating fluorescent wings at the **Valley of Butterflies** on Rhodes (p. 441).
- For a hot night on **Kos** (p. 441), squeeze your sweet self into your tightest pants, then go try to get in somebody else's.

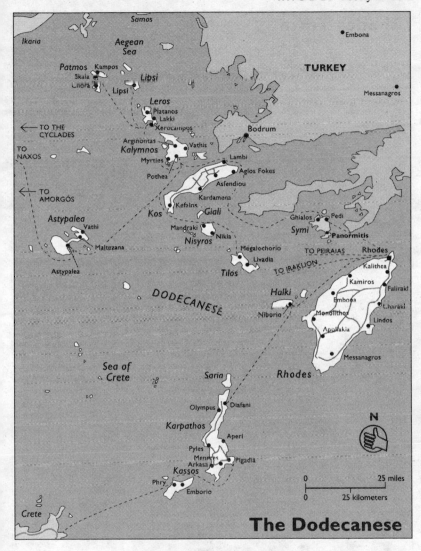

The Dodecanese

RHODES Ροδος

In Rhodes the days drop as softly as fruit from trees.

—Lawrence Durrell

Rhodes is the undisputed tourism capital of the Dodecanese. Yet the sheer size of the island allows the interior regions and many of the smaller coastal towns to retain a sense of serenity. Sandy beaches stretch along the east coast, jagged cliffs skirt the west, and green mountains freckled with villages fill the interior. Kamiros, Ialyssos, and Lindos show the clearest evidence of the island's classical past, while medieval fortresses slumber in Rhodes City and Monolithos. Despite the onslaught of tourism, soothing strolls are still possible in smaller villages and along the cobblestone streets of the Old Town.

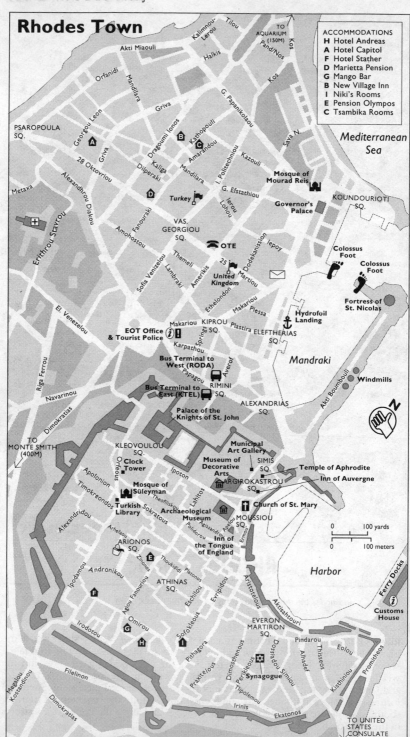

Rhodes Town

ACCOMMODATIONS
H Hotel Andreas
A Hotel Capitol
F Hotel Stather
D Marietta Pension
G Mango Bar
B New Village Inn
I Niki's Rooms
E Pension Olympos
C Tsambika Rooms

PSAROPOULA SQ.

Akti Miaouli

TO AQUARIUM (150M)

Mediterranean Sea

Mosque of Mourad Reis

Governor's Palace

KOUNDOURIOTI SQ.

Colossus Foot

Colossus Foot

Fortress of St. Nicolas

VAS. GEORGIOU SQ.

OTE

United Kingdom

Turkey

Hydrofoil Landing

EOT Office & Tourist Police

KIPROU SQ.

ELEFTHERIAS SQ.

Mandraki

Bus Terminal to West (RODA)

Bus Terminal to East (KTEL)

RIMINI SQ.

ALEXANDRIAS SQ.

Windmills

Palace of the Knights of St. John

TO MONTE SMITH (400M)

KLEOVOULOU SQ.

Clock Tower

Municipal Art Gallery

Museum of Decorative Arts

SIMIS SQ.

Temple of Aphrodite

Inn of Auvergne

Mosque of Süleyman

Turkish Library

ARGIROKASTROU SQ.

Archaeological Museum

Church of St. Mary

MOUSSIOU SQ.

ARIONOS SQ.

Inn of the Tongue of England

ATHINAS SQ.

EVERON MARTIRON SQ.

Harbor

Ferry Docks

Customs House

Synagogue

TO UNITED STATES CONSULATE

0   100 yards
0   100 meters

■ City of Rhodes

Founded in 408 BC by the unification of three city-states, the city of Rhodes has served as the island's capital for over 20 centuries. In terms of regal majesty, the city knows no equal in all of Greece. The exceptional harbor, detailed architecture, and intricate layout—all designed by the architect Hippodamos—made Rhodes one of the ancient world's most beautiful cities. It was the Knights of St. John who left the city's most visible legacy, during their 14th-century occupation. The breathtaking palace and the grand fortress that surrounds the Old Town give the city a medieval flair.

ORIENTATION AND PRACTICAL INFORMATION

The city is divided into two districts: the **New Town,** stretching to the north and west, and the **Old Town,** below it, encapsulated within the medieval fortress walls. There are also three adjacent harbors. Most boat traffic uses the **Mandraki,** the New Town's waterfront. Private yachts, hydrofoils, and excursion boats dock here. International and most domestic ferries use the **Commercial Harbor** outside the Old Town. **Acandia,** the harbor below it, provides a port for cargo ships. Beaches are located north beyond the Mandraki and along the city's west coast. **Rimini Square,** beneath the fortress's turrets at the junction between the Old and New Towns, has the city's tourist office, both bus stations, and a taxi stand. To get here from the vase-shaped Mandraki, walk to the base and head one block inland along the park on the New Town side. The **New Town** is a mecca for nightlife—Orfanidou St. has been popularly dubbed Bar Street.

Transportation

Ferries: Service to Peiraias (14hr., 1-4 per day, 8955dr); Kos (2-3 per day, 3900dr); Kalymnos (1-2 per day, 4265dr); Leros (1 per day, 4662dr); Patmos (1-2 per day, 5366dr); Symi (4 per week, 2000dr); Tilos (4 per week, 2774dr); Nisyros (4 per week, 2778dr); Kastellorizo (3 per week, 2002dr); Thessaloniki (1 per week, 14,554dr); Chalki (1 per week, 1903dr); Astypalea (2 per week, 5035dr); Samos (2 per week, 6504dr); Alexandroupolis (1 per week, 11,544dr) via Chios (1 per week, 7007dr), Lesvos (1 per week, 7603dr), and Limnos (1 per week, 9374dr); Karpathos (3 per week, 4351dr); Kassos (2 per week, 5246dr); Sitia, Crete (1 per week, 5856dr); Ag. Nikolaos, Crete (1 per week, 6156dr); Iraklion, Crete (1 per week, 6221dr); Santorini (1 per week, 5151dr); Paros (1 per week, 6894dr); Milos (1 per week, 8450dr); Amorgos (1 per week, 4644dr); and Mykonos (1 per week, 6732dr). **Daily Excursions** from Mandraki Port to Symi and Panormitis Monastery (4000dr round-trip), Kos (14,000dr round-trip), and Lindos (5000dr round-trip). **International ferries** head to Limassol, Cyprus (17hr., 1 per week, 20,500dr) and Haifa, Israel (36hr., 1 per week, 33,500dr).

Flying Dolphins: Hydrofoil service connects Rhodes with the northeast Aegean islands, Turkey, and the Dodecanese. To Symi (2849dr); Tilos (5293dr); Nisyros (5383dr); Patmos (10,524dr); Leros (9141dr); Chalki (3657dr); Ikaria (12,380dr); and Fourni (12,382dr). Check travel agencies for current schedules.

Buses: Stations lie on opposite sides of Papagou St. at Rimini Sq. **East** station is served by KTEL (tel. 27 706 or 24 268). Service east to Faliraki (20 per day, 350dr); Lindos (13 per day, 950dr); Afandou (15 per day, 360dr); Pefkos (5 per day, 1050dr); Archangelos (14 per day, 600dr); Kolymbia Beach (10 per day, 600dr); Kalithies (8 per day, 350dr); Lardos (6 per day, 950dr); Malona/Massari (4 per day, 700dr); Charaki (2 per day, 750dr); Gennadi (5 per day, 1150dr); Tsambika Beach (1 per day, 650dr); Vliha (2 per day, 950dr); Laerma (1 per day, 1150dr); and Pilona (1 per day, 900dr). **West** station is served by RODA (tel. 26 300). Service west to Kalithea/Calypso (34 per day, 350dr); Paradisi Airport (27 per day, 350dr); Koskinou (16 per day, 350dr); Theologos (19 per day, 360dr); Soroni/Fanes (9 per day, 480dr); Kalavarda (9 per day, 550dr); Salakos (14 per day, 750dr); Embana (3 per day, 1100dr); Kamiros (2 per day, 900dr); Petaloudes (2 per day, 1000dr); Monolithos (1 per day, 1500dr); and Kritinia (1 per day, 950dr).

Flights: Olympic Airways, 9 Lohou St. (tel. 24 571; for reservations 24 555; for the airport counter 92 839), near the central OTE. Open M-F 7:30am-9pm. The **airport** (tel. 91 771) is on the west coast, 17km from town, near Paradisi. Public buses run

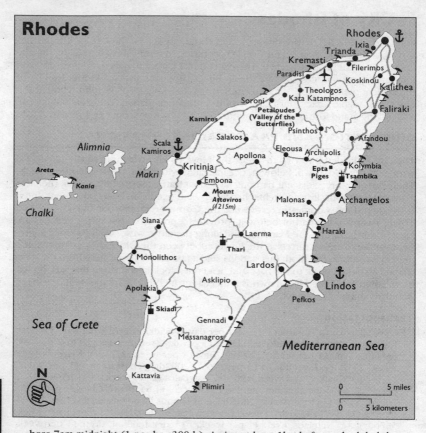

Rhodes

Alimnia

Areta

Kania

Chalki

Makri

Sea of Crete

Rhodes ⚓
Trianda Ixia
Kremasti Filerimos
Paradisi Koskinou Kalithea
Theologos
Soroni Kata Katamonos Faliraki
Petaloudes
Kamiros (Valley of the
Butterflies) Psinthos
Salakos Afandou
Scala Eleousa Archipolis
Kamiros Apollona
Kritinia Epta Kolymbia
Embona Piges Tsambika
Mount
Attaviros Malonas Archangelos
(1215m) Massari
Siana Haraki
Laerma
Thari
Monolithos Lardos
Apolakia Asklipio Lindos ⚓
Skiadi Pefkos
Gennadi
Messanagros *Mediterranean Sea*

N

Kattavia
Plimiri

| 0 | | 5 miles |
| 0 | | 5 kilometers |

DODECANESE

here 7am-midnight (1 per hr., 300dr). Arrive at least 1hr. before scheduled departure. **Domestic flights** to Rhodes are usually booked at least 2 weeks in advance. Flights to Athens (5 per day, 21,500dr); Kos (3 per week, 11,000dr); Karpathos (4 per day, 9400dr); Kassos (1 per day, 10,000dr); Kastellorizo (1 per day, 7500dr); Iraklion, Crete (4 per week, 18,500dr); Thessaloniki (2 per week, 28,500dr); Santorini (3 per week, 19,500dr); and Mykonos (3 per week, 19,500dr). Off-season departures are less frequent and subject to change.

Taxis: (tel. 27 666), in Rimini Sq. Radio taxis also available (tel. 64 712, 64 734, 64 756, 64 778, or 64 790). Check price list for out of town destinations. Open 24hr.

Moped Rental: Mandar Moto, 2 Dimosthenous St. (tel. 34 576), in the Old Town. Take Sokratous St. to Hippokratous Sq. and continue on Aristotelous until Evraion Martiron Sq. Rentals 2500-4000dr per day. Open daily 8am-11pm.

Bike Rental: Mike's Motor Club, 23 I. Kazouli St. (tel. 37 420) in the New Town. Mountain bikes 1500dr per day. Cobblestones in the Old Town and maniacal drivers in the New Town make roads in Rhodes generally unsafe. Open daily 8am-8pm.

Road Emergencies: Dial 104.

Tourist and Financial Services

Tourist Office: (tel. 35 945), in the tiny yellow building in Rimini Sq. Bus, ferry, and excursion schedules, accommodations advice, and **currency exchange.** Open M-Sa 8am-9pm, Su 8am-3pm.

Greek National Tourist Office (EOT): (tel. 23 255 or 23 655), at the corner of Makariou St. and Papagou St. in the New Town. Walk up Papagou a few blocks from Rimini Sq. Extremely helpful for all travel needs. Open M-F 7:30am-3pm.

Budget Travel: Castellania Travel Service (tel. 75 860 or 75 862; fax 75 861), in Hippokratous Sq. at the intersection of Sokratous St. and Aristotelous St. in the Old Town. Low prices on international travel, USIT ticketing, **ISIC** and **GO25 cards** issued (2600dr), international telephones, free **luggage storage**. Open daily in summer 8:30am-11:30pm, in winter 8am-1pm and 4-8pm. **Triton Holidays,** 9 Plastira St. (tel. 21 690), in the New Town, is also well regarded.

Consulates: The Voice of America (tel. 24 731), southeast of the city, just past Sigourou St. Handles insular affairs, especially emergencies. Open M-F 8am-4:30pm. A **British Vice-Consul** is available M-Sa 8am-2pm through **Lloyd's Travel Bureau,** #23 25th Martiou St. (tel. 27 306 or 27 247). **Turkish Consulate,** 10 Iroon Polytechniou St. (tel. 23 362 or 24 603). Open M-F 8am-1pm.

Banks: Ionian Bank, 4 Symi Sq. (tel. 27 434), offers **currency exchange.** Open M-Th 8am-2pm, F 8am-1:30pm, Sa 8:30am-1pm. The **National Bank** has an office in Museum Sq. with an **ATM.** Open M-Th 8am-2pm, F 8am-1:30pm. In the New Town, the **National Bank** (tel. 27 031) in Kyprou Sq. also has **currency exchange.** Open M-Th 8am-2pm, F 8am-1:30pm, Sa 9am-1pm. Many other banks in New Town, but few in Old Town.

American Express: Rhodos Tours Ltd., 23 Ammohostou St., P.O. Box 252 (tel. 24 022). Open M-F 9am-1:30pm and 5-8:30pm, Sa 7:30am-3pm.

Local Services

English Bookstore: Kostas Tornaras Bookstore, 5-7 Soph. Venizelou St. (tel. 32 055), in the New Town. Open M-F 8:30am-1:30pm and 5-9pm, Sa 8am-2pm. **Second Story Book,** 24 Amarantou St., in the New Town, sells second-hand books.

Laundromat: House of Laundry, 2 Er. Stavrou St., (tel. 38 510), near the corner of Octovriou St. and Orfanidou St. in the New Town. 1000dr wash, 500dr dry. Open daily 9am-9pm.

Public Toilets: Strategic locations in the New Town include Rimini Sq., next to the tourist office and the new market. In the Old Town, search out facilities at Orfeos St. and Sokratous St. Free.

Public Baths: Hamam (tel. 27 739), Arionos Sq. in the Old Town. Not your typical shower, but a good way to get clean. Single sex. Admission 500dr. Open Tu 1-6pm, W-F 11am-6pm, Sa 8am-6pm.

Emergency and Communications

Hospital: (tel. 22 222 or 25 555), Erithrou Stavrou St. off El. Venizelou St. Open for emergencies 24hr. **Visitor's clinic** open daily 5-9pm. Be prepared to wait for medical attention; patients line the corridors. **Medical Emergencies:** Dial 100.

Police: (tel. 23 294), Ethelondon Dodekanission St., 1 block behind the post office. Open 24hr. **Lost and found** open M-F 8am-2pm. The **tourist police** (tel. 27 423 or 23 329), in the GNTO building, speak English. The **port authority** (tel. 22 220 or 28 888), or Central Harbor Master is on Mandraki St. just left of the post office. Complete boat schedules. Open 24hr.

Post Office: Main branch (tel. 22 212 or 34 873), on Mandraki St., along the waterfront and next to the Bank of Greece. Open M-F 7am-8pm, Sa 7:30am-3pm, Su 9am-2pm. **Parcel service** daily 7:30am-2pm. **Poste Restante** window takes a lunch hour. Also a **mobile branch** in the Old Town on Orfeos, near the Palace of the Grand Masters. From Museum Sq., head down Ipoton St. Open M-F 7:30am-2pm. **Postal Code:** 85100.

Internet Access: Minoan Palace, 13 Ir. Polytechniou St., at corner of G. Efstathiou St. (tel. 20 210). 1000dr per hour, 30min. minimum. Open daily 9:30am-2am.

OTE: 91 Amerikis St. (tel. 24 599), at the corner of 25th Martiou St. in New Town. Open 6am-11pm. **Telephone Code:** 0241 (for the northern half of the island), 0244 (below Kolymbia on the east), and 0246 (below Kalavarda on the west).

ACCOMMODATIONS

Old Town

Pensions are scattered about the narrow pebbled paths of the Old Town, the preferred resting place for most travelers. Low prices here inevitably mean low luxury,

DODECANESE

so prepare yourself. Winding streets are inconsistently named; bite the bullet and buy a map. Off-season prices run roughly 20-40% less than those in summer.

Hotel Andreas, 28d Omirou St. (tel. 34 156; fax 74 285). Rooms with bunk-beds are ideal for families or groups. Roof terrace and bar hosts barbecues 3 times a month. Fun, friendly atmosphere. Doubles 6000dr, with bath 8000dr; triples with bath 10,000dr; quads with bath 12,000dr.

Pension Olymbos, 56 Ag. Fanouriou St. (tel./fax 33 567). From Hippokratous Sq., go up Sokratous St. and take a left on Ag. Fanouriou St. Look for the archway covered in pots and flowers. Spotless rooms with private baths and common kitchen facilities. Doubles 8000dr; triples 10,000dr.

Rooms above Mango Bar, 3 Dorieos Sq. (tel. 24 877 or 28 324). From Sokratous, take Ag. Fanouriou up to Dorieos Sq. to reach sparkling rooms above a bar with the cheapest draft beer in town (450dr per pint). All rooms with private baths. Singles 4000dr; doubles 6000dr; triples 8000dr.

Hotel Stathis, 60 Omirou St. (tel. 24 357). French and English spoken. Nightly folk music from nearby theater. Noon check-out. Laundry 950dr. Breakfast 500dr. Dorms 2500dr; singles 6000dr; doubles 6000-8000dr.

Niki's Rooms to Let, 39 Sofokleous St. (tel. 25 115). Quiet atmosphere. Singles 5000dr, with private bath 6000dr; doubles 7000dr, with private bath 8000dr.

New Town

The New Town is rather charmless, with its large apartment buildings and commercialized atmosphere; however, it is near the closest swimmable beach and has more than ample nightlife. Expensive hotels overshadow the coast, but affordable pensions can be found along the narrow streets of Rodiou, Dilberaki, Kathopouli, and Amarandou. Information about New Town pensions is available at the tourist office.

Hotel Capitol, 65-67 Dilberaki St. (tel. 62 016 or 74 154), has quiet, spacious rooms with private showers in a house once inhabited by Rhodes's mayor. Breakfast included. Singles 7000dr; doubles 8000dr; triples 12,000dr; quads 14,000dr.

New Village Inn, 10 Konstantopedos St. (tel. 34 937). Couple-owned, well-run hotel delivering exceptional rooms. Singles 5000dr; doubles 8000dr.

Marieta Pension, #52 28 October St. (tel. 36 396), is a charming, family-owned pension in a 60-year-old traditional villa. Rooms have high ceilings and private baths. Doubles 8000dr; triples 12,000dr.

Tsambika Rooms, 38 Kathopouli St. (tel. 26 840), in an alley 1 block east of corner of I. Pragoumi and Mandilara. Peculiar, widely varied set-up—one room has a spiral staircase leading to bath and balcony—but rooms with private bath are large, clean, spacious, and surround a homey courtyard. Proud, friendly owners speak little English. Quiet yet close to New Town nightlife. Doubles 4000-6000dr.

FOOD

The city's large tourism industry means good, local *tavernas* are virtually non-existent. In the Old Town, food tends to be mediocre, the waiters aggressive, and the prices high. In the New Town, you will be overwhelmed by flashing fast food signs and Wendy's burger billboards. However, a burgeoning expat community has created a tasty international palate.

Old Town

L'Auberge Bistrot, 21 Praxileous St. (tel. 34 292). From the synagogue, walk south on Perikleous; take your first right, then second left. The covert location makes discovering this gastronomic gem all the more worthwhile. A friendly French couple has created an unforgettable bistro. Jazz pumps into the gorgeous courtyard and inviting interior lined with art. Two starters from the constantly changing menu make a great meal. Starters 500-1200dr, entrees 1800-2500dr.

Yiannis, 41 Apellou St. (tel. 36 535), just off Sokratous away from the New Town. Food is prepared with care and the portions are huge. *Stifado* 1500dr, *moussaka* 1100dr, and *Elliniko* plate with enough food for 3 people 1800dr.

Mediterraneo, 29 Eshcylou St. Go south on Pythagora St. from Hippocrates Sq., turn right at Platonos St., and left at a small square onto a larger one. Great Italian food. Spaghetti smothered in tomato and basil 1200dr, vegetarian pizza 1600dr.

New Town

Niohorio, 29 I. Kazouli St. (tel. 35 116). Well-priced local grill house serving basic Greek fare (*gyros* 250dr, *souvlaki* 1200dr), salads, and myriad carnivorous plates (sausages 600dr, meatballs 600dr).

7.5 Wonder, 15 Dilberaki St. (tel. 39 805). Euro-hip "7-and-a-half" serves pricey Mediterranean, Scandinavian, and modern Asian cuisine in stunning romantic setting.

Da Capo, 12 G. Leontos St. (tel. 76 790), offers traditional Greek food and an extensive list of pizzas (1500dr) at patio and balcony.

India, 16 Konstantopedos St. (tel. 38 395). Wide selection of Indian food, including vegetarian fare. Slightly expensive, but specials are generally better priced.

Panieri Health Foods, 1 L. Fanouraki (tel. 35 877). Get your *echinacea* fix and stock up on natural grains, pasta, vitamins, skin care products, and yes, Birkenstocks. Open M-F 9am-2pm and 5-9pm, Sa 9am-2pm.

New Market, a stop on the package tour route, houses a panoply of fresh fruit.

ENTERTAINMENT

Old Town

By night, the Old Town contains a number of cultural offerings within and around its walls, including a ridiculous **sound and light show.** *(Admission 1000dr, students 600dr; most of the show can be seen and heard from outside the gate for free.)* This audiovisual evening display at the palace (tel. 36 795) gives an account of the Ottoman siege of the city during the Crusader occupation. It sounds enthralling, but don't expect much. The entrance is on Papagou St. in Rimini Sq. Shows alternate in English, Swedish, German, and French at one-hour intervals. For live music, **St. Francis Church** (tel. 23 605), at Dimokratias and Filellinon St., echoes with sublime organ recitals Wednesday nights at 9pm. Check with the tourist office for performances in the **ancient theater** near Monte Smith. The **National Theatre** (tel. 29 678), off the Mandraki next to the town hall, stages occasional winter productions. **Rodon,** by the National Theatre, shows new flicks and subtitled classics. *(Admission 800dr.)* The **Folk Dance Theater** (tel. 29 085), on Andronikou St. in the Old Town, stages hokey performances featuring dances and songs from all over Greece. *(Shows May-Oct. M, W, and F 9:10pm. Admission 3000dr, students 1500dr.)*

Later in the evening, a few bars and cafes fill up with crowds that are tamer and more sophisticated than their New Town counterparts. **Cafe Havana/Theater Bar** (tel. 27 887) and the alley they share form the focus of Old Town bar life. These lively neighbors, on the corner of Miltiado and Apellou, one block south of Sokratous, are two brilliant answers to the ostensibly difficult question of where to grab a drink in the Old Town. At **Cafe Besara,** 11-13 Sofokleous St. (tel. 30 363), mosaics share wallspace with Coca-Cola paraphernalia and the ebullient owner seems to know everybody. You'll find coffee, beer, wine, *ouzo, meze,* and interior design magazines in a number of languages. From the fountain, take Pythagora St. down towards the mosque, then turn left at Sofokleous St. **Valentino's** (tel. 34 070), off Apellou St., caters to a primary gay clientele.

New Town

The only thing greasier than New Town cafes are the paws of **Bar Street** Romeos, as they slither indiscriminately around members of the fairer sex. Nightlife here is neither shy nor tame. Propriety and shame are checked at the door. Drinking money, dancing shoes, and libidos arrive positively intact, but disappear as nights progress. Although popular bars and clubs are scattered throughout the New Town, crowds flock to Orfanidou St., unanimously referred to as Bar Street. Popular places have expensive drinks, while empty bars will cut deals. The five-minute walk from end to end will give you a feel for each place's atmosphere.

Scorpio, 28 Orfanidou St. (tel. 77 747). The liveliest dance floor on Bar Street.

El Corazon, 27 Orfanidou St. (tel. 75 798). Cultural immersion, Dionysiac style, eased by specials like 4 shots of tequila for 1000dr. Dancing inside, bar outside.

Down Under, 37 Orfanidou St. (tel. 32 982). Good times at this Australian-themed bar playing loud rock. Clientele has a propensity for dancing on bar. G'nite mate.

Boulevard, 44 Orfanidou St. (tel. 78 316). Bar Street's favorite music cafe. More sane, but no less sedate, and just as packed.

Colorado Pub, 57 Orfanidou St. (tel. 75 120). Live band performing covers of songs you probably know the words to. Attracts many despite 1500dr cover.

Bar Berlin (tel. 32 250). Bar Street's most popular gay hangout.

Del Mar, corner of 28th Octovriou St. and E. Stavrou St. Cafe and club for the hip and well-dressed. A touch of class moments away from Bar Street, Del Mar resembles a Mediterranean mansion.

La Scala. A large sprawling complex southwest of town, by the beachside Rodos Palace Hotel in Ixia. The king of Rhodes's nightclubs, accompanied by covers fit for royalty. Watch for special party nights.

The Blue Lagoon, #2 25th Martiou St. (tel. 76 072), near the post office. Sail the Bacchanalian seas at this bar-cum-bizarre Disneyesque pirate-scape. So bad it's good.

Gas, #2 25th Martiou St., next to the Blue Lagoon. Large dance club popular with locals and tourists, spinnin' the usual suspects of dance mixes.

Outside the City

Excursion boats, tracing the beach-filled coast from Rhodes to Lindos, leave the city in the morning and return in the afternoon. They make several stops, including at Faliraki. Schedules and prices are posted at the dock along the lower end of the Mandraki (3500dr round-trip). **Waterhoppers** (tel. 38 146) and **Dive Med Centres** (tel. 61 115) offer **scuba diving** lessons and trips to Kalithea (lessons 12,000dr; non-diving passengers 6000dr; kids under 6 free), as well as trips for certified divers.

Rodini Park is a forested area outside the city with streams, trails, a restaurant, and some small, harmless animals left from the time when Rodini was a zoo. Bus #3 runs to the park regularly. **Kalithea,** 10km south of Rhodes Town, features a deserted spa at the beach cove's meager snack bar (not-so-fresh-looking cheese pie 350dr; soda 250dr). **Buses** run 15 times per day to Faliraki (300dr) and Lindos (900dr).

SIGHTS

Very few other islands can boast of being known for a sight that doesn't exist, and may never have existed. These bragging rights belong to the **Colossus of Rhodes,** a 35m bronze stature of Helios that may have stood astride the island's harbor. It was allegedly destroyed by an earthquake in 237 BC. Considered one of the **seven wonders of the ancient world,** the Colossus has been immortalized in tacky illustrations across the island. Two bronze deer now stand at the entrance to the Mandraki harbor, each claiming a spot previously occupied by an enormous foot.

The Old Town

There is nothing like redecorating to make a place feel more like home. Taking heed of this maxim, the Knights of St. John gave the city of Rhodes an extensive face lift upon their conquest, replacing Hellenistic structures with medieval forts and castles.

The best place to begin exploring the Old Town is **Symi Square,** inside Eleftherias Gate at the base of the Mandraki. To the right, with your back to the arch, is the **Municipal Art Gallery,** featuring contemporary paintings by local artists. *(Open Tu-Sa 8am-2pm. Admission 500dr.)* Behind the 3rd-century BC **Temple of Aphrodite** in the middle of the square stands the 16th-century **Inn of the Tongue of Auvergne,** with an Aegean-style staircase on the facade.

Past Symi Sq. is **Argykastrou Square,** with a relocated Byzantine fountain at its center. The 14th-century **Palace of Armeria,** now the **Archaeological Institute,** is on the right side of the square. Connected to the palace is the **Museum of Decorative Arts** with Dodecanese costumes, carved sea chests, and ceramic plates. *(Open Tu-Su 8:30am-3pm. Admission 600dr, students 300dr.)* **Museum Square** is after the low archway; to its left is the **Church of St. Mary.** *(Open Tu-Su 8:30am-3pm. Admission 500dr, stu-*

dents 300dr.) The Knights of St. John transformed this 11th-century Byzantine structure into a Gothic cathedral. Most of the rich interior frescoes were obliterated when the Ottomans remodeled the building into the Enderoum Mosque. The Italians then remade the mosque into a church, which has since retired to a quiet existence as an icon museum.

Nearby, the **Inn of the Tongue of England** is a 1919 copy of its predecessor, built in 1483 but destroyed in one of the many battles fought to defend the city. Dominating the other side of the square, with its beautiful halls and courtyards, the former **Hospital of the Knights** is now the **Archaeological Museum** (tel. 27 674). *(Open Tu-Su 8:30am-3pm. Admission 800dr, students 400dr, seniors 400dr.)* Its treasures include the small but exquisite *Aphrodite Bathing* from the first century BC and the 4th-century *Apollo.* The **Avenue of the Knights,** or Ipoton St., sloping uphill near the museum, was the main boulevard of the inner city 500 years ago. The Order of the Knights of St. John of Jerusalem consisted of seven different religious orders, called "tongues" because each spoke a different language. Their inns, now government offices that line both sides of Ipoton St., are not open to tourists. Because each tongue was responsible for guarding one segment of the city wall, parts of the wall are labeled "England" or "France" on the map.

At the top of the hill, a second archway leads to Kleovoulou Sq. To the right sits the pride of the city, the **Palace of the Grand Master** (tel. 23 359), with 300 rooms, moats, drawbridges, huge watch towers, and colossal battlements. *(Open Tu-F 8am-7pm, Sa-Su 8:30am-3pm. Admission 1200dr, students 600dr.)* The palace survived the long Ottoman siege of 1522 only to be devastated in 1856 by an explosion of 300-year-old ammunition forgotten in a depot across the street. The Italians began rebuilding the castle at the beginning of this century. Determined to outdo even the industrious Knights, they restored the citadel and embellished many of its floors with mosaics taken from Kos (see p. 441). The interior decoration was completed only a few months before the start of WWII, so the Italians had little chance to savor their fruits of their effort. For an indescribable bird's-eye view of the entire fortified city, wait patiently for a Tuesday or Saturday afternoon. Those with good balance and no fear of heights are permitted to walk along the city walls—an amazing, albeit brief, photo opportunity. *(Open Tu and Sa 2:45-3pm. Admission 1200dr, students 600dr.)*

Several blocks west of the south end of the Old Town off Diagoridon, a **stadium,** a small **theater,** and a **Temple of Apollo** have been partially reconstructed on the hill near Monte Smith. The stadium and theater are quite well preserved, but the temple lies in ruins. The few standing columns can be seen from the ferry; they're just before the last stretch of hotels. The only other pre-Roman site is the ruined 3rd-century BC **Temple of Aphrodite.**

The Hora

To experience a different era of the city's history, turn right into Kleovoulou Sq. after the palace. After passing under several arches, turn left onto Orfeos St., better known as the **Plane Tree Walk.** The large **clock tower** on the left marked the edges of the wall that separated the knights' quarters from the rest of the city. *(Open daily 9am-11pm. Admission 600dr.)* The setup was identical during the Ottoman Era, but the boundaries changed; the Old Town housed the Muslims and Jews, while the Christians lived outside its walls. Climbing the rock tower leads to a small cafe. The **Mosque of Süleyman,** one block from the clock tower, dates from the early 19th century with red-painted plaster walls, a garden, and a stone minaret. The original mosque on this site was built after Sultan Süleyman the Magnificent captured Rhodes in 1522. Its location makes it a good landmark in the Old Town. *(Closed to the public.)*

The **Turkish library,** built in 1793 opposite the mosque, is full of 15th- and 16th-century Persian and Arabic manuscripts. *(Open daily 10am-1pm and 4-7pm. Free, but donation expected.)* The other Ottoman-era buildings and monuments in the Old Town are in various states of decay. One worth your time is the 250-year-old baths, the **hamam** (tel. 27 739) in Arionos Sq. *(Open Tu 1-6pm, W-F 11am-6pm, Sa 8am-6pm. Admission 500dr.)* Notice the dome with small carved stars through which sunlight streams.

Leading downhill from the Mosque of Süleyman is the main shopping strip, **Sokratous St.** Formerly an Ottoman bazaar, today the street is lined with jewelry stores, restaurants, and junkshops, none likely to yield the bargains the former bazaar may once have. Continuing east along Aristotelous St., you'll reach **Martyron Evreon Square** (Square of the Jewish Martyrs) in the heart of the old Jewish Quarter. An integral part of Rhodes's history, the Jewish community had been present since the inception of the city. It was the flight of Sephardic Jews from Spain during the Inquisition that accounts for the Spanish flair in some of the old city's medieval architecture. In 1943, 2000 Jews were taken from this square to Nazi concentration camps; only 50 survived. A little way down Dossiadou St. is the **Shalom Synagogue,** restored by the survivors after the war. *(Services held Friday at 5pm. Modest dress is required.)* It is decorated by Oriental rugs covering the stone mosaic floor and hanging "eternal lamps." To see the interior, ask Lucia (who lives above it) to contact the caretaker, Mr. Soviano.

The New Town and Mandraki

If you look past the tasteless billboards and flashing advertisements, pearls of architectural ingenuity are shrouded behind the overwhelming display of consumer culture. Lush plant life, a rarity in the southern Aegean Islands, and old-growth trees fill parks and line sidewalks. Stately Italian architecture dominates the modern business district. Mussolini-inspired stone buildings preside over wide Eleftherias St. The bank, the town hall, the post office, and the National Theater are the more imposing structures on the inland side of the street. Directly opposite is the majestic **Governor's Palace** and a cathedral built by the Italians in 1925. The cathedral replicates St. John's Church, leveled in an 1856 explosion.

Named after Süleyman's admiral who died trying to capture Rhodes from the Knights of St. John in 1522, the **Mosque of Mourad Reis** is an important remnant of the Ottoman presence. The small, domed building inside is his mausoleum. Turbans indicate male graves, flowers indicate female ones.

Opposite the cemetery, **Villa Kleovoulos** served as author **Lawrence Durrell's** residence from 1945-1947, during his appointment with the Foreign Office. A number of Durrell's books are set in Greece, including his most celebrated *Reflections on a Marine Venus,* which takes place in Rhodes. A small plaque notes his time here.

Three defunct **windmills** stand halfway along the harbor's pier. The **Fortress of St. Nicholas** at the end of the pier, built in 1464, guarded the harbor until the end of WWII. *(Closed to the public.)* Greece's only **aquarium** (tel. 27 308 or 78 320), also a marine research center for the Dodecanese, is at the northern tip of the island. *(Open daily Apr.-Oct. 9am-9pm; Nov.-Mar. 9am-4:30pm. Admission 600dr, students 400dr.)* Various creatures of the Aegean depths are exhibited.

One long **beach** lines the north and west coast of the New Town. Although one of the least inviting on the island, beach-goers flock to the sand and sun, particularly on the west coast.

■ Faliraki Φαλιρακη

A smaller yet more concentrated collection of the modern and tourist-oriented vices that plague the New Town, Faliraki should be sampled in small doses unless you have a strong taste for the young, the restless, and the loud. Characterized by bars named for alcohol-induced impotence (e.g. The Brewer's Droop) or advertising wall-to-wall foam parties, the town attracts an audience that befits the scene. The raucous nightlife brings with it not only a shortage of peace and quiet but also a shortage of available accommodations—yet another reason to visit Faliraki as a daytrip.

ORIENTATION AND PRACTICAL INFORMATION Located 5km south of Kalithea and blessed with a sandy beach, Faliraki is a popular resort town. It consequently draws eager beach bunnies who shuffle between beach and bar throughout the day. Ermou St. is the main thoroughfare connecting the beach with the Rhodes-Lindos highway. There are two main bus stops in Faliraki, one on the Rhodes-Lindos road and one on the waterfront. Directly opposite the waterfront bus stop, to the right of Ermou St., is the **first aid station** (tel. 85 555). Dr. Zanettullis (tel. (094) 582 747) can be reached 24 hours a day if he's not at the station (open daily 8am-6pm). The **pharmacy** (tel. 85 998) is on the main road up to the highway; look for the green cross (open daily 9am-10:30pm). There is a **taxi stand** next to the waterfront bus stop. **Buses** run to Rhodes City (18 per day, 350dr). The bus from Faliraki to Lindos leaves from the waterfront bus stop (14 per day, 800dr). Faliraki is also a base for boat trips to Lindos (4000dr), Kos (11,000dr), and Symi (5000dr). The **Janus Travel Agency** (tel. 86 179 or 86 169), on Ermou St., offers **currency exchange, telephones,** and safe-deposit boxes (open daily 8:30am-10pm). The **Agricultural Bank** is on Ermou St. (open M-Th 8am-2pm, F 8am-1:30pm). A 24-hour **ATM** sits across the street. **Telephone code:** 0241.

ACCOMMODATIONS Lodgings in Faliraki are hard to find, especially in the high season, as most places rent their rooms to British package tour companies. **Hotel Edelweiss** (tel. 85 305; fax 85 944), on Ermou St., is an older hotel, centrally located for the beach and bars, which also offers currency exchange (doubles 8000-10,000dr). **Hotel Faliro** (tel. 85 483 or 85 399) offers rooms farther inland on Ermou St. (doubles 6000-8000dr). Rhodes's only **campsite** (tel. 85 516 or 85 358) is off the main road 1500m north of Faliraki; ask the bus driver to let you off (he may even take you there). Facilities include a TV, a disco/bar, a market, hot showers, and a pool.

FOOD Dining in Faliraki too often means inhaling a burger, greasy fries and a soda at any of the endless stretch of fast-food joints. **Crepes Time** (tel. (093) 288 200), Ermou St., serves a panoply of crepes all day and night (chocolate and banana 850dr, ham and cheese 850dr; open 9am-5am). **Sarantis** (tel. 85 501), on Rhodes-Lindos Ave. where Ermou St. ends, is a family-run restaurant with a seafood focus (dover sole 1950dr, cod 1750dr; open 5pm-midnight). Your other option is sugar—the tiny sweet shop halfway between the main road and the beach, between a tourist shop and a side street, serves the gooey kind of *baklava* that leaves honey dripping down your face (300dr, and worth every penny).

ENTERTAINMENT With each sunset, the sunburnt masses migrate inland from the beach toward uniformly priced beer (600-700dr) at jubilant bars on Ermou St.; later there is a second exodus to a handful of popular dance clubs. **Chaplin's** (tel. 85 662) is on Ermou St. by the beach. The beachside location makes it most popular during the day, especially during Friday afternoon karaoke competitions (shots 500dr). **Jimmy's Pub** (tel. 84 643), inland on Ermou St., is an ultra-British bar with the requisite Guinness on tap. Additional stimuli include soul music and TVs throughout the bar. **The Brewer's Droop** (tel. 85 944), a few doors down from Jimmy's Pub, shows daily movies and is the place to go for frozen margaritas; choose from banana, pineapple, melon, or strawberry (1500dr), or for the truly adventurous, a *frozen orgasm* (screaming or multiple). **Oscars** (tel. 87 450), near the Brewer's Droop, is named after the Faliraki tradition of wedding cinema with alcohol. Movies run all day with Happy Hour from 7 to 9:30pm and midnight to 2am. **Reflexions** (tel. 87 037), on the Rhodes-Faliraki St., attracts a diverse crowd who come for the hopping dance floor, friendly atmosphere, and theme nights. **Millennium** is on the Rhodes-Faliraki St., set back in a shopping center. Posh, new, and large, this is quickly becoming Faliraki's most popular dance club. **Q Club**, on the Rhodes-Faliraki St. closer to town, is a modern club with guest DJs and slightly older clientele.

■ Between Faliraki and Lindos

Eleven kilometers farther south, just before Kolymbia, a road to the right leads to **Epta Piges.** Constructed by Italians seeking potable water for nearby Kolymbia, the aqueduct today quenches thrill-seekers instead of thirst. A trip through the 150-meter pitch-black tunnel incites screams, laughs, and sickness. Both scathed and unscathed (there's no turning around) exit the tunnel into a large freshwater pool—picturesque and refreshing. To skip the tunnel and head straight for the pool, take the path next to the tunnel which is used to return from the pool. A decent streamside *taverna* with peacocks sits at the entrance before the tunnel. There's no direct bus service; ask any Lindos/Archangelos bus driver to let you off there. Continue inland past Epta Piges to visit the Byzantine **Church of Agios Nikolaos Fountoucli,** 3km past Eleousa, which has 13th- and 15th-century frescoes. **Buses** stop at Eleousa (3 per day) on the way to Rhodes. Villagers in **Arthipoli,** 4km away, rent rooms.

Back along the coast road, the turn-off to **Kolymbia** leads to a eucalyptus-lined road, also lined with disappointing tourist shops. At the end of town, a large sandy beach abuts the southern cliff and is popular with the local package tour hotels. From Rhodes, buses reach Kolymbia Beach 10 times a day (600dr).

From the coast road, **Tsambikas Monastery** is best marked by the restaurant that sits below it. A 1km road leads up to the restaurant and the Byzantine cloister and its panoramic views rest 1km farther up a steep walking trail. The monastery was named after sparks (*tsambas*) that locals claimed to have seen atop the hill. Upon climbing to the church, the locals discovered an icon of the Virgin Mary that had mysteriously appeared from Cyprus. Angry Cypriots ordered that the icon be returned, and the locals obliged. This bizarre occurrence repeated itself; by the third time, Cypriots agreed that Rhodes must be the icon's proper home. To this day, infertile women ascend the mountain to pray to the Virgin Mary for fertility. Before attempting this ritual, child-seeking visitors should be aware of a catch: should the prayer prove successful, the baby must be named Tsambikos if a boy, and Tsambika if a girl—perhaps not what you had picked out from your baby name book. One bus runs to the long and flat **Tsambika Beach,** 1km south of the turnoff for the monastery along the coast road (650dr); however, any bus that passes the turnoff should let you off here.

Roughly 10km farther down the road from Tsambikas (15km north of Lindos), take the turn-off to **Charaki.** The beach lies next to a hill topped by the crumbling **Castle of Feracios.** Constructed in 1306, this was the Knights of St. John's first stomping ground on Rhodes. The meager ruins remaining today barely warrant the arduous hike up to reach them. Rooms and restaurants line the beach. **Buses** to Charaki (2 per day, 750dr) leave from Rhodes (Rimini Sq.).

■ Lindos Λινδος

> Nothing in excess.
>
> —Cleoboulos

With whitewashed houses clustered beneath a castle-capped acropolis, Lindos is perhaps the most picturesque town in Rhodes. Vines and flowers line narrow streets, and pebble mosaics carpet courtyards. Charm like this cannot stay a secret for long, and Lindos's hasn't. In summer, Lindos's packed streets make crowds in the City of Rhodes pale in comparison, and shop owners take advantage of the masses by charging astronomical prices for food and services. Lindos is also notoriously hot and short of rooms in the summer and is a better place to visit outside of high season.

ORIENTATION AND PRACTICAL INFORMATION Lindos is a pedestrian-only city. All traffic stops at **Eleftherias Square,** where the bus and taxi stations are situated. **Buses** run to Lindos from Rimini Sq. in Rhodes. Arrive early; they fill quickly. **Excursion boats** from Rhodes depart at 9am and return at 5pm, stopping elsewhere on the coast, including Rhodes City and Turkey. Buses connect Lindos to Rhodes Town (16 per day, 950dr); Faliraki (14 per day, 800dr); Pefkos (9 per day, 250dr); Esperides (3 per day, 800dr); and Kolymbia Beach (2 per day, 650dr).

Past the **Telebank** 24-hour **ATM, Acropolis St.** leads through the eastern part of town and up to the acropolis. **Apostolou Pavlou St.,** another main street, runs perpendicular to Acropolis St. just past the **Church of the Assumption of Madonna,** whose stone belfry rises above the middle of town. Houses are distinguished only by frequently changing numbers.

The rather unhelpful **municipal tourist office** (tel./fax 31 288 or 31 900) in Eleftherias Sq. offers **currency exchange** and sells maps (open daily 8am-9:30pm). Their best selection is the watercolor "Lindos-Illustrated Map" (800dr). **Pallas Travel** (tel. 31 494; fax 31 595), on Acropolis St., has an even better map of Lindos (free), offers currency exchange, and can arrange various excursions (open M-Sa 8am-10pm, Su 9am-1pm and 5-10pm). Critical and not-so-critical services line the intersection of Apostolou Pavlou St. and Acropolis St. The **National Bank** is near this junction on Apostolou Pavlou St. (open M-Th 9am-2pm, F-Sa 9am-1:30pm), as is the **pharmacy** (tel. 31 294; open M-Sa 9am-11pm, Su 9am-3pm), just past Yianni's Bar. Sheila Markiou, an American expat, runs the superb **Lindos Lending Library** (tel. 31 443) with more than 7000 English, Italian, German, French, and Greek books. To get there, walk to Pallas Travel and bear right where the road forks; the library is up and to the left (open M-Sa 9am-8pm, Su 9am-4pm). Sheila also runs a **laundry** service out of the store (1800dr wash, dry, and soap). The **medical clinic** (tel. 31 224) is to the left before the church (open M-Sa 9am-1:30pm and 6-8pm; 24hr. for emergencies). There are **public toilets** across from the information office near the taxi/bus station (100dr). The **police** are at 521 Ap. Pavlou St. (tel. 31 223; open M-F 8am-3pm, 24hr. for emergencies). The **post office** (tel. 31 214) is just uphill and to the right of the donkey stand (open M-F 7:30am-2pm). **Postal code:** 85107. **Telephone code:** 0244.

ACCOMMODATIONS Package tours hog even the tiniest pensions, making Lindos a difficult place to spend the night—virtually impossible in August. One option is to arrive in the morning before the tour buses rumble in and ask the tour companies' offices if they have any empty rooms. **Pension Electra** (tel. 31 266) is on Acropolis St. From the main square, take the first left downhill after the donkey stand and follow signs for the Acropolis; at the end, follow the turn-off with stairs for the Acropolis; continue downhill toward the beach. The pension offers a garden, terrace, and clean rooms. Look past the crumbling exteriors of neighboring buildings. Rooms include private bath, A/C, and fridge (doubles 12,000dr; triples 14,000dr). **Pension Katholiki** sits just above Pension Venus, with more basic rooms. Inquire at 57 Acropolis St. (doubles 10,000dr). **Tereza Hatzinikola Rooms to Let** (tel. 31 765) is next to Milos wine bar on a small street off Apostolou St., past the supermarkets. You'll find clean, homey rooms (doubles 8000dr). To find **"506" Zinovia Houriri Rooms and Studios** (tel. 31 220), from the main square walk along Apostolou St. past the National Bank. Turn left at Lindian House, then right when the road splits. The grandmotherly owner offers basic rooms with shared baths (singles 6000dr; doubles 7000dr).

FOOD AND ENTERTAINMENT Eating on a budget, like sleeping, also poses a challenge in Lindos. Restaurant prices range from expensive to exorbitant. The only cheap alternatives are *souvlaki-pita* bars, *creperies* (crepes start at 600dr), and grocery stores on the two main streets. "Snack bar" shops serve the healthiest option in Lindos (yogurt with honey and fresh fruit 500-700dr). **Cyprus Taverna** (tel. 31 539) has rooftop tables below the acropolis where you can dine on Greek food with a Cypriot twist (*stifado* 1700dr, *hummus* 500dr). **Chinatown** (tel. 31 983), from Apostolou Pavlou St. downhill towards the beach, has a Greek patio with Chinese lamps (sweet and sour chicken 1700dr, *satay* 1700dr, curry 1800dr; open daily 6pm-1am).

To prepare for the climb to the acropolis, or refuel upon your descent, stop off at **Il Forno Bakery** around the corner from the bookstore. Authentic *focaccia* (400dr) and *panzerotti* (700dr) draw constant crowds (open M-Sa 8am-9pm, Su 8am-1pm). In an inviting courtyard near the National Bank of Greece, **Gelo Blu** (tel. 31 761) serves 18 flavors of delicious *gelato* made from natural ingredients (from 600dr). Good—and potent—espresso, cappuccino, and refreshing iced drinks accompany the chocolate fudge cake (open daily 9am-1am). **Ta Mezedakia** (tel. 43 627) is a 10-minute drive south of Lindos in Gennadi. From Lindos, this family-run restaurant requires wheels or a hefty hike, but those who do venture here will find the seafood freshly caught by the owner and the prices cheap (open daily noon-1am).

Lindos's nightlife is relatively tame; municipal law requires music to stop at midnight. If you are not ready to call it a day, head to **Amphitheatre** (tel. (093) 288 549), an open-air nightclub not far out of town. Free cabs shuttle you from Lindos square to the dance floor, where you can rage with a view of both the acropolis and the sea (open daily midnight-4am; 1000dr includes first drink). Less energetic types might try **Antika,** on Apostolou Pavlou St. in the center of town. This beautiful bar, enhanced by a pebble mosaic floor and lush indoor garden, has board games, monthly foreign magazines, and daily papers (pint of beer 500dr; open daily 5pm-1am). The **Museum Bar** (tel. 31 446) is another more subdued option. Watch CNN, MTV, ESPN, or even the Discovery Channel on one of their three televisions. The sangria is fruity and refreshing (1000dr) and the coffee freshly brewed (400-600dr).

SIGHTS Lindos's premier attraction, the ancient **acropolis,** stands amid scaffolding at the top of sheer cliffs 125m above town. *(Open M 12:30-6:40pm, Tu-Sa 8am-7:40pm. Admission 1200dr, students 600dr.)* The walls of a Crusader fortress further enclose the caged structure. Excavations by the Danish Archaeological School between 1902 and 1912 yielded everything from 5000-year-old neolithic tools to a plaque inscribed by a priest of Athena in 99 BC listing the dignitaries who visited Athena's Temple—Hercules, Helen of Troy, Menelaus, Alexander the Great, and the King of Persia. The winding path up to the acropolis is veiled in lace tablecloths sold by local women; the cobwebbed pall makes for a surreal ascent. Right before the final incline, don't miss the ancient Greek *trireme,* which the artist Pythocretos carved into the cliffside as a symbol of Lindos's inextricable ties with the sea. Lined with staircases, the daunting 13th-century **Crusader castle** looms over the entrance to the site. As you leave the castle, make a U-turn to your left to reach the imposing **Doric Stoa** (arcade), whose 13 restored columns dominate the entire level. The arcade, built around 200 BC at the height of Rhodes's glory, originally consisted of 42 columns laid out in the shape of the Greek letter "Π." The large stone blocks arranged against the back wall served as bases for bronze statues which have been long since melted down. The **Temple of the Lindian Athena** comes into view at the top of the steps. According to legend, a temple was built here as early as 1510 BC. All that remains today are parts of the temple built by the tyrant Cleoboulos in the 6th century BC. Once a tremendously important religious site, it's now one of the few ancient temples with inner walls still fairly intact; colonnades flank both sides. Donkey rides to the acropolis are a rip-off (1000dr one way); the 10-minute walk is not too strenuous. Cleoboulos's tomb is across the way, inscribed with his timeless maxim, "Nothing in excess."

The graceful stone bell tower projecting from the middle of town belongs to the **Church of the Assumption of Madonna,** rebuilt by the Knights of St. John in 1489. *(Open daily 9am-1pm and 3-5pm. Modest dress required.)* Brightly colored 18th-century frescoes, retouched by the Italians in 1927, illuminate the interior. At the southwest foot of the acropolis are the remains of the **ancient theater.** The **Voukopion** is on the north side of the rock face, visible from the donkey path. This cave, which the Dorians transformed into a sanctuary for Athena, is believed to date from the 9th century BC and may have been used for special sacrifices that could be performed only outside the acropolis.

■ Western and Southern Rhodes

Ialyssos and Filerimos

A string of high-rise hotels abuts the 8km stretch of sand west of Rhodes. The west end of this luxury hotel district is the town of modern **Ialyssos** (Trianda). The hotels were built in the late 60s and early 70s under Greece's military dictatorship. Along with Lindos and Kamiros, Ialyssos was once one of the three great cities on the island. The ruins, 5km south of present-day Ialyssos, are rather meager. Most impressive are the 4th-century BC **Doric fountain** ornamented with four lion heads, the adjacent **Filerimos monastery,** and the **Church of Our Lady of Filerimos** (actually four conjoined chapels). The church and monastery occupy the site of a 3rd-century BC **Tem-**

ple to Athena and Zeus Polias. *(Open Tu-F 8:30am-2pm, Sa-M 8:30am-3pm. Admission 800dr, students 400dr.)* On the stone floor just inside the doorway of the room to the left rests a remnant of the original Byzantine structure—a fish, the symbol of Christ, carved into one of the red stones. The path past the chapel leads to the ruins of a Byzantine castle. Unfortunately, there is no easily negotiable road to Filerimos, but taxis from Rimini Sq. will make the trek for 3000dr round trip. Aside from a moped or a bike, the only alternative is the bus from Rhodes to Ialyssos (6 per day, 250dr).

Kremasti and Paradisi

Four kilometers along the coast south of modern Ialyssos, **Kremasti** is discernibly wealthier than surrounding towns, thanks to an influx of money from Rhodian expats in the United States. The result is markedly different from towns whose wealth derives from tourism. Evidence includes the stately *platia*, where the church, a playground, and a Greek Orthodox Men's Club bustle around the clock and the free-lined main street with trendy cafes and restaurants. **Paradisi** lies 3km south of Kremasti and next to the Rhodes airport. **Athinea** (tel. 82 762), along the main road, serves some of the island's better Greek food (*kleftiko* 1500dr, octopus 1400dr; open 6pm-2am).

Valley of Butterflies

Six km inland from the village of **Theologos, Petaloudes,** or **Valley of Butterflies,** is a popular visiting spot, whether the fluttering ones are present or not. During the summer, Jersey tiger moths flock to the valley's Styrax trees, attracted to a resin that is also used in making incense. While resting to live out their final days in the trees, the moths fast, living only on water and body fat, in order to conserve energy for rigorous mating sessions. After the deed is done, they die of starvation. The valley is accessible from a lower entrance next to an old mill, or from the main entrance, which is farther uphill. The trail winds around a stream and past miniature waterfalls along cute little bridges. The valley and its many trees are worth a walk throughout the year, but are a particularly welcoming reprieve from summer's sun-beaten coasts. Valley-goers should note that noise interrupts the moths' reproduction process, and should refrain from joining other visitors in clapping or stomping to incite the moths to flight.

Monolithos and the South

Monolithos, on the island's southwest tip, is a tiny collection of scattered houses. The **Castle of Monolithos,** 2km west, is well worth the trip. In ruins, the fortress sits at the summit of a 160m-high rock pillar, and visitors can still walk inside. To get there, follow the only western road out of town. Despite its uninspired name, Monolithos' **Restaurant/Bar Greek Food** has decent entrees. One bus leaves Rhodes daily for Monolithos via Embona and Ag. Isidoros (2½hr., 1500dr). Here in farm and goat-herding country, grassy yellow flatlands slope gradually into hills studded with low-lying shrubs. **Buses** run daily to village of Lardos (6 per day, 950dr).

KOS Κως

> Cos is the spoiled child of the group. You know it at once without even going ashore. It is green, luxuriant, and a little dishevelled.
>
> —Lawrence Durrell

The booming nightclubs and packed bars of modern Kos don't pay adequate tribute to the impressive history of the island. In ancient times, Kos was a major trading power with a population of 160,000—eight times that of today. An episcopal seat of the Byzantine Empire, the island became a target for predatory naval forces. The Knights of St. John prevailed in 1315, seizing control and turning Kos into one of their outposts. Since then, its history has mirrored that of the other Dodecanese in passing under Italian, German, and British governments.

DODECANESE

The citizens of Kos are perhaps the island's biggest claim to fame. As the sacred land of Asclepius, god of healing, it seems appropriate that **Hippocrates,** the father of medicine, would also be from Kos. His 2400-year-old oath to healing is still taken by doctors. Not to be outdone by science, the island has also produced major contributors to literature. Both Theocritus and his teacher Philetas wrote their poetry here.

Today, Kos's secure position as one of the major stops on the tourist island hopping circuit draws an appropriate crowd. Rivalling Rhodes in terms of sheer numbers, it tends to draw a younger, louder, more intoxicated crowd. The raucous bars and mammoth hotels that line the otherwise golden beaches may dismay a casual traveler. Perseverance rewards those who take the time to look in the quiet nooks and glimpse traditional Kos hospitality.

■ Kos Town

In Kos Town, minarets of Ottoman mosques stand beside grand Italian mansions and the massive walls of a Crusader fortress. The town is a repository of Archaic, Classical, Hellenistic, and Roman ruins. Unfortunately, it is also one of the more expensive places to visit in the Dodecanese. Package tour agents have made contracts with many of the pensions, leaving very few rooms for independent travelers. Rooming difficulties aside, the combination of ancient, medieval, and modern styles make Kos a historian's paradise by day, while a profusion of bars and clubs makes it a top destination for travelers focusing on nighttime activity.

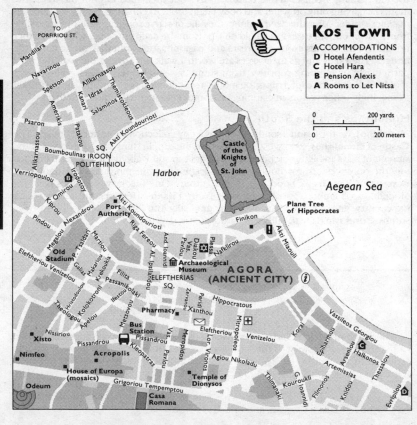

ORIENTATION AND PRACTICAL INFORMATION

The colossal walls of the Castle of the Knights of St. John overwhelm the vista as ferries pull into the harbor of Kos Town. If, facing inland, you walk left from the harbor, the stately trees framing the **Avenue of Palms** (also called Finikon Street) make the island feel less imposing. Continuing along the waterfront past the Palms leads to **Vas. Georgios St.** and the rocky beach alongside it. Turn right onto the Palms and follow it to the next corner of the fortress and you will come upon **Akti Kountouriotou St.**, another waterfront street that wraps around the harbor. The city bus station, boats to Turkey, travel agencies, restaurants, and Kos' thriving nightlife can all be found here. Branching off Akti Koundouriotou St. inland are the town's main arteries. **Venizelou St.** leads through a row of travel agencies directly into the shopping district. **Megalou Alexandrou St.**, a few blocks down, heads to **Palaiologou Square,** the ruins of ancient Kos Town, and eventually to the inland villages. The town's other sandy beach begins near the end of Akti Koundauriotou.

Transportation

Ferries: Service to Peiraias (11-15hr., 2-3 per day, 7536dr); Rhodes (4hr., 2 per day, 3460dr); Kalymnos (1¼hr., 1-3 per day, 2415dr); Leros (2½hr., 1 per day, 2090dr); Patmos (4hr., 1-2 per day, 2768dr); Paros (1 per week, 4331dr); Naxos (1 per week, 4242dr); Syros (1 per week, 6138dr); Mykonos (1 per week, 5078dr); Tinos (1 per week, 5282dr); Nisyros (2 per week, 1766dr); Tilos (1952dr); Symi (2 per week, 2537dr); Astypalea (1 per week, 3040dr); Kastelorizo (1 per week, 4348dr); Ikaria (3753dr); and Amorgos (1 per week, 4195dr). **Greek boats** run to Bodrum, Turkey (near ancient Halicarnassus) every morning (12,000dr round-trip). **Turkish boats** leave in the afternoon and return the next morning (15,000dr round-trip). Since travel is international, it is not regulated by the Greek government—shop around and ask for student discounts. **Port Authority** (tel. 26 594) is at the corner of Negalou Alexandrou St. and Akti Kountouriotou St. Open 24hr.

Flying Dolphins: Two per day to Kalymnos (3150dr); Leros (4325dr); Patmos (5920dr); and Samos (6470dr). Two per week to Tilos (3640dr); Agathonisi (5980dr); and Astypalea (5850dr). Also Symi (1 per week, 4690dr); Lipsi (6 per week, 3600dr); Nisyros (3 per week, 3640dr); Fourni (3 per week, 7080dr); and Rhodes (2 per day, 6950dr).

Flights: Olympic Airways, 22 Vas. Pavlou St. (tel. 28 331 or 28 332). To Athens (2-3 per day, 21,800dr) and Rhodes (2 per week, 9800dr). Open M-F 8am-3:30pm. On Sa-Su, call 51 567. Olympic runs a **bus** (1000dr) from Kos Town to the airport 2-4 times per day. Schedule posted. Kardamena or Kefalos buses can let you off near the airport. Taxis from Kos Town to the airport cost 5000-5500dr.

Buses: (tel. 22 292). Leave from Kleopatras St. near the inland end of Pavlou St. behind the Olympic Airways office. Service to Tigaki (30min., 12 per day, 300dr); Marmari (35min., 11 per day, 300dr); Asfendiou-Zia (40min., 3 per day, 300dr); Pyli (30min., 5 per day, 300dr); Mastihari (35min., 5 per day, 460dr); Antimachia (40min., 6 per day, 370dr); Kardamena (45min., 6 per day, 500dr); and Kefalos/Paradise (1hr., 6 per day, 700dr). Roughly half of the buses run on Sundays. Full schedule posted by the stop. Tickets are purchased on the bus.

City Buses: 7 Akti Kountouriotou St. (tel. 26 276), on the water. Fares 150-250dr, to: Agios Fokas (57 per day); Lampi (25 per day); Thermae (20min., 9 per day); Marmaroto (8 per day); and Asclepion (15min., 16 per day).

Taxis: (tel. 22 777), near the inland end of the Avenue of Palms.

Moped/Bike rentals: Laws restricting rentals to those with proper motorbike licenses are more strictly enforced here than on other islands. However, driving behavior does little to reflect this. Those renting should exert caution when driving, particularly at night when the young and the restless also become inebriated. **Sernikos,** 19 Herodotou St. (tel. 23 670). Take your first right off Megalou Alexandrou St. and go 2 blocks. **Mike's** (tel. 21 729), corner of Amerikis St. and Psaron St. At both service-oriented places, mopeds go from 2500dr; bikes 500-1000dr.

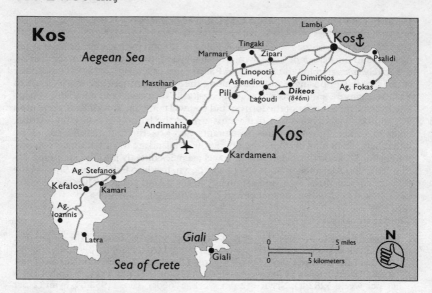

Tourist and Information Services

Tourist Office: (tel. 28 724, 24 460), at Akri Miaouli St., Hippokratous St., and Vas. Georgiou St. Free maps (kiosks sell the same map for 250-300dr), information on excursions, events, lodgings, and ferry and hydrofoil schedules. Open M-F 7:30am-9pm, Sa 7:30am-3pm.

Tourist Agencies: No single agency in Kos has comprehensive boat information. Two large ferry companies (DANE and GA) and two hydrofoil lines (Ilio and Dodecanese) serve Kos and its neighbors. **Pulia Tours,** 3 Vas Pavlou St. (tel. 26 388 or 21 130; fax 26 388), near the waterfront end of this main road, sells DANE and hydrofoil tickets, organizes day excursions, offers **currency exchange** and helps in finding rooms. Open daily 7am-11pm. **GA Office** (tel. 28 545; fax 24 864), on Vas Pavlou St. across from the National Bank, serves the other ferry and hydrofoil lines, and offers similar tourist services. Open daily 8:30am-10pm.

Banks: National Bank (tel. 28 517), in back of the Archaeological Museum, 1 block inland from the water on A.P. Ioannidi. 24hr. Cirrus/MC **ATM.** Open M-Th 8am-2pm, F 8am-1:30pm. **Commercial Bank,** 7 Vas. Pavlou St. (tel. 28 825), inland from the City Bus station, advances money on Visa. Open M-Th 8am-2pm, F 8am-1:30pm. After hours, **exchange currency** at travel agencies along the waterfront.

American Express: (tel. 26 732). Follow Akti Koundouriotou St. to the dolphin fountain and look for it at the corner of Boubouliras St. Full AmEx services for cardholders. Open M-Sa 9am-2pm and 5-9pm.

Laundromat: 124 Alikarnassou St. Walk 2 blocks off Megalou Alexandrou St. on Kyprou St. Wash, dry, and soap 1500dr. Open M-F 8:30am-1:30pm and 5-9:30pm, Sa 8:30am-4pm.

Emergency and Communications

Police: (tel. 22 100). On Akti Miaouli St. in the large yellow building next to the castle. Some English spoken. Open 24hr. **Tourist police** (tel. 22 444), in the same building. Open daily 7:30am-2pm.

Pharmacies: 5 Va. Pavlou St. (tel. 22 346), next to the Commercial Bank. Open M-Tu and Th-F 8:30am-2pm and 5-9:30pm, W and Sa 8:30am-2pm. After hours, check the door for the number and address of the on-call pharmacy.

Hospital: (tel. 28 050). On Mitropoleas St., between El. Venizelou St. and Hippocrates St. **Emergency:** (tel. 22 300). **Information:** (tel. 28 013). Open 24hr.

Post Office: 14 Venizelou St. (tel. 22 250). Follow signs from Vas. Pavlou St., which lead past Eleftherias Sq. and the fruit market, and turn left onto Venizelou St. Open M-F 7:30am-2pm. **Postal Code:** 85300.

Internet Access: Del Mar Internet Cafe, 4a Meg. Alexandrou (tel. 24 244), offers an expensive and limited on-line service.

OTE: (tel. 22 499). Around the corner from post office, at the corner of T Virona and Xanthou. Open M 8a 7:30am-10pm, Su 8am-10pm. **Telephone Code:** 0242.

ACCOMMODATIONS

Hotel vacancies are rare during July and August, so start searching for rooms early. Most inexpensive places are on the right side of town if you're facing inland. It is best to seek out your own room (the dock hawks in Kos are notorious), but if your boat docks in the middle of the night, you may have no choice. Camping on the beach or in the park along the Avenue of Palms is illegal. Prices are 20-40% lower off season.

⊕Pension Alexis, 9 Herodotou St. (tel. 28 798, 25 594), first right off Meg. Alexandrou St., on the back left corner of the first intersection. Incomparable hospitality. If rooms are full, the proprietor will put you up with a mattress and sheets on the patio (1200dr) or cut you a deal at his elegant **Hotel Afendoulis** in the ritzier part of town. Balconies, common baths, and a guest book dating back to 1979. Prices flexible, especially if you are carrying *Let's Go*. Doubles 5500-7000dr; triples 7500dr. Breakfast 800dr.

Hotel Afendoulis, 1 Evrilpilou St. (tel./fax 25 321 or 25 797). Evrilpilou is right down Vas. Georgiou. Well-kept rooms with private baths in a quiet part of town near the beach. Doubles 7500-9000dr. Breakfast 800dr. Ask about the cellar rooms that go for cheaper rates.

Rooms to Let Nitsa, 47 Averof St. (tel. 25 810), near the beach north of town. Super-clean rooms with baths and kitchenettes. Doubles 7000dr; triples 9000dr.

Hotel Hara (tel. 22 500, 23 198), corner of Chalkonos St. and Arseniou St., 1 block inland from the water. All rooms are large; those upstairs are nicer. Private phones, baths, and towels provided. Singles 6600dr; doubles 8500dr; triples 10,500dr. Flash your *Let's Go* for a free room upgrade.

Meropis Hotel, 5 Meropidos St. (tel. 22 789), near the post office. Rooms with shared bath are old and basic, but clean. Singles 3000dr; doubles 4000dr.

Anna Sofou Rooms, 1 Artemisias (tel. 26 158), where Venizelou St. becomes Artemisias St. Rooms with shared bath are even more basic and refurbishing rooms and baths wouldn't hurt, but cheap by Kos Town standards. Doubles 4000-5000dr.

FOOD

As a rule, try to avoid the waterfront cafes and restaurants—any hope of finding good, cheap food lies farther inland. The fruit and vegetable **market** in Eleftherias Sq. on Vas. Pavlou St. is inside a large yellow building with a picture of grapes over the doors. It caters to tourists and is therefore expensive. Cheaper fruit can be found in mini-markets (open M-F 7am-9pm, Sa 7am-6pm, Su 10am-2pm).

Hellas, 7 Psaron St. (tel. 24 790), at corner of Amerikis. Serves immense portions of touristy, yet well-prepared Greek dishes. Lamb *kleftiko* 1500dr, *moussaka* 1200dr. Good vegetarian options available. Open noon-1am.

Ampavris (tel. 25 696). Take the road past the Casa Romana; about 15min. walk from town. A true diamond in the rough and one of the few places on Kos to find authentic cuisine. Stuffed flower buds 900dr, Greek salad 700dr.

To Cohili, 64 Alikarnasou (tel. 25 000), at corner of Amerikis St. Serves self-described "slow-food" in and around a cute pink house. Traditional Greek, octopus (1100dr), and other varied dishes, chick-pea burger (750dr).

Nick the Fisherman, 21 Averof St. (tel. 23 098), at corner of Alikarnasou St. Daily catches straight to your plate. Mussels (1600dr), sea-urchins (1500dr).

Cafe Aenous (tel. 26 044) serves light meals and drinks in a former mosque, with prime outdoor seating in Eleftherias Sq.

Far East, 3 Bouboulinas St. (tel. 20 969), next to the waterfront by the dolphin rotary. The best place in town to get your fix for Chinese food. Try the cashew chicken (1500dr) or sweet 'n' sour spare ribs (1500dr).

ENTERTAINMENT

Kos Town's pub-, bar-, and club-oriented nightlife is famous throughout the Greek islands. Prepare for crowds of people wearing skin-tight clothing and looking for a good time. Most bars are in two districts: the first includes the streets of **Exarhia** between Akti Koundouriotou St. and the ancient *agora,* and the area around Vas. Pavlou St. Beers will cost you 500-800dr at any of these places, and cocktails about 1200dr. Most places open at 9pm, fill by 11pm, and keep kickin' until about 4am. The second district is **Porfiriou St.** in the north near the beach, where drinks are cheaper and the atmosphere is more subdued.

Fashion Club, 2 Kanari St. (tel. 22 592), by the dolphin statue rotary. Kitsch (peanut-vending machines) meets *de rigueur* (elegant candles) at Kos's most ostentatious club. The friendly dance floor isn't nearly as prententious as the bouncers would have you think. 2500dr cover includes first drink. No cover (just attitude) for the large TV-filled cafe in front.

Saloon Tex. If you can squeeze in, this is surely the liveliest place around the *agora* to shake your thing—on the floor, on tables, on the bar. Drinks cost 200-300dr more than elsewhere.

Heaven (tel. 23 874), on Zouroudi St. along the waterfront. Appropriate cabana theme for being opposite the beach. This disco is large, loud, outdoor, and popular. 2000dr cover includes first drink and is sometimes waived early in the evening.

Galatea. A wood-paneled, slightly futuristic setting provides background for the friendly and lively bar near the *agora.*

Hamam Club (tel. 24 938), near the *agora,* next to the taxi station. In a large exotic former bath house, today it refreshes and soothes with happy hour (8-10pm), live acoustic sets until midnight, and a hopping dance club later on.

Ano Otak, 57 Kanari St. (tel. 29 146), a couple blocks north of Fashion Club. Touches of class are wasted on the package tour set, but the club fills up early.

System Bolaget, 3 Porfirou St. The name—Swedish for "liquor store"—aptly sums up this watering hole where blond hair and blue eyes prevail.

Pub Cuckoo's Nest, across from System Bolaget on Porfirou St., is humbler than many of Kos's drinking spots, and prone to deals (free shot with beer, 500dr).

SIGHTS

The panoply of architectural styles here attests to Kos's constant changes in ownership. The field of ruins bounded by Nafklirou St., Hippocrates St., and the waterfront, is the **agora,** now dominated by a thriving cat population that sunbathes among the ruins. *(Open 24hr. Free.)* You will find a **Temple of Aphrodite** and a more impressive 2nd-century AD **Temple of Hercules** here. Two short stairways off Grigoriou St., which runs along the southern edge of town, descend to the ruins. The main roads intersect Grigoriou St. 1km from the sea. The site itself is bordered by two Roman roads: the **Cardo** (axis), perpendicular to Grigoriou St., and the **Decumana** (broadest), parallel to Grigoriou St. and intersecting Cardo St. An ancient gymnasium, a swimming pool from the Roman era, and an early Christian basilica built over a Roman bath are all nearby. At the end of the Decumana, the 3rd-century AD **House of Europa,** protected under a modern wooden shelter, has a mosaic floor depicting Europa's abduction by a bullish Zeus. *(Open 24hr. Free.)*

The **odeum,** a well-preserved ancient Roman theater, is across the street. *(Open 24hr. Free.)* The 3rd-century AD **Casa Romana,** uncovered by an Italian archaeologist in 1933, is down Grigoriou St. These ruins concealed the remnants of an even older (5th century BC) and more striking Hellenic mansion. *(Open Tu-Su 8:30am-3pm. Admission 600dr, students and seniors 300dr.)* The meager ruins of a **Temple of Dionysus** are opposite the Casa Romana.

The 15th-century **Castle of the Knights of St. John** was reinforced with elaborate double walls and inner moats in response to 16th-century Ottoman raids. *(Open Tu-Su 8am-2pm. Admission 800dr, students 400dr.)* As a result, it withstood innumerable attacks and is one of the best preserved examples of medieval architecture in all of Greece. Cross a bridge from the Plane Tree to enter the castle. The Order of St. John on Kos was originally dedicated to healing the sick, but you would never know it from the size of the fortifications.

Before crossing the bridge, between the Palms and the ruins of the agora, you will see the gigantic **Plane Tree of Hippocrates,** allegedly planted by the great physician 2400 years ago. The tree, with a 12m diameter, is actually 500 years old; nonetheless, Hippocrates is said to have taught pupils and written books under its foliage. A spring next to the tree leads to an ancient sarcophagus that the Ottomans used as a cistern for the nearby **Hadji Hassan Mosque.** Behind the tree, the monumental former **Town Hall,** originally the Italian Governor's Palace, now houses police, justice, and governmental offices. The most impressive Ottoman structure is the **Defterdar Mosque** in Eleftherias Sq. Nearby, on Diakou St., is the abandoned Art Deco **Synagogue of Kos,** in use until WWII. The city's Byzantine **Greek Orthodox Cathedral** looms large on the corner of Korai and Agios Nikolaou St.

The **archaeological museum** (tel. 28 326) is on the left in Eleftherias Sq., up Vas. Pavlou St. *(Open Tu-Su 8am-2pm. Admission 800dr, students 400dr. No photographs permitted.)* Highlights include the celebrated statue of Hippocrates found at the Odeon of Kos. It now stands in the northwest room. A 2nd-century AD Roman mosaic in the central courtyard depicts Hippocrates and a colleague entertaining the god Asclepios.

Farmers and claustrophobes will be pleasantly surprised at how quickly Kos Town's urban fracas gives way to a pastoral setting north of town. Much of the island's northern section is flat, and many roads have bike lanes that provide easy access to any number of beaches. If you take the main road east of town, you will pedal past a sandy, crowded stretch on the way to the hot springs of **Thermae,** located near the road's end. **Lampi Beach** is at the northernmost tip of the island. Going west from there will take you all the way to the tourist stripmall of **Tigaki** (10km west of Kos). The waterfront road is interrupted at **Aliki Lake,** so turn inland and cycle past fields with grazing livestock on the road parallel to the highway. **Marmari** and **Mastihari** are pleasant, longer rides away. A hat and map are essential. If cycling does not interest you, buses run to Thermae (9 per day), Lampi (34 per day), Marmari (10 per day), and Mastinari (4 per day), but rides are often snug.

■ Asclepion Ασκληπειον

*4km west of Kos Town. The site is easily reached by **bus** in summer (15min., 16 per day), or by bike or moped, if you follow the sign west off the main road and continue as straight as possible. Taxis cost about 500dr. **Open** June-Sept. Tu-Su 8:30am-7pm. **Admission** 800dr, students 400dr.*

The ancient sanctuary Asclepion is dedicated to the god of healing. In the 5th century BC, Hippocrates opened the world's first medical school and encouraged the development of a precise science of medicine. Combining early priestly techniques with his own, Hippocrates made Kos the foremost medical center in ancient Greece. Many new doctors still travel here to take their oaths.

Most of the ruins at the Asclepion actually date from the 3rd century BC. The complex was built into a hill on five terraces that overlook Kos Town and the Aegean. Remains of the ancient buildings are plentiful; it is easy to envision the structures as they once stood if you can ignore the swarms of tourists. A forest of cypress and pine trees, sacred in ancient times, adjoins the site, and 2nd-century AD Roman baths are inside. Explore the *natatio* (pool), the *tepidarium* (room of intermediate temperature), and the *caldarium* (sauna).

The most interesting remains at Asclepion are in the three stacked levels, called *andirons.* These contain the **School of Medicine,** statues of deities, and a figure of Pan, the mythical half-goat-half-human. Climb the 30 steps to the second *andiron* to see the best-preserved remains of the Asclepion, the elegant columns of the 2nd-century BC **Temple of Apollo,** and the 4th-century BC **Minor Temple of Asclepios.** The 60-step climb to the third *andiron* leads to the forested remains of the **Main Temple of Asclepios** and affords a view of the site, Kos Town, and the Turkish coast.

When going or returning, consider stopping for superlative vegetarian-friendly *taverna* fare at **Arap** (tel. 28 442) in Platanos, by the turn-off for Asclepion. *Yoghurtlu* (mixed vegetables in a yoghurt sauce, 700dr) is among the many great finds here.

■ Central Kos

The impact of package tours seeking "traditional Greek villages" is beginning to wear on the villages south of Kos Town. Where fertile fields once yielded tomatoes and olives, tourism is now the cash crop. Nevertheless, the island's many paved roads make wonderful terrain for short trips by bike or moped. It is possible to go from Kos to Mastihari and then up to Pyli and Zia entirely on back roads. For those who prefer the bus, the main road leads first to the modern village of **Zipari,** which includes the ruins of the early **Christian Basilica of St. Paul,** 11km southwest of Kos Town. From there, a twisting road slowly winds through the green foothills of the Dikeos Mountains to **Asfendiou,** consisting of five small settlements, of which **Lagoudi** is the prettiest. It is easy to hike for hours and not encounter a soul. Buses from Kos go to Asfendiou (40min., 3 per day, 300dr). South of Lagoudi, the road narrows to a mule path and the hills become even less cultivated. A mere 8km farther (although a good portion of it is uphill), you will come to the compact ruins of old Pyli, which are 14th-century frescoes in a Byzantine church built within a castle. Buses go to Pyli from Kos (30min., 5 per day, 300dr). From Pyli, a twisting, potholed paved road climbs over the hills and descends into Kardamena.

A turn-off for the **Castle of Antimachia** is 1km before Antimachia on the main road to the left. Yet another legacy of the Knights of St. John, the fortress sits majestically on an isolated hilltop. For those who can't get enough of medieval architecture, the 20-minute hike up the hill will offer you another opportunity to marvel at medieval ruins. Otherwise, the castle in Kos Town is far more imposing. Antimachia is a relatively uninteresting town, but it does house the island's only operating **windmill,** which you can see to the left of the main road. Next to the windmill and across the street, visit the traditional house to watch the making of a wool carpet. *(Open daily 9am-9pm. Admission 100dr.)* The turn-off for **Plaka** is on the road to Kefalos, 2500m out of Antimachia. The forested park provides refuge from the sun, a scenic setting for picnics, and free admission to the always-playing show of peacocks proudly displaying their plumage.

Mastihari and Kardamena are the two resorts of central Kos. Both offer beaches, streets with few cars, and several restaurants. **Mastihari,** north of Antimachia, is quiet, cozy, and popular among families. If you wish to make this more than a daytrip, try **Hotel Arant** (tel. 51 167; fax 51 168), equidistant from the bus stop and the beach (doubles with bath 8000dr). There are also many pensions and rooms available along the beach (doubles 8000dr). **For You Tourist Services** (tel. 51 149), one block from the bus, helps find rooms (open 9am-9pm). **Boats** go to Kalymnos from Mastihari (3 per day, 810dr). Five **buses** per day leave Kos for Mastihari (45min., 460dr).

■ Southern Kos

Southern Kos is covered by rolling hills, ravines, and occasional cow pastures. **Kefalos,** Kos's ancient capital and the only town of any real substance on the southern half of the island, is neither crowded nor terribly interesting. North of Kefalos is the picturesque little harbor of **Limionas.** Sit down for an excellent maritime meal at Limionas (tel. (0934) 22 002). The fish is cheap and freshly plucked from the store owner's fishing nets (*barbounia* 7500dr per kg, octopus 1200dr, Greek salad 700dr). The beach that stretches from Limionas to Mastihari is gorgeous and deserted.

Agios Theologos, just west of Kefalos, is one of the island's quietest and most beautiful beaches, a 4km hike from town. Because it is so hard to get to, you will probably have it all to yourself. At the Kefalos bus stop, take the dirt path that branches off to the right and begin your descent. It will take you about an hour, but the peace and quiet that awaits is worth the extra toil.

You will find the **best beaches** in all of Kos on the southeast shore of the island along the main road before Kefalos. Closer to Kefalos, where the road dips to sea level, **Ag. Stefanos** beach has been appropriated by Club Med. Private property signs and fenced-off areas make it clear that only paying guests are welcome in the resort; the beach, however, is open to the public and is a scenic place for a swim. The ruins of a Byzantine church meet the waves at the end of the dirt road that goes to the beach. Impressive mosaics lie covered at the moment, but should eventually be revealed for visitors' viewing pleasure. The tiny island of **Kastri** is a short swim from the shore, tempting those who want to explore its rock formations or who want a perfect place to sunbathe. On the stretch up to Kardamene, **Camel** is a beautiful, mildly busy beach; **Paradise** has its own bus stop and is popular and more crowded; **Magic** has a Hawaiian look to it, and is farther north, empty, and enticingly blue. Ask the bus driver to let you out at any of the beaches.

KALYMNOS Καλυμνος

> In Kalymnos the infant's paint-box has been at work again on the milky slopes of the mountain.
>
> —Lawrence Durrell

Although the first inhabitants of Kalymnos have yet to be identified, archaeologists believe that the Phoenicians colonized the island around 2000 BC. The ruins at Embrio and Vathis suggest that this was a prosperous civilization. Doric and Persian tribes, Venetians, Genoese, the Knights of the Order of Saint John, Ottomans, and Italians all followed the Phoenicians.

Kalymnos is well-known not for its ancient history but instead for its sponge-diving industry. In years past, many men would depart for five or six months and dive for sponges in the Libyan Sea, south of Muammar Qadhafi's Line of Death. Sponges still lurk about (in warehouses, tourist kiosks, and restaurant display-cases), hearkening back to the island's glory days as the sponge capital of the world.

Unfortunately, the sponges are dying off, and Kalymnos' former staple industry is now in decline. The island's economy has been partially resuscitated by an influx of tourists on its western beaches, and most of the island's development clings to the coast. However, the interior has been left mysteriously barren. These rugged mountains, cascading into wide beaches and blue-green water, are an unbelievable reward for those willing to step off the beaten track.

■ Pothia Ποθια

During the Italian occupation at the turn of the century, many locals painted their houses blue, Greece's national color, to antagonize the Italians. Pink and green buildings have since infiltrated Pothia's neighborhoods and, although slightly grayed, this relatively large town (population 10,000) remains more colorful than its whitewashed Aegean counterparts. Pothia is not made to accommodate tourists; there are few rooms, few agencies, and few attractions. However, behind the bustle of the busy port, narrow backstreets are lined with stellar examples of classical architecture.

ORIENTATION AND PRACTICAL INFORMATION

Ferries arrive at the far left end of the port (facing inland). The road leading from the dock bends around the waterfront until it runs into the large, cream-colored municipal building, a church, and the town hall. Narrow, shop-lined **Eleftherias St.** heads one-way inland at this point, leading to **Kyprou Square,** home to the **post office,**

OTE, police, and **taxis.** The waterfront road continues past town hall, to a strip of fish *tavernas* and one unparalleled sweet shop. The second most important avenue, **Venizelou St.,** intersects Eleftherias St. at the end of the harbor near Agios Christos Church. Continue on this road to reach the western part of the island. Follow the harbor promenade past the police station to access the road to Vathis. Most streets in Pothia are unnamed, but following the landmarks is relatively easy.

Transportation

Ferries: Sail to Peiraias (13hr., 1-2 per day, 7000dr); Leros (1hr., 1-2 per day, 1850dr); Patmos (3hr., 1-2 per day, 2450dr); Kos (1½hr., 1-2 per day, 1400dr); Rhodes (6hr., 1-2 per day, 4350dr); Astypalea (3hr., 2 per week, 2600dr); Lipsos (3 per week, 2000dr); Tilos (3 per week, 2650dr); Symi (3 per week, 3225dr); Nisyros (3 per week, 1745dr); Thessaloniki (1 per week, 13,500dr); Mykonos (1 per week, 5100dr); Naxos (1 per week, 4600dr); Paros (1 per week, 3800dr); and Samos (1-2 per week, 3800dr). There is also service to Mastihari in Kos near the **airport** (3 per day, 1000dr). Kalymnos sends daily **excursions** to the small island of Pserimos between Kalymnos and Kos (1800dr round-trip), home to superior beaches and a few *tavernas.* **Port Authority** (tel. 24 444), in the yellow building across from the customs house, at the end of the dock. Updated ferry information. Open 24hr.

Flying Dolphins: Fast, expensive, and severely contingent on weather conditions. Daily to Kos (3270dr); Leros (3810dr); Patmos (4900dr); Lipsos (4280dr); Ikaria (6180dr); Fourni (6800dr); Agathonisi (4980dr); Samos (6145dr); Tilos (4075dr); Nisyros (3315dr); Symi (6785dr); and Rhodes (8750dr).

Buses: Every hour on the hour 7am-10pm, buses leave for Kastelli (50min.) via Hora (10min.); Panormos (15min.); Myrties (20min.); and Massouri (25min.). Fares 100-250dr. 6 buses go to Vilhadia, 2 to Emborio, 4 to Vathis, 3 to Argos, and 3 to Plati Gialos. Buses to western towns leave from the town hall in harbor center. Buses to Vathis depart from the northeast corner of the waterfront. Purchase your tickets before boarding at Themis mini-market, next to the town hall, and insert them into the automated validating box on the bus, much like the system in Athens.

Flights: Olympic Airways (tel. 29 265; fax 28 903). Take the first left past the National Bank; it's 50m on the left. Open M-Tu and Th-F 8am-1:30pm and 5-8:30pm, W and Sa 8am-1:30pm.

Taxis: (tel. 24 222, 29 555) Congregate in Kyprou Sq. up Eleftherias St. 7am-9pm. Taxis also operate as taxi buses, for people going in one direction.

Moped Rental: Costas Katrivesis (tel. 50 105), directly behind the port police at the end of the dock. Mopeds range from 2000-4000dr per day, with partial insurance. Open daily 8:30am-9pm.

Tourist and Financial Services

Tourist Office: (tel. 28 583), along the waterfront, in a little white house behind the kiosk and statue of Poseidon, in the shadow of the Olympic Hotel. English-speaking staff helps with rooms, transportation, and sights. Bus schedules and maps. Open M-F 9am-2:30pm and 3-8:30pm, Sa 10am-1:30pm and 6-8:30pm, Su 10am-1:30pm.

Tourist Agencies: There is no one agency to satisfy all your tourist needs—especially if you are looking at boat schedules. **Magos Travel** (tel. 28 777 or 28 652), on the waterfront near the port police, sells hydrofoil tickets and G.A. ferry tickets. Open daily 8:30am-9pm. **DANE Sea Lines** (tel. 23 043, 24 083), next to the tourist office and clearly marked by a yellow flag, represents the other ferry line that serves Kalymnos. Between the two offices, you will find any ferry information you could possibly need. Open daily 8am-2pm and 5-10pm.

Bank: National Bank (tel. 29 794), on the waterfront, has an **ATM,** advances cash (MC and Visa), offers **currency exchange.** Open M-Th 8am-2pm, F 8am-1:30pm.

Emergency and Communications

Pharmacy: (tel. 29 338), near the intersection of Eleftherias and Venizelou. Open M-Tu and Th-F 9am-1pm and 5:30-8:30pm, W 9am-2pm.

Hospital: (tel. 28 851), on the main road to Hora, 1.5km from Pothia. Open 24hr.

Police: (tel. 22 100 or 29 301). Go up Eleftherias St. and take the left inland road from the taxi square. In a blue and yellow Neoclassical building on the right. Open 24hr.

Post Office: (tel. 28 340). On your right, just past the police station. Has **currency exchange.** Open M-F 7:30am-2pm. **Postal Code:** 85200.

OTE: (tel 29 599). From the taxi square up Eleftherias St., take the inland road on the right. Open M-F 7:30am-3:10pm. **Telephone Code:** 0243.

ACCOMMODATIONS

Securing a room in Pothia is hassle-free; pension owners await even late-night ferries, and the tourist office shack is helpful when open.

Katerina (tel. 22 186). Head inland from the waterfront at the National Bank, take the first left, follow the bends, and look for signs to the Panorama Hotel. When the road splits at the embankment wall, go right: the first alley on the left leads to three flights of stairs. At the top, meet a replica of the stereotypical Greek grandmother—welcoming, compassionate, and concerned about your empty stomach. Family members can help you communicate about logistics, but food is a universal language. Katerina rents large, spotless rooms with tile floors, communal baths, and kitchen facilities. Doubles 4000dr; triples 5000dr.

Pension Greek House (tel. 29 559), the flower-covered home on the corner of the final alleyway near Katerina's. Hospitable and comfortable. Rooms have private baths and refrigerators. Doubles 5000dr; triples 7000dr.

Pension Irene (tel. 28 684). From the ferry dock, take the waterfront to P. Maximus, walk inland all the way to the taxi station, head left and turn right at the hairdresser. On left-hand side, next to bakery. Clean rooms in quiet part of town. Communal kitchen. Doubles with shared bath 4000dr.

Villa Themelina (tel. 22 682), next to the Archaeological Museum. A luxurious mansion with swimming pool. Elegant rooms. Doubles 7000dr; triples 8000dr.

FOOD AND ENTERTAINMENT

The typical bars and modest *tavernas* are tightly clustered on Pothia's harbor. Most people enjoy a few drinks on the waterfront before heading to the clubs in Massouri.

Xefteris (tel. 28 642). From the town hall, head up Eleftherias St., take the first right, then the first left directly into the *taverna*'s outdoor garden. Out of the way and not at all touristy. Oldest restaurant on the island. Traditional *laverna* serves authentic Greek cuisine, including island specialties like *dolmathes* (stuffed vine leaves; 1200dr) and stuffed zucchini (1200dr). Dessert is also sinfully good. Do not pass up this opportunity to indulge. Open daily noon-1am.

Navtikos Omilos Restaurant (tel. 29 239), isolated at the end of the harbor, all the way on the left (facing inland). Depending on the season, you will have front row seats facing either an amusement park (June-July) or the ocean. Very inexpensive, but prepare to dine with excursion groups from Kos, especially in afternoon. Spaghetti *neapolitana* 590dr; Greek salad 700dr. Open daily 8am-3pm and 6:30-11pm.

Alachouzou (tel. 29 446), past the church and along the waterfront, is a Greek pastry lover's paradise. The sweet shop has been making only 5 types of desserts for over 35 years and has perfected all 5. *Galactobouri* (custard sandwiched between *phyllo* dough and drenched in sweet syrup; 350dr) is the house and island specialty; try it with homemade ice cream. Open daily 8am-1am.

MacDonuts, on the right-hand side of Eleftherias St. in a storefront with "1899" carved on the edifice. Best doughnuts in the Aegean. Open 8am-midnight.

Apothiki (tel. 23 084), just past the town hall on the waterfront road. Pothia's trendiest nighttime haunt. Chic interior and patio are popular with local youth.

Cine Oasis, just off the waterfront, at the end of a short alleyway plastered with movie posters. When bar-hopping gets old, the outdoor movie starts at 9:30pm. It changes every night; posters announce feature presentations. Adults 1400dr, children 1000dr.

SIGHTS

Learn first-hand about the island's historic **sponge industry.** The sponge shop of **Nikolas Gourlas** is on the waterfront near the port police. Mr. Gourlas speaks English and will be happy to show you around the factory, where sponges are cleaned and chemically treated. *(Sponge mementos from 500dr.)* Follow the blue signs from Venizelou St. to the **Archeological Museum of Kalymnos** (tel. 23 113), housed in the former mansion of Catherine and Nikolaos Vouvalis, turn-of-the-century sponge barons from Kalymnos. *(Open Tu-Su 9am-2pm. Free.)* The **Nautical Museum** (tel. 24 862), a few doors down from the town hall, on the second floor, houses traditional island wares and clothing and explores the life and work of the island's sponge divers. *(Open Tu-Sa 10am-2pm, Su 10am-1pm. Admission 500dr, students 300dr.)* The hilltop **Monastery of Agion Pantes and Agios Savvas** overlooks the town. *(Monastery is free.)* Visitors can enter at the gate on the right side; the first chapel on your left contains the bones of canonized Saint Savvas in a sarcophagus. The nuns there may welcome you with water and an occasional sweet. The monastery is always open, but it is best not to disturb the nuns during their afternoon chores.

From the customs house, take the roads to the left to reach the beach at **Therma,** 2km away. Arthritic patients make pilgrimages to the sanitarium here to wade in its **sulphur mineral baths.** (Doctor's permission is required to bathe. Those without medical problems will probably not want to con a prescription; the baths have a strong odor.) The main beach is crowded, but a short walk around the bend leads to a quiet swimming spot. The tranquil beach at **Vlichadia** (6km from Pothia), the island's only **scuba diving** site, is farther west from Therma (backtrack toward Pothia and then slightly north). Despite this attraction, an inconvenient bus schedule keeps Vlichadia Beach pleasantly peaceful. The rocky bottom is hard on the feet.

■ Western Coast

Kalymnos has two main roads running out of Pothia, one northwest and one northeast. A few kilometers along the northwest road, a side road to the left leads up to a fortress of the Knights of St. John, also called **Chrissocherias Castle.** A number of little chapels are hidden in its remains. Painted sections of wall indicate holes left by privateers in search of treasure. The **Pera Castle,** a Byzantine structure later enlarged and fortified by the Knights, looms north of Chrissocherias across the valley. Nine tiny white churches maintained by elderly Horian women are scattered throughout the ruins. Directly opposite lies the small village of **Argos**—once the ancient city of Argiens, now a suburb of Pothia. Pera Kastro and Argos overlook the town of **Hora,** once Kalymnos's capital but now little more than another one of Pothia's tentacles.

One kilometer or so beyond Hora, just after the road begins to descend into Panormos, a few white steps by the side of the road lead to the shell of the **Church of Christ of Jerusalem.** *(Open 24hr. Free.)* Byzantine Emperor Arcadius built this church to thank God for sparing him in a storm while at sea. The stone blocks with carved inscriptions are from a 4th-century BC temple to Apollo that stood on the same site. By incorporating and subordinating these architectural elements, the church came to be viewed as a symbolic victory over paganism. The road branches at Panormos. One offshoot goes to **Kantouni,** a village with a crowded, less-than-spectacular beach. On the waterfront, the **Domus Restaurant** serves excellent food (Greek salad 800dr), then clears the tables for a night of dancing. Don't miss the rooftop sunset.

The beachside walking path leads to a quiet cove with interesting rock formations. Another road from Panormos leads 2km to the sandy and less-crowded beach of **Plati Gialos.** You may consider staying at **Pension Plati Gialos** (tel. 22 014), perched on a cliff with a memorable view of the coastline (doubles 6000dr); follow the paved road to the top of the hill, where you will find the pension's reception.

An empty beach stretches out at **Arginontas,** at the end of a long, narrow inlet. Both roads to the beach rise dramatically along cliffs that plunge into turquoise water. Although not the cleanest place on the island, **Vanzanelis'** (tel. 47 389), at Arginontas Beach, has a *taverna* and rooms with baths and refrigerators (doubles 7000dr; triples

8000dr). Two buses from Pothia venture this far (250dr). The last village on the west side, **Emborio,** is unruffled and remote. **Harry's Restaurant** (tel. 47 434), 20m from the beach, provides good food and beds (doubles 8000dr; triples 9000dr; all with bath and kitchenette). A small boat makes an **excursion** from Myrties to Emborio daily at 10am (1800dr).

Although most of Kalymnos supports only grass and wildflowers, the valley at **Vathis** (6km northeast of Pothia) is a rich potpourri of mandarins, limes, and grape-vines. The valley starts at the village of **Rina.** There is no beach here (swim off the pier), but the exquisite scenery and lack of tourists compensate for the lack of sand. On the north side of the inlet is **Daskaleios,** a stalagmite cave within swimming range. In Rina, the **Hotel Galini** (tel. 31 241) has decent rooms (doubles with bath and balcony 6500dr). The three *tavernas* on the tiny waterfront also rent rooms, but prices are similar to the hotel's.

Myrties and Telendos

Both the gray-sand beach at **Myrties,** 7km up the coast, and the pebbly one at **Massouri,** the next town, can be quite crowded. Massouri is well-known as the center of the island's nightlife. Establishments open late, and the clientele arrive even later. With only one paved road running through Massouri, all of the bars and clubs are within a five-minute walk of one another. The **Pink Elephant** boasts Guinness on tap (600dr), hard cider (600dr), and an assortment of cocktails (1000dr). The real hotspots are the dance clubs **Forum, Saloon,** and **Club Dorian Tropical.** Each charges a 2000dr cover that includes a free drink. The party starts after midnight.

Myrties's finest attraction, a short boat ride out of town (15min., every 30min., 200dr), is the tiny, rocky islet of **Telendos,** severed from Kalymnos by an earthquake in AD 554. A city occupied the fault line where the island cracked, and traces of it have been found on the ocean floor, but the rift is invisible from the surface. The Roman ruins on Telendos are modest at best, but a few small, secluded beaches fringe the island. (Turn right from the ferry dock for the best beaches.) The Byzantine **Monastery of St. Constantine** is past the beaches to the right (open only for liturgy). Accommodations in Telendos are generally full only for a couple of weeks in August. Most pensions charge 3000-5000dr for a double. **Uncle George's Pension** (tel. 47 502), near the docks, has an excellent restaurant and clean rooms (doubles with bath 4000dr; studios with kitchenette and bath 5000dr). Before leaving Myrties, look back at Telendos. Many claim that a woman's profile is visible in the rock along the left side of the mountain (all right, stretch your imagination). According to residents, she is mourning her lost husband.

PATMOS Πατμος

Declared the "Holy Island" by ministerial decree—signs at the port warn that nudity and other "indecent" behavior will not be tolerated—Patmos's historical and religious significance is evident to any visitor. In ancient times, Patmians worshipped Artemis, goddess of the hunt, who is said to have raised the island from the sea. Orestes built a grand temple to Artemis after seeking refuge on Patmos from the Furies, who were pursuing him for murdering his mother Clytemnestra.

While he was in exile from Ephesus, St. John established a Christian colony here and purportedly wrote the *Book of Revelation* in a grotto overlooking the main town. His words, "I…was on the isle that is called Patmos, for the word of God, and for the testimony of Jesus Christ…" could be considered the island's motto. In the 4th century AD, when the Christian faith spread with the Byzantine Empire, a basilica replaced the razed Temple of Artemis. In the 11th century, the fortified Monastery of St. John was built on a hill overlooking the entire island.

Modern Patmos is lively and sophisticated, and thus far has managed to strike a delicate balance between its current popularity and solemn past. While the island's long religious history makes it popular for spiritual pilgrimage, artisans have also found inspiration in this setting. Galleries and craft stores are abundant in the island's larger towns. The oft-sighted yellow flag with the black two-headed eagle is the age-old banner of the Byzantine Empire and Greek Orthodox Church.

■ Skala Σκαλα

Built along a graceful arc of coastline, the neat, colorful port town of Skala gives only a hint of the island's diverse terrain. The town did not develop until the 19th century, when fear of pirates subsided and people began to live safely by the water. The main administrative buildings, which house the post office and customs house, were constructed during Italian occupation (1912-1943). Today, whitewashed churches are camouflaged among village buildings, but Skala also caters to the secular—cafes, bars, *tavernas,* shops, and galleries line the street. Centrally located, Skala is the most convenient place to stay on the island, particularly for those relying on the inconvenient bus schedule.

ORIENTATION AND PRACTICAL INFORMATION

Skala's amenities are all within a block or two of the waterfront. Small ferries dock opposite the line of cafes and restaurants, while larger vessels park in front of the Italian building that houses the police and post office. The building borders the main square, where banks are located. Skala is on a narrow part of the island; if you walk away from the water you can reach the opposite coast in about 10 minutes.

Transportation
Ferries: Most ferries are run by DANE (tel. 31 314) or GAGA (tel. 31 217), both near the square. Daily service to Peiraias (10hr., 6355dr); Leros (1½hr, 500000dr); Kalymnos (2½hr., 2542dr); Kos (4hr., 2720); and Rhodes (10hr., 5600). Connections also to Lipsi (3 per week, 1106dr); Samos (4 per week, 1700dr); Agathonisi (4 per week, 1522dr); and Mykonos (2 per week, 4000dr). Ferries run once per week to Nisyros (3200dr); Tilos (3200dr); Naxos (3700dr); Paros (4500dr); and in summer Thessaloniki (21hr., 11,500dr). Private **excursion boats** go to Lipsi (daily, 1500dr one-way, 2500dr round-trip) and to different beaches around the island (round-trip 1000dr). Check out the deals posted along the waterfront.

Flying Dolphins: Service to Leros (30min., 2 per day, 3360dr); Kalymnos (1hr., 2 per day, 4900dr); Agathonisi (40min., 2 per week, 3980dr); Lipsi (20min., 2 per week, 2620dr); Samos (50min., 2-3 per day, 3645dr); Ikaria (50min., 1 per day, 3780dr); and Fourni (1hr., 3 per week, 3500dr).

Buses: Across from the little park, left of the police station. 10 per day go to Hora (10min.), 5 of which continue to Grikou (10min.), and 4 to Kampos (15min.). All fares 220dr, children free. Schedule posted at bus stop or tourist office.

Taxis: (tel. 31 225). Congregate in the main square 24hr. in summer, but are difficult to catch in the *après*-disco flurry, and from 3-6:30am. Taxis to Hora 700-1000dr.

Car Rental: Patmos Rent-a-Car (tel. 32 203). Turn left after the post office and look for it on your right (2nd floor). 9000dr and up. Open daily 8am-11pm.

Moped Rental: Abundant throughout Skala. Two are well-guarded, service-oriented, and also rent mountain bikes. **Express Moto** (tel. 32 088); turn left after the tourist office and take the first right. New models 1500-5000dr per day. Open daily 8am-8pm. **Theo Girogio** (tel. 32 066). New models 2000-40000dr per day. Open daily 8:30am-10pm.

Tourist and Financial Services
Tourist Office: (tel. 31 666), in the big Italian building across the dock. Maps, brochures, bus schedules, information on all ferries, and help with accommodations. Ask for the free *Patmos Summertime* guide, which includes maps of Skala and the island. Open M-F 9am-3:30pm and 4-10:30pm, Sa 11am-1:30pm and 6:30-8pm.

Port Authority: (tel. 31 231), to the left of the ferry dock, next to the snack bar. Information on ferries. Open 24hr.; knock forcefully if it's late.

Tourist Agencies: All over the waterfront, but each offers information on only those ferry lines for which they sell tickets. Consult the tourist office or the port police

DODECANESE

for complete schedules and then ask where to buy your particular ticket. **Apollon Tourist and Shipping Agency** (tel. 31 356 or 31 354; fax 31 819) is the local agent for **Olympic Airways.** Open daily 8:30am-8:30pm.

Banks: National Bank (tel. 31 123, 31 774, or 31 591), in the far end of the square. Cash advances on MasterCard and **currency exchange.** Open M-Th 8am-2pm, F 8am-1:30pm. Exchange at the post office and **Apollon Agency** as well.

Laundromat: Just Like Home (tel. 33 170), 5min. from the dock on the waterfront road toward Meloi and Kampos. 3000dr per 5kg load (wash, dry, and soap). Open M-F 9am-1pm and 5-8pm. 24hr. service.

International Bookstore: International Press (tel. 31 427), behind the Pantelis Restaurant—look for the signs. Open daily 8am-9:30pm.

Emergency and Communications

Pharmacy: (tel. 31 500), behind Apollon Travel, on the first street parallel to the waterfront. Open daily 8:30am-1:30pm and approximately 6-9pm. Call 31 083 for after-hours emergencies.

Hospital: (tel. 31 211), on the main road to Hora, across from the monastery Apokalipsi (2km out of Skala). Open daily 8am-2pm. **Emergency:** Call the **police,** who know doctors' schedules and will contact them (tel. 31 087 or 31 571).

Police: (tel. 31 303), upstairs from the tourist office. Open 24hr.

Tourist Police (tel. 31 303), housed with the police above the tourist office.

Post Office: (tel. 31 316), on the main square, next to the police. Open M-F 7:30am-2pm. **Postal Code:** 85500.

Internet Access: Patmos Logic (tel. 33 000), past the OTE, has limited access on one computer (1000dr per hr), Open M-Sa 9am-1pm and 5-9:30pm.

OTE: (tel. 31 399). Follow the signs in the main square. Open M-F 7:30am-3:10pm. The cafe-bar at the boat dock has an international telephone.

Telephone Code: 0247.

ACCOMMODATIONS

Skala's hotels are often full in summer, but finding a room in a pension or private home is usually easy. Even boats arriving at 1am are greeted by a battalion of locals offering rooms (singles 4000dr; doubles 6000dr). Off-season prices are generally lower by 20-40%. Unless hotels are full, bargaining for better prices proves fruitful. There are many rooms on Vas. Georgiou St. and on the street leading to the OTE.

Captain's House Hotel (tel. 31 793; fax 34 077), on the waterfront; from the dock, facing inland, walk left. Attractive room with private bath and balconies offering exceptional views. Breakfast 1000dr. Doubles 6000-7000dr.

Jason's Rooms (tel. 31 832 or 31 838), near the OTE on opposite side of the street. Clean, cheerful rooms and a friendly manager make Jason's popular with backpackers. Singles with shared bath 5000dr; doubles 6000dr, with bath 7500dr.

Maria Paschalidis (tel. 32 152 or 31 347) runs an energetic pension with spotless rooms, permeated by the fragrance of jasmine. Walk left from the ferry dock and right onto Vas. Georgiou St. Roughly 50m on the left, after Pizza Zacharo, across from the basketball court, is Maria's "rooms to let" sign. Doubles 6000dr, with bath 8000dr; triples 8000dr, with bath 10,000dr.

Pension Sofia (tel. 31 501 or 31 876), between Maria's rooms and Pizza Zacharo, above a Tae Kwon Do school. Knock on the second floor or ask at the next door on the right for the immaculate rooms. Friendly Sofia will surely make guests feel at home and is prone to feeding them. Breakfast included. Doubles with bath 7000dr; triples and quads with common baths 5000dr.

Flower Stefanos Camping at Meloi (tel. 31 821), 2km northeast of Skala. This excellent campground has a minimarket, laundry, shower, grill facilities, motorbike rentals, and a tasty budget cafe. It is a 2min. walk from Meloi Beach. Follow the waterfront road all the way to the right, facing inland; look for signs. Or, for free shuttle service, watch for the tie-dye colored van at the port. 1500dr per person; 750dr per tent; 750dr per tent rental.

FOOD

Several seafood restaurants featuring expensive fish entrees line the waterfront. There are several **grocery stores** clustered around the main square, as well as numerous **sweet shops.** Visit a sweet shop and try the Patmian dessert *pouggia,* a ball of honey and nuts (almonds, walnuts, or peanuts) covered in dough and sometimes smothered in powdered sugar (220-300dr), or Patmian cheese pie, a pastry shell filled with local cheese, eggs, milk, and cinnamon (380dr).

Grigoris (tel. 31 515), across from the bus stop at the corner of the road to Hora, has good and reasonably priced fare. Experience the swordfish *souvlaki* or grilled grouper (each 1400dr). Open daily noon-4pm and 6pm-1am.

The Old Harbor Restaurant (tel. 31 170), with woodwork balcony on the waterfront road to Meloi, reputedly serves the island's best seafood—the best, however, does not come cheap. One medium-sized serving of *barbounia* will cost about 2500dr (800dr per kg). Open daily 6pm-midnight.

Pantelis (tel. 31 230), a cheaper but equally delicious option. Behind the central strip of cafes on the street parallel to the waterfront, this family restaurant will overwhelm you with its selection of Greek dishes. Over 50 choices each day, many vegetarian. *Gigantes* 800dr, *kakavia* 1500dr. Open daily 11am-11pm.

Augerinos, on the road to the OTE, has excellent take-out *souvlaki-pita* (350dr).

ENTERTAINMENT

As befits such a sacred island, the nightlife is free of the rowdy excesses of some islands, though Skala is slowly adopting a more lively complement to the promenading and casual cafes that are standard fare here.

Koncolato (tel. 32 323), a bright club popular with regulars and visitors.

Cafe Aman (tel. 32 323), a chic cafe resting below the magnificently lit church a.k.a. Agia Paraskevi. Draws a pre-bar crowd early in the evening, but many stay all night.

Music Club 2000 (tel. 32 405), by the gas station. Five minutes down the road to Melloi. Liveliest dance floor on Patmos. More crowded as the night wears on.

Art Cafe (tel. 33 092). Vibrant paintings liven the inviting cafe-bar where older clientele is prone to leisurely evenings listening to owner Nikos play DJ all night long.

Pépe Nero Bar (tel. 32 231), behind the tourist information office. The younger crowd heads here for Latin, funk, and soul music—everything that makes you shake. Gets a little crowded, so be prepared to become closely acquainted with the person next to you. Open daily 9pm-3am.

Arion (tel. 31 595), next to Apollon Travel. Popular, cavernous cafe-bar, with an ideal patio for awaiting late night ferries. Beer 500-800dr, cocktails 1200dr.

Apocalypse Now?

Most people have read (or heard of) the story in the Book of Revelation that says that in the years before the Second Coming, people will be forced to bear the Sign of the Beast (the number 666). In most of the world, little thought or credence is given to this passage of scripture—but in Greece, all hell has broken loose over it. The furor began when the European Union passed the Schengen Treaty, an agreement which, among other things, called for each person in the EU to be issued an electronic ID card. Pretty harmless, right? Not according to many Greeks, who vehemently declare that the bar codes on the IDs are designed around the infamous three sixes. Each bar code, it seems, possesses three bars corresponding to the number six, one each at the beginning, the exact middle of the code, and at the end. Are these bar codes really the mark of the Antichrist as prophesied by the Book of Revelation? The powerful Greek Orthodox Church, which has called on all believers to shun the new IDs, certainly thinks so. But only time will tell whether the electronic ID cards are merely a sign of modern times—or the apocalyptic Sign of the Beast.

■ Hora Χωρα

From almost any part of Patmos, you can see the white houses of Hora and the majestic gray walls of the nearby Monastery of St. John the Theologian above. View the Patmos shoreline and the outlying archipelago, and roam Hora's labyrinthine streets, where gardens spread out behind grand doors in the shelter of the monastery.

The town's convoluted layout makes it impossible to give precise directions. The map of Patmos available at kiosks and tourist shops comes with a questionable illustration of town. Take care of business before arriving; a few phonecard telephones and a mailbox at the bottom of the hill are the only links between Hora and the outside world. From the bus and taxi station, both the monastery and main square (*platia*) are reached by walking left and following signs. **Buses** travel to Hora from Skala (10min., 10 per day, 190dr). The bus stops at the top of the hill outside the town; this is also the point of departure for buses from Hora to Grikou. A taxi here from Skala costs 1000dr. Walking is also an option as (4km and steep) the steps to Hora are quicker and safer than the road. To reach **Vangelis** (tel. 31 967), head toward the monastery and follow signs to the central square. Home to traditional Greek cuisine, Vangelis is the talk of the town. Peek into the pots and pans; this is what good Greek food looks like (*moussaka* 900dr). Grab a seat on the rooftop garden and enjoy the view (open daily noon-2pm and 6pm-midnight). **Cafe Stoa** (tel. 32 226), in the main square across from Vangelis, is the center of Hora nightlife. Enjoy a cheap cocktail (900dr). Be prepared to take a cab home if you are staying in Skala—the last bus from Hora leaves at 10:30pm, long before you will be ready to leave (open daily 5pm-2am).

Monastery of St. John the Theologian

Monastery and treasure museum **open** *M 8am-1pm, Tu 8am-1pm and 4-6pm, Th 8am-1pm and 4-8pm, W F-Sa 8am-1:30pm, Su 10am noon and 4-6pm.* **Admission** *to treasury 1000dr; monastery is free. Modest dress; no shorts or bare shoulders. Try not to visit the monastery at midday in summer, when it becomes packed with tourists. If you come in the off season, one of the monastery's 20 monks (there were once 1700) may volunteer to show you around. In summer, you will have to tag along with a guided group.*

The turreted walls and imposing gateway of the **Monastery of St. John the Theologian** (tel. 31 398) make it look more like a fortress than a place of worship. St. Christodoulos founded the monastery in 1088, nearly 1000 years after St. John's celebrated stay on the island. Pragmatic considerations proved more important than aesthetic ones, as the monastery was a constant target of pirate raids. The memorial to St. John was transformed into a citadel with battlements and watch towers. As you enter the courtyard, notice the 17th-century frescoes on the left that portray stories from *The Miracles and Travels of St. John the Evangelist,* written by John's disciple Prochoros. To the upper right, a fresco portrays St. John's duel with a local priest of Apollo named Kynops. When the Saint threw Kynops into the water at Skala, the heathen turned into stone. The rock is still in the harbor—ask any local to point it out.

The monastery contains 10 chapels within its walls, constructed to allow maximum prayer, while respecting the Orthodox dictate that restricts masses to one per day per altar. The **Chapel of the Virgin Mary** is covered with 12th-century frescoes; these original works were previously hidden behind the faces of the walls, but were exposed in 1956 by tremors. The **treasury** guards icons, ornamented stoles (some of which were donated by Catherine the Great of Russia), a copy of St. Mark's Gospel, and an 8th-century Book of Job. Look for **Helkomenos,** an icon painted by El Greco, near the end of the exhibit. The **Chapel of the Holy Christodoulos** holds the remains of the monastery's illustrious founder. Shortly after Christodoulos's death, many visitors attempted to appropriate his saintliness by carrying away his remains, so the monks built a marble sarcophagus to contain his sanctity and covered it with a silver reliquary.

Simantiri Mansion

Tel. 31 360. **Open** *M-Sa 9am-2pm and 5-8pm. Free.*

At the opposite end of Hora, next to the convent of Zoodohas Pigi, the **Simantiri Mansion** boasts a versatile collection of heirlooms, icons, and furniture. To get there, turn right by the telephone in the square above the bus station.

Apocalypsis Monastery

Open M 8am-1pm, Tu 8am-1pm and 4-6pm, Th 8am-1pm and 4-8pm, W and F-Sa 8am-1:30pm, Su 10am-noon and 4-6pm. Dress appropriately. Free.

Halfway up the hill on the winding road that connects Hora and Skala (2km from each) is a turn-off for another monastery, the **Apocalypsis,** a large, white complex of interconnected buildings. Most people come here to see the **Sacred Grotto of the Revelation** (tel. 31 234), adjacent to the Church of St. Anne. In this natural cave, St. John dictated the *Book of Revelation,* the last book of the New Testament, after hearing the voice of God proclaim "Now write what you see, what is to take place hereafter" (Rev. 1:19). Christians believe that when God spoke to St. John, he cleft the ceiling of the cave with a three-pronged crack representing the Holy Trinity. Silver plating marks the spot upon which, it is presumed, St. John slept.

■ Around Patmos

Arriving at the port in Skala, visitors are welcomed by a sign across the street—*Patmos: Beautiful Beaches Nestled in Tradition.* As the sign attests, the island has no shortage of great beaches, disparate enough to appease beach bums of all flavors.

Two kilometers north, **Melloi** is the closest beach outside Skala. Large trees flanking the back of the sandy beach allow for sun and shade. A bit farther north is **Kambos,** another pleasant option for beachgoers, with a sandy bottom and frequent bus service (15min., 4 per day, 190dr) Though a bit crowded, it has an inviting square and the Church of Evangelismos just below the beach.

Just over the hill from Kambos, **Vagia Beach** is a world apart—rocky, secluded, and serene. East along the road to Livadia, a path leads down to an attractive, unmarked beach set against a small cliff. A bit farther east, **Livadia** beach and **Livadia Restaurant** share spectacular views of the string of islets that lies just off-shore.

While bus service extends only as far as Kambos, the hikes or bikes required to get to farther beaches pay dividends in solitude and atmosphere. North of Kambos, the beach at **Lambi** is famed for its rare multi-colored pebbles, growing rarer as tourists continue to pocket them as souvenirs.

The town of **Grikou,** only 5km southwest of Skala, is rapidly turning into a family beach resort. The beach itself is less than ideal, and a rocky bottom makes wading uncomfortable, but watersport rentals are available (paddleboats 1300dr per hr., water-skiing 5000dr per 10 min.). Rooms in the area are geared to families, offering kitchens and several bedrooms as a single unit. **O Flisvos** (tel. 31 380 and 31 961) rents studios for up to three people above a shaded *taverna* overlooking the bay (with bath 12,000dr). Mopeds can continue 2km farther to the secluded **Plaki Beach,** where the road degenerates. To reach the island's best beach, **Psili Ammos,** take the road to Grikov from Hora, then take the road that branches off to the right, headed for **Thiakofti.** At Thiakofti, park your moped and proceed down the dirt path, clearly marked with asbestos-painted rocks and handwritten signs. You will be sunbathing on a golden stretch of sandy paradise only 20 minutes later. Excursion boats leaving from Skala at 10am and returning at 4pm provide an easier route to Psili Ammos (1 per day, 1200dr). Although convenient, this option offers little flexibility.

ASTYPALEA Αστυπαλια

Few travelers venture to butterfly-shaped Astypalea, the westernmost of the Dodecanese islands. Jagged hills and secluded orange and lemon groves merit leisurely exploration. It is an excellent place to unwind and let off a little steam—in fact, the island has a historical precedent. Astypalea's most infamous athlete, an Olympic boxer named Kleomedies, returned home after being disqualified from the ancient

Games for fatally defeating his opponent. To vent his frustration, he destroyed the schoolhouse, killed all the children, and committed suicide. Shocking, considering the island's soothing atmosphere.

■ Astypalea Town

Surrounded by tawny hills, Astypalea town is composed of Skala (also known as Pera Yialos) by the port, and Hora, at the top of the hill. It is the only major city on the island, and most of the services and amenities you'll need can be found here.

ORIENTATION AND PRACTICAL INFORMATION Just before the town's small beach, the **police** (tel. 61 207) are in a small building (open daily 8am-7pm). The **port police** (tel. 61 208) are in a white building with a Greek flag, on the waterfront between the town and the port. The **OTE** (tel. 61 212 or 61 215) is at the foot of the Paradissos Hotel (open M-F 7:30am-2pm). **M. Karakosta,** under the Aegean hotel, is an agent of the **National Bank** (tel. 61 236; open M-Th 8am-2pm, F 8am-1:30pm), while the small branch of the **Commercial Bank** on the waterfront has an **ATM** (open M-Th 8am-2pm, F 8am-1:30pm). **Astypalea Tours** (tel. 61 328 or 61 292), on the main road to Hora, can handle transportation questions (open daily 10am-1pm and 6-10pm). The **post office** along with **currency exchange** (tel. 61 223; open M-F 7:30am-2pm) and several **supermarkets** (open 9am-1pm and 5-9pm) are all in this older section of town. In case of **medical emergency,** call the clinic at 61 222. **Ferries** run to Peiraias (13hr., 3 per week, 7000dr); Leros (2 per week, 1850dr); Patmos (2 per week, 2450dr); Kos (3½hr., 1 per week, 1400dr); Kalymnos (3hr., 3 per week, 2790dr); Rhodes (5hr., 2 per week, 4350dr); Mykonos (2 per week, 5100dr); Naxos (5½hr., 2 per week, 4600dr); Paros (7hr., 2 per week, 3800dr); Samos (2 per week, 3800dr); Amorgos (2½hr., 2 per week, 3060dr); and Santorini (4hr., 2 per week, 3400dr). **Flying Dolphins** serve essentially the same islands as the ferries and are roughly twice as fast and twice as expensive. A **pharmacy** (tel. 61 444) is at the end of the main road to Hora (open M, Tu, Th-F 9am-1:30pm and 6-8pm, W and Sa 9am-1:30pm). In case of **emergency,** call 61 544. **Moto Center Astypalea** (tel. 61 263 or 61 541; fax 61 540), on the waterfront near the ferry dock, and **Moto Rent Vergouli** (tel. 61 351), on the main road to Hora, rent **motorbikes** from 2500dr (both open daily 8am-2pm and 4:30-9pm). The ever-changing **bus schedule** is posted daily where the waterfront meets the main road to Hora. **Buses** run as far as Livadia and Analipsi. **Postal code:** 85900. **Telephone code:** 0243.

ACCOMMODATIONS Rooms on the island fill up quickly in July and August with regular summering Athenians, but vacancy is the norm the rest of the year. Astypalea Tours can also help arrange accommodations, though these tend to be more expensive. **Hotel Astynea** (tel. 61 209) offers simple rooms along the waterfront, quite similar to those of **Hotel Paradisso** (tel. 61 236), which is closer to the ferry dock (singles 3000-4000dr; doubles 6000-8000dr). The **Hotel Aegean** (tel. 61 236), on the main road, has clean rooms with baths (singles 3500dr; doubles 4500dr; triples 5500dr). While prices at **Maistrali** (tel. 61 691) jump in the high season, for most of the year these charming rooms with old wooden furniture and kitchen facilities are at competitive prices with other hotels. To get there from the waterfront, walk to the main road and take the first left before Michali's cafe. Ask at the restaurant of the same name on the right-hand side (doubles 12,000dr in high season, 6000dr in low season). **Camping Astypalea** (tel. 61 338) is 2½km east of town near Marmari; follow signs or take a bus toward Maltezana (1000dr per person; 750dr per tent).

FOOD AND ENTERTAINMENT Restaurants sit near the waterfront in Astypalea town and on the square in Hora. At **Albatross** (tel. 61 546), on the waterfront, tapestries and a straw roof create a cozy atmosphere for a tasty but random assortment of Chinese, German, and Italian cuisine (barbecued chicken 1200dr). **Etherio** (tel. 61 419), on the waterfront next to Hotel Astynea, serves Greek standards and hearty pastas on an attractive patio. Try the fisherman's pasta with shrimp, mussels, and codfish (2000dr), pesto (1300dr), or—for the culinary aesthete—*roquefort* (1100dr).

SIGHTS The **Archaeological Museum** houses a small, well-presented collection of archaeological discoveries from throughout the island, including stone inscriptions, early Christian sculptures, and findings from Mycenaean graves. *(Open M-F 8am-2pm. Free.)* Before heading up to the castle, stop here to see some of the better-preserved objects once held within the fortification. The museum is on the main road to Hora, just inland from the waterfront.

In Hora, a striking row of windmills leads to the **castle,** originally an effective bastion of defense for the Knights of St. John, and later, the Turks (who left the most significant architectural presence). The structure is becoming increasingly ramshackle, slowly shedding walls and windows. There is a clear view of the island and its flock of tributary islets from here.

■ Around Astypalea

Two kilometers west of Hora sit the dozens of *tavernas,* accommodations, and the large but unremarkable beach that constitute **Livadia.** Proximity to Hora makes Livadia a logical base of excursion for beach-seeking travelers, although to the east of Astypalea Town the beaches are more plentiful and appealing. A 20-minute hike southwest along the coast, **Tzamaki Beach** is much less crowded, and at times, a refuge for nude bathers. Four kilometers farther along a dirt path, the sand and palm trees at **Agios Konstantinidos** make it the Livadia area's best beach. There is an array of options for eating and sleeping in Livadia. On the right-hand side of the dirt road, leading off the small waterfront bridge, **To Gerani** (tel. 61 484) restaurant has doubles (4000dr) of higher quality than some of Livadia's dingier rooms-to-let.

A right turn after the sixth windmill circuitously leads past a military base to the gated but accessible monastery of **Agios Ioannis,** while the view from the monastery, overlooking a small waterfall, is attractive. The arduous yet bland trek to get here makes this diversion only for die-hard monastery lovers or occasional classicists.

Northeast of Astypalea town, the main road leads toward the other "wing" of the butterfly island, passing the campsite and a number of sandy beaches. Generally, at each point that a sign warning against nudity appears a good beach lies just below the road. As the road is a bus route, drop-offs and pickups occur at designated stops, and sympathetic drivers make informal stops.

Lackluster buildings and ominous construction mar the colorful gardens and gentle landscapes of the fishing villages of **Maltezana** (officially known as **Analipsi**), 10km northeast of Astypalea Town. Home to some largely intact Roman mosaics, Maltezana is accessible by bus (2 per day, 150dr.) Along the coast road out of town, **Analipsi Rooms** offers basic rooms within walking distance of a number of good beaches (singles 3500dr; doubles 4000dr). Inquire at the supermarket in front. In front of the market, Almira (tel. 61 451) serves fresh fish and lobster on a garden patio.

Two kilometers farther, the natural harbor at Vathi is subdivided into **Exo Vathi** and **Mesa Vathi;** there is a decent beach nearby at **Agios Andreas.**

KARPATHOS Καρπαθος

The midpoint between Rhodes and Crete, Karpathos is often seen only at a distance by those taking the overnight ferry. Karpathians personify Greece's famed welcoming spirit—those who disembark will enjoy overwhelming hospitality.

War and conquest define Karpathos' history. Karpathians fought with Sparta in the Peloponnesian War in 431 BC and lost their independence to Rhodes in 400 BC. In 42 BC the island fell to Rome. In the following centuries, Karpathos was ruled in turn by the Arabs, the Genovese pirate Moresco, the Venetians, and the Ottoman Empire. Ottoman rule ended when the Italians conquered the island during WWI. Karpathos even found itself ruled by the Germans for a few years following the end of WWII.

Despite such a scattered past, the last half-century has been pivotal in characterizing the island. A war-ravaged economy sent many a Karpathian to U.S. eastern seaboard cities. Karpathos today has a significant Greek-American constituency who

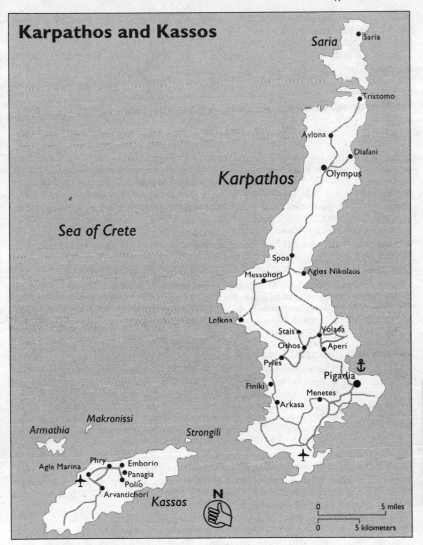

Karpathos and Kassos

Saria

Saria

Tristomo

Avlona

Diafani

Karpathos

Olympus

Sea of Crete

Spoa

Messohori

Agios Nikolaos

Lefkos

Stais

Volada

Othos

Aperi

Pyles

Pigadia

Finiki

Menetes

Arkasa

Makronissi

Armathia

Strongili

Agia Marina

Phry

Emborio

Panagia

Polio

Arvantichori

Kassos

N

0   5 miles

0   5 kilometers

DODECANESE

have returned to their beloved island and invested heavily. As a result, Pigadia and other towns successfully infuse modern elements into a traditional setting. In the mountains north, a world unto itself, residents preserve tradition almost religiously.

■ Pigadia Πηγαδια

Pigadia, literally "the wells," was formerly called Possi, for "Poseidon Polis," but drew objections because the name also meant "drinking about." Today it's known simply as Karpathos Town. While lacking the natural beauty much of the island offers, it may be the best base for accessing it all.

ORIENTATION AND PRACTICAL INFORMATION

The best way to orient yourself in Karpathos Town is to embrace the oh-so-Greek attitude of *laissez-faire*. The streets and square are not named. There are only two main roads. One, running along the water, is lined with *tavernas,* cafes, pharmacies, and the National Bank; the other, a block inland, runs parallel to the first and contains the post office, bakery, and signs for various guest houses. If you insist on buying a map, make sure it is up to date. The best places to purchase maps are **Karpathos Travel** and **Possi Travel** (350dr). Maps of the area in tourist shops are often outdated.

Transportation

Ferries: To Peiraias (21hr., 3 per week, 7800dr); Iraklion (6hr., 2 per week, 3500dr); Kassos (1½hr., 3 per week, 1480dr); Paros (17hr., 2 per week, 5025dr); Rhodes (5hr., 2 per week, 4175dr); and Santorini (12hr., 2 per week, 4860dr). For other Dodecanese islands, Rhodes is a busy connection hub.

Flights: Olympic Airways (tel. 22 150), on the street parallel to the water. Flights to Athens (2 per week, 22,600dr) via Rhodes (4 per day, 9400dr), and to Kassos (1 per week, 3500dr). Open M-F 8am-3:30pm. The **airport** (tel. 22 057) is 5km outside Pigadia. Open M-Sa 8am-8pm.

Buses: 1 block up Dimokratia St. from the town center. Serve most villages in the south (300-1000dr); check the ever-changing schedule at the bus stop or at Karpathos Travel, or call Manolis at 22 192.

Taxis: (tel. 22 705) run 24hr. to the villages (2000dr to nearby villages). Government regulated taxi prices are posted at the station on Dimokratia St.

Car Rental: Circle Rent A Car (tel. 22 690). Cars from 10,000dr per day.

Moped Rental: Moto Carpathos (tel. 22 382) offers reliable service and is run by Karpathos' answer to James Dean. Facing inland from the bus station, walk right 2 blocks, it's on the left hand side. Mopeds start at 3500dr per day. Open 8am-3pm and 5pm-8pm. If motorbiking, ensure you have enough gas for your destination. There are no stations outside Pigadia.

Tourist and Financial Services

Tourist Agencies: Karpathos Travel (tel. 22 148; fax 22 754), Dimokratia St., between the bus station and waterfront. Bus and boat schedules. Arranges accommodations, **rents cars** (43,400dr for 3 days), and **exchanges currency.** Sells tickets for excursions to Lefkos, Diafani, and Olympus. Open M-Sa 8:30am-1pm and 5:30-9pm, Su 9-11am and 6-8pm. Both Karpathos and **Possi Travel** (tel. 22 235; fax 22 252), around the corner on Apodimon Karpathion St., sell maps for 350dr. Open M-Sa 8:30am-1pm and 5:30-8:30pm, Su 9am-noon and 6pm-8pm.

Banks: National Bank (tel. 22 409), opposite Possi Travel. **Currency exchange** and **ATM** that accepts Visa/MC. Open M-Th 8am-2pm, F 8am-1:30pm.

Boat Excursions: Chrisovalandu Lines and **Karpathos I.** Both run daily excursions to Olympus leaving 9am and returning 5:30-6:30pm. For information, both companies advertise nightly at their boats near the ferry docks.

International Bookstore: Caroles Corner of Karpathos (tel. 23 636), on the way to the bus station from the ferry. Has a limited selection of new and used English language books. Open M-Sa 9am-1:30pm and 5:30-10:30pm, Su 5:30-10:30pm.

Emergency and Communications

Pharmacies: 3 near the water. All open M-F 8am-1pm and 5:30-8:30pm.

Medical Assistance: Contact the **Health Center** (tel. 22 239), a large white building 100m past 5 October Sq., on N.K. Matheou St. After 2pm, go directly there and ring the bell in an emergency. No English spoken. Open 8am-1:30pm and 5-9:30pm.

Police: (tel. 22 222). At the corner of Ethn. Anistassis St., next to the post office. They don't speak much English, but they try valiantly. Open 24hr.

Port Police: (tel. 22 227), next to the ferry dock. Open 24hr.

Post Office: (tel. 22 219). Take the uphill road right of the bus station. Open M-F 7:30am-2pm. **Postal Code:** 85700.

OTE: Past the post office, go left uphill. Open M-F 7:30am-3pm. **Telephone Code:** 0245.

ACCOMMODATIONS

Illegal free-lance camping transpires mostly undisturbed on the town beach to the north. *Let's Go* does not recommend free-lance camping. Room prices are 1000-2000dr less in the off season, but can be haggled down for most of the year.

Mertonas Studios (tel. 22 622 or 23 079), 2 blocks left and uphill from the bus station, facing inland. Eva Angelos rents gorgeous, furnished studios with private baths and daily maid service that would make Mr Clean weep. Eva claims to be a "coffee-ground psychic"—ask about her relationship with various international leaders. Doubles with bath 5000-7000dr; winter doubles 50,000dr per month.

Harry's Rooms to Rent (tel. 22 188). Facing inland at the bus station, turn right and take the first left. Has built up a loyal clientele over many years. Modern rooms with balcony and common bath. Singles 3200dr; doubles 4800dr; triples 5000dr.

Elias Rooms for Rent (tel. 22 446). From the bus station, walk up the stairs past the supermarket. Rooms are quiet yet centrally located. Owner is happy to inform guests about the island. Ask about traditional rooms for rent. Singles 4000dr, with private bath 5000dr. Doubles 5000dr, with private bath 6000dr.

Fortoula Rooms for Rent (tel. 22 519). Facing inland at the bus station, turn right, then left at Motor Carpathos, then left at the alley where the road becomes two-way—Fortoula is uphill to the right near the end of the alley. It's easier to reach than it sounds, but Fortoula will probably pick you up if you call. The convivial owner insists she's "crazy about clean." Let her fetish be your benefit. Singles 3000-4000dr; doubles 4000dr-5500dr; triples 6000dr.

Hotel Blue Sky (tel. 22 356 or 22 279). Next to Harry's Rooms to Rent. Simple rooms with private baths and excellent prices. Singles 2500dr; doubles 4000dr.

Odyssey, (tel. 23 240, 23 241, or 23 242), next to Eva's, but farther down the hill. Spotless studios and furnished apartments. Doubles 7000dr; quads 12,000dr.

Hotel Avra (tel. 22 388; fax 23 486). Facing inland at the bus station, turn right. Avra is a few doors down on the right-hand side. Clean, well-located rooms. Singles 3000dr, with private bath 4000dr; doubles 5000dr, with private bath 6000dr.

FOOD AND ENTERTAINMENT

Although waterfront taverns tend to be expensive and bland, better options lie away from the ferry dock, along the paved waterfront road toward the beach. Cafes (fairly touristy) are popular in the evening. Other nightlife may be out of walking distance.

⊛Kali Karthia (tel 22 256), just past the school on the water at the north end of town. Fresh and cheap fish, since the owner's sons stock the restaurant daily. Grade A fish 7500dr per kg, or do like the chef does and order the Lalamari-esque *swpia* (1500dr). Open daily 7am-1am.

The Life of Angels (tel. 22 484). A gem of a dining experience on the road parallel to the main waterfront. Live Greek folk music and tasty Karpathian meals, in a charming old building. Try the *spetsofai* sausages baked with peppers (1600dr) or the *psarokeffedes,* tasty fish cakes (800dr).

Ideal (tel. 23 171), between National Bank and the church. One of the few waterfront *tavernas* with cheaper options. Plate of dips 500dr; pita *gyros* 300-400dr.

Kamarathos' Beehive, next to Karpathos Travel back along the waterfront. Has an endless variety of sweets. Open daily 7am-2am.

The Art Center, located in the center of the town near the mayor's office. For the artistically inclined. Minas Vlahos, the most acclaimed artist on Karpathos, captures the feeling of the island in work displayed in his tranquil studio. Hand-made cards 500dr. Open M-Sa 9am-1pm and 5-9pm.

Ylapi (tel. 22 524), uphill from the post office. The name refers to a meeting place for laborers after work, and what transpires here nightly is play. 1500dr cover includes first drink.

The Rocks (tel. 85 700) mesmerizes with liquid lamps, and is one of 3 waterfront bars that are always crowded and serve beer (800dr) and cocktails (1200-1500dr). Open at 8 or 9pm until late.

Eros (tel. 23 368). Dance to everything from Greek pop to hip-hop. Open 8pm-5am.

DODECANESE

To escape the waterfront and get down with the locals, prepare for an uphill climb or drive. Head straight out of town and follow the aimlessly scattered but carefully painted concrete blocks that mark the path to **Fillagri** (tel. 23 373), a unique bar and dance club. Overlook the island's largest olive grove as you party in an abandoned olive oil mill. With four bars—three indoors and one outdoors—the club handles over 800 thirsty customers each weekend night. For a smaller scene, head upstairs to **Gamma-3**, a bar that plays both Greek and foreign music (beer 700dr, mixed drinks 1000dr). Both places open before midnight, but only pick up around 1 or 2am. Nearby, the newly opened **Pardiso Club by Palladium** (tel. 22 524) is equally popular with the dancing set (cover varies).

■ Southern Karpathos

West of Pigadia, winding roads ascend toward charming villages and cloud-covered mountains before descending into the beach-laden west coast. Even if you're planning to stay in Pigadia, a daytrip around the western loop is not to be missed. Heading northwest of Pigadia, the road leads past sandy Vroundi Beach. There's no shortage of cantinas or sunbeds here. The road then turns west into lush hiking country.

Aperi became the island's capital in medieval times when Arab raids forced the Karpathians to abandon their coastal town. Today, it remains the island's spiritual capital. The church here holds the **Panagia** (Virgin Mary) icon revered throughout Karpathos. *(Open daily 8-11am.)* Legend has it that long ago a monk was chopping wood when blood suddenly spurted from one of the logs. The perplexed monk recognized the log as an icon of the Virgin Mary, and although the object disappeared several times, it always reappeared in an old church in Aperi. The monk understood that the *Panagia* wished to stay in that spot, and in 1886 a bishop's church was built.

Large well kept homes surrounding the fountain and *tavernas* in the middle of the village attest to the area's wealth. The road continues uphill through the old-fashioned villages of Volada and Othos.

Enchanting **Pyles** is the westernmost of the southern mountain villages, winning over visitors with its narrow alleys, small *tavernas,* and famous honey. A walk through the village leads to picturesque groves. Two kilometers west of Pyles, the road hits Karpathos' stunning west coast. **Lefkos,** 12km north, is popular with package tours for its beach and small port. Along the coast to Lefkos, those willing to trade sand for a rocky cove will have a gorgeous stretch of coast to call their own. Inland from the coast, hiking terrain in the forest need only be shared with the goats.

South along the coast, the miniature fishing port of **Finiki** today consists mostly of tourist amusements. **Dimitrios Fisherman's Taverna** (tel. 61 294 or 61365) attains local renown for excellent preparation of Dimitrios's daily catch. The *taverna* is one of a few places which rents rooms throughout Finiki (doubles 6000dr).

In **Arkasa,** south of Finiki, the large windswept remains of five parallel Cyclopean walls flank the coast, all the way to Agios Nikolaos at the southern end of town. Freelance campers can be found on a small beach cove close to the sandy shore of Agios Nikolaos; follow the road from Arkasa to Agios Nikolaos. **Alpha Hotel** (tel. 61 352), at the north end of Arkasa, is one of the few hotels serving independent travelers (singles 4000dr; doubles 5000dr). Roughly halfway between Arkasa and Pigadia, the hillside town leads a quiet existence. A huge church sprouts from the terraced houses below. Its marble pillars were salvaged from the ruins of an early Christian basilica. In the house in front of the church you will find Anna, the keeper of the keys. Ask at **Manolis Kafeneion** (tel. 81 356) for a key to the tiny, free, **folk art museum.** Excellent Karpathian meals can be had at **Two Brothers Restaurant** (tel. 81 396), in the middle of town.

■ Northern Karpathos

No good roads connect the rural north and commercial south of Karpathos. A 1983 fire devastated most of the Aleppo Pine Forests between Spoa and Olympus, eliminating any modernization in this beautiful arid region. Daily **excursion boats** from Karpathos Town are the most reliable and scenic means of transport. Karpathos Travel offers combined boat and bus trips to Diafani (2hr. one way; 4500dr includes round-trip bus to Olympus). A boat journeys to the white beach of **Apela** and to the island of **Saria** north of Karpathos twice per week (from Diafani 1hr., round-trip 2500dr).

Diafani

A stay in languorous Diafani (which means "transparent") allows you to stick close to the beaches of North Karpathos or to explore Olympus at your leisure (2 buses per day, 350dr), but the town itself has nothing more to offer than overpriced *tavernas* and a sleepy port. **Orphanos Travel and Shipping Agents** (tel. 51 410; fax 51 316), on the dock to the right of the *tavernas,* offers **exchange services,** room info, and ferry and excursion tickets. Ask about free boat trips to local beaches (open daily 8am-1pm and 2:30-10pm). There is **no bank** in Diafani. A telecard **phone** is in front of the travel agency. The **police** (tel. 51 213) are in the town center (open 24hr.). There is a **post box,** visited three times per week. Rooms to let abound; expect to pay 3000-4500dr for a single and 5000-7500dr for a double. Diafani's **campsite** (tel. 51 288) starts at 700dr per person, but is rather disorganized, resembling free-lance camping.

Olympus

Olympus is traditional, but no single word can convey the thoroughness of its isolation and insularity. Ethnologists and linguists have lauded the region's preservation of centuries-old customs. Eighty families seeking to escape attacking pirates founded the village, perched 1750m above sea level atop Mt. Profitis Ilias, in the 11th century. Each family built its own windmill, house, and church, which explains the innumerable chapels that dot the area today. The degree of isolation here makes the village and its inhabitants distinct from villages in other areas and from other Karpathians. A history of migrant work that took Olympian men to Rhodes facilitated the **matriarchal tradition** that continues in the village today. Left behind to maintain the property and household while their husbands were away, women took control and responsibility over the family assets; houses are still inherited from mother to daughter. The radiant long-sleeved white shirts and flowered aprons worn by women provide a striking contrast to their weathered skin. Plaster-sculpted nymphs, angels, eagles, and Venetian lions decorate the exteriors of traditional homes, while the interiors are filled with hand-embroidered linens and ceramic plates. Tourist interest and dollars have led Olympians to preserve and, in some cases, rekindle these craft traditions.

To travel between Olympus and Diafani, you can take a taxi or the small bus that leaves both Diafani (when the boat from Karpathos Town arrives) and Olympus daily. A dusty hike along the valley floor is another alternative if you have the time, energy, and drinking water.

Two **working windmills** overlook the cliffs on the west side of the village—here the women of Olympus grind flour for bread, which they bake in huge stone ovens smoldering under the hillside. Meanwhile, the men either play backgammon and musical instruments in the coffeehouses, or lead the overworked donkeys in the right direction. The **folk museum,** beneath one of the windmills (pick your way up the narrow village path), offers a glimpse of a 19th-century home, with tools and adornments. *(Open daily 10am-9pm.)* While you are there, check out the windmill. You can brave the tiny ladder inside and watch one whirl behind the scenes.

Pension Olymbos (tel. 51 252), around to the left of the bus stop near the start of the village, rents traditional Karpathian rooms with hand-carved beds (singles 2500dr; doubles 3000dr, with bath 5000dr). They also serve home-cooked food in the adjacent **taverna;** *pastitsio* and *moussaka* (each 1200dr), are worth every drachma. Farther uphill, **Hotel Astro** (tel. 51 378) has rooms with shared baths (singles 3000dr; doubles 5000dr; triples 7500dr). Unquestionably the best rooms in Olympus are near the windmills at **Hotel Aphrodite** (tel. 51 307 or 51 454), where large, clean rooms offer breathtaking views. Inquire at Parthenonas Taverna along the way.

Surprisingly, some of the best food in Olympus is served at the **Milos Tavern** (tel. 51 333), in the windmill above the museum. Wait for the tour groups to leave, then enjoy the stuffed pitas baked in the wood-burning oven right before your eyes (350dr). For a heartier meal, choose the village's traditional meal, the pasta-like *makarounes*, served with cheese and sprinkled with onion (900dr). The *loukoumades* (honey-glazed doughnut holes) are great for dessert.

If you are willing to bound over stone walls, visit the oldest chapel on Karpathos, **Agia Triada**, one of two adjacent stone chapels easily visible from the town above (look down to the right of the bus stop for earthy red arched roofs). The frescoes inside are 13th- or 14th-century "aniconic" geometric paintings of birds and fish. The largest church in the village, **Kimisi tis Theotokou**, is arguably the most beautiful. Laden in gold foil, the altar is exquisite, and the handpainted Biblical scenes adorning the walls are breathtaking. If the priest isn't around, ask at the folk museum for a key.

One of the few men you will see laboring in Olympus is the cobbler **Nikolaos Kanakis,** who makes the leather boots that are standard footwear in the village. At 60,000dr per pair, these boots are not made for walking.

KASSOS Κασσος

Billed as "the tranquil island," Kassos will surely provide a reprieve from the incessant tourism that characterizes other islands—before August's influx of visiting Greeks and foreigners, "comatose" may be a more appropriate description. Kassos is probably the least-visited island of the Dodecanese. However, despite its stark landscape littered with pock-marked rocks, the island is not as ghastly as it appears; Kassos has several remote beaches, two intriguing caves, and a few humble archaeological sites.

■ Phry Φρυ

The best way to orient yourself is to note the island's layout as you approach it from sea. Virtually all Kassiot civilization is visible from here. The port town of **Phry** is not much to look at, but is nonetheless the main town on the island. Two kilometers east of Phry, **Emborio** is an even smaller town, with an uninviting beach and a few *tavernas*. Above Phry and Emborio, clusters of homes dot the arid hillside. Moving clockwise, these are the villages of **Poli, Panagia, Arvantichori,** and **Agai Marina** respectively. All are connected by desert roads. On the other side of the hill (not visible from the ferry), the villages of Kathistres and **Chroussoulas** lead the way to the island's caves.

ORIENTATION AND PRACTICAL INFORMATION With the cancellation of the island bus service, **taxis** (tel. 41 183 or 41 278) are commonly used for intervillage transit (800-1000dr). **Moto Kasso** (tel. 41 746), on the main street in Phry, rents motorbikes (3500dr per day). Walking is also an option, as the farthest town is less than an hour away. **Ferries** connect Kassos with Karpathos (1½hr., 1760dr); Rhodes (6½hr., 5246dr); Piraeus (19½hr., 7829dr); and all three Cretan ports: Sitia (2½hr., 2511dr); Iraklion (5hr., 3982dr); and Agios Nikolaos (5hr., 2600dr). Weather permitting, they run twice a week. **Boats** land at the port of Phry. **Flights** to and from Rhodes (6 per week, 13,200dr) and Karpathos (3 per week, 3400dr) are twice as expensive but more reliable. A **taxi** from Phry to the airport costs 500dr, but you can easily walk the 5km west. Services on Kassos are sparse but those that do exist are all in Phry. For timetables and information about the island, go to **Kassos Maritime and Tourist Agency**, Iroon Kasou Sq. (tel. 41 323 or 41 495; fax 41 036), right behind the church (open M-Sa 7:30am-2:30pm and 5-9:30pm, Su 7:30am-3pm). The **police station** (tel. 41 422) is on the road to the airport (open 24hr.). The **post office** is off Iroon Kasou Sq. (open M-F 7:30am-2pm). Across the street you'll find the **Olympic Airways** office (tel. 41 555; open 8am-4pm). The **OTE** is several blocks inland (open M-F 8am-2pm). The **hospital** (tel. 41 333) is on Kriti St., past the bus stop (open M-F 8am-3pm).

There is a **National Bank** branch (tel. 412 34) in the supermarket next to the Anesis Hotel (currency exchange M-F 9am-noon). The **port police** (tel. 41 288) is on the road to Emborio (open 24hr.). **Telephone code:** 0245. **Postal code:** 85800.

ACCOMMODATIONS AND FOOD Kassos's two C-class hotels generally have plenty of rooms, except in August. Studio apartments outside Phry are considerably pricier. **Anagenesis** (tel. 41 495 or 41 323), on Iroon Kasou Sq., next to the travel agency, has rooms with seaview balconies. Inquire at the travel agency (singles 4200-6500dr; dou bles 6500-9000dr). **Anesis** (tel. 41 201; fax 41 234) on the main street has rooms with less picturesque balconies. Inquire at the supermarket next door (singles 3000dr, doubles 4000dr). **Blue Sky Apartments,** (tel. 41047; fax 41 747) fully equipped studios on the way to Agia Marina. George, the owner, also runs **excursions** to Karpathos (12,000dr). "Rooms to Let" signs sprout up seasonally throughout town, where clean, simple rooms run 3000-6000dr. For both visitors and locals, many days begin and end at **Zaftava.** The restaurant boasts front-row seats for the island's biggest daily event—boats arriving at the port. **Milos** (tel. 41 825), on the platia, next to Agios Spiridon Church, is a popular local tavern affording good views from its patio. Try the *sitaka* (1100dr), lasagna with Kassos cheese. Supermarkets and bakeries sit on or around the main street.

SIGHTS The rural village above Phry merits leisurely excursions for a taste of Kassiot agricultural life. In Panagia, see the decadent, former homes of sea-captains; Athenians and former Kassiots who summer here are gradually refurbishing these once impressive edifices.

Ten minutes past the village of Kathistres, the entrance to the cave of **Ellinokamara** is partially sealed by a Hellenic wall. Inside, inveterate spelunkers can clamber over slimy stones. On a footpath 1.5km beyond Ellinokamara, the cave of **Selai** bristles with stalactites and stalagmites.

From Poli, the 40-minute hike to **Agios Mamas Monastery** brings you to scenic overlooks of the southeast coast. The boulders you see from the monastery are reputed to be the hulls of three ships, turned to stone by vengeful monks.

Kassos's several beaches are more notable for the solitude they afford than for sand or setting. From Phry the closest beach to the east is in **Emborio,** a small patch of sand next to the port. To the west, a super-abundance of seaweed mars deserted **Ammoudi.** Beaches improve further along both coasts, but the best beaches in the area are on the minuscule island of **Armathia,** only a few nautical miles away and accessible by excursion boats run out of the travel agency in Phry.

SYMI Συμη

The famous **Panormitis Monastery** rests in a remote spot at the Symi's southern end, while the historic port of **Yialos** adorns the northern tip; an uninhabited, hiking-friendly mountain range separates the two. Locals fondly share stories of people coming on daytrips from Rhodes and staying for a month. Others tell of visitors intending to stay a week who could not leave this earthly paradise. Such a trend has created a sense of vested interest among both locals and foreigners in preservation and refurbishing, as opposed to the "live for this summer" ethic of many touristed islands—this mentality is most discernible at night, when sponge-crazy daytrippers have set sail back to Rhodes.

Monasteries were the only dwellings on these steep, barren shores until 19th-century commercial growth led to the construction of the port. During this period, shipbuilding, sponge-diving, fishing, and trade flourished, and Symi received concessions from the Sultans, eventually becoming the capital of the Dodecanese. Ships made in Symi still have a reputation for being fleet and smooth to handle.

Yialos is one of the lovelier ports in Greece. A string of islets leads boats into the harbor, where a rainbow of pastel houses welcomes visitors. To show its apprecia-

DODECANESE

tion of this unique town, the Greek government declared the port of Symi a historic site in 1971. Many of the houses here date from the 19th century, but most were abandoned when the island's sponge-diving industry collapsed.

Symi remains poor while searching for an industry to replace sponge-diving. A growing emphasis on the cultivation of spices has given the island a glimmer of financial stability. In the meantime, locals depend heavily on tourism. The growing population of foreign residents has given the island a slightly cosmopolitan flair to match the colorful mosaic of houses.

■ Symi Town

Symi is one of the most attractive parts throughout the Greek isles and the only significant town on the island. It is divided into two sections—Yialos, the port, has many of the island's visitor services, and Horio, perched hundreds of steps above the port, affords beautiful views of both the port and the fig-orchard-covered mountains.

PRACTICAL INFORMATION

Transportation

Ferries: Two per week to Peiraias (8340dr); Kos (2720dr); Kalymnos (3455dr); Tilos (1835dr); and Nisyros (2470dr). Daily excursion boat from Rhodes can provide access to Rhodes's more comprehensive ferry service (2000dr one way to Rhodes).

Flying Dolphins: 4 per week to Rhodes (2850dr). 1 per week to Kos (5000dr); Kalymnos (6890dr); and Astypalea (8470dr).

Bus: A green van stops on the east waterfront past Ikonomou Square. On-the-hour transportation to Horio (5min., 150dr) and Pedhi (10min., 200dr).

Taxis: (tel. 72 666). Most congregate near the bus stop on the east waterfront.

Tourist and Financial Services

Travel Agency: Symi Tours (tel. 71 307), a block inland from the waterfront gold shop. Sells ferry, hydrofoil, and plane tickets, handles **currency exchange,** and helps find accommodations. Open daily 9am-2pm and 6-10pm.

Banks: National Bank (tel. 72 294), straight ahead from the dock and to the right after the footbridge where the harbor bends left. 24hr. **ATM** services. **Ionian Bank** (tel. 71 122), on the waterfront, a couple of doors down, left of the ferry landing. 24hr. **ATM.** Both banks open M-Th 8am-2pm, F 8am-1:30pm.

International Bookstore: (tel. 71 690; fax 71 773). On the waterfront near the pharmacy. Sells newspapers, magazines, and limited selection of novels in several languages. Fax services available. Open daily 8:30am-2pm and 5pm-midnight.

Public Toilets: Down an alley, left of Taverna Meraklis. Free.

Emergency and Communications

Police: (tel. 71 111), next to the Yialos clock tower, in a big white building on the waterfront. Open 24hr.

Medical Center: (tel. 71 290), next to the church, directly opposite Hotel Kokona. Open M-F 9am-1pm; after hours, call the police.

Pharmacy: (tel. 71 888), on the waterfront, at the left side of the harbor, past Ikonomou Sq. Open M-Sa 9am-2pm and 5-9pm, Su 9am-1pm.

Post Office: (tel. 71 315), in the same building as the police, up the flight of stairs on the left. Offers **currency exchange.** Open M-F 7:30am-2pm. **Postal Code:** 85600.

OTE: inland along the left side of the park in the middle of the harbor; follow signs starting at Neraida restaurant. Open M-F 7:30am-3:10pm. **Telephone Code:** 0241.

ACCOMMODATIONS

Most travelers do not spend the night, but a small herd of dock hawks still awaits the arrival of ferries and hydrofoils. With many empty rooms outside of July and August, you can get miraculous results by asking prices of the hawker, then laughing and responding that you can only afford half that. Throughout town, expensive list prices drop fast with perseverance, though in the high season, rooms can be hard to find.

Hotel Kokona (tel. 72 620, 71 451), over the foot bridge and to the left of the old church tower, has pristine, welcoming rooms with baths and balconies that actually smell clean. Doubles 8000-10,000dr; triples 10,000-12,000dr; quads 12,000-14,000dr. Breakfast 900dr.

Opera House Hotel (tel. 72 034), from the ferry dock walk into town, cross the footbridge, turn right along the park and take the first left after. While doubles run upwards of 12000dr, prices can be bargained down significantly. Clean rooms and large bathrooms around a huge gorgeous garden filled with tables and chairs.

Dallaras Snack Bar (tel. 72 030), on the waterfront, has small but attractive rooms in a nearby house. Doubles with shared bath 7000dr.

Hotel Maria (tel. 71 311), next to Hotel Kokona. Large rooms with kitchen facilities on a cute courtyard. Doubles 7000-9000dr.

Vigla Taverna (tel. 71 932), on the waterfront in the center of town. Rooms with home-like decor and fans. Doubles 7000dr.

FOOD

Taverna Meraklis (tel. 71 003). Piping-hot authentic food. Steer away from the waterfront, walk over the foot bridge, and go one block inland from Symi Tours. Overwhelmingly delicious Greek and island specialties. The *moussaka* and *pastitsio* (each 900dr) are truly fabulous. Open daily 10am-4pm and 6pm-1am.

Georgios' Restaurant (tel. 71 984), at the top of the 200 stairs to the Horio. Authentic family-owned restaurant serves beyond the basic Greek menu. Try the *peppers florini* (red peppers stuffed with feta 1200dr), and lamb *exohiko* (lamb baked in aluminum foil with potatoes, cheese, and oregano 1800dr). Open daily 7pm-2am.

Syllogos (tel. 72 148), up the steps to the Horio. Named for and embodying the village meeting place. Dishes are slightly expensive (1600-2000dr), but superb service, terrace views, and eclectic menu more than compensate. Menu revolves around daily specials like chicken stew with herbs and prunes.

Hellenikon (tel. 72 455), on Ikonomou Sq., near the footbridge. Owner Nikos is an ardent wine aficionado and will try to make you one too. Being on a budget will keep travelers from delving too deep into the extensive cellar. Italian-inflected Greek cuisine is very tasty, if slightly pricey.

Kantirmi Cafe (tel. 71 381), at the waterfront footbridge from which the cafe gets its name. Popular with foreign residents. Excellent daytime sandwiches (avocado and bacon 600dr) give way to beer (400-700dr), liqueurs (650dr), and cocktails (800dr). Also serves ice cream. Open daily 9am-4pm and 6pm-2am.

ENTERTAINMENT

Ⓜ**Jean and Tonic Pub** (tel. 71 819), in Horio, up the hill from George's. Happy hour 8-9pm and friendly conversation all night long. Jean, a British vacationer who loved Symi so much that she never went home, can help with accommodations.

Katoi Bar (tel. 71 752), over the bridge along the east waterfront. Popular among Greek residents. Greek music, good coffee, small tables for good conversation. Beer 600-800dr; long drinks 1000dr; cocktails 1000-1400dr. Open daily 9am-noon and 7pm-2am.

The Club, at the footbridge that seems to shake with the deafening bass beat. Everyone heads to this packed dance club once the music dies down at the bars at midnight). Be prepared for a young and lusty crowd. 2000dr cover includes first drink.

SIGHTS

In Yialos, the **Naval Museum** (tel. 72 363), housed in a yellow Neoclassical building at the back of the main waterfront strip, recounts the history of sponge-diving on the island with equipment, photographs, and maps. *(Open daily 10:30am-3pm. Admission 300dr.)* At the east side of the waterfront, several sets of stairs lead the way to Horio, a 20- to 30-minute hike. Constructed to fortify itself from medieval pirate raids, the vil-

DODECANESE

lage is worth visiting if only for its planning scheme. The shadiest and most straight-forward is the one farthest along the water, close to where the road heads uphill. Follow the road at the top of the stairs and you will see signs for the small but very worthwhile **archaeological museum** (tel. 71 114), housing classical and Byzantine pieces as well as island costumes and utensils. *(Open Tu-Su 8:30am-2:30pm. Admission 500dr, students 300dr, seniors 400dr, under 18 200dr.)* The museum ticket also covers entrance to the nearby **Chatziagapitos Mansion,** which contains objects of everyday life once owned by Symiotes of yesteryear. *(Open Tu-Su 8:30am-2:30pm.)* Signs also lead through a maze of streets to the ruins of the old **castle** where, aside from the church of Megali Panagia, little remains within the Cyclopean walls. A 20-minute walk below Horio, **Pedhi** is the only other village on Symi. Lacking Yialos's stateliness and Horio's historical atmosphere, the small fishing port sports a humble gravelly beach. A more rewarding option is sandy and serene Agios Nikolaos, a 30-minute hike farther east.

Panormitis Monastery, the grand Monastery of the Archangel Michael (friend of travelers), looms at the center of a remarkable horseshoe-shaped harbor in the south-ern part of the island and greets you with its chiming bells. The monastery was built in the 15th century, at the spot where a local woman happened upon an icon of Michael. Although it was brought to Yialos, the icon kept returning to Panormitis. The palatial white buildings of the monastery, dominated by an elegant bell tower in the center, contains two small museums, one with ecclesiastical relics and worship-pers' gifts and one with folkloric exhibits. *(Both open daily 10am-12:30pm and when excursion boats visit. Admission 200dr for both.)*

The small monastery church houses an exceptional wooden altar screen. The screen is famous throughout the Dodecanese for its wish-granting powers, and tokens in the museum represent supplicants' requests. Modest dress is required to enter the monastery. A gate attendant hands women wrap-around skirts to wear inside. No regular buses run to the monastery, but tour buses from Yialos run four times per week (1hr.), and a boat from Yialos heads here as well. Hiking here is rigor-ous and requires a full day. Mopeds are not well-suited to the gravelly terrain closer to the monastery. If Panormitis appears too ambitious take the red paths that mark hik-ing trails off the main road. They will lead you through a forest dedicated to James Brown to a remote monastery and isolated beaches. All excursion boats from Rhodes stop here. There are free toilets to the left of the complex. The bakery under the arch-way to the left has fresh goodies.

Cuckoo for Koukkoumas?

Think singles bars are a difficult way to find a mate? Visit the island during Koukk-oumas for a taste of matchmaking Symi style. Traditionally, Koukkoumas begins on the evening of May 1st. Unmarried girls with living parents silently gather water from seven homes in which the housewife is named Irene. Later that evening, the girls toss their rings into the water and place the water on a roof for the night. The next morning the would-be brides use the gathered water to bake salty pies. All baking must be done with their hands behind their backs. A long day's baking gives way to singing, dancing, and salty pie eating. During the festiv-ities, a young girl whose parents are living takes each ring and utters a male name. Before sleeping that night, the would-be brides, dehydrated from extensive danc-ing and copious salt consumption, go to another house to drink water. If an unmarried male who shares the name spoken by the young girl resides in that house, then she's found her husband.

Nos Beach, a 10-minute walk from Yialos (head north along the waterfront, past the shipyard), is tiny but close to the port. The beach at **Nimborio,** 45 minutes on foot past Nos, is mediocre, but the views make the walk worthwhile. You can also take a taxi boat (800dr round-trip). **Pedi,** a short distance by bus, boasts radiant sands and refreshing water. Symi's tiny coves shelter a few excellent beaches at **Agios Marina, Nanou,** and **Marathounda** on the east side of the island, which are accessible only by boat (daily, round-trip 1000dr). Boats also go to **Sesklia Island,** south of Symi (round-trip 3000dr). Excursion boats do not follow a set schedule. They all line up with destinations and prices posted in the morning.

NISYROS Νισυρος

Greece's *other* volcanic island, Nisyros is not quite as popular and dramatic as Santorini, but Nisyros has to its credit a virgin landscape and an island community not yet infiltrated by the vices of tourism. With its volcano, clifftop monastery, and greenery that endures well into the summer, Nisyros is a latent treasure of the Aegean. Small and unfrequented by travelers, the island allows rowdy backpackers to detox between parties in Kos and Rhodes, and offers picturesque hiking.

■ Mandraki Μανδρακι

Mandraki is Nisyros' tiny, whitewashed port town. While the area where the ferries dock is quite dingy, the winding streets and handsome views of the sea make the city both pleasant and comfortable.

ORIENTATION AND PRACTICAL INFORMATION Virtually all of Mandraki sits to the right of the port. Walking along the waterfront, small alleys lead inland to residential areas and the orchards above them. However, most travelers' hungers can be satiated along the waterfront and on the parallel inland road. The **port authority** (tel. 31 222; open 24hr.), the **police** (tel. 31 201; open 24hr.), and **post office** (tel. 31 249; open M-F 7:30am-2pm), which also offers **currency exchange,** are all housed in the white building on the dock with the Greek flag. The road continuing left around the bend leads into the town. **Enetikon Travel** (tel. 31 180; fax 31 168) is on that road, on the right side in a tiny building on the rocks. A multilingual staff helps with boats, Flying Dolphins, accommodations, excursions, and faxes (open daily 9:30am-1:30pm and 6-9pm). Along the same road, parallel to the waterfront, you'll find **Alfa Rent** (tel. 31 580), in the first waterfront square, which has moped rentals from 2500dr per day (open daily 8:30am-9:30pm). Farther along the same path is the representative of the **National Bank** (tel. 31 459; open M-Th 8am-2pm, F 8am-1:30pm) in **Diakomitalis Tours.** If you take the first left off the road from the dock into town, you'll reach the uptown square. The red cross on the left marks the **pharmacy,** which is usually open in the evenings. In a little office behind the town hall, **Eleni Kendri** sells tickets for ferries to the island and for **Olympic Airways** flights (tel. 31 230; open daily 7-9pm).

Two **ferries** per week serve Nisyros on their way to Rhodes (2340dr), Kalymnos (1450dr), Tilos (1200dr), Symi (2380dr), Kos (1600dr), and Peiraias (6590dr). **Flying Dolphins** speed twice per week to Rhodes (5840dr), Tilos (2800dr), and Kos (3175dr). **Buses** on Nisyros run on their own time, but when they do turn on the engine, two per day head to Loutra (5min.), Pali (10min.), Emborio (20min.), and Nikia (30min.). There are many private buses heading to the crater of the volcano. Ask around when you dock; most wait to meet incoming boats. There are two **taxi services** on the island: **Babis'** (tel. 31 460) and **Irini's** (tel. 31 474). **Postal code:** 85303. **Telephone code:** 0242.

ACCOMMODATIONS In high season, doubles range from 4000-7000dr; in the off season, rates may fall by up to 50%. Rooms are scarce but generally available except in mid-August, during the island's big festival for the Virgin Mary, when prices shoot up with demand. On the road leading left from the dock, **Three Brothers Hotel** (tel. 31 344) offers well-maintained seaside rooms with bath and friendly service from the brothers three (singles 5000-6000dr; doubles 5000-8000dr). Across the street, **Hotel Romantzo** (tel. 31 340) has clean rooms with bath at negotiable prices (singles 3000dr; doubles 4000dr; triples 6000dr). In Mandraki, **Taverna Nisyros** (tel. 31 460) has doubles with bath and kitchenette for 4000dr.

DODECANESE

FOOD It is generally a good idea to wander away from the cafes and *tavernas* that attract most excursion visitors. A small sign points to **Y Fabrika** (tel. 31 552), on one of the little streets leading from the town hall square to the water. Go down the steps for books, music, and superb Greek *mezedes* at this cozy and friendly *ouzeri* (octopus 1000dr, *raki* 200dr, beer 400-500dr). Look for a sign on the road parallel to the waterfront, pointing to **Tavernas Nisyros** (tel. 31 460), where Polyxeni cooks up a storm (Greek salad 700dr, *moussaka* 900dr, lamb chops 12,000dr). **Captain's** (tel. 31 225), at the water's edge, sells the island's delicious specialty, *soumada* (almond juice; 1100dr per bottle), and cheap fish (swordfish fillet 1500dr).

Nights are calm in Nisyros, with a few bars along the waterfront after Captain's restaurant and inland in **Ilikiomenhi Square. Evallaz** music bar (tel. 31 307) on the waterfront dishes out tunes and *ouzo* late into the evening.

■ Around Nisyros

Mandraki Volcano

As soon as you dock, it's obvious that the volcano is the island's main attraction. Tour guides and travel agents toting volcano signs crowd the dock—there's even a model of the island glorifying the volcano on the quay. Trips up to the **Stefanos crater** are often pre-booked, but you can join a group for 1000-1500dr. The bus ride is 20 minutes and you have 45 minutes to wander around in the crater. Another option is renting a moped, but drive carefully, as the roads are narrow. There is no admission fee to the crater. There is a **cafe** on the site (soda 350dr; open daily 9:30am-7pm), and you'll find a public toilet behind the cafe. Inside the crater, you'll see piles of sulphur and jets of scalding steam against the island's almost eerie landscape. Although the volcano has been dormant since 1888, there's audible rumbling in parts of the crater.

A 20-minute walk uphill from its famous and popular neighbor, the **Alexhandros crater** leads a quiet existence. Virtually unvisited but no less spectacular, the Alexhandros crater is accessible via a small walking trail that begins behind the toilets and leads over the mountain.

Panagia Spiliani Monastery

On the cliff at the end of the Mandraki is the Panagia Spiliani Monastery. *(Open daily 10am-3pm. Free.)* The sacred icon of this monastery used to reside in a small cave just above Mandraki's port. It would mysteriously disappear from the sanctuary only to be found on the site of today's monastery. After several disappearing acts, the monks took it as a sign and built a new home for the icon, making a large replica of it in 1798 to display in the new church. The tender gazes of Christ and the Virgin Mary have been known to grant relief from pain. The church also has relics of Agios Charlambos in its antechamber. Recently, on the rear face of the icon of the Virgin Mary, an altar boy discovered the iconographer's hidden portrait of Agios Nikolaos, which had been covered with an old cloth for over two centuries. Pictures of the back of this two-faced icon are displayed in the church as well. To get up to the monastery, climb the narrow uphill steps across from the church with the pink bell tower.

On those same steps up to the monastery is the tiny **Historical and Popular Museum,** with folkloric exhibits on life on Nisyros. *(Open F-W 10:30am-2:30pm and 6-8pm. Free.)* The well-preserved Cyclopean walls, built by the Venetians, are perched at the edge of Mandraki just off the road to the volcano, and extend to the monastery. Stairs built into the walls allow visitors to step up and walk the length of them.

Nikia and Pali

The quiet hillside village of **Nikia** boasts views of the island of Tilos to the southeast, and a bird's-eye view of the volcano. The small square is the center of Nikia life, containing the village church and a few cafes. Halfway between Mandraki and the volcano, a sign marks the turn-off to **Emborio,** 1km away. The once-abandoned village is gradually being refurbished by summering Athenians and foreigners.

On the road past the dock, a 10-minute walk from Mandraki, are the **thermal springs** of Loutra. Because of their therapeutic qualities, these springs are open only to visitors bearing a doctor's prescription.

Four kilometers east of Mandraki, the small fishing village of **Pali** contains a relatively large number of restaurants, accommodations, and motorbike rentals. **Hellinis** (tel. 31 453) and **Aphrodite** (tel. 31 242) are both harborside *tavernas* offering clean rooms with balconies (doubles 4000-6000dr). The **Pali Bakery** carts its wares across the island, but during a visit to the village you can and should hit the source.

Beaches

Nisyros also has few pleasant beaches, thanks to the steaming black volcanic rocks and sand, which torment the feet. Behind the monastery's cliff, along a waterfront path, is a small secluded beach (5min. walk from Mandraki). Past Loutra, on the road to Pali, **White Beach** is anything but white. The island's best beach, 5km east of Pali and just past the **Oasis** *taverna*, is better only in that it's cleaner and larger. Depending on demand, Enetikon Travel organizes trips to the nearby island of **Giali** for its better beaches (2000dr round-trip).

LEROS Λερος

Mental hospitals, military *junta* prisons, and extensive foreign occupation are not the usual stuff of Greek islands—Leros has been a bit hard-pressed to convince others of its virtues. The goddess Artemis, a fleet-footed hunter and otherwise independent woman, may have been the island's first celebrity. Since she chose Leros, so did the Persians, the Knights of St. John, and the Italians, who are most influential on the Leros of today: they saw in Lakki's natural harbor the potential for an ideal naval base during WWII. After the war, the Greek government chose Leros as a site for mental hospitals. In the past, these institutions garnered negative attention for poor treatment of patients, and perhaps impeded the island from being swept onto the tourism bandwagon. In many respects, this has proved its saving grace. Though the island now gains popularity yearly, the government has made a number of quite sane decisions on restricting building associated with tourism. The underdog Leros is positively on the upswing—believing otherwise would be crazy.

■ Lakki Λακκι

Lakki, an uninviting port town and the ferry-goer's introduction to Leros, has borne the brunt of the island's recent turbid past. The waterfront, whose design hails from the era of Italian occupation, has the semblance of an extravagant movie set populated with cast and crew on eternal break. A grand rotary-dotted boulevard fronts large Art Deco buildings that sit untouched and, in the case of the once elegant but now dilapidated Leros Palace Hotel, abandoned. The stately buildings stand in stark contrast to the humble pace of town today. Lakki has done little to cultivate the tourism that has caused neighboring towns to flourish. The town is gradually reviving itself as public sentiment shifts to favor preserving these edifices as a historical reminder, rather than letting them crumble as a political symbol. Still, few people choose to tour or stay in Lakki—all except architectural buffs are eager to find the fastest transit to beaches around Platanos.

ORIENTATION AND PRACTICAL INFORMATION Virtually all tourist services are on or just inland from the waterfront. The closest beach is 1km west in Lovlouki, which makes for a scenic walk along the coast. The mental hospital is 2km to the west. **Ferries** float away to Kos (1 per day, 2090dr); Kalymnos (1-2 per day, 1850dr); Patmos (1 per day, 3240dr); Samos (2 per week, 5160dr). Kos and Patmos connect with more comprehensive ferry service. **Flying Dolphins** leave from Agia Marina. A **taxi station** (tel. 22 500) is next to the police station. **Kostis Travel and Shipping,** 9

King George Ave. (tel. 22 500; fax 22 872), along the waterfront near the police station, offers comprehensive travel assistance. A **National Bank of Greece** is along the waterfront. An **Agricultural Bank** sits inland from the police station, at the left where the road separates (both open M-Th 8am-2pm, F 8am-1:30pm, with 24hr. **ATM**). The **police** (tel. 22 222) are at the far end of the waterfront from where ferries dock (open 24hr. in theory). To find the **port police** (tel. 22 224), head inland by the waterfront school near the ferry dock and take the first left, in a seemingly abandoned building. (Open 24hr. but may require ringing doorbell.) A **hospital** (tel. 23 251 or 23 554) is two blocks inland of the waterfront school (open 24hr.). For a **pharmacy** (tel. 23 782), head inland at the cinema and take the second right (open daily 8am-1pm and 5-9pm). The **post office** (tel. 22 929) is inland from Leros Palace Hotel. **Postal code:** 85400. **Telephone code:** 0247.

ACCOMMODATIONS Few choose Lakki as a base for exploring the island, but ferry schedules may necessitate overnight stays here. Rooms are expensive, but the town's unpopularity can put travelers in a bargaining position. **Hotel Katerina** (tel. 22 460; fax 23 038) is by far the best bet in town, with clean if slightly institutional rooms. Their van may be waiting at the ferry for pickup (singles 6000dr; doubles 7000dr). From the port, walk along the main street, head inland at the cinema, and take the second right. **Hotel Artemis** (tel. 22 416), a few blocks inland before Leros Palace Hotel, is the next best option (singles 6000dr; doubles 7000dr). The large **campground,** 3km southeast, in between the mental hospital and Xero Kampos, has standard facilities (1100dr per person; 700dr per tent; 650dr per tent rental); the owner also runs **Leros Diving Center.**

FOOD AND ENTERTAINMENT There are a couple of notable exceptions to the boring string of restaurants along and just inland of the waterfront. Located next to the post office, inland from Leros Palace Hotel, **To Petrino** (tel. 24 807) serves carefully prepared meals in the sort of setting that keeps you lingering all night. The menu changes but consists of starters (around 700dr) and large carnivorous portions (around 1700dr). **Koulouki** (tel. 24 935), 1km west of town on the coast road, is a beachside *taverna* under a canopy of trees (lamb with pasta 1400dr; prawns 1400dr; open daily 9am-midnight). Aside from the handful of restaurants, Lakki virtually shuts down at night. Those who do venture out go to the Tex-Mex themed and seldom crowded **Puerto Club,** or the newly reopened **outdoor cinema,** showing English language films with Greek subtitles nightly. Both are along the waterfront.

■ Platanos Πλατανος

The island's oldest settlement and present-day capital, Platanos straddles the crest separating the southeast from the northwest portions of the island. As primarily a logistical center, Platanos provides a service hub for the neighboring beach towns it gazes down upon, and steps for walking to the Kastro. A bland but functional *plateia* (square) opens to Agia Marina to the northwest and Pendeli to the southeast, with little clarity as to where the towns separate. Visitors prefer staying in nearby beach towns, but the **Eleftheria Hotel** rents large, clean rooms (7000dr), arranged through **Laskarina Travel** (tel. 23 550), below the *plateia* on the road to Pendeli.

Visible from afar, the imposing **Kastro** was one of the Knights' of St. John many stomping grounds among the Dodecanese (open daily 8:30am-8:30pm; admission 500dr). Although it eventually fell into Turkish hands, the arduous trek involved in reaching the fortification may have you wondering how. For walkers, the Kastro is accessible from a seemingly eternal set of stairs ascending from behind the *platia.* Those with wheels can take a circuitous road from Pendeli that runs along a sheer coastal drop-off. Within the exterior walls rest a small complex of churches and the exceptional **Ecclesiastical Museum.** The first room displays an exquisite collection of censers, chalices, ceremonial dresses, and other religious instruments and vestments. Another room houses artifacts from local shipwrecks. A library in the back holds religious books in a serene setting. The **Panagia tou Kastrou** next door is visited for its gold *iconostasis* of the Virgin Mary.

■ Agia Marina Αγια Μαρινα

Just below Platonos, Agia Marina, with its endearing waterfront, is probably the most charming town in Leros. Accordingly, it has become heavily touristed. Though the town is noted for its nightlife and has the island's only Flying Dolphin service, rooms in Agia Marina are hard to come by. Staying in Alinda is much more common. With no beach in town, Agia Marina lends itself to eating, drinking, and promenading.

Travel agencies, cafes, an **Agricultural Bank** (open M-Th 8am-2pm, F 8am-1:30pm, no ATM), a 24-hour **police station** (tel. 22 226), and a number of moped rentals sit along the waterfront, alongside a burgeoning collection of boutiques and tourist shops. Just inland from the bank, **Captain Michael's Taverna** (tel. 24 987) serves seafood-focused dishes amid modest nautical surroundings. Try the specialty fish soup (1000dr) or swordfish steak (1200dr). When the moon comes up, Agia Marina becomes naughtier and livelier than its daytime calm would intimate. Evenings begin at any of the waterside cafes or the locals' preferred watering hotel, **To Meltemi**, and end at trendy **Apothiki** (tel. 22 968) for Greek music, **La Playa** (tel. 22 934) for British/American tunes, or the funkier **Apocalypse.** All are clustered around the waterfront, and some charge covers (around 1300dr), depending on the evening.

■ Alinda Αλινδα

Two kilometers northwest of Agia Marina, Alinda is a vast assemblage of hotels, rooms for rent, tourist shops, and restaurants scattered along the coast. A paltry stretch of coarse sand that passes for a beach runs the length of the town. Cars whizzing by in frightening proximity don't temper the beach's popularity, which is bizarre, considering the excellent beaches that lie less than one kilometer away.

Rooms abound, though package tours can make availability difficult during high season. **Hotel Alinda** (tel. 23 266), on the waterfront, has large older rooms above a touristy but tasty restaurant (doubles 6000dr, with private bath 7000dr). **Hotel Papofotis** (tel. 22 247) offers large basic pension rooms at the north end of town. Look for signs indicating where to turn. While its rates skyrocket in August, **Effie's Apartment** (tel. 24 459) has competitive rates for much of the year. Large, well-appointed studios surrounding a lush garden may cause you to stay forever. Look for the waterfront "Effie's" sign pointing inland (doubles from 7000dr).

For entertainment, **Cosmopolitan** (tel. 23 564), at the Agia Marina end of town, buzzes all day on the large patio and at night inside at the bar. Also along the waterfront, the Belenis Mansion is a ridiculous looking edifice and home to the island's **Folklore and Historical Museum.** *(Open M-F 9am-noon and 5-8pm. Free.)* A scattered exhibit on the press may interest some. A half-kilometer north along the coast at Panagies, a series of small coves offer attractive beaches without crowds, and in the cave of the farthest cove, without swimsuits. West of Alinda, **Gourna** is host to a long, flat, sandy beach. At the northern end of the crescent-shaped bay, miniature **Agios Issidoros Church** is built on a large rock in the water. A walking path connects the church with the land. North of Alinda, the **Temple of Artemis,** once an important site of worship, is essentially rubble today. More interesting is the small altar behind it, still used on occasion today for Christian services.

CYPRUS Κυπρος

Would that I go to Cyprus, the island of Aphrodite,
Where the Loves who soothe mortal hearts dwell.

—Euripides

Ancient temples, Roman mosaics, remote monasteries, castles, mosques, and the Green Line are monuments to Cyprus' eternal role as both peaceful meeting place and bloody battleground for East and West. The land has passed through the hands of Phoenicians, Greeks, Persians, Ptolomies, Romans, Arabs, Crusaders, Ottomans, and Brits into a strained independence, all the while retaining its own unique if multi-faceted identity. The land abounds in natural beauty from the sandy beaches of Agia Napa to the cool mountain air of the Troodos range. The island caters to diverse travelers and remains generally clean, pleasant, and grime-free, even in its most industrial cities. The people of Cyprus are friendly and hospitable, and the popularity of the island as a tourist destination is on the rise, especially among Brits and Arabs. Most residents speak English. Traveling in Cyprus is generally more expensive than in Greece, but the island has some budget options.

🏛 HIGHLIGHTS OF CYPRUS

- Stare like Narcissus at your crystal clear reflection at the Baths of Aphrodite in **Polis** (p. 499). Sorry no bathing allowed.
- Spend the night in a mosque turned hostel, dine among poets at an art cafe, and see the foundations of one of the world's oldest cities at **Larnaka**.(p. 486).
- Frolic on the beaches of corybantic **Agia Napa** (p. 492), a splashing ground unrivaled in the Mediterranean.
- Cross the Green Line into Turkish-occupied territory in **Nicosia** (p. 510), the world's last divided city.

ESSENTIALS

■ Money

US$1 = C£0.52 (Cypriot Pounds)	**C£1 = US$1.90**
CDN$1 = C£0.34	**C£1 = CDN$2.96**
UK£1 = C£0.87	**C£1 = UK£1.14**
IR£1 = C£0.74	**C£1 = IR£1.35**
AUS$1 = C£0.30	**C£1 = AUS$3.36**
NZ$1 = C£0.26	**C£1 = NZ$3.85**
SAR1 = C£0.14	**C£1 = SAR7.17**
100GRdr = C£0.17	**C£1 = 418GRdr**
TL10,000 = C£0.02	**C£1 = TL533,943**

Note: Cyprus pounds will be indicated by £. Prices quoted were effective in the summer of 1998. As inflation and exchange rates fluctuate, present prices may differ by as much as 30%. For more information, see **Money Matters,** p. 16.

■ Getting There

The third-largest island in the Mediterranean after Sicily and Sardinia, Cyprus lies 64km from Turkey, 160km from Israel and Lebanon, and 480km from the nearest

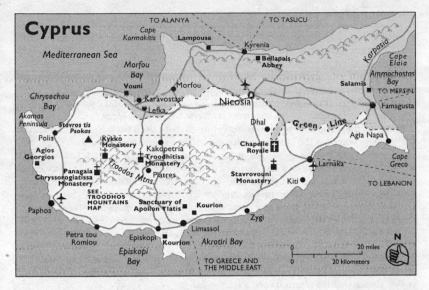

Cyprus

Mediterranean Sea

Greek island. The Republic of Cyprus is accessible from Greece and other European and Middle Eastern countries by airplane or boat. Limassol can be reached by sea from a seemingly unlimited number of points, and finding a boat agency to facilitate your trip should not be difficult. By plane, Cyprus is accessible on **Olympic Airlines** (U.S. tel. (800) 223-1226), **Egypt Air** (U.S. tel. (800) 334-6787), **Cyprus Airways** (U.S. tel. (212) 714-2310), and other airlines. Student fare on Olympic (age 12-28) or Cyprus Airways (age 12-24) is US$190 round-trip from Athens to Larnaka; you'll need to show a letter from your university or an ISIC.

If your travels originate in north Cyprus, and you have a Turkish stamp in your passport, you can never enter the south. Northern authorities may stamp a separate piece of paper if you ask. The quickest way to get to southern Cyprus, therefore, is to first fly to London, and then to the south. This trick will only work if you don't have a Northern Cyprus stamp on your passport. A cheaper, but much slower, way is to go by seabus (or ferry) to Taşucu in Turkey, take a bus from there to Marmaris, from there a ferry to Rhodes, and finally a ferry to southern Cyprus. Travel time: about two days. To be safe, ask the Turkish authorities not to stamp your passport, as a Taşucu stamp gives away that you've been to northern Cyprus.

■ Once There

TOURIST ORGANIZATIONS

Tourist offices in Cyprus are extremely helpful and efficient. There are offices in Limassol, Nicosia, Larnaka, Paphos, Polis, Agia Napa, and Platres. The main office is the **Cyprus Tourism Organization,** P.O. Box 4535, 19 Limassol Ave., Nicosia CY 1390 (tel. (2) 337 715); in the **U.S.,** 13 E. 40th St., New York, NY 10016 (tel. (212) 683-5280). The CTO offices provide excellent free maps and information on buses, museums, events, and other points of interest. A particularly helpful publication available at tourist offices is *The Cyprus Traveler's Handbook* (free). Officials generally speak English, Greek, German, and French.

TRANSPORTATION

A reliable highway system serves much of Cyprus, but caution is required on the winding mountain roads. Cars drive on the left side of the road in the south and on the right in the north. Rented cars may not cross the Green Line. The south also has several British rotaries, some of which can be particularly intimidating for American drivers. Transportation is almost nonexistent after 7pm. Shared **taxis** run regularly Monday through Friday between Limassol, Paphos, Larnaka, and Nicosia (£2-3.50). Hitchhiking is uncommon, and neither locals nor tourists are likely to offer rides.

Buses to the **Troodos Mountains** depart once daily from both Nicosia and Limassol. Renting wheels is the best option for mountain excursions. There is no direct bus connection from Paphos to Nicosia or Larnaka; you must pass through Limassol. Bus service throughout Cyprus is less frequent in the winter. There is one island-wide **bus schedule** available at tourist offices. This schedule provides all necessary information, including prices for buses and private taxi service. All Cypriot rental cars have manual transmission and standardized rental rates. The cheapest compact cars should cost no more than £17 per day, small motorbikes £5, and larger motorcycles £7-8 (most dealers rent two-seat motor bikes, but operating with two riders may result in a fine). Cypriot law requires that seatbelts be worn in front seats, and an international driver's license or a national driver's license from your home country is required. A temporary Cypriot driver's license, good for six months, can be obtained from district police stations with a photo ID and £1.

PRACTICAL INFORMATION

> **Emergencies:** dial 199 for **ambulance, fire,** or **police** in southern Cyprus.

Post offices are open Monday through Friday from 7:30am to 1:30pm (1pm in the summer). Some have afternoon hours from 3:30-5:30pm (summer 4-6pm). *Poste Restante* (see **Keeping in Touch,** p.36) is available only in Nicosia, Larnaka, Paphos, and Limassol (10¢ per piece). Letters from the south must have a 1¢ refugee stamp.

Southern Cyprus has fairly reliable **telephone service** (administered by **CYTA**). Direct overseas calls can be made from nearly all public phones. **Telecards** sold at banks and kiosks make international calls more convenient. They must be used in special phones, and are available in £3, 5, and 10 denominations. Private phones in hotels may have a 10% surcharge.

In general, off-season prices (Oct.-May) are about 20% lower than the rates quoted in this book. Nicosia, Troodos, Paphos, and Larnaka all have **HI youth hostels.** Although Cyprus has few formal campgrounds, some travelers sleep on beaches and in forests. Campers choose their sites discreetly and leave them as clean as they found them. Women should be especially wary and never camp alone.

HISTORY

■ Ancient and Medieval Cyprus

The remains of round stone dwellings indicate settlement on Cyprus as early as neolithic times, dating back to roughly 7000 BC. Cyprus first achieved local importance in the **Bronze Age** due to its wealth of copper ore. Linguists are unsure whether *Kypros,* from which the word "copper" is derived, first referred to the island or the metal itself. The Bronze Age witnessed an increase in Cyprus' trade and cultural exchange with neighboring countries.

The most dramatic change in island culture was fostered by the arrival of the **Mycenaeans** from the Peloponnese in the Middle Bronze Age, initiating a Hellenic tradition that has carried over to the present. From 1400 to the mid-12th century BC, Mycenaean traders visited the island regularly, spreading the use of the Greek language and introducing written notation for commerce. The arrival of **Phoenician** traders and colonists in the first millennium BC introduced yet another fresh cultural impulse to the island. The Phoenicians shared political control with the Greeks until the arrival of the **Assyrians** in the 7th century BC, who dominated the island for 100 years. After the waning of Assyrian power, the Egyptians briefly took hold of the island, but were soon overthrown by the Persian king. There was significant resistance to Persian rule by Cypriots, notably in the efforts of pro-Hellenic Evagoras I, who forced Persians out of Salamis and spread Greek throughout his kingdom.

As Persian expansion stagnated, **Alexander the Great** absorbed Cyprus into his growing empire. In 295 BC, following Alexander's death, Ptolemy claimed Cyprus for Egypt. Cyprus prospered under the succession of **Ptolemies.** While cultural and religious institutions remained unchanged, the Greek alphabet came to replace the local syllabic script. Two centuries later, in 58 BC, Rome took advantage of Ptolemy's misfortunes by annexing Cyprus. **Christianity** was introduced to the island in 45 AD by the apostle Paul and the Cypriot apostle Barnabas. The spread of Christianity continued for the next three centuries, and, with the conversion of the Roman governor in 46 AD, Cyprus became the first territory in the world to be ruled by a Christian.

BYZANTINE RULE TO THE OTTOMAN EMPIRE

When Constantinople was proclaimed the capital of the eastern half of the divided Roman empire, the stage was set for the synthesis of Roman civic thought, Greek philosophy, and the Greek Orthodox tradition in Cyprus. During these centuries, the island endured several disasters—two devastating earthquakes in 332 and 342, a 40-year drought that severely scarred the island, and fierce Arab raids in the 7th century that once again proved the island's vulnerability to foreign attack. At the same time, however, many new towns were founded, and established towns expanded significantly. In 1191, **Richard the Lionheart,** en route to the Crusades in Jerusalem, quickly overran the island, which proved indispensable in provisioning the Christian armies. After robbing the island of its treasures, King Richard sold Cyprus to the **Knights Templar,** who in turn passed responsibility on to Guy de Lusignan, a minor French noble who had been involved in the Crusades.

The **Lusignan Dynasty** (1192-1489) ruled through a feudalistic system of class privileges that oppressed the lower classes and suppressed Cypriot culture and religion. Despite French subjugation of the locals, the Lusignan era left an impressive legacy of Gothic architecture in the form of churches, cathedrals, and castles. As setbacks in Palestine forced the Crusaders into full retreat, the Lusignans invited Crusader families to set up camp on the island. By the late 13th century, Cyprus had become the wealthiest island in the eastern Mediterranean. Yet in 1489 the **Venetians,** profiting from the Lusignans' dynastic intrigues, annexed the island. They strengthened Cypriot military defenses, but were still no match for the Ottoman Empire. In 1570, following a two-month siege, Nicosia surrendered to the Ottomans. The fall of Famagusta one year later marked the beginning of the **Ottoman period** in Cyprus.

Cypriots welcomed the Ottoman abolition of feudalism, and the peasants acquired land under the new system. The Orthodox Church also flourished in this period, serving as a powerful administrative machine for the sultan. As the Empire weakened in the 19th century, Britain found itself defending Ottoman territories in the face of Russian expansionism. In July of 1878, British forces landed peacefully at Larnaka and assumed control of Cyprus as a second military base. **Britain** entered into an arrangement with Turkey in which the island's excess revenue was used to pay off Ottoman war loans. Although Cypriots did not enjoy political self-determination under the British, they benefited from the construction of many public works—roads, bridges, drinking and irrigation water supplies, a railway line, schools, and hospitals.

▓ Cyprus in the 20th Century

In 1954, **General George Grivas,** in conjunction with **Archbishop Makarios,** founded the **EOKA** (National Organization of Cypriot Fighters), an underground *enosist* movement. When the United Nations vetoed the Greek request to grant Cyprus self-government in 1955, General Grivas and the EOKA initiated a round of riots and guerilla warfare aimed at the British government. In response to increased EOKA activity, the underground Volkan (Volcano), under the leadership of **Rauf Denktaş,** founded the TMT (Turkish Resistance Organization). TMT was a paramilitary organization designed to fight the *enosists* and to push for **taksim,** or partition of the island between Greece and Turkey. Weary of the perpetual violence but unconvinced that either *enosis* or *taksim* was viable, Britain, along with the foreign ministers of Greece and Turkey, agreed in 1959 to establish an independent Cypriot republic. On August 16, 1960, Cyprus was granted independence and became a member of the U.N. and the British Commonwealth.

The new constitution stipulated that a Greek Cypriot president and a Turkish Cypriot vice-president were to be appointed through popular election and that the Greek to Turkish ratio in the House of Representatives would be 70:30. In 1959, Archbishop Makarios became the republic's first president, and **Fazıl Küçük,** leader of the Turkish Cypriot community, was elected to the vice presidency without opposition. In 1963, Makarios proposed 13 amendments to the constitution, intended to facilitate bicommunal life, which included the abolition of the president's and vice-president's veto power and the introduction of majority rule. When the Turkish government threatened to use military force if these amendments were implemented, renewed violence broke out between the EOKA and TMT, resulting in the division of Nicosia along the Green Line. In February 1964, the U.N. dispatched a "temporary" peacekeeping force that has been renewed indefinitely.

In 1968, Makarios and Küçük were both re-elected by an overwhelming majority, although in the years following they were subject to several coup plots, notably one by former ally General Grivas who returned to Cyprus in 1971 to found the militant EOKA-B and to revitalize the call for *enosis.* Intermittent violence exploded into an international affair in 1974 when the Greek Cypriot National Guard, assisted by the military **junta** in Greece, overthrew Archbishop Makarios and replaced him with **Nikos Sampson,** a notorious EOKA member who favored immediate *enosis.* Five days later the Turkish army invaded Cyprus from the north in order to protect Turkish Cypriots from the National Guard. Early in 1975, the North declared itself the Turkish Federated State of Cyprus (TFSC), officially partitioning the island.

RECENT YEARS

In November 1983, Turkish-occupied Cyprus proclaimed itself independent as the Turkish Republic of Northern Cyprus (TRNC). Although only Turkey has recognized the new state, the TRNC has established trade relations in Europe and with several Arab states. Led by Rauf Denktaş, northern Cyprus lags far behind the Republic of Cyprus economically, but is generally supported by Turkish-Cypriots who, in recent years, have been joined by thousands of settlers from mainland Turkey. In 1992, the U.N. significantly pared down its peacekeeping mission, leaving Cypriots to resolve their situation without much international intervention.

Glafkos Clerides, former head of the conservative Democratic Rally (DISY), became head of the Republic of Cyprus in 1993. The re-election of Denktaş in the North has helped the negotiation process, and, in conjunction with U.S. involvement, resolution seems possible in the near future. Both Turkey and Greece are eager to win the favor of the U.S. and E.U.

Greek officials are hopeful for the Republic of Cyprus's acceptance into the European Union. Turkey, however, objects to the proposal, warning that it would seek unification with Northern Cyprus if the Republic of Cyprus joins the European

Union. In early August 1997, Turkey and Northern Cyprus had already agreed to work toward partial defense and economic integration. The agreement, which incensed the Greek government, came just five days before U.N.-sponsored talks between the two sides were supposed to yield greater cooperation.

That window of peaceful cooperation deteriorated in late 1997 when the Republic of Cyprus placed an order for a shipment of S-300 missiles from Russia. Both the Turkish government and the Turkish Cypriot government have threatened that the delivery of these weapons will prompt an immediate response in the form of stepped up military presence on the island. The summer of 1998 saw an escalation of tensions concerning the impending delivery, and at the time of writing, the weapons were scheduled to arrive in November of 1998. Periods of tension alternate with periods of relative calm, but there are many points of contention whose balance is crucial for the maintenance of good relations between Greece and Turkey. The announcement in March of 1998 that the E.U. is considering the Republic of Cyprus as a potential member state has catalyzed a host of questions as to the future of the island. Turkey is not a candidate for admission in either the first or second round, and there is some concern about the possible implications for the political status of northern Cyprus in the event of the Republic of Cyprus's admission into the E.U.

In the past few years, negotiations to resolve the situation have stopped and started with periodic U.S. involvement, including the mediation efforts of the current U.S. Ambassador to the U.N. **Richard Holbrooke,** architect of the Bosnian peace treaty. Despite the efforts of Holbrooke and the U.S. government, Turkish-Greek relations over Cyprus are still largely composed of saber-rattling over missiles and fighter planes. The eagerness of Turkey and Greece to strengthen ties with the U.S. and the pending E.U. membership applications of Turkey and the Republic of Cyprus may help provide impetus for some kind of bicommunal settlement in the coming years.

COASTAL CYPRUS

Despite Kourion's beautiful setting, the Dionysiac detail of the Roman floor mosaics at Paphos, and the sheer antiquity of the ancient city of Kitium, nothing on the island draws visitors like the almost magnetic attraction of Cyprus' beaches. Tourism on the coast has helped Cyprus retain the feel of a British colony—in the summer it seems as if Brits outnumber Greeks. Still, as the case is in Paphos, the monuments are often just a block back from the beach, making the transition from marble to sand a quick one.

■ Limassol Λεμεσος

Centrally situated on Cyprus' south coast and 50-70km from other major cities in southern Cyprus, Limassol is the transportation hub of the island. The city is industrial yet cosmopolitan, a cordial introduction to Cyprus as port of entry for most passenger ferries. Accordingly, there is a perpetual barrage of cultural festivities to entertain foreigners and natives. The city's sophisticated restaurants and designer stores, the presence of embassies, and instances of remarkable architecture contribute disparate strands of sophistication lacking in other Cypriot cities; at the same time, rapid growth and a lack of urban planning have taken their toll on the city proper, nurturing an endless row of hotels stretching east along the coast. The region's jewels—a gorgeous beach, and the extensive Roman and Hellenistic ruins of Kourion lie—10km to the west on the Akrotiri Peninsula.

ORIENTATION AND PRACTICAL INFORMATION

Passenger boats arrive at the **new port,** 5km southwest of the town center. As you enter the arrivals terminal, a **tourist desk** to your right has excellent free maps. Bus #1 runs to the port from the station near the Anexartisias St. market and bus #30 runs

Agios
Nikolaos

Archaeological
Museum

Agia Zoni

Art
Museum

Municipal
Gardens

Municipal
Zoo

Agios
Panteleimon

Folk Art
Museum

Police
HQ

Agia Trias

Agia Marina

Mediterranean Sea

Katholiki

Athinon

Eleftherias

Town
Hall

Agios
Androkinos

Agia Napa

Agios
Mamas

Limassol Castle/
Medieval Museum

Djelal Bayar

Agia Thekla

Agios
Antonios

Akrotiri Bay

N

0 ____ 300 yards

0 ____ 300 meters

Limassol
ACCOMMODATIONS
C Continental Hotel
A Guest House Ikaros
D Hotel Metropole
B Luxor Guest House

from the port to downtown Limassol (every 30min., Sa every hr., 35¢). After ships arrive, buses wait near the customs building; otherwise, the stop is outside the port gates. A taxi to town costs £2.50. If you're headed for another major town, call the appropriate *service taxi,* and you'll be picked up at the port at no extra charge. In town, most shops, services, and sights can be found within a few blocks of the waterfront, especially along **Agiou Andreou St.,** which is also called **St. Andrew St.**

Transportation

Ferries: Poseidon Lines (tel. 745 566; fax 745 577) and **Salamis Tours** (tel. 355 555; fax 364 410) run to Haifa, Israel (11hr., 2 per week, £50); Rhodes, Greece (18hr., 2 per week, £44), and Piraeus via Rhodes, (45hr., 2 per week, £47).

Cruises: Salamis Tours (tel. 355 555; fax 364 410), **Louis Tourist Agency** (tel. 363 161; fax 363 174), and **Paradise Island Tours** (tel. 357 604; fax 370 298) stop at Haifa, Israel and Port Said, Egypt.

Buses: KEMEK (tel. 747 532) at the corner of Irinis St. and Enosis St., 400m north of the castle, serves Nicosia (M-F 5 per day, Sa 3 per day, £1.50) and Paphos (10 per week, £1.50). **Kallenos** (tel. 654 850) picks up by the old port, and heads for Larnaka (M-Sa 3-4 per day, £1.70). To reach the Troodos Mountains, contact Kyriakos, 21 Thessalonkis St., which serves Platres (6 per week, £2).

Service Taxis: to Nicosia (£3.45); Larnaka (£3); and Paphos (£2.50). Taxis run 6am-6:30pm. Contact **Kyriakos** (tel. 364 114) or **Makris** (tel. 365 550).

Bike and Moped Rentals: Agencies cluster on the shore road, near the luxury hotels. Motorbikes £6.50 per day. For longer rentals, you'll find lower rates in Polis.

Tourist and Financial Services

Cyprus Tourism Organization: 15 Spiro Araouzos St. (tel. 362 756), on the waterfront 1 block east of the castle. Open M, Th 8:15am-2:15pm and 4-6:30pm, Tu-W and F 8:15am-2:15pm, Sa 8:15am-1:15pm. An office at the **port** (tel. 343 868) is open immediately following arrivals. Another office is in **Dassoudi Beach,** 35 George I Potamos Yermassoylas (tel. 323 211), opposite the Park Beach Hotel, open the same hours as the Limassol office.

Tourist Agencies: Salamis, 28 Octovrion St. (tel 355 555), offers package tours and cruises. **American Express,** 1 Archiepiskopou Kyprianou St. (tel. 362 045), in the offices of **A. L. Mantovani and Sons.** Open for AmEx transactions M-F 8am-12:45pm and 2:30-5:30pm.

Bookstores: Becky's Book Exchange, 51 Kitou Kyprianou St. Open M-Sa 9am-1pm.

Laundromat: (tel. 368 293), on Kaningos St. off Markarios Ave., near the Archaeological Museum. Same-day service or do-it-yourself. Wash £2, dry £1. Open M-Tu and Th-F 7:30am-1pm and 2-5pm.

Emergency and Communications

Police: (tel. 330 411), on Gladstone and Leondios St. next to the hospital.

Hospital: Government General Hospital, outside Limassol near the village Polemidia; take the #15 bus. There are many private doctors and clinics.

Pharmacy: There are pharmacies all over town. Dial 1402 for 24hr. location.

Post Office: Main office (tel. 330 190), Gladstone St., next to the central police station. Open May-Sept. M-Tu, Th-F 7:30am-1:30pm and 4-6pm, W 7:30am-1:30pm, Sa 9-11am. **Postal Code:** 3900.

Internet Access: available at **Cybernet Café,** 79 Eleftherias St. (tel. 745 093; e-mail cafeInfo@zenon.logos.cy.net). Open daily noon-midnight. **Netwave Internet Club** 153 Makarios Ave. (tel. 730 239, email netwave@netwave.com.cy). Open M-F 3:30-midnight, Sa-Su 1pm-midnight. Both charge £2.50 per hour, £1 per additional hour.

CYTA: On the corner of Markos Botsaris St. and Athinon St. All phones in Limassol use telecards except a few in the port. **Telephone Code:** 05.

ACCOMMODATIONS

Without many flats or a youth hostel, Limassol offers its best budget accommodations in a row of quirky guest houses a few blocks inland. Solo travelers, especially women, may prefer the more upscale hotels on the waterfront.

Luxor Guest House, 101 Agiou Andreou St. (tel. 362 265). Hardwood floors and understated decor lend a simple elegance to some rooms. Well located, though proximity to the port can bring a mixed bag of customers. Singles £5; doubles £10.

Guest House Ikaros, 61 Eleftherias St. (tel. 354 348). *Twin Peaks* comes to Limassol. Tapestries, fish tanks, animal skins, and chandeliers. Rooms are large and clean. Shared bath is off a garden; sinks are on the open-air patio. Each day, first shower is free, second is 50¢. Call to reserve in high season. Singles £5; doubles £10.

Continental Hotel, 137 Spiro Araouzos St. (tel. 362 530). Two-star hotel on the waterfront. Some rooms have sea-view balconies. Well-priced compared to other waterfront rooms. A/C £2. Breakfast free. Singles £15; doubles £25; triples £35.

Hotel Metropole, 6 Iphigenias St. (tel. 362 686), off Agiou Andreou St. Centrally located. Rooms are reasonably clean, some with private bath. Port-oriented clientele includes customers from various walks of life. Singles £6; doubles £9.

FOOD

There are a plethora of Cypriot *tavernas,* small *kebab* houses, and cafes throughout the city. The best option for the health- and wealth-conscious traveler is the **Municipal Market.** This huge warehouse spills onto the sidewalk and is filled with fresh produce, meat, seafood, and bread vendors (open M-Tu and Th-F 6am-1pm and 4-6pm, W 6am-1pm). You can put together a cheap, delicious lunch of grapes, a loaf of fresh bread, and local *halloumi* cheese for less than £1.

Mikri Maria, 3 Ankara St. (tel. 357 676). The owner of this endearingly unpretentious restaurant serves exquisite Cypriot food cooked over hot coals. Grilled *lountza* and *halloumi* is delicious, as is the refreshing *tzatziki*. Diners enjoy outside street-side tables and guitar playing inside in winter. Open M-Sa 7pm-10:30 or 11pm.

Pangos, on Sotiri Michaildi St., near Municipal Gardens, just off the touristy water-front. Locals consistently confirm that this counter-only, no frills, *meze* restaurant is their favorite. Pull up a stool and prepare to be full (*meze* £5.50).

Vasilikos, 252 Agiou Andreou St. (tel. 375 972). Known as the place to come for spe-cial events. Tasty renditions of traditional Cypriot fare with stately interior and patio make this worth the splurge.

Ta Kokkina, 239 Agiou Andreou St. (tel. 340 015). The zebra hide isn't likely to win points with animal rights activists, but the exotic garden and bar will please all. Eclectic African menu (curry £4, steak £6).

Sidon, 71-73 Saripolou St. (tel. 342 065), next to Municipal Market. Upscale restau-rant serving Lebanese twist on Cypriot cuisine in stunning stone room and patio. Vegetarian *meze* £5, lamb £3.70, chicken wings £2.50.

Richard and Berengaria, 23 Irinis St. (tel. 363 863), opposite the castle. This tiny *kebab* house serves inexpensive local specialties like *sheftalia* (£1) and *halloumi* sandwiches (75¢). Cypriot brandy sour (65¢).

Edo Lemosos, 111 Irinis St. (tel. 353 378). Traditional Greek guitar music late into the evening; summer outdoor seating in a large tree-covered, candle-lit courtyard. *Meze* £7.75. Half bottle of local brandies £3.75. Musicians inside in winter. Open daily 9:30pm-12:30am.

Skoozi!, 292 Agiou Andreou St. (tel. 642 549), 1 block from the Guest House Luxor. Soups, salads, sandwiches, and pasta for a hip, local clientele. Young Cypriots enjoy jazz, trance, and opera music wafting over the stone floors and Byzantine arches. Delicious crepes (banana with *ganache* £2.60). Many kinds of coffee (65¢).

ENTERTAINMENT

Although not known for its nightlife, Limassol's size allows for a diversity that makes it attractive to travelers looking for variety after the sun goes down. Bars and cafes center around Agiou Andreou St., while clubs are near beaches at the edge of town.

Graffiti, 244 Agiou Andreou St. (tel. 747 552). Well-dressed twenty-somethings con-gregate at this tree-laden open air bar for good music and trendy atmosphere.

Symio, 248 Agiou Andreou St. (tel. 343 090). Painting-lined walls, funky stools, and tables designed by the owner—a painter whose studio is in Limassol. Manages to be both hip and unpretentious.

Passatempo (tel. 342 214), on the corner of Agiou Andreou St. and Souzou St., serves coffees, drinks, and light meals—the *Gucci* and *Rolex* appetizer plates are excessively expensive, but a *cappuccino* (£1.50) is an affordable way to sit in the chic Mediterranean mansion and patio.

Paradozo, 140 Irinis Sr. (tel. 342 288). Largely open air bar with plenty of nooks for conversation or *tavli*. Cologne for males and black for all are prerequisites.

SIGHTS

The **Limassol Castle** is the only building of historical significance in the city, where Richard married Queen Berengaria in 1191. It was then destroyed by earthquakes and Genoese assaults, and the only traces of the old Byzantine fort are in the western wall of the building. In the early 14th century, the Knights Templar fortified the castle's walls and covered the Gothic windows. Later, the Knights of St. John converted the great Western Hall into a Gothic church and the chapel into a series of prison cells. The Ottomans claimed the castle in 1570, and the capacious West Hall was used as a prison under the British regime until 1940. The **Cyprus Medieval Museum** (tel. 330 419) is the present incarnation of the castle and houses a scattered collection of medi-eval armor and religious objects. (*Open M-F 7:30am-5pm, Sa 9am-5pm, Su 10am-1pm; off season M-Sa 7:30am-5pm. Admission £1.*)

The **Archaeological Museum** (tel. 330 132), on the corner of Kaningos and Vyronos, contains an assortment of funerary *stelae*, jewelry, statues, and terra cotta

Goris Gregoriadis at the Green Movement

When he's not out spear-fishing, coordinating the wine festival, or conducting archaeological research, Goris Gregoriadis likes to tend bar every evening at the Limassol chapter of the Green Movement. The consummate Renaissance man, Goris requires little prompting to wax philosophical on fishing, Greek history, or viticulture, or to espouse his own archaeological theories, which have garnered him attention both locally and in academic circles. Two of his more interesting discoveries are the significance of summer solstice at the nearby sanctuary of Apollo (the sun lines up perfectly between the columns at sunset) and the strange relationship between Limassol area sites Kouklia, Kourion, and Amathous (they form an isosceles triangle). Even if Goris is not in, a visit to the Green Movement will not disappoint. The 200-year-old building is testament to Limassol's fine architectural past and serves, at different times of day, as a bar, a stage for spontaneous jam sessions, and a meeting room for political and environmental discussions. Head to 259 Agiou Andreou St. (tel. 369 595).

figurines. (Open M-F 7:30am-5pm, Sa 9am-5pm, Su 10am-1pm. Admission 75¢). The **folk art museum,** 253 Agiou Andreou St. (tel. 362 303), one block east of the intersection of Zenon and Agiou Andreou, houses 19th- and 20th-century embroidery and costumes. (Open M-W, F 8:30am-1:30pm and 3-5:30pm, Th 8:30am-1:30pm. Admission 30¢.) East along the waterfront, between Olympion St. and Vyronos St., the attractive **Municipal Gardens** are home to Cyprus' largest zoo and the **Municipal Open Air Theatre** (check with tourist office for schedule). Limassol's **Reptile House** (tel. 372 779), at the Old Port near Limassol Castle, showcases poisonous scaly critters from around the world. (Open daily 9am-6pm. Admission £1, children 50¢.)

The city's long stone beach might be a little too rocky and too near the busy port for the intensely discerning beachgoer, but a new breakwater has made the area more pleasant for swimming. **Dassoudi Beach,** 3km east of town, is far better; take bus #6 from the market on Kanaris St. (every 15min., 50¢). The ebullient **Ladies Mile Beach,** just west of the new port is also popular (take bus #1).

Limassol is host to a wide array of special events throughout the year. At summer's end, Limassol's gardens are transformed into a modern-day tribute to the ancient wine god, Dionysus. In the Limassol **wine festival,** participants are given a bottle to fill with as much of the local wine as they can handle. (Late Aug. to early Sept. 6-11pm. Admission £1.50.) Between trips to the casks, digestion is aided by music, dance, and theater performances. A bottle of your favorite vintage makes a great souvenir at the evening's close. At the end of June, actors from around the world trek to Limassol to take part in **Shakespeare Nights** (tel. 363 015). **Carnival,** 50 days before Orthodox Easter (usually in February), is celebrated with more vim and vigor in Limassol than anywhere else in Cyprus. Details are available at the tourist office and in This Month's Principal Events.

The **Kolossi Castle** 9km west of Limassol played a crucial role during the Crusades. Both the Knights Templar and the Knights of the Order of St. John briefly made the castle their headquarters. (Open June-Sept. daily 7:30am-7:30pm. Admission 75¢.) When the latter knights moved to Rhodes in 1310, Kolossi, with its wealth of vineyards, remained their richest overseas possession. To reach Kolossi, take bus #16 from the bus station in Limassol (every 20min., 40¢).

■ Akrotiri Peninsula

Outside the British base of Akrotiri, Her Majesty's soldiers frolic year-round in the small resort town of **Pissouri;** the city on a cliff offers enticing views, but no one goes there for sight-seeing. Pissouri has enough watering holes in the main square to appease barflies of all varieties. Trendy **Sultana** (tel. 222 287) and the more down-to-earth **George's Iron Horse Pub** (tel. 221 177) are both popular. The **Bunch of Grapes Inn** has both a restaurant and rooms (doubles £25; breakfast included).

Kourion

The remarkably well-preserved ruins of **Kourion** are 12km west of Limassol. *(Open June-Sept. daily 7:30am-7:30pm; Oct.-May daily 7:30am-5pm. Admission £1.)* First settled during the neolithic period, Achaïans from Argos colonized Kourion during the 14th and 13th centuries BC. It became famous for its **Sanctuary of Apollo** (8th century BC) and its **stadium** (2nd century AD), both west of the main settlement. In the 4th century AD, the same earthquake that destroyed several other Cypriot coastal cities leveled Kourion. The city was rebuilt in the 5th century only to be burned in the 7th century during an Arab raid. As a result, the **Temple of Apollo** and other parts of the Sanctuary of Apollo are largely reconstructed. A photograph of the pre-reconstruction sanctuary hangs in the front office.

The impressive **amphitheater** is used for **Shakespeare Nights** in June, occasional summer concerts and theatrical productions, and weekend theater in September. The earliest structure on the site was a small theater built in the 2nd century BC. During Greek and Roman times, the theater was used for dramas; by the 3rd century AD, civilization on display had degenerated to animal fights and professional wrestling.

Across the road from the basilica lie a group of ruins under excavation. In the northwest corner are the remains of the **House of Gladiators** and its mosaic gladiator pin-ups. The **House of Achilles,** facing the highway at the end of the excavation site, is fenced off, but you can get the key at the ticket office or climb in through the narrow path following the fence along the road. The nearby **Museum of Kourion** in Episkopi village provides clear explanations of the artifacts. *(Open M, W, F 7:30am-2:30pm, Th 7:30am-2:30pm and 3-6pm. Admission £1.)*

Buses leave Limassol Castle bound for ancient Kourion. (Every hr. on the hr., 9am-1pm, return from ancient Kourion 11:50am, 2:50, and 4:50pm. 60¢.) Mopeders to Kourion usually go via Episkopi village. There are no signs for Kourion until you're within about 2km of the site, so a good map is essential.

■ Larnaka Λαρνακα

The remains of **St. Lazarus** lie in the city's central church and give the city its name from the ancient Greek word for coffin: *larnax*. Fortunately, tropical Larnaka isn't as grim as its name. According to tradition, Lazarus came to **Kition** (upon whose ancient ruins Larnaka was built) as the island's first bishop after being resurrected by Christ. Larnaka, one of the oldest continually inhabited cities in the world, retains monuments from each major phase of its long history. A segment of the ancient city walls and some Bronze Age temples can be found in the north of town. Elsewhere in the city, the Hala Sultan Tekke Mosque dates back to the first Arab invasion of Cyprus (647 AD), while the graffiti reading *"Hellas, Enosis, EOKA,"* elicits memories of the violent movement for union with Greece just a few decades ago. Larnaka, however, is curiously indifferent to its long history and has become a modern tourist center, offering visitors a long beach bordered by numerous cafes and restaurants. Quieter and cleaner than Limassol, sunny Larnaka (pop. 65,000) charms visitors, and while it is less expensive than neighboring Agia Napa, rooms are just as scarce in summer.

ORIENTATION AND PRACTICAL INFORMATION

Athinon Avenue, also known as the "Palm Tree Promenade," runs along the waterfront and is Larnaka's most popular attraction. In summer, masses of barefoot young Cypriots and sandal-clad foreigners fill its cafes, restaurants, pubs, and beaches. The kitschy French-style lamp posts illuminate the strip every evening as mobile vendors and amusement rides create a carnival atmosphere. **Vasileos Pavlou Square,** where most practical facilities are located, is a block west of the north end of Athinon Ave.

Transportation

Airport: (tel. 692 700) Most flights into Cyprus land at the Larnaka airport. Bus #19 runs to town. (14 per day in summer, 6:20am-7pm; in winter 6:20am-5:45pm;

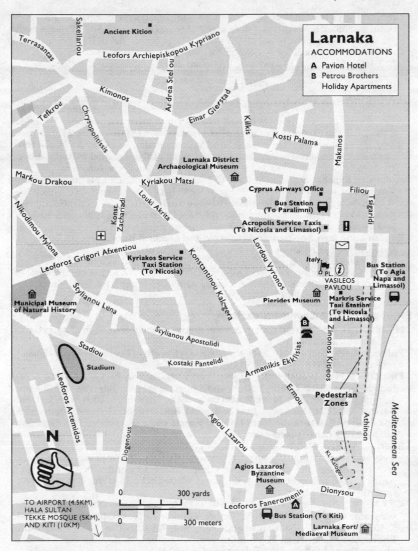

Larnaka
ACCOMMODATIONS
A Pavion Hotel
B Petrou Brothers
  Holiday Apartments

reduced service Saturday afternoons and no service Sundays; 50¢.) Taxis cost £3 to get to St. Lazarus Sq. in the center of town.

Buses: Leave from Athinon Ave. by the marina on the seafront opposite Four Lanterns Hotel. Look for a sandwich board on the sidewalk with the schedule. **Kallenos Buses** (tel. 654 850 or 644 666) go to Nicosia (7 per day M-F 7am-4pm, 4 per day Sa until 1pm, £1.50) and Limassol (4 per day M-F 8am-4pm, 3 per day Sa until 1pm, £1.70). **EMAN** (tel. 721 321) buses to Agia Napa leave from the same spot (M-Sa 8:30am-5:30pm, 4 per day Su until 4:30pm, £1). **A.L.** (tel. 650 477; fax 654 977) bus #19 leaves from St. Lazarus Sq. and stops at St. Helenis, Artemidos Ave., Meneou, Kiti, and Tersefanou (13-14 per day 6:20am-5:45pm and 7pm, 60¢).

Service Taxis: Makris (tel. 652 929 or 655 333), Vasileos Pavlou Sq., opposite the Sun Hall Hotel. **Acropolis** (tel. 655 555), at the corner of Markarios Ave., opposite the police station, and **Kyriakos,** 2C Ermou St. (tel. 655 100). All run to Nicosia (every 30 min., M-F 6am-6pm; £2.40); Acropolis and Makris run to Limassol (every 30min., M-F 6am-6pm; £3). To reach Paphos by service taxi, go to Limassol and connect with a Limassol-Paphos service taxi (£2.50). Service taxis will pick up and

drop off anywhere in the city. Call ahead. On Sundays the companies alternate, running until early afternoon. Prices may be higher (by roughly 50¢). **Private taxis** are shamelessly expensive but offer 24hr. service. Contact Makris for a private taxi.
Car Rental: Phoenix Rent-A-Car, 65 Makarios Ave. (tel. 623 407 or 622 314; fax 650 460). Prices from £10 per day. Unlimited mileage. Minimum age 25.

Tourist and Financial Services

Tourist Office: C.T.O., Vasileos Pavlou Sq. (tel. 654 322). The helpful officers provide information and maps for all Cyprus. Hours vary widely depending on the season, but it is generally open M-Tu and Th-F 8:15am-2:30pm and 3-6:15pm, W and Sa 8:15am-2:30pm. There is also an **airport branch** (tel. 643 000). Open 24hr.

Bank: All 3 major banks are on or around Vasileos Pavlou Sq. 24hr. **ATM** and traveler's checks and currency exchange at the **Bank of Cyprus,** next to AmEx office. Open M-F 8:30am-12:30pm and also M 3:15-4:45pm during the summer.

American Express: Stasinou St. (tel. 652 024), in the office of **Mantovani Plotin Travel,** across from the C.T.O. No traveler's checks or currency exchange. Provides money check forms for those drawing funds from AmEx cards. Guarantees personal checks for acceptance at local banks. Open M-F 8am-1pm and 3:30-7pm, Sa 9am-noon; reduced hours in winter.

English Language Bookstore: Academic and General Bookstore, 41 Ermou St. (tel. 628 401), provides a comprehensive offering of new and used books as well as current magazines in English. Selection includes British and American fiction, Cypriana, classics, English and Greek (in translation) poetry, and a full complement of *Let's Go* books. Offers student discounts. Open M-Tu and Th-F 9am-2pm and 4-7pm, W and Sa 9am-2pm.

Emergency and Communications

Hospital: (tel. 630 300) Off Grigori Afxentiou Ave., at the intersection of Agias Elenis and Konst. Zachariada St.

Police: (tel. 630 200) On Makarios Ave., one block north of the tourist office. English spoken. Open 24hr. **Fire:** tel. 630 199.

Post Office: Main branch (tel. 630 18 or 630 178), Vasileos Pavlou Sq. Open Sept.-June M-Tu and Th-F 7:30am-1:30pm and 3-6pm, Sa 9-11am; July-Aug. M-F 7:30am-1:30pm and 4-7pm, Sa 9-11am. **Postal code:** 6900. There is a branch in **St. Lazarus Sq.** (tel. 630 182). Open Sept.-June M-W and F 8am-1:30pm, Th 8am-1:30pm and 3-6pm; July-Aug. M and F 7:30am-1:30pm. **Postal code:** 6902. Note that each post office has a separate postal code.

Internet Access: Web Internet Cafe, 54 Lordou Vyronou St. (tel. 654 954; email webcafe@webcafe.com.cy; http://www.webcafe.com.cy). Email may be sent and received through the cafe's address. Computer use £2 per hr.; printing 20¢ per page. **Pliktro Internet Cafe,** 1 Klimonas St. (tel. 627 303; email pliktro@pliktro.cy.net) £1.50 per hr.

CYTA: 7-9 Z Pierides St. (tel. 132 or 640 257), follow Lordou Vyronos toward the sea-front. Office is on the right, before Zinonos Kitieos. Open June-Aug. M-F 7:30am-7pm, Sa 7:30am-1pm; Sept.-May M-F 7:30am-6pm, Sa 7:30am-noon. **Phone cards** in £3, 5, or 10 amounts are also available at most kiosks. **Telecard phones** throughout the city. **Telephone Code:** 04.

ACCOMMODATIONS

The town's hotels and pensions tend to fall into three distinct categories—resort hotels, flats, and dives. Cleaner and cooler than the dives, flats are cheaper alternatives to regular hotels in Larnaka. Prices tend to be £5-7 less in winter.

Youth Hostel (HI) (tel. 621 188), Nikolaou Rossou St. in St. Lazarus Sq., housed in a part of a former mosque, has 3 large rooms (all female, all male, and co-ed) with 10 beds each and 1 room for a family. Open 24hr., but front desk is not manned 24hr. Guests can sign in anytime. No luggage storage. Relatively empty, even in summer months, so single rooms may be available. Some kitchen facilities. Bring sheets (or rent them for £1) and bug repellant. £3.50 per person.

⍟**Petrou Bros. Holiday Apartments,** 1 Armenikis Ekklisias St. (tel 650 600 or 650 601; fax 655 122). Centrally located 2 blocks from the sea-front. Offers immaculate and spacious modern flats with bathrooms, showers, telephones, kitchens, A/C, balcony, 24hr. reception, and sun roof. Laundry and travel services, parking, break-fast, and access to a pool are also available (£1-2 each). Doubles £18; quads £28; 6 person suite £35. Mention *Let's Go* for a 30% discount.

Elexenia Hotel Apartments, 1 D. Demetriade St. (tel. 650 666; fax 651 466), at the corner of D. Demetriade St. and Nicholas Rossou St , just off St. Lazarus Sq. Bright, cheerful rooms, many of which are brand new, at bargain rates by Larnaka standards. In-room A/C, TV, and kitchen facilities. Singles £9; doubles £10; triples £12.

Pavlon Hotel, 11 Fancromeni Ave. (tel. 656 688), St. Lazarus Sq , offers clean rooms, most with balconies overlooking St. Lazarus Church. Singles £13; doubles £18; quads £30. Breakfast of toast and coffee included.

FOOD

Most of Larnaka's *tavernas* and bars are on the waterfront. Larnaka also offers an array of international cuisines, including Chinese, Armenian, Lebanese, Italian, French, and Indian. Prices include 10% service charge and 8% V.A.T.

1900 Art Cafe, 6 Stasinou St. (tel. 653 027). Run by a painter and a poet, the cafe fosters the exchange of intellectual and artistic ideas over carafes of local wine (£2.50), tea (90¢), or coffee (50¢-£1). The *milopita,* or apple pie, is their specialty (£1.10). Vegetarian dishes also available (most entrees £3.50). A tasteful and obscure selection of Greek folk music lends sonic ambiance. Friday nights offer performances by Cypriot and Greek folk musicians. Bookshop, bar, fireplace, and display of local artists' works upstairs. Open M-Sa 8:30am-2:30pm and 6pm-1am, Su 6pm-1am.

Mauri Helona (tel. 650 661), at the beginning of Mehmet Ali St., at St. Lazarus Sq. The logo—a booze-swigging turtle—embodies Mauri Helona's two specialties—seafood and alcohol. Offers a variety of *mezedes* (£5-6). The entrance is filled with skeletal marine remains and toy turtles. A group of singers and musicians gather until midnight Tu-Sa nights. Fish £3.75-4.75, chicken £2.75, rabbit £4, pork £2.75. House wines £3-4, beer £1.25. Open for dinner at 6pm, closed Su-M.

Para, 3 Mehmet Ali St. (tel. 626 280), next to Mauri Helona. Caters to a primarily local clientele with delicious and reasonably priced *meze* (£5), salads (£2), kebabs (£3), and vegetarian meals amid wine casks, checkered tablecloths, a working jukebox, and historic photographs of Larnaka.

The Tuck Inn. Open 24hr. and located in the middle of Athinon Ave. This fast food joint and kiosk offers the cheapest meal in town. Kebab, souvlaki, burgers, veggie burgers, and salads £1.75 or less. Eat in or take-out.

Kali Kardia, 8 Zehra St. Cooking out of a small, hut-like room, and serving only a few outside tables in the heart of the old Turkish quarter, Kali Kardia is Cypriot cuisine at its most authentic. Simple menu (kebabs, souvlaki, salads) at low prices (£2-4).

ENTERTAINMENT

Larnaka's nightlife has a split personality: beach-front pubs on Athinon Ave. and cafes in town. Sun-baked tourists compare their package tours over beer and *ouzo* on the waterfront. Located toward the south end of the harbor, the shared patios of **Stone Age Pub, Hard Rock Cafe,** and **Scarlio** form the tripartite soul of the beachfront nightlife. Inland, a number of increasingly popular cafes all provide three basic poisons: alcohol, caffeine, and ice cream. At **Nitro Cafe** (tel. 664 909), on the corner of Grigori Afxentiou St. and Lordou Vyronos St., the DJ spins a soulful mix of house, American R&B, and Greek pop from 10am to 6am so Larnaka's insomniacs never lack a place to chat. **Preserve,** 91 Ermou St. (tel. 659 013), is a posh bar open until 2am.

SIGHTS

The **Larnaka District Archaeological Museum** (tel. 630 169), on Kilkis St., has a small collection of finds from around Larnaka dating from neolithic to Roman times. *(Open M-W 9am-2:30pm, Th 9am-6pm. Admission 75¢.)* The temple complex of the ancient city of **Kition** is the oldest spot in Larnaka, although most of it is now underground. *(Open M-W 9am-2:30pm, Th 9am-6pm. Admission 75¢.)* Settled in the early 13th century BC and abandoned soon after, Kition was rebuilt in 1200 BC by refugees

CYPRUS

from the Peloponnese. The city was damaged in wars with the Phoenicians and Egyptians (4th century BC) and leveled by earthquake and fire in 280 BC. Ruins reveal part of an ancient Cyclopean wall, the **Temple of Astarte** (the Phoenician goddess of fertility), and four small temples. Appreciation of the site requires an active imagination as only barely discernible foundations remain. The site's entrance is difficult to find; walk north from the archaeological museum (with the museum on your left) on Kilkis St., head left on Leontiou Machaira St., left again onto Ioanni Paskirati St., and the entrance is at the end of the road.

The private **Pierides Foundation Museum** (tel. 651 345 or 652 495) on Zinonos St. is the former home of Demetrios Pierides (1811-1895), a cultured man and collector of Cypriot artifacts. *(Open M-F 9am-1pm and 3-6pm, Sa 9am-1pm, Su 10am-1pm. Admission £1.)* His descendants have continued this tradition and still occupy the top floor of the house. Prehistoric Cypriot idols are displayed in china chests. Pots take the place of end tables, and antique maps of Cyprus hang in lieu of wallpaper. Relics abound from 3000 years of Cypriot history, including Byzantine and traditional art. In the adjacent yard, classical and modern sculptures stand side by side.

The **Municipal Museum of Natural History,** on Stadiou St. across from the stadium, houses 5000 individually labeled Cypriot insects. *(Open Tu-Su 10am-1pm and 4-6pm. Admission 20¢.)* Three kinds of extinct snakes have been stuffed, and other preserved local animal species are arranged in panoramic displays. Live versions of turkeys, buzzards, and canaries, plus a flamingo and a peacock. A park for all ages and a playground for children under 10 surrounds the museum.

The **Tornaritis-Pierides Museum of Paleontology** and the **Larnaka Municipal Gallery,** housed in the old customs warehouse at the end of Athinon Ave., are two of Larnaka's best organized museums. *(Museum and gallery tel. 658 848. Open Tu-F 10am-1pm and 5-7pm, Sa-Su 10am-1pm; reduced hours in winter. Admission £1 each. Call in advance to arrange a tour from the curator.)* The paleontology museum boasts fossils from Cyprus and around the Mediterranean. Pieces in the collection date back 500 million years and include the now-extinct pygmy elephant, whose migration to Cyprus is not yet fully understood. The modern Cypriot art in the gallery portrays issues of heritage, ethnicity, politics, and culture alongside a small but impressive set of abstract works and a rotation of featured collections. The curator is more than willing to expound on the art and refer aesthetes to the artists' private galleries throughout the island.

At the south end of the port, a small **medieval fortress** peers over the water's edge. *(Open M-F 7:30am-7:30pm; reduced hours in winter. Admission £1.)* Built by Venetians in the 15th century and rebuilt by Ottomans in 1625, the fort contains artifacts and photographs from local excavations and churches, as well as early Byzantine artifacts and a medieval armory. Across the street stands the medieval mosque of Al Kibir, which is still in use today but allows visitors during most of the day.

The first left north of the fortress leads to the **Church of St. Lazarus,** which is built over the saint's tomb. *(Museum and church tel. 652 498. Open daily 8am-12:30pm and 3:30-6:30pm. Admission 50¢. Greek Orthodox services Su 6-9:30am. Modest dress required.)* In the Gospel story, Christ resurrected Lazarus after the latter had been dead for four days. The revived Lazarus journeyed to Cyprus, became the island's first bishop, and lived in Kition another 30 years before dying again. The church was built in the 9th century and has been burnt and rebuilt several times since then. You can visit St. Lazarus's tomb by descending steps near the iconostasis. The church's belfry was added in 1857. The courtyard holds a small Byzantine museum with ecclesiastical art.

At the north end of Athenon Ave., find Larnaka's **Marina,** upon which couples and families warm up for their *voltas* (nightly strolls) among the palm trees. The **town beach** (a dismal mixture of packed dirt and cigarette butts) manages to satisfy the vacationers who bake there. The bustling beach also offers **water sports:** canoes (£3.50 per hr.), paddleboats (£5.50 per hr.), sail boards (£4.50 per hr.), water-skis (£5.50 per ride; £6 per lesson), jet-skis (£10 per 15min.), mini-boats (£7 per 15min., £12 per 30min.), or banana boats (£3.50 per person). Beautiful, less crowded beaches are farther northeast on the way to Agia Napa.

■ Near Larnaka

The Salt Lake and Tekke
Open in summer daily 7:30am-7:30pm. Free.

In a hauntingly exotic setting, 2km west of Larnaka Airport, the **Hala Sultan Tekke Mosque** looks over the edge of a salt lake surrounded by palm trees. Also called the Tekke of Umm Haram, the mosque, a local pilgrimage site, was constructed in AD 647 during the Arab invasion of Cyprus and rebuilt in 1816 over the site where Umm Haram (Muhammad's maternal aunt) fell off a mule and broke her neck. Three gargantuan stones—reputed to have been quarried in Mecca—surround her grave in back of the mosque. The mosque also houses the tomb of the great-great grandmother of Jordan's King Hussein—she died in exile in Cyprus in 1929. Bus #19, bound for Kiti, leaves St. Lazarus Sq. and travels west to the Hala Sultan Tekke Mosque (15min., 14 per day, 50¢); ask the driver to stop at the mosque or you'll end up in Kiti. To be dropped at the turnoff, tell the bus driver "Tekke." From there, walk along the paved road for 1km. In winter, pink flamingos flock to the lake, but in summer it dries up and the flamingos fly away. Legend has it that St. Lazarus created the lake over an old woman's vineyard as punishment for her lack of hospitality.

Kiti
Open M-F 8am-4pm, Sa 10am-4pm, Su 9am-noon and 2-4pm.

You can also take bus #19 all the way to the village of **Kiti** (25min. from Larnaka) and the church of **Panayia Angeloktisti**, literally "Built by the Angels." Again, ask the driver to stop there. This church was built in the 11th century, but it retains a section built several hundred years earlier. The mosaic in the central apse, representing the Virgin Mary with Christ surrounded by the Archangels Michael and Gabriel, is one of the more important works of art on the island. The narthex of the church was built in the 14th century by the Gibelet family, one of the most prominent Latin noble families of medieval Cyprus.

Stavrovouni Monastery
Open to men daily Apr.-Sept. 8am-noon and 3-6pm; Oct.-Mar. 8am-noon and 2-5pm.

40km from Larnaka and 9km off the main Nicosia-Limassol road is **Stavrovouni Monastery.** According to tradition, the monastery, whose name means "mountain of the cross," was constructed by order of St. Eleni in 327 BC on a site called Olympus, where a pagan temple had stood. At the time, Eleni, mother of the Emperor Constantine, who had recently converted to Christianity and moved his capital to Byzantium, was returning from Palestine where she had found the Holy Cross. She presented a fragment to the monastery, where it is kept in the church's iconostasis. Although their founder was female, the monks do not allow women into the monastery. In general, the brothers of the monastery feel little compulsion to comply with secular timetables and may turn visitors away at a whim.

If allowed to enter, notice the working garden to the right before following the circuitous path up to the monastery. The structure itself is relatively small with a church, a kitchen, a refectory, and dormitory-style beds for the 28 monks who make Stavrovouni their home. The area open to visitors revolves around a courtyard with a sundial and a well. The interior of the church is elaborately frescoed. A peek into the refectory reveals a long wooden table and a fireplace used to combat harsh high altitude winters. The room's rustic charm and a whiff of the kitchen around mealtime suggests that the monks would prove successful in the restaurant business.

The monks themselves receive visitors with widely varied manners. Some are friendly and happy to explain the workings and history of the monastery. Others ignore secular intruders and remain silent even when spoken to. The monastery is essentially accessible only by car, though a hardy few make the hour-plus hike from the nearby village of Karnes. The turn-off to the monastery is well marked from exit 11 off the Nicosia-Limassol highway. A round-trip taxi out of Larnaka costs about £20, including the wait during a visit.

■ Agia Napa Αγια Ναπα

Twenty years ago, Agia Napa was a quiet farming and fishing village. Most tourists flocked to Famagusta, 16km to the north, allowing Agia Napa's ruined monastery and white sandy beaches to lie peacefully vacant. When Turkey occupied Famagusta in 1974, Agia Napa was transformed almost overnight into a tourist resort *par excellance* replete with marble and brass glitz, all the while absorbing a large refugee community from Northern Cyprus. The one quiet village has developed a raucous nightlife popular among foreigners.

ORIENTATION AND PRACTICAL INFORMATION Trying to navigate Agia Napa by addresses and street signs is an exercise in futility; a free map of the town is available at any C.T.O. in Cyprus and will prove extremely helpful. Agia Napa Monastery and the winding streets up the hill from it form the center of town, which houses several bars and *tavernas*. Makarios Ave., in front of the monastery, is the main drag with banks and shops. Uphill Makarios Ave. becomes Dinokratias St., which leads north to Paralimni. Toward the sea, Nissi St. heads west of Makarios Ave. to Larnaka and Nissi beach. Most tourist services are on or around Makarios Ave. The **C.T.O.,** 12 Kyrou Nyrou St. (tel. 721 796), provides those essential maps (open M-Tu and Th-F 8:30am-2:15pm and 3:30-6:30pm; W 8:30am-2:15pm). **The Hellenic Bank** (tel. 721 488; fax 722 636) is on Makarios Ave. (open M-F 8:30am-12:30pm; less often in winter; 24hr. **ATM**). **AirTour-Cyprus,** 28 Makarios Ave. (tel. 721 265; fax 721 776), books flights out of Larnaka airport. (Open in summer M-Tu and Th-Sa 8am-1pm and 4-6:30pm, W and Sa 8am-1pm. Reduced hours in winter.) **EMAN** (tel. 721 321) provides regular service to Larnaka (M-Sa 10 per day, 6:30am-5pm; Su 4 per day, 9am-4pm; £1), Nicosia (M-Sa, 8am; £2), as well as Paralimni and Protaras (M-Sa 10 per day, 6:30am-5pm; Su 5 per day, 9am-6pm; 40¢). Bus transit is reduced in winter. The **bus station** is next to the Hellenic Bank. Expensive but effective for leaving the immediate vicinity of Agia Napa, **Agia Napa Taxi** (tel. 721 111 or 721 888), just uphill from the monastery off Makarios Ave., offers 24hr. service. Bikes and Mopeds are ideal in Agia Napa and the surrounding area. Try **Angelos Motosport,** 15 Nissi St. (tel. 721 695). Walk down Makarios Ave. toward the beach and take the only right back toward Larnaka (open daily 8:30am-6:30pm; motorcycles, mopeds, and bikes £2-7.20 per day). The **police** (tel. 721 553) are north of town on the road to Paralimni. The closest **hospital** (tel. 821 211) is 10km north in Paralimni. The **post office** is on D. Liperti St. (open M-F 7:30am-1:30pm, Sa 9-11am). **Postal code:** 5330. **Telephone code:** 03.

ACCOMMODATIONS Half of the buildings in town are luxury hotels full of tourists on box-lunch tours, making inexpensive rooms elusive at best, and at worst—in August—nearly non-existent. Be prepared for noise at all hours at some of the less glamorous rooming establishments. To get to **Xenis Rooms** (tel. 721 086), go up the road to Paralimni until you have to turn. A left and then a right at Mary's Supermarket will take you there—it's at the top of the hill. Rooms have baths and kitchens (singles £8). Just before Xenis Rooms, across from Mary's Supermarket, is **Paul Marie Hotel Apts.** (tel. 721 067), which boasts currency exchange, its own pool table, bar, and rooftop pool (singles £16; doubles £20; quads £30).

On Makarios Ave., in close proximity to the nightlife, simple but pleasant flats are available above the **Cinderella Leather Shop** (tel. 722 148). They come with kitchen facilities and large balconies; inquire within the shop (singles £13; doubles £15). Don't confuse these flats with the spartan rooms available above **Cinterella Supermarket** (tel. 721 041 or 724 277), just uphill from the monastery on the road to Paralimni. These may be the cheapest rooms in town, located right on top of the nightlife with shared bathroom and kitchen facilities (singles £3; doubles £6).

The **campground** is 3km from town (tel. 721 946; £1.25 per person, £1.50 per tent), near crowded **Nissi Beach.**

FOOD Supermarkets and 24hr. take-out shops, which afford the flexibility of a picnic beside the relatively serene monastery, are generally preferable to Agia Napa's tourist traps, which serve the same food at higher prices. **Raven's Rook** (tel. 722 427), above the Hellenic Bank and near the tourist office, serves meals in a pleasant rooftop garden (tuna salad £2.60, kebab £2.95). **Jasmin Kebab House** (tel. 721 436), on D. Solomou St., offers the cheapest take-out in town, complete with a Cypriot flair (chicken kebab £1.30; open daily 11am-5am).

ENTERTAINMENT After dark, Agia Napa's watering holes and discos make their presence abundantly clear with an incessant barrage of neon and thumping bass. The nightly ritual begins shortly after sundown as intoxicants sample the profusion of pubs; the crowds here dwindle after 1am, however, when the action moves to the dance clubs—which keep pumping until 4am. Pubs are everywhere, but cluster around the footpath uphill from the monastery. **Minos Pub** has a jukebox and music every night, but more important to its patrons are the draft beers (£1-1.60 per pint) and strong drinks (£1.50). The **Makedonas,** within a minute's stumbling distance of Minos, has drinks for just £1 all night. The dance clubs are more scattered, but they're never too far away; follow the inescapable basslines. **Club Mythology, Revival,** and the retro **Starsky & Hutch** draw substantial crowds. **Emporium,** with its newly renovated interior, considers itself Agia Napa's classiest club. A markedly different vibe emanates from **Freedom Reggae Pub,** with its hammock, Caribbean decor, and pseudo-rastafarian jams. While the pubs have no cover, the clubs often charge between £2 and £5 depending on the evening; local coupons or being female can significantly mitigate costs.

SIGHTS Within the walls of the 16th-century Venetian **Monastery of Agia Napa,** you'll find a beautiful courtyard with flowers, plants, trees, and an octagonal, dome-covered, marble fountain. *(Open daily 7:30am-5pm. Services are held every Saturday at 6pm. Free.)* The huge sycamore outside the west entrance is famous in Cyprus. Every summer Sunday at 8pm, locals perform Cypriot **folk dances** in the square near the monastery. The monastery's small chapel is off the main courtyard. While inside, you might hear the well, which still supplies water to the inner chapel built into a cave. The well's appearance is connected to the **Miracle of Panagia** (the Greek name for the Virgin Mary). During pirate attacks, Christians would seek refuge in the chapel's cave. Once, the pirates occupied the town for several days. The people in the cave were on the brink of dehydration, when, according to local Christian belief, Mary appeared to the people and pointed to the fresh water coming from the corner of the cave. Since then, the water has never run dry.

The **Tornaritis-Pierides Municipal Museum of Marine Life,** 1825 Agias Mavris St. (tel. 723 409), hints that Cypriots see more in their coral-reefed beaches than lucrative tourist bait. *(Open M-Sa 9am-2pm, Th 3-6pm. Admission £1, students and soldiers free.)* Located in the basement of the town hall, the museum features giant shells, fossilized fish, and stuffed birds from around the Mediterranean as well as an explanation of local efforts to save sea turtles, which are common victims of beachside development. The **beaches** by the hotels at the east end of town and **Nissi beach** to the west can become extremely crowded but provide occasional gorgeous stretches of sand and water. Closer to Agia Napa, the better beaches are north and south of **Protaras** (10km from Agia Napa).

■ Cape Greco and the Red Villages

For a more solitary communion with Cyprus' southeast coast, take a half-day or day on moped or bicycle to trek around Cape Greco and the Red Villages near the Green Line, which separates the region from the area occupied by the Turks. East of Agia Napa on Kyrou Nerou St., resort hotels give way to an unadorned coast. A number of rough surface roads connect the mainland to the sea and to the mostly unmarked hiking trail, 8km from town, which leads to **Cape Greco.** You'll find no tourists here, no half-built concrete hotels, no *tavernas,* and no sand—just rocky coves cascading into the magnificent blue sea. The cape has remained undeveloped because of a military radar installation, giving James Bond aspirants the chance to swim off the rocks beneath two space-age radar dishes.

Back on the main road, signs point to **Agiou Anargyroi,** a small but remarkable church that stands in splendid isolation over the sea. Next to the church, stairs descend to sea caves that are easily large enough to wander inside. North on the main road, civilization reappears in **Protaras,** where virgin white sands spread across the area's best beaches. Despite its beautiful beaches, Protaras has recently surrendered itself to the strip mall culture of Agia Napa. Northeast of Protaras, the road turns into the drab modern village of **Paralimni.** Two kilometers north of Paralimni, a stone's throw from the Green Line, is the small village of **Dherinia.** Several tourist lookouts nearby provide views of the "ghost" of occupied **Famagusta;** construction cranes stand exactly as they did a quarter of a century ago.

■ Paphos Παφος

When the Ptolemies of Egypt conquered Cyprus, they made Paphos their capital. Under their rule, the city grew fabulously wealthy and developed into a cosmopolitan commercial center. Paphos maintained this exalted position under the Roman conquerors, but a 4th-century earthquake ended its supremacy. The Cypriot capital, and the accompanying political and social prestige, moved to Salamis (near modern Famagusta). Paphos shrunk to a small village until recently, as it has risen again as the tourist capital of the Republic of Cyprus. Sights of historical interest—classical, Byzantine, Venetian, and modern—surround the city, far more than in Agia Napa, its resort rival on the southeastern coast. Paphos also boasts far more scenic beaches than the equally historic Larnaka or Limassol. Paphos has been a place of honor for Aphrodite, goddess of beauty, and its rolling hillsides and finely curved coastline evince her continued blessings since the 12th century BC.

ORIENTATION AND PRACTICAL INFORMATION

The city of Paphos is divided into two sections. The upper **Ktima Paphos** (referred to simply as "Paphos") is centered around Kennedy Sq., where most of the city's shops, budget hotels, and services are located. The lower **Kato Paphos** lies roughly 1km to the south, and hosts luxury hotels, holiday villas, and most of Paphos's nightlife. Everything listed below is in Ktima Paphos, unless otherwise noted.

Transportation

Buses: Nea Amoroza Co., 79 Pallikaridi St. (tel. 236 822), across from the ESSO station in Kennedy Sq. Minibuses run to Polis (weekdays 10 per day, £1). Some continue on to Pomos (£1.10).

City Buses: Municipal buses (#11) run every 15 min. between Ktima Paphos and Kato Paphos (40¢). Catch one in Ktima Paphos, just up the road from the post office, or in Kato Paphos at any of the yellow benches on the road to town. Buses also go to Coral Bay (20 per day, 40¢). Schedules in the tourist office.

Service Taxis: Go to Limassol (every 30 min., M-Sa 6am-6:30pm, Su 7am-5:30pm, £2.50). Contact **Makris** (tel. 232 538) or **Kyriakos** (tel. 232 538). From Limassol both connect with Nicosia service taxis, and **Makris** connects to Larnaka.

Moped Rental: several shops in Kato and Ktima Paphos. £2.50-6.50 per day.

Airport: C.T.O. (tel. 422 641). Contrary to popular belief, there is a second international airport in Cyprus. Although most flights arrive in Larnaka, Paphos International Airport receives various European airlines and many chartered flights. Opens when flights arrive. Offers **currency exchange** and a C.T.O. branch. Private taxis from city center £5, from Kato Paphos £5. No bus service.

Tourist and Financial Services

Tourist Office: C.T.O, 3 Gladstone St. (tel. 232 841), across from Iris Travel. Hours vary. The **airport C.T.O.** (tel. 422 833) is open when flights arrive.

Travel Agency: Iris Travel, 10A Gladstone St. (tel. 237 585), opposite the C.T.O. Ferry tickets to Rhodes, Crete, and Israel (student discounts up to 20%). Airline tickets to London and Greece (student discounts up to 40% if age 24-28, depending on airline). Rents cars (£13-22 per day, unlimited mileage; must be over 25) and apartments (from £5 per person). Open M-F 8am-1pm and 4-7pm, Sa 8am-1pm.

Banks: Many concentrated around Kennedy Sq. **Bank of Cyprus,** Evagorou St., with **ATM.** Open M-F 8:30am-12:30pm.

Bookstore: Axel Bookshop, 62-64 Makarios Ave. (tel. 232 404). Books about Cyprus and novels in English. Open M-Sa 8am-1pm, M-Tu and Th-F 4-7:30pm.

Emergency and Communications

Police: Grivas Digenes Ave. (tel. 240 140) in Kennedy Sq., opposite the Coop Bank. English spoken. Open 24hr. For **emergencies,** dial 199.

Hospital: Paphos General, Neophytos Nicolaides St. (tel. 240 111). Free first aid. English spoken. A long walk; you'll probably want to take a taxi. **St. George's Private Hospital,** 29 El. Venizelou St. (tel. 247 000; fax 241 886), on the way to the youth hostel. Casualty and ambulance services. English spoken. Open 24hr.

Internet Access: Limanaki Bar (tel. 239 616), by Paphos fort in Kato Paphos. £2 per hr. Open daily 5pm-2am. **Surfcafe,** 1 Gladstone St. (tel. 239 239), in Kennedy Sq. £1.50 per hr. Open daily 9am-8pm.

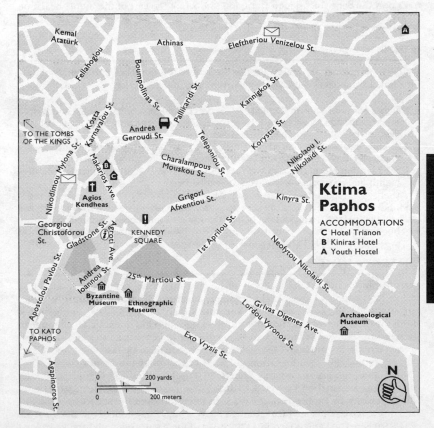

Ktima Paphos

ACCOMMODATIONS
C Hotel Trianon
B Kiniras Hotel
A Youth Hostel

CYPRUS

Post Office: Main branch on Eleftheriou Venizelou St. Open M-Tu, and Th-F 7:30am-1:30pm and 3:30-5:30pm (afternoon hours for stamp purchase only), W 7:30am-1:30pm, Sa 9-11am. Smaller office (tel. 240 223) on Nikodhimou Mylona St. Open M-F 7:30am-1:30pm, Sa 9-11am. The post office in **Kato Paphos** is on Ag. Antoniou St. (tel. 240 226). **Postal Code:** 8900 in Ktima Paphos; 8903 in Kato Paphos. **CYTA:** Grivas Digenes Ave. (tel. 230 228). Open daily 7:30am-7:30pm. **Telephone Code:** 06.

ACCOMMODATIONS

Finding inexpensive accommodations in Paphos is a chore. Solo travelers should stick to the youth hostel or, if finances permit, one of the nicer hotels; groups might try renting a flat. The following are in Ktima (upper) Paphos, unless otherwise noted. Prices are higher in Kato Paphos, where nightlife is better and beaches are closer.

Youth Hostel (HI), 37 Eleftheriou Venizelou St. (tel. 232 588), on a residential street northeast of the town center. From the square, follow Pallikaridi to Venizelou, and turn right—a 10min. walk from town. Sheets £1. Dorms £4.

Kiniras Hotel, 91 Makarios Ave. (tel. 241 604). Clean rooms with private bath and phone in beautiful hotel. Has restaurant and lovely patio. A/C available at £2 per day. Breakfast included. Singles £20; doubles £30.

Violetta Flats, 7 Dionissiou St. in Kato Paphos (tel. 234 109; fax 220 734). Clean, home-like studios with kitchen facilities. Well-situated for enjoying nightlife, poorly situated for avoiding it. Singles £15; doubles £18; Quads £30.

Zenon Gardens Geroskipou Camping (tel. 242 277), east of the tourist beach on the sea, 3km from Paphos Harbor. Minimarket, restaurant, and kitchen. £2 per site; £2 per 3 people; £1 per small tent. Open Mar.-Oct.

FOOD

While most restaurants in Kato Paphos are geared to pound-laden foreigners, dining in Ktima Paphos can be affordable and even elegant.

Peggy's Miranda Cafe, in Kennedy Sq., serves continental breakfast (£2) and hosts a book swap. Run by and for British expatriates, it offers a cultivated local, colonial flavor. Open M-Tu and Th-F 7am-6:30pm.

Surfcafe, 1 Gladstone St. (tel. 239 239), has reasonably priced light meals (sandwiches £1-1.50, beer 80¢) and internet access (£1.50 per hour). Open until 8pm.

Park Mansion Hotel (tel. 245 645) serves grills (from £2.50) and prix-fixe dinners nightly and runs occasional all-you-can-eat barbecues.

Athens, 47 Evagora Pallekaride St. (tel. 232 613). Sweet shop for the sugar-starved.

Hondros, 96 Ap. Pavlou St. (tel. 234 256), in Kato Paphos, is one of the older restaurants in the area, founded long before the town's tourist boom. Sit under the bamboo-covered terrace beneath the grapevines and eat lamb *kleftiko* off the spit (£3.75). Open daily 11am-4pm and 7pm-midnight.

ENTERTAINMENT

Kato Paphos is home to virtually all of the area's nightlife, centering around Agias Napas St., a couple blocks inland from the waterfront. The area is instantly recognizable by bright lights and loud noise. **Summer Cinema** (tel. 632 229), on the waterfront, just past Geroskipou Beach is a trendy open-air club in exotic Mediterranean beachfront setting, just far enough from package hotels that locals can call it their own. To reach **Stigma** from Paphos Beach Hotel, turn inland at Iasonos St. and it is on the right-hand side. Paintings liven the walls of the funky but homey cafe. Coffee, drinks, and *tavli* inside on patio. **Shotts,** 91 Poseidon (tel. 622 616), is a popular dance club despite the £5 cover. A rooftop patio makes **Limanaki** (tel. 239 616), on the waterfront by Paphos Fort, *the* place in town to watch the sunset over the fort and cruise the internet after dark, though many seem to stay until dawn. **Boogies** (tel. 244 810) is an Old Paphos favorite in the heart of the bar district with karaoke kicking off every evening. After 2am, slurred but earnest renditions of Spice Girls songs give way to a hot dance floor.

SIGHTS

Kato Paphos

Apostolou Pavlou St., which connects Kato and Ktima Paphos, must have been just as much traffic centuries ago, as it is clustered with monuments to the Roman, early Christian, Byzantine, and Venetian periods of Cypriot history.

The mosaic floors of the **House of Dionysus,** the **House of Theseus,** and the **House of Aion** (tel. 240 217) are the city's more dazzling ancient spots. *(Admission £1.)* Discovered accidentally by a farmer plowing his fields in 1962 and excavated by a Polish expedition, the largely intact mosaics covered 14 rooms of the expansive Roman House of Dionysus. The floors depict scenes from mythology and daily life with vibrance and a subtle use of the stones' natural hues. Farther toward the water rests the **House of Theseus** complex, dating from the 2nd to the 6th centuries AD. The ruins reveal a luxurious building with marble statues and columns and mosaic floors. The two mosaics of Theseus and Achilles are accessible by walkways.

To the north of the mosaics, you'll find the remnants of an *agora* beside the limestone Roman **odeon**—a small, roofed semi-circular theater. *(Open in summer daily 7:30am-7pm. Admission 50¢.)* Built in the 2nd century AD, the odeon accommodates 3000 and is still used for performances. Built in the late 7th century on a hill overlooking the harbor, the **Byzantine Castle** *(Saranda Kolones)* was intended to protect inhabitants from Arab pirates. To get there, take Sophia Vembo St. off A. Pavlou Ave. When an earthquake destroyed the castle in 1222, the Lusignans built the **Paphos Fort** at the end of the pier, which was later rebuilt by Venetians and the Ottomans. *(Open daily 10am-5:45pm. Admission 75¢.)*

The musty **Catacombs of Agia Solomoni,** along the road between Ktima and Kato Paphos (opposite the Apollo Hotel), include a chapel with deteriorating Byzantine frescoes. *(Open 24hr. Free.)* Dedicated to St. Solomoni (Hannah), the chapel sits on the site of the old synagogue. Part of the deepest chamber is filled with lucent water, which you may not notice until you're drenched in it. A tree with handkerchiefs draped from its branches marks the entrance to the catacombs on A. Pavlos Ave. The tree is said to cure the illnesses of those who tie a cloth to it. St. Paul was allegedly whipped for preaching Christianity at nearby **St. Paul's Pillar.**

Ktima Paphos

The **Archaeological Museum** on Grivas Digenes Ave (tel. 240 215), 1km from Kennedy Sq., houses an array of Bronze Age pottery, tools, sculpture, statues, and artifacts from the House of Dionysus and the House of Theseus. *(Open M-F 7:30am-2:30pm and 3-5pm, Th 7:30am-2:30pm and 3-6pm, Sa-Su 10am-1pm. Admission 75¢.)* Don't miss the **Ethnographic Museum,** 1 Exo Vrysi St. (tel. 232 010), just outside of Kennedy Sq. *(Open M-Sa 9am-6pm, Su 10am-1pm. Admission £1. Guidebooks in English £3.)* The impressive private collection, displayed in the owner's home, depicts different phases of Cyprus's past through a series of rooms devoted to vocational and domestic life. The garden is a highlight of the museum, sporting a 3rd-century BC Hellenistic tomb, Christian catacombs, and *kleftiko* ovens. The **Byzantine Museum,** #26 25th Martiou St. across from the Ethnographic Museum (tel. 232 092), has icons and religious relics from local monasteries and churches. *(Open M-F 9am-5pm, Sa 10am-1pm. Admission £1.)*

West of Ktima Paphos, a signposted road runs 1km to Paleokastra's **Tombs of the Kings** (tel. 240 295)—a misnomer, since those interred in these stone tombs were merely local aristocracy. *(Open M-F 7:30am-5pm, Sa-Su 9am-5pm. Admission 75¢.)* The larger tombs consist of an open court encircled by burial chambers, with Doric columns carved out of the underground rock and stairways leading down to the interiors. The tombs, from the Hellenic and Roman periods, were also used as hideouts by early Christians fleeing persecution. To the north of the tombs lies **Paleoeklisia** (literally "old church"), with fragments of Byzantine frescoes.

■ Near Paphos

Paleopaphos

Tel. 432 180. Museum and temple **open** *M-F 7:30am-5pm, Sa-Su 9am-4pm.* **Admission to** *ruins, city, and museum 75¢. The sites are most easily seen from the excursion buses. Renting a moped is not advisable—the road is very dangerous.*

The area around Paphos contains some of Cyprus's most popular beaches and greater archaeological treasures. Adjacent to the modern village of **Kouklia** lie the ruins of the great **Temple of Aphrodite** and **Paleopaphos** (Old Paphos), once the capital of a kingdom encompassing nearly half of Cyprus. The temple itself was the religious center of the island and a destination for pilgrims from every corner of the Roman world. Built in the 12th century BC, it thrived until the 4th century AD, when the edicts of Emperor Theodosius and a series of earthquakes reduced it to rubble. The scant remains—merely piles of rocks—make little sense without a guide. *A Brief History and Description of Old Paphos,* published by the Department of Antiquities, is available in the adjoining **Paleopaphos Museum.**

Monastery of Agios Neophytos

Take the bus to Tala (6 per day M-F, 4 per day Sa-Su), then walk to the monastery. **Open** *daily 7:30am-noon and 3pm-dusk.* **Admission 50¢.**

The **Monastery of Agios Neophytos,** with icons, Byzantine frescoes, and painted caves and buildings, lies 9km north of Paphos, near Coral Bay Beach. Roughly 100m from the monastery complex are three rock caves carved out by Neophytos and covered with beautiful 12th-century frescoes. Bring a flashlight.

Beaches

The two most popular **beaches** stretch along **Geroskipou** to the east and **Coral Bay** to the north. Geroskipou is well touristed with snack bars, while Coral Bay is sandier and larger. Bus #11 from Ktima Paphos goes to Yeroskipou (3 per hr., 40¢), and #15 goes to Coral Bay from Yeroskipou (every 20min., 40¢). Although there is no public transportation (accessible primarily by jeep excursion or motorbike), **Cape Lara** is host to sandy beaches and is a nesting site for Green and Loggerhead Turtles. As both species have seen a steady decline in population, the Lara Sea Turtle Project was conceived in 1971 to protect the turtles and ensure that nesting continues here. Turtle nests can be viewed in the Project's hatchery enclosure.

Turtles Can't Disco

During their breeding season, June to August, turtles clamber ashore at night and dig holes in the sand using their rear flippers. The amphibians then lay their eggs and bury them in the holes before returning back to sea. When the hatchlings emerge from the sand at sunset, the water's phosphorescence attracts them off terra firma and into the sea. Recently, a turtle's life has become an especially tough one. With the growth of tourism in Cyprus, the evening entertainment industry is creeping over many beaches that were once the turtles' undisturbed breeding grounds. The phosphorescence of the moonlit water can't compete with garish disco lights, and toddling turtles, in their pilgrimage to the sea, can't resist the trap. Traveling inland, most turtlettes die of exhaustion if they're not snapped up by predators first.

■ Polis Πολις

One of this coastal resort's first visitors was Aphrodite, who came to Polis to bathe—the goddess of beauty no longer bathes alone. Tourism has gained a foothold in Polis, which is smaller, cheaper, and more relaxed than Paphos, 37km to the south. Accessible by minibus and taxi and blessed with hiking trails in the nearby Akamas peninsula and some of the country's better beaches, Polis is becoming a popular Cypriot base for budget travel.

ORIENTATION AND PRACTICAL INFORMATION For a small town, Polis can be difficult to navigate. Fortunately traveler necessities are consolidated into particular areas, and those who do get lost will discover some stellar examples of traditional Cypriot architecture—large, rounded wooden doors and stone masonry. At the end of the winding main street is the *platia*, home to several locally flavored cafes and all of the town's tourist services. The **CTO** office (tel. 322 468) is the island's newest, offering enthusiastic advice for daytrips and accommodations (open M-Sa 9am-1pm and 2:30-5:45pm). The **police** (tel. 321 451) roost one block from the square in the direction of the beach and speak some English (open 24hr). Around the *platia* you'll find three **banks** (all open M-F 8:30am-noon). The **post office** (tel. 321 539; open M-F 7:30am-2pm and Th 3-5pm) and **Spirides Taxi Service** (tel. 516 161) are also on the *platia*. The **Lemon Garden** (tel. 321 443), away from square past the Hellenic Bank, rents and sells **sports equipment** such as jet skis, and mountain bikes (£1.50-4 per day) and diving stuff. **Pegasus** (tel. 321 374 or 322 156) in the *platia* rents cars, mopeds (£4 per day), mountain bikes (£3 per day), and apartments. Two **pharmacies** (tel. 321 253 and tel. 321 167) are down the street from the post office. The **hospital** (tel. 321 431) about a six-minute walk from the *platia* toward the campground. For Internet access head to **Polis 2000+**, 10 Makariou St. (tel. 322 736), away from the *platia* past the Hellenic Bank. **Postal code: 8905. Telephone code: 06.**

ACCOMMODATIONS Camping is popular for budget travelers. Beyond the parking lot to the Baths of Aphrodite, a large field provides practically beach-side camping for free. Camping here is illegal but rules are generally ignored as long as the field remains clean. Some campers here seem to have taken up semi-permanent residence. The field also leads to the two main hiking trails of the Akamas peninsula. **Campground** (tel. 321 526), 1km from the town center in a fragrant, seaside eucalyptus grove, is open from March to October; follow signs for the campground. The campground boasts shower facilities, a playground, and a bar that hosts beach parties every Thursday and Sunday in addition to Sunday volleyball and mini-football competitions with alcoholic prizes (£1 per person; £1.50 per tent; tent rental £2). The **Lemon Garden** (tel. 321 443) has a unique combination of quality rooms, food, and atmosphere. All rooms come with kitchenette, private bath, A/C, and view (doubles £14-16; larger rooms £16-20). Don't plan your honeymoon here, but for pretty good hotel accommodations, **Lovers Nest Apartments** (tel. 322 401), on the road to **Latchi**, offers well-kept studios with a large pool and pool-side bar (singles £15; doubles £20; triples £23). Also look for inexpensive rooms in private households on the road to Latchi, along the road to the beach, or inquire at a cafe. Rooms go for about £5-6 per person. Next to the church before Vomos Taverna, **Mrs. Charita Antoniou** (tel. 321 989) rents spacious rooms with access to a common bath and kitchen. The three front rooms open onto a porch (£5 per bed).

FOOD AND ENTERTAINMENT The *platia* cafes and restaurants all serve uniform fare at similar prices and are popular with tourists as well as locals. **Vomos Taverna** (tel. 321 143) serves drinks and snacks by the beach. In town, **Arsinoe** (tel. 321 590), across from the church, is run by a fisherman's family and serves their daily catch (swordfish £3.50, fish *meze* £4.50; open daily 8am-1pm and 7pm-1am). Nearby, the **Kebab House** sells scrumptious *souvlaki* for £1.50. There's a beachside disco, but a more appealing option is to enter the world of **Marios Garden Café** (tel. 321 551), located down a set of stairs, just beyond the Akamas Hotel from the *platia*. Marios has turned this dilapidated Turkish house into a whimsical garden cafe and bar, with statues, quirky furniture, and a bonfire in the middle. Marios serves up daily specials that may be the best meals in town.

SIGHTS The **Baths of Aphrodite,** a shady pool carved out of limestone by natural springs, is 10km west of Polis. It is reportedly where Aphrodite married Akamas, the son of Theseus, and the place to which Aphrodite came to cleanse herself after her nocturnal exploits. According to legend, all who bathe in the pool stays forever young. However, for now, don't look here for immortality, the baths are strictly look but don't swim. Buses run from Polis to the Baths (M-F 9:30, 10:30am, and 2:30pm; 50¢). The church of **Agios Andronikos** in Polis was built in the 15th century, but was converted to a mosque during the latter half of the 16th century by invading Ottomans who plastered over its frescoes. Now the plaster is being removed and the church restored. Ask for a key from the CTO to see the church yourself.

■ Near Polis

To the West
Pristine **beaches** and a small selection of inexpensive lodgings characterize the road from Polis to the baths of Aphrodite. The port town of **Latchi,** 2km west of Polis, offers some hotels and a pleasant stretch of coastline (tel. 32 11 14 or 23 67 40 for more information; bus from Polis 40¢). West of Latchi, a long sand beach stretches at Takkas Bay, and then again below the **Baths of Aphrodite Tourist Pavilion.**

Nature lovers and avid hikers will appreciate the region's self-guided trails, just outside Polis on the **Akamas Peninsula.** Akamas is noted as being the easternmost point for European vegetation and soil to naturally exist and contains a remarkable array of flora and fauna (particularly in the spring), some of which (especially the stationary varieties) are marked along the trails. A guide to hiking the Akamas trails, available at all tourist office, is an invaluable reference.

Next to the Baths of Aphrodite, signs mark the beginning of the two primary hiking trails: the **Aphrodite** and the **Adonis.** Both trips take between two and three hours, although adding the Fontana Amaroza sidetrip from the Aphrodite can take closer to half a day. The trails take the same path for the first 2km, leaving coastal scrub behind in favor of fragrant forest. The two split at the ruins of **Pyrgos tis Rigainas,** believed to be a medieval monastery, where picnic tables and a potable well sit among huge oak trees. From here, the Aphrodite, generally considered the nicer of the two, continues right, ascending Mt. Sotiras before descending towards the coast into a field cleared by forest fire and hugging the coast back towards the starting point.

Near the coast, the turnoff for **Fontana Amaroza** leads towards a shipwreck and sea caves as well as the fountain of love itself. While it may have worked wonders in the past, today the *fontana* is a stagnant pool and anyone bringing a date is likely to walk back alone. From Pyrgos tis Rigainas, the Adonis continues left, running along a series of streams on its way back to the main road just east of the tourist pavilion.

To the East
East of Polis, along the road to Kato Pirgos (65km), placid farming villages preside over deserted stretches of beach that are slightly rockier, but no less appealing than those to the west. By the turnoff for Makounta and Kinousa, shaded picnic tables line a sandy stretch of beach. Trekking east of Pomos demands a 45-minute detour around the village of Kokkina, currently occupied by the Turkish military.

South of Polis, the village of **Androlikou** has been abandoned since the Turkish military forced the Turkish-Cypriots who inhabited the village to evacuate. Today goats wander through the streets and among the crumbling buildings. Ten kilometers south, the story of **Dhrousha** has a happier ending. With its narrow winding streets, beautiful village houses, and panoramic views, Dhrousha is becoming increasingly wealthy and popular. Both villages are best visited by following signs from route E709 which runs south from the road between Polis and Latchi.

It is difficult to tour the area without wheels. **Minibuses** (tel. 236 740 or 236 822) pass through Polis from Paphos (10 per day M-F 6:30am-7pm, 5 per day Sa 9am-4pm, £1). Some minibuses from Paphos continue on to Pomos (£1.15). Two **buses** from Kato Pirgos also stop here. *Let's Go* does not recommend hitchhiking, and passing cars are rare, but those that come by will usually stop.

TROODOS MOUNTAINS

Isolated villages tucked into cool, pine-covered mountains provide refuge from the sun-baked coastal cities. Tiny hamlets and Byzantine churches dot the countryside while remote monasteries and pine forests ward off the summer heat. Hikers and campers in particular will find a small paradise here. What is usually a peaceful and rejuvenating natural experience in June and early July, however, can turn frustrating and costly in August when the urban crowds descend on the area, especially on weekends. From January to March, **Mt. Olympus,** the highest point in Cyprus (1951m), is host to hundreds of skiers.

Public transportation to the area and between the villages runs infrequently, and even scheduled stops can be unreliable. The best way to get around is to rent some wheels or make a friend with a car. Some hitch; *Let's Go* cannot recommend it. It's difficult to maintain a rigid schedule here. In the mountains, no town has motorbike rentals, but you can easily rent mopeds (standard transmission, more than 100cc) or cars in Limassol, Paphos, Polis, or Nicosia if you are over 25. Mountain roads, however, are tortuous, winding, bumpy, and always steep.

■ Platres Πλατρες

Centrally located and the most accessible town in the Troodos by public transportation, **Platres** is a convenient base for exploring the region. Although the town itself lacks character, its forested setting and hiking trails only minutes away make Platres appealing, even with the incessant barrage of tour buses.

ORIENTATION AND PRACTICAL INFORMATION Platres is divided into the **pano** (upper) and **kato** (lower) sections. Pano Platres contains most tourist facilities, while Kato Platres is largely residential. The tourist office has essential maps for hiking trails.

Zingas Bus (tel. (02) 463 989) in Nicosia runs to Platres (M-Sa 1 per day, £2) on a reservation basis, so call ahead. From Limassol, a **Kyriakos** (tel. 421 346) service taxi leaves at 11:30am, returning at 7am (M-Sa, £2). A private **taxi** from either city costs £15-20. Kyriakos has an office in Platres (tel. 364 114) for transit in the area. **Top Hill Souvenirs** (tel. 422 022), on the main street, down the hill from the post office, rents **mountain bikes.** There are some great bike routes in the Troodos, and the staff is happy to help you find them (21-gear bikes £4 per day; open daily 9:30am-6pm).

The **tourist office** (tel. 421 316) is left of the parking lot in the main square (open M-F 9am-3pm, Sa 9am-2pm). The **post office** sits to the left of the tourist office. (Open in summer M-F 7am-noon and 3-5pm, in winter M-F 8-10am and 3-5pm.) The **Bank of Cyprus** is opposite the tourist office and Popular Bank is just uphill and has a 24-hour ATM (open M-F 8:15am-12:30pm). The **hospital** (tel. 421 324) is below Pano Platres (open 24hr.). The nearest **pharmacy** (tel. 922 020) is in Kakopetria (open M-F 8am-2pm, Sa 8am-1:30pm). The **police** (tel. 421 351) are opposite the tourist office in a converted military chapel. The **CYTA,** next to the post office, sells phone cards (open M-F 7:30am-1:30pm). **Postal code:** 4815 in Kato and 4820 in Pano Platres. **Telephone code:** 05.

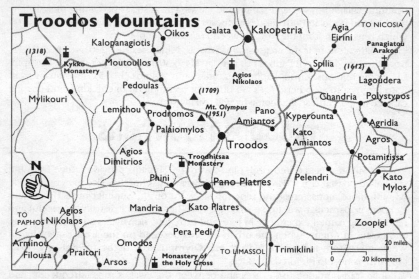

Troodos Mountains

ACCOMMODATIONS At **Kallithea Hotel** (tel. 421 746; fax 422 241), on the right side on the road to Kato Platres, the friendly owner offers clean, simple rooms, some with balcony or patio (doubles £10 including breakfast). Ask about the rooms across the street which are practically in the forest. A large balcony has tables and chairs to enjoy the view and hear nightingales croon (doubles £9 including breakfast). To find **Lanterns** (tel. 422 661), walk downhill from the post office and turn right at the supermarket (doubles £10, including breakfast).

FOOD Psilo Dentro, north of Platres on the road to Troodos (tel. 422 050), serves sumptuous trout from its fish farm under a beautiful canopy of tall trees (whole trout £4.20; open daily 8am-5pm). From the post office walk uphill to **Kilas Ton Harition** (tel. 421 454), at the end of the road. They serve fish late into the evening and the streamside forested setting makes it a local favorite. For picnics, two large **grocery stores** are downhill from the post office. **Soforla Supermarket** (tel. 421 666) and **Cherryland** (tel. 421 414) stock standard supplies and a huge selection of ice cream bars (Soforla open daily 7:30am-9pm; Cherryland open daily 7am-10pm).

■ Near Platres

Platres is well situated for visiting a number of charming villages. Taking side roads to get there affords some beautiful mountain hiking and biking opportunities.

Omodos

Eight kilometers southwest of Kato Platres is the cordial lace and wine village of **Omodos.** Your introduction to the town will be the lively and heavily touristed main square. Here, you can buy a bottle of local, dry wine (£2) or fiery *tsipoura,* a Cypriot whiskey. At the end of the square is the famous **Monastery of the Holy Cross.** Repairs to sections damaged in a 1996 earthquake leave some parts off limits. Many of the structures in the monastery, including the church, are still open. To the left of the main entrance to the monastery, the labyrinthine streets of gentrified Omodos lead past souvenir shops, beautiful whitewashed homes and a restored wine press (*linos*). In the village, the newly opened **Avli Tou Themistoklou** (tel. 422 649) serves *meze* (£5) at dinner and light meals at lunch. For the best breads and pastries in town head to **Cafeteria Croissanterie** (tel. 422 142), behind the square near the parking lot. The in-house bakery also serves sandwiches (£1-1.20; open daily 8:30am-midnight).

Troodhitissa Monastery

Eight monks and myriad animals make their home in the modern **Troodhitissa Monastery,** 5km from Platres on the Prodromos-Platres road. Dedicated to the Virgin Mary, the original monastery was built in 1250 to house one of her miracle-working icons. During the chaos of the iconoclastic movement in the 8th century, a monk hid an icon of the Virgin Mary in Troodos, where a miraculous pillar of fire protected it. More than a century later, a sign revealed the site of the icon; the monastery still stands on the site. As of recently, the monks have called it quits on official visiting hours to better concentrate on religious affairs. Those that do show up, however, may be granted entrance.

Platres Trails

Psilo Dendron Restaurant, just north of Platres, marks the starting point for a number of hiking trails of varying terrain, distance, and difficulty. Most lead toward various vantages of **Kaledonia Falls,** surely the Troodos region's most celebrated spot, and perhaps its most picturesque.

Left of the restaurant, a path accessible by car a and mountain bike reaches the falls early, affording postcard views before continuing through a forested path for 3km. The trail ends by the presidential palace near Troodos, built by, among others, the famous French poet **Arthur Rimbaud.** At the end of the trail, keep veering left to reach the Platres-Troodos road. To the right of the restaurant, a trail joins with an easterly trail before reaching a junction. From here yellow signs lead to either the top of Kaledonia falls or the south shoulders of Mt. Olympus.

Also to the right of the restaurant, the least impressive but most ambitious of the trails is a mountain-bike-accessible 9km dirt track leading to the unremarkable **Mesopotamos Monastery.** Pick up a map of Platres area hikes at the Platres tourist office.

■ Troodos Τροοδος

While the mountains which share its name bear a number of colorful villages, Troodos itself is merely an aggregate of tourist and camping facilities that provide a base for exploring the region. Just 10km north of Platres, **Troodos** is accessible only by **bus** from **Clarios Bus Co.** (tel. 453 234) in Nicosia (M-F 11:30am, returns 6:30am; £1.10) and generally require a reservation. A private **taxi** from Nicosia costs £17. You can either hike (at least 2hr.) or take a taxi (£5) from Platres. The **police** (tel. 421 623), just outside of town, offer **CYTA** info, but keep unreliable hours. For more reliable services, head to Platres, Kakopetria, or Limassol.

The **Troodos campground** (tel. 422 249), 2km north of the main square in a pine forest (£1.50 per person), provides laundry facilities, a minimarket, a bar/restaurant, and a first aid station. The **Jubilee Hotel Bar** (tel. 421 647), just outside of town, is a favorite of British ex-pats. The hotel also rents bicycles. Up a dirt road from the rotary, the **Troodos Youth Hostel** (tel. 422 400) is the roomiest and the most relaxing of the island's hostels (£4 per person, £1 for sheets).

Troodos Trails

Four of the region's more spectacular hikes originate in the Troodos area. Detailed maps are available at all Cyprus tourist offices. From Troodos, **Artemis** is a 15-minute walk along the main road to Prodromos. Beginning 200m up the road, the circular trail wraps around Mt. Olympus for 7km, or roughly ten-and-a-half hours. Although relatively flat and mostly covered in black pines, the hike provides excellent views of Cyprus. From the Troodos post office, the **Atalante** trail essentially mimics the Artemis trail, though at a lower altitude. The trail runs 8½km, ending at the Prodromos-Troodos road, near the chromium mine camp. The 3km **Persephone** trail leaves from the coffee shop in Troodos Sq. and gradually descends to a divine lookout point among huge slabs of limestone rock. The **Kaledonia** trail is the shortest, but perhaps most captivating of the Troodos trails, leading to Kaledonia Falls and ending at Psilo Dendron restaurant, near Platres.

■ Kakopetria Κακοπετρια

Picturesque **Kakopetria,** literally "evil rock," is the most popular town in the northern part of the mountains. According to local legend, the large rock perched on the hillside rolled over and crushed a couple, initiating a tradition in which newlyweds sit on the rock to ensure marital stability.

Lately, indications have been more auspicious. Kakopetria has become a model of the nation's trend towards "agrotourism," tourism co-existing with tradition in which tourists and weekending urban Cypriots are expected to blend in seamlessly with village life. Although contrived, the result is an aesthetic success, ensuring tasteful tourism within its old village and lively public square. Kakopetria, with its old village and abundance of restaurants and accommodations, is an ideal stop over or a base for those that prefer to confine hiking to a daytime activity.

ORIENTATION AND PRACTICAL INFORMATION Clarias (tel. 453 2334) runs to and from Kakopetria out of Nicosia (13 leaving M-F, 2 Su, 9 returning M-F, 2 Su, £1.10), and some continue to Troodos by reservation. All three major banks, **Bank of Cyprus** (tel, 922 525), **Hellenic Bank** (tel. 922 636), and **Popular Bank** (tel. 922 955) are in the public square (open M-F 8:15am-12:30pm), near the **post office** (tel. 422 422; open M-W, F 7:30am-1:30pm, Th 7:30am-1:30pm and 3-6pm). The **police station** (tel. 922 420 or 922 255) is up the street from the bank (open 24hr). A **pharmacy** (tel. 922 020) on Makarios Ave., is towards the Nicosia-Troodos road (open 9:30am-9pm), and a doctor (tel. 923 077) is a few doors down. **Telephone code:** 02.

ACCOMMODATIONS Kakopetria has a number of budget rooms in the form of "rooms to let" above or behind restaurants, which tend to offer rooms along the stream. Package tour hotels and their large pools rest further uphill.

Rooms below Serenity Coffeeshop (tel. 922 602) are on Old Kakopetria St., between the bridge and Linos Inn. In the heart of old Kakopetria where rooms are generally much pricier, this friendly traditional cafe offers rustic rooms with streamside patios. Intimacy with forest and stream accurately account for its name (singles £10; doubles £12). To reach **Hekali Hotel,** 22 Gr. Digenis St. (tel. 992 501; fax 922 503), from the square, follow signs to the police station then turn right—you'll find considerably more substantial rooms with TV, phone, and balcony, than the various "rooms to let." Rooms (singles £13; doubles £20). From Public Square, turn right at Hellenic Bank to reach **Kifissia Hotel,** 20 Aedonin St. (tel. 922 421), which has clean, no-frills rooms with balconies (£8 per person includes breakfast).

FOOD AND ENTERTAINMENT Although it's no gastronomic mecca, Kakopetria has more dining options than neighboring towns. Restaurants center around the public square with those catering to tourists right on the square, and the cheaper *kebab* houses just off the square. At **Maryland at the Mill** (tel. 922 536), conspicuously perched on the hill above a former mill across the bridge from Old Kakopetria St., ponder village life from an upscale patio over tasty meals that run the fiscal gamut (hamburgers £1.30, chicken salad £3.25, trout £5.35; open M-F noon-11, Sa-Su noon-3:30pm and 7:30-11pm). The **Greek Orthodox Club** operates an informal *taverna* serving *kebabs* (£2) and salads (£2), which are probably the cheapest meals in town (no assigned hours, but generally open for lunch and dinner).

Platia Pizza (tel. 922 3352 or 923 661) dishes up what the chef calls distinctly Australian pizza in the charming public square. Choose from vegetarian, south of the border, and others (from £3.40). If a long day's hike has left you incapacitated, Platia delivers throughout town for free (open daily 6-10pm). **Clarion Brand Disco,** 21

Makarios Ave. (tel. 923 470), across the stream from Public Square, next to Lina gas station, lights up the evening groove. Wiggle your weary hiking bones alongside teenagers from neighboring villages who gather for their favorite Greek dance hits (open summer only with £3-5 cover).

SIGHTS The cobbled streets of Old Kakopetria are lined with well-maintained traditional village houses. Kakopetria and its smaller neighbor **Galata** have five Byzantine churches between them; the most beautiful is **Agios Nikolaos tis Stegis**, 4km southwest of Kakopetria on the road to Troodos. The interior of this 14th-century church is painted with strikingly unique frescoes. The caretaker is happy to provide a tour detailing the history of the church and frescoes upon request. *(Open Tu-Sa 9am-4pm and Su 11am-4pm.)* The church of **Panagiatou Arakou,** 16km southeast of Kakopetria, is another repository of elaborate 12th-century frescoes, including Christ Pantokrator (on the inside of the dome). South of the church is the comely vineyard village of **Agros,** with the only rooms in the vicinity.

■ Kykko Monastery Μονη Κυκκο

*From the Leonidou St. station in Nicosia, Kambos sends **buses** to Kykko Monastery (M-Sa one round-trip per day £3).* **Open** *daily 9-6. Supermarket, tourist pavilion with exorbitant prices, and several sweet shops are nearby.* **Video** *available in the gift shop.*

Kykko Monastery, in the northwest part of the mountains, 14km from the village of Pedhoulas, enjoys more wealth and prestige than any other monastery on the island. The monastery was founded in the early 12th century when a hermit, after curing the Byzantine Emperor's daughter, was given the Apostle Luke's **icon of the Virgin Mary.** The monastery has burned down numerous times, but the celebrated icon has survived intact. As the icon is thought too holy to be viewed directly, it is completely ensconced in mother of pearl and silver casing. After entering the monastery's palatial courtyard, you may think you've wandered into a large luxury hotel with 400 beds for visitors. Built in the early 19th century, the buildings seem more suitable for hosting revelry than religion.

The monks' rapport with visitors is friendlier than that of the average group of Greek ascetics-turned-tour guides. This secular side seems to have introduced entrepreneurial leanings: those with cameras in the church are reminded that, in respect for the sanctity of the space, photography in the sanctuary is prohibited, but that a video is available for purchase in the gift shop.

Kykko gained new fame in this century as a communication and supply center during the Cypriot struggle and as the monastic home of Archbishop Makarios III. Only 1.5km away were the secret headquarters of the first military leader of the struggle, "Dighenis," General George Grivas.

The Cypriot Republic's first President **Makarios' tomb** is just 2km away in the high hills west of the monastery. The site, guarded by two Greek Cypriot soldiers, is partially open to the east. Makarios requested the opening so that on the day of Cypriot reunification, sunlight would enter his tomb and he could celebrate with his people. Just above the tomb is a path leading up to an icon of the Virgin, called the *throni* (small throne). The trees behind the path are laden with scarves placed there by sick children hoping to be cured.

NICOSIA Λευκωσια

Landlocked Nicosia is a city of walls. The ramparts and barbed wire of the Green Line separate the Greek capital from the Turkish side of the city, and the imposing Venetian walls separate the new cities from the old. Built on the ancient Roman town of Ledra, Nicosia first prospered under the Lusignan dynasty. When Lusignan power waned, Venetians arrived in 1489. In 1567, they built huge walls to ward off Ottoman cannons. The walls didn't work; three years later the Ottomans conquered Nicosia in seven weeks, and ruled the city for several hundred years. The Ottoman era ended with the British arrival in 1878. When Cyprus won independence in 1960, Nicosia became its capital. As a result of the events of 1974, Nicosia is the last divided city in the world, now that the walls have been torn down in Berlin and Beirut. Passage between the two sides across the Green Line is sanctioned from the Ledra checkpoint on the southern side (see p. 510).

■ South Nicosia

Within the walls, the old city remains cognizant of its past. OutsideN the walls the newer city appears insistent on looking only forward—it's an expanding metropolis and sprawling suburbia embracing all facets of modernization, with mixed results. Greek Cypriots call their city Lefkosia, but use of Nicosia is common and inoffensive.

The city has taken measures to restore the old **Laiki Yitonia,** the pedestrian shopping district, where the cobblestone streets are crammed with shops and restaurants. The recent proliferation of museums and monuments reflects the town's eagerness to maintain its spirit and cultural heritage. Unfortunately, the city still has only one major attraction: the ominous Green Line—south Nicosia is still geared toward bureaucrats rather than backpackers. Still, south Nicosia offers the true Cyprophile a chance to interact with the local population on its own terms, without the frills of tourism, and gives an intimate view of the political strife that has been the primary force shaping modern Cyprus (see p. 480).

ORIENTATION AND PRACTICAL INFORMATION

The easiest way to orient yourself in Nicosia is to refer to the Green Line, running east-west at the north end of the city. This line splits the **Old City** within its circular Venetian walls into the respective Greek and Turkish sectors. When you walk down the streets divided by the border, you are confronted by sheet metal barriers or white and blue dividers. Do *not* ignore the signs forbidding photography that are scattered throughout the area. The southern part of Nicosia within the walls contains most budget lodgings, museums, and sights. From **Eleftherias Square,** Evagoras St. heads southwest into the **New City.** Intersecting Evagoras are Makarios Ave., Diagoras St., and Th. Dervis St., which leads away from the city to the youth hostel. The New City is much busier than the old and is the center of Nicosia's nightlife. Be sure to get the free map from the tourist office.

Transportation

Buses: Kallenos, Solomos Sq. (tel. 654 850), runs connections to Larnaka (M-Sa 3-7 per day, £1.50). **Kemek,** 34 Leonidas St. (tel. 463 989), south of Solomos Sq. and **ALEPA** (tel.625 027), near Solomos Sq., run to Limassol (M-Sa 3-5 per day, £1.50) and to Paphos (M-Sa 1 per day, £3). **EMAN,** at the bus stop 100m east of the post office at Eleftherias Sq., with an office at 2 Eleftherias Sq. (tel. 473 414), runs to Agia Napa during the summer (M-F 1 per day, £2). **Paralimni-Deryneia,** 27 Stasinou St. (tel. 444 141), at Kyriakas Taxi, runs to Parlimni, Protaras, and Agia Napa (M-F 1 per day, £2.50). **Zingas** (tel. 463 989), at the Kemek office, runs to Prodromos, Pedoulas, and if a reservation is made, to Platres (M-Sa 1 per day, £2). **Clarios** (tel. 453 234), at Costanze Bastioon St. 200m east of Eleftherias St., runs to Kakopetria (M-Sa 12 per day, £1.10; Su 2 per day, £1.90) and to Troodos by reservation. **Kambos,** Leonidou St., runs to Kykko Monastery (M-Sa one round-trip per day, £3). **Service Taxis:** To Limassol (£3.45), Paphos (£5.95). Taxis to Larnaka (30min., 2 per hr. 6am-6:30pm, £2.40). **Makris** (tel. 466 200), **Kyriakos** (tel. 444 141), and **Solis** at Tripolis Bastion St. (tel. 466 388), run taxis to Polis (5 per week, £5).

Tourist and Financial Services

C.T.O.: (tel. 444 264) 11 Aristokypros St., in the Laiki Yitonia. Entering Eleftherias Sq., turn right and follow signs from the post office. Route maps, a complete list of

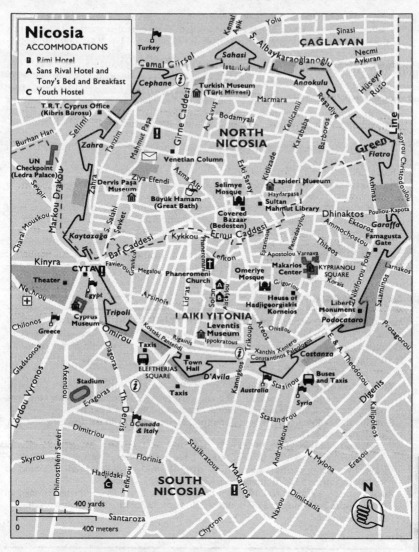

Nicosia
ACCOMMODATIONS
B Rimi Hotel
A Sans Rival Hotel and Tony's Bed and Breakfast
C Youth Hostel

village buses, and free copies of *Nicosia: This Month*. Open M-F 8:30am-4pm, Sa 8:30am-2pm. A free **tour** through the old village of Kaimakli leave from here (conducted in English; 2hr., one tour per week on Monday at 10am). Tours are led in old-fashioned wooden buses and provide a taste of Nicosia before development.

Embassies: Australian High Commission, 4 Annis Comninis St. (tel. 473 001; fax 366 486), 500m east of Eleftherias Sq. off Stasinou Ave. Open in summer M-F 7:30am-3:20pm. **Egypt,** 3 Egypt Ave. (tel. 465 144; fax 462 287), open M-F 8am-2pm. **Greece,** 8 Lordou Vyronos (tel. 441 880; fax 473 990), open M-F 9am-noon. **Israel,** 4 I. Grypari St. (tel. 445 195), open M-F 9am-noon. **Lebanon,** 1 Vas. Olgas (tel. 442 216; fax 467 662), open M-F 9am-noon. **Syria,** 1 Androkleous St. (tel. 474 481; fax 446 963), open M-F 8am-2:30pm. **U.K. High Commission,** Alexanderou Pavlou St. (tel. 473 131; fax 367 198), west of the old city. Open M-F 8-11:30am. **U.S.,** Metochiou and Ploutarchou (tel. 476 100; fax 465 944). Open in summer M-F 8am-4pm; in winter M-F 8am-5pm.

Banks: Bank of Cyprus, 86-88-90 Phaneromeni St. (tel. 477 774), offers **ATM currency exchange.** Open M-F 8:15am-12:30pm. Convenient branch in Laiki Yitonia on Drakos St. (tel. 365 959) with 24hr. **ATM.** Open M-F 8:30am-noon and 3:15-4:45pm, Tu-F 8:30-noon.

American Express: A.L. Mantovani and Sons, 2D Agapinoras St. (tel. 443 777), 1km south of Solomos Sq. down Makarios Ave. Open M-F 8am-12:45pm and 3:30-6:30pm.

Bookstores: Philippides & Son, 10 Paleologos Ave. (tel. 462 984), opposite the post office. Well stocked, slightly pricey resource for travel guides, fiction, and (for the traveling classicist) Greek literature in translation. Emergency and Communications

Police: (tel. 303 090). 150m east of Paphos Gate on Digenis St., inside the wall. Open 24hr. **Emergency:** Dial 199.

Hospital: (tel. 451 111), at Omirou St. and Nechrou St. Open 24hr.

Internet Access: Alphagraphics, at the corner of Mycenae St. and Santa Roza St. in the new city. Open M-F 8am-7pm, Sa 9am-1am.

Post Office: Main Office (tel. 303 231) on Constantinos Paleologos Ave., east of Eleftherias Sq. within the walls. Open M-Tu and Th-F 7:30am-1pm and 4-7pm, W 7:30am-1pm. Branch offices on Digenis St., Palace St., and Loukis Akitas Ave. (tel. 302 531). **Postal Code:** 1903.

CYTA: 14 Egypt Ave. (tel. 470 200). Sells £3 telecards, good for about 30min. of local phone time. Telecards work in pay phones anywhere on the island. Open M-F 7am-7pm. **Telephone Code:** 02.

ACCOMMODATIONS

Most of Nicosia's budget accommodations are within the city walls and are tolerably clean. If you don't like the room you're shown, ask to see another—the degree of cleanliness and comfort tends to vary widely, and there are usually plenty of rooms from which to choose.

Youth Hostel (HI), 1 Hadjidaki St. (tel. 444 808), 1km into the New City. Little supervision and few guests. Kitchen and yard provide meeting spots for travelers. Bring bug repellant. Showers included. Sheets £1. Dorms £4 per person.

Sans Rival, 7 Solon St. (tel. 474383). Simple, modern rooms in the Laiki Yitonia. Singles £10; doubles £13.

Tony's Bed and Breakfast, 13 Solon St. (tel. 466 752; fax. 454 225), in the Laiki Yitonia. Rooms range widely in size, but all have radio, phone, and fridge and some have TVs. Large rooftop patio looks over the old city. Full English breakfast included. Singles £11-15; doubles £18-22; triples £27; quads £32.

Rimi Hotel, 5 Solon St. (tel 463 153; fax 452 816). Recently renovated rooms, all with private bath. Singles £23; doubles £30; triples £36; breakfast at downstairs restaurant included.

FOOD

Dining choices in Nicosia range from *tavernas* with live music to pubs, pizzerias, and full restaurants. The touristy joints around Laiki Yitonia serve Cypriot cuisine in cool surroundings. The smaller restaurants in the Old Town cater more to locals.

Mattheos (tel. 475 846), behind the Phaneromeni Church (near a small mosque). Good food for low prices. Shaded tables outside. *Koupepia* (stuffed grape leaves) and *moussaka* £2.75 each. Open daily 5am-7pm.

Berlin #2 Cafe (tel. 474 935), corner of Lefkon St. Savor your *kebab,* salad, and pita (£2.50) in the shade of the Green Line. A real U.N. guard is in the background. Open M-Tu, Th-F 7:30am-6:30pm, W and Sa closes early.

Lozantras, 67 Phaneromeni St. (tel. 464 136), has established a loyal following who come for their exceptional grills (£3-6). Deep red walls and hardwood floors create an attractive atmosphere.

The Powerhouse, at the Municipal Art Center. Dine next to great art in the gallery's tastefully modern, but slightly expensive restaurant.

Natural Choice, 11 Chytron St. in the new city (tel. 362 674), convenient to the youth hostel. All food is homemade at this fresh foods eatery. Outdoor seating under huge umbrellas; rather institutional interior. Wash down your seasonal stuffed veggies or chicken curry (£2.50) with a huge slab of sugar-free apple pie (75¢). If you don't feel healthy enough after a meal, stock up on vitamins or self-help books in the adjacent health food store.

Byzantine (tel. 477 085), 1 block from the tourist office, is a wooden-beamed restaurant with a shady courtyard. Offers *meze* (£5), *moussaka* (£3.50), and salad (£2.25). Open M-Sa 8am-5pm.

For the most inexpensive eating in Nicosia, head to the **municipal market** on the corner of Digenis Akritas St. and Kallipolis Ave., a huge warehouse filled with a variety of food stands. You can buy fresh feta in blocks and make your own salad. Hanging pigs will make you either ravenous or vegetarian (open daily 6am-1pm and 4-6pm). A colorful streetside **produce market** opens on Wednesdays near Eleftherias Sq. along Constantinos Paleologos Ave. (open W 9am-1pm and 4-6pm).

ENTERTAINMENT

Removed from the coast and most of Cyprus' tourist masses, Nicosia takes on an intensely urban feel by night—Greek, with a cosmopolitan flair.

Ta Kala Kathoumena, 21 Nikokleous St. (tel. 464 654). Beautifully tucked into an alley near Phaneromeni Church. Nicosia's cognascente gather at night for debate, backgammon, and well-priced coffee and drinks. Open 11am-midnight.

⊛**Odyssea Pub,** Eleftherias Sq. (tel. 451 174). Unselfconsciously local, popular watering hole frequented by twenty-something Cypriots. Open daily 8am-4am.

Zebra Bar, in Chapo Galxis shopping center, off Makarios Ave. in new city. Choose your poison and immerse yourself in all things zebra in the funky, dimly lit bar.

SIGHTS

The **Makarios Cultural Center** (tel. 430 008) occupies the Old City buildings of Archbishopric Kyprianos Sq., a former 15th-century Gothic monastery. Several interesting museums are clustered here. The **Byzantine Art Gallery** hosts the island's largest collection of icons. *(Open M-F 9am-4:30pm. Admission £1.)* The **Folk Art Museum** (tel. 463 205) presents Cypriot masterpieces of woodcarving, embroidery, pottery, basketry, and metalwork from the 18th to 20th centuries. *(Open M-F 9am-5pm and Sa 10am-1pm. Admission £1.)* A guide to the collection costs 50¢. The neighboring **Greek Independence War Gallery** (tel. 302 465), founded in 1961, contains photographs and other items from the struggle for *enosis,* the unrealized union of Cyprus with Greece. *(Open M-F 9am-4:30pm and Sa 9am-1pm. Admission 50¢.)* Also in the area is the **St. John Cathedral Church,** built in 1662 by Archbishop Nikiforos. *(Open M-F 8am-noon and 2-4pm, Sa 9am-noon.)*

Near the Archbishopric is the **House of Hadjigeorgiakis Kornesios,** known as **Konak Mansion,** 18 Patriarch Gregory St. (tel. 302 447). *(Open M-F 8am-2pm, Sa 9am-1pm. Admission 75¢.)* A famous dragoman (Ottoman interpreter) lived in this luxurious 18th-century structure. Nearby is the **Ömeriye Mosque,** easily recognizable by its huge minaret. The **Turkish Baths,** 8 Tillirias St. (tel. 477 588), are across from the mosque. *(Open for women W and F 8am-3pm; for men W and F 3-7pm, Tu, Th, and Sa-Su 8am-7pm. Admission £4.)* The **Nicosia Municipal Art Center** demands a visit, with impressive displays of accomplished and up-and-coming artists who garner little attention outside Cyprus. *(Open Tu-Sa 10am-3pm and 5-11pm, Su 10am-4pm. Free.)*

A marble monument depicting 14 Cypriots, each representing a period of the island's history, is down Korais St. from the Archbishopric. Nearby, along the Venetian Walls at the end of Theseus St., is the recently restored **Famagusta Gate,** which served as the main entrance to the medieval city. Built in 1567, it now hosts plays, concerts, and lectures. *(Open M-F 10am-1pm and 4-7pm. Free.)*

In the Laiki Yitonia, the **Leventis Municipal Museum** on Hippocratis St. (tel. 451 475), won the European Museum of the Year award in 1991. *(Open Tu-Su 10am-4:30pm. Free.)* The exhibit chronicles the history of Nicosia, beginning with the modern city, back to 3000 BC. The **Cyprus Jewelers Museum,** 7-9 Odos Praxipou St., is opposite the tourist office. *(Open M-F 10am-4:30pm. Free.)* Though small, it is worth visiting. The 18th- to 20th-century collection includes gold and silver plates, spoons, and jewelry hand-crafted in the *filigree* and *skaleta* techniques.

The **Cyprus Museum** (tel. 302 189) has the most extensive collection of ancient art and artifacts on the island, from the pre-Hellenic periods through the Byzantine era. *(Open M-Sa 9am-5pm, Su 10am-1pm. Admission £1.50.)* Lovers of archaeology may find hours of fun comparing local jewelry from many periods of civilization, while everyone will feel dwarfed by the larger-than-life terra cotta figures of ancient Cypriots. Next to the archaeological museum and behind the Garden cafe are the colorful **botanical gardens,** a popular picnic and leisure site on weekends whose aviaries showcase most of the island's indigenous species. *(Open daily 8am-10pm. Free.)*

■ Crossing the Green Line

The **Green Line** is Nicosia's main attraction. The only spot on the border where photography is permitted is on Ledra St., where the military has erected a makeshift shrine to the north. Crossing the infamous Green Line **from the south** is relatively easy, if you follow the strict regulations. Don't even try to get information on northern Nicosia on the Greek-Cypriot side. Greek-Cypriots have not crossed the line for over 20 years. You will not be permitted to cross if you are a Greek citizen or if you are of Greek descent. Head for the **Ledra Palace Checkpoint** between the Greek-Cypriot and Turkish walls. This former hotel, its interior gutted and its exterior marred by bullet holes, stands on neutral territory and houses U.N. troops.

You will show your passport on the Greek-Cypriot side and again on the Turkish side, where you'll also fill out a general information form in order to receive a special visitor's visa (£3-4, fluctuating based on currency rates). They will not stamp your passport. *Do not let them stamp your passport.* If they stamp your passport, you will not be readmitted to Greek Cyprus. They will, however, give you a form to be stamped by someone at another window. Hold on to this form—you will need it to cross back after your visit.

Some reminders: (1) You may enter Northern Cyprus between 8am and 1pm, but must return by 5pm. No exceptions. It is not possible to start a trip through north Cyprus and Turkey by crossing the Green Line. Guards will not allow those who arrive with large backpacks to cross with their packs. (2) Cars are not allowed—you must cross by foot. (3) As in other areas of Nicosia and Cyprus, do *not* take pictures of anything that has to do with the military or police. (4) As you will be forewarned on the Greek side, you are not allowed to buy anything on the Turkish side. If you wish to buy food, you must exchange your Cypriot pounds for Turkish lira. Also, you can't bring items purchased in the north back to the south—they will be confiscated. (5) If you have a problem, ask the U.N. soldiers with blue berets for assistance.

For **North Nicosia,** because of the fluctuating value of the Turkish lira, prices are listed in U.S. dollars. For an **emergency ambulance** dial 112; for **police** 155; for **fire** 199. At press time, American calling cards (e.g., AT&T, MCI) do not work in northern Cyprus. The post office sells special phonecards that work in all pay phones.

▓ North Nicosia

North Nicosia teems with green-clad troops—all instructed to be kind to tourists. The city's growth has followed a different plan from its severed Siamese twin to the south; modernization, rather than fastidious conservation, has crept into the Old City, but the newer sections outside the walls are not as developed as their southern counterparts. While the Girne Caddesi (Kyrenia Road) has been punctuated with high-rises and even glitzed up a bit for tourists, much of the Old City, especially in the east and along the Green Line, is a ghost town of crumbling walls and stray barbed wire.

ORIENTATION AND PRACTICAL INFORMATION From the **Ledra Palace** crossing (notice patriotic signs reading "Gratitude to the Motherland" and "Gratitude to the Turkish Army"), a roundabout with a Turkish **victory monolith** in the middle is 500m up the street. Follow the city walls to the **Girne Gate** (Kyrenia Gate). From there, **Girne Cad.**, the main street, runs to the main square, **Atatürk Meydanı**, and continues to the Green Line. *Photography of the Green Line is prohibited.*

A **tourist office** is inconveniently situated at the extreme northwest of the city on Bedrettin Demirel Cad., 2km from the Girne Gate (open M 7:30am-2pm and 3:30-6pm, Tu-F 7:30am-2pm; in winter M-F 8am-1pm and 2-5pm). Only **Turkey** has a full embassy (tel. 227 2314) in north Cyprus, at Bedrettin Demirel Cad. (open M-F 9am-noon). The following countries have "representative offices," which offer some consular services: **Australia** (tel. 227 1115), in the Saray Hotel (open Tu and Th 9am-noon); **U.K.,** 9 Shakespeare Ave. (tel. 228 3861; open M-F 8-11:30am); **U.S.,** 20 Güner Türkmen Sok. (tel. 227 2443; open M-F 8am-3:30pm). Several offices along Girne Cad. offer **currency exchange** (open M-F 8am-1pm and 2-4pm). **Banks** close at noon, but those in Atatürk Meydanı reopen at 3:30pm. **ATMs** are near Atatürk Meydanı.

A **hospital** (tel. 228 5441) is on the road to Girne, roughly 700m from the Victory Monument. Look for the *Hastane* sign. The **police** are on Girne Cad. (tel. 228 3311), close to Atatürk Meydanı. **Pembe Telefon,** 30m right of the post office, has metered booths and sells phone cards (open M-F 7:30am-2pm and 3:30-5:30pm). The **Government Telecommunications Department** is on Arif Salim Cad., halfway between Girne Gate and the bus station. Inexpensive **restaurants** crowd the area near the Girne Gate; *döner kebap* and *Öz Amasyalı* are popular lunch options.

SIGHTS The **Selimiye Mosque,** formerly **Agia Sophia Cathedral,** is a bizarre sight: a seemingly ancient cathedral looming in the shadow of its two soaring minarets. Despite the *seccade* (prayer rugs) and Islamic calligraphy, the saints carved in the arches above the door and the flying buttresses testify to the edifice's original purpose. The Roman Catholic cathedral, built by Crusaders in 1326, was gutted and refurbished by the Ottomans in 1570. From Atatürk Meydanı, with Girne Gate at your back, continue down Girne Cad., looking left for the twin minarets. Beside it is the **Bedesten,** formerly the 14th-century Orthodox Cathedral of St. Nicholas. Ottomans converted it into a covered market and later a barn. The Bedesten's modern successor, where fruit and vegetables are available at decent prices, is next door.

With your back to the Selimiye Mosque, head straight for a block and take a left to get to the **Büyük Hamamı,** a traditional Turkish bath once a 14th-century church. *(Open daily 7am-10:30pm. Bath, exfoliation, and massage $16.)* Just a dice throw away is **Kumarcılar Hanı** (Gamblers' Inn), which now houses northern Cyprus's Antiquities Department, along with a small restaurant. *(Open M-F 8am-2pm.)* A block or two to the east and beyond the Selimiye Mosque is the Gothic-era **Haydarpaşa Camii,** once a Lusignan church, and today a gallery. Face the Green Line and follow it to the right to the **Derviş Paşa Museum.** *(Open daily 9am-7pm, but often closes around lunchtime. Admission $3, students 40¢.)* The former mansion of a notable 20th-century Cypriot newspaper owner has been converted into an ethnographic museum with clothing and household goods. The **Mevlevi Tekke,** near the tourist office, once a Sufi *tekke*, is now a small **Turkish Museum** housing life-size models of whirling dervishes and Islamic artifacts. *(Open M-F 7:30am-2pm and 3:30-6pm. Admission $3, students 40¢.)*

CYPRUS

Appendix

■ Holidays and Festivals

GREECE

Jan. 1: Feast of St. Basil. Carrying on a Byzantine tradition, Greeks cut a New Year's sweet bread called *Vassilopita,* baked with a coin inside. The person who gets the slice with the coin is that year's lucky person.

Jan. 6: Epiphany. Celebrated in the West as the day the Magi appeared in Bethlehem to greet the baby Jesus; in the Eastern church Epiphany is recognized as the day Jesus was baptized by St. John. In Greece, *kallikantzaroi* (goblins) appear between Christmas and Epiphany. Village bonfires scare them away. At Epiphany, waters are blessed and evil spirits leave the earth. Crosses are thrown into harbors all around Greece and the young men who fetch them are considered blessed.

Jan. 31-Feb. 22: Carnival. Three weeks of feasting and dancing before the Lenten fast begins on Feb. 22. Notable celebrations occur in Patras and Cephalonia.

March 25: Greek Independence Day. Commemorates the 1821 struggle against the Turkish Ottoman Empire. Also a religious holiday, the Feast of the Annunciation, when the angel Gabriel told Mary of the Incarnation.

Apr. 9: Orthodox Good Friday. People carry candles in a procession through town or around the church in one of the Greek church's most moving liturgies.

Apr. 11: Orthodox Easter. The most holy day in the Greek calendar. After a midnight mass followed by a meal, celebrations on Easter Sunday typically include feasting on spit-roasted lamb and red-dyed hard-boiled eggs, followed by dancing.

April 23: St. George's Day. Celebration in honor of the dragon-slaying knight. Festivities at Limnos, Chania include horse races, wrestling matches, and dances.

May 1: Labor Day. Also Feast of the Flowers. Wreaths of flowers hung outside people's doors. The odd Communist demonstration.

June: The Day of the Holy Spirit. This national religious holiday takes place 40-50 days after Easter and is celebrated differently in each region.

May 30: Pentecost. Celebrated 50 days after Easter.

Aug. 15: Feast of the Assumption of the Virgin Mary. Celebration throughout Greece, particularly on Tinos, in honor of Mary's ascent to Heaven.

Sept. 8: The Virgin's Birthday. In some villages an auction is held to determine who will carry the Virgin's icon. The money is used to provide a village feast.

Oct. 26: Feast of St. Demetrius. Celebrated with particular enthusiasm in Thessaloniki. The feast coincides with the opening of new wine.

Oct. 28: National Anniversary of Greek Independence. Called "*Ohi* Day" in honor of Metaxas's famous "*Ohi*" (No) to Mussolini.

Nov. 17: Commemoration of the rise of the Greek university students against the junta of 1974. Speeches are presented at the University of Athens.

Dec. 24-25: Christmas. As part of the festivities, children traditionally make the rounds singing *kalanda* (Christmas carols).

CYPRUS

Cypriots observe not only Greece's holidays, but also hold their own regional and local festivities; below are a few of the most significant:

Jan. 31-Feb. 22: Carnival. The most notable celebrations are in Limmasol.

Feb. 22: Green Monday, or Lent. In areas of more strict observation this initiates seven meatless weeks of Lenten fasting.

Apr. 1: Southern Republic Day, commemorating the creation of the Republic.

May 31: Kataklismos, or Flood Festivals. Across Cyprus, Pentecost marks the beginning of days of feasting and celebration, remembering Noah and his ark's deliverance from the Flood, as well as paying vague homage to Aphrodite.

Oct. 1: Cyprus Independence Day.

Dec. 26: Boxing Day. In addition to Christmas, Cypriots celebrate Boxing Day, a throwback to the days of British colonization.

■ Climate

Climate is fairly uniform throughout Greece; the islands are a bit milder, and areas of higher altitude in the north are cooler. Summer is sunny and sticky—it's almost impossible to escape the heat and humidity without an air conditioner or a beach. Winter temperatures hover around 12°C; October-March is the rainy season.

Avg. Temp. in °C Rain in mm	January		April		July		October	
	Temp	Rain	Temp	Rain	Temp	Rain	Temp	Rain
Athens	12	62	19	23	33	6	23	51
Nicosia	10	76	18	18	29	1	21	25
Thessaloniki	6	44	15	41	27	22	18	57

■ Conversions

1 centimeter (cm) = 0.4 inch	1 inch = 2.5cm
1 meter (m) = 3.3 feet	1 foot = 0.3m
1 kilometer (km) = 0.62 mile	1 mile = 1.6km
1 kilogram (kg) = 35.5 ounces	1 ounce = 28g
1 kilogram (kg) = 2.21 pounds	1 pound = 0.45kg
1 liter (L) = 0.26 gallon	1 gallon = 3.8L
1 Imperial Gallon (U.K.) = 1.2 gallons	1 gallon = 0.83 Imperial Gallons
°F = (°C x 1.8) + 32	°C = (°F - 32) x .56

Quick-Reference Temperature Conversion

To convert from degrees Fahrenheit to degrees Celsius, subtract 32 and multiply by 5/9. To convert from Celsius to Fahrenheit, multiply by 9/5 and add 32.

°C	-5	0	5	10	15	20	25	30	35	40
°F	23	32	41	50	59	68	77	86	95	104

■ Telephone Codes

See **Keeping in Touch** (p. 36) for full information and advice about telephone calls in Greece and Cyprus, including international access.

INTERNATIONAL CALLING CODES

Australia	Austria	Canada	Cyprus	Greece	Ireland
61	43	1	357	30	353
Japan	N. Z.	S. Africa	Turkey	U. K.	U. S.
81	64	13	90	44	1

CITY CODES

Greece 30

Aegina	0297	**Andros**	0282	**Corfu**	0661
Agia Galini	0832	**Arahova**	0267	**Corinth**	0741
Agios Nikolaos	0841	**Astypalea**	0243	**Delphi**	0265
Agria	0423	**Athens**	01	**Dimitsana**	0795
Alexandropoulis	0551	**Cape Sounion**	0292	**Edessa**	0381
Amorgos	0285	**Cephalonia**	0671	**Epidavros** '	0753
Andritsena	0626	**Chios**	0271	**Eritrea**	0221

APPENDIX

CITY CODES

						Greece 30
Folegandros	0286	Kimi	0222	Petalidio	0722
Galaxidi	0265	Kithnos	0281	Piraeus	01
Gythion	0733	Kos	0242	Poros	0298
Halkida	0221	Kyparissia	0761	Pouri	0422
Hania	0821	Kythera	0735	Pylos	0723
Hersonissos	0897	Lefkada	0645	Rafina	0294
Hora Sfakion	0825	Lesvos	0251	Rethymnon	0831
Ierapetra	0842	Lia	0664	Rhodes	0241
Igoumenitsa	0665	Limni	0227	Samos	0273
Ikaria	0275	Limnos	0254	Samothraki	0551
Ioannina	0651	Litohoro	0352	Serifos	0281
Ios Village	0286	Matala	0892	Sifnos	0284
Iraklion	081	Methoni	0723	Sithonia	0375
Isthmia	0746	Metsovo	0656	Sitia	0843
Limni	0674	Milos	0287	Skiathos	0427
Itilo	0733	Monemvassia	0732	Skopelos	0424
Kalamata	0721	Mt. Athos	0377	Skyros	0222
Kalambaka	0432	Mycenae	0751	Sparta	0731
Kalavrita	0692	Mykonos	0289	Symi	0241
Kalymnos	0243	Nafplion	0752	Syros	0281
Kardamili	0721	Naxos	0285	Thassos	0593
Karpathos	0245	Neapolis	0734	Thebes	0262
Karpenisi	0237	Olympia	0624	Thessaloniki	031
Karystos	0224	Osios Loukas	0267	Tinos	0283
Kassos	0245	Paleochora	0823	Tripoli	071
Kastoria	0467	Parga	0684	Volos	0421
Kavala	051	Paros	0284	Xilokastro	0743
Kea	0288	Patmos	0247	Zagorohoria	0426
Kellini	0623	Patras	061	Zakinthos	0695
					Cyprus 357
Agia Napa	03	Nicosia	02	Platres	05
Larnaka	04	Pano Platres	05	Podromos	0295
Limassol	05	Paphos	06	Polis	06

■ Glossary of Greek Terms

Below are words used frequently in discussions about Greek art, architecture, cultural history and food, as well as in everyday travel speech.

acropolis a fortified high place; a sacred area

aftokinito car

agora a level city square; marketplace

alati salt

angouraki cucumber

apse nook beyond the altar of a church

architrave lintel resting on columns; lower part of the entablature directly below the frieze

astonomaieo police; pigs

Archaic Period 700–480 BC

arnaki lamb

astakos lobster

avga eggs

bouleterion meeting place of an ancient city's legislative council

Byzantine Period AD 324-1453

cella inner sanctum of a classical temple

Classical Period 480-323 BC

Corinthian column ornate with leafy or flowery capital embellishment.

Cyclopian walls massive irregular-cut Minoan and Mycenaean stone walls

dimarchio town hall

dolmades warm stuffed grape vine leaves with egg-lemon sauce

dolmadakia cold stuffed vine leaves

domatia rooms for rent in private homes

Dorian referring to invaders of 1100 BC

Doric column cigar-shaped columns with wide fluted shafts, cushion capitals, and no bases

efimerevon 24-hour pharmacy

entablature upper orders of a temple facade resting on columns

exedra curved recess in classical or Byzantine architecture

exonarthex transverse vestibule in a Byzantine church preceding the facade

feta soft white goat-milk cheese

forum Roman marketplace

frieze middle part of the entablature

frappés whipped, frothing coffee drink

frourio medieval castle

Geometric Period 1100-700 BC

ghala milk

glika sweets

gyro greasy, pita-wrapped love

Hellenistic Period 323-46 BC

herm pillar, usually with an erect phallus, crowned with a bust.

hora village

iconostatis screen bearing icon in a Byzantine church.

Ionic column slender column with twin scrolling spiral capital and fluted base

iperastiko long distance (phone calls, transportation, etc.)

kafeneio cafe and social hub

kalamarakia baby squids

kasseri hard yellow cheese

kastro castle and fortifications

kato hora lower village (spatially)

kotopoulo chicken

ktapodhi octopus

ladhi oil

leoforos avenue

leoforeo bus

logariasmo check

magiritsa tripe soup with rice

metope square block in the Doric frieze, first painted and later sculpted

megaron large hall in a house or palace

melizanes eggplants

meltemi in the Cyclades and Dodecanese an unusually strong north wind

Minoan Period 3000-1250 BC

moni monastery or convent

moschari veal

moustarda mustard

Mycenean Period 1600-1100 BC

narthex vestibule along the west side of a Byzantine church

Neolithic Period 3000-2000 BC

nosokomeio hospital

odeion small semi-circular theater

odos road

oikos house

ouzeri ouzo tavern serving yummy treats

paleochora old town

palaestra classical gymnasium

panagia Virgin Mary

panigiri local festival, often religious

pediment a triangualar space in the facade of an ancient temple

peplos mantle worn by ancient Greek women; Athena's nightie

periptero small street newstand; kiosk

peristyle colonnade around a building

philos friend or homeslice

piperi pepper

plateia town square

pleio ferry

polis city-state

portico colonnade or stoa

pronaos outer columnar temple porch

propylon sanctuary entrance flanked by columns

prytaneion administrative building

psaria fish

psomi bread

rhyton cup shaped like animal's head

Roman period 46 BC-AD 324

satyr erect follower of Dionysus

skala port settlement

souvlaki skish kebab

stele stone slab tomb marker

stoa in ancient marketplaces, an open portico lined with rows of columns.

taverna restaurant or tavern

tholos Mycenean earth-covered circular beehive-shaped tomb

triglyph in the Doric frieze with 3 vertical grooves alternating with metopes

trireme ancient ship with 3 sets of oars

tsoutsoukakia meat balls in tomato sauce

volta esplanade

voutiro butter

zakhari sugar

■ Greek Alphabet

The table of the Greek alphabet (only 24 letters) below will help you decipher signs. The left column gives you the names of the letters in Greek, the middle column shows the printed lower case and capital letters, and the right column provides the approximate pronunciations of the letters.

alpha	α A	*a* as in father	nu	ν N	*n* as in net
beta	β B	*v* as in velvet	ksi	ξ Ξ	*x* as in mix
gamma	γ Γ	*y* as in yo or *g* as in go	omicron	o O	*o* as in row
delta	δ Δ	*th* as in there	pi	π Π	*p* as in peace
epsilon	ε E	*e* as in jet	rho	ρ P	*r* as in roll
zeta	ζ Z	*z* as in zebra	sigma	σ (ς), Σ	*s* as in sense
eta	η H	*ee* as in queen	tau	τ T	*t* as in tent
theta	θ Θ	*th* as in health	upsilon	υ Y	*ee* as in green
iota	ι I	*ee* as in tree	phi	φ Φ	*f* as in fog
kappa	κ K	*k* as in cat	xi	χ X	*ch (h)* as in horse
lambda	λ Λ	*l* as in land	psi	ψ Ψ	*ps* as in oops
mu	μ M	*m* as in moose	omega	ω Ω	*o* as in glow

■ Greek-English Phrases

Greetings and Courtesies

Good morning	Καλημερα	kah-lee-ME-rah
Good evening	Καλησπερα	kah-lee-SPE-rah
Good night	Καληνυχτα	kah-lee-NEE-khtah
yes	Ναι	NEH
no	Οχι	OH-hee
please/you're welcome	Παρακαλω	pah-rah-kah-LO
thank you (very much)	Ευχαριστω	ef-hah-ree-STO (po-LEE)
excuse me	Συγνομη	seeg-NO-mee
hello (polite, plural)	Γεια σας	YAH-sas
hello (familiar)	Γεια σου	YAH-soo
OK	Ενταξι	en-DAHK-see
What is your name?	Πως σε λενε	pos-se-LEH-neh
My name is ...	Με Λενε	me-LEH-neh ...
Would you like some red wine?	Μηπος θελεις λιγο κοκκινο κρασι;	ME-pos THEL-ees LE-go KO-kee-no kra-SEE?
Mr./Sir	Κυριος	kee-REE-os
Ms./Madam	Κυρια	kee-REE-ah

Time

What time is it?	Τι ωρα ειναι;	tee-O-rah EE-neh?
yesterday	χθες	k-THES
today	σημερα	SEE-mer-a
tomorrow	αυριο	AV-ree-o
first	πρωτο	PRO-to
morning	πρωι	pro-EE
evening	βραδι	VRAH-dhee
later tonight	αποψε	ah-PO-pseh
last	τελευταιο	teh-lef-TEH-o

Problems

Do you speak English?	Μιλας αγγλικα;	mee-LAHS ahn-glee-KAH?

I don't speak Greek	Δεν μιλαω ελληνικα	dhen mee-LAHO el-leen-ee-KAH
I don't understand	Δεν καταλαβαινω	dhen kah-tah-lah-VEH-no
I am lost	Χαθηκα	HA-thee-ka
I am ill	Ειμαι αρροστος	EE-meh AH-ross-toss
I love you	Σ'αγαπαω	SAII-gap-AH o
Help!	βοητηεια	vo-EE-thee-ah

Directions

Where is ...?	Που ειναι;	pou-EE-neh ...?
I'm going to ...	Πηγαινω για	pee-YEH-no yah ...
When do we leave?	Τι ωρα φευγουμε;	tee O-rah FEV-goo-meh?
restaurant	εστιατοριο	es-tee-ah-TO-ree-o
post office	ταχυδρομειο	ta-khee-dhro-MEE-o
market	αγορα	ah-go-RAH
museum	μουσειο	mou-SEE-o
pharmacy	φαρμακειο	fahr-mah-KEE-o
bank	τραπεζα	TRAH-peh-zah
church	εκκλησια	eh-klee-SEE-ah
hotel	ξενοδοχειο	kse-no-dho-HEE-o
room	δοματιο	dho-MAH-teeo
suitcase	βαλιτσα	vah-LEE-tsah
airport	αεροδρομειο	ah-e-ro-DHRO-mee o
airplane	αεροπλανο	ah-e-ro-PLAH-no
train	τραινο	TREH-no
bus	λεωφορειο	leh-o-fo-REE-o
ferry	πλοιο	PLEE-o
ticket	εισιτηριο	ee-see-TEE-ree-o
hospital	νοσοκομειο	no-so-ko-ME-o
port	λιμανι	lee-MA-nee
toilet	τουαλετα	twa-LE-ta
police	αστυνομεια	as-tee-no-ME-a
archaeology	αρχαιολογια	ark-ha-o-lo-GEE-a
bar	μπαρ	BAR
doctor	γιατρος	yah-TROS
right	δεξια	dhek-see-AH
left	αριστερα	ah-rees-teh-RAH
here, there	εδω, εκει	eh-DHO, eh-KEE
open, closed	ανοιχτο, κλειστο	ah-nee-KTO, klee-STO

Prices

How much?	Ποσο κανει;	PO-so KAH-nee
I need	Χρειαζομα	khree-AH-zo-meh
I want	Θελω	THEH-lo
I would like ...	Θα ηθελα	thah EE-the-lah ...
I will buy this one	Θα Αγορασω αυτο.	thah ah-go-RAH-so ahf-TO
Do you have?	Εχετε:;	Eh-khe-teh
Can I see a room?	Μπορω να δω ενα δωματιο	bo-RO nah-DHO E-nah dho-MAH-tee-o
bill	λογαριασμο	lo-gahr-yah-SMO
newspaper	εφημεριδα	eh-fee-meh-REE-dha
water	νερο	ne-RO
good	καλο	kah-LO
cheap	φτηνο	ftee-NO
expensive	ακριβο	ah-kree-VO

Numbers

zero	μηδεν	mee-DHEN
one	ενα	Eh-nah
two	δυο	DHEE-o
three	τρια	TREE-ah
four	τεσσερα	TES-ser-ah
five	πεντε	PEN-dheh
six	εξι	E-ksee
seven	επτα	ep-TAH
eight	οκτω	okh-TO
nine	εννια	en-YAH
ten	δεκα	DHEH-kah
eleven	ενδεκα	EN-dheh-kah
twelve	δωδεκα	DHO-dheh-kah
thirteen	δεκα τρια	DHEH-kah TREE-ah
fourteen	δεκατεσσερα	DHEH-kah TES-ser-ah
fifteen	δεκαπεντε	DHEH-kah PEN-dheh
sixteen	δεκαεξι	DHEH-kah E-ksee
seventeen	δεκαεπτα	DHEH-kah ep-TAH
eighteen	δεκαοκτω	DHEH-kah okh-TO
nineteen	δεκαεννια	DHEH-kah en-YAH
twenty	εικοσι	EE-ko-see
thirty	τριαντα	tree-AN-dah
forty	σαραντα	sa-RAN-dah
fifty	πενηντα	pen-EEN-dah
sixty	εξηντα	ex-EEN-dah
seventy	εβδομηντα	ev-dho-MEEN-dah
eighty	ογδοντα	og-DHON-dah
ninety	ενενηντα	en-EEN-dah
hundred	εκατο	ek-ah-TO
thousands	χιλιαδες	hil-ee-AH(dhes)
million	εκατομμυριο	eka-to-MEE-rio

The Way We Were

Five years ago, *Never on Sunday's* Greece became the Greece of *Z.* Nevertheless, some of the early villainy of the regime has vanished, no doubt with an eye toward the country's extraordinary tourist potential, and the hostility toward the counterculture has been tempered by the realization that beneath many a beggarly exterior lies a fat reserve of cash.

It's a country known by its celebrants less as a place than as a state of soul. Most students go to Greece not for the common tourist amenities of ease and grand cuisine, but for the bracing quality of its life, land and light—for the austere Greek arrangement of the world, with its incomparable solitudes, live goats and ten billion olives. Pure black storms rumble over tooth-white island towns, and the old man with the monkey goes to pieces with too much wine and a tambourine. Cretans wear their boots and live out years so strangely rudimentary as to seem half-magical to us. The luxury of everywhere-pruned Italy gives way here to stubble-ground, places that giants and then Turks ransacked, and here and there spookiness and the wind's whistle tell you that you're near oracles' ground.

—*Let's Go: Europe 1972*

Index

Researcher-Writers

Brady Gunderson   *Cyprus, Dodecanese*
The darling of the Cypriot tourist ministry, Brady raced with wheels of fire around the
island of Cyprus. If only the mail traveled so fast! Cognizant of his own past as a burning goat, Brady sojurned in Leros to bring *Let's Go* its first insane asylum listings. The
monks of Stavrovouni begged him to take join the order, Aphrodite rose from her
baths to claim him, Rhodes thought he was the reincarnation of the Colossus, and the
Apocalypse put off the end of the world another year and cowered in fright while
Brady was on Patmos. Brady shunned these diversions, fleeing to Turkey to tease Sufi
silk-worms, buy ink cartridges for his leaking pen, and hammer out those last few
golden batches.

Ashley Kircher   *Cyclades, Sporades, & Northeast Aegean Islands*
Jammin', slammin', rockin', and hoppin', her way across the Aegean, Ashley was a
party trooper, and a true connoisseur of Cycladian and Sporadian club life. Ashley had
an amazing sense of balance, seeking out not only the chic and the hip but also the
chill and the truly quality. She braved the endless ferries, yawned through the
"sleepy towns," jostled by the sweaty masses (on the beaches and off), and withstood
the moschino-clad *kamaki* with an admirable stoicism—partying all night and tanning all day really *was* a tough job! Well done Ashley!

Jeremy Kurzyniec   *Peloponnese, Sterea Ellada, & Ionians*
It is difficult for one to discern whether Jeremy is a reincarnation of the erudite Pausanias or the galant Lord Byron. Perhaps both. Whatever his spiritual past, Jeremy definitely proved himself a Most Intrepid Classicist, weathering *kleftes*, heat, Dorians, and
more *kleftes*, and keeping his copy up to the highest standards of informed research
on the road. With a veneration for the Greek past equal to Schleimann's, Jeremy
wasn't quite as fast and loose with his baubles at Mycenae. But he'd never miss the
latest tragedy at Epidavros. Olympia retains its ancient athletic glory after his well-
applied attentions. And don't think we didn't notice...you were even serious about
your ice cream...

Michele Lee   *Attica, Saronic Gulf Islands, & Crete*
Despite the fact that her dialect dated back to the 5th century, Michele became an
Athenian overnight, skipping from square to square, sipping *frappé* after foamy
frappé. Her overhaul of Athens in our pages, rivalling the civic reforms of a young
Pericles, will set the standard for years to come. Sailing down to Crete like the great
Athenian Theseus, Michele didin't kill any minotaurs and didn't desert anyone on any
beaches, but she did leave behind a special *logos* in the hearts of all those she met on
the *odos*. Good luck in China, Michele! Καλο ταξιδι!

Nick Stephanopoulos   *Northern Greece & Corfu*
The baddest *malaka* this side of Salonica, Nick could write a whole book on the
hedonistic mores of Corfu, then serve it up into a *gyro* with a side of *tzatziki*. We
never had to worry that Nick wasn't getting a real feel for wherever he went; we
knew he was chilling at the *plateia* being mistaken for a native or down at the *ouzeri*
drinking like one. When he wasn't climbing lush verdant mountains, plunging
through gorges, taking monastic vows, or getting hit on by cigarette models, Nick
expanded the book in some of the toughest directions—north to the Albanian border, deep into minaret-laden Thrace and all the way up Mt. Olympus. He did it the
whole time with that magic Grecian style. Just remember to keep your hair nice and
slicked back.

Acknowledgments

Thanks to Allison (good luck in Oz!), our favorite receptionist Eliza, the Map Boys for late-night metaphysics, Nicra, Monica, omnipresent Dan & Heath, Greek Goddess Maryanthe, ultra-typists Michele Guyen Lee and Elena DeCoste, Brian Martin for cookies, Zakaras & the Euro-crew for crunchin' the Turks. Kemalists Mustafs and the Bird,, Måns and his various usurpers, and Bonga. RWs, this is your book.

Thanks to various *malakas* in Athens—Blanes, Fats, and Mike; Anna and Araceleis; Fiona, Josephine, and Mexo-Greco Byron Kelley. Mo'miks. Selçuk in Samsun. In Mass Schliz, Sobol, & dumbism lost. MSPG. My sister a KKE member. Mum & Ted I suppose get some credit. Dan Turk & Waka Goumba. Sonesh my eternal partner in fire safety. Robin Ghetto Diaspora. Don Stefania. Speier a bad man. Branch & Bro more bad men. Lester and Mila, filch that ass. E for Albos. Paloff & Delmore, Last Great. . . Package. R, sooner or later one of us must know. Derek the embodiment of Ghetto. Katie-bird for subtle poetics. Sahi-Buteri, I treasure your friendship like a prized family heirloom. Nelope hereby declared an Official Classicist. Mustafs, I hope our new babies grow up happy. Måns to the Måxx. Angie remembered. Masters Reish, Fowden, Russell, Glavin. I don't beleive in suffering. Σωμα ειναι σημα—**CRL**

Thanks to Ottomåns Ghetto for making *Let's Go* perpetually entertaining (even if you're all nuts) especially Christian for being the fuckin' best at what you do and Saadi for being a tortured genius, classicists, roommates and friends for a great time fitting too much into summer days and nights, parents for understanding about being busy (I miss you), siblings (esp. thanks Bec for L.A.), Ella and Louie Liz Phair Lou Reed Premiums a.f.k.a.Prince Stan Getz-Staples Singers for so often saving the day—**PAC**

>>>>>>>>>>>>>>>>>>>>>>>>>> λογος <<<<<<<<<<<<<<<<<<<<<<<<<<<

christian, the old man the monkey
penelope, the wine the tambourine
to you go the pieces —**SS**

Editor	Christian Reed Lorentzen
Associate Editor	Penelope Carter
Associate Editor	Saadi Soudavar
Managing Editor	M. Allison Arwady
Publishing Director	Caroline R. Sherman
Publishing Director	Anna C. Portnoy
Production Manager	Dan Visel
Associate Production Manager	Maryanthe Malliaris
Cartography Manager	Derek McKee
Design Manager	Bentsion Harder
Editorial Manager	M. Allison Arwady
Editorial Manager	Lisa M. Nosal
Financial Manager	Monica Eileen Eav
Personnel Manager	Nicolas R. Rapold
Publicity Manager	Alexander Z. Speier
New Media Manager	Måns O. Larsson
Map Editors	Matthew R. Daniels, Dan Luskin
Production Associate	Heath Ritchie
Office Coordinators	Tom Moore, Eliza Harrington, Jodie Kirschner
Director of Advertising Sales	Gene Plotkin
Associate Sales Executives	Colleen Gaard, Mateo Jaramillo, Alexandra Price
President	Catherine J. Turco
General Manager	Richard Olken
Assistant General Manager	Anne E. Chisholm

Thanks to Our Readers...

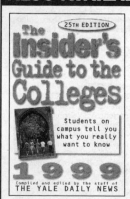

★Let's Go 1999 Reader Questionnaire★

Please fill this out and return it to **Let's Go, St. Martin's Press**, 175 Fifth Ave., New York, NY 10010-7848. All respondents will receive a free subscription to *The Yellowjacket*, the Let's Go Newsletter. You can find a more extensive version of this survey on the web at http://www.letsgo.com.

Name: _____

Address: _____

City: _____ **State:** _____ **Zip/Postal Code:** _____

Email: _____ **Which book(s) did you use?** _____

How old are you? under 19   19-24   25-34   35-44   45-54   55 or over

Are you (circle one)   in high school   in college   in graduate school   employed   retired   between jobs

Have you used Let's Go before? yes no   **Would you use it again?** yes no

How did you first hear about Let's Go? friend   store clerk   television   bookstore display   advertisement/promotion   review   other

Why did you choose Let's Go (circle up to two)? reputation budget focus   price   writing style   annual updating   other: _____

Which other guides have you used, if any? Fodor's   Footprint Handbooks   Frommer's $-a-day   Lonely Planet   Moon Guides   Rick Steve's   Rough Guides   UpClose   other: _____

Which guide do you prefer? _____

Please rank each of the following parts of Let's Go 1 to 5 (1=needs improvement, 5=perfect). packaging/cover   practical information   accommodations   food   cultural introduction   sights   practical introduction ("Essentials")   directions   entertainment   gay/lesbian information   maps   other: _____

How would you like to see the books improved? (continue on separate page, if necessary) _____
_____

How long was your trip? one week   two weeks   three weeks   one month   two months or more

Which countries did you visit? _____

What was your average daily budget, not including flights? _____

Have you traveled extensively before? yes no

Do you buy a separate map when you visit a foreign city? yes no

Have you used a Let's Go Map Guide? yes no

If you have, would you recommend them to others? yes no

Have you visited Let's Go's website? yes no

What would you like to see included on Let's Go's website? _____
_____

What percentage of your trip planning did you do on the Web? _____

Would you use a Let's Go: recreational (e.g. skiing) guide   gay/lesbian guide   adventure/trekking guide   phrasebook   general travel information guide

Which of the following destinations do you hope to visit in the next three to five years (circle one)? Canada   Argentina   Perú   Kenya   Middle East   Caribbean   Scandinavia   other: _____

Where did you buy your guidebook? Internet   independent bookstore   chain bookstore   college bookstore   travel store   other: _____